# Contemporary Authors®

ISSN 0275-7176

# Contemporary Authors®

## A Bio-Bibliographical Guide to Current Writers in Fiction, General Nonfiction, Poetry, Journalism, Drama, Motion Pictures, Television, and Other Fields

*volume* **181**

GALE GROUP

Detroit
San Francisco
London
Boston
Woodbridge, CT

# Staff

Library of Congress Catalog Card Number 62-52046
ISBN 0-7876-3241-4
ISSN 0010-7468
Printed in the United States of America

10 9 8 7 6 5 4 3 2 1

# Contents

**Indexing note:** All *Contemporary Authors* entries are indexed in the *Contemporary Authors* cumulative index, which is published separately and distributed twice a year.

**As always, the most recent *Contemporary Authors* cumulative index continues to be the user's guide to the location of an individual author's listing.**

# Preface

*Contemporary Authors (CA)* provides information on approximately 100,000 writers in a wide range of media, including:

- Current writers of fiction, nonfiction, poetry, and drama whose works have been issued by commercial publishers, risk publishers, or university presses (authors whose books have been published only by known vanity or author-subsidized firms are ordinarily not included)

- Prominent print and broadcast journalists, editors, photojournalists, syndicated cartoonists, graphic novelists, screenwriters, television scriptwriters, and other media people

- Authors who write in languages other than English, provided their works have been published in the United States or translated into English

- Literary greats of the early twentieth century whose works are popular in todays high school and college curriculums and continue to elicit critical attention

A *CA* listing entails no charge or obligation. Authors are included on the basis of the above criteria and their interest to *CA* users. Sources of potential listees include trade periodicals, publishers' catalogs, librarians, and other users.

## How to Get the Most out of *CA*: Use the Index

The key to locating an author's most recent entry is the *CA* cumulative index, which is published separately and distributed twice a year. It provides access to *all* entries in *CA* and *Contemporary Authors New Revision Series (CANR)*. Always consult the latest index to find an authors most recent entry.

For the convenience of users, the *CA* cumulative index also includes references to all entries in these Gale literary series: *Authors and Artists for Young Adults, Authors in the News, Bestsellers, Black Literature Criticism, Black Writers, Children's Literature Review, Concise Dictionary of American Literary Biography, Concise Dictionary of British Literary Biography, Contemporary Authors Autobiography Series, Contemporary Authors Bibliographical Series, Contemporary Literary Criticism, Dictionary of Literary Biography, Dictionary of Literary Biography Documentary Series, Dictionary of Literary Biography Yearbook, DISCovering Authors, DISCovering Authors: British, DISCovering Authors: Canadian, DISCovering Authors: Modules* (including modules for Dramatists, Most-Studied Authors, Multicultural Authors, Novelists, Poets, and Popular/Genre Authors), *Drama Criticism, Hispanic Literature Criticism, Hispanic Writers, Junior DISCovering Authors, Major Authors and Illustrators for Children and Young Adults, Major 20th-Century Writers, Native North American Literature, Poetry Criticism, Short Story Criticism, Something about the Author, Something about the Author Autobiography Series, Twentieth-Century Literary Criticism, World Literature Criticism,* and *Yesterday's Authors of Books for Children.*

## A Sample Index Entry:

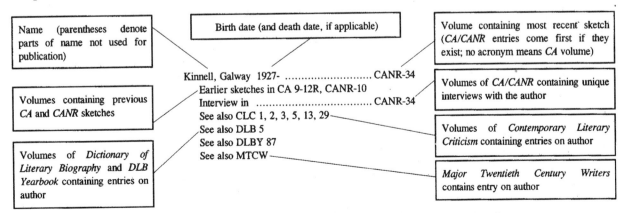

# How Are Entries Compiled?

The editors make every effort to secure new information directly from the authors; listees' responses to our question-naires and query letters provide most of the information featured in *CA*. For deceased writers, or those who fail to reply to requests for data, we consult other reliable biographical sources, such as those indexed in Gale's *Biography and Genealogy Master Index*, and bibliographical sources, including *National Union Catalog*, *LC MARC*, and *British National Bibliography*. Further details come from published interviews, feature stories, and book reviews, as well as information supplied by the authors' publishers and agents.

*An asterisk (\*) at the end of a sketch indicates that the listing has been compiled from secondary sources believed to be reliable but has not been personally verified for this edition by the author sketched.*

# What Kinds of Information Does An Entry Provide?

Sketches in *CA* contain the following biographical and bibliographical information:

- **Entry heading:** the most complete form of author's name, plus any pseudonyms or name variations used for writing

- **Personal information:** author's date and place of birth, family data, ethnicity, educational background, politi-cal and religious affiliations, and hobbies and leisure interests

- **Addresses:** author's home, office, or agent's addresses, plus e-mail and fax numbers, as available

- **Career summary:** name of employer, position, and dates held for each career post; resume of other vocation-al achievements; military service

- **Membership information:** professional, civic, and other association memberships and any official posts held

- **Awards and honors:** military and civic citations, major prizes and nominations, fellowships, grants, and hon-orary degrees

- **Writings:** a comprehensive, chronological list of titles, publishers, dates of original publication and revised editions, and production information for plays, television scripts, and screenplays

- **Adaptations:** a list of films, plays, and other media which have been adapted from the author's work

- **Work in progress:** current or planned projects, with dates of completion and/or publication, and expected publisher, when known

- **Sidelights:** a biographical portrait of the author's development; information about the critical reception of the author's works; revealing comments, often by the author, on personal interests, aspirations, motivations, and thoughts on writing

- **Interview:** a one-on-one discussion with authors conducted especially for *CA*, offering insight into authors' thoughts about their craft

- **Autobiographical Essay:** an original essay written by noted authors for *CA*, a forum in which writers may present themselves, on their own terms, to their audience

- **Photographs:** portraits and personal photographs of notable authors

- **Biographical and critical sources:** a list of books and periodicals in which additional information on an author's life and/or writings appears

- **Obituary Notices** in *CA* provide date and place of birth as well as death information about authors whose full-length sketches appeared in the series before their deaths. The entries also summarize the authors' careers and writings and list other sources of biographical and detah information.

## Related Titles in the *CA* Series

*Contemporary Authors Autobiography Series* complements *CA* original and revised volumes with specially commissioned autobiographical essays by important current authors, illustrated with personal photographs they provide. Common topics include their motivations for writing, the people and experiences that shaped their careers, the rewards they derive from their work, and their impressions of the current literary scene.

*Contemporary Authors Bibliographical Series* surveys writings by and about important American authors since World War II. Each volume concentrates on a specific genre and features approximately ten writers; entries list works written by and about the author and contain a bibliographical essay discussing the merits and deficiencies of major critical and scholarly studies in detail.

## Available in Electronic Formats

**CD-ROM.** Full-text bio-bibliographic entries from the entire *CA* series, covering approximately 100,000 writers, are available on CD-ROM through lease and purchase plans. The disc combines entries from the *CA*, *CANR*, and *Contemporary Authors Permanent Series* (*CAP*) print series to provide the most recent author listing. The *CA CD-ROM* is searchable by name, title, subject/genre, nationality/ethnicity, personal data, and as well as by using Boolean logic. The disc is updated every six months. For more information, call 1-248-699-4253.

*Contemporary Authors* is also available on CD-ROM from SilverPlatter Information, Inc.

**Online.** The *Contemporary Authors* database is made available online to libraries and their patrons through online public access catalog (OPAC) vendors. Currently, *CA* is offered through Ameritech Library Services' Vista Online (formerly Dynix).

**GaleNet.** *CA* is available on a subscription basis through GaleNet, an online information resource that features an easy-to-use end-user interface, the powerful search capabilities of the BRS/Search retrieval software, and ease of access through the World-Wide Web. For more information, call 1-248-699-4253.

**Magnetic Tape.** *CA* is available for licensing on magnetic tape in a fielded format. The database is available for internal data processing and nonpublishing purposes only. For more information, call 1-248-699-4253.

## Suggestions Are Welcome

The editors welcome comments and suggestions from users on any aspect of the *CA* series. If readers would like to recommend authors for inclusion in future volumes of the series, they are cordially invited to write the Editors at *Contemporary Authors*, Gale Group, 27500 Drake Rd., Farmington Hills, MI 48331-3535; or call at 1-248-699-4253; or fax at 1-248-699-8054.

# *CA* Numbering System and Volume Update Chart

Occasionally questions arise about the *CA* numbering system and which volumes, if any, can be discarded. Despite numbers like "29-32R," "97-100" and "180," the entire *CA* print series consists of only 193 physical volumes with the publication of *CA* Volume 181. The following charts note changes in the numbering system and cover design, and indicate which volumes are essential for the most complete, up-to-date coverage.

**CA First Revision**
- 1-4R through 41-44R (11 books)
  *Cover:* Brown with black and gold trim.
  There will be no further First Revision volumes because revised entries are now being handled exclusively through the more efficient *New Revision Series* mentioned below.

**CA Original Volumes**
- 45-48 through 97-100 (14 books)
  *Cover:* Brown with black and gold trim.
- 101 through 181 (81 books)
  *Cover:* Blue and black with orange bands.
  The same as previous *CA* original volumes but with a new, simplified numbering system and new cover design.

**CA Permanent Series**
- *CAP*-1 and *CAP*-2 (2 books)
  *Cover:* Brown with red and gold trim.
  There will be no further Permanent Series volumes because revised entries are now being handled exclusively through the more efficient *New Revision Series* mentioned below.

**CA New Revision Series**
- CANR-1 through CANR-85 (85 books)
  *Cover:* Blue and black with green bands.
  Includes only sketches requiring significant changes; **sketches are taken from any previously published *CA*, *CAP*, or *CANR* volume.**

| If You Have: | You May Discard: |
|---|---|
| *CA* First Revision Volumes 1-4R through 41-44R and *CA Permanent Series* Volumes 1 and 2. | *CA* Original Volumes 1, 2 ,3, 4 Volumes 5-6 through 41-44 |
| *CA* Original Volumes 45-48 through 97-100 and 101 through 181 | **NONE:** These volumes will not be supeseded by corresponding revised volumes. Individual entries from these and all other volumes appearing in the left column of this chart may be revised and included in the various volumes of the *New Revision Series*. |
| *CA New Revision Series* Volumes *CANR*-1 through *CANR*-85 | **NONE:** The *New Revision Series* does not replace any single volume of *CA*. Instead, volumes of *CANR* include entries from many previous *CA* series volumes. All *New Revision Series* volumes must be retained for full coverage. |

# A Sampling of Authors and Media People Featured in This Volume

## Poul Anderson

Known as a writer of "hard" science fiction, or science fiction scrupulously based on scientific fact, Anderson is also recognized as an accomplished creator of fantasy tales based on Nordic mythology, such as the prize winning story "The Queen of Air and Darkness." Many of his science fiction novels and short stories are set in the same universe and document the exploration of outer space by the Technic Civilization. Anderson's use of this "future history" motif in his works, according to some critics, is extensive and extremely well-crafted. Anderson contributes an autobiographical essay to this volume of *CA*.

## Howard Fast

Fast is often referred to as one of the most widely read authors of the twentieth century. Over the course of seven decades he has written novels, screenplays, and works of nonfiction that offer a unique perspective on events in American history. A former member of the communist party, Fast was blacklisted by publishers during the 1950s, resulting in his founding of the Blue Heron Press as an outlet for his work. His fiction often underscores the heroic acts of freedom-loving Americans and sheds light on long-forgotten events in U.S. history. Fast describes his life and work as a writer in an autobiographical essay included in this volume of *CA*.

## Hugo Gernsback

An author, inventor, publisher, and businessman, Gernsback is credited with originating the genre of scientifiction, or what is known today as science fiction. Through such novels as *Ralph 124C41+* and his line of pulp magazines, which included *Amazing Stories* and *Science Wonder Stories*, Gernsback fostered an imaginative vision of the future that was based, at least in part, on science fact. The prestigious Hugo Award, science fiction literature's highest honor, was named in honor of Gernsback.

## Tanino Guerra

Italian screenwriter Guerra initially concentrated his literary career on writing poetry in his native dialect, Romagnol. The recurring themes of his early work, published shortly after World War II, are chaos and death. In the 1950s Guerra began to write screenplays, and was soon collaborating with acclaimed film directors Michelangelo Antonioni and Federico Fellini.

Guerra has worked on over sixty films over five decades, including the U.S.-made *Zabriskie Point*.

## Daniel Keyes

Best known for his novel *Flowers for Algernon*, the story of a retarded man who becomes a genius through psychosurgery only to regress to his former condition, Keyes is recognized by critics for crafting poignant fiction around psychological issues. In addition to his novels and short stories, Keyes has authored several nonfiction volumes, including *The Minds of Billy Milligan*, an account of multiple personality disorder. Keyes discusses his early life as a writer in an autobiographical essay included in this volume of *CA*.

## Jeffrey Meyers

A prominent and prolific biographer of literary figures, Meyers has studied the lives of Ernest Hemingway, Robert Frost, D. H. Lawrence, Katherine Mansfield, Joseph Conrad, Edgar Allan Poe, George Orwell, and others. In regard to his *Robert Frost*, published in 1996, *New York Times* critic Michiko Kakutani deemed it "by far Mr. Meyer's most persuasive and thoughtful biography yet." An autobiographical essay by Meyers is included in this volume of *CA*.

## Adolph S. Ochs

Ochs was owner and publisher of the *New York Times* for forty years, from 1896 until his death in 1935. Beginning his career in journalism as an office boy, Ochs first revitalized the *Chattanooga Times*, then took over management of the *New York Times*, eventually becoming the majority stock holder. He elevated the content of the *Times* from the more sensational newspapers of the 1890s and turned the struggling paper around financially. Under Ochs's leadership, the *Times* adopted the motto "All the News that's Fit to Print."

## Luciano Pavarotti

Acclaimed by many as one of the greatest operatic tenors of all time, Pavarotti is hugely popular throughout the world. Critics have marveled not only at his bell-like clarity of tone and his unmatched ability to achieve exceptionally high notes, but also at his professional longevity and the nearly perfect preservation of his voice after almost forty years of singing. He has also co-authored two volumes of memoirs, *My Own Story* and *Pavarotti: My World*.

## Ida Tarbell

Remembered as a muckraking journalist, Tarbell's most significant work is *The History of the Standard Oil Company*. Published in 1904, the volume exposed the monopoly Standard Oil held over the petroleum industry as well as the devious practices the company employed to maintain its market dominance. It also helped set in motion the U.S. Supreme Court's landmark antitrust decision to break up Standard Oil. Tarbell also authored a number of volumes about Abraham Lincoln, including *The Life of Abraham Lincoln* and *The Early Life of Abraham Lincoln*.

## Brian Warner (Marilyn Manson)

In his persona as the eerie and flamboyant rock musician Marilyn Manson, Warner took "shock rock" to a new level in the 1990s with songs about death, pain, and perversity. The graphic nature of both his lyrics and stage shows, as well as his bizarre androgynous costumes, have created controversy throughout the U.S. In the memoir *The Long Hard Road Out of Hell*, written with Neil Strauss, Warner describes his troubled teenage years, bouts of drug abuse, and eventual success as a rock star.

# Acknowledgements

Grateful acknowledgement is made to those publishers, photographers, and artists whose work appear with these authors' essays.

## Photographs/Art

Alvar Aalto: CORBIS/Bettmann. Reproduced by permission.

Janine Canan: Mary Golden (caption: Reading from *She Rises like the Sun*, A Room of One's Own, New York, 1989).

## Text

Janine Canan: All poems copyright © Janine Canan and reprinted with permission of the author.

Daniel Keyes: Autobiographical essay excerpted from *Algernon, Charlie and I: A Writer's Journey,* Challcrest Press Books, an imprint of Challenge Press, Inc. (Boca Raton, Florida), 2000. Reprinted with permission of Daniel Keyes.

# A

## AALTO, (Hugo) Alvar (Henrik)  1898-1976

*PERSONAL:* Born February 3, 1898, in Kuortane, near Jyvaskyla, Finland; died May 11, 1976; married Aino Marsio, 1924 (died, 1949); married Elissa Makiniemi, 1952; children: (first marriage) two. *Education:* Helsinki Polytechnic, Dip. Arch., 1921.

*CAREER:* Architect. Exhibition designer in Goteborg, Sweden, and with firm of Tampere and Turku, Finland, 1923-27; private practice, Jyvaskyla, Finland, 1923-27, then in Turku, 1927-33, and Helsinki, 1933-76; Massachusetts Institute of Technology, Cambridge, Massachusetts, professor of experimental architecture, 1946-47. *Military service:* Finnish Army, 1939.

*MEMBER:* Academy of Finland, member, 1955; Akademie der Kunste, Berlin, honorary member; American Institute of Architects, honorary fellow.

*AWARDS, HONORS:* Honorary Royal Designer for Industry, Royal Society of Arts, London; first prize, Finland competition, 1923, for Jyvaskyla Workers' Club; first prize, Finland competition, 1927, for Paimio Sanatorium; first prize, competition, 1927, for Viipuri Municipal Library; first prize, Finland competition, 1936, for Finnish Pavilion, World's Fair, Paris; honorary member, Royal Institute of British Architects, 1937; first prize, Finland competition, 1938, for Finnish Pavilion, World's Fair, New York; Chevalier of the Legion d'Honneur, France, 1939; honorary doctorate, Princeton University, New Jersey, 1947; first prize, Finland competition, 1948, for Forum Redivivum: Cultural and Administrative Centre, Helsinki; honorary doctorate, Technical University of Helsinki, 1949.

First prize, Finland competition, 1950, for Lahti Church; first prize, Finland competition, 1950, for

*Alvar Aalto*

Saynatsalo Town Hall; first prize, Finland competition, 1950, for Pedagogical University, Jyvaskyla; senior fellow, Royal College of Arts, London, 1950; first prize, Finland competition, 1951, for Ruatatalo Office Building, Helsinki; first prize, Finland competition, 1951, for Kuopio Regional Theatre; first prize, Finland competition, 1952, for Church, Seinajoki; first prize, Finland competition, 1955, for Town Hall, Goteborg, Sweden; Gold Medal for Architecture, Royal Institute of British Architects, 1957; honorary member, Sodra Sveriges Byggnadsteniska Samfund, Sweden, 1957; honorary member, American Academy of Arts and Sciences, 1957; Kommendors Korset av Dannebrogen, Denmark, 1957; First Prize, competition project, 1958, for Town

1

Hall, Kiruna, Sweden; Honorary Member, Aceademia di Belle Arti, Venice, 1958; honorary member, Association of Finnish Architects, 1958; honorary fellow, American Institute of Architects, 1958; honorary member, Norske Ariktekterns Landsforbund, Norway, 1959; first prize, Finland competition, 1959, for Town Hall, Seinajoki.

Honorary doctorate, Norges Tekniske Hojskole, Trondheim, Norway, 1960; first prize, competition project, 1961, for Opera House, Essen, West Germany; Sonningpriset, Denmark, 1962; honorary doctorate, Eidgenossische Technische Hochschule, Zurich, 1963; fellow, World Academy of Arts and Sciences, Israel, 1963; Gold Medal, American Institute of Architects, 1963; Gold Cube, Svenska Arkitekters Riksforbund, Sweden, 1963; Cordon del Calli de Oro, Sociedad de Arquitetos, Mexico, 1963; honorary doctorate, Columbia University, 1964; honorary doctorate, Politecnico, Milan, 1964; honorary member, Vastmanlands-Dala Nation, Uppsala, Sweden, 1965; honorary member, Colegio de Arquitetos, Peru, 1965; honorary doctorate, Technische Hochschule, Vienna, 1965; Grand Cross of the Lion of Finland, 1965; Bronzeplakette, Freie Akademie der Kunste, Hamburg, West Germany, 1965; Medaglia d'Oro, City of Florence, 1965; Diplome des Palmes d'Or du Merite de l'Europe, 1966; Helsingin Yliopsiton Ylioppilaskunnan Puheenjohtajiston merkki purppuranauhassa, Finland, 1966; honorary member, Engineering Society of Finland, 1966; honorary member, Bund Deutscher Architekten, Germany, 1966; Grande Ufficiale al Merito, Republic of Italy, 1966; first prize, competition project, 1967, for Protestant Parish Centre, Zurich-Altstetten, Switzerland; Thomas Jefferson Medal, University of Virginia, Charlottesville, Virginia, 1967; Alvar Aalto Medal, Finland, 1967; honorary member, American Academy of Arts and Letters, 1968; honorary member, National Institute of Arts and Letters, United States, 1968; honorary doctorate, University of Jyvaskyla, 1969; Litteris et Artibus Medal, Sweden, 1969; Medaille d'Or, Academie d'Architecture, Paris, 1972; Grand Croix de l'Ordre du Faucon, Iceland, 1972; first prize, competition, 1958, for Art Museum, Aalborg, Denmark (with J.J. Baruel); Tapiola Medal, 1975; Outstanding Architect Award, National Arts Foundation, Liechtenstein, 1975; honorary member, Akademie der Bildenden Kunste, Vienna, 1975; honorary member, Royal Scottish Academy, 1975.

## WRITINGS:

*An Experimental Town,* [Cambridge, MA], 1940.

*Post-War Reconstruction: Rehousing Research in Finland,* [New York City], 1941.

*Synopsis,* [Stuttgart], 1970.

*SIDELIGHTS:* Alvar Aalto was a Finnish architect and designer and one of the most important figures of twentieth-century architecture. With a career that spans half a century, Aalto is considered to be one of the masters of modernism, was a leading member of the International Modern school of architecture, and remains known for his skillful balance of formal abstraction, individual expression, and thoughtful humanism. He is also noted for his careful attention to architectural and applied art details and his consideration of textural elements. His style is distinguished by certain variations from the precepts of International Style, among which include a strong interest in Finland's cultural tradition, its woodland and water landscape, and a commitment to the individual human experience. Early works that exemplify these characteristics include the Muurame Parish Church (1927-29) and the Farmers' Cooperative in Turku (1927-28). His later architectural masterworks include Villa Mairea in Noormarkku, Finland (1938-39), the Baker House Dormitory at the Massachusetts Institute of Technology in Cambridge, Massachusetts (1947-48), and Saynatsalo Town Hall, Finland (1950-52). Aalto was also a master of wooden furniture design, and invented the basic bent plywood process in 1932. Stanley Abercrombie, in *Contemporary Architects,* contends that "throughout the whole scope of this work—from stools, vases, and lighting fixtures to the planning of entire urban areas—it is possible to see not only those personal inclinations and poetic 'complexities' that separate Aalto from the mainstream of the modern movement, but also those touches of thoughtfulness and grace that raise his work above the mainstream of the architecture of any period." William C. Miller, in the *International Dictionary of Architects and Architecture,* finds that "through responsive and responsible design, Aalto was able to create an architecture that was extremely humane, yet profoundly tangible." Edgar J. Kaufmann Jr., in *Interior Design* magazine, writes that "Aalto had a remarkably sure touch, a sense of lyrical enjoyment, and repertory of witty details. This allowed his work to maintain an appealing human scale as well as human warmth. He enlarged the horizon of modern architectural design." Almost ninety percent of his buildings are in Finland.

Aalto was born Hugo Alvar Henrik Aalto on February 3, 1898, in Kuortane, near Jyvaskyla, Finland. In 1916, he enrolled at Helsinki Polytechnic, where he studied architecture and became the protege of Armas Lindgren. Polytechnic teachers Carolus Lindberg and Usko

Nystrom also influenced the young architect. He graduated in 1921 and found a position as an exhibition designer with Arvid Bjerke in Goteborg, Sweden. He found subsequent work in the Finnish cities of Tampere and Turku. In 1923, he began a private architectural practice in Jyvaskyla, Finland. The following year, he married the architect Aino Marsio (1894-1949), who became an equal partner in Aalto's work until her death in 1949. Miller notes that Aino "informed building design as well as the creation of furniture and applied art object, and together husband and wife formed a symbiotic unit, complementing and contrasting one another." Lloyd C. Engelbrecht, in *Contemporary Designers,* maintains that "they worked so closely together that it is impossible to identify their separate roles in their joint projects, or even to be certain which were joint projects and which were not."

Neoclassicism and Northern romanticism were the reigning forces in Scandinavian architecture in the early twentieth century. In the beginning of his career, Aalto subscribed to these forms and executed them with skill and grace. Simplicity of form, the use of classical components, a strong application of native Finnish lumbers, and the existence of well-proportioned spaces mark Aalto's early buildings. These buildings include the Workers Club in Jyvaskyla (1924-25), the Seinajoki Civil Guards Complex (1925), the Jyvaskyla Civil Guards Building (1927), and the Muurame Church (1927-29). These designs exhibit Aalto's mastery of the classical revival that was taking place in Scandinavia at the time. However, even in these early works, Miller asserts, there are hints to Aalto's mature designs, such as courtyards that were central to the organizational plan of the building and "a sense of whimsy and playfulness in his details." Aalto never gave up completely on traditional forms; rather he pared them down to the basic, elemental structures and re-worked them in a way that made sense to the world at the time. Mattick asserts that Aalto possessed a "genius for being lucidly romantic about modern experience."

The Aaltos gained prominence in 1927 with their winning design for the Southwestern Agricultural Cooperative Building in Turku. They moved their office to the cosmopolitan Turku, which provided a connection to the European continent and the avant-garde thinkers who lived there. Soon, they made key associations with various important figures, including Gunnar Asplund, Le Corbusier, Sven Markelius and Laszlo Moholy-Nagy. Aalto was a quick learner, absorbing the principles of contemporary and avant-garde architecture as well as "functionalism" (the Finnish term for modernism). In 1928, Aalto joined the Congres Internationaux d'architecture Moderne (CIAM), an association of architects that exposed him to new techniques and styles. His work at this time demonstrated his rapid ideological growth, and reveals that his connection to CIAM influenced the stylistic changes in his vision. Miller states that the 1927 Southwestern Agricultural Cooperative was a rigid work of classicism, while his 1929 Turun Sanomat Newspaper Building was the first building in Finland to incorporate Le Corbusier's "five points of new architecture," and his Paimio Tuberculosis Sanatorium Housing of 1933 showed the influence of Russian constructivism and the Dutch De Stijl. Engelbrecht maintains that "nowhere were the humanistic intentions of the CIAM group more readily apparent than in Aalto's work and in the high regard its members had for his work."

Aalto also developed a style in furniture-making as well, creating a stackable chair for the Agricultural Cooperative and the famous curvy, bent plywood chair for the Paimio Sanatorium. Engelbrecht contends that after his union with CIAM, Aalto's furniture design became "more daring and original." In the 1930s, the Aaltos founded the Artek furniture company with Mairea Gullichson. Artek designed, manufactured and distributed Aalto's outstanding furniture, including the famous three-legged stacking stool. His early furniture shows the influence of eighteenth and early nineteenth-century styles, but he had a desire to refine and purify the essential forms. Engelbrecht contends that "while there was some direct influence on Aalto from CIAM designers, such as Marcel Breuer, who developed a cantilevered chair, the ability of Breuer and others in the group to create a sense of excitement about experimental furniture was more important." Aalto's plywood stacking chair, patented in 1929, was fitted with legs outside seat area, a design that ingeniously allowed for stacking. In the same year, Aalto designed a bent-plywood chair that consisted of one piece of wood mounted on a cantilevered steel base. Some of his furniture was designed for use in his buildings, such as the Paimio Sanatorium and the Viipuri Municipal Library in Russia. In the periodical *American Craft,* Paul Mattick writes, "There is no modern furniture more warmly elegant that Aalto's chairs and tables." Kurt Andersen, writing in *Time* magazine, maintains that "the best pieces are bareboned but sensuous, simultaneously playful and serene."

Aalto's design for the Paimio Sanatorium was the winning entry of a competition in 1929, and he was contracted to construct the building as well as all of its furnishings and equipment. In this building, Aalto demonstrates his humanistic approach to architecture, displaying a keen understanding of people's needs and how they relate to their interior environment. Abercrombie states that "Aalto was more than a master of artistic form and of intelligent planning; he was the master as well of the details that relate a building successfully to its users. He cared for the proper shape of a handrail, for the convenience of storage elements, for the texture of a wall, and for the delights of natural light." It is clear from a study of the Paimio Sanatorium that Aalto was thoughtful down to the smallest details, considerately addressing the psychological relationship people have with their immediate environment. The lighting fixtures were placed outside the field of vision of someone lying down, while the water taps were designed to flow silently. The plywood scroll chair was made without metal parts to prevent noise, and its lack of upholstery and open structure allowed it to remain as sanitary as possible. It remains one if his finest designs, a perfect balance of form and function. Andersen says that "an extreme, almost quixotic regard for the human factor was what separated Aalto from his more renowned contemporaries."

In 1933, the Aaltos' reputation grew to international prominence, with a furniture exhibition in London organized by the *Architectural Review* and another exhibition at Milan's Triennale. In the same year, they again moved their offices, this time to Helsinki. Aalto's work went through a transitional phase in the mid-1930s, when the twisting curvatures and free-form energy of his furniture design appeared in his architecture. Miller asserts that during this period, "Aalto's work assumed a more tactile and picturesque posture, becoming less machine-like in imagery. Coupled with a rekindled interest in Finnish vernacular building traditions and a concern for the alienated individual within modern mass society, these changes signaled Aalto's movement away from the technical functionalism of the early 1930s to a more personal style." Aalto's position as an important architect was also bolstered by the creation of magnificent constructions in cities on the European continent and in the United States. These include the Finnish pavilions for the Paris World's Fair (1937) and the New York World's Fair (1939), which was a joint commission with Aino. The Finnish Pavilion in Paris showcased a conical skylight for the introduction of natural light into the space, an idea that Aalto revisited later in various forms. It also was designed with an interior court that acted as a primary organizing structure for the rest of the building. This courtyard focus became a fundamental theme throughout Aalto's career. The Finnish Pavilion in New York featured a three-story-high display wall that was rendered in a flowing, undulating form. This sinuosity is a significant compositional element that is somewhat of a signature in Aalto's style. Miller states that "exploring the tectonic possibilities of the undulating surface, he demonstrated a unique sensitivity to the dynamics of the sinuous element in architecture . . . the sinuous element is not merely a building element or spatial construct, but assumes another presence as furniture, glassware, light fixture, and door handle and handrail." Andersen says "an Aalto building is apt to swell or zigzag confoundingly, to have lines and textures that seem more botanical and geological than geometrical."

Aalto's remarkable ability to fuse seemingly disparate themes in his work is well illustrated in his 1935 library in Viipuri, Finland (now Vyborg, Russia). Although much of the library showcases the reductivist abstraction central to modernist ideology, there are elements that highlight themes opposed to modernism, such as non-linear organic forms, sensual and tactile considerations, and additive fabrications. Here, Aalto's sinuous lines are manifested in the surging billows of the ceiling of the library's lecture hall, which was fitted with strips of wood to achieve a powerful acoustical environment. Miller finds that the staircases, landings, and handrails of the Viipuri reading room are "dynamic elements celebrating human action and movement." The organic lines are echoed on other, smaller levels, such as lighting fixtures, door handles, and even glassware. However, the exterior of the building in rendered in a strict rectilinear form well within the functionalistic tenets of International Style. The result is a rigid exterior formalism that provides the shell for a warm, relaxing interior, an unusual and highly effective architectural amalgam that Franz Schultze, in *Art in America,* calls "a highly personal union of intention and effect." A 1938 exhibition at the Museum of Modern Art in New York, organized by John McAndrew, solidified Aalto's international preeminence.

After World War II, Artek was revived and Aalto continued his experiments in furniture design. In 1947, he developed the "Y" leg. In the same year, Aalto started work on his first permanent design in the United States, the Baker House dormitory at the Massachusetts Institute of Technology in Cambridge, Massachusetts. Baker House was built of rough brick, and featured Aalto's signature sinuous lines to give variant views of the adjacent river. Abercrombie asserts that this work "was a clear break with modern purity, unity, and planarity," while Mattick enjoys the "eccentric floor plans and . . . idiosyncratically meandering halls." In 1949, his wife Aino passed away. In the same year, he won another competition, this time for the design of the village center of Saynatsalo. From 1950 to 1952, the construction of Saynatsalo Town Hall took place, under the supervision of a young architect named Elissa Maki-niemi. They married in 1952, and, like his previous marriage, the two forged a close collaboration. She managed Artek's production, which was bolstered by Aalto's development of a five-part upright frame in the shape of a fan in the mid-1950s.

The important buildings of Aalto's mature style include Villa Mairea in Noormarkku (1939), the Town Hall in Saynatsalo (1950-52), the Public Pensions Institute in Helsinki (1952-56), the Ruatatalo Office Building in Helsinki (1953-55), Jyvaskyla Teachers College (1953-56), the Helsinki House of Culture (1955-58), the Church of Three Crosses in Vuoksenniska (1956-58), the Technical Institute in Otaniemi (1956-64), and the Cultural Centre in Wolfsburg, Germany (1960-63). Miller finds that his later works "seem to fuse both classical restraint and romantic exuberance."

Though Aalto eschewed some key elements of modernism to create a highly personal style, Abercrombie argues that "in Aalto's differences from other modernists, we should find not a repudiation of modernism, but a demonstration of the breadth and strength of that movement." Mattick believes that Aalto is "the most mysterious of all the major architects." Aalto was an enigmatic creator, and a study of his work reveals some seeming contradictions that only add to the complexity by which he organized his aesthetic principles. On one hand, he was a staunch supporter of the Finnish cultural tradition; on the other hand, he was a global stylist, finding inspiration from international modernists. On one hand, he was a technical virtuoso, creating new methods to execute formal architectural expressions; on the other hand, he was extremely sensitive to the human element. He loved conventional forms, yet he was aggressively experimental. Schultze finds that "duality is the leitmotif of Aalto's architecture." However, in the final analysis of Aalto's work, it is "an honorable and simple humanism," Abercrombie concludes, "that prevails over any stylistic character." Aalto was an intuitive creator who took cues from all sides and created hybrids that seamlessly synthesized form and function, designs that held as their motivating factor the human individual. Utilitarian, comfortable, and pure expressions of personal style, his work remains that of an ultimately modern master.

*BIOGRAPHICAL/CRITICAL SOURCES:*

*BOOKS*

*Contemporary Architects,* St. James Press (London), 1994.
*Contemporary Designers,* 3rd edition, St. James Press (Detroit, MI), 1997.
*International Dictionary of Architects and Architecture,* Volume 1: *Architects,* St. James Press (Detroit, MI), 1993.
Johnson, Donald Leslie and Donald Langmead, editors, *Makers of Twentieth-Century Modern Architecture,* Greenwood Press (Westport, CT), 1997.

*PERIODICALS*

*American Craft,* June-July, 1998, p. 50.
*Architectural Digest,* February, 1990, p. 50.
*Art in America,* May, 1998, p. 110.
*ARTnews,* January, 1985, p. 97; February, 1998, p. 80.
*Gifts and Decorative Accessories,* April, 1998, p. 56.
*House Beautiful,* September, 1995, p. 46; March 1998, p, N66.
*Interior Design,* June, 1984, p. 272; September, 1984, p. 270; August, 1993, p. 84.
*New York Review of Books,* April 9, 1998, p. 16.
*Progressive Architecture,* April 1998, p, 173.
*Time,* November 19, 1984, p. 138.*

\*      \*      \*

## ABEL, Robert   1913(?)-1987

*PERSONAL:* Born c. 1913; died March 22, 1987, in Miami, FL.

*CAREER:* Professional boxer, producer, director, and screenwriter.

*WRITINGS:*

Playwright, including author of the play *The Samson Slasher.* Author of screenplays, including *Roar of the Crowd* and *Breakdown* (based on his play *The Samson Slasher.*

*OBITUARIES:*

*PERIODICALS*

*Philadelphia Inquirer,* April 1, 1987.*

## ADAMS, Mary (Grace Agnes) 1898-1984

*PERSONAL:* Born March 10, 1898, in Hermitage, Berkshire, England; died May 15, 1984, in London, England; daughter of Edward Bloxham (a farmer) and Catherine Elizabeth Mary (Gunter) Campin; married Vyvyan Adams (politician and reformer) on February 23, 1925; children: one daughter. *Education:* Attended Godolphin School, Salisbury, England; University College, Cardiff, Wales, first-class honors in botany, 1921; Newham College, Cambridge, England, research scholar and Bathurst student, 1921-25.

*CAREER:* Cambridge University, Cambridge, England, tutor and lecturer for extramural and board of Civil Service Studies, 1925-30; British Broadcasting Corp. (BBC), England, adult education officer, 1930-36, producer for television service, 1936-39; Ministry of Information, England, director of Home Intelligence, 1939-41; North American Service Broadcasting, England, producer, 1942-45; BBC-TV, England, worked in arts and sciences programming, 1946-48, head of television talks, 1948-54, assistant to the controller of television programs, 1954-58; deputy chair of Consumers' Association, 1958-1970. Member, Independent Television Authority, 1965-70. Consultant to British Broadcasting Corp.

*AWARDS, HONORS:* Order of the British Empire, 1953; Newnham College, Cambridge, associate, 1956-69; University College, Cardiff, fellow, 1983.

*WRITINGS:*

(Editor) *Science in the Changing World,* Appleton-Century, 1933.
(Editor) *The Modern State,* Allen & Unwin, 1944.

Also author of *Six Talks on Heredity,* 1929; contributor to *Punch.*

*SIDELIGHTS:* A pioneer in the fields of broadcasting and television, Mary Adams was the first female television producer in England. She is remembered for the attention her programs brought to topics otherwise left in the realm of professional literature, including medical and health information.

Adams began her broadcasting career in 1928 when she was a tutor and lecturer at Cambridge University. She developed a series, later published as *Six Talks on Heredity,* for the British Broadcasting Corp. (BBC) and it was during this time that she recognized the educational potential of broadcasting. Within two years, Adams

joined the staff of the BBC as its adult education officer. In 1936, Adams accepted a position as a television producer at the company's new television service. Thus, she became the first woman to hold such a position.

As a producer, Adams developed programming in a variety of areas, including education, politics, talk, and culture. The Television Service's operations ended at the onset of World War II, so Adams worked for North American Service broadcasting. Throughout the war, she produced programs aimed at boosting listeners' morale, such as *Transatlantic Quiz.* Adams returned to the BBC in 1946 and produced shows on cooking, gardening, art, science, and world celebrations.

Considered the first producer to bring medical information via television to the public, Adams developed several health-related series, beginning in 1949 with *A Matter of Life and Death.* Her other medical series included *Matters of Medicine, The Hurt Mind,* and *Your Life in Their Hands.* Adams also produced quiz shows—notably *Animal, Vegetable, Mineral?,* which aired during the 1950s—and children's programs such as *Muffin the Mule* and *Andy Pandy.*

Adams retired from the BBC in 1958, although she continued to serve as a consultant for the company many years after her official departure.

*BIOGRAPHICAL/CRITICAL SOURCES:*

*BOOKS*

*The Dictionary of National Biography, 1981-1985,* Oxford University Press, 1990.

*PERIODICALS*

*Times* (London), May 18, 1984.*

\* \* \*

## AKINS, Zoe 1886-1958

*PERSONAL:* Born October 30, 1886, in Humansville, MO; died October 29, 1958, in Los Angeles, CA; married Hugo Rumbold, 1932 (died, 1932). *Politics:* Republican.

*CAREER:* Playwright, screenwriter, poet, and novelist, c. 1912-47. Writer for Paramount and Metro-Goldwyn-Mayer, 1934-38.

*AWARDS, HONORS:* Pulitzer Prize for Drama, 1935, for *The Old Maid.*

*WRITINGS:*

*Interpretations: A Book of First Poems,* M. Kennerley (New York City), 1912.
*Papa,* M. Kennerley, 1913.
*Cake upon the Waters,* Century (New York City), 1919.
*Declassee, Daddy's Gone a-Hunting,* [and] *Greatness,* Boni & Liveright (New York City), 1923.
*Such a Charming Young Man,* Samuel French (New York City), 1924.
*The Old Maid,* Appleton-Century (New York City), 1935.
*The Little Miracle,* Harper (New York City), 1936.
*The Hills Grow Smaller,* Harper, 1937.
*Forever Young,* Scribners (New York City), 1941.
*Mrs. January and Mr. Ex,* Samuel French, 1948.
*In the Shadow of Parnassus: Zoe Akins's Essays on American Poetry,* edited by Catherine N. Parke, Susquehanna University Press, (Selinsgrove, PA), 1994.

PLAYS

*The Magical City,* produced in New York at Bandbox Theatre, 1915.
*Papa,* produced in New York at Little Theatre, April, 1919.
*Footloose,* produced in New York at Greenwich Village Theatre, May, 1919.
*Declassee,* produced in New York at Empire Theatre, October, 1919.
*Daddy's Gone a-Hunting,* produced in New York at Plymouth Theatre, August, 1921.
*The Varying Shore* produced in New York at Hudson Theatre, December, 1921.
*The Texas Nightingale* produced in New York at Empire Theatre, November, 1922.
*A Royal Fandango* produced in New York at Plymouth Theatre, November, 1923.
*The Moon-Flower,* produced in New York at Astor Theatre, February, 1924.
*First Love,* produced in New York at Booth Theatre, November, 1926.
*The Crown Prince,* produced in New York at Forrest Theatre, March, 1927.
*The Furies,* produced in New York at Shubert Theatre, March, 1928.
*The Love Duel,* produced in New York at Ethel Barrymore Theatre, April, 1929.
*The Greeks Had a Word for It,* produced in New York at Sam H. Harris Theatre, September, 1930.

*The Old Maid,* produced in New York at Empire Theatre, January, 1935.
*O Evening Star!,* produced in New York at Empire Theatre, January, 1936.

OTHER

*Sarah and Son* (screenplay), Paramount, 1930.
(With Doris Anderson and G. Morris) *Anybody's Woman* (screenplay), Paramount, 1930.
*The Right to Love* (screenplay), Paramount, 1930.
*Women Love Once* (screenplay), Paramount, 1931.
(With Samuel Hoffenstein) *Once a Lady* (screenplay), Paramount, 1931.
*Working Girls* (screenplay), Paramount, 1931.
*Christopher Strong* (screenplay), RKO, 1933.
*Outcast Lady* (screenplay), Metro-Goldwyn-Mayer, 1934.
(With Frances Marion and James Hilton) *Camille* (screenplay), Metro-Goldwyn-Mayer, 1936.
(Author of dialogue) *Accused,* Criterion/United Artists, 1936.
(With Joseph Anthony) *Lady of Secrets* (screenplay) Columbia, 1936.
*The Toy Wife* (screenplay), Metro-Goldwyn-Mayer, 1938.
*Zaza* (screenplay), Paramount, 1938.
(With Marguerite Roberts) *Desire Me* (screenplay), Metro-Goldwyn-Mayer, 1947.

*SIDELIGHTS:* Author of the Pulitzer Prize-winning play *The Old Maid* (1936), Zoe Akins was known for her comedies in both of her writing careers: she wrote for stage and screen for two decades. Starting in the 1920s, she had sixteen plays on Broadway in as many years. She was skilled at adapting plays and novels for the screen, and several of her plays were made into movies by others. Centered on female characters, and favoring glamorous, elegant settings, her plays and films regarded women's difficulties and peccadillos with a shrewd, humorous eye.

Born into a wealthy Republican family in Missouri, Akins became entranced with the stage from seeing touring companies in St. Louis theaters, and started writing plays when she was only twelve. Her play *Papa,* a comedy in three acts, toured the country before its brief, twelve-performance stint at the Little Theater in New York City in 1919. By the time *Papa* reached New York, Akins had already seen the Washington Square Players perform her one-act verse melodrama *The Magical City* at the Bandbox Theater (1915/16 season).

Akins first tasted success with the play *Declassee,* a society drama produced in 1919 at the Empire Theater and starring Ethel Barrymore. Barrymore played Lady Helen Haden, who calls herself "the last of the mad Varricks" and believes in living recklessly; it was one of Barrymore's most popular roles. The play, which explores the effects of divorce on a woman, draws from trashy magazine romances as well as the writings of Elinor Glyn and Saki. It was adapted to screen as *Her Private Life* in 1929.

On the heels of *Declassee* came *Daddy's Gone a-Hunting* (1921), *The Varying Shore* (1921), *The Moon-Flower* (1924) (filmed by Paramount as *Eve's Secret* in 1925), and *The Furies* (1928). *The Greeks Had a Word for It* (1930), a comedy about three models seeking wealthy husbands, was adapted for the big screen by Sidney Howard as *The Greeks Had a Word for Them* (1932). *How to Marry a Millionaire* (1953) was based upon both *Greeks* and the play *Loco* by Dale Eunson and Katharine Albert.

Akins won the 1935 Pulitzer Prize for drama for her play *The Old Maid,* adapted from Edith Wharton's novella about an unmarried mother and her daughter. Starring Judith Anderson and Helen Menken, it opened at the Empire Theater, New York, in January 1935. In a mixed review, a *New York Times* reviewer called it "a cautious adaptation rather than a vigorous one." In *Books,* W. P. Eaton observed that Akins compensated for being unable to present Wharton's drily humorous prose style "by giving to the two leading actresses opportunities for portraying cool social distinction." When Akins won the Pulitzer—a highly controversial decision—dissenting critics formed the Drama Critics Circle to present their own awards. Akins also wrote the film version starring Bette Davis and Miriam Hopkins.

Within two years of moving to California in 1928, Akins was under contract to Paramount as a screenwriter. Her first screenplay was *Anybody's Woman* (1930), for which she shared credit with G. Morris and Doris Anderson; it starred Ruth Chatterton as a chorus girl married to a wealthy, no-good lawyer. Four of Atkins' first five screenplays were written for Chatterton, who had just come to film from the stage. In *Sarah and Son* (1930), Chatterton played a self-sacrificing woman who sells her baby to a wealthy oil man. And in *The Right to Love* (1930), Chatterton plays two roles: a mother who prevents her daughter from marrying the country boy she loves, and the daughter, who, when she grows up, wants her own daughter to marry for love.

Akins adapted her own *Daddy's Gone a-Hunting* into the screenplay *Women Love Once* (1931). She also adapted *Christopher Strong* (RKO, 1933) from the best-selling novel by Gilbert Frankau. The film, featuring Katherine Hepburn (as an aviatrix in love with a married man) and directed by Dorthy Arzner, was not a great success. Hepburn had fared better in the film based on Atkins' play *Morning Glory,* earlier in the same year; she won her first Academy Award for the role of a naive, egotistical young actress from Kansas, eager to become a star in New York. In addition to collaborating on *Christopher Strong,* director Arzner and writer Akins worked together on *Sarah and Son, Anybody's Woman, and Working Girls* (1931).

Akins moved to Metro-Goldwyn-Mayer, where her first script was *Outcast Lady* (1934), adapted from the novel *The Green Hat* (1924) by Michael Arlin. The novel had already been adapted for the screen in 1928 as the silent film *A Woman of Affairs,* starring Greta Garbo. The story of *Outcast Lady,* which starred Constance Bennett, was considerably weakened by changes made to accommodate the censorship laws imposed by the Hays Office. In 1936, Akins collaborated on the adaptation of Alexandre Dumas *fils' Camille.* The film, directed by George Cukor, starred Greta Garbo as romantic heroine Marguerite Gauthier and Robert Taylor as her lover Armand Duval. It was an enormous box-office success, and was also popular with the critics. Akins then wrote *The Toy Wife* (1938) for Luise Rainer, who had just won Academy Awards for her performances in *The Great Ziegfeld* (1936) and *The Good Earth* (1937). In *The Toy Wife,* Rainer plays a frivolous wife in New Orleans in the 1880s.

Cukor described Akins as one of America's most gifted artists, and the two collaborated on several more occasions. Akins teamed up with Cukor again at Paramount for *Zaza* (1938), starring Claudette Colbert in the third film version of the play. They also worked together on the Metro-Goldwyn-Mayer production of *Pride and Prejudice* (1940), but Cukor was replaced by Robert Z. Leonard and Akins' script was rewritten by Aldous Huxley and Jane Murfin, so she was not credited as a writer. After a six-hear hiatus from the screen, Akins collaborated on *Desire Me* (1947), a Greer Garson vehicle directed by Cukor. Adapted from the novel by Leonhard Frank, it is about a man who pretends his best friend is dead so he can take over his wife and property. Cukor was replaced by Mervyn LeRoy, though neither received screen credit as director.

Akins' talents as a writer extended to poetry and fiction. She published her first poems in the *St. Louis Mirror,* and in 1912 collected her poetry in *Interpretations: A Book of First Poems*. Of her novel *Cake upon the Waters* (1919), about a young widow who becomes cold and stingy when she inherits a fortune, a reviewer for the *New York Evening Post* observed, "Her people are not interesting and the things that happen to them are more exciting than credible. But there is a sense of adventure." In the novel *Forever Young* (1941), a woman reminisces about her first year at school in 1900 as the youngest girl in the class, and recalls how she helped save the school from disgrace. In the *New York Times*, L. M. Field praised it as "very well written, sensitive, intelligent and mature," while in *Books*, Anne Brooks admired the "charming background of the formal old school" but said, "The characters move through [the book] like the dim, romantic figures of a dated novel . . . their emotions and thoughts are so completely conventional that there is nothing to make them understandable as people."

Akins did not receive as much recognition for her screenwriting as she did for her plays, although she appeared to have dedicated herself equally to each. Her light comedies and social dramas failed to break artistic molds: as a critic for *Freeman* observed in a review of a collection of three of her plays, *Declassee, Daddy's Gone a-Hunting,* and *Greatness,* "She never bends completely to the demands of her plots, and still she lacks the courage to flaunt them entirely"; the reviewer called this tendency "at once her bulwark and her undoing." But in Akins' best works, her witty dialogue enabled some of the finest actresses of the 1920s and 1930s to show off their talents, and took an irreverent poke at women's relationships with men, money, family, and each other.

*BIOGRAPHICAL/CRITICAL SOURCES:*

*BOOKS*

*Dictionary of Literary Biography,* Volume 26: *American Screenwriters,* Gale (Detroit, MI), 1994.
*Women Filmmakers and Their Films,* St. James Press (Detroit, MI), 1998.

*PERIODICALS*

*Books,* May 19, 1935, p. 11; April 27, 1941, p. 8.
*Freeman,* November 7, 1923.
*New York Times,* July 28, 1935, p. 17; April 27, 1941, p. 7.
*New York Evening Post,* November 8, 1919, p. 12.*

---

## AL-BISATIE, Mohamed   1937-

*PERSONAL:* Born November 19, 1937, in Sharqiya Province, Egypt; son of Ibrahim (a teacher) and Insaf (Rustum) Al-Bisatie; married Sanaa Abdel Aziz, 1970; children: Rasha, Hisham, Yasser. *Ethnicity:* "Egyptian." *Education:* University of Cairo, B.A. (commerce and accountancy), 1960. *Religion:* Muslim.

*ADDRESSES: Home*—13 Sharia al-Baramika, al-Hayy al-Sabie, Medinat Nasr, Cairo, Egypt.

*CAREER:* Government Auditor's Office, Cairo, Egypt, auditor, 1961-97, undersecretary of state, 1994-97. *Military service:* One year's compulsory service, 1965.

*MEMBER:* Writers Union of Egypt.

*AWARDS, HONORS:* State prize for best novel of 1994.

*WRITINGS:*

*SHORT STORIES*

*Al-Kibar wa-'l-Sighur* (title means "The Old and the Young"), 1967.
*Hadith min al-Tabiq al-Thalith* (title means "Talk from the Third Floor"), 1970.
*Ahlam Rijal Qisar al-Umr* (title means "Dreams of Men Who Didn't Live Long"), 1984.
*Hadha Ma-Kan* (title means "This Is What Happened"), 1988.
*Munhana al-Nahr* (title means "The Turn of the River"), 1992
*Daw' Da'if la Yakshif Shay'a* (title means "Faint Light That Reveals Nothing"), 1993
*Sa'at Maghrib* (title means "The Hour of Sunset"), 1996.
*A Last Glass of Tea and Other Stories,* translated by Denys Johnson-Davies, Lynne Rienner (Boulder, CO), 1998.

Also author of *On the Brink* (stories), American University of Cairo Press.

*NOVELS*

*Al-Tajir wa-l-Naqqash* (title means "The Merchant and the Painter"), 1976.
*Al-Ayyam al-Sa'bah* (title means "Difficult Days"), 1979.
*Al-Maqha al-Zujaji* (title means "The Glass Cafe"), 1979.

*Buyut Wara' al-Ashjar,* 1993, translation by Johnson-Davies published as

*Houses behind the Trees,* University of Texas Press (Austin, TX), 1998.

*Sakhab al-Buhayrah* (title means "The Fury of the Lack"), 1994.

*Aswat al-Layl* (title means "Voices of the Night"), 1998.

*Wa-Ya'ti al-Qitar* (title means " . . . And the Train Comes"), 1999.

Also author of other novels and short story collections. Chief editor of the series "Literary Voices." Works have been translated into Spanish, Italian, and French.

*ADAPTATIONS: Houses behind the Trees* has been filmed.

*WORK IN PROGRESS:* An autobiography.

\*     \*     \*

## ALDANOV, M. A.
### See ALDANOV, Mark (Alexandrovich)

\*     \*     \*

## ALDANOV, Mark (Alexandrovich) 1886(?)-1957
### (M. A. Aldanov, Mark Alexandrovich Landau, Mark Alexandrovich Landau-Aldanov)

*PERSONAL:* Original surname, Landau; some sources transliterate the middle name as "Aleksandrovich"; born November 7, 1886 (some sources cite 1889), in Kiev, Russia; immigrated to France, 1919, and to the United States, 1941; died of a heart ailment, February 25, 1957, in Nice, France. *Education:* Earned university degrees in chemistry and law.

*CAREER:* Novelist.

*WRITINGS:*

(Under name Mark Alexandrovich Landau-Aldanov) *Lenin,* translated from the French by Beatrice Sorchan, Dutton (New York City), 1922.

*Devyatoye termidora* (novel; first volume of the tetralogy "The Thinker"), 1923, published with *Chertov most,* Moskovskiaei raboshiaei (Moscow), 1989,

translation published as *The Ninth Thermidor,* 1926.

*Svyataya Yelena, malenki ostrov* (novel; second volume of "The Thinker"), 1923, published with *Zagovor,* Moskovskiaei raboshiaei, 1989, translation published as *St. Helena, Little Island,* 1924.

*Chertov most* (novel; third volume of "The Thinker"), 1925, published with *Devyatoye termidora,* Moskovskiaei raboshiaei, 1989, translation published as *The Devil's Bridge,* 1928.

*Zagovor* (novel; title means "The Conspiracy;" fourth volume of "The Thinker"), 1927, published with *Svyatava Yelena, malenki ostrov,* Moskovskiaei raboshiaei, 1989.

*Preiyamoe deaeistvie* (stories), with commentary by Andreeiya Chernysheva, Novosti (Moscow), 1994.

*Portrety,* with commentary by Chernysheva, Novosti, 1994.

*Nachalo konyetisa,* with commentary by Chernysheva, Novosti, 1995.

*Zhivi kak khochesh',* with commentary by Chernysheva, Novosti, 1995.

*Ocherki* (essays), with commentary by Chernysheva, Novosti, 1995.

Other writings include *Desyataya Simfoniya* (nonfiction), 1931, translation published as *The Tenth Symphony,* 1950; *Nachalo kontsa* (novel), 1939, translation published as *The Fifth Seal,* 1943; *Mogila voina* (nonfiction), 1940, translation published as *For Thee the Best,* 1945; *A Night at the Airport,* 1949; *The Escape,* 1950; and *Nightmare and Dawn,* 1957. Some writings appear under the names M. A. Aldanov and Mark Alexandrovich Landau.

*BIOGRAPHICAL/CRITICAL SOURCES:*

BOOKS

Lee, C. Nicholas, *The Novels of Mark Aleksandrovich Aldanov,* Mouton (The Hague, Netherlands), 1969.

*PERIODICALS*

*Boston Transcript,* June 10, 1922, p. 4.
*Freeman,* April 5, 1922.
*Literary Review,* March 25, 1922, p. 524.
*New York Times,* July 9, 1922, p. 3.
*Outlook,* July 10, 1922.

*OBITUARIES:*

*PERIODICALS*

*New York Times,* February 26, 1957.

*Times* (London), February 26, 1957.*

\* \* \*

## ALFORD, Terry (L.) 1945-

*PERSONAL:* Born October 7, 1945, in Mobile, AL; son of L. L. and Bess (Horne) Alford; married Jeanette Stewart, 1969; children: Jane, David, Carey. *Education:* Mississippi State University, B.A., 1966, M.A., 1967, Ph.D., 1970. *Avocational interests:* Swimming, collecting rare books and historical documents, hiking.

*ADDRESSES: Office*—Department of History, Northern Virginia Community College, 8333 Little River Turnpike, Annandale, VA 22003. *Agent*—Wendy Weil Agency, 232 Madison Ave., Suite 1300, New York, NY 10016. *E-mail*—talford@nv.cc.va.us

*CAREER:* Students' College of Arts and Sciences, Washington, DC, professor of history and trustee, 1971-72; Northern Virginia Community College, Annandale, professor of history, 1972—. Georgetown University, guest curator, Lincoln Assassination Exhibit, 1985-86, lecturer, 1986—. Expert witness, Booth Exhumation Trial, Baltimore, MD, 1995. Founding board member, Lincoln Institute of the Mid-Atlantic. Consultant to Time-Life Books' "Civil War" series, and to ABC News on assassination topics.

*MEMBER:* Manuscript Society, Organization of American Historians, Surratt Society, Lincoln Group of DC.

*WRITINGS:*

*Prince among Slaves* (biography), Harcourt (New York City), 1977.
(Editor and author of introduction) Asia Booth Clarke, *John Wilkes Booth: A Sister's Memoir,* University Press of Mississippi (Jackson, MS), 1996.

Also author of *This One Mad Act,* 1985. Contributor to history journals. Member of editorial board, *Lincoln Herald.*

*WORK IN PROGRESS:* A biography of John Wilkes Booth.

*SIDELIGHTS:* Terry Alford told *CA:* "I enjoy biography more than any other form of history. It is essentially story-telling, and that's what first gathered the villagers around the fire many years ago."

*BIOGRAPHICAL/CRITICAL SOURCES:*

PERIODICALS

*Best Sellers,* February, 1978.
*New Yorker,* January 16, 1978.
*Washington Post Book World,* December 18, 1977.

\* \* \*

## ANDERSON, Poul (William) 1926-
### (A. A. Craig, Michael Karageorge, Winston P. Sanders)

*PERSONAL:* Born November 25, 1926, in Bristol, PA; son of Anton William and Astrid (Hertz) Anderson; married Karen J. M. Kruse, December 12, 1953; children: Astrid May. *Education:* University of Minnesota, B.S., 1948.

*ADDRESSES: Home*—3 Las Palomas, Orinda, CA 94563. *Agent*—Chichak, Inc., 1040 First Ave., New York, NY 10022.

*CAREER:* Freelance writer, except for occasional temporary jobs, 1948—.

*MEMBER:* Institute for Twenty-First Century Studies, Science Fiction Writers of America (president, 1972-73), American Association for the Advancement of Science, Mystery Writers of America (northern California regional vice chair, 1959) Scowrers (secretary, 1957-62), Baker Street Irregulars, Elves, Gnomes, and Little Men's Science Fiction Chowder and Marching Society, Society for Creative Anachronism.

*AWARDS, HONORS:* First annual Cock Robin Mystery Award, 1959, for *Perish by the Sword;* Guest of Honor, World Science Fiction Convention, 1959; Hugo Award, World Science Fiction Convention, for best short fiction, 1961, for "The Longest Voyage," 1964, for "No Truce with Kings," 1969, for "The Sharing of Flesh," 1972, for "The Queen of Air and Darkness," 1973, for "Goat Song," 1979, for "Hunter's Moon," and 1982, for "The Saturn Game"; Nebula Award, Science Fiction Writers of America, 1971, for "The Queen of Air and Darkness," 1972, for "Goat Song," and 1981, for "The Saturn Game"; August Derleth Award, British Fantasy Society, 1974, for *Hrolf Kraki's Saga;* Mythopoeic Award, 1975; J. R. R. Tolkien Memorial Award and Gandalf Award, Grand Master of Fantasy, World Science Fiction Convention, 1978.

*Poul Anderson*

## WRITINGS:

*Perish by the Sword* (novel), Macmillan, 1959.
*Murder in Black Letter* (novel), Macmillan, 1960.
*The Golden Slave* (novel), Avon, 1960.
*Rogue Sword* (novel), Avon, 1960.
*Murder Bound* (novel), Macmillan, 1962.
*Is There Life on Other Worlds?* (nonfiction), Crowell, 1963.
*Thermonuclear Warfare* (nonfiction), Monarch, 1963.
*The Infinite Voyage: Man's Future in Space* (nonfiction), Macmillan, 1969.

### SCIENCE FICTIQN NOVELS

*Vault of the Ages,* Winston, 1952, reprinted, Avon, 1969.
*Brain Wave,* Ballantine, 1954, reprinted, Ballantine, 1985.
*The Broken Sword,* Abelard, 1954, reprinted, Baen Books, 1988.
*No World of Their Own* (bound with *The 1,000 Year Plan* by Isaac Asimov), Ace Books, 1955, published separately as *The Long Way Home,* Gregg, 1978.

*Planet of No Return,* Ace Books, 1956, published as *Question and Answer,* 1978.
*Star Ways,* Avalon, 1957, published as *The Peregrine,* Ace Books, 1978.
*War of the Wing-Men,* Ace Books, 1958, published as *The Man Who Counts,* 1978.
*The Snows of Ganymede,* Ace Books, 1958.
*Virgin Planet,* Avalon, 1959.
*The Enemy Stars,* Lippincott, 1959.
*The War of Two Worlds,* Ace Books, 1959.
*We Claim These Stars!,* (bound with *The Planet Killers* by Robert Silverberg), Ace Books, 1959.
*Earthman, Go Home!,* (bound with *To the Tombaugh Station* by Wilson Tucker), Ace Books, 1960.
*The High Crusade,* Doubleday, 1960.
*Twilight World,* Torquil, 1960.
*Mayday Orbit,* (bound with *No Man's World* by Kenneth Bulmer), Ace Books, 1961.
*Three Hearts and Three Lions,* Doubleday, 1961.
*Orbit Unlimited,* Pyramid Publications, 1961.
*The Makeshift Rocket,* Ace Books, 1962.
*After Doomsday,* Ballantine, 1962.
*Shield,* Berkley Publishing, 1963.
*Let the Spacemen Beware!* (bound with *The Wizard of Starship Poseidon* by Kenneth Bulmer), Ace Books, 1963, published separately as *The Night Face,* 1978.
*Three Worlds to Conquer,* Pyramid Publications, 1964.
*The Star Fox,* Doubleday, 1965.
*The Corridors of Time,* Doubleday, 1965.
*Ensign Flandry,* Chilton, 1966.
*World without Stars,* Ace Books, 1966.
*Satan's World,* Doubleday, 1969.
*The Rebel Worlds,* Signet, 1969, published in England as *Commander Flandry,* Severn House, 1978.
*A Circus of Hells,* Signet, 1970.
*Tau Zero,* Doubleday, 1970.
*The Byworlder,* Signet, 1971.
*Operation Chaos,* Doubleday, 1971.
*The Dancer from Atlantis,* Doubleday, 1971.
*There Will Be Time,* Doubleday, 1972.
*Hrolf Kraki's Saga,* Ballantine, 1973, reprinted, Baen Books, 1988.
*The Day of Their Return,* Doubleday, 1973.
*The People of the Wind,* Signet, 1973.
*Fire Time,* Doubleday, 1974.
*A Knight of Ghosts and Shadows,* Doubleday, 1974, published in England as *Knight Flandry,* Severn House, 1980.
*A Midsummer Tempest,* Doubleday, 1974.
(With Gordon Ecklund) *Inheritors of Earth,* Chilton, 1974.

*The Worlds of Poul Anderson* (contains *Planet of No Return, The War of Two Worlds,* and *World without Stars*), Ace Books, 1974.

(With Gordon Dickson) *Star Prince Charlie* (juvenile), Putnam, 1975.

*The Winter of the World,* Doubleday, 1975.

*Mirkheim,* Berkley Publishing, 1977.

*The Avatar,* Putnam, 1978.

*Two Worlds* (contains *Question and Answer* and *World without Stars*), Gregg, 1978.

*The Merman's Children,* Putnam, 1979.

*A Stone in Heaven,* Ace Books, 1979.

*The Devil's Game,* Pocket Books, 1980.

*The Road of the Sea Horse,* Zebra Books, 1980.

*Conan the Rebel #5,* Bantam (New York City), 1980.

(With Mildred D. Broxon) *The Demon of Scattery,* Ace Books, 1980.

*The Last Viking: Book One, The Golden Horn,* Zebra Books, 1980.

*The Sign of the Raven,* Zebra Books, 1980.

*Cold Victory,* Pinnacle Books, 1982.

*The Gods Laughed,* Pinnacle Books, 1982.

*Maurai and Kith,* Tor Books (New York City), 1982.

*New America,* Pinnacle Books, 1983.

*The Long Night,* Pinnacle Books, 1983.

*Orion Shall Rise,* Pocket Books, 1983.

*Agent of Vega,* Ace Books, 1983.

*Conflict,* Pinnacle Books, 1983.

*Time Patrolman,* Pinnacle Books, 1983.

*Bat-Twenty-One,* Bantam, 1983.

(With Gordon Dickson) *Hoka!,* Simon & Schuster, 1983.

(With wife, Karen Anderson) *The Unicorn Trade,* Tor Books, 1984.

*Dialogue with Darkness,* Tor Books, 1985.

*The Game of Empire,* Pocket Books, 1985.

*The Psychotechnic League,* Tor Books, 1985.

(With wife, Karen Anderson) *The King of Ys,* Baen Books, Book 1: *Roma Mater,* 1986, Book 2: *Gallicenae,* 1988, Book 3: *Dahut,* 1988, Book 4: *The Dog and the Wolf,* 1988; four volumes revised and published together, Simon & Schuster, 1996.

*The Year of the Ransom,* Walker & Co., 1988.

*Conan the Rebel #17,* Ace Books, c. 1989.

*No Truce with Kings* (bound with *Ship of Shadows* by Fritz Leiber), Tor Books, 1989.

*The Boat of a Million Years,* Tor Books, 1989.

*The Shield of Time,* Tor Books, 1990.

*Inconstant Star* (contains "The Man-Kzin Wars" and "Man-Kzin Wars III"), Baen Books, 1991.

*Murasaki: A Novel in Six Parts,* Bantam, 1992.

*A Harvest of Stars,* Tor Books, 1993.

*Kinship with the Stars,* Severn House, 1993.

*The Stars Are Also Fire,* Tor Books, 1994.

*Harvest the Fire,* Tor Books, 1995.

*The Fleet of Stars,* Tor Books, 1997.

*War of the Gods,* Tor Books, 1997.

*Operation Luna,* Tom Doherty Associates, 1999.

*SHORT STORY COLLECTIONS*

(With Gordon Dickson) *Earthman's Burden,* Gnome Press, 1957.

*Guardians of Time,* Ballantine, 1960, revised edition, Pinnacle Books, 1981.

*Strangers from Earth: Eight Tales of Vaulting Imagination,* Ballantine, 1961.

*Un-Man and Other Novellas* (bound with *The Makeshift Rocket*), Ace Books, 1962.

*Trader to the Stars,* Doubleday, 1964.

*Time and Stars,* Doubleday, 1964.

*Agent of the Terran Empire* (includes *We Claim These Stars!*), Chilton, 1965.

*Flandry of Terra* (includes *Earthman, Go Home!* and *Mayday Orbit*), Chilton, 1965.

*The Trouble Twisters,* Doubleday, 1966.

*The Horn of Time,* Signet, 1968.

*Beyond the Beyond,* Signet, 1969.

*Seven Conquests: An Adventure in Science Fiction,* Macmillan, 1969.

*Tales of the Flying Mountains,* Macmillan, 1970.

*The Queen of Air and Darkness and Other Stories,* Signet, 1973.

*The Many Worlds of Poul Anderson,* Chilton, 1974, published as *The Book of Poul Anderson,* DAW Books, 1975.

*Homeward and Beyond,* Doubleday, 1975.

*Homebrew,* National Education Field Service Association Press, 1976.

*The Best of Poul Anderson,* Pocket Books, 1976.

*The Earth Book of Stormgate,* Putnam, 1978.

*The Night Face and Other Stories,* Gregg, 1978.

*The Dark between the Stars,* Berkley Publications, 1980.

*Explorations,* Pinnacle Books, 1981.

*Fantasy,* Pinnacle Books, 1981.

*Winners,* Pinnacle Books, 1981.

*Starship,* Pinnacle Books, 1982.

*Past Times,* Tor Books, 1984.

*Alight in the Void,* Tor Books, 1991.

*The Armies of Elfland* (contains "The Queen of Air and Darkness"), Tor Books, 1992.

*OTHER*

(Adaptor) Christian Molbech, *The Fox, the Dog, and the Griffin,* Doubleday, 1966.

(Author of introduction) *The Best of L. Sprague de Camp,* Ballantine, 1978.

*Time Wars* (short stories), Tor Books, 1986.

*Space Folk* (short stories), Baen Books, 1989.

*The Time Patrol* (contains short stories and novella "Star of the Sea"), Tor Books, 1991.

(With wife, Karen Anderson) *The Night Fantastic* (anthology), DAW, 1991.

*All One Universe* (contains short stories, essays, and a play), Tor Books, 1996.

Contributor to books, including *All about the Future,* edited by Martin Greenberg, Gnome Press, 1955; *The Day the Sun Stood Still: Three Original Novellas of Science Fiction,* Thomas Nelson, 1972; *Science Fiction: Today and Tomorrow,* edited by Reginald Bretnor, Harper, 1974; *The Craft of Science Fiction,* edited by Bretnor, Harper, 1976; *Turning Points: Essays on the Art of Science Fiction,* edited by Damon Knight, Harper, 1977; *Swords against Darkness,* edited by Andrew J. Offutt, Zebra Books, Volume 1, 1977, Volume 3, 1978, Volume 4, 1979; *The Blade of Conan,* edited by L. Sprague de Camp, Ace Books, 1979; *Space Wars* (short stories), edited by Charles Waugh and Martin H. Greenberg, Tor Books, 1988.

Also contributor to anthologies, including *Possible Worlds of Science Fiction,* edited by Groff Conklin, Vanguard, 1951; *A Treasury of Great Science Fiction,* edited by Anthony Boucher, Doubleday, 1959; *The Hugo Winners,* edited by Isaac Asimov, Doubleday, 1962; *Space, Time, and Crime,* edited by Miriam Allen de Ford, Paperback Library, 1964; *Masters of Science Fiction,* Belmont Books, 1964; *The Science Fiction Hall of Fame,* edited by Ben Bova, Doubleday, 1973; *The Future at War,* edited by Bretnor, Ace Books, 1979. Contributor of short stories, some under pseudonyms A. A. Craig and Winston P. Sanders, to *Magazine of Fantasy and Science Fiction, Galaxy, Analog Science Fiction/Science Fact, Isaac Asimov's Science Fiction Magazine,* and other publications.

*SIDELIGHTS:* Although he is often referred to as a writer of "hard" science fiction—science fiction with a scrupulously accurate scientific basis—Poul Anderson is also known for his creation of plausible fantasy worlds, often based on Nordic mythology. His "recognition of the inevitability of sorrow and death and of the limitations of human powers (but not human spirit) in the face of the immense inhumanity of the universe," Russell Letson of the *Science Fiction and Fantasy Book Review* believes, "lifts Anderson's fiction above its flaws." "It is increasingly clear," writes Michael W. McClintock in the *Dictionary of Literary Biography,*

"that [Anderson] is one of the five or six most important writers to appear during the science-fiction publishing boom of the decade following the end of World War II."

The novel *Tau Zero* is one of Anderson's best works of hard science fiction. It presents a simple scientific possibility—a space ship uncontrollably accelerating at a steady one gravity—and develops the consequences in a relentlessly logical and scientifically plausible manner. Sandra Miesel, writing in her *Against Time's Arrow: The High Crusade of Poul Anderson,* finds the novel's structure a key to its effectiveness. "To convey the numbing immensities of the time and distance traversed [during the novel]," Miesel writes, "Anderson begins slowly, letting a few hours elapse at the normal rate in the first chapter. Thereafter, the tempo quickens at an exponential rate until eons fleet by in heartbeats and the reader unquestioningly accepts all the marvels described." James Blish calls *Tau Zero* "the ultimate 'hard' science fiction novel." Blish goes on, in his review of the book for the *Magazine of Fantasy and Science Fiction,* to say that "everybody else who has been trying to write this kind of thing can now fold up his tent and creep silently away. . . . Overall, [*Tau Zero*] is a monument to what a born novelist and poet can do with authentic scientific materials. And as is usual with recent Anderson, the poet is as important as the novelist."

Anderson's scientific accuracy is reflected in the carefully constructed backgrounds he creates for his stories. He has set about fifty of his science fiction novels and short stories in a consistent "future history" of his own devising. This history concerns the exploration of outer space by the *Technic Civilization,* and each story explores a different event within this history. Although other science fiction writers have also used the future history idea, McClintock believes Anderson "has utilized it more extensively—and arguably to better advantage—than any other writer."

In his fantasy works, too, Anderson constructs imaginary worlds that are logical and coherent. These worlds are often based on Nordic sagas or contain elements from Nordic history. His prize-winning story "The Queen of Air and Darkness" is set in an arctic wilderness that is, Miesel states, "a scientifically plausible Elfland." The story is included in the anthology of eight stories published under the title *The Armies of Elfland,* which Karen L. Ellis in *Kliatt* calls an "entertaining anthology." In *Operation Chaos,* Miesel notes, magic is "a perfectly rational, orderly activity." The novel *The Merman's Children* is based on a medieval Danish ballad about the decline of the world of Faerie. Set in Denmark in the Middle Ages, the novel tells of the struggle between the mermen and the Christian church. The conflict arises because the mermen, an older and less developed species, do not possess souls. "One might guess the book," writes Gerald Jonas in the *New York Times Book Review,* "to be either a fantasy or a 'historical' novel. Yet Poul Anderson . . . has produced a genuine hybrid." Anderson, McClintock states, "is consistent and logical in constructing backgrounds." Anderson's "sensibility is mythic," McClintock further states, "and strongly influenced by the Nordic Edda and sagas that are part of his heritage. . . . At his best, Anderson evokes responses, not unlike those appropriate to *Beowulf* or the *Volsungasaga.*"

The three adventures in *The Shield of Time* also show Anderson's interest in ancient and medieval history. They take place in 200 B.C., the Pleistocene era, and 12th-century Naples. For this book, Anderson resurrects the "Time Patrol" (a squad he first created in the 1950s), whose job it is to travel through time to make sure history is not tampered with. "Anderson play[s] nicely with the idea that history may pivot on one lone individual, though the identity of that individual may not be at all obvious," notes Tom Easton in *Analog Science Fiction/Science Fact.* Tom Whitmore remarks in *LOCUS:* "Anderson has looked closely at several historical points where a small nudge would have made a big difference, and his historical settings (as always) feel grittily believable. But the story struck me as ultimately futile." A new novella, "Star of the Sea," and Anderson's other stories about the Time Patrol are compiled in the book *The Time Patrol.* The stories relate the people and places throughout history that agent Manse Everard encounters during his career. "There is an indefinable 'period' feel to the earlier tales, a 1950s sensibility different from the bleak . . . vision of . . . the stories from the 1980s," Russell Letson contends in *LOCUS.*

Over the years, Anderson has dealt with "overpopulation, conflict between cultures, humankind's biological imperatives, and depleted natural resources," writes Michael Pottow in the *Science Fiction and Fantasy Book Review,* "but in the final analysis each of the stories is about people." A recurring theme in his work is the importance of individual liberty and free will. Anderson admits to Jeffey M. Elliot in *Science Fiction Voices #2:* "If I preach at all, it's probably in the direction of individual liberty, which is a theme that looms large in my work." Miesel sees Anderson as primarily concerned with the question, "How should mortal man in a finite universe act? Rejecting passivity, [Anderson]

asserts that free action is both possible and necessary. . . . Mortals must resist entropy in both its guises, tyrannical stasis or anarchic chaos. The fight is all the more valiant for its utter hopelessness."

In *Harvest of Stars* pilot Kyra Davis travels to North America to rescue her boss, Anson Guthrie, who now exists as a downloaded personality. The continent is governed by religious fanatics known as Avantists, aiming to take over Fireball Enterprises. The book also introduces Earth's intelligent nonhuman species, the Keiki, and the bioengineered human species, the Lunarians. Critics fault the book for changing from an adventure to a vision. In the *New York Times Book Review,* Gerald Jones claims: "*Harvest of Stars* is overwritten, underimagined and fatally flawed with self-satisfied musings on life-according-to-Guthrie that read suspiciously like the author's own self-justifications." Letson notes in *LOCUS:* "[The book] has more of Anderson's strengths than his weaknesses," including "a *genuinely* poetic feeling for the physical universe" and ". . . a capacity for the elegiac and the tragic that are rare in sf."

In the first part of *The Stars Are Also Fire,* Dagny Beynac, a descendant of Anson Guthrie, works to preserve peace on the Moon where she lives with her genetically adapted children. In the second part, two individuals search for the secret to unlocking the Peace Authority's control of their way of life. The two intertwined stories in the book span centuries and multiple worlds. *Harvest the Fire* features the rivalry between humans and cybernetic organisms, while in the *The Fleet of Stars* Anson Guthrie returns to Earth as a personality downloaded onto his spacecraft's computer. On Earth he seeks the secret that keeps artificial intelligences in power. *Publishers Weekly* calls the book "an exciting culmination to an ambitious saga about the future of human evolution."

Anderson provides a running commentary to connect nine stories, six essays, a play, and two other pieces that compose *All One Universe.* Notes a reviewer for *Publishers Weekly,* "Readers tolerant of potpourri may go for this, but Anderson's most pungent work it isn't." However, C. W. comments in *Rapport,* "On the whole, *All One Universe* is a collection which does its creator proud while delighting his fans."

Because of his emphasis on liberty, Anderson has gained a reputation in science-fiction circles "as being fairly far to the right," Charles Platt states in *Dream Makers, Volume 2: The Uncommon Men and Women Who Write Science Fiction,* "and has been called a reactionary." When asked about this, Anderson told Platt to "just look at what I'm reacting against. . . . If I had to call myself something, it would be either a conservative libertarian or a libertarian conservative. . . . Basically, I feel that the concepts of liberty that were expressed . . . by people like the Founding Fathers were actually the radically bold concepts from which people have been retreating ever since. And I don't believe that it's necessarily reactionary to say so."

When asked to comment on the role of science fiction in relation to other types of literature, Anderson told *CA:* "I have written quite a lot of it, and am proud to have done so, because science fiction is and always has been part of literature. Its long isolation, strictly a twentieth-century phenomenon, is ending; its special concepts and techniques are becoming common property, employed not only by the mass media but by some of our most respected writers; in turn, it is shedding artistic parochialism and thus starting to communicate beyond a small circle of enthusiasts. This is good, because the particular concerns of science fiction never have been parochial; they have included, or tried to include, all of space, time, and fate. Not that I wish to make exaggerated claims. I merely set forth that science fiction is one human accomplishment, among countless others, which has something to offer the world. Lest even this sound too pompous let me say that at the very least it is often a lot of fun."

*AUTOBIOGRAPHICAL ESSAY:*

Anderson contributed the following essay to *CA:*

Being asked to contribute to this series was a quite unexpected honor. Even more is it a danger, the risk of boring you. Still, if the life has been quiet, the times have been otherwise, and of course everybody's experience of history is unique. I'll offer a few comments, too. Better crotchety than dull.

Some of my ancestors and living kinfolk would have much more interesting stories to tell, but that is matter for a whole book, or several books. Here I'll simply declare that the lineage of my parents was basically Danish, without going into the complications which lurk behind that "basically," except to observe that one branch has been American for more than a hundred years. My father, Anton William Andersen, was born over here but educated in Denmark. He was the son of a sea captain and no relation to the great Hans Christian. He disliked his first name and never used it, being Will or Willy to his friends. During World War One he came back to join the United States Army. There he grew

tired of explaining the spelling of his surname and Anglicized it to Anderson.

A literary tradition exists on the other side; my mother, Astrid Hertz, was descended from both Carsten Hauch and Henrik Hertz. Her own father was a physician in Copenhagen, where she was born. After a series of jobs and experiences more varied than was usual for a respectable young lady in those days, she crossed the Atlantic to work as a secretary in what was then the Danish legation in Washington. By a most unlikely chance, she met Will Anderson again. They had gone to the same school in the old country but afterward lost touch with each other. Since his discharge from the army he had stayed on in America, working as a civil engineer. Now they started dating, and early in 1926 they were married. I was born on 25 November of that year, in Bristol, Pennsylvania.

Since he had promised her that she could name their first baby, I am called after her father, Poul. The middle name she made William. That first name is a version of "Paul" and I might have Anglicized too, except that in grade school the teachers kept telling me I wasn't spelling my own name right, and I got my back up about it. The proper pronunciation is not an Anglo-Saxon noise; it falls about midway between "powl" and "pole." I'll answer to anything.

Mother's parents came over for the occasion of my birth, and Grandfather was the attending doctor when this happened, at home. She herself was the anesthesiologist. He gave her a cloth soaked in chloroform to hold to her nose when the pains got bad. As consciousness dimmed, her hand naturally fell, so she could not get an overdose. I realize that this wouldn't always work.

Everybody in the apartment building, and quite a few from elsewhere, had to come see the new baby. One person who went "kitchy-kitchy-koo" had a bad cold, which I caught. Grandfather wrote a prescription for an anticongestant which the American druggist misread; it nearly killed me. Much worse was that the illness led to chronic otitis media. This condemned me to many years of recurrent torture, when the middle ear would fill up until the drums ruptured. As a result, I am hard of hearing and was disqualified for military service later on. It seemed that the trouble had finally burned itself out sometime in my thirties, but in my fifties it recurred in the form of mastoiditis on the left side. Death was the least unpleasant of the possibilities which surgery averted. Now I seem all right; but whenever there

*Infant Poul with his parents, 1927*

is the slightest doubt about my state of health, I don't go near any infant.

About the age of six or so, I caught chorea, St. Vitus' dance. It took me years to get my coordination back; I remember how hard it was to master the riding of a bicycle at the venerable age of eleven. I'm still somewhat of a klutz, though I can do most things reasonably well.

This medical history is only worth mentioning, first, as a period piece, since it is happily much less common nowadays; second, as a warning to new parents, since the fact remains that such natural enemies of humankind as the tiger were trivial compared to those natural enemies that swarm everywhere around us to this day; third, because it doubtless had something to do with making my childhood and adolescence as solitary as they were.

Needless to say, it was only a single factor, and not the main one. Most of what I am came from within myself. Besides, I don't want to do an Eeyore number. On the whole, if you consider 99 percent of the human beings who have ever existed, I have been fantastically fortunate in my life. And I'll match my good luck with that of anybody else in the upper 1 percent.

I was less than a year old when a change of job for my father took the family to Port Arthur, Texas. There he advanced to chief estimator at the Texaco plant, and there, in 1930, my brother was born. It was Dad's turn to name a child, and the event caught him flat-footed.

He called his engineers into conference. They came up with John Jerome.

Port Arthur lies near the Louisiana border, on the fringe of the bayou country. It is, therefore, Deep South rather than West, although amply supplied with Texas pridefulness. It was already an industrially progressing city, and canals from the Gulf had made it a seaport. We'd often see a ship apparently steaming over the flat hinterland. Summers are hot and humid; air conditioning and mosquito control were then in the future. Occasionally the waters overflowed. A kayak that my father had built got its first trial in our backyard, while a neighbor boy made a pet of a small alligator he had found in his.

After a few years my parents had saved enough money to build their own house in a suburb. Dad took a hand in the design, using his engineering skill and nautical background to make it a marvel of compactness without being cramped. Behind it was a cottage for servants, generally a maid and her man-of-all-work husband. You didn't have to be rich in those times to afford such a standard of living. Nowadays the government takes too much, before you even see it.

The suburb was a wonderland for boys, full of trees to climb and vacant lots to romp in. Once a pile of bricks lay for weeks next door; we made castles out of it and burrows in it, at considerable risk to our necks. Clay soil could be molded into figures which the sun baked dry. My parents had a good-sized boat, which Dad had built himself, and we were often out on the water, sometimes for a weekend across the state line. The Yacht Club was a fine site for crabbing or for holding a barbecue. On vacations we'd get as far afield as Carlsbad Caverns or the Ozarks—or Europe, about which more later.

The single drawback, but it was enormous, was school. "The twelve-year sentence," somebody has called it. Most of that time stands in my memory as utter emptiness, a purgatory of boredom. I endured it quietly and kept my resentment to myself, aside from the rebellious things that all little boys were expected to say. Now and then a good teacher lit a torch for me, but this was rare.

Doubtless a majority of people have experienced school otherwise. Doubtless a great deal of what I suffered was my fault. There were opportunities, especially social, of which I never took advantage. Once past the cruel small-boy stage of life, hardly anybody ever tried to make trouble for me, and many made efforts to be friendly.

Perhaps this introversion was in part an inheritance from my father. He was a big, handsome man, popular because he was affable toward everybody except those few whom experience caused him to decide were humanly worthless. However, he was not what you would call very sociable. Most of his spare time he spent with his wife and children, or reading, or making things in his workshop. He was good with his hands, also as an artist; he used to draw delightful cartoons for us boys. Some chairs he made for the house were beautiful. One, though, was slyly designed to be uncomfortable; that was the one he offered unwelcome visitors. He had perhaps three or four friends who were close. Those were close indeed, and the friendships outlasted his death.

I've tended to be like that. As a kid, I had only a single real friend, but we were inseparable. The circle of other boys with whom I got along reasonably well was small. We used to model animals out of clay and with them enact long stories. In that sort of game, I could be a leader. A recurring motif was a kind of perpetual cold war between Animal Land and School Land.

Otherwise my physical handicaps caused me to make a poor showing and, during high school, develop a special hatred for physical education. As grade-schoolers, we boys played marbles for keeps, and I was no good at that either. Finally I devised some punchboards and sold chances, one marble per chance, ten to the winner. I soon had more than anybody else. Then others started doing likewise. And then the teachers noticed, and found out who it was that had turned Tyrrell School into a gambling hell.

My brother John was much more normal in every way. A great deal of our mother's lively, outgoing personality was, and is, in him.

Though a mild amount of rampaging was allowed boys, especially at Hallowe'en, they and the girls were raised in the strict code of manners of the old South. You said "Yes, sir" and "Yes, ma'm" to your elders, you rose when a lady entered the room, you never used bad language in her presence, and it was taken for granted that when you, a boy, grew up you would provide for, protect, and honor your own womenfolk.

The exception was black people. Any snot-nosed white kid called any "colored" person of any age by his or her first name. Segregation and subordination were the natural order of things. Yet there was no conscious oppression. If boys of the same race didn't go to school together, they did often play together, at least until puberty set in. White adults felt responsible for the well-being of any blacks who worked for them. Once I heard my father and some friends vow that any Ku Klux Klansman who showed up in town would leave it on a rail, attired in tar and feathers. Otherwise all thought of lynching horrified them.

Affection frequently developed between the races. The day after my father's death, old Jack, caretaker at the Yacht Club, somehow made his way out to our suburb, knocked on our back door, told Mother how sorry he was, and asked if there was anything he could do for her—chop some wood, maybe? I'll agree now that the system was wrong, but never that it was evil.

People in that milieu were generally religious. My parents were not, and didn't attend church; they didn't even have John or me baptized. Nonetheless they arranged for us to go to Sunday school. Later, in Minnesota, we got Wednesday school, on a released-time program that the courts have probably since forbidden. The church happened to be Episcopalian. The idea was to expose us to that part of the heritage of our civilization. I'm glad it happened. Some schools also had prayers or the like. From the age of twelve, if not earlier, I was an agnostic, but I don't remember that these practices hurt any sensitive little soul in me, nor do I see where they violated any rights of mine.

Now John and I were not entirely assimilated to the culture around us. Our parents took care to keep the family bilingual, another deed for which we remain ever grateful. We celebrated Christmas in the Danish style, emphasis on the eve rather than the day. With the selflessness typical of American husbands in that era of male chauvinist piggery, Dad gave his wife several trips back to the old country to visit her folks there, and she took us children along. So we came to address and think of her as Mor, Danish for "Mother."

I sometimes wonder what our lives would have become if they had continued like this. Surely Dad would have gone far, as his associates did. But one fall day in 1937 turned chilly. He started back home to get his overcoat. On the way, his car collided with another. Both drivers were instantly killed.

Long afterward, Mor confessed that, though she tried to keep on doing well by us, for a while she was an automaton. Will Anderson had been the only man in her life. He always would be. Over the years she declined more than one offer of marriage. Grief went away at last, but love never did.

The couple had always considered it a sacred obligation to see their children through college, and had been putting money aside for this. Dad's attitude toward his wife was equally old-fashioned; he carried plenty of insurance. Taxes and inflation had not yet made thrift impossible, so the savings account was in good shape too. Mor was not left rich, but she wasn't badly off.

For several months she tried to carry on in Port Arthur. It was hopeless. The place was too haunted. She longed to go back to Denmark, where she had many friends and relatives, some of them in influential positions. Why not settle there? In the spring of 1938 she put the three of us on a train to upstate New York, where a friend of hers had an artist husband and a son about my age. We spent a while with them before crossing the Atlantic. I was now old enough that I well remember the scenic Hudson valley, and my introduction to Mary Poppins and Oz.

The whole trip stands pretty clear before me. Our passage was on a German liner—third class, though plenty luxurious for the likes of us—which set us off at Bremen, where we overnighted. Soldiers and Nazi functionaries were everywhere; a huge poster reminded people to make sure their gas masks were in order; in a beautiful park where swans swam on a pond, an official bulletin board displayed the International Jew plotting to rob the world.

Denmark, to which we proceeded by rail, was like another planet. If I am not being sentimental, it was still more charming then than now. Everybody was so cheerful and *decent*—including an aunt of mine who had been a Communist since 1917 and her current lover. Grandfather was dead but Grandmother remained very much alive, a tall and imposing lady with a mane of white hair. Mor's cousin Jens was a fabulous Dionysian figure. Cousins of about my own age were a lot more fun than any kids in Texas. All of these persons would later be active in resisting the Nazi occupation, but that was for the future; this was the last golden summer.

For several generations the family had had a lease on an eighteenth-century fisher cottage on the Sound near Elsinore, and there we spent a good deal of the time. Perhaps its accumulation of things my forebears had cherished, within walls older still, had more to do with nourishing a sense of history and tradition in me than did the well-known places which every tourist saw. (Long afterward, when the lease had been lost, I would be the last of us to spend a night there.) We explored Copenhagen itself, of course, and quite a bit of serene rural Denmark, and southern Sweden. I've never gotten this out of my system, nor wanted to.

But . . . it was becoming too obvious that war was on the way. Mor was long since a naturalized American. What concerned her more, though, was that her sons were American born. In fall we returned.

Not to Port Arthur. Not ever, except on a visit or two. While we still had money, it wasn't a lifetime's worth. Through her connections abroad, Mor had gotten back her former secretarial job at the Danish legation. She rented a house in nearby Silver Spring, Maryland. After a while her own mother came over to live with us.

By and large, this became a rather happy time for me. The local junior high school was excellent. The faculty were relaxed and amiable, and believed in encouraging individual potentialities. Simultaneously, they upheld a proud academic standard. Both these features made school, on the whole, actually enjoyable. I soon became close friends with a classmate, Neil Waldrop; we could talk to each other, and about stuff like astronomy and evolutionary biology. Rock Creek Park was grand for a Saturday ramble and amateur geologizing. The Smithsonian was an Aladdin's cave of wonders.

It was different for my brother John. He had adored his father, whose death came at his vulnerable age of seven. Now he didn't get along with Grandmother, Mor's job took most of her time and energy, he had no friends in his grade school. One day Mor came home to see him sitting on the steps in his cowboy suit, aiming his cap pistol at the empty air and saying, "Bang, bang, bang," while tears poured down his face. She decided the time was overpast for getting out of this situation. But where to?

California was a possibility. A friend of her youth had gotten married in the San Diego area, to a businessman who had made himself a fortune. He offered to invest Mor's money for her. Had she accepted, she too would undoubtedly have become wealthy, and John and I would have grown up surrounded by worldly goods and left-wing ideology.

This is as convenient a place as any for some remarks on politics. We have to make an effort, these days, to put ourselves in the minds of people of goodwill, back in 1917 and after. They had seen the grimness of working-class lives. My medical grandfather never presented many a bill, because he knew the patient couldn't afford it; and he would hear workers trudging to the job before sunrise and back after sunset. The vast improvement since is almost entirely due to better technology and to whatever degree government has kept hands off, but that was not generally foreseeable then. Additionally, his generation and his children's witnessed the mass lunacy that was World War One. They were ripe to believe that the October Revolution was the red dawn of a new day. The Edwardian Enlightenment was ironically conducive to that; it amounted to a faith in human rationality, and Marxism claims to be founded on fact and reason.

Mor never became a Communist, but a sister of hers and various friends did, and others were fellow travelers, including the lady now in San Diego. My parents were Democrats, like practically everybody else in the South. They thought the New Deal was actually doing something to relieve the Depression. As a matter of course, I was raised under this idea. I don't know what intensive exposure to the real Left would have done, though it seems plausible that I'd have ended up as a flaming Tory.

In the event, Mor made a different decision. It was to prove financially disastrous. Yet she always believed afterward that it was beneficial for her sons and this was profit enough. Her brother Jakob Hertz—Jack, he called himself—had immigrated too, done well as an engineer, and now for some reason got the notion that he wanted to be a farmer. His wife had kinfolk in southern Minnesota. He wrote to Mor, proposing that they buy adjacent properties, both of which he would operate. Mainly she saw this as a wholesome environment which might heal John. She agreed.

First, after she quit her job, we made a cross-country auto trip. I suspect she meant it as a last fling at freedom. Passing through such marvels as Yellowstone, we ended in a cottage on the ocean shores of Washington state, an area with which I have ever since been in love. There Grandmother said good-bye, took a bus to New York, and thence sailed home to Denmark. It had not worked out, her joining the household. She was a gallant old soul nonetheless; afterward she personally defied and once even outwitted the Germans; it is well for me to recall that she revisited us after the war, and later Mor visited her before her death, and those were happy times.

We three drove back to Minnesota. There Mor bought her farm, forty acres of plowland, pasture, and second-growth woods. It had no buildings, so while the house and barn and the rest were under construction we spent several months, 1939-40, in Northfield. That's a middle-sized town south of Minneapolis, partly a farmer's market, partly the home of two colleges, Carleton and St. Olaf. Carleton in particular enjoys an international

reputation. Northfield is thus an odd, pleasant mixture of Academe and Demos. We acquired friends in both.

We boys were enrolled in its schools. Later, living in the countryside, we should technically have gone to its high school. Concerned for our education, Mor pulled wires to keep us where we were. It meant long bus rides, but is another deed for which we are grateful.

I want to be fair to Northfield High School. It was the best in a wide radius, offering such subjects as physics, chemistry, mathematics through advanced algebra and solid geometry, Latin and living foreign languages, one good course each in world history and sociology. (The ignorance of these last two nowadays, especially among college graduates, is appalling, and goes far toward explaining the Totentanz that has been postwar American politics.) The faculty were dedicated and generally kindly. The student body was amiable. I learned more than I realized at the time.

Yet those years are pretty bad in my memory. I was a total social misfit. It didn't help that the war came along, gasoline was rationed, and I couldn't get into town on my own even if time had permitted after my farm chores or if, for that matter, I had wanted to. My grades were excellent and my deportment got me a name for prissiness among the other boys. They hadn't heard me out on the farm, swearing at a horse or cow or balky piece of machinery; there I earned a certain admiration from hardened men. As for school, except for the occasional fire-kindling teacher, it was something to be outlived.

I regret having to include my English classes. The teachers meant well, and they did get the mechanics of the language firmly into my head, but they were old maids, some nice, some waspish, and their idea of introducing us to literature was to lay a piece of work out on a dissecting table. It took me years afterward to discover that Shakespeare, for instance, is fun; and to this day I generally look upon literary critics as being old maids, of whatever sex.

Let me repeat, the basic misery of those years I brought largely on myself; and it is largely in retrospect that I see how wretched they were. During them, that was just the way life was, and at least I was not in a concentration camp or anything like that. John, always more normal, soon regained emotional equilibrium, went through the same school, and had a generally fine time.

Anyway, I had my private world to retreat to, the world of books and, specifically, science fiction.

I'd kept in touch by mail with my Silver Spring schoolmate Neil Waldrop. Shortly after my arrival in Minnesota, he sent me a bundle of magazines. They seemed to be terrible pulp trash, and I didn't intend to read them, but fell sick abed for a few days and had nothing else. Immediately I was hooked. *Thrilling Wonder Stories; Startling Stories; Amazing Stories;* above all, the cerebral *Astounding Science Fiction . . . .*

As a kid, I'd been a great fan of such imaginative comic strips as "Popeye" and "Alley Oop"—the splendid creations of Segar and Hamlin, not the zombie imitations which have succeeded. I've mentioned Oz and Mary Poppins, and there was also Dr. Dolittle. (They tell me you can't get him anymore. Those books have been banned as racist by the people who so bravely defend the rights of pornographers.) Later came Jules Verne, H. Rider Haggard, Sax Rohmer, a bit of H. G. Wells. And of course stars, planets, dinosaurs, atoms, the whole stuff of science had always been magical. Now here were these magazines, which offered stories of this kind every month!

I spent much of my tiny allowance on subscriptions. These didn't give me enough science fiction, so I started writing my own, in longhand. Neil did likewise for a while, and we'd exchange manuscripts for mutual comments, but presently he stopped and I went on alone, writing for nobody but myself. I didn't intend to make a career of this, but I did daydream about moonlighting at it and perhaps, someday, seeing words of mine in print, right up there with the words of Robert Heinlein, Isaac Asimov, or A. E. van Vogt.

Meanwhile there was reality to get through. I don't want to say anything against my uncle Jack. Suffice it that Pearl Harbor happened, and he went into war industry in Minneapolis, and his wife Jenny must needs take over their farm. She was a dear person, energetic and conscientious, but she and Mor were left essentially alone, dependent on the goodwill of neighbors to keep going.

About one of these, a relative on whom they had counted, I certainly do want to say something, but there might be a legal hazard in that, even at this late date. Enough that he appointed himself an enemy. The rest of the men around were, on the whole, okay. Mor did have to give one of them the knee once, when he got grabby; but he learned his lesson and made no more trouble of that kind. The others never did at all. Their wives were unfailingly kind and helpful.

If these people tended to bore the Anderson family in social situations, quite likely this was our fault. In their ways, they were actually apt to be colorful individualists. I have since encountered far more sheep-like conformity in the thinking of academics and journalists. Nonetheless, we never fitted very well into the community.

We could not isolate ourselves from it. People needed each other to a degree that scarcely exists anymore. For instance, men and boys of the neighborhood got together for such jobs as haying and threshing, farm by farm, while their women prepared communal meals. When a blizzard closed roads, you checked around to make sure nobody was in trouble. It wasn't exactly a pioneer situation, but it was the last remnant of the old yeomanry.

That's long gone. Mor went broke because forty acres are too little to support the equipment you need. Also she, as a widow, had to pay for much of her help—and weren't most of our hired men a succession of weirdos! We were basically chicken farmers, and our dear government slapped wartime price controls on eggs while letting the cost of feed soar.

She never said much afterward about that struggle. It is only my thinking about it that has put me in awe of her. She was worse than alone, she was saddled with a pair of teenage boys, as sullen and selfish as is usual at that age—or perhaps more so, since the war denied us many of the outlets now taken for God-given rights. In any case, school, together with the long commute to and fro, limited what we could do to help.

Those years weren't altogether bad. They may have forced upon us a certain discipline which has stood us in good stead. She always thought so. For my part, I am not sorry to have made the acquaintance of different kinds of animals, and winter and hard labor, and men and women who earned their livings with their hands. Though I would not willingly go back, it is well to have been there.

By 1944, though, Mor was at the end of her resources. The farm had consumed all her money except for the hallowed education fund. Through a friend on the Carleton College faculty, she got a job at its library, which she held until she reached retirement age. Meanwhile, she got rid of the farm.

She became a hell of a great librarian. She mastered the skills fast and, with her background in foreign languages and history, was often the best researcher on hand. Lacking the degree, she could only go so far in grade. Some of academe's characteristic, vicious in-fighting sometimes touched her peripherally. Otherwise, the students and most of the faculty loved her. Not that she was a sweet little old lady—no, always a salty character.

Well, this is getting ahead of the story. After high school graduation in 1944, I tried to enlist in the army—were we not in a glorious crusade which our leaders assured us would bring peace forever after?—but was turned down because of my scarred eardrums. A routine draft call later that year had the same result.

Carleton College had offered me a small scholarship, on the basis of my high school grades, but I chose to enroll at the University of Minnesota. This was because its Institute of Technology offered an almost 100 percent scientific program. (A year of engineering English was required. So was a quarter of literary English, where I breezed through the reading of a few novels and the twaddle I was supposed to write about them. As electives I took some Spanish and some philosophy of science, the latter taught by the brilliant, hard-boiled logical positivist Herbert Feigl.) My aim was to become a physicist.

Suddenly I was free. The old maids and soft young faces of high school were behind me. I was among men, and men whose trade was knowledge. They regarded me as an adult, willingly gave help if asked but never volunteered any, always taking for granted that I was responsible for myself. Minneapolis was a much less interesting city than it has since become, but it was my first city to run about in on my own. Less among classmates than among chance acquaintances out of the entire student body, I made new friends and with them, for the first time, began really deep-going exploration of things that really mattered.

Not that life became uproarious. Aside from an occasional beer bust or the like, it stayed pretty quiet. For the first couple of years I went home most weekends to help out on the farm, till Mor found a buyer. I avoided extracurricular activities. If nothing else was happening, and it usually wasn't, I'd spend my evenings reading, or else writing stories. Regardless, and never mind any missed opportunities, this was a splendid time for me.

The war ended, for the nonce, at Hiroshima and Nagasaki. As a reader of science fiction, perhaps I understood a little better than most folk what this meant. But I don't claim any prophetic insights, and in fact the world has gone down ways that nobody predicted. I suspect it always will.

Abruptly campus was flooded with veterans enrolling on GI benefits. They were generally fine guys, for whom I felt a certain wistful admiration, though they hardly ever boasted of their combat doings. They did, however, overcrowd my classes. It seemed as if everybody wanted to be a nuclear physicist. This was one reason why I moved over more toward astronomy. Another was a growing realization that not only was I awkward in the laboratory, I lacked any mathematical gift. It was easy to learn theorems that somebody else had proven, but where it came to creating a demonstration for myself, I wasn't much.

Unfortunately for me, Minnesota had only a minor astronomy department. Its head, Willem Luyten, was a first-rank scientist, but what he could offer students was quite limited.

Meanwhile, as it happened, Neil Waldrop came to Minnesota in 1946, enrolling in its excellent premedical school. We spent many delighted hours together. Out of conversations about the atomic bomb came the idea for a story, which I thereupon wrote. He said it merited submitting for publication. I borrowed Mor's typewriter, put the thing in proper form, and sent it to *Astounding*—giving Neil a shared byline, since the basic notion had been his.

Months passed. I went off to a summer job in the north woods. I was back at school that fall before a letter came. John Campbell, the editor, had *read* "Tomorrow's Children." He wanted to *buy* and *print* it. That kind of experience comes one to a lifetime.

This first effort of mine appeared in the spring of 1947. In the following year or so I wrote and sold a couple more, for what was then fairly good money. This may have been a factor causing me to run out of academic steam. More and more, my attention went to other things than studies. I did graduate in 1948 "with distinction," my college's equivalent of "cum laude," but my heart was no longer entirely in it.

Another factor has already been mentioned, the slow and reluctant realization that I could never be more than a second-rate scientist. A third, doubtless the main one, was a whole new direction that my life had taken.

This came about through science fiction. Its influence on quite a few lives has been enormous. In some cases the results have been unhealthy, but generally they are straightforward and beneficent. By casting glamour over science and technology, it has recruited many a young person into these fields, and helped him or her get through long, unglamorous years of study and apprenticeship. I have this admission from a number of them, some world-famous, and certainly the influence was there upon me, though in my case it worked itself out along different lines.

Before Pearl Harbor, several boys and a couple of adults, enthusiasts of the literature, had founded what they called the Minneapolis Fantasy Society. Like other such fan groups, it held meetings to discuss its favorite subject, and it put out a mimeographed amateur magazine to exchange for similar publications. Presently most of the members went into uniform, and when they came back they were no longer boys but young men. Just the same, they were as avid for science fiction as ever, and late in 1947 they reconstituted the MFS. Some had died or moved elsewhere, but some new people joined. I was among these.

A letter of mine, published in a professional magazine, led to my being invited to a meeting. What an evening that was! I met a god of mine, Clifford D. Simak, who turned out to be a warm human being. I met a whole clutch of kindred spirits, more or less my age, and after the meeting we went out for beer and talk till the bars closed, and then for coffee and talk, and I rolled back to my lodgings at sunrise full of new worlds and exploding stars.

Thereafter I was a regular member and made friendships, which time and long separations have not dimmed in the least. Whenever we get together again, all too seldom these years, it is as if we had never been apart. Doubtless the best known of these comrades of mine, today, is Gordon R. Dickson, who has long since realized the ambition he had borne since childhood, to be a writer. Especially influential on me was an older man, already a husband and father, Kenneth Gray. We used to sit up half the night at his house, arguing. Self-taught, he knew more history than most professors of the subject, and military service had taken him into far and strange corners of the world. His political conservatism gave my left liberalism of that time a salutary kick in the guts. There were others, most of whom have gone on to distinguish themselves in their chosen fields, but the list would grow too long.

The list of women would not. They were precious few in our circle. Any who appeared and were attractive and intelligent were quickly snapped up by some fellow. I've scant patience with today's paranoid feminism, but it seems undeniable that education and expectations in those days turned most girls into bores. Matters have improved enormously since then.

MFS activities were more than simply fannish. In fact, soon we lost interest in fandom per se, though not in science fiction. We stopped having regular meetings or issuing publications, and "MFS" became a shorthand phrase for a group of people who saw a lot of each other.

Parties, picnics, cross-country junkets . . . softball on summer Sundays, rough touch football in the autumn . . . our favorite downtown bar, where you could nearly always find somebody . . . the German Dinner Club . . . the confidences and desperations of youth. . . . Those were not years of pure bliss, especially not for Gordy and myself, as hand-to-mouth as we were living. We suffered our disappointments in love, the manifold frustrations of being poor, the sight of our work in sleazy paperbacks ineptly copyedited, for in those days a science fiction writer was at the absolute bottom of the totem pole. In just about every way, our lives since have vastly bettered. But still and all, I am glad to have had those years.

This was when I settled into a writing career in earnest. Graduating into a recession, with no money left for further studies, but being a bachelor who had never had a chance to develop expensive tastes, I thought I'd support myself by my stories while I looked around for steady employment. The search was half-hearted, and eventually petered out. I liked too much being my own boss, precarious though the living often was. Only slowly did it dawn on me that writing had, all along, been what nature cut me out to do.

Mostly I was selling to the magazines, especially *Astounding,* as it was then called (nowadays *Analog*). My early pieces there tended to be rather cold and abstract. However, for a brief span I became a mainstay of *Planet Stories,* which featured blood-and-thunder adventure yarns—along with experimental work by such people as Ray Bradbury, which nobody else would touch. And the first novel I wrote which saw print, *The Broken Sword,* is a rather passionate love story among other things. It took years to find a publisher, and meanwhile I did a juvenile book on commission, which was therefore my premier appearance at that length. Occasionally Gordy and I collaborated on a humorous "Hoka" yarn. The first few of these were run in a magazine published in Chicago, whose assistant editor, Bea Mahaffey, was gorgeous. I sometimes took the train there just to date her.

My initial science fiction convention was in Toronto, 1948. Events of this kind were then small, humbly

*Anderson (left) with fellow writer and friend, Gordon R. Dickson, about 1970*

housed, and almost entirely masculine. That was soon to change.

Restlessness grew within me. In the summer of 1949 I went with my brother John to Mesa Verde National Park, where we had jobs. Mine was behind the lunch counter, and ever since then I have felt a perhaps exaggerated sympathy for waiters and such. I quit early and hitchhiked back to Minnesota, to drive with Oliver Saari to the convention in Cincinnati.

Ollie and I traveled cross-country next year to a more professional gathering in New York. That was where I first met Isaac Asimov, L. Sprague de Camp, Willy Ley, and many another giant. All were gracious to this brash newcomer. Later that summer, John and I fared out to the Pacific coast. We looked in on the world convention in Portland, where I enjoyed a lively evening with Anthony Boucher, co-founder and co-editor of *The Magazine of Fantasy and Science Fiction.* He was to become a dear friend.

By the spring of 1951 I had enough money to go to Europe. John came too. We crossed on the old *Empress of Canada*—ah, that last night out, a full moon working its magic on the girls—and bought bicycles in Liverpool. Thence we youth-hosteled our way through a good bit of Britain and the Continent. When John went back to college in fall, I stayed on for a couple of months more, knocking around by myself or in company with chance-met Europeans.

Landing in New York, I took a few days there. One of my high hopes was to meet John W. Campbell, editor of *Astounding,* practically the single-handed creator of modern science fiction. He gave a cordial reply to my telephone call, and I spent an unforgettable afternoon in his office. Our relationship was to become close over the years. It wasn't simply that I was among his most frequent contributors, or that we struck up a lengthy and argumentative correspondence. Gradually it became clear to me that beneath that prickly exterior of his was a gentle, even shy soul. I had begun by worshipping him; I went on to admire and like him; I ended loving him. In his last years, when he was under heavy and often nasty attack from lit'ry types who considered him a reactionary and a has-been, I took every chance to defend him. He didn't bother to do that himself. I doubt he minded very much. But I damn well did.

The story's gotten ahead of itself again. Returning to Minneapolis, I began to find it more and more confining. My dream was to get back to Europe and settle down there, in some base from which to explore the entire eastern hemisphere. However, I was now pretty broke. Not only would passage money be needed, but a stake. I settled down to earn the necessary sum. Trying to save, I did scarcely any traveling in 1952, except to the world convention in Chicago.

That changed my plans.

Chicago's was the first of the big conventions, a thousand or so in attendance. Nowadays the major ones run to several times that number, and camaraderie between professionals and fans has pretty well drowned in the mob. The old bacchanalian, almost orgiastic spirit seems extinct also—this generation of young people is more sober and decorous than mine was—though at my present age that doesn't bother me, while the overcrowding does. I seldom attend any more, except an occasional regional gathering which is of humane size.

In 1952 you weren't yet overwhelmed. It was easy to get together with the individuals you wanted to be with, and to meet new persons whom you found you also wanted to be with.

Among the latter I encountered a young lady by the name of Karen Kruse. Born in Kentucky in 1932, she now lived in the Washington, D.C. area with her widowed mother and two younger brothers. While still in high school, she had founded a Sherlock Holmes society—there is considerable overlap between followers of science fiction and of the great detective—which remains active today in the capital under the thumb-to-nose name she gave it, the Red Circle. Upon graduation she had gone to work for the Army Map Service. With some money saved, she planned to enter Catholic University. She was not of that faith, but it had a fine drama department, and that was where her main interest lay, outside of science fiction and its fandom.

I took her aside for a beer and we became nearly inseparable for the rest of the long weekend, right on through the last party, where Stu Byrne sang Gilbert and Sullivan all night and we, with Tony Boucher, watched the sun rise over Lake Michigan. After going back to our respective homes, we corresponded eagerly. It was a curious courtship, but by spring we knew we were in love.

John had graduated from Carleton College and returned to Denmark on a one-year Fulbright scholarship. His field was history, with an eye to getting into the foreign service. It had been agreed that I would meet him over there when he was finished and we'd travel around, Mor joining us when she got her vacation. I was no longer exactly anxious to go, but people were counting on me. I did manage a few days in Karen's neighborhood and a few more with her in New York, to which her mother drove us, before the *Ryndam* sailed.

Nevertheless, on the whole it became a jolly summer. John and I rented a motorcycle with a sidecar. Czech-made, it kept breaking down along the way, until we had practically rebuilt it, but it did put wheels under three persons. At first the third was a Danish friend. He hitchhiked back from the south of France, and we went north again through Switzerland to England, where Mor landed. Now it was her turn in the sidecar, going to Paris, Holland, and Denmark. That was a rainy year. I remain convinced that a motorcycle is an ingenious combination of the drawbacks of bicycle and automobile. But what the hell.

John and Mor went home in fall. Since I had not originally intended to do so, I had no ticket, and must perforce wait a while; transatlantic passages were nowhere near as available then as now. I would have gone to Norway, but fell sick. My Communist aunt tended me as lovingly, in her tiny apartment, as she had tended her mother during the old lady's long dying.

The Berlin blockade and the Korean War were recent memories, the cold war was in its deepest freeze and a hot one looked imminent. Kenny Gray had gotten me to learn the truth about the Soviet Union and its institutionalized horrors. Among the Danish Communists, neither John nor I made any bones about where our loyalties lay—and our loathings; but personal relationships stayed entirely amicable.

This may be why John realized he could never hope to get into the foreign service. It was the so-called McCarthy era. In retrospect, I must agree that this consisted largely of intellectuals screaming from the rooftops that they were afraid to speak above a whisper. Certainly no one scolded me for my 1953 story "Sam Hall," in which a fascistic American government of the future is violently overthrown. John Campbell, who bought it, was himself a political conservative. Also, Communist espionage and subversion were an ugly fact.

Even so, some cruel and costly mistakes were made. The United States lost a good spokesman in my brother. He wanted a job that would let him travel, so after his army hitch he returned to school and got his degree in geology. Among other things, he later led the first expedition ever made into the Sentinel and Heritage Mountains of Antarctica. Doing field work in Utah, he met one Linda Jones and married her. They have two daughters. Until his retirement, he was professor of his subject at Kent State University in Ohio.

But all that was far in the future. I eventually got a cancelled berth on the *Stockholm* and came back to the States myself. This wasn't to Minnesota, except for farewells. If I couldn't live abroad just yet, I wanted to try something a bit glamorous, and remembered San Francisco from a visit earlier. Besides, Tony Boucher lived and worked right across the Bay, so there was one ready-made friend. Karen felt restless too. We agreed to try our luck yonder. She went and got herself an apartment in Berkeley and a job, and was waiting when I arrived. We were married that December.

For the next several years we lived in Berkeley. In those days the town was civilized, stimulating, amiably wacky. Its climate was better than that of San Francisco, which was only a short drive away anyhow. Here our daughter Astrid was born, in 1954. She tied us down somewhat; doubtless we could have traveled more with her than we did, but in the event decided not to. She was worth it. She still is.

Among people we went around with were Tony Boucher, Reginald Bretnor, Jack Vance, and their wives. Over the years we became closely knitted to them. Besides other writers than these, those who became good friends included members of the Elves', Gnomes', and Little Men's Science Fiction, Chowder, and Marching Society, which met on alternate Friday evenings for a program of some kind followed by beer and conversation till its favorite bar closed, and often threw hellratious parties.

If it seems that our social life has been dominated by persons concerned with science fiction, this is doubtless true, but that doesn't mean it has been narrow. The average reader or writer is uncommonly aware of the real world and active in it, with an uncommonly broad range of interests and knowledge. To give a single example, Jack Vance used to hold jam sessions at his house, which was where I got some understanding and appreciation of jazz. He also taught me most of what I know about carpentry. This was when he and I were building a houseboat for the use of our families. Originally Frank Herbert was a partner in the enterprise, but he was then a newspaperman and a change of jobs caused him to move away. Jack and Frank are among the most widely traveled, as well as widely read individuals I have ever met or heard of.

Besides, Karen and I had more activities. We attended meetings of the Mystery Writers of America, where speakers told fascinating things about crime and police work. We revived the local Sherlock Holmes club. There were all sorts of lectures, movies, and other such events. Mor came out each year for a lengthy visit and charmed everybody.

It wasn't entirely fun or easy. For a while it was damned rough. The science fiction field fell on evil days, a publishing contract on which I'd counted was renegotiated to my disadvantage, sales elsewhere languished, we went into debt. Karen had lost her job soon after I came to join her, and never taken another, in part because of my Southern prejudices about the roles of man and wife. It became clear that I'd better get one.

With a background in both physics and writing, I was offered a good post as a tech writer at the Lawrence Radiation Laboratory. This required a clearance for top secret material. I told the FBI men about my Communist aunt and the rest. If that was disqualifying, I said, they should so inform me and I'd withdraw my application with no hard feelings. They said it wasn't necessarily, and later called me in for another interview. That was obviously just a fishing expedition, full of questions about people I knew scarcely or not at all. I must say the agents were courteous, and it was perhaps not nice of me to start using sesquipedalian words in order that the man with the stenotype must ask me how to spell them.

Time passed. There was no word. Karen and I got broker and broker. Finally I gave up and took another offer. I am told that this was a favorite trick of the government's. If officialdom had no sound reason not to clear somebody, but didn't want to, it stalled him till he could wait no longer and went away. I don't think this exactly expedited defense work.

My job was at a local Department of Agriculture laboratory, as a very junior-grade chemist. Boss and coworkers were likeable, but it was intensely boring, and perhaps this is a reason why, after the nine months of probation usual in civil service, I was gently told that they couldn't use me.

By then, however, that was a deliverance. My paychecks had kept us going. Evenings and weekends I wrote. The earnings from that paid off our debts and gave us a stake. When my mild bondage ended, in 1957, we celebrated by taking Astrid and Mor on a camping trip up the north coast. Ever since, I have been a full-time freelance writer and have done pretty well financially.

The annual world science fiction convention, on Labor Day weekend if held in the United States, traditionally has some professional as its guest of honor. He or she gets a room at the hotel (these days, all expenses) in return for making a keynote speech and being accessible to the fans. In 1959 the convention took place in Detroit, and the honor fell to me.

We put Astrid in the back seat of the Morris Minor we'd bought, as part of the "tailfin rebellion" of that era, and started off. Our trip to Detroit took a couple of months, since we went by way of Tennessee, Washington, New York, and Quebec; afterward we stayed a few weeks with Mor in Minnesota, and as the first snow fell headed home via Arizona. It was a grand trek, but I'll never do that much driving again. Since, we've flown to our basic destination and rented a car.

Less and less were we content in Berkeley. Sleaze and smog were moving in. A filling station replaced the house next door. Besides, it no longer made sense to pay rent when we could be paying off a mortgage and getting a tax break to boot. Early in 1960, we started looking around.

What we eventually found was a house in Orinda. This is a suburb on the eastern flanks of the hills which wall Berkeley and Oakland. It's beautiful and peaceful; a woman can walk its unlighted streets after dark without fear. Though it's fairly well built up, the topography and the many trees give an illusion of being in the countryside, and the air on the upper slopes is always clean. The house we saw is rather small, but sufficed for three, and it stands on one of the half-acre lots for which the area is zoned. A fountain was playing in the patio. We couldn't really afford it, but love generally finds its way. Astrid has since moved to a home of her own—her husband is my colleague Greg Bear—but Karen and I are there still. We now have two grandchildren, who are, of course, incomparable.

As it happened, we moved barely in time. The 1960s' Revolt of the Idealists was getting under way. It changed our funny old Berkeley into a place humorless, dirty, and dangerous. By now the tide of neo-barbarism has receded, though local slang still bespeaks the People's Republic of Berkeley.

That decade scrubbed me free of any last traces of liberalism and, for that matter, intellectual elitism. I saw academe fawn upon the kooks and goons whom its own lies had evoked. As for the Vietnam War, its aftermath suggests to me that perhaps those of us who supported the American effort had a valid point or two to make. With rare exceptions, the people who agitated for our defeat do not admit that they may have done the world a disservice, any more than the average German did after Hitler. Nowadays these leaders seem primarily concerned with saving us from the cleanliness, safety, economy, and abundance of nuclear energy.

I will agree that our government had no business squandering lives and treasure—on both sides—on a war it had no intention of winning. But there is no monstrosity of which a government is incapable. Because a few limitations on it still survive, ours can be endured, most of the time, which is more than can be said for nearly all the rest. The liberals are working hard to change this.

Aside from politics, life remained good for my family. We prospered. Science fiction became respectable, almost too much so. For some years I did a fair amount of lecturing around the country, thereby discovering that most students continued to be clean and reasonable human beings. By 1965 we were able to go abroad for several months, something we've done fairly often since then. Among experiences on this particular trip was a tour of the paleolithic sites in the Dordogne countryside such as the president of France might get if he asked politely, as well as becoming intimate with that whole lovely region. It was courtesy of the prehistorian in charge of work there, the late Francois Bordes, and his wife-colleague. He was still another person we'd met through science fiction. Stories about him could go on for many pages.

We had adventures closer to home. Jerry Pournelle, afterward to become a writer himself, and I attempted to bring a sailboat down from Seattle to Los Angeles. She was a nimble twenty-footer but we were an awful pair of amateurs who hadn't even equipped her with an outboard motor. When a gale hit us off Cape Flattery, I had the helm all night, trying to keep us off a lee shore, while Jerry handled such jobs as taking in reef points. Subsequently we were stormbound, along with the entire fishing fleet, so long that Jerry ran out of time and we had to give up. But I remember things like lying becalmed in an unutterably quiet blue-and-silver dawn, and a pod of killer whales swimming by and one raising himself to look over the rail as if to say good morning. . . .

In the pause between Gemini and Apollo, 1963-64, I got a contract to write the script of a television documentary on the space program for the United States Information Agency. The budget was miserable, but visiting the sites and meeting the people on the project was a tremendous experience. Karen and I have both been quite involved with space, as spectators and as activists. Joe Green, who works at the Cape, used to throw terrific parties for the science fiction types who, armed with press credentials, got together each time a ship was about to leave for the moon.

All three Andersons were in the Society for Creative Anachronism, from its start in a Berkeley backyard, 1966. This organization, which is now nationwide and has overseas branches, goes in for medieval combat with wooden weapons—and if you think that's effete, you haven't been on the receiving end of one—as well as costumery, music, dance, cuisine, poetry, crafts, and everything else needed to revive the Middle Ages "not as they were but as they should have been." It was fine recreation for the whole family. Despite my age, I did well enough in battle to be awarded a knighthood, while Karen served a term as head of the College of Heralds. Since Astrid moved away we haven't attended many events, but the memories are warm.

In 1972-73 I put in a stretch as president of the Science Fiction Writers of America. That proved to be a job still more hard and thankless than I had imagined. In large part this was because of internal chaos. Nobody knew what anybody else was supposed to do. Nobody could so much as find a copy of the bylaws. Such a development is quite common in service organizations staffed by volunteers, and often destroys them. I spent most of my year coaxing forth a consensus for basic structural reforms and, at the end of it, getting them voted in. My successor, Jerry Pournelle, put them into effect and started the machinery working. He deserves most of the credit for saving what has by now evolved into the most active and effective group this side of the Screen Writers' Guild. However, I'm proud of my smaller role.

Mor retired and moved to Ohio to be with John, Linda, and her young granddaughters. She still came out almost every year to us, and sometimes we visited them. Her last stay here was in 1981. Her health had generally been excellent—at the age of seventy-nine, she hiked to the bottom of the Grand Canyon and back on the

same day—but now suddenly it failed, and later that year she died, as gallantly as she had always lived. Both her sons were there.

Inevitably, we have had other losses and sorrows, as well as reverses, but there have been abundant joys too, and on the whole we must reckon ourselves among the luckiest people who have ever lived. Most of this is too personal for public discussion, and in any event has little or nothing to do with my development as a writer, which I suppose this essay is mainly about.

Karen has written professionally too, a few stories and poems. I wish she'd do more. Sometimes she's given me so much in the way of ideas for a piece that I've shared the byline with her. Always she's been my co-thinker or mental spark plug or whatever you want to call a person who'll talk with you, at length and brilliantly, about whatever you have in mind. She can supply information as well, whether right out of her head—she's a lot better at languages than I am, reads more on every conceivable subject, and remembers it more clearly—or looking it up for me. As a manuscript emerges in first draft, she becomes what she calls my resident nitpicker, and has combed out countless solecisms. She's a topnotch proofreader. And, oh, yes, a great cook.

If I don't otherwise say much about my work, it's because of a feeling that it has to speak for itself. As of today, the books total about eighty. That's less impressive than it looks, when you consider how long I've been in the business. Compared to, say, Isaac Asimov, I'm a sluggard—especially as of the past decade or so. Mainly my work is classifiable as science fiction or fantasy, but it also includes historical, mystery, and juvenile fiction, science fact, journalism, essays, verse, and translations.

I've been honored with various awards and such, but am not among those writers who appeal to English departments. No sour grapes here; those who do, like Ursula LeGuin and Frank Herbert, I admire myself, and enjoy reading. It is more than enough for me to know that my following numbers in it scientists, technologists, astronauts, and others of whose doings *I* am a fan. Considering the generally masculine tone of my writing, I've been a little surprised at the high proportion of women among those readers who really like and understand it. The last time I counted, words of mine had appeared in eighteen foreign languages.

I hope I've been improving. Certainly I no longer find the production of my first several years readable, and it's lucky for me that the public in those days was tolerant. Influences upon a writer are often hard to identify, but I think I know what some of the more important ones have been for me. There were editors John Campbell and Tony Boucher, who provided all sorts of inspiration and opportunity while scarcely ever trying to dictate. Besides H. G. Wells and Olaf Stapledon in science fiction, there were the giants of the Campbell Golden Age. Towering elsewhere have been the classical Greeks, the Icelandic Eddas and sagas, the King James Bible, Shakespeare, Mark Twain, Rudyard Kipling, Robinson Jeffers, and a Dane by the name of Johannes V. Jensen. I don't mean that my stuff measures up to any of this, only that I've tried. Science, technology, history, the whole world around us and the whole universe around it, provide endlessly fascinating subject matter.

Over the years I've written in a lot of different veins, from romantic to realistic, adventurous to abstract, somber to slapstick. The last two or three novels seem to be pointed in other directions, new to me. Where this will lead I don't know, but it should be fun along the way.

*BIOGRAPHICAL/CRITICAL SOURCES:*

*BOOKS*

Benson, Gordon, Jr., *Poul Anderson, Myth-Master and Wonder-Weaver: An Interim Bibliography (1947-1982),* G. Benson, Jr., 1982, 5th revised edition published as *Poul Anderson, Myth-Master and Wonder-Weaver: A Working Bibliography,* Borgo Press, 1990.

*Contemporary Authors Autobiography Series,* Volume 2, Gale, 1985.

*Contemporary Literary Criticism,* Volume 15, Gale, 1980.

*Dictionary of Literary Biography,* Volume 8: *Twentieth-Century American Science-Fiction Writers,* Gale, 1981.

Elliot, Jeffrey M., *Science Fiction Voices #2,* Borgo, 1979.

Miesel, Sandra, *Against Time's Arrow: The High Crusade of Poul Anderson,* Borgo, 1978.

Peyton, Roger C., *A Checklist of Poul Anderson,* privately printed, 1965.

Platt, Charles, *Dream Makers, Volume 2: The Uncommon Men and Women Who Write Science Fiction,* Berkley Publishing, 1983.

Stever, David, and Andrew Adams Whyte, *The Collector's Poul Anderson,* privately printed, 1976.

Walker, Paul, *Speaking of Science Fiction: The Paul Walker Interviews,* Luna Publications, 1978.

*PERIODICALS*

*Algol,* summer-fall, 1978.
*Analog: Science Fiction/Science Fact,* February, 1991, p. 176; December, 1993, p. 163; March, 1996, p. 146.
*Booklist,* October 1, 1995, p. 254; February 15, 1996, p. 981.
*Books and Bookmen,* August, 1972.
*Globe and Mail* (Toronto), November 18, 1989.
*Kirkus Reviews,* August 15, 1995, p. 1146; December 1, 1995, p. 1671.
*Kliatt,* September, 1991, p. 19; September, 1992, p. 18; January, 1995, p. 12.
*Library Journal,* October 15, 1995, p. 91; November 15, 1996, p. 42.
*LOCUS,* August, 1990, p. 27; May, 1991, p. 45; October, 1991, p. 19; June, 1993, p. 29; November, 1994, p 25.
*Luna Monthly,* June, 1972.
*Magazine of Fantasy and Science Fiction,* March, 1971; December, 1971; December, 1992, p. 31.
*National Review,* January 2, 1964.
*New York Times Book Review,* October 28, 1979; September 12, 1993, p. 36.
*Publishers Weekly,* September 20, 1991, p. 124; July 26, 1993, p. 62; July 18, 1994, p. 239; January 22, 1996, p. 61; February 24, 1997, p. 69.
*Rapport,* Volume 19, number 3, 1996, p. 31.
*School Library Journal,* April, 1992, p. 170.
*Science Fiction and Fantasy Book Review,* April, 1982.
*Science Fiction Review,* May, 1978.
*Tribune Books* (Chicago), December 30, 1990, p. 6; October 27, 1991, p. 6.
*VOYA,* February, 1995, p. 343.
*Washington Post Book World,* February 24, 1980; May 29, 1983; August 26, 1990, p. 8; March 31, 1991, p. 12.
*Wilson Library Bulletin,* January, 1995, p. 90.

\*    \*    \*

## ANDRIAN, Gustave W(illiam) 1918-

*PERSONAL:* Born September 17, 1918, in Hartford, CT; son of William and Alexandra (Perakos) Andrian; married Margaret Anne Penfield, August 18, 1951; children: Robert, Barbara, William. *Education:* Trinity

College, Hartford, CT, B.A., 1940; Johns Hopkins University, Ph.D., 1946.

*ADDRESSES: Home*—94 Midwell Rd., Wethersfield, CT 06109.

*CAREER:* University of Maryland at College Park, instructor in Army Specialized Training Program, 1943-44, assistant professor of Spanish and French, 1945-46; Trinity College, Hartford, CT, assistant professor, 1946-53, associate professor, 1953-62, professor of Modern Languages, 1962-87, John C. McCook Professor of modern languages, 1980-87, professor emeritus, 1987—.

*MEMBER:* Modern Language Association of America, American Association of Teachers of Spanish and Portuguese, American Association of University Professors.

*WRITINGS:*

*Fondo y Forma: Literature, Language, Grammar Review,* Macmillan (New York City), 1970.

(Editor) *Modern Spanish Prose: An Introductory Reader,* Macmillan, 1964, 2nd edition published as *Modern Spanish Prose: An Introductory Reader, with a Selection of Poetry,* 1969, 3rd edition published as *Modern Spanish Prose: With a Selection of Poetry,* 1977, 6th edition published as *Modern Spanish Prose: Literary Selections from Spain and Latin America,* 2000.

(Editor with Jane Denizot Davies) *Pret a Lire: Prose et Poemes Choisis,* Macmillan, 1980.

\*    \*    \*

## ANTIN, Mary 1881-1949

*PERSONAL:* Born June 13, 1881, in Plotzk, Russia; immigrated to the United States, 1894; died after a long illness, May 15 (one source says May 17), 1949, in Suffern, NY; daughter of Israel (in business) and Esther (a business manager; maiden name, Weltman) Antin; married Amadeus William Grabau (a geologist and paleontologist), October 5, 1901 (separated); children: Josephine Esther Grabau Ross. *Education:* Attended Barnard University. *Religion:* Judaism.

*CAREER:* Activist, lecturer, and writer.

*MEMBER:* Hale House.

*WRITINGS:*

*From Plotzk to Boston,* foreword by Israel Zangwill, W. B. Clarke & Co. (Boston, MA), 1899.

*The Promised Land,* Houghton Mifflin (Boston, MA), 1912, published with a foreword by Oscar Handlin, Houghton Mifflin, 1969, republished with an introduction and notes by Werner Sollors, Penguin (New York City), 1997.

*They Who Knock at Our Gates: A Complete Gospel of Immigration,* illustrations by Joseph Stella, Houghton Mifflin, 1914.

*At School in the Promised Land; or, The Story of a Little Immigrant* (chapters from Antin's *The Promised Land*), Houghton Mifflin, 1916, republished with educational material by Mellie John, Houghton Mifflin, 1928.

*Selected Letters of Mary Antin,* edited by Evelyn Salz, Syracuse University Press (Syracuse, NY), 1999.

Contributor to periodicals, including *American Hebrew, American Magazine, Atlantic Monthly, Berkshire Courier, Common Ground, New York Times, Outlook,* and *Primary Education.* Work also published in German. Antin's letters can be found at the Library of Congress Manuscript Division, Washington, DC.

*ADAPTATIONS:* Author Rosemary Wells and illustrator Dan Andreasen adapted Antin's *The Promised Land* as the children's book *Streets of Gold,* Dial Books for Young Readers (New York City), 1999.

*SIDELIGHTS:* Mary Antin, born to a Russian Jewish family, is known for *From Plotzk to Boston* and *The Promised Land,* two autobiographical accounts of her immigration to North America. Her work offers a vivid glimpse into the geographical and personal journey made by millions of Jews between 1891 and 1914. An ardent patriot, she lectured across the United States, praising her new home and the merits of open immigration. Antin asserted that America needed its immigrants as much as the immigrants needed America.

Born in 1881, Antin grew up in the wake of Czar Alexander III's infamous May Laws, 1882 rulings that led to the expulsion of Jews from southern Russia's Pale region. Her mother, born Esther Weltman, was from a prosperous family, and at the age of ten began to help customers and keep books for the family business. She was also a determined scholar, and was allowed to continue her formal education after her self-taught business skills had impressed her father. In an arranged union, Esther Weltman married Israel Antin, an impoverished man studying to become a rabbi. When he did not become a rabbi, Esther's father stopped supporting the young Antin family.

After unsuccessfully trying a number of occupations, Israel Antin traveled throughout Russia, hoping to establish himself financially so that he could send for Esther and the couple's two daughters, Fetchke (also known as Fannie) and Mary. As Mary Antin recounts in *The Promised Land,* "the ideal of a modern education was the priceless ware that my father brought back with him. . . . He resolved to live . . . the life of a modern man. And he saw no better place to begin than with the education of the children." Meanwhile, Esther Weltman Antin had inherited her father's business. But after she and her husband suffered from lengthy illnesses, the business failed. When they regained their health, they decided to emigrate to America with their family, which now included four children.

Israel Antin arrived in the United States in 1891. Experiencing additional financial problems, he depended upon the help of a Jewish benevolent society to sponsor the journey of his wife and their four children three years later. They lived in a series of immigrant slums in Boston, Massachusetts, finally settling in the city's South End. In *The Promised Land,* Antin writes that her parents viewed free public education as "the essence of American opportunity, the treasure that no thief could touch." Yet the family's financial troubles prevented all the children from enjoying this opportunity. Fetchke went to work in a sweatshop to help support the family when the three younger children started school.

Antin flourished in school. She learned English quickly and covered the first five grades of school in six months. When a teacher helped publish one of her early essays in *Primary Education,* Antin was so excited to see her work in print that she decided to become a writer. Through the Hebrew Industrial School, Antin attracted the interest and sponsorship of prominent families. The Hechts, Jewish philanthropists and social reformers, encouraged her writing, and Antin often visited the home of Lina Hecht.

Through the Hechts, Antin met other people who helped her in her literary career. Reform Rabbi Solomon Schindler helped her translate the letters that she had written to her uncle Moses back in Russia. These letters form the basis for Antin's book *From Plotzk to Boston.* While Schindler helped her to translate the letters from the original Yiddish, Mrs. Philip Cowan helped publish the book, and novelist Israel Zangwill agreed to write its introduction. The letters were first published in *American Hebrew,* the New York-based

periodical of Philip Cowan. The book was dedicated to Hattie Hecht, one of Antin's sponsors and friends.

*From Plotzk to Boston* was published in 1899, just five years after Antin's arrival in America. Its publication introduced Antin to other prominent and reformminded Jewish families. According to Susan Koppelman in the *Dictionary of Literary Biography Yearbook: 1984,* the publication of *From Plotzk to Boston* had two goals: "The proceeds from its sales were destined to keep the girl in school, but the role the book was expected to fill among readers was a propagandistic one." At the time, some Americans were vehemently opposed to immigration, especially to the arrival of more Russian Jews. Antin's book tries to help readers identify with the new immigrants and encourages Americans to view the new arrivals in positive ways.

During high school, Antin attended the Boston Latin School for Girls, the public preparatory school for Radcliffe University. Around this time, she met liberal minister and literary figure Edward Everett Hale and became involved with Hale House, his South End settlement house. Through the Natural History Club at Hale House, Antin met her future husband, Amadeus William Grabau, a German American graduate student at Harvard University. Antin and Grabau were married in Boston in 1901.

When her husband began working at Columbia University in New York City, Antin enrolled at Barnard University. Her chronic ill health worsened, and digestive problems kept her from completing her degree. She continued her education more informally through such mentors as Josephine Lazarus (sister of the poet Emma Lazarus), an essayist who praised *From Plotzk to Boston.* Lazarus encouraged Antin to write her autobiography. When they became parents in 1907, Grabau and Antin named their only child Josephine Esther, after Josephine Lazarus and Esther Weltman Antin, guiding figures in Mary Antin's life.

After Lazarus's death in 1910, Antin began the autobiography that Lazarus had been urging her to write. The *Atlantic Monthly* published sections of it in 1911 and 1912. *The Promised Land* was a tremendous literary success when it was published in 1912. It was reprinted thirty-three times and sold nearly 84,000 copies before Antin's death in 1949. A reviewer in the *Nation* admired its important message and "its direct and vivid style," comparing it to the autobiographies of social reformer and immigrant Jacob Riis, patriot Benjamin Franklin, and educator Booker T. Washington. A *New York Times* contributor wrote: "The argument for immigration—the benefit of America and the immigrant, each to each—is implicit in every chapter of *The Promised Land*." The same critic called the book a "moving, vividly interesting" account, as well as "a unique contribution to our modern literature and to our modern history."

The first half of *The Promised Land* recounts Antin's childhood in Plotzk. The author describes how she understood the world through family stories. The book's second half focuses on life in "the promised land," the United States. Antin discounts her family's suffering by viewing hardships as temporary setbacks that did not dim her enthusiastic view of her new home. She views settlement houses and free education and libraries as the tools immigrants could use to succeed in their new environment.

Although Antin expresses optimism in the title *The Promised Land,* she admits that her mother and sister did not reap the benefits of the promised land. Her father's belief in the need for education did not extend to his wife, and he believed that women should be subservient to their husbands. Fetchke's years in a sweatshop were punctuated by an arranged marriage to a similarly traditional man, and she labored at home much as she did at the factory, without any opportunities to make decisions for herself. Antin was aware that she could have had a life much like her mother or Fetchke's, and the writer recognized all that these women did for her.

*The Promised Land* describes the immigrant experience as a rebirth and a religious experience. Critics who charged that Antin was moving away from her Jewish roots and assimilating into the larger culture were also offended by her critique of Judaism as a patriarchal religion. Yet Antin adamantly identified as a Jew and always observed the Jewish holidays; her ambivalence toward Judaism encompassed both her love for its traditions and her loyalty to the women that she believed it devalued.

Former United States president Theodore Roosevelt recruited Antin to lecture for the Progressive Party, and the author later campaigned for Republican presidential candidate Charles Evans Hughes. Her political speeches were infused with her religious beliefs, and she explained immigration and the "unique spiritual mission of America" at various places, including prisons, Carnegie Hall, and the Tuskegee Institute. While she was giving lectures across the country, traveling for months at a time, her sister Fetchke, now divorced, took care of Antin's household.

In 1914 Antin's *They Who Knock at Our Gates: A Complete Gospel of Immigration* was published. First published as an acclaimed series of articles in *American Magazine,* this treatise on immigration policy argues for open immigration and reveals the ways in which immigrants were victimized. Antin characterizes immigrants as "not the refuse, but the sinew and bone of all the nations." Reviewing the work in the *Dial,* one critic praised Antin's "command of her adopted language," observing that the author's "Americanism is as thorough-going as any true patriot could wish, and her enthusiasm in espousing the cause of both the immigrant and the new land to which he is hastening, is contagious."

By 1918 Antin was an impassioned Zionist, supporting the creation of a new nation for Jews in the Middle East. Her marriage was troubled, due in part to Grabau's career difficulties. He had not received any raises in his $2,500 salary at Columbia University, even though he became a full professor. Antin made six to ten thousand dollars a year on the lecture circuit and received royalties from her books. The discrepancy in their salaries was allegedly a source of marital tension. Columbia University dismissed Grabau in 1919 for vociferously expressing his German sympathies in World War I. Due to their professional and ideological differences and to spare their daughter further anguish, Antin and Grabau separated.

Antin turned from political activism to an interest in health and spirituality when a physical breakdown forced her to retire from the lecture circuit. Throughout her life, her physical problems were attributed to nervous distress. She spent time at the Riggs Institute in Stockbridge, Massachusetts, and through Dr. Riggs met William and Agnes Gould. The Goulds had founded Gould Farm in the Adirondack Mountains in 1913 on the belief that love could lead to spiritual fulfillment. Antin collected material for a book on William Gould, but produced only a single chapter. She studied Christianity because she believed it could help her discuss Gould's work. Her last publications were "The Soundless Trumpet" (1937), an *Atlantic Monthly* essay exploring mystical experiences, and "House of One Father" (1941), an essay affirming her Jewish identity and published in *Common Ground.*

Antin died in 1949 as a result of her ongoing health problems. While the United States did not entirely live up to the promise it had held for her family in their imaginations, it indeed proved to be Antin's promised land. To her, becoming an American meant sharing ideals and an identity with the likes of George Washington and Abraham Lincoln, and even in the face of strong anti-immigrant sentiment, she continued to see her adopted home in a positive light.

*BIOGRAPHICAL/CRITICAL SOURCES:*

BOOKS

Antin, Mary, *The Promised Land,* Houghton Mifflin (Boston, MA), 1912, published with a foreword by Oscar Handlin, Houghton Mifflin, 1969, republished with an introduction and notes by Werner Sollors, Penguin, 1997.

Antin, Mary, *They Who Knock at Our Gates: A Complete Gospel of Immigration,* illustrations by Joseph Stella, Houghton Mifflin, 1914.

*Dictionary of Literary Biography Yearbook: 1984,* Gale (Detroit, MI), 1985.

*PERIODICALS*

*Dial,* June 1, 1914.
*Nation,* May 23, 1912.
*New York Times,* April 14, 1912.*

\*    \*    \*

## ARMYTAGE, Walter Harry Green    1915-1998

*OBITUARY NOTICE*—See index for *CA* sketch: Born November 22, 1915, in Kimberley, South Africa; died of Alzheimer's disease, June 13, 1998. Educator and historian. Armytage devoted his career to education and wrote prodigiously on the subject. After graduating from Downing College of Cambridge in 1937, he continued studying there and received a certificate in education in 1938, followed by a master's degree in 1941. His career was briefly interrupted by World War II, when he served as a member of the London Irish Rifles. After returning from the war he joined the education faculty at the University of Sheffield in 1946. He quickly moved up the ranks, being named senior lecturer and then professor before he was forty. In 1954 he was tapped to serve as chair of the department, a post he maintained until 1982. Through the years he served as visiting faculty at several universities including Kent State and the University of Michigan. His writing continued throughout his career. His first book, *A.J. Mundella: The Liberal Background of the Labour Movement,* was published in 1951, and was followed by numerous books on the topic of education including *Civic Universities: Aspects of a British Tradition, A Social*

*History of Engineering, Four Hundred Years of English Education,* and a series of four books that looked at U.S., French, German and Russian influences on English education.

*OBITUARIES AND OTHER SOURCES:*

BOOKS

*Who's Who,* Marquis, 1998.

*PERIODICALS*

*Times* (London), July 8, 1998.

\*    \*    \*

## ARTHUR, Karl    1952-

*PERSONAL:* Born August 3, 1952, in St. Paul, MN; son of Bernice Ruth Norlemann. *Ethnicity:* "Caucasian." *Education:* Attended college in Hayward, CA; studied natural resource management; attended University of Arizona. *Politics:* "Constitutionalist." *Religion:* Lutheran. *Avocational interests:* Private pilot, training tracking dogs, sailing.

*ADDRESSES: Home*—Tucson, AZ. *Office*—c/o Ravenhawk Books, 7739 East Broadway Blvd., Suite 95, Tucson, AZ 85710; fax 520-886-9885. *E-mail*—76673.3165@compuserve.com.

*CAREER:* 6DOE Investigations, Tucson, AZ, private investigator, 1981—. Worked as government consumer fraud specialist. Executive producer of the documentary film *Searching for the Write Life,* 2000.

*MEMBER:* National Writers Association, Society of Southwestern Authors, International Association of Credit Card Investigators, Arizona Homicide Investigators Association, Lions Club International, North American Conservation Association, Sedona Humane Society.

*WRITINGS:*

*All . . . the Little Bitches* (suspense novel), Ravenhawk Books (Tucson, AZ), 1999.

*Vanquishing the Predator* (nonfiction), Ravenhawk Books, in press.

Author of "Confessions of a Former Republican," a syndicated political opinion column, 1997.

*WORK IN PROGRESS: Bank of Satan,* a mystery novel, publication by Ravenhawk Books expected in 2000; *Desert Dogs,* a novel, completion expected in 2001; *Who's Scamming Whom?,* nonfiction, 2001; *Hiring Strategies for the New Millennium,* 2001.

*SIDELIGHTS:* Karl Arthur told *CA:* "My primary motivation for writing is an effort to entertain myself and relieve boredom; especially from February through August, when there are no football games.

"My efforts in fiction were influenced by Edgar Allan Poe, Herman Melville, and Vincent Price. My nonfiction projects help me come to terms with and, hopefully, validate my life's experiences.

"I am a most undisciplined writer. I do not set aside specific times or days to write. I've tried this, but it just doesn't work for me. I write when I feel the desire, the need, the passion. When that will occur, only God knows. I write when I have something to say, even if it is only to myself."

\* \* \*

**AYRES, Becky**
    **See HICKOX, Rebecca (Ayres)**

# B

**BARONDES, Samuel H(erbert) 1933-**

*PERSONAL:* Born December 21, 1933, in Brooklyn, New York, NY; son of Solomon and Yetta (Kaplow) Barondes; married Ellen Slater, September 1, 1963 (died, November 22, 1971); children: Elizabeth Francesca, Jessica Gabrielle. *Education:* Columbia University, A.B., 1954, M.D., 1958.

*ADDRESSES: Office*—Box 0984, LPPI F 346, Department of Psychiatry, University of California, San Francisco, San Francisco, CA 94143-0984. *E-mail*—barondes@socrates.ucsf.edu.

*CAREER:* Psychiatrist, researcher, and educator. Peter Bent Brigham Hospital, Boston, MA, intern, later assistant resident in medicine, 1958-60; United States Public Health Service, National Institutes of Health, Bethesda, MD, senior assistant surgeon, 1960-63; McLean Hospital and Massachusetts General Hospital, both Boston, resident in psychiatry, 1963-66; Albert Einstein College of Medicine, Bronx, New York City, assistant professor, then associate professor of psychiatry and molecular biology, 1966-69; University of California, San Diego, professor of psychiatry, 1969-86; *Journal of Neurobiology,* associate editor, 1970-77; University of California, San Francisco, professor and chair, department of psychiatry, 1986-94, director of the Langley Porter Psychiatric Institute, 1986-94, director of the Center of Neurobiology and Psychiatry, 1994—, Jeanne and Sanford Robertson professor of neurobiology and psychiatry, 1996—; member of editorial boards of professional journals.

*MEMBER:* National Institutes of Health (member, alcoholism and alcohol problems review committee, 1967-70), National Science Foundation (member, neurobiology review committee, 1970-73), Veterans Administration Central Office (member, neurobiology merit review board, 1972-75), McKnight Foundation (member, scholarship review committee, 1976-89), American Society of Cell Biology (council member, 1981-84), McKnight Endowment Fund for Neuroscience (member, board of directors, 1986—; president, 1989—), Charles E. Culpeper Foundation (member, scientific advisory committee, 1987—).

International Brain Research Organization (member, governing council, 1994), National Institute of Mental Health (chair, genetics workgroup, 1997), Foundation Fund for Research in Psychiatry (member, board of directors), Buck Center for Research in Aging (member, board of scientific advisors), Research America (member, scientific advisory committee), Institute of Medicine-National Academy of Science, Society of Neuroscience, American Society of Biological Chemists, Psychiatric Research Society.

*AWARDS, HONORS:* National Institutes of Health fellow, 1960-63; Harvard University Medical School, Cambridge, MA, teaching fellow in psychiatry, 1963-66; career development award, National Institutes of Health, 1966-69; Research Career Development Award, United States Public Health Service, National Institutes of Health, 1967; Fogarty International Scholar, National Institutes of Health, 1979; J. Elliott Royer Award, 1989; P. H. Stillmark Memorial Medal, Estonia, 1989; fellow, American Association for the Advancement of Science, American Psychiatry Association, and American College of Neuropsychopharmacology.

*WRITINGS:*

(Editor) Symposia of the International Society of Cell Biology, *Cellular Dynamics of the Neuron,* Academic Press (New York City), 1969.

(Editor) *Neuronal Recognition,* Plenum Press (New York City), 1976.

*Molecules and Mental Illness,* Scientific American Library (New York City), 1992.

*Mood Genes: Hunting for Origins of Mania and Depression,* W. H. Freeman (New York City), 1998.

Contributor of articles to professional publications.

*SIDELIGHTS:* An educator and researcher, Samuel H. Barondes is an authority on the genetic factors of mental illness. A professor of psychiatry and other subjects at various schools, he has directed research institutions and has worked with a number of organizations devoted to the study of mental illness. Critics have praised Barondes's books *Molecules and Mental Illness* and *Mood Genes: Hunting for Origins of Mania and Depression,* predicting that the works will interest both scientists and lay readers. In *Mood Genes,* Barondes discusses the research he and others have conducted in order to identify the specific genes that cause severe mental illnesses.

Barondes has also edited studies for professionals in the health sciences, among them *Cellular Dynamics of the Neuron* and *Neuronal Recognition. Science* contributor Bruce McEwen stated that *Cellular Dynamics of the Neuron* (1969) "provides a good insight into cell biological approaches to some of the central problems of neurobiology." McEwen noted that the research in the book could quickly become outdated and that an index would improve the work, yet concluded that *Cellular Dynamics of the Neuron* "is of considerable value both as an introduction to the field for the novice and as an important source of information and reference material for the specialist." As the editor of *Neuronal Recognition* (1976), Barondes crafted a book that "describes some of the evidence for the formation of selective synapses and several biochemical and cellular models for how it may be mediated," according to *Science* contributors Michael Dennis and Regis B. Kelly.

In *Molecules and Mental Illness* (1992), Barondes offers readers a brief but broad look at biological psychiatry. He describes the reemergence of the discipline during the later part of the twentieth century—with the introduction of new psychotherapeutic drugs—and explains how these medications, brain chemicals, and genetics affect mental illnesses. He devotes a chapter

each to schizophrenia, manic-depressive disorder (also known as bipolar disorder), and obsessive-compulsive disorder, and also discusses neurotransmitters and receptors. The book also includes photographs, artwork by mentally ill individuals, diagrams, and poetry.

Reviewing *Molecules and Mental Illness* in *Choice,* S. Shapiro observed that it offers "clear and simple explanations of the basic biology of brain function." In a *Nature* review, Solomon H. Snyder called the book "an exquisitely elegant volume" with "rigorous yet highly readable explanations of the biological underpinnings of mental illness," and deemed it "an important contribution that will interest all thoughtful readers, whether scientists or educated lay people." Philip Morrison, discussing *Molecules and Mental Illness* in *Scientific American,* called Barondes "a gifted expositor and a most cultivated man who has given us a serious, exciting, up-to-date, and compact introduction to biological psychiatry." Morrison added: "It is a pleasure to remark that the chapters devoted to the genetics of behavior, both simple and complex, to the molecular mechanism of the genes themselves and in particular to neurons and their circuitry are as readable and concise accounts as any a reviewer can cite."

Barondes's book *Mood Genes: Hunting for Origins of Mania and Depression* (1998) focuses on the genetic component of mental illnesses. Another multifaceted work, *Mood Genes* includes historical information, a technical explanation of how Barondes and other scientists have tried to identify genes that predispose individuals to mental illness, and personal stories about mentally ill patients and their families. In the book's history section, Barondes discusses the professional and political background of such scientific research. He explains that for years, biological psychiatry had taken a back seat to the Freudian, psychoanalytical treatment of mental illness. The popularity of Freudian theory during the early twentieth century was furthered by the fact that the Nazis appropriated the work of German researchers to validate the sterilization of hundreds of thousands of people, thus tainting the study of biological psychiatry.

Barondes "demonstrates quite elegantly how the principles of genetic research have evolved," wrote Robbie Vickers in a *New Scientist* review of *Mood Genes.* Yet Vickers added that the author makes a "rather extravagant claim about the possible molecular underpinnings of mania and depression" when he argues that genetic findings can help in the development of new behavioral and biological treatments for those types of mental illness. *Nature* contributor George Fink stated that

"Barondes dismisses rather peremptorily the candidate gene approach (looking for genes that appear biologically relevant to the disorder) in the hunt for mood genes." Fink noted that the approach that Barondes does discuss in *Mood Genes,* the linkage approach, "has failed to identify mood genes." Yet Fink admitted that "Barondes lucidly encompasses the development of modern psychiatry and genetics, and shows how the two are coupled in the quest for the genetic basis of mood disorders." *New York Times Book Review* contributor Derek Bickerton wrote that he "found it hard to stop reading *Mood Genes.*" Bickerton added that although the book contains a wealth of scientific terms and concepts, "Barondes unfolds his complex material with such consummate skill—moving simply and logically from one step to the next—that these hurdles can be taken in stride."

*BIOGRAPHICAL/CRITICAL SOURCES:*

*PERIODICALS*

*Choice,* October, 1993, p. 322.
*Nature,* June 17, 1993, p. 594; June 11, 1998, pp. 534-536.
*New Scientist,* June 13, 1998, p. 43.
*New York Times Book Review,* September 20, 1998, p. 19.
*Science,* December 11, 1970, pp. 1187-1188; February 11, 1977, p. 570.
*Scientific American,* November, 1993, pp. 116-117.*

\*          \*          \*

**BARR, Amelia Edith (Huddleston)   1831-1919**
**(J. O. Nugent, C. Kendrick)**

*PERSONAL:* Born March 29, 1831, in Ulverston, Lancashire, England; died March 10, 1919, in Richmond Hill, NY; buried in Sleepy Hollow cemetery; daughter of William Henry (a Methodist minister) and Mary (Singleton) Huddleston; married Robert Barr (a wool merchant), July 11, 1850 (died, 1867); children: Mary, Lilly, Alice, several others. *Education:* Attended Normal School in Glasgow, Scotland. *Religion:* Methodist.

*CAREER:* Teacher, 1847-69. Freelance writer, 1869-1919.

*WRITINGS:*

*Romances and Realities: Tales of Truth and Fancy,* J. B. Ford (New York City), 1876.

*The Young People of Shakespeare's Dramas for Youthful Readers,* Appleton (New York City), 1882.
*Cluny MacPherson: A Tale of Brotherly Love,* Dodd, Mead (New York City), 1883.
*Scottish Sketches,* American Tract Society (New York City), 1883.
*The Hallam Succession,* Dodd, Mead, 1884.
*Jan Vedder's Wife,* Dodd, Mead, 1885.
*The Lost Silver of Briffault,* Philips & Hunt (New York City), 1885.
*Between Two Loves: A Tale of the West Riding,* Harper (New York City), 1886.
*The Bow of Orange Ribbon: A Romance of New York,* Dodd, Mead, 1886.
*A Daughter of Fife,* Dodd, Mead, 1886.
*The Last of the MacAllisters,* Harper, 1886.
*The Squire of Sandal-side,* Dodd, Mead, 1886.
*A Border Shepherdess: A Romance of Eskdale,* Dodd, Mead, 1887.
*Paul and Christina,* Dodd, Mead, 1887.
*Christopher, and other Stories,* Philips & Hunt, 1888.
*In Spite of Himself: A Tale of the West Riding,* Clarke, 1888.
*Master of His Fate,* Dodd, Mead, 1888.
*The Novels of Besant and Rice,* Dodd, Mead, 1888.
*Remember the Alamo,* Dodd, Mead, 1888, published as *Woven of Love and Glory,* Clarke, 1890.
*Feet of Clay,* Dodd, Mead, 1889.
*Friend Olivia,* Dodd, Mead, 1889.
*The Beads of Tasmer,* Dodd, Mead, 1890.
*The Household of MacNeil,* Dodd, Mead, 1890.
*She Loved a Sailor,* Dodd, Mead, 1890.
*Love for an Hour Is Love Forever,* Dodd, Mead, 1891.
*Mrs. Barr's Short Stories,* Bonner (New York City), 1891.
*A Rose of a Hundred Leaves: A Love Story,* Dodd, Mead, 1891.
*A Sister to Esau,* Dodd, Mead, 1891.
*Michael and Theodora: A Russian Story,* Bradley & Woodruff (Boston), 1892.
*The Preacher's Daughter: A Domestic Romance,* Ward & Drummond (New York City), 1892.
(Under pseudonym J. O. Nugent) *Girls of a Feather: A Novel with Illustrations,* Bonner (New York City), 1893.
*The Lone House,* Dodd, Mead, 1893.
*The Mate of the "Easter Belle" and Other Stories,* Bonner, 1893.
*A Singer from the Sea,* Dodd, Mead, 1893.
*Bernicia,* Dodd, Mead, 1895.
(Under pseudonym C. Kendrick) *The Flower of Gala Water: A Novel with Illustrations,* Bonner, 1895.
*A Knight of the Nets,* Dodd, Mead, 1896.

*Winter Evening Tales,* Christian Herald (New York City), 1896.

*The King's Highway,* Dodd, Mead, 1897.

*Prisoners of Conscience,* Century (New York City), 1897.

*Stories of Life and Love,* Christian Herald, 1897.

*Maids, Wives, and Bachelors,* Dodd, Mead, 1898.

*Trinity Bells: A Tale of Old New York,* Taylor, 1898.

*I, Thou, and the Other One: A Love Story,* Dodd, Mead, 1899.

*Was It Right to Forgive? A Domestic Romance,* Stone (New York City), 1899.

*The Maid of Maiden Lane: A Sequel to "The Bow of Orange Ribbon": A Love Story,* Dodd, Mead, 1900.

*The Lion's Whelp: A Story of Cromwell's Time,* Dodd, Mead, 1901.

*Souls of Passage,* Dodd, Mead, 1901.

*A Song of a Single Note: A Love Story,* Dodd, Mead, 1902.

*The Black Shilling: A Tale of Boston Towns,* Dodd, Mead, 1903.

*Thyra Verrick: A Love Story,* Taylor (New York City), 1903.

*The Belle of Bowling Green,* Dodd, Mead, 1904.

*Cecilia's Lovers,* Dodd, Mead, 1905.

*The Man Between: An International Romance,* Authors and Newspapers Association (New York City), 1906, published as *Love Will Venture In,* Chatto & Windus (London), 1907.

*The Heart of Jessy Laurie,* Dodd, Mead, 1907.

*The Strawberry Handkerchief: A Romance of the Stamp Act,* Dodd, Mead, 1908.

*The Hands of Compulsion,* Dodd, Mead, 1909.

*The House on Cherry Street,* Dodd, Mead, 1909.

*A Reconstructed Marriage,* Dodd, Mead, 1910.

*A Maid of Old New York: A Romance of Peter Stuyvesant's Time,* Dodd, Mead, 1911.

*Sheila Vedder,* Dodd, Mead, 1911.

*All the Days of My Life: An Autobiography, the Red Leaves of a Human Heart,* Appleton (New York City), 1913.

*Three Score and Ten: A Book for the Aged,* Appleton, 1913.

*Playing with Fire,* Appleton, 1914.

*The Measure of a Man,* Appleton, 1915.

*The Winning of Lucia: A Love Story,* Appleton, 1915.

*Profit and Loss,* Appleton, 1916.

*Christine, A Fife Fisher Girl,* Appleton, 1917.

*Joan; A Romance of an English Mining Village,* Appleton, 1917.

*An Orkney Maid,* Appleton, 1918.

*The Paper Cap: A Story of Love and Labor,* Appleton, 1918.

*Songs in the Common Chord: Songs for Everyone to Sing, Tuned to the C Major Chord of This Life,* Appleton, 1919.

SIDELIGHTS: Amelia Edith Barr is best known for her historical romances, many of which are set during Colonial times. Barr's work contains hints of her moral and religious background, as well as hints of her appreciation of women's status. As Bruce Guy Chabot noted, in an article for the *Dictionary of Literary Biography:* "Though [Barr's] narratives are often melodramatic and moralistic, containing little real suspense or humor, and her dialogue is not realistic, her characters are interesting and her pacing of events keeps the readers' interest." Barr's tales, which were enormously popular during her lifetime, pleased many because of their rich historical detail, and because of their comfortably preachy moral tone.

Barr, who wrote so prolifically about American history, was actually born in Ulverston, a small town in Lancashire, England. Her parents, William Henry and Mary Singleton Huddleston, were of middling fortune but high education. William Huddleston was a Methodist minister whose wealth enabled Barr to attend private schools early on. She writes in her memoir: "My physical being was cared for by loving parents in a sweet orderly home, and my mental life well fed by books stimulating the imagination." But by the time Barr reached sixteen, her father "lost his fortune," as a contributor to the *Feminist Companion to Literature in English* explained. Accordingly, Barr began to teach at Norfolk, and she then went to the Normal School in Glasgow to train for a lifetime of such work.

While in Scotland, however, Barr met Robert Barr, who was also the child of a minister. As Chabot recounted: "[Barr's] family, who were Scots, opposed the marriage because Huddleston's family was English and poor. Amelia Barr eventually opposed the marriages of her two eldest daughters, and the theme of parents opposing their daughters' marriages is found in many of her novels." Regardless of their parents' disapproval, the two were married on July 11, 1850; thereafter, as the *Feminist Companion* contributor noted, Barr endured an "ambivalent marriage," one which would produce 8 children in all.

By 1853, Barr's husband had gone bankrupt, forcing the two to relocate to the United States. Barr had become acquainted with Harriet Beecher Stowe and Henry Ward Beecher back in Scotland, and she soon began to write for Henry Ward Beecher's newspapers. As Chabot explains, Barr worked both in Chicago and in Memphis, living briefly in Austin, Texas, before settling in Galveston. But in 1867 Barr's husband died, leaving her little to support those of her children who had survived the journey. Barr took Mary, Lilly, and Alice, her three daughters, to Ridgewood, New Jersey in order to begin a new life as a writer.

Barr earned a small but sufficient income through her writing, and is remembered for her sentimental historical novels more than her poetry. Barr's work began to be accepted right away, and by 1876 some of her fiction was published in book form. By the 1880s, Barr had truly found her milieu: romances set in the early years of the United States. In part, this specialty derived from the demands of the market; American novels sold better. But the specialized genre seemed to suit Barr well. Chabot illustrates Barr's typical method: "Barr's practice was to research historical periods in preparation for writing about them. She spent long days studying in the fine arts alcove of the south hall of the Astor Library, which she believed she had seen years earlier in a vision as a 'city of books.' " *Jan Vedder's Wife* (1885), an early novel, was produced in an early version of this practice. As Chabot comments: "[the novel] shows the results of Barr's painstaking research into the backgrounds and lifestyles of her characters, in this case Dutch speech patterns, literary history, domestic life, and clothing styles." *Jan Vedder's Wife* is also, like much of Barr's work, intensely moralistic in tone.

Critics also praised Barr for her realistic descriptions, her intense historical research, and her strong sense of character development. In one of her most famous novels, *Remember the Alamo* (1888), Barr used these gifts to depict Texas history. In the novel, Robert Wolf, a New York doctor, comes to San Antonio only to become swept up in the area's battles over territory. Chabot explains: "Like any historical novelist Barr uses actual historical events as a starting point, inventing what is necessary to flesh out known facts into fiction. Her heroes are larger than life and more legendary than historical, but the work stands as an important reflection of lasting attitudes about the lore surrounding the Alamo and the emotionally charged roles of the major characters." *Remember the Alamo* depicts such American figures as Davy Crockett and General Houston with obvious care; General Houston's son even wrote to Barr after her novel was published to thank her for her impressive reconstruction of his father's character and work.

Because of her skillful depiction of character, her rigid moral code, and her extensive research, Barr's novels became some of the best-selling fiction books of her time. Barr's books were loved by her readers because, through them, she spoke as truly as she could. Moreover, she set high standards for writers of historical romance; her careful research made her books enlightening as well as fun.

*BIOGRAPHICAL/CRITICAL SOURCES:*

*BOOKS*

Blain, Virginia, Clements, Patricia and Grundy, Isobel, *The Feminist Companion to Literature in English,* Yale University Press (New Haven, CT), 1990.
*Bloomsbury Guide to Women's Literature,* Prentice Hall (New York City), 1992.
Bzowski, Frances Diodato, *American Women Playwrights, 1900-1930,* Greenwood Press (Westport, CT), 1992.
*Dictionary of Literary Biography,* Volume 202: *Nineteenth-Century American Fiction Writers,* Gale Research (Detroit, MI), 1999.
*Oxford Companion to American Literature,* Oxford University Press (New York City), 1995.\*

\*    \*    \*

**BAZELL, Robert (Joseph)   1945-**

*PERSONAL:* Born August 21, 1945, in Pittsburgh, PA; son of Irving and Beatrice (Robb) Bazell; married Ilene Tanz, September 11, 1966 (divorced); married Margot Weinshel, July 31, 1979; children: (first marriage) Rebecca, Joshua; (second marriage) Stephanie. *Education:* University of California, Berkeley, B.A. (biochemistry), 1967, Ph.D. (immunology); studied biology at the University of Sussex, England, 1968-69.

*ADDRESSES: Office*—NBC News, 30 Rockefeller Plaza, New York, NY 10112.

*CAREER: Science,* Washington, DC, writer for the News and Comment section, 1971-72; *New York Post,* New York City, reporter, 1972-76; WNBC-TV, New York City, reporter, 1976; NBC News, New York City, 1976—, began as science correspondent, became chief health and science correspondent, chief health and science correspondent for NBC series, including *Dateline NBC, Now,* and *Today.*

*MEMBER:* Phi Beta Kappa.

*AWARDS, HONORS:* George Foster Peabody Broadcasting Award, 1993, for health and science reports for

NBC; Maggie Award, Planned Parenthood, and Alfred I. du Pont-Columbia Award, both for reports on the AIDS epidemic; Emmy Award, outstanding informational or cultural programming, for report on experimental brain surgery, *Now;* Emmy Award, for series of reports on the brain, *NBC Nightly News with Tom Brokaw.*

*WRITINGS:*

*Her-2: The Making of Herceptin, a Revolutionary Treatment for Breast Cancer,* foreword by Dr. Mary-Claire King, Random House (New York City), 1998.

Contributor to periodicals.

*SIDELIGHTS:* The chief health and science correspondent for NBC News, Robert Bazell has been creating nationally televised reports on medical and scientific issues since 1976. He has won Emmy Awards for his reports on the brain and brain surgery, other awards for his stories on the AIDS epidemic, and a prestigious George Foster Peabody Broadcasting Award in 1993. Bazell also wrote a book about the development of a gene-based drug for breast cancer, *Her-2: The Making of Herceptin, a Revolutionary Treatment for Breast Cancer.*

Herceptin is a gene-based medication that has been designed to attack a specific gene. While it does not cause the nausea or hair loss that is associated with chemotherapy and radiation therapy, the drug is associated with an increased risk of stray cancer cells metastasizing to the brain and the potential weakening of the heart muscle. Herceptin is useful in certain cases of breast cancer where the individual produces too much of a protein called Her-2/neu, which leads to excessive cell growth. One-quarter to one-third of breast cancer patients produce such high levels of Her-2/neu.

Authorities at the United States Food and Drug Administration (FDA) approved Herceptin as a treatment for advanced breast cancer during the late 1990s. While *Library Journal* contributor Gail Hendler wrote that FDA authorities "fast-tracked" their approval of Herceptin, *Her-2: The Making of Herceptin* reveals that there was nothing particularly fast or easy about the work leading up to this point. Bazell recounts how the drug's cocreator Dennis Slamon needed exceptional resolve to guide his research past the criticism of scientists and past the poorly devised clinical trials sponsored by its manufacturer. The author introduces readers to women with breast cancer who could not gain access to Herceptin

and who succumbed to the disease, and others who took the drug in its trial stages. The book also includes profiles of individuals and companies who gave financial support to the project.

According to a *Publishers Weekly* reviewer, *Her-2: The Making of Herceptin* is an "admirably objective report," as "Bazell paints a complete picture of the development of the nontoxic 'miracle' drug." *Library Journal* contributor Gail Hendler praised Bazell's "meticulous research." Writing in the *New York Times Book Review,* Robin Marantz Henig described *Her-2: The Making of Herceptin* as "a troubling and fascinating book." Touched by the book's profiles of breast cancer patients, Henig found that these individuals "give *Her-2* its particular sting," but concluded that the book inspires optimism: "*Her-2* leaves the reader with the impression that we might be on the threshold of a new way of understanding and treating one of our most dreaded diseases."

*BIOGRAPHICAL/CRITICAL SOURCES:*

*PERIODICALS*

*Library Journal,* September 15, 1998, p. 102.
*New York Times Book Review,* September 20, 1998, p. 19.
*Publishers Weekly,* August 10, 1998, p. 378.*

\*        \*        \*

**BEAUFORT, Simon**

*PERSONAL: Education:* Studied history.

*ADDRESSES: Agent*—c/o St. Martin's Press, 175 Fifth Ave., Rm. 1715, New York, NY 10010.

*CAREER:* University of Cambridge, Cambridge, England, historian.

*WRITINGS:*

*Murder in the Holy City,* St. Martin's Press (New York City), 1998.

*SIDELIGHTS:* Simon Beaufort is a Cambridge historian and the author of the novel *Murder in the Holy City.* An historical mystery set in Jerusalem in the year 1100, *Murder in the Holy City* introduces the reader to Sir Geoffrey de Mappestone of England, a Crusader who participated in the conquest of Jerusalem. Even though the Christian Crusaders have triumphed over the Greeks, Jews, and Saracens, they are divided into various religious and military factions, all with their own motives. These uneasy allies share a common fear when a serial killer murders two knights and three priests.

Geoffrey finds one of the victims himself when his friend and fellow knight is stabbed in the house of a Greek widow. Geoffrey is in the service of Lord Tancred, who orders him to find the killer, a command seconded by Duke Godfrey of Lorraine, a Catholic religious leader known as the Advocate. The investigation leads Geoffrey into the heart of Jerusalem and into the dangerous arena of conflict between the knights and priests. The knight seeks to satisfy Tancred and to prevent other deaths, complicated tasks that ultimately put his own life at stake.

A *Kirkus Reviews* contributor found that *Murder in the Holy City* will appeal to "readers interested in the place and period," but warned that "puzzle fans must contend with an endlessly repetitive, confusing, and dull slog." A *Publishers Weekly* reviewer noted that Beaufort "neatly captures the particulars of everyday life" in ancient Jerusalem, and deemed the novel to be a "satisfying mystery nestled securely in a well-detailed historical context." Reviewing *Murder in the Holy City* in the *Library Journal,* Rex E. Klett wrote that the work contains "good plotting, abundant action, and close attention to period verisimilitude."

*BIOGRAPHICAL/CRITICAL SOURCES:*

*PERIODICALS*

*Kirkus Reviews,* November 1, 1998.
*Library Journal,* December, 1998, p. 160.
*Publishers Weekly,* November 9, 1998, p. 60.*

\*      \*      \*

## BECHER, Anne 1963-

*PERSONAL:* Surname is pronounced *Beck*-er; born December 19, 1963, in Denver, CO; daughter of Harold T. (a psychiatrist) and Ingrid (an indexer; maiden name, Haymaker) Becher; married Joseph J. Richey, August 16, 1987; children: Jacob Swan, Flora Sol. *Ethnicity:* "European-American." *Education:* Carleton College, B.A. (magna cum laude), 1987; University of Colorado,

M.A., 1992. *Politics:* Democrat. *Religion:* Jewish. *Avocational interests:* Gardening, yoga, music.

*ADDRESSES: Home*—2737 Kalmia Ave., Boulder, CO 80304. *E-mail*—Anne.Becher@colorado.edu.

*CAREER:* University of Colorado, Boulder, instructor in Spanish, 1989, 1990-92, and 1996—. New Horizons Cooperative Preschool, co-chairperson of board of directors, 1998-99.

*MEMBER:* National Writers Union, Phi Beta Kappa.

*AWARDS, HONORS:* Watson Fellow, T. J. Watson Foundation, 1987.

*WRITINGS:*

(With Beatrice Blake) *The New Key to Costa Rica,* Ulysses Press, 1986, 14th edition, 1999.
*Biodiversity: A Reference Handbook,* American Bibliographical Center-Clio Press (Santa Barbara, CA), 1998.
*American Environmental Leaders,* American Bibliographical Center-Clio Press, in press.

Co-editor and co-publisher of the literary magazine *Underground Forest/La Selva Subterranea,* 1986—.

*SIDELIGHTS:* Anne Becher told *CA:* "Having been concerned about the environment and social justice for as long as I can remember, I try to write on these topics or to integrate these issues into whatever I am writing. In *The New Key to Costa Rica,* Beatrice Blake and I cover all types of tourism, but our hearts are really in ecotourism and community-based tourism. We wrote and carried an extensive 'sustainable tourism' survey, in order to recognize lodges that were devoted to conservation, providing good jobs to local people, and sustaining Costa Rica's fragile culture. The lodges that scored high in these three areas were given a star in our book. Our hope is that, by steering our readers to those places, conservation and sustainable development will be given an extra boost.

"Since 1996 I have also been writing reference books for the American Bibliographical Center-Clio Press. *Biodiversity* came out in 1998. It's a book in the 'Contemporary World Issues' series and follows the format of the series: chapters provide an overview, a chronology, biographical sketches, statistics and important documents, a directory of organizations, and print and non-print resources and reviews. Right now I am working on a biographical dictionary of American environmental leaders. It will include four-hundred short biographies of historical and contemporary figures.

"My master's degree is in Hispanic languages, and I teach Spanish because I enjoy doing it. It's much less solitary than writing! It also provides me with a more dependable income. I enjoy the diversity of devoting my work time to both writing and teaching, but it's hard to be doing both in addition to raising my two kids and working with my husband to maintain our home."

*BIOGRAPHICAL/CRITICAL SOURCES:*

PERIODICALS

*Library Journal,* September 1, 1998, p. 168.

\*　　\*　　\*

**BELL, Jadrien**
　　**See GOLDEN, Christie**

\*　　\*　　\*

**BERTOLUCCI, Attilio 1911-**

*PERSONAL:* Born November 18, 1911, in San Prospero, Italy; son of Bernardo (a landowner) and Maria Rossetti (a landowner) Bertolucci; married Ninetta Giovanardi (an elementary-school teacher); children: Bernardo, Giuseppe. *Education:* Attended University of Parma School of Law, 1931-35; University of Bologna, degree in art history, 1935.

*CAREER:* Poet and essayist. High school teacher of art history, late 1930s-54; RAI (Italian Broadcasting Company), beginning 1954. Worked as a translator, editor of literary journals, and founder and director of "La fenice," a series on foreign poets for Gunada Publishers.

*AWARDS, HONORS:* Premio Viareggio, for *La capanna indiana,* 1951; Etna-Taormina Prize, for *Viaggio d'inverno,* 1971; Tarquinia-Cardarelli Prize, for *Viaggio d'inverno,* 1971; Biella Prize, for *La camera da letto,* book 1, 1984.

*WRITINGS:*

*Sirio,* Minardi (Parma), 1929.
*Fuochi in novembre,* Minardi, 1934.
*La capanna indiana,* Sansoni (Florence), 1951, revised and enlarged edition, Garzanti (Milan), 1973.

*Viaggio d'inverno,* Garzanti, 1971.
*Poesie e realta '45-'75,* Savelli (Rome), 1977.
*La camera da letto,* Garzanti, 1984, enlarged edition, 1988.
*Aritmie,* Garzanti, 1991.
*Al fuoco calmo dei giorni: poesie 1929-1990,* edited by Paolo Lagazzi, Biblioteca Universale Rizzoli (Milan), 1991.
*Selected Poems,* translated by Charles Tomlinson, Bloodaxe (Newcastle upon Tyne), 1993.
*Verso le sorgenti del Cinghio,* Garzanti, 1993.
*Una Lunga amicizia: Letters, 1938-1982,* Garzanti, 1994.
*Imitazioni,* Scheiwiller (Milan), 1994.
*La lucertola di Casarola,* Garzanti, 1997.
*All improviso ricordado: Conversazioni,* Guanda (Parma), 1997.

OTHER

(Translator) *Poeti antichi tradotti dai "Lirici nuovi,"* edited by Luciano Anceschi, Balcone (Milan), 1945.
(Translator) Honore de Balzac, *La ragazza dagli occhi d'oro,* Guanda, 1946.
(Translator) D. H. Lawrence, *Classici italiani,* with preface, Bompiani (Milan), 1948.
(Translator) Thomas Love Peacock, *L'abbazia degli incubi,* Guanda, 1952.
(Editor and translator) *Poesia straniera del Novecento,* Garzanti, 1958.
(Editor with Pietro Citati) *Gli umoristi moderni,* Garzanti, 1961.
(Translator with Aldo Rossi) Ernest Hemingway, *Verdi colline d' Africa,* Einaudi (Turin), 1968.
(Translator) Thomas Hardy, *Poesie, in Romanzi,* Mondadori (Milan), 1973.
(Translator) Charles Baudelaire, *I fiori del male,* Garzanti, 1975.

Contributor to various books, including *Artemisia,* Mondadori, 1953, and *Contemporary Italian Poetry,* edited by Carlo Golino, University of California Press, 1962. Bertolucci also contributed to several periodicals, including *Botteghe Oscure, Paragone,* and *Poesia.*

*SIDELIGHTS:* Italian poet Attilio Bertolucci began to write very early in his life. At the age of six he was sent to a boarding school a few miles from his home in Parma, where he began writing verse and other things in order to fill up the time. This early start perhaps prepared him to be ready to publish his first book of poems at the age of eighteen. Upon the encouragement of his friends and former high school teacher, Cesare Zavattini, he published the collection *Sirio* ("Sirius") in 1929. It contains twenty-seven poems that evoke dream-like images of the countryside near Parma where Bertolucci grew up. But Bertolucci himself explained that his landscape images are metaphor, not strict reality.

Bertolucci completed high school in 1931. His work won national acclaim when he took second place in a contest in 1933. Subsequently, he began to publish in journals until his second collection came out in 1934. *Fuochi in novembre* ("Fires in November") exalts everyday objects and colloquial language as he again describes the rural areas of Italy he intimately knows. For example, one poem is about the area his parents moved to when he was just a few months old and is titled "Emilia."

After a failed attempt at law school, Bertolucci attended the University of Bologna in 1935 to study art history under the noted Italian scholar, Roberto Longhi. Upon graduation, he began a career as a high school teacher of art history. During this time, Bertolucci also started writing essays on literature that were published in journals.

In 1939, he founded a series on foreign poets called "La fenice" ("The Phoenix"). For the next few years he directed this program which nurtured his interest in foreign writers whom he had always found more inspirational for his own writing than those closer to home. During the period leading up to and including World War II, Bertolucci did little writing.

When Italy surrendered to the Allies in 1943, Bertolucci left teaching for a while and took refuge in a family residence in an Apennine village. In a 1980 interview with Sara Cherin, Bertolucci explained that he was too depressed about world circumstances to write. Instead, he and his wife went into seclusion for most of the rest of the decade. Bertolucci took up teaching art history again in 1951 after moving with his family to Rome.

His third collection of poetry, *La capanna indiana* ("The Indian Hut") was published the same year. The volume combines poems from his first two books with new works gathered under the section title "Lettera da casa" ("Letter from Home"), as well as the long, three-part poem, "La capanna indiana," and a short piece called "Frammento escluso" ("Excluded Fragment"). The poetry in this award-winning collection is described by Andrea Ciccarelli in the *Dictionary of Italian Literature* as "an elegiac, colloquial analysis of his private history." But the newer poems written between

1935 and 1950 show evidence of change in the poet's outlook. Mark Pietralunga explains in the *Dictionary of Literary Biography,* "The reality of war, the deaths of loved ones, and the sight of his children growing up have affected the serenity of his personal environment. Bertolucci reacts to these changes by retreating further into his protective, conservative space in order to defend himself from the violence of these new experiences."

Bertolucci gave up teaching in 1954 and began pursuing other interests, including working for the RAI (Italian Broadcasting Company), editing literary journals, and consulting for the Garzanti publishing company. In 1955 he published an expanded edition of *La capanna indiana* that included eighteen new poems which deal with the suffering he felt when he left the countryside to settle in Rome. In "Pensieri di casa" ("Thoughts of Home"), for example, he no longer is a witness to the natural wonders he describes in the poem but instead, idealizes them from his memory.

After the publication of this last book, Bertolucci endured personal hardships that kept him from publishing for a time. In 1954 his father died. The poet then began to have anxiety attacks, and in 1958, he went to a mental hospital. His next book of poetry, *Viaggio d'inverno* ("Winter Voyage") was not published until 1971. Eighty-four poems from the period 1955-71 are included in this volume which won Bertolucci both the Etna-Taormina and the Tarquinia-Cardarelli prizes. The poems in *Viaggio d'inverno* reflect the poet's consciousness of his own aging process and again reflects on the personal crisis he feels at being separated from the idyllic countryside. The voice in the poem "I papaveri" ("The Poppies"), for example, is that of an older man who is no longer empowered with the ability to control his environment.

*La camera da letto* ("The Bedroom") is a long narrative poem and also the poet's autobiography. Bertolucci had been writing this work, which chronicles his own history and family, for nearly twenty years prior to publication. It was divided into two volumes: book 1, which included chapters 1 through 29 and appeared in 1984, was followed by chapters 30 through 41 in book 2, published in 1988. The structure is like that of a novel, beginning with the tale of his ancestors' arrival to the region of the Apennines and continuing through to his own departure from Parma to the city of Rome. The prose-like format of this long poem, which Bertolucci called his "private novel," and the complexity of sentence structures and rhythm make this an unusual work without model in Italian literature. Mark Pietralunga writes in the *Dictionary of Literary Biography* that Bertolucci's "decision to attempt a long narrative poem is an exceptional event for contemporary Italian poetry and clearly confirms his position of autonomy among poets in Italy today."

Since *La camera da letto,* Bertolucci has published several works, including the poetry collection *Verso le sorgenti del Cinghio* ("Toward the Springs of Cinghio"), published in 1993, and most recently *La lucertola di Casarola,* released in 1997. He continues to work and live both in Rome and his native region of Parma.

*BIOGRAPHICAL/CRITICAL SOURCES:*

*BOOKS*

Baroni, Gabriella Palli, editor, *Una lunga amicizia: lettere 1938-1982,* Garzanti, 1994.

Cherin, Sara, *Attilio Bertolucci: I giorni di un poeta,* Salamandra, 1980.

Citati, Pietro, *Il te del cappellaio matto,* Mondadori, 1972.

De Robertis, Giuseppe, *Altro Novecento,* Le Monnier, 1962.

*Dictionary of Literary Biography,* Volume 128: *Twentieth-Century Italian Poets,* Gale (Detroit), 1993.

Fortini, Franco, *I poeti del "900,* Laterza, 1977.

Frattarolo, Renzo, *Notizie per una letteratura,* San Marco, 1961.

Iacopetta, Antonio, *Attilio Bertolucci: Lo specchio e la perdita,* Bonacci, 1984.

Jewell, Keala, *The Poiesis of History,* Cornell University Press, 1992.

Lagazzi, Paolo, *Attilio Bertolucci,* Nuova Italia, 1982.

Massini, Giuliana, and Bruno Rivalta, editors, *Sulla poesia: Conversazioni nelle scuole,* Pratiche, 1981.

Mengaldo, Pier Vincenzo, *Poeti italiani del novecento,* Mondadori, 1978.

Pasolini, Pier Paolo, *Passione e Ideologia (1948-1958),* Garzanti, 1960.

Siciliano, Enzo, *Autobiografia letteraria,* Garzanti, 1970.

*PERIODICALS*

*Aurea Parma,* September, 1982, pp. 124-135.

*Fiera Letteraria,* May 25, 1958.

*Milano-Sera,* June, 1951, p. 3.

*Nuovi Argomenti,* July-December, 1971, pp. 221-233.

*Paragone,* no. 20, August, 1951, pp. 40-43; no. 262, December, 1971, pp. 199-124; no. 288, February, 1974, pp. 90-99.

*Rassegna della Letteratura Italiana,* January-December, 1979, pp. 327-338.

*Repubblica,* January 9-10, 1977, p. 16.

*Studi Novecenteschi,* December, 1984, pp. 295-319.

*Tuttolibri,* November 19, 1988.*

\* \* \*

## BINYON, (Robert) Laurence   1869-1943

*PERSONAL:* Born August 10, 1869, in Lancaster, England; died March 10 (some sources say March 11), 1943, in Reading, England; son of Frederick (a clergyman) and Mary (Dockray) Binyon; married Cicely Margaret Powell, 1904; children: three daughters. *Education:* Attended St. Paul's School and Trinity College.

*CAREER:* Art historian, critic, translator, playwright, poet, c. 1890-1943; curator, British Museum; Norton Professor of Poetry at Harvard University; Byron Chair of Letters at the University of Athens.

*AWARDS, HONORS:* Chevalier of the French Legion of Honor; Fellow of the Royal Society

*WRITINGS:*

*Lyric Poems,* Elkin Mathews (London), 1894.
*Poems,* Daniel (Oxford), 1895.
*Dutch Etchers of the Seventeenth Century,* Macmillan (New York City), 1895.
*London Visions,* Elkin Mathews, 1896.
*The Praise of Life: Poems,* Elkin Mathews, 1896.
*John Crone and John Sell Cotman,* Macmillan, 1897.
*Porphyrion and Other Poems,* Richards (London), 1898.
*Second Book of London Visions,* Elkin Mathews, 1899.
*Western Flanders,* Unicorn (London), 1899.
*Thomas Girtin: His Life and Works,* Seeley (London), 1900.
*Odes,* Unicorn, 1901, revised edition, Elkin Mathews, 1913.
*The Death of Adam and Other Poems,* Methuen (London), 1903.
*Dream Come True,* Eragny Press (London), 1905.
*Penthesilea,* Constable (London), 1905.
*Paris and Oenone,* Constable, 1906.
*Attila: A Tragedy in Four Acts,* Murray (London), 1907.
*Painting in the Far East,* Longmans, Green (New York City), 1908.
*England and Other Poems,* Elkin Mathews, 1909.
*The Flight of the Dragon,* Murray, 1911.
*Auguries,* Heinemann (London), 1913, John Lane (New York City), 1914.

*The Winnowing Fan: Poems of the Great War,* Elkin Mathews, 1914, Houghton Mifflin (Boston, MA), 1915.

*The Anvil,* Elkin Mathews, 1916.

*The Cause: Poems of War,* Houghton Mifflin, 1917.

*The New World: Poems,* Elkin Mathews, 1918.

*English Poetry in Its Relation to Painting and the Other Arts; Poetry and Modern Life,* Oxford University Press (London), 1918.

*The Four Years,* Elkin Mathews, 1919.

*The Secret: Sixty Poems,* Elkin Mathews, 1920.

*Arthur: A Tragedy,* Small, Maynard (Boston), 1923.

*Ayuli: A Play in Three Acts and an Epilogue,* Blackwell (Oxford), 1923, Appleton (New York City), 1924.

*The Sirens: An Ode,* Stanton Press (Chelsfield), 1924.

*Tradition and Reaction in Modern Poetry,* Oxford University Press, 1926.

*The Engraved Designs of William Blake,* Benn (London), 1926.

*The Wonder Night,* Faber & Gwyer (London), 1927.

*Boadicea: A Play in Eight Scenes,* Benn, 1927.

*Sophro the Wise: A Play for Children,* Benn, 1927.

*The Idols,* Macmillan (London), 1928.

*Three Short Plays: Godstow Nunnery, Love in the Desert, Memnon,* Sidgwick & Jackson (London), 1930.

*Landscape in English Art and Poetry,* Kenkyushu (Tokyo), 1930, Cobden-Sanderson (London), 1931.

*Collected Poems,* two volumes, Macmillan, 1931.

*Akbar,* Appleton, 1932.

*English Water-Colours,* Black (London), 1933.

*The Case of Christopher Smart,* Oxford University Press, 1934.

*The Young King: A Play,* Goulden (Canterbury), 1934.

*The Burning of the Leaves and Other Poems,* edited by wife, C. M. Binyon, Macmillan, 1934.

*The Spirit of Man in Asian Art,* Harvard University Press (Cambridge), 1935.

*Brief Candles,* Golden Cockerel Press (London), 1938.

*The North Star and Other Poems,* Macmillan, 1941.

*The Madness of Merlin,* edited by Gordon Bottomley, Macmillan, 1947.

*OTHER*

(Translator with Alice Kemp-Welch) Christine de Pisan, *The Book of the Duke of True Lovers,* Chatto & Windus (London), 1909.

(Editor) *The Golden Treasury of Modern Lyrics,* Macmillan, 1924.

(Translator) Dante, *Episodes from the Divine Comedy,* Benn, 1932.

(Translator) Dante, *Inferno,* Macmillan, 1933.

(Translator) Dante, *Purgatorio,* Macmillan, 1938.

(Translator) Dante, *Paradiso,* Macmillan, 1943.

(Translator) *The Portable Dante,* Viking (New York City), 1947.

*SIDELIGHTS:* Robert Laurence Binyon had a long and admirable career in the second tier of English arts and letters. His father, Frederick Binyon, was a clergyman, and his mother, Mary, was the daughter of Robert Benson Dockray, resident engineer of the London and Birmingham Railroad. Binyon showed an early interest in art and poetry. After attending St. Paul's School, he attended Trinity College at Oxford, where his poem "Persephone" was awarded the Newdigate Prize. In 1890 he took a first-class degree in classical moderations, and in 1892, a second-class degree in *litterae humainoires.* In 1890 he also published four poems in a volume called *Primavera: Poems by Four Authors,* which included the work of three other young Oxford undergraduates, one of whom was his cousin, Stephen Phillips, who would also achieve a measure of fame as a poet.

Following his undergraduate education, Binyon took a position at the British Museum, in the department of printed books, and in 1895 moved to the department of prints and drawings where he would stay until retiring in 1933, with promotions to assistant keeper and keeper along the way. He published his first book of poetry in 1894. Called *Lyric Poems,* it was quickly followed by two books on painting, *Dutch Etchers of the Seventeenth Century* in 1895 and *John Crone and John Sell Cotman* in 1897. These two interests would govern his career, as he alternated between poetry and essays on the visual arts. Binyon managed to produce almost a book a year in the span between 1894 and 1944. He was also interested in Oriental art and culture: books such as *Painting in the Far East* (1908) and the book of poems *The Flight of the Dragon* (1911) reflect this interest. Ezra Pound was highly complimentary of the later work, and thought of Binyon as a pioneer in the Western appreciation of Chinese and Japanese art.

Binyon married Cicely Margaret Powell in 1904, and they had three daughters together. When World War I broke out, he became an orderly in the Red Cross, and managed to visit the front in 1916. He turned this experience into numerous books of verse that took the war as a subject. *The Winnowing Fan, The Anvil, The Cause,* and *The New World,* published from 1914 to 1918, all dealt with the war as a noble cause, though his work became progressively less sentimental. One reviewer from *Literature Digest* said "Laurence Binyon's poetry once was somewhat coldly 'literary'—aloof from common human experience, but the war has given him new vigor and new humanity." He produced one poem out of this experience that became a touchstone, "For the Fallen." The poem was frequently anthologized and inscribed on war monuments throughout England. In the most memorable stanza of the poem, Binyon pledges that the living will not forget their sacrifice: "They shall not grow old, as we that are left grow old/Age shall not weary them, nor the years condemn/At the going down of the sun and in the morning/We will remember them." Compared to other war poets such as Seigfried Sassoon and Wilfred Owen, Binyon's efforts lack some of the visceral charge and disillusionment that characterizes much of the response to the war, but his sentiment nevertheless was embraced by the public. Susan Millar Williams, writing in *Dictionary of Literary Biography,* describes his style as "concise and spare . . . [he] was a staid, serious, and scholarly man, he was not humorless and liked a joke."

In the 1920s Binyon wrote *The Sirens* and *The Idols,* two long epic poems that treat man's struggle to come to terms with himself. The latter prompted a *New York Herald Tribune* reviewer to write, "Mr. Binyon's penetration into the centers of ultimate darkness, which takes place in "The Idols,' rewards him with many jewels of his own finding." In the 1930s he traveled and lectured on art and literature at various universities. He followed T. S. Eliot at Harvard as Norton Professor of Poetry, and also lectured in the United States, Holland, China, Scandinavia, Japan, Rome, Berlin, Vienna, and Paris. He was also named a chevalier of the French Foreign Legion and a fellow of the Royal Society. He was appointed to the Byron Chair of Letters at Athens at the age of seventy.

During his career, Binyon became interested in experimental versification. He had been influenced by John Masefield, who argued that verse should be spoken aloud, and, at Oxford, Robert Bridges had shared with him the complex rhythms of Gerard Manley Hopkins's sprung verse, whose poetry could not yet be found in print. His experiments were not as radical, however. Mainly, he was skillful at manipulating verse within narrowly defined limits. This culminated in his translation, done throughout the 1930s, of Dante's *Divine Comedy.* He translated it in its original terza rima, a feat M. J. Alexander, writing for *Reference Guide to English Literature* called "remarkable." Alexander went on to praise Binyon for the quality of the translation, saying "the skills of versification and the profound culture that produced Binyon's poetic language are not likely to be found again in any of his successors to this task (translating Dante) of unique importance for En-

glish literature." The Dante translation was published beginning in 1933, and perhaps stands as his last contribution.

Binyon's poetry was generally thought to be highly refined, and, adjectives such as "stately," "dignified," and "grave" are frequently used to characterize his verse. But such praise has drawbacks for a poet. One reviewer from *Bookman* said of *Selected Poems,* "It is the sort of verse teachers used to like to read aloud in school because of its academic sense and the perfect beat of its feet. Every poem shows traces of careful workmanship which effectively irons out the initial inspiration."

Indeed, while Binyon enjoyed a reputation for craft and elegance, especially among a more conservative audience, this lack of vitality prevented him from being appreciated on a wide scale beyond his own age. Binyon spoke to a late Victorian context from well within its aesthetic, moral and ideological assertions; this is nicely summed up by Archibald MacLeish in a review in *Saturday Review of Literature* of *The Idols,* in which he writes, "the ode is the kind of cultivated, scholarly, well-bred expression of emotion which will certainly receive the praise of well-bred, scholarly and cultivated people, and the praise or dispraise of others can hardly be important to its author."

It is this limited purview that constituted both Binyon's charm and his major flaw as a poet. His poetry was not entirely didactic, though it did have a tendency to contain an uplifting message. Williams quotes James Granville Southworth, writing for the *Sewanee Review:* "In contrast to the poetry of Mr. T. S. Eliot, Mr. Binyon affects a reconstruction of beauty against the forces of disintegration—forces against which Mr. Eliot seems powerless to act. Mr. Eliot's poetry is a balm to the contemporary who lacks the strength to combat the anticultural forces of the present day. Mr. Binyon's poetry is a constant challenge to a fuller life." His distinguished career was exemplary of a certain breed—he was often described as a perfectionist—that slipped out of fashion as the twentieth century gained further distance from Victorian England. The academic remove from which he surveyed his subjects was indeed "cultivated," "scholarly" and "well-bred"; that these adjectives are subtly critical when applied to a poet does not detract from his eminent position as a skilled and respected poet and man of letters in his time.

*BIOGRAPHICAL/CRITICAL SOURCES:*

BOOKS

*Dictionary of Literary Biography,* Volume 19: *British Poets, 1880-1914,* Gale Research (Detroit, MI), 1983.
*Reference Guide to English Literature,* 2nd edition, St. James Press (Detroit, MI), 1991.
Southworth, James Granville, *Sowing the Spring,* Books for Libraries Press (Freeport, NY), 1940.

PERIODICALS

*Bookman,* October 22, 1922.
*Literature Digest,* May 19, 1917.
*New York Herald Tribune,* May 26, 1929, p. 10.
*Saturday Review of Literature,* April 20, 1929.
*Sewanee Review,* July, 1905, pp. 279-291.*

\* \* \*

## BIRRELL, Augustine    1850-1933

*PERSONAL:* Born January 19, 1850, in Wavertree, England; died on November 20, 1933; son of Charles Morton (a Baptist minister) and Harriet Jane (Grey) Birrell; married Margaret Mirrlees, 1878 (died, 1879); married Eleanor Locker Tennyson, 1888; children: two sons. *Education:* Trinity College, Cambridge, B.A., 1872; University of London, L.L.B. *Politics:* Liberal Party. *Religion:* Agnostic. *Avocational interests:* Book collecting.

*CAREER:* British essayist, biographer, and member of Parliament. Admitted to the bar, 1875; appointed Queen's Counsel, 1885.

*AWARDS, HONORS:* Honorary Fellow, Trinity Hall, Cambridge, 1899.

*WRITINGS:*

*Obiter Dicta,* Stock (London), 1884, Scribners (New York City), 1885.
*Obiter Dicta: Second Series,* Stock, 1887, Scribners, 1888.
*Life of Charlotte Bronte,* Scott (London), 1887.
*Res Judicatae: Papers and Essays,* Scribners, 1892.
*Essays about Men, Women, and Books,* Scribners, 1894.
*The Duties and Liabilities of Trustees: Six Lectures,* Macmillan (London), 1896, Macmillan (New York City), 1897.
*Four Lectures on the Law of Employers Liability at Home and Abroad* Macmillan (New York City), 1897.
*Sir Frank Lockwood: A Biographical Sketch,* Smith, Elder (London), 1898.
*Collected Essays,* 2 volumes, Stock, 1899.
*Seven Lectures on the Law and History of Copyright in Books,* Cassell (New York City), 1899.
*Essays and Addresses,* Scribners, 1901.
*Miscellanies,* Stock, 1901.
*William Hazlitt,* Macmillan, 1902.
*Emerson: A Lecture,* Green (London), 1903.
*Andrew Marvell,* Macmillan, 1905.
*In the Name of the Bodleian and Other Essays,* Scribners, 1905.
*Frederick Locker-Lampson: A Character Sketch,* Scribners, 1920.
*The Collected Essays and Addresses of the Rt. Hon. Augustine Birrell, 1880-1920,* 3 volumes, Dent (London), 1922, Scribners, 1923.
*More Obiter Dicta,* Scribners, 1924.
*Augustine Birrell,* edited by Francis Henry Pritchard, Harrap (London), 1926.
*Et Cetera: A Collection,* Chatto & Windus (London), 1930.
*Things Past Redress,* Faber & Faber (London), 1937.

*SIDELIGHTS:* Augustine Birrell began his literary career by falling in love, or rather by finally succumbing to an irrepressible urge to express his love to one Margaret Mirrlees. It was in 1874, two years after Birrell graduated from college and had taken a sober position as a barrister in London, that an anonymous essay titled "A Curious Product" appeared in *Macmillan's Magazine.* The essay expressed the pent-up anguish of a young man suffering from unrequited love. While "A Curious Product" was Birrell's first appearance in print, it was not representative of the works that would later bring him literary recognition.

Indeed, Birrell would never again take pen in hand to effuse about the transports of love. However his more typical works were presaged by yet another anonymous foray into the world of letters. In the early 1880s he put together a collection of his own essays, to which he added a single contribution by a friend, and in 1884 he had the collection published at his own expense. That collection, titled *Obiter Dicta,* quickly found an appreciative audience, much to its authors' (and self-publisher's) surprise. As Christopher Kent reports, writing for *Dictionary of Literary Biography,* "Their success was startling: six editions were called for in a year."

As a result, Birrell would go on to produce several further collections, including *Obiter Dicta: Second Series,* (1887), *Essays about Men, Women, and Books* (1894), two volumes of *Collected Essays* (1899), *More Obiter Dicta* (1924), and *Et Cetera: A Collection* (1930). In all, he would publish five further volumes of essays, as well as several literary biographies and a number of writings on legal topics. One reviewer from the *New York Tribune* described Birrell as "the patron essayist of the 'saving remnant' who make of literature a graceful garment, and who remain now, as always, a constant if not very energetic influence upon the writing and publication of literary criticism."

Birrell was a man of his time and his class: a professional career, particularly in the field of law, was the mark of a properly bred gentleman, as was a career in politics. Having "taken the silk" (become a queen's counsel) in 1885, Birrell duly set about fulfilling the rest of the social requirements of a member of his class. As a widower, he had already set up a household in which his sister, a spinster, ruled as housekeeper, and he prepared to enter politics. In his first two attempts to be elected to Parliament, in 1885 and 1886, he won the Scottish constituency of West Fife and took his seat as a Liberal Member in 1889. There remained but one further step to take; as Kent reports: "To complete his transformation into a personage he married in 1888 Eleanor Locker Tennyson, widow of the poet laureate's second son, . . . and granddaughter of the earl of Elgin."

With his political position firmly established, an elevated social position accruing through his marriage, a profession he greatly enjoyed, and a comfortable income, Birrell now embarked upon a time of his life when he could indulge those things he valued most in life: good books, good conversation, and good company. In the year prior to his marriage he had brought out a second series of *Obiter Dicta* essays and a biography of Charlotte Bronte; now he would have greater leisure to devote to his literary efforts.

Birrell's next writings would be centered upon the subject of the law; he released *Res Judicatae: Papers and Essays* in 1892. In this and in his later legal writings, Birrell approached his subjects with an admirable insistence on clarity. Indeed, as Kent observes "Solicitors. . . complained that making the law so intelligible jeopardized their profession." Birrell's literary interest in the law was varied and wide-ranging: he covered topics as disparate as copyright law and employer liability, leaving aside his writings on particular issues of the law (inspired by his career as barrister).

Birrell's themes were varied as well, and he let his own interests guide his selection of topics, rather than attempt to court the literary trends and fashions of the day. Sometimes he wandered beyond the confines of essays, as in his books on Charlotte Bronte and Andrew Marvell, but he rarely ventured into anything that could be classified as literary criticism. As with his essays, he allowed his personal fancy, not literary fashion, to dictate the subject matter of his books. In a few essays he attempted to take on larger themes, such as religious concerns, but regardless of topic his essays are marked by a firm commitment to plain speaking and a rejection of over-intellectualizing.

At the same time that Birrell was earning his reputation as a man of letters, he was also nurturing his career in politics. He served his first constituency, in Scotland, well throughout the 1890s, but in 1900 he was asked by his party to try instead to win in Manchester. He was unsuccessful, but his absence from Parliament was brief. In 1906 he ran again, this time for North Bristol, and returned to government victorious. In 1906 he was appointed Minister of Education, and his political success seemed assured. But in 1907 he accepted a very difficult appointment, to the position of chief secretary of Ireland. This thankless task could easily have spelled disaster for Birrell, given the contentious relations between England and Ireland then, as now. But Birrell was sympathetic to the Irish people, and by all reports he handled the responsibilities well, at least for his first six years in the post. It was only during the final three years, complicated by the agitations of the Irish Home Rule party and the disruptions of World War I, that things began to go sour. He left the office under something of a cloud in 1916 and retired from Parliament, and political life in general, two years later. From that time onward, he would concentrate solely on his literary endeavors. Ultimately, Birrell's reputation as a meticulous chronicler of the Victorian life was well deserved.

*BIOGRAPHICAL/CRITICAL SOURCES:*

*BOOKS*

*Dictionary of Literary Biography,* Volume 98, Gale, 1999.

Gardiner, A. G., *Prophets, Priests, and Kings,* Dent (London), 1914.

Gross, John, *The Rise and Fall of a Man of Letters,* Weidenfeld & Nicolson (London), 1969.

Mortimer, Raymond, *Channel Packet,* Hogarth (London), 1942.

O'Broin, Leon, *The Chief Secretary: Augustine Birrell in Ireland,* Chatto & Windus (London), 1969.
Tennyson, Sir Charles, *Stars and Markets,* Chatto & Windus, 1957.

*PERIODICALS*

*Historical Journal,* June, 1976, pp. 421-452.
*New York Tribune,* September 21, 1924, p. 5.*

\*　　\*　　\*

**BLACK, Ivory**
　　**See JANVIER, Thomas A(llibone)**

\*　　\*　　\*

**BLANC, Suzanne**

*PERSONAL:* Female.

*ADDRESSES: Agent*—c/o Doubleday Publicity, 1540 Broadway, New York, NY 10036.

*CAREER:* Writer.

*AWARDS, HONORS:* Edgar Allan Poe Award, Mystery Writers of America, 1961, for *The Green Stone.*

*WRITINGS:*

*MYSTERY NOVELS*

*The Green Stone,* Harper (New York City), 1961.
*The Yellow Villa,* Doubleday (Garden City, NY), 1964.
*The Rose Window,* Doubleday, 1967.
*The Sea Troll,* Doubleday, 1969.

Contributor of short stories to books, including *Merchants of Menace,* edited by Hillary Waugh, Doubleday, 1969; and *Men and Malice,* edited by Dean Dickensheet, Doubleday, 1973. Contributor of short stories to periodicals, including *Ellery Queen's Mystery Magazine.*

*SIDELIGHTS:* According to Jane S. Bakerman in *Twentieth-Century Crime and Mystery Writers,* Suzanne Blanc's mystery novels depict characters who feel emotionally isolated from others. In the works *The Green Stone, The Yellow Villa,* and *The Rose Window,*

Blanc places her vulnerable female characters in Mexico, a foreign land. The American women travel to Mexico in order to resolve their personal crises. Bakerman observed that the women's "personal problems and their progress toward solutions of them provide interesting and realistic sub-plots for the crime stories."

Bureau of Tourism investigator Miguel Menendez must solve the murders in the *The Green Stone, The Yellow Villa,* and *The Rose Window.* Menendez himself feels isolated, since he is the member of a Indian minority within the larger Mexican culture. The investigator's feelings of isolation are heightened by his deteriorating relationship with his wife. This breakdown provides another continuing subplot for the novels. Even Blanc's villains feel isolated. Early in the novels, readers discover their identities and crimes and even some of the motivations behind their crimes. The villains "are isolated by their backgrounds and by their crimes," commented Bakerman in *Twentieth-Century Crime and Mystery Writers.*

Set on a ship sailing the Pacific Ocean, Blanc's *The Sea Troll* features passengers, freight, and an alcoholic captain who may be a murderer. Though missing Miguel Menendez, *The Sea Troll* does have similarities to Blanc's other novels. It features a young American woman, unaccustomed to travel, who seeks unfamiliar surroundings to deal with personal turmoil. Critics gave *The Sea Troll* mixed reviews. Bakerman deemed it to be Blanc's "least successful" novel, but concluded that the author "is a good writer whose canon, though slender, is strong."

*BIOGRAPHICAL/CRITICAL SOURCES:*

*BOOKS*

*Twentieth-Century Crime and Mystery Writers,* St. James Press (Chicago, IL), 1991.

*PERIODICALS*

*Kirkus Reviews,* February 1, 1969, p. 140.
*Publishers Weekly,* February 3, 1969, p. 59.*

\*　　\*　　\*

**BOAS, Franz　1858-1942**

*PERSONAL:* Born July 9, 1858, in Minden, North Rhine-Westphalia, Germany; immigrated to United

**Franz Boas**

States, 1887, naturalized citizen, 1892; died of a heart attack, December 21, 1942, in New York,NY. *Education:* Studied physics and mathematics at the universities of Heidelberg and Bonn, 1877-81; University of Kiel, Ph.D., 1882. *Religion:* Jewish.

*CAREER:* Geographer, educator, linguist, anthropologist, editor, and author. Clark University, Worcester, MA, anthropology instructor, 1888-92; employed by World's Columbian Exposition, 1893, and Field Museum of Natural History; Columbia University, New York City, first professor of anthropology, 1896-1936; American Museum of Natural History, curator of anthropology, 1896-1905.

*MEMBER:* American Anthropological Association (founder), American Folk-Lore Society.

*WRITINGS:*

*Vocabularies of the Tlingit, Haida and Tsimshian Languages,* [Philadelphia], 1892.
*The Social Organization and the Secret Societies of the Kwakiutl Indians,* [Washington, DC], 1897.
*Facial Painting of the Indians of Northern British Columbia,* [New York City], 1898.

*American Committee for Democracy and Intellectual Freedom,* [New York City], 1939.
*The Vocabulary of the Chinook Language,* New Era Printing Company (Lancaster, PA), 1904.
*Vocabularies from the Northwest Coast of America,* [Worcester, MA], 1916.
*Folk-Tales of Salishan and Sahaptin Tribes,* American Folk-Lore Society (New York City), 1917.
*Grammatical Notes on the Language of the Tlingit Indians,* University Museum (Philadelphia), 1917.
*Kultur und rasse,* Vereinigung wissenschaftlicher verleger (Berlin), 1922.
*The Mind of a Primitive Man,* Macmillan (New York City), 1931.
*Keresan Texts,* G. E. Stechert & Co. (New York City), 1928.

Also author of *Ethnography of Franz Boas: Letters and Diaries Written on the Northwest Coast from 1886 to 1949,* 1969. Editor, *American Folk-Lore Society Journal,* 1908-25, *Publications of the American Ethnological Society,* 1907-42, and *Columbia University Contributions to Anthropology,* 1913-36; editor and founder, *International Journal of American Linguistics,* 1917-39; editor, *American Anthropologist* and *Journal of American Folklore;* assistant editor, *Science* magazine. Also edited reports of the Morris K. Jesup North Pacific Expedition, 1898-1930.

*SIDELIGHTS:* Known as the "founding father of American anthropology," Franz Boas was a German-born American educator, linguist, geographer, editor, author, and most important, anthropologist. As a Jewish immigrant from Germany, and a scholar of many different peoples, Boas took a vigorous stand against racism. He insisted that culture, not heredity, be the basis for contemporary anthropological study. He believed that scientific means could bring a greater understanding of social problems, and in his most famous book, *The Mind of Primitive Man* (1911), he revolutionized thought about primitive people's mentality. Columbia University's first professor of anthropology, Boas remained active even after retirement as both a writer and an emeritus professor until his death in 1942.

Boas was born into a cultured, Jewish family in Minden, North Rhine-Westphalia, Germany, on July 9, 1858. He began his studies in 1877 in physics and mathematics at the universities of Heidelberg and Bonn, and received a Ph.D. from the University of Kiel in 1882. His dissertation was on the coloration of sea water, and he intended to be a geographer. By the time he immigrated to the United States at the age of twenty-nine, he had changed his interest from the earth to humanity.

On the first of many expeditions, Boas traveled as a geographer to the Baffin Island in the Canadian Arctic. This was an especially dangerous journey. At one point, he and his traveling companion missed their meeting with a supply sled and became lost on their way back to the nearest settlement, Anarnitung. In sub-zero temperatures their dogs refused to move, and they were forced to trek on foot for twenty-six hours without food or fuel through the freezing air, fog, and deep snow. By the time they reached Anarnitung, Boas's nose and fingers were frostbitten. Though he did not let this brush with death deter him, Boas did become much more interested in the Inuit people of Baffin than in the land itself. Douglas Cole writes in an article in the *Beaver,* "Retrospectively, the most significant aspect of Boas's experience in Baffin Island was his ethnographic immersion among the Inuit. His life and reputation were to be made in anthropology, and this was his initiation. A shift of interest was already evident by the end of the Cumberland Sound trip. . . . Participation in the life of the Intuit also sharpened his social sense and his belief in the equality of virtue among peoples." Boas wrote about his observations in Baffin-Land in his book, *The Central Eskimo* (1888) and later in *The Eskimo of Baffin-Land and Hudson Bay, 1901-1907.* A reviewer of *The Central Eskimo* in *Choice* described Boas's writing style: "While it now [in 1965] seems a little old-fashioned in organization and in its preoccupation with artifacts, houses, and tools, it still reads well. The author's approach to one of the world's most popular people, the Eskimo, is factual, coldly detached, and severely neutral."

Following this expedition, Boas returned to Berlin where he taught geography at the University of Berlin and held a post at the Royal Museum of Ethnology. In 1886 he traveled to Vancouver Island, where he studied the Pacific Northwestern Indian tribes. He then decided to settle in the United States and moved to New York, where he was married (Boas became a naturalized citizen in 1892). He was an assistant editor for *Science* magazine, and later edited *American Anthropologist,* the *Journal of American Folklore,* and the *International Journal of American Linguistics* (which he also founded). From 1888 to 1892 Boas taught anthropology at Clark University in Worcester, Massachusetts, and studied Native Americans in British Columbia, Canada. He left the Northeast for Chicago in 1893 to work at the World's Columbian Exposition and the Field Museum of Natural History.

In 1896 Boas began teaching at Columbia University, thereby becoming the first professor of anthropology in the United States. Throughout the rest of his career he remained at Columbia, building the anthropology department himself and training the next generation of anthropologists, including Alfred L. Kroeber and Melville Herskovits. Acclaimed writer Zora Neale Hurston also studied under Boas while at Barnard College. Boas began as an exacting and demanding teacher, but through the years he softened enough for his students and colleagues to call him "Papa Franz." Even after his retirement in 1936, he continued teaching as an emeritus professor until his death in 1942.

For the most part, Boas wrote for academic readers rather than for general readers, and his over six hundred monographs or articles were published by scientific or government organizations. He also worked at the American Museum of Natural History as a curator of anthropology from 1896 to 1905, and edited reports of the Morris K. Jesup North Pacific Expedition from 1898 to 1930.

Boas's primary interests were the cultures of North American Indians, particularly the Pacific Northwestern Kwakiutl. He endured great physical hardships through his numerous trips to document Kwakiutl art, literature and language. In 1966 his field notes were compiled into *Kwakiutl Ethnography.* Boas's interests in American Indian language families eventually brought about the study of structural linguistics. They also culminated in the book, *Handbook of American Indian Languages* (1911), which he edited. Among the findings of other anthropologists, Boas included his own field notes on Tsimshian, Kwakiutl, and Chinook Indians. He also collected Indian folklore, and published a study of Tsimshian myth in 1916. Andrew Wiget, in an article in *Choice,* describes why Boas studied languages: "His interest in transcribing and translating texts was twofold. He saw them first as records of cultural documents that recorded forever practices soon to vanish; second, he understood the necessity for the study of Native languages of recording entire texts, not merely lexicons or elicited statements."

Throughout his life, Boas remained skeptical of generalizations and theories, relying instead on concrete scientific observations. But he did rely on anthropological methods and previous finding to study social problems. Boas refuted the popularly held notion that heredity was the sole determinant of character and intelligence, insisting that one had to consider culture and variations of individuals within cultures. He took this approach in *Anthropology and Modern Life* (1928), in *Race, Lan-*

guage, and Culture (1940), and in his most famous book, *The Mind of Primitive Man.* This last book was written for a general audience, unlike the bulk of his writings. From 1910 he began conducting an anthropometric study for the U.S. Immigration Commission. As documented in *Changes in Bodily Form of Descendants of Immigrants,* he discovered that the longer an immigrant resided in the United States, the greater their physical differences tended toward American "norms."

"Papa Franz" died of a heart attack on December 21, 1942, in New York City. Following his death, his works continued to be published, including *Ethnography of Franz Boas; Letters and Diaries of Franz Boas Written on the Northwest Coast from 1886 to 1941* in 1969. His influence perpetuated itself for generations afterwards; anthropologist Margaret Mead, for example, was the student of Ruth Benedict, a student of Boas.

### BIOGRAPHICAL/CRITICAL SOURCES:

#### BOOKS

*Dictionary of American Biography,* Supplement 3: *1941-1945,* Scribner, 1973.

Herskovits, Melville, J., *Franz Boas: The Science of Man in the Making,* Scribner, 1953.

Stocking, George W., Jr., editor, *The Shaping of American Anthropology, 1883-1911: A Franz Boas Reader,* Basic Books, 1974.

#### PERIODICALS

*Beaver,* August/September, 1986.
*Choice,* March, 1965; June, 1986.
*New York Times,* December 22, 1942.*

\* \* \*

### BONK, Ecke

*PERSONAL:* Citizen of Austria.

*ADDRESSES: Agent*—c/o Goldie Paley Gallery, Moore College of Art and Design, 20th St. and the Parkway, Philadelphia, PA 19103-1179.

*CAREER:* Art historian, typographer, designer, and musician. Designer of graphic concepts for record albums, including *Azurety, L'Histoire de Mme. Tasco,* and *A Notion of Perpetual Motion.*

### WRITINGS:

(With Helmut Draxler and Robert Fleck) *Brigitte Kowanz, Franz Graf: Oktober 1983* (exhibit catalog), Delphin Druck (Vienna, Austria), 1984.

*Marcel Duchamp—The Box in a Valise: The Making of the Boite-en-Valise de ou par Marcel Duchamp ou Rrose Selavy,* translated by David Britt and published as *Marcel Duchamp, The Box in a Valise,* Rizzoli (New York City), 1989.

*Marcel Duchamp: The Portable Museum. An Inventory,* Thames and Hudson (London, England), 1989.

*Maschinenzeichen,* Passagen (Vienna, Austria), 1991.

(With Christian Kravagna and Sabine B. Vogel) *Brigitte Kowanz: Wiener Secession, 8.9-17.10.1993* (exhibit catalog), edited by Doris Rothauer, with Gabriele Grabler, Die Secession (Vienna, Austria), 1993.

*Thomas N. Pauli: GEN: die Evolution der Stille* (exhibit catalog), Triton (Vienna, Austria), 1995.

(With Anne d'Harnoncourt and Rebecca Rickman) *Jacqueline Matisse: Kitetail Cocktail,* Goldie Paley Gallery, Moore College of Art and Design (Philadelphia, PA), 1999.

Other work includes *Allgemeine Typosophie: Ein Handbuch zur Arbeit von Ecke Bonk.* Contributor to books, including *Joseph Cornell/Marcel Duchamp . . . in Resonance,* chronology by Susan Davidson, Cantz (Stuttgart, Germany), 1998.

*SIDELIGHTS:* Ecke Bonk has written studies on Marcel Duchamp, the modernist artist whose works reflect the influence of Cubism and Futurism and who became one of the leading exponents of Dadaism. Bonk's work on Duchamp focuses on the Portable Museum, a project also known as *Boite en Valise* or the Box in a Valise. The Portable Museum is a series of boxes created by Duchamp and his assistants. These boxes contain miniature replicas of Duchamp's paintings and sculptures. After the first edition appeared in 1941, Duchamp created and exhibited more boxes until his 1968 death. Bonk discusses Duchamp's work in the monograph *Marcel Duchamp—The Box in a Valise: The Making of the Boite-en-Valise de ou par Marcel Duchamp ou Rrose Selavy,* a book translated by David Britt and published as *Marcel Duchamp, The Box in a Valise.* He also discusses Duchamp's project in *Marcel Duchamp: The Portable Museum. An Inventory.*

"It is pointless to produce commentary on Duchamp's work or document it in anything but the most fastidious way and Ecke Bonk's unraveling of the history of each of the editions and the manufacture of each of the many items follows in the exemplary footsteps of Duchamp's most masterly disciple and exegete, Richard Hamilton," explained Tom Phillips in a *Times Literary Supplement* review of *Marcel Duchamp: The Portable Museum. An Inventory.* Phillips likened Duchamp's installment of his works of art in miniature museums to moves in a vast chess game—a game at which the artist excelled. *Art in America* contributor Charles F. Stuckey observed that art historians have identified Duchamp's project either "as a deconstructed form of *catalogue raisonne* or as a portfolio of replica prints and sculptures."

Critics praised Bonk's scholarship in *Marcel Duchamp: The Portable Museum. An Inventory.* They noted the many complications involved in cataloguing the minute variations in Duchamp's various techniques and the reproductions in the various boxes, and of documenting the art works that Duchamp included in the boxes. *Art in America* contributor Stuckey concluded: "As a result of Bonk's investigations, Duchamp's Boxes can no longer be overlooked as some scholar's playthings but now must be counted among the most fascinating and technically demanding print/sculpture editions in the history of art."

*BIOGRAPHICAL/CRITICAL SOURCES:*

PERIODICALS

*Apollo,* May, 1990, pp. 354-355.
*Art in America,* June, 1990, pp. 51, 53, 55.
*Burlington Magazine,* July, 1992, p. 459.
*Library Journal,* January, 1999, p. 89.
*Times Literary Supplement,* March 16-22, 1990, p. 281.*

\*     \*     \*

**BORAH, Timm**
  **See ZECH, Paul**

\*     \*     \*

**BORLEY, Lester   1931-**

*PERSONAL:* Born April 7, 1931; son of Edwin Richard and Mary Dorena (Davies) Borley; married Mary Alison Pearce; children: three daughters. *Ethnicity:* British. *Education:* Attended Queen Mary College, London, and Birkbeck College, London. *Politics:* Social Democrat. *Religion:* Anglican. *Avocational interests:* Listening to music, gardening, looking at pictures.

*ADDRESSES: Home*—4 Belford Pl., Edinburgh EH4 3DH, Scotland.

*CAREER:* British Travel Association, member of staff, 1955-57, assistant to the general manager for the United States, 1957-61, manager of Chicago office, 1961-64, assigned to Australia, 1964-67, and West Germany, 1967-69; Scottish Tourist Board, chief executive, 1970-75; English Tourist Board, chief executive, 1975-83; National Trust for Scotland, director, 1983-93; Europa Nostra, The Hague, Netherlands, secretary general, 1993-97. Member of council, Scotland's Garden Scheme (member of executive committee, 1970-75 and 1983-93); National Gardens Scheme, member of council, 1975-83; International Council of Monuments and Sites, member of international cultural tourism committee, 1990—, chairperson of cultural tourism committee for ICOMOS (UK), 1993—. Edinburgh Film House, member of board of governors, 1987-96, honorary vice-president, 1996—; Cromarty Arts Trust, member, 1995—. Academia Istropolitana, Bratislava, visiting lecturer, 1995—; International Cultural Center summer school, Krakow, Poland, visiting lecturer. Advisor to World Monuments Fund (New York). *Military service:* Royal Air Force, 1945-51; RAF Voluntary Reserve, 1951-55.

*MEMBER:* Royal Society of Arts (fellow), Royal Scottish Geographical Society (fellow), Tourism Society (fellow).

*AWARDS, HONORS:* Honorary Kentucky Colonel, 1963; D.Litt., Robert Gordon Institute of Technology, 1991; commander, Order of the British Empire, 1993.

*WRITINGS:*

(Editor) *Dear Maurice: Culture and Identity in Late Twentieth-Century Scotland; A Tribute to Maurice Lindsay on His Eightieth Birthday,* Tuckwell Press (East Linton, England), 1998.

Also contributor to academic publications on the management of cultural heritage and the development of cultural tradition. General editor, Jamie Stormonth Darling and Robin Prentice, *Culzean: The Continuing Challenge; The Story of the Restoration and Presentation of Culzean Castle and Country Park since 1945* (pamphlet), Scottish Heritage USA, 1985.

*BIOGRAPHICAL/CRITICAL SOURCES:*

*PERIODICALS*

*Times Literary Supplement,* August 14, 1998, p. 36.

\*    \*    \*

## BOROFKA, David 1954-

*PERSONAL:* Born in 1954.

*ADDRESSES: Agent*—c/o MacMurray & Beck Communications, 1649 Downing St., Denver, CO 80218.

*CAREER:* Novelist and short story writer.

*AWARDS, HONORS:* Iowa Short Fiction Award, 1996, for *Hints of His Mortality.*

*WRITINGS:*

*Hints of His Mortality* (short stories), University of Iowa Press (Iowa City, IA), 1996.
*The Island* (novel), MacMurray & Beck (Denver, CO), 1997.

*SIDELIGHTS:* David Borofka is the author of two books: *Hints of His Mortality,* a 1996 collection of short stories, and *The Island,* a 1997 novel. All fourteen stories in the 1996 volume examine the consequences of failure in men's lives. Borofka's flawed protagonists—a suicidal clergyman, an unsuccessful writer-turned-insurance salesman, a college professor trapped in a mediocre career, and others—struggle with the repercussions—for themselves and their loved ones—of their inability to realize private hopes and professional aspirations. A reviewer for *Publishers Weekly* called *Hints of His Mortality* an "accomplished collection," remarking that even though "Borofka's writing is sometimes prissy and inert . . . the intensity of his stories is almost palpable." *Library Journal* contributor Christine DeZelar-Tiedman commented that Borofka's "clear prose often sparkles with unexpected metaphor and insight." Elizabeth Gaffney of the *New York Times Book Review* praised Borofka for "the deftness, subtlety and humor with which he makes . . . many bedeviled lives cohere in a single vision." Gaffney also enthused that the collection's "narrative power . . . rivals a swiftly plotted novel."

*The Island,* a coming-of-age tale set in Portland, Oregon, in 1968, is narrated by fourteen-year-old Calvin "Fish" Becker. When his parents travel to Europe in an attempt to rescue their marriage, Calvin is sent to spend the summer with family friends, the wealthy and eccentric Lamberts. Over the course of the summer Calvin experiments with sex and alcohol, confronts the implications of his parents' failing marriage, and gradually becomes aware of the intricacies of the adult world. A reviewer in *Publishers Weekly* pronounced this first novel "gentle though occasionally hackneyed," adding that "at their best, Borofka's vivid, humble word-pictures . . . resonate and linger in the reader's mind." In *Booklist,* Nancy Pearl complained that the novel is poorly structured. To her, it almost seemed that Borofka "had stitched together some of his short stories." She did, however, conclude that the characters are well drawn, and the writing "frequently lyrical."

*BIOGRAPHICAL/CRITICAL SOURCES:*

*PERIODICALS*

*Antioch Review,* fall, 1997, p. 496.
*Booklist,* November 15, 1997, pp. 540-41.
*Christian Century,* December 17, 1997, p. 1204.
*Library Journal,* January, 1997, p. 151.
*New York Times Book Review,* January 19, 1997, p. 9.
*Publishers Weekly,* October 7, 1996, p. 62; September 8, 1997, p. 56.
*Virginia Quarterly Review,* summer, 1997, p. 93.\*

\*    \*    \*

## BRADY, Jane 1934-
### (Jane White)

*PERSONAL:* Born in 1934, in Cambridge, England; daughter of a historian. *Education:* Studied English.

*ADDRESSES: Agent*—c/o Hamish Hamilton, Penguin Books, Ltd., Bath Rd., Harmondsworth, Middlesex UB7 ODA, England.

*CAREER:* Novelist. Worked in the news department of the British Broadcasting Corporation's Overseas Service.

*WRITINGS:*

*UNDER PSEUDONYM JANE WHITE*

*Quarry,* Michael Joseph (London, England), 1967.
*Beatrice, Falling,* Michael Joseph, 1968.
*Proxy,* Michael Joseph, 1968.

*Retreat in Good Order,* Michael Joseph, 1970.
*Left for Dead,* Michael Joseph, 1971.
*Norfolk Child,* Michael Joseph, 1973.
*Comet: A Novel,* Hamish Hamilton (London, England), 1975.
*Benjamin's Open Day,* Hamish Hamilton, 1979.

SIDELIGHTS: Jane Brady's has written psychological thrillers using the pseudonym Jane White. Critics compared Brady's novel *Quarry* to the classic novel *Lord of the Flies* by William Golding because both depict young boys committing violent acts. In *Quarry,* three boys, Carter, Randy, and Todd, kidnap and imprison a fourth boy. Carter, Randy, and Todd each use the fourth boy to fulfill their needs: Carter's need for rough games, Randy's need for cruelty, and Todd's need for love. Although their victim willingly submits to all of their demands, the three judge the victim guilty, kill him, and blow up the quarry where he has been imprisoned.

Reviewing *Quarry* in the *New York Times Book Review,* George Grella wrote that White attempts to draw parallels between the life and suffering of Jesus to the novel's victim and his death but does not quite succeed: "Had Miss White taken advantage of the virtues of her supple and economical prose, and allowed her abstractions to grow organically from a convincingly created reality, her novel might have succeeded both as fiction and as parable. Trying to be both, it ends being neither." Other critics praised Brady for her characterizations. The author's "insights into the behavior of children are extraordinarily good," wrote a reviewer in the *Nation,* who also praised Brady's depiction of the boys' relatives.

In Brady's novel *Proxy,* fifteen-year-old Patch suffers under the attentions of his overly possessive mother, Judith, during a long convalescence. Patch's father then hires a young tutor who diverts Judith's attention away from her son. Brady "confirms the talent she showed for scene-setting" in *Quarry,* wrote a reviewer in the *Times Literary Supplement,* "and there are moments when the uneasy manner and gawky conversation of adolescence are admirably conveyed," but added that the character of Judith "never comes alive enough to frighten." A *Publishers Weekly* contributor admitted that even though the character of Judith "overshadows" the other characters, she "is one of the more seductive and spooky mothers in fictional guise."

Brady's novel *Beatrice, Falling* features a man undergoing a prolonged mental breakdown after the suicide of his wife. Critics compared *Beatrice, Falling* to

Brady's previous novels and commented on the stylistic similarities among the three. "Necessary as it is for any good novelist to use particular hallmarks, to be *sui generis* a recognizable stylist, these may be dubious assets to so prolific a writer as Miss White," commented a reviewer in the *Times Literary Supplement.* The reviewer wrote that Brady establishes "a splendidly straightforward kind of suspense" story but abandons it in favor of creating "a symbolic purgatory for her hero." A *Publishers Weekly* reviewer disliked the novel's protagonist but deemed *Beatrice, Falling* to be "an intriguing semi-Gothic tale."

With *Retreat in Good Order,* Brady returns to character-driven plots. A married couple, Sarah and Robert, take in Sarah's teenage niece, who has been living in a convent school in Italy. Like some of Brady's other adolescent characters, Maria strikes out at those around her in response to her own internal conflicts. She accuses her uncle of seducing her, and the allegation causes her grandfather to have a stroke and die. Yet this crisis strengthens Sarah and Robert's marriage, and Maria returns to the convent. *Library Journal* contributor Jean Drabbe Barnett observed that *Retreat in Good Order* "is entertaining, although not provocative." Stuart Hood, writing in the *Listener,* wrote that the novel "is well-written in a quiet, even style, observant and polished—too polished perhaps."

Brady's futuristic *Comet: A Novel* is set on a world experiencing a nuclear holocaust. A *Publishers Weekly* contributor reviewing *Comet: A Novel* warned readers that "you won't believe a word of it," while Dan Miller called the novel "fast-moving fiction with dozens of unanswered questions," in his *Booklist* review. In *Benjamin's Open Day,* Brady again explores the dysfunctional mother-son relationships and violence that she writes about in *Quarry* and *Proxy.* In this novel, unlikable protagonist Benjamin suffers psychological damage at the hands of his adulterous mother and his cruel classmates. Benjamin ultimately burns down his school and his mother dies of a drug overdose. "As in the best Hitchcock, simplistic psychology is the excuse for some very effective spine-chilling," noted Emma Fisher in her *Spectator* review of *Benjamin's Open Day.*

BIOGRAPHICAL/CRITICAL SOURCES:

PERIODICALS

*Booklist,* March 15, 1971, p. 586; May 1, 1976, p. 1246.
*Kirkus Reviews,* January 15, 1976, p. 96.
*Library Journal,* April 1, 1969, p. 1525; February 15, 1971, p. 659.

*Listener,* June 11, 1970, p. 794.

*Nation,* October 2, 1967, pp. 317-318.

*New Statesman,* February 9, 1968, p. 177; September 10, 1971, p. 340.

*New York Times Book Review,* September 24, 1967, p. 49.

*Publishers Weekly,* January 29, 1968, p. 91; January 27, 1969, p. 90; February 9, 1976, p. 96.

*Spectator,* March 10, 1979, p. 23.

*Times Literary Supplement,* March 9, 1967, p. 199; February 8, 1968, p. 141; November 28, 1968, p. 1329; October 22, 1971, p. 1340.*

\*   \*   \*

## BRENNAN, Timothy (Andres) 1953-

*PERSONAL:* Born September 13, 1953, in Milwaukee, WI; son of Joseph Killorin (an attorney) and Virginia Mae (a homemaker; maiden name, Andres) Brennan; married Keya Ganguly (a professor), January 4, 1997. *Education:* University of Wisconsin—Madison, B.A., 1976; Columbia University, M.A., 1981, Ph.D., 1987. *Politics:* Socialist. *Religion:* None. *Avocational interests:* Piano, swimming, singing.

*ADDRESSES: Home*—111 East Seventh St., #54, New York, NY 10009; and 313 Laurel Ave., St. Paul, MN 55102. *Office*—343 Folwell Hall, University of Minnesota, Minneapolis, MN 55455. *E-mail*—tbrennan@ ccmail.sunysb.edu.

*CAREER:* Purdue University, Purdue, IN, assistant professor of English and comparative literature, 1986-90; State University of New York—Stony Brook, assistant professor, 1990-94, associate professor of English, 1994-98; University of Minnesota—Twin Cities, associate professor, 1998-2000, professor of comparative literature and English, 2000—. Visiting professor at University of Michigan, 1989-90, Rutgers University, 1993-94, and Cornell University, 1996-97.

*MEMBER:* International Association of Philosophy and Literature, Modern Language Association, American Comparative Literature Association, Latin-American Studies Association, Teachers for a Democratic Culture, Intercampus Faculty Committee for Peace and Justice.

*AWARDS, HONORS:* Fulbright fellow, Berlin; Society for the Humanities, Cornell University; senior fellow, CCACC, Rutgers University; Humanities Research Institute, University of California—Irvine; ACLS grant-in-aid, Center for Cuban Studies.

*WRITINGS:*

*Salman Rushdie and the Third World: Myths of the Nation,* St. Martin's Press (New York City), 1989.

*At Home in the World: Cosmopolitanism Now,* Harvard University Press (Cambridge, MA), 1997.

(Editor and co-translator with Alan Wast and Richard Schwartz) Alejo Carpentier, *Music in Cuba,* University of Minnesota Press, 2000.

Contributor to books, including *Between Languages and Cultures: Translation and Cross-cultural Texts,* edited by Anuradha Dingweney and Carol Maier, Pittsburgh University Press, 1985; *Nation and Narration: Post-structuralism and the Culture of National Identity,* edited by Houri Bhabha, Routledge, 1990; *Edward Said: A Critical Reader,* edited by Michael Sprinker, Basil Blackwell, 1992; *Postcolonial Studies Reader,* edited by Bill Ashcroft, Gareth Criffiths, and Helene Tiffin, Routledge, 1995; *Multiculturalism in Transit: Germany and the United States,* edited by Jeffrey Peck and Klaus Milich, Berghahn, 1997; *Class Issues: Pedagogy and the Public Sphere,* edited by Amitava Kumar, New York University Press, 1997; *A Practical Reader in Post-colonial Theory and English Literature,* edited by Peter Childs, Edinburgh University Press, 1998.

*WORK IN PROGRESS: Cultures of Belief: Avant Gardes, Communists, Colonies, and Culture, 1910-1945.*

*SIDELIGHTS:* Timothy Brennan is an associate professor of cultural studies and comparative literature at the University of Minnesota—Twin Cities. Brennan's expertise is in the areas of twentieth-century literary and cultural theory, especially theories of culture, the German philosophical tradition, and theories of colonialism, European modernity and its relationship to the New World. He also has researched the triangular relationship between Latin America and the Caribbean, the United States, and postwar Britain.

Commenting on *Salman Rushdie and the Third World: Myths of the Nation,* Anuradha Dingwaney Needham wrote in *Modern Fiction Studies,* that Brennan "has written an important book; its frames of reference . . . and terms for discussing Rushdie . . . will resonate in critical debates on 'Third' world texts and cultures." "What Brennan does best is to illustrate the coherence of Rushdie's work," commented Abdulrazak Gurnah in the *Times Literary Supplement.* "His discussion of it is assured and well informed, adding to our understanding of the novels' achievement by revealing their complexities." Gurnah referred to Rushdie's "hybrid" background, influenced by India, Pakistan, and England, and said that "one of the achievements" of Rushdie's *The Satanic Verses* "is its celebration of hybrids." Brennan includes Rushdie in the group of Third World writers he describes as "cosmopolitan" or "world writers." Mario Vargas Llosa, Gabriel Garcia Marquez, Isabel Allende, Bharati Mukherjee, and Derek Walcott also fall into this category.

In discussing "cosmopolitanism," *Times Literary Supplement* reviewer John Kerrigan wrote, "Overall, the suspicion grows that, as postcolonial criticism acquires the international reach which it needs if it is to understand the workings of empire, it risks losing touch with the disadvantaged communities of the developing world." Kerrigan noted that Brennan first addressed this controversy in *Salman Rushdie and the Third World.* In *At Home in the World: Cosmopolitanism Now,* Kerrigan added, Brennan "elaborates this diagnosis, extending the account of 'cosmopolitanism' to include the internationally informed academics, journalists, and policy advisers who are (in his view) stifling the message of liberation movements and clearing the way for a globalism, which is American capitalism writ large. . . . He has fresh, provocative things to say about the role of intellectuals in the New World Order." Brennan maintains that postcolonial critics "advance the interests of Western pluralism when they celebrate 'hybridity' or 'problematize' situations which are exploitative," in Kerrigan's view; He also "finds it astonishing that postcolonial studies should be so present-minded as to be indifferent to the leftist intellectualism which helped make decolonization possible. . . . [and allow] the 'dumbification of American mass culture' which Adorno identified in the 1940s [to] sweep the world."

Brennan told *CA:* "I am interested in the margins as expressed through the 'center'—that is, the role of the minority arts and movements of cultural belief in defining a collective modernity. One example of this complicated process can be seen in the part played by colonial intellectuals (often based in Europe or New York) in the exchange between European theories of history and language and non-Western forms of art and cultural practice. My work deals with the history and elaboration of imperialism as a cultural fact and as a persistent structure of feeling; the history and origins of 'cultural studies' from the young Hegelians, through utopian socialism, early Freud, to the colonial motifs found in the interwar avant-gardes—the study, in other words, of the genealogy of culture as an 'opaque' entity. My areas of special interest include cultural theory, theories of colonialism, translation theory, Latin America, and the

twentieth century Marxist tradition (Lukacs, Gramsci, Adorno, Brecht, Lefebvre, Williams, Jameson). Apart from this lineage, my interests extend to critics such as Bataille, Heidegger, and to the cross-section of institutional critiques of the media and discursive or aesthetic accounts of social being. My literary interests are found in the comparative literature of the 20th century, particularly the historical European and American novel, and narratives of African and Afro-Latin diasporas in the Caribbean basin, the United States, and postwar Britain."

*BIOGRAPHICAL/CRITICAL SOURCES:*

*PERIODICALS*

*American Book Review,* April, 1991, p. 25.
*Booklist,* October 15, 1989, p. 419.
*Choice,* January, 1990, p. 788.
*London Review of Books,* October 26, 1989, p. 11.
*Modern Fiction Studies,* winter, 1990, p. 655.
*Times Literary Supplement,* March 2, 1990, p. 221; August 21, 1998, p. 8.
*World Literature Today,* winter, 1991, p. 197.

\*    \*    \*

## BRINER, Bob  1935-1999

*OBITUARY NOTICE*—See index for *CA* sketch: Born August, 28, 1935, in Dallas, TX; died of abdominal cancer, June 18, 1999, in Greenville, IL. Sports executive and author. Briner spent most of his career in the sports field, coaching high school teams before moving into college sports administration. He worked for both the Miami Dolphins football club and the Dallas Chaparrals basketball team (later known as the San Antonio Spurs), but was best-known for his impact on the world of tennis. Briner helped merge tennis and television, first with World Championship Tennis, and then with the Association of Tennis Professionals players' union, of which he was executive director from 1975 to 1979. He was instrumental in opening major international tournaments such as Wimbledon and the French Open to professionals, a move that forever changed the sport. In 1979 he co-founded ProServe Television, from which he retired in 1996. During his career Briner, a Methodist, wrote several books that dealt with Christianity among them *Roaring Lambs, The Management Methods of Jesus,* and *The Leadership Lessons of Jesus.*

*OBITUARIES AND OTHER SOURCES:*

PERIODICALS

*New York Times,* June 20, 1999, p. A39.
*Times* (London), July 9, 1999.

\*       \*       \*

**BROWN, Byron 1952-**

*PERSONAL:* Born March 2, 1952, in Ottawa, Ontario, Canada; naturalized U.S. citizen; son of Quentin (a film director and producer) and Louise (Stumberg) Brown; married Sata Sheton Mann, May 21, 1983 (marriage ended October 15, 1985); married Ellen Friedman (a psychotherapist), July 19, 1992. *Ethnicity:* "Caucasian." *Education:* Swarthmore College, B.A. *Religion:* None.

*ADDRESSES: Home and Office*—1516 Beverly Pl., Albany, CA 94706; fax 510-524-6278. *E-mail*—ByB@ aol.com.

*CAREER:* Mangrove Collective, San Francisco, CA, movement teacher and performer, 1976-80; improvisational teacher of voice and movement, San Francisco, 1980-85; owner of a desktop publishing business in Macao, 1986-99. DHAT Institute, Berkeley, CA, member of board of directors and spiritual teacher, 1992—; Ridhwan Foundation, member.

*MEMBER:* National Writers Union.

*WRITINGS:*

*Soul without Shame,* Shambhala (Boston, MA), 1999.

*SIDELIGHTS:* Byron Brown told *CA:* "I have been a teacher for much of my adult life, though it has not been in traditional schools. One of my great loves has been communicating ideas, concepts, and perspectives to people through speaking or writing. I have always had a certain facility at translating challenging notions into understandable language and helping people appreciate the subtleties in their experience. This was true in the field of improvisational dance and voice work that I pursued for ten years, and it is now the case in spiritual practice.

"I am sure that part of my interest in the spoken and written word comes from my father, who used to read to us out loud and then later would develop word games and make up songs. When I was an adolescent, he and I would read Shakespeare's plays out loud together, and he encouraged me in the enjoyment of the English language and in using it well. As I went through school and college, I wrote papers for classes and kept a journal off and on. The one other outlet for writing over the years has been letters. For a period of time I wrote extended letters to numerous friends, in which I described at length many aspects of my life in a generally stream-of-consciousness style.

"Always I had in the back of my mind the desire to write in some more significant way. Because of my interest in articulating what I was experiencing and communicating my excitement about things I was seeing, I have always gravitated toward nonfiction exposition rather than storytelling. When I was in my twenties, while I was being a performer, I practiced writing reviews of many of the performances in theater and dance that I attended. If I knew the performers, I might later send them a copy; one or two were published in a dance magazine.

"But the project of actually writing a book did not come to the foreground until I was in my forties, after I had worked as a desktop publisher for many years. In that job I typeset books for others, including my spiritual teacher, A. H. Almaas. I became familiar with what went into publishing a book, and the prospect became less daunting. I think the fact that I knew I could publish my own book, even if no other publisher was interested, gave me impetus to go ahead and see the project through.

"*Soul without Shame* was a labor of love that resulted from many years of teaching people to work with their inner critics, as an adjunct to my work as a spiritual teacher in the Ridhwan School of A. H. Almaas. Initially I began to write the book so I could stop teaching workshops—if I put all I knew down on paper, then people could just buy the book! However, as the project unfolded it became much more than that. My understanding of the material itself deepened immensely through the need to articulate clearly and thoroughly. I learned much in developing interesting and effective ways to present the material, and I realized I had a growing desire to help people who were beyond the reach of the Ridhwan School. Finally I discovered I had much to learn about embracing myself in a fuller way as I allowed my love for the truth and the richness of the soul to be fully expressed in my writing."

**BROWN, Reeve Lindbergh**
   **See LINDBERGH, Reeve**


* * *


## BRUCE, Philip Alexander   1856-1933

*PERSONAL:* Born March 7, 1856, in the Staunton Hill plantation, Charlotte County, VA; died, August 16, 1933, in Charlottesville, VA; buried in cemetery at the University of Virginia, Charlottesville, VA; son of Charles (a plantation owner) and Sarah (Seddon) Bruce; married Elizabeth Turnstall Taylor Newton, October, 1896; children: Philippa Alexander. *Education:* Studied history and literature at the University of Virginia; Harvard University, LL.B., 1878. *Politics:* Moderate.

*CAREER:* Vulcan Iron Works, Richmond, VA, secretary-treasurer, 1887-90; *Richmond Times,* Richmond, VA, writer, 1890-92; *Virginia Magazine of History and Biography,* cofounder, 1893, editor, 1893-98; University of Virginia, Charlottesville, VA, centennial historian, beginning 1916; historian of Virginia and the American South; also worked as a lawyer.

*MEMBER:* Virginia Historical Society (corresponding secretary, 1892-98).

*WRITINGS:*

*NONFICTION*

*The Social History of Virginia,* 1881.
*The Plantation Negro as a Freeman; Observations on His Character, Condition, and Prospects in Virginia,* Putnam (New York City), 1889.
*Economic History of Virginia in the Seventeenth Century. An Inquiry into the Material Condition of the People, Based upon Original and Contemporaneous Records,* two volumes, Macmillan (New York City), 1895-96.
*A School History of the United States,* American Book Company (New York City), 1903.
*The Rise of the New South,* G. Barrie & Sons (Philadelphia, PA), 1905.
*Robert E. Lee,* G. W. Jacobs & Company (Philadelphia, PA), 1907.
*Social Life of Virginia in the Seventeenth Century. An Inquiry into the Origin of the Higher Planting Class, Together with an Account of the Habits, Customs, and Diversions of the People,* Whittet &

Shepperson (Richmond, VA), 1907, revised and enlarged edition, Bell (Lynchburg, VA), 1927.
*Institutional History of Virginia in the Seventeenth Century. An Inquiry into the Religious, Moral, Educational, Legal, Military, and Political Condition of the People, Based on Original and Contemporaneous Records,* two volumes, Putnam, 1910.
*Brave Deeds of Confederate Soldiers,* G. W. Jacobs & Company, 1916.
*History of the University of Virginia, 1819-1919: The Lengthened Shadow of One Man,* five volumes, Macmillan, 1920-22.
(Editor with Lyon Gardiner Tyler) *History of Virginia,* six volumes, American Historical Society (Chicago), 1924.
*History of Virginia, Volume One: The Colonial Period,* American Historical Society, 1924.
*The Virginia Plutarch,* two volumes, University of North Carolina Press (Chapel Hill, NC), 1929.
(Editor) *Virginia: Rebirth of the Old Dominion,* five volumes, Lewis (Chicago), 1929.

Contributor to books, including *Library of Southern Literature,* seventeen volumes, edited by E. A. Alderman and others, Hoyt (New Orleans), 1907-23; and *The South in the Building of the Nation,* edited by J. A. C. Chandler and others, thirteen volumes, Southern Historical Publications Society (Richmond, VA), 1909-13. Contributor to periodicals, including the *Contemporary Review, New York Evening Post, Richmond Times,* and the *South Atlantic Quarterly.* Bruce's papers are at the Virginia Historical Society, Richmond, VA, and the Alderman Library at the University of Virginia.


*POETRY*

*Pocahontas and Other Sonnets,* [Norfolk, VA], 1912.

*SIDELIGHTS:* Born into a prominent Virginia family just five years before the outbreak of the Civil War, Philip Alexander Bruce became a prolific social historian of the South. Although trained for a career in law, Bruce abandoned a legal career to research the role of the free black person in the Southern economy. Bruce then became the secretary-treasurer for Vulcan Iron Works, the firm owned by his brother in Richmond, Virginia. Like the law, this career failed to hold Bruce's interest.

Bruce penned a series of articles on the impact of the end of slavery on the Southern economy for the *New York Evening Post* in 1884. He used these articles and his previous research on the free black to write the 1889 book *The Plantation Negro as a Freeman; Observa-*

tions on *His Character, Condition, and Prospects in Virginia.* Bruce joined the staff of the *Richmond Times* in 1890, where he contributed articles about topical issues important to many Southerners. As his scholarly interest in the history of the South grew, Bruce spent more time researching the antebellum era, the period of time before the American Civil War. He left the *Richmond Times* in 1892.

To further his interests in history, Bruce joined the Virginia Historical Society and served as its corresponding secretary. With other members of the Society, he founded the *Virginia Magazine of History and Biography* and served as its editor from 1893 to 1898. Believing that antebellum Southern society had its earliest roots in its colonial heritage, Bruce envisioned a sweeping history of the colonial enterprise in the region, beginning with the economic underpinnings and eventually covering all aspects of social, economic, and political life in the region. He distilled the first several years of his exhaustive research into the *Economic History of Virginia in the Seventeenth Century. An Inquiry into the Material Condition of the People, Based upon Original and Contemporaneous Records,* a work published in two volumes in 1895 and 1896.

Bruce married Elizabeth Turnstall Taylor Newton in 1896, and the couple later had a daughter, Philippa Alexander. The Bruces traveled through Europe from 1898 to 1907 so Bruce could conduct archival research on the American colonies. During this time, he wrote a textbook, *A School History of the United States* (1893). Two years later, Bruce's *The Rise of the New South* was published. It focuses on how the American South had changed since 1877.

Bruce and his family returned to the United States in 1907, settling in Norfolk, Virginia. The historian's next work, *Robert E. Lee* (1907), chronicles the life of the famed American Civil War general. That same year, Bruce's *Social Life of Virginia in the Seventeenth Century. An Inquiry into the Origin of the Higher Planting Class, Together with an Account of the Habits, Customs, and Diversions of the People* was published. In 1910, the *Institutional History of Virginia in the Seventeenth Century. An Inquiry into the Religious, Moral, Educational, Legal, Military, and Political Condition of the People, Based on Original and Contemporaneous Records* was published. Bruce's trilogy of Virginia history contains *Economic History of Virginia in the Seventeenth Century, Social Life of Virginia in the Seventeenth Century,* and *Institutional History of Virginia in the Seventeenth Century.*

After the completion of his historical project on Virginia, Bruce returned to Europe, living with his family in England from 1913 to 1916. L. Moody Simms, Jr., writing in the *Dictionary of Literary Biography,* noted: "The outbreak of World War I pulled [Bruce] once again into the twentieth century, focusing his attention on contemporary affairs for several years." Bruce initially took an isolationist stance on the war, but later believed that the United States should enter the war. Yet this realization did not prevent Bruce from becoming a vocal critic of Woodrow Wilson's efforts to establish the League of Nations.

In 1916 the Bruces relocated to Charlottesville, Virginia. Bruce accepted a position as the centennial historian at the University of Virginia, and began to research the university's history. His five-volume *History of the University of Virginia, 1819-1919: The Lengthened Shadow of One Man* (1920-22) emphasizes the influence of the university's founder, U.S. president Thomas Jefferson. Bruce edited *History of Virginia,* a six-volume history published in 1924, with Lyon Gardiner Tyler and wrote the first volume of the work, *History of Virginia: The Colonial Period.* In 1929 Bruce edited a five-volume collection of historical essays on Virginia's history, *Virginia: Rebirth of the Old Dominion.* That same year, Bruce produced *The Virginia Plutarch,* a two-volume study of important and influential Virginians. Bruce died in Charlottesville, Virginia, in 1933.

*BIOGRAPHICAL/CRITICAL SOURCES:*

BOOKS

*Dictionary of Literary Biography,* Volume 47: *American Historians,* Gale (Detroit, MI), 1986.*

\*    \*    \*

## BULANDA, Susan 1946-

*PERSONAL:* Born December 19, 1946, in New York, NY; daughter of Charles and Helen (Ross) van den Broek; married Larry S. Bulanda; children: Thomas. *Education:* William Paterson College of New Jersey (now William Paterson University), B.A., 1977; Monmouth College (now University), M.A., 1987. *Avocational interests:* Gardening, bonsai, search and rescue, research.

*ADDRESSES: Home*—Pottstown, PA. *E-mail*—Susanb21@juno.com.

*CAREER:* Dog trainer and ethologist, 1961—. Coventry Canine Search and Rescue Unit, cofounder and head trainer, 1989-92; Phoenixville Fire Department, head trainer for K-9 Search and Rescue Unit, 1992—; United Kennel Club, senior conformation judge, 1995—. Worked as systems analyst and project leader, 1977-85; consultant to Indoor Air Solutions.

*MEMBER:* National League of American Pen Women (president of Chester County branch, 1996-98), Association of Pet Dog Trainers, Dog Writers Association of America, Cat Writers Association of America, National Association for Search and Rescue, North American Beauceron Club (founding member; member of board of directors, 1987-97), U.S. Border Collie Club.

*AWARDS, HONORS:* George Washington Medal of Honor, Freedoms Foundation, 1991; National League of American Pen Women, Norman E. and Marjorie J. Roller First Place Award, 1996, for *Ready!,* and special merit award, 1996, for the article "Life and Death: What It's Like When It's All up to You and Your Dog."

*WRITINGS:*

*The Canine Source Book,* Doral Publishing, 1990.
*Ready! The Training of the Search and Rescue Dog,* Doral Publishing, 1994.
*Boston Terriers,* Barron's (Woodbury, NJ), 1994.
*Ready to Serve, Ready to Save: Strategies of Real-Life Search and Rescue Missions,* Doral Publishing, 1999.
*On the Wind: Scent Work for the Hunting Dog,* Doral Publishing, 1999.

Contributor to magazines and newspapers, including *Dog World, Alpenhorn, Main Line Times, Rare Breeds Journal, SAR Dog Alert,* and *Good Dog.* Editor-in-chief, *Beauceron News,* 1987-96.

*WORK IN PROGRESS:* A dog training book; a book about animals in religion; continuing research on theology and animals.

*SIDELIGHTS:* Susan Bulanda told *CA:* "I have always loved to write and have been writing since I can remember. B.C. (Before Computers) I limited my writing to short stories and articles. After I purchased my first computer, I started to write books.

"Currently most of my writing is nonfiction. It has always been my goal to inform and entertain my reading audience. I like to present complex topics and information in a manner that is easy to understand and enjoy-

able to read. My most popular books are about search and rescue. When I wrote my first search-and-rescue book, there was little published on the topic. Since I was experienced in search and rescue and have been an ethologist and dog trainer for many years, some of the old-timers asked me to write a book. Now I have completed two books on the subject. *Ready! The Training of the Search and Rescue Dog* has been translated into Japanese and adopted worldwide as a bible for search-and-rescue dog training. *Ready to Serve, Ready to Save: Strategies of Real Life Search and Rescue Missions* has already gone international. It is a unique book because it is written for the professional who wants to learn about the strategies used by some of the top experts in the United States, yet it is also written for the general public to enjoy and to gain insight about search and rescue. It shares some of the feelings and experiences that search-and-rescue people typically do not discuss outside the professional community.

"Occasionally I teach an adult creative writing class in our local school system. The two most important things that I stress to my students are to read and to write every day, even if it is only for thirty minutes. A writer must learn to write on demand, not only when in the mood."

\* \* \*

## BULGYA, Alexander Alexandrovich 1901-1956
### (A. Fadeyev, Alexander Fadeyev)

*PERSONAL:* First and middle names are sometimes transliterated as "Aleksandr Aleksandrovich;" pseudonymous surname is sometimes transliterated as "Fadeev;" born December 24, 1901, in Kimry, Russia; committed suicide, May 13 (some sources cite May 14), 1956, in Moscow, U.S.S.R. (now Russia).

*CAREER:* Writer. Served as representative of Communist party (member of Central Committee and Supreme Soviet) and secretary of Union of Soviet Writers.

*AWARDS, HONORS:* Stalin Prize, for *Molodaia Gvardiia.*

*WRITINGS:*

*UNDER PSEUDONYM FADEYEV*

*Molodaia Gvardiia* (novel), 1945, translation published as *The Young Guard,* 1959, translation by Violet Dutt, Progress Publishers (Moscow), 1973.

Other writings include *Razgrom* (novel), 1927, translation published as *The Nineteen,* 1929; *Poslednii iz Udege* (title means "The Last of the Udegs"), four volumes, 1929-36; and *Leningrad in the Days of the Blockade,* 1946.

*OBITUARIES:*

PERIODICALS

*Times* (London), May 15, 1956.*

\*     \*     \*

## BUZZI, Aldo   1910-

*PERSONAL:* Born August 10, 1910, in Como, Lombardy, Italy; son of Paolo and Kathe (Mueller) Buzzi. *Education:* Graduated from Milan School of Architecture, 1938.

*ADDRESSES: Home*—Via Bassini 39, 20133 Milan, Italy.

*CAREER:* Architect, Milan, Italy, 1939-42; assistant director, scene writer, and screenwriter for various film production companies, the former Yugoslavia, Rome, Italy, and France, 1942-66; Rizzoli Publishers, Milan, Italy, editor, 1966-76. Editor of films, including *La Kermesse eroica, Ridolini e la collana della suocera e Ridolini esploratore,* and *Sette anni di guai,* all produced by Editoriale Domus, 1945.

*WRITINGS:*

NONFICTION

*Piccolo diario americano,* illustrated by Saul Steinberg, All'insegna del pesce d'oro (Milan, Italy), 1974.
*L'uovo alla kok: ricette, curiosita, segreti di alta e bassa cucina: dall'insalata all'acqua alla pastina in brodo della pensione, da Apicio a Michel Guerard, da Alexandre Dumas a Carlo Emilio Gadda, dal generale Bisson a san Nicolao della Flue,* illustrated by Saul Steinberg, Adelphi (Milan, Italy), 1979.
*Viaggio in Terra delle mosche e altri viaggi,* 1987, published with *Cechov a Sondrio: appunti sulla Russia* in *Cechov a Sondrio; e, Altri viaggi,* A. Mondadori (Milan, Italy), 1994, translated into English by Ann Goldstein and published as *Journey to the Land of*

*the Flies and Other Travels,* Random House (New York City), 1996.
*Cechov a Sondrio: appunti sulla Russia,* Scheiwiller (Milan, Italy), 1991, published with *Viaggio in Terra delle mosche e altri viaggi* in *Cechov a Sondrio; e, Altri viaggi,* A. Mondadori, 1994, translated into English by Goldstein and published as *Journey to the Land of the Flies and Other Travels,* Random House, 1996.

SCREENPLAYS

*Amore in citta* (also known as *Love in the City*), D.C.N./ Italian Film Export, 1953.
*L'imprevisto* (also known as *L'imprevu*), Orsay Films, 1961.

OTHER

*Taccuindo dell'Aiuto-Regista,* 1946.
*Quando la Pantera Rugge,* 1972.

Contributor to periodicals.

*SIDELIGHTS:* Writer Aldo Buzzi has worked as an architect, editor, and in various capacities in the film industry. His writings include screenplays as well as books about travel and other subjects. Ann Goldstein translated Buzzi's books *Viaggio in Terra delle mosche e altri viaggi* and *Cechov a Sondrio: appunti, sulla Russia* as *Journey to the Land of the Flies and Other Travels* (1996). Buzzi uses his travel experiences to discuss history, literature, food, and other topics in the essays in *Journey to the Land of the Flies and Other Travels.* James Marcus, reviewing the work in *Salon,* observed that Buzzi "relies on his stockpile of sensations and squirreled-away facts to evoke a place, or more to the point, his experience of it."

A *Publishers Weekly* reviewer called *Journey to the Land of the Flies* "a droll jaunt through the well-stocked mind of an Italian architect, cineaste, and publisher in whom places arouse extraordinary ruminations." A *Kirkus Reviews* contributor also noted Buzzi's talents and interests, stating that "erudition and wit characterize these travels into the past with an Italian publisher, writer, gourmand, and lover of women." Harlow Robinson, reviewing the work in the *New York Times Book Review,* also mentioned the author's diversity, writing that "the reader cannot always be sure of Mr. Buzzi's whereabouts on any given page." Robinson called Buzzi's book a "quirky, dreamy, and poetic collection of travel and literary impressions." *Washington Post Book World* contributor Michael Mewshaw concluded: "*Journey to the Land of the Flies* reiterates in its elusive rococo fashion that the richest reward of traveling resides in the process, not the destination, just as the greatest pleasure of reading lies in the discovery not of new places, but of sensibilities one hadn't previously known existed."

*BIOGRAPHICAL/CRITICAL SOURCES:*

*PERIODICALS*

*Kirkus Reviews,* December 1, 1995, p. 1679.
*Library Journal,* February 15, 1996, p. 167.
*New York Times Book Review,* April 21, 1996, p. 40.
*Publishers Weekly,* November 27, 1995, p. 57.
*Washington Post Book World,* May 26, 1996, p. 7.

*OTHER*

*Salon,* (webzine), March 18, 1999.*

# C

## CANAN, Janine 1942-

*PERSONAL:* Born November 2, 1942, in Los Angeles, CA; daughter of Lewis Marion (a restaurateur and entrepreneur) and Mary Athene (Clay) Burford; married Michael James Canan, August 31, 1963 (divorced). *Education:* Stanford, 1960-63; University of California, Berkeley; New York University; University of California, San Francisco.

*ADDRESSES: Home*—772 Earnest Dr., Sonoma, CA 95476.

*CAREER:* Poet and private practice psychiatrist.

*AWARDS, HONORS:* Susan Koppelman Award for best-edited feminist work, 1990, for *She Rises Like the Sun: Invocations of the Goddess by Contemporary American Women Poets.*

*WRITINGS:*

POETRY

*Of Your Seed,* Oyez Press (Berkeley, CA), 1977.
*The Hunger,* Oyez Press, 1979.
*Who Buried the Breast of Dreams,* Emily Dickinson Press (Berkeley, CA), 1981.
*Daughter,* illustrated by Donna Brookman, Emily Dickinson Press, 1981.
*Shapes of Self,* Emily Dickinson Press, 1982.
*Her Magnificent Body: New and Selected Poems,* Manroot Press (San Francisco, CA), 1986.
(Editor) *She Rises like the Sun: Invocations of the Goddess by Contemporary American Women Poets,* The Crossing Press (Freedom, CA), 1989.
*Goddess Poems,* Sagittarius Press (Port Townsend, WA), 1997.

**Janine Canan**

*Love, Enter,* Open Bone Press (Port Angeles, WA), 1998.
(Editor) Lynn Londier, *The Rhyme of the Ag-Ed Mariness: Last Poems of Lynn Londier,* Station Hill Press (Barrytown, NY), 1999.
(Translator) Else Lasker-Shueler, *Star in My Forehead: Poems by Else Lasker-Schueler,* bilingual German/English edition, Holy Cow! Press (Duluth, MN), 1999.

Canan's poetry has been included in anthologies, including *Pointing Outward; Anthology of Underground Poetry; Women Poets of the World; State of Peace: The Women Speak; We Speak of Peace; Sirius Verse; Of Frogs and Toads; Heal Your Soul, Heal the World;*

*Women Celebrate: Breaking Silence into Joy;* three volumes of *Return of the Goddess;* and many others. Her work has also been published in numerous periodicals, including *The Acorn, Alternative Harmonies, California Quarterly, The Creative Woman Quarterly, The Cypress Review, Deserted Times, Focus, The Laureate Letter, Manhattan Poetry Review, Minotaur, Of the People, Open Bone Review, Pandora, Poetry USA, The San Francisco Chronicle, Visions,* and *Writer's Gazette.*

Several of Canan's poems have also been published as keepsakes, broadsides, and greeting cards. *Janine Canan Reads,* a reading of selected poetry, was released on audio cassette from Heaven Productions.

*WORK IN PROGRESS:* Two books of poetry, *Changing Woman* and *The One I Love: Selected Poems;* and two books of prose, *Goddesses, Goddesses: Essays by Janine Canan* and *Journeys with Justine.*

*SIDELIGHTS:* Janine Canan is the author of several volumes of feminist poetry, including *Of Your Seed, Who Buried the Breast of Dreams,* and *Goddess Poems.* She has also translated the poems of German writer Else Lasker-Shueler into English, and edited two poetry collections. The first collection she edited, *She Rises like the Sun: Invocations of the Goddess by Contemporary American Women Poets,* won the 1990 Susan Koppelman Award for best-edited feminist work.

*AUTOBIOGRAPHICAL ESSAY:*

Canan contributed the following essay to *CA:*

*I—Childhood in the City of the Queen of Angels*

In 1942 I was born (again ?), in the City of the Queen of Angels amidst the worldwide violence of World War II. My father, Lewis, who owned restaurants classified as "essential business," was spared the horror of the war. At his *Wich Stand* drive-in, he courted my mother, Mary, a beautiful twenty-year-old with poignant dark eyes, who was taking singing lessons and temporarily working as a car-hop.

Lewis Marion Burford was a slender and handsome twenty-eight year old living with his mother, Flora. Flora Agnes Cox (1887-1973), daughter of Lou Eva (Pike) Perkins (1867-1922) and John Exum Cox (1849-1926), was a Quaker whose family had emigrated from the British Isles in the seventeenth and eighteenth centuries to Pennsylvania and then North Carolina, where they settled as plantation farmers in Dobbs (then called

Wayne) County. Lou Eva and John moved west to Kansas, where redheaded Flora met and married Benjamin Simpson Burford (1883-1919), whose ancestors had come to America from the medieval village of Burford, England. The young couple left Kansas to farm in Colorado, and there gave birth to four children: Lucille, Glen, Louis (later changed to Lewis) and Hazel.

Louis (born in 1912) was seven and sick at home with his mother the day his father's Ford skidded over treacherous winter ice into the tree that took his life. Flora remarried. She, her four children, and new husband drove west to Los Angeles, where little Louis was unforgettably awed by the immense Pacific Ocean. Frugal Flora and her second husband, ever struggling to find work, eventually divorced, and the children went to work, picking fruit and operating a fruit beverage stand. Somehow my father managed to save enough money for piano lessons. By the age of seventeen, the Depression had taught him the necessity of making money. For his education, he realized he would have to read "the books of experience."

My mother, Mary Alene Clay, was born in Los Angeles in 1920, third-generation Californian. Although the history of her family of flamboyant storytellers may never be known, ancestral stories point to heritages from Germans, the English and Spanish, probably Jews, and possibly Native Americans. I have often wondered from whom my grandmother, my mother, my sisters, and I inherited our marked epicanthic oriental eyelids. My great-grandmother Jesse Hawthorne, born in California, had married Jacob Kircher, a Mormon blacksmith and Carlsbad, New Mexico, mayor with several wives, who was said to have descended from German Jews converted to Catholicism. Jesse eventually left Jacob and her children in New Mexico, returning to Los Angeles to open a cleaning business. Lela, the younger of their children, born in California in 1897, was sent east to a Catholic convent school in the midwest, and returned to California to marry Everett Clay and give birth to two daughters, June and Mary. Soon after Mary's birth, Clay departed, taking little June with him, and Mary never knew either her father or her sister.

Temperamental Lela, a good storyteller and a phenomenal crocheter, for awhile a nurse and a Communist, was not a good mother. Frequently moving and occasionally changing partners, she neglected and mistreated her daughter. Mary sometimes stayed with her Aunt Marguerite, and briefly lived with a foster family. Changing schools constantly, with no father or siblings and a difficult mother, Mary found a place for herself in the larger world of books, and at her new schools entertained her schoolmates with plays which she herself wrote.

Both of my parents, having lost their fathers early, grew up poor during the twenties and the Great Depression. But by the spring of 1940, my father and his brother owned two flourishing drive-ins, and he and my mother were in love. A year later the striking dark-haired couple, while attending a wedding, spontaneously drove to Las Vegas and married. The next winter, as Mary and Lewis made love in their cozy house on Adale Place, I was conceived. On the second day of November, the second *Dia de los Muertos* (the day dead children visit the living), I was born at noon in Saint Vincent's Hospital. "Nuns rushed in the halls. Mother wore a silk bedjacket. The nipple was rubber," I wrote in the stream-of-consciousness prose poem "Childhood" in 1977, dictated during my psychoanalytically-oriented psychiatric residency. But twenty years later, in "Introduction to the Poet" from *Changing Woman*, it seemed more like this:

I slipped out of my mother's anesthetized womb into Saint Vincent's hospital in the City of the Queen of Angels (where my great-grandmother, my grandmother and my mother had arrived before me). The welcoming hands of a white-coifed nun tucked me into a safe niche in her long black gown that rustled, as she rushed down the corridor, with all the untold feminine mysteries of the millennia.

> Mother gave me the name Janine, which comes from a Hebrew root and means *God is gracious, God is merciful.* She tried to nurse me, but her milk, like that of most American mothers during the nineteen-forties and subsequent decades, "dried up" within a week. I was changed to formula milk and fed on a pediatric schedule. A photograph of my parents with their newborn daughter Janine Ann, reveals a joyful father tenderly rocking his new baby in the crook of his arm, her tiny face tilted toward his, with a confused-looking woman standing at his side.

After my birth, my father bought an orange grove on Pomona in Brea, south of Los Angeles. Mother, Father, and I moved into a cream-colored cottage surrounded by thousands of fragrant orange trees. There my father, with the help of Mr. Birch, also raised chickens to produce eggs for his war-rationed restaurants. Every day he drove into the city to work, and I remained with my mother. Mary started stitching a baby quilt for my bed which was never finished, but the soft stuffed golden

*As infant, with parents, Mary and Lewis Burford, about 1942*

bear who was to ride in the appliqued donkey-cart became my dearest companion, loved to pieces.

Before I could even sit, Mother had me propped next to her, reading me stories and rhymes out of books like Olive Beaupre's beautifully illustrated *My Little Book House*. One afternoon a war plane crashed into the orange grove and blazed into pieces among the trees. The pilot strolled out of the wreckage unscathed, and lit a cigarette. By the age of five months (as documented by one of my favorite photographs), I had already developed a detached and thoughtful gaze upon the world. Amidst the sweet scents of the orange trees I sat, contemplating. One day I suddenly stood and began to walk. My first sentence, says my mother, was an agreeably formed "May I have drink of water, please."

When I was about two years old, my parents decided to move back to Los Angeles, in time for my sister Dianne Louise's birth. After a short stay in an apartment on Bronson, we moved into the large three-story house on Palmero Street that was to be my childhood home. 4338 Palmero was located in the View Park hills, overlooking the palm trees of the Los Angeles basin, midway between Hollywood, downtown, and the beach, and only minutes from my father's drive-in at Slauson and Overhill. Lewis had chosen a house that was a white traditional-modern blend, sturdily built into the hillside on half an acre, copiously planted with roses, begonias and bougainvillea; peach, lemon, lime, apricot, kumquat, loquat, fig, and pomegranate trees; a southern magnolia, a towering avocado, and a tumbling hillside of pink, white and lavender geraniums mingled with ivy.

Dianne and I shared a bedroom lovingly decorated by Mother. At bedtime she sang us beautiful tunes such as Brahms's "Lullabye," "Spring-time in the Rockies," and "Rockabye Baby," or told us amusing rhymes such as "The Little Girl with a Curl in the Middle of her Forehead." And we always clamored (I especially) for more! Shortly before I turned three, Patriarchy's World War II reached its grand finale with America's unforgettable explosion of atomic bombs over Japan. And I entered Dr. Sooling's School for Little Folks, a pleasant place where I recall being scolded, to my deep humiliation, for reaching into Dr. Sooling's generous bosom while blissfully floating upon her lap.

When I turned six—"a stocky six year old in pink organdy . . . with intelligence in her voice" ("Some of Each," *Shapes of Self*)—I was allowed to choose my own bedroom. I picked the sunny room on the southwestern corner over the garage, with a small dressing room adjacent to a bathroom that interconnected with our loved Irish housekeeper's bedroom. In my room the windows were surrounded with bright magenta bougainvillea. At night the great avocado tree shadow-danced on the ceiling. The room had floral peach wallpaper and old-fashioned colonial maple furniture, including a small writing desk which I chose. This beloved room, which I shared with my dolls—baby Didi-Doll, Jocko Lover Boy, a furry monkey with long arms and felt hands, and many others—was the setting for the rich inner life that occupied me throughout my childhood.

In the backyard, Dianne and I played on the swing, slide, and sandbox, built forts under the peach trees, and played croquet and badminton with the neighbor children. In the street we played tag, with the old gray catalpa tree, shedding its pods in front of our house as home base. We had a big collie dog named Michael of Tamarack (later heartbreakingly hit by a car), and several cats. Our gracious neighborhood included old Mrs. French, who watched over us from her upper window, the gentle Wilsons next door—a professor, his schoolteacher wife, and their son—and two large Irish Catholic families, whose vivacious daughters wore dark-blue pinafore uniforms that I envied.

Mother, though often preoccupied, took good care of our physical needs, braiding our hair into tidy brown braids looped behind our ears; dressing us well in outfits I still remember: matching handknit red wool sweaters, caps, and mittens or pale-blue chiffon dresses with countless ruffles; and taking us on enjoyable outings to the doctor and dentist. We were given all kinds of lessons in the arts—tap dancing at four, piano lessons at five. As I poured over my fingers on the big white and black keyboard, fragile graying Mary Martha Hart sat beside me, while Mother, seated on our curved rose sofa with her perennial cup of coffee and cigarette in hand, periodically bubbled praise. After tap came ballet, then oil painting lessons, and marimba and flamenco lessons, but the piano lessons never stopped. When I was about five, Mother completed her own high school education, and our whole family proudly attended her graduation, where she sang "Ah Sweet Mystery of Life" in her lovely tremulous alto voice. Above all, what mother passed on to me was her love of beauty in art and nature.

At six I entered first grade at Forty-Second-Street Elementary School. There I painted a vivid colorful cow, and met my little friends Toni, Suzanne, Frannie, Maggie, David, Allen, and my first boyfriend Archie. Our class memorized Longfellow's "The Children's Hour," and played Louisa May Alcott's *Little Women,* with myself as the narrator. Immersed in the magic of childhood, pulling our handcrafted wagons and carrying our baby dolls, wearing hand-sewn skirts—mine with pink and black dragonflies—and large bonnets, we were pioneers. Dreamily weaving our long crepe-paper ribbons around the maypole, we danced the May.

At home our family plugged in the first television on the block, built by my inventor-uncle, Glen. Dianne and I eagerly watched Beany and Cecil the Seasick Sea Serpent inside the big box on our playroom floor. By the time I was eight, and Dianne was six, my second sister, Michele Marie, was born. After spending her first days in an incubator, Michele emerged in a soft yellow blanket, soon learning to smile with a calming humor, which was to protect her from many of the painful dramas that overshadowed Dianne's and my early years.

In those days, I typically waited long lonely hours to be picked up after school, and getting to school—waking up mother—was a similar ordeal. On Sundays, however, a family friend took me to Sunday school at the local, friendly Presbyterian church where I had been baptized, and which my whole family attended on Christmas and Easter. Occasionally I spent Saturday night at Grandmother Burford's and attended a big

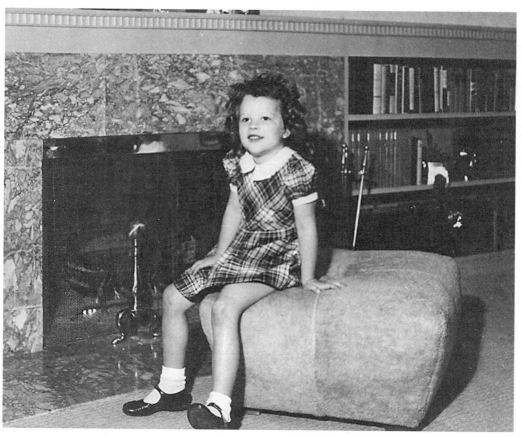

*Five years old, about 1947*

evangelical church with her on Sunday. Christmases at our house were major events. On Christmas eve my family performed music for each other—even my father played a piano piece remembered from his teens—and we caroled with neighbors. On Christmas day there were many wonderful gifts gorgeously wrapped, and the entire Burford family—uncles, aunts, and cousins—came to our house for dinner and gifts. "A Beautiful Meal" in *Shapes of Self* describes Mother's traditional Christmas dinner.

A good pupil, I formed strong attachments to my dedicated teachers throughout my school years. Because my mother was unpredictable and sometimes hypercritical, and my father was always at work, my teachers were all the more significant. In fact, they were crucial. My early poetry collections contain memorials to some of these teachers, like "Bosom," which fuses my nurturing fourth grade teacher Helen Hum with my equally nurturing high school English teacher Blanche Garrison:

> Helen Hum and Blanche Garrison have their large arm around me and I am being pressed against the massive slope of their bosom. I am

looking up at their silvery shingles of hair and their broad roll of chin. Don't be afraid of the paint, says Helen Hum. Just write what comes to mind, Blanche Garrison adds.

My school friends were equally important to me. We all formed a Brownie troop that evolved into a Girl Scout and later a Mariner troop, affording us innumerable opportunities to get together for exuberant birthday and slumber parties, craft sessions, volleyball games, and campouts under the brilliantly pulsing stars. "My Book" (*Shapes of Self*), sums up the atmosphere of puberty that came over me and my friends:

> Karen knows about sex—she has hair down there. Carol is bouncing on her ball in the swimming pool, having her first magical experience. She is rocking in the bathtub bargaining with God. I am floating in my inner tube with my book. Karen passes me a note—a figure with breasts. I add some lines and pass it back. Karen is busy with our drawing. My heart stops. Miss Smith is stalking down the aisle, snatching the drawing and crushing it in her

fist. Her eyes are bulging out. Carol is crying at the blackboard. She is the only one who knows how to have one. At night she will dream of me—*You were a rebel, you were mysterious, you were a powerful figure; together we would have made a perfect person.* I was always in my book.

Indeed, I often had my nose stuck in a book as I devoured *Heidi,* the Laura Ingalls Wilder books, and all the Nancy Drew mysteries given me by a neighbor. A school painting I made of the pilgrim's first Thanksgiving shows a girl praying at a table spread with food, her mind filled with dual, transforming images of barren winter and abundant harvest autumn—unconsciously illustrating, perhaps, the vivid contrasts of my own alternatingly happy and unhappy childhood.

Managing his restaurants and other businesses—a popcorn company, a shopping center, even a small desert airport—Dad worked endless days. He came home for Mother's tasty dinners—such as creamed tuna on toast with spinach—which we ate together in the coral kitchen booth, and returned to work. Occasionally, he would come home again for a midnight snack, when to my delight I was awakened so I could join in. My father often took us out to dinner, driving long distances throughout the county for a delicious meal—Southern fried chicken at Knott's Berry Farm, prime rib at Lowry's in Beverly Hills, or chili-size with lots of onions at Joe's downtown. When home, he always found a way to be helpful, whether bathing us, adjusting windows for fresh air, or bringing food for breakfast. Strongly dedicated to supporting his family, he set an example of modesty, discipline and devotion.

Terribly shy in the early years of adolescence, my focus was on school and my dreams. I had a voracious appetite to learn, combined with an aching longing for love. Many hours were spent reading and daydreaming as I sprawled across my jade-quilted bed. The short poem "Burning" (*Shapes of Self*), based on a real-life encounter with vanilla, one of my favorite scents, sums up the sort of personality I was developing:

> No one is in the kitchen and I am climbing up
> to the top shelf. Where the vanilla is kept. The
> vanilla of vanilla pudding, the vanilla of warm
> bread custard, the vanilla of vanilla frosting,
> the vanilla of banana cream pie. I am holding
> the flat dark flask, untwisting its tight little lid.
> No one is coming as I bend to sniff its secret
> juice, place its mouth on my lips, tilt my head

back and let it run in. *You promised*! I swallow, burning.

For my twelfth birthday, my mother took me to see the opera *La Boheme.* I will never forget romantic Mimi dying over and over again on her chaise lounge. Often ecstatically merged into the world around me, I was given my own first vision. One night mysterious shadows agitating upon my bedroom ceiling suddenly revealed the massive, all-consuming waves of Creation, crashing and rolling forever onward through time. From then on, I was acutely aware of the reality of *transience,* and I knew there was no going back.

Whereas my conservative father lived in a world called "At Work," and my mother seemed to float in an interior world with her cup of black coffee and a cigarette, I lived increasingly in my glowing room. As my relationship with my mother became more difficult, even stormy during adolescence, I spent more time than ever there. And one night, doors slamming, the whole world seemed to shake apart as a major earthquake hit our City of the Queen of Angels. My budding independence, mounting energy, and passionate hopes were more than Mother, house bound by inner conflicts, could tolerate. Wounding scenes, criticisms, punishments, forgotten promises, gifts taken back, and threats to send me away to private school were painfully common occurrences.

Throughout childhood, I often jotted down the thoughts that came to me in some significant and conclusive way—spoken to me by a growing inner voice—and slipped them into the maple drawer by my bed. At thirteen I entered Audubon Junior High School, and wrote my first (as far as I know) poetic stanza, a pulsing pubescent love call. I also started playing the harp. "Her Strings" (*Shapes of Self*) tells how it came about:

> Over Grandmother's sofa hung a large picture
> of a beautiful young woman in a long blue
> dress, playing the harp; next to her, a woman
> in a gold dress stood singing. Then when I was
> eleven, Maureen Love moved in next door—
> she played the harp. I used to go over to her big
> white house, and watch her, at the end of a long
> red-carpeted room, pluck and strum the
> strings—thin Maureen in her pink dress with
> her pink cheeks. And so it was that, year after
> year, I asked for a harp. One Christmas, waking before everyone else, I crept downstairs
> with my gifts—down the rose wool stairs,
> down the beige stairs onto the cold linoleum.
> And my eyes, rounding the corner, flew to the

harp: Tall regal golden lover. Circling around,
I breathed upon her, and wherever I touched—
her strings resounded.

My sublimely beautiful, golden 1917 Wurlitzer harp, generously given to me by my parents, was chosen by my harp teacher, the encouraging and eccentric Catherine Jackson, remembered in "Whatever You Want" *(Shapes of Self):*

> Catherine Jackson is seated at the harp. With frizzy gray hair, dangling earrings and her long powdered nose. Long bare arms, over satiny skirt with hand-painted flowers spread over her knees: *My mother said I'd never amount to a hill of beans.* Her strong callused fingers press into the strings. Then she swishes out the door, her high laugh *glissandoing.* Lifts her foot— the one in the elevated red leather shoe—into her yellow jeep, and vanishes over the hill. Her writing swirls gaily over the page: *You can do whatever you want.*

Junior high school graduation at age fourteen was an important rite of passage. I wore a grown-up tailored beige suit that announced that I had entered womanhood. My parents took me on a wonderful trip to New York and New England. By fourteen, having dipped into my mother's college psychology books and novels like *The Snake Pit,* I was scouting the local library for further psychology texts. Whereas at thirteen I had dreamed of becoming an architect who would renovate old houses, by fourteen—to the surprise of teachers and friends with more ordinary fantasies—I wanted to become a psychiatrist. What being a psychiatrist meant to me at that age, I am not sure, but it must have had to do with desiring the blessing of real intimacy, and being able to guide those who are lost out of the dark.

One day my close friend Carol Bredenbeck brought me a copy an interesting book of Hatha yoga postures, which I tried out first on myself, before engaging neighbor kids in building a yogic pyramid. An activist streak in me took the form of going round the neighborhood collecting donations for the Multiple Sclerosis Society. On our bookshelves I discovered the romantic world of Jane Eyre and the English Bronte sisters—Charlotte, Emily, and Anne. In American Literature class, the summer before high school, I eagerly met my first poets—T. S. Eliot, Emily Dickinson, and Edna St. Vincent Millay.

At Susan Miller Dorsey High School, a unique school whose population in the late 1950s was one-third European, one-third Asian, and one-third African American, I had excellent teachers. On the other hand, I was crushed when I failed to be admitted into a popular social club. Now I focused increasingly on preparations for college, becoming active in all kinds of organizations—French Club, Dorsey High Chorus, Girls' Letter Society, Ladies (a service organization), and the California Scholarship Federation. I edited the Girls' Athletic Association newsletter, and in senior year was class treasurer. My neighborhood friend Maureen Love and I occasionally played harp duets for school concerts, weddings, and television programs. A zealous student, I took any extra classes I could, such as early morning World History and Creative Writing. It was in the latter that I wrote my first published poem, "The Distance Is Great," about the gap between the old and the young, published in our high school literary magazine *Trial Flights.*

At this time my religious search began. Visits to Catholic mass and Jewish synagogue, and fantasies of becoming a nun, intermingled with visits with friends to Venice coffeehouses where poetry was read to jazz, foreign movie houses, Oscar Levant's live television show, record shops, and bookstores, such as the wonderful Pickwick Books in Hollywood. I rode across the wide valley on the bus until my father gave me a little black Studebaker with red leather upholstery. While my sister Dianne, attending Marlborough School for Girls, became more and more immersed in a world of boys, I had many free-floating crushes but only a few dates. Nights when my father was at work, I did homework, watched old movies on television with Mother, and listened to her lengthy entertaining stories. I was more immersed in literature than ever, and for my graduation my parents gave me—to my vast joy—Harvard's new three-volume *Poems of Emily Dickinson,* annotated with all known variants, along with a fat volume of Edna St. Vincent Millay's *Complete Poems.*

My psychoanalytically-oriented poem "Childhood" ended:

> . . . I was walking down Hollywood Boulevard into Pickwick Books, the record stores. I was watching Madame Bovary in the small dark theater, their legs touching under the table. I was running away, down the block past the McDermotts', the Barys', up the hill to the house with the low brick wall where I sat drying my tears, watching the clouds, the moon. I was walking home. I was wading through waist-deep flood-waters in my home-made woolen skirt. I was going away to college.

Indeed, I was extremely excited about the prospect of college, getting my books and wardrobe together and packing them into a big green trunk, reading recommended books such as H. G. Wells's Outline of *History,* and visiting college campuses like Pomona and Stanford. Selected by American Field Service to be a yearlong foreign student to France, I was not sent since a family could not be found. As a graduation surprise, my father secretly arranged for me to travel for a month with my friend Carol to visit her family in Sweden, then join a group of schoolteachers making a grand tour of Europe by bus through England, France, Holland, Germany, Italy, Switzerland, and Spain. This was a momentous life experience, which left many deep impressions upon me and greatly expanded my view of the world.

My childhood had been one of loneliness and bounty. Now approaching college, I sensed with longing a new beginning.

### II—Youth in the Sixties

I entered Stanford University in the fall of 1960, when Stanford was a slumberous, tree-lined campus where the occasional student strolled by with a stack of books, lost deep in thoughts of Western Civilization, a challenging English essay, or an upcoming date. In a German class in the first month, I met my husband-to-be, Michael James Canan, a highly literate economics major also from Los Angeles. Our first date, a dance sponsored by his "eating club," was taken up with a pressing discussion of politics—his obsession—followed by a surprising goodnight kiss. Mike and I soon became inseparable, studying and eating together, eventually becoming engaged.

I entered college as a pre-med major intending to become a psychiatrist. But after an overpowering 8 A.M. chemistry class, repeated discouragement from my pre-med advisor (known in the future as a notorious sexist), and a year of wheeling a library cart through the back wards of Agnews' State Mental Hospital as a Stanford volunteer, I changed my major to French. Thanks to four years of well-taught high school French, I immediately entered advanced courses in French linguistics and literature—Villon, Hugo, Valery, Baudelaire, Rimbaud, Claudel, Prevert, etc. In those days it didn't strike me as odd that all the writers we studied were male—I was so happy to be able to read them, however awkwardly, in their native tongue. I was writing a few poems myself, which I showed to no one. About this time, sadly my mother's mother died of tuberculosis, while she herself was hospitalized in a mental hospital.

At Stanford I received a superb classical Western education, for which I have always been grateful. The most outstanding courses were Theodore Roszak's Western Civilization section, which met at his home; Frederick Spiegelberg's popular lecture course on comparative religion (I especially remember his lively demonstration of Tibetan ghost traps); and charming Professor Georges Lemaitre's wittily entertaining courses on Sartre and Existentialism. I played harp in the Stanford Symphony, and took harpsichord lessons. During the summers Mike was building me a harpsichord.

Because I took summer music courses on Bach—whose music I have always adored—at UCLA, I graduated from Stanford with distinction in three years, at the same time as Mike, who was a year ahead. As usual, Mike worked that summer in the Pacific Palisades bank near his parents' home, and I talked my father into letting me work in his restaurant as a waitress. I was growing closer and closer to Mike's warm and literate Irish-Anglo family, and it was Mike's mother Molly who gave me e. e. cummings' *Collected Poems,* precious love lyrics that I often carried with me, savoring for many years. On August 31, 1963, Mike and I were married in a Presbyterian Church in Brentwood, I was twenty, Mike twenty-one. After a honeymoon in Mexico, we arrived in Berkeley to begin graduate school—he in the law school his father had attended, and I in the German department. Why German? Because by now I needed to read Rilke.

My first day on the UC campus, I was stunned by the umpteen political flyers shoved into my hands as I walked through Sather Gate. Photographs of napalmed Vietnamese women and children shocked me, and it took me several weeks to absorb what I was seeing for the first time, and to know what I felt about it. Meanwhile, I had to struggle with my UC advisor, just as I had with my Stanford pre-med advisor, but this time I didn't give up. In spite of his disapproval, I was able to take the Rilke course, along with *Minnesang,* a course on German medieval love poetry, in my first semester.

I walked into the Rilke class, and at first sight fell totally in love with my professor—a Hungarian Jew slumped at the podium, glasses sliding down his nose, cigarette in one of his graceful hands. A mystic philosopher writing an endless ontology, Andrew O. Jaszi, son of a Hungarian counter-revolutionary leader and a Hungarian artist, became my teacher for the next several years. I took all the courses he taught, which were precisely those courses I wanted to take: Goethe, Romantic German Drama, Modern German Poetry, as well as

Rilke. Through these courses Professor Jaszi passed on to me his deeply thoughtful and mystical vision of wholeness.

In 1964, the student Free Speech Movement began, synchronized with student rebellions against patriarchal madness round the world. Attending protest gatherings, marches, and sit-ins, I canceled German classes I was teaching in order to join my students and professors in vociferous anti-war demonstrations. My husband was absent. One day my old Stanford Western Civ instructor, Ted Roszak, appeared on Telegraph Avenue, pointedly quizzing me about the scene. He and his family had moved to Berkeley, Ted was working on his brilliant *Making of A Counterculture,* and we soon became staunch friends. Through student friends Jane and Steve Sokolow, I was "turned on" to the magical wonders of marijuana—Mike, again, abstained. Following a recipe published by Aldous Huxley's wife Laura for "Heavenly Blue" morning glory seeds, a friend and I had our first psychedelic experience—for me a taste of infinite oneness, culminating in a vision of the entire cosmos revolving in the corner of our apartment ceiling.

I described the cultural atmosphere of Berkeley in the sixties in my autobiographical introduction to *Changing Woman:*

> In the Sixties the Bay Area throbbed with poetry, effervesced with poetry, *was* poetry. Robert Duncan was often seen flying down The Avenue in his magic cape. Julia Vinograd, dressed in black and yellow robe and cap, limped into Telegragh Avenue cafes peddling booklets of poems for a dollar. At the Berkeley Community Theater Janis Joplin, in a sexy short black dress, belted out cosmic lyrics to the accompaniment of Big Brother and the Holding Company; while Ram Dass pontificated afterwards. In San Francisco Glenn Gould hovered over his piano, humming indecipherable chants. At the Jazz Workshop, all night long John Coltrane poured out his heart through his saxophone. Ali Akbar Khan and Ravi Shankar arrived in the Berkeley Amphitheater with their soulful sarod and sitar. And at the Golden Gate Park Love-In, Allen Ginsberg sang of the fall of America, transcendently stoned—but by then I was too in-love with my Rilke professor to make the scene.

> . . . Standing in Cody's Books on Telegraph Avenue, I read every new poetry edition that arrived on the shelf—from Robert Duncan's pulsing *Opening of the Field,* to Michael McClure's mysterious *Dark Brown.* In the joyous Summer of 1965, an unforgettable Berkeley Poetry Conference presented one-eyed Creeley, howling Ginsberg, raging Le Roi Jones; Olson as a humongous drunken bear, lively lisping Levertov in a striped tee-shirt, ascetic Snyder with a goatee, and Duncan overpowered by his incessant visions. A yogi arrived from India proclaiming Berkeley the heartbeat of the world.

Just before I was to take my master's examination, and Mike was to graduate from law school, and together we were to join the Peace Corps in Venezuela (which Mike had chosen in preference to war in Vietnam), we found ourselves spontaneously deciding to split up. Our paths certainly seemed to be leading in different directions. Mike already had his life mapped out on a staid and conventional track as lawyer and family man. But my life—*my search*—was just beginning. I was twenty-three and the whole world lay before me as an unknown. I was ready to embark on my journey. A chance meeting that night with novelist Gunther Grass, passing through Berkeley on a lecture tour for his novel *The Tin Drum,* seemed to whirl me forever out of the academic orbit I had been circling in for six years.

Fairly amicably, Mike and I split our minimal worldly goods, arguing only over the lovely walnut harpsichord that he had built for me as a wedding gift, and signed the do-it-yourself divorce agreement. My master's exams forgotten, I was suddenly in Paris, on my way to a friend's whitewashed eighteenth-century ruin on the tiny scorched Greek island of Hydra, suspended in the exquisite azure of the Aegean. Mike remained in Berkeley, studying for bar exams before his own departure for Venezuela, where he was inducted into the Vietnam War anyway, and then escaped by signing up for officer training in an inactive branch of the armed forces, safe in Montana. After a sad month in romantic, sunny Greece, I took a train to Munich—where I took in the vivid, colorful, angular paintings—and then on to Berlin.

Lovely Myrna from Canada, whom I had met in the German department and who would later become a journalist, was already settled in Berlin when I arrived. She helped me find a job, where I lasted only a matter of weeks, as a secretary in the small avant-garde Gerhardt publishing house, run by Frau Gerhardt herself. There I was, in the historical capital of Germany, the heart of German Nazism, where heaps and heaps of bomb-rubble alternated with glossy new American buildings that stood proud in celebration of capitalism. Young people with children migrated to West Germany, and war-disabled elders waited for death. The Free University of Berlin, Von Karajan's sublime Philharmonic, diverse avant-garde chamber music groups, the classical Schiller Theatre, and the nightlife were among the most sophisticated in the world. For a few dollars I went to a concert almost every night; danced in the decadent red and black disco clubs; met massive Charles Olson, drunkenly womanizing in a dark bar after his reading; attended lectures; dated another lawyer; and had painful dreams about my aborted marriage.

One afternoon in a bookstore on the Kurfuerstendam, I discovered a new red volume of Expressionist Else Lasker-Schueler's *Gesammelte Gedichte,* released by Koesel Verlag in celebration of the German-Jewish poet's birth-centennial. I tried a few translations, embarking on a project that was to occupy me intermittently for three decades. And one wintry day, I woke in my narrow cot next to the smoking charcoal oven, looked at the matching lithographs of Goethe and Schiller, listened to the old landlady—who still remembered the rape and looting by Russians—as she shuffled down the hall, saw snow all over the ground below, and knew it was time to go home. The mauve heather, she had complained was proper for a grave, I left on the windowsill.

Back in Berkeley I moved into a household of graduate students, who coincidentally included political writer Jonathan Schell. Berkeley was bulging with writers in those days. Almost immediately, I entered into a deeply affecting but inevitably heartbreaking relationship with my now also divorced, former German professor Andrew Jaszi—my philosopher. These were days of Coltrane all night at North Beach's Jazz Workshop, Glenn Gould humming on stage to melodies of Bach, Ginsberg pouring out his cosmic Jewish soul, crowded love-ins and be-ins in Golden Gate and other parks. One windy afternoon, as I stood at the window of City Lights Books, an intoxicated old Afro-American man insisted on giving me his tiny, red, battered and scribbled-in Robert Burns—and it felt like a sign.

Working on a high school teaching credential at UC so I could get a job, I decided to take Peter Dale Scott's poetry workshop. Professor Scott, a Canadian-born poet and political writer, gathered some of our workshop poems together in *Pointing Outward,* and persuaded me to start teaching creative writing at UC myself, in a special program for student participation in university education. In one class I met an impressive, effervescent, unpublished poet named Dennis Walton, who introduced me to the work of Kenneth Rexroth—translator of the great Chinese lyricist Tu Fu, and a magnificent love and nature poet himself. About this time I also taught English to foreign students at UC, and was a reader for a rhetorics professor.

Eventually, I taught high school as a substitute. For a year or so I lived with a lively group-utopian economist Don Shakow and his wife Carol; poet David Taylor, worshipper of Kenneth Patchen; and writer Greta Kimball and her husband Jim—in a pleasant house with large windows looking onto the oak-strewn hills of Lafayette, and a central fireplace round which we often gathered. In "Protest" (*Journeys with Justine*), I tell the story of my 1968 arrest in a campus demonstration, protesting the university's refusal to allow black revolutionary parolee Eldridge Cleaver, author of a compelling book called *Soul on Ice,* to teach a course. "Protest" is a kind of love story that ends with the two protagonists getting handcuffed and stepping up into the bus that will take them to jail. In my case, the jail was Santa Rita, where I was incarcerated in a large room with dozens of other rebellious female students. The last night, noisy and giddy during dishwashing, I was put into solitary confinement. Seated next to the toilet under a bright light that never went off, I absorbed the poignant and enigmatic graffiti smeared on the walls and read several books of the Bible, frightened I wouldn't be released. The next day I walked out of jail with pages of minuscule journals rolled into an inserted tampax tube. My conservative father, appalled by my politics, disowned me.

After 1968 the Women's Movement really took off. Provocative guerrilla street theater cropped up around town, and in the bookstores stapled chapbooks containing the tender and explosive secrets of new and original female voices appeared. Hungrily, I devoured every syllable of Alta, Susan Griffin, and Judy Grahn. I joined Women for Peace. I was always in love, it seemed, but my love life was unsettled. For awhile, living in a cottage on Wheeler Street and working as a teacher in the public schools and a private school, I dated the enigmatic sculptor Sidney Gordon. Still crushed by the failure of my relationship with Jaszi, I wisely decided to enter therapy with a British-school psychiatrist, Dr. Hella Fluss. Thanks to her wonderful modeling, I suddenly found myself deciding to do the long-postponed pre-med work and finally applied to medical school. I hated the idea of indefinitely postponing having children, for which I longed. But I still wanted to be a psychiatrist—or maybe even an obstetrical gynecologist (one way or another I wanted birth!) I was nearly thirty—the time was now or never.

While working as a home teacher, I completed the two years of required pre-medical courses at Merritt Community College and University of California, applied to a large number of medical schools, and miraculously was accepted at New York University, then ranked fifth among American medical schools. Shortly after my acceptance, however, a tragic event occurred. I discovered that my sister Dianne, unbeknownst to my family, had suffered a schizophrenic break. Dianne received considerable treatment, but never fully recovered. I was devastated, but had to carry on with finishing my premed work anyway.

Just before leaving Berkeley, I experienced one of the most joyful events of my life: I was present at the home-birth of the first baby of my friends Jane and Steve Sokolow, who then lived in a commune. The experience is described in my poem "Birth," later read at the 1971 opening of the University of California Art Museum, and blessed with the somber praise of the august poet William Everson, as he rose to the podium after me.

> . . . A sleeper you wake,
> you stretch, you wail,
> beautiful breather you pale—
> from florid fish to flesh
> your fluid skin dries out to touch.
> Your eyes look round, stagger, still widen.
> Your ears are spiraling, your mouth untwists.
> Oh, you are open now.

Throughout my twenties, I had searched and sampled. I had rejected conventional married life. And like the woman in a later prose poem, I had "cultivated a life of eager waiting" ("Eager Waiting," *Shapes of Self*). Now it was time to choose my path. I spent a sunny summer among friends and evergreens on wooded Vashon Island in Washington where I completed the first version of an Else Lasker-Schueler manuscript, prefaced by David Meltzer who had published some of my translations in his beautiful journal *Tree*. Then I set out for the East coast, and another new beginning.

### III—Becoming a Psychiatrist and a Poet

A month before my thirtieth birthday, I arrived in New York City with eight hundred dollars in my purse from the sale of my scant furniture and little Morris Minor. The high cost of medical school was to be met by a scholarship and loan from NYU that I just learned had been granted. From a large, noisy, cockroach-infested apartment on the West Side, I soon moved to a shared apartment on Murray Hill near the medical center.

"Roach Hunts," "A Queen," "Gloria," and other poems about New York and medical school, later collected in *Of Your Seed,* were written there.

Medical school was the most demanding situation I had encountered so far. The intellectual and emotional load was daunting, and I felt as pressured as all the other students. Even so, I could not resist the allure of the great cultural center gyrating round me. I ran off to concerts, plays, poetry readings and art museums to refresh my soul, which felt caged, rather like the Haitian woman who turns into a panther "flashing teeth of white ivory / and eyes of heavy gold" in the poem "Panther in New York." I went regularly to the Metropolitan just to experience two sublimely peaceful Vermeers—the woman in blue reading a letter by the window, and the woman lifting a shining brass pitcher. Or I took refuge at the ninety-second Street Y Poetry Series, the Saint Mark's Poetry Project, or Louise Bernikow's Manhattan Poetry Club. During my New York years, I had the good fortune to hear Denise Levertov, Adrienne Rich, Muriel Rukeyser, and Stephen Spender, along with master musicians like violinist Yehudi Menuhin, singer Dietrich Fischer-Diskau, pianist Alfred Brendel, and more jazz greats than I can remember: Betty Carter, Marylou Williams, Yusef Lateef, and many more.

In the spring of my first year, my beloved grandmother Burford, then in her mid-eighties, suffered a heart attack and passed on. "On the verge of spring / you bent like a vine / and went . . .", I wrote. "Loved wine of communion, / we drank you thirsty / for a memory. . . . You were the past / and returned to it / leaving the small green sprouts of your seed." Thirsty for memories of my own past, I was painting word-portraits of many of the people who had been significant to me since childhood.

After a summer in Berkeley, I returned to a studio in Greenwich Village across from Edna St. Vincent Millay's "narrowest house in the city." In that building, flooded with a symphony of tenants' music, a well-read copy of Denise Levertov's latest volume lay on the floor by my borrowed mattress. In a crate under my TV lived my black-and-white rabbit, who co-existed with my black cat Astatine (who actually dragged the bunny into the closet with her the night she gave birth to a litter of kittens). And one morning I missed all my lectures, glued to the television during a marathon festival of Greta Garbo's entire filmic *oeuvre*. Riding the bus daily, back and forth from the medical center to the Village, knitting squares for an afghan in New York, autumn colors, inspired the poem "Afghan":

Like the leaves in Vermont in October. Squares knitted on the bus going cross-town, squares knitted on the train heading north, squares knitted on the plane flying west. Before the television, during lectures, while conversing on my bed. Then painstakingly crocheted together with brown of tree, with brown of soil. A blanket, a colorful blanket. Like a pile of leaves you can bury yourself in. Heaping them for bonfires. Raising them, hundreds of brilliant flags.

In medical school, as everywhere in the seventies, the Women's Movement was heating up, and a women's group formed at the medical center. Appalled by the shocking sexist and racist display encountered at our Anatomy exam—a voluptuous black female cadaver with an ice pick through her navel, indicating anatomical structures we were to name—we were psychologically prepared for our lecture on the human gait: a young woman in a leotard and net stockings prancing on a tabletop, while the professor discoursed on her anatomy, in particular her *gluteus maximus.* Sitting in the front row of the large lecture hall, I instantly stood and turned round to see, midway back, my friend Gloria's broad cape flapping behind her as we synchronously marched out of the hall, followed by a large portion of the class, including one of the anatomy professors, a granddaughter of the great anatomist Cunningham. This was a precious moment of victory, and the lecture was never given again.

And on the afternoon that my classmates coldly dissected frogs in physiology class, I squatted stubbornly and immovably on the desk, and poured out a poem to our "Frog": "your eyes / two polished memories of the stream / where you leapt from stone to stone / don't blink. Down on slippery tile you don't kick. . . ./ But as they untie you, your legs begin to wave—one green and spotted / like the gut of the river, the other carved in the image of human squalor." By the time a batch of dogs had been ordered for us to dissect and kill, a group of us had organized ourselves and sent a moral statement concerning the sanctity of life, demanding that the dogs ordered for us be spared: we would not participate.

When I took my first course in psychiatry, it was instantly clear that I had arrived at my destiny. I felt an incredible energy, a profound engagement with the enormous range of human problems presented, and composed a few poems triggered by particularly stunning encounters with unhappy patients at Bellevue, hospital of New York's poor, as well as at University Hospital, the hospital of the wealthy.

I spent my third year of medical school in California, living with my friend Sam Case, an occasional writer, and continuing my studies in obstetrics and psychiatry at the University of California in San Francisco. Uncertain about how I would manage the dual careers of poetry and psychiatry, I wanted time to write and establish my commitment to writing. Around the corner from the house Sam and I were subletting stood Joanna Griffin's (Susan Griffin's sister) *Bacchanal,* a poetry and art bar on Solano Avenue, where Judy Chicago, Lynn Lonidier, Madeline Gleason and various other feminist artists performed, and where I too gave a reading. At this time I set to work gathering poems for my first collection, *Of Your Seed.* My dear friend Carolyn Verlinden, from pre-med days, brought the manuscript to the attention of librarian Dorothy Hawley, who in turn passed it on to her husband, Robert Hawley, publisher and editor of Oyez Press. Oyez had published Duncan, Levertov, Di Prima, Olson, Everson, McClure, and other fine poets. I couldn't believe my ears when Robert, staring with his coal-black eyes, told me he would like to publish my little collection.

I returned to New York and rented a studio apartment in Tudor City, one block away from the UN, which I furnished with things salvaged from the cornucopia of New York garbage bins. Arriving home at ten or eleven o'clock at night from the hospital, I would pour a glass of wine, sit down at my old, rock-heavy, black Royal typewriter, anchored on plywood and orange crates, and tap out the dreamy lyrical poems of *Daughter.* Or I read the masterful English poet W. H. Auden, a doctor's son. And either I had a clairvoyant experience or I actually heard Helen Adams read her magic poetry somewhere one night. A new friend, Paula Bromberg, radical lesbian feminist Gestalt therapist and founder of the Women's Therapy Center in Greenwich Village, introduced me to the street and theatrical world of the Village. Paula led me to the brilliant and poetic psychoanalyst Harold Searles's presentation on schizophrenia, and to the Women's Salon, where I heard talks by Kate Millett and Barbara Demming. At NYU, Dr. Elisabeth Kuebler-Ross talked to us on death and dying. At the UN one afternoon, I had the transcendent experience of hearing Mother Teresa speak about caring for the world's poor. And during a happy getaway to Mystic Seaport at the end of the four years, I experienced an epiphany: "Like a madwoman she swims, flailing at the hard stuff that forever gives way: It is all hers and she belongs to it. . . . Over her the sky is an enormous mystery she'll forever be turning to." ("A Hand," *Shapes of Self*).

*Graduation from NYU School of Medicine, 1976*

Although the years in New York were exciting ones, I was homesick for the heartwarming sunbeams of California, the land of my birth, the land of beauteous Calafia, the black Amazon Queen. I invited my parents to New York for my graduation. We had grown farther and farther apart, and it was only as we walked toward my New York apartment that it slowly dawned on me my father could hardly walk. I was distressed to learn he was suffering from the awful disease of emphysema—the destruction of his lungs caused by years of smoking, topped by a case of "walking pneumonia."

I returned to Berkeley for a psychoanalytically-oriented psychiatric residency at Herrick Hospital. I loved the Herrick program and the patient work, and enjoyed a number of outstanding mentors, including outrageous and gorgeous Cherokee psychoanalyst Bryce Boyer, who wore turquoise jewels and taught us all about early human development. It was Dr. Boyer who introduced me to the work not only of Melanie Klein, Anna Freud,

and Phyllis Greenacre, but more importantly to the crucial work of Margaret Mahler, *The Psychological Birth of the Human Infant,* a book that more than any other has helped me for two decades to understand and help my patients' psychological development at the profoundest level. But for my own growth, I now chose Jungian analysis with Ann Miller.

During my Herrick years I wrote the poems "Rain," "Doom," and "The Singer," and assembled my second collection of poetry, *Who Buried the Breast of Dreams.* Robert Hawley, no longer actively publishing but ever supportive of my work, published in 1979 an elegant letterpress keepsake of five poems entitled *The Hunger.* It elicited some encouraging words from New Directions publisher James Laughlin: "These are distinguished poems. You must send me some for my anthology."

At this time I helped Peter Scott edit his forthcoming *Rumors of No Law* (which included a few of his sixties portraits of me), and he in turn invited me to join a Berkeley poetry group that included himself, Diana O'Hehir, future poet laureate Robert Pinsky, and Josephine Miles who from her wheelchair seemed amazingly able to mend anything made of words. I also joined a lively group of San Francisco State University women writers whose work influenced me, including Phyllis Koestenbaum, Frances Jaffer, Kathleen Frazer, Beverly Dahlen, and Nellie Wong. During this period I was also deeply moved by the publication of Adrienne Rich's beautiful *Twenty-One Sonnets.*

My development as a poet and psychiatrist had, for some reason, always gone hand in hand. In the second year of my residency I gave a talk that explored the relationship of the two:

> Long long ago the poet and the healer were one and the same person. Even in today's tribal societies, the shaman sings, dances, paints, administers drugs and personal advice. All of the arts are combined to heal. During the course of Western history, the arts have separated. . . . Today it is not the psychotherapist or the patient who sings the actual power songs of beauty and healing, but the poet. And often it is to the poet that we go—in moments of suffering and other extremities—for consolation, diversion, illumination, and healing. But when even art is not sufficient to console, divert, illumine, and heal, it is to the psychotherapist that we turn. For the therapist nurtures the healing speech in others. Psychotherapy is the art of so

listening and so responding, that the deepest levels of speech are liberated in a healing "song," that arises from the truest self of the sufferer, and ultimately reveals the power and beauty of what it is to be human. ("The Poetry of Psychotherapy," *Goddesses, Goddesses: Essays by Janine Canan*)

Frustrated that the Herrick program, though excellent in teaching about psychopathology, stopped short of teaching about the healthy personality, I transferred to Mt. Zion Hospital in San Francisco for the final year of my nine-year training. There I participated in an innovative adolescent program devised by much-loved Sullivanian analyst Otto Will, with Anna Freud's protege Erik Erickson, and Erickson's wife Joan, who created a new arts program. I was in a highly creative state myself, reading with passion Dickinson, Rexroth, Anderson, Lawrence, and Murdoch, and pouring out, between 1978 and 1980, one hundred sixty prose poems. These visionary poems came out of an intoxicating state in which I seemed to have palpable access to the endless, luminous web of Creation. "Ecstatic" sums up the mood:

> I'm ecstatic—have written four poems, listening to Bach, and now will do the dishes. Then shower and go over to Helen's to hear her tape on self-love and the levels of love. At five I'll do my shopping at the Co-op, buy two new tires and get my car washed, then come home and get ready—uh oh, the phone is ringing and it's Carol asking about the party and I say, Come over at ten, we'll smoke a joint, then go on over to Steve's. She says, That's perfect, and I say, I'm writing a poem and if I hurry and hang up I can get you in the poem too. I'm beginning to realize that everything really does belong in the poem and this poem could go on forever.

Out of the one hundred sixty poems, eighty were selected by me and sequenced by Betty Roszak to create *Shapes of Self.* The title came from a line in an Indian *Upanishad: One who has seen the shapes of self, runs after them everywhere.* These poems, I believe, convey a strong sense of spiritual destination—my own "destination on the enthralling road" ("Destination"). Though I am sometimes "like a beetle pinned against a burning sky" ("Foggy City"), they brim with joy, love, and light. There are love poems like "Molten Earth": "You I love, like my life. Sunshine cold, pure, streaming down into the pit of my body, all my senses budding hard, unquestionable, untouched rainbows of blos-

soms. . . ." There are portraits like "Vermilion Flower": "Emily Dickinson is staying at home. She's wearing her white eyelet dress, wandering in her night-garden, composing a poem. . . ." There are poems about poems like "About to Speak": "I love the unspoken words in things, their meanings gleaned, their secret initiate choruses held in the little human ear-coil for a moment of bright Spring. . . ." There are hymns to nature like "Blossom": "Magnolia blossom, cupped and quivering in the frost, purple on the outside, white on the inside, little feather tongues licking deep within. . . ." And there are, in *Shapes of Self,* pure songs of the soul like "She's In":

> You follow a character along and at a certain moment she opens up and splashes out light: She's golden, sparkling, sleep and overflowing, all blond, all silk, cascading, phosphorescent like waves at night, shimmering and shaking, she's all resonance, all response, an instrument arched and vibrating, light as wood, elegant as bone. She's laughing, she's blinking and twinkling. She's flowing. She's curving like oil, like gold. She wants you, calls you, collects and reflects you. She's ringing. She's squirming and swinging. She's plucked. She's touched—alive. She's over your head. She's eager. She's ready. She's on—within. She's in—gorgeous. She's in!

Upon completion of my residency, I traveled to Greece for a month. Recovering from medical training, and consolidating my own identity as a poet, I ferried to Lesbos in search of the great great Sappho, whose fewest words are worth thousands of volumes by others. My wanderings and musings there inspired a longish prose poem, "Sappho of Eressos" (*Her Magnificent Body*). It opens, "Sappho looks up, angry about the myths . . . that wish to enclose her name. But she laughs, glowing like the evening. A pink and orange smile crosses the sky. . . . She touches those dry roads and sees herself strolling in a dusty dream, seven-string lyre hung at her side, dress twined like the olive-tree, whose upper arms are jubilantly silver." From Lesbos I took the ferry to Crete, where I visited Knossos, the glorious temple of an ancient Goddess civilization, and stared at pure azure from my cafe chair, occasionally rising to dip in its divine clarity, and then jot down a few words about "The Sea."

I returned to Berkeley to open a practice in general psychiatry in a brown-shingled house hidden by acacias on Carleton Street.

*IV—In the Divine Mother*

On the evening of October 16, 1980, I walked into my living room and threw myself down on my stuffed oak couch, as a voice from within proclaimed, "I give up." One of the things I surely had to give up was an impossible infatuation that had been occupying me for some time. And I wondered—with despair that was heading toward horror—would I have to give up children too?

Granted, I was exhausted from the decade of training. The "conservative era" was underway, cuts in education and social programs were affecting people everywhere, including many of my patients. My flat on Carleton had been put up for sale, and I had moved to Grizzly Peak atop the Berkeley hills. Now the mountain I had been climbing for a decade, as I completed my medical training, turned inside out. Before me lay an abyss; I would have to descend to its depths. Some days were so dark that when I woke in the morning, I groaned to realize that I had another day to live through. Great waves were carrying me—whither? One of my favorite books at this time was Virginia Woolf's poetic novel *The Waves,* which appears in my poem "Birthday":

> Sitting in the bathtub, re-reading
> *The Waves,* telephone
> on the floor, I think:
> My birthday—I'll write a poem.
>
> . . . . Andrew calls and asks me how I am.
>    "Nervous,"
> I reply. "Nervous jubilant or nervous afraid?"
> '*Not jubilant.*' Yes, Marcia says you think
> you have reached the middle of your life."
> In the dark restaurant I had told her,
> "It all seems so small now," and her eyes
>    flamed.
> Now to Andrew I say, "No, I'll live longer
> than that. Grandmother lived to be eighty-five
> and I have more to do than she did."
> "You don't know," he says.
>
> Dunking my head, I hear our conversation
> throbbing in the waves. Definitely
> a middle-aged poem, my new self says,
> stepping from the bath, dripping.
>                           (*Her Magnificent Body*)

I was thirty-eight, and the Dark Night of my soul had fallen. I needed a guide and decided to do Jungian dream-work with Ruth Collins. "Valley of Death", about the grim reality of nuclear destructiveness, ex-

presses the horror I felt at forces around and within me: "Shaft rising, head of the sacred phallus explodes over the valley in awesome blinding light: Jornada del Muerte—Heaven fills with radiation, Earth craters like the Moon." The darkness demanded more light, and I wrote "The Duck," which begins:

> Mother Father Heaven, can't I have
> your pure spirit, your pure blue?
> I'm thirsty, can't You carry me?
> I want to sleep, can't I lie down
> in your arms, these lakes—You have so
>    much!
> Mother Father Heaven, can't I have You?

In "Dance" I wrote: "Soul that has no face, peers out from everything: the bottoms of her feet, the underside of the car, the smoky figure of Mother leaving. In a long dress that sweeps the floor, hair swinging beyond her, she dances it—like sex she dances it. Like stars."

Meanwhile, I decided to establish my own press. Laughlin, who had published one of my poems in *New Directions 42,* was not interested in doing a whole collection, nor was another publisher I contacted. My Emily Dickinson Press published *Who Buried the Breast of Dreams,* followed by *Daughter* (illustrated by Donna Brookman) in 1981, and *Shapes of Self* in 1982. The first two books were not reviewed, and the latter received its only—fortunately positive—review from fellow—poet Andrei Codrescu. "Told with that lulling incantatory charm of the *Arabian Nights,* a joyous and lusty book, remarkably free from guilt," he wrote in the *Baltimore Sun.* Else Gidlow, whom I met about this time, responded warmly: "Remarkable—searing—portraits. You are a perceptive writer—original, too." And poet Phyllis Koestenbaum, whose rhythmic, prose poems, along with the lush prose style of Iris Murdoch, had inspired my own, added her kind words: "The language is stunning. It flows—."

In 1982 I attended Stanford University's Conference on Women and Poetry, where I listened excitedly to dynamic readings by fifteen American women poets, including Denise Levertov, Carolyn Kizer, Judy Grahn, Audre Lorde, Josephine Miles, and Alma Villanueva, whose passionate visionary work I encountered for the first time. I took a valuable course at the University of California on *Revising the Poem,* taught by the *grande dame* of poetry herself, Carolyn Kizer, and I learned to disassemble and rebuild a poem as if it were an automobile engine. Longing to study with the musical, English-born poet Denise Levertov, I was forever deeply disappointed when a workshop with the poet was canceled due to an airline strike which Levertov wished to honor.

In 1983 I began a long prayer, stimulated by a conversation with one of my patients, a nun: "Lady, how can I speak, my mouth silent / as the hills, dumb with fear and desire? Lady of the Myriad Names, your beauty and destruction / freeze my heart. How can I approach You. . . ." ("Our Lady," *She Rises like the Sun*). "Beautiful Mother of Words," written in 1975 and published in *Daughter,* had perhaps been my first Goddess poem, but now the poems to Her began to flow in an unending stream. "Inanna's Descent" (*Her Magnificent Body*), inspired by second millennium BC Sumerian poetry, came next, and then "Our Lady," in which I invoked the Goddess by all the names I knew.

In 1984 I met Anglo-Irish novelist Iris Murdoch, in whose powerful and searching work I had become profoundly immersed, when she came to Berkeley to give a lecture. The story of our encounter was later written in "Irises, Irises: A Visit from Iris Murdoch" (*Goddesses, Goddesses*). This meeting was the beginning of a precious friendship by correspondence which continued until the novelist's tragic Alzheimer's illness in the nineties. But in general, this was a difficult time. My adored first Samoyed dog, Orlando, not yet two years old, suddenly died of an undiagnosable illness. A sociopathic patient crossed my path, bringing with her years of personal and professional harassment. And once again the house I was renting was put up for sale, and I was forced to move.

My father, though ill, kindly and generously helped me purchase a lovely meditative Spanish-style house on Avis Road in Berkeley. The first poem I received after the move into my new home was the often anthologized "Dear Body," which came in seven seven-line stanzas as I swam in a nearby public swimming pool. It ends:

> . . . . With your delicate, hyper-sensitive
> nerves—
> painstakingly cultivated by erratic Mother
> Karma
> who one moment forgets, the next grips
> violently,
>
> so aware everything irritates or gives you
> overwhelming pleasure, ecstatic wicked Body,
> maniacally driven from one unreachable
> extreme
> to another, isn't it obvious how, torn
> between joy and terror, you became a poet,
> passionately vibrating instrument, house

of the certain yet doubting, ever shifting eye.

> Earthbody, brief spouse, what a strangely
> inconvenient marriage. Yet you are my only
> true support. And though you may never
> fathom what I secretly am, may you—
> who accepted the nature of existence itself—
> stay with me in your lovely halo of death
> till I depart, dearest Body, my slave, my
> queen.

At the Berkeley Zen Center, I learned how to sit zazen. Taking up Sufi dancing, I began to follow Sufi teacher Pir Vilayat, whose spiritual teachings gracefully bridged Eastern and Western psychology. At Joanna Griffin's I had met avant-garde poet Lynn Lonidier. Working on *Clitoris Lost* at the time, Lynn was obsessed with Greece, and, after intensely quizzing me that evening about my travels to Crete and Lesbos, had gone home and written "Isle of Lesbos," the first in a series of poems inspired by our friendship. Lynn loved and supported my work. She created a moving rendition of "Our Lady" on her synthesizer. And in her San Francisco cottage on Vernal Heights, she introduced me to visionary genius Robert Duncan, whose sing-song readings I had attended since the sixties. She pressed me to read him my own "Harp" poems from *Shapes of Self,* poems which symbolize the saintly function of art. But I was then too shy to do so.

Later on, when Robert came to my house for dinner, he talked that stream of language that was his way of being, his "mouth in which the heart rises / pouring itself into liquid and fiery speech" ("Circulations of the Song"). Though Robert had lost his mother at birth, and his father soon after, he had gained a relationship to the whole cosmos. At a small gathering at the Roszaks' where, ill with kidney disease, he read from his masterpiece "Circulations of the Song," I finally read before him my long narrative poem "Passion of Georgia O'Keeffe" (*Her Magnificent Body*) which, said Lynn, stunned him:

> . . . . I know what I must paint now—I paint
> what I love. Flowers, stones, bones
> instruct me. Details are confusing.
> I observe, select, eliminate—ruthlessly
>
> I search for meaning inside things.
> Tearing roots from my heart,
> arrange in ever broadening light: ikons,
> offerings,
> blessings that come from, return to life. . . .

Lynn also introduced my work to her publisher Paul Mariah, founder of Manroot Press. Paul, who had previously published Duncan, Broughton, Cocteau, Fisher, Gunn, and Grahn, was eager do a volume of my selected poems. *Her Magnificent Body* was the result. It came out at a very difficult time for him, for his beloved longtime partner Ken, the main funder of Manroot, died of AIDS during production, and Paul was deeply shaken. Nevertheless we completed the book, which was one of the last books he published. Paul firmly believed that my work would be remembered for its elegiac achievement. Through Paul, I became friends with the wonderful and witty mystical poet James Broughton, and his partner Joel Singer, a photographer and collage artist. And round this time I also met poet and critic Jack Foley, a lively supporter of many poets. Jack interviewed me with Lynn on his KPFA Poetry Program, and published my work in *Poetry USA*.

In the mid-eighties I met Professor Margaret Clark, then director of the Medical Anthropology Department at the University of California in San Francisco. To this warm and brilliant, and charismatic woman I was deeply drawn, and eventually she moved into my home. Around this time I also began to study Vedanta, India's philosophy of non-dualism, with Carol Whitfield, a devotee of Swami Dayananda. At the same time I was inspired by the exuberant Goddess imagery emerging, it seemed, everywhere, and I dove into compiling an anthology of Goddess poetry. *She Rises like the Sun: Invocations of the Goddess by Contemporary American Women Poets,* gathered the work of twenty-nine poets, among them Maya Angelou, Meridel Le Sueur, Joy Harjo, Audre Lorde, Ntozake Shange, Anne Waldman, Paula Gunn Allen, Judy Grahn, May Sarton, Marge Piercy, Robin Morgan, Julia Vinograd, Diane Wakoski, Denise Levertov, Carolyn Kizer, Linda Hogan, Jana Harris, Susan Griffin, Elsa Gidlow, and Diane Di Prima.

At the same time, my father was dying of emphysema. I had visited him occasionally in Lake Havasu, Arizona, where he and my mother had moved because of his health, and later in southern California, where they had returned as he became more gravely ill. We had some close talks that were moving and reconciling for me; in one he gave his blessing to my poetry (although he never read any of it). In early 1988, Margaret and I bought a beautiful larger home on Tamalpais Road, with a magical tower, a mahogany staircase that spiraled upward, and a magnificent view of the San Francisco Bay. We moved in together but it was to be a heartbreaking move. On April 16, my father died. After his death, I worked on the final stages of the anthology,

and Margaret, in the process of retiring from academic life, lent her sensitive ear to help me. At this time, I was also doing consultation with Jungian analyst Joseph Henderson, who had been analyzed by and worked with Carl Jung himself.

In the spring of 1989, *She Rises like the Sun* was released by The Crossing Press. Poets Mary Mackey, Alma Villanueva, Jana Harris, Diane Di Prima, Judy Grahn, Lynn Lonidier, and Mary Koerte joined me in a joyous reading-tour at bookstores and colleges along the West and East coasts, and on radio and television. Alone, I traveled on to Paris. Naturally I was delighted when *She Rises* received the 1990 Susan Koppelman Award for best-edited feminist work and was acknowledged by *Booklist* as "one of the best books to come from the Women's Spirituality Movement." But I was even more moved when, over the years, many women expressed to me individually how much the book meant to them. Only my mother, ironically, could find something with which to be displeased. *She Rises like the Sun* sold ten thousand copies before it went out of print seven years later.

Margaret and I were now having problems, and I rented a small writing cabin in Bolinas on the coast where I spent weekends and wrote some of the stories that would eventually become *Journeys with Justine.* In 1990, Margaret, who had been my anchor, and so deeply loved, moved to San Raphael. At the end of 1991, with great sadness I sold our magical Tamalpais house. In spite of my agony, I somehow managed to write a couple of reviews during these months, one of Diane Di Prima's long overdue *Pieces of a Song: Selected Poems* for the *San Francisco Chronicle,* the other of James Broughton's wondrous *Special Deliveries: Selected Poems* for Andrei Codrescu's *Exquisite Corpse.* A prolific occasional poet and a sibling-Scorpio, James reciprocated with a poem for my thirty-ninth birthday, which I have treasured. "What would it mean," he ponders, "to be a Janine? / To be beheld / in the sheen serene / of a Scorpio queen / like Janine?"—concluding with "umpteen bangs on a tambourine / for velveteeny evergreen / Janine."

During a subsequent visit to James and Joel's woodsy home in the idyllic seaport of Port Townsend, Washington, I was enthusiastically presented with English novelist Andrew Harvey's latest book, *Hidden Journey: A Spiritual Awakening.* Harvey's account of his sublime spiritual journey to a young Indian woman considered an incarnation of the Divine Mother mesmerized me. At James's insistence, I introduced myself to Harvey when he came to Berkeley not long afterward. Jane Heaven invited the two of us to converse about spirituality on her midnight KPFA program, "Magic in the Air," and Andrew and I were soon friends. On the heels of Andrew's visit came Mark, Andrew's friend, who had just seen his best friend Carol through her death from AIDS. Arriving on my forty-ninth birthday, Mark presented me with Carol's picture of Mother Meera, smiling radiantly, and a tiny statue of Ganesh, the elephant God who removes obstacles, especially for poets.

Now I packed my possessions, giving many things away and putting the rest in storage in a friend's basement. I closed my psychiatric practice and my various accounts, sent my dear cat and dog to friends, and bought a one-way ticket to Bali. "Bird Mother," I wrote, "You greet me at the gate. / You show me the scaly pine's height. / You offer me the sky's vast freedom. / Now give me Your blessing, wherever I fly" (*Changing Woman*). Carrying a few light clothes, the photo of Mother Meera, and my portable typewriter, I boarded the airplane that lifted me up to the brilliant pink evening sun, rising perpetually as we flew toward the beckoning East. Into the warm wet womb that is Bali, I collapsed for two months, until I was revived by the mysterious prodding and gesticulating incantations of a beautiful Balinese shaman.

From Bali I traveled on, through Singapore, where I awaited my visa, to Madras, India. It was mid-March, and boiling hot. Completely disoriented by India's exotic poverty and dust, I roamed the Madras museum, with its many exquisite bronze deities, the carved sandstone temple at Mahabalipuram beach, and other powerful places like the Shakti Temple, from which I was tearfully shooed away as a contaminated non-Hindu. I flew to Coimbatore, and drove to Swami Dayananda's ashram in the hills. Swamiji greeted me warmly, and in the days to come worked his insightful and comical spiritual chiropractic on my neglected self. At one point I actually fainted, and when I woke up, I was in a world with which I had a different, fuller relationship. I knew where my soul was (and wasn't), and that it was my true me.

More travel in India: to Belur and Halebid temples, congested Delhi, and exotic Rajastan, where I contracted mycoplasmic pneumonia. Only semi-recovered, I flew westward on to Paris. The flight over the startlingly green continent of Europe followed by our arrival over the divinely beautiful garden of *la belle France,* is something I will never forget. In my fresh eyes, Paris seemed so pristine, so lovely; and the quiet, in contrast to India, seemed surreal. At *Le Prince Albert* on the Right Bank, I joined my former neighbor Phyllis

Schaefer, the widow of Chinese scholar Edward Schaefer (author of *The Divine Woman: Dragon Ladies and Rain Maidens in T'ang Literature*). After some pleasant travel in fragrant Provence, we returned to Paris, and I rented a studio in a seventeenth-century building on an ancient street near the Pompidou. I began to work on organizing the poetry I had written since my last book, *Her Magnificent Body,* published in 1986.

When Andrew Harvey returned from a stay with Mother Meera in Thalheim, Germany, we met at his jewel-like, sixth-floor studio overlooking the courtyard of a count. Andrew urged me to visit Mother Meera right away and on my return move into his atmospheric apartment, wallpapered with the pictures of saints, while he traveled to India to be with Mother there. Andrew, well known for his spiritual journey writings, high-strung, and luminously inspired, whether bubbling with bliss or raging against the world's evils, opened a number of spiritual doors for me. Some of the dramatic moments I spent with him—whether amusing, intimidating or miraculously inspiring—reappeared in "City of Our Lady" in *Journeys with Justine.* But my 1992 and subsequent visits to Mother Meera herself gave me firsthand experiences of divinity that were truly awesome. These I tried to convey in the short stanzas of "Revelations at Thalheim," which came to me at each *darshan.*

When, at last, I returned to the United States to the Bay Area—my inner voice questioned impatiently: "What is the point of all this!?" Since I had no answer, I drove north and decided to settle, at least for a time, in the Pacific Northwest, on the Olympic Peninsula, in the quaint Victorian town of Port Townsend, situated on a narrow finger of land that protrudes into the deep blue straits of Juan de Fuca, boundary between the United States and Canada. I picked up my cat Marianne—who was glad to see me—and my dazed but loyal, dear dog Sophia on the way. "Welcome to the end of the road," quipped James, who with Joel greeted me with open arms. Struck by James's exceptional productivity out on the edge of nowhere, I was hoping for the same for myself. Above all, I wanted quiet time for further reflection, meditation, and healing. Port Townsend turned out to be the perfect place to fulfill all my intentions.

But more astounding, it was here that I finally found my ultimate teacher. I had first encountered Mata Amritanandamayi's extreme spiritual power in Berkeley, during the painful time with Margaret. Her sizzling blessing, her stunning embrace, her burning chant, "Ma, Ma, Ma, Ma," had been crucial to my survival. But then I had no context for such an experience. Now I learned

*Reading from She Rises like the Sun, A Room of One's Own, New York, 1989*

And the Moon comes sowing
diamonds down the darkened strait,
and kneels beneath
Your mighty feet.

Now You lean out
over the crumbling abyss
and gather us back
into Your molting red limbs.

*Changing Woman* unfolds in three movements. It is introduced by an autobiographical essay, "I Introduction to the Poet." The second section, "Fathers' Night," offers poems of political despair over Patriarchy's relentless march in the wrong direction, and hopeful visions of a more sensitive and feminine orientation toward life. The third section, "Journey to the Root," contains a long sequence of love poems that follow the nuanced coming undone of a relationship. It includes translations as well, from the French and German of Francis Jammes, Marguerite Yourcenar, Guillaume Apollinaire, Heinrich Heine, and Simone Weil. The final movement of *Changing Woman* contains spiritual poems: a retelling of the story of the Navajo Creation Goddess, Changing Woman; recreations of poems by sixteenth-century Indian poet Mirabai; many Goddess poems; and poems written through the inspiration of the Divine Mothers of India.

that Ammachi, as this *mahatma* or great soul and incarnation of the Divine Mother was lovingly known in India and throughout the world, began her annual world tour just twenty minutes from my house. And so it was perfectly natural that during the six years I lived in Port Townsend, writing constantly and conducting my small psychiatric practice, I became ever more deeply involved in Amma's spiritual practice of devotion, song, meditation, and service. In Amma I found the manifestation of the maternal love lacking in my own life, as in the lives of most people in the male-dominated and ego-oriented Western world.

The natural setting of Port Townsend was deeply nurturing to my soul: her tall cedars, firs, and red-skinned madronas; her eagles, herons, finches, chickadees, and shiny crows; her nearby shore where I walked nearly every day, in all kinds of weather, over glowing rocks with Sophia and later on our new Samoyed puppy, Devi (meaning "Goddess"). It inspired many poems that were eventually collected with all the poetry written from 1986 to 1998 in *Changing Woman.* "Madrona Mother" captures, I believe, the feeling of that gentle place:

At the cliff 's edge
I sit upon Your deepening root,
Your foliage vast
above my wondering head.

While living in Port Townsend I received, by telephone, a great deal of invaluable criticism and support from my friend, writer Kris Brandenburger. Besides working on *Changing Woman,* I also worked on a series of short stories, *Journeys with Justine,* which recount a woman's epiphanies over several decades. I finally brought to completion my translations, *Star in My Forehead: Poems by Else Lasker-Schueler,* which found a home with publisher Jim Perlman at Holy Cow! Press in Minnesota. Many of my poems, as well as stories and essays, were taken for publication in a wide variety of journals, and numerous anthologies such as *Her Words, Heal Your Soul—Heal the World, American Poets Say Good-bye to the Twentieth Century,* and *The Divine Feminine: Exploring the Feminine Face of God Around the World.*

During this time Marija Gimbutas died, the great archeomythologist who had published landmark works on the matricentric, neolithic European civilization of the Goddess. Her assistant Joan Marler, on whose KPFA radio program *Brainstorm* I had read my poetry in the eighties, asked me to write an essay about the relationship of my poetry to Gimbutas's archeomythology for a *festschrift, From the Realm of the An-*

*cestors: Essays in Honor of Marija Gimbutas.* The result was "Goddesses, Goddesses: From Archeology to Poetry of the Feminine," later collected with my other essays in *Goddesses, Goddesses: A Poet's Journey* (unpublished). With drum, tambourine, and bells, I performed poetry in celebration of the Goddess at conferences honoring Gimbutas's work on the Goddess civilization held at the Smithsonian in Washington, D.C.; in San Francisco, sponsored by the California Institute of Integral Studies; and at Greek poet Nanos Valaoritis's ancestral home on Madhouri Island.

My friend Lynn Lonidier also died during this period by tragically stepping off a cliff and falling to her death on a San Francisco beach. I knew that Lynn had left much unpublished poetry, some of which I had seen, and I felt strongly motivated to see this work into publication. From her archive, transferred to the Hormel Gay and Lesbian Center at the San Francisco Public Library, I uncovered as much of the work as I could, wrote an introductory biography, gathered together a preface from her old friend Jerome Rothenberg, photographs from her brother, Professor Fred Lonidier, and a collage cover from her dear friend Jess (Duncan's partner). *The Rhyme of the Ag-Ed Mariness: Last Poems of Lynn Lonidier* was accepted for 1999 publication by Station Hill Press in New York.

From Port Townsend I made some significant trips: back to Paris (where I met the *enfant terrible* of French literature, novelist Bruno Guy-Lussac), and to India (where again I became sick, and yet was blessed to meet Mother Teresa in Calcutta, visit the ancient temples at Khajuraho, Ellora and Ajanta, see Swami Dayananda in Bombay, and spend powerfully transforming time with Ammachi at her ashram in Kerala), and of course to California (where I met another saint, Sri Ma, visited Ammachi again, and saw old friends, usually staying with childhood friend, Carol Fabric). One-armed Rusty North, publisher of Sagittarius Press in Port Townsend, handset a tiny, blood-red chapbook of poems she selected from *Changing Woman,* named *Goddess Poems.*

In 1998 I decided to return to California—for which I was longing—in order to be closer to old friends and family, the rich cultural life of the San Francisco Bay Area, the women's spirituality network, and in particular Ammachi's ashram in nearby San Ramon. Although my years in Port Townsend had been peaceful and productive, I missed the warmer California spirit and higher energy. I bought a small house in lovely Sonoma, once (for three weeks) the capital of the renegade Republic of California and home of the northern-most Franciscan Mission. Situated amidst rolling green and golden vineyards, Sonoma was graciously built around a large and spacious Mexican plaza, now a park full of every kind of tree imaginable, a busy pond with ducks, and freely wandering colorful chickens.

Once again I opened my psychiatric practice, now clearly focused on integrating psychology, spirituality, and medicine. Susan Hahn, poet, friend, and editor of *Open Bone Review,* selected poems from *Changing Woman* for a lavender chapbook entitled *Love, Enter.* My noble Oyez publisher Bob Hawley, now terminally ill, published a letterpress keepsake of the poem "And I Release You," also from *Changing Woman.* And I, meanwhile, turned my attention to collecting from the ten volumes of Mata Amritanandamayi's *Awaken, Children,* her sublime words for a *Songs of the Divine Mother.*

To be a poet is a calling, a gift, a devotion, a duty, and, finally, a mystery. I feel graced and grateful to be a woman and a poet, to have known the intimacies of both poetry and psychiatry. And I am thankful for all the many teachers along the way. My life feels like a rich and intricate weave of abundance and beauty, incessant change and transformation. In masculine and materialistic America—fascinated with the slick, the empty and the deadly—the image of the poet is often confused with the soul of poetry. My own somewhat mystical work—focused on the feminine, in love with the feminine, insistent on the feminine—is perhaps an anomaly. Yet my work alone, better than any biography, documents my journey. While the Divine Mother has been writing my life, I have been copying it onto paper. The ink I use is the light within me, my writing a shimmer-strand in the infinite web of Her bliss. Not long ago, as I whirled in the embrace of the Ionian Sea, came these words, "In Your Miracle":

> Alone in the aqua blue water of Your body,
> I whirl my prayer of love.
>
> Green rocks greet me
> and greeny red fish swim by.
>
> As I float on Your liquid bliss skin,
> above me Your umbrella of light,
>
> I am
> Your starfish daughter—
>
> in Your undulating clear blue belly,
> in the aquamarine of Your heart.

**CHATEAUCLAIR, Wilfrid**
    **See LIGHTHALL, William Douw**

\*    \*    \*

**CLEVE, John**
    **See PROCTOR, Geo(rge W.)**

\*    \*    \*

**CLOUD, Yvonne**
    **See KAPP, Yvonne (Mayer)**

\*    \*    \*

**COOKSON, Catherine (McMullen)   1906-1998**
    **(Catherine Marchant)**

*OBITUARY NOTICE*—See index for *CA* sketch: Born June 20, 1906, in Tyne Dock, South Shields, England; died June 11, 1998, in Jesmond Dene, England. Novelist. Cookson's hardscrabble life began in the northeast part of England where she was the illegitimate daughter of a drunken mother and a father she never knew. She believed her father was a gentleman and thought she should act accordingly as a lady. This led to her reading voraciously and taking elocution lessons to improve herself, all the while fetching beer for her mother from the local pub or taking items to hock at a pawnshop. When she was old enough to leave home she headed for the seaside town of Hastings, where she bought a home with her meager salary as a laundress and opened a rooming house for men. One of her boarders, teacher Tom Cookson, caught her eye and they married in 1940. Three miscarriages and a stillborn resulted in a nearly crippling depression for Cookson and her husband suggested she start writing to work through her grief. Her first book, *Kate Hannigan,* was published in 1950 and after that she averaged two books a year. Most of her stories took place in the area where she had grown up and featured salty characters one might find near the docks and beach where she spent her youth. Two of Cookson's best-known books are *Our Kate: An Autobiography* and *Katie Mulholland,* both published in the late 1960s. Other popular books include *The Glass Virgin, The Dwelling Place,* and the *Mallen* novels trilogy. She also wrote several books under the pseudonym Catherine Marchant. Two of her works

were made into movies for television and, by the time of her death, she was one of England's most-read authors with some 100 million copies of her books sold. Her books also made up one-third of the most-borrowed from English libraries and by 1997 she had written nine out of ten books on the most-circulated list.

*OBITUARIES AND OTHER SOURCES:*

*PERIODICALS*

*Chicago Tribune,* June 12, 1998, sec. 1, p. 12.
*Los Angeles Times,* June 12, 1998, p. A22.
*New York Times,* June 12, 1998, p. A19.
*Times* (London), June 12, 1998.
*Washington Post,* June 12, 1998, p. C9.

\*    \*    \*

**CRAIG, A. A.**
    **See ANDERSON, Poul (William)**

\*    \*    \*

**CRICHTON, Judy   1929-**

*PERSONAL:* Born November 25, 1929, in New York, NY; daughter of Benjamin F. (a television producer) and Edith (Lansburgh) Feiner; married Robert Crichton (a novelist), 1951 (deceased); children: Sarah, Rob, Jennifer, Susan (deceased). *Education:* Attended high school.

*ADDRESSES: Office*—320 West 71st St., New York, NY 10023. *Agent*—Melanie Jackson, 250 West 57th St., New York, NY 10107.

*CAREER: This Week* (magazine), New York City, clerk/typist, 1946-48; *Argosy* (magazine), cartoon and assistant articles editor, 1948-50; worked in television as producer and writer, including such programs as *I've Got a Secret* and *What's the Story* for Columbia Broadcasting System (CBS); CBS, producer and writer for documentaries, including *The CIA's Secret Army, The Defense of the United States, The Nuclear Battlefield,* and *The Battle for South Africa,* beginning 1974; producer and writer, then senior producer for American Broadcasting Company (ABC) documentary series *Closeup,* to 1985; producer for Public Broadcasting System (PBS), beginning c. 1986, producer of *The*

*American Experience,* c. 1989-96, consultant, 1996—; freelance writer, c. 1996—.

*AWARDS, HONORS:* Received several Emmy Awards for work in television.

*WRITINGS:*

SELECTED TELEVISION DOCUMENTARIES

(With others) *ABC News Closeup: To Save Our Schools, to Save Our Children,* ABC, September, 1984.
(With others) *ABC News Closeup: After the Sexual Revolution,* ABC, July 30, 1986.
(With Thomas Lennon) *ABC News Closeup: At a Loss for Words . . . Illiterate in America,* ABC, September 3, 1986.

Contributing writer for several television documentaries, including (with David Grubin)*America—1900.*

NONFICTION

(With Marshall Frady and others) *To Save Our Schools, to Save Our Children: The Approaching Crisis in America's Public Schools,* introduction by Robert Coles, New Horizon Press (Far Hills, NJ), 1985.
(With David Grubin) *America 1900: The Turning Point,* Holt (New York City), 1998.

*SIDELIGHTS:* Television writer and producer Judy Crichton has had a career in television for over five decades. Her father, Ben Feiner, was a pioneering television producer in New York City, and by the late 1940s, Crichton had followed in his footsteps. She worked at first on game shows for CBS, including *I've Got a Secret* and *What's the Story?* During the 1970s, still at CBS, Crichton began producing the documentaries for which she has become known. *The CIA's Secret Army, The American Way of Cancer,* and *The Defense of the United States* are all part of her body of work for CBS. She moved to ABC to work on that network's *Closeup* documentary series, where she was instrumental in the writing and production of such programs as *To Save Our Schools, to Save Our Children* and *After the Sexual Revolution.* In the mid-1980s, Crichton settled at PBS, working out of its large Boston affiliate, WGHB. There she served as the executive producer of *The American Experience,* a documentary series that "aims to do for our nation's past what 'Nova' does for science," in the words of Harry F. Waters in *Newsweek.* When Crichton retired in 1996, she continued as a consultant and writer for *The American Experience.* She has garnered several

Emmy Awards for her work in television, and two of the projects she has helped bring to the small screen have been turned into books—1985's *To Save Our Schools, to Save Our Children: The Approaching Crisis in America's Public Schools,* which she helped write under the leadership of Marshall Frady, and 1998's *America 1900: The Turning Point.*

While still working on *Closeup,* Crichton helped write and produce *To Save Our Schools, to Save Our Children,* which was first broadcast in 1984. The documentary warned of declining literacy rates and SAT scores, and discussed both parental absence due to the rise in two-income families as well as the ways in which teachers' unions protect incompetent instructors from being fired. Though a *Variety* reviewer would have liked to see "an examination of the best and the brightest among students" to find out "what makes them tick? What motivates them to work so hard?," the critic concluded that "the three-hour effort was a noble one" and *To Save Our Schools, to Save Our Children* proved "a major triumph for ABC News."

*America 1900: The Turning Point* is the book version of a documentary Crichton wrote for PBS's *The American Experience* after she retired as its executive producer. In it, she looks at the year that began the twentieth century, a year that saw such events as the Galveston hurricane and the first billion-dollar corporation. She examines personalities who were influential in 1900, such as Theodore Roosevelt, who was elected U.S. vice president that year and was destined to become president upon the assassination of his running mate. She also provides the perspectives of men and women who would go on to become influential in American culture, but who were young in 1900—these include U.S. President Harry S Truman and poet Carl Sandburg. *America 1900* in print found favor with critics; for instance, a *Publishers Weekly* reviewer hailed it as "a vivid, beautifully illustrated account of the U.S. at the turn of the century." Brooks D. Simpson in the *Library Journal* was less effusive, affirming that the volume "is a pleasant . . . overview of the nation as it stood on the verge of a new century."

*BIOGRAPHICAL/CRITICAL SOURCES:*

PERIODICALS

*Boston Globe,* December 5, 1998.
*Library Journal,* October 1, 1998, pp. 108, 110.
*Newsweek,* November 13, 1989, pp. 101-102.
*Publishers Weekly,* September 21, 1998, p. 33.
*Savvy,* March, 1987, p. 10.

*Variety,* September 12, 1984, p. 66; August 6, 1986, p. 66; September 10, 1986, p. 80.

\* \* \*

**CUNNINGHAM, E. V.**
  **See FAST, Howard (Melvin)**

# D-E

## DARRID, Diana Douglas 1923-

*PERSONAL:* Born January 22, 1923, in Bermuda; naturalized U.S. citizen; daughter of Thomas M. (attorney general of Bermuda) and Ruth (a homemaker; maiden name, Neilson) Dill; married Kirk Douglas (an actor), November 2, 1943 (marriage ended); married William Darrid (an actor, producer, and novelist, December 14, 1956 (died, 1992); children: (first marriage) Michael, Joel. *Ethnicity:* "Caucasian." *Education:* Attended American Academy of Dramatic Art. *Politics:* Democrat. *Religion:* Agnostic. *Avocational interests:* Art, opera, travel, tennis, golf.

*ADDRESSES: Home*—4035 Madelia Ave., Sherman Oaks, CA 91403.

*CAREER:* Professional actress on stage, screen, and television, 1941-46; writer, 1994—. American Academy of Dramatic Arts, member of board of trustees.

*MEMBER:* Academy of Motion Picture Arts and Sciences.

*AWARDS, HONORS:* Drama-Logue Award, 1979, for *Old Times.*

*WRITINGS:*

*In the Wings: A Memoir,* preface by Michael Douglas, Barricade Books (New York City), 1999.

*WORK IN PROGRESS:* A suspense novel about the aftermath of the French underground; research on the Maquis and the rescue of downed pilots of the Royal Air Force.

*SIDELIGHTS:* Diana Douglas Darrid told *CA:* "*In the Wings* was started as a memoir for my grandson, Cameron Douglas, at the request of his father. As I progressed, I realized that I was writing for myself and had to get it all down as honestly as possible. I wrote mostly on impulse, as the scenes popped into my mind. I would then fiddle around with them a bit on the computer until I knew exactly what I wanted to express.

"I had written two screenplays earlier, but they were never produced. I read continually—history, biography, the *New York Times,* anything I can get my hand on. The capture and trial of Klaus Barbie was the inspiration for my novel in progress."

*BIOGRAPHICAL/CRITICAL SOURCES:*

*PERIODICALS*

*People,* September 6, 1999.
*Publishers Weekly,* July, 1999.

*       *       *

## DAVES, Delmer (Lawrence) 1904-1977

*PERSONAL:* Born July 24, 1904, in San Francisco, CA; died of a heart condition, August 17, 1977, in La Jolla, CA; son of Arthur Lawrence (a businessman), and Nan (maiden name, Funge) Daves; married Mary Lawrence (an actress), 1938. *Education:* Stanford University, studied engineering; law degree, 1927.

*CAREER:* Draftsman, screenwriter, actor, technical adviser, director, and producer. University of California, San Diego, Regents' Lecturer.

*MEMBER:* National Cowboy Hall of Fame, Delta Kappa Alpha (honorary member, 1976).

*AWARDS, HONORS:* Received "hommage" from *Cinematheque Francaise;* honorary film retrospective, Oberhausen Film Festival, 1972; special trustee's award, Western Heritage Association.

*WRITINGS:*

SCREENPLAYS

(With Al Boasberg) *So This Is College,* (and story), Metro-Goldwyn-Mayer, 1929.

(Author of adaptation with Lou Edelman and of dialogue with Malcolm S. Boylan) *Shipmates,* Metro-Goldwyn-Mayer, 1931.

(With Maurice Rapf) *Divorce in the Family* (and story), Metro-Goldwyn-Mayer, 1932.

*Clear All Wires* (continuity), Metro-Goldwyn-Mayer, 1933.

(Author of story with Grant Leenhouts and of screenplay with Loy Breslow) *No More Women,* Paramount, 1934.

(With Robert Lord) *Dames,* Warner Brothers, 1934.

(With Edelman) *Flirtation Walk* (and story), Warner Brothers/ First National, 1934.

*Stranded,* Warner Brothers, 1935.

(With Lord) *Page Miss Glory,* Cosmopolitan/Warner Brothers, 1935.

*Shipmates Forever* (and story), Warner Brothers, 1935.

(With Charles Kenyon) *The Petrified Forest,* Warner Brothers, 1936.

*The Go-Getter,* Warner Brothers, 1937.

*The Singing Marine* (and story), Warner Brothers, 1937.

(With Gladys Lehman) *She Married An Artist,* Columbia, 1937.

*Professor Beware,* Paramount, 1938.

(With Donald Ogden Stewart) *Love Affair,* RKO, 1939, revised with Leo McCarey as *An Affair to Remember,* Twentieth Century-Fox, 1957.

*$1,000 a Touchdown* (and story), Paramount, 1939.

*The Farmer's Daughter* (story), Paramount, 1940.

*Safari,* Paramount, 1940.

(With Noel Langley) *Unexpected Uncle,* RKO, 1941.

(With Robert Pirosh and Eve Greene) *The Night of January 16th,* Paramount, 1941.

(With Michael Fessier and Ernest Pagano) *You Were Never Lovelier,* Columbia, 1942.

(With Albert Maltz) *Destination Tokyo,* Warner Brothers, 1943.

*Stage Door Canteen* (and story), United Artists, 1943.

(With Alvah Bessie) *The Very Thought of You,* Warner Brothers, 1944.

*Hollywood Canteen* (and story), Warner Brothers, 1944.

*The Red House,* United Artists, 1947.

*Dark Passage,* Warner Brothers, 1947, CBS/ Fox Video, 1987.

*Task Force* (and story), Warner Brothers, 1949.

*Bird of Paradise* (and story), Twentieth Century-Fox, 1951.

*Treasure of the Golden Condor,* Twentieth Century-Fox, 1953.

*Drum Beat* (and story), Warner Brothers, 1954.

(With Leo Townsend) *White Feather,* Twentieth Century-Fox, 1955.

(With Russell S. Hughes) *Jubal,* Columbia, 1956.

(With James Edward Grant and Gwen Bagni Gielgud) *The Last Wagon,* Twentieth Century-Fox, 1956.

*A Summer Place,* Warner Brothers, 1959.

*Parrish,* Warner Brothers, 1961.

*Susan Slade,* Warner Brothers, 1961.

*Rome Adventure,* Warner Brothers, 1962.

*Spencer's Mountain,* Warner Brothers, 1963.

*Youngblood Hawke,* Warner Brothers, 1964.

*The Battle of the Villa Fiorita,* Warner Brothers, 1965.

*SIDELIGHTS:* Delmer Daves was born with not only a knack for storytelling, but also an interest in the creation of words. Displaying artistic sensibilities from childhood, Daves began reproducing the Gothic calligraphy he found in his church hymnals at age eleven. As an adult, Daves would use his creative abilities to pay his way through law school before focusing his energies on the film industry. Whether he was acting, writing, directing, or producing, Daves was always utilizing his artistic background. Few people can boast of a successful film career in their own country, but Daves not only found acclaim in America, he also received accolades from foreign countries. In short, Delmer Daves utilized his unique talents to his advantage, making him a success in all he endeavored.

Daves was born in San Francisco, California, in 1904. An early interest in calligraphy led him to jobs as a teacher, draftsman, and designer. He received his law degree from Stanford in 1927, having paid his way through school via his artistic abilities. In addition to his interest in lettering, Daves was also active in drama during these early years. That interest led him to theater productions, as well as bit parts in numerous films.

Upon graduating from law school, Daves moved to Los Angeles to pursue a career in film. Armed only with an introduction from a classmate at Stanford, Daves approached James Cruze, a director/producer who was currently working on a film titled *The Covered Wagon.* Daves impressed Cruze enough to hire him as an assistant in the prop department. From there, Daves's career in film bloomed. Soon he was working at Metro-Goldwyn-Mayer, first in the props department, and then as an actor and advisor on the 1929 film *The Duke Steps Out.* To get his next job as a technical advisor on the film *So This Is College,* Daves had to submit ideas for the film to its director Sam Wood. Not only did he create ideas, but Daves also wrote a part for himself, so impressing Wood that he hired Daves to become a staff writer. From here, Daves would focus his energies, between 1929 to 1943, to screenwriting for various studios.

Daves' early work reflects his basic understanding of how Hollywood operated. According to Joy Boyer, writing for *Dictionary of Literary Biography,* "Daves learned that movies were a commercial product necessarily crafted within the limitations of technical facilities, time, and budget. A good film was one that showed a profit; a good script, one that gave the public the story they wanted. His early scripts . . . reflected this awareness. They risk little and remain faithful to tried-and-true conventions."

Most of Daves's early work focused on the romantic genre. His most successful scripts of this period were the films of Dick Powell and Ruby Keeler. In these films, the formula was good vs. evil, with a definite struggle and evident personal growth. What they lacked in variety, they made up for in box office success, providing Daves with a track record to continue writing. Some of these films include *Dames* and *Flirtation Walk,* both made in 1934, and *Shipmates Forever,* filmed in 1935.

After 1936, Daves's writing became less formulaic, and more confident. He covered a variety of genres, including musicals, mysteries, romances, and gangster films. Daves' strong suit was in his characters, and their relations to one another. The best films of this era were 1936's *The Petrified Forest,* 1939's *Love Affair,* and 1942's *You Were Never Lovelier.* In these movies, Daves focuses his efforts on his main character, usually a middle-aged man who, up to this point in his life, has allowed fate to control his world. During the course of the film, however, the man meets a woman and the two somehow find themselves in a situation where they must make decisions for themselves, thus redefining who they really are. 1939's *Love Affair* provided the basis for the later film *An Affair to Remember.* In the earlier film, the plot was sacrificed to character devel-

opment. To this end, Daves provided a model for films of the romantic genre to follow. The romantic comedies of today still rely on character development, more than plot, paying homage to Daves' formula.

In addition to his screenwriting career, Daves began working as a director in 1943. His first effort was the war film, *Destination Tokyo,* which he also wrote. However, he did direct a few films that he didn't write. These films include *To The Victor, Broken Arrow,* and *The Badlanders.* He also began producing his films in 1959, providing him with greater creative freedom.

Boyer considers Daves's Westerns of the 1950s to be his strongest writing. It is in these films that, "plot, character, and theme complement one another gracefully. These films are generally set in the last quarter of the nineteenth century, when a rugged frontier was gradually giving way to modern America . . . protagonists are frequently men caught between nineteenth- and twentieth-century values and, consequently, between a private code of honor and a code premised on the good of the community. Right and wrong are not easily distinguished . . . and most stereotypes of the Western are blurred in favor of moral and personal ambiguities."

Perhaps the reason that Daves' westerns are considered some of his best work is that they represented a piece of his own history. His ancestors had traveled west in covered wagons. More recently, Boyer adds, "his grandfather served in the Union army and became one of the first Pony Express riders.

In the late 1950s, and early 1960s, Daves began writing romantic films with an air of melodrama. These films include *A Summer Place, Parrish,* and *Rome Adventure.* While these were not his best films, they nonetheless reflected his literary talent. When other writers failed to please studio executives, Daves was called in to fix an ailing script. This was the case with 1959's *A Summer Place.* No one else had produced a satisfactory draft of Sloan Wilson's novel, so Daves was called in to doctor the script. He turned in such a successful draft that he not only received writing credit, but he also got the opportunity to direct and produce.

In the 1970s, Daves received numerous accolades from his peers, both locally, and abroad. While his work possessed certain flaws, over the course of his career, Daves continually improved as both a writer and a director. His best films reflect his creativity and enthusiasm for his subject matter. His worst ones show a writer still honing his talent. Overall, his impressive career is one to be applauded, and his talent should not be forgotten.

BIOGRAPHICAL/CRITICAL SOURCES:

BOOKS

*Dictionary of Literary Biography,* Volume 26: *American Screenwriters,* Gale (Detroit), 1984.
*International Dictionary of Films and Filmmakers,* 2nd edition, St. James Press (Detroit), 1991.*

\*   \*   \*

DAVIS, Kenneth S(idney)   1912-1999

*OBITUARY NOTICE*—See index for *CA* sketch: Born September 29, 1912, in Salina, KS; died of cancer, June 10, 1999. Writer. Davis is best known for his four-volume history on President Franklin D. Roosevelt but worked a variety of jobs in the communications field before settling on writing as his full-time vocation. After graduating from Kansas State University of Agriculture and Applied Science (now Kansas State University) in 1934 and receiving a master's from the University of Wisconsin, he served as an information specialist for the U.S. Soil Conservation Service, then spent two years as a journalism teacher at New York University. He worked on the public relations staff of Milton Eisenhower in the 1940s. In 1951 he began his long career as a full-time author and continued writing up until his death. Many of his works focus on well-known figures such as Dwight D. Eisenhower and Charles Lindbergh. In addition to his works on Roosevelt, Davis also wrote *A Prophet in His Own Country: The Triumphs and Defeats of Adlai E. Stevenson, Experience of War: The United States in World War II, The Cautionary Scientists: Priestly, Lavoisier, and the Founding of Modern Chemistry,* and *Kansas: A Bicentennial History.* His volumes on Roosevelt are *The Beckoning of Destiny, 1882-1928; The New York Years, 1928-1933; The New Deal Years, 1933-1937;* and *Into the Storm, 1937-1940.* Shortly before his death Davis completed a fifth installment, *The War President.* The books took more than three decades to research and write. Unlike some biographers who are hesitant to criticize their subjects, Davis's study is balanced in its assessments, critics say, and the first volume won the Francis Parkman Prize from the Society of American Historians.

OBITUARIES AND OTHER SOURCES:

PERIODICALS

*New York Times,* June 15, 1999, p. B14.
*Washington Post,* June 13, 1999, p. C5.

\*   \*   \*

DENT, Thomas C(ovington)   1932-1998

*OBITUARY NOTICE*—See index for *CA* sketch: Born March 20, 1932, in New Orleans, LA; died following surgery for a heart ailment, June 6, 1998, in New Orleans, LA. Civil rights activist, poet, and essayist. Dent grew up in a socially aware southern family and graduated from Morehouse College in 1952. His writing career began around that time when he was hired at the *Houston Informer* and he later wrote for *New York Age.* In 1961 he became a public information worker for the National Association for the Advancement of Colored People Legal Defense and Educational Fund. Through that assignment he became deeply involved in the civil rights movement and the importance of the struggle was reflected in some of his writings. Dent helped publish the newspaper *On Guard for Freedom* and co-founded New York City's Umbra Workshop. In addition he also co-published the poetry magazine *Umbra.* He wrote two poetry books, *Magnolia Street,* and *Blue Lights and River Songs: Poems.* He wrote several one-act plays including *Snapshot* and *Ritual Murder.* For four years in the late 1960s he helped run the Free Southern Theater, which traveled throughout the south performing plays with racial themes in poor areas. The troupe sometimes performed Dent's work. His most recent book, published in 1996, brought his passion for writing together with his interest in the civil rights movement. *Southern Journey: My Return to the Civil Rights Movement,* tells of his 1991 visits to cities that were instrumental in the movement.

OBITUARIES AND OTHER SOURCES:

BOOKS

*Who's Who Among African Americans,* Marquis, 1998-99.

PERIODICALS

*New York Times,* June 11, 1998, p. B12.
*Washington Post,* June 11, 1998, p. D8.

## de YOUNG, M(ichael) H(arry)  1849-1925

*PERSONAL:* Born September 39, 1849 in St. Louis, MO; died February 15, 1925; son of Michael H. and Amelia de Young; married Kate I. Dean, 1880; children: four daughters, one son. *Education:* Attended high school in San Francisco.

*CAREER:* Businessman and politician. *San Francisco Chronicle,* San Francisco, CA, co-founder and co-publisher with brother Charles, 1865-79, publisher, 1880-1925. Delegate to Republican National Convention, 1888, 1892, and 1908; chairman of the California delegation to the Republican National Convention, 1888; United States representative to Paris Exposition, 1889; national commissioner to World's Columbian Exposition, Chicago, 1892; organizer of San Francisco Midwinter Fair, 1894; founder of Golden Gate Park Memorial Museum (now the M. H. de Young Memorial Museum); commissioner-general to Trans-Mississippi Exposition in Omaha, NE, 1898; Red Cross executive committee, 1906; vice president, Panama-Pacific International Exposition, San Francisco, 1915.

*WRITINGS:*

Founder and co-publisher of the *San Francisco Chronicle,* 1865-79, and publisher, 1880-1925.

*SIDELIGHTS:* M. H. de Young, Jr., is remembered as the man who built northern California's largest-circulation newspaper, the *San Francisco Chronicle.* For approximately sixty years, De Young headed the paper, and it, along with the *Los Angeles Times,* stood as the preeminent conservative view for California. In addition to his publishing duties, de Young devoted much of his time and energy to the city of San Francisco, helping to develop it into the thriving city it is today.

De Young was born on September 30, 1849, in St. Louis, Missouri, and moved with his family to San Francisco in 1854. During their high school years, de Young's interest in journalism was evident as he and his older brother, Charles, put out a small paper called the *School Circle.* In addition to that, while de Young was still in high school and Charles was nineteen, the brothers borrowed money from their landlord and rented space in a printing shop to produce a four-page newspaper that they called the *Dramatic Chronicle.* The *Dramatic Chronicle,* which first appeared on January 17, 1865, was comprised of notices about shows at local theatres. After its first issue, the paper was subsidized by local theatre owners, and it was distributed free throughout the city. By the end of its first month, the *Dramatic Chronicle* had a circulation of 2,000 copies. The spirited writing in the *Dramatic Chronicle* caught the attention of Mark Twain, who contributed some pieces, and then of Bret Harte, who did the same. Soon, it became fashionable for noted local writers to get a byline in the paper.

In the meantime, Michael and Charles pored over copies of the nation's leading newspaper of the time, the *New York Herald,* carefully taking note of the paper's style, substance, tone, and format, which they proceeded to copy diligently, and with great success. Within two years, they were able to afford their own offices and printing equipment. Years later, de Young said, as quoted in Stephen D. Bray's essay in *Dictionary of Literary Biography,* that the early *Dramatic Chronicle* had "just enough reading matter for men to read during lunch, and it was of a character to attract special attention. There were criticisms of public men, crisp references to important events, shots at conspicuous people, and other such information."

By September of 1868, the *Dramatic Chronicle* had a circulation of over 10,000, and changed its name to the *Daily Morning Chronicle.* The paper was no longer free, but it sold for just five cents a copy. In its new form, the editors promised "what will prove a novelty in San Francisco journalism, a bold, bright, fearless and truly independent newspaper." The *Chronicle* proceeded to take a vehement activist stance against utility monopolies and to run scandalizing articles about well-known people, particularly the very wealthy. Though the de Youngs were sued for libel no less than a dozen times by 1871, the paper's popularity blossomed, and the brothers prospered.

During the 1870s, Charles de Young formed a close political bond with Denis Kearney, a labor agitator and leader of the Workingmen's Party. Together they advocated on behalf of a new state constitution that was more favorable to the interests of workers, and which was opposed by most other newspapers and by most of the large corporations in California. De Young and Kearney ultimately prevailed with the voters, who approved the new constitution. However, after this triumph the two men found themselves at odds. De Young was incensed by Kearney's support for the candidate for mayor of San Francisco, the Reverend Isaac S. Kallach. He wrote against Kallach vociferously in the *Chronicle,* and actually shot him. Kallach recovered from his gunshot wounds and won the election. Shortly thereafter, on April 23, 1880, Kallach's son shot and killed Charles de Young in the *Chronicle* offices.

In the wake of his brother's assassination, M. H. de Young found a wife, Kate Dean, who would later bear him five children. Tragically, one of his children, de Young's only son, was to die of typhus in 1913. Around the same time, de Young gained full control of the *Chronicle* and took it in a more conservative, less activist direction, and the reporting focus became more business-oriented. Within a few years, the paper became identified with the philosophy of the Republican party, and in 1888, 1892, and 1908, de Young served as a delegate to the Republican national convention. De Young himself ran for the Senate in 1892 but lost.

In 1892, President Harrison appointed him a national commissioner to the World's Columbian Exposition, held in Chicago the following year. In Chicago, de Young conceived the idea of a Midwinter Fair in San Francisco, which took place in Golden Gate Park in 1894. The Midwinter Fair was a tremendous success for de Young and the city; it provided hundreds of jobs for unemployed San Franciscans during a time of national economic depression. Not long thereafter, de Young founded the Golden Gate Park Memorial Museum, which began in the Fine Arts building that had been constructed for the Midwinter Fair. He not only founded the museum, but he began to fill it as well. De Young proceeded to travel the world, collecting fine art that he donated to the museum. The museum has since been renamed the M. H. de Young Memorial Museum.

De Young continued to receive various ambassadorial appointments, including commissioner-general to the Trans-Mississippi Exposition in Omaha, Nebraska, in 1898, national commissioner to the Paris Exposition in 1900, and vice president and director of concessions at the Panama-Pacific International Exposition in San Francisco in 1915. He died on February 15, 1925, at the age of seventy-five. De Young was mourned and eulogized by journalists, newspaper editors, and statesmen across the country. Particularly after the death of Charles, de Young seldom expressed his own opinions directly in the *Chronicle*. He did not write editorials with the flair and savvy of an editor such as his primary competitor, William Randolph Hearst, editor of the *San Francisco Examiner*. Yet de Young is remembered today as a highly charismatic journalist who built a great newspaper and indelibly stamped it with the mark of his distinctive personality and character.

*BIOGRAPHICAL/CRITICAL SOURCES:*

BOOKS

Bruce, John, *Gaudy Century,* Random House (New York City), 1948.

*Dictionary of Literary Biography,* Volume 25: *American Newspaper Journalists, 1901-1925,* Gale (Detroit), 1984.

Young, John P., *Journalism in California,* Chronicle Publishing (San Francisco, CA), 1915.

*PERIODICALS*

*Pacific Historical Review,* August 16, 1947, pp. 271-284.

*San Francisco Chronicle,* February 16, 1925, pp. 2-9.*

\*        \*        \*

## DOWDEN, Edward    1843(?)-1913

*PERSONAL:* Born May 13, 1843(?), in Mentenotte, Ireland; died April 4, 1913, in Dublin, Ireland; son of John Wheeler (a merchant and landowner) and Alicia (Benett) Dowden; married Mary Clerke, 1866 (died, 1892); married Elizabeth Dickinson West, 1895; children: four (first marriage). *Education:* Attended Queen's College, Cork, and Trinity College, Dublin.

*CAREER:* Poet, scholar, and critic. Alexandra College, Dublin, Ireland, professor of English Literature, 1866; University of Dublin, Dublin, Ireland, professor of oratory and English literature, 1867; Trinity College, Dublin, chair of oratory and English, 1867, professor of English literature, 1867-1913.

*MEMBER:* Undergraduates' Philosophical Society (president, 1863), English Goethe Society (president 1888-1911), Irish National Library (trustee), Irish Liberal Union (secretary), Irish Unionist Alliance (vice-president).

*AWARDS, HONORS:* LL.D., University of Edinburgh and Princeton University; DC.L., Oxford University; D.Litt., Cambridge University.

*WRITINGS:*

NONFICTION

*Shakspere: A Critical Study of His Mind and Art,* King (London), 1875, Harper (New York City), 1880.
*Shakespeare,* Macmillan (London), 1877, Appleton (New York City), 1878.
*Studies in Literature, 1789-1877,* Kegan Paul (London), 1878.
*Southey,* Macmillan, 1879, Harper, 1880.

*Spenser the Poet and Teacher,* Volume 1 of *The Complete Works of Edmund Spenser,* edited by A. B. Grosart, privately printed, 1882.

*The Life of Percy Bysshe* Shelley, two volumes, Kegan Paul, 1886, Lippincott (Philadelphia) 1892.

*Transcripts and Studies,* Kegan Paul, 1887.

*New Studies in Literature,* Houghton (Boston), 1895.

*The French Revolution and English Literature,* Scribner (New York City), 1897.

*A History of French Literature,* Appleton, 1897.

*Puritan and Anglican: Studies in Literature,* Holt (New York City), 1900.

*Robert Browning,* Dutton (New York City), 1904, published as *The Life of Robert Browning,* Dutton, 1915.

*Michel de Montaigne,* Lippincott, 1905.

*Essays Modern and Elizabethan,* Dutton, 1910.

*A Woman's Reliquary,* privately printed, 1913, Dent, 1914.

*OTHER*

*Poems,* King, 1876, enlarged edition, Dent (London), 1914.

*Letters of Edward Dowden and His Correspondents,* edited by Elizabeth D. Dowden and Hilda M. Dowden, Dutton, 1914.

*Fragments from Old Letters, E. D. to E. D. W., 1869-1892,* edited by wife, Elizabeth D. Dowden, Dutton, 1914.

*Letters about Shelley, Interchanged by Three Friends-Edward Dowden, Richard Garnett, and W. Michael Rossetti,* edited by R. S. Garnett, Hodder & Stoughton (London), 1917.

*SIDELIGHTS:* Those who knew him often described Edward Dowden as "mature". He was brought up in a home rich with culture and tradition. Although his affluent middle-class family was of English and Scottish origin, they had been living in Ireland for two hundred years. Dowden's education began at a young age in the public library. As he grew older, he was privately tutored before attending classes in Queen's College in Cork. At the age of sixteen, Dowden attended Trinity College and impressed teachers and classmates with his intelligence. He received his M.A. in 1867 and then attended divinity school. Dowden went on to create a reputation for himself as a poet, scholar, and critic, as well as expand his professional study of English letters. In a time when English literature was considered a relatively new field, Dowden's writings helped to bring the discipline a great deal of respect. As stated in the *Oxford Companion to Irish Literature,* "Chiefly [Dowden] is remembered for pioneering academic work in the first Chair dedicated to English literature alone."

In 1866 Dowden married, and in 1867 he accepted a position at Trinity College. Dowden was criticized for marrying at such a young age. It was thought his early marriage and academic position at Trinity College would hinder his creativity as a poet and prevent him from fully committing to poetry. Despite the criticisms, Dowden did continue to write poetry all through his life and even published poetry books. He is, however, mostly remembered as a biographer and literary critic.

Dowden's first publication and his most recognized work was *Shakspere: A Critical Study of His Mind and Art,* published in 1875. A. R. Jones, writing for *Dictionary of Literary Biography,* states "There can be no doubt that his work was a landmark in Shakespearian criticism and established him in the front rank of Shakespearian critics." With *Shakspere,* Dowden did something that no critic had done before—he showed Shakespeare as a person and did not focus on him solely as a writer. Through his interpretation of Shakespeare's work, he was able to show readers Shakespeare's views on people, morals, and life in general. As Richard Eaton notes in *Dictionary of Literary Biography,* "His was the first effort to try to take the measure of Shakespeare's personality from the plays and poems." Jones notes that "[Dowden's] interpretation is the first attempt in English to trace the growth of Shakespeare's intellect and character from youth to full maturity." As reviewed in the *Nation,* "The book has an established place in Shakespearean criticism."

In 1877, Dowden went on to publish his primer called *Shakespeare,* a basic book aimed at nonacademic readers. Although the book came under criticism from some for being too simplistic, it enhanced Dowden's popularity among readers. In addition to writing, Dowden also traveled extensively, including two trips to America. He also lectured outside Dublin frequently. He lectured at Oxford in 1889, at Cambridge between 1892 and 1896, and at Princeton in 1896. But no matter how often or how far he traveled, Dublin was always Dowden's home and his source of inspiration. He also remained true to Trinity College and stayed there all his life, despite offers from other universities.

Dowden's next project, a two-volume biography on the poet Percy Bysshe Shelly, was an ambitious undertaking. Published in 1886, *Life of Percy Bysshe Shelley* confirmed Dowden's reputation as a pioneer scholar of his time. For Dowden, writing the biography proved very difficult. Dowden had the delicate task of dealing with a scandal from Shelley's past. It seemed that Shelley left his first wife, Harriet Westbrook, and married another woman, Mary Godwin. It was Shelley and Godwin's son and daughter-in-law who commissioned Dowden to write the biography and gave him access to Shelley's private collection of work. With both families trying to impose their views on his work, Dowden was determined to achieve a neutral tone that was fair to both families. He also feared that the public would think that he was showing favoritism toward the Shelleys because he was working for them. However, after some changes at the behest of the Shelley family, Dowden's final manuscript met with the approval of both families.

Although *Life of Percy Bysshe Shelley* was generally reviewed well, it also came under attack, not for Dowden's writing, but for the manner in which he dealt with the matter involving Shelley's abandonment of his first wife. Reviewers perceived his neutral presentation of the situation as a condoning of Shelley's actions. The book did not sell well, but Jones notes that "[Dowden's] biography remains the first scholarly biography of the poet and is a monument to Dowden's scrupulous respect for veracity and his ability to deal with the tangled lives involved with objectivity and compassion."

Dowden went on to write several more biographies, including *Southey,* published in 1879. Dowden greatly admired and identified with Robert Southey both as a man and a writer. Dowden was also an admirer of French literature and in 1905, he published *Michel de Montaigne.* Using a combination of research of the letters left by Montaigne, his writings, and other facts Dowden was able to capture the essence of Montaigne as a writer and a person. A *Dial* reviewer wrote, "It is no cut-and-dried biography, but an illuminated record of the mind and soul of the man whom Sainte-Beuve called 'the wisest Frenchman that ever lived.' "

Dowden's interest in English literature—modern and Elizabethan—led him to issue *Essays Modern and Elizabethan.* Published in 1910, this book included sixteen essays reprinted from reviews on such various topics as Shakespeare and Elizabethan romance. According to a review in the *Saturday Review,* "Professor Dowden wears his erudition as lightly as a Frenchman, and he spices his chapters with the stories that are always new."

Dowden suffered a great loss when his first wife died in 1892; he was soon able to find inspiration in another woman. In 1895 he married Elizabeth Dickinson West, who had been a friend for many years. In 1913, he even

published a collection of love poems dedicated to her called *A Woman's Reliquary.* Toward the end of Dowden's life, his health was faltering as the bronchial problems that he had had for years began to worsen. With his death in 1913, Dublin and the rest of the world lost a great literary figure. As Eaton notes, "[Dowden] brought stature to his discipline by applying to it the spirit and some of the tools of more traditional studies (careful editing, scrupulous handling of materials), as well as by his graceful writing style and immense industry."

*BIOGRAPHICAL/CRITICAL SOURCES:*

*BOOKS*

*Dictionary of Literary Biography,* Volume 149: *Late Nineteenth-and Early Twentieth-Century British Literary Biographers,* Gale (Detroit), 1985.
Eastman, Arthur M., *A Short History of Shakespearean Criticism,* Random House (New York), 1968.
Stavisky, Aron Y., *Shakespeare and the Victorians: Roots of Modern Criticism,* University of Oklahoma Press, 1969.

*PERIODICALS*

*Dial,* September 16, 1905.
*Nation,* June 20, 1912.
*Saturday Review,* July 16, 1910.*

\*        \*        \*

### DUNNE, George H(arold)   1905-1998

*OBITUARY NOTICE*—See index for *CA* sketch: Born March 11, 1905, in St. Louis, MO; died June 30, 1998, in Los Gatos, CA. Priest and author. An outspoken critic of segregation, Dunne's belief in racial equality led him to be the first director of the ecumenical Committee on Society, Development, and Peace. His views on society had begun to take shape when he was a missionary in China in the 1930s and he began openly criticizing segregation in the 1940s. Dunne said racial segregation was a sin and frequently spoke out against Roman Catholic institutions that endorsed it, making him one of the first prominent Catholics to do so. His criticism led to him being fired from the Institute of Social Order at St. Louis University, but he later found teaching posts at Loyola University in Los Angeles and at Santa Clara University. He was active in the civil rights movement and marched with the Reverend Martin Luther King on several occasions. Dunne's best-known work, *Generation of Giants,* related to the early Jesuit missions in China. Other works include the books *Religion and Democracy* and *The Right to Development,* as well as the play *Trial by Fire,* which described the bombing of a black family that chose to live in a Los Angeles area that had been all-white until their arrival. His memoirs, *The King's Pawn: The Memoirs of George Dunne, S.J.,* were published in 1990.

*OBITUARIES AND OTHER SOURCES:*

*PERIODICALS*

*Los Angeles Times,* July 11, 1998, p. B8.
*New York Times,* July 14, 1998, p. B10.
*Washington Post,* July 17, 1998, p. C8.

\*    \*    \*

**DUVALL, Aimee**
   **See THURLO, David**

\*    \*    \*

**ECKSTEIN, Harry   1924-1999**

*OBITUARY NOTICE*—See index for *CA* sketch: Born January 26, 1924, in Schotten, Germany; immigrated to the United States, 1936; died of heart failure, June 22, 1999, in Newport Beach, CA. Educator and author. Eckstein spent his first twelve years in Nazi Germany before his family settled in Columbus, Ohio, in 1936. He received bachelor's, master's and doctoral degrees from Harvard University, where he was hired after receiving his Ph.D. in 1954. After serving on Harvard's political science faculty for four years, he moved to Princeton. Eckstein was considered influential for his theory that political culture plays a large role in the success of a democracy and in 1980 he was hired at the University of California at Irvine. He was a Distinguished Research Professor in the political science department there when he died. Eckstein's area of expertise was democratic stability and he wrote several books about government and politics, including *Patterns of Government, Pressure Group Politics,* and *Division and Cohesion in Democracy.*

*OBITUARIES AND OTHER SOURCES:*

*BOOKS*

*American Men and Women of Science: Social and Behavioral Sciences,* 13th edition, R.R. Bowker Company, 1978.
*Who's Who,* 49th edition, Marquis, 1995.

*PERIODICALS*

*New York Times,* July 11, 1999, p. A31.

\*    \*    \*

**EDDY, Edward D(anforth, Jr.)   1921-1998**

*OBITUARY NOTICE*—See index for *CA* sketch: Born May 10, 1921, in Saratoga Springs, NY; died of prostate cancer, June 28, 1998, in South Kingstown, RI. Educator and author. Eddy came from a well-educated family—his father was a lawyer and his mother was a university professor—and he chose to make education his career. He received bachelor's and doctoral degrees from Cornell University and a master's of divinity from Yale. His first position was as associate director of the interfaith office at Cornell, where he stayed until 1949 before moving to the University of New Hampshire, where he was an instructor in English and assistant to the president. He continued moving upward there, serving as acting president and provost in 1955. He later served at both Chatham College and Pennsylvania State University. He contributed articles to several professional journals and wrote books on education, including the academic classic *Colleges for Our Land and Time,* as well as *The College Influence on Student Character* and *The Twelve-College Cost-Quality Study.* He continued his activity in a number of education-related ventures such as the Providence Blueprint for Education after his retirement from the presidency at the University of Rhode Island in 1991.

*OBITUARIES AND OTHER SOURCES:*

*PERIODICALS*

*New York Times,* July 2, 1998, p. B9.

## EDWARDS, John Carver 1939-

*PERSONAL:* Born December 8, 1939, in Charleston, SC; son of John Pelham and Elizabeth (Carver) Edwards; married Lorraine Spann (a public relations director), in 1972 (divorced, September, 1992); children: Leigh, John. *Education:* Wofford College, A.B., 1964 (with honors); University of Georgia, M.A., 1967, Ph.D., 1975. *Politics:* Independent. *Religion:* Episcopalian. *Avocational interests:* Military modeling, walking, fishing, baseball.

*ADDRESSES: Home*—385 Greencrest Dr., Athens, GA 30605. *Office*—Richard B. Russell Library, University of Georgia, Athens, GA 30602. *E-mail*—jedwards@ arches.uga.edu. *Agent*—Aleta M. Daley, Maximilian Becker Agency, 444 East 82nd St., New York, NY 10025.

*CAREER:* Georgia Department of Archives and History, Atlanta, head of Manuscripts Division, 1970-72; University of Georgia Libraries, Athens, records officer, 1972-77, university archivist, 1977-93, special projects archivist, 1993—.

*MEMBER:* Academy of Certified Archivists, Society of American Archivists, Authors Guild, Phi Kappa Phi, Phi Alpha Theta, Pi Gamma Mu, Delta Tau Kappa.

*WRITINGS:*

*Patriots in Pinstripe: Men of the National Security League,* University Press of America, 1982.
*Berlin Calling: American Broadcasters in Service to the Third Reich,* Praeger (Westport, CT), 1991.
*Airmen without Portfolio: U.S. Mercenaries in Civil War Spain,* Praeger, 1997.

Contributor of numerous articles to scholarly journals, including *Atlanta Historical Bulletin, Georgia Historical Quarterly, Georgia Magazine, Illinois Quarterly, International Behavioral Scientist, Military Affairs, North Dakota Quarterly, Research Studies, South Carolina History Illustrated, Southern Studies,* and *Studies in History and Society.* Preparer of various archival exhibits.

*ADAPTATIONS: Berlin Calling* and *Airmen without Portfolio* were adapted for radio documentaries for National Public Radio.

*WORK IN PROGRESS: The Two Worlds of Howard Max Rinehart: Aerial Pioneer.*

*SIDELIGHTS:* American archivist and historian John Carver Edwards has mined scores of records repositories to write about unusual and oft-neglected topics. Among his works are *Patriots in Pinstripe,* about a World War I military organization, *Berlin Calling,* a book about U.S. radio broadcasters who served the Nazis, and *Airmen without Portfolio,* about U.S. pilots who fought in the Spanish Civil War. In his work, Edwards delves into human motivational factors for individuals' actions.

Edwards grew up in Spartanburg, South Carolina, where he heard local whispers about a prominent banker whose brother, Robert Henry Best, had committed treason against the United States during World War II. When Edwards attended Wofford College, a small liberal arts Methodist college in his hometown, he became even more interested in the traitorous Best, who had graduated from Wofford some forty-eight years earlier. Edwards' profile of Best led to his writing another profile, and yet another, until he had chronicled the lives of eight expatriate turncoats in *Berlin Calling.* These short-wave radio propagandists included Jane Anderson, Max Otto Koischwitz, Best, Douglas Chandler, and Donald Day. Trying to understand the broadcasters' reasons for their actions, Edwards studied letters, transcripts from treason trials, and documents from the British Broadcasting Corporation and the Federal Bureau of Investigation.

Judging *Berlin Calling* to be a "fine book," Robert Herzstein, writing in the *Journal of American History,* added, "His thorough use of all important archival sources correctly portrays the so-called radio traitors as arrogant but pathetic victims, not of society, but of themselves and their twisted visions of reality." Edwards' "fascinating book is a model for historians," concluded Joseph P. Hobbs in *Choice.*

Military historian Jon Guttman, writing for the *History Network* online, commented on Edwards' penchant for writing about such colorful and bizarre historical characters in his review of *Airmen without Portfolio.* In this work, which is based on aviators' memoirs and secondary sources, Edwards described the political motivations and day-to-day activities of twelve American mercenary pilots who fought for the Spanish Republican government during the Spanish Civil War. "As with his 1991 book, *Berlin Calling,* . . . Edwards is fascinated by the individual stories of Americans who volunteered for causes that went beyond the policies of their own country," wrote Guttman. "Drawing on a wealth of international documentation to shed light on the volunteers' comrades in arms and opponents, Edwards cuts through decades of popular myth to present the often grim realities of their war—one in which airmen on both sides were learning from scratch the techniques that would be devastatingly commonplace in World War II. What emerges from his study is the portrait of a small, committed and courageous band of unique characters whose deeds, even stripped of mythos, can stand on their own merit."

*BIOGRAPHICAL/CRITICAL SOURCES:*

PERIODICALS

*Athens Magazine,* December, 1991, pp. 64-70.
*Choice,* November, 1991, p. 508.
*Georgia Review,* spring, 1992, pp. 173-174.
*History Today,* September, 1992, pp. 54-55.
*Journalism Quarterly,* summer, 1992, p. 482.
*Journal of American History,* September, 1983, p. 447.
*Journal of Communication,* winter, 1992, pp. 147-148.
*Library Journal,* May 1, 1991.
*Washington Post Book World,* July 14, 1991, p. 8.

OTHER

*History Network,* http://thehistorynet.com/reviews/ bk—airmercen.htm (September 1, 1998).

\*    \*    \*

## ELDREDGE, Dirk Chase 1932-

*PERSONAL:* Born June 30, 1932, in Salt Lake City, UT; married Donna M. Beavers, August 14, 1954; children: Kim D. Gibler, Dirk C. Eldredge II. *Education:* University of Southern California, B.S. (cum laude), 1956. *Politics:* Republican. *Avocational interests:* Reading.

*ADDRESSES: Home and Office*—6121 Capri Court, Long Beach, CA 90803.

*CAREER:* IBM, Los Angeles, CA, and Portland, OR, marketing manager, 1957-70; National Office Supply, president/owner, and Condo Resorts International, president, 1971—. Co-chairman of Ronald Reagan's campaign for governor of California, 1966-67. *Military service:* U.S. Air Force, 1951-52, enlisted man.

*MEMBER:* Round Table of Orange County (founder; chair, 1981-82), Drug Policy Foundation.

*WRITINGS:*

*Ending the War on Drugs: A Solution for America,* Bridge Works (Bridgehampton, NY), 1998.

Contributor to various journals, including the *Washington Times* magazine.

*WORK IN PROGRESS: Immigration: Policies with No Purpose,* a book on U.S. immigration policies; *The Seven Secular Laws of Recuperation,* a book about physical and psychological recovery from major illnesses and injuries; *The Category Killers in Retail,* a study of the sociological effects of the demise of small businesses at the hands of huge retail outlets.

*SIDELIGHTS:* Although he became a published author relatively late in life, Dirk Chase Eldredge brings a wealth of experience in business to his writing. In his book *Ending the War on Drugs,* Eldredge delivers an attack on America's controlled-substances policy. The author's views on drugs were shaped by two important experiences: the pain he suffered as the child of an alcoholic, and the research he undertook after hearing a judge speak out on the unintended consequences of the government's doomed efforts to eradicate drug use.

*Ending the War on Drugs* gives a grim account of these consequences, including increased criminal activity, widespread corruption, glutted courtrooms and jails, the introduction of ever-more-potent drugs, a coercive and alienating foreign policy, the erosion of civil liberties, and a sense of persecution within the black underclass. Pointing to the lessons of the Prohibition era, Eldredge argues that drugs should be decriminalized and distributed through state-owned outlets like the ones some states use to regulate the sale of alcohol. In this way drugs could be sold at well below their current street value, eliminating the black market and with it the violence and gang activity associated with drug dealing. At the same time, profits could be directed toward education and treatment programs.

Despite its controversial recommendations, *Ending the War on Drugs* has been generally well received. A writer for *Kirkus Reviews* called it "[a] good summary of and introduction to a libertarian perspective on drugs, freedom, and the role of the state," while the Hon. John L. Kane, Jr., writing in the *Denver Post,* noted that the book "will appeal to the business-oriented reader; it is long on facts and short on preaching. It is pragmatic rather than theoretical. It contains enough anecdotal information to keep the pages turning and still covers issues as diverse as domestic and international politics, law enforcement, race relations, public health, ethics, penology and economics. . . . It is not for the reader who wants bland assurances and hand-holding, but for those who demand a pungent description of the most troubling crisis of our time."

Eldredge told *CA:* "My primary motivation in writing is a desire to serve my country and its people. Politics has always been exciting and interesting to me, but I have never had the courage and resources to seek public office. Writing with the objective of bringing common sense and focus to public policy affords me an opportunity to fill this void in my life.

"Research is the keystone of the writing process for me. I love the excitement of the search for facts and ideas. I liken it to panning for gold. You sift through much sand and silt until you come across that nugget of information or that glistening idea which enriches your work."The book I am currently working on concerns the immigration issue. I was drawn to this subject because of my concern over the lack of focus of our hodgepodge of immigration laws and policies. I see them as 'policy by pressure group' rather than sound public policy with clear priorities and objectives.

"My pending book on recuperation was inspired by my personal experience of recovery from five major surgeries between my forty-fourth and sixty-fourth birthdays. In it I will recount the experience of myself and others. I will set forth in a secular context what has worked well physically and attitudinally.

"My thirty years of experience as a retailer plus much research will form the basis of my book on the sociological effects of what retailers call 'category killers.' These are large national chains such as Home Depot, Office Club, and Wal Mart against which small, local hardware stores, office supply dealers and other specialty stores have little chance. The coming of these behemoths has caused the shuttering of many Main Streets in small-town America as well as countless small retailers in metropolitan areas. This has changed the lives of entrepreneurs, employees, and their families throughout our nation."

*BIOGRAPHICAL/CRITICAL SOURCES:*

*PERIODICALS*

*Denver Post,* September 27, 1998.

*Foreign Affairs,* November, 1998, p. 153.
*Kirkus Reviews,* June 15, 1998, p. 869.

\*　　\*　　\*

## ENGLISH, David    1931-1998

*OBITUARY NOTICE*—See index for *CA* sketch: Born May 26, 1931; died of a stroke, June 10, 1998, in London, England. Journalist. English was one of the most influential newspapermen of his time, serving as editor of England's *Daily Mail* for twenty years and then as chairman of Associated Newspapers in the 1990s. English's rise to fame was the result of endless reporting assignments that first began in 1951 when he was hired by *the Daily Mirror.* He then moved on to positions at the *Daily Sketch, Sunday Dispatch,* and *Daily Express.* He was a foreign correspondent and foreign editor for the *Express,* which led to him covering the 1968 United States presidential election. That assignment resulted in the book *Divided They Stand,* which he wrote with other *Daily Express* staffers. English joined Associated Newspapers, owner of *The Daily Mail,* in 1969 and was named editor in 1971. He took the paper from its position as a struggling tabloid to a must-read for the middle class and along the way he founded a chain of free papers that he eventually sold to Rupert Murdoch for a good sum. English was a strong supporter of former British prime minister Margaret Thatcher and was knighted by her in 1982.

*OBITUARIES AND OTHER SOURCES:*

*PERIODICALS*

*Los Angeles Times,* June 13, 1998, p. A14.
*New York Times,* June 12, 1998, p. A19.
*Times* (London), June 11, 1998.
*Washington Post,* June 12, 1998, p. C8.

\*　　\*　　\*

**ERICSON, Walter**
**See FAST, Howard (Melvin)**

# F

**FADEYEV, A.**
See BULGYA, Alexander Alexandrovich

\*   \*   \*

**FADEYEV, Alexander**
See BULGYA, Alexander Alexandrovich

\*   \*   \*

## FADIMAN, Clifton (Paul)   1904-1999

*OBITUARY NOTICE*—See index for *CA* sketch: Born May 15, 1904, in Brooklyn, NY; died of pancreatic cancer, June 20, 1999, on Sanibel Island, FL. Radio show host, editor, and author. Fadiman helped establish the Book-of-the-Month Club and spent more than five decades reviewing books for the group. He loved the written word, having read his first book at age four, and continued his hobby until well into his eighties when he became blind due to acute retinal necrosis. He estimated he had read about 25,000 books in his lifetime and although he lost his sight, he did not lose his interest in books. As a member of the editorial board for Book-of-the-Month he continued reviewing books after listening to them on tape. Fadiman's career contained a brief stint as a teacher before he moved to publisher Simon & Schuster where he was an editor from 1927 to 1935. From there he moved to *New Yorker* magazine where he was book editor. During his tenure there he became involved in radio and hosted the *Information Please* show, which ran from 1938 to 1948. The show featured four intellectuals (including Fadiman) who would answer questions sent in by listeners. Anyone who could stump the stars received a free set of *Encyclopedia Britannica.* The show was a success and at one time could claim nine million listeners. Other broadcasts of which Fadiman was host include *Conversation, Mathematics, What's in a Word?*, *This Is Show Business,* and *Quiz Kids.* In 1944 he joined the Book-of-the-Month Club staff and served in a variety of positions until he was named chairman emeritus in 1997. He served on the editorial board for Encyclopaedia Britannica beginning in 1955 and created *Treasury of the Encyclopaedia Britannica,* condensing the company's editions into one volume. A fan of anthologies and treasuries, Fadiman edited more than thirty, including *The Three Readers: An Omnibus of Novels, Stories, Essays and Poems, The Short Stories of Henry James,* and *Party of Twenty: Informal Essays from Holiday Magazine.* Not content to simply edit other people's works and write introductions to them, Fadiman was an author in his own right, having written *The Lifetime Reading Plan, Enter, Conversing,* and, with Sam Aaron, *The Joys of Wine* and *The Wine Buyer's Guide.*

*OBITUARIES AND OTHER SOURCES:*

*PERIODICALS*

*Chicago Tribune,* June 21, 1999, sec. 2, p. 7.
*Los Angeles Times,* June 22, 1999, p. A24.
*New York Times,* June 21, 1999, p. B8.
*USA Today,* June 21, 1999.
*Washington Post,* June 22, 1999, p. B7.

## FAST, Howard (Melvin) 1914-
### (E. V. Cunningham, Walter Ericson)

*PERSONAL:* Born November 11, 1914, in New York, NY; son of Barney (an ironworker, cable car gripper, tin factory worker, and dress factory cutter) and Ida (a homemaker; maiden name, Miller) Fast; married Bette Cohen (a painter and sculptor), June 6, 1937; children: Rachel, Jonathan. *Education:* Attended National Academy of Design. *Religion:* Jewish. *Avocational interests:* "Home, my family, the theater, the film, and the proper study of ancient history. And the follies of mankind."

*ADDRESSES: Home*—Greenwich, CT. *Agent*—Sterling Lord Agency, 65 Bleeker St., New York, NY 10012.

*CAREER:* Worked at several odd jobs and as a page in the New York Public Library prior to 1932; writer, 1932—. Foreign correspondent for *Esquire* and *Coronet,* 1945. Taught at Indiana University, 1947; member of World Peace Council, 1950-55; American Labor Party candidate for U.S. Congress, 23rd New York District, 1952; owner, Blue Heron Press, New York, 1952-57; film writer, 1958-67; chief news writer, Voice of America, 1982-88. Has given numerous lectures and made numerous appearances on radio and television programs. *Military service:* Affiliated with U.S. Office of War Information, 1942-44; correspondent with special Signal Corps unit and war correspondent in China-India-Burma theater, 1945.

*MEMBER:* Century Club, Fellowship for Reconciliation.

*AWARDS, HONORS:* Bread Loaf Literary Award, 1937; Schomburg Award for Race Relations, 1944, for *Freedom Road;* Newspaper Guild award, 1947; National Jewish Book Award, Jewish Book Council, 1949, for *My Glorious Brothers;* International Peace Prize from the Soviet Union, 1954; Screenwriters annual award, 1960; Secondary Education Board annual book award, 1962; American Library Association "notable book" citation, 1972, for *The Hessian;* Emmy Award for outstanding writing in a drama series, American Academy of Television Arts and Sciences, 1975, for episode "The Ambassador," *Benjamin Franklin;* Literary Lions Award, New York Public Library, 1985; Prix de la Policia Award (France), for books under name E. V. Cunningham.

**Howard Fast**

*WRITINGS:*

*Two Valleys,* Dial (New York City), 1933, Lovat Dickson, 1933.

*Strange Yesterday,* Dodd (New York City), 1934.

*Place in the City,* Harcourt (New York City), 1937.

*Conceived in Liberty: A Novel of Valley Forge,* Simon & Schuster (New York City), 1939, Michael Joseph (London), 1939.

*The Last Frontier,* Duell, Sloan & Pearce (New York City), 1941, Bodley Head (London), 1948.

*The Romance of a People,* Hebrew Publishing (New York City), 1941.

*Lord Baden-Powell of the Boy Scouts,* Messner (New York City), 1941.

*Haym Salomon, Son of Liberty,* Messner, 1941.

*The Unvanquished,* Duell, Sloan & Pearce, 1942, John Lane (London), 1947.

*The Tall Hunter,* Harper (New York City), 1942, Harper (London), 1942.

(With wife, Bette Fast) *The Picture-Book History of the Jews,* Hebrew Publishing,1942.

*Goethals and the Panama Canal,* Messner, 1942.

*Citizen Tom Paine,* Duell, Sloan & Pearce, 1943, John Lane, 1945.

*The Incredible Tito,* Magazine House (New York City), 1944.

*Freedom Road,* Duell, Sloan & Pearce, 1944, new edition with foreword by W. E. B. DuBois, introduction by Eric Foner, M. E. Sharpe (Armonk, NY), 1995.

*Patrick Henry and the Frigate's Keel and Other Stories of a Young Nation,* Duell, Sloan & Pearce, 1945.

*The American: A Middle Western Legend,* Duell, Sloan & Pearce, 1946.

(With William Gropper) *Never Forget: The Story of the Warsaw Ghetto,* Book League of the Jewish Fraternal Order, 1946.

(Editor) Thomas Paine, *The Selected Works of Tom Paine,* Modern Library (New York City), 1946.

*The Children,* Duell, Sloan & Pearce, 1947.

(Editor) Theodore Dreiser, *Best Short Stories of Theodore Dreiser,* World Publishing, 1947.

*Clarkton,* Duell, Sloan & Pearce, 1947.

*Tito and His People,* Contemporary Publishers (Winnipeg, Canada), 1948.

*My Glorious Brothers,* Little, Brown (Boston), 1948, new edition, Hebrew Publications, 1977, Bodley Head, 1950.

*Departure and Other Stories,* Little, Brown, 1949.

*Intellectuals in the Fight for Peace,* Masses & Mainstream (New York City), 1949.

*The Proud and the Free,* Little, Brown, 1950.

*Literature and Reality,* International Publishers (New York City), 1950.

*Spartacus,* Blue Heron (New York City), 1951, Citadel (Secaucus, NJ), 1952, Bodley Head, 1952, reprinted with new introduction, North Castle Books (Armonk, NY), 1996.

*Peekskill, U.S.A.: A Personal Experience,* Civil Rights Congress (New York City), 1951.

*Tony and the Wonderful Door,* Blue Heron, 1952.

*Spain and Peace,* Joint Anti-Fascist Refugee Committee, 1952.

*The Passion of Sacco and Vanzetti: A New England Legend,* Blue Heron, 1953, Bodley Head, 1954.

*Silas Timberman,* Blue Heron, 1954, Bodley Head, 1954.

*The Last Supper, and Other Stories,* Blue Heron, 1955, Bodley Head, 1956.

*The Story of Lola Gregg,* Blue Heron, 1956, Bodley Head, 1957.

*The Naked God: The Writer and the Communist Party* (memoir), Praeger (New York City), 1957, Bodley Head, 1958.

*Moses, Prince of Egypt,* Crown (New York City), 1958, Methuen (London), 1960.

*The Winston Affair,* Crown, 1959, Methuen, 1960.

*The Howard Fast Reader,* Crown, 1960.

*April Morning,* Crown, 1961, Methuen, 1961.

*The Edge of Tomorrow* (stories), Bantam (New York City), 1961.

*Power,* Doubleday (New York City), 1962, Methuen, 1963.

*Agrippa's Daughter,* Doubleday, 1964, Methuen, 1965.

*The Hill,* Doubleday, 1964.

*Torquemada,* Doubleday, 1966, Methuen, 1967.

*The Hunter and the Trap,* Dial, 1967.

*The Jews: Story of a People,* Dial, 1968, Cassell (London), 1960.

*The General Zapped an Angel,* Morrow (New York City), 1970.

*The Crossing* (based on his play of the same title), Morrow, 1971, Eyre Methuen (London), 1972, New Jersey Historical Society, 1985.

*The Hessian* (based on his screenplay of the same title), Morrow, 1972, Hodder & Stoughton, 1975, reprinted with new foreword, North Castle Books (Armonk, NY), 1996.

*A Touch of Infinity: Thirteen Stories of Fantasy and Science Fiction,* Morrow, 1973.

*Mohawk* (screenplay; short film), Paulist Productions, 1974.

*Time & the Riddle: Thirty-One Zen Stories,* Ward Richie Press, 1975.

*The Immigrants,* Houghton (Boston), 1977, Hodder & Stoughton (London), 1978.

*The Art of Zen Meditation,* Peace Press (Culver City, CA), 1977.

*The Second Generation,* Houghton, 1978, Hodder & Stoughton, 1979.

*The Establishment,* Houghton, 1979, Hodder & Stoughton, 1979.

*The Legacy,* Houghton, 1980.

*The Magic Door* (juvenile), Avon (New York City), 1980.

*Max,* Houghton, 1982.

*The Outsider,* Houghton, 1984.

*The Immigrant's Daughter,* Houghton, 1985.

*The Dinner Party,* Houghton, 1987.

*The Call of Fife and Drum: Three Novels of the Revolution* (contains *The Unvanquished, Conceived in Liberty,* and *The Proud and the Free*), Citadel, 1987.

*The Pledge,* Houghton, 1988.

*The Confession of Joe Cullen,* Houghton, 1989.

*Being Red: A Memoir,* Houghton, 1990.

*The Trial of Abigail Goodman: A Novel,* Crown, 1993.

*War and Peace: Observations on Our Times,* M. E. Sharpe, 1993.

*Seven Days in June: A Novel of the American Revolution,* Carol (Secaucus, NJ), 1994.

*The Bridge Builder's Story,* M. E. Sharpe, 1995.

*An Independent Woman,* Harcourt Brace and Co. (New York City), 1997.

*Redemption,* Harcourt Brace and Co. (New York City), 1999.

Author of weekly column, *New York Observer,* 1989-92; also columnist for *Greenwich Time* and *Stamford Advocate.*

PLAYS

*The Hammer,* produced in New York, 1950.

*Thirty Pieces of Silver* (produced in Melbourne, 1951), Blue Heron, 1954.

*George Washington and the Water Witch,* Bodley Head (London), 1956.

*The Crossing,* produced in Dallas, TX, 1962.

*The Hill* (screenplay), Doubleday, 1964.

*David and Paula,* produced in New York City at American Jewish Theater, November 20, 1982.

*Citizen Tom Paine: A Play in Two Acts* (produced in Williamstown, MA, then in Washington, DC, at the John F. Kennedy Center for the Performing Arts, 1987), Houghton, 1986.

*The Novelist* (produced in Williamstown, MA, then Mamaroneck, NY, 1991), published as *The Novelist: A Romantic Portrait of Jane Austen,* Samuel French (New York City), 1992.

Also author of *The Hessian,* 1971. Also wrote episode "The Ambassador," *Benjamin Franklin,* CBS, 1974, as well as for the television series *How the West Was Won,* ABC, 1978-79.

NOVELS; UNDER PSEUDONYM E. V. CUNNINGHAM

*Sylvia,* Doubleday, 1960, published under name Howard Fast, Carol, 1992.

*Phyllis,* Doubleday, 1962.

*Alice,* Doubleday, 1963.

*Shirley,* Doubleday, 1963.

*Lydia,* Doubleday, 1964.

*Penelope,* Doubleday, 1965.

*Helen,* Doubleday, 1966.

*Margie,* Morrow, 1966.

*Sally,* Morrow, 1967, published under name Howard Fast, Chivers, 1994.

*Samantha,* Morrow, 1967.

*Cynthia,* Morrow, 1968.

*The Assassin Who Gave Up His Gun,* Morrow, 1969.

*Millie,* Morrow, 1973.

*The Case of the One-Penny Orange,* Holt (New York City), 1977.

*The Case of the Russian Diplomat,* Holt, 1978.

*The Case of the Poisoned Eclairs,* Holt, 1979.

*The Case of the Sliding Pool,* Delacorte (New York City), 1981.

*The Case of the Kidnapped Angel,* Delacorte, 1982.

*The Case of the Angry Actress,* Delacorte, 1984.

*The Case of the Murdered Mackenzie,* Delacorte, 1984.

*The Wabash Factor,* Doubleday, 1986.

NOVELS; UNDER PSEUDONYM WALTER ERICSON

*Fallen Angel,* Little, Brown, 1951.

AUTHOR OF INTRODUCTION

Isabella Leitner and Irving A. Leitner, *Saving the Fragments: From Auschwitz to New York,* New American Library, 1985.

Arthur J. Sabin, *Red Scare in Court: New York versus the International Workers Order,* University of Pennsylvania Press, 1993.

*The Sculpture of Bette Fast,* M. E. Sharpe, 1995.

*ADAPTATIONS:* The film *Rachel and the Stranger,* RKO Radio Pictures, 1948, was based on the novels *Rachel* and *Neighbor Sam; Spartacus* was filmed in 1960 by Universal Pictures, directed by Stanley Kubrick and Anthony Mann, starring Kirk Douglas, Laurence Olivier, Tony Curtis, Jean Simmons, Charles Laughton, and Peter Ustinov; other works by Fast have been adapted to film, including *Man in the Middle,* Twentieth Century-Fox, 1964, based on his novel *The Winston Affair, Mirage,* Universal, 1965, based the novel *Fallen Angel* written under the pseudonym Walter Ericson, *Sylvia,* Paramount, 1965, based on the novel of the same title, *Penelope,* Metro-Goldwyn-Mayer, 1966, based on the novel of the same title written under the pseudonym E. V. Cunningham, and *Jigsaw,* Universal, 1968, based on the screenplay for *Mirage* which was based on Fast's novel *Fallen Angel;* writings by Fast have also been adapted for television, including *The Face of Fear,* CBS, 1971, based on the novel *Sally* written under the pseudonym E. V. Cunningham, *What's a Nice Girl Like You . . .?,* ABC, 1971, based on his novel *Shirley, 21 Hours at Munich,* ABC, 1976, based on a story by Fast, *The Immigrants,* syndicated, 1978, was based on his novel of the same title, *Freedom Road,* NBC, 1979, based on his novel of the same title, *April Morning,* broadcast as a *Hallmark Hall of Fame* movie, CBS, 1988, based on the novel of the same title, and *The Crossing,* Arts and Entertainment, 2000, based his novel of the same name; *The Crossing* was recorded on cassette, narrated by Norman Dietz, Recorded Books, 1988; and *The Immigrant's Daughter* was recorded on cassette, narrated by Sandra Burr, Brilliance Corporation, 1991.

*SIDELIGHTS:* Howard Fast has published novels, plays, screenplays, stories, historical fiction, and biographies in a career that dates from the early days of the Great Depression. Fast's works have been translated into some eighty-two languages and have sold millions of copies worldwide; some observers feel that he may be the most widely read writer of the twentieth century. *Los Angeles Times* contributor Elaine Kendall writes: "For half a century, Fast's novels, histories and biographies have appeared at frequent intervals, a moveable feast with a distinct political flavor." *Washington Post* correspondent Joseph McLellan finds Fast's work "easy to read and relatively nourishing," adding that the author "demands little of the reader, beyond a willingness to keep turning the pages, and he supplies enough activity and suspense to make this exercise worthwhile."

The grandson of Ukrainian immigrants and son of a British mother, Fast was raised in New York City. His family struggled to make ends meet, so Fast went to work as a teen and found time to indulge his passion-writing-in his spare moments. His first published novel, *Two Valleys,* was released in 1933 when he was only eighteen. Thereafter Fast began writing full time, and within a decade he had earned a considerable reputation as a historical novelist with his realistic tales of American frontier life.

Fast found himself drawn to the downtrodden peoples in America's history—the Cheyenne Indians and their tragic attempt to regain their homeland (*The Last Frontier*), the starving soldiers at Valley Forge (*Conceived in Liberty: A Novel of Valley Forge*), and black Americans trying to survive the Reconstruction era in the South (*Freedom Road*). In *Publishers Weekly,* John F. Baker calls these works "books on which a whole generation of radicals was brought up." A *Christian Science Monitor* contributor likewise notes: "Human nature rather than history is Howard Fast's field. In presenting these harassed human beings without any heroics he makes us all the more respectful of the price paid for American liberty." *Freedom Road* in particular was praised by the nation's black leaders for its depiction of one race's struggle for liberation; the book became a bestseller and won the Schomberg Award for Race Relations in 1944.

During the Second World War, Fast worked as a correspondent for several periodicals and for the Office of War Information. After the conflict ended he found himself at odds with the Cold War mentality developing in the United States. At the time Fast was a member of the Communist Party and a contributor of time and money to a number of anti-fascist causes. His writing during the period addressed such issues as the abuse of power, the suppression of labor unions, and communism as the basis for a utopian future. Works such as *Clarkton, My Glorious Brothers,* and *The Proud and the Free* were widely translated behind the Iron Curtain and earned Fast the International Peace Prize in 1954.

Baker notes that Fast's political views "made him for a time in the 1950s a pariah of the publishing world." The author was jailed for three months on a contempt of Congress charge for refusing to testify about his political activities. Worse, he found himself blacklisted to such an extent that no publishing house would accept his manuscripts. Fast's persecution seemed ironic to some observers, because in the historical and biographical novels he had already published—like *Conceived in Liberty: A Novel of Valley Forge* and *The Unvanquished*—as well as in his work for the Office of War Information, Fast emphasized the importance of freedom and illuminated the heroic acts that had built American society. He made the relatively unknown or forgotten history of the United States accessible to millions of Americans in books like *The Last Frontier,* and as a correspondent for the radio program that would become the Voice of America, he was entrusted with the job of assuring millions of foreigners of the country's greatness and benevolence during World War II. Yet even after Fast learned of Stalin's atrocities, which convinced him that he had been betrayed by the Communist Party and caused him to break his ties with it, he did not regret the decision he had made in 1944. His experience as the target of political persecution evoked some of his best and most popular works. It also led Fast to establish his own publishing house, the Blue Heron Press.

Fast published *Spartacus* under the Blue Heron imprint in 1951. A fictional account of a slave revolt in ancient Rome, *Spartacus* became a bestseller after it was made into a feature film in 1960, starring Kirk Douglas, Sir Laurence Olivier, and Tony Curtis. By that time Fast had grown disenchanted with the Communist Party and had formally renounced his ties to it in 1956. In a discussion of Fast's fiction from 1944 through 1959, *Nation* correspondent Stanley Meisler contends that the "older writings must not be ignored. They document a unique political record, a depressing American waste. They describe a man who distorted his vision of America to fit a vision of communism, and then lost both."

Fast published five books chronicling the fictional Lavette family, beginning with *The Immigrants* in 1977. *The Immigrant's Daughter* (1995), relates the story of

Barbara Lavette, Dan Lavette's daughter, and her political aspirations. Denise Gess in the *New York Times Book Review* calls *The Immigrant's Daughter* "satisfying, old-fashioned story-telling" despite finding the novel occasionally "soap-operatic and uneven." Barbara Conaty, reviewing the novel in *Library Journal,* calls Fast a "smooth and assured writer." A reviewer for *Publishers Weekly* concurs, commenting that "smoothly written, fast-paced, alive with plots and subplots, the story reads easily." The Barbara Lavette saga ended with the publication of *An Independent Woman* in 1997.

The prolific Fast published another politically charged novel in 1989, with *The Confession of Joe Cullen.* Focusing on U.S. military involvement in Central America, *The Confession of Joe Cullen* is the story of a C.I.A. pilot who confesses to New York City police that, among other things, he murdered a priest in Honduras, and has been smuggling cocaine into the United States. Arguing that the conspiracy theory that implicates the federal government in drug trafficking and gun running has never been proved, Morton Kondracke in the *New York Times Book Review* has reservations about the "political propaganda" involved in *The Confession of Joe Cullen.* Robert H. Donahugh, however, highly recommends the novel in *Library Journal,* calling it "unexpected and welcome," and lauding both the "fast-moving" storyline and the philosophical probing into Catholicism. Denise Perry Donavin, in *Booklist,* concurs, finding the politics suiting the characters "without lessening the pace of a powerful tale."

Fast focuses on another controversial subject, the issue of abortion, in his 1993 novel *The Trial of Abigail Goodman.* As a *Publishers Weekly* critic notes, Fast views America's attitude toward abortion as "parochial" and is sympathetic to his protagonist, a college professor who has an abortion during the third trimester in a southern state with a retroactive law forbidding such acts. Critical reaction to the novel was mixed. Ray Olson in *Booklist* argues that "every anti-abortion character" is stereotyped, and that Fast "undermines . . . any pretensions to evenhandedness," calling the novel "an execrable work." The *Publishers Weekly* critic, on the other hand, finds *The Trial of Abigail Goodman* "electrifying" and calls Fast "a master of courtroom pyrotechnics." Many critics, including Susan Dooley in the *Washington Post,* view the novel as too polemical, failing to flesh out the characters and the story. Dooley argues that Fast "has not really written a novel; his book is a tract for a cause, and like other similar endeavors, it concentrates more on making converts than creating characters." A reviewer for *Armchair Detective* con-

curs, concluding that the novel would have been much stronger if "there were some real sincerity and some well-expressed arguments from the antagonists." A *Rapport* reviewer agrees as well, and comments: "Fast is more than capable of compelling character studies. There's a kernel of a powerful trial novel here, but this prestigious writer chooses not to flesh it out."

Fast returned to the topic of the American Revolution in his 1994 novel *Seven Days in June: A Novel of the American Revolution.* A *Publishers Weekly* critic summarizes: "Fictionalizing the experiences of British commanders, loyalists to the crown and a motley collection of American revolutionaries, Fast . . . fashions this dramatic look at a week of profound tension that will erupt [into] the battle of Bunker Hill." Some critics see *Seven Days in June* as inferior to Fast's *April Morning,* considered by some to be a minor masterpiece. Charles Michaud in *Library Journal* finds that *Seven Days* "is very readable pop history, but as a novel it is not as involving as . . . April Morning." A *Kirkus Reviews* critic faults the novel for repetitiveness and a disproportionate amount of focus on the sexual exploits of the British commanders, concluding that *Seven Days* "has a slipshod, slapdash feel, cluttered with hurried, lazy characterizations." The critic for *Publishers Weekly,* however, argues that the novel "ekes genuine suspense" and lauds Fast's "accomplished storytelling."

*The Bridge Builder's Story* tells of Scott Waring and his young bride, Martha, who honeymoon in Europe during the Nazi era and find themselves persecuted by Hitler's thuggish minions. After Martha is killed by the Gestapo, Scott makes his way to New York, where his ensuing sessions with a psychiatrist provide much of the narrative. While Albert Wilheim, writing in *Library Journal,* finds this novel to perhaps "test the limits of credibility," he praises Fast's "skillful narration." And Alice Joyce, in *Booklist,* opines that in *The Bridge Builder's Story* "Fast's remarkable prowess for storytelling" results in a "riveting tale, sure to satisfy readers."

Fast's time as a Communist in Cold War America provided him with an extraordinary story to share in his autobiographical works, including *Being Red: A Memoir.* Charles C. Nash of *Library Journal* calls *Being Red* "indispensable to the . . . literature on America's terrifying postwar Red Scare." Fast explained to Jean W. Ross in an interview for *Contemporary Authors:* "There is no way to imagine war or to imagine jail or to imagine being a father or a mother. These things can only be understood if you live through them. Maybe that's a price that a writer should pay." Fast tells Ken Gross in *People Weekly* that he wrote the book with the inspiration of his son, Jonathan, who wanted to show it to his own children. Rhoda Koenig of *New York* magazine remarks that Fast's story is "a lively and gripping one," and that he "brings alive the days of parochial-school children carrying signs that read 'KILL A COMMIE FOR CHRIST'."

With a critical eye, Ronald Radosh asserts in *Commentary* that *Being Red* contains information and perspectives that contradict portions of Fast's 1957 memoir, *The Naked God: The Writer and the Communist Party.* In Radosh's opinion, *Being Red* was the author's attempt to "rehabilitate" the Communist Party he had admonished in *The Naked God.* "Now, nearly thirty-five years later, it almost sounds as though Fast wants to end his days winning back the admiration of those unreconstructed Communists," Radosh claims, even calling them "some of the noblest human beings I have ever known."

Fast has also published a number of detective novels under the pseudonym E. V. Cunningham, for which he received a Prix de la Policia Award. Many of these feature a fictional Japanese-American detective named Masao Masuto who works with the Beverly Hills Police Department. Fast tells *Publishers Weekly,* "Critics can't stand my mainline books, maybe because they sell so well, [but] they love Cunningham. Even the *New Yorker* has reviewed him, and they've never reviewed me." In the *New York Times Book Review,* Newgate Callendar calls detective Masuto "a well-conceived character whose further exploits should gain him a wide audience." *Toronto Globe and Mail* contributor Derrick Murdoch also finds Masuto "a welcome addition to the lighter side of crime fiction." "Functional and efficient, Fast's prose is a machine in which plot and ideals mesh, turn and clash," Kendall concludes. "The reader is constantly being instructed, but the manner is so disarming and the hectic activity so absorbing that the didacticism seldom intrudes upon the entertainment."

Fast's voice has interpreted America's past and present and helped shape its reputation at home and abroad. One of his own favorites among his novels, *April Morning,* has been standard reading about the American Revolution in public schools for generations, the film *Spartacus* has become a popular classic, and *Being Red* offers an account of American history that Americans may never want to forget, whether or not they agree with Fast's perspectives. As Victor Howes comments in *Christian Science Monitor,* if Howard Fast "is a chronicler of some of mankind's most glorious mo-

ments, he is also a register of some of our more senseless deeds."

*AUTOBIOGRAPHICAL ESSAY:*

Fast contributed the following essay to *CA:*

My father, Barney Fast, was a workingman all of his life. He was born in 1869 in the town of Fastov in the Ukraine and was brought to the United States in 1878, aged nine, by his older brother, Edward. Immigration shortened Fastov to Fast, gave it to him as a last name, and so it remained.

In 1897, working in a tin factory in Whitestone, Long Island, my father made friends with a young man named Daniel Miller. Miller's family had moved from Lithuania to London a generation before, and Daniel, one of a family of five sons and two daughters, had made his way to America alone. When the war with Spain began, Barney and Dan and a few other Jewish boys working at the tin factory organized a regiment to fight in Cuba and thereby revenge themselves for the expulsion of Jews from Spain in 1492. They persuaded enough non-Jews to join up to make a regiment of three hundred men, and one of the bookkeepers at the plant, a man in his middle sixties named Charlie Hensen, who claimed to have been a cavalry officer during the Civil War, offered to train the three hundred as a cavalry regiment. That was not as loony a proposition as it sounds, for the war in Cuba was disorganized, with all sorts of citizens getting into the act—as witness Theodore Roosevelt and his Rough Riders.

Hensen collected twenty-five percent of each man's pay, with which he proposed to buy uniforms, sabers, and horses. But after a few months, Hensen and the money disappeared, and Barney never did get to Cuba. He did, however, become bosom pals with Danny Miller, and Danny showed Barney a picture of his beautiful sister. My father fell in love with the picture, began to correspond with Ida Miller, saved his money, sent her a steamship ticket for passage to America, and in due time married her. In 1904 their first child, Rena, was born, and in 1906 they had a son named Arthur, a sensitive, beautiful boy that I know only from photographs. He died of diphtheria six years later. My brother Jerome was born in March of 1913, and I came in November of the following year. My mother's last child, Julius, was born in 1919. My mother died of pernicious anemia in the spring of 1923, when I was eight-and-a-half years old.

We were always poor, but while my mother lived, we children never realized that we were poor. My father, at the age of fourteen, had been an ironworker in the open-shed furnaces on the East River below Fourteenth Street. There the wrought iron that festooned the city was hammered into shape at open forges. As a kid, Barney had run for beer for the big, heavy-muscled men who hammered out the iron at the blazing forges, and there was nothing else he wanted to do. But the iron sheds disappeared as fashions in building changed, and Barney went to work as a gripper man on one of the last cable cars in the city. From there to the tin factory and finally to being a cutter in a dress factory. He never earned more than forty dollars a week during my mother's lifetime, yet with this forty dollars my mother made do. She was a wise woman, and if a wretched tenement was less than her dream of America, she would not surrender. She scrubbed and sewed and knitted. She made all of the clothes for all of her children, cutting little suits out of velvet and fine wools and silks; she cooked and cleaned with a vengeance, and to me she seemed a sort of princess, with her stories of London and Kew and Kensington Gardens and the excitement and tumult of Petticoat Lane and Covent Garden. Memories of this beautiful lady, whose speech was so different from the speech of others around me, were wiped out in the moment of her death. I remember my father coming into the tiny bedroom where I slept with Jerome, waking us gently, and saying, "Momma died last night." Although I was very young, I must have known what death meant—my mother had been sick for over a year—for at that moment my mind had to choose between memory and madness, and forgetfulness and sanity. My mind chose forgetfulness so that I could remain sane. The process is not uncommon and is called infantile amnesia; it was not until years later that my memories of my mother began to return.

Because my memories of my mother were wiped out in a flash, the dark-haired woman who lay in the open coffin in our tiny living room—packed with family and curious neighbors—was strange to me. I wept dutifully. My mother's brother Gerry, a young physician and the only solvent member of the family, pressed a silver dollar into my hand, and it quieted my tears. I had never seen anything like it before.

All the dismal business of a death in poverty, of the tragedy of my poor father left with three small children and a nineteen-year-old girl who had been coddled and treasured by her mother to the point of becoming a spoiled child, shattered by her mother's death, does remain in my memory. For a few months after my mother's death, my sister tried to keep the family together, but more and more she saw herself trapped, doomed to spinsterhood by the responsibility of caring for three little boys. So acute was her fear that she plunged into marriage, compounding the tragedy and leaving my bewildered father to take care of the three small children. Jerome and I hated the man she married. His only virtue in our eyes was that he was British, somehow distantly related to us by marriage, but he was insensitive and stupid.

I loved my sister—and did so to the day of her death—but my father was shattered by her departure. My maternal grandmother—I never saw my father's parents—took my brother Julius to live with her in Long Island. He was only four years old, and there was no way my father could take care of him. Indeed, there was no way my father could take care of Jerome and me.

My father was a dear and gentle man, a gentleman in every sense of the word, but his own mother had died when he was seven years old, and the death of his wife threw him into a deep depression. I know that several women loved him, but he never married again. If he had, possibly my life would have been different, but as it was, my brother and I were left from morning to night on our own, with no one to turn to, no one to care for or feed us—with a father who was depressed and disoriented and often did not come home until well past midnight, plunging Jerome and me into periods of terror that were to be repeated again and again.

The years that followed provided an experience in poverty and misery that was burned into my soul. In time, nothing much changed in the scheme of poverty; what did change was my ability to face and alter circumstances. I ceased to be wholly a victim. The place where we lived was a wretched slum apartment, made lovely by the wit and skill and determination of my mother; but after her death and the departure of my sister, the place simply disintegrated. Jerome and I, two small boys essentially on our own, had to be mother and father and brother to each other. Jerome cared for me; to the best of my ability, I cared for him. My father disappeared each morning at 8 A.M. and rarely did he return until after midnight; periodically, he was out of work. We made some efforts to keep the apartment clean, but that's not within the scope of small boys. The apartment became dirty; the cheap furniture began to come apart; trash accumulated. In his depression, my father seemed unaware of what was happening. We had holes in our clothes, our shoes were coming apart, and Pop made only an occasional effort to rectify things.

In actuality, we had no childhood; it slipped away. When I was ten and Jerome was eleven, we decided to take things in hand. My brother was like a rock, and without him I surely would have perished. We needed money, and Jerome had heard somewhere that you could make money delivering newspapers, in particular the *Bronx Home News,* which existed entirely on home delivery with a system worked out by a man named Keneally. I don't recall his first name, and there's no way I can find it, but I remember him with great fondness. He had an office in Washington Heights, and one day after school, Jerry and I made our way there and presented ourselves to Mr. Keneally, a tall, lean, long-faced man.

I can imagine how we appeared to him, two ragged kids with long, shaggy hair, holes in our shoes, holes in our stockings. "We can do it!" Jerry pleaded, and Keneally said okay, he'd give us a chance, even though we were too young to do a proper route. But one of his boys had left, and maybe the two of us together could do one route. He was very kind. He was of the generation of Irish who had fought their way up from the starkest poverty, and he understood. We were given a book of some ninety customers who took daily papers, including Saturday and Sunday, and each week we had to collect twelve cents from each customer. We paid a straight price for our bundle, and it amounted to about two out of every twelve cents—a price we paid whether we were able to collect or not.

So my working life began, at age ten, and from then until I was twenty-two years old I had one job or another: for three years delivering the *Bronx Home News,* then working for a cigarmaker on Avenue B on the East Side, then a hatmaker on West Thirty-eighth Street, then making deliveries and cleaning at an uptown butcher shop, and then at the 115th Street branch of the New York Public Library. When I left the library, I worked for a year in a dress factory, first as a shipping clerk and then as a presser—at least a presser in training. Meanwhile, I finished grade school, went to high school, got a scholarship to the National Academy of Design, and worked there for a year. I gave it up when, at the age of seventeen, I sold my first short story.

The first toll poverty takes is human dignity, and no family in abject poverty lives like the Crachits in Charles Dickens's *A Christmas Carol.* He was faulted on that, and he wrote *The Chimes* to show the other side of the coin, but he left out the sense that every poverty-stricken family has of a world put together wrong. It was particularly evident in New York, where the poor lived cheek by jowl with the rich. The rich were always evident, the people I so catalogued then, those who lived on Riverside Drive and Fort Washington Avenue. They were middle-class people, but we had nothing,

and to us they were wealthy in the only way we knew wealth. In those days of the 1920s, there was no safety net beneath the poor, no welfare, no churches handing out free dinners. Survival in poverty was your own affair. I have tried to explain this to people who expressed indignant wonder at the fact that I joined the Communist party. The absence of unemployment insurance is educational in a way that nothing else is.

One of the main reasons, perhaps, for our survival as a family unit was the place where we lived. The anti-Semitism that prevailed was maniacal; there is no other way to describe it. And this crazed Christian sickness forced Jerry and me at first, then Julius with us, into a closed, defensive unit. Aside from my uncle's family in the summer, no relative held out a hand to us. Some of them were well-to-do; all of them lived comfortably, but my father's pride forbade his asking for help, and none was offered. They were a lousy crew, and I'll say no more about them.

We didn't complain, Jerry and I, and in a sense the challenge of keeping the family alive was a game we played. We lived in two worlds, the wretched world of reality and the marvelous, endlessly exciting world of the books we read. In those days, bread, milk, and cheese were delivered very early in the morning to the doors of the prosperous. When we had no food, we'd be up at six in the morning to find bread and milk and cheese that would keep us alive. We did not consider it stealing; we never questioned our right to remain alive. Once, we appropriated—a better word—an entire stalk of bananas from a truck. Some we kept for ourselves, eating bananas until we could not face another. The rest we sold for a nickel a hand. When we were utterly penniless and my father was unemployed, we scoured the neighborhood for milk bottles, a nickel for each returned. We knew the back way into every house in the area; we knew the rooftops.

When I turned fourteen, in 1928, I reached an age of maturity, the difference from childhood being, to my mind, the difference between being a victim without recourse and a sort of adult with recourse. My brother and I had arrived at an age where we could change things. Filth was no longer a permanent part of our existence; it could be dealt with and done away with. We were working and Barney was working, making fifty dollars a week, the most he had ever earned per week in all his life. Julius was living with us now, aged nine years old, and both Jerry and I felt a sense of responsibility toward him. We informed Barney that we were going to move out of that miserable slum apartment, and when he put up a storm of protest—he was incapable of altering his living place—we said that we'd move without him. Jerry and I were both working for the New York Public Library at that point, paid thirty cents an hour, a sum that was reduced to twenty-five cents an hour after the great stock market crash; and with extra time on Wednesday and Saturday, I took home nine dollars a week and Jerry eleven. Twenty dollars was not to be sneezed at—indeed, in our world it was a princely sum—and it bought us food and clothes. With Barney's fifty dollars added to our twenty, there was an income of seventy dollars a week, unimaginable riches. It did not last very long, but long enough to get us out of 159th Street and up to Inwood at the northern tip of Manhattan.

I began to think. From the time when the street became my life, I had plotted, schemed, maneuvered, manipulated, cozened, and, when the need arose, pleaded; and these are all mental activities, but by thinking I mean putting one fact against another and trying to measure the result. This kind of thinking is a very special thing.

The winter of 1929-1930 I worked at the public library in lower Harlem, at 203 West 115th Street. I was poorly paid—down to twenty-five cents an hour that winter—but I loved working in the library. The walls of books gave me a sense of history, of order, of meaning in this strange world, and I could easily pick up two, three, sometimes four hours of overtime in a week. I worked from four to nine, closing time, for five days and on Saturday from nine to one. Since we did checking and arranging on Saturdays, I could pick up the overtime there, and I could always slip down to the closed reference shelves in the basement to get my homework done. My wages averaged between seven and eight dollars a week, but in the shattered prices of deflation, that was decent money. The important thing was the world of books around me. I read everything without discrimination—psychology, astronomy, physics, history, and more history—and some of it I understood and some of it I didn't.

And I began to think.

The subway ride I took to my home was a nickel. At the uptown end of the subway, where I left the train, a man in a blue serge suit, jacket and vest and tie—a man of some fifty years—stood out on the street and sold apples for a nickel each. Every night on my way home I bought an apple, a large, shiny Washington State Delicious apple. I bought the apple because I was hungry, because the man touched something very deep inside of me, and because I had begun to think. This went on for several weeks. I was a kid with a job; he was a ma-

ture man, a businessman or an accountant or something of the sort to my guess. I thought of my father. Barney was a workingman; this was a middle-class educated man, and one night he stopped me.

"Hey, kid," he said, "what's your name?"

"Howard Fast."

"That's an odd name," he said. "Do they call you a fast worker?"

I stared at him without answering, and then I blurted out, "Do you have kids, mister?"

Now he stared at me, and then he began to cry. Tears—real tears. I don't know whether I had ever seen a grown man cry, and it remains in my memory as one of the most woeful moments of my life.

I grabbed my apple, pressed a nickel into his hand, and ran. I ran all the way home. He was gone the next day, and I never saw him again. There are theories that the level of consciousness varies from time to time and that most of our lives are lived at a very low level of consciousness, almost like a walking sleep. Memory is sharpest when it recalls the highest moments of consciousness; I believe this, and that moment scared my mind.

Other things were working on my personal mental schematic. I had seen my father on strike; I had seen him locked out; I had seen his head bloodied on a picket line. I had watched the economy of my own country collapse; I had seen the packing-crate villages grow on the riverfront. I did not have to be instructed about poverty or hunger; I had lived them both. I had fought and been beaten innumerable times, not because of my religion—Barney never imposed religion on us, for which I am eternally grateful—but because I was Jewish, and all of it worked together to create in my mind a simple plea, that somewhere, somehow, there was in this world an explanation that made sense.

That was my way. I never faulted the other ways. I knew kids who were arrested, who turned into thieves or ran with the gangs—it was the time of Prohibition—and I understood this, and often enough I said to myself, "There but for the grace of God goes Howard Fast." I was lucky. One of the kids ended up in the electric chair. Oh, I was damned lucky.

Jerry found a copy of *The Iron Heel* by Jack London. At that time, Jack London stood first among our literary heroes. Today, I find his prose flowery and too mannered, but our taste was less demanding then, and we read and reread every book of his on the library shelves—except for *The Iron Heel.* We never could find a copy in the library. The head librarian at 115th Street was a Mrs. Lindsay, a very dignified and tall woman, a distant relative I think of the man who was to become our mayor. I got up the courage to ask her why we didn't have *The Iron Heel,* and she informed me that it was considered a Bolshevik book. She had never read it, and she hoped I was not interested in such things.

How could I not be interested? *Bolshevik* was a wild word at that time; it was not so long before that the Bolsheviks had burst into history. You couldn't pick up a copy of the *Daily News,* the *Mirror,* or the *Graphic* without having the infamies of the Bolsheviks scream at you from the front page. The word, Russian for "majority," has gone out of use today, but then it was the number one synonym for evil.

*The Iron Heel* was my first real contact with socialism; the book was passed around among the kids I knew at high school. If I had lived on the Lower East Side or in one of Brooklyn's immigrant enclaves, I would have had a taste of socialism with my mother's milk, but in this solidly Irish-Italian block there was no hint of it, and at that time George Washington High School was middle-class, filled with well-dressed boys and girls who had allowances and money for a decent lunch in the school cafeteria. Against this background, *The Iron Heel* had a tremendous effect on me. London anticipated fascism as no writer of the time did; indeed no historian or social scientist of the time had even an inkling of the blueprint Jack London laid out, which came into being a few decades after his death. In it, he drew the struggle against fascism by an underground socialist movement, and he did it so convincingly that we were not quite sure that what he wrote of had not already happened.

It was the beginning of my trying to understand why society was structured as I saw it to be structured. Communist bashing became so pervasive in the 1960s and 1970s that few people even attempted to understand or inquire into the forces that produced socialist thinking and, out of it, the Communist movement.

And then, one day, arranging books in the library, I came upon Shaw's *The Intelligent Woman's Guide to Socialism and Capitalism,* and the die was cast.

I think I read somewhere that Shaw had so named his book to excite the curiosity of men, and I had also heard

that he believed women to be more intelligent than men—a belief I share. In any case, *The Intelligent Woman's Guide to Socialism and Capitalism* is the clearest exposition of the subject I know of. I was then sixteen, and the book provided me with a new way of thinking about poverty, inequality, and injustice. Shaw had opened an enormous Pandora's box, and never in my lifetime would I be able to close it. The book also set me off in a new direction in my reading, and in quick succession I read Thorstein Veblen's *The Theory of the Leisure Class,* Bellamy's *Looking Backward,* and Engels's *The Origin of the Family.* My mind exploded with ideas. I hurt dear Hallie Jamison, my wonderful high school English teacher, by engaging her in a discussion of whether any nation involved in World War One had been fighting a just war—her beloved having died on the western front—and I made a general nuisance of myself because of my obsession for knowing everything there was to know. In his novel *Martin Eden,* Jack London had stated unequivocally that a writer must have a total knowledge of science. I believed him and set out to gain just that, even reading a bit of Herbert Spencer—recommended by London—in the process. Still in high school, I found psychology, read the Watsonians and rejected them, read the Gestalt theorists and liked them a little better, read the Binet-Simon book on testing, gave intelligence tests to everyone I could corner, and thereby washed myself out of the process, for when it came time for me to be tested at school, I explained that I knew the tests forward and backward. Result—I never knew my own IQ and took comfort in that.

I decided to become a writer. There was no problem in making this decision. It was the only way of life I ever considered, from as far back as my memory goes. I decided to be a writer, to write stories and books, and to illustrate them myself. I had no desire to become an easel painter—only to be able to illustrate what I wrote in the manner of Howard Pyle and N. C. Wyeth. They were my idols; the marvelous illustrations they did for books and magazines constituted my approach to art.

We had pulled the family together and out of the wretched morass of poverty and misery. Jerry and I were earning enough to keep the family going on a decent basis even when Barney was out of work. You didn't need much to get by in the early thirties. Jerry rooted jobs out of everywhere and nowhere, and when I graduated from high school I was earning nine dollars a week as a page at the 115th Street library. The Morris Plan gave small loans on the strength of co-workers, without collateral. Their interest amounted to twenty-seven percent, but we somehow got Jerry through his first year of college and paid back the loan. I applied to both Cooper Union and the National Academy, then a sprawl of old-fashioned studio buildings at 110th Street, just east of the Cathedral of St. John the Divine. The waiting list at Cooper Union was years in length; the National Academy accepted me for immediate entrance.

I enrolled at the National Academy. By God, I had done it. I was seventeen years old, and I was alive and healthy, when by all the odds I should have been either dead or hopelessly weak and sick. With my brothers and my father, I had a clean, proper home, a bed without bedbugs—as a kid they had made my life in bed a nightmare—books of my own, shoes without holes, a warm winter overcoat, and above all, I was a scholarship student at what was then the most prestigious art school in America. And as yet, I had done no time in jail, and that was not the least of my accomplishments, for I was not a quiet or contemplative kid, but one of those irritating, impossible, doubting, questioning mavericks, full of anger and invention and wild notions, accepting nothing, driving my peers to bitter arguments and driving my elders to annoyance, rage, and despair. I probably had some good points as well.

And I was innocent—not simply unsophisticated, but innocent in the sense that I was free of hate. That applied to both of my brothers too; we were without hate. As far as sophistication was concerned, that was a quality you had to pick up along the way.

I had become a writer and I would remain a writer. The question of ever being anything else never entered my mind; there was only one thing I could be in this life and that was what I was. Each morning I arose at six and wrote. Two hours later, I left for the National Academy, where I practiced cast and figure drawing in the severe and tedious classical manner. I completed a story every few days and as promptly dispatched it to one magazine or another. It's hard to recall and believe in my own naivete, for all those first stories were handwritten in ink, and my altered handwriting—I was left-handed—was not easily read. After sending out about a dozen stories, I happened to mention to one of the librarians what I was doing, and to my dismay she informed me that no magazine would bother to read a handwritten story. Either I typed out my stories or forgot the whole matter.

We had a family discussion. After all, since I read each story aloud to my brothers once it was done, they had a sort of vested interest, and it was agreed that we would put out $1.75 to rent a typewriter for a month.

I had to learn to use it, and while I made a few attempts at touch typing, I soon gave that up and settled into the two-finger method, which I continue to use. I kept the typewriter for a second and then a third month, and then, incredibly, I sold a story.

Looking back, I find it astonishing; at the time, I felt it to be a miracle. It was not that I had no expectations of selling stories—I was supremely confident that one day I would—but it was a date in the indefinite future, and here, miracle of miracles, it had happened. The story was titled "Wrath of the Purple," and the purchaser, for thirty-seven dollars in honest American money, was *Amazing Stories* magazine, the first of the science-fiction magazines.

In 1931, thirty-seven dollars was a substantial sum of money—at least at my level of society. I was still working at the library, going there directly from the academy, but the best I could do at the library, even with all the overtime I could squeeze out of the job, was nine dollars a week, and here one story had brought me more than a month's pay. Now that I had reached my full height of five feet, ten-and-one-half inches, my work at the library changed. Rather than rearranging books, putting returned books back on the shelves, and seeing that all the reference numbers read in proper sequence, I was put to the business of tracking down overdue books, going to the apartments of the people who had borrowed them, and reclaiming them—and if possible collecting the fines. The fine, I recall, was two cents per day per book.

I wrote my first novel when I was sixteen. I had never heard of anyone having a novel published at sixteen, but I said to myself, "Why not a first time?" I finished it, read it through, and decided that it was so bad the best thing I could do with it was consign it to the trash can. The second novel dealt with my year at the academy. It was titled "To Be an Artist." I brought it by hand to three publishers; each one asked me to come and get it—without comment. I was not deterred. I sold a story to a pulp magazine, and it brought me forty dollars.

I wrote my heart out every morning, and I went to work for the hatmaker. As the months passed, I discovered something that I had suspected for many years but had been unable to come to grips with: that the most wonderful, beautiful, and desirable of God's creatures was called a woman. To a boy of seventeen, this phenomenon is shrouded in frustration and ineptitude. I fell passionately in love with a girl named Marjorie. The problem was that, what with working at a job, writing, trying to educate myself, and sharing in the housekeeping, cleaning and cooking, of our male menage, I had no time to deal with young love.

I learned about the bookstalls on lower Fourth Avenue (now Park Avenue South), hundreds of open stalls, thousands of books, and for forty cents I bought a battered copy of *Das Kapital* by one Karl Marx. Not too many years before, I had regarded books as things that existed only in the New York Public Library; now I was creating my own library, but as far as *Das Kapital* was concerned, I fought my way through two hundred pages or so and then surrendered. George Bernard Shaw did much better with explanation. *The Communist Manifesto,* which I bought for ten cents, a worn pamphlet, was full of brimstone and fire and much more to my taste. I fell in love with a girl named Thelma. I fell in love with a girl named Maxine.

When someone asks me how and why I became a Socialist and a Communist, the answer is always inadequate. Intellectuals deal with ideas and abstractions. Never having had enough education to become a proper intellectual, I have spent my life dealing with facts and events, and this journey has burned itself into my memory. I have tried to write these events as I experienced them, with no broader perspective than I had at the time and without giving them too much importance. I left home and spent a month wandering through the South, looking for work, seeing a land as different from New York City as night from day. I journeyed through a society in disintegration, saved from inner destruction by World War Two, still six years in the future. And through all this, I never whimpered or turned a thought against this land which I had come to love so, nor can I ever think of the South without recalling not the jails and the guns but the wonderful slow wagon ride through the Peedee Swamp, arguing the Civil War with the southern kids. But I had reached an age where the innocence, born not of faith but of intolerable poverty, was beginning to crumble and where I began to understand that society could be planned and function in another way, called socialism; and because I came to believe that the only serious socialist party in America was the Communist party, I was bitterly attacked and slandered for fifteen years of my life.

I went to work. I found work as a shipping clerk in a dress factory in the heart of the garment center, and I wrote, morning and evening, six, seven, eight hours a day. I had written three complete unpublished novels before I took off for the South. I wrote two more in the few months after I returned. Five novels—one a five-hundred-page opus. They are best unremembered. The sixth novel, which I called *Two Valleys,* found a publisher.

This first publisher was the old original Dial Press, and the man who accepted the book was the editor in chief of that distinguished publishing house, a gentleman by the name of Grenville Vernon. I received a one-hundred-dollar advance, and the book was sold to the British publishing house Michael Joseph. The fact that the author was not yet nineteen was made much of, and while the novel was no great work of art, it was a gentle and readable book, a love story set in Colonial times in the mountains of what is today West Virginia. The reviews were decent and kind, with many bows to my age, but sales were inconsequential because the owner of the company, Lincoln MacVeagh, had put the house up for sale. For all that, I was recognized as a bright new hope on the literary horizon. I was given a Bread Loaf Award, and I spent two weeks at that lovely spot in the Green Mountains eating marvelous food, learning the finer points in the use of knives and forks, watching the critic John Mason Brown and his colleagues drink more martinis than I had ever imagined human beings could consume and make sense, and falling moderately but romantically in love with Gladys Hasty Carroll, a very popular and beautiful writer of the time and about ten years older than I. I actually gathered the courage to tell her I loved her before the session finished, but that was as far as it went, and I never saw her again. She was very kind to me.

Suddenly everything dried up and I stopped writing. Months went by and I wrote nothing. I continued to work in the garment factory. I trundled trucks through the streets and packed cases and learned to use a pressing machine and a felling machine, and worked my way up to twelve and then fourteen dollars a week, and dated a beautiful girl who worked in a publishing house; we parted because beyond subway fare to work and back, a nickel each way, and fifteen cents more for lunch at the Automat, brown beans and coffee, I had nothing, not even a decent pair of pants. Jerry was in his third year of college—we managed that somehow— and Julius was in high school, and everybody worked, and our need to hold the family together, now that two of us were adults and my younger brother was pushing adulthood, was almost demonic. Barney could rarely get better than the lowest paid job, but we managed, with a kind of crazy pride that we took no welfare or outside help of any kind. Interestingly, my father, a loyal Democrat and for years a county commissioner who worshipped Al Smith, was always reminded by the local Democratic boss that if worse came to worst, the party would step in. I think of how many times he came around to check Pop's vote, have a shot of bootleg gin, and say to him, "You know, Barney, that the party will never let you or the kids go hungry." Well, there were times when we were hungry, but we never dunned the party, and Barney always rejected their annual turkey, with instructions that they give it to some poor family.

And then I went back to writing. Up each morning at six, dress, chew a sweet roll, drink a glass of milk, and write. Two more pulp stories were sold, and I paid a semester of Jerry's tuition. On and off, as I would hit a short-story sale, I would pay tuition. I fought for my writing now, so the two hours before I went to work were daily agony. More and more deeply aware of my own position, I struggled to write about myself. I put together a story about a little boy, living in the street I lived on, whom I called Ishky. I coined the name because it sounded very Jewish, and I had his mother speak only the most broken English; but when his mother's Yiddish was translated formally, it emerged as classical English, full of *thee*'s and *thou*'s. I got the idea from Henry Roth's wonderful book, *Call It Sleep.* Ishky had one friend, a little Italian boy, my friend then, who played the fiddle and who, because he was a shoemaker's son, we called Shoemake. The body of the story concerned the lynching of a black kid. My story would be called *The Children,* and I wrote and rewrote, and tore up what I had and wrote it again, and drank coffee and smoked. Drink had no allure for me; nicotine had.

But cigarettes cost money. The factory where I did my eight or nine hours of survival work each day had a solidly Jewish-immigrant working force—cutters, machine operators, everyone—and the chatter and gossip that never stopped were carried on in Yiddish. On my first day there, when I had to have orders translated, they named me *goy,* Yiddish for Gentile. I had picked up the cigarette habit from a waiter I worked with one summer, but brand cigarettes were twelve cents a pack—even the lowly Wings were eight or ten cents a pack, depending on where you bought them—and this cut into food money. Therefore I bought one pack a week, treasured it at home as a crutch for writing, and depended on my bumming talents for daytime smoking. And since I never smoked more than two or three cigarettes during working time, and since practically everyone in the factory smoked, I could always find a butt. But only if I asked for it in Yiddish, and thereby my first Yiddish word was *papiros,* Yiddish for cigarette. Whatever my question, the workers would fling back at me, "Freg mir in Yidish" (Ask me in Yiddish).

*The author in 1946*

Then a day came when I decided that *The Children* was as finished as it would ever be. My two published books and my handful of sold stories had persuaded a literary agency to accept me as one of its writers. The agency was McIntosh and Otis and was run by three pleasant ladies, Mavis McIntosh, Elizabeth Otis, and Mary Abbott. They were middle-class literary types, good agents, and to me characters out of an Edwardian novel. An additional attraction for me was that on the little table in their waiting room they kept a wooden box of cigarettes. I gave them *The Children*—forty-five thousand words of it—and washed my hands of it. I decided that I would continue as a writer, but there would be no more about myself and my childhood. It was too close, too confusing, and too filled with pain.

Whit Burnett, publisher of *Story* magazine, bought *The Children* and published it. *Story* was the most distinguished magazine of the short story in America at a time when the short story was at its peak as an art form internationally and when American short stories were read and admired the world over—which says nothing for the finances of *Story.* Burnett paid fifty dollars for forty-five thousand words, by word count—still the practice at the time—one tenth of a cent per word. I was absolutely enraged when Mary Abbott telephoned to give me this offer, and I fumed and ranted until she convinced me that Whit Burnett published at a loss and that such was the reputation and distinction of *Story* that it could only profit me even if he paid me not a penny. Mary felt that it was a very good thing for young writers to struggle and make do, but the young writers she knew came from proper middle-class families and good universities with fallback. I had no fallback whatsoever. Nevertheless, she convinced me that *Story* was the proper place for the short novel I had written. I told her to go ahead, but it would have to be one hundred dollars. On and off, I had put a year into the book, and even as a newspaper delivery boy at the age of ten, I had not worked for two dollars a week. Also, since I had received an advance of one hundred dollars for each of my two published books, I might as well keep my price up. (That's a joke; I would not want it misunderstood.)

*The Children* was published in the March issue of *Story,* a year and a half after Bette, my wife to be, and I met. Since it was so long a piece, it took practically all of the magazine. James J. Fee, the police inspector of Lynn, Massachusetts, was put onto it, and he read the first copy of *Story* he had ever read, and probably the first book he had ever read. He proclaimed that *The Children* was "the rottenest thing I ever read!" Only two copies of *Story* went to the local news dealer, and Inspector Fee immediately confiscated them. The next day it was banned in Waterbury, Connecticut, and an order for six hundred extra copies promptly came in from news dealers in that town. Whit Burnett danced with delight, and Mary Abbott called to congratulate me, telling me that I was so lucky, since having a work banned was the best thing that could happen to sales, and if only it was banned in Boston, sales would skyrocket. It was banned in Boston and in six other New England cities, and *Story* had the largest press run in all its history. The book was hailed as a small masterpiece and lauded to the skies, and Whit Burnett said that *The Children* saved *Story,* at least for the time being. But saving Howard Fast was another matter, and when my agent suggested to Burnett that he let me share in the prosperity by adding another one hundred dollars to the sum he had paid, he turned her down flat.

A writer is a strange creature. He is a delicate sheet of foil on which the world prints its impressions, and he is self-serving and self-oriented and yet utterly vulnerable, and when I say "he," I mean "she" as well, and for a woman it holds true even more painfully, for whatever a man suffers, a woman suffers more and feels more deeply; and though everyone may believe that he or she can write, in these United States of over two hundred and fifty million people, only a handful can claim the title of writer in its highest sense. I married a gifted, beautiful woman who would one day be one of the finest sculptors we have, and she put aside her own need for my need. I don't know whether it was worth it, or how wise she was to follow me down the paths I took. If one grows old and a little bit wise, all the symbols of greatness and importance and glory shrivel to almost nothing.

By the time Bette and I married, I had finished *Place in the City,* and the book had been published with less than earthshaking results, selling perhaps five thousand copies; but now I was selling short stories for anywhere from five hundred to one thousand dollars each. Such sales every six months, though, did not pay the rent, and we filled in the low spots every way we could. We wrote term papers for college students who had money and no brains; I did pulp stories for fifty dollars each—anything, since once I married I gave up factory work to be a full-time writer.

Bette and I had invested in a 1931 Ford convertible, which cost us forty dollars. Not only did it run, but the clutch was so worn that no one else could start the car. A semimagical way of working clutch and gas pedal allowed me to put it into motion, and even though one of the tires had a hole the size of a fifty-cent piece, through which the inner tube protruded in a threatening bubble, we ran it for thousands of miles with no trouble. When something broke, it never cost more than a dollar to replace. We parked it on the street, and of course no thief in his right mind would have touched it.

We drove it everywhere, and on one of our journeys we went to Valley Forge in Pennsylvania and spent one afternoon there, moved deeply by the reconstruction of the old revolutionary war encampment. I decided then and there that I'd write a book about the army's winter in Valley Forge, and for the next six months I read American history and wrote the book I would call *Conceived in Liberty;* it became my first real breakthrough as a novelist.

With Sam Sloan, my editor, gone from Harcourt, Brace, and with his replacement there less than thrilled with the sales of *Place in the City,* Mary Abbott sent my new novel to Simon and Schuster. They accepted it immediately, published it, and sold fifteen thousand copies, a decent record for my writing. The book, which dealt with the American Revolution somewhat in the realistic manner of Erich Maria Remarque's novel *All Quiet on the Western Front,* about World War One—a treatment never before applied to our revolt—was received with great enthusiasm by the critics. James T. Farrell reviewed it for the *New York Times,* kindly and constructively, and I was unusually thrilled by his guess that when I got the "lightning bugs," as he called them, out of my writing, I might become a very important writer indeed.

During the years between 1937, when I got married, and 1942, when I took over the Voice of America at the Office of War Information, I withdrew completely from active political involvement. For the first time in my life, I was tasting financial security, minimal but actual. Our first year was difficult. I had read bits and pieces, never a full story, of the magnificent running battle and flight to freedom of Chief Little Wolf and his Cheyenne Indians. I wanted desperately to write about it, but the only way I could do so would be to go to Oklahoma, where the old Cheyenne reservation had been, and talk to some of the old Cheyennes still there. Also, in Norman, Oklahoma, at the university, there were Indian students and, on the faculty, a man named Stanley Vestal, who knew more about the Cheyennes than any white man in America. I told the story to Simon and Schuster and talked them into paying me one hundred dollars a month for an entire year. We had two hundred dollars in our bank account. Ninety dollars bought us an ancient Pontiac to replace our Ford, and with $110 to live on, we set off for Oklahoma. It was a wonderful trip; the Pontiac was fine as long as one didn't push it too hard, and the world of the Great Plains was an incredible change for this survivor of the city streets.

Back in New York, we were dead broke once again, but with the guarantee of one hundred dollars a month from Simon and Schuster. It took nine months for me to write *The Last Frontier,* and when I finished it, neither Bette nor I was particularly thrilled with the result. The editors at Simon and Schuster were less than thrilled, and they returned the manuscript with a note that cancelled the unpaid two hundred dollars of my advance and let me understand that the prompt repayment of the ten months' stipend already spent would be expected. But none too soon, I assured them, since our next meal was the major problem.

Meanwhile, Sam Sloan's new publishing house, Duell, Sloan and Pearce, had begun to function, and when I told him that Simon and Schuster had dumped *The Last Frontier,* he asked to read the manuscript. He read it promptly and asked to see me, and the first thing he put to me was whether I knew how I went wrong. I didn't know, and then he explained, gently, that I had tried to tell the story from the Indians' point of view. "You

can't," he said. "You can't get inside Little Wolf's head, and you can't translate Indian speech into English and make it believable." Then what to do with what I had? That was when Sam told me to throw it away and begin again and tell the story from the white man's point of view. When I explained that I had carfare home and not much more, he immediately gave me a check for two thousand dollars as an advance.

The publication of *The Last Frontier* marked the end of our time of poverty and intermittent small riches. Suddenly, Bette and I had enough money for all our modest desires, and I was hailed as a bright new star on the literary horizon. Carl Van Doren, writing a lead review of the book, said, *"The Last Frontier* is an amazing restoration and recreation. The characters breathe, the landscape is solid ground and sky, and the story runs flexibly along the zigzag trail of a people driven by a deep instinct to their ancient home. I do not know of any other episode of Western history that has been so truly and subtly perpetuated as this one. A great story has been found again, and as here told promises to live for generations."

Of course it was all too much. The literary world is never restrained in either its praise or its condemnation. There were no bad reviews, nor would there be any bad reviews for my next book, *The Unvanquished,* which I wrote and completed in the months between my giving the manuscript of *The Last Frontier* to Sam Sloan and its publication.

Years later, when I complained to my Zen teacher that my being a member of the Communist party had thrust me into literary obscurity and made me the hate target of the literary elite who ruled the weekly book section of the *New York Times* and other such reviews, he looked at me with contempt and said, "You dare to complain of something that saved your own soul!"

Perhaps he was right.

As for my books, they were reviled once I became a Communist, but they were read and read, and at no time during the fifty-six years that followed the publication of my first novel did efforts to suppress them actually succeed.

Pearl Harbor had happened, and the world was at war, and the United States joined the forces that faced Adolph Hitler and his fascist allies. It was 1942, and in the desperate rush by America to turn a peaceful nation into a war machine, many things were quickly if loosely put together. One of these was a propaganda and informa-

*Recipient of the International Peace Prize, with daughter, Rachel, and wife, Bette, 1951*

tion center, something that the country had done well enough without in the past but that now was a necessity in this era of radio. This propaganda and information center, so hastily thrown together, was called the Office of War Information, or OWI; and feeling that the only available pool of talent to man it was in New York City, the government took over the General Motors Building at Fifty-seventh Street and Broadway. In the first few months after Pearl Harbor, the government set to it in a sort of frenzy to remake the building according to its needs, staff it, and somehow learn the art—if such it was—of war propaganda.

Howard Fast, meanwhile, was living the ultimate fulfillment of a poor boy's dream. At this point, 1942, I was sitting right on top of eighteen pots of honey. My novel *The Last Frontier,* published a year earlier, had been greeted as a "masterpiece," praised to the skies by Alexander Woollcott and Rex Stout, and chosen as a selection by the esteemed Readers Club; and my new novel, *The Unvanquished,* just published, the story of the Continental army's most desperate moment, had been called by *Time* magazine, who found in it a parallel for the grim present, "the best book about World War Two." I was twenty-seven years old, about to turn twenty-eight, and five years earlier I had married the wonderful blue-eyed, flaxen-haired Bette, an artist by every right, and still my wife and companion fifty-three years later. We had survived the first hard years nicely enough, and we had just put down five hundred dollars for an acre of land on the Old Sleepy Hollow Road near Tarrytown, in Pochantico Hills.

At Sears, Roebuck we purchased for twelve dollars a set of blueprints, and with a mortgage of eight thousand dollars and one thousand dollars in cash, we built a small, lovely two-bedroom cottage. Bette became pregnant, we acquired a wonderful mongrel named Ginger, and I finished writing a book I would call *Citizen Tom Paine.* I cleared the land myself, Bette learned to bake and cook and sew small clothes, and I saw a rewarding, gentle future, in which we would have many children and Bette would paint and I would write my books and earn fame and fortune. And then came the war, and it all turned to dust.

In quick succession, my father died; my younger brother, close to me and my dearest friend, enlisted in the army; I drew a low draft number; and Bette miscarried our first child and sank into gloom. The future that we had planned so carefully was cast aside; Ginger was given to my older brother and promptly ran away and disappeared; the house was put up for sale; we moved into a one-room studio in New York; and Bette, convinced that my orders would be cut in a matter of weeks at the most, leaving her to face the possibility of years alone, joined the Signal Corps as a civilian artist making animated training films.

When I argued with my wife that it made more sense for me to enlist, as my brother had, than to wait around for a summons by the draft board, she strenuously and angrily objected, guided by the sensible feminine hope that the board would somehow miss me. Then one midday, on West Fifty-seventh Street, I met Louis Untermeyer, and my life changed and nothing would ever again be what we had dreamed our lives might be. Whether it works that way, where a chance meeting can turn existence upside down, or whether what happened to me would have happened in any case, I don't know.

Louis Untermeyer, at that time in his middle fifties, had a national reputation as a poet and anthologist. His knowledge of poetry was encyclopedic, his critical sense wise and balanced, and his wit delightful. He would become a major figure in my life, a beloved friend as well as surrogate father, but at that time I knew him only slightly.

On this day in 1942 I greeted Louis Untermeyer as my savior and eagerly accepted his invitation to lunch. Any meal with Louis was a delight. He would bring a gourmet's appreciation to a boiled egg, and his wit was so much a part of him that he had no existence without it. During lunch I poured out my tale of boredom and frustration, and he offered a solution. The solution was the Office of War Information, and it was located down the street, two blocks from where we were eating.

Elmer Davis, newly appointed head of the Office of War Information, was trying to whip a massive, short-wave radio operation into shape, setting up speaking and translation units for every country of occupied Europe. The feeling at the State Department and the War

Department was that we must somehow reach the medium-wave receivers in European households, and since the only part of the European community that was free and allied to us was Great Britain, our people cast their covetous eyes on the British Broadcasting Company. The British were none too happy at the thought of the Yanks putting their grubby fingers on the precious BBC, but their dependence on these same Yanks was enormous, so there was no way they could shunt our demands. Elmer Davis, a one-time correspondent for the *New York Times* and later a radio news commentator, was at that time the most respected man in the field of radio news transmission. Joseph Barnes, a veteran newspaperman, talented and respected, was brought in by Davis to work with him. Both of them understood the importance of medium wave as opposed to short-wave, and they persuaded our government to lean on the British; the result was that the British agreed to turn over their BBC medium-wave transmitters to us for four hours a day, from 2:00 A.M. to 6:00 A.M. our time, which was 7:00 A.M. to 11:00 A.M. London time. AT&T set up a triple transatlantic telephone transmission to London; it would take our voices across the ocean with practically no loss in quality.

So now we had it, a transmitting facility that would cover Europe with our propaganda and could be tuned in by every home on the continent. Now it remained only to find someone to prepare the basic fifteen-minute program that would be translated into eleven languages and repeated several times in French and German. My knowledge of what happened in this search came from John Houseman, who headed up the shortwave operation—dramatic radio propaganda—and whom I later came to know and like enormously. John—or Jack as we called him—had given up his work as a successful producer to come to the OWI, and according to him, three men were hired in succession to be BBC anchor writer, and each of the three served from a week to two weeks and then was fired. One was the head of the second-largest ad agency in New York; the other two were newspapermen.

During a meeting with Houseman on another subject, Davis and Barnes raised the question of whom to hire for the BBC and where to find him. They told Houseman how desperate they were and what a letdown the three candidates had been, all of them highly recommended and men of experience. There were other men—it was before the time when they might have turned to women—whom they wanted, men in good positions who would not give up their careers even for the OWI. Houseman asked Davis and Barnes exactly what they wanted, to which they answered someone who

*Celebrating Louis Untermeyer's ninety-second birthday in Weston, Connecticut. Top row: from left, Bette, Jon, Howard Fast, and Untermeyer's son. Bottom row: Brynn Untermeyer, Louis Untermeyer, and Erica Jong Fast*

could write clean, straightforward prose, someone who was literate yet simple and direct.

To this, Houseman answered that he had just read the proofs of a book called *Citizen Tom Paine,* clean, colorful political writing by a kid name of Howard Fast. And how old was this kid? Twenty-seven or twenty-eight. And how do they get in touch with him? He's right here in this building, top floor, writing a pamphlet about the American Revolution. And what in hell was he or anyone else doing sitting up there and writing a pamphlet about the American Revolution? Didn't anyone up there understand that this was World War Two, and not the American Revolution? A few minutes after this discussion, the head of the pamphlet department came to my desk and told me that Elmer Davis, chief of the operation, wanted me downstairs in the radio section.

In Elmer Davis's office, Davis and Barnes and Houseman awaited me. I walked into the room, and the three cold-eyed, hard-faced men stared at me as if I were an insect on a pin, and then Elmer Davis asked, "Are you Fast?"

Of course, they were not hard-faced or cold-eyed, but I was scared and unsure of myself and convinced that I was to be fired for some awful foul-up in my pamphlet, which must have been brought to them as proof of my culpability. I can recall the conversation that followed fairly well, by no means exactly after all these years. Jack Houseman, my entry angel into this strange new world, began by spelling out the nature of what would be called from then on simply the BBC, how the deal with the British had come about, and what it was intended to do. Then Elmer Davis picked up and said to me, "That's why you're here, Fast. Jack says you can write."

They were all standing. Suddenly, they all sat down. No one asked me to sit down, so I remained standing. They kept looking at me as if I were distinctive in some way. I wasn't. I was five-feet, ten-and-a-half inches. I still had plenty of hair, and I had round cheeks that embarrassed the hell out of me because they turned pink at my slightest unease. Brown eyes and heavy, horn-rimmed glasses completed the picture.

"Do you follow me?" Davis asked.

I shook my head.

"What he means," Houseman said kindly, "is that he wants you to take over the BBC and write the fifteen-minute blueprint every day."

I shook my head again. If I had unclasped my hands, they would have been shaking like leaves. I was not being fired. This was worse.

"I can't do that," I said.

"Why not?"

"I just don't know how. I never wrote for radio. I never wrote for a newspaper."

"We're not asking for references," Barnes said. "Mr. Houseman here says you can write simply and well and that you can think politically. We're asking you to write a fifteen-minute news program that will tell people in occupied Europe how the war goes, what our army has done, and what our hopes and intentions are. We want you to do it plainly and honestly, to tell the truth and not mince words. You are not to lie or invent. You will have a pool of some twenty actors available, and you will choose three each night to speak your words for the English section. Other actors will speak the foreign translations."

"It's no use," I pleaded. "I'm going to be drafted. I have a low number."

Elmer Davis came to me and lifted off my glasses. Staring at them, he said, "You're technically blind in your right eye, aren't you?"

"Oh, no," I said. "No. I see quite well out of that eye."

"You won't be drafted," Elmer Davis said.

"Suppose I botch the whole thing?" I said.

"We'll give you a week, and if you botch it, we'll dump you."

"And if you're drafted," Barnes assured me, "you'll be back here in a uniform—unless we toss you out first."

They didn't fire me. The weeks stretched into months, and they didn't fire me. My number came up a few weeks after my BBC job began, and I was still of the belief that if you were going to fight fascism, the way to do it was with a gun in your hands. I wasn't worried about my bad right eye, because during the physical, standing on line to have my eyes examined, I simply memorized the chart. When my turn came and I handed my papers to the eye doctor, he studied them a bit longer than he had to and then consulted some notes on his desk.

"Fast?" He handed me a card to cover my right eye. No problem there. "The other eye now." I began to call off the chart, and the doctor grinned and held up three fingers.

"Forget the chart. How many fingers?"

I guessed two.

"Actually, three. Come on, mister—go back to where you were."

"They set me up, didn't they? Who was it? Barnes? Davis?"

I stomped out of there in a fury and went back to the nightmare that they called the American BBC—and a nightmare it was. I had never driven myself like that before or since, and I was no stranger to hard work, physical or mental. I would get into my office at eight in the morning, usually to find someone from some branch of the government waiting for me. The White House wanted to stress the numbers of tank production because the Germans were saying that in no way would we ever match their numbers. Or Whitehall wanted us to play down the invasion of the continent. Or why wasn't I putting more emphasis on food production? This gentleman is from the Department of Agriculture. I could plead that he didn't have to come up from Washington in person and kill a precious hour of my morning. The secretary so instructed him. The secretary felt that I did not understand that a war was fought with food as well as bullets. The people on the continent were starving. Did I understand what it meant for them to know that there would be ample food? Nobody made appointments with me; they just poured in. The Cham-

*Howard Fast*

ber of Commerce—how on earth did the U.S. Chamber of Commerce know what I was writing? No one publicized that we had four hours of BBC each morning, but everyone appeared to know. Ordnance has this new carbine; eight in the morning, they're there with the carbine. What in hell am I to do with a carbine? How did I get here? I'm a kid, and I know practically nothing about anything. Ten P.M. I get back to my office, and a distinguished-looking gentleman tells me that he has been waiting two hours. He represents the shipyard owners of America. Do I know what shipyards mean in this war? Do I understand that without ships we would lose this war?

So much for the first thirty years of my life. As with any truncated autobiographical memoir, this account deals only with bits and snatches of my life. One searches one's memory for mileposts, so to speak, for moments

of decision that point to one or another of the paths that might have been taken. My tenure with the Office of War Information was finished in 1944, when the entire operation of the new Voice of America, which I had created and brought to fruition, was moved to North Africa. I desperately wanted to go with it, but J. Edgar Hoover decided otherwise—by informing my superiors at the OWI that I was a Communist, which at that time I was not. I was offered another post in the organization, an assignment to write a pamphlet on American history. I refused it indignantly and resigned. I had only one purpose in mind, to go overseas and play some part in the war—if only to report on it.

My wife had become pregnant, and our first child, a daughter, was born that year. At the same time, I took two steps that were to change the course of my life. I joined the Communist party, and I went overseas to the

China-Burma-India Theater of Operation as a correspondent for the magazine *Coronet* and for the newspaper *P.M.* My journey overseas and my experiences in North Africa, Saudi Arabia, and India resulted in little of major importance for either the war effort or the periodicals that had engaged me, but indeed they were very important in my education and development as a writer and observer of the tragedies and obscenities of the human race. I had a firsthand look at the waste and horror of war, and of the crime that mankind inflicts upon itself.

My part as a reporter overseas was short-lived; my membership in the Communist party, on the other hand, extended from 1944 to 1956. It changed my life, and even to the date of this writing, in April of 1993, almost forty years after leaving the party in sorrow and anger, its effects upon my career still continue. My reasons for joining the party are too complex to put down here. I have spelled them out in great detail in a memoir called *Being Red,* published by Houghton Mifflin in 1990. Suffice it to say that during my time at the OWI, I watched and wrote of the Soviet Union's struggle against the armies of Adolph Hitler. I worked with Communists, among others. I met Communists whom I admired. In the 1930s, almost every American writer or artist or musician whom I admired was either a member of the party or a friend of the party.

But for myself and my family, those twelve years became an unending parade of persecution and isolation. *Freedom Road,* a story of the struggle of the newly freed slaves after the Civil War, was the last book of mine to be published before it was generally known that I was a Communist. It appeared in 1944 to a chorus of critical praise such as few books have ever received. It sold more than a million copies worldwide, becoming during the next ten years perhaps one of the most widely read serious novels of the time. But that was the end of the critical praise. My next novel, *The American,* was denounced as Communist propaganda, the fate of book after book as the years of my party membership continued.

With the writing of *Spartacus,* things came to a head. The manuscript was submitted to my then publisher, Little, Brown and Company, welcomed and highly praised by my editor, Angus Cameron, then vice president of the company, and scheduled for publication. J. Edgar Hoover, head of the FBI, then decided to intervene personally, sending an agent to Little, Brown and Company with a decree that they were not to publish the book. Similar instructions were sent to every other publisher to whom the book was submitted. After seven leading publishers had declined the book, I published it myself. It sold forty thousand copies in hardcover and another million in paper reprint—but those reprint sales took place after I had left the party, as did the making of the motion picture.

In the course of those years in the party, every book I wrote was viciously attacked and denounced, a situation that reversed itself to a degree after I resigned from the Communist party in 1956.

In those Communist party years, I was sent to prison for three months for contempt of Congress, the act of refusing to surrender lists of names of people who had supported medical aid to Republican Spain.

In 1952, I was a candidate for Congress in the twenty-third congressional district in New York. I ran on the American Labor party ticket—a ticket denounced as pro-Communist—and I was soundly defeated.

When I look back on the years I spent as a member of the Communist party, I am torn between a sense of twelve years of frustration and repression, and a sense of twelve years of struggle and growth in social understanding. I don't regret them, but I deeply regret that I lacked the understanding that would have allowed me to balance my passion for social justice with a clearer judgement of the Communist party, which, instead of bringing us closer to socialism, turned a generation away from it.

When I left the party in 1956, after the monstrous revelations of Joseph Stalin's maniacal cruelties, I had a raging anger against a movement I felt betrayed by. I put some of my feelings into a bitter book called *The Naked God,* published in 1957, and subtitled *The Writer and the Communist Party.* But this feeling of rage and bitterness soon passed, eased by the fact that the world I once knew as a young writer opened up to me again. Two of my books, written under the shadow of my party membership, were immediately bought by film producers. *Spartacus* became not only an enormously successful film, but a best-selling novel ten years after its initial publication, and the novels written after leaving the party found a new generation and a new audience.

For my wife, my daughter, and my son, it was the beginning of a new life, a life without constant fear and persecution. In a nation where so much is easily forgotten, where history is almost meaningless, the years of the witch-hunt are hardly remembered at all, but they were agonizing years, not only for myself as an actual party member, but for liberals as well.

During the years of the blacklist, I decided to do what so many other blacklisted writers had done, to write under another name. My first attempt was a book called *The Fallen Angel,* which I published under the pseudonym of Walter Ericson. It was subsequently made into a film called *Mirage.* Later, my new agent, Paul Reynolds, suggested the name of E. V. Cunningham. I wrote twenty books under that name, published here and immensely successful in Europe.

Indeed, my release—it can be called that—from the party resulted in an explosion of repressed creativity on my part. Only the first of the E. V. Cunningham books was written during the blacklist; however, the pleasures of writing half-serious suspense stories became so captivating that I wrote, as I said, nineteen more. Nor did I limit myself to the novel. I had always loved California, and in 1974, we moved to Los Angeles, where my wife and I lived for six years. I did screenplays for three films, only one of which was produced. I turned my novel *Citizen Tom Paine* into a theatrical play, done first in Williamstown and eventually in Kennedy Center in Washington, D.C. I wrote a play based on the life of Jane Austen, called *The Novelist.* It was done at Williamstown, at Theater West in Springfield, Massachusetts, in Mamaroneck, and for a short run in New York.

While living in California, I decided to write a book about a woman whose life and experience would parallel my own, having her born the year and month of my own birth, namely November in 1914. I enjoy writing about women. I called her Barbara Lavette, and eventually the story of Barbara Lavette, from her birth to her sixty-eighth year, ran to five books that sold over ten million copies.

No matter what direction my writing took, I could never give up a social outlook and a position against hypocrisy and oppression. This has been a theme that runs through all of my writing. Some five years ago, I undertook a weekly column for the New York *Observer.* Selections from this column were published in a book of essays called *War and Peace.* The book was published by M. E. Sharpe.

All in all, I have lived the life of a writer, a man of letters, a life I chose and which I followed doggedly through the seventy-eight years of my life. I have been fortunate and unfortunate—but more fortunate than unfortunate. I have been married for fifty-six years to a wonderful woman, with whom I fell in love at the age

of twenty. We have two children and three grandchildren, and we live very quietly in Connecticut, a place where we have lived for many years and which we love dearly.

I cannot close this short survey of my life as a writer without mentioning a book I wrote called *April Morning.* I wrote this book in 1960, the story of a young adolescent who was witness to the battles of Concord and Lexington at the beginning of the American Revolution. Quietly published by Crown Books, without fuss or fanfare, it went through almost fifty editions in hardcover and literally millions of copies in softcover, mass-market reprint. Generations of middle-school children have read this book, which is used as a text in most of the fifty American state school systems, and have taken from it a deep feeling of what America is and how it came into being.

[*Editor's Note:* Portions of this essay are excerpted from the author's memoir, *Being Red.*]

*Postscript (March, 1999)*

A few days before my eightieth birthday, in 1994, my wife passed away after a seven-month struggle with cancer. We had been married more than fifty years, and her death was a terrible blow to me. I was plunged into gloom and acute depression, and for the following year I wrote almost nothing.

We then lived in a large house in Greenwich, most of it devoted to my wife's sculpture and painting and to my office space. The house was filled with her presence, her work, her paintings and sculpture. Wherever I turned, her work faced me. My wife had been a beautiful young woman, and the beauty stayed with her until her seventy-eighth year. To my mind, she was a great sculptor, and I still treasure much of her work.

Seven months after her death, when my son was looking for a house in Old Greenwich, I saw the small house where I live today. I had come only to advise him, but when I saw this house, I made my first step out of gloom and sorrow. I bid for it and bought it, and a few months later I moved into it, spreading my excess furniture among my children.

My emergence from depression was a slow and agonizing process. I was living alone, managing to write two columns a week for my local newspaper and the *Times-Mirror* wire. I needed help with research and other matters, but more than that, I found it almost impossible for me to live alone. Then, in April of 1996, I met a young woman—I say young because she was approaching fifty, and I was some thirty-two years older than she.

Her name is Mercedes O'Connor. She had been recently divorced and needed a job. I had been successful enough as a writer to afford her wages, and she took me up on my offer—and thereby gave me an entirely new creative life. She is a literate, well-read and remarkable woman, and within a week after the relationship began, I put aside the gloom and began another book. This was to be called *An Independent Woman* and became the sixth and final book of the long series I had written about Barbara Lavette and the Lavette family.

To go back some years to 1974: it was then that I decided to write a book about a woman and her family. It became a very long project, and by the time I published the sixth and final book, it comprised almost two thousand pages. Each of the books became a best seller of sorts. An odd fact that I should note here is that this book, *An Independent Woman,* was published by Harcourt Brace, the same company that had published my first serious novel, *Place in the City,* some sixty years before.

My relationship with Ms. O'Connor not only took me out of depression, but evolved into a close and loving relationship. I was back at work now, doing the one thing I loved best, writing. A second novel, *Redemption,* was completed and will be published in July of 1999. *An Independent Woman* was published in June of 1997. And I am now in the process of completing still another novel to be called: *Greenwich, Connecticut,* and will probably be published in the year 2000.

Along with this, a screenplay of mine called *The Crossing* is in the process of filming as a television film by the Arts and Entertainment cable channel.

So you might say that I have begun another life of literary work at the rather ripe age of eighty-one. I remain in good health, and so far my memory serves me well. I look forward cheerfully to the future. Certainly, it can be no worse than the past.

*BIOGRAPHICAL/CRITICAL SOURCES:*

*BOOKS*

MacDonald, Andrew, *Howard Fast: A Critical Companion,* Greenwood (Westport, CT), 1996.

Meyer, Hershel, D., *History and Conscience: The Case of Howard Fast,* Anvil-Atlas (New York City), 1958.

*PERIODICALS*

*Armchair Detective,* spring, 1994, p. 218.
*Atlantic Monthly,* September, 1944; June, 1970.
*Best Sellers,* February 1, 1971; September 1, 1973; January, 1979; November, 1979.
*Booklist,* June 15, 1989, p. 1739; July, 1993, p. 1916; October 1, 1995, p. 252.
*Book Week,* May 9, 1943.
*Chicago Tribune,* February 8, 1987, pp. 6-7; April 21, 1987; January 20, 1991, section 14, p. 7.
*Christian Science Monitor,* July 8, 1939; August 23, 1972, p. 11; November 7, 1977, p. 18; November 1, 1991, p. 12.
*Commentary,* March, 1991, pp. 62-64.
*Detroit News,* October 31, 1982.
*Globe and Mail* (Toronto), September 15, 1984; March 1, 1986.
*Kirkus Reviews,* June 15, 1994, p. 793.
*Library Journal,* November 15, 1978; September 15, 1985, p. 92; May 15, 1989, p. 88; October 1, 1990, p. 96; August, 1991, p. 162; July, 1994, p. 126; September 1, 1995, p. 206.
*Los Angeles Times,* November 11, 1982; November 11, 1985; November 21, 1988.
*Los Angeles Times Book Review,* December 9, 1990.
*Nation,* April 5, 1952; May 30, 1959.
*New Republic,* August 17, 1942, p. 203; August 14, 1944; November 4, 1978; May 27, 1992.
*New Statesman,* August 8, 1959.
*New York,* November 5, 1990, pp. 124-125.
*New Yorker,* July 1, 1939; May 1, 1943.
*New York Herald Tribune Book Review,* July 21, 1963.
*New York Herald Tribune Books,* July 27, 1941, p. 3.
*New York Times,* October 15, 1933; June 25, 1939; April 25, 1943; February 3, 1952; September 24, 1984; February 9, 1987, p. C16; March 10, 1987; April 21, 1991, pp. 20-21; October 23, 1991, p. C19; November 19, 1993, p. A2.
*New York Times Book Review,* October 13, 1933; April 25, 1943; February 3, 1952; March 4, 1962; July 14, 1963; February 6, 1966; October 2, 1977, p. 24; October 30, 1977; May 14, 1978; June 10, 1979; September 15, 1985, p. 24; March 29, 1987, p. 22; August 20, 1989, p. 23.
*People Weekly,* January 28, 1991, pp. 75-79.
*Publishers Weekly,* August 6, 1979; April 1, 1983; July 19, 1985, p. 48; November 28, 1986, p. 66; July 22, 1988, p. 41; June 30, 1989, p. 84; June 21, 1993, p. 83; July 11, 1994, p. 66.
*Rapport,* Number 1, 1994, p.38.
*Saturday Review,* March 8, 1952; January 22, 1966; September 17, 1977.

*Saturday Review of Literature,* July 1, 1939; July 26, 1941, p. 5; May 1, 1943; December 24, 1949.

*Time,* November 6, 1977.

*Times Literary Supplement,* November 11, 1939.

*Tribune Books* (Chicago), February 8, 1987, p. 6.

*Washington Post,* October 4, 1979; September 26, 1981; September 25, 1982; September 3, 1985; February 9, 1987; March 3, 1987; September 6, 1993, p. C2.

*Washington Post Book World,* October 23, 1988; November 25, 1990.

\* \* \*

## FELTON, Keith Spencer 1942-

*PERSONAL:* Born May 3, 1942, in San Francisco, CA; son of Jean Spencer (a physician) and Janet Elizabeth (a social activist; maiden name, Birnbaum) Felton; married Susan L. Kennedy, October 18, 1981 (divorced, 1998); children: Peter Spencer, Laurens Kennedy. *Education:* Grinnell College, B.A., 1964; University of California, Los Angeles, M.F.A., 1967. *Politics:* "Cynical liberal Democrat." *Religion:* "Lapsed Unitarian." *Avocational interests:* Photography, boating, camping, bicycling, music (string bass, guitar).

*ADDRESSES: Home*—29 Acevedo Ave., San Francisco, CA 94132. *Office*—P.O. Box 6808, San Mateo, CA 94403-6808. *E-mail*—ksfelton@Pacbell.net.

*CAREER:* Critic for regional arts publications, Los Angeles, CA, 1968-70; book reviewer, critic, and editor, 1969-80; Cinema Dix-Francs (documentary film company), Los Angeles, founder, 1975, executive producer of films, including *The Box,* 1975-86; writer and researcher, 1987—. Copy editor for entertainment magazines, 1970-71. Photographer, with exhibitions in the San Francisco area.

*AWARDS, HONORS:* Drama Selection, National Collegiate Players, 1964, for *Daniel Prince;* creative writing award, Music Corporation of America, 1967; Discovery Award, Four Winds Press, 1968, and prize from San Joaquin Delta College, 1971, both for the play *The Last Lost Weekend of Missionary Peale;* James D. Phelan Award in Literature, 1977, for *Maddie and Vince;* award from Ann Arbor Film Festival, 1982, for *The Box.*

*WRITINGS:*

*Warriors' Words: A Consideration of Language and Leadership,* Praeger (Westport, CT), 1995.

Author of the plays *Daniel Prince* and *The Last Lost Weekend of Missionary Peale,* 1968, and the novel *Maddie and Vince,* 1977. Contributor to periodicals, including *Coast, FM,* and *Fine Arts.*

*WORK IN PROGRESS: Lars and Little Olduvai,* in which a father and son solve anthropological mysteries buried in their own back yard; *Anthem of the Aching Heart,* "a sojourn through the poetic mystery of divorce;" *A Writer's Guide to Hand Tools: A Practical Cognate for the Creative Mind; A Wordcrafter's Daybook: Confessions of a Language Lover.*

*SIDELIGHTS:* Keith Spencer Felton told *CA:* "In a career which has spanned more than thirty-five years and multiple art forms, I have focused upon the power of language as both the subject of a book and the *raison d'etre* of a host of other writings. I was a child actor who began a literary career as a playwright. It was inescapable that language would play an important part in my viewpoint and artistic expression. Achieving awards, productions, and publication of some of my early plays, I turned to longer forms of fiction and continued to expand my writing into journalism and filmmaking. During the decade of the 1970s, I wrote regularly for the *Los Angeles Times Book Review* and ran a documentary film company specializing in exemplary subjects in the visual and performing arts.

"The creativity of fiction and the plasticity of films led ultimately to nonfiction forms and to a series of books about language. My work of the 1990s owes a great debt to the dozen earlier years I spent reviewing books. Working with Digby Diehl, and under the prodigious and awe-inspiring Robert Kirsch, I was exposed to the rigor of the task of absorption and analysis of a literary work and the subsequent discipline of shaping interpretation and commentary in a cogent and responsible way to guide a readership. Researching my own books and letting the expression of their ideas unfold has never seemed so difficult following that apprenticeship.

"For my most recent book research, my ten-year-old son Lars and I set out to unearth a story in the literal sense. *Lars and Little Olduvai* charts an archaeological experience we undertook in the southern stretches of the San Francisco Bay, once replete with Native American settlements. The book's abiding concern is to promote the reader's awareness of history and, through the inducement to participate, excite a new way of thinking about oneself and one's environment. Exposing the vivid culture of a once-thriving and now long-decimated tribe (the Ohlone), the text provides a philosophical premise that the community spirit which enlivened the Ohlones has motivated these new archaeologists as well and has the power to motivate others; that the locus for discovery needn't be exotic, but can be local; and that the best artifact one can excavate is a connection with the human spirit.

"My current project involves a personal incident concerning the renowned actress Lotte Lenya. Our encounter forms a touchstone for a literary grappling with the vicissitudes of seeking love---an emotional enterprise at which Lotte spent her life, mostly unsuccessfully. What might have been tragic to others was manageable by her only in the way, for example, that the characters of Beckett found ways to prevail. Her lifelong 'Tunnel of Love' was a subterranean labyrinth; living it was one of the glorious expressions of existential survival. My book attempts to illuminate some of that tunnel's interstices, as negotiated by Lenya."

\*     \*     \*

## FENNARIO, David 1947-

*PERSONAL:* Born David William Wiper, on April 26, 1947, in Verdun, Quebec, Canada; son of James (a house painter) and Margaret (Kerr) Wiper; married, wife's name Elizabeth; children: one son. *Education:* Attended Dawson College, early 1970s. *Politics:* Socialist Labor Party.

*CAREER:* Worked as a shipper and mail clerk in Canada; employed as a packer and releaser in a Montreal, Canada, dress factory, 1969; writer, 1972—, playwright, 1975—; Centaur Theatre, Montreal, playwright-in-residence, 1975-76; affiliated with the Black Rock Community Centre Theatre group, Verdun, Quebec, Canada, after 1981.

*AWARDS, HONORS:* Chalmers Award, 1979, for *Balconville*.

*WRITINGS:*

*Without a Parachute* (journal; adapted by the author and first produced at the Theater Passe Muraille, Toronto, February 6, 1979; revised version produced as *Changes,* Ottawa, 1980), Dawson College (Montreal), 1972.

*On the Job* (play; first produced at the Centaur Theater, Montreal, January 29, 1975), Talonbooks (Vancouver), 1976.

*Nothing to Lose* (play; first produced at the Centaur Theater, Montreal, November 11, 1976), Talonbooks, 1977.

*Balconville* (play; first produced at the Centaur Theatre, Montreal, January 4, 1979), Talonbooks, 1980.

*Moving* (play), produced at the Centaur Theatre, Montreal, February 2, 1983.

*Blue Mondays* (with poems by Daniel Adams and illustrations by Sheila Salmel), Black Rock Creations (Verdun, Quebec), 1984.

*The Murder of Susan Parr* (play), produced in Montreal, 1989.

*The Death of Rene Levesque* (play), produced in Montreal, 1991.

*Joe Beef: A History of Pointe Saint Charles* (play; first produced in Montreal, 1985), Talonbooks, 1991.

*Doctor Thomas Neill Cream: Mystery at McGill* (play; produced as *Neil Cream: Mysteries of McGill,* produced at McGill University, Montreal, October 17, 1985), Talonbooks, 1993.

*Without a Parachute* has been translated into French.

*SIDELIGHTS:* Since the mid-1970s David Fennario has become one of Canada's best-known political playwrights in English. Fennario's work reflects several strong Marxist ideas and his plays, primarily set in the working-class neighborhoods of Montreal where he was raised, portray economic, linguistic, and class tensions among the region's struggling, often systematically tyrannized inhabitants. Fennario's interest in this section of society was first evident in his 1972 memoir, written when he was only in his mid-twenties: "Where do these people get the strength to keep on living in the face of such despair and hopelessness?," he wrote in *Without a Parachute.* "The whole area stinks of broken dreams and insanity. Little taverns hugging the corners of the street. Factory chimneys, match-box houses, solitary street lamps. Secondhand, everything is second-hand, including their lives."

Fennario was born David William Wiper in 1947 in Verdun, Quebec, a poor section of Montreal whose residents were both English- and French-speaking laborers. "In this subculture he learned to be streetwise in a city divided between French and English factions and further stressed by an increasingly obvious and vocal ethnic mosaic," explained Reid Gilbert in *Contemporary Dramatists.* He changed his name as a young adult to "Fennario" after a Bob Dylan song, "Pretty Peggy-O." After dropping out of high school, Fennario hitchhiked across the United States and held a succession of menial jobs. He lived in Toronto in the mid-1960s during its counterculture heyday, when it was home to a large population of American draft-dodgers, and he was even jailed for a month on vagrancy charges. In 1969 he took a job in a dress factory in Montreal as a packer and shipper.

A voracious reader from an early age, Fennario began studying at Dawson College, where a teacher encouraged his writing and helped arrange the publication of *Without a Parachute.* This coming-of-age memoir brought Fennario sudden success upon publication in 1972. "The vigorous dramatic situations, dialogue, and strong characterizations in the work," noted Aviva Ravel in an essay on the playwright for *Dictionary of Literary Biography,* landed Fennario a playwright-in-residence post at Montreal's Centaur Theatre. Though he had never seen a live theater performance until that point, Fennario quickly wrote his first play, *On the Job,* based on his experiences in the dress factory a few years before.

Produced at the Centaur in early 1975, *On the Job* takes place on Christmas Eve in the packing room much like the one in which Fennario worked a half-dozen years before. Its employees, scheduled for a half-day because of the holiday, are told they must stay much later in order to fill a rush order from a famous Canadian department store, Eaton's, "a megabusiness that is a symbol of the Canadian establishment," explained Gilbert in *Contemporary Dramatists.* Overhead the workers can hear the management Christmas party; the owner visits the packing room and, in a burst of holiday cheer, gives them the rest of the day off. Their foreman rescinds the order after he leaves. *On the Job*'s characters include an older man, much resigned to the misery and powerlessness of his employment situation; a combative, shirker punk; and a former hippie with radical political beliefs who convinces his co-workers to strike in protest. Instead, all are fired. "The play progresses at a brisk pace, the dialogue is lively and trenchant, and the characters are recognizable and sympathetic," noted Ravel in *Dictionary of Literary Biography.*

*On the Job* was a hit in Montreal, enjoyed success in other Canadian cities as well, was filmed for television, and even translated into a French-language version. "Fennario has an ear for the dialects of Montreal, and in large part the accurate, powerful vernacular accounts for his early local success," wrote Gilbert.

November of 1976 saw the debut of Fennario's second play at the Centaur, *Nothing to Lose.* The work is set in a Montreal tavern to which a suddenly successful young playwright has returned for a few beers; his fellow drinkers are truckers who discuss a possible strike action. Murray, their union representative, tries to dissuade them, and Jackie, the writer Jerry's old friend,

soon begins drinking far too much. "The main conflict is between Jerry and Murray, with Jackie caught between the two but eventually deciding to lead the workers in a takeover of the warehouse," wrote Ravel. All pity the tragicomic alcoholic who is eventually ejected, and fear that his fate may one day be theirs.

For a time Fennario relocated to Canada's largest city, and wrote his 1978 stage work, *Toronto,* there. The drama takes place in a Toronto hotel room where the artistic director of a theater, a playwright, and a director are attempting to cast the writer's second play. A journalist comes to interview the new literary sensation, and there is much discussion of leftist politics. The work, Fennario's only one set outside of Quebec, was termed by Gilbert "his least convincing play," a sentiment echoed by Ravel. "Despite the occasional comic antics, the play, arising out of the playwright's experiences in the theater, succeeds neither as satire nor comedy and strains to maintain the momentum of his previous work," assessed the *Dictionary of Literary Biography* essayist.

Fennario's next play, however, was a great success in Montreal. *Balconville* takes place in the Pointe St. Charles neighborhood, another working-class district, and the "balconies" of its title are part of the tenement apartment buildings inhabited by French- and English-speaking residents who live in too-close proximity, filled as they are with prejudices against the other. "Here each observes the other, and petty jealousies and language barriers explode under pressure into family and social hatreds," wrote Gilbert. At one point two male characters make an obvious display of their respective flags on the balconies: the Quebecois's blue and white fleur-de-lis, and the red and white maple leaf. But as Fennario shows, Balconvill'e factions are all truly in the same socio-economic situation.

The Francophone characters of *Balconville* are Cecile and her husband Claude, who is about to be laid off from his job. Across the way live Muriel and her rebellious son Johnny, a resentful recipient of unemployment benefits; Johnny's wife is a waitress but is becoming increasingly feminist in her views and threatens to leave him. Despite the tensions between neighbors, "a moment of reconciliation occurs when they both realize they share similar problems—untrustworthy politicians, slum landlords, and capitalists exploit workers regardless of nationality," wrote Ravel. "The play culminates with a fire set by the landlord to collect insurance. As *Balconville* goes up in flames, the characters unite to rescue their possessions."

*Balconville* was one of the first Canadian plays to use bilingual dialogue as an element of its production. That it is untranslated for the audience plays an important role in the efficacy of the work: "the viewer is trapped by the text into participating in a dramatic distillation of the frustrations of the nation," noted Gilbert in *Contemporary Dramatists.* Its first run at the Centaur Theatre set box-office records in 1979, was a favorite that year of local drama critics, and even won a Toronto-area award for best new Canadian play.

That same year, Fennario adapted his first book, *Without a Parachute,* into a one-man play, *Changes,* that premiered in Toronto. He eventually left the Centaur, disillusioned with the pitfalls of commercial success, and became a founding member of a smaller theater company in Verdun called Black Rock Community Centre. The first work that premiered with it was *Joe Beef: A History of Pointe Saint Charles* in the mid-1980s. The play is based upon a supposedly true incident from Montreal's past: during a six-week strike in 1887, one waterfront tavernkeeper generously fed a thousand canal workers and their wives and children. Fennario casts that tavernkeeper as the emcee who takes the audience on a working-class version of Montreal history. "French explorers, Indians, priests, farmers, workers, and landowners of English, French, Irish, and Scottish origins, all in class and social conflict, appear in a series of vignettes," wrote Ravel. "The loosely connected skits, songs, and dances often parody current political issues." *Joe Beef* failed to achieve the success of his earlier works, however. "The revue is lively, sometimes funny, and often moving," wrote Gilbert, ". . .but it does not offer much to audiences in the late 20th century."

Several later works by Fennario failed to achieve the critical and commercial success of his earlier works. One of them was the 1985 drama *Doctor Thomas Neill Cream: Mystery at McGill,* produced at McGill University in Montreal and published in book form in 1993. Another play, *The Death of Rene Levesque,* chronicles the life and times of one of French-speaking Quebec's most prominent leaders in the separatist fight. The work was not favorably received in Montreal, "partly because it insulted some Francophone viewers," remarked Gilbert.

Fennario is also the author of the fictionalized journal/novel of one David Wiper, *Blue Mondays.* The 1984 volume, set in the late 1960s and early '70s, includes poems by Daniel Adams and illustrations from Sheila Salmela. Ravel described it as "a political manifesto. . . . Many of the episodes, skillfully rendered,

present those personal experiences which have had a strong impact on Fennario's life. The journal is a good introduction to the plays which also draw on the author's experiences at work, at home, and in the Verdun working-class community."

*BIOGRAPHICAL/CRITICAL SOURCES:*

*BOOKS*

*Canada's Playwrights: A Biographical Guide,* edited by Don Rubin and Alison Cranmer-Byng, Canadian Theatre Review Publications, 1980.
*Contemporary Dramatists,* St. James Press, 1999.
David Fennario, *Without a Parachute,* Dawson College, 1972.
*Dictionary of Literary Biography,* Volume 60: *Canadian Writers since 1960,* Gale (Detroit, MI), 1987.
*The Work: Conversations with English-Canadian Playwrights,* edited by Cynthia Zimmerman and Robert Wallace, Coach House Press, 1982.

*PERIODICALS*

*Books in Canada,* May, 1984, p. 4.
*Canadian Forum,* February, 1981, pp. 14-17; April, 1983, pp. 38-39.
*Matrix,* fall, 1984, pp. 25-34.
*Performing Arts,* summer, 1980, pp. 22-25.
*Saturday Night,* April, 1978, pp. 59-60, 62; November, 1979, pp. 101, 103-104.*

\*          \*          \*

**FERRIS, Scott R.   1956-**

*PERSONAL:* Born December 22, 1956, in Constableville, NY. *Education:* Attended Community College of the Finger Lakes, 1975-76; studied in Copenhagen, Denmark, 1977; attended University of Pisa, 1977; State University of New York College at Plattsburgh, B.A., 1978.

*ADDRESSES: Home and Office*—P.O. Box 73, Franklin Springs, NY 13341. *E-mail*—kentiana@dream scape.com.

*CAREER:* State University of New York College at Plattsburgh, curatorial assistant at Rockwell Kent Gallery, 1979-80; Old Sturbridge Village, Sturbridge, MA, historical interpreter, 1980; Kent Estate, Au Sable Forks, NY, director of Rockwell Kent Legacies,

1980-82; Plains Art Museum, Moorhead, MN, curator of collections and exhibitions at Rourke Gallery, 1983-84; Katie Gingrass Gallery, Milwaukee, WI, exhibit designer and preparer, 1984; J. and R. Ferris Antiques, Madison, NY, antiques dealer, specializing in Civil War-era medical and scientific instruments, military objects, and Americana, 1985—. Adirondack Museum, Blue Mountain Lake, NY, guest curator, 1996-99. Lecturer at seminars, museums, and educational institutions, including State University of New York College at Plattsburgh and Library of Congress; consultant to art collections and auction houses, including Christie's and Leslie Hindman Auctioneers. Cedarlands Scout Reservation, director of rock climbing and rappeling, 1985—.

*MEMBER:* American Association of Museums, College Art Association of America, Catalogue Raisonne Scholars Association.

*WRITINGS:*

(With Ellen Pearce) *Rockwell Kent's Forgotten Landscapes,* Down East Books (Camden, ME), 1998.
(With Caroline M. Welsh) *The View from Asgaard: Rockwell Kent's Adirondack Legacy,* Adirondack Museum (Blue Mountain Lake, NY), 1999.

Author of "News from the Legacies," a quarterly column in *Kent Collector,* 1981-82. Contributor to periodicals, including *Art and Antiques Northeast.* Contributing editor, *Kent Collector.*

\*    \*    \*

## FIELD, Marshall III  1893-1956

*PERSONAL:* Born September 28, 1893, in Chicago, IL; died of a brain tumor, November 8, 1956, in New York, NY; son of Marshall II and Albertine (Huck) Field; married Evelyn Marshall, 1915 (divorced, 1930); married Audrey James Coats, 1930 (divorced, 1934); married Ruth Pruyn Phipps, 1936; children: (first marriage) Marshall IV, Barbara, Bettine; (third marriage) Phyllis, Fiona. *Education:* Attended Eton and Trinity College, Cambridge.

*CAREER:* Field, Glore, and Company, senior partner, c. 1920s-35; *PM,* New York City, publisher, 1940-48; *Chicago Sun* (later *Sun-Times*), Chicago, IL, publisher, 1941-50; Field Enterprises, chief executive, 1944-1956. *Military service:* U.S. Army Field artillery, World War I, became captain; received Silver Star for gallantry in action.

*WRITINGS:*

*Freedom Is More than a Word,* University of Chicago Press (Chicago), 1945.

*SIDELIGHTS:* Grandson to the founder of the Marshall Field department store and heir to his vast fortune, Marshall Field III distinguished himself in the world of journalism. But it was a career that he did not become involved in until later in his life. Born in Chicago in 1893, Field spent much of his youth in England after his father's death from an apparent suicide in 1909. He returned to the United States as an adult in 1914, at which time he began to dabble in a variety of business ventures as well as serving as a soldier in a field artillery unit during World War I. In the 1930s he began to take an interest in politics and abandoned his business dealings, leaving the investment-banking firm of Field, Glore and Company where he was a senior partner in 1936. He became a staunch supporter of Roosevelt's New Deal and of U.S. involvement in World War II.

It was perhaps his burgeoning concern for political and social issues that inspired Field to turn to journalism. Using the money he had inherited, he invested in a New York newspaper called *PM* in 1940. This first foray into the newspaper business happened when he was forty-six year old. Later the same year he bought out most of the paper's other investors, becoming its chief source of financial support even though it was struggling to survive. But to Field, that did not matter much. As Mary Ann Weston writes in the *Dictionary of Literary Biography,* "For Field, journalism was the culmination of a remarkable personal transformation that took him far from the role expected of one of his lineage—a sheltered life of wealth and privilege—to the unabashed liberalism that led some, according to author John Tebbel, to brand him a 'traitor to his class.' " *PM* was a leftist paper started by Ralph Ingersoll, who had been the publisher of *Time* magazine. It accepted no advertising and Ingersoll was even accused of having communists on the payroll. Field was a frequent visitor to the paper's offices and often supported its liberal take on the news, but he remained just the moneyman, leaving all editorial decisions up to Ingersoll.

*PM* folded in 1948 after Field had invested about $5 million. But Field had never been as interested in the paper's financial success as he was about the ideals it promoted, and his dealings with *PM* do reveal some of Field's own philosophy in his approach to journalism. In 1945 he wrote a book titled *Freedom Is More than a Word* in which he explains his belief that "the American public learned that *PM* is the place where people can get a hearing if they have a just cause. This is true whether they represent racial or religious minorities, pro-labor groups, independent businessmen fighting the monopolists, consumers or individuals deprived of civil liberties in one way or another. *PM* became and remains the focus of whatever cries out for courage against injustice."

In addition to explaining his journalistic policies, this first and only book by Field talks about democracy, education, and the responsibilities that come with having money. Reviewing the book for the *Weekly Book Review,* Joseph Barnes wrote, "Its strengths are its author's open-minded belief in trial and error as a social and political principle, and a healthy optimism about the future. [Field] is aware of the formidable problems our democracy faces, but confident that there is nothing wrong with us that more democracy won't cure."

In his book, Field also talks about his choice to back a second newspaper, the *Chicago Sun.* With the paper from its creation, this time Field took a more hand's on approach to running the business. First appearing in late 1941, the *Sun* took an early stance, upon Field's urging, on the beginning of World War II. Field believed that the United States should take part in the conflict and supported the positions of Roosevelt and his administration.

Although partisan issues such as these got the paper off to a slow start, Field maintained his view that the *Sun* fulfilled Chicago's crying need for an independent morning paper to rival the right-wing *Tribune.* Run by Colonel Robert R. McCormick, the *Tribune* attacked its new competitor. McCormick wrote an editorial in his paper accusing Field of being a "slacker" because he did not volunteer for military service during World War II. The colonel also managed to keep the *Sun* from having access to the Associated Press wire service, the country's largest new-gathering agency. This difficulty was eventually settled in a lawsuit. Despite these and other early hardships, Field was determined to make the Chicago *Sun* into an independent paper that, unlike *PM,* paid its own way. With an eye to this goal, he bought the fledgling afternoon tabloid, the *Chicago Times,* in August of 1947 for a sum in excess of $5 million, not including the $2.5 million of the paper's past debt which he then assumed. The following year Field merged the two papers into a morning tabloid called the *Sun-Times.*

Field decided to retire from the newspaper business in 1950, turning control of the Chicago *Sun-Times* over to his son, Marshall Field IV. He continued to support the

paper financially, reportedly investing $25 million into it before it started to turn a profit. During his era in journalism, Field had established a corporation called Field Enterprises. Among the projects this company worked on were the publication of World Book Encyclopedias and the Sunday magazine supplement *Parade.* This company's broad interests in the field of communications also included four radio stations, the publishing houses Simon & Schuster and Pocket Books, as well as Childcraft children books.

In addition to business ventures, Field was quite active with a number of social and charitable causes. He established the Field Foundation to provide financial aid to resolve issues relating to child welfare and race relations. He helped found the Roosevelt University in Chicago and was a philanthropist to a number of organizations, including the New York Philharmonic Society, the Metropolitan Opera Association of New York, the University of Chicago, and the Chicago Museum of Natural History, which was later renamed the Field Museum because of his support. Field died of a brain tumor in 1956 at the age of sixty-three. Both his sons and his grandson went on to have careers in the Chicago newspaper industry.

## BIOGRAPHICAL/CRITICAL SOURCES:

### BOOKS

Becker, Stephan, *Marshall Field III: A Biography,* Simon & Schuster (New York City), 1964.
*Cambridge Dictionary of American Biography,* Cambridge University Press (Cambridge), 1995.
Darby, Edwin, *The Fortune Builders,* Doubleday (New York City), 1986.
*Dictionary of Literary Biography,* Volume 127: *American Newspaper Publishers, 1950-1990,* Gale (Detroit, MI), 1993.
Downs, Robert B., and Jane B. Downs, *Journalists of the United States,* McFarland & Co. (Jefferson, NC), 1991.
Tebbel, John, *The Marshall Fields: A Study in Wealth,* Dutton (New York City), 1947.

### PERIODICALS

*American Political Science Review,* August, 1945.
*Book Week,* April 15, 1945, p. 3.
*Booklist,* May 1, 1945.
*Business Week,* February 28, 1959, pp. 56-63.
*Canadian Forum,* September, 1945.
*Chicago,* September, 1983, pp. 179-185.
*Christian Century,* April 25, 1945.
*Christian Science Monitor,* April 25, 1945, p. 14.

*Commonweal,* April 20, 1945.
*Editor & Publisher,* November 25, 1961.
*Ethics,* April, 1945.
*Foreign Affairs,* October, 1945.
*Kirkus Reviews,* April 15, 1945.
*Library Journal,* April 15, 1945.
*New Republic,* November 3, 1941, pp. 581-583; April 30, 1945.
*New York Times,* April 29, 1945, p. 4; November 9, 1956, p. 29.
*New Yorker,* November 13, 1943, pp. 20-21.
*Newsweek,* August 4, 1947, pp. 82-84.
*Printer's Ink,* August 26, 1960, pp. 40-42.
*Saturday Review,* October 9, 1965, p. 72.
*Time,* August 10, 1942, p. 51; October 1, 1965, p. 69.
*Wall Street Journal,* August 17, 1978, pp. 1, 17.
*Weekly Book Review,* April 15, 1945, p. 2.*

\* \* \*

## FIELDS, Rick   1942-1999

*OBITUARY NOTICE*—See index for *CA* sketch: Born May 16, 1942, in Manhattan, NY; died of lung cancer, June 6, 1999, in Fairfax, CA. Writer. Fields worked a variety of odd jobs such as apple picker, plumber's assistant and furniture mover before settling on a writing career. He helped found *Tricycle: The Buddhist Review* and the *Loka Journal,* and contributed articles to many publications, several of which related to Buddhism and New Age thinking. He also edited *Yoga Journal* and was a contributing editor at *New Age Journal.* Fields became interested in Buddhism in the early 1970s, studying both the Zen and Tibetan traditions, and wrote several books on the topic. His best-known work is *How the Swans Came to the Lake: A Narrative History of Buddhism in America.* His other titles include *Taking Refuge in LA: Life in a Vietnamese Buddhist Temple* and *Chop Wood, Carry Water: A Guide to Spiritual Fulfillment in Everyday Life,* which he wrote with Peggy Taylor, Rex Weyler, and Rick Ingrasci. A recent work, *Instructions to the Cook: A Zen Master's Lessons in Living a Life that Matters,* co-authored with Bernard Glassman, was published in 1996 and his book of poetry, *F--- You, Cancer and Other Poems,* came out in 1998.

*OBITUARIES AND OTHER SOURCES:*

*PERIODICALS*

*Los Angeles Times,* June 13, 1999, p. B5.
*New York Times,* June 11, 1999, p. A31.

*Washington Post,* June 13, 1999, p. C5.

\* \* \*

## FLOINN, Criostoir O
### See O'FLYNN, Criostoir

\* \* \*

## FREEMAN, Legh Richmond   1842-1915
### (Horatio Vattel)

*PERSONAL:* Born December 4, 1842, in Culpeper, VA; died of Bright's disease, February 7, 1915; son of Arthur Ryland and Mary (Kemper) Freeman; married Ada Virginia Miller (died, 1878); married Janie Nicholas Ward, 1886 (died, 1897); married Mary Rose Genevieve Whitaker, 1900; children: (first marriage) three sons, (second marriage) two. *Politics:* Liberal, later a "John Brown Republican," Populist, Republican. *Avocational interests:* Exploring.

*CAREER: Kearney Herald,* Fort Kearney, NE, publisher and reporter, 1865-66; *Yellowstone Country,* reporter, 1866-67; *Frontier Index,* Dakota Territory, editor, 1868-70s; *Ogden Freeman,* Ogden, UT, editor; *Washington Farmer,* editor. Worked variously as a telegraph operator in Fort Kearney, NE, telegrapher in Rock Island, IL, and coal miner in Rock Springs, WY. Populist Party delegate, 1896. *Military service:* Confederate Army, Civil War, 1864, Cavalry, served as telegrapher; captured and imprisoned by Union troops; joined United States Army.

*WRITINGS:*

Journalist associated as reporter or editor with various newspapers, including *Kearney Herald, Yellowstone Country, Frontier Index, Ogden Freeman,* and *Washington Farmer.* Some articles published under pseudonym Horatio Vattel. The major repository of Freeman's early newspapers is in the Bancroft Library at the University of California, Berkeley; family letters are in the James Lawson Kemper file of the Alderman Library Manuscripts Department at the University of Virginia, Charlottesville.

*SIDELIGHTS:* Legh Richmond Freeman spent his life publishing newspapers on the American frontier, but he was born in the eastern state of Virginia. In the East,

Freeman's family had strong political connections. It was believed in the family that John Hoomes Freeman (Legh's grandfather) was Thomas Jefferson's private secretary; the truth is that he had a lesser role as one of Jefferson's overseers. Freeman was also the nephew of the former governor of Virginia, James Lawson Kemper. Despite the influence of the Freeman family in the East, Freeman journeyed westward and eventually became a major voice for the West.

As a young man, Freeman joined the Confederate Army. Serving as a Confederate private in a Kentucky Cavalry regiment, Freeman was captured and imprisoned in 1864. His specialty was working as a telegrapher and it is thought that he may have been gathering intelligence in the Kentucky Appalachians when captured. Freeman was detained at Rock Island military prison in the Mississippi River between Davenport, Iowa, and Rock Island, Illinois, and was eventually released when he volunteered to serve in the U.S. Army out west. According to Thomas H. Heuterman, writing in the *Dictionary of Literary Biography,* Freeman envisioned himself as "Horatio Vattel, Lightning Scout of the Mountains," and he would come to embody this fantasy in his adult life.

Traveling within a regiment of Unionized Southerners, he reached Fort Kearney, Nebraska, the day Southern troops surrendered at Appomattox (April 9, 1865). Freeman took the position of telegraph operator at the fort. He earned as much as $150 per month in this capacity. Freeman used money from his salary, along with equipment at Fort Kearney, to initiate his own publication: the *Kearney Herald.* Freeman's equipment consisted mainly of makeshift materials, even whittling needed letters from small blocks of wood. Each issue of the *Kearney Herald* consisted of four pages measuring nine by fourteen inches with two columns. Under the name of the paper was the large motto, "Independence in All Things, Neutrality in Nothing." He may have taken this saying from another nearby newspaper, the *Huntsman's Echo.* Freeman charged $6 for an annual subscription and $4 for half a year.

Freeman's reporting focused upon numerous minor events, though he did know how to discern notable news stories. He once interviewed mountain man Jim Bridger. An admirer of explorers, Freeman decided to follow Bridger west. Asking his brother, Frederick Kemper Freeman, to assume control of the *Herald,* Freeman went to satisfy his attraction toward gold fields and Native Americans. Freeman soon ventured to country that was primarily populated by the Native Americans. He experienced Yellowstone country, writing tales of geysers and other natural phenomena.

Freeman lived in Yellowstone from the summer of 1866 until the spring of the following year. At that time, the *Herald* was renamed the *Frontier Index,* as Freeman's brother moved the paper to frontier territories, such as North Platte and Julesburg, Nebraska Territory, and Fort Sanders and Laramie, Dakota Territory. In 1868, Freeman resumed his position as editor of the newspaper. The *Frontier Index* entertained readers with "a mixture of tall tales, anecdotes, humorous essays, and travel narratives in columns adjacent to news of railroad construction and booming towns," states Heuterman. One of his yarns claims that a sheep he shot that rolled into a hot spring and became cooked breakfast. He once noted, "The Yellowstone Lake, in Wyoming Territory, is so clear and deep, that by looking into it you can see them making tea in China."

Racial references were not uncommon in the *Index,* where Freeman revealed his antipathy toward blacks, Asians, and Native Americans. He went so far as to refer to these groups as "species of the animal kingdom." As Heuterman explains, Freeman believed in "a widely held Western view" that "Chinese coolies threatened the jobs of whites, and Indian depredations justified the red man's extinction." Freeman also could not stomach Ulysses S. Grant; he referred to the president as a "whiskey bloated, squaw ravishing adulterer, monkey ridden, nigger worshipping mogul."

Also an alienator of criminals, Freeman wrote an article that resulted in the burning of his newspaper office. In this article, Freeman zestfully reported the deaths of three robbers hung by vigilantes who had broken into the town jail. One week later, on November 20, 1868, friends of the victims destroyed the *Frontier Index* office. Freeman escaped, but at least fourteen others were killed in the riot.

Freeman married Ada Virginia Miller of Strasburg, Virginia, and moved to Rock Island, Illinois, to once again work as a telegrapher. He soon left for Rock Springs, Wyoming, to mine coal (the Union Pacific railroad was converting from wood- to coal-burning furnaces). In 1875, Freeman took his pregnant wife and two children to Ogden, Utah, to start another paper: the *Ogden Freeman.* After unsuccessfully attempting to befriend the Mormon population, he turned against the group, relying on outside sales and advertising. Freeman then re-released the *Frontier Index* in Butte, Montana, in 1878. His wife was killed on her way to meet Freeman there, when a shotgun fell from her wagon and fired. Freeman reacted by considering mysticism and shifting his political stance from Liberal to "John Brown Republican."

Freeman spent the next five years in Montana, putting out six different periodicals. During this period, he successfully weathered a lawsuit against himself, but his business ventures did not fare well. He later took his three sons to Yakima in the Washington Territory, lured by the news of a new railroad line. There he printed the *Washington Farmer,* but soon faced several legal entanglements, which he won.

In 1886, he married again, this time to a woman from Georgia named Janie Nicholas Ward. He then attempted to set up a publishing operation in the Puget Sound area by promoting a new town. Though the benefits were not what he had hoped, he and his family did remain in Washington.

Freeman joined the Populist Party in the hopes of economic assistance through politics; he also eyed, but did not attain, a congressional nomination. He also organized a People's Party that won no seats. He even dutifully tried in 1897, to no avail, to persuade state representatives to launch him into the U.S. Senate.

Freeman faced some difficult times in later life. His elder sons left him, and his second wife passed away in 1897. In 1900, he married a third time, to Mary Rose Genevieve Whitaker. Freeman was influential in the 1906 passage of irrigation legislation in Yakima, Washington. Once more, Freeman attempted a U.S. Senate seat, and later a mayoral post in North Yakima, but gathered few votes. Just three months after the mayoral election, Freeman died on February 7, 1915. He lived the life of his nom de plume, Horatio Vattel, but wealth and notoriety alluded him. It is noteworthy that his *Washington Farmer* did survive and thrive after his passing.

### BIOGRAPHICAL/CRITICAL SOURCES:

*BOOKS*

*Dictionary of Literary Biography,* Volume 23: *American Newspaper Journalists, 1873-1900,* Gale, 1983.

Heuterman, Thomas H., *Movable Type: Biography of Legh R. Freeman,* Iowa State University Press, 1979.

Wright, Elizabeth, *Independence in All Things, Neutrality in Nothing,* Miller Freeman, 1973.*

# G

## GASPERETTI, David 1952-

*PERSONAL:* Born December 4, 1952, in Milwaukee, WI; son of Emil J. and Connie Gasperetti. *Education:* Lawrence University, B.A. (magna cum laude), 1976; University of California, Los Angeles, M.A., 1978, Ph.D. (Russian litertature), 1985.

*ADDRESSES: Office*—University of Notre Dame, Department of German and Russian, 318 O'Shaughnessy Hall, Notre Dame, IN 46556. *E-mail*—gasperetti.2@ nd.edu.

*CAREER:* University of Tulsa, Tulsa, OK, assistant professor, 1985-89; University of Notre Dame, Notre Dame, IN, assistant professor of Russian, 1989-96, associate professor of Russian, 1996—.

*MEMBER:* American Association for the Advancement of Slavic Studies, American Association of the Teachers of Slavic and East European Languages, Phi Beta Kappa.

*AWARDS, HONORS:* Outstanding academic book award, *Choice,* 1998, for *The Rise of the Russian Novel: Carnival, Stylization, and Mockery of the West;* Teacher of the Year award, University of Tulsa College of Arts and Sciences; Social Science Research Council fellowship; Kaneb Center Traching Award, University of Notre Dame.

*WRITINGS:*

*The Rise of the Russian Novel: Carnival, Stylization, and Mockery of the West,* Northern Illinois University Press (DeKalb, IL), 1998.

Contributor to periodicals, including *Russian Literature, Slavic and East European Journal,* and *Russian Review,* and to *Dictionary of Literary Biography:* Volume 150: *Early Modern Russian Writers, Late Seventeenth and Eighteenth Centuries,* edited by Marcus C. Levitt, Gale (Detroit), 1995.

*WORK IN PROGRESS:* Research of the Russian novel of the 1830s to 1850s and its cultural context.

*SIDELIGHTS:* David Gasperetti is an associate professor of Russian at Notre Dame University, where his courses include "Surveys of Nineteenth and Twentieth-Century Russian Literature," "Pushkin and His Time," "Tolstoy," "*The Brothers Karamazov,*" and "Revolution in the Russian Novel." Gasperetti is also the author of *The Rise of the Russian Novel: Carnival, Stylization, and Mockery of the West.* Prior to 1775, there were only twelve original Russian novels. The government's monopoly on printing ended in 1783, but this did not result in a ground swell of creativity, and fiction continued to be mistrusted. In his book Gasperetti shows how reader interest increased because of the work of three important writers who set the trend in literature during the era of Catherine the Great and led to the development of Russian prose fiction during the 1840s. "Acknowledging their unpolished artistry, he convincingly applies Bakhtin's theory of carnival to demonstrate their use of Russian popular culture to subvert prevailing European conventions," wrote N. Tittler for *Yankee Book Peddlar* online.

These three authors include Matvei Komarov, who wrote *Milord George,* a romance adventure in which hero and heroine travel over high seas to Turkey, Sardinia, Copenhagen, and Venice where they meet at a carnival. Hidden by her disguise, she tests his fidelity.

In Komarov's *Vanka Kain,* a bandit is sentenced to hard labor. Andrew Kahn wrote in the *Times Literary Supplement* that "the hero's winning villainy reflects the Russian love of underdogs, and is in the spirit of the folkloric and literary texts that celebrate figures like the bandit Stepan Razin and the rebel Pugachev."

The second author is Mikhail Chulkov, an actor at the court theatre in St. Petersburg, a civil servant in the Department of Commerce, and a writer who was not a part of the literary establishment. His *The Mocker* is a collection of stories and legends through which "he simultaneously parodied serious prose and pursued utopian fantasy," wrote Kahn. Kahn said Chulkov created "a hybrid and open genre that looks forward to Dostoevsky's *Diary of a Writer.*" Kahn called Chulkov's *Comely Cook* "a cross between Moll Flanders and Molly Bloom." It is a rags-to-riches story of a seductress, and although the monologue has been praised by scholars, Gasperetti contends it is merely a prop to undermine the conventions of serious literature. Kahn said the works of Komarov and Chulkov "revel in comic reversals and wantonness, champion the poor over the privileged, the serf over the master, and even the reader over the author." These popular works were circulated through a type of wood-block book, called a *lubok,* which had been in use since the seventeenth century.

Gasperetti's third subject is Fedor Emin, and Kahn compared him to Komarov and Chulkov. "By contrast, the novels of Fedor Emin roll didacticism, adventure, and the sentimental into one," wrote Kahn. Emin was a Turk who lived a colorful life. In his *The Adventures of Themistocles,* the first Russian philosophical novel, the hero comments on the nature of the ideal state. Abduction and rescue figure in the plot of *The Marquis de Toledo,* which takes place in the Orient. Gasperetti describes Emin's works as examples of early realism. Kahn concluded that Gasperetti "makes an excellent case for the artistic value of a pioneering set of novels whose significance outweighs their small number."

*BIOGRAPHICAL/CRITICAL SOURCES:*

*PERIODICALS*

*Choice,* October, 1998, pp. 323-24.
*Russian Review,* January, 1999, pp. 133-34.
*Slavic and East European Journal,* spring, 1999, pp. 204-06.
*Slavic Review,* winter 1998, pp. 937-38.
*Times Literary Supplement,* August 7, 1998, p. 13.

*OTHER*

*Yankee Book Peddlar,* http://www.ybp.com/choice/ Choice98HumLang%26Literature.htm (1999).*

\*   \*   \*

**GELBART, Nina Rattner**

*PERSONAL:* Female.

*ADDRESSES: Agent*—University of California Press, 2120 Berkeley Way, Berkeley, CA 94720.

*CAREER:* Writer and historian. Occidental College, Los Angeles, professor of science and history of science.

*AWARDS, HONORS:* Recipient of awards, including the Sierra Prize, for *Feminine and Opposition Journalism in Old Regime France.*

*WRITINGS:*

*HISTORY AND BIOGRAPHY*

*Feminine and Opposition Journalism in Old Regime France,* University of California Press (Berkeley), 1987.
*The King's Midwife: A History and Mystery of Madame du Coudray,* University of California Press, 1998.

Also author of *Science in Enlightenment Utopias: Power and Purpose in Eighteenth-Century French "Voyages Imaginaires,"* 1974.

*SIDELIGHTS:* Professor and historian Nina Gelbart explores the roots of French feminism and its basis in journalism during the eighteenth century in her book *Feminine and Opposition Journalism in Old Regime France.* Specifically the book recounts the history of the periodical *Journal des Dames,* which existed from 1759 until 1778, and which started out as a light and inconsequential magazine for women. According to Gelbart the publication evolved to walk a fine line between what was considered legitimate and what was being published underground. Of its nine editors during its publication, three were women.

The author demonstrates how the magazine grew from its rather conservative beginnings to a paper that questioned the role of women in French society and suggested that women's roles needed to change. Editors with different philosophical bents helped shaped the paper. For example, one woman who served between 1761-1763 (Madame de Beaumer) had extremely radical leanings which were reflected in the paper. Formerly the publication had been guided by men who were sympathetic to the plight of women but who did not want to upset the status quo. De Beaumer faced pressure from French censors and was eventually ousted for her attempts to place female equality on a level with oppression in general. The two women editors who followed made progress for feminists, according to Gelbart, but worked better within the existing social system. The final female editor was a follower of the philosopher Jean-Jaques Rousseau and worked to portray motherhood as an elevated ideal and a "renewed social purpose."

Gelbart claims that the evolution of the *Journal des Dames* sheds light on the roots of French feminism and also influenced the French revolution. Margriet Bruijn Lacy of *French Review* calls the author an "excellent storyteller" and praises Gelbart's assiduous research, even thought Lacy claims that Gelbart uses too many arguments to make her points. Carolyn Chappell Lougee of the *American Historical Review* is also complementary, and praises the author's balance of "biography, intellectual analysis, and institutional profile." *Choice* reviewer H.S. Vyverberg calls the book significant for its survey of eighteenth century feminism.

In *The King's Midwife: A History and Mystery of Madame du Coudray* Gelbart attempts to piece together what is known about this interesting figure in French history. Du Coudray was of obscure origins, but her midwifery skills were noticed by French king Louis XV, who was convinced that his country was decreasing in population. Inspired by the Enlightenment and in hopes of creating a strong France, the King commissioned du Coudray to travel to rural France and teach poor, illiterate women the art of midwifery. Du Coudray was credited with training more than 10,000 midwives on her trips through rural France. She also authored and updated a book on midwifery for the medical profession and created the first model (using skeleton bones and sponged blood) of a female pelvis and uterus so that her trainees could get hands-on experience.

Little is known about du Coudray's personal life or thoughts, but one reviewer notes that Gelbart has done an admirable job of collecting any available biographical research and letting the reader make their own conclusions. Some of the research suggests that du Cou-

dray was motivated by self promotion and income rather than a kindred sympathy for fellow French women. Pamela June Weatherill of the *American Scientist* calls the book an "exciting read" and relevant for readers in many professions, including medicine, biography, and politics. A *Publishers Weekly* reviewer finds Gelbart's method of presentation effective, using "brief dated sections that describe du Coudray's activities in the present tense."

*BIOGRAPHICAL/CRITICAL SOURCES:*

*PERIODICALS*

*American Historical Review,* October, 1989, pp. 1109-1110; October, 1991, p. 1206; December, 1996, p. 1552.
*American Scientist,* July-August, 1998, p. 390.
*Choice,* January, 1988, p. 820.
*French Review,* December, 1989, pp. 370-371.
*New York Times Book Review,* July 26, 1998, p. 29.
*Publishers Weekly,* April 6, 1998, p. 66.
*Southern Economic Journal,* January, 1997, p. 823.

\*    \*    \*

## GELFAND, Mark I.

*PERSONAL: Education:* Columbia University, Ph.D., 1972.

*ADDRESSES: Home*—Brookline, MA. *Office*—Department of History, Boston College, Chestnut Hill, MA 02467; fax: 617-552-2478. *Agent*—c/o Northeastern University Press, 416 Columbus Place, 360 Huntington Ave., Boston, MA 02115.

*CAREER:* Writer. Boston College, Boston, MA, associate professor of history.

*WRITINGS:*

*A Nation of Cities: The Federal Government and Urban America, 1933-1965,* Oxford University Press (New York City), 1975.
(Editor with Robert E. Lester) *The War on Poverty, 1964-1968,* University Publications of America (Frederick, MD), 1986.
*Trustee for a City: Ralph Lowell of Boston,* Northeastern University Press (Boston, MA), 1998.

Contributor to books, including *Exploring the Johnson Years,* 1981; *Reshaping America: Society and Institu-*

*tions, 1945-60,* 1982; *American Choices: Social Dilemmas and Public Policy Since 1960,* 1986; *Snowbelt Cities: Metropolitan Politics in the Northeast and Midwest Since World War II,* 1990; and *Metropolitan Governance Revisited,* 1998. Also coeditor of collection of essays *The War on Poverty, 1964-1968.* Contributor of articles and reviews to periodicals, including *American Historical Review, Business History Review* and the *Annals of the American Academy of Political and Social Science.*

*SIDELIGHTS:* Mark Gelfand, an associate professor at Boston College, has focused on issues of modern American urban development and policy in his two monographs. *A Nation of Cities: The Federal Government and Urban America, 1933-1965* explores the relationship that developed between big cities and the federal government during the 1930s, when rural interests generally controlled state legislatures. Since these bodies were not inclined to support programs for big cities, urban leaders formed the United States Conference of Mayors to convince the U.S. Congress to authorize direct federal aid to cities. How this aid affected urban growth, wrote Joseph L. Arnold in *The Journal of American History,* is an important subject that had been relatively neglected until Gelfand's study, which Arnold hailed as an "excellent straightforward narrative" that presents the first "detailed overview of these vast, complex [federal] programs." Arnold noted that Gelfand's judgments in the book were "cautious and tentative," and further observed that ambiguous definitions of "the city" can lead to different conclusions as to the long-term effects of federal aid to cities. Arnold concludes that Gelfand's view of urbanization "lends credence to the assertion that our late-twentieth-century cities . . . are accurate physical expressions of the dominant values and modes of thought of the American people."

Gelfand's second monograph focused not on urbanization in general but on a specific city, Boston, and in particular the contributions of its distinguished resident Ralph Lowell. *Trustee for a City: Ralph Lowell of Boston* (1998), which *Library Journal* reviewer Thomas McMullin considered well-written, examines Lowell's role in supporting such institutions as Massachusetts General Hospital, the Museum of Fine Arts, and Harvard University, and his part in creating Boston's public television station, WGBH. "Gelfand . . . sees Lowell's biography as a means of exploring continuity and change in Boston during this century," wrote McMullin, who also appreciated the book's treatment of the "dynamics of the postwar urban elite" and American philanthropy. These dynamics were particularly complicated in Boston, where the Yankee elite still dominated civic institutions. *Boston Globe* reviewer Michael Kenney pointed out that Gelfand rightly emphasizes the radical changes Lowell advanced at many Boston institutions, including the appointment of women as well as Irish, Jewish, and nonwhite members. Kenney noted that Gelfand suggests that Lowell's most important contribution to Boston was "that he broke out of his class and social position to further efforts to improve racial and religious tolerance."

*BIOGRAPHICAL/CRITICAL SOURCES:*

*PERIODICALS*

*Boston Globe,* November 16, 1998, p. D14.
*Journal of American History,* June 1982, pp. 218-220.
*Library Journal,* October 1, 1998, p. 102.

*OTHER*

*Boston College History Department,* http://www.bc.edu/bc—org/avp/cas/his/history/gelfand.html (November 11, 1999).*

\*        \*        \*

## GEORGE, Anne

*PERSONAL:* Married.

*ADDRESSES: Home*—Birmingham, AL. *Agent*—c/o Avon Books, 1350 Avenue of the Americas, New York, NY 10019; fax 212-261-6895.

*CAREER:* Writer, editor, and former school teacher.

*AWARDS, HONORS:* 1997 Agatha Award for Best First Mystery for *Murder on a Girls' Night Out;* former Alabama State Poet; nominated for the Pulitzer Prize; recipient of other writing awards.

*WRITINGS:*

*Wild Goose Chase,* Druid Press (Birmingham, AL), 1982.
(Editor with Jerri Beck) *A Baker's Dozen: Contemporary Women Poets of Alabama* (anthology), Druid Press, 1988.
*Murder on a Girls' Night Out,* Avon (New York City), 1996.
*Murder on a Bad Hair Day,* Avon, 1996.
*Murder Runs in the Family,* Avon, 1997.

*Murder Makes Waves,* Avon, 1997.
*Murder Gets a Life: A Southern Sisters Mystery,* Avon, 1998.

Also contributor to literary journals.

*SIDELIGHTS:* Anne George began her writing career with a book titled *Wild Goose Chase,* published by a small Alabama publishing house, Druid Press, in 1982. Six years later, George teamed up with Jerri Beck to edit the poetry anthology *A Baker's Dozen: Contemporary Women Poets of Alabama,* also for Druid. This southern state is also the setting for George's mystery novels, which include *Murder on a Girls' Night Out,* published in 1996.

*Murder on a Girls' Night Out* features unlikely sleuth Patricia Anne Hollowell, a retired teacher suddenly drawn into the world of murder investigation when her flamboyant sister Mary Alice becomes proprietor of a country-music nightclub. George constructs a plot that centers around the slaying of the club's former owner and the prime suspect in the deed—coincidentally, one of Hollowell's favorite students from her classroom days. A review of *Murder on a Girls' Night Out* in *Publishers Weekly* offered a mixed assessment: as a crime novel, its solution involved too many flimsy links and long-dormant secrets, but the magazine gave praise to George's capacity for "sprightly dialogue and a humorous eye for detail."

Patricia Anne and Mary Alice return in 1997's *Murder Runs in the Family,* which begins with the wedding of Mary Alice's daughter. At the festivities, the sisters strike up a friendship with genealogist Meg Ryan, but are later shocked to learn she has committed suicide. The Hollowells suspect foul play in Ryan's improbable jump from a courthouse window. The more the sisters dig, the more intrigue they uncover, and learn that Ryan was not the person she seemed. A contributor to *Publishers Weekly* found that the story line of *Murder Runs in the Family* "spins out of control," but granted that George creates "wonderful dialogue," exceptional characterizations of even minor players, and an engaging party scene that opens the novel. George has penned other mysteries, including *Murder on a Bad Hair Day* and *Murder Makes Waves.*

*BIOGRAPHICAL/CRITICAL SOURCES:*

*PERIODICALS*

*Publishers Weekly,* January 22, 1996, p. 66; April 14, 1997, p. 71.
*References Services Review,* summer 1995.

*OTHER*

*Avon Books,* http://www.avonbooks.com (November 11, 1999).
*Mystery Awards,* http://www.slip.net/cluelass/Awards.html.*

\*        \*        \*

## GERNSBACK, Hugo   1884-1967

*PERSONAL:* Born August 16, 1884, in Luxembourg; immigrated to the United States, February, 1904; died August 19, 1967, in New York, NY; son of Maurice (a wine wholesaler) and Berta (Durlacher) Gernsback; married three times; third wife, Marn Hancher; children: two daughters, one son, from first two marriages. *Education:* Attended the Ecole Industrielle Luxembourg, and the Technikum Bingen, Germany. *Avocational interests:* Inventing, radio.

*CAREER:* Inventor, businessman, editor, writer, and publisher.

*MEMBER:* Officer of the Oaken Crown, Luxembourg (1954).

*AWARDS, HONORS:* Hugo Special Award, 1960; Hugo Award for science fiction is named for Hugo Gernsback; Michigan Institute of Radio Engineers/Radio Relay League, 1957, for inventions in the field of radio communications.

*WRITINGS:*

*The Wireless Telephone,* Modern Electrics (New York City), 1910.
*Wireless Hook-ups,* Modern Electrics (New York City), 1911.
*Radio for All,* Lippincott (Philadelphia), 1922.
*Ralph 124C 41+,* Stratford (Boston), 1925.
*How to Build and Operate Short Wave Receivers,* Short Wave Craft (New York City), 1932.
*Evolution of Modern Science Fiction,* (New York City), 1952.
*Ultimate World,* edited by Sam Moskowitz, Walker (New York City), 1972.
(Contributor) Frederik Pohl, editor, *The Science Fiction Roll of Honor,* Random House (New York City), 1975.
*Official Radio Service Manual and Complete Directory of All Commercial Wiring Diagrams, 1930,* Vestral (New York City), 1984.

*SIDELIGHTS:* Although today's fans of science fiction are unlikely to know Hugo Gernsback's novels, they most certainly will know his name—the prestigious Hugo Award for science-fiction writing was named after him. He is perhaps the single most influential individual in the development of the science fiction short-story genre in the United States, although that career arose almost accidentally. While still quite young, Gernsback showed great promise as a scientist and technician and, as Garyn G. Roberts writes in *Dictionary of Literary Biography,* he was "never satisfied with the limits of existing scientific knowledge." In the first years of the 1900s, his inventive mind came up with the prototype of a new kind of battery, but by 1904 the European-born Gernsback had failed to secure a patent for his invention in Germany or France, and so decided to immigrate to the United States, where he hoped to patent and market it.

Gernsback's hopes were dashed—his invention was powerful, but impractical to manufacture. However he was not without options in his newly adopted homeland: he took a research position with New York manufacturer William Roche. This job lasted less than a day; Roche suddenly took it into his head to suspect Gernsback of industrial espionage and fired him on the spot. Gernsback then became a partner in the Gee-Cee Dry Battery Company, an unsatisfactory situation that he left when he discovered that his partner was siphoning off the company's profits. He then went into business on his own, producing automobile batteries, and did well until hard economic times wiped out his wholesale distributor in 1907.

Gernsback turned his considerable skills and interest to other technical fields, ultimately entering into a partnership that specialized in importing specialized scientific equipment from Europe. This venture led Gernsback to explore the then still-young field of radio communications, and he invented the walkie-talkie in about 1909. From this point on, Gernsback's influence in radio grew immensely, largely as a result of his first publishing venture: he founded *Modern Electrics* in 1908. The first radio magazine published anywhere in the world, *Modern Electrics* was important for its role in popularizing radio—within two years of first publication, Gernsback had organized 10,000 amateur radio operators—but also because it provided Gernsback with an outlet for his first efforts at science-fiction writing, which he called "scientifiction."

His novel *Ralph 124C41+,* set in the year 2600, was introduced to his readership in serialized form in the pages of *Modern Electrics* from April, 1911, to March, 1912. (It was brought out in book form in 1925). Heartened by the popular success of *Ralph 124C41+,* Gernsback began a new serialized tale, based on the Rudolf Erich Raspe character, Baron Munchausen, who first appeared in print in 1785. Like the first novel, these tales were printed in Gernsback's magazine, now retitled the *Electrical Experimenter,* and they ran from May, 1915, to February, 1917. Soon, Gernsbeck was accepting stories from other authors as well. By 1923, his magazine—once again retitled, this time as *Science and Invention*—was publishing some of the most innovative fiction of the day. His nearest competitors in this genre were two pulp magazines, *Weird Tales* and *Argosy,* but they had, up to this time, concentrated on far more fanciful tales. The success of Gernsback's authors changed the face of the genre, introducing a trend toward stories that drew more directly on legitimate scientific advances and attempted to extrapolate from them into the future.

In April of 1926, Gernsback entered the pulp magazine arena himself, when he produced the first issue of *Amazing Stories.* Gernsback was a science fiction purist—he had little use for the fantasy-oriented stories that had, up to the 1920s, dominated the pulp fiction market. Instead, as Roberts notes, "The stories he published and encouraged authors to write were based on 'real,' 'possible' scientific achievements." Among the authors who saw their first stories published in this landmark magazine and Gernsback's *Scientific Detective Monthly* are some of the classic names in the pantheon of early science fiction writing: Ray Cummings, E. E. "Doc" Smith, David H. Keller, Stanton A. Coblentz, and Jack Williamson.

By this point, Gernsback had formed the Experimenter Publishing Company, under which auspices he also published *French Humor,* a weekly, *Tidbits,* a monthly, and *Your Body,* a quarterly magazine devoted to health topics of popular interest. In 1929, however, Gernsback's empire was due for a fall. With *Your Body,* he entered into head-to-head competition with another highly successful publisher, Bernarr MacFadden, prompting the latter to try to buy him out. Roberts reports what happened next: "Suddenly, on 20 February, 1929, apparently at McFadden's instigation, Gernsback was sued for payment by three creditors." Gernsback's Experimenter Publishing Company was forced into bankruptcy under then-extant legal provisions in the state of New York. Gernsback was not down for long: in mid-1929 he was back in business at the helm of the newly founded Stellar Publishing Company, which issued *Everyday Mechanics, Science Wonder Stories,* and *Air Wonder Stories* before the summer was out. By

December of that same year, *Scientific Detective Monthly* (later retitled *Amazing Detective Tales*) hit the magazine stands. He soon returned to the field of popular health publishing as well, bringing out the monthly *Sexology* in 1933.

Gernsback's role in defining the fiction genre that we know today as "science fiction" cannot be underestimated. His publications supported and nourished the talents of the genre's earliest writers, and his own stories, editorials, and essays helped define the terms of the field. Little wonder, then that he was invited to the World Science Fiction Convention in 1952 as guest of honor, or that, the following year, the Convention's annual achievement awards became known as "Hugos." He died in 1967 at the age of eighty-three. As Bill Blackbeard concludes in *Dictionary of Literary Biography*, "Hugo Gernsback is secure in his position of honor in the field of science fiction as a man who saw how to package identifiably his favorite form of reading matter and focus the attention of its many followers on a single outlet—with the results we all know today."

*BIOGRAPHICAL/CRITICAL SOURCES:*

BOOKS

*Dictionary of Literary Biography*, Gale (Detroit, MI), Volume 8: *Twentieth-Century American Science-Fiction Writers*, 1981, Volume 137: *American Magazine Journalists, 1900-1960*, 1994.
Aldiss, Brian W., and David Wingrove, *Trillion Year Spree: The True History of Science Fiction*, Atheneum, 1986.

PERIODICALS

*Algol*, winter, 1978, pp. 23-27.*

*       *       *

# GIST, John   1963-

*PERSONAL:* Born October 26, 1963, in Denver, CO; son of Christopher (a teacher) and Phyllis Angeline (Jozuik) Gist; married, wife's name, Wendy, August, 1998. *Ethnicity:* "Multi." *Education:* University of Wyoming, B.A., 1992; University of Alaska, M.F.A., 1996. *Politics;* "Individual." *Religion:* "Esoteric." *Avocational interests:* Quantum physics, the occult.

*ADDRESSES: Home*—Mills, WY. *Office*—Andmar Press, P.O. Box 217, Mills, WY 82644.

*CAREER:* University of Alaska, Fairbanks, English teacher, 1992-96; Andmar Press, Mills, WY, editor-in-chief, 1996—.

*WRITINGS:*

*Crowheart* (fiction), Andmar Press (Mills, WY), 1999.

*WORK IN PROGRESS: The Pale Criminal,* a novel.

*SIDELIGHTS:* John Gist told *CA:* "I write best in the mornings, before the mundane tendencies of the day have had a chance to cement into my consciousness. Most importantly, I attempt to write at least five days per week; this process keeps the project simmering in my subconscious.

"I write because I must. My greatest influences are Nietzsche, Faulkner, Ouspensky, *Beowulf,* Tolkien, Castaneda, and Camus."

*       *       *

# GLASSMAN, Maxine

*PERSONAL: Education:* Studied the harp at the Eastern School of Music. *Avocational interests:* Playing the harp.

*ADDRESSES: Home*—Andover, MA. *Agent*—c/o Donald I. Fine Books, 275 Hudson St., New York, NY 10014.

*CAREER:* Author. Worked in a carpet store in Boston, MA, for eighteen years; book reviewer for the *Worcester Telegram Gazette,* Worcester, MA.

*WRITINGS:*

*Love among the Orientals,* Fine (New York City), 1998.

*SIDELIGHTS:* Author Maxine Glassman lives in Amherst, Massachusetts. She reviewed books for twenty years and for eighteen years worked in an oriental carpet store in Boston's Back Bay. In her debut novel, *Love among the Orientals,* Doris and Jake Seagull own such a store, Classic Designs, in the Back Bay neighborhood. A *Publishers Weekly* reviewer said, "The comic, supernatural story line of this debut starts with a sexy conceit but then fizzles." Doris is the daughter of a mobster, and her love for her rugs is such that she grieves when she sells one. Jake runs the business and secretly sells rugs from Doris's private collection. A spell from the Kama Sutra has been cast on the rugs, which heightens the libidos of everyone in the shop, employees and customers alike. The staff includes Lesley, who is having a lunchtime affair with a widower; and Jon and Sarah, both married, but not to each other, who are also involved in a torrid romance.

Carpets begin disappearing from the homes of Classic Design's clients, and detective Mike Hannagan of the Boston Police Department is on the case. He and Sarah are attracted, she leaves her husband, wins eleven million dollars in the lottery, and begins a romance with Mike, who solves the mystery of the missing carpets. "So many clues point to the thief that untangling the machinations behind the crimes seems beside the point," wrote Malachy Duffy in the *New York Times Book Review.* A *Kirkus Reviews* contributor said, "Glassman's knowledge of and fondness for rugs is the singular strength of an otherwise wan debut outing, in which the sex is more busy than erotic and the rug-theft subplot is a half-woven afterthought." However, *Library Journal* reviewer Ellen R. Cohen called *Love among the Orientals* a "delightful, sensual tale."

*BIOGRAPHICAL/CRITICAL SOURCES:*

*PERIODICALS*

*Booklist,* June 1, 1998, p. 1732.
*Kirkus Reviews,* April 15, 1998, pp. 514-515.
*Library Journal,* May 1, 1998, p. 137.
*New York Times Book Review,* September 20, 1998, p. 24.
*Publishers Weekly,* April 20, 1998, p. 47.*

\*    \*    \*

## GODDARD, Morrill   1865-1937

*PERSONAL:* Surname pronounced "*go*-dard"; born October 7, 1865, in Auburn, ME; died of a heart attack, July 1, 1937, in ME; son of Charles William (a lawyer and public official) and Rowena Caroline (Morrill) Goddard; married Jessamine Rugg, 1889; children: five. *Education:* Attended Bowdoin College; Dartmouth College, B.A., 1885 (at age nineteen). *Avocational interests:* Yachting.

*CAREER: New York World,* reporter, 1885-87, city editor, 1887-89, Sunday editor, 1889-96; *New York Jour-*

*nal* (renamed the *American*), Sunday editor, 1896-1922; *American Magazine* (renamed *American Weekly*), editor, 1896-1937.

*WRITINGS:*

*What Interests People—and Why,* American Weekly (New York City), 1932.

*SIDELIGHTS:* Morrill Goddard's contribution to the field of journalism was an injection of sensationalism and color. One of the pioneers of so-called "yellow journalism," his talents induced a bidding war between Joseph Pulitzer and William Randolph Hearst. Goddard's influence is still evident in many newspapers, particularly in their Sunday editions.

Goddard was born on October 7, 1865 in Auburn, Maine; his family hailed from Portland. His father, Charles William Goddard, was an attorney who had served as United States consul in Constantinople during the Civil War and eventually became a state judge. Goddard's mother, Rowena Caroline Morrill Goddard, was the daughter of a governor of Maine. A graduate of the Portland public school system, Goddard followed his father and enrolled in Bowdoin College. During his sophomore year, he was expelled for taking part in freshman hazing activities. Transferring to Dartmouth College, he completed his undergraduate studies without drawing much attention to himself, though he did take an avid interest in school publications.

In 1885, Goddard graduated at the very young age of nineteen and immediately moved to New York. He did not even wait to receive his diploma. Goddard set his sights on a full-time position at Pulitzer's *New York World,* and worked diligently to attain one. Like most young reporters, Goddard had to produce his own news stories, receiving remuneration only for material that appeared in the paper. Goddard remedied this situation by befriending the city morgue's manager, "a peg-legged Civil War veteran" as James Boylan stated in the *Dictionary of Literary Biography,* with gifts. Prowling about the morgue enabled Goddard to write intriguing copy; he was made a full staff member of the *World* in a matter of weeks.

Goddard didn't stop his aggressive efforts until after he became the paper's city editor at the age of twenty-one. Boylan noted, "His feats of aggression and intrusion as a reporter, strangely contrasting with his quiet personality, became legend." He mounted a funeral carriage to observe the family of Ulysses S. Grant during his funeral procession. He learned Latin phrases to interview a delegate from the Vatican. He used his connections in Maine to interview James G. Blaine, a candidate for the presidency from that state. When President Grover Cleveland honeymooned in 1886, Goddard was among the many reporters who hounded the newlyweds. His work ethic so astounded Ballard Smith, managing editor of the *World,* that Goddard advanced after only two years on the job. Goddard preferred "hard news," Boylan explained, but Pulitzer wanted him for Sunday editor. Goddard was convinced when Pulitzer uncharacteristically offered him the freedom to assemble his own staff. Goddard took his position so seriously that he stirred unrest in other departments of the *World,* and in 1892, Pulitzer terminated his editorship.

After some time off in Paris, Goddard traveled back to New York City and resumed his work. Goddard then proceeded to amend the Sunday edition. In 1893, Goddard assembled a 100-page edition in honor of Pulitzer's tenth anniversary with the *World.* In November of 1894, Goddard produced (with the help of artist Richard F. Outcault) the first color comics section in an American newspaper. Some historians contend that Goddard first fashioned the banner headline. He was known often to employ "the cutaway drawing," enabling readers to peer inside a body or object. One of Goddard's more risque articles, titled "The Girl in the Pie," piqued the interest of William Randolph Hearst. Having just bought the *Morning Journal* of New York, he was on a secret staff hunt. Goddard received an offer from Hearst in January of 1896, but was hesitant. As Boylan detailed, Goddard had two misgivings: "Hearst might not last in New York and . . . he did not want to leave the staff he had built at the *World.*" A usually frugal man, Hearst promised Goddard an annual salary of $35,000. Hearst then proceeded to net virtually the entire *World* Sunday edition staff. What followed was a seesaw battle: Pulitzer took the staff back with a higher offer, but within a day Hearst reclaimed the staff for good.

At the *Journal,* Goddard found himself with greater editorial freedom. Enticing headlines, Boylan explained, such as MARS PEOPLED BY ONE VAST THINKING VEGETABLE, DOES MODERN PHOTOGRAPHY INCITE WOMEN TO BRUTALITY?, and A SOUTH SEA ADAMLESS EDEN WHERE HUSBANDS ARE WELCOME, coupled with large illustrations and short articles, helped expand the readership of the Sunday *Journal* dramatically.

Goddard's journalistic philosophy rested in his love of "true life stories." Addressing his critics by noting that, "The great events of history have been sensational,"

Goddard believed that actual events are far more fascinating than fictional tales. Boylan quotes a reviewer at *Tide* magazine, "He knew, possibly, with greater surety than any editor of his time, what interested people and why." In spite of his high-profile position, Goddard kept a surprisingly low profile. A private man, he spurned celebrity and avoided "professional journalism activities." In 1937 Goddard died of a heart attack while vacationing in Maine with his family. He was generally regarded as a brilliant and tenacious man, who undoubtedly helped to set the pace to all journalists to follow in the tradition of the American Sunday paper.

*BIOGRAPHICAL/CRITICAL SOURCES:*

*BOOKS*

Bleyer, Willard Grosvenor, *Main Currents in the History of American Journalism,* Houghton Mifflin, 1927.
*Dictionary of Literary Biography,* Volume 25: *American Newspaper Journalists, 1901-1925,* Gale (Detroit, MI), 1984.
Mott, Frank Luther, *American Journalism: A History: 1690-1960,* Macmillan, 1962.
Swanberg, W. A., *Pulitzer,* Scribners, 1967.
Winkler, John K., *W. R. Hearst: An American Phenomenon,* Simon & Schuster, 1928.

*PERIODICALS*

*Collier's,* January-July, 1911.
*Columbia Journalism Review,* summer, 1963, pp. 24-28.
*Dartmouth Alumni Magazine,* October, 1937, pp. 13-14, 33-34.
*Journalism Quarterly,* autumn, 1971, p. 466.*

\*    \*    \*

**GOFFEE, Robert (Edward)   1952-**

*PERSONAL:* Born April 18, 1952, in London, England; son of Edward William and Rose Elizabeth (Jones) Goffee; married Victoria Julie Marriott, October 14, 1978; children: Hannah Naomi, Tom Robert. *Education:* University of Kent, B.A. (with honors), 1973, Ph.D., 1978.

*ADDRESSES: Office*—London Business School, Sussex Pl., Regent's Park, London NW1 4SA, England.

*CAREER:* Organizational behavior educator, consultant, and author. University of Surrey, Surrey, England, lecturer, 1981-83; London Business School, London, England, professor, 1983-95, department head, 1995—; Creative Management Associates, London, managing partner, 1990—. London Business School board of governors, 1991-94.

*MEMBER:* Academy of Management.

*AWARDS, HONORS:* University of Bath, research fellow, 1976-78; University of Kent, research fellow, 1978-81; Society for the Encouragement of the Arts, Manufacturers and Commerce, Royal Fellow.

*WRITINGS:*

(With Richard Scase) *The Real World of the Small Business Owner,* Croom Helm (London), 1980, Croom Helm (New York City), 1987.

(With Richard Scase) *The Entrepreneurial Middle Class,* Croom Helm (London), 1982.

(With Richard Scase) *Women in Charge: The Experiences of Female Entrepreneurs,* Allen & Unwin (Boston, MA), 1985.

(With Richard Scase) *Entrepreneurship in Europe: The Social Processes,* Croom Helm (New York City), 1987.

(With Richard Scase) *Reluctant Managers: Their Work and Lifestyles,* Unwin Hyman (Boston, MA), 1989.

(With Richard Scase) *Corporate Realities: The Dynamics of Large and Small Organizations,* Routledge (New York City), 1995.

(With Gareth Jones) *The Character of a Corporation: How Your Company's Culture Can Make or Break Your Business,* HarperBusiness (New York City), 1998.

Contributor of articles to professional journals and newspapers.

*SIDELIGHTS:* Robert Goffee is a management consultant and cofounder, with Gareth Jones, of Creative Management Associates in London, England. Goffee is the author of several books, including *Women in Charge: The Experiences of Female Entrepreneurs,* written with Richard Scase. Goffee and Scase interviewed fifty-four British women who began their own businesses and grouped them in four classifications. They define "Innovative Entrepreneurs" as highly qualified women who struck out on their own because of negative experiences in their jobs. They say these women consider their businesses their top priority. "Conventional Businesswomen" are less qualified and start businesses to supplement other income. Their families and homes are of the highest priority, with their

businesses ranking lower. "Radical Proprietors" are wealthy and highly qualified women whose go into business to help other women. Profit is not the main motive. The authors say "Domestic Traders" are similar to "Conventional Businesswomen" but start businesses to gain independence rather than income. They say the businesses of these women are hobbies, and their homes and families also come first.

Goffee and Scase present empirical evidence to support their conclusions in the first half of the book. The results of the interviews are presented in the second half. The authors demonstrate the difficulties women face when working for others and in managing their own businesses. Their reason for conducting the study and writing the book was to focus on women. Other studies on men have been applied to women, but Goffee and Scase feel that because women work for different reasons than men, these generalizations are not appropriate. Goffee and Scase indicate that the British women marry at a younger age, live longer, and have fewer children. Joyce M. Beggs reviewed the book in *Journal of Small Business Management.* Beggs pointed out that other findings show "that American women of the 'baby boom' continue to postpone both marriage and childbearing." Beggs said that in applying the results of the study of British women to American and other women, the comparison "could be as inaccurate as generalizing from men to women."

Goffee and Jones wrote the *Character of a Corporation: How Your Company's Culture Can Make or Break Your Business* based on fifteen years of research and their experiences as consultants to companies such as Johnson & Johnson, Polygram, Heinekin, and Unilever. The authors discuss the corporate culture which can be directly linked to corporate profits, increased performance, and improved lives of employees. They employ the two sociological concepts of solidarity and sociability in exploring the human dynamics of corporations. Managers can determine which of the four basic cultural forms noted in the book—networked, mercenary, fragmented, and communal—exist within their teams, departments, and organizations. The book profiles large and small companies and examines how their cultures have affected these businesses. Companies that include Coca-Cola, Disney, Hewlett-Packard, and Nike each enjoy a positive corporate culture. In a *Library Journal* review Susan C. Awe concluded that Goffee and Jones show "how a company's particular culture affects performance and how that culture can be changed."

*BIOGRAPHICAL/CRITICAL SOURCES:*

*PERIODICALS*

*Journal of Small Business Management,* January, 1989, p. 64.
*Library Journal,* October 1, 1998, p. 106.*

\*    \*    \*

**GOLDEN, Christie 1963-**
   **(Jadrien Bell)**

*PERSONAL:* Born November 21,1963, in Atlanta, GA; married an artist. *Education:* University of Virginia, B.A. (English), 1985. *Avocational interests:* Herbalism, making soap.

*ADDRESSES: Home*—Colorado. *Agent*—c/o Ace Books, Putnam Berkley Group, Inc., 200 Madison Ave., New York, NY 10016.

*CAREER:* Author.

*MEMBER:* Science Fiction Writers of America, Horror Writers of America, Society for Creative Anachronism.

*WRITINGS:*

*Ravenloft: Vampire of the Mists* (novel in the "Ravenloft Game" series), TSR (Geneva, WI), 1991.
*Dance of the Dead* (novel in the "Ravenloft Game" series), TSR, 1992.
*The Enemy Within* (novel in the "Ravenloft Game" series), TSR, 1994.
*Instrument of Fate,* Ace (New York City), 1996.
*Star Trek Voyager: The Murdered Sun,* Pocket Books, 1996.
*Star Trek Voyager: Marooned,* Pocket Books, 1997.
*King's Man and Thief,* Ace (New York City), 1997.
*Star Trek Voyager: Seven of Nine,* Pocket Books, 1998.
*Invasion America,* ROC, 1998.
*Invasion America: On the Run,* ROC, 1998.
(With Michael Jan Friedman) *Star Trek the Next Generation: Double Helix: The First Virtue* (sixth book in a series), Pocket Books, 1999.
(Under pseudonym Jadrien Bell) *A.D. 999,* Ace (New York City), 1999.

Also contributor to anthologies, including *Realms of Valor,* TSR, *Realms of Infamy,* TSR, *Realms of Magic,* TSR, *Blood Muse, Urban Nightmares,* and *Lammas Night, Otherwhere,* and *Highwaymen: Robbers and Rogues.*

*SIDELIGHTS:* Christie Golden combines elements of Gothic horror, fantasy, and science fiction in her work. *Ravenloft: Vampire of the Mists* is intended to complement the "Ravenloft" game. The story concerns the horror-laden realm of Ravenloft, which is packed with ghosts and werewolves and ruled by the Count Strahd Von Zarovich. The plot revolves around a vampire elf who is forced out of the Forgotten Realm and into Ravenwolf, where he must confront the Count.

Golden continues the saga of Ravenloft in *Dance of the Dead,* the story of a young dancer named Larisa Snowmane who travels by ship through Ravenloft seemingly unplagued by all the sinister possibilities there. The ship is manned by an evil captain with a chilling secret. When the ship arrives at a Ravenloft island full of zombies, Larisa must enlist the help of its residents and perform the magic Dance of the Dead in order to save herself from the evil that the Captain represents.

Golden mixes aspects of romantic literature, fantasy, and history in *King's Man and Thief.* The main character, Deveran, has two identities. Publicly he is a benefactor of the arts and privately he rules the city's thieves. While he is attempting to take the thieves further from evil and make them better people, factions within his group oppose him and launch a plan to make every inhabitant of the city capable of new levels of evil and darkness. Deveran romantically encounters the Goddess Health, who holds the key for him to save the city. Margaret Miles, writing in *Voice of Youth Advocates,* enjoyed "the elaborate religious system" that Golden creates in the book, but felt that the relationship between Deveran and Health was not truly important enough to the story "to satisfy romance fans." But Miles thought that Golden bore future watching for readers who enjoy such a blend of fantasy, horror, and romance.

*BIOGRAPHICAL/CRITICAL SOURCES:*

*BOOKS*

Reginald, Robert, *Science Fiction and Fantasy Literature, 1975-1991,* Gale, 1992.

*PERIODICALS*

*Locus,* October, 1991, p. 46; November, 1991, p. 35.
*Rapport,* April, 1992, p. 21.
*Voice of Youth Advocates,* August, 1997, p. 192.*

## GONZALES, Rodolfo 1928-

*PERSONAL:* Born June 18, 1928, in Denver, CO; son of migrant workers. *Education:* Attended high school in Denver, CO.

*ADDRESSES: Agent*—c/o Crusade for Justice, Denver, CO.

*CAREER:* Professional boxer, 1947-55; former bail bondsman; political activist and businessperson (including ownership of a neighborhood bar), beginning in 1955. Denver Democratic Party, captain of Chicano district, 1957, coordinator of Colorado Viva Kennedy presidential campaign, 1960. Los Voluntarios (civic organization), founder, 1963; Crusade for Justice, founder, 1966; War on Poverty, chairperson, 1966, and publisher of the newspaper *El Gallo.*

*WRITINGS:*

*I Am Joaquin/Yo Soy Joaquin: An Epic Poem,* illustrated by Yermo Vasquez, Crusade for Justice (Denver, CO), 1967.

Also author of the unpublished plays *The Revolutionist* and *A Cross for Maclovio.*

*SIDELIGHTS:* Rodolfo Gonzales rose from humble origins to become a prominent activist and spokesperson for the Chicano movement in the United States. The son of itinerant farm laborers, Gonzales began his career in the boxing ring, later becoming a bar owner in Denver, Colorado. By 1966 his only career was that of promoting Chicago culture and self-improvement. Gonzales founded the Crusade for Justice, which became the home of a cultural center, a formal school for all ages of children and adults, the dance company Ballet Folklorico de Aztlan, and the newspaper *El Gallo.* The Crusade for Justice also became a national voice for a distinctly Chicano identity.

During the 1968 Poor People's March, Gonzales announced his "Plan of the Barrio," described by David Conde in the *Dictionary of Literary Biography* as "a declaration of issues demanding improvement of housing and education that took into account the Chicano social and linguistic heritage, land reform, political rights, and the redistribution of wealth and resources." A year later Gonzales participated in the first annual Chicano Youth Conference, whose manifesto, "El Plan Espiritual de Aztlan," according to Conde "established the concept of Aztlan, that is, the American Southwest, as a national homeland" for Chicano Americans.

The vision that fueled Gonzales's activism is revealed in his sole published work, the long, epic poem *I Am Joaquin/Yo Soy Joaquin,* first printed in 1967. The poem has been applauded not only for its social value, but also for its literary artistry and epic proportions. Conde wrote: "There is little doubt that *I Am Joaquin* was written as a social document that sought to instill Chicano pride and identity as well as encourage community activism. . . . The literary merit of the work comes from the manner in which the poem is constructed and how theme and structure come together to produce a superior artistic experience. Its epic quality comes from the depiction of a dual journey into the postclassic world of pre-Columbian meso-America as well as into the contradictions of the Chicano heritage."

The epic journey is both historical and interior; Joaquin personified the heroes of Chicano history as individuals at war with the contrasting aspects of their personal identities, a conflict that Chicanos continue to wage today. Joaquin's journey reaches as far back into the past as the Aztec empire, with its heroic kings and emperors, who were both victors and vanquished. It weaves through the Spanish colonial period to the cultural and political upheavals of the nineteenth century that led to the dominance of such leaders as Father Miguel Hidalgo, Benito Juarez, and Joaquin Murrieta, who appear in the poem as both martyr and executioner, both statesman and revolutionary, both outlaw and victim. In the twentieth century Joaquin fights in World War II and Vietnam, and he struggles in the streets of today's cities to resolve what Conde called "the contradictions of the cultural and spiritual reality that is Chicano identity." In this present time, the critic noted, *I Am Joaquin* "recapitulates the negative condition of the Chicano in the contemporary world before ending on an optimistic note." The poem is now regarded as one of the most widely read and important representations of Chicano literature and of the Chicano movement itself.

*BIOGRAPHICAL/CRITICAL SOURCES:*

*BOOKS*

*Dictionary of Literary Biography,* Volume 122: *Chicano Writers, Second Series,* Gale (Detroit, MI), 1992.*

## GOODENOUGH, Ursula (Wiltshire) 1943-

*PERSONAL:* Born March 16, 1943, in Queens Village, NY; daughter of Erwin Ramsdell Goodenough and Evelyn (Wiltshire) Pitcher; married Robert Paul Levine, August 10, 1969 (divorced, 1980); married John Edward Heuser, July 29, 1980; children: (first marriage) Jason, Mathea; (second marriage) Jessica, Thomas, James. *Education:* Attended Radcliffe College, 1960-61; Barnard College, B.A., 1963; Columbia University, M.A., 65; Harvard University, Ph.D., 1969.

*ADDRESSES: Office*—Washington University, Department of Biology, St. Louis, MO 63130.

*CAREER:* Biologist, researcher, and author. Harvard University, Cambridge, MA, assistant professor, 1971-76, associate professor of biology, 1976-78; Washington University, St. Louis, MO, professor of biology, 1981—.

*MEMBER:* American Society of Cellular Biologists (president).

*AWARDS, HONORS:* Grants from the National Institutes of Health and the National Science Foundation.

*WRITINGS:*

*Genetics,* Holt (New York City), 1974, revised edition, 1984.
*The Sacred Depths of Nature,* Oxford University Press (New York City), 1998.

Also author of academic papers and articles published in professional journals.

*SIDELIGHTS:* Ursula Goodenough is a noted molecular biologist and professor at Washington University in St. Louis, Missouri. The first edition of Goodenough's *Genetics* was called "comprehensive, up to date, and readable" by a *Choice* reviewer. D. J. Cove reviewed the third edition in *Nature.* Cove called *Genetics* a " 'Let's start with DNA' book." Cove noted that Goodenough includes a chapter on Mendelian inheritance and a history. Goodenough addresses population and evolutionary genetics in her text. Cove felt that because of advances in genetics "at the molecular level" these subjects should be integrated "into the general body of genetics teaching." Cove said Goodenough provides up-to-date information on the analysis and handling of DNA "building on the strength of the molecular and microbial side of her earlier editions."

*Booklist* reviewer Gilbert Taylor wrote that in *The Sacred Depths of Nature,* Goodenough "ruminates on how a religious sensibility is compatible with reductionist science." Goodenough offers basic instruction in the life sciences, including biochemistry, Darwinian biology, population dynamics, and chaos theory in a work that offers her own insights into the mysteries of science and religion. "Goodenough forges a kind of religious naturalism that will not be unfamiliar to readers of New Age literature," wrote Gregory McNamee for *Amazon.com.* Goodenough draws on the observations of authorities such as Stephen Hawking and Edward O. Wilson, and delves into the spirituality of Taoism and Transcendentalism. The subjects of her chapters included astrophysics, cosmology, evolutionary theory, cell biology, sexuality, and death, and each ends in a reflection. A *Publishers Weekly* reviewer wrote that Goodenough "offers a scientist's insight into the dialogue between science and religion." The reviewer noted that the book is structured like a devotional, "but with a decidedly broader approach to the vast ontological questions being pursued."

*BIOGRAPHICAL/CRITICAL SOURCES:*

*PERIODICALS*

*Booklist,* November 1, 1998.
*Choice,* September, 1974, p. 971.
*Nature,* March 7, 1985, p. 44.
*Publishers Weekly,* October 26, 1998, p. 56.

*OTHER*

*Amazon.com,* http://www.amazon.com (1999).*

\* \* \*

## GOODWIN, Karin

*PERSONAL:* Female.

*ADDRESSES: Home*—Richmond, VA. *Agent*—c/o Chronicle Books, 85 Second St., San Francisco, CA 94105.

*CAREER:* Author. Has worked as a DJ, a house painter, a nude model, a gymnastics coach, and a licensed private investigator.

*WRITINGS:*

*Sleeping with Random Beasts* (novel), Chronicle (San Francisco), 1998.

*SIDELIGHTS:* Karin Goodwin's first novel, *Sleeping with Random Beasts,* saw print in 1998. It tells the story of a female protagonist named Eleanor May Shank, whose nickname is Bean. As the book opens, Bean decides she has had enough of her current boyfriend, an alcoholic who cheats on her with other women. She is also less than thrilled with her dull employment in a bank, and decides to abandon both significant other and job to begin a cross-country journey of self-discovery while working on her photography. One of her stops is at the home of her father, who is upset at his daughter's willingness to give up gainful work. Along the course of Bean's trip, which eventually leads to her estranged mother in Seattle, she sleeps with many men. Some are old boyfriends, others are acquaintances she makes along the way. By the end of the novel, she is pregnant, and has no idea who the father is. Yet, during the course of her journey, she has also told readers much about her childhood and adolescence, allowing for understanding of her behavior.

*Sleeping with Random Beasts* met with mixed critical responses. A *Publishers Weekly* reviewer noted that "by the time one character advises, 'Have some backbone!' You're not thirteen anymore,' the reader has already been there, thought that." On the other hand, *Booklist* contributor Ted Leventhal speculated that "perhaps a sign of *Beasts'* success is the reader's constant desire to give Bean a kick in the butt and tell her to get a job." Barbara Maslekoff concluded in a *Library Journal* appraisal that "Goodwin's first novel is so real that it sometimes sounds like talking out loud."

*BIOGRAPHICAL/CRITICAL SOURCES:*

*PERIODICALS*

*Booklist,* January 1, 1998, pp. 774, 776.
*Library Journal,* January, 1998, p. 140.
*Publishers Weekly,* January 5, 1998, p. 58.*

\*          \*          \*

**GOURDIN, Amalia**
   **See LINDAL, Amalia**

\*          \*          \*

**GOW, James**

*PERSONAL: Education:* School of East European and Slavonic Studies, received Ph.D.

*CAREER:* Has held teaching and research positions at Hatfield Polytechnic and the Centre for Defence Studies.

*WRITINGS:*

*NONFICTION*

*Legitimacy and the Military: The Yugoslav Crisis,* St. Martin's (New York City), 1992.
(Editor) *Iraq, the Gulf Conflict, and the World Community,* Macmillan (New York City), 1993.
*Triumph of the Lack of Will: International Diplomacy and the Yugoslav War,* Columbia University Press (New York City), 1997.

Also author of monographs for Brassey's Centre for Defence Studies, including *The Gulf Crisis: Politico-Military Implications,* 1990; *Yugoslav Endgames: Civil Strife and Inter-State Conflict,* 1991; and *Peace-Making, Peace-Keeping: European Security and the Yugoslav Wars,* 1992. Contributor to *Encyclopaedia of Conflicts, Disputes, and Flashpoints in Eastern Europe, Russia, and the Successor States,* by Bogdan Szajkowski, Longman (Harlow, Essex, England), 1993.

*SIDELIGHTS:* James Gow has penned several books and monographs on the breakup of the former Yugoslavia into several different states and the subsequent wars that have erupted between them. Among his efforts are *Legitimacy and the Military: The Yugoslav Crisis* and *Triumph of the Lack of Will: International Diplomacy and the Yugoslav War.* He has also edited a volume and written a monograph on the Gulf War.

*Triumph of the Lack of Will* discusses the implications the troubles of the former Yugoslavia have for Europe and the rest of the Western world. Mark Danner included the volume in a group critique of books about the region in the *New York Review of Books,* and, in a footnote, quoted Gow: "The Yugoslav war moved from being an important question for European stability and security and a test of the then CSCE's brand new Conflict Prevention Centre, to being a test of the future of E[uropean] U[nion] Common Foreign and Security Policy." Then, Gow continued, "from that it moved to being a test of U[nited] N[ations] diplomacy and UN peacekeeping; from that, it became a test of European, Transatlantic and East-West relations and post-Cold War cooperative security." The author concluded: "finally, it became a test of N[orth] A[tlantic] T[reaty] O[rganization] credibility and with that of international and particularly American credibility. . . . [D]espite the commitments that went with these tests, for four years international diplomacy struggled to end the war." Danner praised *Triumph of the Lack of Will* as a "detailed accounting" of the escalation of hostilities between the states of the former Yugoslavia.

*BIOGRAPHICAL/CRITICAL SOURCES:*

PERIODICALS

*New York Review of Books,* November 20, 1997, pp. 56-64.*

\*      \*      \*

**GRAY, Ellington**
**See JACOB, Naomi (Ellington)**

\*      \*      \*

**GRAY, Pat   1953-**

*PERSONAL:* Born July 1, 1953, in Belfast, Northern Ireland; son of Jack (a lecturer) and Helen (Nichol-Smith) Gray; married Jane Klauber (an attorney), March 26, 1988; children: Laura, Daniel. *Education:* University of Leeds, B.A., 1974; Birkbeck College, London, M.Sc., 1979. *Avocational interests:* Cycling, fresh air.

*ADDRESSES: Home*—38 Kestrel Ave., London SE24 0EB, England. *Office*—University of Luton, Park Sq., Luton, Bedfordshire, England. *Agent*—Juri Gabriel, 35 Camberwell Grove, London SE5 8JA, England. *E-mail*—pat.gray@luton.ac.uk.

*CAREER:* University of Luton, Luton, England, senior lecturer in politics, 1991—.

*AWARDS, HONORS:* Winner of World One-Day Novel Cup.

*WRITINGS:*

*Mr. Narrator* (novel), Dedalus (England), 1989.
*The Political Map of the Heart* (novel), Images (England), 1995.
(Editor) *Policy Disasters in Western Europe* (nonfiction), Routledge, 1998.
*The Cat* (novel), Ecco Press (Hopewell, NJ), 1999.

Also author of short stories. Contributor to academic journals.

*WORK IN PROGRESS:* Research on responsibility and blame.

*SIDELIGHTS:* Pat Gray told *CA:* "My upbringing in Northern Ireland has made me interested in political and moral issues and the connection between fact, fantasy, and fiction in general. I am also interested in comic writing of the dark or macabre variety, which I suppose my life has prepared me for."

*BIOGRAPHICAL/CRITICAL SOURCES:*

PERIODICALS

*Kirkus Reviews,* September 1, 1998.
*Publishers Weekly,* August 24, 1998, p. 44.

\*      \*      \*

**GRAZER, Brian   1951(?)-**

*PERSONAL:* Born July 12, 1951 (one source says 1953), in Los Angeles, CA; children: Sage, Riley. *Education:* Attended the University of California; studied law, early 1980s. *Avocational interests:* Surfing.

*ADDRESSES: Office*—Imagine Films Entertainment Inc., 9465 Wilshire Blvd., 7th Floor, Beverly Hills, CA 90212.

*CAREER:* Intern in Warner Brothers' legal department during the early 1980s; script reader for Brut/Faberge; talent agent; affiliated with Edgar J. Scherick-Daniel Blatt Col; Imagine Films Entertainment Inc. (independent movie and television production company), co-chief executive with filmmaker Ron Howard, c. 1986-1992; film producer, 1982—.

Producer of films, including *Night Shift,* Warner Bros., 1982; (also story author) *Splash,* Buena Vista, 1984; *Real Genius,* Tri-Star, 1985; (with George Folsey Jr.) *Spies Like Us,* Warner Bros., 1985; (with James Keach; also story author) *Armed and Dangerous,* Columbia, 1986; (with David Valdes) *Like Father, Like Son,* Tri-Star, 1987; *Vibes,* Columbia, 1988; *The 'Burbs,* Universal, 1989; *Parenthood,* Universal, 1989; (executive producer with Jim Abrahams), *Cry-Baby,* Universal, 1990; *Kindergarten Cop,* Universal, 1990; (executive producer) *Closet Land,* Universal, 1991; *My Girl,* Columbia, 1991; (executive producer) *The Doors,* Tri-Star, 1991; *Housesitter,* Universal, 1992; (with Ron Howard) *Far and Away,* Universal, 1992; *Boomerang,* Paramount, 1992; (also story author) *House Sitter,* 1992; (executive producer) *CB4,* 1993; *For Love or Money,* 1993; *Greedy,* 1994; *The Paper,* 1994; *The Cowboy Way,* 1994; *My Girl 2,* 1994; *Apollo 13,* 1995; *The Chamber,* 1996; *Sgt. Bilko,* 1996; *Fear,* 1996; *The Nutty Professor,* 1996; *Ransom,* 1996; *Love for Hire,* 1997; *Liar Liar,* 1997; *Inventing the Abbotts,* 1997; and *Mercury Rising,* 1998.

Producer of television films, shows, and series, including (with S. Bryan Hickox), *Thou Shalt Not Commit Adultery,* National Broadcasting Company (NBC), 1978; (with Bruce Cohn Curtis), *Zuma Beach,* NBC, 1978; (executive producer) *Shadow Chasers,* American Broadcasting Corporation (ABC), 1985; (executive producer) *Ask Max* ("Disney Sunday Movie"), ABC, 1986; (executive producer) *Take Five,* Columbia Broadcasting System (CBS), 1987; (executive producer) *Ohara,* ABC, 1987; (executive producer) *Splash, Too* ("Disney Sunday Movie"), ABC, 1988; *Poison,* Showtime, 1988; (executive producer) *Mutts,* ABC, 1988; (executive producer) *Smart Guys,* NBC, 1988; (executive producer) *Parenthood* (based on the 1989 film of the same name), NBC, 1990; *Hiller and Diller,* 1997; and *From the Earth to the Moon,* 1998.

Film actor in *Splash,* Buena Vista, 1984; appeared on television programs, including *The New Hollywood,* NBC, 1990; and *Naked Hollywood,* Arts & Entertainment Network (A&E), 1991.

*AWARDS, HONORS:* Academy Award nomination (with Lowell Ganz, Babaloo Mandel, and Bruce Jay Friedman), outstanding original screenplay, 1984, for *Splash;* named Producer of the Year, National Association of Theatre Owners and ShoWest, 1992; Academy Award nomination for best picture, 1996, for *Apollo 13.*

*WRITINGS:*

*STORY TREATMENTS FOR FILM AND TELEVISION*

*Splash,* Buena Vista, 1984.
*Shadow Chasers,* ABC, 1985.
*Armed and Dangerous,* Columbia, 1986.
*House Sitter,* 1992.

Also creator of the story for television's short-lived *Shadow Chasers.*

*SIDELIGHTS:* Brian Grazer is perhaps best known as a motion picture producer. With acclaimed director Ron Howard, Grazer formed the production company Imagine Films Entertainment Inc.; even after the business was dissolved in 1992, however, Grazer and Howard continued to work together in the film industry. Grazer's production credits include *Night Shift, Splash, Parenthood, Apollo 13,* and *Liar Liar. Apollo 13,* on which Grazer worked with Howard, received an Academy Award nomination for best picture in 1995. Grazer has also done production work for television programs and has been responsible for the story ideas for some of his successful films as well—his story for *Splash* gave him a share in the Academy Award nomination garnered in 1984 for outstanding original screenplay. The original stories for the 1986 film *Armed and Dangerous* and the 1992 film *House Sitter* are also at least partially the product of Grazer's imagination.

*Splash* is a comedic film about a man's love affair with a mermaid. The movie opens with an eight-year-old boy named Allen Bauer diving from a tourist boat because he is attracted by something he sees beneath the waves. Though he is quickly rescued, he manages a fleeting glimpse of a child mermaid. When Allen becomes an adult (portrayed by Tom Hanks), he has another boating accident and this time is rescued by the mermaid (portrayed by Daryl Hannah). She retains his wallet, with his identification, and arrives in New York City to look for him, sprouting legs in order to cope with its streets—from one of which she takes her name, Madison. At first Allen does not realize Madison is a mermaid, and their blooming relationship is further complicated because she is pursued by a mad scientist obsessed with the idea of capturing her and dissecting her in a lab. To escape the scientist, the pair eventually escape back into the ocean, where Allen is able to breathe as long as he sticks close to Madison.

*Splash* proved popular with film audiences but received mixed response from critics. John Simon of *National Review,* for instance, did not care for it and advised potential viewers who hadn't read Hans Christian Andersen's fairy tale "The Little Mermaid" to "do so, and forget this stupid movie." He further criticized *Splash* as "not so much a fairy tale as a large, sophomoric wet dream." Stanley Kauffmann in the *New Republic* was much more positive in his opinion of *Splash.* "Except when it tries too hard to amuse," he declared, "it's amusing." Kauffmann added, "What's best about the picture is that the fantasy element is never explained; it's taken for granted."

Critics have also been well-disposed towards what many consider Grazer's biggest success as a producer, *Apollo 13.* Also starring Hanks as astronaut Jim Lovell, the film depicted the moon mission that had to be abandoned due to equipment failure and nearly ended in tragedy. David Denby in *New York* gratefully hailed the film's "square-jawed integrity."

*BIOGRAPHICAL/CRITICAL SOURCES:*

BOOKS

*Contemporary Theatre, Film, and Television,* Gale Research (Detroit, MI), 1993.

PERIODICALS

*National Review,* May 4, 1984, pp. 54-56.
*New Republic,* April 9, 1984, p. 24.
*New York,* July 10, 1995, pp. 50-51.
*Variety,* May 4, 1992, p. 5.*

\*     \*     \*

**GRIFFITHS, Anne M(arjorie) O(rd)   1953-**

*PERSONAL:* Born December 30, 1953. *Education:* Edinburgh University, LL.B., 1978; University of London, Ph.D., 1988.

*ADDRESSES: Agent*—c/o University of Chicago Press, 5801 Ellis Ave., Chicago, IL 60637.

*CAREER:* Admitted as solicitor, Law Society of Scotland, 1980; Department of Scots Law, lecturer, 1980-92, senior lecturer, 1992—; E.S.R.C. research fellow in Botswana, 1982; Wolfson College, Oxford, England, Centre for Socio-Legal Studies, visiting scholar, 1985; Cornell University, Ithaca, NY, visiting associate professor of law, spring, 1988; American Bar Foundation, Chicago, IL, research scholar, 1990-91; University of Witwatersrand, South Africa, South African human sciences research fellow, summer, 1992; University of Texas at Austin, visiting professor of law, 1996, 1998. Board member of the International Commission on Folk Law and Legal Pluralism, 1983—; member of International Committee on Crimes of Violence against Women, Commonwealth Secretariat, London, 1985; member of several other university committees; member of Commonwealth Legal Education Group.

*MEMBER:* European Association of Social Anthropologists, French Society of Legal Anthropologists, Royal African Society.

*WRITINGS:*

*Development of Tests of Cognitive Functioning for Use with an Adult, Illiterate, Rural Zambian Population,* University of Zambia (Lusaka, Zambia), 1978.
*In the Shadow of Marriage: Gender and Justice in an African Community,* University of Chicago Press (Chicago, IL), 1998.

*SIDELIGHTS:* Scottish law professor Anne M. O. Griffiths presented her findings about the legal system in Botswana, Africa, in her study *In the Shadow of Marriage: Gender and Justice in an African Community.* Focusing on rules and laws that pertain to the family, procreation, marriage, and divorce, Griffiths studied observations of court cases and other legal negotiations, as well as interviews with participants of legal cases in Botswana during the 1980s. In Botswana, as in much of Africa, a dual legal system exists. Tribal law based in an African oral tradition and a government legal system based on British common law (Botswana was once a British colony) provide different opportunities for justice. Most local disputes find resolution in the *kgota,* or chiefs' courts, while appeals and broad-based disputes end up in the government courts.

Writing in the *Women's Review of Books,* Kathleen Sheldon found *In the Shadow of Marriage* to be a difficult but worthwhile read. "Unfortunately, for a non-specialist reader, much of this interesting story is obscured by markedly academic language; in the case studies this is combined with local terms and people's names which will be unfamiliar to most Western readers, so that reading takes some effort. There is no glossary for the Tswana terms," she commented, adding, "Yet these kinds of obstacles are worth struggling with for any reader interested in the application of law in the daily lives of African men and women, in how women of different status understand and use the legal systems available to them, and in the gendered aspects of women's lives as they live in the shadow of marriage."

*BIOGRAPHICAL/CRITICAL SOURCES:*

PERIODICALS

*Women's Review of Books,* September, 1998, pp. 25-27.

## GRIPPANDO, James M. 1958-

*PERSONAL:* Born January 27, 1958, in Waukegon, IL. *Education:* Received B.A. and J.D. from University of Florida. *Avocational interests:* Cycling, in-line skating, golf, sailing.

*ADDRESSES: Agent*—Arthur and Richard Pine, Arthur Pine Associates, 250 West Fifth St., New York, NY.

*CAREER:* Writer, c. 1994—. Admitted to Florida Bar; worked as a trial attorney in Miami, FL, 1984-96. Law clerk to Honorable Thomas Clark, U.S. Court of Appeals, 1983.

*MEMBER:* Mystery Writers of America, Phi Beta Kappa.

*AWARDS, HONORS:* University of Florida Outstanding Leadership Award; cited by *Florida Trend* as one of their "Emerging Leaders under 40"; Best Novels of 1998 citation, *Bookman News,* for *The Advocate.*

*WRITINGS:*

*The Pardon,* HarperCollins (New York City), 1994.
*The Informant,* HarperCollins, 1996.
*The Abduction,* HarperCollins, 1998.
*Found Money,* HarperCollins, 1999.
*Under Cover of Darkness,* HarperCollins, 2000.

Also author of numerous scholarly articles for law reviews and legal journals; contributor to nursing textbooks.

*SIDELIGHTS:* Crime and suspense author James Grippando was a trial lawyer and partner at one of Florida's leading law firms before bringing his knowledge of crime to several mystery novels that he has authored. *The Informant* involves a series of seemingly unrelated and gruesome killings happening across the United States. An informant has begun to leak clues to a reporter at a Miami paper, but the anonymous caller demands cash for the information, which the FBI agrees to provide. The informant claims to think exactly like the killer and to be able to predict the killer's next move. In the meantime the reporter and one FBI agent, Victoria Santos, cross paths—unlike many on the case, Santos is convinced that the informant and the killer are separate individuals. Marilyn Stasio, reviewing the novel for the *New York Times Book Review,* noted that Grippando's book started out "with an air of credibility," while the *Publishers Weekly* contributor described it as possessing "an unusually cerebral and low-key beginning to a thriller, emphasizing procedures, forensics, and professional ethics rather than shock or even suspense." But after the question regarding the identity of informant and killer is resolved, the *Publishers Weekly* contributor continued, Grippando moves the story into the more familiar territory of the thriller genre. In what Stasio called "a nice flair for the grotesque," Grippando picks up the pace and features additional murders at the hands of sharks and pythons. The final climax takes place on a cruise ship and brings all main characters together.

Grippando writes about the manipulative and many-layered world of politics in *The Abduction.* It is the year 2000 and Allison Leahy is the first female in the United States to run for president. Opposing her is an African American candidate named Lincoln Howe. Howe's granddaughter Kristen has just been mysteriously abducted, and Leahy experienced a similar tragedy years ago when her newly adopted baby girl was abducted and never returned. Leahy is torn as to whether to become involved in the investigation of Kristen's disappearance, and wonders whether the recent abduction is a manipulative plot by her political opponents. Others wonder whether Leahy's supporters orchestrated the abduction. Leahy ends up working with Kristen's mother to investigate the abduction, and the actions of both women cause repercussions in the political arena.

Grippando's novel *Found Money* offers a "cautionary tale of greed, family secrets, and the dangers of getting what you wish for," according to a *Publishers Weekly* critic. Main character Ryan learns that his recently deceased father has two million dollars hidden in the attic, the money obtained through blackmail. Ryan decides to do nothing about the money until he can learn more about its origin, which leads to a flurry of investigations by the FBI and other officials. In the meantime, after Amy Parkins receives a $200,000 cash gift that she traces back to Ryan's deceased father, Ryan and Amy work together to uncover a much larger conspiracy than expected, with involvement from huge corporations and high-level political figures.

Grippando told *CA:* "I love to write. That's why I do it. I spent four years writing a novel that was never published, and I have never once looked back on it as a waste of time. I enjoyed the process, and that's the one piece of advice I give all aspiring writers—keep it fun."

*BIOGRAPHICAL/CRITICAL SOURCES:*

*PERIODICALS*

*Booklist,* August, 1996, p. 1854; February 15, 1998, p. 998.
*Library Journal,* April 1, 1997, p. 145; March 15, 1998, p. 93; January, 1999, p. 150.
*New York Times Book Review,* October 13, 1996, p. 29.
*Publishers Weekly,* July 22, 1996, p. 227; February 9, 1998, pp. 71-72; January 11, 1999, p. 57.*

\* \* \*

**GUERRA, Antonio**
   **See GUERRA, Tonino**

\* \* \*

**GUERRA, Tonino   1920-**
   **(Antonio Guerra)**

*PERSONAL:* Born March 16, 1920, in Sant' Arcangelo, Romagna, Italy; married Lara Iabloskina (marriage ended); married Eleanora Kreindlina, 1977. *Education:* University of Urbino, degree in education, 1946.

*ADDRESSES: Agent*—c/o Edizioni del Girasole srl, Via Paolo Costa 10, 481000, Ravenna, Italy.

*CAREER:* Poet, screenwriter, fiction writer, and artist. Secondary school teacher, 1940s-53.

*AWARDS, HONORS:* Premio Argentario, for *L'uomo parellelo,* 1969; Premio Friulano "Resit d'aur," 1984; Premio Comisso, 1986; Pasolini Poetry Prize, 1988.

*WRITINGS:*

*I scarabocc,* Lega (Faenza), 1946.
*La s-ciupteda,* Lega, 1950.
*La storia di Fortunato,* Einaudi (Turin), 1952.
*Lunario,* Benedetti (Faenza), 1954.
*Dopo i leoni,* Einaudi, 1956.
(With Elio Petri) *L'assassino,* Zibetti (Milan), 1962.
(With Michelangelo Antonioni) *Il deserto rosso,* edited by Carlo di Carlo, Cappelli (Bologna), 1964.
*L'equilibrio,* Bompiani (Milan), 1967, translated as *Equilibrium,* Chatto & Windus (London), 1969, Walker (New York City), 1970.
*L'uomo parallelo,* Bompiani, 1969.

(With Luigi Malerba) *Millemosche senza cavallo,* Bompiani, 1969.
(With Malerba) *Millemosche mercenario,* Bompiani, 1969.
(With Malerba) *Millemosche fuoco e fiamme,* Bompiani, 1970.
(With Malerba) *Millemosche innamorato,* Bompiani, 1971.
*I bu: Poesie romagnole,* Rizzoli (Milan), 1972.
(With Lucile Laks) *Il cannocchiale e altri testi,* Bompiani, 1972.
(With Malerba) *Millemosche e il leone,* Bompiani, 1973.
(With Federico Fellini) *Amarcord,* Rizzoli, 1973, translated as *Amarcord: Portrait of a Town,* Abelard-Schuman (London), 1974, Berkley (New York City), 1975.
*Millemosche e la fine del mondo,* Bompiani, 1973.
*I cento uccelli,* Bompiani, 1974.
(With Malerba) *Millemosche alla ventura,* Bompiani, 1974.
(With Luigi Malerba) *Storie dell'anno Mille,* Bompiani, 1977.
*Il polverone: Storie per una notte quieta,* Bompiani, 1978.
*I guardatori della luna,* Bompiani, 1981.
*Il miele,* Maggioli (Rimini), 1981.
(With Michelangelo Antonioni) *L'aquilone: Una favola del nostro tempo,* Maggioli, 1982.
*Il leone barba bianca,* Emme (Milan), 1983.
*La pioggia tiepida,* Rusconi (Milan), 1984.
*La capanna,* Maggioli, 1985.
(Contributor) Hermann W. Haller, editor, *The Hidden Italy: A Bilingual Edition of Italian Dialect Poetry,* Wayne State University Press (Detroit, MI), 1986.
*Il viaggio,* Maggioli, 1987.
*Il libro delle chiese abbandonate,* Maggioli, 1988.
*L'orto d'Eliseo,* Maggioli, 1989.
*Il profilo del conte,* Maggioli, 1990.
*Cenere,* S. Lazzaro, 1990.
*Il vecchio con un piede in Oriente,* Maggioli, 1990.
*L'impiccagione dei pesi grossi,* Il girasole (Valverde), 1991.
*A Pechino fa la neve: una cosa teatrale,* Maggioli, 1992.
*L'albero dell'acqua: Dedicato soprattutto a Ezra Pound,* edited by Luca Cesari, Scheiwiller (Milan), 1992.
*E' caval d'Ulisse,* Moby Dick (Faenza), 1996.

*SCREENPLAYS*

*Uomini e lupi,* 1956.
*Un ettaro di cielo,* 1957.

*Cesta duga godinu dana*, 1958.
*L'avventura*, 1959.
*Le signore*, 1960*La notte*, 1960.
*Il carro armata dell' otto settembre*, 1960.
*L'assassino*, 1961.
*I giorni contati*, 1962.
*L'eclisse*, 1962.
*La noia*, 1963.
*Gli invincibili sette*, 1964.
*Deserto rosso*, 1964.
*La Donna e une cosa meravigliosa*, 1964.
*Le ore nude*, 1964.
*Matrimonio all' italiana*, 1964.
*Contrrosesso*, 1964.
*Saul e David*, 1964.
*Casanova '70*, 1965.
*I grandi condottieri*, 1965.
*La decima vittima*, 1965.
*Blow-up*, 1966.
*Le fate*, 1966.
*C'era una volta*, 1967.
*Le scatenato*, 1967.
*L'occhio selvaggio*, 1967.
*Un tranquillo posto in campagna*, 1968.
*Sissignore*, 1968.
*Amanti*, 1968.
*L'Invitee*, 1969.
*In Search of Gregory Wood*, 1969.
*I girasoli*, 1970.
*Zabriskie Point*, 1970.
*Tre nel mille*, 1970.
*Uomini contro*, 1970.
*Giochi particolari*, 1970.
*La supertestimone*, 1971.
*Il caso Mattei*, 1972.
*Gli ordini sono ordini*, 1972.
*Bianco, rosso, e . . .* , 1972.
*A proposito Lucky Luciano*, 1973.
*Carne per Frankenstein*, 1973.
*Amarcord*, 1974.
*Dites-le avec les fleurs*, 1974.
*Quarante gradi sotto il lenzuolo*, 1975.
*Cadaveri eccellenti*, 1976.
*Caro Michele*, 1976.
*Un Papillon sur l'epaule*, 1978.
*Letti selvaggi*, 1978.
*Cristo si e fermato a Eboli*, 1979.
*Il mistero di Oberwald*, 1979.
*La notte di San Lorenzo*, 1981.
*Identificazione di una donna*, 1982.
*E la nave va*, 1983.
*Nostalgia*, 1983.
*Carmen*, 1984.
*Kaos*, 1984.

*Henry IV*, 1985.
*Taxidi sta kythera*, 1985.
*Good Morning Babilonia*, 1986.
*Ginger e Fred*, 1986.
*O Melissokomos*, 1986.
*Cronaca di una morte annunciata*, 1987.
*Topio stin omichli*, 1988.
*La Femme de mes amours*, 1988.
*Burro*, 1989.
*Dimenticare Palermo*, 1990.
*Il sole anche di notte*, 1990.
*Stanno tutti bene*, 1990.
*Viaggio d'amore*, 1991.
*To meteoro vima to Pelargou*, 1991.
*La Domenica specialmente*, 1991.

*SIDELIGHTS:* In 1944 at the age of twenty-four, Tonino Guerra was arrested by the Fascist government in his homeland of Italy and sent to the concentration camp, Troisdorf, in Germany. It was while he was there that he began writing poetry in his native dialect, Romagnol. Many of his fellow prisoners were from the same region of northern Italy as he was and were diverted and comforted by his poems.

Upon his return to Italy, these poems were published under the title *I scarabocc* ("The Scribbles") in 1946. In the *Dictionary of Literary Biography*, Hermann W. Haller explains Guerra's use of his native dialect in composing these poems, writing "it is consonant with his rebellious opposition to the Fascist threats and policies of the time." Guerra's second book of poetry, *La Sciupteda* ("The Gunshot") was published in 1950, followed by *Lunario* ("Almanac") in 1954. His poetry from this early period paints a bleak picture of a chaotic and decaying world that is filled with conflict and tension. One of the poet's recurring themes is death, as can be seen in the poem "I bu." This poem appeared in a 1972 collection of the same name, which gathered poetry from Guerra's first three collections along with a few previously unpublished works.

In 1953 Guerra moved to Rome and began a career as a screenwriter. His first script was a collaboration with Elio Petri for director Giuseppe De Santis called *Uomini e lupi* ("Men and Wolves"), released in 1956. Three years later he began a partnership with the acclaimed director Michelangelo Antonioni, beginning with the script for *L'avventura* (1959). In 1969 the duo traveled to the United States to make the film *Zabriskie Point*. Afterward, Guerra had a breakdown, an experience that he recorded in the novel *L'uomo parallelo* (Parallel Man), published in 1969. The work won him his first official recognition when he received the Premio Argentario the same year.

Guerra began an ongoing collaboration with director Francesco Rosi in 1967. For him, Guerra wrote screenplays for the noted films *Il caso Mattei* ("The Mattei Affair," 1972), *A proposito: Lucky Luciano* ("Re: Lucky Luciano," 1973), and *Cadaveri eccellenti* ("Illustrious Corpses," 1976). Guerra continued his partnership with Rosi into the 1990s. Another notable association began in 1973, this one with Federico Fellini. The motivation for such top-notch filmmakers such as these to want to work with Guerra may have been because of his poetic style. Guerra would work with twenty-six different directors on over sixty films during the course of his career.

In addition to poetry and scripts, Guerra wrote a number of prose works. In the 1970s and 1980s, he published three books of prose—*I cento uccelli* ("The Hundred Birds") published in 1974, and *I guardatori della luna* ("The Moon Watchers") published in 1981. In 1977 he also published a series of short stories written with Luigi Malerba titled *Storie dell' anno Mille* ("Stories from the Year One Thousand"). These popular stories tell takes of a medieval knight named Millemosche.

In the 1980s Guerra turned his attentions back to writing poetry. In 1981 he published *Il miele* ("Honey"), a long prose poem. The work is divided into thirty-six cantos of free verse that tell a story of the final years of life for two brothers. Set in the region of northern Italy where Guerra is from, the town where these brothers live is all but abandoned. Like his earlier poetry, this and his subsequent three published poems were all written in his native dialect.

*La capanna* ("The Cabin") was published in 1985. This poem centers on a huge cabin near the ocean in Galilea. The history of this cabin is recounted beginning with its creator, Zangala, a sanitation worker who abandoned the cabin. A stranger named Homer then moves in and lives in solitude until he receives an unexpected visit from a woman, Isolina, who wants to help him with the house. The two end up having an affair, though Isolina is married. Homer responds to this by disappearing. In explanation of the meaning of this unusual poem, Guerra once commented that it was inspired by his relationship with his second wife, Eleanora Kreindlina, whom he met on a trip to the Soviet Union and married in 1977.

In 1987 Guerra published *Il viaggio* ("The Journey"), an account of an old couple's honeymoon trip to the seashore. In the *Dictionary of Literary Biography*, Hermann W. Haller describes it as "a trip of life and memory, a search for truth, yet also a journey toward death." This work was followed by *Il libro delle chiese abbandonate* ("The Book of Abandoned Churches") published in 1988. In it, the poet takes his reader on a tour of decaying churches and convents, each with its own unique history.

These four works from the 1980s have in common their evocations of death and decay. The modern world has taken over the countryside of the poet's birth, permanently changing society and culture to the extent that the region's history is being erased. At the same time, however, Guerra's poems reveal a sense of hope and even some humor, qualities that temper the morbid mood.

Guerra ended the decade with two works—*L'orto d'Eliseo* ("Eliseo's Garden"), published in 1989, and *Il profilo del conto* ("The Count's Profile"), published in 1990. *L'orto d'Eliseo* relates a story of an old man's conflict with a mole in his garden. *Il profilo del canto* is about the last remaining count in the Marecchia valley. Something of a Renaissance man, Guerra has written stories for children and worked as a schoolteacher. He is also an artist whose paintings are inspired by Asian and Russian art. He has received numerous awards including the Pasolini Prize in 1988 for his distinguished career as a poet.

## BIOGRAPHICAL/CRITICAL SOURCES:

### BOOKS

Bondanella, Peter, and Julia Conaway Bondanella, editors, *Dictionary of Italian Literature,* Greenwood Press, 1996.
*Dictionary of Literary Biography,* Volume 128: *Twentieth-Century Italian Poets,* Gale Research (Detroit, MI), 1993.
*International Dictionary of Films and Filmmakers,* 2nd edition, Volume 4: *Writers and Production Artists,* St. James Press (Detroit, MI), 1993.
*Lingua, dialetto, poesia: Atti del Seminario popolare su Tonino Guerra e la poesia dialettale romagnola,* Girasole, 1976.
*Tonino Guerra,* Maggioli, 1985.

### PERIODICALS

*Annali d'Italianistica,* Volume 6, 1988, pp. 162-178.
*Best Sellers,* February 15, 1970.
*Library Journal,* December 15, 1969.
*New Republic,* February 7, 1970.

*Stampa,* October 29, 1972.*

\*     \*     \*

## GUSSOW, Adam 1958-

*PERSONAL:* Surname is pronounced "gus-oh"; born April 3, 1958, in New York, NY; son of Alan (an artist and environmentalist) and Joan (a nutrition educator; maiden name, Dye) Gussow. *Education:* Princeton University, B.A. (English; magna cum laude), 1979; Columbia University, M.A. (English), 1983; Princeton University, Ph.D. (English), 2000. *Politics:* "Liberal with occasional left and centrist leanings." *Religion:* "Agnostic half-Jew." *Avocational interests:* Music, cooking, running, table tennis.

*ADDRESSES: Home*—261 Seaman Ave., #F8, New York, NY 10034. *Agent*—Tina Bennett, Janklow and Nesbit Associates, 598 Madison Ave., New York, NY. *E-mail*—asgussow@aol.com.

*CAREER:* Guitar Study Center, New York, NY, blues harmonica instructor, 1988-91, 1999; Princeton University, Princeton, NJ, lecturer, English, 1998-99; The New School, New York, NY, adjunct professor of humanities, 1999.

*MEMBER:* Modern Language Association, American Studies Association.

*AWARDS, HONORS:* Essay on Jack Kerouac and Malcolm Cowley included in *Pushcart Prize X,* 1985.

*WRITINGS:*

*Mr. Satan's Apprentice,* Pantheon, 1998.

Also contributor of essays and reviews to periodicals, including *Georgia Review, Boston Review,* and *Village Voice.* Author of column, "Journeyman's Road," *Blues Access* magazine, 1995—.

*WORK IN PROGRESS:* Research on blues literature and southern violence for Ph.D. dissertation.

*SIDELIGHTS:* Adam Gussow is an adjunct professor of humanities at The New School in New York City and a blues harmonica player and instructor. Gussow's memoir *Mister Satan's Apprentice* begins in 1975 in suburban New York, where the smart, lonely sixteen-year-old buys his first harmonica after being inspired by a record of Magic Dick playing "Whammer Jammer" with the J. Geils Band. A first girlfriend is gained and lost, a heart is broken, and a young white bluesman-in-training is thrown onto the thorns of life. A parallel narrative begins almost immediately: nine summers down the road, abandoned by another girlfriend and broken-hearted once again, Gussow falls in with harp player Nat Riddles—a charismatic, wily, and musically gifted young New Yorker, an African-American big brother to Gussow's hungry blues apprentice. Riddles, who has transformed street-harp playing into a kind of living theater, introduces Gussow to the downtown blues scene, centered around an East Village juke-joint called Dan Lynch's Blues Bar.

When Riddles is shot in the chest outside Dan Lynch's under mysterious circumstances and flees to Virginia, Gussow is forced to find another blues-master. This happens in the unlikeliest possible way. Gussow is driving through Harlem one day in 1986 when he notices a greybearded older black man set up in front of a phone company office, playing thrash-funk guitar, crashing on a stomp-cymbal, and rasping out gutbucket blues. His name turns out to be Satan—'*Mister* Satan to you!' he roars at the surrounding crowd.

*Mister Satan's Apprentice* documents the highs and lows of this unlikely but weirdly symbiotic duo as they hone their Harlem sound before being picked up by Bo Diddley's manager and thrust onto European concert states. Satan and Adam hit the streets of Times Square—the ragged, pre-Disney Times Square—and Morningside Heights. Gussow also takes a sabbatical to play harmonica in the orchestra of a touring company of *Big River,* Broadway's musical version of *The Adventures of Huckleberry Finn.* A *Publishers Weekly* reviewer called this "the book's centerpiece . . . a humorous foil to his freewheeling life on the street and the racial prejudices he observes. But the heart of the book is the luminous portrait of Mr. Satan." "Throughout this memoir there is mainly love for his mentor, Mister Satan; yet there is hardly rage about being cast out from this community while Gussow himself is its fondest champion," wrote P. J. Rondinone in *American Book Review.* "It's politics like this that create more racial hatred than necessary. . . . There is still much work to do before a whitey can truly make it in the hood." "Gussow shows an English major's love of words . . . and he can sometimes strain a metaphor to the point of breaking," wrote a *Kirkus Reviews* reviewer. "But for the most part, he's a fine writer. . . . You don't have to be a blues fan to love this tale."

Gussow told *CA:* "For roughly ten years (1984-1994), I divided my time between successive drafts of a failed first novel and an increasingly lucrative, wildly improbable career as a blues harmonica player on the streets of Harlem with a Mississippi-born guitar man named Mister Satan. In 1995, an article I wrote for *Harpers* about the partnership ('Winter Blues') caught the eye of a literary agent. I put the novel aside, worked up a proposal, and, amazingly, was handed a contract and an advance. I'd kept voluminous journals during the preceding decade; they were a primary resource in reconstructing my progressive entrance into Harlem streetside society. I'd also kept cassette recordings of harmonica lessons with harp mentor Nat Riddles, street and club gigs, and radio interviews (Mister Satan and I had risen from the streets in the early 1990s to becoming Flying Fish recordings artists Satan and Adam). Working from these materials and the flimsiest of outlines, I wrote *Mister Satan's Apprentice* in roughly fifteen months. They were wonderful months, shadowed by not the slightest trace of writers's block. My writing method is simple: I write (well, type) two double-spaced pages a day, generally in the morning. I revise later in the day. By the time I put those two pages aside that night, the prose is as clean as I can make it. Later line editing is rarely needed. Two pages a day, ten pages a week, forty pages a month. Keep that up and a book happens.

"Stylistically, I was trying to find a middle ground between the spontaneous, centripetal, endlessly unfolding (blowing) sentences of Kerouac and Hemmingway's ruthless economy. Writing about music in a context of soul-depth as I was, I also looked to Ralph Ellison. His narrator's description at the beginning of *Invisible Man* of a marijuana-prompted descent into the deeper levels of African-American experience with the help of Louis Armstrong's trumpet playing on *Black and Blue* offered me a useful model, both existential and literary, for fleeting epiphanies I'd been graced with as a Harlem street blues harmonica player.

"I wrote the book, above all, to honor as best I could the two older men—African-American musicians both—who saw something like artistic promise in me and firmly, by example, taught me how to make the most of it."

## BIOGRAPHICAL/CRITICAL SOURCES:

### PERIODICALS

*American Book Review,* March-April, 1999, p. 1.
*Kirkus Reviews,* October 1, 1998, pp. 1432-1433.
*Living Blues,* May/June, 1999, pp. 109-110.
*Philadelphia Inquirer,* December 6, 1998, p. Q7.
*Publishers Weekly,* September 21, 1998, p. 61.
*Wall Street Journal,* November 13, 1998, p. W12.
*Washington Post Book World,* November 23, 1998, pp. 1, 7.

# H

## HALL, Patricia

*PERSONAL:* Born in Great Britain.

*ADDRESSES: Agent*—c/o St. Martin's Press, 175 Fifth Ave., Rm. 1715, New York, NY 10010.

*CAREER:* Investigative reporter.

*WRITINGS:*

*MYSTERY NOVELS*

*The Poison Pool,* Crime Club (London, England), 1991.
*Death by Election,* Little, Brown (London), 1993.
*Dying Fall,* Little, Brown, 1994.
*In the Bleak Midwinter,* Little, Brown, 1997, published as *Dead of Winter,* St. Martin's Press (New York City), 1997.
*Dead on Arrival,* Constable (London), 1999.
*Perils of the Night,* Constable, 1999.

*SIDELIGHTS:* Investigative reporter Patricia Hall draws on her journalistic experience to write mysteries known for their subtle characterizations and social realism. Hall complicates the conventions of a typical murder mystery by exploring social justice issues and the chasm between social classes. Hall's novels *The Poison Pool, Death by Election, Dying Fall,* and *Dead of Winter* depict environmental pollution, political corruption, sexual molestation, and uneasy relations between the police and the people they are supposed to protect.

In Hall's novel *The Poison Pool,* a brain-damaged teenager, Joey Macready, confesses to the murder of an elderly gentleman in Yorkshire, England. After his arrest and imprisonment, Macready dies in jail, an apparent suicide. Detective-Inspector Alex Sinclair and social worker Kate Weston both doubt that Macready's death is a suicide. Weston and Sinclair then work to expose a far-reaching cover-up involving influential people. Sybil S. Steinberg, writing in *Publishers Weekly,* called Hall's novel an "auspicious debut" and Weston and Sinclair "a pair readers will root for and hope to see again." In another review of the novel, *Los Angeles Times Book Review* contributor Charles Champlin praised the "crisp story" and the author's "ear for Yorkshire speech and her feeling for village life." *New York Times Book Review* contributor Marilyn Stasio wrote that *The Poison Pool* contains "an interesting setting, presentable characters, and a decent puzzle."

Hall's novel *Death by Election* is the first of a series of novels featuring Laura Ackroyd, a reporter for the *Bradfield Gazette,* and Chief Inspector Michael Thackeray, a recent transplant to the town of Bradfield, Yorkshire, England. *Death by Election* blends murder, blackmail, suicide, and sex in "a satisfyingly ugly study of English local politics," according to a *Kirkus Reviews* contributor. After a member of Parliament dies, sociology professor Richard Thurston decides to run for office as a candidate of the Labour Party. The death of Harvey Lingard, one of Richard's former students, threatens Richard's candidacy. It appears that Lingard, who had AIDS, was murdered. The police believe that Thurston killed Harvey and a journalist. While Chief Inspector Thackeray is eager to arrest the professor, Laura Ackroyd, one of Thurston's former students, works to prove his innocence. In *Death by Election,* Hall "has planted the seeds of a complex, involving series," wrote Mary Carroll in *Booklist.*

Moving beyond parliamentary politics and university life, Hall's *Dying Fall* centers on the Heights, a grim housing project in Bradfield. Alleged police corruption aggravates an already troubled relationship between the police and Heights residents, and a new crime wave intensifies community anger about a murdered child. In the wake of a series of sexual assaults on the children who live in the Heights, producers of a television series ask *Bradfield Gazette* reporter Laura Ackroyd to research the homicide of young Tracy Miller. Although Miller's half brother, Stephen Webster, was convicted of this crime, others question his guilt. When Chief Inspector Michael Thackeray begins investigating Webster's conviction, he encounters Laura Ackroyd and helps with her own investigation. A riot, attacks on the elderly, death threats, and muggings all occur before the book's conclusion.

Reviewing *Dying Fall* in the *Armchair Detective*, Rick Mattos observed that "Hall shines in portraying the emotions of those who feel trapped in a decaying, unsafe environment." A *Kirkus Reviews* critic called the novel "an equally unsparing sequel to *Death by Election*," while *Booklist* contributor Mary Carroll applauded "Hall's vivid portrait of the witches' brew of troubles besetting the Heights' residents."

Hall's novel *In the Bleak Midwinter* was published in the United States as *Dead of Winter*. In *Dead of Winter*, Chief Inspector Thackeray investigates the death of Linda Wright, a sales agent for a successful real estate company. While Wright's death initially appears to be the result of a car accident, Thackeray and his colleague, Sergeant Kevin Mower, suspect that she was murdered. Thackeray and Mower immediately suspect Jimmy Townsend, Wright's companion and coworker. Townsend, under investigation for mortgage fraud, mysteriously vanishes, thus compounding the officers' suspicions.

This is a difficult time for Thackeray on a personal level as well. His sometime lover, journalist Laura Ackroyd, is spending the winter in the town of Arnedale working on the local weekly newspaper. Thackeray avoids Arnedale and its neighboring towns for personal reasons relating to his troubled past. Soon after Ackroyd arrives in Arnedale, a fatal truck crash reveals local hostilities toward an unpopular development scheme and serious corruption in the village. When a village woman who protested the development scheme is murdered, Thackeray travels to Arnedale to investigate whether this murder is related to the death of Linda Wright. Hall "once again delivers an insightful, well-paced tale of lives infected by greed and ambition," wrote a reviewer in *Publishers Weekly,* while a *Kirkus Reviews* contributor called *Dead of Winter* "psychologically acute" and "absorbing stuff."

*BIOGRAPHICAL/CRITICAL SOURCES:*

*PERIODICALS*

*Armchair Detective,* spring, 1996, p. 229.
*Booklist,* September 1, 1994, pp. 26-27; September 1, 1995, p. 45; February 1, 1997.
*Kirkus Reviews,* July 1, 1994, p. 888; August 1, 1995, p. 1062; January 1, 1997.
*Los Angeles Times Book Review,* December 12, 1993, p. 11.
*New York Times Book Review,* December 26, 1993, p. 22.
*Publishers Weekly,* October 4, 1993, p. 66; January 6, 1997, p. 68.
*Times Literary Supplement,* November 22, 1991, p. 20.
*Wilson Library Bulletin,* January, 1994, pp. 107-108.*

\* \* \*

## HALLIWELL, Ruth

*PERSONAL:* Female.

*ADDRESSES: Agent*—c/o Oxford University Press, Clarendon Publicity, 198 Madison Ave., New York, NY 10016.

*CAREER:* Freelance writer.

*WRITINGS:*

*The Mozart Family: Four Lives in a Social Context,* Clarendon Press (New York City), 1997.

*SIDELIGHTS:* Ruth Halliwell is the author of *The Mozart Family: Four Lives in a Social Context,* a biography of the family of the great musical composer, Wolfgang Amadeus Mozart. The book examines the Mozart family through the accounts of intimates of the family, chambermaids, princes, and assorted onlookers in Salzburg.

Halliwell presents a Mozart family that is very different from the one depicted in previous books. Centering on Leopold Mozart, Wolfgang's father, and to a lesser extent on mother Maria Anna and sister Nannerl, Halliwell attempts to debunk some of the myths that accompany the memory of Wolfgang Mozart. The letters written by Mozart's parents and sister, never before translated into English, reveal how these myths came about.

Mozart's father, Leopold, was an accomplished violinist and was respected throughout Europe for a book that he had written about playing the violin. Although Leopold was a distinguished celebrity among musicians, he was not considered a genius. Nevertheless, Leopold felt that he had never received the kind of compensation that he deserved, and he endeavored to ensure that his young son would be paid well. Leopold recognized early in Wolfgang's life that his son had exceptional talent, and he tried to nurture that talent.

The letters that appear in the book were saved by Leopold. They reveal much about the Mozart clan, including the considerable power of Wolfgang's widow, Constanze, and the importance of Nannerl in Wolfgang's success. According to *Contemporary Review* writer Richard Mullen, *The Mozart Family* is "a superbly researched, well-written and thoroughly enjoyable work."

*BIOGRAPHICAL/CRITICAL SOURCES:*

*PERIODICALS*

*Contemporary Review*, July, 1998, pp. 51-52.*

\*　　\*　　\*

**HALPERT, Sam   1920-**

*PERSONAL:* Born in 1920. *Avocational interests:* Reading.

*ADDRESSES: Agent*—c/o Southern Heritage Press, P.O. Box 10937, St. Petersburg, FL 33733. *E-mail*—sampert@aol.com.

*CAREER:* Writer. Also worked as a typesetter. *Military service:* Army Air Force, served as a B-17 navigator, served in Europe in World War II.

*WRITINGS:*

(Editor) . . . *When We Talk about Raymond Carver,* Peregrine Smith (Layton, UT), 1991, expanded edition published as *Raymond Carver: An Oral Bi-*

*ography,* University of Iowa Press (Iowa City, IA), 1995.
*A Real Good War,* Southern Heritage Press (St. Petersburg, FL), 1998.

Author of short stories.

*SIDELIGHTS:* Sam Halpert has edited an oral biography of the highly regarded American writer Raymond Carver. He has also written an autobiographical novel about World War II. Both books have been critically praised.

Published in 1991, . . . *When We Talk about Raymond Carver* is a book of reminiscences by Carver's lovers, close friends, and associates. The interviewees include Maryann Carver, Carver's wife of twenty-five years, Carver's companion, the poet Tess Gallagher, and the writers Tobias Wolff, Richard Ford, and Jay McInerney. Russell Banks, discussing . . . *When We Talk about Raymond Carver* in the *Atlantic,* called the book "an old-fashioned Irish kind of wake, in which dear friends and family members gather and recollect and tell stories and lies, make their confessions and renew loyalties, offer toasts, and sing songs of praise and lamentation, one hard upon another." When Carver died at the age of fifty in 1988, "it was widely agreed then that he had already made a major contribution to American literature," wrote Banks.

"Like so many Carver fans, Halpert may have forgotten that not everybody in the world has heard of him, yet, one of the strongest aspects of the book is that Halpert simply lets his subjects talk and tell their stories," stated Stephen Schugart in the *Bloomsbury Review.* Halpert also produced an expanded edition of . . . *When We Talk about Raymond Carver, Raymond Carver: An Oral Biography* (1995). *Library Journal* contributor Peter Dollard judged *Raymond Carver: An Oral Biography* to be "highly readable" as well as "an engrossing, touching, and insightful remembrance of Carver."

Halpert's World War II novel *A Real Good War* (1998) chronicles the wartime experiences of the young American crew members of a bomber plane. Stationed in Europe, the soldiers can return home after completing thirty-five dangerous bombing missions over Nazi Germany. The novel's unnamed narrator, a navigator like Halpert, wonders who will die next. A *Kirkus Reviews* contributor stated that the novel's battle scenes have "a fresh and bracing realism," and called the book "an inspiring debut: nostalgic, ironic, and respectful of a harrowing moment in America's history." A *Publishers Weekly* reviewer deemed *A Really Good War* to be "gripping fiction," while *New York Times Book Review* contributor Peter Bricklebank noted that it depicts "the fine line between a close call and a tragedy, not to mention the way guilt is detonated by war's deadly absurdity."

BIOGRAPHICAL/CRITICAL SOURCES:

PERIODICALS

*American Literature,* December, 1995, p. 901.
*Atlantic,* August, 1991, pp. 99-103.
*Bloomsbury Review,* October/November, 1991, p. 17.
*Kirkus Reviews,* November 15, 1997.
*Library Journal,* April 15, 1995, p. 76.
*New York Times Book Review,* April 26, 1998, p. 22.
*Publishers Weekly,* October 13, 1997, pp. 55-56.

OTHER

*Salon,*     http://www.salon.com/books/log/1999/07/08/ halpert/index.html (November 4, 1999).*

\*          \*          \*

## HAMILTON, Dakota

PERSONAL: *Avocational interests:* Volunteer work.

ADDRESSES: *Home*—Vancouver, British Columbia, Canada. *Agent*—c/o Author Mail, Seventh Floor, HarperCollins Publishers, 10 East 53rd St., New York, NY 10022.

CAREER: Writer.

WRITINGS:

*Freedom's Just Another Word* (novel), HarperCollins (New York City), 1998.

SIDELIGHTS: Dakota Hamilton is a writer who makes her home in Vancouver, British Columbia, Canada, and volunteers at a prison for women. In the novel *Freedom's Just Another Word,* Hamilton presents the world of the women's prison through Margaret Hoffer. Margaret has been convicted of killing her husband Mongrel, a biker and drug dealer, but maintains her innocence and claims that Mongrel committed suicide. She spends her time in jail by reminiscing about her past with Mongrel, reading tarot cards, and recalling favorite recipes.

Margaret is part of a close-knit cadre of inmates who form a twelve-step group. Instead of dedicating their meetings to self-improvement, this twelve-step group uses the time to plan their escape. After their successful escape, the women travel across the country in search of their own personal freedom. Toronto *Globe and Mail* contributor Lisa Godfrey faulted the novel's "careless writing," but admitted that "in its finer moments, Hamilton's novel is as amiable and unrepentant as the story's jailed narrator." Reviewing *Freedom's Just Another Word* in the online *Herald Book Club,* Paula White called the book "refreshing, poignant, and knock-down funny," and judged the characters to be "endearing, challenging, and unforgettable."

BIOGRAPHICAL/CRITICAL SOURCES:

PERIODICALS

*Globe and Mail* (Toronto), April 4, 1998.

OTHER

*Herald Book Club,* http://www.telusplanet.net/public/ lethher/archive/feature16.html     (October     13, 1998).*

\*          \*          \*

## HAMILTON, Laurell K.

PERSONAL: Married. *Education:* Received degree in English.

ADDRESSES: *Agent*—c/o Marian Montgomery, 375 Hudson St., New York, NY 10014.

CAREER: Writer.

WRITINGS:

*Nightseer,* Ace Books (New York City), 1992.
*Nightshade* ("Star Trek, the Next Generation" series), Pocket Books (New York City), 1992.
*Guilty Pleasures* ("Anita Blake, Vampire Hunter" series), Ace Books, 1993.
*The Laughing Corpse,* Ace Books, 1994.
*Death of a Darklord* ("Ravenloft" series), TSR, 1995.
*Circus of the Damned,* Ace Books, 1995.
*Lunatic Cafe,* Ace Books, 1996.
*Bloody Bones,* Ace Books, 1996.
*Killing Dance,* Ace Books, 1997.
*Burnt Offerings,* Ace Books, 1998.

*SIDELIGHTS:* Laurell K. Hamilton's novels bridge the genres of science-fiction, mystery, and horror. She writes about vampires, elves, private eyes, magi, and sentient trees, and has been rewarded with one of the highest compliments for such a writer: numerous reviewers have praised her writing and the worlds that she has imagined as being convincing and rich.

Hamilton's first novel, *Nightseer,* sets the tone for her entire body of work, laying out a world where the existence of magic, demons, and other supernatural phenomena are taken as ordinary. The story itself recounts the adventures of Keleios, described by one reviewer as "a grown woman, master enchanter, prophetic dreamer, and experienced demon fighter, herself tainted with a touch of demonic evil." After discovering a latent ability in sorcery, Keleios is (humiliatingly) sent back to school to learn to control these powers. This return to education is hardly smooth, though, and soon Keleios is embroiled in a fierce struggle against a witch with a vendetta against Keleios and her family. The plot deepens when the school itself becomes the target of political revenge by marauding demons. Keleios is at the center of these many battles, with and without allies, and sees them through to their conclusion.

Reviews of *Nightseer* were tepid; unlike her later novels, where Hamilton creates a vivid, unusual new world for her characters to explore, this world is described by Carolyn Cushman of *Locus* as "working within a standard fantasy scenario." "Once the battles start," Cushman adds, "the novel is all action with little point beyond revenge . . . [While] a bit of reluctant but inevitable romance helps tie the plot together,. . . . [Keleios's] companions, however important, come and go from one battle to the next, a process ruinous to the convincing development of relationships." For all of these problems, however, Cushman still finds much to praise in the novel, and notes that "for a newcomer [Hamilton] demonstrates a real feel for the most popular elements of genre fantasy."

Hamilton's next book is part of the popular "Star Trek: The Next Generation" series. Based on the popular *Star Trek* television series of the same name, *Nightshade* follows the exploits of the *U.S.S. Enterprise* crew as they encounter a planet completely polluted by its inhabitants. To make matters even worse, the natives are engaged in a war of mutual annihilation. The crew of the *Enterprise* become enmeshed in the planet's warlike politics when Captain Picard is wrongly accused of murdering one of the planet's delegates. Picard is sentenced to death, and the remainder of the *Enterprise* crew must rush to rescue him by finding the real killer.

Reviewers noted that Hamilton's book sits well within the "Star Trek" series, even though her style is at times heavy-handed. As Hugh M. Flick Jr. writes in *Kliatt,* "The horrors of runway pollution are clearly spelled out to even the most undiscerning reader."

*Guilty Pleasures,* Hamilton's next offering, kicked off what would become her signature series. The novel introduces an alternate Earth, similar enough to have recognizable brand names, but with a few important differences. Not only does this alternate Earth include a grisly variety of undead creatures—vampires, zombies, ghouls, and worse are part of the story—but in this parallel universe, humans have accepted the presence of these creatures and have legalized their existence. So long as they can peacefully coexist with living creatures, the undead are legally free to roam.

While most of the undead are surprisingly willing to live by these rules, some of their brethren are up to no good. To handle these criminal undead, the humans have set up special police teams—dubbed "spook squads"—to handle and eliminate the bad apples. As in our world, there are some cases that the police cannot solve, and in their place private investigators fill the gap. Anita Blake, heroine of the series, is just such a private eye. Petite but tough, her primary interest is professional animation (raising zombies), but she's also an accomplished vampire hunter. She's so good at this "hobby," in fact, that she's known among the undead as "the Executioner." The title of *Guilty Pleasures* refers to a vampire strip club popular with daring humans seeking the titillating experiences of rubbing elbows with the undead. Blake visits the nightclub for a bachelorette party and ends up unwilling coerced into accepting a case to stop a serial killer of vampires.

Several reviewers praised Hamilton for her creative vision. Don D'Ammassa writes in a *Science Fiction Chronicle* review that Hamilton's alternate world makes "all the setting for a tough detective story that works reasonably well." Cushman comments in *Locus:* "About all that's missing is real romantic tension, but the characters are generally too unpleasant to be involving. Still, there are plenty of kinky plot twists, lots of dark humor, and a slap-dash pace to keep things going." Samantha Hunt, writing in *Voice of Youth Advocates,* has perhaps the highest praise for the book. Not only is *Guilty Pleasures* "a fast-paced delight, with its strange characters, snappy dialogue, and brutal action," but Hunt suggests that readers "look forward to a sequel—the author can not possibly leave us hanging at ' . . . I don't date vampires. I kill them.' "

In answer to Hunt's wish, Anita Blake returns in *The Laughing Corpse,* the second book in the "Anita Blake, Vampire Hunter" series. This time through, Anita's arm is twisted by a millionaire who desires to have a certain corpse raised from the dead. Anita refuses him, protesting that, due to the extensive deterioration of the body, a human sacrifice would be required, and she doesn't do sacrifices. The millionaire doesn't take no for an answer. Before she can resolve that problem, the police call her in to investigate a grisly series of murders apparently committed by a zombie. To add to her problems, handsome vampire Jean-Claude becomes increasingly assertive in expressing his romantic interest in Blake.

Critics hailed *The Laughing Corpse* as brilliantly balanced between suspense and hilarity. A reviewer in the *Science Fiction Chronicle* calls it "a major improvement over the series opener, which took so much time establishing the background of a world where supernatural creatures are taken for granted that the story often faltered. Now our attention is firmly centered on the main character and the mystery she's involved with, with great results." Samantha Hunt, writing in *Voice of Youth Advocates,* calls the book "gross, grisly, gruesome, and one heck of an evening's read for those who relish same." Impressed by Hamilton's continuing installments to the series, Cushman, again writing for *Locus,* notes that "the creepy and the mundane alternate constantly in these novels, for often hilarious contract. . . . But there's also plenty of intriguing detection, edge-of-the-seat excitement, and grue for the hardcore [sic] buffs."

Blake returns for a third engagement in Hamilton's *Circus of the Damned.* Here the vampire hunter gets caught in the middle ground when two vampire lords fight for pre-eminence. Reviews for this continuation of the series continued to be excellent. A *Library Journal* review reports that "fans of hard-boiled detective stories and vampire fiction will enjoy this well-written, fast-paced dark fantasy." A *Science Fiction Chronicle* contributor goes further, opining that "Hamilton has created a genuinely interested alternate world, people it with fascinating characters, and given us a protagonist we can really care about."

*Death of a Darklord,* Hamilton's next novel, marked a brief respite from the Anita Blake series. The story is set within the framework of the popular "Ravenloft" role-playing game. Not surprisingly, Ravenloft is a game system based on a hearty blend of horror and fantasy, subjects Hamilton seems to relish. The story centers around a village under attack by armies of zombies raised from the earth by some unknown malefactor. A mage finder is hired to restore things to normal, and the book follows his travels to the root of the problem. A *Science Fiction Chronicle* reviewer asserts that Hamilton "does a good job at evoking the atmosphere of her setting, and her characters are reasonably well drawn."

Hamilton has since returned to the adventures of trusty Anita Blake. *The Lunatic Cafe* revolves, not surprisingly, around a set of killings that Blake must investigate. This time through, the police are unsure whether the killer is mortal or undead, so Blake has even less than usual to rely on. Romance is again a sticky point for Blake, as old friend Jean-Claude, the local Master Vampire from the earlier novels, surfaces to challenge Blake's latest boyfriend for the sleuth's hand in marriage. Joseph R. DeMarco, writing in *Kliatt,* praises the novel, calling Hamilton "a writer who combines elements of everything in her work: police procedural, wry sense of humor, detailed knowledge of the supernatural, and much more. Her writing is smooth and beautiful. Her Anita Blake is intelligent, witty, strong, clever and lots of fun."

*BIOGRAPHICAL/CRITICAL SOURCES:*

*BOOKS*

*Detecting Women 2,* Purple Moon Press (Dearborn, MI), 1996.

*PERIODICALS*

*Kliatt,* May 1993, p. 16; May 1996, p. 16.
*Library Journal,* May 15, 1995, p. 99; June 15, 1995, p. 98.
*Locus,* February 1992, p. 30; October 1993, p. 27; October 1994, p. 33.
*Science Fiction Chronicle,* September 1993, p. 32; January 1995, pp. 37-38; June 1995, p. 37; July 1995, p. 37; May 1997, pp. 127-128.
*Voice of Youth Advocates,* February 1994, p. 381; February 1995, p. 348.*

\*    \*    \*

**HARCOURT, Wendy**

*PERSONAL:* Female.

*ADDRESSES: Office*—c/o *Development,* The Society for International Development, 207 via Panisperna, 00184, Rome, Italy. *E-mail*—wharcourt@agira.stm.it.

*CAREER:* Society for International Development, editor of *Development* (journal); lecturer at colleges including Schumacher College, Dartington, England, 1997.

*WRITINGS:*

(Editor) *Feminist Perspectives on Sustainable Development,* Zed/Society for International Development (London), 1994.
(Editor) *Power, Reproduction, and Gender: The Intergenerational Transfer of Knowledge,* Zed/Society for International Development (London), 1997.

*SIDELIGHTS:* Feminist economist and editor Wendy Harcourt produces *Development,* the quarterly journal of the Society for International Development. As Harcourt notes on the journal's website, *Development* focuses on informing readers about "the cutting edge issues of sustainable human development. From views on development, alternatives to strategies at the local level and reports on the inside debates at the [United Nations], *Development* provides a provocative broad survey of today's development debates."

The Society for International Development is a global network of people interested in diverse, sustainable, and inclusive development. Harcourt's interest in these issues, and in the elimination of gender bias in economics and development, is apparent in the two anthologies she edited. *Power, Reproduction, and Gender: The Intergenerational Transfer of Knowledge* presents case studies exploring people's sexual behavior in a variety of nations, including Brazil, Italy, Pakistan, Switzerland, Ghana, Tanzania, and Sri Lanka. The book examines how, when, and why people change their sexual and reproductive behavior, and how sexual and reproductive knowledge is handed down from one generation to the next or from one person to another.

*Feminist Perspectives on Sustainable Development,* a collection of seventeen papers edited by Harcourt, provides a feminist view of sustainable development and examines the connection between women, the environment, and development.

*BIOGRAPHICAL/CRITICAL SOURCES:*

*PERIODICALS*

*Environmental Politics,* spring, 1995, p. 144; summer, 1995, p. 337.
*Geographical Journal,* July, 1995, p. 227.
*Journal of Economic Literature,* March, 1995, p. 365.

*OTHER*

*Development* Website, http://www.sagepub.co.uk/journals/usdetails/j0152.html (June 12, 1998).*

\*      \*      \*

**HARPER, Christopher**

*PERSONAL: Education:* University of Nebraska, B.A. (English literature and journalism), 1973; Northwestern University, M.S.J. (journalism), 1974.

*ADDRESSES: Office*—311 Park Hall, Ithaca College, Ithaca, NY 14850.

*CAREER:* Associated Press, Chicago, IL, reporter, 1974-75; *Newsweek* Magazine, correspondent in Chicago, 1975-77, correspondent in Washington, DC, 1977-79, bureau chief in Beirut, Lebanon, 1979-81; *ABC News,* bureau chief in Cairo, Egypt, 1981, correspondent in Rome, Italy, 1981-83, bureau chief in Rome, 1983-86; *20/20* (ABC television news program), reporter, 1986-95; New York University, journalism department faculty member, 1994-97; Ithaca College, Ithaca, NY, Roy H. Park Distinguished Chair, 1997—.

*MEMBER:* Society of Professional Journalists, Online News Association, Association of Education in Journalism and Mass Communication.

*WRITINGS:*

*And That's the Way It Will Be: News and Information in a Digital World,* New York University Press (New York), 1998.

Also author of *What's Next in Mass Communications,* St. Martin's; *Journalism 2001;* and *The New Mass Media,* Houghton.

*SIDELIGHTS:* In *And That's the Way It Will Be: News and Information in a Digital World,* Christopher Harper writes about the impact of the internet on communications, particularly from a journalistic standpoint. According to Scott Rosenberg in the *New York Times Book Review,* Harper's basic premise is that the internet has and will change the means by which news communications are disseminated. Harper also states that the internet phenomenon inherently changes the status of journalists. Not only has their formerly exclusive role changed (now they must share information distribution with a variety of others who can disseminate information easily to thousands of people), but the quality of information on the internet is often never tested or verified before it reaches the masses.

One example that Harper cites involved information regarding the TWA Flight 800 crash which newsman Pierre Salinger supposedly obtained from the internet. While Salinger was initially excited by the scoop and presented it as news-breaking information, it later turned out that the information had circulated on the internet for weeks before and that it was inaccurate. This incident prompted newsman and peer Walter Cronkite to describe the use of the internet as a "frightful danger to all of us." Cronkite was referring to the double-edged sword that the internet provides; while it has the ability to disseminate information at unheard of speeds and to great numbers of people, it also has the power to quickly spread false rumors. Harper advises journalists and internet users to approach information found online with healthy skepticism.

Rosenberg objected to the progression of information in Harper's book, which he called "a casual and haphazard survey" of the topics, akin to "information nuggets on a shoddy Web site." For example, Rosenberg claimed that the book moves disjointedly from a description of people's preferences for obtaining news to quotes from internet experts to profiles of "digital journalists," or those who publish news and articles on the internet. Rosenberg cited instances where the author has provided misinformation (in one case, stating that the simplest way for a computer to get a virus is through e-mail), and value-laden if well-intentioned advice for banning hate literature and discriminatory material from the internet. The reviewer also faulted Harper for not addressing the commercial players responsible for the migration of news to the internet, and what these players are doing to shape the trend.

Rosenberg maintained that Harper's journalistic bent causes him to not fully address the internet as a communications medium. Instead, the author focuses on the internet's publishing implications. By narrowing his focus, Harper also misses an analysis of some of the grassroots and informal news services that have sprung up online—for an example, Rosenberg used gossip columnist Matt Drudge. Rosenberg concluded that while Harper focuses only on the internet's impact on the established journalism profession, larger changes are already occurring in the medium that will impact information dissemination beyond typical news providers' control. *Library Journal*'s Judy Solberg gave a more positive analysis of Harper's work, commenting that the author has an "engaging writing style" and is optimistic about the future of internet journalism.

*BIOGRAPHICAL/CRITICAL SOURCES:*

*PERIODICALS*

*Library Journal,* June 15, 1998, p. 87.
*New York Times Book Review,* July 12, 1998.

*OTHER*

*Ithaca College Web site,* http://www.ithaca.edu/faculty/charper/resume.htm (November 17, 1999).*

* * *

## HARPER, Linda Lee

*PERSONAL: Education:* B.A., 1982; M.F.A., 1985.

*ADDRESSES: Office*—Department of Community Programs, University of Tennessee, Knoxville, TN. *Agent*—c/o Nightshade Press, P.O. Box 76, Troy, ME 04987.

*CAREER:* University of Tennessee, Knoxville, instructor in community programs; writer.

*AWARDS, HONORS:* First Prize from Academy of American Poets; William and Kingman Page Chapbook Award, Nightshade Press, for *A Failure of Loveliness;* Washington Prize for Poetry for *Toward Desire;* Writer's Voice Hibiscus Award for *Cataloguing.*

*WRITINGS:*

*A Failure of Loveliness* (poetry), Nightshade Press, 1994.
*Toward Desire* (poetry), Word Works, 1996.

Also author of *Blue Flute* and *Cataloguing.* Contributor to periodicals, including *America, Georgia Review, International Quarterly,* and *Passages North.*

*SIDELIGHTS:* Linda Lee Harper received the William and Kingman Page Award for *A Failure of Loveliness,* a collection of poems comprising what Phebe Davidson described in *Belles Lettres* as a chronicle of various family members who realize "near-mythic significance." Davidson, acknowledged the sexual and violent nature of some of the poems and noted their "narrative strength," but she added that "it is Harper's lyrical strength that gives the book . . . its quality of endurance."

*BIOGRAPHICAL/CRITICAL SOURCES:*

*PERIODICALS*

*Belles Lettres,* January, 1996, pp. 37-38.*

\* \* \*

## HARRIS, Ronald W(alter)   1916-1999

*OBITUARY NOTICE*—See index for *CA* sketch: Born August 19, 1916, in Wiltshire, England; died June 17, 1999. Educator and author. Harris devoted his life to education, serving as a schoolmaster for more than thirty-five years. A history teacher at the King's School at Canterbury, Harris demanded excellence from his students and was rewarded during his career with the knowledge that nearly two hundred scholarships or exhibitions were awarded to students under his tutelage. His area of expertise was political history and he wrote several textbooks on the subject including *Latin for Historians, England in the Eighteenth Century, An Historical Introduction to the Twentieth Century,* and *The Philosophy of Politics.* Prior to joining the staff at King's School, where he was head of the history department, Harris taught briefly in Jamaica.

*OBITUARIES AND OTHER SOURCES:*

*PERIODICALS*

*Times* (London), July 16, 1999.*

\* \* \*

## HARSCH, Joseph C(lose)   1905-1998

*OBITUARY NOTICE*—See index for *CA* sketch: Born May 25, 1905, in Toledo, OH; died June 3, 1998, in Jamestown, RI. Journalist. Harsch's career was devoted to reporting the news, whether from the homefront or a far-flung location. After receiving his first bachelor's degree from Williams College in 1927 he followed that with a second bachelor's from Corpus Christi College at Cambridge in 1929 and promptly was hired at the *Christian Science Monitor.* He stayed at the *Monitor* for nearly fifty years and filed stories from Washington, D.C., Rome, Berlin and other locations. For many of the years between 1943 and 1971 he also worked for the three major television networks, sometimes as a correspondent, other times providing commentary. He saw many historical events as they unfolded, from the bombing of Pearl Harbor to the Soviet Union during the early years of the Cold War. Harsch wrote several books based on what he had covered for the *Monitor,* including *Pattern of Conquest, The Curtain Isn't Iron* and *At the Hinge of History.*

*OBITUARIES AND OTHER SOURCES:*

*PERIODICALS*

*Chicago Tribune,* June 5, 1998, sec. 1, p. 10.
*New York Times,* June 5, 1998, p. D21.*

\* \* \*

## HARSTAD, Donald

*PERSONAL:* Married; wife's name, Mary.

*ADDRESSES: Home*—Elkader, IA. *Agent*—c/o Doubleday, 1540 Broadway, New York, NY 10036.

*CAREER:* Worked in law enforcement for twenty-six years. Served as deputy sheriff in Iowa.

*WRITINGS:*

*CRIME NOVELS*

*Eleven Days,* Doubleday (Garden City, NY), 1998.
*Known Dead,* Doubleday, 1999.

*SIDELIGHTS:* Author Donald Harstad was a deputy sheriff and worked in law enforcement for twenty-six years in Iowa before he published his first book, *Eleven Days.* In the book Harstad makes use of his law enforcement background and the technicalities from a case he worked on to weave his plot. The story is set in a small, seemingly peaceful and innocent Iowa country town. The town is shaken when protagonist Carl Houseman receives a 911 emergency call leading to a location with multiple murder victims. As Houseman and his peers dig into the evidence, their investigation points to the existence of a satanic cult in town and suggests that some victims may have been sacrificed (including a baby) and that others will follow. Further work on the case leads Houseman to believe that the town pastor and his wife are prime suspects in the murders. The book peaks with a charged confrontation at a town church.

A *Publishers Weekly* reviewer praised the book, commenting on the author's "deceptively sparse style" which won out even when Harstad "crowd[ed] the plot" with too many details. This reviewer compared Harstad with Joseph Wambaugh (another author of cop thrillers), praised the tightness of Harstad's action scenes, and looked forward to Harstad continuing his new career as an author. *Booklist* writer David Pitt, who called the author's style "[n]either as coarse as Joseph Wambaugh nor as strictly procedural as Ed McBain—but, in terms of skill, on a par with both," liked Harstad's reliance on investigation techniques to tell the story, rather than made-for-TV type plotting.

*BIOGRAPHICAL/CRITICAL SOURCES:*

PERIODICALS

*Booklist,* April 15, 1998, p. 1383.
*Publishers Weekly,* May 25, 1998, p. 61.*

\*   \*   \*

## HASSAM, Andrew

*PERSONAL: Education:* Holds a Ph.D.

*ADDRESSES: Office*—University of Wales, Lampeter, Ceredigion SA48 7ED, England.

*CAREER:* Director of B.A. in Australian Studies program at the University of Wales, Lampeter; visiting scholar at Queensland University of Technology, 1999. Member of the Centre for Australian Studies in Wales.

*AWARDS, HONORS:* Has held a number of research fellowships in Australia, including the Harold White Fellowship, 1992; Australian Bicentennial Fellowship, 1994; C. H. Currey Memorial Fellowship, 1995; and Visiting Fellowship at the Australian National University, Canberra, 1998.

*WRITINGS:*

FICTION

*To the Edge of the Page* (short stories), Spectrum (London), 1988.

NONFICTION

*Writing and Reality: A Study of Modern British Diary Fiction,* Greenwood Press (Westport, CT), 1993.
*Sailing to Australia: Shipboard Diaries by Nineteenth-Century British Emigrants,* Manchester University Press (Manchester, England), 1995.
(Editor) *No Privacy for Writing: Shipboard Diaries 1852-1879,* Melbourne University Press (Melbourne, Australia), 1995.

Also international editorial advisor for *Electronic Journal of Australian and New Zealand History, Journal of Australian Studies,* and *Australian Humanities Review.*

*WORK IN PROGRESS: Through Australian Eyes,* a study of letters and diaries written by Australians visiting England.

*SIDELIGHTS:* Andrew Hassam has written a volume of short stories, 1988's *To the Edge of the Page,* as well as three works of analyzing diary writings and how they reveal cultural differences. In his 1993 book, *Writing and Reality: A Study of Modern British Diary Fiction,* Hassam explores modern and postmodern diary novels written by British writers, including John Berger, William Golding, and Doris Lessing, from the mid-1950s through the mid-1970s. His focus is on the authors' textual strategies in representing the reality of the diary in fictional form; he also examines the relationship between individual and social reality, and the questioning, by the diaristic novels, of culturally imposed notions of reality. Delineating limits which the culture had placed around the genre, and around the relationship between writing and reality, Hassam theorizes about ways in which the novels had transgressed those limits. For *Choice* reviewer B. Braendlin this makes for a "valuable" discussion of "narrative issues involving 'facticity, history, autobiography, and gender.' "

More widely reviewed was Hassam's 1995 book, *Sailing to Australia: Shipboard Entries by Nineteenth-Century British Emigrants,* in which he turns his attention to diary texts written by real, though uncelebrated, Britons. Some 1,300,000 people from Great Britain immigrated to Australia in the nineteenth century, according to W. W. Reinhardt, writing in *Choice;* of those, the memories of about 850 have been preserved in the form of shipboard diaries. Hassam studied around a hundred of these, available at the National Library of Australia, through the prism of poststructuralist literary theory.

The first chapter of his book is devoted to an historical recounting of the shipboard experience. Passengers were divided into first, second, and third-class compartments; female first-class passengers remained mostly in their cabins, an equivalent of the safe havens they found in the Victorian home; third class, or steerage, was arranged into sexually segregated quarters. A lowest class—stowaways—was hounded by passengers and crew alike. There was much crowding, much idle drinking and eating, and much passivity. The rigid social class barriers of England were largely preserved on the ship, as reflected in the diaries. The diaries, predominantly the artless creations of amateur writers, are often bare and factual, though they sometimes contain attempts at imitating the prevailing literary style. The first sighting of Australia was typically a high point of poignancy in a diary; and most diaries ended very soon after the landing.

Hassam, analyzing the diaries, found that they revealed for him the ways in which culture determines both behavior and literary form. As critic Graham Little expressed it in *Australian Book Review,* for Hassam, "[N]arrative convention . . . shapes the experience of the emigration, not the other way around." In Hassam's view, "[T]he emigrants didn't write them [the diaries] at all; the culture did," Little said. Little declared his skepticism about this postmodern approach to literature and to experience; he preferred to see, in the diaries' manifestations of spontaneous, genuinely felt, human experiences; and in the shaping of the diaries, he discerned a parallel to the shape of the actual emigrant voyage itself rather than to a literary convention of the voyage narrative. Nevertheless, Little found in some of the diaries "wonderful descriptions of embarkation . . . , vividly coloured images of confusion and excitement," and more. For *Choice*'s Reinhardt, *Sailing to Australia* was "[s]cholarly, well-documented . . . , a solid contribution." Very high praise was accorded Hassam by a *Times Literary Supplement* critic, who called his analysis "exceptionally rich and fruitful" and his theoretical grasp of the diary form (and related forms) "firm." While the physical emigration to Australia did not always live up to its promise, this reviewer observed, "*Sailing to Australia* . . . richly fulfills its own promise and deserves every success."

*BIOGRAPHICAL/CRITICAL SOURCES:*

*PERIODICALS*

*Australian Book Review,* May, 1995, pp. 14-15.
*Choice,* June, 1993, p. 1626; May, 1995, p. 1502.
*Times Literary Supplement,* December 15, 1995, p. 28.*

## HAWKE, David Freeman   1923-1999

*OBITUARY NOTICE*—See index for *CA* sketch: Born December 14, 1923, in Philadelphia, PA; died of heart disease, June 20, 1999, in Madison, CT. Historian, author. Hawke, a scholar of American history, wrote several books relating to the American Revolution, including *In the Midst of a Revolution* and *Honorable Treason: The Declaration of Independence and the Men Who Signed It.* He focused on well-known historical figures in works such as *Benjamin Rush, Paine,* and *Franklin.* His love of history translated into his chosen profession of education and he worked at a number of schools including Long Island University and Pace University before settling in at the Herbert H. Lehman College of the City University of New York in 1972. In 1986 he was named professor emeritus. Although he said his books fell short of pleasing both historians and casual readers, his joy from writing was enough to make him get out of bed each day, he said.

*OBITUARIES AND OTHER SOURCES:*

*PERIODICALS*

*New York Times,* June 25, 1999, p. B9.

\*          \*          \*

## HAYES, Elizabeth T.

*PERSONAL: Education:* Holds a Ph.D.

*ADDRESSES: Office*—LeMoyne College, English Department, LeMoyne Heights, Syracuse, NY, 13214.

*CAREER:* LeMoyne College, Syracuse, NY, chair of English Department.

*WRITINGS:*

(Editor) *Images of Persephone: Feminist Readings in Western Literature,* University Press of Florida, 1994.

*SIDELIGHTS:* Elizabeth T. Hayes is the editor and contributor to a collection of eleven scholarly essays titled *Images of Persephone: Feminist Readings in Western Literature.* These readings, which treat the evolution of the Greek Persephone myth in French, American, and English literary works, provide close textual analyses of pieces by such writers as Geoffrey Chaucer, William

Shakespeare, Nathaniel Hawthorne, D. H. Lawrence, Samuel Beckett, Margaret Atwood, Helene Cixous, Zora Neal Hurston, Toni Morrison, and Alice Walker, among others. Hayes' introductory essay, "The Persephone Myth in Western Literature," provides an overview of the Greek sources of the Persephone myth, and four renderings of the myth are provided in an appendix. According to B. M. McNeal, writing for *Choice, Images of Persephone* "would be useful" in a variety of lower or upper level college courses, particularly those dealing with women's studies, feminist or mythic criticism, or cultural studies.

*BIOGRAPHICAL/CRITICAL SOURCES:*

PERIODICALS

*Choice,* December, 1994, p. 595.*

\*     \*     \*

# HAYWARD, John (Davy) 1905-1965

*PERSONAL:* Born February 2, 1905; died September 17, 1965; son of John Arthur (a surgeon) and Rosamond Grace Rolleston Hayward. *Education:* Attended King's College, Cambridge.

*CAREER:* Writer, c. 1926-65; taught at a girls' school in Cambridge.

*WRITINGS:*

(Editor) *Collected Works of John Wilmot, Earl of Rochester,* Nonesuch Press (London), 1926.

(Editor) *Complete Poetry and Selected Prose of John Donne,* Nonesuch Press (London), 1929.

(Editor and author of introduction and notes) *The Letters of Saint-Evremond, Charles Marguetel de Saint Denis, Seigneur de Saint-Evremond,* Routledge (London), 1930.

*Charles II,* Duckworth (London), 1933.

(Editor) *Nineteenth-Century Poetry, An Anthology,* Chatto & Windus (London), 1932.

(Editor) Jonathan Swift, *Gulliver's Travels and Selected Writings in Prose & Verse,* Nonesuch Press (London), 1934.

(Editor) *Silver Tongues: Famous Speeches from Burke to Baldwin,* Joseph (London), 1937.

(With T. S. Eliot, G. C. Faber, and F. V. Morley) *Noctes Binanianae: Certain Voluntary and Satyrical Verses and Compliments as Were Lately Ex-*

*chang'd between Some of the Wits of the Age,* privately printed (London), 1939.

(Arranger and editor) *Love's Helicon or the Progress of Love Described in English Verse,* Duckworth (London), 1940.

(Selector and editor) T. S. Eliot, *Points of View,* Faber & Faber (London), 1941.

*A Catalogue of Printed Books and Manuscripts by Jonathan Swift, D.D. Exhibited in the Old Schools in the University of Cambridge. To Commemorate the 200th Anniversary of His Death, October 19, 1745,* Cambridge University Press (Cambridge), 1945.

*Prose Literature Since 1939: A Survey of English Prose Literature Other Than Fiction from 1939 to 1945,* Longmans, Green (London), 1947.

*English Poetry: A Catalogue of First & Early Editions of Works of the English Poets from Chaucer to the Present Day Exhibited by the National Book League at 7 Albemarle Street, London, 1947,* Cambridge University Press (Cambridge), 1947.

(Selector) Samuel Johnson, *Dr. Johnson. Some Observations and Judgements upon Life and Letters,* Zodiac Books, no. 5, Lighthouse Books (London), 1948.

(Selector) *Seventeenth-Century Poetry: An Anthology,* Chatto & Windus (London), 1948.

(Editor and author of introduction) Swift, *Selected Prose Works of Jonathan Swift,* Cresset (London), 1949.

(Contributor with R. W. Chapman, John Carter, and Michael Sadleir) *Book Collection: Four Broadcast Talks,* Bowes & Bowes (Cambridge), 1950.

(Compiler and author of introduction) *T. S. Eliot: Poems Written in Early Youth,* privately printed (Stockholm), Farrar, Straus (New York City), 1967.

(Editor and author of introduction) *John Donne: A Selection of His Poetry,* Penguin (Harmondsworth, UK), 1950.

(Author of introduction) Edmund Spenser, *The Faerie Queene,* 2 volumes, Oxford University Press (Oxford), 1953, republished in one volume as *The Coronation Edition of the Faerie Queene,* Heritage Press (New York City), 1953.

(Editor) *T. S. Eliot: Selected Prose,* Penguin, 1953.

(Editor) *The Penguin Book of English Verse,* Penguin, 1956, republished as *The Faber Book of English Verse,* Faber & Faber (London), 1958.

(Editor) Robert Herrick, *Herrick: Poems,* Penguin, 1961.

(Selector and author of preface) *The Oxford Book of Nineteenth-Century Verse,* Clarendon Press (Oxford), 1964.

*Catalogue of the Collection of English and French Literature of the Sixteenth to Nineteenth Century, the Property of the Late John Hayward, Esq., C.B.E.,* Sotheby (London), 1966.

*Hand-List of the Literary Manuscripts in the T. S. Eliot Collection Bequeathed to King's College, Cambridge by John Davy Hayward in 1965,* King's College Library (Cambridge), 1973.

Editor of *The Book Collector.* Hayward's papers are at King's College, Cambridge, in the Hayward Papers and the T. S. Eliot Collection of Manuscripts.

*SIDELIGHTS:* John Hayward is best known for his editorial leadership of the periodical *The Book Collector* as well as his relationship to author T. S. Eliot. Hayward was a meticulous and extremely knowledgeable scholar, collector, editor, and critic. He brought this knowledge to *The Book Collector,* and from 1952 to 1965, Hayward was the visionary for the journal. According to P. H. Muir, a former member of the editorial board of the *Collector,* as quoted from the winter 1965 issue of the *Collector,* "the journal became avowedly . . . the exclusive product of John Hayward's fertile brain. . . . No journal of its kind has lasted so long and none has achieved such eminence and authority." Many writers, especially Eliot, looked to Hayward for his critical thoughts on their work. In his American edition of *Four Quartets,* Eliot mentions Hayward's contributions to the volume, "I wish to acknowledge a particular debt to Mr. John Hayward for general criticism and specific suggestions during the composition of these poems." Throughout his life, Hayward had a love for literature and this showed in both his work and his personal relationships. Elizabeth Icenhower, writing in *Dictionary of Literary Biography,* stated, "He was devoted to books and their readers; to literature, especially poetry; to his friends; to lively conversation and social interchange; and, perhaps above all, to extraordinary and uncompromising standards in writing and publishing."

As a young boy, Hayward was diagnosed with muscular dystrophy. As he grew older, he would be confined to a wheelchair. His physical condition, however, did not affect his ambition in life. He attended King's College at Cambridge and graduated in 1927. Even before graduation, he would edit his first collection, the *Collected Works of John Wilmot, Earl of Rochester.* Hayward went on to compile poetry and prose of John Donne as well as letters of Saint-Evremond. For both achievements, *Complete Poetry and Selected Prose of John Donne* (1929) and *The Letters of Saint-Evremond, Charles Marguetel de Saint Denis, Seigneur de Saint-Evremond* (1930), Hayward received accolades. For the

Donne volume, a reviewer for *Times Literary Supplement* commented, "Mr. Hayward makes it as easy as is possible for the reader . . . 'to unravel' the complicated threads of Donne's thought." Another *Times Literary Supplement* lauded *The Letters of Saint-Evremond* as "a model of good editing in an elegant and readable essay."

In 1932, Hayward completed *Nineteenth-Century Poetry, An Anthology,* and in 1933, a biography about Charles II. Both titles were well-received. *Charles II,* specifically, was described in the *Spectator* as "a brilliant and satisfying character study . . . an extraordinary achievement." At the same time as editing and compiling the works of others, he wrote literary reviews. Icenhower pointed out, "These articles make good reading in themselves, and in passing they offer insights into Hayward's opinions and emotions. His writing is reflective and yet to the point, graceful and witty, and always in a style appropriate to the matter discussed." In 1941, Hayward took on his first task of editing one of Eliot's collections; it would be published as *Points of View* and is a compilation of Eliot's critical essays. This experience must have proved successful for they would continue the writer/editor relationship on two more titles: *T. S. Eliot: Poems Written in Early Youth* and *T. S. Eliot: Selected Prose.* The two litterateurs would also live together for more than a decade following Eliot's first marriage.

As well as Eliot's work, Hayward would continue to compile and edit the work of Donne, Samuel Johnson, Jonathan Swift, Edmund Spenser, and Robert Herrick, among others. He would also edit and write for *The Book Collector* until his death in 1965. Icenhower related, "Sitting at the center of his international bibliographic network, he knew the day-by-day events of the book world and brought to bear all his experience and knowledge of books and readers," as he shaped each issue of *The Book Collector.* Hayward's final compilation was *The Oxford Book of Nineteenth-Century Verse.* A critic writing in the *New York Times Book Review* found that "The selection as a whole prompts a new look at 19th-century poetry as a single movement."

The following year, Hayward passed away after sixty years of life, fifty of which had him fighting a debilitating illness. In his *Prose Literature since 1939: A Survey of English Prose Literature Other Than Fiction from 1939 to 1945,* Hayward pointed out his lifelong beliefs on writing: "If literature is to continue to be a civilising element in society, it must do more than preserve a tradition; it must develop its capacities with the needs of the times." In the same book, he revealed that he hoped for "a scheme of values . . . to arise and out of disillusionment a dynamic faith in the power of the printed word to express the finest operations of human thought and sensibility."

*BIOGRAPHICAL/CRITICAL SOURCES:*

BOOKS

*Dictionary of Literary Biography,* Volume 201: *Twentieth-Century British Book Collectors and Bibliographers, First Series,* Gale Research (Detroit, MI), 1999.

Gardner, Helen, *The Composition of Four Quartets,* Faber & Faber, 1978.

Hayward, John, *Prose Literature Since 1939: A Survey of English Prose Literature Other Than Fiction from 1939 to 1945,* Longmans, Green (London), 1947.

PERIODICALS

*Book Collector,* winter, 1965.
*London Magazine,* December, 1956.
*New York Times Book Review,* August 16, 1964.
*Spectator,* March 31, 1933.
*Times Literary Supplement,* June 27, 1929; December 18, 1930; March 20, 1930; June 19, 1948.*

\*     \*     \*

**HEAD, William P(ace) 1949-**

*PERSONAL:* Born October 15, 1949, in Miami, FL; son of Downer Pace (a sales/express agent) and Ella Margueritte (a librarian; maiden name, Crittenden) Head; married Randee Lynn Geigis, June 6, 1975; children: Matthew, Brian, Evan. *Ethnicity:* "Caucasian." *Education:* Florida State University, B.A., 1971; University of Miami, M.A., 1974; Florida State University, Ph.D., 1980; completed U.S. Army TRA DOC Course, 1985, and Aerospace Historian Course, U.S. Air Force, 1989. *Politics:* Democrat. *Religion:* Methodist. *Avocational interests:* History.

*ADDRESSES: Home*—111 Chantilly Dr., Warner Robins, GA 31088. *Office*—955 Robins Pkwy., Ste. 200, WR-ALC/HO, Robins AFB, GA 31088. *E-mail*—william.head@robins.af.mil; billhead@juno.com.

*CAREER:* University of Alabama, Huntsville, assistant professor of history, 1981-84; U.S. Air Force, Robins

Air Force Base, historian, 1984-96, chief, Office of History, 1996—. Adjunct professor of history, Mercer University, 1985-90, Mason State College, 1987—, and Georgia Military College, 1989-94.

*MEMBER:* Association of Third World Studies, Association of Asian Studies, Society for Military History, Georgian Association of Historians, Society for the History of the Federal Government, Phi Kappa Phi.

*AWARDS, HONORS:* Received special recognition from Alabama Senate for leadership in 1984 History/Humanities Festival; was twice the recipient of most outstanding articles award for *Journal of Air Force Logistics,* 1992; named Most Outstanding Historian, United States Air Force, 1994.

*WRITINGS:*

*America's China Sojourn,* University Press of America (Lanham, MD), 1983.
*Yenan,* Documentary Publications (Chapel Hill, NC), 1987.
*Looking Back on the Vietnam War,* Greenwood Press (Wesport, CT), 1993.
*Every Inch a Soldier,* Texas A & M University Press (College Station), 1995.
*The Eagle in the Desert,* Praeger (Westport, CT), 1996.
*The Tet Offensive,* Praeger, 1996.
*Weaving an New Tapestry,* Praeger, 1999.

Associate editor of *Journal of Third World Studies,* 1985-98.

*WORK IN PROGRESS: Fifty Years of Air Force Theory, Doctrine, and Operations,* due in 2000.

*SIDELIGHTS:* A military historian, William P. Head has written several books on the Vietnam conflict, including *Looking Back on the Vietnam War* and *The Tet Offensive.* His first historical study, based on his doctoral dissertation, was *America's China Sojourn.* Head researched primary and secondary sources for this survey of American-Chinese foreign policy during the 1942-1948 period. "Overall," wrote Col. Phillip S. Meilinger in *Airpower Journal, "Every Inch a Soldier* is an excellent addition to the literature on airpower biography."

Head told *CA:* "I write on history because it fascinates me and I was trained to do so. My current position is designed for me to research and write on items relevant to the Air Force and my installation. Having been trained in U.S./Asian (modern) diplomatic history, I still have a fascination for that subject too. Since I work for the military, I am now also a military historian. It is particularly interesting (to me) to examine how the U.S. military affects, and is in turn affected by, our democratic society. Luckily, I have had a wide latitude of topics about which I can write. All have been worthwhile since they not only fit my job but my interests. I am also fortunate that most of my research materials are in my own base archives or nearby at AFHRA, Maxwell Air Force Base, Alabama."

*BIOGRAPHICAL/CRITICAL SOURCES:*

PERIODICALS

*Airpower Journal,* winter, 1995, pp. 114-115.
*American Historical Review,* April, 1984, p. 539.
*Choice,* November, 1983, p. 486.
*Journal of Asian Studies,* May, 1985, p. 590.
*Pacific Historical Review,* May, 1986, p. 333.

\*    \*    \*

**HEAP, Desmond    1907-1998**

*OBITUARY NOTICE*—See index for *CA* sketch: Born September 17, 1907, in Burnley, England; died June 27, 1998. Solicitor and author. Heap was considered a brilliant legal scholar and served as comptroller and city solicitor to the corporation of London for more than twenty-five years. However, he may be best known for helping to arrange in 1968 the sale of London Bridge to an American oil company. Heap's law career began in 1933 when he was admitted as a solicitor after graduating from Victoria University of Manchester. He had successively important jobs ranging from assistant to prosecuting solicitor and deputy town clerk for the city of Leeds before being named to his London post in 1947. Throughout his years practicing law he also lectured on the subject at universities in the United States including Harvard, Cornell, the University of North Carolina and the Georgia Institute of Technology. He spoke on town planning in Uganda, Trinidad and Botswana. He had been active in town planning and was a member of the Royal Town Planning Institute from 1947 to 1977. Heap's interest in planning led him to write numerous texts, including *Planning Law for Town and Country, Development Plans—Their Status, Making, Review and Effect,* and *The New Town Planning Procedures: How They Affect You.* He was knighted in 1970 and retired in 1973. He later received the Gold Medal Award from the Lincoln Institute of Land Policy in Cambridge, MA, and a Gold Medal from the Royal Town Planning Institute.

*OBITUARIES AND OTHER SOURCES:*

PERIODICALS

*Times* (London), July 1, 1998.

\*    \*    \*

**HECHT, Daniel**

*PERSONAL: Education:* Iowa Writers' Workshop, M.F.A. (writing).

*ADDRESSES: Home*—Vermont. *Agent*—c/o Viking Penguin USA, 375 Hudson St., New York, NY 10014.

*CAREER:* Writer. Has also worked as a guitarist and recording artist, performing twice at Carnegie Hall and releasing the album *Willow,* Windham Hill Records, 1980.

*WRITINGS:*

*Skull Session,* Viking (New York City), 1998.

Contributor to periodicals, including *Guitar Player.*

*SIDELIGHTS:* Daniel Hecht was a musician before he wrote his first novel, but a hand injury ended his fifteen-year career as a guitarist. While a musician, however, he specialized in New Age Guitar music which was described in *New Age Music Guide* as "melodic, and lyrical."

In 1991, he wrote about a memorable performance in China in *Guitar Player.* The performance took place several months after the Tienanmen Square massacre of students by the Chinese government and tensions were still volatile during Hecht's visit. Hecht told of one unique moment after a performance when he was duped by government officials into shaking the hands of two old men. A second later, he realized that the old men were also government officials and that the event had been staged to make it appear that he supported the Chinese government. As he recalled, "I dropped the old men's hands as if they were dead fish, realizing I'd just been used." When he left the stage, he gave a raised fist salute to the crowd, which he called his "real encore." Later during his Chinese visit when the government tried to get Hecht's Chinese agent to return to his home village and leave Hecht's tour, Hecht took another stand and objected, pleading illness for the rest of the government tour. He later traveled with his agent and performed in many other towns in China. Though Hecht described difficulties in performing in China (unsanitary conditions, red tape, and unpredictable power outages), he called it an "adventure that touches and challenges a musician's body, heart, mind and soul," and "the opportunity to build a connection between nations and cultures."

Hecht published his first book, *Skull Session,* in 1998. The book features protagonist Paul Skoglund, a man whose work, life, and mind have been compromised by his Tourette's Syndrome. Paul, whose father committed suicide and whose son also has neurological problems, decides to leave the work world and restore his aunt's old house. The house has been vandalized, either by local teenagers, or as Hecht suggests, a more sinister source which may be linked to Skoglund's father's death. As Skoglund delves into the mystery with his girlfriend Lia, he also explores the workings of his own mind. *Library Review* critic Elsa Pendleton called the book "a marvelous mix of modern Gothic horror and romance." A *Publishers Weekly* reviewer noted that after Hecht's fifteen-year musical career, "he has brought welcome artistry and elegance to his new field."

*BIOGRAPHICAL/CRITICAL SOURCES:*

*BOOKS*

Birosik, Patti Jean, *The New Age Music Guide,* Colliers Books, Macmillan Publishing Co. (New York City), 1989.

*PERIODICALS*

*Guitar Player,* January, 1991, pp. 73-75; September, 1991, pp. 17-19.
*Library Journal,* November 15, 1997, p. 76.
*Publishers Weekly,* November 17, 1997, pp. 54-55.

*OTHER*

*Penguin Putnam Online* web site, http://www.penguin putnam.com (November 11, 1999).*

**HEYM, Georg (Theodor Franz Arthur)   1887-1912**

*PERSONAL:* Born October 30, 1887, in Hirschberg, Silesia (now Jelenia Gora, Poland); drowned, January 16, 1912, in Berlin, Germany.

*CAREER:* Poet.

*WRITINGS:*

*Der ewige Tag* (poems), 1911, reprinted, Aufbau-Verlag (Berlin, Germany), 1969.
*Ubra vitae* (poems), 1912, reprinted, Insel-Verlag (Frankfurt am Main, Germany), 1962.
*The Thief, and Other Stories,* translated by Susan Bennett, Libris, 1994.

*BIOGRAPHICAL/CRITICAL SOURCES:*

*BOOKS*

Bridgwater, Patrick, *Poet of Expressionist Berlin: The Life and Work of Georg Heym,* Libris (London, England), 1991.
Krispyn, Egbert, *Georg Heym: A Reluctant Rebel,* University of Florida Press (Gainesville, FL), 1968.*

*       *       *

**HICKOX, Rebecca (Ayres)
(Becky Ayres)**

*PERSONAL:* Female.

*ADDRESSES: Agent*—c/o Holiday House, Inc., 425 Madison Ave., New York, NY 10017.

*CAREER:* Children's book author.

*AWARDS, HONORS:* Oregon Book Award for young readers, 1993, for *Matreshka.*

*WRITINGS:*

*FOR CHILDREN*

(As Becky Ayres) *Victoria Flies High,* Cobblehill Books (New York City), 1990.
*Matreshka,* illustrated by Alexi Natchev, Doubleday (Garden City, NY), 1992.
*Per and the Dala Horse,* illustrated by Yvonne Gilbert, Doubleday (Garden City, NY), 1995.

*Zorro and Quwi: Tales of a Trickster Guinea Pig,* illustrated by Kim Howard, Doubleday (Garden City, NY), 1997.

*The Golden Sandal: A Middle Eastern Cinderella,* illustrated by Will Hillenbrand, Holiday House (New York City), 1998.

OTHER

*Salt Lake City,* Dillon Press (Minneapolis, MN), 1990.

*SIDELIGHTS:* Rebecca Hickox made a niche for herself retelling folktales and creating her own folktale-like stories in such picture books as *Matreshka, Per and the Dala Horse, Zorro and Quwi,* and *The Golden Sandal.* Employing the colorfully painted, nesting Russian dolls called "Matreshka" as her first picture-book subject, Hickox tells the story of Kata, who takes refuge from a snow storm in the house of Baba Yaga, a Russian witch. When the witch is out of sight, the magical dolls come alive and help Kata escape before Baba Yaga can turn her into a goose and cook her for dinner. *Matreshka* elicited mixed reviews. A *Publishers Weekly* commentator thought the plot lacked suspense and was "bland." Conversely, a *Kirkus Reviews* critic, noting the colloquial tone and use of rhyming chants, called *Matreshka* a "lively retelling" and a "winning" tale.

Hickox was inspired to write about a Dala horse after she bought one of these Swedish children's toys. When she could find no existing tales about this toy, she made up one of her own, which Joanne Schott of *Quill and Quire* judged to be "solidly in the folktale spirit." In what Cynthia K. Rickey called in *School Library Journal* a "vigorous" text, Hickox tells the story of three brothers who, upon their father's death, are each given a different kind of horse. The eldest son gets a strong workhorse, the second son a fine riding horse, and the third son a wooden Dala horse. Although the two older brothers poke fun at their youngest sibling, Per, he recognizes that the Dala horse may someday prove its usefulness, and, indeed, it does. An "appealing adventure story," asserted *Booklist* commentator Carolyn Phelan.

Hickox turned to the common figure of the trickster for her next picture book, *Zorro and Quwi.* Adapting material from the Peruvian Andes, Hickox recounted four episodes about Quwi, a guinea pig who continually outfoxes Zorro, the red fox. Reviewers found much to like about *Zorro and Quwi.* In *Kirkus Reviews,* a critic called the episodes "delightful," and in *Publishers Weekly* a commentator judged Hickox to be a "master of comic timing."

Although the Cinderella story has been retold many times, Hickox decided to tell an Iraqi version in the picture book *The Golden Sandal.* This time the heroine is Maha, the daughter of a widowed Iraqi fisherman, while the fairy godmother is a little red fish whose life Maha has spared. In the view of contributor Karen Morgan in *Booklist,* Hickox gave the tale a "whole new look," so new that some readers might not understand why, for example, the young man Tariq would want to marry someone he has never met. According to a writer for *Kirkus Reviews,* the "unusual setting, comic characters," and universal emotions give the story its appeal, an opinion seconded by a *Publishers Weekly* critic, who deemed the work an "able retelling" of the Cinderella fable. Writing in *Horn Book,* Susan P. Bloom called *The Golden Sandal* a "new and appealing version" of the tale. "Charmingly told," added a critic for the *New York Times Book Review.*

*BIOGRAPHICAL/CRITICAL SOURCES:*

*PERIODICALS*

*Booklist,* January 15, 1993, p. 910; December 15, 1996, p. 730; April 1, 1998, p. 1326.
*Horn Book,* spring, 1996, pp. 30-31; March-April, 1998, p. 227.
*Kirkus Reviews,* October 15, 1992, p. 1306; December 1, 1996, p. 1738; February 15, 1998, p. 267.
*New York Times Book Review,* September 20, 1998, p. 32.
*Publishers Weekly,* November 9, 1992, p. 84; November 18, 1996, p. 78; December 9, 1996, p. 68; January 26, 1998, p. 91.
*Quill and Quire,* January, 1996, p. 45.
*School Library Journal,* January, 1996, pp. 84-85; February, 1997, pp. 92-93; April, 1998, pp. 117-18.*

\*      \*      \*

**HIRSCH, Alan**

*PERSONAL:* Son of Shula Hirsch.

*ADDRESSES: Agent*—c/o Free Press, 866 Third Ave., New York, NY 10022.

*CAREER:* Writer and attorney.

*WRITINGS:*

NONFICTION

(With Pippa Green) *The Impact of Resettlement in the Ciskei: Three Case Studies,* Southern Africa Labour and Development Research Unit (Cape Town, South Africa), 1983.

(With William W. Schwarzer and David J. Barrans) *The Analysis and Decision of Summary Judgment Motions: A Monograph on Rule 56 of the Federal Rules of Civil Procedure,* Federal Judicial Center (Washington, DC), 1991.

(With Diane Sheehey) *Awarding Attorneys' Fees and Managing Fee Litigation,* Federal Judicial Center, 1991.

(With William W. Schwarzer) *The Elements of Case Management,* Federal Judicial Center, 1991.

*Talking Heads: Political Talk Shows and Their Star Pundits,* St. Martin' (New York City), 1991.

(With Akhil Reed Amar) *For the People: What the Constitution Really Says about Your Rights,* Free Press, 1998.

YOUNG ADULT FICTION

(With mother, Shula Hirsch) *Off the Mat,* Northwest Publishing, 1995.

*SIDELIGHTS:* Alan Hirsch, a lawyer by trade, began his writing career in the 1980s with a series of academic monographs that would be of interest primarily to other lawyers or to those interested in the crossroads where the practice of law and public policy meet. In the 1990s, however, Hirsch tried to reach a wider audience with two books. One is a young adult novel written in collaboration with his mother, Shula Hirsch. Called *Off the Mat,* the book tells the story of the friendship between two boys—one white, the other African American—who meet in the eighth grade and share a love of school wrestling. When the two attend different high schools, however, they become dogged adversaries, particularly because the reward for their duel for the county wrestling championship is a college scholarship. *Off the Mat* was not an especially successful debut novel; one *Publishers Weekly* critic called the effort "plodding" and "[b]y turns preachy and melodramatic."

In contrast, the warm reception critics gave to Hirsch's book *Talking Heads* testifies to his skill with nonfiction. In the *Washington Post Book World,* for example, Jonathan Yardley called *Talking Heads* "provocative and useful," and a *Publishers Weekly* reviewer praised the book's analysis as "a model of its kind." In *Talking*

*Heads* Hirsch trained his sights on television talk shows that feature animated ideological exchanges between journalists of contrasting political stripes. These shows include *The McLaughlin Group, Crossfire, The Capital Gang,* and others, and their "stars" include such well-known figures as William F. Buckley Jr., George Will, Sam Donaldson, and Patrick J. Buchanan.

Hirsch is highly critical of these shows for several reasons. In his view they reduce political commentary to "aggressive, bite-size chunks." He finds the "talking heads" presumptuous in their willingness to express settled opinions about virtually any subject. He disdains the "locker-room machismo" of otherwise serious and thoughtful journalists during their noisy debates. And he argues that "the participants, rather than the issues they are discussing, become the central drama." What troubles Hirsch about these shows is that they trivialize debate and substitute celebrity for substance. The result, says Hirsch, is a debasement of on-air political debate, where everything is staged for show and effect with a view to higher ratings, and therefore bigger advertising dollars.

*BIOGRAPHICAL/CRITICAL SOURCES:*

PERIODICALS

*New York Times Book Review,* March 3, 1991, p. 18.
*Publishers Weekly,* December 7, 1990, p. 68; January 8, 1996, p. 70.
*Washington Post Book World,* February 3, 1991, p. 3.*

\*      \*      \*

## HIXSON, William F.

*PERSONAL: Avocational interests:* Economics.

*ADDRESSES: Agent*—c/o Praeger Publications, 1 Madison Ave., 11th Floor, New York, NY 10010-3603.

*CAREER:* Retired businessman and engineer.

*WRITINGS:*

*A Matter of Interest: Reexamining Money, Debt, and Real Economic Growth,* foreword by John H. Hotson, Praeger (New York), 1991.
*Triumph of the Bankers: Money and Banking in the Eighteenth and Nineteenth Centuries,* Praeger (Westport, CT), 1993.

Contributor to periodicals, including *Eastern Economic Journal, The History of Economics Society Bulletin,* and *Economies et Societes.*

*SIDELIGHTS:* After retiring from a career as a businessman and engineer, William F. Hixson went on to make a contribution to the field of economics with two books. The first, *A Matter of Interest: Re-examining Money, Debt, and Real Economic Growth* was published in 1991, and analyzed the American economy from World War I to the time of writing. In Hixson's view, as told by a reviewer in the *Journal of Economic Literature,* the American economy was a laissez-faire one before 1933, the year of Franklin D. Roosevelt's New Deal, and a mixed economy since then: that is, a capitalist economy in which government spending is an important factor. Hixson believed that although the Great Depression was inevitable given the economic arrangements of the laissez-faire era, the present system is untenable as well, and must be replaced within the next few decades or even sooner. H. I. Liebling, writing in *Choice,* lamented Hixson's gloomy assessment that the leading indicator was the ever-rising percentage of the economic product that is devoted to paying off the interest on borrowings. An economy increasingly burdened by interest payments, Hixson feels, cannot long sustain itself.

Further, Hixson quarrels with the current practice by which the Federal Reserve Board manipulates interest rates in order to moderate growth and thus, in theory, curb inflation. Liebling explained Hixson's argument that when higher interest rates are used as an anti-inflationary tool, they in themselves lead to inflation. He posits also that corporations should finance themselves through equity rather than debt. Most dramatically, in the view of *Monthly Review* critic Robert Pollin, Hixson argues that the federal government ought to cease engaging in debt financing. Instead, Hixson feels the government should finance its operations solely through its money-creating power, printing more money when the economy needs stimulation and less when it does not. As a corollary, Hixson declares that private lending institutions must no longer have the power to create money by lending out the great majority of their deposits at interest. In a banking system in which banks were required to keep one hundred percent of their deposits on hand, there would be far less reliance on debt, and no need for federal deposit insurance, Hixson declares.

The simplification of the financial system, and the lower reliance on debt, which these changes would create, are, in Pollin's opinion, "obviously desirable ends," but when it came to the practicality and theoretical solidity of Hixson's suggestions, Pollin felt that Hixson has "overstated his case on some crucial points." Pollin felt it would be unrealistic to expect the U.S. government to convert back to a less liquid economic system, when in reality over the past generation or more the thrust of economic changes has been for banks to create ever-newer ways of making depositors' money both highly liquid and highly profitable. Even if a massive political mobilization were to occur, Pollin asserted, Hixson's reforms might not receive highest priority. Further, Pollin advised that relying exclusively on the government's money-creating power can itself lead to inflationary pressure, if the money created exceeds what is justified by the tax base. Massive new creation of money could only overcome inflationary pressures if the projects on which the money was spent were productive enough to create strong development.

This is a political question, Pollin implied, the answer of which would depend on the wisdom of progressive thinkers in mapping out the institutional framework for such a system. Reservations aside, Pollin expressed considerable respect for Hixson's work, which he called "a stimulating effort at providing an explanation for the economy's fundamental financial difficulties," and "a serious attempt at advancing policy ideas for overcoming these problems." Pollin praised Hixson for his "creative" use of statistics and for drawing "fruitfully" upon the ideas of diverse economists, notably Henry Simons, a predecessor of Milton Friedman at the University of Chicago. Concluded Pollin, "Regardless of how one responds to the details of Hixson's proposals, *A Matter of Interest* is a serious attempt to grapple with the issues before us. As such, it should become a useful resource in building both the economic understanding and political will necessary for constructing a more equitable and viable financial system." Liebling declared, "This volume should provoke educated general readers as well as others to compare these views with standard principles of macroeconomics on the debt burden issue."

Hixson's second book, the 1993 *Triumph of the Bankers: Money and Banking in the Eighteenth and Nineteenth Centuries,* explored the evil (in Hixson's view) effects of banks' having usurped the governmental function of money-creation through such means as paper money, checking accounts, and credit cards. John J. McCusker, writing in the *Journal of American History,* opined, "This 'call to arms' is very much in the spirit of William Jennings Bryan."

*BIOGRAPHICAL/CRITICAL SOURCES:*

*PERIODICALS*

*Choice,* April, 1992, p. 1270.
*Journal of American History,* December, 1994, pp. 1280-81.
*Journal of Economic Literature,* March, 1993, p. 305.
*Monthly Review,* October, 1993, p. 57.*

\*    \*    \*

## HO, Anh Thai   1960-

*PERSONAL:* Born October 18, 1960, in Hanoi, Vietnam; son of Ho Si Lang and Ho Thi Diep. *Education:* Vietnam College of Diplomacy, M.A., 1983; University of Delhi, Ph.D., 1994.

*ADDRESSES: Office*—Ministry of Foreign Affairs, 6-Chu Van An, Hanoi, Vietnam; fax 84-4-8234-169. *Agent*—Wayne Karlin, P.O. Box 239, St. Mary's City, MD 20686. *E-mail*—thaiha@hn.vnm.vn.

*CAREER:* Ministry of Foreign Affairs, Hanoi, Vietnam, cultural expert, 1983-88; Embassy of Vietnam, New Delhi, India, third secretary, 1988-94; Ministry of Foreign Affairs, Hanoi, cultural expert, 1994—.

*MEMBER:* Vietnamese Writers Association, Hanoi Writers Association (member of executive committee).

*AWARDS, HONORS:* Award from Vietnamese Writers Association.

*WRITINGS:*

*L'Ile aux femmes* (novel; title means "The Women on the Island"), L'Aube (France), 1997.
*Behind the Red Mist* (novella and stories), Curbstone Press (Willimantic, CT), 1998.

Author of seven other novels and six collections of stories.

\*    \*    \*

## HOBDAY, Jose
### (Sister Jose Hobday)

*PERSONAL:* Daughter of a Seneca mother and Seminole father. *Religion:* Roman Catholic.

*ADDRESSES: Home*—Gallup, NM. *Agent*—c/o Continuum Publishing Group, 370 Lexington Ave., Suite 1700, New York, NY 10017-6503.

*CAREER:* Roman Catholic nun, Franciscan order. Has taught students at all levels, from elementary school through college.

*WRITINGS:*

*Stories of Awe and Abundance* (essays), Sheed & Ward (Kansas City, MO), 1995.
*Simple Living: The Path to Joy and Freedom,* Continuum (New York City), 1998.

Also author of text for inspirational tape recordings. Contributor of articles to the magazine *Praying.*

*SIDELIGHTS:* Sister Jose Hobday, a Native American and a Sister of St. Francis, has championed the cause of voluntary simplicity. In 1996 she published a collection of forty-nine short essays, which had previously appeared in the magazine *Praying.* Throughout the book, titled *Stories of Awe and Abundance,* Hobday describes how God was present to her as she grew up in the American Southwest.

Two years after the appearance of her debut book, Hobday published *Simple Living.* In this introduction to the concept of spiritual simplicity, Hobday deals with six particular areas of concern: shelter, food, clothing, work, transportation, and recreation. The first step she counsels in moving toward simple living is to determine one's level of need for these things, from true necessity to luxury. Hobday strongly asserts that simplifying life is crucial for a person to achieve true freedom, both physical and spiritual. According to a *Publishers Weekly* contributor, *Simple Living,* with its short chapters, "accessible style," and "devotional tone," is an "ideal introduction" to the idea of voluntary simplicity.

*BIOGRAPHICAL/CRITICAL SOURCES:*

*PERIODICALS*

*National Catholic Reporter,* January 12, 1996, p. 17.
*Publishers Weekly,* October 26, 1998, p. 60.*

\*    \*    \*

## HOBDAY, Sister Jose
### See HOBDAY, Jose

## HOHL, Ludwig   1904(?)-1980

*PERSONAL:* Born April 9, 1904 (some sources say 1901), in Netstal, Ganton Glarus, Switzerland; died November 3, 1980; son of Arnold (a Protestant minister) and Magda Zweifel Hohl; married Henriette Adelheid Charlotte von Mayenburg, March 7, 1935 (divorced March 8, 1945); married Johanna-Katharina Fries, February 18, 1946 (divorced January 13, 1948); married Heidy Antoine, March 18, 1948 (divorced October 23, 1951); married Erna Erika Tschanz, November 21, 1963 (divorced November 17, 1970); married Madeleine-Jeanne de Weiss, September 8, 1980; children: (third marriage) Adele. *Education:* Attended Gymnasium at Frauenfeld.

*CAREER:* Writer, c. 1939—.

*AWARDS, HONORS:* Literary award from Lions' Club, 1965, and from Schiller Foundation, 1970; Robert Walser Centenary Prize, 1978; Petrarca Prize, 1980.

*WRITINGS:*

*Nuancen und Details* (title means "Nuances and Details"), 2 volumes, Oprecht (Zurich), 1939-42.

*Naechtlicher Weg* (title means "Night Path"), Morgarten (Zurich), 1943, revised, Suhrkamp (Frankfurt am Main), 1971.

*Die Notizen; oder, Von der unvoreiligen Versoehnung* (title means "The Notes; or, Concerning the Not Overhasty Reconciliation"), 2 volumes, volume 1, Artemis (Zurich), 1944, volume 2, Artemis (Zurich), 1954, Part II republished as *Vom Erreichbarren und vom Unerreichbaren* (title means "Concerning the Attainable and the Unattainable"), Suhrkamp, 1972, Part VII republished as *Varia* (title means "Odds and Ends"), Suhrkamp, 1977, Parts I and XII republished as *Vom Arbeiten: Bild,* Suhrkamp, 1978, Part IX republished as *Das Wort fasst nicht jeden: ueber Literatur,* Suhrkamp, 1980.

*Dass fast alles anders ist* (title means "That Almost Everything Is Different"), Walter (Olten & Freiburg), 1967.

*Bergfahrt* (title means "Mountain Climb"), Suhrkamp, 1975.

*Von den hereinbrechenden Raendern: Nachnotizen* (title means "Concerning the Edges That Are Giving Way"), Suhrkamp, 1986.

*Und eine neue Erde,* Suhrkamp, 1990.

*Jugendtagebuch,* Suhrkamp, 1998.

*SIDELIGHTS:* Author Ludwig Hohl is best known for his compilation of short prose pieces in *Die Notizen:* *oder, Von der unvoreiligen Versoehnung* ("The Notes: or, Concerning the Not Overhasty Reconciliation"). This work is separated in twelve parts with each part focusing on a different theme. Some of the topics include literature and art, human capabilities, communication, dreams, and more. For example, the first part features the subject of work while Part XI comments on death. In the first part, Hohl suggests that the human potential for changing the world occurs in three stages. The process begins with the first stage, which is the idea. The second stage is the breaking down of the idea into smaller ideas, and the third stage is the completion of tasks toward the realization of the ideas. H. M. Waidson of *Dictionary of Literary Biography* finds that "Hohl's pieces in *Die Notizen* are not always of a consistent quality; the generalizations are sometimes sweeping and sometimes provocative." Hohl's final version of *Die Notizen* was published in two volumes, the first in 1944 and the second in 1954. Individual parts have also been published on their own at varying times.

Hohl's other work also consists of shorter writings. His first publication, *Nuancen und Details* ("Nuances and Details"), is, the title suggests, a combination of short prose that may highlight or provide greater insight into Hohl's inner thoughts or beliefs. In the two volumes of this work, the prose takes the various forms of notes, comments, stories, memories, and more. Even though the first volume of *Nuances and Details* wasn't published until 1939 and the second volume in 1942, Hohl had written the text for both in the early 1930s, between 1931 and 1935. This was typical for Hohl whose most prolific writing period was the 1930s with most of his work not appearing in print until the 1940s and later.

Another literary achievement by Hohl, and considered by Waidson to be "the most immediately accessible of his writings," is the short story compilation *Naechtlicher Weg* ("Night Path"). This volume contains thirteen stories with the title story being the most acclaimed. In "Naechtlicher Weg," a man's death along the road on a cold night seems to have been related to the main character's dream of the night before. Another story, "Das Blatt" ("The Leaf") portrays a man whose thoughts are centered on the leaf he is holding, and "Optimismus" ("Optimism") relates the final days of an artist, who eventually dies, in a hospital. *Die Notizen* followed *Naechtlicher Weg,* and Hohl's *Dass fast alles anders ist* ("That Almost Everything Is Different"), another compilation featuring Hohl's thoughts and dreams, as well as stories, appeared in 1967.

Almost ten years later, in 1975, Hohl published his last work, *Bergfahrt* ("Mountain Climb"), which is one story instead of a typical Hohl compilation. In the tale, two men decide to go on a climb together, but as they encounter tough times, they part ways and soon meet their deaths. Five years after this final achievement appeared in print, Hohl passed away, leaving behind what one critic, Carl Seelig, described, as quoted in *Dictionary of Literary Biography*, as "a dazzling crystal collection of intellectual and spiritual insights into man's complex nature, life today, and the realm of dreams and death."

*BIOGRAPHICAL/CRITICAL SOURCES:*

BOOKS

*Dictionary of Literary Biography,* Volume 56: *German Fiction Writers, 1914-1945,* Gale (Detroit, MI), 1987.*

\*       \*       \*

**HOLLAND, Isabelle   1920-**
   **(Francesca Hunt)**

*PERSONAL:* Born June 16, 1920, in Basel, Switzerland; daughter of Philip (a U.S. Foreign Service officer) and Corabelle (Anderson) Holland. *Education:* Attended University of Liverpool; Tulane University of Louisiana, B.A., 1942. *Religion:* Christian. *Avocational interests:* "All things Spanish—music, fiestas, the sound of the language; cats."

*ADDRESSES: Home*—1199 Park Ave., New York, NY 10028. *Agent*—JCA Literary Agency Inc., 242 West 27th St., New York, NY 10001.

*CAREER:* Freelance author of novels and short stories for adults, young adults, and children. Worked for various publications, including as a fiction editor for *Tomorrow;* a copy writer for a book advertising agency, beginning in 1949; *McCall's,* New York City, until 1956; Crown Publishers, Inc., New York City, publicity director, 1956-60; J. B. Lippincott Co., New York City, publicity director, 1960-66; *Harper's,* New York City, assistant to publisher, 1967-68; G. P. Putnam's Sons, New York City, publicity director, 1968-69.

*MEMBER:* Authors Guild, Authors League of America, PEN.

*AWARDS, HONORS:* National Book Award nomination, 1976, for *Of Love and Death and Other Journeys;*

*Isabelle Holland*

Ott Award, Church and Synagogue Library Association, 1983, for *Abbie's God Book* and *God, Mrs. Muskrat, and Aunt Dot.*

*WRITINGS:*

FOR CHILDREN; FICTION

*Amanda's Choice,* Lippincott, 1970.
*The Mystery of Castle Rinaldi,* American Educational Publications, 1972.
*Journey for Three,* illustrated by Charles Robinson, American Publications/Houghton Mifflin, 1974.
*Alan and the Animal Kingdom,* Lippincott, 1977.
*Dinah and the Green Fat Kingdom,* Lippincott, 1978.
*Now Is Not Too Late,* Lothrop, Lee & Shepard/Bantam, 1980.
*A Horse Named Peaceable,* Lothrop, 1982.
*Abbie's God Book,* illustrated by James McLaughlin, Westminster, 1982.
*God, Mrs. Muskrat, and Aunt Dot,* illustrated by Beth and Joe Krush, Westminster, 1983.
*Green Andrew Green,* Westminster, 1984.
*Kevin's Hat,* illustrated by Leonard Lubin, Lothrop, 1984.
*Henry and Grudge,* illustrated by Lisa Chauncy Guida, Walker Co., 1986.
*The Christmas Cat,* illustrated by Kathy Mitchell, Western Publishing, 1987.

*The Easter Donkey,* Golden, 1989.

*FOR YOUNG ADULTS; FICTION*

*The Man Without a Face,* Lippincott-Harper, 1972.
*Heads You Win, Tails I Lose,* Lippincott/Fawcett, 1973.
*Of Love and Death and Other Journeys,* Lippincott/
    Fawcett, 1975.
*Hitchhike,* Lippincott/Fawcett, 1977.
*Summer of My First Love,* Fawcett. 1981.
*Perdita,* Little Brown/Fawcett, 1981.
*The Empty House,* Lippincott-Harper, 1983.
*After the First Love,* Fawcett, 1983.
*The Island,* Little Brown/Fawcett, 1984.
*Jenny Kiss'd Me,* Fawcett, 1985.
*Love and The Genetic Factor,* Fawcett, 1987.
*Toby the Splendid,* Walker, 1987.
*Thief,* Fawcett, 1989.
*The Unfrightened Dark,* Little Brown/Fawcett, 1989.
*The Journey Home,* Scholastic (New York City), 1990.
*The House in the Woods,* Little Brown/Fawcett, 1991.
*The Search,* Fawcett, 1991.
*Behind the Lines,* Scholastic, 1994.
*The Promised Land,* Scholastic, 1996.

*FOR ADULTS; FICTION*

*Cecily,* Lippincott, 1967.
*Kilgaren,* Weybright & Talley/Bantam, 1974.
*Trelawny,* Weybright & Talley/Bantam, 1974.
*Moncrieff,* Weybright & Talley/Fawcett, 1975.
*Darcourt,* Weybright & Talley/Fawcett, 1976.
*Grenelle,* Rawson-Wade/Fawcett, 1976.
*The deMaury Papers,* Rawson-Wade/Fawcett, 1977.
*Tower Abbey,* Rawson-Wade/Fawcett , 1978.
*The Marchington Inheritance,* Rawson-Wade/Fawcett,
    1980.
*Counterpoint,* Rawson-Wade/Fawcett, 1980.
*The Lost Madonna,* Rawson-Wade/Fawcett,, 1981.
*A Death at St. Anselm's,* Doubleday/Fawcett, 1984.
*Flight of the Archangel,* Doubleday/Fawcett, 1985.
*A Lover Scorned,* Doubleday/Fawcett, 1986.
*Bump in the Night,* Doubleday/Fawcett, 1988.
*A Fatal Advent,* Doubleday/Fawcett, 1989.
*The Long Search,* Doubleday/Fawcett, 1990.
*The House in the Woods,* Little, Brown, 1991.
*Search,* Fawcett Book Group, 1991.
*Behind the Lines,* Scholastic, 1994.
*Family Trust,* NAL/Dutton, 1994, Thorndike Press
    (Thorndike, ME), 1995.
*The Promised Land,* Scholastic, 1996.

*OTHER*

Contributor of short stories to periodicals, including *Collier's* and *Country Gentleman.* Holland's papers are kept in the Kerlan Collection at the University of Minnesota, Minneapolis, and in the deGrummond Collection at the University of Southern Mississippi, Hattiesburg. Also author of writings under the name Francesca Hunt.

*ADAPTATIONS:* In 1993, *The Man without a Face* was adapted to film directed by and starring Mel Gibson, produced by Icon Entertainment International.

*SIDELIGHTS:* Isabelle Holland is a respected author of books for a wide range of readers. Her work for children and young adults is known internationally and is cited for its realism. In this genre, she deals with topics that, while common to the average teenager, are often seen by critics as controversial. Characters in these books deal with social ostracization, parental neglect, and sexual awakenings. As a mystery writer, Holland has also created novels that have been described as well-written gothic fiction. Despite the inclusion of often sensational material—haunted houses, murder, and drugs—these volumes for adults, like Holland's young adult fiction, have been praised for their realistic characters. Some reviewers of her books have speculated that the author's primary concern is with creating believable protagonists. Holland confirmed this in *Speaking for Ourselves,* stating that "all my books, whatever the category or form, deal, most importantly, with the inner journey of the central character."

"I think of myself as a storyteller," Holland wrote in *Speaking for Ourselves,* "and for this I am indebted to my mother." Holland's mother was often faced with the task of keeping her daughter entertained. To this end she turned to storytelling, creating tales that held Holland in rapt attention. As she grew older, Holland discovered that many of her mother's stories had roots in history and legend. She also found that in addition to being exciting and entertaining, these stories provided insight regarding real life situations. Holland was attracted to creating stories that could address genuine problems while simultaneously regaling a reader. This became an important goal in her writing. As she declared in *Speaking for Ourselves,* "Stories, however long . . . should above all be interesting."

Using her experiences in English boarding schools, Holland created her first novel, 1967's *Cecily.* One of the two key characters is Elizabeth, a young woman who teaches at the Langley School, a prestigious English boarding academy. While the emphasis at Langley is on academics, proper feminine etiquette is also a priority, and there is an unspoken ideal that determines a student's success. The most accomplished girls at the school are the ones who are tall, good-looking, and cheerful. Into this environment comes thirteen-year-old Cecily. Cecily is awkward, overweight, and miserable, the opposite of the perfect Langley girl. This unhappy young girl's presence has a devastating effect on Elizabeth.

At the time *Cecily* appeared, most publishers did not have a separate category for young adults, the genre with which the book is most closely identified. As a result, the semi-autobiographical tale was published as an adult novel. Critics, however, had no trouble discerning the book as a valuable addition to the growing library of literature for young adults. *Horn Book* reviewer Ruth Hill Viguers described *Cecily* as "a beautifully polished gem of a novel." Edith C. Howley wrote in *Best Sellers* that the book is "tightly knit and plausible," cited the characters as clearly defined, and appraised the book overall as "well done."

Holland's next book, *Amanda's Choice,* was written for children but addresses problems that are universal to people in relationships. Amanda is an unhappy young girl whose father has recently remarried. Preoccupied with his new wife and other matters, her father does not pay enough attention to her. In an attempt to amend this situation, Amanda adopts vulgar language and mischievous behavior. This tactic earns her father's attention, but it is not the positive recognition that she craves. Alice Low wrote in the *New York Times Book Review* that Holland "understands child-rearing, psychological nuances and social problems, but she uses her characters to carry messages rather than to tell their flesh and blood stories." Reviewing *Amanda's Choice* in the Bulletin of the Center for Children's Books, Zena Sutherland lauded the book for its "memorable characterization" and "good style."

Holland's third novel, 1972's *The Man without a Face,* was appraised as "deeply affecting" by *Children's Literature in Education* contributor Corine Hirsch, who calls the book Holland's "most interesting novel to date." The book is one of Holland's best known, primarily because of its controversial subject matter. Charles is a fourteen-year-old whose father has died. Since that time, his mother has remarried and divorced four times. He lives with her and his sisters. Viewing his mother's marriages as a betrayal to his father, Charles's attitude toward women in general is mis-

ognistic. Having loved and lost his father, he is also fearful of close relationships.

As the story begins, Charles and his family are spending their summer on an upper-class resort island. Because his grades have slipped considerably, Charles must enlist the aid of a tutor to gain entrance to an exclusive boarding school. He seeks the help of Justin McLeod, a reclusive native of the island. Justin's restrained manner poses little threat to Charles's fear of close emotional ties. With the tutor's positive influence, Charles begins to face his own feelings and becomes sensitive to the needs of others. The crucial and controversial event in the story, however, comes when Charles's cat is kicked to death by the delinquent boyfriend of one of his sisters. He goes to Justin for comfort and ends up spending the night in his tutor's bed. Holland implies that an act of homosexual love occurs between Charles and Justin. Soon after, Justin dies of a heart attack, leaving all of his possessions to Charles. Charles grieves his mentor's passing, but he realizes that his relationship with Justin has helped him face his life and has enabled him to be open with others.

The inclusion of the homosexual element in *The Man without a Face* often sparked more discussion among critics than the novel's narrative quality. Many reviewers commented on Holland's motives, speculating on the novel's moral lessons. Sheryl B. Andrews wrote in *Horn Book* that "the author handles the homosexual experience with taste and discretion; the act of love between Justin and Charles is a necessary emotional catharsis for the boy within the context of his story, and is developed with perception and restraint." In an adverse response to the book, Frances Hanckel and John Cunningham, writing in the *Wilson Library Bulletin,* complained of potential anti-gay sentiment. Hanckel and Cunningham felt that "in light of such limited coverage of the gay experience in YA [young adult] fiction, the possible identification of such a major character as a corrupter of children is grossly unfair." While Hirsch disagreed with Holland's stance on parenting, complaining that "character and plot are manipulated in order to illustrate the dangers of permissiveness and the value of discipline," she praised the author's use of homosexual themes, writing that "the novel's strength lies . . . in the development of [Justin and Charles's] intense emotional relationship and the corresponding enrichment of Charles' sensibilities."

*Lion and the Unicorn* contributor Kate Fincke saw a deeper meaning in *The Man without a Face:* "Holland seems to have a twofold purpose. One is to speak some psychological truth on the matter of homosexuality; the other is to alleviate anxiety and to absolve guilt in the young adolescent reader about his own homosexual inclinations or acts." Comparing the fates of Justin and Charles at the novel's end, Fincke further interpreted that "what Holland implies is that the transient adolescent homosexual is acceptable, but the mature homosexual is doomed."

Holland stated in the *Horn Book* that she "didn't set out to write about homosexuality" in *The Man without a Face.* "I started this book with only the idea of a fatherless boy who experiences with a man some of the forms of companionship and love that have been nonexistent in his life." Holland wrote that the character of Justin possesses "qualities that mythologically as well as psychologically have always been the archetypes of fatherhood." These qualities, which include masculinity and kindness, filled a void in Charles and eventually helped the boy lead a better life. This, Holland stated, was more important "than the almost incidental fact that the book is about love between two people of the same sex."

Holland returned to writing novels for young adults in 1975, producing the National Book Award nominee *Of Love and Death and Other Journeys.* The central character, Meg Grant, is a teenager who is coming to a crossroads in her life. She is at an age where the adulthood she so desperately craves is within her reach, but she is also repeatedly reminded of her proximity to childhood. Her priorities change significantly when she learns that her mother has cancer. When her mother dies, Meg must learn how to deal with her grief. She falls in love with a boy named Cotton but is rejected by him. Oddly, Cotton's rejection triggers a realization in Meg that, although her mother is gone, she can survive on her own and lead a happy life.

Holland was praised for accurately evoking teenage emotion in *Of Love and Death.* "What makes the book really entertaining is Isabelle Holland's ability to capture all the precarious qualities of teenhood," lauded Anne Marie Stamford in *Best Sellers.* Stamford also admired Holland's skill in depicting real life. She concluded her review by stating that "the author's straightforward sense of humor when describing people and situations made me laugh out loud, a response rare indeed to novels these days." A critic for *Kirkus Reviews* praised the novel as "genuinely moving," and assessed *Of Love and Death* as containing "real emotion . . . that can't be ignored."

Holland wrote another children's book in 1982, *Abbie's God Book,* in which twelve-year-old Abbie conveys her thoughts on God, her family, and friends. In 1983 Holland published a related volume, *God, Mrs. Muskrat, and Aunt Dot.* The story centers around young Rebecca, a recent orphan. After the loss of her parents, Rebecca has come to live with her aunt and uncle. Told through a letter to God, Rebecca relates how her relationship with her imaginary friend, Mrs. Muskrat, has helped her adjust to her new life and surroundings. *Abbie's God Book* and *God, Mrs. Muskrat, and Aunt Dot* were jointly honored with the Church and Synagogue Library Association Ott Award in 1983.

Holland's career as a writer spans more than three decades. Beginning with the publication of Cecily in 1967, she has received considerable praise from critics, teachers, librarians, and readers. Holland's handling of often sensitive material has been continually praised, as has her distinct portrayals of young people. As Sutherland stated in the *Bulletin of the Center for Children's Books,* "It is . . . in insight into motivations and relationships that the author excels." Kaye echoed this sentiment in *Booklist,* opining that "Holland writes with compassion and a sensitive understanding of human nature and its idiosyncrasies."

"My books have always dealt with the relationship between the child or adolescent and the adult or adults who live in and dominate the young person's portrait of self," Holland stated in *Literature for Today's Young Adults.* She continued: "It is that struggle between the child and the adult in the creating of that self-portrait that often preoccupies my writing."

Holland believes that parents or other adults will often unintentionally inflict mental damage on a young person, damage that can scar the child for many years. While Holland's books criticize the mistreatment of young people, she also views them as a means to make people aware of, and hopefully address and correct, these problems. She summarized by stating, "If my books are about the wounds given . . . they are also about the healing that can take place, given the right adult at the right time."

*AUTOBIOGRAPHICAL ESSAY:*

Holland contributed the following essay to *CA:*

Probably the most influential fact of my childhood is that though my parents were from Tennessee I never lived in the United States till I was twenty and had almost all my schooling abroad. I was born in 1920 in Basel, Switzerland, where my father was American Consul. He and my mother and my brother, Philip, known to the family as Pito, had been there since 1913 and spent the four years of World War I there. Pito, born in 1911, was nine years older than I. He was actually born in Jackson, Tennessee, my mother's home town, but was taken almost immediately to Saltio, Mexico, where my father was then U.S. consul. Shortly after they arrived, a young woman turned up at the consulate looking for a way back to the States. Mindful of a wife with an infected wisdom tooth and an infant son who had somehow also contracted blood poisoning (or so I was always told), Father said this young woman looked like an angel of light. "Would you like a job now?" he asked. "Yes," she said. She went home with him that day and was with us from sometime in 1911 to 1927, first bringing up my brother, then me.

We called her Dolly all the years she was with us, but her name was Bridget Moore. She was born in New York City and brought up in the New York Foundling Hospital. She had gone down to Mexico with an American family and left for reasons not entirely clear. The version I always heard was that they no longer needed her. My brother told me many years later that she had left the family abruptly because the father of the household had made advances to her, and she, a good Catholic girl, was having none of it.

Some of my earliest memories, in Guatemala City, Guatemala, were loitering around a Catholic church while Dolly was in the confessional. With nothing better to do, I dabbled in the holy water, which was in a font well above my head. When Dolly emerged from the confessional, she found me on my toes playing in the holy water. She wiped my hands off firmly, then slapped them, telling me I shouldn't be playing in holy water. I held no grudge against her for this or the occasional spanking. My memory of such punishments was that I usually knew I had done wrong and had deliberately risked it. Often she would say, "If you do that after I've told you not to, Isabelle, I'll spank you." When I did it anyway, she spanked me. But neither she nor I held any grudge about it afterwards. In later years after Dolly had left, when I did something I knew or should have known was wrong, my mother never spanked me, but would tell me how much I had hurt her and how badly she felt about it. This, of course, filled me with guilt and made me feel terrible. The rages my father would fly into were mainly on two grounds: One, that I was too fat because I ate too much, and two, that I received low marks because a) I was stupid and b) hadn't studied.

As I write this, I realize how much I have painted both parents as monsters, which they weren't. They, too, were products of their backgrounds. I loved my mother, who was a wonderful storyteller and had a great sense of fun and humor. But we didn't know each other really well until I was seven. Up to that time I was brought up by Dolly, who had brought up my brother before me.

One of the stories my mother told me was about her father. When he was sixteen, he joined the Confederate Army and fought in the last year of the Civil War and was, I think, present at the battle of Franklin. In one of the lesser skirmishes he was in, the Confederates won. According to the customs of the day, the commander of the losing army would turn over his sword (or pistol) to the commander of the winning army. My grandfather, who was frequently used as a messenger by his commanding officer, was standing up there beside him when the Union Commander proceeded to surrender his sword and belt. He gave his sword to the Confederate commander, then looked at my grandfather. "I'm going to give my belt to this kid here," he said. "He reminds me of my son back home." And he, a huge man who towered above my grandfather, proceeded to try and buckle his belt around my grandfather's waist. It fell off, of course, but my grandfather, enormously proud, took it back home with him to Jackson, Tennessee, and put it in the attic.

Many decades later, when my grandfather, then the owner of a hardware store in Jackson, was a widower, he would stroll downtown in the afternoon and sometimes sit and chat with the drummers (salesmen) staying there in the hotels and rooming houses. One day one of the drummers said, "The last time I was down here, I was with the Union army. We lost that day, and I gave my belt to a kid who reminded me of my son back home. I often wonder what happened to him."

My grandfather didn't say a word. He simply got up, went home to his attic, got the belt, came back to the hotel or rooming house where he'd seen the drummer and laid the belt across his knees. The man jumped up and embraced him, and they had a grand reunion.

My grandfather died before I was born, so I never met him. But in the last years of his life he stayed often with my family in Basel, Switzerland, and there are some charming photographs of him, an elderly man, with my brother, who was a young child. One of the pictures showed them on a sled, my grandfather with my brother between his knees, going down a snowy slope. Whenever I see one of those photographs, I think of the story my mother told me.

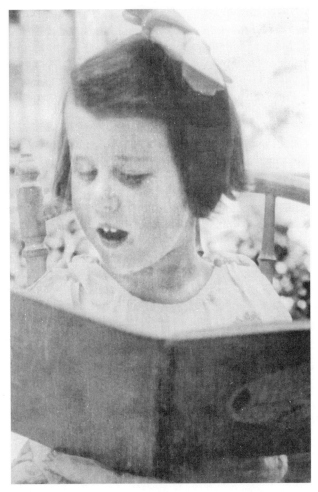

*Isabelle Holland, five years old in Guatemala*

I have come to realize that my father had a remarkable boyhood and youth, a product of a far older America than the one I finally came to when I was twenty and have lived in ever since. He was born in Kentucky. When he was three his family moved to Martin, Tennessee, where he lived until he was nineteen. At that time Martin was a very small town. According to stories he told me, when he was three he took a walk by himself and kept on walking until he was well out of town and decided to come back.

As he described it to me later, an old countryman in a cart came along going back towards Martin, and my father asked him for a ride. As they passed each farmhouse the man would say, "Do you live there, son?" My father would shake his head and say "no." As the man later told my father's mother, he had just about decided that they must have passed the three-year-old's house when Father pointed and said, "That's where I live." His mother was out, worriedly scanning the road. The

countryman told her he had picked up my father three miles from there.

When he was five his older brother, who was seven, started to their little country school. My father announced he was going too. My grandmother told him he couldn't, he was too young. But it didn't stop him. He trotted along beside his brother. The principal called on his mother a few days later, and my father told me he overheard his mother apologizing for not having been able to stop her younger son from going.

"Don't worry," the principal reassured her, "he'll get tired in a few days and quit."

He didn't miss a day for nine years, and he had had all the public education the state of Tennessee had to offer at that time. In addition to that, one of his chores was to milk the family cow every morning before school. I learned this in Wales where we used to go for vacation while my father was American Consul, later Consul General, in Liverpool, England. His passion was fly fishing, and he used to put a sandwich in his satchel and fish in a local stream. Once, when I was with him, he went to see if the farmer on whose land he was fishing could give him some milk. We found the farmer in the cowshed, milking.

"May I try?" my father asked, after a minute.

The farmer got up from the stool and my father sat down and started milking. I was enormously impressed. His rural background and upbringing had always seemed unreal to me.

"Can I try?" I asked.

"All right," my father said. He looked up at me. "You do it this way, pulling on the teat like this." And he demonstrated.

Eager to try, I sat down with my back to the front of the cow as my father had been sitting. As I pulled the teat I heard a funny blowing noise behind me. The cow had turned its head and was looking at me. "No, no," my father said, "you do it this way," and he showed me again. The cow seemed mollified. So I pulled again. Something made me leap up and just in time. The cow, making an ominous noise, had kicked the bucket and the stool over.

"You just don't know how to do it," my father said disgustedly.

(I used this scene in my book, *The Journey Home,* published by Scholastic in 1990.)

From Switzerland he was transferred in 1923 to Guatemala City, Guatemala. I was three, and on our way to Guatemala visited the United States for the first time, meeting and staying with various relatives.

The American Consulate was a one storey building—which all buildings in Guatemala City were at that time, because the city was surrounded by volcanoes, some of which were active. Earthquakes were common and frequent. I remember once walking with Dolly to the barrancas, or ravines, at the edge of the city and seeing flames shooting up from one of the cone shaped peaks beyond the barrancas.

The consulate and the residence attached spread over a large block. We had three patios in which were two parrots, three parakeets, a fountain containing goldfish, two dogs and a horse. When we were having an earthquake my mother would herd the family into one of the patios, and once I remember seeing a roof flying through the air.

My memories of Guatemala are like a vividly illustrated child's picture book. Guatemala City, the capital where we lived, was only thirteen degrees from the equator but five thousand feet in altitude. There was a rainy season and a dry season. When the sun shone, which was all the time except when it rained in the rainy season, it was brilliant. Because it was so high, the nights were cool. My days consisted of going to what we called Christopher Columbus park with Dolly where I played with my best friends, Ralphie and Moisie Piccoto, whose nanny, Nurse Roberts, an Englishwoman, was a great friend of Dolly's. Ralphie and Moisie were Orthodox Jews. Their father came from Palestine, their mother from Manchester, England.

The other children I played with were Guatemalan, German and English. At that time the Germans owned most of the coffee fincas (plantations), the Americans were in charge of the engineering works, and the English ran the railways. To accommodate their children, there was a German school, an English school and an American school. My brother, who was twelve when we reached Guatemala, was sent by my parents to the German school because up to that time his education had been in German in Switzerland, and they thought it would be easier for him to go on with the same system. Whether they were right or not I don't know. The three schools took the children up to the age of fourteen. After that most children were sent back to their own countries. And my brother, who had not lived in the States since he was a few months old, was sent at fourteen to a military school in Missouri and then to a boarding school in Bell Buckle, Tennessee.

When I was six I insisted on going to school, backed by my father. So I was sent to school with the wife of the chief Presbyterian missionary who had taught school in the States and was teaching her own children. For much of the year I was there, my teacher was Jessie Margaret Sullenberger, aged twelve. Already I knew how to read. I had a book about a dog named Spot which I proudly read aloud to anyone who would listen, mostly to Ralphie Piccoto to impress him.

In 1927 my father developed amoebic dysentery from which he probably would have died, had not one of the doctors from the Rockefeller Foundation, who was there at the time, given him an experimental drug which pulled him from death's door. He recovered, but he was told he could never again live in the tropics. So he was transferred to Liverpool, England.

Mother, Father and I sailed back to the States the autumn I was seven. Dolly, who had been courted over the years in a desultory way by an English carpenter living in Guatemala City, finally decided to marry him. I was a flower girl at the wedding. It was only there, at the wedding, that the fact that I was going to lose her finally sank in. When it did I burst into tears and cried desolately while Dolly, still in her wedding gown, stopped everything to comfort me.

When the ship reached New York, my father left almost immediately for Liverpool to find a house. Mother and I stayed in the States that winter, mostly in St. Louis, where my mother's sister, her husband and daughter lived. And I attended the elementary school there where I was taught the Palmer method of writing (from which I was rapidly untaught the moment I reached an English school).

Mother and I sailed for Liverpool the following spring when I was not quite eight. My father had rented a house in Birkdale, a suburb about twenty miles from Liverpool.

I remember the following year as the most desolate of my life. I felt totally alone. I had lost Dolly. Because he was the new consul, my father and mother had to be out a great deal. They would not, of course, have left me by myself. There were maids in the kitchen. But they wanted nothing to do with me. Just for company I would ring the bell in the living room and when the maid appeared asked her to bring me a sandwich. (It was probably about this time I started putting on weight!) At whatever hour my mother had said was my bedtime, one of the maids would come in and tell me I had to go to bed. I would insist that she come up and sit on my feet so I could know she was there, and to stay until I went to sleep. It was spring, and daylight went on and on. But even during the day in that far northern hemisphere, the daylight was often gray.

When I finally went to a small private school I was, and remained during the twelve years I was in England, the only American in every school I went to. Everything about me was wrong. I was short, fat, noisy and eager to please in a culture where the belle ideal was to be tall, blonde, flat chested, good at games and reserved. I was none of those things.

On the other side, I got an excellent education in the basics and developed a love for English history and literature that has stayed with me. Needless to say, at that time in pre-World War II English schools—or at least the ones I went to—American history and literature were not even touched on. One class, a geography class, stays in my mind. We did the British Isles, which was fair enough, then we did the British Empire which in the thirties was enormous and included vast chunks on almost every continent. In the course of this, of course, we studied Canada. Then we did Europe, Asia and Africa. Finally we arrived at the Americas (less those parts that had been dealt with as parts of the British Empire).

"There are forty-eight states in the United States of America," the geography mistress said, which there were then. "The most important state is the state of Maine, which is the one nearest to Canada. The capital city of the United States is Washington, which is on the POTomac River."

I took these bits of information home that night to my Tennessee parents. My mother was indignant over the undeserved (in her view) prominence given the state of Maine. My father brushed that aside. "Listen, Isabelle," he said to me. "You go back tomorrow and tell her that is pronounced PotOmac!" So, probably foolishly, I did. I raised my hand and said, "Please Miss (whatever her name was), that is pronounced PotOmac."

The woman looked at me with eyes of gray ice and said, "In England we call it POTomac."

Her reply came to represent to me, for the rest of my life, the irritating arrogance, but also the strength of the English. When the rest of Europe collapsed under the advance of Hitler's army, in some cases preferring surrender to having their cities bombed, the English stuck it out, bombed cities and all. And, to be fair, England was an island, a fact that has shaped its history as well as its psychology. There was the English Channel between her and the marching armies of the Reich and, since the Norman conquest, the rest of the world.

Sometimes I did well in school, sometimes I did disastrously, a result, I finally came to realize, of how happy I was in that particular class or that particular school, which meant how popular or unpopular I was.

I had never heard of Freud, nor, for any useful purpose, had my parents. And I don't think they would have agreed with Wordsworth's lines about ". . .trailing clouds of glory do we come / From God, who is our home: / Heaven lies about us in our infancy!/ Shades of the prison-house begin to close / Upon the growing boy. . . ." They were both forty-three when I was born and, though well educated, they were not, I have come to realize, sophisticated about some things. They grew up with the belief, probably held by most of their contemporaries, that children were an extension of their parents, and should be treated and judged as such.

One of my foibles is quoting poetry, something I'm inclined to do the way other people meditate or recite mantras. I inherited this from my mother who could also do it, though our choice of quotable poets was different. For her it was mostly Tennyson and various American poets, for me Keats and Shelley with some Kipling and A. A. Milne, plus (occasionally) Shakespeare thrown in. I owe this, again, to the English schools where large segments of poetry had to be learned by heart.

To this day poetry is something I sometimes mumble to myself as I walk down the street. Once, after I had undergone an unpleasant medical procedure for which I had been sedated, I asked the doctor if I had said anything while half conscious—imagining a string of four letter words floating out of my mouth. He laughed. "You quoted poetry," he said.

My mother, a Methodist child of the South, could also quote chunks from the Bible. I have never known any lay person who knew the Bible as she did. Thanks to her, to this day I think of the Bible, quite apart from any theological considerations, as the greatest collection of stories I have ever known. And one of the things for which I am eternally grateful to her is that she entertained me by telling me so many of the stories long before I actually read them.

I had my first publication when I was thirteen. I was an avid reader of a children's paper/magazine called *Tiger Tim,* a publication of which my father disapproved. He thought I should be reading great literature. "Never read anything for the story, Isabelle," he said to me, "Read it for the philosophy behind it." I thought it was a rotten idea then and I still think so.

In *Tiger Tim* one week it said, "Write a story of three hundred words and send it to us. If we publish it, we'll send you a prize." So I wrote my first story, adapting it from an incident in my own life, and called it "Naughty Betty." (Betty, of course, is the nickname for Elizabeth, and in Spanish-speaking Guatemala, the country I had previously lived in, Isabelle was considered another version of, and often used in place of, Elizabeth.) Like me, Betty hated to practice the piano. In real life I would often just bang on the keys in irritation and more than once was caught by my father, who was not pleased. In "Naughty Betty," Betty also banged on the keys, but in her case one of the keys broke, turned out to be hollow and contained a little note which led to a map which led to a treasure buried in the bottom of her garden, and she was able to help her family in all their financial woes. (This story came out during the Depression, and there was much talk of financial woes!)

The story was published and I received a book as my prize. My father was enormously proud and went around buying all the copies of *Tiger Tim* he could find, something he did fifteen years later when I sold my second story.

I went to private girls' day schools and for two unhappy years from fourteen to sixteen to a boarding school. It was my own fault. My parents had no desire for me to go, and of course it was more expensive. But I had been consuming vast numbers of boarding school stories in various magazines and girls' and boys' annuals and wanted desperately to go. I had also read and reread E. F. Benson's *David Blaize* and *David of Kings,* two books in a trilogy about a boy's first year at a "public" (in the English sense) school and later at Cambridge, books which were tremendously popular in the schools I went to.

But for me boarding school was an unmitigated disaster: I looked wrong, sounded wrong, acted wrong. I had no friends the first year and only one the second. Probably as a result of those years, I have never had any illusions about the capacity for cruelty and gang mentality among teenagers towards an unpopular target, regardless of class or education. Needless to say, unhappy as

I was, I failed everything and was removed from the school by my parents.

I went back to one of the day schools I had been to before, worked hard, and the following year sat again for the School Certificate examination and achieved an honors matriculation which guaranteed my entrance to university. (The whole school system in England is different now, I gather.)

A year later I attended the University of Liverpool, reading history (still my favorite subject). The courses were in Mediaeval English History, Modern English History, Modern European History, French, and English literature. I also acquired my first boyfriend, an architectural student at the university. When I tell my young friends today that eighteen was then considered normal for this cataclysmic event, I can see from their faces they mentally put me back in the nineteenth century with Jane Austen and George Eliot.

During my second year at university, World War II started. The year after that The American Ambassador in London, Joseph Kennedy, the ranking U.S. State Department representative in Great Britain, ordered all wives and minor children of State Department officers out of the British Isles. Neither Mother nor I wanted to go. Mother had no desire to leave her husband and her home, and I had a strong desire not to leave my fiance, who was now serving in the Royal Navy Voluntary Reserve. (Our engagement had been announced the previous year.)

But the ambassador was adamant, so Mother and I travelled by train across Ireland and left on the last neutral ship to leave Europe, an American vessel anchored in Galway Bay. Every light in the ship was blazing and arc lights were trained on the American flag flying from the mast and the one painted on the side of the ship. The U.S. was not yet at war, and the ship's command was determined that no German submarine lurking in the vicinity could claim ignorance of its neutral status.

It was a memorable voyage. The cabins were packed full with the American wives of American diplomats, foreign wives of American diplomats and the American wives of foreign diplomats, most, if not all of whom, seemed to have babies and small children.

The panelled corridors of the ship were crisscrossed with ropes and strings from which hung diapers (this was before the days of disposable diapers). And, since the ship was traveling west and we lost an hour each day, the poor mothers had to rise and push their prams and baby carriages around the deck an hour earlier each morning, because, of course, the babies were unaware of the change in time. The resulting noise was awesome and gave me an anti-baby stance which shocked my dormitory mates when I finally entered college in the States. (One afternoon I came back from class to find pictures of babies from every known magazine pinned and taped to the walls of my room. Apparently the girls in the dormitory, shocked at my anti-baby attitude, had been collecting them for weeks just for this purpose. To this day I'm not sentimental about babies—animals yes, babies no.)

I loitered in the New York area for a few weeks, then joined my mother who had gone down to New Orleans to stay with her brother, a neurosurgeon, and her sister-in-law.

That fall I entered Newcomb College of Tulane University. It was a period of adjustment. I was neither a foreigner nor a native. My parents were American, and because my father was with the State Department I had the status of native birth. (This was an oddity that brought pens screeching to a halt when I first registered to vote. "Where were you born?" the voting registrar asked. "Basel, Switzerland," I replied. "When were you naturalized?" "I didn't have to be," I said, piously quoting my father. "By virtue of an act of Congress I have the status of native birth." That's when the pens stopped. The questioner got up, checked in some volume, then pointed to the open book and said in some wonderment to his fellow registrars, "She's right.")

The fact remained that I had never lived in the United States and was as much a stranger in a strange land as though I were an immigrant. In some ways I felt I had some things worse than an authentic immigrant who would be expected to be different. Despite my slightly English accent I was not, which sometimes made things a little difficult. I spent a long time, many years after that, trying to decide for myself what I was. In the meantime I set out to enjoy myself, which I did with enthusiasm, and New Orleans was a wonderful town in which to do it. After I was accepted at Newcomb on the strength of the letter from the Dean of the Faculty of Arts of Liverpool University, it was discovered I had never had either American history or any form of science. (In the schools I had gone to you could take either some branch of science or. . . And I always took whatever the "or" was, neatly avoiding all science.) I was assigned to U.S. history and physics classes. I managed to flunk them both (enjoying myself came first!) and had to take them over in summer school.

At this point, the dean, no longer impressed by my travels and European education, called me in and announced flatly that if I wanted to (eventually) graduate, I'd have to take make-up classes in summer school and achieve acceptable grades in all the courses I'd flunked. With the gun at my head, I did this, making As in various literary courses and even a B in physics. The physics exam consisted of seven questions, each one divided into two parts, one a definition, the other an equation. Curiously, I enjoyed the equations and was reasonably good at them. Before the exam the professor said to me, "Isabelle, whatever you do, choose the equation. You're better at that and you always try to change the wording of the definition. In science you can't do that."

For the first six questions I followed her strong suggestion. But in the seventh, the equation looked so complicated and the definition so easy, I ignored her suggestion for that one. A few days later she said to me, "I told you not to do any of the definitions!"

"Did I get it wrong?" I said unbelievingly.

"Yes. You rewrote it—as you always do! The other six questions you did fine!" I got a B. That has been my one brush with science. For two years after I graduated, I worked in New Orleans with the Censorship Bureau of the War Department. Because I had no foreign languages good enough to read any letters not written in English, I was stuck with those that were and found the job unspeakably boring. It cured me of any tendency I might ever have of reading other people's mail. There was only one exception I remember: An English officer stationed in New Orleans who wrote literate, witty and tender letters to his wife every week. When letters to be opened and censored were passed out, all of us seated at the table I was at fought to get his letters.

In the evenings I continued to enjoy myself, an easy task in New Orleans at that time. By then the U.S. was at war and we had the army, the navy, the air corps, the British and the French all stationed there. And I belonged to an organization patriotically dedicated to see that none of these young fighting officers would feel neglected. Once a week we gave a cocktail dance to ensure that.

My father had retired by then and bought a house in New Orleans and I lived at home. The main bone of contention between us was the hideously late hours I would come home, always tiptoeing in, hoping against hope he would be asleep. He never was. I remember around three or four one morning, trying to ease the door open silently, hearing his voice floating down the stairs, "Good morning, bright eyes!" Since I had to be at the office at eight I was, needless to say, pretty short of sleep. To make up for this I frequently dozed across two chairs in the lunch hour at work.

At this time I had been planning my return to England where I wanted to join the WRENS (women's voluntary navy) and more or less keeping up through letters with my fiance and friends. I knew my father would not countenance the idea of my returning to England, and my mother claimed she would be ill with worry if I left home. Again this makes my parents sound mediaeval in their attitude, but times then were different. My parents were born around 1879 or '80. They reflected the attitudes with which they had grown up. I once said to her indignantly, "If I were married and my husband were transferred to central China, wouldn't you expect me to go?"

"Of course, dear. But that's different."

I did tell them I wanted to go to New York to get a job in publishing, which I considered a first step on the way back to England. Finally, the wife of the British Consul General in New Orleans with whom I had made friends, invited me to join her and her daughters for six weeks in Canada, where she had taken a cottage by a lake. I accepted, knowing full well I had no intention of returning to New Orleans, but I did not say that to my parents.

The six weeks in Canada were fun. When I left I took a ticket to New York where I had been invited to stay with the daughter of friends my parents had made in Switzerland. The father was an American, the mother English, and they had come over here in about 1935. I stayed with my friend for five days. I remember one morning looking out the window of the high floored apartment at the roofs and skyscrapers of upper east side and midtown New York and thinking exultantly, "It's mine!" (temporarily forgetting that I considered myself on my way back to England).

At the end of five days my friend said apologetically there was only one spare room, and another guest was due to arrive. Without a moment's hesitation I moved into the Biltmore Hotel. (While I had had a good education in the liberal arts, the practical aspects of life had slid past me unnoticed and pretty much untaught.)

It was a few days before Labor Day of 1944, and I spent the intervening days looking for a job (it would take money to get back to England!). I had an impressive background and wasn't above referring casually (and inaccurately) to my father, the ambassador. And I had

an English accent. All these combined to get me a job as a corresponding secretary at *Life* magazine. I had had one week in New Orleans of typing school, which enabled me to lie cheerfully when asked if I could type and say emphatically, "Of course."

About a week or ten days later, my bill from the Biltmore came in. Even with the student rate I had been given, it shocked and scared me. I went to my boss and asked airily when we would be paid.

She explained that we were paid twice a month, but since I had arrived in the middle of one pay period, my paycheck wouldn't appear for another two weeks. "Why?" she asked.

I explained about my bill from the Biltmore.

A horrified expression came over her face as she realized what a dummy, in practical terms, she had hired. "You're staying at the Biltmore?"

By that evening she had me in a room in an apartment on East Eighty-sixth Street. For the next year I lived in a variety of places, sharing rooms, sleeping on pull-out sofa-beds. Finally, more by good luck than good management, I got myself into the Barbizon Hotel for women, in those more puritanical times a place noted for its glamorous models who took their possessions around in hat boxes. With some notion now of what I could not afford, I had a small single room with a bath around the corner. And I lived there for the next five years.

During that time I had a variety of jobs. I worked for a magazine published by the National Council of the Protestant Episcopal Church, writing a column about the hot news from various dioceses. I was fiction editor at *Tomorrow,* a literary magazine published by Eileen Garrett, who was also a noted psychic and founder of the American Society of Psychical Research. Finally in 1949 I got a job as copywriter at a book advertising agency and learned there more about writing than at any time before or since. Publishers in those days had little money to spend on advertisements, and what they did have had to be most effectively used in small spaces. "Use short, direct words, Isabelle," the copy chief taught me. "Avoid adjectives, put the strength of the sentence in the verb." To this day I think that's the best advice about writing I was ever given.

In the meantime, and mostly on weekends, I tried to write magazine stories. I remember magazine fiction as a lot commoner then than it is now. I got a lot of my

*Holland making a point in New York, about 1952*

efforts back, but the agent I had acquired finally sold a story to a Curtis magazine, *Country Gentleman,* published in Philadelphia. My story, "The Professor's Butterfly," appeared in 1948. My only other published story, "A Matter of Pride," was published in *Collier's* in 1951.

Finally, in the midfifties, I had the money to go back to England. When I arrived in London I asked a friend who had been British Vice Consul in New York and was now at the Foreign Office if he could get me a work permit, because at that time the British were very strict about allowing foreigners to work.

He said, "Ask me before you leave, Isabelle."

I stayed a month in London with an American friend I had made at one of my jobs and who now worked for the London bureau of *Time* magazine. After that I went to Scotland and stayed for a month outside of Inverness with the same lady whose husband had been British Consul General in New Orleans. Since then he had been

British Ambassador in either Ecuador or Venezuela, and had since retired to his native Scotland. At the end of the month I returned to London and asked my Foreign Office friend and his wife to dinner.

"Well, Isabelle," he asked, "what about that permit to work here?" To my own astonishment I heard myself say, "No, I am going back to New York."

It was some kind of milestone.

I returned to New York with my rent paid and five dollars in my pocket. With such an obvious and pressing need to find employment immediately, I landed a temporary job reading manuscripts from the slush pile at McGraw Hill. After a few weeks I got my first full-time job in book publishing as Publicity Agent at Crown Publishers.

When the job agency to whom I had gone to offered me this job interview, I said indignantly, "But I want an editorial job."

"Go anyway," they said.

I knew I needed their help in finding a job, so, grumbling, I did. It was one of the best things that happened to me. I was, I found, far better suited temperamentally to be a publicity director than an editor. I took the job and stayed in it for four years. My work consisted in writing book releases and sometimes book jacket copy and taking book reviewers and TV and radio people out for lunch or meeting them after work for cocktails and telling them about the books Crown was publishing and arranging interviews for the authors. I went from Crown to J. B. Lippincott in 1960. One of the first books I handled there was *To Kill A Mockingbird* by Harper Lee, though I can claim no credit whatever for the justified acclaim the book received then and since, including, of course, the Pulitzer Prize.

It was during the six years I was at Lippincott that I started writing my first novel. *Cecily* was about a short, fat, unhappy thirteen-year-old in an English boarding school, and contained, of course, a large autobiographical element, since I had indeed been a short, fat thirteen-year-old in an English boarding school. The antagonist was her opposite, a tall, slim, very popular though rather reserved teacher named Elizabeth. The story revolved around the tension between them, instigated by Cecily's need for attention and Elizabeth's antagonism to the needy child.

I was much taken at that time with the Harper Novel of Suspense which was then very popular. So into this rather simple story I started pouring a complicated plot involving spies and foreign intrigue. When I finished I took the manuscript to one of the editors at Lippincott and asked him to read it. He was very kind and gentle. When he called me in he said, "Isabelle, you have two books here, one about the child and her teacher and the other this mishmash of spies and dark intrigue. If I were you I'd stick with the child."

I took it home and cried a little, and proceeded to do exactly the same thing changing only the location to Long Island—a thoroughly unlikely place, considering the subject matter. Then I took the second manuscript to another editor in the house. She echoed almost word for word what the first editor had said, only more emphatically and on yellow lined paper. This time I believed her. So I took *Cecily* home and returned it to its original simplicity. That summer I took a trip to England and carried *Cecily* to my English agent. The day before I left London she came to my hotel and said, "Isabelle, this is a perfectly publishable book, but you have no descriptions! And you have to have some."

The reason, of course, was that all my life I had skipped descriptions in novels, preferring action and dialogue, which was one reason why I barely skimmed through such masters as Sir Walter Scott with his many lyric portraits of the highland with its heather and moors. So I came back to New York and spent the next three months putting in descriptions, using my own boarding school as a model. Then I sent the novel off to my American agent. Unknown to me the second editor at Lippincott to whom I had shown the manuscript had told the agent, "If Isabelle ever finishes that book, I want to see it." *Cecily* was published by Lippincott in 1967.

Shortly after it came out, the children's book editor at Lippincott said, "I think you could write me a children's novel." Out of that came my first children's book, *Amanda's Choice.*

I have written in all thirty-three children's and young adult books, as well as eighteen adult books. Most of the latter are mystery or suspense novels, the exceptions being *Cecily* and a family saga, *Family Trust,* published in 1994 by Dutton.

I was attracted to the genre of romantic suspense by such wonderful writers as Mary Stewart, Daphne du Maurier, Velda Johnson and others. Of course the great masters of this genre are *Jane Eyre* by Charlotte Bronte and, in this century, du Maurier's *Rebecca.* I suppose I reflect my generation in preferring the tension and

*The author in 1958*

suspense of romance to the more contemporary into bed at the first encounter, followed by explicit sex. Although certainly not a "romantic suspense" in the strict meaning of the term, the classic, *Pride and Prejudice,* has many of the best qualities of romantic suspense. Some of my romantic suspense novels include *Kilgaren, Trelawny, Moncreiff* (my own favorite), *Darcourt, Grenelle, The deMaury Papers, Tower Abbey, The Marchington Inheritance, Counterpoint,* and *The Lost Madonna.* These were followed by the St. Anselm's mystery series. Looking back, I have come to see that the theme of most of my middle range children's and young adult novels is the emotional tension and resulting relationship between the central character—the child or young adult—and the adult most important in his or her life. In my own opinion my three best books are *The Man Without A Face* (from which, twenty-one years later, the movie directed by and starring Mel Gibson was made), *Of Love and Death and Other Journeys,* nominated for the National Book Award (Children's Books), in 1976, and *The Journey Home,* a story about two Irish Catholic orphans in New York City who went out on the orphan train in the

1870s and were adopted by a Protestant farming couple in Kansas. *The Journey Home* received several regional awards.

People I meet and students in the class I teach, "Writing for Children," at New York University School of Continuing and Professional Studies, frequently ask me "Where do you get your ideas?" My answer is probably more or less the same as many other writers': From my own life and experience and the problems and situations that preoccupied me. Except for my first year at Mrs. Sollenbergers' in Guatemala, and the few months I spent in the St. Louis elementary school, I was the only American in every school I went to. So many of my stories have dealt with children or young adults who are different in some way or other from the schoolmates around them. When I have been asked where the idea for *The Man Without A Face* came from, I go back to two things: my poor relationship with my father, and the school stories I grew up reading. Many of these at that time dealt with the relationship in their "public schools"—in reality big (and expensive and extremely selective) private schools such as Eton, Harrow, Rugby and Winchester—between the older prefects and the younger boys whose job it was to wait on them and make tea for them in their studies, among which were the aforementioned *David Blaize* and *David of Kings* I read and reread and still have on my bookshelf. It is, of course, an England and a school system long gone.

*Of Love and Death and Other Journeys* sprang from a question a school librarian asked me at a school where I was giving a talk.

"Miss Holland," she said, "the fathers in your books are wonderful but the mothers are terrible. Why?"

Stricken with guilt I tried to stumble out with some answer, but my editor at the time supplied the best reply: "Because Isabelle keeps on creating the father she wished she had, and so, having to have a family villain, has put the blame on the mothers." It was probably a good answer and undoubtedly true, but I decided at that point I had to create a lovable mother. However, since I hadn't grown up with the typical homemaking, cookie-baking mother, I made the mother in *Of Love and Death and Other Journeys* a charming and lovable ditsy woman who runs tatty little tours over Europe.

The story is told from the point of view of fifteen-year-old Meg, who accompanies her mother, and takes place mostly in Italy where I had been many times, staying in a castle near Perugia rented by the same woman with whom I had stayed the first days I was in New York.

The castle was owned by a cousin of hers, and for thirty years she has rented it for four months during the summer. The place was always full to overflowing with guests, mostly from various European countries where she had many friends, and we drove around and visited other towns and villages and art museums from there. It is now also a summer artists' colony. The opening line of the novel is "I met my father for the first time when I was fifteen." The reason Meg finally meets her father is that her mother comes to realize she is dying and has summoned her former husband to meet the daughter he's never seen.

In the last few years New York City, or rather Manhattan, itself has become my main hobby. This started when I took a course at the New School on Manhattan history. The course included walking tours, and I became addicted to them after the course ended and spent Saturday and Sunday afternoons over the next several years going on walking tours conducted by various groups. I learned among other things that the famed Wall Street is on the exact location of, and was named for, the wall built in 1653 by the Dutch settlers across the southern tip of Manhattan, some say to protect the Dutch from the Indians, others say from the English settlers of the Massachusetts Bay Colony whom they feared might come down and raid them.

Springing from this interest I wrote *Behind the Lines*, published in 1994, a young adult novel about the New York City draft riots of 1863, reportedly the worst riot this country has ever seen. The heroine is Katy O' Farrell, a fourteen-year-old kitchen maid in one of the great houses on Washington Square, whose brother, to her relief, is a year too young to be drafted. But the twenty-one-year-old son of the household where she works is within draft age. When her master and mistress learn about Katy's brother, they try to take advantage of a clause in the draft law: anyone who did not want to be drafted could buy his way out by paying three hundred dollars to the government. Or he or his family could find someone to take his place. Naturally, but to Katy's horror and anger, the family wants to offer Katy's brother the three hundred dollars to take Master Christopher's place.

*The Promised Land,* published in 1996, was a sequel to *The Journey Home.* It takes place three years after *The Journey Home* and sprang from a newspaper article appearing in 1874, shown me by the archivist of the Children's Aid Society which had sent out the orphan trains. The first train went out in 1853 and the last in 1929. According to the records, some 100,000 children were sent out on the trains and were adopted.

The article the archivist showed me appeared in the paper, the *Irish World*. At that time the Irish, pouring over here after the famine had destroyed their land, were, in effect, the underclass. Many of the parents, their bodies wasted by the devastation of the famine, died shortly after their arrival, leaving their children without parents or homes. Sometime after 1850 the Reverend Charles Loring Brace, a young Presbyterian minister, came down to New York to take up his ministry. But he was devastated by the sight of all the homeless children living on the streets and in doorways and devised the idea of sending them out on trains where people might be interested in adopting them.

Today, people express horror at the thought of the orphans, lined up on station platforms or in church halls, while those who had expressed an interest to the Society's agent sent out ahead of time, pointed and said "I'll take that one or that one."

While it may sound grim and somewhat heartless, what people now don't realize is that the fate of those children, homeless orphans from the New York streets, were far better off on a farm or in a small town west of the Hudson, than back in the city. There were few orphanages at that time, and, if they were to survive at all, a life of crime, or, for a girl, prostitution was the only prospect.

Unfortunately, to many of the Catholic Irish, the orphan trains were seen as part of a Protestant plot to evangelize the children to Protestantism. And the article in the *Irish World* strongly and indignantly stated this view.

In *The Promised Land* Uncle Michael, the children's uncle just over from Ireland and trying to find his nieces, reads this article and hears the same viewpoint expressed by many of his sister's Irish neighbors. So, finding out from the Children's Aid Society where the girls are, he goes to Kansas to find them and bring them back to restore them to their faith and heritage. Needless to say, he finds them given far better care by the Protestant adoptive parents than he could possibly supply if he took them back with him to New York.

Animals appear in most of my stories. I grew up with pets, but I never consciously realized how important they were to me until I got my first apartment to myself, a studio, in New York City. I moved in in the fall of 1956. Not too long after that, without consciously thinking about it, I went to an animal shelter and adopted my first cat, whom I named Francesca (after, of course, St. Francis, patron saint of animals). Not too long after that a plump black kitten joined the family.

*Lunching with Gale editor Motoko Huthwaite at the New York Metropolitan Museum of Art, January 2, 1999*

Francesca, who had been sole cat for a while, deeply resented it and would beat up on him from time to time. Seeing this, my then current boyfriend (a Civil War buff) said, "There he stands like a stone wall." So I named him Stonewall Jackson. Francesca and Stonewall were the first of many cats. Another dark kitten who had been brought up to New York in a pillowcase from Philadelphia was named Amanda after my first children's book heroine.

My favorite and most prized picture of myself was taken by the distinguished photographer, Jill Krementz, and shows me holding my beloved cat, Waldo (named after my favorite hero in one of Georgette Heyer's regency novels). One summer when I was visiting a friend in England, I found myself trying to find reasons to return to New York earlier than planned. As I mentioned one excuse after another, my hostess looked at me sternly and said, "I think you want to get back to Waldo."

She was right.

In the intervening years I have had many cats, sometimes as many as five at once. As the years passed, of course, some cats have died. I now have three: Emily, found at the age of four weeks on a road in Rockland County; Tobias, found on West Seventieth Street; and Henry, who was going to be euthanatized by an owner who had become pregnant. I have never actually bought a cat. All of mine have come to me through shelters or because someone was going to get rid of them or from my vet. I cannot imagine life without them! And when I attend a meeting or gathering in a public space and someone announces that "children are welcome, but no pets, please," I have been caught mumbling to myself, "it should be the other way around." C. S. Lewis once said to a friend, "People always say to me, 'Professor Lewis, you must love children, you write for them so wonderfully.' What they do not realize is that writers of children's books do not necessarily do so because they love children. Frequently they don't even like them. But on some level they have never stopped being children." He was absolutely right!

I have now lived in New York fifty-four years and have moved many times. For thirteen years I lived in Chelsea on the lower west side of Manhattan, in an apartment of a house built in 1846 by the son-in-law of Clement Clarke Moore, who wrote "A Visit from St. Nicholas" (popularly known as "The Night Before Christmas") and who taught in the Episcopal Seminary across from where I lived. I now live on what is generally called the upper east side.

As always, I am working on something, this time a young adult book about a German girl who, with her father and younger sister, emigrated to New York in the 1850s, following the defeat of the 1848 Revolution in Germany, when many intellectuals, radicals and socialists, outraged at the return to power of the conservatives, started coming over here (and were and still are called the forty righters). It was they who established Kleine Deutschland (Little Germany) in what today is called the Lower East Side.

I have another book, *Paper Boy,* about a twelve-year-old Irish immigrant boy, Kevin, who comes over here with his father and younger sister in the 1890s, coming out from Holiday House in the spring of 1999.

I have sometimes been asked what advice I'd give to aspiring writers. I can only quote two very important anecdotes from my own life and experience. After I'd published my short stories I ran into a self-created wall. I was working then and I kept waiting for the perfect weekend for me to write a full chapter of my first novel. It never came. I didn't write for about five years until one day I had the thought: If I ask of myself, not a chapter, but a shorter and therefore less frightening amount, I might do it. So I lowered my demand of myself to one page a day. I set my alarm for five-thirty, put some water on for coffee and sat down at my desk in my nightgown and robe.

I did a page, and the next day I did another. Nor did I make the mistake of upping my quota to two pages. If I got carried away and did two or more pages, I went back to one page for the next day. Five years and many revisions later that became my first novel *Cecily.*

The next anecdote occurred when I was no longer working in an office and was freelancing. I had written two thirds of a page and got stuck. Never one to suffer silently, I called various friends and asked their advice. All of them said, "Declare yourself a holiday and go to a movie." Finally I called a fellow writer, the author of a Pulitzer Prize-winning play, and asked him. He gave me unforgettable counsel. "Don't leave that chair, Isabelle, until you've finished that page."

"If I could finish the page I would never have called you in the first place," I said indignantly.

Then he said, "It doesn't matter what you write, Isabelle. If you can't write anything else, write your name, BUT DON'T GET UP UNTIL YOU FINISH THE PAGE."

Grumbling, I did as he told me. I wrote, "My name is Isabelle Holland, my name is Isabelle Holland, now is the time for all good men to come to the aid of the party, etc., etc." And then the miracle happened. The block broke and I was able to finish the page. From that I learned that writing is not only an art or a craft, it is also a physical habit.

I still think about and use those two pieces of advice.

*BIOGRAPHICAL/CRITICAL SOURCES:*

*BOOKS*

*Authors & Artists for Young Adults,* Volume 11, Gale, 1993.

*Contemporary Literary Criticism,* Volume 21, Gale, 1982.

Gallo, Donald R., editor, *Speaking for Ourselves,* National Council of Teachers of English, 1990, pp. 97-98.

Nilsen, Pace, *Literature for Today's Young Adults,* Scott, Foresman, 1980.

*Something about the Author,* Volume 70, Gale, 1993.

*Twentieth-Century Children's Writers,* 4th edition, St. James Press, 1995.

*PERIODICALS*

*Best Sellers,* April 1, 1967, p. 7; December 1, 1974, pp. 382-383; May, 1975, p. 33; January, 1976, pp. 306-

307; September, 1977, p. 174; June, 1979, pp. 111-112.

*Booklist,* January 1, 1980, p. 667.

*Bulletin of the Center for Children's Books,* September, 1970, pp. 9-10; April, 1979, p. 138; March, 1980, p. 135.

*Children's Literature in Education,* spring, 1979, pp. 25-34.

*Christian Science Monitor,* June 12, 1974, p. F5; August 3, 1977, p. 23.

*Horn Book,* June, 1967, p. 353; August, 1972, pp. 375-376; June, 1973, pp. 299-305; June, 1980, p. 297.

*Junior Bookshelf,* June, 1980, pp. 143-144.

*Kirkus Reviews,* April 1, 1975, pp. 383-384; March 15, 1977, p. 285.

*Lion and the Unicorn,* winter, 1979-80, pp. 86-95.

*New York Times Book Review,* May 3, 1970, p. 23; October 30, 1977, pp. 34, 36.

*School Library Journal,* September, 1977, p. 145.

\*   \*   \*

## HOLMES, Larry  1949-

*PERSONAL:* Born November 3, 1949, in Cuthbert, GA; son of John and Flossie (a cotton picker) Holmes; married; wife's name, Diane; children: Listy, Lisa, Larry. *Ethnicity:* "African American." *Education:* Attended public schools.

*ADDRESSES: Office*—c/o Holmes Enterprises Inc., 704 Alpha Bldg., Easton, PA 18042. *E-mail*—holmsl@hotmail.com.

*CAREER:* Worked at various jobs in early years, including car washes, at rock quarries, rug mills, foundries, construction, and janitorial; sparring partner for Muhammed Ali; Round 1 Bar & Disco, owner; sportswear store, owner; professional boxer.

*AWARDS, HONORS:* Heavyweight champion, World Boxing Council, 1978-83; International Boxing Federation 1983-85; named one of ten Outstanding Men in America by Junior Chamber or Commerce, 1980.

*WRITINGS:*

(With Phil Berger) *Larry Holmes: Against the Odds,* St. Martin's (New York City), 1998.

*SIDELIGHTS:* Boxer Larry Holmes overcame an impoverished childhood and consistent lack of profes-sional support to emerge finally as a champion fighter in 1978, when he took the World Boxing Council heavyweight title from Ken Norton. He successfully defended his title 21 times, and built subsequent business interests into a fortune worth $40 million. Yet Holmes's life was filled with struggle. His autobiography, *Larry Holmes: Against the Odds,* co-written with New York Times boxing writer Phil Berger, chronicles the obstacles he faced and the triumphs he earned both inside and outside the ring.

Holmes was born on November 3, 1949, in Cuthbert, GA. One of 12 children, he was raised by his mother, Flossie, a cotton picker. The family moved north to Easton, Pennsylvania, when Larry was six years old. Life was difficult for the family, and Holmes remembers feeling embarrassed by his Salvation Army clothes and humiliated by the family's dependence on welfare. He dropped out of school in seventh grade, and worked at various low-skilled jobs including car washes, rock quarries, factories, and janitorial work. At the beginning of his boxing career, Holmes struggled to obtain financial backing. Unlike contemporaries like Muhammed Ali or George Frazier, who had large syndicates behind them, Holmes had to fight for purses of only $125 to $200. The situation only improved after Ali invited Holmes to become his sparring partner at his new training camp in Deer Lake, Pennsylvania. The relationship was good for Holmes, who was soon earning $500 per week during Ali's training season and who used the opportunity to develop and mature as a boxer. Nevertheless, promoters were reluctant to advance Holmes's career, and he had few opportunities to make his mark.

Finally, in 1978, Holmes got a title fight. He beat Ken Norton for the World Boxing Council heavyweight championship, and defended his title 21 times before relinquishing it to become International Boxing Federation champion from 1983 to 1985. But success was not without its darker side. After defeating Muhammed Ali in a 1980 title fight, Holmes's reputation began to dim. As *New York* writer Mark Jacobson put it, "Holmes kept winning, but audiences found his highly mobile jab-overhand-right technique more workmanlike than inspiring. Neither hated nor loved, he was a fighter for the cognoscenti." He also had his share of bad luck. In 1985, one fight away from tying Rocky Marciano's record for consecutive wins (49), Holmes lost to Michael Spinks—in a close decision that he felt reflected prejudice against a black athlete's surpassing a white athlete's record. This attitude earned him a reputation—inaccurate, in the view of some sports writers—as a complainer.

This blunt honesty emerges again in his memoir, *Larry Holmes: Against the Odds.* In the book, Holmes is particularly outspoken in his unflattering portraits of promoter Don King and other celebrities in the boxing world. Though some reviewers felt that this critical tone detracted from the book's more generally positive message, others felt the comments were well deserved. A reviewer for *Publishers Weekly* noted that the negativity in the book was depressing but honest, and concluded that the memoir "is by turns saddening and inspiring. Holmes comes across as a heroic American athlete." And David Davis, in the *New York Times Book Review,* appreciated Holmes's story as "a series of lessons in persistence." Reviewers praised the book's account of Holmes's difficult early life and his determination to succeed.

After retiring from boxing, Holmes concentrated on various business ventures. He speaks proudly of how he developed unused land in a run-down section of Easton, Pennsylvania, and built it into a thriving business complex. His holdings include a disco, a restaurant and lounge, a training and recreation center, a motel, and two office buildings. In 1997, Holmes, then aged 47, surprised the boxing world by challenging 21-year-old Maurice Harris to a fight at New York City's Madison Square Garden. Promoters hoped the event would stimulate interest in a future Holmes bout with aging superstar George Foreman. But, though Holmes beat Harris in a decision after ten rounds, the fight was hardly a distinguished one. As David Remnick put it in the *New Yorker,* Holmes was badly out of shape and "could not have beaten Maurice if he had been handed a baseball bat. . . . But boxing being boxing, of course, the judges awarded him the fight. . . . The Champ was at his end, and so, too, it seemed was boxing."

*BIOGRAPHICAL/CRITICAL SOURCES:*

*BOOKS*

Hickok, Ralph, *A Who's Who of Sports Champions,* Houghton Mifflin (New York City), 1995.

*PERIODICALS*

*Booklist,* September 1, 1998, p. 52.
*Library Journal,* October 1, 1998, p. 101.
*New York,* July 28, 1997, p. 32.
*New Yorker,* August 11, 1997, p. 25.
*New York Times Book Review,* November 15, 1998, p. 62.
*Publishers Weekly,* October 19, 1998, p. 69.
*Sports Illustrated,* April 17, 1995, p. 11; June 3, 1996, p. 16; October 28, 1996, p. 29.

*OTHER*

*Larry Holmes Web site,* http://www.larryholmes.com/ (November, 1999).*

\* \* \*

## HOLOCH, Naomi

*PERSONAL: Education:* Oberlin College, B.A., 1961; University of Aix-en-Provence, France, Licence es Lettres, 1965; Columbia University, Ph.D., 1972.

*ADDRESSES: Office*—Purchase College, State University of New York, Purchase, NY 10577.

*CAREER:* Instructor at New York University, 1968-72; Purchase College, State University of New York, assistant professor, 1975-82, associate professor, 1982—.

*AWARDS, HONORS:* Fulbright teaching assistantship, 1964-65; National Endowment for the Humanities grant, 1990-92; Lambda Award, 1990, for *Women on Women* anthology series.

*WRITINGS:*

(Editor with Joan Nestle) *Women on Women: An Anthology of American Lesbian Short Fiction,* Plume (New York), 1990.
(Editor with Joan Nestle) *Women on Women 2: An Anthology of American Lesbian Short Fiction,* Plume, 1993.
(Editor with Joan Nestle) *Women on Women 3: A New Anthology of American Lesbian Short Fiction,* Plume, 1996.
*Offseason: A Novel,* Faber (Boston), 1997.
(Co-editor) *Worlds Unspoken: An International Anthology of Lesbian Fiction,* Vintage/Random House (New York), 1998.

*SIDELIGHTS:* Naomi Holoch is an academic and co-editor, with Joan Nestle, of the *Women on Women* series—anthologies of short fiction written by American lesbian women. The writers whose works appear in the series run the gamut from the unfamiliar to the well-established; the works are short stories (some published for the first time) and excerpts from novels. The writers address themes and topics such as love and relationships, sex, families, friendship, gender identity, accepting matters of life and death, and finding solutions to everyday problems.

The first in the series, *Women on Women: An Anthology of American Lesbian Short Fiction,* contains selections by writers like Becky Birtha, Leslea Newman, Joanna Russ, Teya Schaffer, and Jess Wells. Acknowledging this first collection's limited mainstream appeal and branding it "uneven in scope and quality," a *Publishers Weekly* critic nevertheless declared the wide range of lesbian characters depicted in the pieces "surprising."

Writers with works appearing in *Women on Women 2: An Anthology of American Lesbian Short Fiction* include Madelyn Arnold, Lucy Jane Bledsoe, Rebecca Brown, Michelle Cliff, Ellen Frye, Helen Hull, Edith Konecky, Mary Wings, and Jacqueline Woodson. Because *Women on Women 2* reprints some stories written early in this century, this collection "proves that the struggle for sexual freedom is more than a contemporary issue," noted the contributor to *Publishers Weekly.* This volume includes "the widest diversity possible" of lesbian writers, the critic continued. Marie Kuda, writing in *Booklist,* appraised the pieces in this anthology as "definitely diverse" and "uniformly excellent," judging this collection "every bit as good as the first *Women on Women.*"

*Women on Women 3: A New Anthology of American Lesbian Short Fiction* includes pieces by Bledsoe, Brown, Cliff, Nisa Donelly, Frye, Frankie Huddenbroich, Kate Millet, Lu Vicker, and others. This third compilation "boldly challenges any notion of lesbian writing as a homogeneous genre," proclaimed a reviewer for *Publishers Weekly.*

*Offseason: A Novel,* Holoch's first book, tells the story of the long-distance relationship between Miriam, a lesbian translator based in New York, and Gabriella, a married bisexual editor living in Paris. Miriam has been in love with Gabriella for years and flies to her friend in France when she senses that something is wrong with Gabriella. During their week-long visit, the two women begin an affair, full of stress and complications. A contributor to *Publishers Weekly* considered *Offseason* "ambitious" and "intelligent, but fatally disorganized." This reviewer found the novel's best scenes "so convincing that one wishes the whole could live up to these parts." Judith Akalaitis opined in *Library Journal:* "Holoch's superb description of the women's relationship" results in characterizations "both love[d] and loathe[d]" by readers. *Booklist* writer Whitney Scott labeled *Offseason* a "beautifully crafted novel . . . full of delicately shaded nuances." Scott concluded: "Holoch traces the intermingling of friendship and desire with a sure, sensitive hand."

*BIOGRAPHICAL/CRITICAL SOURCES:*

PERIODICALS

*Booklist,* June 1 & 15, 1993, p. 1789; May 15, 1996, p. 1571; January 1, 1998, p. 776.
*Library Journal,* January, 1998, p. 141.
*Publishers Weekly,* April 6, 1990, p. 111; May 10, 1993, p. 70; May 20, 1996, p. 252; November 24, 1997, p. 53.*

\*    \*    \*

## HOPKINS, Brian A.   1960-

*PERSONAL:* Born in December, 1960; married; children: Derek, Summer. *Education:* Memphis State University, B.S., 1983. *Avocational interests:* Book collecting, carpentry, firearms.

*ADDRESSES: E-mail*—brian—a—hopkins@sff.net.

*CAREER:* Writer, 1995—. United States Air Force, Tinker Air Force Base, Oklahoma City, OK, electronics engineer (civilian).

*MEMBER:* Science Fiction and Fantasy Writers of America, Horror Writers Association.

*AWARDS, HONORS:* Honorable mention, L. Ron Hubbard Writers of the Future contest, 1989, for "Ivory in the Blood"; honorable mention, *Year's Best Fantasy and Horror, Vol. 6,* for "The Night Was Kind to Loretta"; honorable mention, *Year's Best Fantasy and Horror, Vol. 8,* for "And Though a Million Stars Were Shining"; honorable mention, *Year's Best Fantasy and Horror, Vol. 9,* for "Gaffed", and *Year's Best Fantasy and Horror, Vol. 10,* for "Dead Art"; nomination (with David Niall Wilson) for Horror Writers Association Bram Stoker Award, for "La Belle Dame Sans Merci"; nomination for Bram Stoker Award, long fiction category, for *Cold at Heart;* nomination for Science Fiction and Fantasy Writers of America Nebula Award, for *Cold at Heart;* Story of the Year, *Eternity* magazine, 1998, for "All Colors Bleed to Red"; fourth place (with Wilson), World Horror Con short story contest, 1999, for "The Poem of Adrian, Grey."

*WRITINGS:*

*Something Haunts Us All* (short story collection), illustrated by Donald Schank, Macabre, Inc., 1995.
*The Endless Masquerade and Other Vignettes of the Fantastique* (electronic publication), photographs

by Susan Burgard, Lone Wolf (Oklahoma City), 1996-97.

*Cold at Heart* (novella), illustrated by Donald Schank, Starlance (Pasco, WA), 1997.

*Flesh Wounds* (limited edition CD-ROM, short stories and artwork), photographs by Susan Burgard, instroduction by Ken Abner, Lone Wolf, 1999.

(With David Niall Wilson) *Joined at the Muse* (short story collection), in press.

Contributor of short stories to science-fiction, fantasy and horror anthologies; author of stories, poems, and essays in numerous print and electronic magazines.

*SIDELIGHTS:* Brian A. Hopkins is an electronics engineer living in the Oklahoma City area. Captivated by writers like Harlan Ellison and George R. R. Martin, he dabbled in science-fiction and horror writing while attending Memphis State University on a U.S. Air Force scholarship, and published his first piece, "Ivory in the Blood," in 1990; it has since been reprinted and has been translated into German. Currently over fifty of Hopkins' stories have been published or are forthcoming in various print and on-line magazines (including *Midnight Zoo, Tome, Aberations,* and *Millenium Science Fiction and Fantasy*), and in anthologies such as *Best of the Midwest's Science Fiction, Fantasy and Horror*. His pieces are routinely reprinted, and several have been recognized in such forums as *Year's Best Fantasy and Horror*. Some of his best work was collected and issued in a 1995 limited edition, *Something Haunts Us All;* this was followed by an electronic volume, *The Endless Masquerade and Other Vignettes of the Fantastique,* in 1996-97. Hopkins has also collaborated on stories with fellow "dark fantasists" James Van Pelt and David Niall Wilson, and has published poetry and essays on technical aspects of science-fiction writing.

*Cold at Heart,* a stand-alone novella, is Hopkins' first effort at longer fiction. The narrative cuts back and forth between two story lines. In one, the author puts a supernatural spin on the tale of Sir John Franklin's ill-fated attempt to find the Northwest Passage in the 1840s, as expedition member John Torrington uncovers the secret of the Arctic wolf—a secret that claims his life and results in disaster for his companions who investigate. In the other, present-day biologist David Snow, his daughter Julie and wildlife photographer Peter Burke (who is recovering from a personal tragedy) undertake their own journey to the Arctic, where they encounter the sinister cunning of a shapeshifting creature. Burke soon finds that he is involved in more than a simple research mission. At the same time that

he develops romantic feelings for Julie, he begins to realize that she, and her abnormally low body temperature, bare some kind of hidden connection to the wolves they are supposedly studying.

Reviewers of *Cold at Heart* have praised Hopkins' evocative and atmospheric use of the Arctic wasteland setting, and his thorough research on topics like anthropology in Canada, the Franklin expedition and historical accounts of werewolves. Jeff Ahrens wrote in *Booklist* that puzzling over the novella's mysteries "will be a delightful undertaking for horror connoisseurs," while *Amazon.com*'s horror editor, Fiona Webster, calls Hopkins' writing "a welcome throwback to the best of the horror/fantasy/adventure tales that used to appear in American pulp magazines from the 1930s through the 1950s. He adheres to the same storytelling principles of economical characterization, vivid descriptions, lots of action, and a bang-up ending." The book was nominated for two important prizes in the science fiction and horror genres: the Nebula and the Bram Stoker Awards. Hopkins has since returned to publishing in electronic format with a CD-ROM, *Flesh Wounds,* combining his fiction and his original artwork.

*BIOGRAPHICAL/CRITICAL SOURCES:*

*PERIODICALS*

*Booklist,* November 1, 1997, p. 454.

*OTHER*

*Amazon.com,* http://www.amazon.com (1999).*

\*          \*          \*

**HOWIE, Betsy**

*PERSONAL:* Divorced. *Education:* Attended drama courses at New York University.

*ADDRESSES: Agent*—c/o Harcourt Brace & Co., 525 B. St., Suite 1900, San Diego, CA 92101.

*CAREER:* Actress, novelist, and playwright. Has worked in a wide variety of positions, including as Santa's elf at Macy's, speech writer for Ronald Reagan, hot dog street vendor, assistant to Stella Adler, nanny for New York Attorney General Robert Abrams, golf cart driver for Walter Cronkite's Governor's Island, publicist for the Dalai Lama, PSA producer for Lauren

Hutton, tour coordinator for author Ann M. Martin, producer for Dr. Ruth, publicist for Ingrid Craven, and as an associate producer for the reopening of Ellis Island.

*WRITINGS:*

*Cowgirls* (musical play; first produced off-Broadway, 1996), music and lyrics by Mary Murfitt, Dramatists Play Service (New York City), 1997.
*Snow* (novel), Harcourt Brace (New York City), 1998.

Also author of plays *Big Stella, Yours Truly,* and *The Bridal Fit.*

*SIDELIGHTS:* Despite her hectic schedule as a New York City stage actress, Betsy Howie found time to be a novelist and playwright. In collaboration with musician and lyricist Mary Murfitt, she wrote the book for the musical play *Cowgirls,* which opened off-Broadway in 1996 to largely favorable reviews. The story concerns Jo, who has just twenty-four hours to find a way to save her father's country-western saloon, called Hiram Hall, from foreclosure. She needs a paying crowd—and she needs one fast. Her wise-cracking waitress, Mickey, and her cook/cashier, Mo (played by Howie), offer to get up on stage and help, but Jo has a better plan: She has booked the Cowgirl Trio, convinced they will attract a big audience. The catch is that there is no Cowgirl Trio; because of a telephone misunderstanding, she has booked the Coghill Trio, three *classical* musicians on a reunion tour. When the trio arrives, they have one day to transform themselves from classical longhairs to foot-stompin' honky-tonk country-and-western musicians.

Howie turned to fiction with her debut novel, *Snow.* The novel's unnamed, thirty-something narrator has problems with men, including her husband, Ray. Tormented by her sense that she does not know "how to be a girl," she packs up and heads to a snowbound cabin in the north with her two cats. There ensues a merger of fantasy and self-analysis. The first cat, Vinnie, talks to the narrator, lecturing her and helping her sort out her insecurities; the other cat, Sophie, makes up expressive dances. During a three-day journey in the snow to find firewood, the narrator faces her anxieties in the form of an annoying polar bear, who helps her release her childhood memories through an old wound in her thigh (at the time she wrote the novel, the author was suffering from a cancerous tumor in her thigh). She finally finds a kind of equilibrium in her life through the ministrations of a mysterious visitor who comes to the cabin to tend her. *Snow* met with mixed reviews. While a *Publishers Weekly* reviewer criticized the novel for "silli-

ness" and "sophomoric prattle," a *Library Journal* contributor found the book "intriguing, imaginative, and compulsively readable."

*BIOGRAPHICAL/CRITICAL SOURCES:*

*PERIODICALS*

*Library Journal,* October 1, 1997, p. 122.
*Publishers Weekly,* October 6, 1997, p. 72.
*Variety,* April 8-14, 1996, p. 68.*

\* \* \*

**HUBBELL, Helene Johnson**
**See JOHNSON, Helene**

\* \* \*

**HUME, George Haliburton   1923-1999**

*OBITUARY NOTICE*—See index for *CA* sketch: Born March 2, 1923, in Newcastle upon Tyne, England; died of cancer, June 17, 1999, in London, England. Theologian, educator, and author. Hume, named George Haliburton at birth, said he decided to become a monk around age eleven. He took on the name Basil in 1942 after entering a Benedictine monastery and made the vows of a monk. He was ordained a Roman Catholic priest five years later. Hume began teaching in 1950 at the monastery's secondary school for boys, where he stayed until 1963. For much of that time he was head of the modern languages department and coach of the rugby team. In 1963 he was named abbot of Ampleforth and then archbishop of Westminster, London. The pope named him cardinal in 1976, which was an unexpected election. Hume proved popular for many reasons—the ability to make other people comfortable, he defended Rome vigorously and he seemed never to forget he was first and foremost a monk. He helped pull England's Catholics together and also won legions of supporters among non-Catholics, including Queen Elizabeth, head of the Church of England. She honored him shortly before his death with the Order of Merit. Hume's first book, *Searching for God,* was a collection of short talks he had given and he followed that with *In Praise of Benedict* and *To Be a Pilgrim: A Spiritual Notebook.* His work, both written and in action, helped make the Catholic Church an accepted part of English life in country whose majority of citizens are Protestants.

*OBITUARIES AND OTHER SOURCES:*

PERIODICALS

*Chicago Tribune,* June 18, 1999, sec. 2, p. 11.
*New York Times,* June 18, 1999, p. A33.
*Times* (London; electronic), June 18, 1999.
*Washington Post,* June 18, 1999, p. B8.

OTHER

*CNN Interactive,* June 17, 1999.

\*   \*   \*

**HUNEVEN, Michelle**

*PERSONAL:* Born in Altadena, CA. *Education:* Iowa Writers Workshop, M.F.A. (creative writing).

*ADDRESSES: Agent*—c/o Alfred A. Knopf Inc., 201 East 50th St., New York, NY 10022.

*CAREER:* Journalist. Associate faculty member of Antioch University—Los Angeles.

*WRITINGS:*

*Round Rock,* Knopf (New York City), 1997.

*SIDELIGHTS:* The reviews of Michelle Huneven's first novel, *Round Rock,* speak to the talent of this West Coast-based writer. Throughout the novel Huneven shows in myriad ways how true the opening line of the book is: "Among the inhabitants of the Santa Bernita Valley, it is commonly believed that nothing there ever goes according to plan." Despite the best-laid intentions of the cast of characters—including Red Ray, an ex-lawyer and recovering alcoholic who runs a shelter for recovering drunks; Libby Daw, a talented musician whose shattering desertion by her husband has left her out of touch with her gift; and Lewis Fletcher, a denial-ridden former hotshot whose alcoholic and drug tinged exploits have landed him unwillingly in Red's care—things just do not seem to work out the way they intend. Characters recover from their addictions and then slip laughingly back into them. Trusts are made and broken. People fall in love, and people form hatreds. The book makes it painfully clear that life in a small town, even a pretty one like Santa Bernita, can be brutish, nasty, and short.

Reviews of *Round Rock* were generally positive. A *Publishers Weekly* reviewer called it a "delightful, bittersweet first novel," and praised Huneven as having "a gift for rendering grownup characters who keep growing up credibly (and quickly) before our eyes." Similarly, Valerie Miner noted in the *Los Angeles Times Book Review* that Huneven "introduces readers to this tight, fractious community as if they were newcomers, free to form their own fresh allegiances." While Miner does find a few faults with Huneven's style—"The dialogue gets stiff; some of the spiritual insights are embarrassingly pedantic. And Huneven, in her eagerness for a broad social canvas, occasionally sacrifices character depth for stereotypes"—Miner admitted that these problems were minor. A *Kirkus Reviews* contributor offered similar praise, calling the novel "deftly managed" and "long, slow, intelligent, and humane."

*BIOGRAPHICAL/CRITICAL SOURCES:*

PERIODICALS

*Esquire,* July, 1997, p. 28.
*Kirkus Reviews,* May 15, 1997, p. 742.
*Los Angeles Times Book Review,* August 3, 1997, p. 2.
*New York Times Book Review,* August 3, 1997, p. 9.
*Publishers Weekly,* June 30, 1997, p. 69.\*

\*   \*   \*

**HUNT, Francesca**
**See HOLLAND, Isabel**

\*   \*   \*

**HUO, T. C.**

*PERSONAL:* Born in Laos; naturalized U.S. citizen. *Education:* University of California, Berkeley, B.A., 1988; University of California, Irvine, M.F.A., 1994.

*ADDRESSES: Agent*—Marie Brown, Marie Brown & Associates, 625 Broadway, New York, NY 10012. *E-mail*—TKHUO@hotmail.com.

*CAREER:* Writer, c. 1998—.

*WRITINGS:*

*A Thousand Wings,* Dutton (New York City), 1998.

Contributor of short story, "Those Years," to *Asian American Literature,* edited by Shawn Wong, Harper-Collins, 1995.

*WORK IN PROGRESS:* Another book about life in the Thai refugee camps.

*SIDELIGHTS:* T. C. Huo belongs to an emerging generation of writers who are transforming American fiction through their focus on the experiences of Southeast Asians and Asian Americans. A native Laotian who immigrated to the United States, studying English at the University of California at Berkeley and earning a graduate degree in creative writing at University of California Irvine, Huo draws on his firsthand knowledge of life on both sides of the Pacific in his debut novel, *A Thousand Wings.* The story is that of Fong Mun, a Laotian of Chinese descent leading a comfortable but rather disconnected life as a caterer and cookbook author in San Francisco. Hoping for an end to his loneliness when he finds himself attracted to Raymond, also a Laotian and a victim of family tragedy, Fong Mun goes about preparing a series of traditional dishes for the younger man.

Prompted by Raymond and by his return to the recipes taught to him long ago by his grandmother, Fong Mun bit by bit reveals the complicated course of his life. With the Communist takeover of Laos during the Vietnam War, the young Fong Mun and his family fled to Thailand. There he spent time in a refugee camp before making his way to America, where he lived in an Oakland housing project. Along the way he had to come to terms with the loss of his own culture, the disappearance of his mother, the death of his grandmother, and the recognition of his own homosexuality. The narrative alternates between Fong Mun's memories and his present-time conversations with Raymond as the two become lovers.

As a writer for *Kirkus Reviews* remarked, "[t]he novel's central concept—that reconstructing recipes from memory is Fong Mun's way of recapturing and preserving the culture taken from him—is a moving one, and when Huo sticks closely to it, we're absorbed and persuaded by his story." The reviewer for *Publishers Weekly* called *A Thousand Wings* "[v]ery informative on the modern history of Laos, and enlivened by wonderful glimpses into a Laotian kitchen," while Whitney Scott, writing in *Booklist,* said that "Huo movingly conjures one man's experience as a person at two removes [as a refugee and a gay man] from the elusive mainstream."

*BIOGRAPHICAL/CRITICAL SOURCES:*

*PERIODICALS*

*Booklist,* March 15, 1998, p. 1201.

*Kirkus Reviews,* February 1, 1998.
*Library Journal,* March 15, 1998, p. 93.
*Publishers Weekly,* February 9, 1998, p. 72.*

\*　　\*　　\*

## HURD, Paul DeHart   1905-

*PERSONAL:* Born December 25, 1905, in Denver, CO; son of Henry C. (a printer) and Katherine (a dietician; maiden name, Renfro) Hurd; married Elizabeth Kelly, 1947; children: Greg, Philip. *Education:* Northern Colorado University, A.B., 1929, M.A., 1933; Stanford University, Ed.D., 1949. *Avocational interests:* Horticulture.

*ADDRESSES: Office*—c/o Teachers College Press, 1234 Amsterdam Ave., New York, NY 10027.

*CAREER:* Teacher and author.

*AWARDS, HONORS:* Honorary Doctorats in Science, Drake University, 1974, Ball State University, 1979, and University of Northern Colorado, 1980.

*WRITINGS:*

*New Directions in Elementary Science Teaching,* Wadsworth, 1968.
*New Directions in Teaching Secondary School Science,* Rand-McNally (Chicago), 1969.
*Inventing Science Education for the New Millennium,* Teachers College Press (New York City), 1997.

Also author of *New Curriculum Perspectives for Junior High School Science* and other books. Contributor of numerous articles to education periodicals, including *Education Digest, Science News,* and *Technology Review.*

Author's manuscripts are housed at the Hoover Institution on War, Revolution, and Peace, Stanford University, Stanford, California.

*SIDELIGHTS:* Author and educator Paul DeHart Hurd has had a long and productive career in teaching young people. Specializing in science education, he has published over three hundred articles in professional journals and has authored a dozen books. Hurd told *CA:* "All of my writings depend upon research. Most of my work is based on a historical and philosophical analysis and interpretation. The primary focus of all my writings has been on education in the sciences."

In 1969 Hurd published two books discussing several of the new experimental programs for teaching science: *New Directions in Elementary Science Teaching* and *New Directions in Teaching Secondary School Science.* After analyzing the need for change in the methods customarily used to teach science, in *New Directions in Elementary Science Teaching* he describes the new approaches used to inspire youngsters with an interest in science, and discusses the curricula designed to integrate these approaches with existing requirements. According to a *Choice* reviewer, *New Directions in Elementary Science Teaching* is an "excellent reference."

At the turn of another decade, Hurd published *Inventing Science Education for the New Millennium.* In this volume, he gives an overview of the history of science teaching. Hurd noted changing trends: for example, the late twentieth-century emphasis upon teaching technology and biology over other science-related subjects. Finally, he recommends further changes to science curricula. Writing in *Choice,* G. E. Hein criticized what he considered to be Hurd's superficial treatment of the topics covered in *Inventing Science Education for the New Millennium.* He also asserted that a number of references and examples Hurd employed are "inappropriate or inaccurate."

*BIOGRAPHICAL/CRITICAL SOURCES:*

*PERIODICALS*

*Choice,* June, 1969, p. 554; April, 1998, p. 1423.
*Library Journal,* June 1, 1969, p. 2229.
*Science Books and Films,* March, 1969, p. 264; December, 1969, p. 209; May, 1970, p. 10.*

\*      \*      \*

## HURLEY, Graham

*PERSONAL:* Male.

*ADDRESSES: Agent*—c/o Macmillan Publishers Ltd., 25 Eccleston Place, London SW1W 9NF, England.

*CAREER:* Author.

*WRITINGS:*

*Rules of Engagement,* Pan Books, 1990.

*Thunder in the Blood,* Macmillan, 1994.
*Sabbathman,* Macmillan, 1995.
*The Perfect Soldier,* Macmillan, 1996.

Also author of *Lucky Break?,* 1983; *Reaper,* 1992; *The Devil's Breath,* 1993; *Heaven's Light,* 1997; *Airshow,* 1998; *Nocturne,* 1998; and *Permissible Limits,* 1999.

*SIDELIGHTS:* Graham Hurley is a novelist who specializes in thrillers set in England. In *Rules of Engagement* he envisions a world on the brink of war when a disabled American submarine drifts into Soviet waters. Hurley focuses on the effect of the threat on England, with the imposition of martial law and the rise to power in one city of the sinister Martin Goodman. In *Thunder in the Blood,* Hurley shifts to the aftermath of the Gulf War. His protagonist is a woman, an underling in the MI5, the British version of the American Central Intelligence Agency, who is assigned to work with a journalist who believes he has uncovered evidence proving that the war in the Persian Gulf was a fraud. "This is a fascinating book because it sets everything the wrong way round," commented a reviewer for *Books,* adding, "but it certainly works."

In *Heaven's Light* Hurley imagines an England strangled by a conservative government and the creation of a third political party by a lawyer and an advertising executive who nearly manage to inspire a revolution for independence in Portsmouth. "Within this accomplished thriller is a serious political novel," remarked Steve Boyd in the London *Times.*

Hurley again steps into the shoes of a female protagonist with *The Perfect Soldier,* in which the mother of an aid worker killed by a land mine in Angola travels to the war-torn country to uncover what really happened to her son. Critics focused on Hurley's anti-war theme, which parses out the responsibility for the death of Molly's son, and untold numbers of others, among the soldiers who planted the mines and their commanding officers, the manufacturers and dealers of land mines, and the governments that have failed to outlaw this cheap means of conducting warfare which ultimately injures far more civilians than military personnel. Edward French, a reviewer for *Books,* called this "a powerful story, thought provoking and exciting, and a worthy successor to Hurley's earlier books."

*BIOGRAPHICAL/CRITICAL SOURCES:*

*PERIODICALS*

*Books,* September/October, 1990, p. 24; May/June, 1994, p. 27; April/May, 1996, p. 8.

*Times* (London), June 28, 1998.*

# I

## IMHOF, Arthur E(rwin)

*PERSONAL:* Born in Switzerland.

*ADDRESSES: Office*—Free University of Berlin, Berlin, Germany. *Agent*—Duncker und Homblot GmbH, Carl-Heinrich-Becker-Weg 9, 12165, Berlin, Germany.

*CAREER:* Free University of Berlin, Berlin, Germany, professor of social history.

*WRITINGS:*

### SOCIAL HISTORY

(With Oivind Larsen) *Sozialgeschichte und Medizin: Probleme der quantifizierenden Quellenbearbeitung in der Sozial- und Medizingeschichte,* Gustav Fischer (Stuttgart, Germany), 1975.

*Aspekte der Bevolkerungsentwicklung in den nordischen Landern, 1720-1750,* two volumes, Francke (Bern, Switzerland), 1976.

*Einfuhrung in die historische Demographie,* C. H. Beck (Munich, Germany), 1977.

*Die gewonnenen Jahre: Von der Zunahme unserer Lebenspanne seit dreihundert Jahren oder von der Notwendigkeit einer neuen Einstellung zu Leben und Sterben: Ein Historicher Essay,* C. H. Beck, 1981.

*Die verlorenen Welten: Alltagsbewaltigung durch unsere Vorfahren—und weshalb wir uns heute so schwer damit tun,* C. H. Beck , 1984, translated by Thomas Roboisheaux as *Lost Worlds: How Our European Ancestors Coped with Everyday Life and Why Life Is So Hard Today,* University Press of Virginia (Charlottesville, VA), 1996.

(With Rolf Gehrmann, Ines E. Kloke, Maureen Roycroft, and Herbert Wintrich; also author of introduction in German and English) *Lebenserwartungen in Deutschland vom 17. bis 19. Jahrhundert,* with tables in German and English, VCH, Acta Humaniora (Weinheim, Germany), 1990.

### EDITOR

*Mensch und Gesundheit in der Geschichte,* Matthiesen (Husum), 1980.

(With Rita Weinknecht) *Erfullt leben—in Gelessanheit sterben Geschichte und Gegenwart,* Duncker und Humbolt (Berlin), 1994.

Also author of *Biologie des Menschen in der Geschichte,* 1978.

*SIDELIGHTS:* Since the 1970s, German-Swiss social historian Arthur E. Imhof has made an important contribution to the burgeoning field of demographic history: the understanding of the past through the quantitative study of vital statistics. This specialty, which was begun in Germany shortly after the beginning of the twentieth century, suffered a setback in that nation during the Nazi years, but it has been revived there through the efforts of Imhof and others. His 1975 book, *Sozialgeschichte und Medizin: Probleme der quantifizierenden Quellenbearbeitung in der Sozial—und Medizingeschichte,* co-authored with Oivind Larsen, is a guide to demographic methods and sources for historians, but it is also a work of demographic historical analysis in itself. The two authors delved into the records of the Scandinavian countries in the eighteenth and nineteenth centuries for their examples. This resulted in what Paul Slack termed in the *English Historical Review* "a precise historical focus" that offered "stimulating suggestions" for further research, as well as being "a useful manual and work of reference for social and medical historians."

Imhof's next book, 1976's *Aspekte der Bevolkerungsentwicklung in den nordischen Landern, 1720-1750,* continued his investigation of Scandinavia, this time on his own. Imhof not only probed into the statistical records of all five Scandinavian countries (which were more complete, on the whole, than those for the rest of Europe), but also learned all the Scandinavian languages, including Finnish and Icelandic, in three years. (A fourth year was spent writing the book.) In the *English Historical Review,* M. W. Flinn called this a "monumental venture" and an "amazingly comprehensive survey," which researchers of Scandinavian origin would "have to work hard and fast to emulate." In the 1,100 pages of the two volumes, which included two hundred tables, Imhof explores macrohistorical variables such as changes in disease patterns, public health policies, methods of contraception, migrations, labor shortages, childbearing, child mortality, and much more, all in the context of pre-industrial economies and pre-vaccination medicine.

In 1977, Imhof wrote a much shorter book with a much different focus. *Einfuhrung in die historische Demographie* is a 150-page opus designed to introduce German students to the methods of historical demographics, and in particular of family reconstitution based on parish records. It was "a modest book with modest aims," observed Michael R. Haines in the *Journal of Economic History,* and Imhof, Haines declared, was "well qualified to write it." The book contains four chapters: an introduction to the field and its interdisciplinary nature, a history of the discipline, specific problems and issues as illustrated by Imhof's own field research, and methods. For one reviewer, John Knodel in the *American Historical Review,* Imhof's treatment of German approaches in the second chapter is "the most fascinating and original contribution of the volume." For Knodel, "Imhof's enthusiastic style" is another factor that would arouse the interest of German-reading students and professionals.

Imhof's quantitative, interdisciplinary approach was combined with a feeling for the real, underlying lives of the people who became statistics. This was made evident in his 1981 volume, *Die gewonnenen Jahre: Von der Zunahme unserer Lebensspanne seit dreihundert Jahren oder von der Notwendigkeit einer neuen Einstellung zu Leben und Sterben: Ein Historicher Essay,* in which he attempted to analyze the increase in life expectancy in Europe since 1600 and, in addition, to call for a new attitude toward life and death on the part of the contemporary West. A reviewer for the *Journal of Modern History,* Charles Tilly, felt that the book was overflowingly abundant in its illustrative materials from Germany, Scandinavia, and other parts of the world: "[H]e delivers great bundles of historical material in attractive wrappings, and calls his readers . . . to unpack this material thoughtfully, deliberately, and often with pleasure." Gerald J. Gruman wrote in the *American Historical Review,* "It is reassuring to read quantitative history 'from below' that really becomes vivid, moving, and even eloquent. Moreover, Imhof's style often is appealing in its modesty, directness, and, at times, humor."

Imhof continued to use quantitative evidence for the purpose of arriving at qualitative understanding in his 1984 volume, *Die verlorenen Welten: Alltagsbewaltigung durch unsere Vorfahren—und weshalb wir uns heute so schwer damit tun,* which was published in the United States in 1996 as *Lost Worlds: How Our European Ancestors Coped with Everyday Life and Why Life Is So Hard Today.* Here, Imhof tries to reconstruct the life of a single German farmer named Johannes Hooss, who lived between 1670 and 1755 in north Hessen. Hooss's life *per se* was the focus of two early chapters, with later chapters venturing into broader fields such as the threat of famine, plague, and war in Hooss's time. This led to Imhof's central thesis: that preindustrial life, although often shorter and more pain-filled than modern life, was less anxiety-laden, because it was organized around a coherent religious worldview. Reviewer Joachim Whaley, writing in the *American Historical Review,* saw the volumes as "a tract for the times . . . [,] often lively and informative but incline[d] to facile generalizations and dubious parallels. Yet it provides intriguing insights into contemporary anxieties. Future scholars may well look back on it as an example of 'Green history.' " A *Publishers Weekly* writer enjoyed Imhof's presentation of the life of four hundred years ago, and his "charming style" but was less convinced by his apparent preference for the seventeenth and eighteenth centuries over the twentieth.

In 1990, Imhof, along with several junior researchers, produced the massive results of a large-scale quantitative analysis of German mortality statistics from the seventeenth to the nineteenth centuries. The focus was on records of 135,000 individuals living between 1740 and 1860 in seven small regions of western Germany; investigations were also made for inhabitants of a previous generation, when statistics were not as carefully kept. The computerized data themselves were available from the Zentralarchiv fur Empirische Sozialforschung in Cologne, Germany; the book was "a necessary companion" to the data, in the opinion of Steve Hochstadt in the *American Historical Review.* The authors disavowed any intention of analyzing or interpreting their data; the presentation itself was their aim, as a service to future scholars who might want to make further studies and interpretations. The book was, in short, a research tool. Hochstadt called the creation of this database "a remarkable achievement, which, if taken full advantage of, will influence historical demographic research for years to come." Another reviewer, *Journal of Social History* contributor John Komlos, alluded to the "awe-inspiring patience" and the organizational, as well as intellectual, skill involved in steering this well-funded project. The bilingual nature of Imhof's introduction, and of the book's tables, made it even more useful, Komlos added.

During his distinguished career, Imhof has also been the editor of some volumes of collected essays. The 1980 *Mensch und Gesundheit in der Geschichte* is a collection of seventeen articles written for an international, interdisciplinary conference held in Berlin in 1978. The conference dealt with medical care and the experience of the individual patient in Europe between the sixteenth and early twentieth centuries. Mary Jo Maynes, reviewing the collection for the *Journal of Interdisciplinary History,* called it "impressive and significant" as a step on the path to "a human-centered, interdisciplinary approach to health in the past."

A 1994 collection edited by Imhof with Rita Weinknecht, *Erfullt leben—in Gelessanheit sterben Geschichte und Gegenwart,* contains papers by specialists in a wide variety of disciplines on the subject of the increase in life expectancy after 1600. Aimed at both a professional and a general audience, the volume sets forth three major reasons for the change: decreased infant mortality, decreased maternal death, and decreased accidental death for young male workers. Imhof says it was necessary to re-examine the Western world's way of life, particularly in old age, to adjust to the new luxury of a longer life span. He recommends primarily that people should reserve the final stages of their lives for study, travel, reading, and reflection. Reviewing the collection for the *Journal of Social History,* Peter K. Taylor called it "both exciting and promising" and "an important challenge" and commented favorably on the relative absence of "difficult German academic language."

## BIOGRAPHICAL/CRITICAL SOURCES:

*PERIODICALS*

*American Historical Review,* October, 1977, p. 992; October, 1978, pp. 967-968; April, 1984, pp. 409-410; June, 1985, pp. 710-711; February, 1992, pp. 224-225.
*English Historical Review,* October, 1977, pp. 907, 909; January, 1983, pp. 206-207; June, 1994, pp. 733-734.
*Journal of Economic History,* December, 1978, pp. 1007-1008.
*Journal of Interdisciplinary History,* autumn, 1981, pp. 351-353.
*Journal of Modern History,* September, 1983, pp. 506-507.
*Journal of Social History,* winter, 1992, pp. 390-91; spring, 1996, pp. 708-710.
*Publishers Weekly,* August 5, 1996, p. 423.\*

\*　　　\*　　　\*

## INGOLDBY, Grace

*PERSONAL:* Female.

*ADDRESSES: Agent*—c/o William Heinemann Ltd., 20 Vauxhall Bridge Rd., London, SW1V 2SA, England.

*CAREER:* Author.

*WRITINGS:*

*Last Dance with You,* M. Joseph (London), 1986.
*Out of Call or Cry: The Island of Sark,* Heinemann (London), 1990.
*Candles and Dark Night,* Heinemann, 1992.
*Bring Out Your Dead,* Dufour Editions, 1999.

Also author of *Across the Water* and *Head of the Corner* for M. Joseph.

*SIDELIGHTS:* Grace Ingoldby's first novel, *Across the Water,* takes place against the background of the Irish Troubles. The story begins in 1976 in a decrepit house in Enniskillen, where Aimee Hamilton and her son have been sent for the summer to reside with her in-laws. Aimee is not happy with these developments; her brother-in-law is heading toward a nervous breakdown. When her playwright husband arrives, she revenges herself by having an affair with a visiting captain. *New*

*Statesman* contributor Colin Greenland found Ingold-by's characters cartoon-like, but with enough inner fire to make them realistic. Ingoldby's wit, according to the reviewer, is sharply focused and "cuts through to an underbelly that is soft and ugly and sad." *Listener* critic Vernon Bogdanor remarked on the strength of the work, and called it the first effort of a "writer with considerable imagination and talent." *Times Literary Supplement* reviewer Patricia Craig called Ingoldby's eclectic writing style (including an overuse of commas) clumsy but gives the author accolades for "avoiding banality."

*Last Dance with You* uses the symbolism of a round house to suggest the conundrum of sadness and deceit that occur among its occupants. The old archeologist Richard Fox inexplicably commits suicide by jumping into the sea. His forty-year-old son is left behind, detached from life and considering himself technically dead. Peter remains in the house for a year after his father's death, aimlessly sorting through materials and trying to make sense of it all. Along the way he confronts the indiscretions of his father (who had an affair with his sister-in-law) and the deceits and sad lives of others in the novel. When a writer appears wishing to complete a biography of his father, Peter is forced to gather information for her and move on. A former woman in his life—Kate—also appears, reminding Peter that he practiced detachment too well and alienated her in the past. Elizabeth Barry commented in the *Times Literary Supplement* on the novel's English style, full of "missed opportunities, unstated longings, and blighted lives." The reviewer commented on Ingoldby's detached tone and found it a little too heartless in this "celebration of the sadness of life." While *New Statesman* writer Liz Heron also found the author's detachment "chilling," she commented on a poignant final scene that has Peter taking to the streets with a tram full of Kate's paintings. *Listener* reviewer Kate Cruise O'Brien called the final image one of "brave and comic pathos."

Reviewers similarly remarked that one of Ingoldby's strengths is her depiction of her characters. She gathers her cast at a convent on the Irish island of Innishcarra in *Head of the Corner,* an exploration of "middle-aged angst," according to Anne Haverty in the *Times Literary Supplement.* Haverty remarked that Ingoldby fails to tap her characters for their best potential, preferring instead to "stay with the mundane." Haverty also appreciated the conciseness of the prose, but found the setting too depressing and the depression not convincing enough. However, reviewer Gillian Wilce, writing in *New Statesman,* admired the "tragic intensity and wit"

of the story, even though she noted a lack of a single vision throughout the work. According to *Times Literary Supplement* reviewer Margot Livesey, the author's strength in *Bring Out Your Dead* is her ability to see inside her characters, and to expose their "small pleasures and meanesses."

In *Candles and Dark Night* Ingoldby returns to the theme of the Irish civil war, though the story is presented as occurring in an imaginary country and, in the words of Deborah Singmaster in a *Times Literary Supplement* article, in a "more expressionistic" version than the realism of the author's first novel. Dora and Stephen are to live in Carver Hill, a surrealistic and rural farm settlement. Dora's sense of foreboding is enhanced by medieval rituals practiced in the town. Meanwhile, the war interferes—Dora's brother becomes a casualty, and a peace-keeping force sets up militaristic presence in the country. Singmaster claimed that the novel neither completely works as a love story or a war story and calls the book "intensely serious."

*BIOGRAPHICAL/CRITICAL SOURCES:*

PERIODICALS

*British Book News,* April, 1985, p. 237; May, 1986, p. 310.
*Listener,* May 23, 1985, p. 32; February 27, 1986, p. 27.
*New Statesman,* February 22, 1985, p. 30; February 28, 1986, p. 27; March 4, 1988, p. 27.
*Observer,* February 23, 1986, p. 28; February 21, 1988, p. 27; April 5, 1992, p. 62.
*Times Literary Supplement,* March 1, 1985, p. 226; March 7, 1986, p. 256; April 8, 1988, p. 384; April 3, 1992, p. 9; December 4, 1992, p. 9; July 3, 1998, p. 21.*

\*   \*   \*

## INNIS, Harold Adams   1894-1952

*PERSONAL:* Born November 5, 1894, in Oxford County, Ontario, Canada; died of cancer, November 8, 1952; son of William (a farmer) and Mary (Adams) Innis; married Mary Emma Quayle, May 10, 1921; children: Mary, Anne, Hugh, Donald. *Education:* Mc-Master Univeristy, B.A., 1916, M.A., 1918; University of Chicago, PhD, 1920.

*CAREER:* Author, editor, and translator, c. 1923-52. University of Toronto, Department of Political Economy, teacher, 1920-29, associate professor, 1929-36, professor, 1936-37, department chairman, 1937-47, dean of graduate school, 1947-52. *Military service:* Canadian Army, World War I.

*MEMBER:* American Economic History Association (president, 1940s).

*AWARDS, HONORS:* Royal Society of Canada, fellowship; University of Glasgow, honorary degree; University of New Brunswick, honorary degree, 1944; McMaster University, honorary degree, 1945; Universite Laval, honorary degree, 1947; University of Manitoba, honorary degree, 1947.

*WRITINGS:*

*A History of the Canadian Pacific Railway,* King (London) 1923.

*The Fur-Trade of Canada,* University of Toronto Library (Toronto), 1927.

*The Fur Trade in Canada: An Introduction to Canadian Economic History,* Yale University Press (New Haven) 1930.

*Peter Pond: Fur Trader and Adventurer,* Irwin & Gordon (Toronto), 1930.

*Problems of Staple Production in Canada,* Ryerson (Toronto), 1933.

*Settlement and the Mining Frontier,* Macmillan (Toronto), 1936.

*The Cod Fisheries: The History of an International Economy,* Yale University Press, 1940.

*Political Economy and the Modern State,* Ryerson, 1946.

(With J. E. Dales) *Engineering and Society, Part 2,* University of Toronto Press (Toronto), 1946.

*Empire and Communications,* Clarendon Press (Oxford), 1950.

*The Bias of Communication,* University of Toronto Press, 1951.

*Changing Concepts of Time,* University of Toronto Press, 1952.

*Essays in Canadian Economic History,* edited by M. Q. Innis, University of Toronto Press, 1956.

*The Idea File of Harold Adams Innis,* edited by William Christian University of Toronto Press (Toronto & Buffalo), 1980.

*Innis on Russia: The Russian Diary and Other Writings,* edited by William Christian, Harold Innis Foundation, 1981.

*OTHER*

(Translator with Alexnder H. Smith) Henry Laurys, *The Foreign Trade of Canada,* Macmillan, 1929.

(Editor) *Select Documents in Canadian Economic History, 1497-1783,* University of Toronto Press, 1929.

(Editor with A. R. M. Lower) *Select Documents in Canadian Economic History, 1783-1885,* University of Toronto Press, 1933.

(Editor with A. F. W. Plumptre) *The Canadian Economy and Its Problems: Papers and Proceedings of Study Groups of Members of the Canadian Institute of International Affairs, 1933-1934,* Canadian Institute of International Affairs (Toronto), 1934.

(Editor) *The Dairy Industry in Canada,* Yale University Press, 1937.

(Editor) Norman J. Ware, *Labor in Canadian-American Relations: The History of Labor Interactions,* Yale University Press, 1937.

(Editor) H. A. Logan, *Labor Costs and Labor Standards,* Yale University Press, 1937.

(Editor) *Essays in Political Economy in Honour of E. J. Urwick,* University of Toronto Press, 1938.

(Editor) Charles H. Young, Helen R. Y. Reid, and W. A. Carrothers, *The Japanese Canadians,* University of Toronto Press, 1938.

(Editor) *The Diary of Alexander James McPhail,* University of Toronto Press, 1940.

(Editor) *Essays in Transportation in Honour of W. T. Jackman,* University of Toronto Press, 1941.

(Editor) *The Diary of Simeon Perkins, 1766-1780,* with an introduction and notes, Champlain Society (Toronto), 1948.

*SIDELIGHTS:* Harold Adams Innis was, according to William Christian writing in the *Dictionary of Literary Biography,* "one of the world's leading economic historians" during the first half of the twentieth century. A Canadian academic who spent his career in the Department of Political Economy at the University of Toronto, Innis's writings on the economic history of his native country and on communication had a tremendous influence on the world of Canadian scholarship.

Innis joined the army for a brief time during World War I after having received a bachelor's degree from McMaster University in Toronto. His military service abruptly ended, however, when he was badly wounded at Vimy Ridge. From that point on Innis dedicated his life exclusively to scholarly pursuits, and he began work right away on his master's thesis while still recuperating in the hospital for a year following his injury.

Innis earned a master's degree from McMaster University and then a doctorate from the University of Chicago in 1920, where he wrote his dissertation on the history of the Canadian Pacific Railway (which was later published in 1923). Fresh out of school, Innis was given a job as a teacher in the political economy department at the University of Toronto where he stayed until his death in 1952.

Innis's major scholarly work was *The Fur Trade in Canada: An Introduction to Canadian Economic History,* published in 1930. This work introduced a new way of looking at Canadian economy: the staple theory. This theory proposed that the economy of the country evolved as the primary staple product shifted from one thing to another. This development began with the fur trade, which was the main source of income for early European settlers to Canada. Innis points out that the unique characteristics of a beaver pelt allowed trade to develop in certain patterns. The products of different industries—fish, timber, wheat, etc.—had different characteristics and subsequently resulted in their own distinct economic patterns and systems.

Innis continued his look at the fur trade industry with the biography of *Peter Pond: Fur Trader and Adventurer,* published in 1930. Innis followed this work with further explorations of the staple theory through examinations of different industries. *Settlement and the Mining Frontier* appeared in 1936, followed by *The Cod Fisheries: The History of an International Economy* in 1940. This latter book discussed the ties between Canadian economy and its European model. As E. P. Hohman wrote in his review of *The Cod Fisheries* for the *Journal of Politics and Economics,* "this works is a monument of erudition in the field of meticulous, factual economic history. The reader is always impressed and sometimes overwhelmed by the evidences of beaver-like industry displayed in the uninterrupted flow of facts and figures in the hundreds upon hundreds of footnote references to little-known source materials."

During World War II, Innis was inspired to concentrate on a new set of topics. As a veteran of World War I, he had returned to his country hoping to continue his studies. Although he did go on to receive a master's degree and then a Ph.D., Innis, unfortunately, found his country and the university system in particular, ill equipped to handle the waves of returning soldiers. Based on this experience, he vowed to help the University of Toronto and other Canadian universities become more prepared for the end of the Second World War. As handbooks to be utilized by veterans, Innis wrote a series of essays that were assembled under the title *Political Economy and the Modern State* published in 1946. He also contributed essays along with C. R. Young and J. E. Dales to *Engineering and Society,* published the same year.

During the war years Innis was also selected to attend the Russian Academy of Sciences 220th anniversary celebration in the Soviet Union. While there, he kept a detailed journal of his experiences and observations. Published years later in 1981 under the title *Innis on Russia,* this account reveals Innis's prescient belief that Westerners had an inadequate understanding of Russia and the ways its people thought.

Innis's experience of writing about Russia was the beginning of a new kind of academic discipline for him to explore. As William Christian writes in the *Dictionary of Literary Biography,* "It was at this time that Innis began to undertake his most innovative work, the research that leads many to credit him with founding the field of communications studies." In 1950 he published *Empire and Communications,* which contains the texts a series of lectures that he had delivered at Oxford on this subject. This was followed by more essays collected in volumes entitled *The Bias of Communication* (1951) and *Changing Concepts of Time* (1952). In these works Innis attempts to articulate the profound influence that communications, in its varying forms, upon western civilization.

At the end of Innis's life, he was mostly concerned with this subject of communications. In the *Dictionary of Literary Biography,* William Christian explains Innis's interest in the topic: "Casting his reflections over all the major civilizations from ancient Egypt to his contemporary world, Innis advanced the hypothesis that the various media of communication influenced the territorial extent and the duration of political organizations." In this way, Innis's interest in communications paralleled his views on staple products. For both areas of study, Innis was intrigued with how these things effect the larger workings, systems, and values of an entire society.

In addition to authoring books, Innis became the chairman of his department at the University of Toronto and then in 1947, became dean of the graduate school. He was active with several societies, doing research and giving speeches for organizations like the Royal Society of Canada and the American Economic History Association. He also translated and edited a number of books on topics that were associated with his areas of study. Upon his death from cancer at the age of fifty-eight, Innis had left a varied and important legacy of scholarship. His staple theory and writings continued to be of interest to Canadian students of politics, economics, and culture well into the 1970s. In 1980, a collection of his notes, sayings, and theories on a range of topics was published under the title *The Idea File of Harold Adams Innis.*

BIOGRAPHICAL/CRITICAL SOURCES:

*BOOKS*

Creighton, Donald, *Harold Adams Innis: Portrait of a Scholar,* University of Toronto Press, 1957.

*Dictionary of Literary Biography,* Volume 88: *Canadian Writers, 1920-1959,* Gale Research (Detroit, MI), 1989.

*Encyclopedia of World Biography,* 2nd edition, Gale Research, 1998.

Havelock, Eric A., *Harold A. Innis: A Memoir,* Harold Innis Foundation, 1982.

Kroker, Arthur, *Technology and the Canadian Mind,* New World Perspectives, 1982.

Melody, William H., Liora Salter, and Paul Weyer, editors, *Culture, Communication, and Dependency: The Tradition of H. A. Innis,* Ablex, 1981.

Neill, Robin, *A New Theory of Value,* University of Toronto Press, 1972.

*PERIODICALS*

*American Economy Review,* March, 1938; March, 1939; September, 1940.

*American Political Science Review,* April, 1938; June, 1940.

*Boston Transcript,* June 29, 1940, p. 2.

*Canadian Forum,* December, 1937; August, 1938.

*Canadian History Review,* December, 1937; March, 1938.

*Canadian Literature,* winter, 1979, pp. 118-130.

*Economist,* October 9, 1937.

*Foreign Affairs,* April, 1938.

*Journal of Politics and Economics,* June, 1938; December, 1940.*

# J

## JACKSON, John W.

*PERSONAL:* Male.

*ADDRESSES: Agent*—c/o Presidio Press, 505-B San Marin Dr., Suite 300, Novato, CA 94945-1340.

*CAREER:* Retired businessman and former curator of the Philadelphia Maritime Museum

*WRITINGS:*

*The Pennsylvania Navy, 1775-1781: The Defense of the Delaware,* Rutgers University Press (New Brunswick, NJ), 1974.
*With the British Army in Philadelphia, 1777-1778.* Presidio Press (San Rafael, CA), 1978.

*SIDELIGHTS:* John W. Jackson, a retired businessman and former curator of the Philadelphia Maritime Museum, shared his historical expertise with readers in two detailed studies: *The Pennsylvania Navy, 1775-1781,* and *With the British Army in Philadelphia, 1777-1778.* In his work on the navy in Pennsylvania, "he adeptly maneuvers the reader through detailed engineering feats. . . . [H]e enumerates the maritime forces comprising rowed galleys, fire boats, and other guard craft; and he enflames our senses with the futile yet heroic deeds of land defenders in Forts Mifflin and Mercer," wrote Benjamin Franklin Cooling in *American Historical Review.* "One hopes that such a book will lead to modern treatment of the other state navies of the Revolution," Cooling added. Several reviewers recommended the work to an audience of history and military specialists. "It is an enormously detailed and heavily documented study, written in a spartan and sometimes plain style," commented William M. Fowler in *William and Mary Quarterly.* "Few people other than the specialist in the military-naval history of the Revolution are apt to read this book." A *Choice* critic suggested that students of the Revolution and of naval history would appreciate this ground-breaking account of the Pennsylvania state navy. "Anyone at all interested in the Revolution should give the book a try."

*With the British Army in Philadelphia,* in which Jackson chronicled a pivotal year in the occupation of Philadelphia by the British, garnered similar reviews. A *Choice* commentator judged the work of particular interest to readers fascinated by the history of Philadelphia, praising the "excellent, often unfamiliar illustrations" and the author's "thorough research" of primary sources. "All in all, Jackson has written an entertaining and useful book," declared Paul David Nelson in a review for *Historian.* "His style is crisp and well paced. His research is copious and comprehensive. . . . His choice of topics for discussion seems inclusive. In addition, he has incorporated a number of maps, an index, and two informative appendixes." Concluded Nelson, "Both the scholar and the general reader will find much to commend in this handsome volume."

*BIOGRAPHICAL/CRITICAL SOURCES:*

*PERIODICALS*

*American Historical Review,* December, 1975, p. 1385.
*Choice,* December, 1974, p. 1538; September, 1979, p. 908.
*Historian,* November, 1980, pp. 140-141.
*William and Mary Quarterly,* April, 1975, pp. 363-364.*

## JACKSON-OPOKU, Sandra

*PERSONAL:* Children: Kimathi Opoku, Adjoa Opoku. *Education:* Attended college; studied with Chinua Achebe and Michael Thelwell.

*ADDRESSES: Home*—Chicago, IL. *Agent*—c/o Ballantine Publishing Group, 201 East 50th St., New York, NY 10022.

*CAREER:* Journalist and writer. Also worked as a lecturer.

*AWARDS, HONORS:* Recipient of awards for her writing.

*WRITINGS:*

*The River Where Blood Is Born* (novel), One World/ Ballantine (New York City), 1997.

Author of poetry and screenplays. Contributor of articles to periodicals, including *Black Enterprise.*

*WORK IN PROGRESS: Tales of Hot Johnny,* a novel; a book for children.

*SIDELIGHTS:* Sandra Jackson-Opoku's novel *The River Where Blood Is Born* was published in 1997. She worked on the book for over twenty years after being inspired by a 1975 trip to Africa. Spanning three hundred years, *The River Where Blood Is Born* tells the stories of a notable African woman and her many female descendants. Some of these descendants become slaves in the United States and on the island of Barbados. Later progeny live in rural areas and in the cities of Chicago, Illinois, London, England, and Montreal, Quebec, Canada. Almost as if she is completing a cycle, a member of one of the later generations returns to Africa to attain spiritual fulfillment and a sense of her history.

Elements of African myths and spirituality accompany the life details of these African and African American women in *The River Where Blood Is Born.* The book features Ananse the spider, a storyteller in African mythology, and dead ancestors worry about and aid their living relatives. Names and symbolism also play a large role in the novel. One of the matriarch's descendents is named Diaspora, representing how Africans were kidnapped from their home continent and brought as slaves to various places in the New World. In addition, all of the women are attracted to water in various forms and by fabrics and needlework.

"The historical Caribbean and Africa come to life in this cleverly constructed but somewhat overwritten tale," wrote a *Publishers Weekly* reviewer. *Booklist* contributor Alice Joyce hailed *The River Where Blood Is Born* as "an expansive tale," adding that Jackson-Opoku chronicles "a richly lyrical panoply of lives." Ellen Flexman, discussing the novel in the *Library Journal,* noted how the author "molds many diverse voices into a powerful chorus" to create "a magical family saga."

*BIOGRAPHICAL/CRITICAL SOURCES:*

*PERIODICALS*

*Booklist,* September 1, 1997, p. 58.
*Library Journal,* August, 1997, p. 130.
*Publishers Weekly,* July 7, 1997, pp. 48-49.

*OTHER*

*Random House.com,* http://www.randomhouse.com/ BB/readerscircle/jackson-opoku/guidep.html (November 4, 1999).*

\*     \*     \*

## JACOB, Naomi (Ellington)   1884(?)-1964 ## (Ellington Gray)

*PERSONAL:* Born July 8, 1884 (some sources say 1889), in Ripon, Yorkshire, England; daughter of Nina Ellington Collinson (a novelist under the name Nina Abbott); died August 26, 1964, in Sirmione, Italy. *Politics:* Conservative Socialist; Labour Party; pacifist. *Religion:* Catholic. *Avocational interests:* Italian opera, antiques.

*CAREER:* Teacher in North of England, 1899-1902; vaudevillian and secretary to vaudevillians Marguerite Broadfoote and Eva Moore, 1902-13; hospitalized for consumption, 1919-20; actress, 1920-47; novelist, 1925-64. *Military service:* Officer in the Women's Legion (superintendent at munitions factory); worked for the Entertainments National Service Association.

*MEMBER:* Actresses Franchise League, Women's Emergency Corps, Three Arts Employment Fund.

*WRITINGS:*

*Jacob Ussher,* Butterworth (London), 1925.
*Rock and Sand,* Butterworth, 1926.

*Power,* Butterworth, 1927.

*The Plough,* Butterworth, 1928.

(Under pseudonym Ellington Gray) *Saffroned Bride-sails,* Butterworth, 1928.

*"That Wild Lie,"* Hutchinson (London), 1930.

*Roots,* Hutchinson, 1931.

*"Seen Unknown . . . ,"* Hutchinson, 1931.

*Props,* Hutchinson, 1932.

*Young Emmanuel,* Hutchinson, 1932.

*A Novel, Groping,* Hutchinson, 1933.

*Poor Straws!,* Hutchinson, 1933.

*Me—a Chronicle about Other People,* Hutchinson, 1933.

*Four Generations,* Macmillan (New York City), 1934.

*The Loaded Stick,* Hutchinson, 1934; Macmillan, 1935.

*"Honour Come Back,"* Macmillan, 1935.

*Me—in the Kitchen,* Hutchinson, 1935.

*"Our Marie": Marie Lloyd: A Biography,* Hutchinson, 1936.

*Barren Metal,* Macmillan, 1936.

*The Founder of the House,* Macmillan, 1936.

*Time Piece,* Hutchinson, 1936.

*Me—Again,* Hutchinson, 1937.

*Fade Out,* Macmillan, 1937.

*The Lenient God,* Hutchinson, 1937, Macmillan, 1938.

*No Easy Way,* Hutchinson, 1938.

*Straws in Amber,* Hutchinson, 1938, Macmillan, 1939.

*More about Me,* Hutchinson, 1939.

*Full Meridian,* Hutchinson, 1939; Macmillan, 1940.

*This Porcelain Clay,* Macmillan, 1939.

*Me—in War-time* Hutchinson, 1940.

*Sally Scarth,* Hutchinson, 1940.

*They Left the Land,* Macmillan, 1940.

*The Cap of Youth,* Macmillan, 1941.

*Under New Management,* Hutchinson, 1941.

*Leopards and Spots,* Hutchinson, 1942.

*Private Gollantz,* Hutchinson, 1943.

*White Wool,* Hutchinson, 1943.

*Me and the Mediterranean,* Hutchinson, 1945.

*Susan Crowther,* Hutchinson, 1945.

*Me—over There,* Hutchinson, 1947.

*Honour's a Mistress,* Hutchinson, 1947.

*A Passage Perilous,* Hutchinson, 1947.

(Contributor) jacob and James C. Robertson, *Opera in Italy,* Hutchinson, 1948.

*Gollantz: London, Paris, Milan,* Hutchinson, 1948.

*Mary of Delight,* Hutchinson, 1949.

*Me and Mine (You and Yours),* preface by W. H. Elliott, Hutchinson, 1949.

*Me—Looking Back,* foreword by Bransby Williams, Hutchinson, 1950.

*The Heart of the House,* Hutchinson, 1951.

*Robert, Nana, and Me: A Family Chronicle,* Hutchinson, 1952.

*The Gollantz Saga* (contains *The Founder of the House, "That Wild Lie,"* and *Young Emmanuel*), 2 volumes, Hutchinson, 1952-53.

*Just about Us,* Hutchinson, 1953.

*The Morning Will Come,* Hutchinson, 1953.

*Me—Likes and Dislikes,* Hutchinson, 1954.

*Antonia,* Hutchinson, 1954.

*Second Harvest,* Hutchinson, 1954.

*The Irish Boy: A Romantic Biography,* Hutchinson, 1955.

*Prince China, by Himself but Dictated to Naomi Jacob,* Hutchinson, 1955.

*Tales of the Broad Acres: Comprising Sally Scarth, The Loaded Stick, Roots,* Hutchinson, 1955.

*Wind on the Heath,* Hutchinson, 1956.

*Me—Yesterday and To-day,* Hutchinson, 1957.

*Late Lark Singing,* Hutchinson, 1957.

*Gollantz and Partners,* Hutchinson, 1958.

*What's to Come,* Hutchinson, 1958.

*Search for a Background,* Hutchinson, 1960.

*Three Men and Jennie,* Hutchinson, 1960.

*Strange Beginning,* Hale, 1961.

*Great Black Oxen,* Hale, 1962.

*Yolanda,* Hale, 1963.

*Me—and the Swans,* Kimber (London), 1963.

*Me—and the Stags,* Kimber, 1964.

*Me—Thinking Things Over,* Kimber, 1964.

*Long Shadows,* Hale, 1964.

*Flavia,* Hale, 1965.

*The Gollantz Saga* (includes *The Founder of the House, "That Wild Lie," Young Emmanuel, Four Generations, Private Gollantz, Gollantz: London, Paris, Milan,* and *Gollantz and Partners*) 7 volumes, New American Library (New York City), 1973-74.

*SIDELIGHTS:* Naomi Jacob was best known for her light, romantic writing and her flamboyant, laughing lifestyle. As an actress and writer, Jacob made a small showing, but as an entertainer and personality she loomed large. Her most famous and readable books, unsurprisingly for such a personage, are her *Me* books, autobiographical musings in an intimate, informal mood.

Jacob was born on July 8, 1884 (or 1889) in Ripon, Yorkshire. Jacob's mother, Nina Ellington Collinson, wrote novels under the pen name "Nina Abbott." Jacob said little about her father, however, causing some to speculate that he may have been as brutal as the men in her fiction. Nevertheless, as Michael Jasper hypothesized in *Dictionary of Literary Biography:* "From her father's side of the family she obtained the pride in the Jewish people and hatred for anti-Semitism and fascism that would form the second major theme of her fiction and would also thread through her many *Me* volumes."

Indeed, some of her most successful novels, the seven novels chronicling the Gollantz family, focus specifically on the experience of Jews in England.

This engagement with her Jewish heritage, however, seems to have developed after she enjoyed a relatively comfortable, Anglican childhood. Despite her delight in the simple pleasures of polished kitchenware, however, Jacob seems to have felt somewhat persecuted in her schools; though she attended several private schools in Yorkshire, Jacob recalls only feeling unwanted in classes. As Jasper comments: "Jacob was a large, gawky, and masculine child, and her teachers and classmates seem to have been put off by her appearance and her assertive, sometimes acerbic, 'mannish' personality."

Jacob's education was sufficient, however, to allow her to teach at the age of fifteen, after what she calls "family reverses." During this period, Jacob both performed and acted as secretary to Marguerite Broadfoote; she converted to Catholicism; and she also became politically active, fighting for women's suffrage and joining the Labour Party. With these artistic and political skills in place, Jacob was poised to join in the war effort in full force. She enlisted in the Women's Emergency Corps (for which she acted as superintendent for a munitions factory), and soon developed the Three Arts Employment Fund, which provided war work for artists.

Jacob's career began in earnest after her work in the war effort brought her notoriety among artists in London. As Jasper explained: "it is fair to say that it is because of her wartime activities in the Entertainments National Service Association (ENSA) rather than for her novels that her name is recognized today . . . It was in ENSA that Jacob brokered a moderate literary and theatrical standing into full membership in the British cult of personality. Cropping her hair into a near crewcut and adopting what would become her signatory affectation, a monocle, she became famous both at home and abroad for her flamboyantly masculine appearance and aggressive behavior." While in the thick of this "cult of personality," Jacob published her first novel, *Jacob Ussher* (1925), and thereafter produced works at an extraordinary rate.

When Jacob began writing, she produced a book or two every year until she died. In 1930, Jacob moved to Sirmione, Italy where she lived for the rest of her life. Just prior to this move, Jacob had begun an intimate correspondence with Radclyffe Hall, whose novel about lesbian identity seems to have encouraged Jacob to move

to the Mediterranean. Jasper suggested, "Freed from the restrictive social atmosphere of England, Jacob openly displayed her sexual identity. She adopted the nickname of Mike or Mickie (Hall was known as John) and began to wear men's suits and cut her hair in a short, masculine style." Nevertheless, as Jasper later explained, "Jacob never wrote openly about lesbianism either in her novels or in her memoirs." Her writing tends, instead, to share fleeting impressions with her readers, gleefully or fiercely relating stories about her world.

While critics generally allow that Jacob's novels are stylistically average, she engages through her loving delineation of character. A *Christian Science Monitor* contributor, describing her work, remarked, "Her character drawing is deft and accurate—not flattering, but warm and fair. She writes a sound English novel, in the realistic tradition." Despite her novels' flaws, however, Jacob won a cheering audience for herself mainly through force of her vigorous, warm personality. Though most of her novels follow the same plot—woman is married, loses husband, finds soul mate afterward—they are enlivened by Jacob's obvious affection for human bravery and human foibles. The thrust of Jacob's warm, flamboyant, familiar, loving personality enlisted legions of fans, for whom her books were, certainly, "very well worth while." She died in 1964.

*BIOGRAPHICAL/CRITICAL SOURCES:*

*BOOKS*

*Dictionary of Literary Biography,* Volume 191: *British Novelists between the Wars,* Gale (Detroit, MI), 1998.
*Twentieth-Century Romance and Historical Writers,* St. James Press (Detroit, MI), 1994.

*PERIODICALS*

*Christian Science Monitor,* August 6, 1935.*

\*      \*      \*

**JAKOBER, Marie   1941-**

*PERSONAL:* Born in 1941.

*ADDRESSES: Agent*—c/o Gullveig Books, Calgary, Alberta, Canada; New Star Books Ltd., 2504 York Ave., Vancouver, British Columbia V6K 1E3, Canada.

*CAREER:* Writer.

*WRITINGS:*

*The Mind Gods: A Novel of the Future,* Macmillan (Toronto), 1976.
*Sandinista: A Novel of Nicaragua,* New Star Books (Vancouver), 1985.
*A People in Arms,* New Star Books, 1990.
*High Kamilan,* Gullveig Books (Calgary, Alberta, Canada), 1993.

*SIDELIGHTS:* The writing career of Marie Jakober underwent a change in the late 1970s. Jakober's first novel, *The Mind Gods,* is a story with science-fiction overtones. Published in 1976, the book follows the demise of Utopia and fleshes out the characters who bring about Utopia's fall. According to T. A. Shippey of the *Times Literary Supplement* the book contains "a well articulated personal philosophy." In 1982 and 1983, Jakober, a Canadian, traveled to Nicaragua to witness firsthand the political upheaval that was occurring there. The result of these visits was *Sandinista: A Novel of Nicaragua,* a radical departure from the fantasy style of Jakober's first published work. Although the plots and characters are fiction, the essential topic of the novel is the reality of revolution—the last months of the oppressive, oligarchical regime of Nicaraguan President Anastasio Somoza.

Jakober tells the story of Nicaragua's civil war through composite characters. The rich Zelaya family is a family that has benefited from the Somoza presidency. A poor revolutionary, Daniel Chillan, stands in as one of the losers in Somoza's regime. Jadine, an innocent Canadian traveler, describes the action as Daniel woos Clariz, the wealthy family's daughter. To the horror of the Zelaya family, Daniel eventually converts Clariz to the Sandinistas and the cause of political revolution. Writing for *Queen's Quarterly,* reviewer Larry Towell calls *Sandinista* "a tightly systematic novel" that is "poetic and thematically accurate."

Jakober continued the story of Nicaragua's revolution with *A People in Arms,* published in 1990. The main themes of the novel are the political messages contained in the words and deeds of the characters. Rich persons in Nicaragua, for example, welcome the influences of the United States, view poor persons as constitutionally passive and mindless, and consider political uprisings to be the product of degenerates. According to *Canadian Literature* reviewer Sue Thomas, Jakober succeeds in *A People in Arms* when she presents the differences between the rich and poor in Nicaragua and the way that power and "unreflective machismo are used to assert and bolster the semiotic reality of the rich."

*BIOGRAPHICAL/CRITICAL SOURCES:*

BOOKS

*Science Fiction & Fantasy Literature, 1975-1991,* Gale Research (Detroit, MI), 1992.

*PERIODICALS*

*Canadian Literature,* spring/summer, 1990, pp. 378-80.
*Queen's Quarterly,* autumn, 1987, pp. 696-98.
*Quill & Quire,* December, 1986, pp. 37, 39.
*Times Literary Supplement,* July 30, 1976, p. 951.*

\*          \*          \*

**JAMES, Frank**
   **See LALA, Frank James John, Jr.**

\*          \*          \*

**JAMIESON, Bill**

*PERSONAL: Education:* Manchester University, graduated with a degree in economics.

*ADDRESSES: Agent*—c/o Gerald Duckworth & Co. Ltd., 61 Friltstr, London, W1B 5TA, England.

*CAREER:* Economics editor for the *Sunday Telegraph.* Has worked as a business journalist for twenty-five years. Member of the Economics Research Council.

*MEMBER:* Royal Society of Arts, Manufacturers, and Commerce (fellow).

*WRITINGS:*

*Goldstrike! The Oppenheimer Empire in Crisis,* Hutchinson Business Books, 1990.
*Britain beyond Europe,* Duckworth (London), 1994.
*The Bemused Investor's Guide to Company Accounts,* Shoal Bay Press (Christchurch, New Zealand), 1997.
*UBS: Guide to Emerging Markets,* Books Britain, 1997.
*The Illustrated Guide to the British Economy,* Duckworth, 1997.
(Editor with Helen Szamuely) *A "Coming Home" or Poisoned Chalice,* Centre for Research into Postcommunist Economies (London), 1998.

Contributor to periodicals, including *Public Management* and *Australian Financial Review*.

*SIDELIGHTS:* Bill Jamieson is an editor with the *Sunday Telegraph* and author of articles and books about economics and politics in Great Britain and Europe. In *Goldstrike! The Oppenheimer Empire in Crisis* Jamieson writes about the 1988-89 takeover fight between Minorca and Consolidated Gold Fields. He said the winners were consultants, the media, and Hanson, which eventually acquired Consolidated Gold. An *Economist* reviewer called it a "bitter struggle between Harry Oppenheimer's Anglo American Corporation and Consolidated Gold Fields. . . . Mr. Jamieson . . . has a journalist's nose for the details of the contested bid. He is less strong, indeed rather superficial, when he comes to the final part of his book, an analysis of the challenges facing the Oppenheimer empire in the 1990s."

In reviewing *Britain Beyond Europe* in the *New Statesman* Stephen Howe noted the trend toward "the growth of political Europhilia," that included "a genuine idealism about prospects of a federal European entity that would be culturally and emotionally as well as economically integrated. . . . During the 1990s, that idealism has dwindled and become more than a little defensive. Again, this reversal has had several causes, not least the shock of revived, often violent nationalist movements across the continent. . . . It rests too . . . on a widespread feeling that almost anything is preferable to the present structures of the United Kingdom." Howe said the value of Jamieson's outrage over national decline is in reminding readers "just how passionate . . . are the emotions that drive hardline Euroscepticism."

In *A "Coming Home" or Poisoned Chalice* Jamieson and Helen Szamuely discuss the establishment of the European Monetary Union's (EMU) global-friendly fixed exchange rate system. Alan S. Milward wrote in the *Times Literary Supplement* that Jamieson and Szamuely feel "the EU (European Union) is an economic disaster, which EMU will make more disastrous." Milward noted the slow growth of the EU's gross national product (GNP) and forecasted that if trends continue, the Far East will overtake European incomes. "For Szamuely and Jamieson, enlargement of the EU will eliminate all chance of the faster income growth which the next round of candidates from the Easter Bloc, Poland, the Czech Republic, Hungary, and Slovenia, are seeking. They should stay out of 'a regime almost as oppressive and dysfunctional as the one from which the beggared Central and East European countries have only recently escaped.' "

Milward stated that the question is whether the GNPs of the richer countries would be slowed to preserve the EMU "and whether the EU will be extended, with the promise of monetary union, into the Eastern Bloc. . . . An EMU which imposes a ceiling on growth and employment will lead, probably, to a breakout by a least one country, but only after longer and more bitter social tensions than exist at present." Milward said that Szamuely and Jamieson predict that by then, the Eastern Bloc members "will be as far behind the present member states as they are now. Membership will eliminate the competitive advantage of their cheap, skilled industrial labour. Far from winning a market for their agricultural products, they will be eating subsidized German and French food exports."

*BIOGRAPHICAL/CRITICAL SOURCES:*

*PERIODICALS*

*Economist,* April 28, 1990, p. 95.
*New Statesman,* June 10, 1994, p. 36.
*Times Literary Supplement,* September 25, 1998.*

\*          \*          \*

**JANOWITZ, Anne F.**

*PERSONAL: Education:* Received doctorate.

*ADDRESSES: Office*—c/o Humanities Research Centre, University of Warwick, Coventry CV4 7AL England.

*CAREER:* English instructor at the University of Warwick; World Education Group, director of Humanities Research Centre.

*WRITINGS:*

(Editor with Nancy J. Peters) *UnAmerican Activities: The Campaign against the Underground Press,* City Lights Books (San Francisco, CA), 1981.
*England's Ruins: Poetic Purpose and the National Landscape,* Blackwell (Cambridge, MA), 1990.
*Lyric and Labour in the Romantic Tradition,* Cambridge University Press (New York City), 1998.
(Editor) *Romanticism and Gender,* Boydell and Brew (Woodbridge, England), 1998.

*SIDELIGHTS:* Anne F. Janowitz, a professor at the University of Warwick, is the author of a couple of literary studies and the editor of several others. Her *England's Ruins: Poetic Purpose and the National Landscape* is a "rewarding study that traces the imaginative and ideological significances of the ruin motif through the thematic and structural manifestations of ruins in English poetry," according to Nicholas Roe in the *Review of English Studies.*

Writing in *Modern Language Review,* David Worrall noted that "Janowitz's cultural history is derived from Martin Wiener, Benedict Anderson, and Ernest Gellner, shot through with highly eclectic literary criticism and theory." In her analysis, Janowitz discusses Old English poetry, modern poetry, the human as a ruin, and the ruinous state of inner-city London. In the *Times Literary Supplement,* John Barrell questioned Janowitz's choice of works to be discussed. "The decision to include these various objects in a genre based on an aesthetics of incompletion is in some cases triumphantly justified, in others more or less unexplained, and the exclusions can be as arbitrary as the inclusions." Nevertheless, Barrell deemed the work "remarkable," adding that the chapter on Wordsworth "is one of the best things written on his politics." Asserting that Janowitz "persuasively" argued her thesis, Worrall concluded that *England's Ruins* is extremely accomplished: dismayingly broad minded, witheringly polished, enviably up-to-date, and steadfast to its strikingly coherent argument."

## BIOGRAPHICAL/CRITICAL SOURCES:

### PERIODICALS

*CoEvolution Quarterly,* winter, 1981, p. 103.
*Library Journal,* December 1, 1981, p. 2310.
*Modern Language Review,* July, 1992, pp. 709-710.
*Review of English Studies,* May, 1992, pp. 289-290.
*Times Literary Supplement,* September 28, 1990, p. 1043; September 25, 1998, p. 33.

### OTHER

*Humanities Research Centre,* http://www.weg.com.tw/england/w99/index-10.htm (November 17, 1999).*

\*    \*    \*

## JANVIER, Thomas A(llibone)  1849-1913
### (Ivory Black)

*PERSONAL:* Born July 16, 1849, in Philadelphia, PA; died June 18, 1913, in New York, NY; buried in Moorestown, NJ; son of Frances de Haes (a poet) and Emma (a writer of children's stories) Janvier; married Catherine Ann Drinker (a painter and author), 1878. *Education:* Attended common school.

*CAREER:* Worked as journalist for *Philadelphia Times, Evening Bulletin,* and the *Press,* 1871-80; traveled as journalist, 1881-84; novelist and short story writer. Also worked briefly in business.

*MEMBER:* Society of the Felibrige (honorary member).

*WRITINGS:*

*Color Studies,* Scribners (New York City), 1885, enlarged edition published as *Color Studies and a Mexican Campaign,* Scribners, 1891.
*The Mexican Guide,* Scribners, 1886.
*The Aztec Treasure-House: A Romance of Contemporaneous Antiquity,* Harper (New York City), 1890.
*Stories of Old New Spain,* Appleton (New York City), 1891.
*The Uncle of an Angel and Other Stories,* Harper, 1891.
*The Armies of To-Day: A Description of the Armies of the Leading Nations at the Present Time,* Harper, 1893.
*An Embassy to Provence,* Century (New York City), 1893.
*The Women's Conquest of New-York. Being an Account of the Rise and Progress of the Women's Rights Movement . . . By a Member of the Committee of Safety of 1908,* Harper, 1894.
*In Old New York,* Harper, 1894.
*Saint Antonio of the Gardens,* with Provencal translation by Mary Girard, Roumanille (Avignon), 1895.
*In the Sargasso Sea,* Harper, 1898.
*The Passing of Thomas; In the St. Peter's Set; At the Grand Hotel du Paadis; The Fish of Monsieur Quissard; Le Bon Oncle d'Amerique; Five Stories,* Harper, 1900.
*In Great Waters: Four Stories,* Harper, 1901.
*The Christmas Kalends of Provence and Some Other Provencal Festivals,* Harper, 1902.
*The Dutch Founding of New York,* Harper, 1903.
*Santa Fe's Partner: Being Some Memorials of Events in a New-Mexican Track-End Town,* Harper, 1907.
*Henry Hudson, a Brief Statement of His Aims and His Achievements,* Harper, 1909.
*Legends of the City of Mexico,* Harper, 1910.
*From the South of France: The Roses of Monsieur Alphonse, The Poodle of Monsieur Gaillard, The Recrudescence of Madame Vic, Madame Jolicoeur's Cat, A Consolate Giantess,* Harper, 1912.

*At the Casa Napoleon,* Harper, 1914.

Also contributor to *Harper's Magazine.* Janvier's papers are housed in a collection by the Clifton Waller Barrett Library at the University of Virginia.

*SIDELIGHTS:* American Thomas A. Janvier is best known for his regional fiction that portrays the lives of New Yorkers of the nineteenth century, especially those of artists in Greenwich Village. Author of nonfiction, a novel, and short stories, Janvier portrayed other settings in his work as well, including Mexico and the south of France, and has been praised for his use of dialect and descriptive writing. *Dictionary of Literary Biography*'s Layne Neeper opines, "Janvier's regionalist preoccupations with place, manners and dialect impart to his work some small measure of historical significance in reflecting certain late-nineteenth-century tendencies in American fiction."

Janvier was born to writers: his father, Frances de Haes, wrote poetry and his mother, Emma, children's stories. To begin his own writing pursuits, Janvier wrote journalism for various periodicals and eventually parlayed his writing into books of nonfiction and fiction. Some of his first pieces of fiction—initially appearing in magazines under the pseudonym Ivory Black—were compiled into 1885's *Color Studies.* This volume was Janvier's first published book and Neeper calls it "his most enduring work." The stories that make up *Color Studies* focus mainly on artisans of Greenwich Village. In "Roberson's Medium," Violet Carmine is an independent young girl from Mexico who is in New York visiting her cousin Mangan Brown. During her visit, she is determined to be free of social protocols befitting women of her time. This includes engaging in an unescorted escapade with a young artist named Rowney Mauve, who becomes enamored with Violet. Rowney, however, is not without a competitor for Violet's affection. Roberson, a fellow artist, reveals his tender feelings for Violet to Rowney. Thus, the competition for Violet ensues. Rowney, to show his place in Violet's affections, plans an event that has him kissing Violet in front of Roberson, who in turn makes the kiss known to others, hoping to sully Violet's reputation. Roberson's plan doesn't work, however. Upon hearing of the disclosure of the kiss, Rowney proposes to Violet and, with her father's approval, the two are wed. Neeper cites this story as "a more interesting story in the . . . collection."

Janvier's next work would move from New York to Mexico. *The Mexican Guide,* which was published in 1886, is a guidebook based on his extensive travels through Mexico. *The Aztec Treasure-House: A Romance of Contemporaneous Antiquity* and *Stories of Old New Spain* both continue the Mexican theme and appeared in 1890 and 1891 respectively. Following the early Mexican titles, Janvier produced *The Uncle of an Angel and Other Stories.* The title story features eighteen-year-old Dorothy, an insolent teenager who takes control of her uncle's home and travel plans.

After *The Uncle of an Angel and Other Stories,* Janvier produced nonfiction on various topics, such as the army, the south of France, the women's movement, and, once again, New York. His next work of fiction was his sea adventure novel, *In the Sargasso Sea.* In this tale, the protagonist, Roger Stetworth, boards a ship hoping for passage to Africa. However, he gets more than he anticipated. At sea, the captain and the first-mate reveal they are slavers and they want Stetworth to join their efforts. When he refuses, Stetworth is beaten and thrown overboard. He survives and is rescued by another ship that soon meets its demise in a storm. Janvier details much of Stetworth's time aboard abandoned ships in the Sargasso Sea as the protagonist explores his surroundings. During his exploration, Stetworth discovers valuables, such as gold and gems. After procuring some jewels, Stetworth builds a suitable craft and leaves the graveyard of ships and is soon rescued.

Following his novel, Janvier returned to writing short stories and nonfiction. He produced *The Passing of Thomas; In the St. Peter's Set; At the Grand Hotel du Paadis; The Fish of Monsieur Quissard; Le Bon Oncle d'Amerique; Five Stories* in 1900, and *In Great Waters: Four Stories* in 1901. He then published more books on Provence, the South of France, and New York, as well as the American Southwest and Mexico. He also penned a volume about English navigator and explorer Henry Hudson. Janvier ended his literary career with a final compilation of stories, *At the Casa Napoleon,* which centers on the lives of recent immigrants to America who are adjusting to their New York setting. According to Neeper, "Janvier's reputation has not withstood the passing of time," but the writer does acknowledge he was "one of the dozens of regionalist writers who flourished at the end of the nineteenth century."

*BIOGRAPHICAL/CRITICAL SOURCES:*

*BOOKS*

*Benet's Reader's Encyclopedia of American Literature,* 1st edition, HarperCollins, 1991.
*Dictionary of Literary Biography,* Volume 202: *Nineteenth-Century American Fiction Writers,* Gale Research (Detroit, MI), 1999.

*Oxford Companion to American Literature,* sixth edition, Oxford University Press, 1995.*

\*    \*    \*

### JENKINS, Elizabeth B.

*PERSONAL: Education:* Earned a doctorate in clinical psychology.

*ADDRESSES: Agent*—c/o Putnam Berkley Publishing Group, 200 Madison Ave., New York, NY 10016.

*CAREER:* Has worked as a family counselor in the San Francisco area.

*WRITINGS:*

*Initiation: A Woman's Spiritual Adventure in the Heart of the Andes* (autobiography), Putnam (New York City), 1997.

*SIDELIGHTS:* During the 1980s, Elizabeth B. Jenkins was working as a family counselor in San Francisco, California, and finishing up her doctorate in psychology when she decided to take a break from these activities by traveling to the Peruvian Andes. She sojourned to the region of Cuzco, and the mountain of Machu Picchu, where she encountered Peru's Q'ero people. In the words of a *Publishers Weekly* critic, the Q'ero are "the keepers of Incan mysticism." Jenkins experienced this mysticism, and made a pilgrimage to various Incan temples during her visit. The effects upon her were so profound that she decided to sell most of her possessions and move from San Francisco to Peru, though she did return to the city to finish her degree.

Jenkins wrote about her encounters with the Q'ero and her mystic experiences in her first book, 1997's *Initiation: A Woman's Spiritual Adventure in the Heart of the Andes.* In *Initiation,* Jenkins describes seeing the Q'ero mountain spirits called *apus,* which look like condors with the heads of human beings. She also provides readers with dialogues which took place between herself and her Q'ero guides, verbal depictions of the beautiful mountain landscapes, and explanations about the animist beliefs of the Q'eros—whose tenents include both the basic unity of the natural world and the notion that humanity as a whole entered in 1993 an auspicious period for spiritual development which is scheduled to end in 2012. Jenkins also frankly discusses the way she

needed to put aside some of her scientific and scholarly training in order to participate in the Q'ero's mysticism.

Many reviewers of *Initiation* have pointed out, however, that Jenkins' scholarly training has shown through in her writing, and most have seen this as a positive enhancement of the book's mystic subject matter. "She employs her rationalist, academic background to evaluate her paranormal experiences," assured a reviewer for *Publishers Weekly,* who felt that this would render readers unable to doubt her sincerity. The critic went on to affirm "the value of the teachings she transmits." Patricia Monaghan, discussing *Initiation* in *Booklist,* put forth the opinion that Jenkins was perhaps the most worthy of many contenders for the "position of female Carlos Castenada" (Castenada having authored many accounts during the 1970s of his mystical experiences with Native American Yaqui shaman Don Juan), and was especially favorable when comparing Jenkins with another New Age author of similar subject matter, Lynn V. Andrews. Monaghan, who felt that Andrews' various tales of her adventures lacked absolute credibility, declared that Jenkins' account "has the ring of truth and is crafted in compelling prose." Gail Wood, writing in the *Library Journal,* expressed positive opinions about *Initiation* as well. This critic cited the "honor and respect" with which Jenkins portrays the culture and beliefs of her Q'ero acquaintances, and hailed her book as "a fine addition to the growing genre exploring indigenous spirituality."

*BIOGRAPHICAL/CRITICAL SOURCES:*

PERIODICALS

*Booklist,* September 1, 1997, p. 10.
*Library Journal,* September 1, 1997, pp. 185-186.
*Publishers Weekly,* August 18, 1997, p. 82.*

\*    \*    \*

### JENNINGS, John M(ark) 1962-

*PERSONAL:* Born November 26, 1962, in Philadelphia, PA; son of Thomas R. and Elizabeth A. (Safko) Jennings; married Kayoko Hatanaka, January 6, 1989; children: Thomas Katsumi, James Katsuya. *Education:* Pennsylvania State University, B.A., 1985; University of Hawaii, Manoa, M.A., 1988, Ph.D., 1995. *Avocational interests:* Reading, surf fishing, Kendo.

*ADDRESSES: Home*—3839 Point of the Rocks Dr., Colorado Springs, CO 80918. *Office*—Department of

History, United States Air Force Academy, 2354 Fairchild Dr., Suite 6F37, Colorado Springs, CO 80840. *E-mail*—JenningsJM@aol.com.

*CAREER:* Suburban Publications, Inc., Wayne, PA, reporter and film reviewer, 1985-86; Sophia University, Tokyo, Japan, visiting researcher, 1992-95; Old Dominion University, Norfolk, VA, assistant professor, 1995-96; United States Air Force Academy, Colorado Springs, CO, assistant professor, 1997—.

*MEMBER:* Association for Asian Studies, Society for Historians of American Foreign Relations, Rocky Mountain World History Association (member of the steering committee, 1997—).

*WRITINGS:*

*The Opium Empire: Japanese Imperialism and Drug Trafficking in Asia, 1895-1945* (history), Praeger (Westport, CT), 1997.

*WORK IN PROGRESS:* An English translation of the Russian memoirs of Grigorii Semenov, an anti-Bolshevik leader in the Russian Civil War; researching higher education and ideology in Manchuria under Japanese rule, 1932-45.

*SIDELIGHTS:* John M. Jennings is an historian and an assistant professor at the United States Air Force Academy. His book *The Opium Empire: Japanese Imperialism and Drug Trafficking in Asia, 1895-1945* traces the history of the drug opium in relation to Japan's rise to power. Reviewing the book in the *American Historical Review,* Michael A. Barnhart wrote that *The Opium Empire* "sheds much light on a neglected aspect of imperial Japan's overseas endeavors."

Jennings writes that Japan's Meiji leaders of the late 1800s and early 1900s established a government monopoly to distribute opium for medicinal uses only. Japan then stopped both producing the drug domestically and importing it. When Japan acquired the island of Taiwan and 200,000 addicts living there, Japanese officials started registering opium users and giving them the drug through the government monopoly. Japan hoped this would curtail and eventually eliminate opium use. Yet the numbers of addicts did not significantly decrease. Japan controlled the production and distribution of opium throughout its colonies, overseeing opium production in Korea after World War I and sending the drug to such places as Taiwan and Manchuria. Despite the government monopoly, the opium trade proved lucrative for some. Jennings argues that the decline of Japan's empire following a war with China and its involvement in World War II parallels Japan's diminishing role in the opium trade.

In his *American Historical Review* discussion of *The Opium Empire,* Michael A. Barnhart commented: "Jennings's story is often colorful and always fascinating. It is to his credit that he has written it from hard-to-find sources. His reluctance to be bolder in his judgements and his refusal to be more forceful in advocating his own hypothesis of the dominance of market forces are the only, minor weaknesses." While *Choice* contributor J. C. Perry observed that *The Opium Empire* may interest specialists more than the general reader, the reviewer noted that the work "is a product of impressively diligent scholarship. It is well organized, succinct, and soundly reasoned." Discussing *The Opium Empire* in *Pacific Affairs,* Joyce A. Madancy concluded: "Jennings's work substantially expands our knowledge of the complexity of Japan's 'Opium Empire,' particularly with regards to the workings of Japan's opium monopolies in Taiwan, Korea, and Manchukuo [Manchuria], and his concise and cogently written volume will be extremely useful for students and scholars interested in untangling the web of complicity in the East Asian opium trade."

*BIOGRAPHICAL/CRITICAL SOURCES:*

*PERIODICALS*

*American Historical Review,* October, 1998, pp. 1299-1300.
*Choice,* November, 1997, p. 541.
*Pacific Affairs,* fall, 1998, pp. 425-426.
*Reference & Research Book News,* August, 1997, p. 101.

\*　\*　\*

**JOHNSON, Helene   1907-**
**(Helene Johnson Hubbell)**

*PERSONAL:* Born July 7, 1907, in Boston, MA; married William Hubbell in 1934; children: one daughter. *Education:* Attended Boston University.

*CAREER:* Writer, c. 1927—. Member of staff of *Consumer Reports.*

*MEMBER:* Fellowship of Reconciliation, Saturday Evening Quill Club of Boston.

*AWARDS, HONORS:* Short story first prize from *Boston Chronicle;* honorable mention for "Trees at Night" in *Opportunity*'s first literary contest; honorable mention for poems "Fulfillment," "Magalu," and "The Road" in *Opportunity*'s second contest; Holstein Poetry Section, Second Prize, for "Summer Matures," Fourth Prize for "Sonnet to a Negro in Harlem."

*WRITINGS:*

(Contributor) *Caroling Dusk: An Anthology of Verse by Negro Poets,* edited by Countee Cullen, Harper & Row (New York City), 1927.

(Contributor) *The Book of American Negro Poetry,* revised edition, edited by James Weldon Johnson, Harcourt, Brace (New York City), 1931.

(Contributor) *The Poetry of the Negro 1746-1970,* edited by Langston Hughes and Arna Bontemps, Anchor/Doubleday (Garden City, NY), 1970.

*SIDELIGHTS:* Helene Johnson is best known for the poems she published in the 1920s and 1930s. One of the youngest and most promising poets of the Harlem Renaissance movement, Johnson seems to have been a modest and shy woman who allowed little of her personal life to be made public. Following her marriage to William Hubbell in 1934, Johnson vanished from the public sphere almost entirely, preferring to raise her daughter in a quiet way. Johnson's early work remains of interest to those investigating the Harlem Renaissance, however; as Lorraine Elena Roses and Ruth Elizabeth Randolph explain in *Harlem and Beyond,* "Johnson's verse captures the concern and excitement inherent in the [Harlem Renaissance] movement."

Johnson was born on July 7, 1907, and was schooled in Boston. She attended Boston University briefly, but left Boston in 1926 to join the cultural movements in Harlem. By that time, Johnson had already won awards for her poetic work; in 1925 she won first prize in a short story contest at the *Boston Chronicle* and had won honorable mention in an *Opportunity* magazine contest, for her first published poem, "Trees at Night." By 1926, Johnson again won honorable mention in the *Opportunity* contest for three of her poems: "Fulfillment," "Magalu," and "The Road." William Stanley Braithwaite reprinted two of these poems in his 1926 *Anthology of Magazine Verse,* remarking that Johnson's early work showed "the lyrical sincerity and insight of her generation." Critic Charles S. Johnson said of the poem "Fulfillment": "Helene Johnson has a lyric penetration which belies her years, and a rich and impetuous power." Raymond R. Patterson, writing for the *Dictionary of Literary Biography,* explains: " 'Fulfillment' is

a Whitmanesque celebration of life and its varied experiences, ranging from climbing 'a hill that hungers for the sky' to riding a crowded trolley car, 'Squeezed next to a patent-leather Negro dreaming/ Of a wrinkled river and a minnow net.' Yet like many of her poems, 'Fulfillment,' perhaps influenced by her interest in Shelley and her romanticism, is based on a paradox that is given focus in the concluding lines: 'Ah, Life, let your stabbing beauty pierce me . . .' and the poet is left 'to die bleeding—consummate with Life.' " With her earliest work so avidly welcomed, Johnson moved into the thick of the Harlem Renaissance cultural circles with her cousin, Dorothy West.

Though little is known of Johnson's time among the major figures of the Harlem Renaissance—she apparently knew Zora Neale Hurston, James Weldon Johnson, Langston Hughes, and others—her presence among those figures is recorded in Wallace Thurman's novel, *Infants of the Spring* (1932). Johnson was swept up into literary fame so quickly, and at such a young age, that her work was not given much time to mature. Roses and Randolph explain: "In retrospect, her talent can be considered only that of a minor poet of the period, for the bulk of her work was produced over a short time and was very similar. She never ventured further, nor did she continue with her writing long enough to grow and develop." But some of the poems Johnson published are quite remarkable, worthy of her early accolades.

Much of Johnson's poetry from the late twenties and early thirties reveals a striking sensual perceptiveness bent to the precise, strict forms she admired. In "Sonnet to a Negro in Harlem," for example, Johnson turns the sonnet form to praise of a young man's body, twisting the form from its origins to create a witty but vaguely sorrowful image of her subject. The speaker ruefully admires the sensual loveliness of a young man who is himself lost in a sensual daydream of "palm trees and mangoes." As both the speaker and the subject are united in sensual daydreams, however, the precision of the rhyme scheme seems to chastise the young man. He has become a passive ideal of beauty, while the speaker seems both delighted and dismayed to find herself his laboring admirer.

In 1929, Johnson returned to Boston, and within a few years had stopped publishing her poetry. Her verse, which had been so overwhelmingly praised and welcomed just a few years before, almost disappeared. But the poems she published during that time are valuable in themselves, not only as records of the energy of the time, but as verses.

*BIOGRAPHICAL/CRITICAL SOURCES:*

*BOOKS*

*Dictionary of Literary Biography,* Volume 51: *Afro-American Writers from the Harlem Renaissance to 1940,* Gale Research (Detroit, MI), 1987.

*Oxford Companion to Women's Writing in the United States,* Oxford University Press (New York City), 1995.

Roses, Lorraine Elena, and Ruth Elizabeth Randolph, *Harlem Renaissance and Beyond,* G. K. Hall (Boston, MA), 1990.

Wagner, Jean, *Black Poets of the United States,* University of Illinois Press (Urbana), 1973.*

# K

## KADISH, Rachel Susan 1969-

*PERSONAL:* Born August 12, 1969, in Bronx, NY; daughter of Lawrence Jerome and Anna (Stein) Kadish. *Education:* Princeton University, A.B. (summa cum laude), 1991; New York University, M.A., 1994. *Religion:* Jewish.

*ADDRESSES: E-mail*—kadish@radcliffe.harvard.edu.

*CAREER:* Goldwater Hospital, New York City, creative writing instructor, 1993; Bunting Institute, Radcliffe College, Cambridge, MA, fiction fellow, 199495; Radio Play Media Foundation, Boston, literary editor, 1995; Harvard University Extension School, creative writing instructor, 1996.

*MEMBER:* PEN.

*AWARDS, HONORS:* Barbara Deming award in fiction, Deming Foundation, 1993; grant for emerging writers, Rona Jaffe Foundation, 1994; grant for writers of exceptional promise, Whiting Foundation, 1994; Pushcart Prize, 1997; Open Voice award, Writers Voice of the West Side, New York, 1997; nominated for a national magazine award.

*WRITINGS:*

*From a Sealed Room* (novel), Putnam (New York City), 1998.

Also author of short stories and articles. Contributor of fiction to periodicals, including *Story, Prairie Schooner,* and *Modern Maturity.* Contributor of book reviews to *Lilith* magazine, 1991. Editor of *Israel Women's Network* (newsletter), Jerusalem, 1991. Contributor to *Pushcart Prize Anthology* and other books, including *Daughters of Kings* and *Travelling Souls.*

*SIDELIGHTS:* The debut novel of Rachel Kadish was first published in 1998. The book, *From a Sealed Room,* thoroughly explores the Israeli society as it follows three women dealing with "feeling hopelessly bound by a painful past," remarked a *Publishers Weekly* critic. The critic went on to praise the work as "wise" and "perceptive," and complimented Kadish for presenting "characters with fine compassion, psychological penetration and attention to detail."

Shifra, "the novel's soul" according to Maggie Galehouse in the *New York Times Book Review,* is an old Polish women struggling with memories of the Holocaust. She lives in Jerusalem and is the neighbor of Maya, the focal point of the "action" in the novel, according to Galehouse. An American student at Hebrew University, Maya lacks emotional support and is in a relationship with a mentally ill, abusive artist who was kicked out of the army. Maya's cousin, Tami is also dealing with an unhappy relationship she and her husband have drifted apart. This "intense, ambitious story . . . explores the chasms between truth and falsehood, past and present," summarized Galehouse. *Library Journal* contributor Molly Abramowitz also referred to *From a Sealed Room* as "ambitious"; however, she maintained that in the book's "series of crises psychological, physical, emotional, and medical. . . . too much is going on."

*BIOGRAPHICAL/CRITICAL SOURCES:*

*PERIODICALS*

*Library Journal,* October 1, 1998.
*New York Times Book Review,* January 10, 1999.

*Publishers Weekly,* September 7, 1998.

\*    \*    \*

## KAMBER, Victor S.

*PERSONAL: Education:* University of Illinois, B.A. (history and political science); University of New Mexico, M.A. (rhetoric and public address; with honors); American University, J.D.; George Washington University, L.L.M. (with highest honors). *Politics:* Democrat.

*ADDRESSES: Office*—c/o The Kamber Group, 1920 L St. NW, Suite 700, Washington, DC 20036-5004.

*CAREER:* Administrative assistant to United States Representative Seymour Halpern (Republican-New York); American Federation of Labor and Congress of Industrial Organizations (AFL-CIO), Building and Construction Trades Department, research director, then assistant to the president, later director of the Task Force on Labor Law Reform; The Kamber Group (communications consulting and public relations firm), Washington, DC, founder, 1980, president, 1980—. Instructor at Georgetown University Business School, American University, and Howard University, all Washington, DC; attorney in private practice; political consultant and commentator. Appeared on numerous television and radio shows, including *ABC News Nightline* (also known as *Nightline*), ABC; *The Big Show,* MSNBC; *Business Insiders,* CNBC; *CBS Morning News,* CBS; *Crossfire,* CNN; *Fox Morning News,* Fox; *Larry King Live,* CNN; and *Rivera Live,* CNBC. Also appeared on C-SPAN and National Public Radio.

*MEMBER:* National Press Club, Newspaper Guild, American Civil Liberties Union, Americans for Democratic Action (national vice president), Economic Club of Washington, International Association of Political Consultants, American League of Lobbyists (member of the senior advisory board), Industrial Relations Research Association, Coalition of Labor Union Women, American University President's Circle, Franklin National Bank (member of the board of directors), Washington Project for the Arts, Phi Gamma Delta (national convention chair at the international convention).

*AWARDS, HONORS:* Several awards for public relations services and audiovisual and print media products.

*WRITINGS:*

*Giving up on Democracy: Why Term Limits Are Bad for America,* Regnery Publishing (Washington, DC), 1995.
(With Brad O'Leary) *Are You a Conservative or a Liberal?,* Boru Publishing (Austin, TX), 1996.
*Poison Politics: Are Negative Campaigns Destroying Democracy?,* Insight Books/Plenum Press (New York City), 1997.
(With Brad O'Leary) *Are You a Democrat or a Republican?,* Boru Publishing, 1998.

Contributor to periodicals, including *Advertising Age, Arkansas Democrat-Gazette, Atlanta Constitution, Boston Globe, Business and Society Review, Chicago Tribune, Christian Science Monitor, Houston Chronicle, Houston Post, Los Angeles Times, Miami Herald, Newsweek, New York Times, Pittsburgh Post-Gazette, Plain Dealer* (Cleveland), *Public Relations Quarterly, St. Louis Post-Dispatch, Sun-Times* (Chicago), *USA Today, USA Weekend* magazine, and *U.S. News & World Report.*

*SIDELIGHTS:* An active participant in the arena of politics, Victor Kamber is the founder and president of the Kamber Group, a public relations and consulting firm. Founded in 1980, the successful company is just one of Kamber's activities. In addition to working as a lawyer and university instructor, Kamber has worked in various capacities at the American Federation of Labor and Congress of Industrial Organizations (AFL-CIO), served as a member of various organizations, and supported a number of causes. He has appeared on television and radio shows, including *ABC News Nightline, CBS Morning News, Crossfire, Larry King Live,* and *Rivera Live,* and has appeared on C-SPAN and National Public Radio. His contributions to periodicals include pieces published in *U.S. News & World Report,* the *New York Times,* the *Christian Science Monitor, USA Today, Advertising Age,* and *Newsweek.*

In *Giving up on Democracy: Why Term Limits Are Bad for America* (1995), Kamber offers convincing arguments against establishing term limits for members of the United States Congress, according to *Booklist* contributor Ray Olson. Olson wrote that Kamber provides "persuasive" evidence as to why "experienced politicians make the best legislators," and writes why term limits are "profoundly antidemocratic." Kamber, a Democrat, wrote *Are You a Conservative or a Liberal?* (1996) with Republican political consultant Brad O'Leary. Another Kamber and O'Leary collaboration, *Are You a Democrat or a Republican?,* was published in 1998. Both books explain the major political groups in the United States and help readers explore their own political leanings.

In *Poison Politics: Are Negative Campaigns Destroying Democracy?* (1997), political consultant and commentator Kamber gives an "erudite analysis of whether negative campaigns—mud slinging—are destroying democracy," commented a *RapportOn* contributor. Steven E. Schier, reviewing the book in *Washington Monthly,* wrote that Kamber gives ample evidence of negative campaigning, as he "points out how far is too far when going negative, offering vivid examples from recent campaigns of attacks on candidates' character, race, gender, or sexual orientation that will make most readers' stomachs turn."

"Kamber takes a valiant stab at providing insight into our political process, but ultimately comes up short because his arguments need more elaboration and his book lacks a disciplined scope," observed Schier in his *Washington Monthly* review of *Poison Politics.* While the *RapportOn* contributor commented that Kamber could elaborate on his arguments in *Poison Politics,* the critic praised the author's "down-to-earth style." Discussing *Poison Politics: Are Negative Campaigns Destroying Democracy?* in the *Washington Post Book World,* a reviewer noted that readers who have followed "recent campaigns will probably appreciate the question raised in Victor Kamber's subtitle."

*BIOGRAPHICAL/CRITICAL SOURCES:*

*PERIODICALS*

*Booklist,* October 1, 1995, p. 237.
*Choice,* April, 1996; July, 1998.
*Library Journal,* October 15, 1995.
*RapportOn,* Volume 20, number 3, 1998, p. 32.
*Washington Monthly,* November, 1997, p. 60.
*Washington Post Book World,* March 1, 1998, p. 13.

\*    \*    \*

## KAPP, Yvonne (Mayer) 1903-1999
### (Yvonne Cloud, a pseudonym)

*OBITUARY NOTICE—See index for CA sketch:* Born 1903, in London, England; died June 23, 1999. Writer. Kapp grew up in London and by some accounts was a rebellious child before going off to King's College in London. At the age of twenty-three and under the pen name Yvonne Cloud she wrote the book that was to bring her early success, *Nobody Asked You.* The novel dealt with the then-shocking subjects of incest and pandering in a French family and received warm endorsements from authors like Graham Green and Rebecca West. Although she wrote a trio of books after self-publishing *Nobody Asked You,* it wasn't until 1972 that she again met with success as the author of a two-volume biography of Eleanor Marx, daughter of Karl Marx. *Eleanor Marx,* Volume I: *Family Life* and *Eleanor Marx,* Volume II: *The Crowded Years,* were lauded for their thoroughness. Reviewer E. J. Hobsbawm said Kapp had the three qualifications needed for a biographer: exact scholarship, a clever and loving eye, and a knowledge of the world. Between her two greatest works Kapp continued writing and editing books. In addition to novels *Mediterranean Blues* and *The Houses in Between: A Domestic Comedy in Several Districts,* she also helped translate *The First Clash* and *Julio Jurenito.*

*OBITUARIES AND OTHER SOURCES:*

*PERIODICALS*

*Times* (London), August 2, 1999.\*

\*    \*    \*

## KARAGEORGE, Michael
### See ANDERSON, Poul (William)

\*    \*    \*

## KENDRICK, C.
### See BARR, Amelia Edith (Huddleston)

\*    \*    \*

## KEYES, Daniel 1927-

*PERSONAL:* Born August 9, 1927, in Brooklyn, NY; son of William and Betty (Alicke) Keyes; married Aurea Vazquez (a fashion stylist, photographer, and artist), October 14, 1952; children: Hillary Ann, Leslie Joan. *Education:* Studied pre-med for one year at New York University; Brooklyn College (now Brooklyn College of the City University of New York), A.B.

*Daniel Keyes*

(psychology), 1950, A.M., 1961; attended a postgraduate course taught by psychiatrist Kurt Goldstein at the City College of New York.

*ADDRESSES: Agent*—Marcy Posner, William Morris Agency, 1325 Avenue of the Americas, New York, NY 10019.

*CAREER:* Stadium Publishing Co., New York City, associate fiction editor, 1950-52; Fenko & Keyes Photography, Inc., New York City, co-owner, 1953; high school teacher of English, Brooklyn, NY, 1954-55, 1957-62; Wayne State University, Detroit, MI, instructor in English, 1962-66; Ohio University, Athens, lecturer, 1966-72, professor of English and Creative Writing, 1972—, director of creative writing center, 1973-74, 1977-78. Supervising producer of television movie *The Mad Housers,* 1990. *Military service:* U.S. Maritime Service, senior assistant purser, June, 1945-December, 1946.

*MEMBER:* PEN, Societe des Auteurs et Compositeurs Dramatiques, Authors Guild, Authors League of America, Dramatists Guild (full voting member), Mystery Writers of America, MacDowell Colony Fellows.

*AWARDS, HONORS:* Hugo Award, World Science Fiction Convention, 1959, for "Flowers for Algernon" (short story); Nebula Award, Science Fiction Writers of America, 1966, for *Flowers for Algernon* (novel); fellow, Yaddo artist colony, 1967; fellow, MacDowell artist colony, 1967; special award, Mystery Writers of America, 1981, for *The Minds of Billy Milligan;* Kurd Lasswitz Award for best book by a foreign author, 1986, for *Die Leben des Billy Milligan,* the German translation of *The Minds of Billy Milligan;* Edgar Allan Poe Award nomination, Mystery Writers of America, 1986, for *Unveiling Claudia: A True Story of a Serial Murder;* individual artists fellowship, Ohio Arts Council, 1986-87; Baker Fund Award, Ohio University, 1986; Award of Honor, Distinguished Alumnus Brooklyn College, 1988.

*WRITINGS:*

*FICTION*

*Flowers for Algernon* (novel), Harcourt (New York City), 1966, Modern Classics Edition, 1995.
*The Touch* (novel), Harcourt, 1968, published in England as *The Contaminated Man,* Mayflower (London), 1973.
*The Fifth Sally* (novel), Houghton (Boston), 1980.
*Daniel Keyes Collected Stories,* Hayakawa (Tokyo), 1993.
*Daniel Keyes Reader,* Hayakawa, 1994.

*NONFICTION*

*The Minds of Billy Milligan* (Book-of-the-Month Club selection), Random House, 1981, revised edition, with afterword, Bantam (New York City), 1982.
*Unveiling Claudia: A True Story of a Serial Murder,* Bantam, 1986.
*The Milligan Wars* (sequel to *The Minds of Billy Milligan;* also known as *The Milligan Wars: A True-Story Sequel*), Hayakawa, 1993, Bantam, 1996.
*Algernon, Charlie and I: A Writer's Journey,* Challcrest Press Books (Boca Raton, FL), 2000.

Author of short stories, including "Flowers for Algernon." Also contributor to numerous anthologies, including *Ten Top Stories,* edited by David A. Sohn, Bantam, 1964. Contributor of fiction to periodicals. Associate editor, *Marvel Science Fiction,* 1951.

"The Daniel Keyes Collection," a repository of papers and manuscripts, is housed at the Alden Library, Ohio University, Athens, OH.

*ADAPTATIONS:* Television play "The Two Worlds of Charlie Gordon," based on the short story "Flowers for Algernon," CBS Playhouse, February 22, 1961; feature film *Charly,* based on the novel *Flowers for Algernon,* starring Cliff Robertson, winner of an Academy Award for this role, Cinerama, 1968; two-act play *Flowers for Algernon,* adapted by David Rogers, Dramatic Publishing, 1969; dramatic musical *Charlie and Algernon,* first produced at Citadel Theater, Alberta, Canada, December 21, 1978, produced at Queens Theater, London, England, June 14, 1979, first produced in the United States at Terrace Theater, Kennedy Center, Washington, DC, March 8, 1980, produced on Broadway at Helen Hayes Theater, September 4, 1980; other adaptations of *Flowers for Algernon* include: French stage play, first produced at Theater Espace Massalia, Marseille, France, October 11, 1982; Irish radio monodrama, first broadcast by Radio Telefis Eireann, Dublin, Ireland, October 25, 1983; Australian stage-play, produced by Jigsaw Theater Company, March, 1984; Polish stage play, adapted by Jerzy Gudejka, first produced at W. Horzyca Memorial Theater of Torun, Torun, Poland, March 3, 1985; Japanese stage play, first produced at Kinokuniya Theater, Tokyo, Japan, January 20, 1987; and a radio play, Czechoslovak Radio Prague, 1988.

*SIDELIGHTS:* The author of several works focusing on psychological themes, Daniel Keyes told *CA* that he is "fascinated by the complexities of the human mind." Keyes is perhaps best known for his novel *Flowers for Algernon,* the story of Charlie, a mentally retarded man who is transformed into a genius by psychosurgery, only to eventually regress. *Flowers for Algernon,* which originally appeared as a short story in the *Magazine of Fantasy and Science Fiction,* is viewed by a *Times Literary Supplement* contributor as "a good example of that kind of science fiction which uses a persuasive hypothesis to explore emotional and moral issues. . . ." The reviewer continues that Keyes's ideas and speculations on the relationship between maturity and intelligence make *Flowers for Algernon* "a far more intelligent book than the vast majority of 'straight' novels. . . . Charlie's hopeless knowledge that he is destined to end in a home for the feeble-minded, a moron who knows that he is a moron, is painful, and Mr. Keyes has the technical equipment to prevent us from shrugging off the pain."

Two of Keyes's works, *The Fifth Sally* and *The Minds of Billy Milligan,* deal with the subject of multiple personalities and are dramatic recreations of factual cases. The title character of *The Fifth Sally* is Sally Porter, a woman who harbors four personalities that embody her emotional states: Nola, an intellectual artist; Derry, a free-spirited tomboy; Bella, a promiscuous woman; and Jinx, a murderous personality. The novel examines the efforts of Sally and her doctor to fuse the four beings into one complete person. "This is an intriguing story," wrote Mel Gilden in the *Los Angeles Times,* "but the reader is able to remain an observer rather than becoming emotionally involved. . . . Despite the intellectual distance maintained between Sally and reader, the book will reward almost anyone who reads it."

*The Minds of Billy Milligan* is based on the case of Billy Milligan, who was arrested on rape charges in Ohio in 1977 and who later became the first person in U.S. history to be acquitted of a major felony by reason of a multiple personality disorder. At the time of his arrest, Billy Milligan was found to possess no fewer than twenty-four personalities—three of them female—with ages ranging from three to twenty-four years old. Among Milligan's dominant personalities were Arthur, an Englishman in charge of all the others; Ragen, a violent Yugoslav who acted as physical protector; and Adalana, a nineteen-year-old lesbian who confessed to instituting the three rapes with which Milligan was charged. According to Keyes, these personalities, along with all the rest, would share "the spot"—control of Milligan's consciousness—whenever their distinctive qualities were needed.

The circumstances under which Keyes was contracted to write Milligan's story proved unusual: It was only after several of Milligan's selves read *Flowers for Algernon* that they agreed among themselves to work with the author. In *The Minds of Billy Milligan,* Keyes writes of a personality known as "The Teacher." The Teacher kept the memory of all the other beings in Milligan and provided much of the book's background information. Through the different personas, the author describes the life of a young man who had suffered years of mental and physical abuse at the hands of his stepfather, and how Milligan had sought solace and protection from the various people existing in him. After Milligan was arrested and sent to a correctional institution for observation, debate surfaced as to how to best classify his mental state. According to Robert Coles in the *New York Times Book Review,* "Keyes makes quite evident in *The Minds of Billy Milligan,* [that] historical tensions within the [medical] profession have yet to be resolved, and have, in fact, been given new expression in this instance. . . ." While the prosecuting attorneys insisted that Milligan be jailed, doctors and psychologists in

Ohio debated the location and terms of such a patient's incarceration. "When he was found 'insane,' " Coles continues, "the arguments did not by any means abate. Was he a 'sociopath'—a liar, an impostor? . . . Was he a severely disturbed and dangerous 'psychotic' who required careful watching, lots of medication, maybe a course or two of electric shock treatment?"

Coles ultimately commended Keyes for telling "this complicated story well. It reads like a play: Billy's 'personalities' come onstage, leave to be replaced by others and then reappear." Peter Gorner found this distracting; in a *Chicago Tribune* review of the book, he stated that the author "interviews everybody, reconstructs, flashes back, and confuses the story in a chatty, conversational style. The alter egos seem to dance before our eyes like a stroboscope." However, in the opinion of David Johnston in the *Los Angeles Times,* "telling the stories of twenty-four different personalities would be a difficult task for any writer. To tell of two dozen personalities in one human body is an extremely complex task. Keyes, on balance, carries it off quite well. While it shortchanges the reader by limiting explanation of motives almost exclusively to Milligan's personalities, [*The Minds of Billy Milligan*] is nonetheless a fascinating work." Finally, *Washington Post Book World,* reviewer Joseph McLellan pointed out that "complexity is . . . the keynote of the Billy phenomenon and equally of its treatment by Daniel Keyes. The challenge of first unearthing this story . . . and then telling it intelligibly was a daunting one. He has carried it off brilliantly, bringing to the assignment not only a fine clarity but a special warmth, and empathy for the victim of circumstances and mental failings that made *Flowers for Algernon* one of the most memorable novels of the 1960s."

As in his two previous works, Keyes unravels the bizarre incidents in a mentally ill person's life in *Unveiling Claudia: A True Story of a Serial Murder.* Claudia Elaine Yasko, having known both the victims and the murderers in three Ohio killings in the late 1970s, fantasized herself as the murderer. She confessed to the homicides in 1978 but the charges were dropped once the real killers were accidentally discovered. Keyes's book records the incidents and attempts to explain why Yasko knew so much about the killings. Gregor A. Preston wrote in the *Library Journal:* "while not as intriguing as Billy Milligan, this is a masterfully told, absorbing story."

*AUTOBIOGRAPHICAL ESSAY:*

Keyes contributed the following essay to *CA:*

## I: THE MAZE OF TIME

### My Writing Cellar

I never thought it would happen to me.

When I was very young and very nearsighted—20/400 vision, everything blurred without my eyeglasses—I believed that someday I'd go blind. So I planned ahead. I strove to be neat, a place for everything and everything in its place. I blindfolded myself and practiced retrieving things without seeing, and I was proud that I could find anything quickly in the dark.

I didn't go blind. In fact, with eyeglasses my vision is excellent.

I can still put my hands on most things I possess. Not because I remember where I put them, but because I take the time to put them away carefully, in logical places. I just have to remember where they belong. What's happening to me is something I never considered. I start out to do something, go somewhere, walk into another room to get something, but then I have to pause. What am I looking for? Then it quickly clicks into place. It's momentary but frightening. And I think of Charlie Gordon at the end of *Flowers for Algernon,* saying, *"I remember I did something but I don't remember what."*

Why am I thinking of the fictional character I created more than forty years ago? I try to put him out of my mind, but he won't let me.

Charlie is haunting me, and I've got to find out why.

I've decided the only way I can put him to rest is to go back through the maze of time, search for his origins and exorcise the ghosts of memories past. Perhaps, along the way, I'll also learn when, how and why I became a writer.

Getting started is the hardest thing. I tell myself, you've got the material. You don't have to make it up—just remember it, shape it. And you don't have to create a fictional narrator's voice the way you did for the story and then the novel. This is you, writing about writing, and remembering the secrets of your own life that became the life of Charlie Gordon.

The opening of the story echoes in my mind. *"Dr. Strauss says I shud rite down what I think and evrey thing that happins to me from now on. I don't know why but he says its importint so they will see if they will use me. I hope they use me. Miss Kinnian says maybe they can make me smart. I want to be smart. My name is Charlie Gordon . . ."*

Although the original novelette begins with those words, that's not how it all started. Nor are his final words about putting *"flowrs . . . in the bak yard"* the end of his story. I remember clearly where I was the day the ideas that sparked the story first occurred to me.

One crisp April morning in 1945, I climbed the steps to the elevated platform of the Sutter Avenue BMT station in Brownsville, Brooklyn. I'd have a ten- or fifteen-minute wait for the train that would take me to Manhattan, where I would change for the local to the Washington Square branch of New York University.

I recall wondering where I would get the money for the fall semester. My freshman year had used up most of the savings I'd accumulated by working at several jobs, and there wouldn't be enough left to pay for three more years at NYU.

As I took the nickel fare out of my pocket and glanced at it, I remembered my father, Willie, once admitting to me that when he had been looking for work during The Great Depression, he would walk the ten miles from our two-room apartment, through Brooklyn and across the Manhattan Bridge each morning and back home each night, to save two nickels.

Often, Dad would leave while it was still dark before I awoke, but sometimes I would be up early enough to catch a glimpse of him at the kitchen table, dipping a roll into his coffee. That was his breakfast. For me there was always hot cereal, and sometimes an egg.

Watching him stare into space, I assumed his mind was blank. Now, I realize he was trying to figure out ways to pay our debts. Then he would get up from the table, pat me on the head, tell me to be good in school and study hard. Back then, I thought he was going to his job. I didn't learn until much later that he was ashamed of being out of work.

Maybe this nickel in my hand was one of those he saved.

I dropped it into the slot and pushed through the turnstile. Someday, perhaps I'd retrace his footsteps, walking from Brownsville to Manhattan, to know what it had been like for him. I thought about it, but I never did it.

I think of experiences and images like these as being stored in the *root cellar* of my mind, hibernating in the dark until they are ready for stories.

Most writers have their own metaphors for stored-away scraps and memories. William Faulkner called his writing place a *workshop* and referred to his mental storage place as a *lumber room,* to which he'd go when he needed odds and ends for the fiction he was building.

My mental storage place was in a part of our landlord's cellar, near the coalbin, in the space under the stairs which he allowed my parents to use for storage. Once, when I was big enough to climb down the cellar stairs, I discovered that's where my parents hid my old toys.

I see my brown teddy bear and stuffed giraffe, and Tinker Toy, and Erector Set, and tricycle, and roller skates and childhood books—some of them coloring books with line drawings still to fill in with crayons. For me it solved a mystery of toys that vanished when I'd grown tired of them and others that reappeared in their place.

Even now, I can smell the dank air and the odor of coal in the nearby bin beside the furnace. I see the steel shaft from the coal truck inserted through the cellar window and then, almost immediately, I hear coal clattering down the slide into the coalbin. Our landlord, Mr. Pincus, opens the cast-iron door of the furnace and stokes it with a poker. I smell wet coal as he shovels it in, and feel heat from the blaze.

Somewhere between the coal bin and the furnace—in the root cellar of my mind—ideas, images, scenes and dreams wait in the dark until I need them.

Remembering my childhood toy hiding place, as I waited for the train, I thought of my mother and father. I mused over the coincidence that both of their parents—unknown to each other—had made their way across Europe to Canada to New York City. There, Betty and Willie met for the first time. They soon married and had me, their first child, in 1927: the year Lindbergh flew nonstop from New York to Paris and Al Jolson played the Jazz Singer in the first talking movie.

During those years of hope and excess that later became known as "The Jazz Age," my parents, like many other new Americans, went to parties and danced the "Charleston" at speak-easies where they could be served illegal gin.

I often wonder what happened to the sepia photograph of my mother, with her bobbed hair and sad dark eyes.

I loved to hear her sing popular songs from two-cent lyric sheets and, sometimes, I would sing along with her, our favorite, "Smoke Gets in Your Eyes."

As a boy, in Quebec, Willie had worked for trappers and learned to speak English, French, Russian and enough Canadian Indian phrases to trade furs. Although he and my mother had little formal schooling, it became clear to me early in childhood that they respected education, and demanded that I excel in school.

Yet, in my adolescence, I discovered the more I read and learned, the less I could communicate with them. I was losing them—drifting away into my world of books and stories.

Ever since I was a child, they had decided I would become a doctor. When I asked why, my father answered, "Because a doctor is like God. He cures people and saves lives."

My mother added, "When you were a baby, you had an infected mastoid and double pneumonia. A wonderful doctor saved your life."

My father said, "We want you to cure people and save lives."

I accepted their reasons and their obligation. I would work hard, take part-time jobs to earn money and go to college and medical school. I would become a doctor. Since I loved my parents, I buried my dream of becoming a writer. I declared pre-med as my major.

Secretly, I wondered if I could become both doctor and writer. I'd read that Somerset Maugham had been educated as a physician and went to sea as a ship's doctor. Chekhov had studied medicine and published his early stories and sketches in journals and papers under the pen name "The Doctor Without Patients." Conan Doyle, unable to support himself as an eye specialist, used his empty consulting room during visiting hours to write the stories of Sherlock Holmes.

An Englishman, a Russian and a Scotsman had started as physicians and then crossed over into the writing life. By following in their footsteps, perhaps I would be able to fulfill my parents' dream as well as my own.

Almost immediately, I saw the flaw in my solution. Before they became successful authors, all three had failed as doctors.

The crowded train pulled into the station, and I got on, not bothering to look for a seat. It was rush hour, and I would have to stand during the half-hour trip to Union Square. I reached through the crush of work-bound commuters for the white enamel pole in the center of the aisle to steady myself in the lurching train. Most people stared up to avoid eye contact. Feeling depressed, I did the same.

My first year at NYU was nearing an end, and I thought: *"My education is driving a wedge between me and the people I love."* And then I wondered: *"What would happen if it were possible to increase a person's intelligence?"*

That morning, as the train clackety-clacked through the tunnel to Manhattan, I stored away those two ideas: *education could force a wedge between people, and the storyteller's "What would happen if . . . ?"*

Later that day, the white mouse happened.

### The White Mouse

The train pulled into the Eighth Street station, a short walk from Broadway to the Washington Square branch of New York University.

I stopped at a doughnut and coffee shop across from the entrance to the main building and saw a friend at the counter. He waved me to an empty stool beside him. We had been at Thomas Jefferson High School in Brooklyn together but had little to do with each other. He was over six feet tall. I was five-foot-five.

It was only after we discovered we were both pre-med and found each other in the same biology course at NYU that we became friends. We studied together, testing each other to prepare for exams. Because of the difference in our height, people who saw us called us "Mutt and Jeff" like the characters in a comic strip popular at the time. I called him "Stretch."

I was dunking my doughnut when Stretch said, "Hey, you see the notice? If you volunteer for the military you get exempt from finals."

"You're kidding."

"In Friday's paper," he said. "Any student signing up for duty at least three months before he turns eighteen can enter the service of his choice. After that, it's the infantry. I'm gonna join the navy."

"I'll be eighteen on August ninth," I said, "just three months from now. But with my bad eyes, I don't think the army will draft me."

"You want to take the chance? Lots of guys have been killed. They'll take anyone who breathes."

We paid our checks and headed across the street to the main entrance of NYU.

I knew Stretch would be accepted into the navy, and I envied him. I loved the sea, or at least the idea of the seafaring life. At sixteen, during my last year in high school, I'd joined the Sea Scouts of America. Our Scout ship, the SSS *Flying Dutchman III,* was an old liberty boat converted into a cabin cruiser. During the spring break, we scraped and primed and painted her hull, and the following summer we cruised up and down the East River.

At meetings during which new Sea Scouts were sworn in, the captain would tell the story of the legendary vessel after which we were named. The SS *Flying Dutch-man* had carried a cargo of gold, and there had been a brutal murder aboard. After that, a plague broke out among the crew, and no port would allow the ship to enter. According to seamen's stories, the spectral ship still drifts sea-tossed, its men never to return home. It is said that, to this day, the ship can be seen in stormy weather off the Cape of Good Hope, an eternal omen of bad luck.

The captain embellished the story each time he told it, and I'd become curious and looked it up on my own. What he didn't tell us were some of the other legends, like the one that says the curse can be lifted if the captain finds a woman willing to sacrifice everything for his sake.

I told that version to some of the other Sea Scouts, and it became our quest when we cruised for girls in Brooklyn's Prospect Park. We were looking for what were then called "Victory Girls," young women willing to sacrifice everything for young men going off to war.

We pretended to be sailors. There were only two differences between our uniforms and the navy's: the anchors on the back corners of our collars instead of stars, and over the front left pocket the letters BSA to identify us as Boy Scouts of America. When some of the girls questioned our lack of height, we explained that we were sub-mariners, and when they asked what "BSA" referred to, we told them, "Battle Squadron A."

None of them ever questioned the anchors.

We picked up lots of patriotic V-girls in Prospect Park, but unlike some of the more experienced and handsome

Sea Scouts, I couldn't find one willing to sacrifice everything for my sake.

"I wish I could join the navy, too," I said to Stretch, as we took the elevator up to our lockers that morning at NYU, "but with my bad vision, I guess it's the infantry for me."

"You can always join the maritime service. They don't have high physical requirements, and merchant marine duty would exempt you from the draft."

"I guess that way I'd still be serving my country."

"Sure. Considering the mines and torpedoes, it's hazardous duty. I read somewhere that more merchant seamen were killed on the Murmansk run than navy sailors."

We took our lab coats from our lockers and headed for class. "My folks would never sign the papers."

"They would if you explained the alternative."

As we entered the biology lab and each moved to our different sections, I was surprised at the smell of formaldehyde. On the marble worktable in front of each student's station lay a covered tray. I reached out to uncover it, but the prof's voice called out: *"Do not touch the tray in front of you!"*

His lab assistant was moving from student to student dropping off a rolled-up dissection kit and a pair of rubber gloves in front of each tray. When he was done, the prof called out, "Put on the gloves and then uncover the trays."

I peeled back the cover, startled to see a dead white mouse on its side.

"Today," he announced, "you will dissect a real specimen."

I knew the bio lab required dissection, but I'd expected a warning. Obviously, the professor enjoyed springing this as a surprise on his students. Not that it bothered me. I was taking bio as a pre-med requirement because I was going to be a surgeon.

In the Boy Scouts I had taken the Advanced First Aid Merit Badge, and in the Sea Scouts during cruises, I was considered "ship's doctor." I treated wounds, boils and abrasions and had become used to the sight and smell of blood. I had hardened myself.

On one *Dutchman* weekend trip up the East River, the crew nearly mutinied over the terrible meals. Since I'd held part-time jobs as a sandwich man in a luncheonette, I was drafted into being "ship's cook" as well. The joke on that voyage was that if I didn't kill them as doctor I'd poison them as cook.

Dissecting a mouse would be no problem.

"Open your dissection kits." He pulled down a chart in front of the blackboard. It showed a mouse's internal organs. "Now, with the scalpel, make an incision in your specimen from the neck through the abdomen to the tail, then pull the skin back with the forceps."

I followed his instructions. The incision was quick and neat and revealed that my specimen was female.

"Proceed to remove the organs, placing them into the petri dishes and labelling each one."

My specimen's uterus was distended. I cut it open, stared in disbelief and backed away from the table. It contained a cluster of tiny fetuses curled up, eyes shut.

"You look pale," my neighbor across the table said. "What's the matter?"

What had startled me at first now saddened me. Several tiny lives had been snuffed out so that I could have a hands-on dissection experience.

A young woman on my left leaned forward to look. Before I could catch her she fainted, knocking over her stool with a loud crash. The lab assistant rushed to revive her with smelling salts, and the prof told us to continue dissections on our own as he and his assistant took her to the infirmary.

But I, great surgeon-to-be, was paralyzed. The thought of removing the fetuses sickened me. I dashed out of the lab into the lavatory, washed my face and hands, and stared at myself in the mirror. I had to go back and finish what I'd started.

After a few minutes, I returned to the lab.

Embarrassed at having fled, I covered up my over-reaction by blurting out, "As the proud godfather of a litter, I'm handing out cigarettes in lieu of cigars."

Laughter, pats on the back and mock congratulations steadied me, but as I finished the dissection a jingle went through my mind:

*Three blind mice, see how they run.*
*They all run after the farmer's wife,*
*Who cut off their tails with a carving knife.*
*You never saw such a sight in your life,*
*    As three blind mice.*

"Good job," the prof said, as he examined my work. "I'm giving you an A."

On the way out, Stretch punched me playfully. "Lucky guy, getting the pregnant one."

That night, as I opened my English lit anthology for the next day's quiz on British poets, I scanned the table of contents and saw *Algernon Charles Swinburne.* I thought, what an unusual first name.

*Second Acting*

Although I'd always wanted to become a writer, I wasn't sure what kind of writing. After I read Nathanael West's horror story of Hollywood—*The Day of the Locust*—I ruled out screenwriting.

That left plays, short stories or novels. I'd read hundreds of each, but my only experience with live theater was student performances in school. I was on stage once, in third grade, and I played an Oracle. In a deep voice, full of portent, I said to the king of the Aztecs, "Thy days are numbered, Montezuma."

That was the extent of my acting experience.

In my teens, I glorified Manhattan. It was Bagdad-on-the-Hudson, city of the arts, of publishing, and Broadway theater. I could reach that Mecca for a nickel and see two-thirds of a show free of charge. All I had to do was mingle with the crowd that stepped out for a smoke after the first-act curtain. When the buzzer announced the second-act warning, I would drift in among them and quickly find a seat before the lights dimmed. I called it *second acting.*

The year was 1942. I was fifteen, and the play was *The Skin of Our Teeth.* Since I had read *Our Town* in high school, and seen the movie, the thought of second acting a Thornton Wilder play excited me.

I was clever enough never to try it on weekends. On a midweek evening, I put on my navy blue suit, a conservative tie, and took the subway to Times Square. I was early that night as I walked to the theater district, so I lingered outside Lindy's Restaurant for a while and peered through the window. I imagined Damon Runyon's hustlers, gamblers and gangsters, guys and dolls hanging out at the restaurant. Runyon called it *Mindy's*. When I could afford to splurge, I'd go inside, sit near the window looking out at the Broadway passersby and gorge myself on the cheesecake Runyon had immortalized.

I stopped daydreaming and focused on the task at hand. I didn't mind missing the first act of *The Skin of Our Teeth*. I could usually figure out the opening situation, but even if I couldn't, it didn't matter. I would develop the opening in my mind, write a beginning that brought the characters and the story together. In those days, I saw many second and third acts, but never any firsts.

Always after the final curtain, I would applaud with the others and visualize the glories of a playwright's life. Curtain calls on opening night of a smash hit. Shouts of "Author! Author!" Bows and bouquets. Then to Sardi's for celebration with champagne and caviar as everyone waited for the early *Times* review.

That night started out the same as usual. I blended in with the crowd of smokers that spilled out of the theater onto the sidewalk, took a cigarette from my imitation gold case and lit up. I mingled with the paying customers and listened to the chatter about the first act, picking up clues about the opening.

When the second-act warning buzzer sounded, I merged with them into the lobby. Above their heads, I caught a glimpse of the faces of Fredric March and Tallulah Bankhead on the life-size poster. I'd seen them both in the movies, of course. Tonight, I would see them live, on stage, in a Thornton Wilder play.

Once inside, I hung back at the rear, scanning the rows for an empty seat, ready to slide into it before the lights dimmed. I saw two in the center of the aisle, but as I made my move I was jostled aside by the latecomers.

Only then did I realize that the crowd was larger than usual. I moved to the wall, peering through the dimming light, my eyes growing used to the dark. Every seat was occupied. Did I dare try the balcony? I'd come this far. Might as well. I went back and headed upstairs two steps at a time. I found a *Playbill,* slipped it into my jacket pocket and headed for an empty seat in the center of a row.

As I sat down, a woman glared at me. "What are you doing? That's my husband's seat!"

"Sorry," I said. "Wrong row."

I jumped up and squeezed my way back to the aisle as a huge man headed towards me. I'd waited too long. I had to backtrack to the other end. People grumbled as I stepped on their feet.

An usher with a flashlight was waiting for me. "May I see your ticket stub? The curtain is about to go up."

Heart pounding, I pretended to search my pockets. "I must have dropped it somewhere. I had it right here."

She looked at me suspiciously. "There are no empty seats in the balcony."

"I'll go down to the lobby and see if I can find it."

"Let me light your way."

"Not necessary," I whispered, moving quickly. But I missed the last step and fell.

"Sir, are you hurt? Let me take you to the manager's office."

"No. No. That's all right. I'm fine."

I ran down the steps two at a time into the empty lobby. There, I saw the full length of the poster with a banner announcement that had been hidden by the crowd heading inside for the second act: *TONIGHT'S PERFORMANCE SOLD OUT!*

Stupid! Stupid! Stupid!

Out of the lobby, into the street. Only then did I look back at the marquee at the play's title that now mocked my close call: *The Skin of Our Teeth.*

I walked north on Broadway to Central Park South, telling myself I might find an adventure along the way. Since it was late, I didn't enter the park, just sat on one of the benches and looked up at the luxury hotels. The name "Essex House" impressed me and I wondered about the lives of wealthy people who lived there. Some day, I would look down from one of those windows to where I was sitting now.

As I passed the theater district on the way back to the subway, I saw the street filled with the exiting theater crowd. Some people entered waiting limos or hailed taxis. Others walked towards brightly lit Broadway.

Once again, I merged into the crowd, as if by being among them I could be part of them. Many held the

*Playbill* in their hands. I pulled mine out of my pocket and held it as a badge that showed I belonged in their world.

One group turned off into Sardi's. I followed them in and looked around. After they were seated, I saw the headwaiter approach. I waved my *Playbill* at him and asked for directions to the men's room.

When I left Sardi's and continued on to the subway, I tried to imagine what the play I had not seen might be like. I couldn't. So on the ride back to Brooklyn, I made one up, about a boy who had a great adventure, a narrow escape—by the skin of his teeth—as he tried to second act a Broadway play.

Twenty-five years later, in 1967, I received a fellowship to the MacDowell Colony for creative artists in Peterborough, New Hampshire, to work on my second novel, *The Touch.*

I was assigned a luxurious studio deep in the woods. On the first day, I was told that to preserve solitude for creativity, the only distraction would occur at noon each day when a car would drive up the gravel path and someone would leave my lunch basket at the door.

Exploring the studio, I noticed a piece of wood in the shape of a paddle on the fireplace mantel. It was inscribed with a list of names of former visitors, some at the top faded, others at the bottom fresh. As I glanced up the long list, I saw the name: *Thornton Wilder.* In 1936 or 1937, he had written *Our Town* in the same studio where I would be working on *The Touch* for the next month.

Remembering my failed evening at the theater, I added my name at the bottom of the paddle.

### Breaking Dishes

It was obvious to me in my youth that my parents wouldn't be able to send me to college, much less medical school. If I was to get a higher education, I would have to work and save.

During summer vacations, when I was eight or nine, I quickly graduated from street corner lemonade stands to selling soda pop and sandwiches. I bought rye bread and salami at a delicatessen and made sandwiches. I bought bottles of soda pop from a nearby wholesaler and packed them in ice in my little red wagon. I sold lunches to women who worked in a garment factory on Van Sinderen Avenue, the borderline between Brownsville and East New York.

I did very well until I was squeezed out by the owner of the delicatessen. Able to gauge my success by the increase in the size of my orders, he put his nephew to work on my route, undercut my prices, and drove me out of business.

In the years that followed, I delivered tuxedos for weddings, assembled screwdrivers in a factory and worked the first *frozen custard* machine in Brownsville. None of them paid much, but I had to save for college.

Two other jobs that I stored away in what I later called my mental root cellar—working as a baker's boy and later as waiter in a luncheonette—stayed hidden in deep memory until "Flowers for Algernon" needed them.

When I was fourteen, I went to work as a delivery man's assistant for The East New York Bagel Bakery, beneath the elevated train, around the corner from where I lived. To start at four in the morning, I had to get up at three a.m. I worked until seven a.m. until the driver dropped me off at Junior High School 149. Out of school at three in the afternoon, homework, dinner and then to bed while it was still daylight.

At first, my job was to help the driver load the back of his van with baskets of hot bagels, some plain, some with poppy or sesame seeds, some with salt. I would sit beside him in the passenger seat while we drove to groceries and restaurants that had not yet opened for business.

As we approached each location in the pre-dawn hours, the driver consulted his order list and called out the size of the order. "Two dozen. One plain, one poppy."

The back of the passenger seat had been removed, so I would turn, grasp three still-hot bagels in each hand and call out "Six! A dozen! Six! Two dozen!" There were no *baker's dozens* then. Poppy and sesame-seeded bagels were painful because they scraped my fingers. But the salt-covered bagels hurt most of all when they touched my raw skin. I bagged them, and as the driver pulled to the curb I jumped out and left them in still-dark doorways.

I remember the day he changed the route to deliver to a new customer. As we passed the corner of Livonia and Saratoga Avenues, I saw lights on in a candy store. "That's strange," I said. "Maybe it's being robbed."

He laughed. "Midnight Rose is open twenty-four hours a day. Nobody in his right mind would rob that store."

When I asked why, he shook his head and said it wasn't too smart to ask questions about the wise guys who hung out at Midnight Rose's place.

At about this time, I got to know an older boy whose family moved in across the street from my home on Snediker Avenue. He was training to become a boxer, he said, but since he was actually too young to box, he confided in me that he planned to use his older brother's nickname, "Kid Twist." He would fight as "The Kid."

I told him I wished I had enough money to pay for the Atlas Dynamic Tension Method so that I could put on muscles like Mr. Atlas in the magazines and comic books and learn to defend myself against some of the bullies who picked on me.

The Kid weight-lifted at the Adonis Club on Livonia Avenue, and one day he took me with him and introduced me around. Some of the muscle men laughed when they saw how skinny I was, but they were very polite to The Kid and gave me advice on how to pump iron. I see them clearly in my mind now, standing in front of mirrors after lifting weights, flexing oiled muscles, the smell of sweat filling the air.

Hoboes dropped in from time to time, to wash up and sometimes to sleep in the back for a night or two. I listened with fascination at their stories of hopping freight trains across the country and meeting old friends with strange names at hobo camps. I thought of quitting school and hopping a freight in the nearby rail yards, to see America. Then I'd have something to write about.

Later, I learned about "Kid" Reles's brother. I still have the newspaper clip from November 13, 1941.

### ABE RELES KILLED TRYING TO ESCAPE

*Abe "Kid Twist" Reles, a major hit man for a murder-for-hire ring, had been testifying against his confederates, and the Mafia who used their services. Early . . . Wednesday, November 12, 1941, although closely guarded by five detectives, Abe Reles either jumped, fell or was pushed out of the sixth floor window of the Half Moon Hotel on the Coney Island boardwalk. Reporters dubbed him "the canary that could sing but couldn't fly."*

Then I understood what the bagel delivery driver had told me about the men who hung out at Midnight Rose's Candy Store. They were the Mafia's execution squad, and reporters called them *"Murder Inc."*

The killers operated right in my neighborhood and received their hit contracts from the bosses in Manhattan who phoned them at the candy store. My boxer friend's brother, Abe "Kid Twist" Reles, had been one of their most feared killers. Shortly after the article appeared, my friend and his family moved from the neighborhood without warning, and I never saw him again.

I was soon promoted from the bagel delivery van to an inside job as baker's helper. Later, when I was practicing writing scenes from my own experiences, I wrote a brief sketch of my impressions of the bakery. Here, unedited, is that memory.

> The bagel factory—the smell of raw dough, and the whitened floors and walls . . . working and kneading the dough in circular motions. Rolling it into long thin tubes, and then with a quick twist of the wrist making them into little circles . . . another [baker] laying these out neatly in a huge shallow wooden tray . . . stacking them high . . . to be wheeled over to the urn and oven. There a boy stands lifting them out of the tray three at a time and throwing them into the bubbling urn . . . then scooping them out, dripping and slimy, with a wire net . . . dumping them on the baker's table. The baker spreads them neatly along the long wooden oar, slides them into the kiln, leaving long deep rows of bagels on wooden paddles while he fills up the next oar . . . Pulls out an oar covered with browned bagels, and runs a string along beneath the bagels to separate them from the wood . . . finally, dumping them into huge wicker baskets where they will be taken out into the waiting truck for delivery in the early dawn. The baker with the lame foot . . . the one who has the rasping voice . . .

Many years later, I used that setting in the novel version of *Flowers for Algernon.*

The night shift at the bakery interfered with sleep and study and my grades suffered, so I took a job as dishwasher in "Parkie's" ice cream parlor on Sutter Avenue. He soon promoted me to soda jerk, then to sandwich maker, counterman, and short-order cook. At sixteen, I found a better job on Pitkin Avenue, a more prestigious location near the Lowes' Pitkin Theater, to wait tables in "Meyer's Goody Shoppe."

There was no longer a Meyer at "Meyer's Goody Shoppe." The luncheonette and ice cream parlor was owned by Mr. Goldstein and Mr. Sohn, both of whom nearly drove all us waiters crazy.

Sweet and gentle Mr. Goldstein always spoke of his desire to help poor boys who were working their way through college. Near the entrance, on the wall behind the cash register, he'd hung photographs from former waiters who had, as he said, "made good." Some were in army, navy or marine uniforms. Others were wearing graduation robes. Goldstein spoke of "his boys" with affection. When I had first applied for the job and told him my parents wanted me to go to medical school, he patted my head and said I was a good boy to listen to my parents.

During the nights he was on duty, if business was slow, he was calm and would sit at the counter and discuss issues of the day with the idle short-order cooks. But when things got busy, he became transformed. Reflective Mr. Goldstein became a screamer, shouting orders at us over the customers' heads.

Mr. Sohn was a different sort of character. When business was good, he stuck to the cash register. We were free to handle our tables in quiet dignity. But during slow periods, before the crowds came in, or between the dinner rush and the after-movie rush, Mr. Sohn would slip into the dining room and, under the pretext of inspecting our stations, he would take possession of most sugar dispensers, ketchup bottles and salt shakers and hide them on the shelves below the cash register.

One of the veteran waiters explained that it was Sohn's reaction to one traumatic day when vandals had emptied all the salt shakers into the sugar dispensers. Sohn was also convinced that someone was stealing knives, forks and spoons, and he intended to find the culprit. He made frequent sorties from behind the cash register to the dishwasher's station and removed much of the flatware. This led to a shortage of every kind of cutlery whenever Sohn was on duty.

At first, it created intense rivalry among the waiters. None of us wanted to tell our customers there were no spoons for their ice cream and coffee, no forks for their chocolate cake. Irate customers would storm out without tipping and without paying, and it was no use trying to explain to Sohn that it was his fault.

I learned from the veterans how to survive. During Sohn nights we prepared ourselves by slipping flatware into our pockets, under our belts and beneath our shirts.

We occasionally joined forces to divert Sohn's attention and penetrated his fortress to liberate sugar, ketchup and salt.

*Quiet Sohn* and *Screaming Goldstein* kept us waiters on our toes—sometimes on each other's toes.

In the two years I'd worked there, I accumulated enough tips for my first year's tuition at NYU. Then one evening my life turned a corner.

The after-movie crowd started arriving at ten o'clock. The place filled up quickly, and soon there was a crowd waiting outside. When four couples arrived and broke through the line, Goldstein did something I'd never seen before. He greeted them, smiling and fawning, led them past the other protesting customers and directed them to my station.

As I went to get water and menus, Goldstein suddenly showed up with glasses of water on a tray. "How come there are no napkins on the tables?" he shouted at me. "Where's the silverware? Why don't they have menus?"

"Mr. Goldstein, they just sat down."

Explaining was useless, so I tried to ignore him as I took their orders. He bustled around, smiling at them. A few minutes later, when he passed me near the kitchen, he said, "What's taking you so long?"

"I just put my orders in, Mr. Goldstein."

"They're ready. On the counter."

I turned to look and, sure enough, the normally lethargic countermen had gone into action and given my new customers' orders of sandwiches and waffles priority.

"What's going on?" I asked one of the older waiters.

"Give 'em good service," he whispered. "Those guys hang out at Midnight Rose's."

I carried two cups of coffee with glass creamers balanced on the edges of the saucers in my left hand and three sandwiches and waffles spread across my right arm.

Goldstein again reappeared from between two aisles. "What's taking you so long?"

"I'm delivering their orders."

"These are special customers."

"I've figured that out already. Mr. Goldstein, please give me a chance . . ."

He blocked my path. "Watch those creamers!"

I looked, and saw that my trembling hands were making the glass creamers alongside the coffee cups jiggle on the edges of the saucers. He walked backwards, facing me, shouting at me. The more he shouted, the more they jiggled. I had learned that a glass creamer, if dropped, would break on the third bounce. If you could kick it to one side before that, you could prevent it from shattering.

Jiggle. Jiggle. One dropped and bounced twice. I tried to kick it aside before the third hit, but failed. It shattered. I attempted to block-kick the second creamer: Bounce . . . bounce . . . *break!* By now I was off balance and the sandwich plates nestled along my right arm wobbled. I tried to grab them but it was too late. Everything else I was carrying crashed to the floor.

"*Mazeltov!*" someone shouted, amidst laughter. Then a couple of others took up the cry, laughing and applauding as if I were a bridegroom stomping the wine glass at a wedding. Someone called out. "The kid ain't stupid! That's easier than washing them!"

Goldstein's face turned red and menacing. "What's the matter with you?" He addressed the mocking customers. "A college boy, and he can't even wait on tables." And then to me, "Clean it up, moron!"

His expression of disgust said it all. He'd given me a chance to work because I needed money for college, and I had betrayed him by breaking his dishes in front of his special customers. He walked away and didn't speak to me for the rest of the evening. But my Murder, Inc. customers left me big tips.

At closing time, I finished cleaning up, refilling sugar bowls and ketchup bottles and mopping the floors around my tables. Then I went up to him and said, "Good-bye, Mr. Goldstein. I'll send you a photograph for your mailing wall as a token of my appreciation."

His brow furrowed. "What do you mean?"

"You've helped me make a decision. I can't put up with this crap any more. I'm enlisting in the merchant marine."

"What about college?"

"That'll have to wait until after the war is over."

He looked at me long and hard. His voice was cold as he said, "Good luck." And as I headed for the door, he shouted so that everyone would hear, "Hey, moron!"

I didn't turn.

"Hey, smart college boy!"

I looked back at him.

"Try not to break everything on the ship!"

That's how, years later, I could imagine what Charlie Gordon felt during the scene in a restaurant when he sees a mentally handicapped busboy drop and break a tray of dishes, and the owner shouts: *"All right, you dope, don't just stand there! Get a broom and sweep up that mess. A broom . . . a broom! you idiot!"*

Suddenly, I was furious at myself and all those who were smirking at him. I wanted to pick up the dishes and throw them. I wanted to smash their laughing faces. I jumped up and shouted: "Shut up! Leave him alone! He can't understand. He can't help what he is . . . but for God's sake, have some respect! He's a human being!"

I was able to see it through Charlie's eyes and feel his emotions. I was able to write it, because it happened to me.

### *I Become Ship's Doctor*

I knew that joining the U.S. Maritime Service would be a turning point. I would be away from my parents, living my own life, pursuing my own dreams. But because I was three months short of my eighteenth birthday, to enlist I needed one of my parents' signatures.

My mother insisted that I was too young, too thin, too short and too nearsighted.

"They don't care," I said. "I can pass the physical."

My father asked, "What about college?"

"A lot of other guys are in the same boat, Dad. They enacted a new law last year—the G.I. Bill—to pay college tuition for servicemen. After my discharge, I'll be able to continue my education free of charge."

I didn't know at the time that maritime service duty would not make me eligible for G.I. benefits.

"You'll still become a doctor?" she asked. "Doctors save lives."

"Of course, I'll become a doctor."

My father frowned. "What about that writer stuff?"

I told them about Somerset Maugham and Chekhov and Conan Doyle having been physicians who later became famous authors, and that I wasn't foolish enough to believe I'd be able to support myself by writing. I didn't mention that as doctors, my three heroes had failed.

"Practicing medicine will be my profession," I said. "Writing will be my hobby."

"You're only seventeen," my mother sobbed. "You're still my baby."

I thought, but didn't tell them, that at seventeen, Jack London had shipped out for a year on a seal-hunting schooner and later used his adventures to write *The Sea Wolf.* I believed that, like London, writing of my own seafaring experiences would launch my career as an author, but what I said was, "I promise I'll be a doctor."

My father signed the enlistment papers and set me free.

After six weeks of basic training at Sheepshead Bay, I was transferred to Radio Officers' Training School on Hoffman Island, in New York Harbor. I liked the thought of sending messages in Morse code and being called Sparks. Perhaps that would be my pen name.

My only memory of Hoffman Island is meeting Morton Klass, who was to become my lifelong friend. Our last names began with K, and so we marched, ate and sat in classes side by side. Since Mort's bunk was across from mine, we argued politics, philosophy and literature, often long after lights-out, until some of the men threw their boots across the barracks to shut us up.

After Germany surrendered on May 7, 1945, the U.S. Maritime Service discovered they had a surplus of radio operators and closed the Hoffman Island Radio Officers' School. Mort sailed as an engine room *wiper,* and I was shipped out a week later to Le Havre, as *army utility* aboard a luxury liner that had been converted into a troopship.

My ship traveled back and forth to France carrying fresh troops to the replacement depot—the men called it *repo depo*—and bringing back G.I.'s who had completed their European tours of duty. They slept in bunks stacked five high in the hold that reeked of sweat, booze and vomit. The poker games went on twenty-four hours a day.

Shore leave in Le Havre was short, and all I remember is the mud and destruction and poverty—images I stored away.

After my second voyage on the troopship, I learned that although the War Shipping Administration had a surplus of radio officers, there was a shortage of pursers. They put out a call for seamen with clerical experience.

As it turned out, one of the most useful courses I had taken in junior high school was touch-typing. Long before it helped me as a writer, I had been able to get clerical jobs during summer breaks. With recommendations from former employers and a successful series of tests, I was granted a purser's license from the War Shipping Administration.

Now, with a U.S. Maritime Service rank of ensign, I no longer wore bell bottoms. A staff officer's uniform with crossed quills above one gold stripe on each sleeve designated my rating. Instead of being called *Sparks,* I would be called *Purser.*

Planning to write of my experiences, I changed the name of the ship and the shipping company in the records I kept, and I avoided using the real names of officers and crew. Except for those changes, what follows really happened.

My first duties as ship's purser took place at the New York office of International Tankers, Inc., where I drew up the ship's manifest and crew lists for the SS *Polestar* and supervised the men's signing of Ship's Articles in the presence of the shipping commissioner.

The navy told us only that it was to be a short coastwise voyage. When I questioned one company official, he pointed to a sign on the office wall showing a flaming ship disappearing into the ocean. Beneath it were the words "A Slip of the Lip Can Sink a Ship."

The men and I were told only that the *Polestar* would depart some time within the next two days from Bayonne, New Jersey, and that I would meet the captain—now on leave to visit his family in Philadelphia—just before sailing. As a matter of security, I learned, we would not be informed of the port of call or the duration of the voyage until after the tugs had escorted us out of New York Harbor and the harbor pilot had left the ship. Only after we were out to sea would the captain open his sailing orders and inform us of our destination.

It was a freezing January morning in 1946 when I finally got to the Bayonne docks. The taxi pulled up as close to the pier as possible, and I made my way along the ice-caked earth, stepping over networks of pipes and ducking under suspended hoses that creaked and swayed in their slings. Finally, I made out the name of my T-2 tanker, at the end of the dock—SS *Polestar.*

Empty of cargo, the ship rode high, looming over the dock, and the gangway tilted up at a forty-five-degree angle. Slipping one of my bags under my arm, I grabbed the railing and climbed up to the well deck. It was littered with papers and empty beer cans. The smell of oil was overpowering, and I had to stop at the windward side for swallows of air before climbing the ladder to the main deck. I could hear the ship creaking as she rose and fell with the wash. Other than that, no sounds. It felt like a ghost ship.

I found my way to the purser's cabin, unpacked and stowed my books: Homer, Plato and Shakespeare, as well as *War and Peace,* and *Moby Dick* in the rack above the desk. Hearing a rustling, I turned to see a baby-faced officer leaning against the open door, watching me. He had four gold stripes on his sleeves.

"Welcome aboard, Purser. I see you're a reader."

"Yes, Captain."

"We have a pretty good ship's library. You'll be in charge of lending out books. Mostly donations, of course, but if there are any special books you want let me know. We have a petty cash fund."

"Glad to hear that."

"But I think you should check out the dispensary and ship's hospital in case you need to order any additional medication or supplies. The last purser was pretty lackadaisical, and he was always running out of stuff."

"Ship's hospital? I don't understand. What's that got to do with me?"

He glanced at my jacket hanging over the back of the chair and frowned, pointing to my sleeve embroidered with gold braid crossed quills. "Where's the caduceus?"

Then I realized he was referring to the winged staff entwined with a snake which, along with crossed quills, would have denoted the usual dual rating of purser/pharmacist mate.

"I'm a purser, Captain, but not a pharmacist mate."

His face reddened. "I told the shipping commissioner I needed a replacement purser who was also a medic!"

"They told me there's a shortage of pursers, especially purser/pharmacist mates. That's why they hired me."

"This won't do, Keyes. I've got forty men aboard ship whose medical needs must be attended to."

Without thinking of the consequences, I blurted out, "I've got First Aid Expert merit badges in both the Boy Scouts and Sea Scouts. I served as ship's doctor on a few of our sailing trips. I was pre-med at college, and I'm planning to become a surgeon."

He studied me for a long time. "Okay, Keyes. You'll have to do. As soon as we're at sea—beyond coastal limits—I'll use my authority to designate you our pharmacist mate. In addition to your regular purser's duties, you'll run the dispensary and hospital, handle sick call, and do short-arm inspections after every shore leave."

"But, Captain—"

"No *buts* about it! You're ship's doctor." On his way out, he asked, "Play chess?"

"Yes, Sir."

"How good?"

"Average."

"Fine. We'll have a game tonight after dinner."

When he was gone, I slumped on my settee. Me and my big mouth. Wrapping and taping down bandages and dispensing aspirin on a Sea Scout weekend voyage up the East River was a far cry from being a physician to forty men at sea.

I beat the captain at chess that evening, but when I saw the annoyance in his blue eyes, I decided not to let that happen too often.

Next morning, the throbbing engines woke me, and I rushed out on deck to watch us weigh anchor and leave port. But I was too late. I climbed one of the ladders to an empty gun-tub, where anti-aircraft cannon had once been mounted, and from that position I could scan the horizon all around me. Unlike sailing along the East River on the *Dutchman III,* now there was no land in sight anywhere.

Suddenly, I had cast off all earthbound duties, plans, responsibilities. Worries and conflicts sloughed off like dead skin, giving way to deep relaxation. Without land in sight, there was no reality—no life, no death—nothing of importance but the here and now of the sea.

For the first time in my life, surrounded by sky and water I experienced "the oceanic feeling," and I understood why men, like an old seaman I'd visited in Sailor's Snug Harbor, followed the sea.

At sixteen, shortly after I had joined the Sea Scouts, I'd made a pilgrimage to the old sailors' home in Staten Island that provided a haven for retired seamen. There I visited one weather-beaten old salt. We sat in the visiting room silently for a while smoking our pipes, I in my pressed Sea Scout uniform and crisp peacoat, he with his black watch cap and threadbare peacoat pulled tight against the drafts.

Then, gripping my wrist and fixing me with his rheumy-eyed stare, he reminisced about his seafaring days. Images from "The Ancient Mariner" flooded my mind: *"He holds him with his skinny hand . . . He holds him with his glittering eye—"*

Like the Ancient Mariner, my old sailor held me captive as he described how his ship had been blown off course and was then becalmed among the Gulf weed drifting in currents into the great whirl in the North Atlantic to which all the sargasso weed in the world flowed. It was known as the Sargasso Sea.

"The island of lost ships and lost souls," he said.

He spoke of ships trapped in the weeds, as well as wrecked vessels that drifted into this watery graveyard, with crews of corpses waiting to be freed from the sargasso weed. He spoke of his own crew surviving there on the worms and tiny crabs, shrimps and octopuses that had changed color and shape, taking on camouflage to look like the floating, bulbous seaweed they lived on. Of mosquitoes big as birds.

"That's where the eels return to," he said, "millions of slimy snakes of the sea, from thousands of miles, from faraway waters coming back to mate, spawn and die."

He was a good storyteller, and I sat there spellbound, listening to him for a long time, pipe smoke curling between us. Then he nodded off to sleep, and I slipped away.

Looking at the ocean now from the deck of the *Polestar* I felt lonely and sad, and then an idea surfaced. In "The Ancient Mariner," Coleridge must have been describing the Sargasso when he wrote: *"We were the first that ever burst / Into that silent sea"* and *"Yea, slimy things did crawl with legs / Upon the slimy sea."*

The engines throbbing beneath my feet brought me back to reality. I turned away from the railing, climbed down from the gun-tub and crossed the catwalk to the officers' dining saloon.

There, at breakfast, I was introduced to the chief mate, who looked like a wrestler, and to the chief engineer, a huge, red-faced Georgian who sported pearl-handled six-guns, and to Sparks, the radio operator, whose eyes stared in different directions.

The captain informed us that he had opened the navy's sealed orders. "The *Polestar*'s destination is Aruba," he said. "There we take on bunkers for our own fuel supply. Then to Caracas, loading a full cargo of Venezuelan heating oil and off-loading it in Philadelphia. Expected duration of voyage, three weeks."

After breakfast, he motioned for me to stay behind.

"The men will get overnight shore-leave in Aruba and two days in Caracas," he said. "The last purser was supposed to lay in a good supply of condoms and prophylaxis ointment kits, but he slipped up. Normally, you'd conduct short-arm inspection for gonorrhea after the men come back aboard from each port, but since most of the crew signed on again in New York, you'd better do your first short-arm tomorrow."

I reminded him that he was to officially appoint me ship's doctor.

"Consider yourself so appointed."

I thought a moment. "I'd like it in writing, Captain."

He glared at me. "Eh?" Which I mentally translated as *Smart Ass?*

But then he softened, scribbled a note on a napkin and handed it to me. I folded it carefully and put it into my wallet for safekeeping beside my staff officer's papers.

Several of the men showed the green-pus symptoms of gonorrhea, and I put them on a regimen of penicillin shots every four hours around the clock for two days. For the night shots, I had to go down to the men's quarters with a flashlight, shine it into their eyes to waken them and roll them over. I gave each one a slap on the butt before punching in the needle, and few of them felt it going in.

I splinted one man's broken left arm—a simple fracture that could be set after we returned to the States.

My other duties included once-a-week openings of the Slop Chest for candy, cigarettes and sundries. We were running low on most supplies so I had to ration them. It confirmed what the captain had said about the last purser. He'd been sloppy about provisioning the Slop Chest.

Other than medical duties and tending the store, I was financial officer. I would have to give the men a draw, advancing them local currency for shore leave in each port. To prevent them from jumping ship in mid-voyage, the advance was limited to one half the money they'd already earned. All I needed to do was multiply each man's rate of pay by the number of days at sea. They could draw up to one-half that amount. I couldn't begin to calculate the draw until the captain told me the date of arrival.

That left me lots of time to read and write. I used my office typewriter to try my hand at writing sketches from my past and keeping my personal journal for material to store away for the sea novel I knew I would write someday.

I realized I had to train myself in the craft of writing. I had studied every book on the subject I could get my hands on. Somerset Maugham, in his autobiographical *The Summing Up,* describes how he taught himself to write by spending days in the library copying passages of authors he admired. That shocked me, at first, but then I understood. Now, with books from the ship's library, I did the same.

I believed that, like Maugham, I would eventually outgrow imitation, but by then I would have learned to shape words into sentences, and to mold them into paragraphs. I trusted myself to develop an ear for language, and to find my own voice and personal style, as well as those of my characters. Since Maugham hadn't been too proud to learn to write as children do—by imitation—neither was I.

From Hemingway, I learned to write simple declarative sentences devoid of figures of speech, in the down-to-earth, transparent style he had learned from Mark Twain. *Huckleberry Finn,* Hemingway said, is the book from which all American fiction descended, and I believe it was the poet Archibald MacLeish who said that

Hemingway had fashioned "a style for his time," playing on the title of Hemingway's first published collection of short stories, *In Our Time.*

From Faulkner, I learned to break those chains, freeing myself to write long, complex sentences and parenthetical paragraphs, often with imagery that explodes into metaphor.

Eventually, I weaned myself from both of them.

In the beginning of "Flowers for Algernon," Charlie's style is direct, childlike and free of metaphors, but as he changes, his simple declarative sentences become compound and then complex, then intricate and metaphoric. As his ability to write deteriorates, his style becomes simple again, until he reverts to near illiteracy.

I learned from the masters in the ship's library.

After refueling in Aruba, the *Polestar* sailed to Caracas for a cargo of heating oil. Then we were homeward bound, with little for me to do until the captain gave me our arrival date in Philadelphia.

Sparks and I were playing chess in my office when, suddenly, there was a furious banging at my door and a distraught seaman burst into my cabin, "Purser! Come quick! Something's wrong with one of the deck hands."

"What is it?"

"I dunno, but he's been puking, and now there's dark stuff coming out of his mouth and nose."

I grabbed my black bag and shouted to Sparks to alert the captain or chief mate. Then I followed the seaman along the catwalk to the men's quarters on the forward deck. A crowd outside the fo'c'sle parted to make way for me. As I reached the doorway and smelled a mixture of sweet lemony syrup and vomit, I started to gag, but I braced myself and went inside.

A heavy-set man was lying on his back across a bottom bunk, with his head halfway to the deck, his face covered with dark, bloody ooze. He was sucking it in and out of his nostrils and mouth, gurgling and gasping for air.

I had seen this middle-aged seaman, from time to time, mopping oil from the well deck, or on a scaffold over the side, painting or chipping. He'd come to the dispensary a couple of times for aspirin to dull his hangovers, and once he mentioned a large family in Philadelphia.

I had no idea what was wrong with him, but I realized he was drowning in his own blood-filled vomit.

"Help me roll him over!"

Two men jumped forward and we turned him face down to keep him from choking.

"Anyone know what happened? What's that sweet smell?"

"He ran out of booze, after we left Caracas," one of the seamen said. "Broke into the galley after Cookie closed it and stole a quart of lemon extract. I think he drank it all."

I shook my head. What was I going to do? Even face down, he was still choking, sucking fluid back up his nose.

Sparks showed up. "What a stink! Need help, Purse?"

"Get the captain!"

"Orders not to wake him. First Mate's on watch in the wheelhouse."

"This guy's drowning in his own bloody vomit. I'll give him artificial respiration to see if I can clear his lungs. Get on the radio and try to contact the nearest navy ship with a doctor aboard. Tell them this guy drank a quart of lemon extract."

Sparks nodded and dashed out.

I took off my shoes, straddled the seaman and turned his head to the left. Then I began pumping him as I'd learned in the Sea Scouts.

"Out goes the bad air . . ." pressing down on his back, "In comes the good air . . ." releasing to let the lungs fill. "Out goes the bad air . . . in comes the good air."

I sat astride him for nearly half an hour, pumping and releasing, wondering if I was helping him or killing him.

A messman showed up with a radio message Sparks had received from a navy ship. It read, *"Give artificial respiration."*

I felt better knowing I was doing the right thing. I showed one of the seamen how to spell me, and he began by imitating my movements and then taking

over. "Out goes the bad air . . . In comes the good . . ."

When I could no longer find a pulse, I sent word back to Sparks to radio the navy doctor for instructions.

A few minutes later the captain showed up with a radio message in his hand. "How's it going, Purser?"

"I think he's a goner."

"The navy doctor says to give your patient a shot of adrenaline to the heart."

I balked at that. *"He's not my patient."*

"He damned well is. You're ship's doctor."

"Only under your orders."

"Then I order you to give your patient a shot of adrenaline to the heart."

"I wouldn't know how to do it. I might kill him."

"It's a direct order, Purser. Do it, or I'll throw you in the brig and bring you up on charges when we get back."

I looked around at my witnesses. "Put the order in writing, Captain."

He found someone with pen and paper and wrote it out.

"Okay," I said, "but I'm sure he's dead already."

I got the adrenaline out of the medicine bag, found a hypodermic and fresh needle and prepared the injection. I looked up at the captain one more time. "You sure?"

"If he's dead, there's nothing to lose."

"But I'm not sure."

"Do it!"

The men rolled him onto his back at my instruction.

With no heartbeat to guide me, I searched for where I hoped this man's heart would be. I shoved the hypo in and jammed the plunger.

Nothing.

The captain told the messenger to have Sparks notify the navy doctor. Minutes later, the man returned with the message. The captain read it aloud. "Continue artificial respiration until midnight. Then declare the sailor dead."

"But he's dead already!"

"There's going to be a naval inquest. Go ahead, Purse, follow the doctor's orders."

"Why me?"

"Because you're the duly appointed doctor on this ship, and he's your patient and you've got your order in writing."

We rolled the dead seaman back onto his stomach, and for the next hour and a half I sat astride a stiffening corpse whispering, "Out goes the bad air. In comes the good."

At midnight, I declared him dead. After we wrapped him in canvas, I asked the captain if we would bury him at sea.

"Can't do it. We're two days off the Florida coast. I have to bring him in for the inquiry."

"Where do we keep him until then?"

The captain shrugged. "Put him into the refrigerator."

A murmur of disapproval at the captain's words traveled from the seamen at the entrance to the fo'c'sle all the way back to the catwalk. The bosun stepped through the crowd, pushed the onlookers outside and closed the hatch.

"Cap'n, with all respects . . ."

"What is it, Boats?"

"The men don't take to the idea of having a dead man stored in with their food. A lot of them are real superstitious. I think you'd have a mutiny on your hands."

The captain looked at me. "Any suggestions, *Doctor*?"

I winced at the word. "We've got him wrapped in waterproof canvas. Why don't we just put him on some boards in one of the empty cargo holds and pile dry ice around him?"

The bosun nodded. "That won't bother them."

"Okay, Boats," the captain said, "Have the deck crew take care of it." Then he turned on his heel and climbed the ladder to the catwalk and back to officers' quarters.

We anchored off Fort Lauderdale, and I watched from the railing as a launch brought navy officers out to the *Polestar*. Although I had done the best I could under the captain's direct orders, I was frightened and nervous about the inquiry. I put his written orders into my briefcase and congratulated myself on my foresight. What would have happened to me without them? Might I have been accused of practicing medicine without a license? Manslaughter? Well, aboard ship, a captain was all-powerful. He had said I was a doctor, and that made it so.

It was a perfunctory inquiry. The ruling was something like "self-inflicted accidental death," and I was cleared.

After we arrived in port, my job was to assist the shipping commissioner who brought aboard Ship's Articles for the sign-off. I gave each man his official "U.S. Coast Guard Certificate of Discharge."

But when the time came to sign Ship's Articles for the next voyage, only the officers signed on, none of the crew. As the bosun had said, most seamen were superstitious, and a ship aboard which a sailor had died was considered a vessel of doom. Despite my having been cleared at the inquest, they had all seen or heard how I had sat astride the dead man, and the word spread that I was a Jonah who urged him on with my incantation of good and bad air, squeezing the breath out of him as I had ridden his soul down to hell.

Out on deck, I ran into the bosun and some of the crew ready to go ashore. Feeling guilty under the stare of the dead man's shipmates, I said, "Sorry I couldn't save him."

The bosun put his hand on my shoulder. "You did all you could, Purse. Most doctors lose a patient now and then."

As I watched them go down the gangway, his words hit home. I'd kept my promise to my parents and practiced medicine, but I'd lost a patient. I knew that when my eighteen-month tour of duty was over and I signed off the *Polestar,* that would end my medical career.

Like Somerset Maugham and Chekhov and Conan Doyle, I had been a doctor for a while, and like them I had failed. Now, I would keep following in their footsteps and try to become a writer.

## II: FROM SHIP TO SHRINK

### Inkblots

I shipped out on the *Polestar* a second time, a planned one-year voyage from Newport News, Virginia, to Naples, and then a shuttle run carrying oil from Bahrein, Arabia, to the naval station on Okinawa. However, the navy changed our orders three times, and we ended up circling the globe in ninety-one days. When I signed off the *Polestar,* I said good-bye and good-riddance to my seagoing medical career.

During six more voyages on other ships, I never once mentioned to any of the captains that I was first aid expert. Then, finally, after eighteen months of sea duty, I signed off my last oil tanker on December 6, 1946, with a "Certificate of Continuous Service" and a letter under presidential seal from the White House.

> To you who answered the call of your country and served in its Merchant Marine to bring about the total defeat of the enemy, I extend the heartfelt thanks of the Nation. You undertook a most severe task—one which called for courage and fortitude. Because you demonstrated the resourcefulness and calm judgment necessary to carry out that task, we now look to you for leadership and example in further serving our country in peace.
>
> [signed] Harry Truman

I went back to my parents' home in Brooklyn where I planned to live while I continued my college education.

My first day home after my discharge, Mom made a large dinner and invited relatives and guests to celebrate my sister Gail's ninth birthday and my return. The nineteen-year-old prodigal son, my parents assumed, would now go on to become a doctor. I hadn't yet gotten up the courage to tell them I had already fulfilled my promise by practicing medicine aboard ship and I had no intention of continuing pre-med or going to medical school.

After dinner, I headed down to my cellar library for a novel to read in bed. But as I opened the door—even before I took the stairs down—I sensed something was missing. Where was the smell of wet coal?

I turned on the light and saw that my bookshelves, books and all, were gone. I tasted panic in my throat as I walked quickly to the alcove behind the steps. The coal bin was gone, and the old furnace had been replaced by an oil-burner.

No books. No coal. No toys in the bin. All the real things were gone. I wanted to dash upstairs and ask my parents, "Why?"

But it wasn't necessary. I understood. They had decided I was no longer a child. I had left as a seventeen-year-old surrogate to their dreams and they had gotten rid of my childish things. They could never have known that their son's ideas and memories and dreams—things he would use to make himself a writer—would always occupy the hideaway beneath the cellar steps.

At breakfast next morning, I told them I had already tasted a doctor's life, and like Maugham and Chekhov and Doyle, I had failed at it. I was not cut out to practice medicine. I was going to become a writer, I said, and now I had to leave Brooklyn to do it.

My mother wept and my father walked out of the room.

I moved from my parents' apartment to an inexpensive furnished room on the West Side of Manhattan, in the neighborhood called Hell's Kitchen. What money I had left from my service pay would have to support me while I wrote my first novel. It was about a seventeen-year-old purser's adventures at sea.

The novel was rejected by a dozen publishers. The last one had left a reader's coverage behind in the manuscript. By mistake? On purpose? Only two lines remain in my memory. The critique began: "It isn't as bad as some unsolicited manuscripts, but it's not good enough . . ." And the last line: "The basic story is good, but it is all on the surface and the characters' motivations are never too clear."

Like most writers, I took solace in the opening and closing phrases, putting the two *buts* out of my mind.

I reread the novel and saw how amateurish it was, how much I had to learn before I could call myself an author: how to get beneath the surface, how to understand a character's motivation, how to revise. I put the manuscript aside, knowing I would have to find another profession to support myself while I learned how to write.

Many writers began as reporters, among them Twain, Hemingway and Stephen Crane. Well, why not?

A few days after my novel was rejected, I went to *The New York Times* building in Times Square and asked to speak to the publisher. Only now do I realize how presumptuous it was of me to approach Mr. Ochs without an appointment or introduction, how amazing it was that I actually got in to see him and how generous it was of him to give me the time.

"I'd like to start as a cub reporter," I told him, "then to become a foreign correspondent."

"Has that always been your goal?"

I squirmed as I searched for the right words. "Well, not exactly. My real goal is to be an author."

He nodded gravely and turned a framed picture on his desk to show me a photograph of a young man. "I'm going to tell you the same thing I told my son," he said. "In the immortal words of the famous journalist and author Horace Greeley, 'Go west, young man. Go west.' "

I suspected that Mr. Ochs interpreted Greeley as advising young would-be authors and journalists to hone their skills and seek their opportunities away from New York, somewhere in the minor leagues.

I thanked him for his advice, but I didn't follow it. Instead, I enrolled in a summer-session journalism course at NYU. I sat in a crowded lecture hall for two weeks before I realized that I would have to devote all my time, energy and single-minded striving to become a good reporter. Using words constantly in newspaper work, I realized, would leave me too tired to create fiction at night. I dropped the course, got back part of my tuition and searched for another career that wouldn't interfere with writing.

I applied to Brooklyn College which, at that time, was free for those whose high school records showed a B average, or who achieved a B or higher in an admissions examination. Unfortunately, I had been a C+ student. In high school, my English teachers had always given me A for creativity and D for grammar and usage. But I placed high on the entrance exam, was accepted for tuition-free admission, and resumed my college education at night.

I was still trying to decide what profession might leave me energy and time to write. I enrolled in an introductory psychology course and found the subject matter fascinating, the instructor stimulating. I was surprised to learn that he was a lay psychoanalyst—not a psychiatrist with an M.D.—and that with only a master of arts degree he had developed a clinical practice.

Here, I decided, was my solution.

As a lay psychoanalyst, I would be able to set my own hours for therapy sessions and charge reasonable fees for helping people deal with their mental problems. I would learn about people's motives, and come to understand their conflicts. And I imagined how that would help me create believable characters—living, suffering, changing characters—for my stories and novels.

As Faulkner said in 1950 when he accepted the Nobel Prize for literature: ". . . the young man or woman writing today has forgotten the problems of the human heart in conflict with itself which alone can make good writing because only that is worth writing about, worth the agony and the sweat . . . leaving no room in his workshop for anything but the old verities and truths of the heart, the old universal truths lacking which any story is ephemeral and doomed . . ."

Instead of exploring "the human heart in conflict with itself," I decided I would write about the *human mind* in conflict with itself, and psychology would be my path. I declared it my major.

I took a daytime job selling encyclopedias from door to door. I hated the cold-calling, high-pressure selling, but I was good at it and the commissions stopped the hemorrhaging from my savings account.

During this time, I took psychology, sociology and anthropology courses, but the more courses I took, the more disillusioned I became. Not about the subject matter, but with the professors. Except for that first instructor who had inspired me, I found most of them dull, pedantic and pompous, and their research trivial.

In my senior year, I confided some personal anxieties to my advisor, a professor of "Psychological Tests and Measurements." She gave me the Rorschach test, and as I responded to the inkblots, a memory flooded my mind.

. . . I see a little first or second grader sitting at the kitchen table doing his homework, dipping a steel-nibbed pen into a bottle of black ink and scratching cursive letters in a black-and-white, marble-covered notebook. As he nears the end of the page, the boy's hand trembles. He presses too hard on the pen. A blob of ink flows down the nib, and before he can lift it from the page, an inkblot drips onto the paper.

He knows what will happen. For the third time that evening—after two errors and now one inkblot—a hand comes out of the shadows, over his shoulder, and rips the page from the notebook.

"Do it over," his mother says. "It has to be perfect."

After the Rorschach, my advisor, the Professor of Tests and Measurements, refused to discuss the results and never spoke to me again. I thought of going to another Rorschach specialist to find out what those inkblots had revealed, but I decided I was better off not knowing.

Years later, I satirized some of my psych professors in *Flowers for Algernon.* Digging up that old homework inkblot memory and my mother's hand tearing out the pages, I transformed my frustrating Tests and Measurements advisor into Burt the Tester whom Charlie Gordon frustrates with his responses to the inkblots.

Writers get even.

### The Boy on Book Mountain

After graduating *summa cum ordinary* in 1950, I took a one-year, postgraduate course at CCNY, City College of New York. The course, called "The Organismic Approach to Psychopathology," was given by the world-famous psychiatrist Kurt Goldstein. His method of teaching, both semesters, was to read to us—word for word, with an impenetrable German accent—his book *The Organismic Approach to Psychopathology.*

During the same period, I began what was called a *didactic analysis.* Anyone who hoped to practice pure psychoanalysis was expected to plumb his or her own depths to unearth biases, traumas and personality defects, and to be able to compensate for them when treating clients. I went twice a week, Mondays and Fridays, at the reduced rate of ten dollars for each fifty-minute hour.

My analyst was short, middle-aged, with a thick Austrian accent difficult to understand. He used the Freudian method—me stretched out on the couch, him sitting in a chair behind me, out of sight.

He laid down the ground rules, which I thought of as the Four Commandments. During the course of my analysis, I was to avoid making any major alterations in my life: I was not to change jobs, move, get married or divorced, or—and this was especially important—I was not to quit therapy. These restrictions, he explained, were based on the theory that painful self-awareness surfacing during depth therapy, along with transference with the analyst, often leads people to find creative ways of dumping their therapists. And therapists have reasons for not wanting that to happen.

I accepted the rules. Actually, I felt I'd be getting my money's worth. In addition to becoming trained as a psychoanalyst, I'd be getting an insight into myself and—at the same time—I'd learn how to use the process of free association as a writing tool.

Three goals for the price of one was a bargain, but at first it didn't work.

Although the dynamics of psychoanalysis require the analyst to sit passively and merely facilitate free association, I became frustrated. Each time I lay on the couch, the first five or ten minutes of the fifty-minute hour came up blank or with inconsequential talk about what was currently going on in my life. One afternoon, I sat up and faced him.

He looked startled.

"I seem to be wasting your time and my money," I said.

He cleared his throat to prepare it for the unorthodox procedure of actually *talking to a client.* "Daniel, let me to you something explain. Is perfectly usual what you are experiencing. You see, in Vienna, the analysand to therapy comes six days a week. Only on Sundays are there no sessions. Is common experience that after a day with no free association, the psychic wound a protective layer forms, and on Monday, it takes a great deal of work to break through to real, substantial association. This blankness, or garbage, you experiencing are, we call, *The Monday Morning Crust.*"

"I don't understand."

"Since you only twice a week to sessions come, with off-days in between, it always some time takes to break through the *The Monday Morning Crust.*"

Although it seemed wasteful to spend ten minutes of each fifty-minute hour in silence or spewing out expensive emotional garbage before penetrating my mental crust, I lay back on the couch again. After ten minutes I began really free-associating. And I remembered.

. . . *Betty's Beauty Parlor,* near the railroad depot of freight sidings, beneath the elevated trains . . . my mother Betty, a self-trained beautician, washing, curling and setting women's hair . . . We live in one room above the beauty parlor, my bed beside the window close to theirs, and I wake up every time the elevated train thunders by . . .

. . . circus season . . . Ringling Brothers Barnum and Bailey Circus trains have pulled into the nearby freight yards. Sideshow people and lady performers come to *Betty's Beauty Parlor* to have their hair and nails done. Some of them wait out on the stone porch, sitting on the steps, playing with me, doing tricks and telling stories. The bearded lady and the tattooed lady are my mother's customers. They say I am a cute little boy.

A lady trapeze artist comes to have her hair done. Her little girl, about five or six with blonde Shirley Temple curls, is crying as her mother drags her inside kicking and screaming.

My mother calls out to me to let the little girl play with my toys. I hand her a train engine from my toy box, but she flings it and it breaks.

"Danny," my mother says, "play with her."

No matter what I do the brat keeps crying.

"Danny . . ." my mother pleads.

I run upstairs and come back with an armload of my books. I open one and begin: "Once upon a time, there was a beautiful princess . . ."

Though the girl keeps crying, I don't stop. Eventually, she grows silent and listens. Of course, I can't really read at that age, but my mother has read the stories to me so often that I know them by heart.

"He can read!" one of the customers says.

The girl's mother asks, "How old is he?"

"Three and a half," my mother says proudly.

"He must be a genius." She opens her purse and takes out a penny. "That was very clever, Danny. Here, buy a piece of candy."

I tilt back my head and try to see my analyst's face. "I guess that's when I first learned I could be paid for telling stories."

I can't make out his face, and he makes no comment.

I must have been three or four years old when those memories were locked in, because Wall Street collapsed in 1929 when I was two, and President Roosevelt closed the banks in 1933 when I was five. Some time between those two dates, my parents were forced to close *Betty's Beauty Parlor* and move to Snediker

Avenue, where they rented two first-floor rooms from Mr. Pincus.

When the hard times came, since my mother had no time to read me to sleep, I taught myself the alphabet. Sounding out the words came easily, and I was a reader long before I entered first grade at the age of six. The teachers at P.S. 63 convinced my mother that there was no point in sending a five-year-old who could read as well as I did to kindergarten.

I associate the connections of memory to the age of six or seven when I first learned what it meant to be a story-teller.

On a humid summer evening, as my parents and I sat on the front porch, I discovered a group of neighborhood kids congregated under the street lamp in front of the local grocery store.

With my mother's permission, I ran to see what was going on. Most of the boys were older, and they were in front of the store sitting on large wooden crates the grocer used to keep milk bottles cold in the wintertime. Someone boosted me up to sit with them so I could watch and hear.

A boy named Sammy stood on the sidewalk telling a story. I still see him clearly, his uncut hair falling over his ears, his shirt patched, his scuffed black shoes unlaced.

He told of Joan of Arc being attacked by the Frankenstein monster, saved in the nick of time by the Hunchback of Notre Dame. And then King Kong captured Mae West and dragged her out into the jungle, but Charlie Chaplin had a sword in his cane, and he killed the huge ape and wandered off twirling his cane.

Everyone sitting on the wooden boxes listened intently as Sammy unfolded his tales. They screamed with disappointment when he stopped with the hated words: "To be continued . . ."

Tony, the next storyteller, tried to imitate Sammy, but he didn't have it. He rambled and lost track of his plots, and the audience showed their disapproval by banging their heels on the sides of the empty milk boxes.

In the summer evenings that followed, I was always there to listen, and to learn what kinds of stories made them kick and what kept them silent. I wanted to join in, to show that I, too, could be a storyteller, but at six or seven I was the youngest and too frightened to perform in front of this audience of tough critics.

I couldn't seem to memorize anything. At home, before joining the group in front of the grocery store, I planned my plots and visualized how I would tell the stories. But when it was my turn, I became confused.

It was the same at school. I did poorly on tests that relied on memory. My mother would get me up early in the morning before a math test to review the multiplication tables, but by the time I got to class it was all gone.

Years earlier, I'd been able to memorize stories from children's books word for word, without even trying, but later, in school, I couldn't recall anything. I guessed I wasn't very bright.

Then one night, in bed, with my eyes closed, I tried to review for the next day's arithmetic test, going over the material again and again. Nothing. Forcing myself to stay awake, I tried to see the numbers. I couldn't add or subtract without counting on my fingers. But next morning, while washing my face with icy water, I stared into the mirror over the sink, eyes stinging with soap. I knew that I knew it all. I rattled off the eight and nine times tables to my reflection.

Between night and morning, no matter how hard I'd struggled, after failing to get this stuff straight in my head, something or someone *had learned it in my sleep.*

I applied the system to the grocery storytelling group: struggle with the material hard before sleep, then put it out of my mind. In the morning I face the other me in the mirror and discover I've got it.

It took me a long time to get up the nerve to perform, but with sleep learning, I had my stories down cold. My plots were dramatic, filled with menace and conflict, and my audience never banged their heels against the boxes.

Years later, I published a short story about Sammy—called "The Spellbinder"—in the *North American Review.* And I transformed my memory of learning during sleep into the sleep-learning machine that Charlie Gordon struggles with during the experiment to increase his intelligence and knowledge.

"I loved storytelling almost as much as I loved books," I told my analyst.

"And what does that make you think of?" he asked in one of his more talkative moments.

"It reminds me of climbing Book Mountain . . ."

"Yes? . . ."

I remembered.

By the time I was in third grade, my father had worked out a partnership deal with a pot-bellied, bald man whose name I don't remember. They opened a junk shop in Brownsville and bought and sold scrap metal, old clothing and newspapers. Junkmen would pull up to the warehouse with horses and wagons and unload their day's accumulation onto the huge scale.

From time to time, my father would take me with him and let me play in the shop. What interested me most was the mountain of books . . .

It's a hot August day, the summer I turn eight . . . My father explains that he and his partner pay a few cents for boxes of old books to be baled and pulped into cheap paper. "You can take some books home."

"To keep?"

"Sure."

"How many?"

He hands me a small burlap sack. "As many as you can carry."

I can still visualize the books piled up to the ceiling. I see three huge men, stripped to the waist, bodies glistening with sweat, bandanas around their foreheads, loading books into two baling presses.

One worker grabs an armful from the base of the huge pile, rips off the covers and hands the naked pages to a second worker who dumps them into the baler. The third tamps them down and sets the baler's press lid.

Then the first man punches the button that crushes the books, and I hear the grinding sound. The second man inserts wires into the machine that will make wirebound bales encased in cardboard from old boxes. The third man opens the machine and pulls the bale out with a hand truck and deposits it on the street with the others so the truck will be able to back up, load them and drive them away to pulp them into rolls of paper.

Suddenly, I know what I have to do. I climb up to the top of Book Mountain and make a place to sit. I grab a book, read a few passages, and either toss it down to the base or put it into my bag. Quickly, I go through as many as I can, desperately sampling enough of a book to decide if it's worth rescuing from the sweating book-destroyers who will feed them to the baler below.

When I've got six or seven books, I slide down the other side of the mountain and load the sack into my bicycle basket.

At home most evenings, when schoolwork is done, instead of listening to the radio serials, I read and read and read. Many of the books are too advanced for me, but I know that someday I will understand them. Someday I will learn what they have to teach.

The image of myself as a boy going up and then coming down Book Mountain is fixed in my memory as the icon of my love of reading and learning.

It was clear to me as I wrote *Flowers for Algernon* where the shape of it came from. As Charlie's intelligence increases, I visualize him ascending a mountain. The higher he climbs, the farther he sees, until at the peak, he turns and sees all around him the world of knowledge—of good and evil.

But then he must come down the other side.

### *Silence of the Psychoanalysts*

My psychoanalyst's lack of any kind of response began to oppress me, and I found myself wondering about him. Like that "Tests and Measurements" advisor who avoided me after the inkblot test, this shrink never talked to me either!

Without confiding in him, I quit selling encyclopedias from door to door and found a new job at Acme Advertising selling direct-mail advertising—mailers with attached return order envelopes. The company called us *Account Executives,* but it was still cold-calling—just one notch above ringing doorbells.

When I told my analyst that I had violated his first commandment against making changes in my life, he said nothing.

During my first *executive* meeting at Acme Advertising, I met Bergie, a tall, heavyset man who knew the good local restaurants and enjoyed talking about books. When he referred to the company as *Acne* instead of *Acme,* I knew I had found a friend.

One day, he asked me to join him for a brown-bag lunch at the Peter Fland Photographic Studio between Broad-

way and Sixth Avenue—a block from the 42nd Street library. He and two Austrian friends who worked at Fland's as retouchers of photographic negatives had formed a chamber music trio, and they played in the studio after their lunch break.

Fland was a jolly, bouncing photographer, with an Austrian accent, whose every comment conveyed good-natured irony. The luncheon concert was followed by a photo shoot, and he invited me to watch. Three tall fashion models came in and lounged about, waiting, looking bored, almost glum. The redhead sipped coffee out of a paper cup, the brunette chain-smoked cigarettes, the third, a blonde, was filing her fingernails.

A few minutes later, a short, dark-haired young woman entered the studio. Her boss was studying a still-wet, eight-by-ten, black-and-white print.

"Ahh, Aurea!" he said, "You were right about the backlight!"

Aurea rearranged the lighting, then slipped out of her shoes to step onto the set and called the models back. She styled the dresses, pulling the brunette's out to flare. When the blonde's dress wouldn't stay put, Aurea took a spool of fine thread out of her pocket, pinned one thread to each side of the hem, pulled them out and pinned the other ends of the threads to the floor. The redhead's dress was too tight, so Aurea slit it down the back and arranged the front folds to drape naturally. Then she stepped aside.

"Perfect!" Fland shouted. "Lights!"

She threw the switches.

The instant the set was illuminated by floodlights the models were transformed. Wet lips glistened, eyes opened wide. They came alive, exciting and alluring under the lights, as Fland took dozens of shots.

"Okay!" he called out. "That's beautiful, ladies."

The moment Aurea switched off the lights, the three models drooped like puppets whose strings had been released. They were bored again, glum, almost plain.

I nodded. Few things were what they appeared to be.

I stopped by the Fland Studio often, before my evening graduate psych courses at CCNY, trying to work up the nerve to invite Aurea out to dinner, or to the theater—for the full three acts, of course.

One Friday afternoon, I got a call from a writer-acquaintance named Lester del Rey. He wanted to know if I was interested in a job as associate fiction editor for a chain of pulps. These were the popular fiction magazines of the day, printed on cheap, untrimmed stock that left paper dandruff all over your dark clothing.

"I don't understand," I said.

"Well, my agent, Scott Meredith, has heard of an opening at Stadium Publications. He's close to the editor, and Scott would like to have the job filled by someone who'd buy stories from Meredith clients. I told him that even though you haven't published yet, you've got a good story sense and might be able to handle the job. It pays fifty dollars a week. Interested?"

Thinking I'd be violating my analyst's First Commandment about not changing jobs a second time, I hesitated, but I said yes.

"Okay, come down to Scott's office. By the time you get here, he'll have a letter of recommendation typed up, and he'll call ahead and set up a meeting between you and Bob Erisman."

"How can Meredith recommend me? He's never met me."

Lester paused. "Don't ask any questions. If you want the job, just get over here quick."

By the time I arrived at the Scott Meredith Literary Agency, Lester had left, but fast-talking Meredith filled me in on the situation.

"Bob Erisman works at his home in Connecticut and comes into New York only on Fridays to pick up the edited stories. His associate fiction editor quit without notice, and he's desperate for a replacement."

He handed me a note: "From the desk of SCOTT MEREDITH—September 1, 1950." It introduced me as an excellent candidate for the position. It said I'd worked at his literary agency for about six months on a temporary job and had experience doing pulp reading for another periodical. They'd sold a few of my baseball, football and science-fiction stories.

I swallowed hard. We'd never get away with this.

His note praised me as a fast reader and typist, familiar with general magazine practice. The quoted salary, he wrote, was acceptable.

When I said nothing, Meredith asked what I thought of the letter.

I shrugged. "The last line is true."

"Good," he said. "Then you'd better get over there before Bob leaves for the week."

Martin Goodman Publications, and its pulp magazine subsidiary, Stadium Publications, were on the sixteenth floor of the Empire State Building. I got there at three o'clock, and Bob Erisman, the editor, was waiting for me.

He got up from behind his desk to greet me, took the letter of recommendation and nodded as he read it. "Good. Scott Meredith is a great judge of people. You start a two-week trial period on Monday."

He led me to the adjoining office that held two desks. At the one near the window, a portly old gentleman with horn-rimmed glasses halfway down his nose was puffing away at a pipe clenched between his teeth.

"This is the editor of our true crime and fact detective lines," Erisman said, introducing us. "Daniel Keyes is trying out for the associate fiction editor's job."

The old gentleman peered at me over his glasses, saluted with his blue pencil, grunted his approval and went back to editing through his pipe smoke.

Erisman led me to a smaller desk against the other wall and pointed to different colored binders stacked on shelves. "Those are the agents' submissions. Dirk Wylie Agency, Lenninger Agency, Matson, and so forth. As you know, the grey ones are from Scott."

I nodded, starting to sweat.

He pointed to a garish red and yellow magazine cover on the wall. The May issue of *Best Western* highlighted a damsel in distress held hostage by a mean-faced, unshaven cowpoke, while the hero's white horse reared as a rifle shot exploded across the yellow background. The blurb read: *"WHERE THE GUNHAWKS GATHER, A filed .45 was the kid's only friend in vengeance valley . . . Smash feature-length novel."* Near the top, a banner heading read *"3 Brand New Novels Plus Short Stories."*

Erisman said, "You'll go through the agents' manuscripts and select and edit the stories to go with the novels."

I picked up the slender magazine. "Three novels?"

He shrugged. "They're really long stories, or short novelettes, but readers like to think they're getting their twenty-five cents worth."

"I don't select those?"

"Novels are commissioned from our top writers in each field, and I edit them. I also write the blurbs, the titles, and describe the drawings for the artists. You buy and edit the short stories. We have nine monthly magazines. Four westerns, four sports and one science fiction. Why don't you take a few of each and get a feeling for the kind of material our readers like."

He looked at his watch. "I've got to catch my train. See you next Friday. Before you leave, drop in at the business office, and they'll put you on the payroll."

After he was gone, I sat down at my new desk and tried out the swivel chair. The true crime editor was too deep in his work to notice me. I picked up copies of *Complete Sports, Complete Westerns, Western Novels and Stories* and *Marvel Science Fiction.*

"So long," I said to my office mate. "Nice meeting you. Have a good weekend."

He waved his blue pencil at me without looking up.

I glanced around the offices on my way out. I was actually going to be paid a regular weekly salary of fifty dollars to read, buy and edit stories. I had landed on the first step of a career that would support me while I wrote fiction. Then I was through the door, down the elevator, and out onto Fifth Avenue to catch the bus that would take me to my psychoanalyst's office. I was apprehensive. I had violated the first of his Four Commandments twice in a matter of months.

I got there a few minutes early, and as I waited I flipped through *Complete Western.* Almost immediately, I saw two typographical errors. That's when I realized that, despite Scott Meredith's recommendation attesting to my familiarity with general magazine practice, I didn't know the first thing about *editing* a manuscript.

As I held the magazine, my hands trembled, and I started to sweat. Something was coming into my mind. Something deep and frightening. The memory of my mother's hand ripping out my homework page. Her words, echoing . . . "It has to be perfect."

When I finally got on the couch, I said, "I've got a new job. I'm quitting *Acme Advertising.* I'm going to edit a chain of pulp magazines."

I expected him to say something like: Oh, you've quit another job? But he didn't respond.

I said, "I must admit I feel guilty at breaking one of the rules you laid down—not once but twice—but I hate cold-call selling, and I'm excited about climbing the first rung up the literary ladder."

After fifty minutes, filled with long periods of silence, I got off the couch, paid him and left. As much as his lack of response irritated me, I realized his method was working. There in his consulting room, I had just associated my new editing job with the earlier inkblot memory of my mother's demand for writing perfection.

Although I felt confident about finding and correcting mistakes, editing paragraphs and sentences and fixing errors, I suddenly wondered, what about editorial notations and proofreaders marks?

Well, I thought, mumbling the cliche that has served me all my life, "Where there's a will there's a way." Instead of going to my room, I took a Fifth Avenue bus to the 42nd Street Library to read up on editing and proofreading marks.

No movies, or ball games or working up the nerve to ask Aurea for a date—not for a while. Erisman would come into the office next Friday to pick up the stories. I had just one week to learn to be an editor.

[*Author's Note:* These are the first eight chapters of my book: *Algernon, Charlie and I: A Writer's Journey.* This story-behind-the-story memoir (including the original novelette version of "Flowers for Algernon") published in full by Challcrest Press Books (an imprint of Challenge Press), February, 2000.]

## BIOGRAPHICAL/CRITICAL SOURCES:

### BOOKS

Scholes, Robert, *Structural Fabulation,* University of Notre Dame Press (Notre Dame, IN), 1975.

### PERIODICALS

*Chicago Tribune,* November 11, 1981.
*Library Journal,* July, 1986.
*Los Angeles Times,* December 12, 1980.
*Los Angeles Times Book Review,* January 3, 1982.

*New York Times Book Review,* November 15, 1981;
August 24, 1986.
*Saturday Review,* March 26, 1966.
*Times Literary Supplement,* July 21, 1966.
*Voice Literary Supplement,* October, 1981.
*Washington Post Book World,* November 29, 1981.

OTHER

*Daniel Keyes Homepage,* http://in.flite.net/dkeyes/
index.html, November 29, 1999.

\*　　\*　　\*

## KEYES, Greg
### See KEYES, J. Gregory

\*　　\*　　\*

## KEYES, J. Gregory 1963-
### (Greg Keyes)

*PERSONAL:* Born in 1963; married; wife's name, Nell
(a jewelry maker). *Education:* University of Georgia,
Athens, M.A. (anthropology).

*ADDRESSES: Agent*—c/o Ballantine Publishing
Group, 201 East 50th St., New York, NY 10022. *E-
mail*—gkeyes@uga.cc.uga.edu.

*CAREER:* Author, 1996—. University of Georgia, Athens, instructor.

*WRITINGS:*

*The Waterborn* (first novel in "Chosen of the Changeling" series), Ballantine (New York City), 1996.
*The Blackgod* (second novel in "Chosen of the Changeling" series), Ballantine, 1997.
*Newton's Cannon* (first novel in "The Age of Unreason" series), Ballantine, 1998.
*A Calculus of Angels* (second novel in "The Age of Unreason" series), Ballantine, 1999.

*SIDELIGHTS:* J. Gregory Keyes is an author and instructor at the University of Georgia, in Athens. When
Keyes was a child, his father's job took the family to
an Arizona Navajo reservation. Keyes became bilingual
and fascinated by language. As an undergraduate, he
studied Russian, French, Mandarin, Japanese, and old

Norse. On the reservation he was exposed to the storytelling that led to his first writings, the retelling of
Southeastern Indian legends and myths. After receiving
an M.A. in anthropology, he began teaching and researching folklore and mythology in addition to subjects relevant to his class.

Keyes was inspired to write his first fantasy, *The
Waterborn,* because of a world history class he took as
an undergraduate and discussion of ancient civilizations, such as Mesopotamia and Egypt, that were organized around the control of water. *The Waterborn* is the
first book of Keyes's series, *Chosen of the Changeling.*
A *Publishers Weekly* reviewer called it "a satisfying,
robust, impressive debut that offers some genuine sur-
prises." Two young people make their way in separate
plots that interweave in a tale of mythical beasts, gods,
and fantasy. Hezhi is a young princess, the daughter of
the emperor of Nhol. Her blood carries the seed of the
powerful River god who controls Nhol. Hezhi is searching for her cousin who was taken away by priests. In
the distant land of the Forest Lord, Perkar, son of a
chieftain, falls in love with a Stream Goddess who is
threatened by the River. Perkar vows to kill the River
and is drawn toward Nohl, where Hezhi lives, after
dreaming of a girl calling to him. In his quest, he encounters monsters and magic and engages in sword
fights. "Keyes has created a memorable world," said
Sally Estes in *Booklist.* Estes called *The Waterborn* a
"richly detailed tapestry, steeped in American Indian
myth and lore." *Voice of Youth Advocates* reviewer
Sandra M. Lee wrote that Keyes "provides engaging
battles, strong characterization, and solid relationships
to tie blood and quest into final confrontation and matu-
ration."

*The Blackgod* is Keyes's sequel to *The Waterborn.*
Hezhi flees from the River, who sends a ghoul to find
her. She and her bodyguard take refuge with the horse-
worshipping Mangs, where Brother Horse teaches her
how to bring forth her own powers. Blackgod the
Raven reveals to Hezhi how she can defeat River at its
source. River sends the ghoul Ghe into the mountains
to kill Hezhi. A *Publishers Weekly* reviewer called Ghe
"a wonderful, Dostoyevskian character, at once repelling and touching," and noted Keyes's "mastery of the
internal lives of his characters and his artful, theatrical
shifts of point of view." *Library Journal* reviewer
Susan Hamburger said the book is "enriched by spiritu-
alism, mystery, and cultural detail." *Booklist* reviewer
Sally Estes called *The Blackgod* "a richly developed
page-turner for the fantasy cognoscenti."

*Newton's Cannon* is the first book of Keyes's alternate history series, *The Age of Unreason.* The book begins in 1715 when the young Boston printer's apprentice Ben Franklin studies alchemic devices invented by Isaac Newton. One of Newton's discoveries is used as a weapon, and a struggle ensues between England and France, whose Louis XIV has been prolonging his life with elixers. Franklin's discoveries put him in danger, and he turns to Newton for protection. Jackie Cassada said in a *Library Journal* review that *Newton's Cannon* is "intricately crafted, elegantly delivered." A *Kirkus* reviewer said the book "is colorful, intriguing, and well handled, if somewhat difficult to swallow." "Eminently worthwhile reading for both fantasy and alternate-history lovers," wrote Roland Green in *Booklist.*

In the next book in the series, *A Calculus of Angels,* cold has shrouded Earth after its collision with an asteroid. Franklin and Newton are in Prague, looking for the secrets of the beings whose science and powers have nearly destroyed the world. Other historical figures woven into the story include Peter the Great, Cotton Mather, and Blackbeard, the pirate. *Amazon.com* reviewer Nona Vero said that each book of the series "has been exciting, suspenseful, and beautifully written."

*BIOGRAPHICAL/CRITICAL SOURCES:*

*PERIODICALS*

*Booklist,* April 1, 1996, p. 1324; March 1, 1997, p. 1068; May 15, 1998, p. 1601.
*Kirkus Reviews,* April 15, 1998, p. 537.
*Library Journal,* June 15, 1996, p. 96; April 15, 1997, p. 123; May 15, 1998, p. 118.
*Magazine of Fantasy and Science Fiction,* April, 1997, p. 130; March, 1999, p. 35.
*Publishers Weekly,* June 10, 1996, p. 90; March 24, 1997, p. 63; April 13, 1998, p. 57.
*Voice of Youth Advocates,* October, 1997, p. 252.

*OTHER*

*Amazon.com,* http://www.amazon.com (1999).*

\*     \*     \*

## KLAUS, Marshall H.   1927-

*PERSONAL:* Born in 1927.

*ADDRESSES: Agent*—c/o Perseus Books, Reading, MA.

*CAREER:* Writer, c. 1976—.

*WRITINGS:*

(With John H. Kennell) *Maternal-Infant Bonding: The Impact of Early Separation or Loss on Family Development,* Mosby (St. Louis), 1976.
(With John H. Kennell) *Parent-Infant Bonding,* Mosby, 1982.
(With John H. Kennell) *Bonding: The Beginnings of Parent-Infant Attachment,* New American Library (New York City), 1983.
(With Phyllis H. Klaus) *The Amazing Newborn,* Addison-Wesley (Reading, MA), 1985.
(With John H. Kennell and Phyllis H. Klaus) *Mothering the Mother: How a Doula Can Help You Have a Shorter, Easier, and Healthier Birth,* photographs by Suzanne Arms, Addison-Wesley, 1993.
(With John H. Kennell and Phyllis H. Klaus) *Bonding: Building the Foundations of Secure Attachment and Independence,* Addison-Wesley, 1995.
(With Phyllis H. Klaus) *Your Amazing Newborn,* Perseus (Reading, MA), 1998.

*EDITOR*

(With Avroy A. Fanaroff) *Care of the High-Risk Neonate,* Saunders (Philadelphia, PA), 1973.
(With Treville Leger and Mary Anne Trause) *Maternal Attachment and Mothering Disorders,* Johnson & Johnson Baby Products Company (Skillman, NJ), 1982.
(With Martha Oschrin Robertson) *Birth, Interaction, and Attachment: Exploring the Foundations for Modern Perinatal Care,* Johnson & Johnson Baby Products, 1982.

*SIDELIGHTS:* Marshall H. Klaus is a neonatologist and the author and editor of many books on childbirth and parents' relationships with their new babies. *Booklist* reviewer Margaret Flanagan said *The Amazing Newborn,* written by Klaus with psychotherapist and social worker Phyllis H. Klaus, is a "lucid explanation of the fascinating process of sensory development." The authors explore a newborn baby's ability to communicate, using facial expressions and movements. *Library Journal* reviewer Diane K. Harvey said the book "will fascinate prospective parents." The book contains 125 photographs of babies younger than ten days old. In reviewing the book in the *Los Angeles Times Book Review,* Jonathan Kirsch called *The Amazing Newborn* an "elegant, compassionate and enchanting little book . . . a lyrical celebration of the unsuspected gifts of the newborn baby."

Co-authored by Klaus and John H. Kennell, *Bonding: Building the Foundations of Secure Attachment and Independence* is a follow-up to the authors' *Parent-Infant Bond*. They discuss bonding that takes place during pregnancy, labor, birth, breastfeeding, and the early months. Studies are cited that show that children who bond well have more success in school and in life. They discuss postpartum depression, parental expectations, and special situations with the birth of premature infants and those with birth defects. A *Publishers Weekly* reviewer said that in their discussion of the relationship between parent and child, Klaus and Kennell "fit together the myriad pieces." Brian McCombie, in reviewing *Bonding* in *Booklist*, called the volume "cleanly written and free of jargon. A fine aid for all soon-to-be parents." *Library Journal* reviewer Marty D. Evensvold called the book "must reading for new parents."

Klaus and Klaus incorporated material from their *The Amazing Newborn* in writing *Your Amazing Newborn*. The book includes more than one hundred new photographs and research on baby behavior during the first weeks. *Library Journal* reviewer KellyJo Houtz Griffin said, "The photos alone are worth the price of the book." The authors note the six states of a newborn's consciousness: quiet alert, active alert, crying, drowsy, quiet sleep, and active sleep. Their recommendations based on new findings are directed at parents and professionals. These include avoiding loud noise at the moment of birth and immediate washing of the baby, which they say eliminates the chemical signals between mother and baby. A *Publishers Weekly* reviewer called *Your Amazing Newborn* "an insightful book. . . . A wonderful primer for new parents."

### BIOGRAPHICAL/CRITICAL SOURCES:

*PERIODICALS*

*American Baby,* May, 1988, p. 116.
*Booklist,* October 15, 1985, p. 292; November 1, 1995, p. 441.
*Library Journal,* November 15, 1985, p. 106; December, 1995, p. 137; October 1, 1998, p. 126.
*Los Angeles Times Book Review,* January 26, 1986, p. 13.
*Publishers Weekly,* September 6, 1985, p. 64; November 6, 1995, p. 92; September 7, 1998, p. 91.*

## KLINGHOFFER, David   1965-

*PERSONAL:* Born October 31, 1965, in Santa Monica, CA; son of Paul and Carol (Bernstein) Klinghoffer; biological son of Harriet Lund. *Education:* Brown University, A.B. (magna cum laude), 1987; also attended the Jewish Theological Seminary. *Politics:* Democratic Socialists of America. *Religion:* Judaism.

*ADDRESSES: Office*—National Review, 215 Lexington Ave., New York, NY 10016-6023.

*CAREER: National Review,* New York City, editorial assistant, 1987, assistant book editor, 1987-89, literary editor, 1992—, later became senior editor; *Washington Times,* Washington, DC, film and television critic, 1990-92.

*WRITINGS:*

*The Lord Will Gather Me In: My Journey to Jewish Orthodoxy,* Free Press (New York City), 1999.

Contributor to periodicals, including *Commentary.*

*SIDELIGHTS:* David Klinghoffer works as a senior editor for the *National Review.* He chronicles his search for religious identity in *The Lord Will Gather Me In: My Journey to Jewish Orthodoxy* (1999). *The Lord Will Gather Me In* is an "intimate and classic tale of spiritual self-discovery and religious rebirth, a book so entertaining, intelligent, and compelling that it is must reading for thinking, morally alive persons of every faith and of no faith," wrote John J. DiIulio Jr. in the *National Review.*

As an eighth grader, Klinghoffer discovered that *halakha*—traditional Jewish laws—classify him as a non-Jew because his birth mother is not Jewish, even though his adoptive parents were Jewish. Later, a young Klinghoffer recircumcised himself in the hopes that the symbolic action would make him a Jew. In *The Lord Will Gather Me In,* the author writes that he entered Brown University as a "secular Jew and a political liberal." Still seeking his spiritual identity during his college years, Klinghoffer met religious Christians and Jews who influenced him.

After college, Klinghoffer began searching for his birth mother. He discovered that his biological mother is a Swedish woman who was abandoned by Klinghoffer's biological father, a man from Kansas. Klinghoffer's birth mother told him that one of her maternal great-grandfathers was a Jew. This statement elated the author, who writes that he realized that "if this was true, I was part Jewish by blood." Klinghoffer then traveled to Sweden to study his Jewish ancestry. Gaining a better sense of his religious heritage, he became an Orthodox Jew.

"Klinghoffer's account of this rebirth as a Jew is barbed at times, poignant at others; it is modest in its religious learning, but thoughtful and informed in those few places where Klinghoffer does tackle theological questions," stated Richard Bernstein in his *New York Times Book Review* discussion of *The Lord Will Gather Me In.* Klinghoffer's book documents an "intellectually fascinating, devilishly funny, and spiritually challenging journey to Jewish orthodoxy," observed DiIulio.

Occasionally, "Klinghoffer's text takes on an annoyed, uncharitable, unkindly tone, especially when he speaks of the varieties of the Jewish experience that he does not find authentic," commented *New York Times Book Review* contributor Bernstein, who also noted that "Klinghoffer is eloquent and stubborn as he makes his case for orthodoxy as the only authentic Jewish practice and identity." In his discussion of *The Lord Will Gather Me In, National Review* contributor DiIulio found that "Klinghoffer's zeal-of-the-convert tone and conclusions are bound to offend many Jews, both religious and secular, both liberal and conservative. His book will also upset many Christians." DiIulio conceded that Klinghoffer deserves praise for "offering a simplified, illuminating rationale for life-affirming Jewish laws" and "for shredding the stereotype of Orthodox Judaism as slavish adherence to inane, hairsplitting laws."

*BIOGRAPHICAL/CRITICAL SOURCES:*

*BOOKS*

Klinghoffer, David, *The Lord Will Gather Me In: My Journey to Jewish Orthodoxy,* Free Press, 1999.

*PERIODICALS*

*National Review,* December 21, 1998, p. 57.
*New York Times Book Review,* December 16, 1998.*

\*          \*          \*

**KNOX, Buddy**
    **See KNOX, Wayne**

**KNOX, Wayne   1933-1999**
    **(Buddy Knox)**

*PERSONAL:* Born April 14, 1933, in Happy, TX; immigrated to Canada, 1974, naturalized Canadian citizen; died of cancer, February 14, 1999, in Bremerton, WA. *Education:* Attended West Texas State College (now University).

*CAREER:* Singer and songwriter. Rhythm Orchids, band member, beginning in the 1950s; worked as record producer for Chancellor and Reprise; MCA Records, Nashville, TN, president in the 1980s; Capitol/Liberty Records, associate in the 1990s. Appeared in the film *Traveling Light,* 1972; record albums include *Buddy Knox,* Roulette, 1957; *Gypsy Man,* United Artists Records, 1968; and *Liberty Takes,* Charly, 1986. *Military service:* U.S. Army Reserve, Tank Corps, active duty, 1957; became lieutenant.

*WRITINGS:*

Author of song lyrics, including lyrics to "Party Doll," 1957, "Lovey Dovey," 1960, "Hula Love," and "I Think I'm Gonna Kill Myself."

*OBITUARIES:*

*PERIODICALS*

*Washington Post,* February 19, 1999.*

\*          \*          \*

**KOCOUR, Ruth Anne   1947-**

*PERSONAL:* Born April 26, 1947, in St. Paul, MN; daughter of Max Gregory and Ruth Heloise (Hillbrand) Kocour; married Robert E. Hall, July 30, 1976. *Education:* University of Colorado, B.S. (environmental zoology), 1969; University of Utah, postgraduate studies, 1972.

*ADDRESSES: Office*—1250 Douglas Fir Dr., Reno, NV 89511.

*CAREER:* Writer, c. 1998—. Ski instructor in Vail, CO, 1969-71; freelance medical illustrator. One-person shows at Fine Arts Gallery, Reno, NV, 1978, and Gallery NAGA, Boston, MA, 1984, 1986, 1987; group shows at Terrence Gallery, Palenville, NY, 1981, Nevada Western Gallery, Reno, NV, 1981, University of

North Dakota, Grand Forks, 1981, Butler Institute of American Art, Youngstown, OH, 1981, and Sierra Nevada Museum of Art, Reno, NV, 1982, 1986.

*MEMBER:* Sierra Arts Foundation.

*WRITINGS:*

(With Michael Hodgson) *Facing the Extreme: One Woman's Story of True Courage, Death-defying Survival, and Her Quest for the Summit,* St. Martin's (New York City), 1998.

Contributor to professional journals.

*SIDELIGHTS:* Ruth Anne Kocour is an artist, medical illustrator, and experienced mountaineer. She was the only woman of a ten-person team that climbed the highest peak in North America, Alaska's Denali (Mt. McKinley), in 1992. Outdoor editor Michael Hodgson assisted Kocour in documenting the treacherous climb to the summit. The worst storm in recorded history struck when the team was at fourteen thousand feet. Winds of up to 120 miles an hour and temperatures that dipped to forty degrees below zero stranded them for over a week. The ten team members survived to go on to the summit, where they stopped for just minutes before quickly descending in the face of more brutal weather. During the same month, eleven climbers were killed on Denali.

Kocour's skin and fingers were blackened with frostbite. In an interview with *Borders.com,* she said that one of her greatest fears was of freezing to death in her sleep. An experienced guide sleeping near the team died this way. The interviewer noted that Kocour credited their guides with much of their survival. Kocour said, "The guides really helped with the decision-making process based on their experience, specifically Robert Link. He'd been there eight times and summited five times. He knew the mountain and the conditions. He had been on Everest three times, once leading Jim Whittaker's international climb. Even still, at the end of the climb, it was the worst experience he had ever had in his mountaineering career." Kocour said she managed "minute to minute. . . . What I attribute my survival to was that ability to stay focused on the moment. You couldn't allow anything—emotions, connections with loved ones, fear, which is a projection into the future and is a result of distraction from the moment—you could allow nothing to take you out of the moment, because it was such a full-time job staying alive, and the moment was endless."

Although Kocour suffered post-traumatic stress syndrome, which kept her from remembering many of the details of the climb, she had kept a journal with a micro-cassette recorder which she transcribed into ninety pages when she returned home. She had mentally blacked out two pages and couldn't remember many of the images contained in her slides. As memories came back to her, she added them. Many of these were revealed to Kocour in nightmares. When she awoke in cold sweats, she would jot down what she had remembered. She feels that by waiting until some time passed before writing her story, she has been able to provide a more complete experience. A year and a half had passed before she had 230 pages, still in a journal format. With Hodgson's help, she was able to complete the book. In the afterword Kocour writes of her climb on Cho Oyu, Everest's sister peak in Tibet.

A *Kirkus Reviews* reviewer said, "There is little delineation of the landscape; the authors appear far more interested in raunch. . . . What might have been a story of mountain savvy, courage, and luck turns into an embarrassment of cliches." Pamela W. Bellows wrote in *Library Journal* that the lack of details of the climb might leave some readers disappointed, "but those looking for a human adventure story of extreme physical and mental challenges will not be." A *Publishers Weekly* reviewer said "Kocour tells of what mountain climbing means to her, ably conveying her passion for the challenge."

*BIOGRAPHICAL/CRITICAL SOURCES:*

*PERIODICALS*

*Harper's Bazaar,* June, 1994, p. 146.
*Kirkus Reviews,* November 1, 1997, p. 1625.
*Library Journal,* February 15, 1998, p. 164.
*Publishers Weekly,* November 10, 1997, p. 62.

*OTHER*

*Borders Books,* www.borders.com/features/mmk980 26.html (1998).*

\* \* \*

**KOTLER, Steven   1967-**

*PERSONAL:* Born May 25, 1967, in Chicago, IL; son of Harvey (in business) and Norma (a teacher) Kotler. *Ethnicity:* "White." *Education:* University of Wisconsin, B.A.; Johns Hopkins University, M.A. *Politics:* "Not at present, but open to new ideas." *Religion:* "See politics."

*ADDRESSES: Agent*—May Evans, May Evans, Inc., 242 East Fifth Ave., New York, NY 10003.

*CAREER:* Freelance journalist.

*WRITINGS:*

*The Angle Quickest for Flight* (novel), Four Walls Eight Windows (New York City), 1999.

Contributor to periodicals, including *Gentleman's Quarterly, Details, Wired, Blue, Travel and Leisure, Self,* and *Men's Journal.*

*WORK IN PROGRESS: Quiat,* a novel; research on entomology in Madagascar, the history of dictionaries, and fallen angels, all for a book, *A Small Green Prayer.*

\*      \*      \*

**KRISTELLER, Paul Oskar    1905-1999**

*OBITUARY NOTICE*—See index for *CA* sketch: Born May 22, 1905, in Berlin, Germany; immigrated to United States, 1939; naturalized citizen, 1945; died June 7, 1999, in Manhattan, NY. Educator and author. Kristeller, a scholar of the Renaissance, grew up in Germany and graduated from the University of Heidelberg in 1928. He completed postdoctoral studies at the University of Berlin and University of Freiburg in the early 1930s, just before the Nazis came to power. Kristeller moved to Italy and was a lecturer at Instituto Superiore di Magistero in Florence and at the University of Pisa before emigrating to the United States and joining the staff at Columbia University. By that time he had already begun writing what would eventually total more than eight hundred books and articles. His best-known work was a seven-volume catalogue, *Iter Italicum,* which was a compilation of Italian Renaissance documents and their locations. Kristeller helped popularize

Renaissance studies and wrote other books on the topic, including *The Classics and Renaissance Thought, Studies in Renaissance Thought and Letters,* and *Eight Philosophers of the Italian Renaissance.* He contributed articles and chapters to books and periodicals, all the while continuing to teach at Columbia, where he was named Woodbridge Professor of philosophy in 1968. He retired in 1973.

*OBITUARIES AND OTHER SOURCES:*

*PERIODICALS*

*New York Times,* June 10, 1999, p. B12.

\*      \*      \*

**KUHLMAN, Erika A.   1961-**

*PERSONAL:* Born January 4, 1961, in Billings, MT; daughter of Paul (an accountant) and Dolores (a homemaker) Kuhlman; married Kevin R. Marsh, July 10, 1999. *Ethnicity:* "Caucasian." *Education:* University of Montana, M.A., 1987; Washington State University, Ph.D., 1995. *Religion:* Unitarian-Universalist.

*ADDRESSES: Office*—Department of History, Washington State University, Pullman, WA 99164. *E-mail*—erika@completebbs.com.

*CAREER:* Washington State University, Pullman, instructor in history, 1998—. Koppel Farm Community Gardens, member of board of directors, 1998—.

*WRITINGS:*

*Petticoats and White Feathers: Gender Conformity, Race, the Progressive Peace Movement, and the Debate over War, 1895-1919,* Greenwood Press (Westport, CT), 1997.

*WORK IN PROGRESS: Women's International Biographical Dictionary,* for Facts on File (New York City), completion expected in 2001.

# L

## LABOWITZ, Shoni

*PERSONAL:* Married Phillip Labowitz (a rabbi).

*ADDRESSES: Agent*—c/o Simon & Schuster, 1230 Avenue of the Americas, New York, NY 10020.

*CAREER:* Rabbi, lecturer, spiritual guide, author, c. 1996—. Temple Adath Or, Fort Lauderdale, FL, rabbi; owner of Living Waters Spa Retreats, FL.

*WRITINGS:*

*Miraculous Living: A Guided Journey in Kabbalah through the Ten Gates of the Tree of Life,* Simon & Schuster (New York City), 1996.
*God, Sex, and Women of the Bible: Discovering Our Sensual, Spiritual Selves,* Simon & Schuster, 1998.

Sound recording, *Kabbalah Yoga, with Rabbi Shoni Labowitz and Carol Parvati Cohen: The Tree of Life in 10 Postures,* Living Waters (Davie, FL), 1996. Host of *Spiritual Focus,* radio program.

*SIDELIGHTS:* Shoni Labowitz is a rabbi, with her husband Phillip Labowitz, at Temple Adath Or, in Fort Lauderdale, Florida. She owns Living Waters Spa Retreats and is a leader in the Jewish renewal movement. Labowitz draws on the teachings of the Kabbalah in her *Miraculous Living: A Guided Journey in Kabbalah Through the Ten Gates of the Tree of Life.* These include intention, wisdom, understanding, compassion, strength, harmony, success, glory, creativity, and nobility. The book includes insights into Taoism and Buddhism as well as mystical Judaism in framing an understanding of and steps to a spiritual life. Meditations are included in each chapter. *Booklist* reviewer George

Cohen said *Miraculous Living* "will attract interest." A *Publishers Weekly* reviewer described it as being "between a workbook for a spiritual journey and a commentary on the wisdom tradition of the Tree of Life." "All readers, regardless of religious faith, will benefit from this meditative approach," wrote a *Library Journal* reviewer.

In *God, Sex, and Women of the Bible: Discovering Our Sensual, Spiritual Selves,* Labowitz offers personal anecdotes and experiences of women who attend her workshops as she explores the lives of women of the Bible and their significance to women today. The eight women are Eve, Leah, Rachel, Jochebed, Deborah, Miriam, Ruth, and Naomi. Labowitz examines the translations of these women's stories and uses them to explain female sexuality in the context of menstruation, pregnancy, childbirth, menopause, and masturbation, and how each of these can provide a spiritual connection with God. A *Library Journal* reviewer recommended *God, Sex, and Women of the Bible* to those "who want a fresh look at the key women in the Old Testament." "Labowitz's penetrating readings provide fresh insights into oft-told biblical tales," wrote a *Publishers Weekly* reviewer.

*BIOGRAPHICAL/CRITICAL SOURCES:*

*PERIODICALS*

*Booklist,* September 15, 1996, p. 182.
*Library Journal,* October 1, 1996, p. 86; October 1, 1998, p. 100.
*Publishers Weekly,* September 2, 1996, p. 126; August 17, 1998, p. 65.*

## LALA, Frank James John, Jr.
### (Frank James)

*PERSONAL:* Born in Los Angeles, CA; son of Frank James John and Isabel Grace (Lackey) Lala. *Ethnicity:* "Italian." *Education:* California State University, Northridge, B.S.; Western Maryland College, M.Ed.; University of California, Los Angeles, M.F.A. and certificates in acting and in alcohol and drug abuse counseling; Columbia Pacific University, Ph.D. *Avocational interests:* Mental health, martial arts (black belt in karate), weight training, performing arts (acting).

*ADDRESSES: Home*—Torrance, CA. *Office*—c/o Midas Management Co., P.O. Box 27740, Las Vegas, NV 89126. *E-mail*—Frank—James3rd@hotmail.com.

*CAREER:* Awakenings Program (for deaf alcoholics and drug abusers), Los Angeles, CA, peer counselor, 1988-90, cofounder of programs in Downey and Whittier, 1988; Midas Co., Las Vegas, NV, substance abuse consultant, 1994—.

*MEMBER:* International Martial Arts Federation of the Deaf, International Narcotic Enforcement Officers Association, National Association of the Deaf, American Public Health Association, National Mental Health Association.

*AWARDS, HONORS:* Named Karate Athlete of the Year, 1993; Outstanding Community Achievement Alumnus Award, California School for the Deaf; Special Award of Honor, Drug Enforcement Administration; Distinguished Achievement in Public Service Award, National Rehabilitation Association; Bell Greve Memorial Award, Western Maryland College; named Kentucky Colonel.

*WRITINGS:*

*Counseling the Deaf Substance Abuser,* Adams Press, 1998.

Contributor to periodicals, including *American Annals of the Deaf* and *NarcOfficer.* Some writings appear under the name Frank James.

*BIOGRAPHICAL/CRITICAL SOURCES:*

*PERIODICALS*

*Community Ear,* January, 1999, p. 4B.
*Silent News,* September, 1999, p. 20.

## LANDAU, Mark Alexandrovich
### See ALDANOV, Mark (Alexandrovich)

*      *      *

## LANDAU-ALDANOV, Mark Alexandrovich
### See ALDANOV, Mark (Alexandrovich)

*      *      *

## LAWSON, Henry (Archibald Hertzberg)   1867-1922

*PERSONAL:* Born June 17, 1867, near Grenfell, New South Wales, Australia; died September 2, 1922, at Abbotsford, in Sydney, New South Wales, Australia; son of Niels Larsen (a Norwegian seaman and laborer, changed name to Peter Lawson in 1867) and Louise Albury Lawson; married Bertha Bredt, April 1896 (formally separated, June, 1903); children: Joseph Lawson, Bertha Lawson. *Education:* Attended Eurunderee Public School in Mudgee area, 1876-80. *Avocational interests:* Socialism.

*CAREER:* Short story writer, poet, c. 1894-1922. Sydney *Republican,* Brisbane *Boomerang,* and Sydney *Worker,* journalist; teacher, 1897-98; builder, apprentice to a railway contractor, house painter, clerk, telegraph lineman, and gold prospector.

*AWARDS, HONORS:* Commonwealth Literary Fund pension, 1920.

*WRITINGS:*

*In the Days When the World Was Wide and Other Verses,* Angus & Robertson (Sydney), 1896.
*Verses, Popular and Humorous,* Angus & Robertson, 1900.
*When I Was King and Other Verses,* Angus & Robertson, 1905.
*The Elder Son,* 1905
*The Skyline Riders and Other Verses,* 1910.
*A Coronation Ode and Retrospect,* 1911.
*For Australia and Other Poems,* 1913.
*My Army, O, My Army! And Other Songs,* 1915, published as *Song of the Dardanelles and Other Verses,* G. G. Harrap (London), 1916.
*Selected Poems of Henry Lawson,* Angus & Robertson, 1918.
*The Auld Shop and the New,* 1923.

*Joseph's Dream,* 1923.
*Winnowed Verse,* 1924.
*Popular Verses,* 1924.
*Humorous Verses,* 1924.
*Poetical Works of Henry Lawson,* Angus & Robertson, 1925.
*The Men Who Made Australia,* 1950.

*SHORT STORIES*

*Short Stories in Prose and Verse,* 1894.
*While the Billy Boils,* Angus & Robertson, 1896.
*On the Track and Over the Sliprails,* Angus & Robertson, 1900.
*The Country I Come From,* Blackwood (Sydney), 1901.
*Joe Wilson and His Mates,* Blackwood, 1901.
*Children of the Bush,* 1902.
*The Rising of the Court and Other Sketches in Prose and Verse,* Angus & Robertson, 1910.
*Mateship: A Discursive Yarn,* 1911.
*The Strangers' Friend,* 1911.
*Triangles of Life and Other Stories,* 1913.

*OTHER*

*A Selection from the Prose Works,* edited by George Mackaness, 1928.
*Prose Works of Henry Lawson,* Angus & Robertson, 1940.
*Stories,* edited by Cecil Mann, 1964.
*Collected Verse,* edited by Colin Roderick, 1967-69.
*Short Stories and Sketches 1888-1922,* edited by Colin Roderick, 1972.
*Autobiographical and Other Writings 1887-1922,* edited by Colin Roderick, 1972.
*The World of Lawson,* edited by Walter Stone, 1974.
*The Essential Lawson,* edited by Brian Kiernan, 1982.
*The Penguin Lawson,* edited by John Barnes, 1986.

*SIDELIGHTS:* Australia's early twentieth-century outback, at its most unromantically bleak and harsh, has been immortalized by the short stories and poetry of Henry Lawson. With his flat, deprecating humor and understated style, Lawson used his own experience in the outback to refute the more exotic depictions that had been written by previous Australians. John Farrell in a review of *While the Billy Boils,* describes the effect of Lawson's realism: "In his versified writings, Mr. Lawson did not let his imagination run far away from the realities in the case, as there may be a temptation to do. In these sketches imagination never obtrudes as a disturbing element. The thing seen or heard is, in such parts of it as are striking and characteristic, reproduced with an exactitude not marred by over-coloring or over-

striving for effect." Lawson also helped define (and often satirized) "mateship." As described in *Twentieth Century Literary Criticism,* mateship "involves a strong bond of loyalty and trust which makes desertion in adversity, selfishness, or failure to defend a 'mate' unthinkable, yet in practice carries few of the trappings of the chivalry it implies and, in its attention to form, can be as cruel as the outback itself."

With all his realism and severity, however, Lawson was above all a storyteller. Cecil Mann writes, in an introduction to *The Stories of Henry Lawson,* "Many people have been misled by taking him always with a solemn literalness. He was, first and last, a fictionizer, a master story-teller—one, moreover, whose inspiration was often necessity—and where fact was troublesome in any of his work the semblance was near enough. . . . Apparent careless casualness is just what Lawson chiefly deliberately aimed at; as much an element of his storytelling as his first-person method, which, in story after story, leaves the impression of listening to one relating a simple factual account, instead of an impression of reading artfully contrived fiction."

Legend has it that Lawson's father, Niels Larsen, a Norwegian seaman, jumped ship at Melbourne, Australia, traveled to Mudgee, and proposed to Louise Albury at first sight; she accepted, and they married on July 7, 1866 at the Wesleyan Parsonage. She was eighteen, and he was thirty-four. Within their first month of marriage they were quarreling frequently and eventually separated in 1883. Meanwhile they established their first home in a tent at the Grenfell diggings. Henry, born June 17, 1867, was their first child. Shortly afterwards, Niels Larsen changed his name to Peter Lawson. The family moved to Eurundaree and then Guglgong, and again to Eurunderee. The Lawsons had four additional children (unwanted by Louise), one of whom died in 1879. In addition to his parents' contentious relationship, Henry Lawson's childhood was also troubled by his hearing loss, first detected when Lawson was nine years old, which became total by the age of fourteen. These early experiences influenced his work as an adult; Lawson always cared about the underdog. Remarkably, his deafness did not impair his ear for dialogue. Laurie Clancy, in *Reference Guide to Short Fiction,* writes that "Despite his deafness, Lawson had an extraordinary ability to capture the rhythms and intonations of idiomatic Australian speech and many of the stories . . . are basically dependent upon some form of oral tradition."

After the Lawsons separated, Peter continued following gold rushes (he died in the Blue Mountains in late 1888) and Louise moved to Sydney, founded the first women's newspaper in Australia, and became a noted feminist. After working as a house painter with his father until 1884, Henry Lawson joined his mother, apprenticed as a painter, and attended a night school where he failed his last exam. Despite this failure, he pursued his writing and published his first poem, "A Song of the Republic" and his short story, "His Father's Mate," in the *Bulletin* in 1887. Lawson's mother nurtured him as a writer; she had raised her son on the works of Dickens and Defoe, as well as Australian writers such as Marcus Clarke and Rolf Boldrewood. The *Bulletin*'s editor, Archibald, also encouraged him. In addition to his contributions to the *Bulletin,* Lawson worked that year as a journalist for the Sydney *Republican,* and later for the Sydney *Worker.*

After a year in Albany, Western Australia, Lawson began writing under the pen name "Joe Swallow" for the Brisbane *Boomerang* in October, 1890. In 1891 he took another trip to the outback, this time to Bourke, and then moved to Wellington, New Zealand in 1893 where his low income cause him to spend his nights on park benches. A year later he left this life for a job at the *Sydney Worker* and published *Short Stories in Prose and Verse* on his mother's press.

Lawson married Bertha Bredt in 1896, Mangamaunu, New Zealand. Also in 1896, Lawson published *In the Days When the World Was Wide, and Other Verses,* a book of poetry, and the short story volume *While the Billy Boils.* This latter book projected Lawson into national fame. A year later they moved to Wellington where Bertha gave birth to a son, Jim, on February 10. The next month they moved to Sydney, where they had their second child, Bertha, in 1899. That spring the family moved to London. Lawson published two short story books, *On the Track* and *Over the Sliprails* (also published as a compilation titled *On the Track and Over the Sliprails*), and a poetry volume, *Verses Popular and Humorous,* in 1900. The following year he published *Joe Wilson and His Mates,* a collection of short stories considered his finest.

Despite these successes Lawson's alcoholism intensified, straining his marriage. His "Joe Wilson" stories are based on his failed marriage with Mary, and focus on male and female sexual relations and madness. His bleak Australian landscape, "Where God ought to be," personifies his nihilistic feelings. Laurie Clancy, writing in the *Reference Guide to Short Fiction* writes that Lawson's random collisions "have no possibility of developing into anything more enduring, though they are

often suffused with the warmth and gentleness of the man himself."

Bertha left with her two children for Sydney in April of 1902; Henry traveled separately. Shortly after their return to Australia, Bertha moved in with her mother after Henry failed to support the family financially. Throughout the years Bertha would repeatedly have Henry imprisoned at Darlinghurst Gaol for failing to provide child support and alimony. During the first winter of their separation, Lawson fell down a cliff while intoxicated and was hospitalized. From this hospital stay he moved to the Royal Prince Alfred Hospital to treat his alcoholism, and then briefly reconciled with his wife. A stillborn child followed, the couple separated again, and Lawson returned to the hospital. During this time, when Lawson's alcoholism kept him rebounding between the jail and the hospital, his work suffered. Though he received financial support at this time from Earl Beauchamp, governor of New South Wales, he was still unable to earn very much money (though he continued to publish poetry and short stories) and became delinquent in his maintenance payments to Bertha. She pressed charges again.

After a brief trip to Victoria, Canada, Lawson was admitted to Darlingurst Gaol's adjoining mental hospital. In 1916 he was given a post in Leeton, writing stories that became *The Yanco Book.* But he relapsed into a month-long drinking binge. Despite the efforts of his friends to divert him, Lawson returned to the Darlinghurst hospital in 1920. A year later he suffered a cerebral hemorrhage which partially paralyzed him, and the following year, on September 2, 1920, he died at his Abbotsford home.

Australian Prime Minister Morris Hughes honored Lawson with a full state funeral at St. Andrew's church on September 4, 1922. Lawson was buried at Waverly Cemetery. Chris Wallace Crabbe, in *Australian Literary Studies* writes: "Henry Lawson remains unquestionably our greatest short story writer. Indeed he is one of our greatest prose writers, a man whose achievement stands there in the *Prose Works,* square and solid and unmistakable. At the same time, we cannot pretend not to notice his limitations, which are considerable; to put it simply, Lawson worked within a very limited range in terms of form, of emotional variety, of the kinds of experience he could grasp and set down clearly. Within these narrow bounds his remarkable art came to fruition and, in time, fell away." Stephen Murray-Smith, in his biography *Henry Lawson,* appears to hold a similar view of Lawson's tragic underachievement: "Lawson had genius, but not the driving ambition or staying power that takes genius to its goal. To put it another way, he had the insights of genius but not its perspectives." Still, Murray-Smith insists that Lawson merits a place in literary history: "While it is true that—as A. G. Stephens several times remarked—Lawson's engagement covered only a small arc of the Australian horizon, within that arc he demonstrated time and time again his deep and pervasive understanding and insight into people."

## BIOGRAPHICAL/CRITICAL SOURCES:

### BOOKS

*Henry Lawson Criticism, 1894-1971,* Angus and Robertson, 1972.
Mann, Cecil, introduction to *The Stories of Henry Lawson,* Angus and Robertson, 1964.
Murray-Smith, Stephen, *Henry Lawson,* Lansdowne Press, 1962.
*Reference Guide to Short Fiction,* St. James Press (Detroit, MI), 1994.
*Short Story Criticism,* Volume 18, Gale Research (Detroit, MI), 1995.
*Twentieth-Century Literary Criticism,* Volume 27, Gale Research, 1988.
*Who Was Who in Literature, 1906-1934,* Gale Research, 1979.

### PERIODICALS

*Australian Literary Studies,* Volume 1, number 3, June, 1964, pp. 147-154, Volume 11, number 2, October, 1983, pp. 152-161.*

\*       \*       \*

## LEAMON, Warren (Coleman) 1938-

*PERSONAL:* Born May 6, 1938, in Atlanta, GA; married in 1967; children: three. *Education:* University of Georgia, A.B., 1960; Vanderbilt University, M.A., 1961; University College, Dublin, Ph.D. (English), 1973.

*ADDRESSES: Office*—Department of English, University of Georgia, Athens, GA 30602.

*CAREER:* University of Georgia, Athens, instructor, 1962-73, associate professor of English, 1979—; University College, Dublin, Ireland, assistant professor of English, 1973-79.

*WRITINGS:*

*Unheard Melodies,* Longstreet Press (Atlanta, GA), 1990.
*Harry Mathews,* Twayne (New York City), 1993.

Also contributor of articles to professional journals, including *Modern Drama, Southwest Review,* and *Southern Review.*

*SIDELIGHTS:* English professor Warren Leamon is the author of the novel *Unheard Melodies,* as well as of the first book-length study of contemporary U.S. novelist Harry Mathews. *Unheard Melodies* is a coming-of-age novel that takes place in post-World War II Atlanta. The anonymous narrator describes his bewildering life, one full of strange relatives and childhood experiences, and how he puzzles these experiences out as he grows from being a fourth grader to a high school graduate. The work garnered praise from reviewers. In the *Christian Science Monitor,* Karla Vallance judged the *Unheard Melodies'* forte to be its universal themes and Leamon's evocation of the past. "He has written a haunting book," she asserted. "It haunts partly because it is a story of a place that is no longer—and of a man who is no longer the boy he used to be. Another reason is the vivid sense of place it evokes." "The story is firmly anchored in a time and place. It feels tangible, real, solid," continued Vallance. "But like any good novel that relies on a given locale, it transcends place. This novel works because it is so humanly present, because it keys so uncannily into the deepest thoughts of a young person." Viewing the work as a whole, Richard Moore in *Sewanee Review* cited Leamon's "finely observed and ironic memories," and concluded of *Unheard Melodies,* "This is a superb novel."

In his biographical and critical study *Harry Mathews,* Leamon introduces readers to Mathews's fiction, which includes short stories and four novels. The work also includes the text of an interview Leamon conducted with Mathews by mail. Steven Moore, writing in *Review of Contemporary Fiction,* found much to like about the study. "Leamon's readings of the novels and stories are extremely useful, both for first-time readers and for longtime admirers, and his book will clearly be the starting-point for subsequent Mathews criticism," Moore maintained. "Intelligent," "well written," and "revealing" were the words D. W. Madden used to describe the work in *Choice.*

*BIOGRAPHICAL/CRITICAL SOURCES:*

*PERIODICALS*

*Booklist,* May 15, 1990, p. 1778.
*Choice,* April, 1994, p. 1293.
*Christian Science Monitor,* July 20, 1990, p. 12.
*Kirkus Reviews,* April 15, 1990, p. 522.
*New York Times Book Review,* July 29, 1990, p. 26.
*Publishers Weekly,* March 16, 1990, p. 63.
*Review of Contemporary Fiction,* spring, 1994, p. 240.
*Sewanee Review,* July, 1991, p. R78.
*School Library Journal,* October, 1990, p. 150.*

\*    \*    \*

## LECLERC, Felix 1914-

*PERSONAL:* Born August 2, 1914, in La Turque, Quebec, Canada; son of Leo and Fabiola (Parrot) Leclerc; married Andree Vien, 1942; children: Martin Leclerc. *Education:* Attended University of Ottawa, 1932. *Politics:* Identified with the independence movement in the 1970s. *Religion:* Catholic. *Avocational interests:* Music, especially playing guitar and singing.

*CAREER:* Poet, novelist, playwright, short story writer, singer, and songwriter. Unexpectedly got a job in Quebec City as a radio announcer, where he worked from 1934-37; returned to the family farm but then took a job at a radio station in Trois-Rivieres, 1937-39; moved on to Radio-Canada in Montreal in 1939, and began acting and singing in public and established himself as a writer by 1941; published his first collection of stories in 1943, and commenced writing poems, plays, stories and novels, and even wrote for television; helped found the VLM theater in 1949; enjoyed a few successful years in Paris performing and making records, 1950-53.

*AWARDS, HONORS:* Book-of-the-month citation, Institut de la Nouvelle-France, for *Adagio;* Grand Prix du Disque, Academie Charles-Cros, 1951; voted most important French-Canadian writer in 1963 by twenty of thirty-four classical colleges; Prix Calixa Lavallee, Society Saint-Jean-Baptiste, 1976; honored with a medal offered by the Movement National des Quebecois, 1980.

*WRITINGS:*

*Adagio,* Fides (Montreal), 1943.
*Allegro,* Fides, 1944, translated by Linda Hutcheon, McClelland & Stewart (Toronto), 1974.

*Andante,* illustrated by Nicole Benoit, Fides, 1944, 1975.
*Pieds nus dans l'aube,* Fides, 1946.
*Dialogues d'hommes et de betes,* Fides, 1949.
*Les Chansons de Felix Leclerc-Le Canadien,* Raoul Breton (Paris), 1950.
*Theatre de village,* Fides, 1951.
*Le Hamac dans les voiles,* Fides, 1951.
*Moi, mes souliers. Journal d'un lievre a deux pattes,* Amiot-Dumont (Paris), 1955.
*Le Fou de l'ile,* Denoel (Paris), 1958, translation by Philip Stratford published as *The Madman, the Kite, and the Island,* Oberon (Ottawa), 1976.
*Douze chansons nouvelles,* Archambault (Montreal), 1958.
*Le P'tit Bonheur, Sonnez les Matines,* Beauchemin, 1959.
*Le Calepin d'un flaneur,* Fides, 1961.
*L'Auberge des morts subites,* Beauchemin, 1964.
*Chansons pour tes yeux,* Robert Laffont (Paris), 1968.
*Cent chansons,* Fides, 1970.
*Carcajou ou le diable des bois,* Editions du Jour (Montreal), 1973.
*L'Ancetre,* Nantel (Quebec), 1974.
*Bonjour de l'ile,* Nantel, 1975.
*Qui est le pere?,* Lemeac (Montreal), 1977.
*Un Matin,* Nantel, 1977.
*Le Petit Livre bleu de Felix, ou, Nouveau calepin du meme flaneur,* Nouvelles Editions de l'Arc (Montreal), 1978.
*Le Tour de l'ile,* illustrated by Gilles Tibo, Editions la Courte Echelle (Montreal), 1980.
*Le Choix de Felix Leclerc dans l'oeuvre de Felix Leclerc,* Presses Laurentiennes (Quebec), 1983.
*Reves a vendre ou Troisieme du meme flaneur,* Nouvelles Editions de l'Arc, 1984.
*Dernier calepin,* Nouvelles editions de l'Arc, 1988.
*Les oeuvres de Felix Leclerc,* edited by Henri Rivard, H. Rivard (Quebec), 1994.

*PLAYS*

*Maluron,* produced in Montreal at Compagnons de Notre Dame Theatre du Gesu, 1947.
*Le P'tit Bonheur,* produced in Montreal at Theatre du Gesu, 1948.
*Caverne des splendeurs,* produced in Montreal at Theatre du Gesu, 1949.
*Voyages de noces,* produced in Montreal at Theatre du Gesu, 1949.
*La Petite Misere,* produced in Montreal at the salle du Gesu, 1950.
*Cantique,* produced in Sudbury, ON at Festival-concours, 1953.

*Sonnez les Matines,* produced in Montreal at Theatre du Rideau Vert, 1956.

*L'Auberge des morts subites,* produced in Montreal at Theatre Quebec at Theatre du Gesu, 1963.

*Les Temples,* produced in Montreal at Comedie Canadienne, 1966.

*P'tit bonheur a trois,* produced in Montreal at Theatre de l'Egregore, 1966.

*L'Eau qui coule, troupe des Gestaux,* Spectacle du Vieux Quebec, 1968.

*Qui est le pere?, Saint-Pierre (Ile d'Orleans),* produced in Quebec at Theatre Le Galendor, 1973.

*SIDELIGHTS:* There is a unique defining nationalism evident repeatedly throughout Quebec history. Many talented individuals were motivated by their pride and convictions to define themselves as singularly French-Canadian. Felix Leclerc was no exception. His talents were numerous, expressed through music, poetry, writing, theater and even political activism later in life. However, his talents primarily stemmed from his fierce loyalty and affection for his native land. In the preface to a play he produced in 1964, Paul Socken, writing for *Dictionary of Literary Biography,* acknowledged Leclerc's identification with both his French Canadian and his Catholic backgrounds, "which are to him two warm garments needed in his harsh land. He may stain them, he may even alter them slightly, he declares, but they fit."

Although Leclerc was without a doubt one of the most prolific and multi-faceted artists in Canada during the twentieth century, there has been no consistency of opinion with regard to his achievements and contributions. In fact, his ranking among literary and artistic circles has elicited fervent debates among critics and scholars alike. His admirers declare him as a man of divine talent and influence, while his critics admit no value or credit to his work. Regardless, the fact remains that he enjoyed a long, successful career, and his efforts reflect a vitally creative period in French Canadian history. Socken went as far as to offer that "Leclerc has embodied and expressed, perhaps more than any other single artist, Quebec's complex evolution."

Leclerc exhibited his personal ambition early on, as he left home at the age of fourteen to indulge academic pursuits in Ottowa. While he was at the University of Ottawa at the age of eighteen, he began to experiment with his musical talents by writing songs, the contents of which ultimately parlayed into some of his writing. His affection for life and his love of music was in large part due to the loving, nurturing home environment created by his mother. In reminiscences of youth, Leclerc

has been known to claim that he and his ten siblings communicated in song more than they talked. One of the most devastating periods in Leclerc's life came when his mother died in 1946. His attempt to deal with his heartache was funneled into two works. First, he wrote a short novel, *Le Fou de l'ile,* which was not published until 1958. Then he wrote a memoir, *Pieds nus dans l'aube,* which celebrated his formative years, especially his family life, and was published the year of his mother's death.

Although *Le Fou de l'ile* was not published until 1958, Socken said that some critics have hailed it as "unjustifiably ignored." The novel is a passionate allegory of the individual's quest for beatitude and spiritual fulfillment. Jean-Noel Samson, who wrote Leclerc's biography in 1967, commented that one can see Leclerc in the novel as "this madman grappling with the anguish of existence, haunted by the memory of a paradise lost, and who passionately searches for happiness in a world that has lost flavor and meaning."

Despite Leclerc's pain during this period of his life, most of his efforts were forms of creative celebrations and testimonies of the human capacity for rapture while on earth. Whereas the subjective virtues of humility and submission often seem to represent inherent limits to personal exaltation, Leclerc asserts that joy and passion can coexist with said Christian virtues, not only individually, but also throughout society. He goes further and asserts that such interdependence and universal compassion among humans is absolutely achievable and, in effect, the key to consummate joy. Leclerc holds that one need only to open himself up to the reality of God's presence to experience divine fulfillment. Paul Socken summarizes Leclerc's philosophies when he says, "Life, in particular rural life, is a symphony composed by the Creator."

Leclerc's professional fate was jump-started when, while traveling with his godfather at the age of twenty, he got a job as a radio announcer in Quebec City. During the three years in that capacity, he submerged himself in the arts and played his guitar whenever and wherever he had the chance. In 1937 he began working at a radio station in Trois-Rivieres, and by 1939 he started singing in public, acting, and writing consistently. That same year he began working at Radio-Canada in Montreal, and by 1941, despite brief detours in which he worked odd, unrelated jobs, he earned the reputation as an established writer. In 1943 Leclerc was encouraged to publish *Adagio,* a collection of stories that broke records by selling more than 4,000 in the first month. His second published work, *Andante,* appeared in 1944 and was released to critical acclaim.

Leclerc took his artistic journey to a new level in 1947 when he shifted his talents to writing for and performing in the theater. By 1950 his talents had caught the attention of the French impresario Jacques Canetti, and Canetti invited Leclerc to share his gifts with Parisians. Leclerc accepted the invitation and spent the next three years enjoying a successful run in France. During his sojourn, Leclerc produced a record, accompanied by a twenty-eight-piece orchestra, that won the prestigious Grand Prix du Disque in 1951. After traveling and performing throughout Europe and Africa, Leclerc returned to Quebec in 1953 with two more such awards. He attributed his success in France to the fortune of his timing, specifically referring to the fact that the years after World War II in France were exceptionally chaotic. Upon his return, Leclerc exercised his talents as a writer for stage and then television, and he continued to give concerts throughout the region. He was extremely popular, and continued to receive honors and accolades for his work, which he produced through 1980. Perhaps the best capsulation of his career, though not necessarily his best work, can be seen in his 1961 *Le Calepin d'un flaneur,* a casual collection of ruminations which cover a wide range of subjects. Some of the topics include relationships between men and women, patriotism, human nature, and the differences between city life and rural life. Socken remarks that "the feeling expressed, not new but refreshingly rendered, is that humanity is trapped by its own conventions and that only the privileged few—the poets, the 'flaneurs' (loafers)—are free."

*BIOGRAPHICAL/CRITICAL SOURCES:*

*BOOKS*

*Dictionary of Literary Biography,* Volume 60: *Canadian Writers since 1960,* Gale (Detroit, MI), 1987.
Samson, Jean-Noel, editor, *Felix Leclerc,* Fides (Montreal), 1967.*

\*     \*     \*

## LEDERER, Ivo J(ohn)   1929-1998

*OBITUARY NOTICE*—See index for *CA* sketch: Born December 11, 1929, in Zagreb, Croatia; immigrated to the United States, 1944; naturalized citizen, 1952; died of pancreatic cancer, June 18, 1998, in the Bronx, NY.

Educator and author. Lederer, a professor of contemporary Russian and Eastern European history, began his career in Europe but ended up in America as a result of the Nazi invasion of his homeland. His family first fled to Italy, where they remained in hiding for three years before immigrating to the United States in 1944. Lederer graduated from the University of Colorado in 1951 and received master's and doctoral degrees from Princeton University. He taught at Princeton and Yale universities before joining the faculty at Stanford in 1965. His scholarly career resulted in numerous awards, including fellowships from the Ford Foundation, the Social Science Research Council and the Rockefeller Foundation. He also received the George Louis Beer Prize in 1964 from the American Historical Association. He wrote *Yugoslavia at the Paris Peace Conference: A Study in Frontiermaking,* and helped edit *The Versailles Settlement: Was It Foredoomed to Failure?* and *Nationalism in Eastern Europe.* At the time of his death he had basically finished his autobiography, *I Have Seen the Mississippi,* and was working at a consulting firm, directing its global business policy council.

*OBITUARIES AND OTHER SOURCES:*

*PERIODICALS*

*New York Times,* June 25, 1998, p. B10.

\*     \*     \*

## LEE, Mary Effie
### See NEWSOME, (Mary) Effie Lee

\*     \*     \*

## LEMAY, Pamphile   1837-1918

*PERSONAL:* Born January 5, 1837, in Lotbiniere, Quebec, Canada; died June 11, 1918; son of Leon (a merchant farmer) and Louise (Auger) Lemay; married Celima Robitaille, 1865; children: fourteen. *Education:* Attended primary school with the Freres des Ecoles Chretiennes at Trois Rivieres and preparatory studies with the notary of Lotviniere; began classical studies in 1846 at the Seminaire de Quebec, graduated, 1850; attended seminary at University of Ottawa; studied law, 1860. *Religion:* Catholic.

*CAREER:* Poet, writer, and lawyer. Called to the bar, 1865; worked as a translator for the legislative assembly at Quebec, then as a translator for Parliament in Ottawa; parliamentary librarian in Quebec, 1867-92.

*MEMBER:* Royal Society of Canada (founding member, 1882).

*AWARDS, HONORS:* Winner of a poetry contest at Laval University with his entry "La Decouverte du Canada" in 1867, a contest he won again in 1869 with "Hymne pour la fete nationale des Canadiens francais"; awarded an honorary doctrate from Laval University in 1888; honored with the official medallion of an officer of L'Instruction Publique of France in 1910.

*WRITINGS:*

*Essais poetiques,* Desbarats (Quebec), 1865.

*Deux Poemes couronnes par l'Universite Laval,* Delisle (Quebec), 1870.

*Catalogue de la bibliotheque de la Legislature de Quebec,* Levis (Quebec), 1873.

*Les Vengeances,* Darveau (Quebec), 1875, republished as *Tonkourou,* Darveau, 1888, published as *Les Vengeances: Poeme rustique,* Granger (Montreal), 1930.

*Le Pelerin de Sainte-Anne* (2 volumes), Darveau, 1877, abridged edition (1 volume), Beauchemin (Montreal), 1893.

*Picounoc le maudit* (2 volumes), Darveau, 1878, modern edition, HMH (Montreal), 1972.

*La Chaine d'or,* Darveau, 1879.

*Une Gerbe,* Darveau, 1879.

*Fables canadiennes,* Darveau, 1882, revised edition, Granger, 1903, abridged edition, 1925.

*Petits Poemes,* Darveau, 1883.

*L'Affaire Sougraine,* Darveau, 1884.

*Fetes et corvees,* Roy (Quebec), 1898.

*Contes vrais,* Soleil (Quebec), 1899, revised and enlarged edition, Beauchemin, 1907.

*Les Gouttelettes,* Beauchemin, 1904.

*Les Epis* (includes *Poesies fugitives et petits poemes*), Guay (Montreal), 1914.

*Reflets d'antan,* Granger, 1916.

*PLAYS*

*Les Vengeances* (produced in Quebec at L'Academie de Musique, 1876), Bossue-Lyonnais (Quebec), 1876.

*Rouge et bleu* (produced in Quebec at L'Academie de Musique, 1889), Darveau, 1891.

*TRANSLATIONS*

Henry Wadsworth Longfellow, *Evangeline,* Delisle (Quebec), 1870, revised and enlarged edition published as *Evangeline et autres poemes de Longfellow,* Guay (Montreal), 1912.

William Kirby, *Le Chien D'or,* Etendard (Quebec), 1884.

*SIDELIGHTS:* Pamphile Lemay, a prolific poet, essayist and spiritual truth seeker, gathered his thoughts on the circumstances of his life and molded them into a purposeful and meritorious creative legacy. Admired for his aptitude for balancing civism with personal tenderness, spirituality with folk tales, and reflection with thoughtful guidance, Lemay incorporated all aspects of his experiences in a way that promoted his own perspectives, as well as provided a forum for his soul's distinct expression and literary melody.

Born at Lotbiniere, Quebec in 1837, Lemay was the oldest child of a merchant farmer, and was one of fourteen children. That in itself must have elicited a strong sense of family and responsibility, and it is an achievement that Lemay even had time or energy to devote to his intellectual pursuits. His primary and preparatory education was ensconced in religion, and in 1846 he entered the Seminaire de Quebec to further submerge himself in classical studies. After four years of intense philosophical, intellectual and spiritual application, Lemay became overwhelmed with his choices and embarked on his own journey to determine his next professional commitment. Though he had originally considered a career in law, after working at odd jobs throughout the United States and Canada he recognized an inner longing to become a priest. Lemay entered the seminary at the University of Ottawa, but was unable to complete his instruction because of severe stomach pains that affected him throughout his life. However, instead of surrendering his passion, Lemay was determined to invent an alternative route on which to follow his calling. Thus, as Barbara Godard stated in *Dictionary of Literary Biography,* "Literature became his pulpit."

In 1860, Lemay once again applied himself to the study of law, and consequently worked as a translator for the legislative assembly at Quebec, and then for Parliament in Ottawa. In 1865 he published *Essais poetiques,* his first volume of verse. Some of his early themes can be detected in this freshman work. The themes include God, nature, respect for tradition, love of country, and the poet's need to express the insides of his soul to the best of his ability. However, much of his eventual defining talents and proficiency was missing from these first efforts. His images were somewhat flat, his tone was hesitant and unsure, and his personal style had yet to emerge. As credit to his character, Lemay recognized these shortcomings and noted them in the preface to the volume. His ability to detach himself from his work in order to gain new perspectives that served to improve his talents was an essential contributing factor of his ultimate success. Lemay did not abandon his early efforts, but instead revisited them and revised them steadily throughout his life. Thus, although he was humble and realistic, he was loyal to his vision, and the frequent revisions of his work indicated a definite attachment, respect and fondness for his craft.

In 1867 Lemay made a career move that ultimately served to launch his writing career, though not in the typical fashion. He accepted a position as the parliamentary librarian at Quebec, and remained at that post for twenty-five years. This career decision invited a financial comfort and daily stability that allowed his creativity to flourish and embark on its own ambitious journey. During those twenty-five years, Lemay was able to break through personal and spiritual barriers and ascend to new creative heights. The stability, as well as the stimulating cerebral environment, provided a sanctuary for his spirituality to grow and prosper. He wrote an epic poem about the war against the Indians called "La Decouverte du Canada," which won in a poetry contest sponsored by Laval University.

It was during this time that he began to contemplate one of his favorite concepts, the notion of the Christian miracle. Essentially, this notion combines the belief of divine intervention with the ability to reflect on one's life and finally observe the reasons and universal rationality for personal struggles and victories alike. After winning the poetry contest at Laval University again in 1869 with "Hymne pour la fete nationale des Canadiens francais," he produced *Les Vengeances* ("The Revenges," 1875). This was, according to Godard, "a didactic poem illustrating sin and redemption, [and dealing with] the separation of parents and children and the coincidences of fate leading to their union, which reveal that 'heaven has its secrets: its greatness crushes us.' " *Les Vengeances* was republished in 1888 as *Tonkourou,* which was the name of the Indian villian who kidnapped the child and was eventually brought to justice. Lemay built upon the dramatic themes and effective conflicts of the poem and restructured it for the stage in 1876.

Lemay also wrote detective novels, which were the first of their kind to be set in the region. Despite the change in genre, his three detective novels maintained the cen-

tral themes of much of his prose and poetry, where the protagonist is necessarily separated from his family and must conquer most of man's lesser qualities in various forms, such as greed and envy. Godard summarizes his plots in the following manner: "Hypocrisy is unmasked, vice punished, and good rewarded: after a struggle and a thousand digressions happiness is obtained."

Challenging his literary potential even further, Lemay spent some time trying his hand at writing comedies, but his efforts were deemed comparably weak. However, during this period he produced one of his most critically acclaimed works, which was an essay he wrote in 1880 for St. Jean Baptiste Day. In this essay, Godard said that Lemay boldly "proclaims the sacred nature of the writer's function-to lead his people toward God and help them maintain their culture." Certainly, the assumption of such a task is a mammoth one, and it was obviously a prime motivating factor for his prolific literary endeavors.

Whereas many writers and artists hit a high point in their career and eventually taper off, Lemay continued to reach new and impressive peaks. In fact, in 1899 he produced what is generally regarded as his prose masterpiece, a weaving of reality, spirituality and folktale called *Contes vrais*. In this he integrated aphoristic legends in real-time with actual historical events. The versatility of his style and stories, as well as his resplendent language, earned him a grateful following and devoted audience. On the heels of the success of *Contes vrais* came what is hailed as his poetic magnum opus, *Les Gouttelettes* ("The Droplets"), a collection of sonnets which was published in 1904. In these sonnets, Lemay's talents truly surfaced, as he showcased his ability to balance simplicity while carefully imposing levels of restraint that can only be learned over time through years of exhaustive writing. Godard summarizes by commenting that "Lemay's subject matter remains familiar, religious or rustic scenes transfused with emotion. His taste for dreaming and habit of moral meditation are here mated with a mature technique to produce delicate poetry."

*BIOGRAPHICAL/CRITICAL SOURCES:*

*BOOKS*

*Dictionary of Literary Biography,* Volume 99: *Canadian Writers before 1890,* Gale (Detroit, MI), 1990.*

## LeROY, (Lemuel) David   1920-1998

*OBITUARY NOTICE*—See index for *CA* sketch: Born January 2, 1920, in Tignall, GA; died of cardiac arrest, June 27, 1998, in Kearneysville, WV. Journalist. After serving five years in the U.S. Army during World War II, LeRoy spent most of his career working with the press. Following his discharge he joined the staff of the *Air Force Times* and served as managing editor from 1951 to 1953. Later that year he took a post as a copy editor with *U.S. News & World Report.* In 1964 he moved to the magazine's Capitol Hill staff and stayed there until 1970. After leaving the publication he worked on the public relations staff of the Republican Congressional Committee and was named executive director of the National Press Foundation in 1977. He wrote *Gerald Ford—Untold Story,* a biography, in 1974, and *Out-doorsman's Guide to Government Surplus* in 1978. He co-authored, with Jack Brosius, *Building and Repairing Canoes and Kayaks,* and *Canoes and Kayaks: A Complete Buyer's Guide.*

*OBITUARIES AND OTHER SOURCES:*

*PERIODICALS*

*Washington Post,* July 1, 1998, p. B6.

*       *       *

## LEVY, Frank   1941-

*PERSONAL:* Born in 1941. *Politics:* Moderate conservative.

*ADDRESSES: Office*—Massachusetts Institute of Technology, 9-515 Urban Studies and Planning Dept., 77 Massachusetts Ave., Cambridge, MA 02139-4307.

*CAREER:* Massachusetts Institute of Technology, Cambridge, professor of urban economics.

*WRITINGS:*

*Northern Schools and Civil Rights: The Racial Imbalance Act of Massachusetts,* Markham Publishing (Chicago), 1971.
(With Arnold J. Meltsner and Aaron Wildavsky) *Urban Outcomes: Schools, Streets, and Libraries,* University of California Press (Oakland), 1974.
*The Harried Staffer's Guide to Current Welfare Reform,* Urban Institute Press (Washington, DC), 1978.

*Dollars and Dreams: The Changing American Income Distribution,* Russell Sage Foundation (New York City), 1987.
*The Economic Future of American Families: Income and Wealth Trends,* Urban Institute Press (Washington, DC), 1991.
(With Richard J. Murnane) *Teaching the New Basic Skills: Principles for Educating Children to Thrive in a Changing Economy,* Free Press (New York City), 1996.
*The New Dollars and Dreams,* Russell Sage Foundation (New York City), 1998.

*SIDELIGHTS:* Frank Levy is a leading researcher in economics and social policy. As early as 1971 he published *Northern Schools and Civil Rights.* In this study, an off-shoot of Levy's doctoral dissertation, the author examines the 1965 Massachusetts law that mandated racial balance in public schools. Levy presents a history of the act and also discusses the problems the United States faces when it tries to change a multiracial society. In the words of a *Choice* reviewer, the entire work, an "important monograph, is acutely relevant, and the final section is a "wonderfully rich" discussion of the urban politics that have prevented desegregation. John J. Fox, writing in *Library Journal,* judged the study to be "interesting and timely," though not outstanding.

With Arnold J. Meltsner and Aaron Wildavsky, Levy conducted a detailed policy analysis of the public schools and library, street department, and budgeting in Oakland, California. The authors presented their findings about the distribution of goods and services to various groups in *Urban Outcomes,* which *Library Journal* reviewer Robert E. Will described as "fascinating" and "well documented," predicting that it would become a model for decision makers in other cities. Likewise, a *Choice* reviewer predicted that the study would greatly interest policy makers elsewhere.

In *Dollars and Dreams* Levy analyzes the performance of the U.S. economy from 1947 to 1984. He determines that a shift to service jobs, coupled with a stagnant economy, caused declining living standards for the white male wage earner beginning a career in 1970. Levy considers income distribution from many perspectives: by race, gender, age, region, occupation, and family status. "When all these movements are taken together, they have not dramatically changed the inequality of current income," Levy concludes. "But they surely have increased the inequality of 'permanent income,' a family's average income over its lifetime."

Critics found much to praise about *Dollars and Dreams.* In a review for *Choice,* contributor H. I. Liebling pointed out the work's accessibility for specialists and lay readers alike. Though he found some "weaknesses" in Levy's macro-[economic] reasoning, Liebling recommended the work for its "fact-filled discussion" of income distribution in the United States. "One can take issue with bits and pieces of Levy's analysis, depending on one's own prejudices," wrote Robert Kuttner in *Washington Post Book World,* "but the book as a whole is very well done, accessible to both specialist and lay reader, chock full of both statistics and insights, and just plain interesting." "This is a notable piece of writing, for its good humor, intellectual keenness and above all for its willingness to let the chips fall," Kuttner added. "Economics generally suffers from its tendency to make things impenetrably complicated but without quite capturing life's actual complexity. Levy not only offers useful insights about dollars and dreams; he points the way to a much more satisfying and recognizable economics."

Levy revisited the topic of *Dollars and Dreams* in *The Economic Future of American Families,* in which he and co-author Richard C. Michel describe the trends in income distribution in the United States from 1960 to 1986. The authors then posit their hypothesis regarding the very slow rate of growth. "This book provides a clear interpretation of the factors influencing both absolute and relative changes in income and wealth among various segments of the population over the past 20 to 25 years," maintained Dan Goldhaber in *Industrial and Labor Relations Review.* "The section on the intergenerational effect of changes in the housing market is especially illuminating," the critic added. Gary Burtless, writing in *Journal of Policy Analysis and Management,* remarked on the continuing timeliness of the authors' work. He applauded Levy and Michel for writing a "clear and even-handed summary of many aspects of the debate over income, earnings, and wealth trends," a study that "should be of value to the much wider class of readers who are interested in understanding the basic facts behind the class-warfare headlines." "Readers looking for a rigorous microeconomic treatment of the subject, however, may be disappointed," added Goldhaber. "Levy and Michel do not break any truly new ground, and the level of their analysis is not extremely technical. Nevertheless, their book provides a thorough overview of family income and wealth trends that will enlighten anyone seeking a nontechnical discussion of topics relating to economic inequality." Burtless concurred: "Specialists in labor economics and public finance might be left hungry for more detail, but general

readers will find this book a sound introduction to a hotly debated subject."

Levy and Richard Murnane turned put their intellect to bear on the U.S. educational system in *Teaching the New Basic Skills.* The authors maintain that the gap between performance by workers and the education system is growing because educators need to teach new skills to make students good workers in a more technological economy. Furthermore, according to Levy and Murnane, the performance gap has contributed to greater differences in income for college-educated and non-college-educated workers. Third, the authors proposed ways that the business world can help local U.S. school systems turn out more employable workers, and pinpoint skills that high school graduates often lack but which are crucial. These new basis skills include math; problem solving; reading at more advanced levels; interpersonal and communications skills; and the ability to use computers. "They argue, quite persuasively, that the current path will threaten America's future," commented Robert Berne in *Journal of Policy Analysis and Management.* "The development of this problem statement is a strong part of the book, but the strongest part is the articulation of what needs to change in public education to produce graduates who have these new basis skills." A *Publishers Weekly* critic noted that the authors present some "interesting points," but they do not always show how their principles should be applied in the real world. Berne, too, pointed out several flaws in *Teaching New Basic Skills,* including the lack of discussion of such issues as current education reform, the influence of local teachers' unions, or principal and teacher accountability and discretion. Nevertheless, judging that the "shortcomings of the book pale in comparison to its strengths," Berne concluded that Levy and Murnane "have written an elegant, thoughtful, and important book that says more about the public education system in the United States than many of the endless debates that take place in the world of politics, the op-ed pages, and even in some of the academic literature."

Levy revisited *Dollars and Dreams* with his 1999 study, *The New Dollars and Dreams.* In this work he updated the statistics for the 1990s and the economic recovery, which he did "brilliantly," according to Mark Levinson of the *New York Times Book Review.* Levy asserts that the primarily reason for the growing gap in incomes is the need for more technologically adept workers, and he suggests that the education system needs improvement. Believing Levy "less successful" in his explanations of what causes growing inequality, in his review of *The New Dollars and Dreams* Levinson countered by citing economists refuting the book's premise. Finally, Levy suggests that a decrease in globalization and shareholder power has reduced workers' bargaining power. The author's "failure to pursue the implications of this statement—that the problem is not that workers lack skills, but that they lack power—is the main flaw in an otherwise thoughtful and meticulously researched book," concluded Levinson.

*BIOGRAPHICAL/CRITICAL SOURCES:*

*PERIODICALS*

*Atlantic Monthly,* September, 1997, pp. 112-115.
*Choice,* February, 1972, pp. 1623-1624; February, 1975, p. 1810; March, 1988, p. 1143.
*Harvard Business Review,* May-June, 1988, pp. 22-28.
*Industrial and Labor Relations Review,* October, 1992, pp. 198-199.
*Journal of Economic Literature,* March, 1990, pp. 92-93.
*Journal of Policy Analysis and Management,* summer, 1992, pp. 528-531; winter, 1998, pp. 125-127.
*Labor Studies Journal,* fall, 1988, pp. 70-72.
*Library Journal,* February 15, 1972, p. 688; June 15, 1974, p. 1689.
*New York Times Book Review,* January 31, 1988, p. 15; January 10, 1999, p. 19.
*Publishers Weekly,* June 24, 1996, p. 38.
*Washington Post Book World,* October 11, 1987, p. 5.*

\*    \*    \*

**LEWIS, Dorothy Otnow   1937-**

*PERSONAL:* Born July 23, 1937, in New York, NY; married Melvin Lewis (a psychiatrist and writer); children: Gillian, Eric. *Education:* Radcliffe College, B.A. (magna cum laude), 1959; Yale University, M.D., 1963; American Board of Psychiatry and Neurology, diplomate (general psychiatry), 1972.

*ADDRESSES: Office*—New York University, NB1S25, 550 First Ave., New York, NY 10016-6402.

*CAREER:* Yale University-New Haven Hospital, New Haven, CT, intern, 1964-65, attending psychiatrist, 1972-93, associate in child psychiatry, beginning 1989, and other positions; Yale University School of Medicine, Department of Psychiatry, New Haven, CT, assistant resident, 1965-67, fellow in child psychiatry, 1968-69, clinical instructor of psychiatry, 1970-71, as-

sistant clinical professor, 1971-75, associate clinical professor, 1975-79, clinical professor of psychiatry, beginning 1979; Serious Youthful Offender Project, Long Lane School, project director, c. 1978; New York University-Bellevue Medical Center, attending psychiatrist, beginning 1979; New York University School of Medicine, New York City, research professor, 1979-81, professor of psychiatry, beginning 1981; member of the editorial board of the *Journal of the American Academy of Child Psychiatry,* 1981-86; Queens University, Flushing, Queens, New York City, visiting scholar, 1986; Tisch Hospital, New York University, New York City, attending psychiatrist, beginning 1990; licensed physician in Connecticut, California, and New York; expert witness on psychiatric matters for legal cases.

*MEMBER:* American Psychiatry Association, American Academy of Child Psychiatry (member of the council, 1979-82), National Institute on Abuse/Addiction Research Center (member of the board of science counselors in the alcohol/drug abuse and mental health administration, 1986-88), National Academy of Sciences (member of the panel on child abuse and neglect, 1992-93), Connecticut Justice Commission (member of the juvenile justice advisory committee, 1975-79), Phi Beta Kappa, Sigma Xi.

*AWARDS, HONORS:* Fellow, American Psychiatry Association, 1970; Blanche F. Ittleson Award for Research in Child Psychiatry, American Psychiatry Association, 1982; Wilfred C. Hulse Award, New York Council of Child and Adolescent Psychiatry, 1988; Rieger Award, American Academy of Child Psychiatry, 1992; grants from the National Institute of Mental Health, 1963-64, Connecticut Planning Commission on Criminal Administration, 1974, Ford Foundation, 1976-81, Law Enforcement Assistance Administration, 1978, Field Foundation, 1981 and 1983, Grove Foundation, 1982, Ittleson Foundation, 1983, Hycliff Foundation, 1983, Kenworth-Swift Foundation, 1983-86 and 1991, Office of Juvenile Justice and Delinquency Prevention, 1985 and 1988-89, National Institute of Justice, 1988, Public Welfare Foundation, 1990, and others.

*WRITINGS:*

(With Melvin Lewis) *The Pediatric Management of Psychologic Crisis,* 1973.
(With David A. Balla) *Delinquency and Psychopathology,* assisted by Shelley S. Shanok, forewords by Justine Wise Polier and Dennis P. Cantwell, W. B. Saunders (St. Louis, MO), 1976.

(Editor) *Vulnerabilities to Delinquency,* Robert B. Luce (Fairfield, CT), 1981.

*Guilty by Reason of Insanity: A Psychiatrist Probes the Minds of Killers,* M.D. Fawcett Columbine (New York City), 1998.

Contributor to periodicals.

*SIDELIGHTS:* When Dorothy Otnow Lewis entered medicine during the 1960s, Freudian theory dominated the field of psychiatry, and there was little interest in searching for a possible biological basis for criminal behavior. While Lewis was studying for her board exams in psychiatry, she reviewed the medical histories of delinquent juvenile patients and found that many had suffered physical injuries prior to their delinquency. She began to wonder if there was a connection between neurological and psychiatric problems.

Lewis wrote *Delinquency and Psychopathology* with David A. Balla. They base the book on their three-year study of more than 200 delinquent children at a psychiatric clinic attached to a juvenile court. "*Delinquency and Psychopathology* is a unique attempt to blend humanism, research, and clinical application to the problem of youthful crime," wrote Arnold W. Rachman in *Contemporary Psychology.* Although Rachman warned that the findings in *Delinquency and Psychopathology* "must be viewed as suggestive, not conclusive," he noted that the work "will appeal to professionals oriented toward treatment and rehabilitation." *Social Casework* contributor Jerome Cohen remarked that "the social perspective receives more attention than the psychodynamic theories" in *Delinquency and Psychopathology,* but admitted that the book "would be worth reading if only to remind the reader that he must not lose sight of the variable causes that underlie any particular piece of psychosocial behavior thought to be problematic to individuals and the society of which they are a part."

In 1981, Lewis edited *Vulnerabilities to Delinquency,* a study of students at a Connecticut correctional school. Lewis and other researchers divided the students into two groups which reflected the nature of their crimes. Lewis found that three-quarters of the delinquents in the more violent group had been abused as children and almost four-fifths had witnessed graphic violence. One-third of the children in the less violent group had been abused, while one-fifth had witnessed brutal behavior. The researchers also found that "virtually all of the more violent offenders had neurological disorders," wrote David Kelley in *Harper's.*

Interviewing a number of juvenile and adult criminals, Lewis has worked with neurologist Jonathan Pincus to study whether neurological disorders lead to psychiatric ones. Based on their research, Lewis has become a vocal opponent of the death penalty. She states that a number of death row inmates should not be held fully responsible for their crimes and argues that many of these people exhibit serious psychiatric problems stemming from the effects of child abuse, brain injuries, or both.

*New Yorker* contributor Malcolm Gladwell wrote that Lewis's manner is "so approachable and so unthreatening that it's no wonder she gets hardened criminals to tell her their secrets." Her conversations with these offenders form the basis of her 1998 book, *Guilty by Reason of Insanity: A Psychiatrist Probes the Minds of Killers.* Abandoning a statistical approach to the subject, Lewis instead offers anecdotal evidence of the abuse and injuries that convicted murderers have suffered. She discusses problems in the judicial system and argues against the death penalty. "By book's end, Lewis makes sure readers are asking themselves whether an eye for an eye is the proper standard by which to approach killers," wrote a *Publishers Weekly* contributor. In *Guilty by Reason of Insanity,* Lewis also contends that every human being is a potential murderer, an assertion that "is frightening, perhaps controversial, and always interesting," stated Sue-Ellen Beauregard in *Booklist.*

*BIOGRAPHICAL/CRITICAL SOURCES:*

*PERIODICALS*

*Booklist,* March 15, 1998, p. 1186.
*Contemporary Psychology,* May, 1978, pp. 325-326.
*Harper's,* August, 1985, pp. 56, 59.
*New Yorker,* February 24 and March 3, 1997, pp. 132-145.
*Publishers Weekly,* March 16, 1998, pp. 45-46.
*Science News,* August 2, 1986, p. 77.
*Social Casework,* March, 1978, pp. 183-184.*

\*    \*    \*

## LIGHTHALL, William Douw   1857-1954
## (Wilfrid Chateauclair)

*PERSONAL:* Born December 27, 1857, in Hamilton, Ontario, Canada; died August 3, 1954; son of William and Margaret Lighthall; married Cybel Wilkes, 1890;

three children. *Education:* McGill University, B.A. (English literature), 1879, B.A. (civil law), 1881, M.A., 1885. *Politics:* Loyalist.

*CAREER:* Lawyer, historian, novelist, poet, philosopher and editor, c. 1887-1933. Served as mayor of Westmount (suburb of Montreal), 1900-03; practiced law in Montreal, 1881-1944. *Military service:* Served with the Prince of Wales Regiment from 1877-78, the Victoria Rifles from 1881-83, and the Victoria Rifles reserve from 1914-17; founded the Canadian Association of Retired Soldiers in 1915.

*MEMBER:* Royal Society of Canada (fellow), Canadian Association of Retired Soldiers (founding member, 1915), Canadian Authors Association (president, 1930).

*AWARDS, HONORS:* Shakespeare Gold Medal from McGill University, 1879; honorary LL.D., McGill University; King's Council, 1915.

*WRITINGS:*

*Thoughts, Moods and Ideals: Crimes of Leisure,* Witness (Montreal), 1887.

(Under pseudonym Wilfrid Chateauclair) *The Young Seigneur; or, Nation-making,* Drysdale (Montreal), 1888.

*An Account of the Battle of Chateauguay: Being a Lecture Delivered at Ormstown, March 8th, 1889,* Drysdale, 1889.

*Montreal after 250 Years,* Grafton (Montreal), 1892, published as *Sights and Shrines of Montreal: A Topographical, Romantic, and Historical Description of the City and Environs,* 1892.

*The False Chevalier; or, The Lifeguard of Marie Antoinette,* Arnold (New York City), 1898.

*A New Hochelagan Burying-Ground Discovered at Westmount on the Western Spur of Mount Royal, Montreal, July-September 1898,* Pelletier (Montreal), 1898.

*Hochelagans and Mohawks: A Link in Iroquois History,* Hope (Ottawa), 1899.

(Under pseudonym Chateauclair) *Hiawatha the Great,* Royal Society of Literature Transactions (London), 1901, published under own name as *The Master of Life: A Romance of the Five Nations and of Prehistoric Montreal,* Musson (Toronto), 1908, McClung (Chicago), 1909.

*Canada: A Modern Nation,* Witness, 1904.

*Thomas Pownall: His Part in the Conquest of Canada,* Hope, 1904.

*The Land of Manitou,* Desbarats (Montreal), 1916.

*Old Measures: Collected Verse,* Chapman (Montreal), Musson, 1922.

*The Outer Consciousness,* 8 volumes, privately printed (Montreal), 1923-30, revised and published in one volume, Macmillan (Toronto), 1933.

*OTHER*

(Editor and author of introduction) *Songs of the Great Dominion: Voices from the Forests and Waters, the Settlements and Cities of Canada,* Scott (London), 1889, abridged edition published as *Canadian Poems and Lays: Selections of Native Verse, Reflecting the Seasons, Legends, and Life of the Dominion,* Musson, 1891.

(Editor) *Canadian Songs and Poems: Voices from the Forests and Waters, the Settlements and Cities of Canada,* Scott, 1892.

Also contributor to periodical publications including *Royal Society of Literature of the United Kingdom, University of Toronto Studies, Canada and Its Provinces, National Municipal Review,* and *Canadian Author and Bookman.*

*SIDELIGHTS:* William Douw Lighthall—intellect, civil servant, and devout Canadian—attempted to integrate his scientific proclivities with his romanticized, ethereal ruminations of the human condition. Especially attentive to the history and development of Montreal and Quebec, Lighthall absorbed his surroundings, exercised a rare, soulful compassion, and applied his natural wisdom and learned knowledge to the world in which he lived. In one of his first historical accounts, published in 1889 and concerning the 1813 Battle of Chateauguay, Lighthall draws a conclusion that encapsulates the tone of much of his non-fictional endeavors. According to Paul Matthew St. Pierre, writing for *Dictionary of Literary Biography,* Lighthall resolves "that we shall always be able to preserve ourselves free in our course of development towards our own idea of a nation."

Born in Hamilton, Ontario, in 1857, Lighthall excelled in his studies and commenced to a long and challenging multi-disciplinary academic career at McGill University. First, he earned a B.A. in English literature, while simultaneously being awarded the Shakespeare Gold Medal, in 1879. Then, Lighthall moved to the study of law, earning his B.A. in civil law over the course of the next two years. This second degree paved the way for what was to become a sixty-three year profession practicing law in Montreal, making him the second of three generations of barristers in the Canadian hub. Evidently still not satisfied with his intellectual evolution, Lighthall pursued and in 1885 received a master of arts degree. These aggressive academic pursuits prompted McGill University to grant him an honorary LL.D. They were probably also instrumental in his winning the election to serve as mayor of Westmount, a post he held from 1900 to 1903.

Lighthall was forever attempting to carve or determine the defining characteristics of his native region. Canada underwent enormous sociopolitical transformations during the nineteenth and twentieth centuries, and Lighthall assumed as his purpose the task of sorting through the peripheral changes to identify the essence of his country. It was his strong belief that an unwavering adherence to core values and patriotic vision would provide Canadians with a strength and ability to conquer all challenges that came their way. His first novel, *The Young Seigneur,* was published in 1888 under the pseudonym Wilfrid Chateauclair, and it promoted his nationalistic themes. It was Lighthall's contention that Canadians must be willing to compromise and even occasionally sacrifice personal interests for the sake of their nation's future. In this novel, St. Pierre posits "his own idiosyncratic concepts of ideal nationhood realized through idealism itself, and of a nation that, once set in motion, can survive all corruption, whether expressed through state, community or the individual." Lighthall asseverated that the only way to propagate such ideals was for Canadians to adhere to the principles of the Loyalist movement.

Lighthall believed in the power and glory of Canada's destiny. He continued to write fiction and nonfiction that was often underscored with moral lessons and/or nationalistic themes which encouraged faith and devotion from his fellow citizens. However, his work and beliefs were truly singular. Specifically, Lighthall found ways to combine the linear thinking involved with writing historical accounts with romanticized philosophies and intangible speculations regarding spirituality and universal truth. In addition to his content, his writing style particularly evidenced the dichotomy of his efforts. For example, in 1889 he published a collection of songs and poetry titled *Songs of the Great Dominion: Voices from the Forests and Waters, the Settlements and Cities of Canada.* The title itself helps to illustrate the dichotomy, as it combines Canadian culture and development with the notion of a living, breathing natural environment that has its own stories to tell. However, further representation of his arguably obscure literary alliances is readily available in his use of language.

As Lighthall aged, his focus was redirected to philosophical analysis. In 1933 he published an eight-volume treatise called *Outer Consciousness,* which he developed from 1923 through 1930. Undeniably, his efforts were colossal and well-intended, but they fell a bit short of life-altering. Building upon his original nationalistic themes, Lighthall developed a theory that supported his platform for communal cooperation. A reviewer for the *Times* of London best summarizes this endeavor, which proposes an ideology called "Superpersonalism." It explains that "Superpersonalism is 'the docrine that the protoplasmic race is a living unit of which all its individuals are organs, and that the individual cell and that living unit act on the same organic plan'. . . . He goes further than to emphasize the solidarity of life . . . the whole of the protoplasmic race 'is inspired by an indwelling, independent, directive Superperson—the Person of Evolution'." Admitting that much of his content was "speculative," the *Times* reviewer goes on to call Lighthall's speculations "as interesting as they are bold." In *Journal of Philosophy,* D. M. Allan reviews *Outer Conciousness,* offering one possible bit of advice that might have been useful for Lighthall during his editing process. "One can only regret that Dr. Lighthall did not spend ten more years out of the evolutionary eternity patiently evolving his rich teleological insights into a rigorously logical argument. Ever pertinent is Pascal's dictum that if he had had more time, he would have written less." Despite this gentle criticism, Allan does commend Lighthall for his intellectual interests and undertaking.

Despite his occasionally discursive literary efforts, Lighthall must be applauded for actively pursuing working philosophies for life and existence. The *Outer Consciousness* series suggests the existence of psychic absolutes, or "hypersych" and the interesting possibility that there is an internal human consciousness that leads us and can only be fulfilled through human solidarity. Whether or not Lighthall managed to perfect his theories, he surely was respected for his ambitious philosophical attempts.

## BIOGRAPHICAL/CRITICAL SOURCES:

### BOOKS

*Dictionary of Literary Biography,* Volume 92: *Canadian Writers, 1890-1920,* Gale (Detroit, MI), 1990.

### PERIODICALS

*Boston Transcript,* April 15, 1931.
*Journal of Philosophy,* June 18, 1931.
*Times Literary Supplement,* August 20, 1931, p. 635.*

## LIMA BARRETO, Afonso Henrique de   1881-1922

*PERSONAL:* Given name is sometimes spelled "Affonso"; born in 1881, in Rio de Janeiro, Brazil; died, 1922.

*CAREER:* Fiction writer.

*WRITINGS:*

*O Triste Fim de Policarpo Quaresma* (novel), 1915, T. F. de Campos y Cia (Sao Paulo, Brazil), 1943, translation published as *The Patriot,* 1978.
*Historias e Sonhos,* 1920, Editora Brasiliense (Sao Paulo), 1956.
*Clara dos Anjos* (novel), Editora Mrito (Rio de Janeiro, Brazil), 1948.
*Marginalia,* Editora Mrito, 1953.
*Tres contos,* Cem Bibliofilos do Brasil (Rio de Janeiro), 1955.
*Diario intimo,* Editora Brasiliense, 1956.
*Os Bruzundangas: Satira,* Editora Brasiliense, 1956.
*O cemit rio dos vivos,* Editora Brasiliense, 1956.

Other writings include *Recordacoes do Escrivo Isaias Caminha* (novel), 1909; *Numa e a Ninfa,* 1915; *Vida e Morte de M. J. Gonzaga de Sa,* 1919; *Bagatelas,* 1922; and *Lima Barreto: Bibliography and Translations* (includes *Clara dos Anjos* and *Vide e Morte de M. J. Gonzaga de Sa*), 1979.*

\*          \*          \*

## LINDAL, Amalia   1926-1989
### (Amalia Gourdin)

*PERSONAL:* Born May 19, 1926, in Quincy, MA; died of cancer, November, 1989, in Guelph, Ontario, Canada; daughter of Edvard O. Gourdin (a lawyer); married Baldur Lindal (a chemical engineer); children: five, including Tryggvi V. *Education:* Boston University, B.A., 1949.

*CAREER:* Freelance journalist, 1942-72; Canadian National Red Cross, Toronto, Ontario, information officer, c. 1973-76; Canadian Diabetics Association, Toronto, public relations manager and editor, 1977-81; *Reader's Choice,* Toronto, editor, 1982-83; teacher of evening classes in short-story writing, 1983-89. English teacher in Reykjavik, Iceland; Statistical Bureau of Iceland, statistician, c. 1968-71.

*AWARDS, HONORS:* Winner of short story contests sponsored by Ontario newspapers in the 1980s.

*WRITINGS:*

*Ripples from Iceland* (autobiography), Norton (New York City), 1962, updated edition, Bokaforlag Odds Bjornssonar (Akureyri, Iceland), 1988.
(Contributor) Tryggvi V. Lindal, editor, *Tromet og fiol* (poems), [Reykjavik, Iceland], 1992.
*Cross-Cultural Fiction of Amalia Lindal,* edited by son, T. V. Lindal, [Reykjavik], 1999.

Contributor of articles and stories to periodicals, including *Christian Science Monitor.* Editor, *65 Degrees: Reader's Quarterly on Icelandic Life,* 1967-70; editor, *Diabetes Dialogue,* c. 1977-81. Stories published prior to 1945 appeared under the name Amalia Gourdin.*

\*          \*          \*

## LINDAL, Tryggvi V(altyr)   1951-

*PERSONAL:* Born May 3, 1951, in Reykjavik, Iceland; son of Baldur (a chemical engineer) and Amalia (a writer and journalist; maiden name, Gourdin) Lindal, *Education:* University of Toronto, B.A., 1978; graduate study at University of Manitoba, 1978-80; University of Iceland, teacher's certificate, 1984.

*ADDRESSES: Home*—Skeggjagata 3, 105 Reykjavik, Iceland.

*CAREER:* Teacher, 1980-92; writer, 1993—.

*MEMBER:* Writers Union of Iceland, Hellas Group of Poets, Iceland-Canada Friendship Society (president, 1995—).

*AWARDS, HONORS:* Jean Monnet European Literary Award, 1998, for poetry.

*WRITINGS:*

*Naeturvordurinn* (poems), [Reykjavik, Iceland], 1989.
(Editor) *Tromet og fiol* (poems), [Reykjavik], 1992.
*Lindal og Lorca* (poems), [Reykjavik], 1997.
*An Icelandic Poet* (poems), Eiginutgafa (Reykjavik), 1998.
(Editor) *Cross-Cultural Fiction of Amalia Lindal,* [Reykjavik], 1999.

Contributor of several hundred essays, poems, and stories to Icelandic periodicals.

## LINDBERGH, Reeve 1945-
### (Reeve Lindbergh Brown)

*PERSONAL:* Born in 1945; daughter of Charles (an aviator) and Anne (an author; maiden name, Morrow) Lindbergh; married Richard Brown (a photographer and teacher; divorced); married Nat Tripp (a writer); children: (first marriage) Elizabeth, Susannah, John (died 1985); (second marriage) Benjamin. *Education:* Radcliffe College, Cambridge, M.A.

*ADDRESSES: Agent*—c/o Simon & Schuster, 1230 Avenue of the Americas, New York, NY 10020.

*CAREER:* Author. Taught in Vermont.

*WRITINGS:*

(Under name Reeve Lindbergh Brown) *Moving to the Country* (novel), Doubleday (Garden City, NY), 1983.

*The View From the Kingdom: A New England Album* (essays), photographs by Richard Brown, introduction by Noel Perrin, Harcourt Brace Jovanovich (San Diego, CA), 1987.

*The Names of the Mountains: A Novel,* Simon & Schuster (New York City), 1992.

*John's Apples* (poems), illustrated by John Wilde, Perishable Press (Mt. Horeb, WI), 1995.

*Under a Wing: A Memoir,* Simon & Schuster, 1998.

*JUVENILE*

*The Midnight Farm,* illustrated by Susan Jeffers, Dial (New York City), 1987.

*Benjamin's Barn,* illustrated by Susan Jeffers, Dial, 1990.

*The Day the Goose Got Loose,* illustrated by Steven Kellogg, Dial, 1990.

*Johnny Appleseed: A Poem,* illustrated by Kathy Jakobsen, Joy Street (Boston, MA), 1990.

*A View From the Air: Charles Lindbergh's Earth and Sky,* photographs by Richard Brown, Viking (New York City), 1992.

*Grandfather's Love Song,* illustrated by Rachel Isadora, Viking, 1993.

*There's a Cow in the Road!,* illustrated by Tracey Campbell Pearson, Dial, 1993.

*If I'd Known Then What I Know Now,* illustrated by Kimberly Bulcken Root, Viking, 1994.

*What Is the Sun?,* illustrated by Stephen Lambert, Candlewick (Cambridge, MA), 1994.

*Nobody Owns the Sky: The Story of "Brave Bessie" Coleman,* illustrated by Pamela Paparone, Candlewick, 1996.

*The Awful Aardvarks Go to School,* illustrated by Tracey Campbell Pearson, Viking, 1997.

*The Circle of Days,* illustrated by Cathie Felstead, Candlewick, 1997.

*North Country Spring,* illustrated by Liz Sivertson, Houghton Mifflin (Boston, MA), 1997.

*SIDELIGHTS:* Author Reeve Lindbergh is the daughter and one of the five surviving children of Charles and Anne Morrow Lindbergh. The first son born to Charles and Anne, Charles Augustus Jr., was kidnapped and killed in 1932, when he was twenty months old. In 1927, Charles Sr. flew the first solo transatlantic flight, traveling from New York to Paris. Charles, who authored the Pulitzer Prize-winning *Spirit of St. Louis,* later came under attack for his position that the United States should remain neutral in the war in Europe and was charged with being anti-Semitic. These incidents kept the Lindbergh family in the spotlight, and the famous parents protected their children from public scrutiny as best they could. Lindbergh and her brothers and sister went on to lead private lives.

Lindbergh and her first husband, Richard Brown, moved from Cambridge, Massachusetts to Vermont, where they both taught school and had four children. Their son John died of encephalitis in 1985, at age twenty months. Lindbergh began writing children's books after John's death. Prior to that time, she had published her autobiographical novel *Moving to the Country.* The book is the story of Nancy and Tom King, who move with their two daughters from a Massachusetts suburb to rural Vermont. Tom is a progressive high school English teacher who faces students lacking basic skills. Nancy is dealing with an unplanned pregnancy. The couple's marriage is strained as they adapt to life in the country and slow acceptance by their neighbors. Nancy loses the baby, and Tom worries about the security of his job. They eventually overcome their internal and external obstacles and gain the support of the townspeople. A *Publishers Weekly* reviewer called *Moving to the Country* "comforting, hopeful, sensitively written, an honest and believable portrayal of marriage, change, and putting down roots." It was described as "an old-fashioned ode to country pleasure and domestic love" by Diane Cole in the *New York Times Book Review.*

In her autobiographical novel *The Names of the Mountains,* Lindbergh reveals what life as a Lindbergh was like after the death of her father through her fictional family headed by aviator Cal Linley and his wife Alicia. Paula Chin wrote in *People Weekly* that Lindbergh wrote the book "to dispel previous notions about their family and the tragedies that have beset it." The story is told through the eyes of Cress Linley, youngest daughter of the couple, who spends a weekend with her siblings and their elderly mother Alicia, who is suffering from memory loss. In real life, the Lindbergh children were caring for their own mother, eighty-six at the time of the book's publication, who was suffering from similar memory lapses and strokes. "Lindbergh's prose has a gentle cadence and charm," wrote a *Kirkus Reviews* reviewer. *Library Journal* reviewer Jan Blodgett wrote that Lindbergh "gently and perceptively unfolds this complex family history." The children of Charles and Anne Morrow Lindbergh and often gather at the farm of Lindbergh, her husband, writer Nat Tripp, and their son Benjamin, in Passumpsic, Vermont.

*Under a Wing: A Memoir* reveals Lindbergh's life as a child growing up in Darien, Connecticut. "This gentle memoir shows a unique and uniquely poignant family life," wrote a *Publishers Weekly* reviewer. Charles was a loving but stern father. He would not allow his children to drink soda or eat candy, marshmallow fluff, or grape jelly. He favored discussion over television and protected his family with his rules. Lindbergh said "There were only two ways of doing things—Father's way and the wrong way." Geoffrey C. Ward wrote in the *New York Times Book Review* that Lindbergh's *Under a Wing* "beautifully recaptures the determinedly ordered life her father insisted his family lead in their Connecticut home after the war."

Lindbergh has written many children's books. Her first, *The Midnight Farm,* is a counting book. A young child is unable to sleep, and his mother takes him for a walk around their farm, where they observe the activities of the animals as night descends. The child grows tired and peacefully slips back into slumber. *Times Literary Supplement* reviewer Jane Doonan called *The Midnight Farm* "a gentle progression from disturbed waking to sleeping worlds." "This warm, loving story will comfort any child afraid of the dark," wrote Eve Bunting in the *Los Angeles Times Book Review.*

In *Benjamin's Barn,* a young boy carries his teddy bear into a big, red barn, to find not only the usual farm animals, but jungle and prehistoric creatures, pirate ships, a princess, and a brass band. A *Publishers Weekly* reviewer found the art and text to be "lackluster and flat." "The rhyming text has a comforting circular flow, well-suited to Benjamin's flight of fancy and . . . return to reality," wrote Anna DeWind in *School Library Journal. Booklist* reviewer Barbara Elleman called the book "a highly pleasing complement to . . . *Midnight Farm.*"

In *The Day the Goose Got Loose,* a goose who sees the wild geese flying overhead creates chaos in the barnyard. The boy who knows the reason for the goose's behavior later dreams of geese and magical lands. A *Publishers Weekly* reviewer said the "soothing, exquisitely illustrated dream sequence . . . offsets the frenzy of the rest of the tale." "The satisfying rhyme and rhythm of this book make it a good choice for reading aloud," wrote Anne Price in *School Library Journal.*

*Horn Book* reviewer Mary M. Burns called *Johnny Appleseed* "a splendid production." The story is of John Chapman, the American folk hero who planted his seeds from the East Coast to the Midwest. "This work shows him as a gentle, religious man on a mission, a lover of the land," wrote a *Publishers Weekly* reviewer. The book includes a map tracing Johnny's journey from Massachusetts to Indiana.

Lindbergh expresses her father's love of the natural world in *A View From the Air: Charles Lindbergh's Earth and Sky.* Her long poem is accompanied by photographs taken by Richard Brown, when he flew with Charles Lindbergh over northern New England in the early 1970s. A *Publishers Weekly* reviewer felt "the presentation . . . seems to distance the reader from Charles Lindbergh's voice." *Booklist* reviewer Deborah Abbott wrote that the verses "capture the pilot's awe and respect for the natural beauty of our land." A reviewer wrote in *Kirkus Reviews* that Lindbergh's poetry "makes an eloquent plea for preservation." A *Publishers Weekly* reviewer said Lindbergh's *Grandfather's Lovesong* "tenderly expresses a man's love for his grandchild." Seasonal scenes of rural Maine are depicted, each accompanied by a quatrain. "Fall and winter scenes are especially captivating," wrote Leda Schubert in *School Library Journal.*

In *There's a Cow in the Road,* as a little girl rushes to get ready for school, she looks through her Vermont farmhouse window to see a cow who is then joined by other barnyard animals until there's a "crowd in the road." By the time the girl and the other children board the school bus, a goat, sheep, horse, pig, and goose have joined to see them off. "The story has warmth and vitality and a sense of community," wrote Hazel Rochman in *Booklist.* A *Publishers Weekly* reviewer noted the details and action not described in the text. "The result is a great deal of kid-pleasing, between-the-lines action." A *Kirkus* reviewer called *There's a Cow in the Road* "a joyous, comical pacesetter for a busy morning."

A man's inept do-it-yourself projects in building and maintaining a farm are the focus of *If I'd Known Then*

*What I Know Now.* Sally R. Dow wrote in *School Library Journal* that the book's "tall-tale humor . . . will appeal to all those 'just learning how.' " In *What Is the Sun* a young boy questions his grandmother, and each answer leads to another question. Patricia Crawford noted in *Language Arts* that the text demonstrates the "comfort" provided to young children "through their interactions with a caring, older adult." *Nobody Owns the Sky* is an account of how Bessie Coleman became the first African American aviator in the world. A *Kirkus* reviewer called it "homage to a brave and dedicated aviation pioneer." Coleman was denied entrance to flying schools in the United States and obtained her pilot's license in France. She then worked as a stunt pilot in the United States and Europe during the 1920s and died in a plane accident in Jacksonville, Florida, in 1926. A *Publishers Weekly* reviewer said Lindbergh "chooses the elements likeliest to inspire a young audience." *Washington Post Book World* reviewer John Cech called *Nobody Owns the Sky* "an important book for the little ones who might think they can't and for those who are learning that they can."

A *Publishers Weekly* reviewer called Lindbergh's *The Awful Aardvarks Go to School* a "witty, giddy alphabet book." The aardvarks terrorize the animals that attend the school, angering anteaters, eating ants, bullying a bunny, and tossing turtles. A *Kirkus* reviewer noted that the aardvarks "are more gleeful than rude," and "come across as much ado about nothing." *School Library Journal* reviewer called *The Awful Aardvarks Go to School* "a flying success." *The Circle of Days* is Lindbergh's adaptation of Francis of Assisi's *Canticle of the Sun,* written in 1225. *School Library Journal* reviewer Patricia Lothrop-Green called it a book "for the eye, if not the ear." "The gentle, rhyming text follows the form of a prayer in praise of brother sun, sister moon, and mother earth and in gratitude to the Lord for providing such wondrous gifts," wrote a *Publishers Weekly* reviewer. Janice M. Del Negro wrote in *The Bulletin of the Center for Children's Books* that in *The Circle of Days,* "Francis of Assisi's hymn of thanks to the Creator is granted glowing life."

Lindbergh uses rhyming couplets in describing how spring unfolds in New England in *North Country Spring.* The book includes a glossary of the fourteen animals included. A *Kirkus Reviews* reviewer felt the text "never captures the anticipation of the season." Kay Weisman wrote in *Booklist* that junior high students will find *North Country Spring* to be "a springboard for writing seasonal poetry." "Lindbergh's ebullient verse is a triumph song of spring's melting, sensory flush," wrote a *Publishers Weekly* reviewer.

## BIOGRAPHICAL/CRITICAL SOURCES:

*PERIODICALS*

*Booklist,* September 1, 1987, p. 65; March 1, 1989, p. 1200; April 15, 1990, p. 1634; September 1, 1990, p. 58; September 15, 1990, p. 171; November 15, 1991, p. 633; August, 1992, p. 2015; November 15, 1992, p. 579; January 15, 1993, p. 915; July, 1993, p. 1975; January, 1997, p. 869; May 15, 1997, p. 1580; October 15, 1997, p. 402; April, 1998, p. 1325.

*Books,* December, 1987, p. 24.

*Bulletin of the Center for Children's Books,* April, 1998, p. 286.

*Children's Book Review Service,* November, 1987, p. 26; August, 1990, p. 160; October, 1990, p. 20; November, 1990, p. 26; October, 1992, p. 20; February, 1997, p. 76; May 1997, p. 111.

*Children's Book Watch,* April, 1991, p. 1; May, 1993, p. 3; January, 1997, p. 5.

*Christian Science Monitor,* November 6, 1987, p. B6; January 4, 1993, p. 12.

*Horn Book,* September, 1990, p. 593; November, 1990, p. 729, pp. 774-75.

*Horn Book Guide,* January, 1990, p. 219; July, 1990, p. 29, 32; spring, 1993, p. 37; spring, 1997, p. 36; fall, 1997, p. 272.

*Junior Bookshelf,* April, 1988, p. 84; June, 1991, p. 95; August, 1993, p. 129.

*Kirkus Reviews,* September 1, 1987, p. 1323; July 1, 1990, p. 933; September 1, 1992, p. 1140; October 1, 1992, p. 1208; July 1, 1993, p. 863; November 1, 1996, p. 1603; February 15, 1997, p. 302; September 15, 1997, p. 1459.

*Kliatt,* September, 1996, p. 24.

*Language Arts,* September, 1996, p. 354.

*Library Journal,* November 15, 1992, p. 102; October 1, 1998, p. 104.

*Los Angeles Times Book Review,* November 22, 1987, p. 6.

*Maclean's,* November 9, 1998, p. 86.

*Magpies,* September, 1991, p. 28; March, 1997, p. 23.

*Minneapolis-St. Paul Magazine,* November, 1987, p. 156.

*New York Times Book Review,* January 1, 1984, pp. 20-22; December 13, 1987, p. 29; April 3, 1988, p. 16; December 2, 1988, p. 38; December 2, 1990, p. 38; March 7, 1993, p. 12; May 16, 1993, p. 31; November 14, 1993, p. 58; May 11, 1997, p. 24; September 27, 1998, pp. 14-15.

*People Weekly,* January 25, 1993, p. 63; September 28, 1998, p. 157.

*Publishers Weekly,* July 22, 1983, p. 118; July 10, 1987, p. 66; June 8, 1990, p. 52; July 13, 1990, pp. 53-54; July 13, 1992, p. 53; October 12, 1992, p. 65; April 19, 1993, p. 59; June 21, 1993, p. 103; May 9, 1994, p. 71; January 29, 1996, p. 101; June 17, 1996, p. 67; November 18, 1996, p. 74; March 24, 1997, p. 82; August 25, 1997, p. 70; January 19, 1998, p. 380; March 23, 1998, p. 95; August 24, 1998, p. 38.

*School Library Journal,* October, 1987, p. 115; June, 1990, p. 103; August, 1990, p. 122; September, 1990, p. 206; September, 1992, p. 222; April, 1993, p. 100; July, 1994, p. 79; August, 1994, p. 140; November, 1996, p. 98; February, 1997, p. 113; April, 1997, p. 113; December, 1997, p. 96; April, 1998, p. 119.

*Skipping Stones,* March, 1997, p. 8.

*Times Literary Supplement,* November 20, 1987, p. 1284.

*Washington Post Book World,* December 8, 1996, p. 23.

*Wilson Library Bulletin,* May, 1988, p. 72.*

\*     \*     \*

## LOMBREGLIA, Ralph

*PERSONAL:* Married; children: a daughter.

*ADDRESSES: Home*—Boston, MA. *Office*—Arlington, MA. *Agent*—c/o Farrar, Straus & Giroux, 19 Union Square West, New York, NY 10003. *E-mail*—Lombreglia@aol.com.

*CAREER:* Writer.

*AWARDS, HONORS:* Guggenheim fellowship, 1996.

*WRITINGS:*

*Men Under Water* (stories), Doubleday (New York City), 1990.

*Make Me Work* (stories), Farrar, Straus (New York City), 1994.

Contributor to magazines, including *Atlantic Monthly* and *New Yorker.* His work has appeared in the anthologies *The Best American Short Stories* (1987 and 1988), *The Vintage Book of Contemporary American Short Stories, American Stories II: Fiction from The Atlantic Monthly,* and *Prize Stories 1996: The O. Henry Awards.* Co-producer of CD-ROM *A Jack Kerouac ROMnibus,* Penguin Electronic (1995), and co-

publisher of Internet newsletter for multimedia developers. His made-for-television movie, *The Last Ferry Home,* aired in 1992.

*SIDELIGHTS:* Short story writer Ralph Lombreglia has been widely published in magazines, anthologies, and in his own pair of short story collections *Men Under Water* and *Make Me Work.* For his stories, Lombreglia often draws on experiences and anecdotes recorded in journals, and as an expert in computers makes technology a deliberate presence in many of his stories. "With 300 TV channels, why should they choose me?" Lombreglia told Louis B. Jones of the *New York Times Book Review.* "I feel I have a real responsibility to my readers to give them something as stylish, as contemporary and as electric as what you might find out there."

*Men Under Water* is full of stories of bright young men who are sensitive and reasonable and trying to make their way in a world that is fraught with confusion. A "powerful first collection of stories," declared *New York Times Book Review* critic William Ferguson, who singled out the title story for special praise. Moreover, in a collective review of short fiction for the *New York Review of Books,* Robert Towers wrote that *Men Under Water* had "received enthusiastic comments" from other writers, including John Barth, Amy Hempel, and Ann Beattie. Although his work differs from theirs, "[t]here is nothing 'postmodernist' or 'minimalist' or 'self-reflective' . . . in his approach." Towers praised Lombreglia's "odd yet persuasive characters, the zany situations that he invents for them, [and] his jazzy prose rhythms," calling him "a very funny man." Towers faulted Lombreglia for being, at times, "too farcical," but commended his ability to portray not only "the crazed desperation of the characters but the weirdness and dislocations that dominate so much American life, public and private."

Lombreglia's second collection of short stories, *Make Me Work,* "veers inward to face directly what turns out to be the human planet," to quote Jones, who enthused, "It is a wonderful visit. From the first sentence, you find yourself relaxing. Soon you find yourself loving his world, wanting to meet his friends." "Mr. Lombreglia's new batch of stories takes a much more complicated view of human nature and society. These stories are both funny and profound, highlighted by lights and deep darks," continued Jones. In a review for *Washington Post Book World,* George Packer found Lombreglia's gift to be "for the kinetic and the absurd," and according to Richard Eder of the *Los Angeles Times Book Review,* Lombreglia "writes in an odd mix of parody and melodrama of characters who submit to the deformities they are confined in, paradoxically, by today's technological and cultural unconstraints." In Eder's view, Lombreglia is "on the rebound from what he sees around him. Fortunately he is made extensively of Silly Putty. His rebounds, at their best, are extravagant and far-fetching. It is in his soberer moments, exploring the straight line of a moral or a plot, that he flounders. He flounders oftener in *Make Me Work* than in his splendid first collection, *Men Under Water.* Lombreglia is all treble obbligato; when he tries for resonance and undertones they seem patched in." Eder particularly called reader's attention to the story "Late Early Man" for its "balance between his characters, zany but disturbingly credible, and his disconcerting moral message," which is "gracefully achieved. None of the other stories quite manages such a balance." Finally, "plot summaries don't really do justice to good writing," explained Jones. "Whatever kind of thing you're already thinking these stories are, they are not. My bet is they're better than anyone anticipates."

*BIOGRAPHICAL/CRITICAL SOURCES:*

*PERIODICALS*

*Los Angeles Times Book Review,* January 2, 1994, pp. 3, 7.
*New York Review of Books,* May 17, 1990, pp. 38-39.
*New York Times Book Review,* April 15, 1990, p. 14; January 2, 1994.
*Washington Post Book World,* March 6, 1994, p. 9.

*OTHER*

*Atlantic Monthly,* http://www.theatlantic.com (February 1, 1999).*

\* \* \*

## LORANGER, Jean-Aubert 1896-1942

*PERSONAL:* Born October 16, 1896, in Montreal, Quebec, Canada; died October 28, 1942, in Montreal, Quebec, Canada; son of Joseph Thomas (a medical student) and Lucie (Beaudry) Loranger; married Alice Tetreau, February 5, 1920; children: Jean De Gaspe, Lucie-Blanche, Francois Jean Aubert. *Education:* Attended Mont Saint Louis, Le Plateau.

*CAREER:* Quebec liquor commissioner, 1922-23; *La Patrie,* journalist, 1923-27; *La Presse,* associate director of information, 1927-30; private secretary to minis-

ter of the navy, 1930-32; served Port of Montreal, 1932-34; *La Patrie,* journalist, 1939-42; *Montreal Matin,* journalist, 1942.

*MEMBER:* Canadian Authors' Association (creator, 1921).

*WRITINGS:*

*Les Atmospheres,* Morissette (Montreal), 1920.
*Poemes,* Morissette, 1922.
*L'Orange* (play), produced at Theatre Parisian, Montreal, January, 1923.
*A La Recherche du Regionalisme: Le Village, Contes et Nouvelles du Terroir,* Garand (Montreal), 1925.
*Les Atmospheres, Suivi des Poemes,* edited by Gilles Marcotte, HMH (Montreal), 1970.
*Contes: Du Passeur a Joe Folcu; Il Le Marchand du Tabac en Feuilles,* two volumes, edited by Bernadette Guilmette, Fides (Montreal), 1978.

Contibutor to periodicals, including *Le Jour.*

*SIDELIGHTS:* French Canadian writer Jean-Aubert Loranger led an interesting and varied existence. A prolific writer, Loranger was published in numerous periodicals, magazines, and newspapers during his lifetime. He also wrote several books, and two volumes of poetry. In addition to his literary output, Loranger held down a series of odd jobs including working as a liquor commissioner, private secretary, and at the Port of Montreal. He took these jobs to care for his young family, possibly hoping to spare them the hardships he and his mother had encountered when his father passed away during his childhood. His difficult upbringing greatly shaped Loranger, perhaps molding him into the great literary talent that he was. In spite of the hardships, his talents and interests were evident early on. According to Maurice Lebel, writing for *Dictionary of Literary Biography,* "The education of the now-fatherless boy was entrusted to tutors, so that he attended neither primary or secondary school, though he did go to Mont Saint-Louis and Le Plateau for some higher education. By then, however, he was already passionately in love with art and French literature, especially the work of Marcel Proust."

Loranger was born in 1896 in Montreal, Canada. His father, a medical student, died of typhoid fever when Loranger was just four years old. The ensuing years were difficult ones for mother and son. Loranger, however, found solace in his studies, especially in art and French literature. Drawing upon his French heritage, Loranger embraced the work of fellow Frenchman

Marcel Proust. He was particularly interested in Proust's study of the psychological development of character and the irrational nature of love. In comparison to the internal strife experienced during much of the nineteenth century, Canada was emerging, in the new century, into a stable country. With the expansion of territory came greater industrialization and commercial growth. While resentments between French and British Canadians still existed, the open hostility between the two ethnic groups appeared to wane as the twentieth century progressed. Greater opportunities existed on all levels, including literature. As a result, Loranger found his work accepted in a variety of literary publications, including the review called *Le Nigog.*

During *Le Nigog*'s brief, thirteen-issue run, Roquebrune published two pieces of Loranger's writing. The first, an article titled "Le Pays laurentien" ("Laurentian Countryside") delved into one of Loranger's favorite subjects: the natural beauty of Quebec. The second article, "A Saint-Sulpice; Causerie de M. Dupuy sur Verhaeren" ("A Chat about the Celebrated Belgian Poet") addressed his literary influences. According to Lebel, these early articles "showed Loranger's two centers of interest: Quebec and the exotic," and established him as a literary force.

In the 1920s, Loranger's life took on a dramatic turn. He married Alice Tetreau in 1920, and together, they had three children in just six years. While raising a family filled a void left by his father's early death, Loranger also clearly felt the pressure of providing for his new clan. Thus in 1922, just two years after his first book *Les Atmospheres* was published, Loranger took a non-literary job as the liquor commissioner of Quebec. His second book, *Poemes,* came out in the same year. A one-act farce followed in 1923, and another book, this one a collection of stories titled *A la recherche du regionalisme* ("In Search of Regionalism") appeared in 1925. Regardless of Loranger's literary successes, however, he continued making a steady living via bizarre occupations. In the early 1930s, Loranger took a personal secretary job, assisting the minister of Ottowa's navy, Alfred Duranleau. From 1932 to 1934, he held an administrative position in the Port of Montreal. These seemingly random occupations must have fulfilled his need to provide for his family, although they clearly did not satiate his creative drive. As always, he continued writing.

In the late 1930s, Loranger appeared to have made a career shift, focusing his "steady" jobs on the literary profession. His early experience in the 1920s on the publication *La Patrie* served him well. From 1932 to 1934,

Loranger contributed regularly to the newspaper *Le Jour,* and eventually went back to work for *La Patrie* in the final years of his life. Additionally, he continued writing other articles that appeared with frequency in numerous publications throughout Canada. According to Lebel, "He wrote actively, from 1920 to 1942. Outside of two collections of poetry, his work consists of more than 150 stories, most of which Bernadette Guilmette collected in 1978 in two volumes."

During the course of his career, Loranger appears to have gone through two distinct literary phases. In both, according to Lebel, "he is in full possession of his medium, writing precisely and energetically . . . his first style . . . anecdotal; those in the second pay attention to social mores. Small villages and their inhabitants, water, fire, tobacco, money, liquor, women, strong men, weak men, solitude, and death are the major motifs the author develops. A good many stories are unclassifiable: biting, irrational, and based on folk sayings. But altogether they reveal a whole philosophy of life, a sincere love, a penetrating observation, and a deep knowledge of the country and its people." Like most French Canadians, Loranger was fiercely loyal to his lineage. He paid literary homage to Canada's struggles of the past decade, in addition to recognizing the major strides Canada as a whole had taken during the twentieth century to become a unified country.

In the early 1920s, Loranger focused his efforts on his poetry. He published two volumes, *Les Atmospheres* in 1920, and *Poemes* in 1922, neither of which earned him much praise from critics of the day. Lebel states, "A marginal poet like Marcel Dugas, Loranger wrote in free verse and experimented with brief poetic forms inspired by the Japanese haiku and tanka. . . . Loranger broke with various received traditions, broke with the alexandrine, and with the orotund patriotic verse." While the critics of his day were skeptical, contemporary critics have been much kinder. A new collection, titled *Les Atmospheres, suivi des Poemes,* was published in 1970, and was well received.

*BIOGRAPHICAL/CRITICAL SOURCES:*

*BOOKS*

*Dictionary of Literary Biography,* Volume 92: *Canadian Writers, 1890-1920,* Gale, 1990.*

## LOUNSBURY, Ruth Ozeki
### See OZEKI, Ruth L.

\*     \*     \*

## LUCAS, Phil 1942-

*PERSONAL:* Born January 15, 1942, in Phoenix, AZ; son of Charles W. (an athletic-equipment manager) and Sally Lucas. *Education:* Atttended Phoenix Community College, 1960-61, and Mesa Community College, 1966; Western Washington University, B.S., 1970.

*ADDRESSES: Agent*—c/o Public Broadcasting Service, 1320 Braddock Place, Alexandria, VA 22314.

*CAREER:* Producer, director, and writer of documentaries and feature films. Producer of television series *Native Indians: Images of Reality,* 1989-90, and television film *Broken Chain,* 1993. Worked as photographer in New York City in early 1970s; trainer in filmmaking at United Indians of All Tribes Foundation, beginning 1974; founding president of Phil Lucas Production Co., 1980. Actor in television series *Northern Exposure,* CBS-TV, 1990-91. Technical and cultural content advisor for television series *Northern Exposure* and *MacGyver.*

*AWARDS, HONORS:* Special achievement award for documentary film from American Indian Film Institute, 1980, and Prix Italia, 1981, both for *Images of Indians;* INPUT Award, 1988, for *The Honor of All;* awards for best animated short subject from American Indian Film Institute, 1984, for *The Great Wolf and Little Mouse Sister* and *Walking with Grandfather.*

*WRITINGS:*

*DOCUMENTARY SCREENPLAYS, AND DIRECTING*

*An Act of Self-Determination,* Bureau of Indian Affairs, 1974.
(With Robert Hagopian; and director with Hagopian) *Images of Indians* (five episodes), PBS-TV, 1979-80.
*Nez Perce: Portrait of a People,* National Park Service, 1982.
*Beyond Hunting and Fishing,* 1989.
(With Janet Tanaka and Peter von Puttkamer) *The Honor of All: The Story of Alkali Lake* (three episodes), PBS-TV, 1985-86.
*I'm Not Afraid of Me,* 1990.
*Healing the Nation,* 1992.

*ANIMATED FILMS; AND DIRECTOR*

*The Great Wolf and Little Mouse Sister,* PBS-TV, 1984.
*Walking with Grandfather,* PBS-TV, 1984, expanded version broadcast as six-episode series, PBS-TV, 1988.

*OTHER FILMS*

Also director of *Voyage of Discovery.*

*SIDELIGHTS:* Phil Lucas is a prominent Native American filmmaker who has won recognition as writer, producer, and director of documentaries on contemporary issues and themes. Lucas began his filmmaking career in 1974 while teaching at the United Indians of All Tribes Foundation in Seattle, Washington. Among his films from this period is *An Act of Self-Determination,* which he made for the Bureau of Indian Affairs.

In 1979 Lucas commenced work on *Images of Indians,* an ambitious, five-part series examining the stereotypical depiction of Native Americans in American films and television shows. In addition, the series explored the negative impact of those stereotypes on the self-perceptions of Native Americans. A *Variety* reviewer noted that the series features "apt examples . . . from many westerns." *Images of Indians* won a special prize in 1980 from the American Indian Film Institute. In the mid-1980s Lucas addressed the prevalence of substance abuse among Native Americans. He wrote and directed *The Honor of All: The Story of Alkali Lake,* which concerns the successful overcoming of alcoholism by members of the Alkali Lake Band. Lucas examined another positive subject in his 1989 production *Beyond Hunting and Fishing,* which describes the economic achievements of Indians from British Columbia. That same year Lucas completed the first fifteen episodes of *Native Indians: Images of Reality* for Canadian television. This series was followed the next year by eleven more episodes examining various aspects of self-perspective among Native Americans.

Among Lucas's other films is *Voyage of Rediscovery,* a feature production—which Lucas wrote, produced, and directed—about a boy who attains a greater understanding and appreciation of his Indian culture after a judge banishes him to an island for eight months. Lucas has also been involved in animated filmmaking. He served as writer, producer, and director of two 1984 animated shorts, *The Great Wolf and Little Mouse Sister* and *Walking with Grandfather,* both of which were broadcast on PBS-TV.

*BIOGRAPHICAL/CRITICAL SOURCES:*

PERIODICALS

*Film Comment,* May-June, 1992, pp. 64-67.
*Variety,* July 16, 1980, p. 70.*

\* \* \*

## LUDWIG, William   1912-1999

*PERSONAL:* Born May 26, 1912, in New York, NY; died of complications from Parkinson's disease, February 7, 1999; son of Charles and Pearl (Zieph) Ludwig; married Susan E. Riesenfeld, October 2, 1938; children: Richard John. *Education:* Columbia University, A.B., 1932, LL.B., 1934.

*CAREER:* Attorney for New York City law firms, including Prince & Loeb and Nathan Burkan, 1934-36; Metro-Goldwyn-Mayer Studios, Los Angeles, staff screenwriter, 1937-59; freelance writer, beginning in 1958. Producer-Writers Guild Pension Trust, chairperson of board of trustees; Writers Guild Industry Health Fund, chairperson of board of trustees; Motion Pictures and Television Fund, member of board of trustees.

*AWARDS, HONORS:* Shared Academy Award, best story and screenplay, Academy of Motion Picture Arts and Sciences, 1955, for *Innocent Melody;* Writers Guild of America West, Valentine Davies Award, 1973, Morgan Cox Award, 1976, and Edmund H. North Award, 1993; Founders Award, Writers Guild Foundation, 1992; Box Office Blue Ribbons for *Love Finds Andy Hardy, Out West with the Hardys,* and *Hardys Ride High;* medal from *Parents'* magazine for *The Hills of Home;* Screen Writers Guild Awards for *The Great Caruso* and *Oklahoma.*

*WRITINGS:*

SCREENPLAYS

*Love Finds Andy Hardy*, MGM, 1938.
*Out West with the Hardys*, MGM, 1938.
*Hardys Ride High*, MGM, 1939.
*Journey for Margaret*, MGM, 1942.
*Oklahoma*, Magna Theatres, 1945.
*The Hills of Home*, MGM, 1948
*Challenge to Lassie*, MGM, 1949.
*Shadow on the Wall*, MGM, 1950.
*The Great Caruso*, MGM, 1951.
*The Student Prince*, MGM, 1954.

(With Sonya Levien) *Interrupted Melody*, MGM, 1955.
*Back Street*, Universal, 1961.

Contributor to law journals.

*OBITUARIES:*

PERIODICALS

*Los Angeles Times,* February 14, 1999, p. B5.*

\* \* \*

## LUERA, Yolanda   1953-

*PERSONAL:* Born March 4, 1953, in Mexicali, Mexico; daughter of Pedro and Amada (Salas) Luera; married Ernesto Padilla, August 26, 1972; children: Mayela, Gabriela, Santiago. *Education:* Attended secretarial school in Mexico; attended San Diego State University, 1972, and California Polytechnic, San Luis Obispo.

*ADDRESSES: Agent*—c/o Lalo Press, Bilingual Press/ Editorial Bilingue, P.O. Box 872702, Hispanic Research Center, Arizona State University, Tempe AZ 85287-2702.

*CAREER:* Poet and fiction writer, 1977—. Also worked in a lithography shop, 1967-68, and for a paint manufacturer and wholesaler, 1969.

*WRITINGS:*

*Solitaria J,* Lalo (La Jolla, CA), 1986.

Also contributor of poems to anthologies, including *Second Chicano Literary Prize: Irvine 1976-1976,* University of California (Irvine), 1977; and *Antologia Historica y literaria,* ed. Tino Villanueva, Fondo de Cultura Economica, (Mexico City), 1980. Contributor of stories to anthologies, including *Second Chicano Literary Prize: Irvine 1985-1987,* University of California (Irvine), 1988.

*SIDELIGHTS:* Poet and fiction writer Yolanda Luera comes from the distinctive culture of the Mexican-American border, growing up in Mexicali and Tijuana, then settling in San Ysidro, California, before moving north to San Luis Obispo, on the California coast. She has produced one book of poetry, numerous uncollected poems, and several stories, all written in Spanish.

According to the profile by Cesar A. Gonzales-T published in the *Dictionary of Literary Biography,* Luera "has a keen sense of the pain of the life of the poor, especially of women, and of the language and wisdom of the common people, as well as [of] their will to endure."

Luera attended secretarial school for six months in Mexicali and found work in a lithography shop and then a paint manufacturing plant—all by the end of her sixteenth year. Two years later, now in California, she earned her high school General Education Diploma; shortly after that, she was newly-enrolled at San Diego State University when a serious automobile accident left her unable to walk for a year. She married when she was 20, and subsequently had three children. Her first book of poetry—*Solitaria J*—appeared in 1986, when she was 33.

*Solitaria J* focuses on Chicanas in families living along the border between the United States and Mexico. The poetry volume's title symbolizes the isolation and lost identity of border life; as Carmen Tafolla writes in the introduction, "That uncommon letter 'J,' once the proud Mexicano 'X,' then changed, so arbitrarily, so colonizingly, from the rhythmic sonete-sound of 'sh' to the forced breath of a 'J,' . . . is a reflection of our own personal history; we have had our Indian 'X' conquered, we stand alone, without our heritage."

*BIOGRAPHICAL/CRITICAL SOURCES:*

*BOOKS*

*Dictionary of Literary Biography,* Volume 122: *Chicano Writers, Second Series,* Gale (Detroit, MI), 1992.*

\*    \*    \*

## LYND, Robert 1879-1949
### (Y. Y.)

*PERSONAL:* Born April 20, 1879, in Belfast, Ireland; died October 6, 1949; son of Robert John (a Presbyterian minister) and Sarah (Rentoul) Lynd; married Sylvia Dryhurst (a poet), 1909; *Education:* Attended Royal Academical Institution, Belfast; Queen's College, graduated, 1899.

*CAREER:* Worked for *Daily Dispatch,* Manchester, England, 1901, and *Today,* London; *Daily News* (became *News Chronicle*), London, assistant literary editor, 1908-12, literary editor, 1912-49.

*WRITINGS:*

(With Ladbroke D. Black) *The Mantle of the Emperor,* Griffiths (London), 1906.

*Irish and English: Portraits and Impressions,* Griffiths, 1908.

*Home Life in Ireland,* Mills & Boon (London), 1909, McClurg (Chicago), 1912.

*Rambles in Ireland,* Estes (Boston), 1912.

*The Book of This and That,* Mills & Boon, 1915.

*If the Germans Conquered England, and Other Essays,* Maunsel (Dublin & London), 1917.

*Ireland a Nation,* Richards (London), 1919, Dodd, Mead (New York City), 1920.

*Old and New Masters,* Scribners (New York City), 1919.

*The Art of Letters,* Unwin (London), 1920, Scribners, 1921, revised edition, Duckworth (London), 1928.

*The Passion of Labour,* Bell (London), 1920, Scribners, 1921.

*The Pleasures of Ignorance,* Scribners, 1921.

*The Sporting Life and Other Trifles,* Scribners, 1922.

*Books and Authors,* Cobden-Sanderson (London), 1922, Putnam's (New York City), 1923.

*Solomon in All His Glory,* Richards, 1922, Putnam's, 1923.

*Selected Essays Chosen by the Author,* Dutton (New York City), 1923.

*The Blue Lion, and Other Essays,* Appleton (New York City), 1923.

*The Peal of Bells,* Methuen (London), 1924, Appleton, 1925.

*The Money-Box,* Methuen, 1925, Appleton, 1926.

*The Orange Tree,* Methuen, 1926.

*The Little Angel,* Methuen, 1926.

*The Goldfish,* Methuen, 1927.

*Dr. Johnson and Company,* Hodder & Stoughton (London), 1927, Doubleday, Doran (Garden City, NY), 1928.

*The Green Man,* Methuen, 1928.

*It's a Fine World,* Methuen, 1930.

*Rain, Rain, Go to Spain,* Methuen, 1931.

*The Cockleshell,* Methuen, 1933.

*"Y. Y.": An Anthology of Essays,* edited by Eileen Squire, Methuen, 1933.

*Both Sides of the Road,* Methuen, 1934.

*I Tremble to Think,* Dent, 1936.

*In Defence of Pink,* Dent, 1937.

*Searchlights and Nightingales,* Dent, 1939.

*Life's Little Oddities,* Dent, 1941.

*Things One Hears,* Dent, 1945.

*Essays on Life and Literature,* Dutton, 1951.

*Books and Writers,* Dent, 1952.

*Galway of the Races: Selected Essays,* edited with an introduction by Sean McMahon, Lilliput Press (Dublin), 1990

*OTHER*

(Editor and author of introduction) *The Silver Book of English Sonnets: A Selection of Lesser-Known Sonnets,* Pleaid (London), 1927.

(Editor and author of introduction) *Collected Essays of Charles Lamb,* 2 volumes, Dutton, 1929.

(Editor) *Great Love Stories of All Nations,* Harrap (London), 1932, published as *Love throughout the Ages,* Coward-McCann (New York City), 1932.

(Compiler) *Modern Poetry,* Nelson (New York City), 1939.

Contributor of essays to periodicals, including the *Nation;* author of weekly column for *New Statesman* under the pseudonym Y.Y.

*SIDELIGHTS:* Robert Lynd was an early twentieth-century Irish belletrist and a literary and political essayist. He was a committed Irish nationalist, and a supporter of the Sinn Fein movement. His declaration of his socialist politics was viewed as anti-British in the province of Ulster, the region of much of his ancestry. A true essayist, his writings displayed his diverse interests and his ability to write intelligently on any subject, with a charming style. His nationalistic fervor for Ireland led to some of his best work.

Lynd's primary employer was the *Daily News,* where he remained for over forty years. He published thirty-three books between the years of 1906 to 1945, and three books were published posthumously. He also published essays in periodicals such as the *Nation* and the *New Statesman,* for which he wrote a weekly column, using the initials "Y.Y." In *Dictionary of Literary Biography,* Alan Thomas writes that "in reflective and humorous temper, [Lynd] took up and examined features of the times, both trivial and momentous, in a light manner and with refreshing freedom from the tyrannies of received opinion." He often wrote about the society of his time, with a style marked by candor, charm, wit and intelligence. A writer for the *New Statesmen,* in reviewing *The Blue Lion, and Other Essays* (1923), noted that Lynd was "one of those rare artists who believe that other men's tastes are worthy of attention, and that other men are as real and as important as himself. There you have the secret of his popularity."

Lynd was born on April 20, 1879 in Belfast, Ireland to Presbyterian minister Robert John and Sarah Rentoul Lynd. His father was one of a long line of ministers of Ulster-Presbyterian origins. He was educated at the Royal Academical Institution in Belfast and then attended Queen's College, graduating in 1899. In 1901, he moved to Manchester, England, to work at the *Daily Dispatch.* After a few months, he moved to London and worked as a freelance journalist, and received regular work from *Today,* edited by Ladbroke D. Black. In 1906, he published *The Mantle of the Emperor* as a co-author with Black. Two years later, he found employment at the *Daily News* as an assistant literary editor. In the same year, he published his first book on his own, *Irish and English: Portraits and Impressions.* Known for its support of the literary essay form (Charles Dickens was the paper's first editor), the *Daily News* provided an encouraging environment for Lang to nurture his talents. In 1909, he married Sylvia Dryhurst, who later became a poet, critic, and esteemed member of the Book Society. Three years later, Lynd became the literary editor of the *Daily News* and remained at the paper, and its successor, the *News Chronicle,* writing a regular weekly essay, until his death.

Lynd's earliest publications of significance were written about Ireland. These include *Irish and English* (1908), *Home Life in Ireland* (1909), and *Rambles in Ireland* (1912). A writer for the *Athenaeum,* reviewing *Home Life in Ireland,* wrote that the work was written "with the laudable object of showing that the differences and contrasts and quarrels of Irishmen are not essential, as resulting from an ineradicable difference of race, but temporary and curable," adding that Lynd "has strong hopes that with the allaying of these causes of dissension the future of Ireland will be different from the past, and that a new patriotism will combine all the forces of the nation into a noble harmony by resolving the present discords." A *Spectator* reviewer reported that "it is the work of a close and interested observer." His books on Ireland were written in a journalistic style that varies from dry reportage to impressionistic personal observations. He was able to observe scenes and report on them with a literary manner, portraying his personal impressions in such a way that they reveal what Thomas calls the "peculiarities of mass psychology."

In 1917, Lynd published *If the Germans Conquered England,* a collection of political essays. This work demonstrates that, although Lynd was an avowed nationalist, as a writer he was able to remain tolerant and humanistic in his treatment of those with opposing viewpoints. Lynd discusses the two nations' clashing value systems during a time of war. While in the end his position remains patriotic, he never succumbs to jingoism. Maintaining a neutral tone, he hypothesizes the benefits that would arise from a German conquest. It is only at the end of the essay that the pro-German attitude switches to the other side, when Lynd deftly utilizes literary quotation and indirect historical and cultural references to support his patriotic point. Thomas pointed out Lynd's literary control through the quoting of a sonnet by Wordsworth asserting the bitterness that fueled Spanish resistance against Napoleon: "He dares to speak / Of benefits and of a future day, / When our enlightened minds shall bless his sway."

Though he was always an adept writer of significant stylistic talent and depth of knowledge, Lynd's early works on Ireland remain his best work. In 1919, he published *Old and New Masters,* a review of literary greats such as Jane Austen, Fyodor Dostoevsky, Henry James, John Keats, Rudyard Kipling and William Wordsworth. Reviewing the book for *Athenaeum,* T. S. Eliot wrote that although Lynd was "educated, and he is, usually and on the whole, on the right side . . . his method, his whole structure of thought, is wrong for a book." A critic for London's *Times Literary Supplement* admitted that while Lynd in a "graceful essayist and an excellent critic; but it is impossible to regard his latest volume, all chapters of which have appeared in periodicals, as more than literary journalism." However, Thomas saw that "the presence in Lynd's writing of the thinking man, able in a phrase to enlarge a perspective, justifies the term essayist rather than reporter. His openness and willingness to use himself and his experiences, and to think out loud, marks with a confident stamp Lynd's informal manner as an essayist."

In that same year, Lynd published *Ireland a Nation,* a thorough examination of the Irish problem, in which he discussed, among other things, the reasons behind Irish sovereignty, the Sinn Fein, the Insurrection of 1916, and the English in Ireland. A reviewer for *Catholic World* wrote that the book "is devoid of all appearances of sentimentality, yet the very calmness with which the argument is followed gives a force to the book which passion itself could hardly sustain." A critic for the *Nation* found that the work "stands above and apart from the vast majority of books on the subject. It owes this distinction . . . primarily to the fact that he lifts the issue to a new and higher plane. Where other writers take it for granted that the dispute is one between two nations, Mr. Lynd confronts the rulers of Great Britain with their pledges not to Ireland but to the civilized world, and insists that an Irish settlement is to England's allies, no less than her enemies, the 'acid test' of whether these pledges are more than mere empty words." Critic H. L. Stewart, writing on the book for the

*Review,* stated that "if his pages have at times the intractable vehemence which belong to his nationality, they are no less lit up with the wit and sparkle that seldom desert a man of his race."

Lynd produced two books in 1920 that were published the following year in New York: *The Art of Letters* and *The Passion of Labour.* A collection of literary essays, *The Art of Letters* contains Lynd's appreciation of several authors, including Thomas Campion, Samuel Taylor Coleridge, Percy Shelley, and Alfred, Lord Tennyson. It also features other essays of varying topics, such as Elizabethan plays, the labor of authorship and the theory of poetry. Brander Matthews, reviewing the work for the *New York Times,* found that Lynd possesses a "wide sympathy," noting that "he loves books and he enjoys talking about them; indeed, he talks about them with so much gusto that makes the reader share his enjoyment." A writer for the *Times Literary Supplement* asserted that "the reason why Mr. Lynd is both graphic and helpful is that, for all his abstention from the philosophy of criticism, he has the soundest views of art." A reviewer writing for the *Boston Transcript* found that Lynd's "sudden, illuminating characterizations reveal knowledge and understanding. *The Art of Letters* is finally discriminative, sanely independent, justly sound, a touchstone and a keystone to much in English literature." However, critic Mark Van Doren was not as enthusiastic in his review for the *Nation,* remarking that "Mr. Lynd continues as the undefiled and healthy British critic, succeeding by his gusto and good sense in making the books live that he talks about but professing no definite or difficult principles. He is not thoughtful; after superb beginnings at the surface he fails to go deep; yet while the illusion lasts that we are in the presence of his authors it is a perfect illusion." A reviewer for *Athenaeum* presented a similarly balanced report: "It shows at once, we think, the merits and demerits of Mr. Lynd's conception of criticism that, while we enjoy his account of authors we have not read, we gain very little from him when he discusses literature with which we are familiar."

*The Passion of Labour* consists of brief discussions of the economic, political and sociological elements of the time. His support of labor does not include the espousal of force, and describes his essays as "appeals to reason," which are meant to avert a sudden movement of labor that may lead to a disastrous end. Lynd touches on a variety of topics, including the middle class, the working man and his sense of duty, the British coalition government, the nouveau riche, and the moral case against prohibition. A critic for the *New Statesman* declared that "anyone today who craves for a wider vision, for a clearer air and for hints at a saner conduct of public affairs may turn to this book. It has eminently qualities which are desperately needed today, honesty and disinterestedness." A *New York Times* reviewer wrote that "the reading is so entertaining, the irony so disarming, and the paradox frequently apparent that we prefer to enjoy the author's method than to quarrel with his opinions." A *New Republic* critic found that "Mr. Lynd's writing is always characterized by clarity of vision and breadth of understanding. His book is replete with sanity and tolerance and good will, qualities that are sorely needed if the world is to recover from its late debauch of unreasoning hate and passion."

In 1921, Lynd published a book of essays titled *The Pleasures of Ignorance,* which was simultaneously published in London and New York and acts as a companion volume to *The Passion of Labour.* A reviewer for the *Literary Review* claimed that "Robert Lynd is a past master in the art of writing those 'middles' which are one of the best features of the English weekly reviews, as they are usually the weakest feature of similar American periodicals. The real test of this sort of writing is republication in book form. Mr. Lynd emerges from that test with the successful few among his innumerable colleagues in the art." A critic for the *New Statesman* found Lynd to be "a beguiling writer; whether he writes shrewd sense or shrewd nonsense, the reader is soothed and tickled into a complacency which is of all moods the most enjoyable."

*Books and Authors,* published in 1922, is another collection of essay concerning other writers. In this volume, Lynd writes on various authors throughout history, including Hans Andersen, Max Beerbohm, Arnold Bennett, Lord Byron, Victor Hugo, and Vachel Lindsay. He maintains that valuable literary criticism needs not only analysis, but also synthesis. He believes that the task of criticism is to first create a writer's genius in one's mind, and then to clear the minds of one's readers so that the image is reflected in theirs. Mindful to Lynd's extensive knowledge of his divergent topics, a critic for the *Nation* claimed that he "sometimes slips; but his slips are surprisingly light and infrequent when we take into account the wide range of his subjects, and the extreme difficulty of preserving both enthusiasm and discretion in writing of authors still alive. In nothing does he show his quality better than in his invariable application to modern authors of the standards which can only be secured by a wide acquaintance with the greatest art of the past." A reviewer for the *Spectator* found Lynd to be "eminently quotable, and that this should be so is a sure sign of a certain kind of excellence." Burton Rascoe, writing for the *New York Tri-*

*bune,* affirmed that Lynd was "unfailingly interesting and stimulating. He is informal, breezy, chatty, and sociable. He does not stand aloof. He has ideas, opinions, notions to impart and he imparts them with grace, good humor, camaraderie . . . he is a man of taste."

During the interwar years, Lynd was primarily a writer of literary entertainment as opposed to scholarly investigation. One of his two 1927 publications, *Dr. Johnson and Company,* does not delve into the writing of Johnson; rather he notes his subject's look, his eating habits and his method of speech. Lynd's preoccupation with a person rather than their work stemmed from his own life as a socialite: his Hampstead home was a social center for the literary class of his time. In 1942, Lynd was struck by a motorbike and never fully recovered. He died on October 6, 1949.

*BIOGRAPHICAL/CRITICAL SOURCES:*

*BOOKS*

*Dictionary of Literary Biography,* Volume 98: *Modern British Essayists,* Gale Research (Detroit, MI), 1990.

*PERIODICALS*

*Athenaeum,* June 13, 1919; October 23, 1909; December 24, 1920; January 28, 1922; October 28, 1922.
*Boston Transcript,* March 23, 1921; June 18, 1924.
*Catholic World,* November 1920; July, 1921.
*Literary Review,* February 19, 1921; December 24, 1921.
*London Mercury,* February, 1921.
*Nation,* May 4, 1921; January 28, 1922; October 28, 1922.
*New Statesman,* November 13, 1920; April 8, 1922; December 22, 1923; December 12, 1925; December 24, 1927; January 7, 1928.
*New York Herald Tribune Books,* June 17, 1928.
*New York Times,* April 3, 1921; April 24, 1921; June 18, 1922; April 12, 1925; April 11, 1926; April 15, 1928.
*New York Tribune,* March 4, 1923; April 19, 1925.
*New York World,* March 25, 1923; April 12, 1925.
*Review,* May 1, 1920.
*Saturday Review of Literature,* August 26, 1922; January 17, 1925; December 12, 1925; May 22, 1926.
*Spectator,* October 23, 1909; October 7, 1922; January 10, 1925; May 22, 1926.
*Times Literary Supplement,* June, 1909; October 28, 1920; November 25, 1920; January 5, 1922; August 10, 1922; November 15, 1923; January 14, 1926.*

# M

## MACHAR, Agnes Maule 1837-1927

*PERSONAL:* Born January 23, 1837, in Kingston, Ontario, Canada; died January 24, 1927; daughter of John (a church minister and principal of Queen's College) and Margaret (Maule) Machar. *Politics:* "Social reformer." *Religion:* Scottish Presbyterian.

*CAREER:* Novelist, poet, and fiction writer, c. 1859-1919.

*WRITINGS:*

*Faithful unto Death: A Memorial of John Anderson, Late Janitor of Queen's College, Kingston, C.W.* Creighton (Kingston, Ontario), 1859.
*Katie Johnstone's Cross: A Canadian Tale,* Campbell (Toronto), 1870.
*Lucy Raymond; or, The Children's Watchword. By a Lady of Ontario,* Campbell (Toronto), n.d., American Tract Society (New York City), 1871.
*Memorials of the Life and Ministry of the Rev. John Machar, D.D., Late Minister of St. Andrew's Church, Kingston,* Campbell, 1873.
*For King and Country: A Story of 1812,* Adam, Stevenson (Toronto), 1874.
(First series) *Stories of New France; Being Tales of Adventure and Heroism from the Early History of Canada,* Lothrop (Boston), 1890.
*Roland Graeme, Knight: A Novel of Our Time,* Fords, Howard & Hulbert (New York City), 1892.
*Marjorie's Canadian Winter; A Story of the Northern Lights,* Lothrop, 1892.
(With Marquis) *Heroes of Canada,* Copp, Clark (Toronto), 1893.
*The Heir of Fairmount Grange,* Copp, Clark, 1895.

*Lays of the "True North" and Other Canadian Poems,* Copp, Clark, 1899, revised and enlarged edition, Musson (Toronto), 1902, Stock, 1902.
*The Story of Old Kingston,* Musson, 1908.
*Stories of the British Empire for Young Folks and Busy Folks* (2 volumes), Stock, 1913, (1 volume), Briggs, 1914.
(Editor and translator) *Young Soldier Hearts of France: A Wreath of Immortelles,* Musson, 1919.
*The Thousand Islands,* Ryerson (Toronto), 1935.

Also contributor to periodical publications such as *Canadian Monthly* and *National Review and Week.*

*SIDELIGHTS:* Canadian authoress Agnes Maule Machar set the pace for feminism in the twentieth century. A staunch supporter of not only women, but of other social causes, she was greatly influenced by her Christian upbringing and demonstrated throughout her life the heroism necessary to evoke major social change. She was a prolific writer, churning out volumes of essays, articles, and other fiction. Whether through her writing or via activism, Machar fought for the rights of women, her country, and social reform. According to Carole Gerson, writing in *Dictionary of Literary Biography,* "Machar wrote more than half a dozen novels, some poetry, and several volumes of the country's major cultural periodicals, with more than sixty-five pieces of prose and poetry published in the *Canadian Monthly* and its successor, *Rose Belford's Canadian Monthly,* and more than one hundred items in the *Week.* She was an outstanding crusader for the causes of temperance, labor, reform, feminism, and in the defense of Christianity."

Machar's parents deserve recognition for their positive influence on their daughter's early years. In a time when girls did not receive formal education, Machar's father, a Scottish Presbyterian minister, strongly encouraged his daughter's personal growth. Thus, he took on much of the schooling responsibilities himself. As a result, the young Machar became extremely well read. She even started writing at an early age, although much of her early work is not clearly identified as she often wrote under various pseudonyms.

In 1846, when Machar was just nine years old, her father became the principal of Queen's College. He remained at the college for the next eight years, greatly impressing upon Machar the importance of higher education. Queen's College later became a university and, according to Gerson, "a Canadian center of the social gospel movement which strongly influenced Agnes Machar's writings."

In 1861, when Machar was just nine years old, her father became the principal of Queen's College. He would remain at the college for the next eight years, greatly impressing upon Machar the importance of higher education. Queen's College would later become a university and, according to Gerson, "a Canadian center of the social gospel movement which strongly influenced Agnes Machar's writings."

Machar's work is characterized by a constant reference to Canadian nationalism. In the year of her birth, a series of insurrections occurred in her native country known as the Rebellions of 1837. In the end, colonial rule once again prevailed, and the resentments between French and British Canadians grew all the more bitter. Growing up, Machar was probably very aware of the ongoing friction between French and British Canadians. While the Act of Union, carried out by British forces in 1841, strove to merge the two Canadas by assimilating the French Canadians, it only created greater tension. In rebellion, the French Canadians retained their language and identity, their bitterness toward their British neighbors palpable.

Britain, fearing that the United States would absorb all of North America if they did not act quickly, looked to Parliament for answers. British Parliament responded by passing the British North America Act in 1867. This act formed all Canadian colonies into a union called the Dominion of Canada. As a result of the ongoing strife, British Canadians experienced a wave of nationalism. This wave spilled over into various art forms, literature being one of them. Machar found herself at the forefront of this new literary era, and she embraced it. Her earliest publications were nationalistic poetry and Christian stories geared toward children. She received

great praise for much of this early work. Gerson states that "her first novel, *Katie Johnstone's Cross: A Canadian Tale* (1870), won a competition sponsored by a Toronto publisher for 'the book best suited to the needs of the Sunday School library.' Describing the religious enlightenment of a fourteen-year-old girl, it set the pattern that was to shape most of Machar's subsequent fiction." In response to the French-Canadian dislike of Canada's British population, Machar herself grew increasingly loyal to her country. She saw the benefits of the British Empire, infusing her nationalistic views into her literary work. Gerson goes on to say, "She later expressed her patriotism in *Stories of New France; Being Tales of Adventure and Heroism from the Early History of Canada* (1890), a collaboration with Thomas G. Marquis, the first of several books of historical anecdotes intended to imbue young readers with a love of country and Empire."

During the last decade of the nineteenth century, in addition to her nationalistic writings, Machar also delved into social and economic criticism. Of the four novels she produced during the period, *Roland Graeme, Knight: A Novel of Our Time* is her most poignant. Gerson states, "Although not set in Canada, *Rolande Graeme . . .* is one of the few pieces of nineteenth century Canadian fiction to examine some of the social and economic problems arising from industrialization. Heroic Roland joins the Knights of Labour in an American mill town, intending 'To ride abroad redressing human wrongs.' Indignant about social injustice yet fearful of class warfare, Machar equally castigates greedy capitalists and sanctimonious clergymen, advocating selflessness and active Christian brotherhood as the solution to conflicts between workers and their employers. In this book, as in all her fiction, didacticism overrides artistry and romance overpowers realism." Throughout her life, Machar criticized numerous social injustices. She was most concerned with poverty, temperance, and the plight of women. According to the *Feminist Companion* contributor, Machar " . . . saw the need for workers to organize justice." Perhaps Machar saw women as the leaders of social reform because they had the most to gain. On a personal level, Machar, in fighting for what she believed in, had gained recognition and literary success. She paved the way for many women that followed in the twentieth century.

### BIOGRAPHICAL/CRITICAL SOURCES:

#### BOOKS

Blain, Virginia, Patricia Clements, and Isobel Grundy, editors, *Feminist Companion to Literature in En-*

*glish,* Yale University Press (New Haven, CT), 1990.

Cook, Ramsay, *The Regenerators: Social Criticism in Late Victorian English Canada,* University of Toronto Press (Toronto), 1985.

*Dictionary of Literary Biography,* Volume 92: *Canadian Writers, 1890-1920,* Gale (Detroit, MI), 1990.

Lecker, Robert, Jack David, and Ellen Quigley, editors, *Canadian Writers and Their Works,* Volume 1, ECW (Toronto), 1983.

PERIODICALS

*Canadian Historical Review,* September 1984, pp. 347-370.

*Journal of Canadian Studies,* August 1975, pp. 32-43.*

\*     \*     \*

## MANN, (Luiz) Heinrich   1871-1950

*PERSONAL:* Born March 27, 1871, in Luebeck, Germany; died March 12, 1950, in Santa Monica, CA; son of Thomas Johann Heinrich (a grain merchant) and Julia (da Silva-Bruhns) Mann; married Maria (Mimi) Kanova (an actress), 1914 (divorced, 1930); married Nelly Kroeger (a nurse), 1939 (died, 1944); children: (first marriage) Leonie. *Education:* Attended Katharineum, Luebeck, and University of Berlin, 1890-91.

*CAREER:* Worked as bookseller apprentice, Dresden, 1889, and at Samuel Fischer-Verlag (publisher), Berlin, 1891; *Das zwanzigste Jahrhundert,* Munich, editor, 1894.

*AWARDS, HONORS:* National Prize of the German Democratic Republic, 1949; offered presidency of the East German Academy of the Arts, 1950.

*WRITINGS:*

*In einer Familie: Roman,* Albert (Munich), 1894, revised edition, Ullstein (Berlin), 1924.

*Das Wunderbare und andere Novellen,* Langen (Munich), 1897.

*Ein Verbrechen und andere Geschichten,* Baum (Leipzig-Reudnitz), 1898.

*Im Schlaraffenland: Ein Roman unter feinen Leuten,* Langen, 1900, translation by Axton D. B. Clark published as *In the Land of Cockaigne,* Macauley (New York City), 1929, published as *Berlin: The Land of Cockaigne,* Gollancz (London), 1929.

*Die Goettinnen oder Die drei Romane der Herzogin von Assy,* 3 volumes, Langen, 1903, translation of volume 1 by Erich Posselt and Emmet Glore published as *Diana,* Coward-McCann (New York City), 1929.

*Die Jagd nach Liebe: Roman,* Langen, 1903.

*Professor Unrat oder das Ende eines Tyrannen: Roman,* Langen, 1905, published as *Der blaue Engel,* Weichert (Berlin), 1951, translated anonymously and published as *The Blue Angel,* Reader's Library (London), 1931, translation also published as *Small Town Tyrant,* Creative Age Press (New York City), 1944, translation by Wirt Williams published as *The Blue Angel,* New American Library (New York City), 1959.

*Floeten und Dolche: Novellen,* Langen, 1905, "Pippo Spano" translated by Basil Creighton and published in *Tellers of Tales,* edited by W. Somerset Maugham, Doubleday, Doran (New York City), 1939, "Drei-Minuten-Roman" translated by Victor Lange as "Three Minute Novel," and published in *Great German Short Novels and Stories,* Random House (New York City), 1952.

*Eine Freundschaft: Gustav Flaubert und George Sand,* Bonsels (Munich), 1905.

*Mnais und Ginevra,* Piper (Munich), 1906.

*Schauspielerin: Novelle,* Wiener Verlag (Vienna), 1906.

*Stuermische Morgen: Novellen,* Langen, 1906, ("Abdankung" translated by Rolf N. Linn and published as "Abdication," Spectrum, 1960), Langen, 1906,

*Zwischen den Rassen: Ein Roman,* Langen, 1907.

*Die Boesen,* Insel (Leipzig), 1908.

*Die kleine Stadt: Roman,* Insel, 1909, translation by Winifred Ray published as *The Little Town,* Secker (London), 1930, Houghton Mifflin (Boston), 1931.

*Gesammelte Werke,* 4 volumes, Cassirer (Berlin), 1909.

*Variete: Ein Akt,* Cassirer, 1910.

*Das Herz: Novellen,* Insel, 1910.

*Die Rueckkehr vom Hades: Novellen,* Insel, 1911.

*Schauspielerin: Drama in 3 Akten,* Cassirer, 1911.

*Die groe Liebe: Drama in 4 Akten,* Cassirer, 1912.

*Auferstehung: Novelle,* Insel, 1913.

*Madame Legros: Drama in 3 Akten,* Cassirer, 1913.

*Brabach: Drama in 3 Akten,* Wolff (Leipzig), 1917.

*Gesammelte Romane und Novellen,* 10 volumes, Wolff, 1917.

*Die Novellen,* 2 volumes, Wolff (Munich), 1917.

*Die Armen: Roman,* Wolff, 1917.

*Bunte Gesellschaft: Novellen,* Langen, 1917.

*Der Untertan: Roman,* Wolff, 1918, translation by Ernest Boyd as *The Patrioteer,* Harcourt (New York City), 1929, published as *Little Superman,* Creative Age Press, 1945, published as *Man of Straw,* Hutchinson (London), 1947.

*Drei Akte: Der Tyrann; Die Unschuldige; Variete,* Wolff, 1918.

*Der Weg zur Macht: Drama in 3 Akten,* Wolff, 1919.

*Der Sohn: Novelle,* Steegemann (Hannover), 1919.

*Macht und Mensch,* Wolff, 1919.

*Die Ehrgeizige: Novelle,* Roland (Munich), 1920.

*Die Tote und andere Novellen,* Recht (Munich), 1920.

*Diktatur der Vernunft,* Die Schmiede (Berlin), 1923.

*Abrechnungen: Sieben Novellen,* Propylaeen (Berlin), 1924.

*Der Juengling: Novellen,* Langes (Munich), 1924.

*Das gastliche Haus; Komoedie in 3 Akten,* Langes, 1924.

*Der Kopf: Roman,* Zsolnay (Berlin), 1925.

*Kobes: Mit 10 Lithographien von Georg Grosz,* Propylaeen, 1925.

*Gesammelte Werke,* 13 volumes, Zsolnay, 1925-32.

*Liliane und Paul: Novelle,* Zsolnay, 1926.

*Suturp,* Wegweiser-Verlag, 1928.

*Mutter Marie: Roman,* Zsolnay, 1927, translation by Whittaker Chambers published as *Mother Mary,* Simon & Schuster (New York City), 1928.

*Eugenie oder die Buergerzeit: Roman,* Zsolnay, 1928, translation by Arthur J. Ashton as *The Royal Woman,* Macauley (New York City), 1930.

*Sieben Jahre: Chronik der Gedanken und Vorgaenge,* Zsolnay, 1929.

*Sie sind jung,* Zsolnay, 1929.

*Der Tyrann; Die Branzilla: Novellen,* Reclam (Leipzig), 1929.

*Die groe Sache: Roman,* Kiepenheuer (Berlin), 1930.

*Geist und Tat: Franzosen 1780-1930,* Kiepenheuer, 1931.

*Ein ernstes Leben: Roman,* Zsolnay, 1932, translation by Edwin and Willa Muir published as *The Hill of Lies,* Jarrolds (London), 1934, Dutton (New York City), 1935.

*Das Oeffentliche Leben,* Zsolnay, 1932.

*Die Welt der Herzen: Novellen,* Kiepenheuer, 1932.

*Das Bekenntnis zum Uebernationalen,* Zsolnay, 1933.

*Der Ha: Deutsche Zeitgeschichte,* Querido (Amsterdam), 1933.

*Heinrich Mann und ein junger Deutscher: Der Sinn dieser Emigration,* Europaeischer Merkur (Paris), 1934.

*Die Jugend des Koenigs Henri Quatre: Roman,* Querido, 1935, translation by Eric Sutton published as *Young Henry of Navarre,* Knopf, 1937, published as *King Wren: The Youth of Henri IV,* Secker & Warburg (London), 1937.

*Es kommt der Tag: Deutsches Lesebuch,* Europa-Verlag (Zurich), 1936.

*Hilfe fuer die Opfer des Faschismus: Rede 1937,* Ueberparteilicher deutscher Hilfsausschub, 1937.

*Die Vollendung des Koenigs Henri Quatre,* State Press for National Minorities of the USSR (Kiev) 1938, translation by Sutton published as *Henri Quatre, King of France,* 2 volumes, Secker & Warburg, 1938-1939, published as *Henry, King of France,* Knopf, 1939.

*Mut: Essays,* Editions du 10 mai (Paris), 1939.

*Lidice: Roman,* Editorial "El Libro Libre," (Mexico City), 1943.

*Ein Zeitalter wird besichtigt,* Neuer Verlag (Stockholm), 1945.

*Voltaire-Goethe,* Verlag Werden und Wirken (Weimar), 1947.

*Der Atem: Roman,* Querido, 1949.

*Ausgewaehlte Werke in Einzelausgaben,* edited by Alfred Kantorowicz, 13 volumes, Aufbau (Berlin), 1951-62.

*Geist und Tat Ein Brevier,* edited by Kantorowicz, Aufbau, 1953.

*Eine Liebesgeschichte: Novelle,* Weismann (Munich), 1953.

*Empfang bei der Welt: Roman,* Aufbau, 1956.

*Das gestohlene Dokument und andere Novellen,* Aufbau, 1957.

*Gesammelte Werke in Einzelausgaben* (14 volumes), Claassen (Hamburg), 1958- 66.

*Die traurige Geschichte von Friedrich dem Groen: Fragment,* Aufbau, 1960.

*Das Stelldichein; Die roten Schuhen,* Dobbeck (Munich), 1960.

*Gesammelte Werke,* edited by the Akademie der Kuenste der DDR, 24 volumes, Aufbau, 1965.

*Werkauswahl in zehn Baenden,* 10 volumes, Claassen, 1976.

*OTHER*

(Translator) *Wer zuletzt lacht: Roman. Aus dem Franzoesischen,* by Alfred Capus, Langen, 1901.

(Translator) Anatole France, *Komoediantengeschichte: Roman. Aus dem Franzoesischen,* Langen, 1904.

(Translator) Pierre Ambroise Francois Choderlos de Laclos, *Gefaehrliche Freundschaften,* 2 volumes, Verlag der Funken (Berlin), 1905, published as *Schlimme Liebschaften,* Insel, 1920.

(Author of foreword) Albert Jamet, *Der Unbekannte Soldat spricht,* translated by Hermynia zur Muehlen, Prager (Vienna), 1932.

(Author of foreword) Gerhart Seger, *Oranienburg: Erster authentischer Bericht eines aus dem Konzentrationslager Gefluechteten,* Graphia (Karlsbad), 1934.

(Author of afterword) Hans A. Joachim, *Die Stimme Victor Hugos: Hoerspiel,* Editions du Phenix (Paris), 1935.

(Author of foreword) Felix Fechenbach, *Mein Herz schlaegt weiter: Briefe aus der Schutzhaft,* Kulturverlag (St. Gallen), 1936.

(Author of foreword) Manuel Humbert, *Adolf Hitlers "Mein Kampf": Dichtung und Wahrheit,* Pariser Tageblatt (Paris), 1936.

(Editor) *The Living Thought of Nietzsche,* Cassell, 1939.

(Author of foreword) *Der Pogrom,* Verlag fuer soziale Literatur (Zurich), 1939.

(Author of foreword) *Deutsche Stimmen zu 1789,* Deutsches Kulturkartell (Paris), 1939.

(Author of foreword) Ernst Busch, *Lied der Zeit: Lieder, Balladen und Kantaten aus Deutschland von 1914 bis 1945,* Verlag Lied der Zeit (Berlin-Niederschoenhausen), 1946.

(Author of introduction) *Morgenroete: Ein Lesebuch,* Aurora, 1947.

(Author of afterword) Victor Hugo, *Dreiundneunzig,* List, 1949.

*Thomas Mann/Heinrich Mann, Briefwechsel 1900-1949 (letters),* edited by Hans Wysling, Fischer (Frankfurt am Main), 1984.

*SIDELIGHTS:* Heinrich Mann was a German writer, whose career has been customarily eclipsed by the importance of his younger brother, the renowned twentieth-century writer Thomas Mann. However, Heinrich Mann penned a handful of significant works, and achieved some measure of stature in Germany. He received the National Prize of the German Democratic Republic in 1949 and was offered the presidency of the German Academy of the Arts in 1950. He gained international celebrity when his novel, *Professor Unrat oder das Ende eines Tyrannen* (1905; translated as *Small Town Tyrant,* 1944), was made into the film *Der blaue Engel* (*The Blue Angel,* 1930), starring Marlene Dietrich and directed by Josef von Sternberg.

A principal representative of the German intellectual left, Mann was strongly opposed to Germany's extreme nationalism and participation in World War I. He espoused his antiwar ideology in "Zola," an article that appeared in the journal *Weiss Blatter* ("White Papers") in 1915. "Zola" stood in total opposition to Mann's conservative brother's warhawk essay on Frederick the Great. The brothers' ideological differences ended in a rift that lasted until 1922. Keenly aware of the cultural and ideological degradation that plagued Germany before and during World War I, Mann was an outspoken critic of social inequality, the abuses of power, and Na-

tional Socialism. Though primarily a novelist, Mann also wrote and staged several theater productions. While his contributions to German drama are minimal, Hans Wagener, writing in *Dictionary of Literary Biography,* maintains that the psychological drama *Schauspielerin* ("Actress," performed 1911), the French Revolutionary tale *Madame Legros* (performed 1917), and *Der Weg zur Macht* (performed 1920) are "powerful and insightful dramas and remain worthy of attention."

Mann was born on March 27, 1871, in Luebeck, Germany, the eldest son of Thomas Johann Heinrich Mann, a well-known grain merchant, and the Brazilian-born Julia da Silva-Bruhns Mann. He was educated in Lubeck at the Katherineum and at the age of eighteen, declining involvement in the family's corn business, Mann apprenticed with a bookseller in Dresden. The following year, he took a position at the then-new publishing house in Berlin, Samuel Fischer-Verlag. In 1890, he started a short stay at the University of Berlin. The following year, his father died and the family business was sold, leaving Mann financially independent. Mann spent some time moving around, living in Munich, Florence, Palestrina and Switzerland. He lived in Italy with his brother Thomas from 1893 to 1898. In 1894, he edited *Das zwanzigste Jahrhundert* in Berlin. In 1914, he settled in Munich and married a Czech actress named Maria (Mimi) Kanova. They had a daughter, Leonie, two years later. They were divorced in 1930. He married Nelly Kroeger in 1939, shortly before his arrival in the United States. She committed suicide in 1944.

Mann's first important work, patterned after Maupassant's *Bel Ami,* was *Im Schlaraffenland* (1900, translated as *In the Land of Cockaigne,* 1925), a satire that reveals the decadence and immorality of Berlin's bourgeois elite. A reviewer for the *New York Times* says, "Its exaggerated, though romantically naive, realism, its rather patent attempt to shock in matters that have long since become literary commonplaces, frequently appear ridiculous unless the reader reminds himself continuously that the scene is laid nearly thirty years ago in a Germany that was just awakening to the abuses of the capitalistic system. Yet the student will find it doubly interesting because it indicates the then unfulfilled promise of literary movements that have since been born, flourished and died."

After the publication of the naturalistic *Im Schlaraffenland,* his next important work was the trilogy *Die Gottinnen oder Die drei Romane der Herzogin von Assy* ("The Goddesses," 1903). These collected volumes, titled *Diana, Minerva* and *Venus,* portray the life of the beautiful Duchess Violante d'Assy, as she makes hopeless attempts to make sense of her life in politics, art and love. His writing style is heavily inspired by the work of d'Annunzio and Nietzsche, an influence that serves to skillfully depict the Duchess in an erotic caricature while maintaining a reverence for the aesthetic impulse. Writing in *Dictionary of Literary Biography,* Michael M. Metzger describes the Duchess's struggle as suffering from "a life whose ambivalence between artistic grandeur and moral revulsion not even she could reconcile." The other early notable work of his early period is the ironic *Die Jagd nach Liebe* (The Pursuit of Love, 1903), which explores the nature of love and decadence among the upper class, and which some critics believe is a counterpart to *Im Schlaraffenland.*

Mann's penchant for satire and caricature gained a strong voice in his 1905 work, *Professor Unrat,* which was turned into the film *Der blaue Engel* (The Blue Angel) in 1930. Probably due to the renown of the film based upon it, this work remains his best known. The story presents a caricature of a corrupt and tyrannical schoolteacher and his relationship with a beautiful dancer and singer of the lower class. It marks a change in Mann's literary interest from aesthetic concerns to political discourse. Metzger finds the novel "a trenchant study of a man driven even in love by frustrated aggression, as both agent and victim of a hypocritical, repressive society." Peter De Vries, reviewing the work for *Book Week,* says, "It is all sound fiction—soundly conceived, soundly thought out. It happens to be done with a certain heaviness, the writing being often rather densely explicit . . . but on the whole this is an intelligent and absorbing tale."

In 1909, Mann published *Die klein Stadt* (1909, translated as *The Little Town,* 1930), which depicts the lives of an opera troupe in an Italian village, a setting which was inspired by his time in Italy. The theme of *Die klein Stadt* upholds the notion that the most effective art serves a social function and becomes more powerful when integrated into life." A critic for the *Times Literary Supplement* asserts that "beneath this vivid, pulsating comedy and its amusing dialogue there lies much philosophy for those who like to seek it."

For much of his vision, Mann looked outside of Germany for insight and inspiration. In addition to Maupassant, Mann found bond to other French writers of the nineteenth century, including Balzac, Flaubert, Stendahl, and Zola. Of Mann's connection to these novelists, Metzger writes that "Mann admired the French authors for their clarity and intellectual conviction, their grasp of an individual's fate as arising not only from his own ideas and volition but also from the historical era and society in which he lives."

Mann first gained real notoriety with his powerful novel *Der Untertan* ("The Underling," 1918; translated as *The Patrioteer,* 1929; translation republished as *Little Superman,* 1945; translation republished as *Man of the Straw,* 1946). It is the first volume of *Das Kaissereich* ("The [German] Empire," 1914), a trilogy that acutely criticizes the society of prewar Prussia, and established Mann as an important social critic of the time. This work explores the situation of the German bourgeoisie, and was criticized by members of the right wing, who claimed it supported a defeatist attitude. Banned during World War I, it achieved great success in the Weimar Republic. He portrayed other facets of German society under the Empire in the two other novels of the trilogy: *Die Armen* ("The Poor," 1917) looked at the proletariat and exposed the corruption and evil of the oligarchy, while *Der Kopf* ("The Chief," 1925) investigated the bureaucracy of the ruling class. The amoral hero of the trilogy, driven by greed and opportunism, squashes the attempts of a few intelligent and caring people to prevent society's downward spiral while under the rule of Wilhelm II. The trilogy remains his greatest success, and some critics have called it a masterpiece. Metzger goes on to say that "most pernicious to Mann was an intellectual tradition in which freedom and justice were abstractions to be striven for by certain individuals through self-improvement; these ideals were held to be achievable by the whole society, if at all, only through a lengthy evolutionary process." A critic reviewing *The Patrioteer* for *Dial* writes that Mann "has exposed Imperialistic Germany as neatly as Sinclair Lewis exposed Main Street—he is an artist of distinction, a negligent artist, perhaps, like the later Tolstoy. The characters are handled with easy competence, the plot moves convincingly." F. C. Weiskopf, reviewing *Little Superman* for the *Saturday Review of Literature,* says, "*Little Superman* is a book of lasting importance, wit, satire, irony, and wisdom."

Mann moved to Berlin in 1928 and published *Eugenie; oder, Die Burgerzeit* (1928, translated as *The Royal Woman,* 1930). Set in France in the 1870s, it is a social comedy about Empress Eugenie that explores the machinations and artifice of Napoleon III's court during the period leading up to the Franco-Prussian War. A critic for the *Saturday Review of Literature* writes that "the narrative contains many interesting and subtle passages though as a whole it lacks the tragic effectiveness of Thomas Mann's often more lurid style. It will appeal to a quieter and no doubt smaller public." Two years later, he enjoyed the success of the film *Der blaue Engel*. Other notable publications during this period include *Mutter Marie* (*Mother Marie*, 1927), which depicts the conspiratorial activities of a general's wife, and *Ein ernstes Leben* (*The Hill of Lies*, 1932), which adeptly illustrates the state of morality in Germany at the time. A critic reviewing *Mother Marie* for the *New York Times* writes that "Herr Mann shows great cleverness in places; a certain richness of worldly knowledge keeps his book from being no more than the mere theatricalism it comes close to being." Florence Milner, reviewing *The Hill of Lies* for the *Boston Transcript,* says, "On the whole it is an amazingly interesting story, full of action, and a fascinating psychological study."

In 1931, he was appointed to the presidency of the poetry section of the Academy of Arts in Berlin. Two years later, the National Socialists burned his books, expelled him from the Prussian Academy, and he lost his German citizenship. Fleeing the Nazi takeover, Mann was granted Czech citizenship while living in Prague and then immigrated to France, where he penned two major historical and psychological works based on the sixteenth-century French king Henry IV: *Die Jugend des Konigs Henri Quatre* (1935, translated as *Young Henry of Navarre*, 1937) and *Die Vollendung des Konigs Henri Quatre* (1938, translated as *Henry, King of France*, 1939). In the *Encyclopedia of World Literature in the Twentieth Century,* Marion Faber writes that these two novels "are an optimistic demonstration of how political ideals can find pragmatic realization . . . us[ing] the high-minded realism of his historical pageant to address the abstract issues of power." Katherine Woods, reviewing *Young Henry of Navarre* for the *New York Times,* writes that "Mann has recreated the young Henry of Navarre in a novel so sharply and tensely alive, so dramatic, so profound and beautiful, as to touch every chord of interest and significance and appreciation in the reader's mind." He remained in France until the German occupation in 1940, fleeing again to the United States, via Spain and Portugal. He settled in Santa Monica, California, near his brother Thomas.

The United States did not provide as conducive an environment for his creative output as did France, and his output during this period reflects a loss of the literary power that marked his mid-career works. Novels from this time include *Lidice* (1943), a poorly described story of the Nazi atrocities surrounding the annihilation of a Czech town, *Der Atem* ("The Breath," 1949), which suffered from an ineffective framework, and the unfinished *Die traurige Geschichte von Friedrich dem Grossen* ("The Sad History of Frederick the Great"),

which was posthumously published in 1960. His final two books, *Empfang bei der Welt* (1943) and *Ein Zeitalter wird besichtigt* ("Review of an Age," 1945), were partially autobiographical.

After World War II, Mann's hopes of returning to Germany were bolstered by his appointment to the presidency of the German Academy of the Arts in East Berlin. However, he died on March 12, 1950 in California, just before assuming the post. Faber asserts that Mann was "a lifelong critic of authoritarianism, militarism, and bourgeois complacency, a supporter of the 1918 revolution in Germany, [and] a friend of socialism," adding that "Mann is more and more recognized as one of the most acute political critics of his day." Although his career existed in the shadow of his brother's renown, she notes that even Thomas "acknowledged Mann's greater political sagacity."

## BIOGRAPHICAL/CRITICAL SOURCES:

### BOOKS

*Dictionary of Literary Biography,* Gale (Detroit, MI), Volume 66: *German Fiction Writers, 1885-1913,* 1988, Volume 118: *Twentieth-Century German Dramatists, 1889-1918,* 1992.
*Encyclopedia of World Biography,* 2nd edition, Gale, 1998.
*Encyclopedia of World Literature in the Twentieth Century,* 3rd edition, St. James Press (Detroit, MI), 1999.
*Reference Guide to World Literature,* 2nd edition, St. James Press, 1995.

### PERIODICALS

*Book Week,* May 21, 1944.
*Boston Transcript,* December 8, 1928, p. 4; April 6, 1935.
*Dial,* March, 1922.
*Literary Review,* February 4, 1922.
*New York Herald Tribune Books,* November 4, 1928, p. 11; April 28, 1929, p. 7.
*New York Times,* November 25, 1928, p. 31; June 9, 1929; September 26, 1937.
*Saturday Review of Literature,* August 2, 1930.
*Times Literary Supplement,* September 18, 1930, p. 732.

### OTHER

*German Exiles in Southern California: Heinrich Mann (1871-1950),* from the University of Southern California Feuchtwanger Memorial Library, at http://www.usc.edu/isd/locations/collections/fml/H—Mann.html.*

\* \* \*

**MANSON, Marilyn**
  **See WARNER, Brian**

\* \* \*

**MARCHANT, Catherine**
  **See COOKSON, Catherine (McMullen**

\* \* \*

**MARTEL, Aimee**
  **See THURLO, David**

\* \* \*

**MATTHEWS, (James) Brander    1852-1929**
  **(Arthur Penn)**

*PERSONAL:* Born February 21, 1852, in New Orleans, LA; died March 31, 1929; son of Edward and Virginia (Brander)Matthews; married Ada Smith (an actress; known on stage as Ada Harland), 1873; children: Edith Virginia Brander Matthews. *Education:* Columbia College, 1868-71; Columbia Law School, LL.B., 1873.

*CAREER:* Teacher, critic, essayist, novelist, and playwright. Columbia University, professor of English, 1892-1900, professor of dramatic literature, 1900-24.

*MEMBER:* Modern Language Association (president, 1910), Simplified Spelling Board (chairman), National Institute of Arts and Letters (original member, president, 1913-14), American Copyright League (founder), Grolier Club, Authors Club, Kinsmen, Nineteenth Century Club, Savile Club, Rabelais Club, Atheneum (nominated by Matthew Arnold).

*AWARDS, HONORS:* Legion of Honor, 1907.

*WRITINGS:*

(As Arthur Penn) *Too Much Smith: Or, Heredity, A Physiological and Psychological Absurdity in One*

*Act,* adapted from *La Posterite d'arun Bourgmestre,* by Mario Uchard, Werner (New York), 1879.

*The Theaters of Paris,* Scribners (New York), 1880.

*French Dramatists of the Nineteenth Century,* Scribners, 1881, 1882, revised and enlarged, Scribners, 1891, 1901.

(As Arthur Penn) *The Home Library,* Appleton (New York), 1883.

(With H. C. Bunner) *In Partnership; Studies in Storytelling,* Scribners, 1884.

*The Last Meeting (A Story),* Scribners, 1885.

*A Secret of the Sea,* Scribners, 1886, enlarged edition, Chatto & Windus (London), 1886.

*Ballads of Books,* G. J. Coombes (New York), 1887.

*Cheap Books and Good Books,* American Copyright League (New York), 1888.

(With George H. Jessop) *Check and Counter-Check, A Tale of Twenty-five Hours,* Arrowsmith (Bristol), 1888, republished as *A Tale of Twenty-five Hours,* Appleton, 1892.

*Pen and Ink; Papers on Subjects of More or Less Importance,* Longmans, Green (New York), 1888, revised and enlarged edition, Scribners, 1902.

*American Authors and British Pirates,* American Copyright League, 1889.

*A Family Tree, and Other Stories,* Longmans, Green, 1889.

*With My Friend: Tales Told in Partnership,* Longmans, Green, 1891.

*Americanisms and Briticisms* (includes essays on other "Isms'), Harper (New York), 1892.

*In the Vestibule Limited,* Harper, 1892.

*Tom Paulding: The Story of a Search for Buried Treasure in the Streets of New York,* Century (New York), 1892.

*The Decision of the Court* (a comedy), Harper, 1893.

*The Story of a Story, and Other Stories,* Harper, 1893.

*The Royal Marine: An Idyl of Narragansett Pier,* Harper, 1894.

*Studies of the Stage,* Harper, 1894.

*This Picture and That* (a comedy), Harper, 1894.

*Vignettes of Manhattan,* Harper, 1894.

*Bookbindings Old and New: Notes of a Booklover,* Macmillan (New York), 1895.

*Books and Play-books* (Essays on Literature and the Drama), Osgood, McIlvane (London), 1895.

*His Father's Son,* Harper, 1895.

*Aspects of Fiction and Other Ventures in Criticism,* Harper, 1896, enlarged edition, Scribners, 1902.

*An Introduction to the Study of American Literature,* American Book Co. (New York), 1896, enlarged, 1911.

*Tales of Fantasy and Fact,* Harper, 1896.

*Outlines in Local Color,* Harper, 1898.

*The Action and the Word: A Novel of New York,* Harper, 1900.

*A Confident Tomorrow: A Novel of New York,* Harper, 1900.

*The Historical Novel, and Other Essays,* Scribners, 1901.

*Notes on Speech-making,* Longmans, Green, 1901.

*Parts of Speech; Essays on English,* Scribners, 1901.

*The Philosophy of the Short Story,* Longmans, Green, 1901, R. West, 1977.

*Cuttyback's Thunder; Or, Frank Wylde* (one-act comedy), adapted from *Serment d'Horace,* by Henry Muerger, Baker (Boston), 1902.

*The Development of the Drama,* Scribners, 1903.

*Recreations of an Anthologist,* Dodd, Mead (New York), 1904.

*American Character,* Crowell (New York), 1906.

*The Spelling of Yesterday and the Spelling of Tomorrow* (circular no. 4), Simplified Spelling Board (New York), 1906.

*Inquiries and Opinions,* Scribners, 1907.

(With Jessop) *A Gold Mine* (three act play), French (New York), 1908.

*The Spelling of the Poets* (circular no. 21), Simplified Spelling Board, 1908.

*The American of the Future, and Other Essays,* Scribners, 1909.

*Moliere, His Life and His Works,* Scribners, 1910.

*A Study of the Drama,* Houghton Mifflin (Boston), 1910.

*A Study of Versification,* Houghton Mifflin, 1911.

*Fugitives from Justice,* Corlies, Macy (New York), 1912.

*Gateways to Literature, and Other Essays,* Scribners, 1912.

*Vistas of New York,* Harper, 1912.

*Shakspeare as a Playwright,* Scribners, 1913.

*On Acting,* Scribners, 1914.

*A Book about the Theater,* Scribners, 1916.

*These Many Years, Recollections of a New Yorker,* Scribners, 1917.

*The Principles of Playmaking; and Other Discussions of the Drama,* Scribners, 1919.

*The Englishing of French Words,* published with *The Dialectal Words in Blunden's Poems,* by Robert Bridges, Clarendon (Oxford), 1921.

*Essays on English,* Scribners, 1921.

*The Tocsin of Revolt, and Other Essays,* Scribners, 1922.

*Playwrights on Playmaking, and Other Studies of the Stage,* Scribners, 1923.

*The Clown: In History, Romance, and Drama,* Crowell, 1924.

*Suggestions for Teachers of American Literature,* American Book Co., 1925.

*Rip Van Winkle Goes to the Play, and Other Essays on Plays and Players,* Scribners, 1926.

*Papers on Playmaking,* edited, with a preface, by Henry W. Wells, Hill & Wang (New York), 1957.

*Papers on Acting,* edited, with a preface, by Wells, Hill & Wang, 1958.

(With others) *Stories of the Army,* Books for Libraries Press (New York), 1970.

*PLAYS*

*Very Odd,* produced in Indianapolis at the Academy of Music, 1871.

*Edged Tools* (four-act play), French (New York), 1873.

*Marjory's Lovers,* produced in New York at Madison Square Theatre, 1887.

(With George H. Jessop) *A Gold Mine,* produced in Memphis at New Memphis Theatre, 1887.

*This Picture and That,* produced in Denver at Lyceum Theatre, 1887.

(With Jessop) *On Probation,* produced in Decatur, IL, 1889.

*Decision of the Court,* produced in New York at Hermann's Theatre, 1893.

*Frank Wylde,* produced in Denver at Lyceum Theatre, 1894.

(With Bronson Howard) *Peter Stuyvesant, Governor of New Amsterdam,* produced in Providence, RI, 1899; produced at Wallack's, New York, 1899.

*EDITOR*

(With a prefatory note) *Comedies for Amateur Acting,* Appleton, 1880.

*Poems of American Patriotism,* Scribners, 1882, revised and enlarged, 1922.

(And author of introduction, notes, and a biographical sketch) *Sheridan's Comedies* (contains "The Rivals" and "The School for Scandal"), by Richard Sheridan, Osgood, 1885.

(With Laurence Hutton) *Actors and Actresses of Great Britain and the United States, from the Days of David Garrick to the Present Time,* Volume 1: *Garrick and His Contemporaries,* Volume 2: *The Kembles and Their Contemporaries,* Volume 3: *Kean and Booth and Their Contemporaries,* Volume 4: *Macready and Forrest and Their Contemporaries,* Volume 5: *The Present Time,* Cassell, 1886; Volume 5 revised and republished as *The Life and Art of Edwin Booth and His Contemporaries,* Page (Boston), 1900.

(With introduction and notes) *The Dramatic Essays of Charles Lamb,* Dodd, Mead, 1891.

(With introduction) *Washington Irving's Tales of a Traveller,* Longmans, Green, 1895.

(With introduction and notes) *Great Plays* (French and German), by Corneille, Moliere, Racine, Lessing, Schiller, and Hugo, Appleton, 1901.

(With introduction) *American Familiar Verse, Vers de Societe,* Longmans, Green, 1904.

(With introduction and notes) *The Short Story; Specimens Illustrating Its Development,* American Book Co., 1907.

*The Oxford Book of American Essays,* Oxford University Press (New York), 1914.

(With notes, biographies, and bibliographies) *The Chief European Dramatists; Twenty-one Plays from the Drama of Greece, Rome, Spain, France, Italy, Germany, Denmark, and Norway, from 500 B.C. to 1879 A.D.,* Houghton Mifflin, 1916.

*The Poems of H. C. Bunner,,* Scribners, 1917.

(With Paul Robert Lieder: with notes, bibliographies, and biographies) *The Chief British Dramatists, Excluding Shakespeare,* Houghton Mifflin, 1924.

### OTHER

Wrote introductions to several books, including *Andre (A Tragedy in Five Acts),* by William Dunlap, Dunlap Society (New York), 1887; *Ten Tales,* by Francois Coppee, Harper, 1890; *Mes. Siddons as Lady Macbeth and as Queen Katherine,* by H. C. Fleeming Jenkins, printed for the Dramatic Museum of Columbia University (New York), 1915; and *The Book of Play Production for Little Theaters, Schools, and Colleges,* by Milton Smith, Appleton, 1926. Contributor to periodical publications including: *Molieriste, Lippincott's, Cosmopolitan, Chap Book, Forum, North American Review, Bookman, Munsey's, Atlantic Monthly, Harper's, Outlook,* and *Mentor.* Matthews' papers are located at the Butler Library, Columbia University.

*SIDELIGHTS:* A contemporary reviewer of his autobiography published in the *Independent* had this to say of Brander Matthews: "If the reader is envious of the author's fortune in knowing so many men of distinction, at least he may be glad that the privilege fell to a man who could write so charmingly about them." Though virtually unknown today, Brander Matthews counted among his close friends such luminaries as Mark Twain, William Dean Howells, James Russell Lowell, Matthew Arnold, Thomas Hardy, Edmund Gosse, Theodore Roosevelt, and Rudyard Kipling. A major critical voice of his generation, he was eulogized in the *New York Times,* writes Nancy Warner Barrineau in *Dictionary of Literary Biography,* as "one of the last of the eminent Victorians of American origin."

Matthews' American origins were indeed impressive; he was descended on his father's side from William Brewster of Plymouth and on his mother's from one of Virginia's oldest families. Matthews studied law at Columbia Law School, but it became clear while he was still a student that his interests were literary. He started writing essays for the magazines of the day, such as the *Atlantic Monthly,* the *Galaxy,* and *Harper's Monthly,* publishing his first play, *Edged Tools* (1873) the year he earned his degree. The young Matthews was stage struck; drama became his great passion, although he received more recognition initially as a critic than as a playwright. Barrineau reports that his first book of criticism, *French Dramatists of the Nineteenth Century* (1881), was described twenty years later by William Peterfield Trent as "the best single volume on its subject." Matthews even wrote an essay in French on the subject of Moliere titled "Moliere en Amerique" (1881). His devotion to French drama, which he considered superior to that of any other country, eventually earned him the Legion of Honor in 1907 for his service to French literature.

Matthews' contributions, however, are certainly not limited to the literature of France. In his *Shakespeare as a Playwright* (1913), Matthews sought to focus attention on Shakespeare in a way that had been neglected. He saw him as a playwright speaking to contemporary audiences, rather than as a poet, psychologist, or philosopher. A reviewer for *Bookman* wrote that Bernard Shaw "will be delighted that the English race is one book the nearer to a rational treatment of their national idol." The approach of the Shakespeare volume was typical of Matthews. In general, writes Barrineau, "Matthews's plays and criticism of the stage are governed by his appreciation of what the audience of a particular place and time demands."

During the 1880s, Matthews began to receive attention for the plays he had written, including the comedy *Margery's Lovers* (1884) and two other plays written with H.C. Bunner, *A Gold Mine* (1887) and *On Probation* (1889). As his comedies and one-act plays were being produced, he took up writing novels and short stories. He wrote several collections of short stories characterized by clever plotting and began to show a promise that would be fulfilled in three later collections that dealt solely with New York. *Vignettes of Manhattan* (1894), *Outlines in Local Color* (1898), and *Vistas of New York* (1912) are praiseworthy, writes Perry D. Westbrook in *Dictionary of Literary Biography,* for "catching the strangeness and variety of the city's life through a series of brief but vivid glimpses of episodes, places, and persons."

The contribution to the art of the short story for which Matthews is best known, however, is a book in which he outlined a theory of the genre, *The Philosophy of the Short Story*. "Matthews' essay" reports Westbrook, "for many years was considered authoritative on its subject." According to the *Oxford Companion to American Literature,* Brander's "influence on playwrights, criticism, and public taste was great."

An energetic, social man, he became involved in movements dedicated to simplified spelling, defining international copyright law, and produced, reports *Benet's Reader's Encyclopedia of American Literature,* essays on topics ranging from "the antiquity of jests to the serious subject of poker." His fame as a critic as well as his presence in numerous creative clubs of the day eventually earned him an appointment to Columbia University as a professor of literature. Eight years later he became professor of dramatic literature, the first position of its kind.

Matthews continued to produce authoritative works on drama, including *The Development of Drama* (1903), *Moliere, His Life and His Works* (1910), *A Book About the Theater* (1916), and *The Principles of Playmaking; and Other Discussions of Drama* (1919). A popular five-volume work of biographical essays Matthews coedited with Hutton, *Actors and Actresses of Great Britain and the United States, from The Days of David Garrick to the Present Time,* sought to link the drama of England and the United States and make stage actors through history accessible to readers. "This mammoth undertaking," writes Barrineau, constituted a "weaving together of biography, criticism, and anecdotes from contemporary periodicals, historical sources, and memoirs." Matthews was instrumental in shaping attitudes toward drama in his time. Barrineau writes that one critic called him "the Father of Our Interest in Drama in this country." "His goal as a critic," comments Barrineau, "was to show how drama of succeeding eras was different from, not necessarily superior or inferior to, what preceded it and to help the reader understand plays in their proper context." The fact that Matthews was a playwright himself is important to his understanding of theatre as a living art form that should be accessible to everyone, not just the highbrow academic. Barrineau quotes a telling line from Matthews' autobiography: "the critic who has himself attempted art is likely to be more competent, to have a keener insight into [drama's] principles and its practices, its traditions

and its technic, than the critic who has never adventured himself into the studio and the stage."

*BIOGRAPHICAL/CRITICAL SOURCES:*

*BOOKS*

*Benet's Reader's Encyclopedia of American Literature,* HarperCollins, 1991.
*Dictionary of Literary Biography,* Gale, Volume 71: *American Literary Critics and Scholars, 1880-1900,* 1988; Volume 78: *American Short Story Writers,* 1880-1910, 1989.
*Oxford Companion to American Literature,* Oxford University Press, 1995.

*PERIODICALS*

*Bookman,* December, 1913.
*Independent,* January, 1918.*

\*    \*    \*

## MCCLUNG, Nellie Letitia   1873-1951

*PERSONAL:* Born October 20, 1873, in Chatsworth, Ontario, Canada; died September 1, 1951, in Victoria, British Columbia, Canada; daughter of John and Letitia (McCurdy) Mooney; married Robert Wesley McClung, 1896; children: five. *Education:* Attended Winnipeg Normal School, Manitoba, 1889. *Religion:* Liberal Protestant.

*CAREER:* Novelist, c. 1908-45. Teacher in rural Manitoba, 1889-96; Political Equality League, Winnipeg, co-founder; Alberta provincial assembly, 1921-25; Victoria, British Columbia, Canadian Broadcasting Corporation, board of governors, 1936.

*MEMBER:* Canadian Women's Press Club, League of Nations, Canadian Authors' Association.

*WRITINGS:*

*Sowing Seeds in Danny,*, Doubleday, Page (New York City), 1908, published as *Danny and the Pink Lady,* Hodder & Stoughton (London), 1908.
*The Second Chance,* Doubleday, 1910.
*The Black Creek Stopping-House and Other Stories,* Briggs, 1912.
*In Times Like These,* Appleton (New York City), 1915.
*The Next of Kin: Stories of Those Who Wait and Wonder,* Houghton Mifflin (Boston), 1917.

(With Mervin C. Simmons) *Three Times and Out: Told by Private Simmons,* Houghton Mifflin, 1918.

*Purple Springs,* Allen, 1921, Houghton Mifflin, 1922, reprinted with an introduction by Randi R. Warne, University of Toronto Press (Toronto), 1992.

*The Beauty of Martha,* Hutchinson, 1923.

*When Christmas Crossed "The Peace,"* Allen, 1923.

*Painted Fires,* Dodd, Mead (New York City), 1925.

*All We like Sheep and Other Stories,* Allen, 1926.

*Be Good to Yourself: A Book of Short Stories,* Allen, 1930.

*Flowers for the Living: A Book of Short Stories,* Allen, 1931.

*Clearing in the West: My Own Story* (volume 1), Allen, 1935, Revell (New York City), 1936.

*Leaves from Lantern Lane,* Allen, 1936.

*More Leaves from Lantern Lane,* Allen, 1937.

*The Stream Runs Fast: My Own Story* (volume 2), Allen, 1945.

(Contributor) *Pomegranate: A Selected Anthology of Vancouver Poetry,* Intermedia Press (Vancouver), 1975.

*Baraka: the Poems of Nellie McClung,* Intermedia Press, 1978.

*Tea with the Queen,* Intermedia Press, 1980.

(Marilyn I. Davis, editor) *Stories Subversive: Through the Field with Gloves Off,* University of Ottawa Press (Ottawa), 1996.


*SIDELIGHTS:* Nettie McClung published sixteen books in her lifetime, but she is known more for her political efforts in Canada's women's suffrage movement than for her literary accomplishments (which were prolific but not critically successful). Laura Goodman Salverson writes in the *Bloomsbury Guide to Women's Literature* that "McClung's social messages do intrude on her fiction, but it is difficult to resist the spirited impulse of her writing. . . . McClung was a powerful tonic for the time that she lived in, and she made her mark on the political configuration of western Canada, especially in terms of the rights of women." McClung's many novels, short stories, and essays were enormously popular with the women of her time, and they helped to galvanize support for McClung's political ideas. She also became a lecturer in great demand, touring the entirety of Canada before visiting United States, England, and Scotland. This was another effective arena in which McClung accomplished her work as a social reformer. Her speaking skills were formidable. Heidi Jacobs, in *Feminist Writers,* defends McClung's often maligned writing for its power in moving people to support social change: "one can see McClung as a skilled rhetorician and her work as well-crafted rhetoric."

Born Nellie Letitica Mooney in Chatsworth, Ontario, in 1873, McClung and her family moved to Manitoba when she was seven years old. Her mother was a strict Scottish Presbyterian and her father an Irish Methodist; this religious upbringing had a significant effect on McClung, who remained religious and defended traditional morals throughout her life. A quick learner, she began attending rural schools at the age of ten and graduated from Winnipeg Normal School in Manitoba in 1889. Thereafter she began teaching all grades in the rural schools of the area until she married pharmacist Robert Wesley McClung in 1896. The McClungs moved to Manitou, Manitoba, and eventually had five children.

In Manitou, McClung became involved in the women's suffrage movement and the Women's Christian Temperance Movement; at this time, the temperance movement was closely linked with the women's movement. *Sowing Seeds in Danny* (1908), a story of an Irish girl and her brother, Danny, growing up on a farm, was McClung's first published novel. It was based on a short story she wrote for a magazine contest in *Woman's Home Companion.* McClung began the project when she was seventeen, inspired by Charles Dickens' use of fiction for social change. She said in her autobiography *Clearing in the West: My Own Story* that she wished "to do for the people around me what Dickens had done for his people." In *Sowing Seeds in Danny,* a rather romantic version of farming life, McClung introduced the themes that would characterize her following work: temperance, liberal Protestantism, and feminism. The novel was a commercial success, selling over 100,000 copies. A critic from the *New York Times* echoed the sentiment of the readers, saying "The humor and sentiment which the members of [a very interesting Irish] family exhibit in their homely lives are what make the book worth while."

Pearlie Watson, the main character in *Sowing,* appears in McClung's second novel, *The Second Chance* (1911) and later in the suffragist novel, *Purple Springs* (1921). A *New York Times* reviewer criticized the work for being "saccharine" and lambasted the work, saying "There is nothing of particular interest in the plot or setting, the characters are not real people, and the incidents all hang in exactly the right way in favor of the good and lovely heroine." In 1911, the McClungs moved to Winnipeg where McClung founded the Political Equity League. She also took part in the Canadian Women's Press Club. McClung discovered that she was good with hecklers and naysayers because of her sharp wit and warm humor. An example of this effective tool is her burlesque, *Women's Parliament,* performed at Winnipeg's Walker Theater on January 1914. Staged by the

Political Equity League, Women's Parliament was a mock court hearing in which men argued before women for their right to vote. This clever reversal revealed the absurdity of arguments against women's suffrage. She wrote in the second volume of her autobiography, *The Stream Runs Fast* (1945), "We had but one desire: to make the attitude of the government ridiculous and set the whole province laughing at the old concept of chivalry, when it takes the form of hat lifting, giving up seats in street cars, opening doors and picking up handkerchiefs, pretending that this can ever be a substitute for common, old-fashioned justice!"

A frequent target of derision and criticism in the Conservative press, McClung kept fighting and kept her humor. After women in Canada finally won the vote during World War I, McClung continued working in women's interest, urging reforms in factory safety, rural health care, and wages, as well as equality under the Divorce Act and equal opportunities for women in education and employment. In 1914, the McClungs moved to Edmonton, Alberta, where McClung was elected as a Liberal member of Alberta's legislature in 1921. She was defeated in 1926, partly because of her temperance views. She did not run for office again, but she stayed active in politics. She was one the "Famous Five," women who joined Emily Murphy's "Person's Case" against the Supreme Court of Canada's unanimous 1928 ruling against women holding public office. The court had ruled that women were not "persons." Murphy, McClung, and their collaborators took this case all the way to the Privy Council in London. The Privy Council overruled the Supreme Court's ruling, calling it "a relic of days more barbarous than ours." As a result, under the British North America Act Canadian, women were proclaimed "persons." McClung wryly remarks in her autobiography that this "Came as a surprise to many women in Canada . . . who had not known that they were not persons until they heard it stated that they were."

McClung was also a syndicated newspaper columnist, and these writings have been collected in *Be Good to Yourself* (1930), *Flowers for the Living* (1931), *Leaves from Lantern Lane* (1936) and *More Leaves from Lantern Lane* (1937). She published the first volume of her autobiography, *Clearing in the West,* in 1935. McClung then moved to Victoria, British Columbia, in the 1930s, and became a member of the Canadian Authors' Association. In 1936, she became the first woman member of the board of governors of the Canadian Broadcasting Corporation, and in 1938 became a Canadian delegate to the League of Nations. McClung retired from public life in 1943, due to poor health.

McClung's fiction was not generally applauded by critics. Northrop Frye called hers a "non-literary career." Yet even her fiction is considered by some contemporary scholars as valuable. Hilda Thomas in the *Dictionary of Literary Biography* writes, "Her characters are stereotypes, her work loosely structured, sentimental, and consciously designed for moral uplift. But her work remains readable for its shrewd observation of human absurdity and its detailed description of the rural countryside and people; and although she never achieves the comic inventiveness of the writers she most admires . . . in her life if not in her art she was, as she claimed in *Clearing the West,* 'a voice for the voiceless .. a defender of the weak.' " Forgotten in the 1950s, feminists in the 1960s rediscovered McClung and championed her feminist writings.

## BIOGRAPHICAL/CRITICAL SOURCES:

### BOOKS

Benham, Mary Lile, *Nellie McClung,* Fitzhenry & Whiteside (Don Mills, ON), 1975.

Blain, Virginia, Patricia Clements, and Isobel Grundy, *The Feminist Companion to Literature in English, Women Writers from the Middle Ages to the Present,* Yale University Press (New Haven, CT), 1990.

*Bloomsbury Guide to Women's Literature,* Prentice Hall (New York City), 1992.

*Cambridge Biographical Encyclopedia,* Second Edition, Cambridge University Press (Cambridge, MA), 1998.

*Dictionary of Literary Biography,* Volume 92: *Canadian Writers, 1890-1920,* Gale (Detroit, MI), 1990.

*Feminist Writers,* St. James Press (Detroit, MI), 1996.

Hallet, Mary, and Marilyn Davis, *Firing the Heather: The Life and Times of Nellie McClung,* Fifth House (Saskatoon), 1993.

Innis, Mary Quayle, editor, *The Clear Spirit,* University of Toronto Press (Toronto), 1966.

Klinck, Carl. F., editor, *Literary History of Canada,* Volume 3, University of Toronto Press, 1976.

Matheson, Given, *Women in the Canadian Mosaic,* Martin (Toronto), 1976.

McClung, Nellie Letitia, *Clearing in the West: My Own Story,* Volume 1, Allen (Toronto), 1935, Revell (New York City), 1936.

McClung, *The Stream Runs Fast: My Own Story,* Volume 2, Allen, 1945.

Savage, Candace, *Our Nell: A Scrapbook Biography of Nellie L. McClung,* Western Producer (Saskatoon), 1979.

*PERIODICALS*

*New York Times,* August 15, 1908, p. 13; March 5, 1922, p. 16.*

\*   \*   \*

## McKIBBIN, Ross

*PERSONAL: Education:* Received doctorate.

*ADDRESSES: Office*—St. John's College, Oxford, England. *E-mail*—ross.mckibbin@sjc.ox.ac.uk.

*CAREER:* St. John's College, Oxford, England, fellow and tutor in modern history.

*WRITINGS:*

*The Evolution of the Labour Party, 1910-1924,* Oxford University Press (London), 1974.
*The Ideologies of Class: Social Relations in Britain, 1880-1950,* Clarendon Press (Oxford), 1990.
(Editor with John Rowett) *Twentieth-Century British History,* Oxford University Press, 1990.
*Classes and Cultures: England 1918-1951,* Oxford University Press, 1998.

*SIDELIGHTS:* Ross McKibbin outlines the development of the British Labour party in *The Evolution of the Labour Party, 1910-1924.* According to *New Statesman* reviewer Robert Rhodes James, many previous histories of the Labour party had "lacked detachment" in their tone. More importantly, the reviewer claimed, they had not addressed the political or social context that helped to shape the party. James objected to McKibbin's description of the book as a "study of the Labour party in its formative years," and noted that McKibbin fails to describe what might be considered important historical events such as the "great schism" of December, 1916, and the disputes between Labour and the Liberal party in the beginning of the century. In James's opinion, McKibbin fails to explore the impact of World War I on the party and to consider parliamentary procedure—elements which, James felt, would have enhanced the volume. Nonetheless, James calls the book "a solid contribution."

*Listener* critic John P. Mackintosh called *The Evolution of the Labour Party* a "serious historical analysis" and claimed that it does a good job of helping the reader understand how the Labour Party came to replace the Liberal Party as a popular alternative to the Conservative Party. One of the main influences in the change, according to McKibbin, was a need to change "the way political affiliations were decided." McKibbin illustrates how, over time, wage earners became more aware of their power to influence policy. The existing class system in Britain helped the workers to consider themselves a cohesive group, even though there was no established Labour Party ideology. McKibbin states that the Labour party, because of its intentional lack of ideology, was not designed to serve as a front for socialism or even to represent the "true" or total voice of the British working class. The Labour Party's lack of an official platform caused some to fear that it might be swallowed up by the Liberal party rather than maintaining its own identity.

Reviewer Kenneth O. Morgan praised McKibbin's work in the *Times Literary Supplement* for bringing new understanding to the history of the Labour party and for his scholarship and perseverance in collecting research for the subject. Morgan noted that the book is laid out in three sections. The first section deals with the structure of the party (at national and local levels) in the years before World War II; the second section addresses the creation of the party constitution in 1918; and the third section illustrates the party's evolution as a central institution. Morgan agreed with McKibbin's emphasis on the continuity of the party as it evolved, including the contribution on union militancy to the growth of the party. According to the author, the occurrence of the war only helped party growth rather than interrupting it. The reviewer concluded by suggesting that McKibbin could have supplemented the work with an analysis of future political developments stemming from party growth.

In *The Ideologies of Class: Social Relations in Britain, 1880-1950* McKibbin challenges the often touted premise that the "labour process breeds militancy and radicalism in the same way . . . that a nuclear reactor breeds fissionable material." To McKibbin, the working class attitude is not primarily political. For example, in an essay titled "Why Was There No Marxism in Great Britain?," McKibbin answers the question by explaining that the working class was too fragmented by the many demands of life and society in Britain, including diverse influences ranging from small workplaces, family life, civic pursuits and clubs, and the varying ideologies of royalty and nationalism. Marxism, according to McKibbin, would require a more unified working class to succeed on a large scale in Britain. McKibbin also looks closely at the everyday life of the British working class, which includes an emphasis on hobbies, gambling with an intellectual bent, and the "resilience of the unemployed" (between the World Wars) who disregarded the five theoretical steps of unemployment wished upon them by theoreticians.

McKibbin's essay also touches on British politics and the rise and fall of parties from the beginning of the twentieth century into the 1950s. *Times Literary Supplement* reviewer Harold Perkin praised McKibbin's use of his fluent research and knowledge to challenge many of the assumptions made about the British working class. *London Review of Books* critic W. C. Runciman pointed out that McKibbin dispels the myth that the working class and the state are always at odds with each other. Runciman called the collection "uniformly excellent," even though noting that McKibbin includes no study of industrial relations or of the growing class of British civil servants, which could be considered a future form of "the state."

McKibbin's 1990 publication *Twentieth-Century British History* was co-edited with John Rowett and is an attempt to add to the perceived scarcity of material on the subject. According to the editors, not only has the subject not adequately been addressed, but much of the data available has not been synthesized. Additionally, historians have failed to work together to create cohesive material on this topic and others. The book contains articles and book reviews on a variety of topics that address British history from an international context.

According to R. W. Johnson in the *London Review of Books*, McKibbin offers a look at the trends and effects on British classes in *Classes and Cultures: England 1918-1951*. The author looks at these influences on the country as a whole, rather than attempting to ferret out various regional influences. He also integrates interesting examples from society that arose because of class conflict or evolution. For example, the working class gained new social and political power after World War I and, according to McKibbin, prices and wages reacted to lessen the differences between the classes. As one result of this more level society, clubs for sporting and commerce arose that allowed the middle class to seek respite, maintain their sense of a separate class, and serve as "neutral territory where social elites could meet unencumbered by other ties like religion."

Johnson complimented McKibbin for his "sharp eye and wonderful sensitivity to nuance" that allow the author to bring some interesting results of class evolution to these pages. According to the author, the middle class continued to change into the 1950s—these people increasingly worked for others and found themselves in newly created professions. In another of McKibbin's example, many members of the upper-class had most of their assets tied up in land. When land values dropped, these people were forced into the middle class. McKibbin integrates cultural markers into his explanation of class trends in the twentieth century—such as sexual repression and the country's growing excellence in sports. A reviewer for the *Economist* stated that the work was "sure to establish itself as the commanding study of its subject."

*BIOGRAPHICAL/CRITICAL SOURCES:*

*PERIODICALS*

*American Historical Review,* June, 1976, p. 594; April, 1992, p. 556.
*Choice,* September, 1975, p. 901; March, 1991, p. 1204.
*Economist,* June 13, 1998, p. S13.
*English Historical Review,* January, 1976, p. 157; October, 1990, p. 1101.
*History Today,* November, 1990, p. 56; February, 1994, p. 56.
*Listener,* March 6, 1975, p. 315.
*London Review of Books,* May 24, 1990, p. 5; May 21, 1998. pp. 12-13.
*New Statesman,* March 28, 1975, pp. 419-420.
*New York Review of Books,* December 17, 1992, pp. 52.
*Observer (London),* August 11, 1991, p. 51.
*Spectator,* February 22, 1975, p. 210.
*Times Literary Supplement,* March 14, 1975, pp. 267-268; April 20, 1984, p. 443; June 15, 1990. p. 637.*

\* \* \*

## McLEAN, Alan A(ngus)  1925-1999

*OBITUARY NOTICE*—See index for *CA* sketch: Born August 18, 1925, in Fenchow, China; died of cancer, June 28, 1999, in Connecticut. Psychiatrist and author. McLean's book, *Mental Health in Industry,* co-written with Graham C. Taylor, was an important work that helped managers understand how they could foster good mental health in their employees. Although that title was one of his best-known, McLean wrote several other books such as *Occupational Mental Health: An Emerging Art, Work Stress,* and *High Tech Survival Kit: Managing Your Stress.* Born in China, McLean grew up in Washington State and graduated from the State University of New York. After receiving his medical degree he served in the U.S. Naval Reserve and continued professional training on the West Coast before returning to the east in 1957 for a job at Cornell University. He wrote while practicing psychiatry at New York Hospital and University Hospital in New York City. McLean served as a faculty member at New York University and Cornell University Medical College, where he was director of the Center for Occupational Mental Health. He managed the medical program and was chief psychiatric consultant for IBM in a professional capacity that lasted nearly three decades. In addition to books he co-wrote or edited, McLean also contributed chapters and to other books and articles to numerous periodicals.

*OBITUARIES AND OTHER SOURCES:*

*PERIODICALS*

*New York Times,* July 4, 1999, p. A24.

\*   \*   \*

## MERVOSH, Edward M.   1941(?)-1998

*PERSONAL:* Born c. 1941; died of heart failure, December 29, 1998, in New York, NY; children: Heather Mervosh Carson.

*CAREER:* Worked as economist for Research Institute of America, Chase Manhattan Bank, and American Importers Association; *Business Week,* began as contributing editor, 1971, became associate economics editor, senior economics correspondent, and European economics correspondent from Brussels, Belgium, 1971-80, economics editor, 1980-85; *U.S. News & World Report,* worked as senior editor and columnist; Financial News Network, correspondent and commentator; Columbia Broadcasting System, correspondent and commentator; *International Business,* editor in chief, beginning in 1993; Economist Group, managing director, until 1995; *Global Business* (Internet publication), cofounder; KPMG Peat Marwick, managing editor of online banking publication, c. 1998.

*WRITINGS:*

(Editor) *The Global Financial Handbook,* Business International Corp. (New York City), 1992.

*OBITUARIES:*

*PERIODICALS*

*New York Times,* January 2, 1999, p. C6.\*

\*   \*   \*

## MEYERS, Jeffrey   1939-

*PERSONAL:* Born April 1, 1939, in New York, NY; son of Rubin and Judith Meyers; married Valerie Froggatt (a teacher), October 12, 1965; children: Rachel. *Education:* University of Michigan, B.A., 1959; attended University of Pennsylvania and Harvard Law School; studied in Edinburgh, Scotland; University of California, Berkeley, M.A., 1961, Ph.D., 1967. *Politics:* Socialist. *Religion:* None. *Avocational interests:* Travel (Asia, Africa, the Near East, Europe), tennis.

*ADDRESSES: Agent*—Sandra Dijkstra Literary Agency, 1155 Camino Del Mar, Suite 515, Del Mar, CA 92014.

*CAREER:* University of California, Los Angeles, assistant professor of English, 1963-65; University of Maryland, Far East Division, Tokyo, Japan, lecturer in English, 1965-66; Tufts University, Boston, MA, assistant professor of English, 1967-71; writer in London, England, 1971-74; Christie's, London, in rare books department, 1974; University of Colorado, Boulder, associate professor of English, 1975—; University of Kent, Canterbury, 1979-80; University of Massachusetts, Amherst, 1982-83.

*MEMBER:* Royal Society of Literature (fellow).

*AWARDS, HONORS:* Fellowships from American Council of Learned Societies, 1970, and Huntington Library, 1971; Fulbright fellowship, 1977-78; Guggenheim fellowship, 1978.

*WRITINGS:*

*Fiction and the Colonial Experience,* Rowman & Littlefield (Totowa, NJ), 1973.
*The Wounded Spirit: A Study of 'Seven Pillars of Wisdom',* Martin, Brian & O'Keeffe (London), 1973; revised edition, *The Wounded Spirit: T. E. Lawrence's Seven Pillars of Wisdom,* St. Martin's (New York City), 1989.
*T. E. Lawrence: A Bibliography,* Garland Publishing (New York City), 1974.

*Jeffrey Meyers*

*A Reader's Guide to George Orwell,* Thames & Hudson (London), 1975, Littlefield (Totowa, NJ), 1977.

(Editor and author of introduction and notes) *George Orwell: The Critical Heritage,* Routledge & Kegan Paul (Boston), 1975.

*Painting and the Novel,* Barnes & Noble (New York City), 1975.

*Catalogue of the Library of the Late Siegfried Sassoon,* Christie's (London), 1975.

*A Fever at the Core: The Idealist in Politics,* Barnes & Noble, 1976.

*George Orwell: An Annotated Bibliography of Criticism,* Garland Publishing, 1977.

*Homosexuality and Literature, 1890-1930,* Athlone Press, 1977.

*Married to Genius,* Barnes & Noble, 1977.

*Katherine Mansfield: A Biography,* Hamish Hamilton, 1978, New Directions Publishing (New York City), 1980.

(Editor and author of introduction) *Four Poems,* by Katherine Mansfield, Stevens, 1980.

*The Enemy: A Biography of Wyndham Lewis,* Routledge & Kegan Paul, 1980, Routledge & Kegan Paul, (Boston), 1982.

(Editor) *Wyndham Lewis: A Revaluation: New Essays,* McGill-Queen's University Press (Montreal), 1980.

*D. H. Lawrence and the Experience of Italy,* University of Pennsylvania Press (Philadelphia), 1982.

(Editor and author of introduction and notes) *Hemingway: The Critical Heritage,* Routledge & Kegan Paul, 1982.

(Editor and author of introduction and chapter) *The Craft of Literary Biography,* Schocken (New York City), 1985.

(Editor and author of introduction) *D. H. Lawrence and Tradition,* University of Massachusetts Press (Amherst), 1985.

*Disease and the Novel, 1880-1960,* St. Martin's, 1985.

*Hemingway: A Biography,* Harper (New York City), 1985.

(Editor and author of introduction) *Wyndham Lewis,* by Roy Campbell, University of Natal Press (Pietermaritzburg, South Africa), 1985.

(Editor and author of introduction and chapter) *The Legacy of D. H. Lawrence: New Essays,* St. Martin's, 1987.

*Manic Power: Robert Lowell and His Circle,* Arbor House (New York City), 1987.

(Editor and author of introduction and notes) *Robert Lowell: Interviews and Memoirs,* University of Michigan Press (Ann Arbor), 1988.

(Editor and author of introduction and chapter) *The Biographer's Art: New Essays,* New Amsterdam Books (New York City), 1989.

*The Spirit of Biography* (selected essays), UMI Research Press (Ann Arbor), 1989.

(Editor) *T. E. Lawrence: Soldier, Writer, Legend: New Essays,* St. Martin's, 1989.

*D. H. Lawrence: A Biography,* Knopf (New York City), 1990.

(Editor) *Graham Greene: A Revaluation: New Essays,* St. Martin's, 1990.

*Joseph Conrad: A Biography,* Scribner (New York City), 1991.

*Edgar Allan Poe: His Life and Legacy,* Scribner, 1992.

*Scott Fitzgerald: A Biography,* HarperCollins (New York City), 1994.

*Edmund Wilson: A Biography,* Houghton (Boston), 1995.

*Robert Frost: A Biography,* Houghton, 1996.

(Editor) *Early Frost: The First Three Books,* Ecco Press (New York City), 1996.

*Bogart: A Life in Hollywood,* Houghton, 1997.

*Gary Cooper: American Hero,* William Morrow, 1998.

*George Orwell: A Biography,* Norton, 2000.

Contributor to books, including *Essays by Divers Hands,* volume 44, edited by Angus Wilson, Boydell & Brewer, 1986; and periodicals, including *London, Sewanee Review,* and *Virginia Quarterly Review.*

Meyers' books have been translated into French, German, Italian, Japanese, Korean, Polish, and Portuguese.

*SIDELIGHTS:* Jeffrey Meyers is a prominent and prolific biographer of literary figures. The frequency with which his books appear leads critic James Atlas, in the *New York Times Book Review,* to call him "indefatigable" and his output "prodigious," although Atlas finds the quality of Meyers's books inconsistent. Meyers, who has likened his work to that of an investigative journalist, turned to literary biography after a significant career in literary criticism. "Meyers began writing primarily as a literary critic who used biography to explicate texts," writes Mark Allister in *Dictionary of Literary Biography,* "and he has since become primarily a biographer who occasionally interprets literature." Allister sees Meyers's use of information on writers' lives in his critical works as foreshadowing his emergence as an author of full-fledged biographies. For instance, *The Wounded Spirit: A Study of 'Seven Pillars of Wisdom'* analyzes British soldier-adventurer T. E. Lawrence's memoir as a work of literature, but explores aspects of Lawrence's life as well.

Meyers's penchant for telling life stories became further apparent in two group biographies. *A Fever at the Core: The Idealist in Politics* deals with people involved in both the arts and political activism, while *Married to Genius* looks at the marriages of several authors. One of these authors was the influential British short-story writer and poet Katherine Mansfield, who subsequently became the subject of Meyers's first full-length biographical work. *Katherine Mansfield: A Biography* provides details on areas of Mansfield's life that had been covered either superficially or not at all by her previous biographers, including her husband, John Middleton Murry. While Murry had depicted Mansfield and their relationship in only the most flattering manner, Meyers discusses Mansfield's numerous love affairs with both men and women, as well as her husband's infidelities and coldness. Some reviewers find the book cruel to Mansfield, while others contend Murry was not as evil as he was portrayed by Meyers. Still others praise Meyers's extensive research—he interviewed every person acquainted with Mansfield—and find that his work casts new light on this literary life.

In the Mansfield book, Meyers did not write extensively about the times in which she lived or provide much opinion on her work. However, *The Enemy: A Biography of Wyndham Lewis,* "is rich in such details," according to Allister. Lewis produced many works of poetry, fiction, and nonfiction (in addition to numerous paintings and drawings), but is not as well known as his early-twentieth-century contemporaries, such as T. S. Eliot, D. H. Lawrence, and Ezra Pound, and is frequently confused with another writer, D. B. Wyndham Lewis. Lewis's reputation also has suffered because of his early support of Adolf Hitler, although he later turned against Hitler. Meyers's biography, several reviewers say, contributes to a greater understanding of Lewis. The book is "richly informative, fair, lively, and in every good sense disinterested," writes Denis Donoghue in *New York Review of Books.* Bernard Bergonzi in *Times Literary Supplement* notes that Meyers is by no means a Lewis partisan, but has written a biography that is "solid and well documented, without being pointlessly massive or tediously long." However, while Bergonzi finds Meyers's evaluation of Lewis's writings "cautious and sensible," he also considers it "quietly dismissive of a good part of the oeuvre."

For his next biographical work, Meyers chose as his subject a writer far more famous than Mansfield or Lewis—one of the giants of twentieth-century American literature, Ernest Hemingway. *Hemingway: A Biography* was the first full-fledged biography of the writer to appear since Carlos Baker's *Ernest Hemingway: A Life Story* in 1969. Meyers made an effort to gather material that had not been included in Baker's book; among his finds was a Federal Bureau of Investigation dossier on Hemingway, indicating the agency's head, J. Edgar Hoover, wished to destroy Hemingway's standing as a writer (Hoover thought Hemingway was a communist). Christopher Lehmann-Haupt, a reviewer for the *New York Times,* finds Meyers's book well organized, "a relief . . . after Professor Baker's shapeless gathering of a million facts." Meyers, according to Lehmann-Haupt, "is able to illuminate what he considers the major turning points of Hemingway's life" and produce "an absorbing tragic portrait." In *Voice Literary Supplement,* Mario Vargas Llosa says the book "adds to as well as corrects" the Baker work and "is the most complete biography" of Hemingway.

Raymond Carver, writing in the *New York Times Book Review,* has a different view: "There's little in this book that Carlos Baker . . . didn't say better. Mr. Baker, despite his blind spots, was far more sympathetic to the work and, finally, more understanding of the man." Carver also asserts, "Adulation is not a requirement for biographers, but Mr. Meyers's book fairly bristles with disapproval of his subject." Carver notes that Meyers devotes much space to Hemingway's large ego (which Meyers claims affected his work adversely), excessive drinking, and ill treatment of his loved ones. *Los Angeles Times Book Review* contributor Irving Marder does not object to Meyers's discussion of Hemingway's personal failings, but sees other flaws in the book: "One is a style so graceless and so imprecise that, at crucial points, there is only ambiguity." Vargas Llosa, while admiring the book's thoroughness, argues that Meyers does not really explain how Hemingway was able to distill the events of his life and various aspects of his personality into literature—including works that Vargas Llosa considers Hemingway's best, the novels *The Sun Also Rises* and *A Farewell to Arms,* "and a handful of outstanding stories." Lehmann-Haupt is bothered by Meyers's dismissal of the possibility that Hemingway's ultramasculine persona was a reaction to insecurity about his sexual identity. "This peculiar bias . . . leaves a gaping hole at the very heart of his otherwise impressive treatment," Lehmann-Haupt says.

Meyers returned to group biography with *Manic Power: Robert Lowell and His Circle.* He deals with Lowell and three other poets who were his contemporaries: John Berryman, Randall Jarrell, and Theodore Roethke, adding an epilogue on Sylvia Plath. All had significant personal problems that informed their poetry. Mark Allister considers the book successful as biography, less so as a study of the poets' art. *Times Literary Supplement* critic Michael Hofmann, however, lambasts Meyers's work as "witless, censorious, treacherous and sloppy."

British writer D. H. Lawrence, whose art and life had figured in some of Meyers's previous works, was the author's next biographical subject. In *Times Literary Supplement,* Julian Symons calls *D. H. Lawrence: A Biography* a "robust, energetic book" and "probably the best biography" of the controversial Lawrence, once vilified for the sexual explicitness of his novels, later condemned as displaying a supremacist attitude toward women. *New York Review of Books* critic Noel Annan praises Meyers's work in sorting out the various versions of events in Lawrence's life and refers to the book as "dispassionate . . . a cool, not cold, analysis." Paul Delany, writing for *London Review of Books,* finds Meyers's assertion that Lawrence's problems in life were due to his relationship with his mother far too facile, but terms the book as a whole "readable, judicious and authoritative." Christopher Hawtree's *Spectator* review, however, criticizes the book as having "a perfunctory air" and "lacking all rhythm and underplaying

much of the subject's existence." Nancy Mairs of *Los Angeles Times Book Review* lauds Meyers for illuminating the relationship between Lawrence's life and his work, while finding Lawrence's work too plentiful to allow the biographer to do so in all cases. The book, though, is an "admirable introduction" to Lawrence, she says.

*Joseph Conrad: A Biography,* featuring the Polish-descended seaman who became a highly regarded British novelist, fulfills the need for a book "that makes overall sense of the myriad, often contradictory, facts of Conrad's life," according to Jay Parini in *Los Angeles Times Book Review.* Parini finds the book's second half "beautifully focused on the author's life of writing," providing insight into the creative process that produced such works as *Heart of Darkness* and *Lord Jim,* and also praises the account of Conrad's little-known love affair with Jane Anderson, an American newspaper reporter. To Peter Kemp of *Times Literary Supplement,* however, the story of the relationship is "wonky erotic conjecture"; he finds Meyers's evidence that the affair was consummated quite unconvincing. Kemp also sees little that sheds new light on any other aspect of Conrad's life or work: "Meyers is happiest with the obvious," he asserts. J. A. Bryant, Jr., while calling the book "neatly crafted" in *Sewanee Review,* terms it "most interesting when [Meyers] is presenting the details of Conrad's life, least interesting when he is reviewing or analyzing the novels." Joyce Carol Oates, writing for *New York Times Book Review,* pronounces *Joseph Conrad* "never less than a workmanlike amalgam of known and new material; at its best, it is sensitively written, and clearly inspired by a great admiration for its subject."

*Edgar Allan Poe: His Life and Legacy* brought a reaction from some critics that was similar to a reaction to the Conrad book: that it fills a void. This book and Kenneth Silverman's *Edgar Allan Poe: Mournful and Never-Ending Remembrance,* published shortly before Meyers's work, are entries in the "relatively new field" of mature, balanced, Poe biographies, writes Lloyd Rose in *Washington Post Book World.* Previously, Rose says, biographers tended either to damn or to idealize Poe, known both for his self-destructive way of life and his still-popular stories and poems of the supernatural. According to Rose, "Meyers is sympathetic but dispassionate towards his subject, which strikes me as exactly the right approach towards such a difficult man." Chicago *Tribune Books* reviewer Colin Harrison terms Meyers's chronicle a "solid, thoughtful biography" and *New Statesman and Society* contributor Robert Carver finds it "elegantly written, important and endlessly fascinating." Carver praises Meyers's insights into Poe's work and his influence as well as his life. In *Times Literary Supplement,* Arthur Krystal considers both Meyers's and Silverman's books "admirably executed" but writes that "it is Meyers who, untempted by psychoanalytic theories, better conveys Poe's . . . literary travails." But Erik Rieselbach, in *American Spectator,* compares Meyers's work unfavorably to Silverman's. Meyers "includes almost nothing that can't be found more fully discussed in Silverman," Rieselbach contends.

Meyers chronicled the life of another self-destructive writer in *Scott Fitzgerald: A Biography.* Merle Rubin, reviewing the book for *Christian Science Monitor,* says it "focuses on the aspects of [Fitzgerald's] personality that made it hard for him to achieve his full potential as an artist"; these aspects include his alcoholism and his troubled marriage to Zelda Sayre. While Meyers, according to Rubin, does not fully reconcile Fitzgerald's flaws with his virtues, the biographer manages to "allow the pathos and curious heroism of his subject to merge for themselves." Some other reviewers find Meyers's portrayal of Fitzgerald less tolerant, even unkind. The book has an "all but sneering tone," writes John Updike in *New Yorker.* Updike asserts that "Mr. Meyers, like the practitioners of celebrity-centered tabloid journalism, shows his subjects no respect." Similarly, Michiko Kakutani of *New York Times* faults Meyers for taking "a snide, patronizing tone" and pronounces the biography "an ugly and superfluous book about a major American artist who deserves a better biographical fate." Kakutani sees value in Meyers's discussion of how Fitzgerald was influenced by numerous writers (including two of Meyers's previous subjects, Poe and Conrad) but on the whole finds the book gives short shrift to Fitzgerald's writing, especially to his "masterpiece, *The Great Gatsby.*"

Brad Leithauser, though, in *New York Review of Books,* expects that Meyers will "take some knocks for focusing so insistently on Fitzgerald's dissipations" but deems such a focus justified: "Fitzgerald's ruinous life-style . . . was not something tangential or supplemental to his work." Fitzgerald's novels and short stories are based to a great degree on his own experiences, Leithauser notes, and Fitzgerald's nemesis, liquor, figures largely in the makeup of his two most famous characters—the bootlegger Gatsby and the alcoholic psychiatrist Dick Diver of *Tender Is the Night.* Leithauser finds that Meyers has drawn "an appealingly pitiful portrait" and, while offering little in the way of new interpretations of Fitzgerald's life or work, has provided

"an encyclopedic enumeration of the real-life counterparts that stood behind Fitzgerald's creations."

Meyers's next subject was a contemporary and friend of Fitzgerald's, Edmund Wilson, who was a literary critic, essayist, historian, poet, fiction writer, and general man of letters. *Edmund Wilson: A Biography* was the first full-scale biography of Wilson, a fact that is not surprising, according to Elizabeth Hardwick in *New Yorker,* because Wilson wrote so extensively about himself; his voluminous diaries and journals, she asserts, are daunting competition for any biographer, and she does not find Meyers's work wholly satisfactory. "Meyers has brought together the grand flow of Wilson's work and life, including all the flirtations, the drinking, and the marital discord," Hardwick writes. "But he has not been able to recreate in his own pages the subject's brilliant mind and spirit."

In *New York Times Book Review,* James Atlas also notes the challenge that Wilson's autobiographical writings pose, but concludes that "somehow Mr. Meyers has produced a highly engaging book. Lively, well proportioned, insightful about the life and work, his brisk narrative puts it all together." *New York Times* reviewer Christopher Lehmann-Haupt considers the book "fascinating" and worthwhile in its assessment of Wilson's literary significance, but is "leery of a tendency on Mr. Meyers's part to emphasize the negative" in his subject's personal life. "Perhaps because [Meyers] wrote this intensely detailed book in a single year . . . he was unable to bring to his story a perspective that might have prevented some of his material from coming across as nasty gossip," Lehmann-Haupt comments.

In 1996, Meyers came out with *Robert Frost: A Biography,* which some reviewers see as a necessary corrective to Lawrance Thompson's highly unflattering biography of this major American poet. Michiko Kakutani of *New York Times* calls Meyers's work "a judicious book that serves as a welcome antidote to Thompson's angry screed and to [Meyers's] own earlier exercises in literary destruction." In *New York Times Book Review,* however, Miranda Seymour contends that Meyers "is not at his thorough and disciplined best in this book . . . [He] seems to have been unable to get under his subject's skin. The Frost he offers is no less an egotistical monster than the man described by Thompson." She also questions the value of Meyers's detailed recounting of Frost's extramarital affair with Kathleen Morrison. Joseph Parisi, a critic for Chicago *Tribune Books,* deems the biography balanced: Meyers, he says, does not hesitate to point out Frost's personal flaws, but also gives "sympathetic explanations" for them. Parisi judges the book's discussion of Frost's poems to be somewhat superficial, but Kakutani praises many of the insights Meyers offers—such as his discussion of the life experiences Frost reflected in one of his best-known poems, "The Road Not Taken." *Robert Frost,* Kakutani adds, "is by far Mr. Meyers's most persuasive and thoughtful biography yet."

*AUTOBIOGRAPHICAL ESSAY:*

Meyers contributed the following essay, "An Itinerant Education: Michigan to Berkeley," to *CA:*

I

In September 1955, age sixteen, I flew from New York to Ann Arbor to begin my freshman year at the University of Michigan. As soon as I left, my mother charged twenty-five thousand dollars to her department store accounts and sued for divorce. My parents' long, unhappy marriage broke up, and their house on Long Island was sold. My father, before embarking on his second and third marriages, shifted into a cheap Manhattan hotel (my photo standing, pathetically, on his dresser). My mother (who's been getting alimony for the last half-century) moved into a decent apartment and cut my father's face out of all the family photos. For the next five years, until he went to Tulane, she subjected my brother to her manic obsessions.

In going to college so young I escaped the worst my mother could do, but I still suffered emotionally from her overbearing personality. Impatient with institutions and regulations, I frequently came into conflict with those in authority. The transition from my teens to midtwenties, from freshman to graduate student to college teacher, coincided with the radical social change from the fifties to the sixties. I longed for intellectual and sexual companionship, and searched for the ideal place that would supply them. I changed from college to college, and traveled abroad as much as I could.

Though I'd been down to Florida and up to Maine, I'd never left the East Coast. Ann Arbor and the sprawling campus were attractive, but I immediately felt the contrast between the warmth and vitality of New Yorkers and the bland, white-bread culture of the provincial Midwest. The farm boys from the remote Upper Peninsula of the state, in their lumberjack shirts and heavy boots, seemed as strange to me as Martians. My roommate, a senior who still lived in the dorms, was even weirder. Pale and skinny, with a large nose, thick glasses, squeaky voice, and damp hands, Martin came

from Grand Rapids, Michigan. In the hot summers, off to work in his father's cold storage vaults, he'd astonish people on the city bus by wearing heavy winter clothing. When things got tense between us, we'd work off our aggressions in a wrestling match. As my hands slid around his wiry hair and sweaty skin, Martin—five years older and slightly stronger—would pin me to the ground. A gauche virgin, he was timidly courting an excruciatingly unattractive girl whom he eventually married. Though fussy and pedantic, Martin was also intelligent, provocative, and stimulating. Our discussions—or arguments—were an important part of my education. I'd spent my high school years fooling around in class, playing sports, and chasing girls; he strengthened my resolve to work hard and do well in college. Most other students, by comparison, seemed frivolous and superficial.

My parents, along with their relatives and friends, I had never found interesting, and my high school teachers seemed ludicrous. So my college professors were the first intelligent adults I'd ever met. The teaching was not exceptional, yet I profited from an advanced-placement English class and two eye-opening courses in Great Books, which introduced me to the classics, Dante, Dostoyevsky, and my lifelong favorite, Thomas Mann. But, even as a freshman, I was opposed to distribution requirements, which forced students to take courses that bored them instead of allowing them to concentrate (as in English universities) on subjects that really interested them and would help their professional careers. I took six college courses in science and logic, but got absolutely nothing out of them. I certainly did not, as teachers claimed, learn scientific method or logical thought.

My freshman year, though I didn't realize it at the time, was a struggle against conformity. Well before my sixteenth year I strongly resisted my parents' attempts to instill family feeling (I always called them by their first names), music lessons, and religious education. But in college I pretended to like several things I basically despised: big band dances (except for the chance to hold a girl close and look down the front of her low-cut dress), football games (cavemen bashing their heads together on a frozen field), and fraternities (with their philistine values and humiliating initiation rites). I also pursued the prettiest girls—shallow and selfish Ice Maidens—rather than those with more character and intelligence.

Pledging a fraternity wasted several days a week in meaningless activities, like making floats for the homecoming parade, which took time away from books and ended in a degrading and pointless "hell week." This was not, I felt, a promising prelude to lasting friendships, which, in any case, were as bogus as the parties were boring. I was also horrified at the prospect of sleeping in the long, thirty-bed, prison-like dormitory of the fraternity house, which stretched in one open space across the top of the entire building and gave ample opportunity for snores, farts, and drunken bestiality. I preferred to spend time with a few close friends, playing tennis and then going to an all-you-can eat dinner at a local restaurant. On one occasion, when we ate every shrimp in the house and kept asking for more, the proprietor ordered us to leave and never return.

In the Eisenhower fifties the university regulated the lives of first-year students to an unconscionable degree. Even if you found the rare, willing girl, alcohol was prohibited, condoms were unavailable and the Arctic weather prevented outdoor dalliance. Dances were strictly chaperoned by housemothers, and girls were forbidden to enter boys' rooms. Just before curfew on Saturdays everyone kissed their dates in front of the dorm, in a mob scene that resembled the departure lounge of a crowded airport. The main release was the springtime panty raids in which girls, chastely hanging out of upper-story windows and frantically waving their small-cup bras and narrow-waisted undies, aroused the demonically driven boys, who had no hope of scaling their fortress of virginity.

As an easterner, I'd been taught from the cradle to admire Ivy League colleges but, idling my way through high school, had not done well enough to gain admission. My good freshman grades now got me into the University of Pennsylvania. Disappointed with Michigan, one of the Big Ten but too big for me, I transferred to Philadelphia for my second year.

A Michigan friend had told me about the Experiment in International Living, which placed American students in European families to increase international understanding. Keen to get to Europe, I signed up—with nine other American college students—to live with families in Genoa. My father (who'd wanted me to go to CCNY because it was free) refused to pay for the trip, so I used the money I'd saved from high school jobs. I missed the orientation period in Vermont and almost missed the ship, which sailed from Quebec City to Le Havre. My last-minute dash annoyed the group leaders, Vince Milone, a young MIT-trained architect, and his wife, Paula. They were angry with me again when they found me necking with one of the girls as the train pulled into Genoa, hardly ready to get off before

it left the station. But we became good friends and kept in touch for the next forty years.

The summer of 1956 in Italy, which literally opened a new world to me, was the greatest experience of my college years. I lived for the first time with kind and contented people, and liked the Innocentis (the father was an accountant, the mother a superb cook, and they had a boy and girl of about my age) much better than my own family. I learned to speak Italian, began to drink wine and eat exotic new foods, saw an opera for the first time (in the Roman Baths of Caracalla), and began to appreciate painting and architecture. I explored Genoa (birthplace of Columbus), with its peach-colored, green-shuttered houses in the hills overlooking the old port. I was fascinated by the elegant shops on the Via XX Settembre, by the secluded villages of the Cinque Terre (accessible only by train), and by the dazzling sea and sky around Portofino and Santa Margherita on the Riviera.

After a month in Genoa, twenty Italians and Americans took a two-week bus trip to Florence, Rome, and Venice, where, without my passport to prove my age, I was denied admission to a law-abiding whorehouse. Going to museums, strolling the streets, and eating outdoors were all exciting experiences. The American students in the group were stimulating and sympathetic (many of them later became doctors, lawyers, and professors), and I also formed close friendships with several Italians outside my "family." I learned more that summer than I did in my academic studies, and Italy became a permanent passion. I later returned a dozen more times and met my Genoese friends all over the country—from Cortina in the Dolomites to Taormina in Sicily.

My year at the University of Pennsylvania began badly. I was given a terrible dorm room, right on a noisy city street—in a dreary part of town—and directly above the sweltering in-house laundry. I persuaded the dean to let me move into the fraternity house, but here again, as a latecomer, I got the noisiest room at the top of the first-floor staircase. Since cliques had already formed during the freshman year, I was resented as an outsider who had pledged elsewhere, and I was subjected to a certain amount of delayed hazing. After my bed was messed up once too often, I put a lock on my door and ended the conflict by dangling the ringleader over the banister and threatening to throw him down the stairs. I won respect at the fraternity in strange ways: by doing a lot of chin-ups in the bathroom, by playing well on the baseball team, and by bringing to dinner several attractive, white-uniformed nursing students—reputedly free with sexual favors.

I met the nurses through my part-time job, transporting patients from the wards to the radiology department at the university hospital. This I found more interesting than my classes. I watched operations on closed-circuit television and had some bizarre experiences. I saw patients rip off their bandages to expose their ghastly wounds. When a nurse asked me to help lift a patient out of bed, saying "you take the legs, I'll take the arms," I reached for the legs, couldn't find them, and was puzzled until the patient explained they'd been amputated. On another occasion a nurse extended my arm and took my blood pressure. Impulsively I stroked her breast as she leaned toward me. To my surprise she allowed it, and my heart beat faster and faster.

Penn was dominated by money and by the desire for more money. Most of my fraternity brothers were in the Wharton School of Business, preparing, in their narrow studies, to take over their fathers' prosperous companies. They were well off and didn't have to worry about the future. I was in the college of liberal arts, the poor stepchild, had to support myself and make my own career. So our values clashed, and I felt depressed by the materialistic ethos of the place.

Despite Penn's Ivy League prestige, the teaching and students were no better than at Michigan. I set up a small personal business, writing English papers for the lazier students. I offered to return the fee if they did not earn at least a B, and I never had to do so. I had an excellent Shakespeare seminar, in which we carefully analyzed three major plays. But I had a lot of trouble with the badly taught and unbearably tedious courses in botany and chemistry. The gunnery and ordnance courses in Naval ROTC, which I'd joined to avoid being drafted after college, were also extremely difficult. Trying to figure out, in those precomputer days, how to fire massive guns while taking account of the ship's speed, wind velocity, sea currents, pitch and roll, shell weight, and movement of the (sometimes out of sight) target baffled everyone but the engineering students. To prevent the entire class from failing the exams, the instructor left the room and allowed everyone to cheat. I was therefore surprised that the captain of the unit raised no objections when I asked to drop out and take my junior year abroad. The main benefit of NROTC was wearing the handsome uniform and getting a half-price fare on the train when I returned to New York each month to be with my high school girlfriend.

My happiest memories at Penn were of listening to Eugene Ormandy and the Philadelphia Symphony, and appearing as a "super" (a monk and a soldier) with the Metropolitan Opera, in *Don Carlo* with the stolid but resonant Jussi Bjorling and in *Il Trovatore* with the dashing Mario del Monaco. I was thrilled to stand on the brightly lit stage and face a packed house, and had to suppress a strange impulse to push aside the tenor—like an *espont neo* at a bullfight—and have a go at the difficult aria in front of several thousand fans. I was so pleased with my elaborate makeup that I wore it home on the bus and drew quite a few stares.

In the summer of 1956 I worked at a Long Island beach club, whose martinet manager did not allow me to sit down or read when there was nothing else to do. I used to return home exhausted after standing in the sun all day and fall asleep right after dinner. My humiliating duties included crawling under the low deck to retrieve fallen playing cards and cleaning the tar off the patrons' disgusting feet. But there were ample rewards: swimming in the ocean and talking to my amusing co-workers, fooling around with girls in their revealing bathing suits, and playing endless pranks. I once locked the manager in a cabin when he was taking a surreptitious nap. We spied through a cunningly concealed hole when the girls were changing their clothes. On a bet with friends, I took a large bite out of a hamburger, served it to a patron and persuaded him that the chef had cut it in a special way. There was, unfortunately, no tipping at the club, and the beach boys were supposed to get a substantial bonus at the end of the season. I had to leave a few days early to start my junior year at the University of Edinburgh. Though I desperately needed the money, I never received it. This was a vivid lesson in the petty ways the rich cheat those who work for them.

The main reason for going to Edinburgh was to travel as much as possible in Europe. With Martin (my freshman roommate, now a graduate student and enrolled in the same university) I bought a tiny Renault 4CV—a photo shows us buried amidst a herd of cows—and drove down to see my "family" in Genoa before starting classes in October. Despite my travels, I was still a hapless eighteen-year-old. In a restaurant in France on the way back, I was served a pot of coffee with an individual filter. Unaware that I had to press down the plunger, I spilled it all over the table. On the same trip I was amazed to see a man casually grab and hold the waitress's behind as he ordered a meal. During the Christmas holiday we drove through Spain, where I saw the first of many bullfights, and Morocco, where Martin, going native, acquired a ludicrous skullcap and tortoise-shell mandolin.

Driving alone to London in the spring, I hit an unexpected patch of ice in Berwick-upon-Tweed, near the

English border, skidded off the road, turned over, and crashed through a fence. The farmer who rushed to my rescue thought I was surely dead, but I walked away unharmed. A few days later in Paris I suffered delayed shock and panic. I traveled on my own through Italy (the Genoese thought I had *scappato per miracolo*) and across the Adriatic to Greece. In Hydra I met an American painter who worked outside on his sun-filled patio. He was the first embodiment I'd seen of the good intellectual life. I thought of him later on, when I lived in a Spanish village in the early 1970s and wrote at a little poolside table overlooking the Mediterranean. At the end of the academic year I took an overnight ferry from Newcastle to Bergen, Norway, woke up as we entered the glacial fjord and traveled through Scandinavia.

Though Edinburgh is a handsome Georgian city, life there was rather dreary. The weather was horrible, the food (especially after Italy) atrocious. Darkness fell at midafternoon in winter, there was a sickly sweet smell from the breweries at night, and the whole country closed down on the strict Sundays. I lived with Martin and six other students in a boarding house, where we were fed insufficient quantities of peas and boiled potatoes every night. When I refused to eat the repulsive dessert, rhubarb and custard, my companions fought for my portion. My freezing room was inadequately heated by a small gas fire that ate up shillings by the hour. It was actually cheaper, I found, to take a long walk to Princes Street, buy a cinema ticket and walk home than to feed the meter all evening. When I bought an electric blanket and got into bed right after the workhouse dinner, the landlord complained about the extra electricity and raised my weekly rent.

The teaching at Edinburgh was terrible, partly because two professors (too old and feeble to stand and deliver their lectures) were about to retire, and my English tutor was inexperienced and terrified. By American standards the Scottish students were socially backward individuals. En masse, they were terribly rude. They trampled on the floor whenever the horrendously dull linguistics teacher tried to speak and actually threw rotten fruit at Prince Philip when he came to give the rectorial address. The academic year ended with a traditionally violent brawl in the main courtyard.

I went out with an American girl who'd found rooms in a real castle, complete with a gallery of armored figures, and with a Scottish girl who worked in the American Consulate and whom I taught to pronounce place names, like Schenectady and Poughkeepsie. I was ecstatic when she invited me to dinner with her family and I could finally satisfy my constant hunger by eating the frugal repast at my digs before wolfing down a decent meal at her house.

In Edinburgh I discovered the first of several minor but crucial books in my college career: Colin Wilson's *The Outsider* (1956), an inquiry into the sickness of modern man. I eagerly read all the extremist authors that seemed so fascinating: Barbusse, Wells, Sartre, Camus, Hemingway, Joyce, Hesse, T. E. Lawrence, Nijinsky, William James, Conrad, Kafka, Kierkegaard, Nietzsche, Blake, Tolstoy, and Rilke. That year I began to keep a list of all the books I'd read and have continued to keep this summary of my intellectual interests. During the last forty years, I've read about eight thousand books, or two hundred each year.

I desperately wanted to spend the summer in Europe but had run out of money and had to return to a job in America. I worked as a counselor in a summer camp on Lake Winnipesaukee in New Hampshire, where I'd been a camper during my adolescent years. Now nineteen, I was only a year older than the senior boys. Too eager to join in the athletic events, I had trouble maintaining discipline and found the work, communal life, and isolation from the world rather tedious. Unaware that the owners of the camp could listen in to private telephone conversations, I unwisely told my parents that I was planning to leave halfway through the season, after I'd received my tips on parents' weekend. I was promptly fired and lost my tips. On the way down to New York, between North and South Station in Boston, I got into a furious row with a taxi driver, and I have avoided taxis (my only phobia) ever since.

I had now attended three different universities in three years and been dissatisfied with all of them. But I had to return to either Michigan or Penn to graduate. Unaware that my two D's in science courses at Penn were not transferable and that I'd have to take six more credits of science, I returned to Michigan, to this and another unpleasant surprise: an oral exam to confirm the credits for my work at Edinburgh. This was conducted by the great economist Kenneth Boulding, whom I'd never heard of. Fortunately, he was in a genial mood. When he found that my economics professor had once been his pupil, he dispensed with further questions and gave me full credit. Nevertheless, I had to take seven courses each term, while working part-time in the library, in order to graduate. Unwisely putting off my science courses till the last term, I got my best grades that fall: five A's and two B's.

I took classes in Renaissance and French Impressionist painting from the witty and dynamic Marvin Eisenberg, by far the most brilliant teacher and most dazzling conversationalist I've ever known. I sat in the front row, absorbing every word, as he flicked the images on the screen and illuminated them with his perceptive comments. One day, as he tried to recall a passage from Auden's "Muse des Beaux Arts," I had my finest hour, supplying from memory the lines he'd been searching for. Over the years I've kept in touch with the elusive Marvin by letter and phone, though I've only managed to see him a few times in Ann Arbor and when I invited him to speak at Colorado. He inspired me to write *Painting and the Novel* and my life of Wyndham Lewis.

When I told Eisenberg about my all-consuming interest in Thomas Mann, he suggested I see Hans Meisel, a professor of political science, who had been Mann's secretary at Princeton in the late 1930s. Impressed at first by my intense curiosity, Meisel patiently answered all my questions. But—puffing on a cigarette while holding it, European fashion, between his thumb and index finger—he eventually became weary of my all-too-frequent visits to his office. To get rid of me for a month or so, he would tell me to read some long and difficult books. But this only fueled my appetite, and he was astonished when, my happy task completed, I appeared the following week with a great many more questions. His reading lists got longer and longer until, with my classes and job, I was unable to cope with them. Though Meisel finally got rid of me, he was inordinately tolerant.

After the tedium of the dorm, the frat house, and the Scottish digs, it was a great pleasure to share an apartment with friends and learn how to cook. In the spring term I went out with Carol, a girl from Detroit, who had creamy skin, perfect features, and a stunning figure. She also had horrible parents and was ultraconventional, fanatically Catholic and an ironclad virgin, who wore tight, passion-stopper knickers down to her knees. I expected her to settle into a respectable life in the suburbs, but she abandoned her religion and her children, got divorced twice, and had a career in business.

Though I tried to learn genetics (supposed to be relatively easy), I was bored and baffled by the course, did poorly on the final, and was in serious danger of failing. To fend off disaster, I wrote a long letter to the teacher at the end of the bluebook, explaining that I'd lost my Penn science credits, had to take seven courses each term, was a serious student, had already been admitted to Michigan Law School, and needed a D (but certainly not an F) in order to graduate from college and continue my brilliant career. I passed the course but never discovered if I managed it from merit or compassion.

After graduating at the age of twenty, I skipped commencement and got a job with a Reading Services company in Greenwich, Connecticut, which quickly taught me to improve the reading skills of prep school students. In the summer of 1959 I taught and lived at the Harvard School in Coldwater Canyon, above Los Angeles, where the students (Gregory Peck's son among them) were bright and respectful. This job, and later ones in Kansas City and Menlo Park, gave me valuable teaching experience while I was still in grad school.

Back at Michigan, I'd settled into my free-room job as dorm counselor, bought my textbooks, and actually started classes. Suddenly, I got a last-minute offer from Harvard Law School, where I'd been languishing on the waiting list. Once again, I was drawn by the irresistible prestige of an Ivy League school, immediately dropped everything (including the goody-goody Carol) and took the train to Boston. She wrote me a poignant love letter, but I didn't see her again till after her first marriage.

As at Penn, my fate at Harvard would be sealed by a room—or lack of one. I signed a lease with two other law students, both called Jim and both from the South, for an apartment that was supposed to be ready in a few weeks but never became ready at all. In the meantime, we were all three housed in a cramped single room in a sleazy hotel in Boston (an unenticing older woman left her door open and walked around naked), cut off from the other students who lived in Cambridge. This greatly contributed to my discontent at Harvard. Years later I met one of these roommates, the giant Jim, at the faculty club at the University of Colorado and was surprised to find he'd become a law professor at Boston University. Later still, I read in a newspaper that he'd saved many lives when he overpowered a hijacker in a small commuter plane that was going into a dive.

The prevailing ethos at Harvard Law School was like the Wharton School—only worse. Most students wore three-piece suits, carried an attache case, and read the *Wall Street Journal*. They wanted to practice corporate law and make as much money as possible. Rumors spread like brushfire about their intense competition for grades and status. If anyone fell asleep with their study light on, the whole dorm, afraid to fall behind, would stay awake and read through the night. Friends took showers together for stand-up-in-stall quizzes. Some mole-like drudges, it was said, entered the underground passageways that connected the dorms, classrooms, and library in September and never emerged again till June.

The teaching, supposed to be the best in the country, was dreadful. Each large class had 125 students, any one of whom could suddenly be called on to recite. At the beginning, at least, when no one knew anything about the law, we were all clever enough to give some sort of bluffing answer. This deceived the students, but not, of course, the remote, arrogant, and sarcastic teachers. We read and summarized hundreds of detailed, hairsplitting cases, which had been reversed on a 3-2 appeal; reversed again, 4-3, by a higher court; and finally reversed in a 5-4 Supreme Court decision. I was idealistic—and naive—enough to believe in some sort of absolute justice. I was disillusioned to discover that whoever had enough money to hire the cleverest lawyer and keep litigating would eventually wear down the opposition and win the case. Worst of all, the casebook system had no apparent connection to the actual practice of law. During the entire three years, the Harvard students never once went out of the classroom and into the courts.

Unlike most students, I hated the classes, wanted to have some sort of life outside of law school, and was more interested in the social value than the financial rewards of the law. When I expressed my unhappiness, everyone advised me to stick it out and earn the prestigious degree that would guarantee a prosperous future. But I knew that the law, at least as it was taught at Harvard, was not for me. At the end of the first term, when I told the fat and florid Dean Griswold (soon to become solicitor general in Lyndon Johnson's administration) that I wanted to leave, he listened with complete indifference and (like the NROTC captain at Penn) abruptly waved me out of the office. Harvard was quite happy to have an attrition rate, by the end of the first year, of about 25 percent.

I later reflected that if I'd stayed at Michigan Law, a gentler and more humane place, or gone to Yale, which was more interested in the philosophical aspects of the law, I might have become a lawyer. Practicing law would have given me more money, power and influence, and been more intellectually demanding, but being an English professor gave me the freedom to travel and to write. Around this time I was invited to an elegant weekend with a friend on Cape Cod and had another glimpse of the good life, relaxed and humane, that seemed unattainable for the driven maniacs at Harvard Law School.

I've been pleased to see that my criticism of law school was far ahead of its time. The teaching of law has now shifted away from the casebook method; professors take a more personal interest in their students; and the students, much more interested in social causes, from opposing capital punishment to protecting the environment, spend a significant amount of time as interns in law offices and courts. When I urged my daughter to work harder at the University of California Law School, she tartly replied: "I'm going to graduate, Dad; you dropped out!" She also entered the Foreign Service and thus fulfilled two of my early ambitions.

I thought of going to grad school in art history. I passed the Foreign Service exams but refused their offer to enter the cultural branch (USIS) instead of the political section. Remembering that Henry James had dropped out of Harvard Law, in January 1960 I transferred to the English department at Harvard. I took violin lessons as an antidote to law and helped a Korean professor translate Chinese poetry into English. But I was, yet again, greatly disappointed in the stuffy atmosphere and narrow-minded professionalism of the English department.

Two foreign and one classical language were essential for the Ph.D. I'd studied Latin in high school, Spanish and French in college, picked up Italian in Genoa, and learned a lot from my double-credit course in German at Harvard. (Later on, in my travels, I learned several hundred words each of Greek, Swahili, and Japanese—enough to ask basic questions and understand simple answers, find a room, and order food.) I also took a dry but solid course in Milton from the short, bald, and prissy Douglas Bush, and became very keen on Renaissance poetry. Edgar Rosenberg's course in the English novel from Sterne to Scott was stimulating but chaotic, and he digressed so frequently that we covered only half the works on the syllabus. The cold, dignified, white-haired Kenneth Murdock, who looked like a portrait of a puritan ancestor, taught the early American novel, which included utterly worthless works by H. H. Brackenridge and Robert Montgomery Bird.

I knew that Edmund Wilson (subject of my future biography) was at Harvard that year, but I had no interest in his course on the literature of the Civil War, the basis of *Patriotic Gore,* and could find no excuse to see him. I attended a lecture by W. H. Auden, whose corrugated face did indeed (as he said) resemble a wedding cake left out in the rain. He seemed drunk, kept leaning forward, pushing his papers off the edge of the lectern and watching them flutter down to the students in the audience, who gathered them up and returned them in chaotic order.

Theodore Roethke, introduced by a trembling Harry Levin (why was the great professor so nervous?), was a jowly, blubbery bear of a man, who read with passion and delighted his audience. Most effective of all was Isaac Bashevis Singer, who slyly assumed a folksy manner and spoke with a strong Yiddish accent. Pale and frail, with a shiny dome and bright blue eyes, he was an extremely effective performer. He said that it was appropriate to use Yiddish, a dying language, to write about ghosts, *dybbuks,* and demons.

Harvard's English department provided me with another key book: A Tutorial Bibliography of *English Literature* (2nd edition, 1953). This forty-five-page pamphlet listed the essential texts and major critical works in English and American literature from Anglo-Saxon to the present. By the time I took my Ph.D. oral exam, I'd read nearly everything in it. This list not only defined the field, but also taught me to compile an exhaustive bibliography of the subject and read *everything* in print before writing a book. I found a great deal of new material for my recently completed life of George Orwell in printed sources (as well as in interviews and unpublished material) that no one else had ever used.

After a year at Harvard I taught again for the Reading Services at the Pembroke School in Kansas City. I liked the eager students, lived in the headmaster's house, and was taken up by the country club set. I read through the Bible and Durrell's *Alexandria Quartet,* was impressed by the oriental art at the Nelson museum, and enjoyed swimming in a muddy cow pond on a sprawling Kansas farm. Having attended three universities, two law schools, and a graduate school in five years (has anyone ever equaled this record?), and still searching for the perfect place, I headed west to the University of California. Berkeley cost much less than Harvard, and the low fees would be reduced a year later when I became a state resident.

## II

I spent the first days with Vince and Paula, the group leaders in Italy, at their apartment in North Beach. We had breakfast on their rooftop patio overlooking the Bay and drove across the Golden Gate Bridge in their convertible. Here I got my third glimpse of the good life. Struck by the physical beauty, I felt I was in paradise. The smell of eucalyptus trees was exotic and Telegraph Avenue elegant. Roger Barber had an expensive furniture store, the Bank of America had a glass instead of a barricaded front, and in one of the shop windows I saw a ceramic plate, hand-painted by Picasso, for only fifty dollars (which, alas, I didn't have). Before Governor Reagan tried to destroy the university by slashing funds, the buildings were in good repair and the campus beautifully tended. The library, staffed by professionals rather than students, was much more efficient in the good old card catalog days.

In my first year at Berkeley I lived alone on Vine Street, just below Shattuck, in a one-room apartment with a bed that pulled down from the wall (I feared it would spring back and pin me upside down), and biked to campus. At that time there were only a few shops on Vine Street and no good places to eat on Shattuck or anywhere else in Berkeley (Spenger's, an old-fashioned fish restaurant, set the standard). If you wanted to eat well you had to go to San Francisco. The store that's now Andronico's was then a co-op and gave its members annual refunds.

Berkeley brought me into contact with several kinds of people I had never known before. My closest friend, Morris Brownell, the son of a Harvard-educated bank president, had gone to prep school and Princeton, had a trust fund and dated, for a time, the heiress to the Marshall Field fortune. Morris had been an NCAA squash champion, crossed the Atlantic on a sailboat, and taken piano lessons from Nadia Boulanger. A few years older than me, he'd also been, by his own account, a hopeless army officer. Though Morris had more money than me, he had a lower standard of living. After boarding school and the army, he was willing to eat almost anything. He rented a room in a house, shared a kitchen, and each week cooked a huge pot of stew that he wolfed down, bit by bit, each day.

At Thanksgiving Morris impulsively invited me to the house of his aunt and uncle (an executive of the Matson shipping line), whom we called the King and Queen, and who lived in splendor in Belvedere, across the bay in Marin County. He did not tell me, however, that he was too shy to ask their permission. Though they welcomed me, it was agony when we sat down. There was one chair short, but they somehow squeezed me in. After the feast, when it was already snowing on the East Coast, I swam in an outdoor pool with a magnificent view.

Morris and I went out with two Stanford graduates, who lived in a secluded hillside cottage we called (after Spenser) the Bower of Bliss, and he later married one of them. At their wedding in 1963, held in a garden as a chamber group played Mozart, his *bon vivant* father, an unwise choice as best man, dominated the speechmaking and festivities, and seemed ready to run off with the bride. On the way to the Seattle World's Fair that summer I followed the honeymooners' path and tracked them down in Dungeness. Spotting their car in the street, I pounded on their hotel room door and yelled: "Open up! Police!" We celebrated our reunion with a luxurious crab dinner. I realized that friends with impressive fathers had to compete unequally with them

*Meyers flanked by colleague Carlos (left) and Morris (right), Berkeley, 1964*

while I, the first in my family to go to college, surpassed my parents when I became a freshman.

In the summer of 1961, with Richard (a high school buddy), Carol (a girl I met in Edinburgh, who also studied English at Berkeley and later became a lawyer and a lesbian), and her sensual friend Pamela, I drove someone's car to Miami, had a few days in Puerto Rico, and spent the rest of the summer working and living on a sailing yacht in the American Virgin Islands. When I asked the boy I was replacing what it was like on the ship, he described it as "a floating whorehouse and rum factory." The captain, a former petty officer, was drunk and unpleasant most of the time—barking out orders that we landlubbers failed to understand.

We had to clean cockroaches out of the disgusting galley, fetch ice from the shore and row it out to the mooring. I was astonished when Richard dropped a huge block of ice, which floated out of reach instead of sinking. The captain would also wake us up in the middle of the night to row him and his latest girlfriend out to the ship. Though we were a serious contender for victory in the round-the-island race, he took a wildly wide turn around one cape and we were jeered at by the drunken crowd when we came in last.

The next year I shared the top floor of a house on Spruce Street, near Vine, with an Italian count and graduate student, who was the same age as my mother. It was amusing to see the bald, gray-haired Carlo creep up to the box office of Pauline Kael's arty movie theater

and ask for a student discount. His grandfather had translated Shakespeare into Italian, and his father, a notorious womanizer, was the director of the Convento di San Marco in Florence, which had the great Fra Angelico frescoes. Since Carlo had no brothers and no children, I urged him to adopt me so I could inherit his title. I thought Count Jeffrey would look good on my job applications, and I planned to paint a coat of arms on the door of my car.

The oddest of odd couples, we both hoped my efficiency and energy would jolt him out of a lifetime of lethargy. But my vitality merely exhausted him. Carlo was born to lie on a couch and eat grapes—preferably peeled by a servant. When *I* peeled an orange for him (the effort would have made him weary), he reproachfully said, "Chafe," his way of pronouncing my name, "you left the white bits." Since he was extremely fastidious about food, on Thanksgiving I had to hide the fact that a friend was serving us duck instead of turkey. Carlo was dining contentedly when the friend's little boy, sworn to secrecy, pointed to the bird, exclaimed "Duck!" and drove him, gagging, from the table. At the end of the year a friend found (or stole) some classical pillars from a wrecked building. We set them up in our garden, decorated them with vines, and had what we considered a refined party. The King and Queen and one or two professors attended, and the ladies wore hats for the grand occasion.

An expert in slow motion, Carlo was a living example of how not to be a graduate student. He could take half an hour to smooth butter and Hero jam on his toast, a full hour to look up a perplexing word in a dictionary. His hopeless inability to complete any practical task turned me into his houseboy, though I drew the line when he wanted his aged mother to come over from Italy and move in with us. Asking him to wash the dishes or take out the garbage invited disaster. If I sent him out with a shopping list, he'd forget all the staples and return with an assortment of luxury items. On the last day of our lease, he hadn't even begun to pack. Faced with a deadline, he resorted to his old ruse and, pleading illness, called up friends who did the work for him. Carlo never finished, scarcely even started, his Ph.D. Ariosto's *Orlando Furioso* was too heavy to lift, let alone read. But he finally convinced a small college in upstate New York that his undergraduate *Dottore in Lettere* degree was roughly equivalent to an American doctorate and got his first job just before he retired. At the end of his first semester there a puzzled student wrote on one of his class evaluations, "Is this guy for real?" "Chafe," he protested, "I *am* real!"

Filled with weak longings and strong repressions, and devoted to his sainted mother, Carlo was also a closet homosexual. His platonic boyfriend turned up every weekend to sponge on us, tormented Carlo by boasting of his sexual exploits, and later became a street hustler. Carlo spent long hours gazing at the naked youths in the changing room of the Strawberry Canyon pool. This seemed most unfair, since the ladies' room was out of bounds to me. But he remained frustrated while I, considered queer by some for living with him, enjoyed the camouflage and was free to play the field. For all his weaknesses, Carlo was utterly charming and lovable. A sensitive and highly civilized man—right out of the decadent society portrayed by my favorites, Proust and Lampedusa—he enhanced my understanding of Italy and taught me a good deal about European culture.

Carlo's friend Marcus—whom he called "Mar-goose" and I called "The Goose"—was another foreign student who had difficulty adjusting to American life. A tall, thin, beak-nosed, intense and brooding Czech, about ten years older than me, he would have been perfect in the role of Hamlet. The Goose had served in both the Russian and American air force, and his past experience had given him a dark outlook. He once startled me by exclaiming that freedom was a luxury people in Eastern Europe could not afford. To them, he explained, work and bread were more important. Looking across the Bay at the glittering lights of San Francisco, I asked him, "Isn't it spectacular?" "Yes," he replied mournfully, "but it has no *heart.*"

The Goose tried to stay continental by hanging out in the Cafe Mediterraneo, and eked out a marginal existence, dining mainly on nuts and raisins, in a shabby room. In our house he once devoured a whole bunch of bananas. His mother worked in a factory in Pilsen, and he went in for proletarian sports like soccer, criticizing me for playing the "elitist" game of tennis.

In contrast to Carlo, who symbolized inertia, The Goose worked extremely hard—but also got nowhere. As soon as he acquired one M.A., he'd change fields and get another one. In my time, he collected degrees in political science, mathematics, and philosophy, and had just enrolled in Classics. His quest for knowledge was impressive but, from a practical viewpoint, quite pointless. Carlo later told me that Mar-goose, tiring of nuts and raisins, had finally given up graduate studies and taken a job with a gigantic corporation that was the quintessence of ruthless capitalism. He prospered in this stricter regime and, abandoning his Socialist views, joined the yacht and polo clubs.

In my second year I bought a horrendously unreliable Morris Minor, which kept breaking down and finally packed it in as I was descending Oxford Street. A legendary mechanic, Jack Suttle, long before NPR's "Car Talk," could diagnose problems long-distance. He'd tell clients to start the engine and then put the phone next to it. But even Jack couldn't save that car. I replaced it with a sturdy Plymouth that had, hidden under the back seat, the tattered briefcase of the great Italian scholar Leonardo Olschki. Treating it as a sacred relic, I used it till it fell apart.

My education at Berkeley was sexual and political as well as academic. According to Philip Larkin, sexual intercourse began in 1963, between the end of the *Chatterley* ban and the Beatles' first LP. But in Berkeley—always ahead of its time—it came a bit sooner, and just at the right time for me. After the fierce constraints imposed on college students in the conservative 1950s—house mothers and chaperones, strict visiting hours, and rules against cars—the new sexual freedom was wildly exciting. The years when girls coyly resisted panty raids, demanded an engagement ring before having sex, or, worse still, "saved it" for marriage, were now over.

The girls—well dressed and pretty—suddenly seemed willing, even eager, to go to bed. It was quite common, with condoms but not AIDS, to meet an attractive girl while standing in line for a movie and become her lover that night. When one girl suggestively said, "I never sleep with anyone on a first date," I immediately asked her out for the following night. When another new girlfriend asked me to drive her to the airport, I jokingly suggested we could get an early start if she spent the night with me—and to my surprise she readily agreed. One friend, studying Asian history, acquired a Japanese girlfriend (rare in those days) to help him with the language. Looking rather peaked on campus, he complained: "I seduced that virgin and created a monster. Her sexual demands are insatiable!"

Two brief contacts between my girlfriends and my teachers revealed the lingering effects of the old constraints. On one occasion I'd spent a pleasant afternoon in bed with a girl who was also in my class in Renaissance literature. I had boldly invited the professor to dinner that night and prepared my only special dish: chicken casserole with mushrooms and artichokes. Instead of asking her to join us, which would have made the evening more enjoyable, I somehow felt it was unseemly to invite my girl at the same time as my teacher. One term I was a reader in the large American literature class of the amiable John Gerber, a visiting professor from Iowa. As I walked out of class with him, a blond buxom girlfriend rushed up and gave me a kiss. As Gerber observed us, I felt more embarrassed than pleased. But now that I am as old as he was then, I realize he must have envied my youthful good fortune.

During my first term I became infatuated with a girl who had an exotic Hungarian background and a lot of money, wore colorful Marimekko dresses and drove a red MG, had long strawberry blond hair and a breathtaking figure—the most beautiful girl I'd ever seen. On my first visit to her flat, in an odd triangular building at the corner of College and Claremont (I still think of her every time I pass it), we talked till after midnight and wound up first in her bathtub and then in her bed. We spent the next weekend at Yosemite.

But my relations with her, like those with my teachers, were filled with minefields. Her family was anti-Semitic, she was sexually frigid. She was absorbed in long-term psychoanalysis, and everything I said was repeated to and interpreted by her doctor. She was also having a simultaneous affair with a limping professor of philosophy who had a heavy German accent and considerable *Schmerz,* both *Welt* and personal. She encouraged our rivalry, and I found it hard to compete with a man whose wealth, position, and reputation I lacked.

I made my first false step when she phoned me one midnight, said she was lonely, and (though she had the red car) urged me to come over. It was cold and rainy, I was tired and had an exam the next day, and couldn't face bicycling across Berkeley and into Oakland. My refusal hurt her feelings and was interpreted, in her sessions with the shrink, as a crucial failure to respond to her needs. (Later on, when lonely and without a girl, I wondered how I could ever have turned down such an offer.) I had persuaded her to stop smoking. But after I'd returned disconsolate from a Christmas trip to Mexico, where my pocket was picked on a crowded bus, she lit a cigarette, and I knew it was all over. These experiences, however painful, were liberating. As I began to understand my own emotions, I learned to appreciate passionate writers like William Blake, D. H. Lawrence, and Norman Mailer.

My third year, still upwardly mobile, I lived with a girlfriend in a charming house, with balcony and view, at the first sharp bend on Panoramic Way. Unlike the well-born Morris and Carlo, she came from a working-class family in Long Beach. We once had a bitter quarrel and she took off, planning (I knew) to exact revenge by spending the night with someone else. I remembered her mentioning, in passing, a handsome and very blond grad student in architecture and instinctively felt she'd

go to him. So I called a friend, also studying architecture, and was able to identify the fellow. I found his address in the phone book, went to his apartment, and, when he opened the door, pushed my way in. Hearing my voice, she hid on the floor of a closet, but I soon found her, half-dressed and with a strange smile on her face. I dragged her home and our reconciliation, fired by jealousy, was sweet. She later joined the Peace Corps, married a South American engineer, became a tax lawyer, and accumulated wealth and weight.

My three houses and many other places—from Tilden Park to Point Reyes—where I had convivial dinners, uninhibited parties, and amorous adventures evoked powerful memories whenever I revisited Berkeley and still do now that I've returned to live and write here.

Once I discovered where I wanted to be and what I wanted to do, my intellectual life focused on the English department. In 1960 about four hundred students studied English in graduate school. Since so many of them milled around anonymously, I distinguished them by nicknames: The Face (very ugly), The Sneer (contemptuous expression), Fussy Joe (extremely neurotic), The Georgia Peach (smooth southerner), The Queen of the Ptolemies (Egyptian), The Blessed Damozel (the cool, distant class beauty), and The Famous Footnote (a legendary figure who'd published a textual emendation of Shakespeare). Only about twelve got their Ph.D.s at the end of each year.

Unlike Harvard, Berkeley didn't hire its own students, and getting a job often meant suffering Midwestern exile and a Siberian climate. So most students, surviving on a modest teaching assistant's stipend, lingered in the library and the coffee shops for years—even decades. Such were the rigors of the Ph.D. that even those who finished remained mired in their routine. I once saw an acquaintance, right after he'd completed the long haul on his dissertation, heading mechanically into the library. Wondering why he didn't take a day off, I asked what he was up to. He replied sadly, "I didn't know what else to do."

I had several good teachers my first year. Charles Muscatine conveyed great enthusiasm for Chaucer. John Traugott imitated the ironic wit of the Augustan satirists. Morris and I shared a passion for the eighteenth century. After Traugott's class we became enchanted by the substitution of "f" for "s" in eighteenth-century printed books and would ask each other, "Will you fuffer me to fing you a fong?" We used Augustan diction in our conversation and tried to outdo one another with quotations from Swift and Pope. Fascinated by the fierce intellectual combats and the darker side of the period, in the Bancroft Library I read the scurrilous attacks on Pope and the Earl of Rochester's obscene play *Sodom*—with pornographic stage directions—which was actually performed at the court of Charles II.

Stephen Orgel shocked me by criticizing the sacred authors of the Oxford histories of Renaissance literature: not only C. S. Lewis, but also the learned Canadian Douglas Bush, who'd taught me Milton at Harvard. I regret that I did not take a class with the brilliant modernist Mark Schorer, though he was then bogged down in a life of Sinclair Lewis, smoking and drinking himself into oblivion. I once went to Muscatine's house with Carlo, who had known him in Florence, and attended a meeting at the home of John Raleigh before seeking a job at the Modern Language Association conference. Apart from these brief encounters I had very little personal contact with my teachers and a lot of trouble with them.

Grad school, in fact, often seemed more like Marine basic training, with teachers like drill sergeants rather than Virgilian guides through the groves of academe. The Anglo-Saxon requirement had, mercifully, been abolished the year before I arrived. I managed to pass the French reading test, though it included a tricky pun on Giorgione and Georges Ohnet—a writer I'd never heard of before and have never come across since then. I made the mistake of taking a required medieval literature course from Charles Jones, who gave pedestrian, stupefying lectures. While Jones was on leave, I passed the difficult Latin exam (Caesar, Virgil, and Horace) administered by the Oxford-trained (and then untenured) Hugh Richmond. When Jones returned, he looked over the exams and decided to fail me. Though this was grossly unfair, no one would listen to my protest, and I had to take it again the following term.

I took a seminar on Yeats and Joyce from the arrogant, imperious Ian Watt, famous for *The Rise of the Novel*, who took pleasure in ordering his students to erase the blackboard. A handsome Englishman with a gasping laugh, he'd been captured after the fall of Singapore and been a prisoner of war on the River Kwai. As graduate chairman, he dealt with all applications from Japanese students by throwing them in the wastepaper basket. Masao Miyoshi could not have taught at Berkeley while Watt was there. When I challenged and even contradicted some of Watt's ex cathedra pronouncements, he got furious and made sure (his young secretary, a friend of mine, later told me) that I did not get a teaching assistantship.

Watt was extremely unpopular with both faculty and students. After he'd left for the University of East Anglia and then wanted to return, Berkeley wouldn't take him back, and he had to go to Stanford. Nearly twenty years later, when Watt's book and my biography of Katherine Mansfield were both reviewed on the same front page of the *New York Times Book Review*, he sent me a postcard with a backhanded compliment, saying that I was, apparently, not quite as dim as he had thought. In 1989, when I was writing a life of Conrad, Tom Moser arranged a dinner at Stanford with Watt and Albert Guerard so I could pick the brains of three leading Conradians. Watt was quite civil and even came to my lecture at Stanford. A few years later, when I met him again at the house of Joseph Frank, the great biographer of Dostoyevsky, Watt was almost affable. Shortly afterwards he had a near-fatal stroke that ended his intellectual life. Though I could not like Watt, I respected his work and valued his grudging praise of my own. Such is the hold teachers have on their students.

Since I could not be a TA, I did other kinds of work. One of my first jobs was at Ed Hunolt's bookstore, just across from campus. If we clocked in at 8:46, he'd begin to pay at 9:00; if we punched in at 9:01, pay would start at 9:15. When I complained about this injustice, I was immediately fired. Some students made up for the pay cuts by taking advantage of the two store entrances, on Bancroft and Telegraph, to steal books. I took revenge by calling Hunolt in the middle of the night from a pay phone across the street and telling him that his store was on fire. I watched him race down, raincoat over his pajamas, expecting to see the place engulfed in flames.

I then began tutoring students and often found, when they cancelled a Friday session, that I had absolutely no money for the weekend. I found more steady work by tutoring two high school football players every weekday for a year and a half, and by teaching Great Books to adults at Berkeley Evening High School. The class needed a minimum of twenty to continue. As the term progressed and the students were distracted by more pressing needs—from family problems to a big game on television—attendance inevitably dropped. So the faithful brought friends to sign in and leave, and even resorted to faking signatures so the class could go on.

Unlike the TAs, who could take only two courses a term while teaching, I had no such restrictions and progressed very fast. I took my M.A. exam at the end of the first year and my three-hour Ph.D. oral, conducted by six professors, at the end of the second. The oral included a half hour on Old French and French literature, and I forcefully rejected the French professor's offer to conduct his part in his native tongue. The Ph.D. oral demanded a knowledge of all the major works of English and American literature. This suited my voracious desire to read everything, but it took great discipline to plow through dreadfully tedious books like *Piers Plowman* and *The Faerie Queene.*

Though one nun had nervously thrown up after the first question, I was pretty confident when I entered the room. I greatly enjoyed answering everything they asked me, including two curveballs on Thomas Burnet's *Sacred Theory of the Earth* and Colley Cibber's *Apology.* One examiner, testing the limits of my knowledge, asked me to identify Bulkington—a minor character, he later told me while apologizing for his trivial pursuit, in *Moby-Dick.* I reassured my friends, anxiously waiting in the corridors, and after the ordeal felt wonderfully relieved—as if I'd just completed a massive psychiatric treatment or emptied myself in a vomitorium after a Roman feast.

Many students, churned up by the demanding and heartless system, got depressed and fell by the wayside. I once had dinner with a gloomy stranger who killed himself the next day. And after several students jumped off the Campanile, plate glass was installed at the top. Many of my close friends left grad school and chose, instead, careers in medicine, law, and business. One composer dried up and became a clerk in the Rad Lab. One finished his degree at Tufts, another married two suicidal wives and languished in Midwestern obscurity.

My problems with Watt and Jones were minor compared to the disastrous things to come. Inspired by W. B. C. *Watkins's Perilous Balance: The Tragic Genius of Swift, Johnson and Sterne* (1939), who all waged a lifelong battle against disease and madness, I wrote my overambitious dissertation on the moral and political ideas of Swift and Johnson. These ideas, I argued, represented a significant strain of conservative thought in the eighteenth century. My director was the grave, dignified, and stone-faced Bertrand "Bud" Bronson, the leading scholar of the department, who was so intimidating that in the men's room junior colleagues would step aside when he approached the urinals. Bronson was rumored to have lockjaw and, indeed, there was a jaundiced tinge to his forbidding face.

It was customary, when flying to New York for the MLA conference and job market, to have a scholarly project that enabled you to apply for a travel grant, which would pay the air fare. I planned to study some of Swift's manuscripts at Yale. But when I brought the

application form for Bronson to sign, he said my research wasn't really necessary. I argued with him about this, explaining that I didn't have the plane fare, and finally persuaded him to support the project. Like Watt, he resented my cheekiness—I can't imagine why—and decided to teach me a dreadful lesson.

He'd always praised my work and given me A's on the chapters I wrote for him in two dissertation courses. But in my thesis defense in June 1963 the committee (of which he was the senior member) rejected the dissertation. Devastated by this setback, I asked Bronson for guidance and direction, and wondered what I could do to salvage the wreck. Like Pilate, he refused to take responsibility and coldly replied: "I wash my hands of the entire matter." I didn't understand what had happened until a friendly assistant professor later told me, after my defense, that Bronson had voted against me.

At the MLA the previous December, my old Shakespeare teacher, Matthias Shaaber, had offered me a job as an instructor at Penn. But now, hooked on California, I accepted a position at UCLA. I idled away the summer of 1963 in the Greek islands. In September, at the age of twenty-four, I grew a mustache to look older and drove down to Los Angeles in my new Triumph sports car. Hiding the dissertation debacle, I took up my all-too-well-named post of acting assistant professor.

But I was now burnt out, and no matter how hard I acted I couldn't be very professional. I drove around town, went to the beach, and spent the next summer hitchhiking around East Africa. I got considerable satisfaction in publishing three chapters of my thesis but knew I could never satisfy Bronson, and I never found a way to pick up the pieces. Acting more like the playboy of the Western world than a serious scholar, I never dreamed I'd eventually write 480 articles and 39 books—many of them based on research I did in the Berkeley library.

During my second year at UCLA, when Tom Parkinson (whom I'd known slightly at Berkeley) came down to give a lecture, I put him up for the night and told him my sad story. By that time, bloody but unbowed, I'd sold my engraving of Sir Joshua Reynolds's great portrait of Samuel Johnson, which seemed to stare down at me censoriously, and decided to abandon the eighteenth century. Instead, influenced by the African students I met at UCLA and on my trip to Africa, I planned to write a second dissertation on colonial novels by Kipling, Forster, Conrad, Cary, Greene, and Achebe, which dealt with political and cultural conflicts. Parkinson, though intellectually inferior to Watt and Bronson,

*With wife, Valerie, in Santa Monica, 1964*

seemed sympathetic and offered to direct my new thesis. So I seemed back on track . . . sort of.

I didn't much like the English department at UCLA, which was very conservative and hierarchical (assistant professors, especially acting ones, had no social relations with the tenured faculty), and the undergraduates were even less serious than I was. Ignoring the excellent advice of a colleague, I made the greatest mistake of my professional life. I naively thought great job offers would last forever and made no arrangements to return to UCLA when I finally finished my degree. In fact, with its good grad students, excellent library, and ample research grants, UCLA would have been an ideal place for a productive scholar. Ironically, I got the best job I ever had before I earned my doctorate or published a word, and never again had such a great opportunity.

My initial appointment at UCLA ended after two years. Since I wasn't ready to return to Berkeley and couldn't get a job without the Ph.D., I spent the next year teaching university courses for the air force in Okinawa, Japan, and Korea. In my second year at UCLA I'd courted Valerie, an English girl who'd graduated from Cambridge and had a fellowship from the English-Speaking Union. We drove around the West that summer, and in September she followed me across the Pacific. We got married, alone and in a Japanese civil ceremony, at the town hall in Naha. The certificate they gave us turned out to be a permit to open a house of ill fame, and we had to get remarried by the American consul.

During my year in the Orient I read and took notes on all the novels of the authors I was planning to write about. Since we traveled home via Southeast Asia, India, Russia, and Europe, I sent back all my papers, including a precious letter from E. M. Forster, on an air force plane. But my luggage, with some suits handmade in Hong Kong, was stolen, and I was never compensated for the papers, which had "no value."

Settling into a house on Spruce Street next door to the one I'd shared with Carlo (who was, of course, still carefully buttering his toast and slowly looking up words in his dictionary), I was fortified and supported by my wife, who got a teaching job in Walnut Creek. Wanting to learn more about political affairs, I went to public lectures by Alexandr Kerensky, a tall, dignified man who'd headed the Provisional Government in Russia between the overthrow of the czar and the seizure of power by the Bolsheviks. A key figure at a turning point in history, he lamented his inability to resist the onslaught of Lenin, saying apologetically, "If only I'd done this; if only I'd done that." I also heard Alger Hiss convincingly defend himself against Whittaker Chambers's accusations of treason.

Mario Savio's Free Speech Movement had taken off in the fall of 1964 when I was teaching at UCLA. And the strong student protest against the Vietnam War continued when I returned from Japan in 1966 to complete my degree. I was passionately opposed to the war and had a fierce argument with some Foreign Service officers who'd served in Laos and upheld the domino theory. But I also found the radical cant and interminable speeches quite boring and—keen to get on with my work—never took part in the continuous sit-ins, marches, and demonstrations.

After writing all morning I'd walk to campus to see what was going on. I'd watch police, on the roof of the Student Union, firing canisters of tear gas into the peaceful mass of students in Spoul Plaza, then read in the *New York Times* the following day about how the students' violent behavior had forced the police to smother them with gas. I was amazed to see that political bias could make the country's leading newspaper publish such lies. And I never imagined that the Free Speech Movement would play a decisive role in changing public opinion, arouse the whole nation and help to end the Vietnam War. Visionaries like Allen Ginsberg, far from being paranoid, had been instinctively right in the 1960s about the genocidal war and the diabolical machinations of the FBI and CIA. It took Robert McNamara, then secretary of defense, more than thirty years to grasp what men like Ginsberg knew while the war was going on.

Earlier, a potentially violent incident had taught me how much the police hated the students. On the day that President Kennedy gave a speech at the Greek Theater, which I did not attend, I brought my car to a garage near campus for a routine check. When I came to pick it up, the Chinese owner, thinking I'd left it there while I heard the speech, wanted to charge me for parking as well as for repairs. I refused and we had a vehement argument. Suddenly, he pulled a rifle from under the counter, pointed it at my chest, and threatened to kill me. Calm in the face of such absurdity, I told him to shoot, and he slowly lowered the gun. When I complained to the police that I'd been threatened with a deadly weapon, they accused me of provoking a respectable businessman. In any case, they added, they could not press charges until he'd actually pulled the trigger. No wonder the students revolted. Betrayed by teachers, cheated by employers, threatened with guns, tear-gassed by police—they had plenty to react against.

*At daughter Rachel's high school graduation, 1990*

I soon discovered that Parkinson (a hulking giant, six feet six inches tall, a fan of the Beat poets and noted campus radical), was not nearly as sympathetic as he had seemed. A right-wing maniac, who claimed to have "declared World War III," had entered his office and shot off his jaw, killing at the same time the student who happened to be with him. Scarred and embittered, with new teeth and jawbone, "Tom," as I'd called him in Los Angeles, now insisted on being addressed as Professor Parkinson.

Cockier than ever after teaching college for three years and publishing my first seven articles, I now knew what I was doing and didn't need much help. Victor Brombert's *The Intellectual Hero: Studies in the French Novel* (1960) taught me how to structure my *Fiction and the Colonial Experience.* But Parkinson was so rude to me when I had to see him, keeping me waiting in the hallway for half an hour after our appointment while, huge feet on his desk, he chatted with bearded undergraduates, that I eventually sought help from Fred Crews. He agreed to take over the dissertation, but only if Parkinson would release me. When I asked him to let me go, he seemed surprised by my complaints and promised to be more civil.

He had very few grad students and wanted credit for directing a dissertation that was nearly done and would someday be published. Like Bronson, he made no comments on my work, apart from adding one missing French accent. But I was so disgusted by his laziness and hostility that when I went in to get his final signature of approval (there was no longer a thesis defense), I didn't even shake hands or say goodbye. Angry when I questioned their authority, Watt, Bronson, and Parkinson, instead of teaching me, felt they had to cut me down to size. So, after passing two Latin exams, writing two dissertations, spending a year in Japan, and losing all my notes, I finally earned my degree. Bloodied but unbowed, I became, in 1967, a real assistant professor at Tufts University.

The harsh, even brutal treatment by the English department prepared me for the cutthroat competition of academic life. Faculty members, bitching about committee work, low salaries, and department politics, rarely talked about their subject. Despite everything, my years at Berkeley were undoubtedly the most intellectually exciting time of my life. The close friendships, rich social life, and passionate discussions about literature were never equalled when I became a professor.

At Berkeley I also became interested in biographical research—and my first subject was myself. During those years, I tracked down Morris traveling on his honeymoon and my errant girlfriend hiding in the closet, discovered that Watt had blackballed me and Bronson had betrayed me. I also arranged, through well-placed contacts, to obtain a copy of a confidential report of my M.A. and Ph.D. exams.

For all their brilliance, the high-flyers in grad school— The Queen of the Ptolemies, The Famous Footnote and The Georgia Peach, who got a job at Yale—in the end accomplished very little. With rare exceptions, graduate school tore their guts out and turned them into harmless drudges. For me, however, Berkeley in the sixties was the ideal place to be. I respected my professors for their learning and prestige, even when they were dullards. And there was no question then, as there is now, of filling out otiose teacher evaluation forms or trying to con professors into giving good grades for inferior work. Though English studies at Berkeley was then dominated by the New Criticism, which demanded a close analysis of the text, I was also taught bibliography, literary biography, and literary history. The students were bright, the classes stimulating, the standards high. I was expected to know three foreign languages, to master the whole of English literature, and to write a publishable dissertation. I'm still restless, as my books show, and prefer to write a biography each year rather than spend a decade on one subject. The first-rate education I received at Berkeley and the intellectual interests fostered there have been the basis of my writing career.

**BIOGRAPHICAL/CRITICAL SOURCES:**

*PERIODICALS*

*American Spectator,* March, 1993, pp. 58-59.
*Bloomsbury Review,* November-December, 1995.
*Christian Science Monitor,* August 7, 1990, p. 13; April 22, 1991, p. 13; May 10, 1994, p. 15.
*Journal and Constitution* (Atlanta), May 8, 1994, p. N10.
*London Review of Books,* January 24, 1991, pp. 22-23; November 10, 1994.
*Los Angeles Times Book Review,* May 23, 1982, p. 16; December 8, 1985, p. 2, 6; July 22, 1990, pp. 1, 13; June 23, 1991, p. 10.
*Nation,* June 12, 1995, pp. 840-44.
*New Statesman and Society,* October 16, 1992, pp. 39-40.
*New Yorker,* May 3, 1989, pp. 166-67; June 27, 1994, pp. 186-94; May 8, 1995, pp. 85-89.
*New York Review of Books,* April 29, 1982, pp. 28-30; January 17, 1991, pp. 10-14; August 11, 1994, pp. 14-16.
*New York Times,* April 15, 1994, p. C29; May 1, 1995, p. C15; May 17, 1995, p. C18; October 21, 1995, p. C22; April 23, 1996, p. C16.
*New York Times Book Review,* November 17, 1985, pp. 3, 51-52; April 14, 1991, pp. 15-16; April 30, 1995, pp. 6-7; May 19, 1996, p. 8.
*Observer,* June 9, 1985, p. 25.
*Publishers Weekly,* September 27, 1985, p. 90; September 18, 1987, p. 166, May 22, 1995, p. 38.
*Sewanee Review,* summer, 1992, pp. 461-66.
*Spectator,* September 1, 1990, p. 30; June 4, 1994, p. 37.
*Times Literary Supplement,* October 31, 1980, pp. 1215-16; July 19, 1985, p. 795; October 18, 1985, pp. 1171-72; December 13, 1985, pp. 1415-16; August 1, 1986, pp. 837-38; May 26-June 1, 1989, p. 578; September 7-13, 1990, p. 940; November 15, 1991, pp. 3-4; October 16, 1992, p. 28.
*Tribune Books* (Chicago), October 18, 1992, pp. 1, 7; May 29, 1994, pp. 3, 10; May 26, 1996, pp. 1, 11.
*Voice Literary Supplement,* March, 1986, pp. 6-7.
*Washington Post Book World,* September 6, 1992, pp. 3, 7.

\*   \*   \*

**MIFFLIN, Margot**

*PERSONAL:* Female.

ADDRESSES: Home—New York, NY. Agent—c/o Juno Books, New York, NY.

CAREER: Journalist.

WRITINGS:

Bodies of Subversion: A Secret History of Women and Tattoo, Juno Books (New York City), 1997.

Contributor of articles on art, women's issues, and books to periodicals, including *Elle, Ms., Entertainment Weekly, New York Times Book Review, Vogue, Cosmopolitan, ARTnews,* and *House Beautiful.*

SIDELIGHTS: In her book *Bodies of Subversion: A Secret History of Women and Tattoo,* Margot Mifflin explores women as both examples of tattoo art and tattoo artists from the nineteenth century to the present. Mifflin delves into issues, including contest nudity and job discrimination, in interviews with tattooed women and artists in the United States, Argentina, and Spain. The book contains one hundred photographs. *Women's Wire* online reviewer Margo Carn noted that although Mifflin presents women tattoo collectors and artists as "renegades of the flesh," she "sometimes falls short," because most of the women were tattooed with designs created by men. Carn did feel that Mifflin "deftly places tattooing within a recognizable cultural and historical context." Carn also felt Mifflin fails to cover modern-day class implications as completely as she did for the earlier history of tattoo art. Finally, Carn would have liked more extensive coverage of racial implications, but she called the book "well written, compelling. . . . And you get the added bonus of spectacular photos."

Mifflin documents early collectors, including sideshow attractions and women such as Betty Broadbent, who entered a beauty contest at the first televised World's Fair in 1939 covered with tattoos. Some of the women learned the art from male artists or from husbands who were artists. Society women who collected tattoos included Winston Churchill's mother, who had a serpent on her wrist. Mifflin notes the rise in female tattooing with the rise in cosmetic surgery during the 1980s. Breast cancer survivors sometimes have art tattooed over their scars, and take pride in their badges of survival and courage. Jacqui Gresham of New Orleans has developed black Betty Boop tattoos for her black customers. Mike Mosher wrote in *Leonardo Electronic Almanac* online that these figures "drawn with devilish horns, bat wings, tail and pitchfork, this visual meme (both babylike and very sexual) from the 1930s has been newly re-ethnicized to be taken up by a new com-munity." Mosher said the subjects of *Bodies of Subversion* reflect "their skin's rich gamut of imagery," and noted the variety of tattoos, from portraits of Malcolm X and Native American imagery to "graphic testaments of lesbian commitment." Mosher said "it is the book's pictures that indelibly etch themselves upon the reader's memory."

BIOGRAPHICAL/CRITICAL SOURCES:

OTHER

*Leonardo Electronic Almanac,* http://www-mitpress.mit.edu/e-journals/LEA/CURRENT/ldr—6-8-9curr.html#bod (1999).

*Weekend All Things Considered,* National Public Radio, http://www.npr.org (May 31, 1998).

*Women's Wire,* http://www.womenswire.com/books/d0304books.html (1999).*

\*　　\*　　\*

## MILLER, Harvey 1935-1999

PERSONAL: Born June 15, 1935, in New York, NY; died of heart failure, January 8, 1999, in Los Angeles, CA.

CAREER: Film director, producer, writer, and actor. Producer of the film *Private Benjamin,* 1980. Producer, executive producer, and director of the television series *The Odd Couple;* associated with the television series *Hey Landlord!,* 1967, *Taxi,* and *The Tracy Ullman Show.* Appeared in films, including *Big,* 1988, *Beaches,* 1988, and *Awakenings,* 1990; actor in the solo show *A Cheap Date with Harvey Miller: The Comedic Life of a Legendary Unknown,* presented at Court Theater, Los Angeles, CA, c. 1998. Writer for comedians Dick Gregory, Shecky Greene, Alan King, and Sandy Baron. *Military service:* U.S. Army, c. 1950s; served in Germany.

AWARDS, HONORS: Emmy Award nomination for, best comedy series, Academy of Television Arts and Sciences, 1974, for *The Odd Couple;* Academy Award nomination, Academy of Motion Picture Arts and Sciences, and award for best original screenplay, Writers Guild of America, both 1980, both for *Private Benjamin.*

*WRITINGS:*

(And director) *Bad Medicine* (feature film), Twentieth Century-Fox, 1985.
(And director) *Getting Away with Murder* (film), Home Box Office, 1996.

Co-author of the screenplays *Private Benjamin,* 1980, and *Cannonball Run II,* 1984. Writer for television series, including *The Odd Couple.*

*BIOGRAPHICAL/CRITICAL SOURCES:*

PERIODICALS

*Back Stage West,* June 4, 1998, p. 18.

*OBITUARIES:*

PERIODICALS

*Los Angeles Times,* January 13, 1999, p. A12.
*TV Guide,* April 10, 1999, p. 4.*

\* \* \*

**MILLER, Sasha**

*PERSONAL:* Born in Oklahoma; married.

*ADDRESSES: Home*—Colorado. *Agent*—c/o Tor Books, St. Martin's Press, 175 Fifth Ave., New York, NY 10010.

*CAREER:* Freelance editor and writer. Also runs an online writing workshop in the SF/Fantasy Literature Forum on CompuServe.

*MEMBER:* Science Fiction Writers of America.

*WRITINGS:*

*Falcon Magic,* published with novel by Andre Norton and Patricia Mathews *On Wings of Magic,* T. Doherty Associates (New York City), 1994.
*Ladylord* (novel), Tor (New York City), 1996.

Her short story "Jamie Burke and the Queen of England" was published in *Magazine of Fantasy and Science Fiction.*

*SIDELIGHTS:* Fantasy writer Sasha Miller made her writing debut with the novel *Falcon Magic.* It appeared in tandem with another novel in the third volume of a trade paperback series called "Witch World: The Turning" and was jointly titled *On Wings of Magic.* On her own, Miller published *Ladylord,* a fantasy novel set in medieval Japan. The story is set in the Third Province, where the ruler Lord Qai prepares to die. Without a male heir, he names his daughter, Lady Javerri, as "son," and grants her his many titles. Lady Javerri becomes known as Ladylord, but until her title is approved by the leader of the First Province, she may be ousted by other contenders for the throne. Ladylord and her new husband, along with a few trusted colleagues, undertake a perilous journey to the First Province. Once there, they are sent on an improbable quest to prove Ladylord's worthiness to rule Third Province. Intrigue abounds as Ladylord tries to collect an egg from a non-human Dragon-warrior. Reviewers judged the work to be successful. In *Publishers Weekly,* a commentator praised Miller for her creation of a "socially complex world" and "captivating characters." A *Kirkus Reviews* critic asserted that *Ladylord* is "well-handled" and "solidly engrossing."

*BIOGRAPHICAL/CRITICAL SOURCES:*

PERIODICALS

*Kirkus Reviews,* January 15, 1996, p. 105.
*Magazine of Fantasy and Science Fiction,* October, 1996, p. 66.
*Publishers Weekly,* March 4, 1996, p. 58.*

\* \* \*

**MILLER, William R. 1959-**

*PERSONAL:* Born February 8, 1959, in Anniston, AL; son of William R. Sr. (an insurance executive) and Joyce Summerlin (Bartley) Miller; married Jill Anderson, 1984 (divorced 1998); children: Julian Wilson. *Education:* Eckerd College, B.A., 1982; Hollins College, M.A., 1983; Binghamton University, Ph.D., 1989. *Politics:* Independent. *Religion:* Episcopalian.

*ADDRESSES: Home*—182-G Dew Drop Rd., York, PA 17402. *Office*—English Department, York College, York, PA 17405.

*CAREER:* Jacksonville State University, Jacksonville, AL, instructor in English, 1984-87; York College, York, PA, associate professor of literature. Visiting associate professor in master's program in writing for children at Hollins College.

*AWARDS, HONORS:* Patterson Prize for Poetry, 1997; Reading Rainbow selection for *Zora Hurston and the China Berry Tree.*

*WRITINGS:*

*Old Faith* (poetry), Mellen Press, 1992.
*Breathed on Glass* (poetry), Druid Press, 1993.
*Zora Hurston and the Chinaberry Tree* (for children), illustrated by Cornelius Van Wright and Ying-Hwa Hu, Lee & Low, 1994.
*Frederick Douglass: The Last Day of Slavery* (for children), illustrated by Cedric Lucas, Lee & Low, 1995.
*The Knee-high Man* (for children), illustrated by Roberta Glidden, Gibbs Smith, 1996.
*The Conjure Woman* (for children), illustrated by Terea D. Shaffer, Atheneum, 1996.
*A House by the River* (for children), illustrated by Cornelius Van Wright and Ying-Hwa Hu, Lee & Low, 1997.
*Richard Wright and the Library Card* (for children), illustrated by Gregory Christie, Lee & Low, 1997.
*The Bus Ride* (for children), illustrated by John Ward, Lee & Low, 1998.
*Jenny and the Peddler* (for children), illustrated by Rod Brown, Dial Books for Young Readers, 1998.
*Night Golf* (for children), illustrated by Cedric Lucas, Lee & Low, 1999.

*SIDELIGHTS:* William R. Miller has written a number of books for children that feature African Americans, and has authored two volumes of poetry. His first published children's story, *Zora Hurston and the Chinaberry Tree,* appeared in 1995. This picture book depicts a period in the life of celebrated author and folklorist Zora Neale Hurston, who is well known for her African American literature. It is an inspirational story intended to show children they can be whatever they want to be no matter their circumstances in life. As a child, Zora had an overbearing father and a mother from whom she gained great strength. However, Zora suffered the loss of her mother when she was only nine years old. Miller portrays the tension between Zora and her father, as well as the independent, resilient nature Zora developed under her mother's influence. The tale ends following the death of Zora's mother. Zora is seen climbing a chinaberry tree (one Zora's mother taught her to climb) and she vows to "never stop climbing" in life. "Readers will embrace this book . . . for its lyrical affirmation

of life's unlimited potential," concluded Ellen Fader in a review for *Horn Book.*

Miller followed *Zora Hurston and the Chinaberry Tree* with 1995's *Frederick Douglass: The Last Day of Slavery.* Another biographical portrait of a famous African American, *Frederick Douglass* describes the early life of abolitionist Frederick Douglass and his rebellion against a slave holder. *School Library Journal* contributor Carol Jones Collins proclaimed, "Miller's narrative is movingly rendered," while *Horn Book* writer Margaret A. Bush deemed it a "thought-provoking biographical tale."

" Miller's *The Knee-high Man* was published in 1996. A *Publishers Weekly* writer judged it as a "well-paced, amiable retelling of [a] folktale." The story features a very small African American man who is even shorter than a rabbit. Tormented by his small stature, the man seeks ways—all unsuccessful—to grow bigger until an owl shows him the importance of accepting who he really is.

In 1996 Miller also produced *The Conjure Woman.* In this story, a young boy named Toby, stricken with a fever, is taken to a conjure woman, Madame Zina, in the hopes that she can heal his illness. During his treatment, Toby and Madame Zina travel to their homeland of Africa, where the boy is healed by his ancestors—the Nakani people of Ghana. After he is healed, Toby is returned to his gladdened parents. Hazel Rochman, a contributor to *Booklist,* wrote, "this picture book makes dramatic use of magic realism." *School Library Journal* reviewer Martha Rosen believed that "young readers and listeners will make the leap between illusion and reality, and the happy ending will please and satisfy them."

Another children's story by Miller, 1997's *A House by the River,* portrays a young girl who is disappointed by her home that is far from town and is threatened by a river. It is not until a storm rages that the young girl, with the help of her mother, gains an appreciation for the protection that her home provides. Carolyn Phelan said in her *Booklist* review, "words and pictures alike depict this . . . household with warmth and dignity." That same year Miller also published *Richard Wright and the Library Card,* which recounts the true tale of another African American writer, Richard Wright, who wanted access to the whites-only library in Memphis at a time when segregation was lawful. The story, which is based on Wright's account in his autobiography *Black Boy,* relates how Wright had to find a Caucasian to write him a note stating Wright was checking books out for a white person and not for himself. Even with the note, Wright experienced resistance from the librarian. However, he was able to check out books, and Miller's story goes on to portray the positive influence books can have on readers. Hazel Rochman wrote in *Booklist,* "words and pictures express . . . the power [Wright] found in books." And a *Kirkus Reviews* critic praised it as "a challenging endeavor, and an accomplished one."

In 1998 Miller introduced *The Bus Ride* to his young readers. This story is based on the real life experience of civil rights activist Rosa Parks, whose landmark decision to not give up her seat on the bus to a white person changed the course of history. In the tale, a young African American girl, Sara, wants to know what it is like to sit at the front of the bus during a time when black people are not allowed to sit in that section. One day she decides to defy the law, and she sits in the front seat. Her action gets her removed from the bus by a police officer, but it also eventually results in the reversal of the law. *Booklist* writer Kathleen Squires determined *The Bus Ride* to be "a fine example of a child taking a stand and making a difference."

*Night Golf,* a 1999 title, has a young African American boy, James, as the protagonist. James enjoys the game of golf and wishes he could play, but the golf course near him is for whites only. In order to gain access to the golf course, James becomes a caddy, and he is soon able to play golf on the course, but only after it is closed at night. The story also provides James with the opportunity to show the white men his talent as a golfer when he is faced with a challenge from one of them. A reviewer for *Publishers Weekly* called the story a "hefty but well-paced text."

For his young readers, Miller has developed a group of strong, independent, and intelligent characters who have dealt with and survived adversity. Many critics resoundingly applaud his accomplishments, especially his ability to write convincing and inspirational stories.

*BIOGRAPHICAL/CRITICAL SOURCES:*

*PERIODICALS*

*Booklist,* October 15, 1994; March 15, 1995; February 15, 1996; May 15, 1997; December 1, 1997; August, 1998.
*Bulletin of the Center for Children's Books,* July-August, 1995, p. 392.
*Horn Book,* January-February, 1995; September-October, 1995; July-August, 1997.

*Kirkus Reviews,* January 1, 1996; May 15, 1997; November 15, 1997; July 15, 1998, p. 1039.
*Library Journal,* November 1, 1991.
*Library Quarterly,* January, 1999, p. 90.
*Nation,* September 11, 1982.
*National Review,* September 17, 1982.
*New York Times Book Review,* February 12, 1995.
*Publishers Weekly,* August 29, 1994; March 20, 1995; January 22, 1996; April 28, 1997; November 17, 1997; July 6, 1998; May 24, 1999, p. 79.
*School Library Journal,* December, 1994, pp. 100-101; June, 1995, p. 103; March, 1996, p. 179; July, 1997, p. 71; February, 1998; October, 1998, p. 108.*

\*   \*   \*

## MILLS, Kay

*PERSONAL: Education:* Received B.App.Sc. (occupational therapy) and graduate diploma in health education promotion.

*ADDRESSES: Home*—Santa Monica, CA. *Agent*—c/o Dutton, 275 Hudson St., New York, NY 10014.

*CAREER:* Journalist and author.

*AWARDS, HONORS: This Little Light of Mine: The Life of Fannie Lou Hamer* was named an American Library Association Best Book in 1993; recipient of numerous awards for work.

*WRITINGS:*

*A Place in the News: From the Women's Pages to the Front Page,* Dodd, Mead (New York), 1988.
*This Little Light of Mine: The Life of Fannie Lou Hamer,* Dutton (New York), 1993.
*From Pocahontas to Power Suits: Everything You Need to Know about Women's History in America,* Plume (New York), 1995.
*Something Better for My Children: The History and People of Head Start,* Dutton, 1998.

Contributor to periodicals, including *Mother Jones, Progressive,* and *New York Times.*

*SIDELIGHTS:* Journalist Kay Mills has published works that deal with social issues in America, particularly feminist social issues. In her "lively, authoritative history of American newspaperwomen," to quote Marie

Shear of *Women's Review of Books,* Mills describes the early work of newspaperwomen and their lengthy struggle for equality in the news room. Mills was quoted in the *New York Times Book Review* as saying, "One overriding reason I wrote the book was that I was trying to sort out why this profession I cared so much about really didn't return the favor for women—and I might add, minorities—for such a long time." "Paradoxically, as you gasp at instance after instance of obstructionism and ignominy visited on newspaperwomen, you exult," declared Shear. "Thanks to Mills, female reality is being validated. It is entering history, where it can no longer be denied. Thus the horror stories are oddly comforting. They tell us that we are not alone, and they can teach savvy younger women about the nasty facts." "*A Place in the News* makes tastier reading than Marion Marzolf 's 1977 history of women journalists, *Up from the Footnote,*" judged Shear. "Mills' generous use of quotes and anecdotes drawn from 150 interviews lends her work the vitality of oral history, while a clear structure keeps the book from rambling. Her writing is clean, unmannered and crisp. . . . The yarns are gorgeous."

During one of her reporting assignments, Mills met civil rights pioneer Fannie Lou Hamer. It was a memorable experience, one that led Mills to eventually write a biography of Hamer titled *This Little Light of Mine.* In it Mills tells the story of Hamer's rise from Mississippi sharecropper, the youngest of twenty children, to a nationally known speaker and organizer for civil rights. Mills's biography of Hamer garnered favorable reviews. "Mills's well-written, well-researched biography comes at an opportune time, for it is hard to believe that a generation has grown up almost ignorant of the work and lives of ordinary men and women like Hamer," declared Leon Dash in *Washington Post Book World.* "Kay Mills, in writing the first full-length biography of this Mississippi sharecropper, has transformed her from something that is at most a faded symbol to a younger generation back into the powerful voice for justice she was in her lifetime," maintained Arlyn Diamond in *Women's Review of Books.* "*This Little Light of Mine* sometimes suffers from information overload, reading less like a biography than an excellent term paper," wrote Phyllis Theroux in *Chicago's Tribune Books.* "But while the author clearly admires Hamer," Theroux observed, "she rarely lets her emotions run away with reality." Diamond added, "Based on extensive research, including a number of interviews with people who knew Hamer personally, this is a very accessible and useful book." "This is an important biography, even for those of us who lived through the civil rights movement: All of us can benefit from being re-

minded of Hamer's struggle, sacrifice and spirit" concluded Dash.

Mills's later works include *From Pocahontas to Power Suits,* a compendium of information about influential American women from the seventeenth, eighteenth, and twentieth centuries. In it Mills touches on such issues as education, women's organizations, workplace roles, and contributions to American society. She also provides a timeline of significant events dealing with women. Mary Carroll described *From Pocahontas to Power Suits* in *Booklist* as an "accessible introduction" to the history of American women.

After visiting Head Start centers around the country, Mills penned *Something Better for My Children,* a "revealing look," according to *Library Journal* critic Samuel T. Huang, at the program's history, successes, and failures. Huang recommended the work to all Congress members who hold the fate of this federally funded educational program in their hands.

*BIOGRAPHICAL/CRITICAL SOURCES:*

*PERIODICALS*

*Booklist,* March 15, 1995, p. 1290.
*Library Journal,* February 1, 1998, p. 97.
*New York Times Book Review,* August 7, 1988, p. 10.
*Tribune Books* (Chicago), January 31, 1993, p. 6.
*Washington Post Book World,* June 26, 1988, pp. 4-5; January 24, 1993, pp. 1, 10-11; July 16, 1995, pp. 1, 10.
*Women's Review of Books,* January, 1989, pp. 7-8; April, 1993, pp. 1, 3-4.

*OTHER*

*Penguin Putnam Catalog Biography,* http://www.penguinputnam.com/catalog/nfiction/authors/4069—biography.html (November 17, 1999).
*Victorian Public Health Training Scheme,* http://www.nwhcn.org.au/VPHTS/records.htm (November 17, 1999).*

\*          \*          \*

**MOELLER, Susan D.**

*PERSONAL: Education:* Yale University, B.A. (cum laude); Harvard University, A.M. (history), Ph.D. (history of American civilization).

*ADDRESSES: Office*—American Studies Department, Brown 206, Brandeis University, 415 South Street, Waltham, MA 02454-9110. *E-mail*—moeller@ binah.cc.brandeis.edu.

*CAREER:* Brandeis University, Waltham, MA, director of journalism department. Has also taught at Pacific Lutheran University and Princeton University.

*WRITINGS:*

*Shooting War: Photography and the American Experience of Combat,* Basic Books (New York City), 1989.
*Compassion Fatigue: How the Media Sell Disease, Famine, and Death,* Routledge (New York City), 1999.

Contributor of writing, illustration, and photography to periodicals, including *Boston Globe, Atlanta Journal/ Constitution, Philadelphi Inquirer, Washington Post,* and *Seattle Times.*

*SIDELIGHTS:* Journalism is an important field for Susan D. Moeller. The director of Brandeis University's journalism department, Moeller has written about the effects of journalism on the population of the United States. With *Shooting War: Photography and the American Experience of Combat,* the former working photojournalist reports on the relationship between Americans and the photojournalistic coverage of five of the United States' most recent wars, including the Spanish-American War, World Wars I and II, the Korean War, and the Vietnam War. In preparation for "this evocative, interesting and disturbing study," wrote Howard Simons in a review for the *Washington Post Book World,* Moeller did "a prodigious amount of research."

Giving a summary of each war's political mood and the particular circumstances that affected its journalistic and photographic coverage, "Moeller builds a solid case for her thesis," remarked J. I. Deutsch in a *Choice* assessment. Deutsch praised *Shooting War* as "an insightful and well-written study of photographic and cultural history." Noting Moeller's contention that early photography of wartime distorted and exaggerated the evils of warfare, *Commonweal* contributor Dennis O'Brien assessed: "Moeller's subject is fascinating, her thesis is basically correct, and she has executed the work fastidiously. Nevertheless," O'Brien cautioned, "the respective worth of words and picture remains a problems." The critic specified an overwhelming lack of quantity and quality of photographs selected for in-

clusion in *Shooting War,* an oversimplification of "judgment about both public mood and political events" as a result "of the heavy 'revisionist' flavor of the historical account," and the inclusion of "irrelevant" historical details merely emphasizing the well-known notion that "War is hell."

Simons identified different flaws: "Moeller's book is laden with polemical moments, such as when she expresses her strong anti-war views. She also has an annoying habit, for a historian, of failing to include the alloy of facts that would harden the steel of some of her contentions. By the same token, she sometimes engages in seriously blemished overgeneralizations, such as her assertion about the journalists in Vietnam that the 'critics are accurate in their assessment of the majority of the press as leftist.' " In addition to noting Moeller's apparent sense of "disappointment that combat photographs . . . have not been more effective in helping to prevent war," Simons concluded his assessment of *Shooting War:* "There is much to argue with . . . and much to provoke thought and much to agree with."

In 1999, a decade after the publication of *Shooting War,* readers were presented with Moeller's analysis of the U.S. media's affect on citizens' general attitude toward world disasters such as the famine in Ethiopia and the spread of the Ebola virus in Africa. In *Compassion Fatigue: How the Media Sell Disease, Famine, and Death,* Moeller asserts that the media's "formulaic and sensationalistic . . . coverage" has resulted in the condition labeled in the book's title, " 'compassion fatigue'—the dulled public sensitivity toward crisis," reported a *Publishers Weekly* contributor. The critic also stated that Moeller's "case studies" were "belabored" and her ending "earnest but pollyannaish." While some reviewers remarked that Moeller offers little in the way of solutions, Judy Solberg, writing in *Library Journal,* judged *Compassion Fatigue* to be both interesting and "well-written."

*BIOGRAPHICAL/CRITICAL SOURCES:*

PERIODICALS

*American Historical Review,* February, 1991.
*American Photographer,* May, 1989.
*Booklist,* March 1, 1989.
*Choice,* September, 1989.
*Commonweal,* June 16, 1989.
*Journal of American History,* March, 1990.
*Kirkus Reviews,* January 1, 1989.
*Library Journal,* March 1, 1989; October 15, 1998.
*Publishers Weekly,* October 26, 1998.
*School Library Journal,* December, 1989.

*Washington Post Book World,* March 26, 1989.

OTHER

*Brandeis University: American Studies faculty biographies,* http://www.brandeis.edu/departments/amer—studies/bios.html (November 17, 1999).*

\*   \*   \*

## MOORE, John L.

*PERSONAL: Religion:* Christian.

*ADDRESSES: Agent*—c/o Thomas Nelson Inc., Nelson Place at Elm Hill Pike, Nashville, TN 37214.

*CAREER:* Has been a rancher and a lay minister; freelance writer.

*AWARDS, HONORS:* Runner-up for the Golden Spur Award from the Western Writers of America; Critics Choice Award from *Christianity Today;* nominated for the Western Heritage Award from the National Cowboy Hall of Fame.

*WRITINGS:*

CHRISTIAN NOVELS

*The Breaking of Ezra Riley,* Lion, 1990.
*Leaving the Land,* Thomas Nelson (Nashville, TN), 1995.
*The Limits of Mercy,* Thomas Nelson, 1996.

OTHER

Also author of Western novels *Bitter Roots* and *Loosening the Reins.* Has contributed work to periodicals, including *Reader's Digest* and *New York Times Magazine.*

*SIDELIGHTS:* John L. Moore has distinguished himself in both the Christian and Western genres. His writing has brought him honors such as the Critics Choice Award from *Christianity Today;* and he was also a runner-up for the Western Writers of America's Golden Spur Award. Moore is perhaps best known for his three novels about Montana rancher Ezra Riley—*The Breaking of Ezra Riley, Leaving the Land,* and *The Limits of Mercy.* His other titles include *Bitter Roots* and *Loosening the Reins.*

*The Breaking of Ezra Riley,* which saw print in 1990, sees the title character striving to save the ranch his fa-

ther left him in his will. Prior to his father's death, Ezra had left the ranch as a young man, hopelessly at odds with the man who sired him. Once the ranch is his responsibility, however, he desperately tries to live up to the paternal expectations he had previously rejected. Critics in general applauded *The Breaking of Ezra Riley,* and frequently remarked upon its superiority to the average Christian novel. Discussing Moore's work, a *Christianity Today* reviewer observed: "It is good to see evangelical novels come of age—writers choosing to write about real people with real conflicts rather than hiding behind cardboard characters and sloppy, overwritten craft." The critic also lauded Moore's ability to make "a character out of a region"—that is, the area around Miles City, Montana, in which the author lives. "That character," the critic continued, "pulls on the lives of the actors as profoundly and unpredictably as God. It is not an easy place."

In 1995's *Leaving the Land,* Moore continued the story of Ezra Riley. This time, Ezra is dealing with a man named Jubal Lee Walker. In Moore's 1996 effort, *The Limits of Mercy,* Ezra must cope with the difficulties which ensue when his wife brings home an abused woman who is confused about the best way to change her situation. While the woman tries to seduce Ezra, he and his family are also the target of an environmental terrorist. "Moore weaves together engaging characters, a strong plot, and a firm sense of place to bring to life the story of one heroic man standing up for what he believes in," observed a reviewer for an Internet site called *Inspired Choices.*

*BIOGRAPHICAL/CRITICAL SOURCES:*

PERIODICALS

*Christianity Today,* September 24, 1990, pp. 37-38.

OTHER

*Inspired Choices,* http://www/acloserlook.com/9612acl/inspiredchoices/fiction/limitsofmercy.html.*

\*   \*   \*

## MORCK, Irene

*PERSONAL:* Born September 20, in St. John, New Brunswick, Canada; married Mogens Nielsen (a farmer). *Education:* University of Alberta, B.Sc. (chemistry; with honors); University of Calgary, teaching certificate. *Avocational interests:* Horse and mule riding, traveling, learning Spanish, hiking.

*ADDRESSES: Home*—Spruce View, Alberta, Canada. *Agent*—c/o Red Deer College Press, 56th Ave. & 32nd St., Box 5005, Red Deer, Alberta T4N 5H5, Canada.

*CAREER:* Has taught science at boys' schools in Kingston, Jamaica, and Barbados; worked for two years as a biochemistry researcher at the University of the West Indies; currently works as a substitute teacher, writer, and farmer.

*WRITINGS:*

*A Question of Courage* (for young adults), Western Producer Prairie Books (Saskatoon, Sascatchewan), 1988.
*Between Brothers* (for young adults), Stoddart (Toronto, Ontario) 1992.
*Touch Trails* (for young adults), Maxwell Macmillan, 1994.
*Tiger's New Cowboy Boots* (for children), illustrated by Georgia Graham, Red Deer College Press, 1996.

*SIDELIGHTS:* Irene Morck is a writer of young adult and children's books. Her first work, *A Question of Courage,* is set in Alberta. Fifteen-year-old Keri is a coward who is unable to canter her horse or handle the beginners' slope on a skiing trip. She feels she is not liked by her classmates and exposes a class cheat to draw attention away from her own problems. Critic Dinah Gough said in *Canadian Children's Literature* that "Morck's initial idea is good and she has patches of confident writing, but she often strains her credibility." Gough said that Keri's introspections "seem contrived" and resolutions of fears are "unbelievable" because they do not come about as an "evolution of character." Eva Martin, writing in *Books for Young People,* went so far as to say the story has "an overblown style with sentiment and purple prose." But Dave Jenkinson wrote in *Canadian Materials* that Morck's strength "resides in her portrayal of teen interactions, particularly those focusing on Keri's rejection by peers."

*Between Brothers,* also set in Alberta and featuring a horse antagonist, was called a "Cain and Abel-type struggle," by a *Quill & Quire* reviewer, who also said that this book and Morck's first are "works of character development rather than of plot." Seventeen year old Greg is continually at odds with his easygoing, sixteen-year-old brother, Michael. During a trail ride, a borrowed horse is lost because of Michael's carelessness.

Greg resents missing a party to join the search, which also includes their father and sixteen-year-old Holly, the owner of the missing animal. During the five-day rescue effort, the brothers fight, first verbally, then physically. A *Canadian Children's Literature* reviewer said, "The central character, Greg, is simply neither likable nor realistic" and observed that Greg's personality "is largely eclipsed" by the characters of Michael and Holly. The reviewer felt that Greg's dilemma "pales into pointless frivolity."

In *Tough Trails,* Ambrose Metford attends a horse auction to buy a pack animal but takes home an older mare who is unsuitable for the job. Ambrose gives the horse to a lonely young boy. Anne Louise Mahoney wrote in *Quill & Quire* that Morck knows "how to tell a story" and said that *Tough Trails* contains "realistic, well-rounded characters" in a story that is neatly balanced with "adventure, drama, and humour."

*Tiger's New Cowboy Boots* is Morck's first picture book. It is the tale of young Tyler, a city boy who travels to the Rocky Mountain foothills to join his uncle's cattle drive. In preparation, Tyler buys new boots, but no one notices them as the animals are driven to their meadow destination. The boots become worn and comfortable along the way and then are noticed by his cousin Jessica and the cowboys. Annette Goldsmith, reviewing the book in *Quill & Quire,* said, "Much of the book's appeal lies in its verisimilitude and subject matter: the rancher's unsentimental and pragmatic approach to animals and work rings true." "The camaraderie shared on a cattle drive is well portrayed throughout this story," wrote Ethel King-Shaw in *Canadian Book Review Annual.*

*BIOGRAPHICAL/CRITICAL SOURCES:*

*BOOKS*

Wilson, Joyce M., editor, *Canadian Book Review Annual,* University of Toronto Press, 1996.

*PERIODICALS*

*Books for Young People,* October, 1988, pp. 17-18.
*Canadian Children's Literature,* 1989, pp. 77-78; winter, 1994, p. 72.
*Canadian Materials,* January, 1989, p. 18.
*Children's Literature Association Quarterly,* winter, 1990, p. 205.
*Emergency Librarian,* March, 1989, p. 22; March, 1993, p. 62.
*Quill & Quire,* December, 1992, p. 26; June, 1994, p. 49-50; January, 1997, p. 39.*

## MOSS, Arthur   1889-1969

*PERSONAL:* Born in 1889, in Greenwich Village, NY; died February 20, 1969, in Neuilly, France. *Education:* Attended Cornell University.

*CAREER:* Freelance writer and magazine publisher, 1921-69.

*WRITINGS:*

(With Hiler Harzberg) *Slapstick and Dumbbell: A Casual Survey of Clowns and Clowning,* Lawren (New York City), 1924.

(With Evalyn Marvel) *The Legend of the Latin Quarter: Henry Murger and the Birth of Bohemia,* Beechhurst (New York City), 1947.

*Second Childhood in Villefranche,* Editions de la Rade (Villefranche), 1952.

(With Marvel) *Cancan and Barcarolle: The Life and Times of Jacques Offenbach,* Exposition Press (New York City), 1954.

*Tale of Twelve Cities and Other Poems,* Two Cities Editions (Paris), 1963.

Also contributor of column, "Books and the Left Bank," to *Boulevardier,* 1927-32.

*SIDELIGHTS:* Arthur Moss is best known for his participation in the early twentieth-century Parisian scene, the expatriate community of American letters. From 1921 onward, Moss was able to mingle with writers like Ernest Hemingway and James Thurber; moreover, he helped to publish their work in several of the journals he and his longtime partner, Florence Gilliam, established. His own writing combined a graceful prose style with solid research.

Moss was born in 1889 in New York City's Greenwich Village. His parents were immigrants involved in the downtown scene: his mother was Turkish and his father German-Jewish. As Moss was growing up, the family assimilated more and more into American life, but Moss nonetheless identified with the European roots of his parents. He briefly attended Cornell University, but left in order to join the rakish world of turn-of-the-century journalism. He worked as a reporter in upstate New York for a time, but soon returned to the more cosmopolitan world of New York City and Greenwich Village in order to edit a literary journal called *Quill.* Moss was from the first deeply connected to an international literary world, deeply committed to developing broad audiences. Moss included in this "new audience" not only men of all nations, but women, too. According to

Florence Gilliam in *Lost Generation Journal,* Moss had an unusual respect for the equality of all human beings. She wrote: "Aside from romantic attachments (he was married several times), he had a notable gift of treating men and women equally as human beings. This endeared him to the feminists of his day, and he marched with the earliest Suffragettes in America."

Gilliam had met Moss when she was a shopgirl in a local bookstore Moss frequented; the two soon found common interests, and Moss put Gilliam to work on *Quill* in September of 1920. But the two soon discovered that the wide audience they hoped to reach was only to be found in miniature in New York City. Eager to find a more international literary community, Gilliam and Moss moved to Paris in 1921.

Within a few months, Moss and Gilliam had set up housekeeping in a small apartment on the Rue Campagne Premiere. They began to publish a magazine called *Gargoyle,* designed to reach an artistic international community. As Jean W. Ross, writing for the *Dictionary of Literary Biography,* remarked, "Commentary in *Gargoyle* focused on the avant-garde in art and letters. Art reproductions represented the work of Pablo Picasso, Henri Matisse, Georges Bracque, Andre Derain, Amedeo Modigliani, Paul Cezanne, Albert Gleizes, Juan Gris, Max Weber, and others. Among the writers who contributed to the magazine were [Malcolm] Cowley, [Robert] Coates, Laurence Vail, Hart Crane, Edna St. Vincent Millay, Sinclair Lewis, Matthew Josephson, Stephen Vincent Benet, Gorham Munson, John Reed, H. D. (Hilda Doolittle), and Bryher (Winifred Ellerman)." As this partial list suggests, Gilliam and Moss were able to find the very best authors and artists, and were able to bring the greatest voices and images of modernism together in an almost unbelievable proximity. What is more remarkable is that Gilliam and Moss were able to find such artists even as they were emerging; they were able to recognize and give opportunities to the phenomenal ex-patriot artistic community in its nascent stage.

Moss and Gilliam were enormously successful in nurturing talent, but they succeeded less as salesmen: *Gargoyle* was a high-quality journal, but it never made a profit and folded one short year after its inception. But Moss's experience with the journal put him at the center of the ex-patriot artistic community. As Al Laney, an editor at the Paris *Herald* described it, Moss was "perhaps the first Boswell of the postwar Quarter . . . , an energetic little man who seemed to know what everybody was doing at all times." In the next years, Moss reported on what "everybody was doing" in a column he wrote for the Paris *Herald,* entitled "Over the River." During this period, too, Moss began to write his first book, *Slapstick and Dumbbell: A Casual Survey of Clowns and Clowning* (1924). The book was written in collaboration with Hiler Harzberg, an American painter whom the ex-patriots sometimes called Hilaire Hiler. Harzberg was, himself, a key figure in the Parisian artistic community: his nightclub, The Jockey, was a congenial watering hole for artists and expatriates and many of Moss's friend congregated there. For a time, Moss even worked as a cashier in The Jockey, keeping tabs on folks for his column and earning a bit of extra money. The spot encouraged the intellectuals who gathered there to relax in an atmosphere of fun. Harzberg provided some illustrations for the text, and Moss also found pictorial work from Heuze, a clown, and from the artist Leger.

Moss also wrote an introduction to his friend Robert Coates's novel, *The Eater of Darkness* (1926) before he began his next publishing effort. With *Boulevardier,* established in 1927, Moss again catered to the modernist, ex-patriot community, but now his focus had switched to the amusements that held the group together. *Boulevardier* was a bit of a social sheet, with plenty of juicy gossip and news about the goings-on of the Left Bank. As Ross comments, *Boulevardier* was "patterned after *The New Yorker* but much inferior." Nonetheless, the journal was cheerfully readable in a way that the more intense *Gargoyle* was not, and it managed to keep afloat until 1932. During those years, Moss also snuck in some genuinely literate news and stories: his own column, "Books and the Left Bank," was always up to date on literary modes, and he also garnered stories from such notable writers as Michael Arlen, Noel Coward, Louis Bromfield, Sinclair Lewis, and Ernest Hemingway. Ross tells an entertaining anecdote from the early days of the magazine: "Jed Kiley, Moss's assistant editor, solicited a story from Hemingway, 'The Real Spaniard,' which was a parody of Louis Bromfield's 'The Real French,' an earlier *Boulevardier* feature. Moss thought the story could be improved and added his own

ending, which angered Hemingway when he saw it in the October 1927 issue." The magazine proved fairly successful, however, by bringing together Moss's excellent contacts, his immaculate taste in literature, and his sense of community fun.

Moss published several more books—two of them co-authored with friend Evalyn Marvel—during his sojourn in Paris. Aside from his final volume, a collection of poems titled *Tale of Twelve Cities and Other Poems* (1963), Moss's writing was predominantly nonfiction. His works include *The Legend of the Latin Quarter: Henry Murger and the Birth of Bohemia* (1946), *Second Childhood in Villefranche* (1952), and *Cancan and Barcarolle: The Life and Times of Jacques Offenbach* (1954). In his memoirs and his biographies, Moss gave his reader a strong sense of how the spirit of a place can engender intense experiences, can even change lives entirely. Moss's own life was certainly changed by the crazy, intense mood of modernist Paris. At the same time, his involvement with the artistic community there—as publisher, barkeep or friend—created the crazy and intense community that fueled so many artists' work. He died on February 20, 1969 in the American Hospital in Neuilly.

*BIOGRAPHICAL/CRITICAL SOURCES:*

*BOOKS*

*Dictionary of Literary Biography,* Volume 4: *American Writers in Paris, 1920-1939,* Gale (Detroit, MI), 1980.
Ford, Hugh, *Published in Paris: American and British Writers, Printers, and Publishers in Paris, 1920-1939,* Macmillan (New York City), 1975.

*PERIODICALS*

*Lost Generation Journal,* fall, 1974, pp. 10-13, 32-33.
*New York Times,* February 22, 1969.
*Paris Herald,* 1947.*

# N

## NAJERA, Rick

*PERSONAL:* Male. *Ethnicity:* Latino.

*ADDRESSES: Agent*—c/o Arte Publico Press, Billingual Press/Editorial Bilingue, P.O. Box 872702, Hispanic Research Center, Arizona State University, Tempe, AZ 85287.

*CAREER:* Playwright, comedy writer, performer, film producer, and director. Televisa, Mexico, translator and writer of soap opera episodes; *Kiki Desde Hollywood* (bilingual television program), executive producer. Latins Anonymous (comedy troupe), founding member.

*WRITINGS:*

*The Pain of the Macho and Other Plays* (includes *The Pain of the Macho, A Quiet Love,* and *Latinologues*), Arte Publico (Houston, TX), 1997.

Author of comedy shows and plays; Writer for the television series *In Living Color,* broadcast on Fox.

*BIOGRAPHICAL/CRITICAL SOURCES:*

*PERIODICALS*

*Library Journal,* August, 1997, p. 87.

*OTHER*

*Nosotros News,* http://www.nosotros.org/news/march1999/latinologues.html (November 17, 1999).*

## NAWROCKI, Sarah   1966-

*PERSONAL:* Born October 3, 1966, in St. Paul, MN; daughter of A. David (a social worker) and Susanna (a bookstore manager; maiden name, Mull) Nawrocki; married Brian Carroll, June 24, 1995. *Ethnicity:* "White." *Education:* Brown University, B.A., 1989; University of North Carolina at Greensboro, M.F.A., 1991.

*ADDRESSES: Home*—515 Brightwood Pl., San Antonio, TX 78209. *Office*—University of Texas at San Antonio, 6900 North Loop, No. 1604 W., San Antonio, TX 78249. *E-mail*—snawrocki@utsa.edu.

*CAREER:* University of North Carolina Press, Chapel Hill, assistant editor, 1993-95; University of Texas at San Antonio, publications editor, 1995-97, assistant director of editorial services, 1997-99, associate director of editorial services, 1999—. Teacher of creative writing, editing, and fiction workshops, including classes at Our Lady of the Lake University.

*MEMBER:* International Association of Business Communicators, Austin Writers League.

*AWARDS, HONORS:* Fellow, National Council for the Arts, 1993; Violet Crown Award, Austin Writers League, 1999.

*WRITINGS:*

*Camping with Strangers* (stories), Boaz Publishing (Albany, CA), 1999.

*WORK IN PROGRESS:* A novel.

## NEILL, Michael

*PERSONAL: Education:* Studied literature.

*ADDRESSES: Agent*—c/o Clarendon Press, Oxford University Press, Great Clarendon St., Oxford OX2 6DP, England.

*CAREER:* Writer and editor.

*WRITINGS:*

*Issues of Death: Mortality and Identity in English Renaissance Tragedy,* Clarendon Press (Oxford, England), 1997.

Contributor to periodicals, including *New York Review of Books.*

*EDITOR*

(With MacDonald P. Jackson) *The Selected Plays of John Marston,* Cambridge University Press (New York City), 1986.
*John Ford: Critical Re-visions,* Cambridge University Press, 1988.
William Shakespeare, *The Tragedy of Antony and Cleopatra,* Clarendon Press, 1994.

*SIDELIGHTS:* Michael Neill edited *John Ford: Critical Re-visions,* a collection of scholarly essays that discuss the work of seventeenth-century English playwright John Ford. "*Re-visions* offers a number of essays that are helpful in assessing not only Ford's work, but the other drama of the period also," wrote R. H. Peake in *Choice.* In one of the essays, Jean Howard examines how Ford's play *Perkin Warbeck* subverts the history plays of Ford's famous contemporary, English playwright and poet William Shakespeare. In another essay, Brian Opie argues how Ford's plays *Love's Sacrifice* and *The Lady's Trial* reflect changes in English society, while Roger Warren's essay examines the treatment of Ford's plays on stage, in film, and on television. "So many of the essays deal with Shakespeare, Fletcher, Middleton, Webster, the playhouses, and the Caroline era, that the book is worthwhile reading for anyone who cares about early modern theatre," observed *Theatre Journal* contributor Sara Jayne Steen, who called *John Ford: Critical Re-visions* "an important contribution to Ford studies."

Neill edited a 1994 edition of Shakespeare's *The Tragedy of Antony and Cleopatra.* Neill's version contains many illustrations, including a "Map of the World of the Play," reproduced images from previous volumes, and illustrations from some of its stage productions. The volume lists previous editions of the play, from the seventeenth century to a 1990 edition. To help readers better understand *The Tragedy of Antony and Cleopatra,* Neill's edition also includes a chronology of historical events relating to the play. Molly E. Smith, discussing the edition in *Sixteenth Century Journal,* praised "Neill's detailed introduction which takes us through all the conceivable topics that one might associate with the play." In the introduction, Neill traces how the play has been received, staged, and criticized. "In short," wrote Smith, "Neill's edition makes a valuable contribution to scholarship on the play while also providing an eminently useful text appropriate both in the classroom and for scholarly work on the play."

*BIOGRAPHICAL/CRITICAL SOURCES:*

*PERIODICALS*

*Choice,* September, 1989, p. 124.
*Sixteenth Century Journal,* spring, 1996, pp. 246-247.
*Theatre Journal,* December, 1990, pp. 516-518.*

\* \* \*

## NELSON, Shirley

*PERSONAL: Female.*

*ADDRESSES: Home*—295 Qual St., Albany, NY, 12210.

*CAREER:* Writer.

*WRITINGS:*

*The Last Year of the War,* Harper & Row (New York City), 1978.
*Fair, Clear, and Terrible: The Story of Shiloh, Maine,* British American (Latham, NY), 1989.

Book reviewer for periodicals, including *Christian Century.*

*SIDELIGHTS:* Shirley Nelson's 1978 debut book, *The Last Year of the War,* is the story of Jo Fuller, a girl who has grown up in a family of agnostics during the early part of the century. During World War II, Jo begins to develop deep religious beliefs. When Jo turns eighteen, she learns that her brother has been shot down over the

Adriatic Sea and is listed as missing in action. She finally comes to grips with the fact that she belongs at home, and must face the terrible guilt she feels about her brother. Critic Don Halberstadt recommended the book in *Library Journal,* calling it a "perceptive first novel." Likewise, a *Publishers Weekly* contributor called the book a "strong and unusually perceptive portrait" that brings the main character's "ambiguities, searchings and confusions to life." A contributor for the *New Yorker* felt that Nelson's writing "radiates the graceful confidence of a seasoned writer."

In 1896, a Freewill Baptist minister named Frank Weston Sandiford convinced hundreds of people, including Nelson's parents, to give up their businesses and homes and found a utopian community called the Shiloh society near Durham, Maine. The Shiloh society gained notoriety because of its claim that the members were preparing the world for the second coming of Jesus Christ. Basing her monograph on the evidence provided by diaries, letters, court records, newspaper articles, and other available sources, Nelson paints a vivid picture of Sandiford and Shiloh. *Fair, Clear, and Terrible* is not only an historical account of Shiloh, but also a cautionary tale of the damaging influence that cult-like leaders can have on society, both then and now. Denise Perry Donavin, reviewing the book for *Booklist,* called it an "intriguing addition to the literature on cults." *Choice* critic T. D. Bozeman felt it was "meticulously researched and well-written." Likewise, a contributor for *Kirkus Reviews* believed it to be a "well-told and painstakingly researched story" that was written with "sensitivity and respect."

*BIOGRAPHICAL/CRITICAL SOURCES:*

PERIODICALS

*Booklist,* June 1, 1989, p.1678.
*Choice,* May 17, 1990, p. 1522.
*Christian Century,* August 26, 1992, pp. 785-86; January 5, 1994, p. 24.
*Kirkus Reviews,* April 1, 1989, pp. 528-29.
*Library Journal,* September 15, 1978, pp. 1767-68.
*New Yorker,* August 28, 1978, p. 93.
*Publishers Weekly,* May 29, 1978, p. 41.*

\*      \*      \*

## NESTLE, Joan   1940-

*PERSONAL:* Born May 12, 1940, in New York, NY; daughter of Regina Nestle (a bookkeeper). *Education:* Queens College, B.A. (English), 1963; New York University, M.A. (English), 1968, doctoral work. *Religion:* Judaism.

*ADDRESSES: Home*—215 West 92nd St., No. 13A, New York, NY 10025.

*CAREER:* Queens College, Flushing, Queens, New York City, professor of English and creative writing and instructor in the SEEK Program; Lesbian Herstory Archives, Park Slope, Brooklyn, New York City, co-founder; lecturer at various venues.

*MEMBER:* Lesbian Liberation Committee, Gay Academic Union (co-founder).

*AWARDS, HONORS:* Gay/Lesbian Book Award, American Library Association, 1988, for *A Restricted Country;* Lambda Literary Award, best fiction anthology, 1997, for *Women on Women 3: A New Anthology of American Lesbian Short Fiction;* Gay, Lesbian, and Bisexual Book Award nomination, American Library Association, 1999, for *A Fragile Union: New and Selected Writings.*

*WRITINGS:*

*A Restricted Country,* Firebrand Books (Ithaca, NY), 1987.
*A Fragile Union: New and Selected Writings,* Cleis Press (San Francisco, CA), 1998.

EDITOR

(With Naomi Holoch) *Women on Women: An Anthology of American Lesbian Short Fiction,* Plume (New York City), 1990.
*The Persistent Desire: A Femme-Butch Reader,* Alyson Publications (Boston, MA), 1992.
(Editor with Naomi Holoch) *Women on Women 2: An Anthology of American Lesbian Short Fiction,* Plume, 1993.
(Editor with John Preston) *Sister and Brother: Lesbians and Gay Men Write about Their Lives Together,* HarperSanFrancisco (San Francisco, CA), 1994.
(Editor with Naomi Holoch) *Women on Women 3: A New Anthology of American Lesbian Short Fiction,* Plume, 1996.
*The Vintage Book of International Lesbian Fiction,* Vintage (New York City), 1999.

Contributor to books and periodicals.

*SIDELIGHTS:* Joan Nestle is a prominent activist in the lesbian community. Her writings include books as well as contributions to various anthologies and periodicals. One of the founders of the Lesbian Herstory Archives, Nestle has edited a number of anthologies with gay and lesbian themes. While Nestle's writings and lectures educate the general public about lesbianism in an attempt to foster tolerance, the author also addresses the tensions and controversies within the lesbian community.

Nestle was born in New York City in 1940. In her autobiographical writings, Nestle cites the influence of her mother, Regina, who liked to write and inspired her daughter's "undeniable right to enjoy sex," as Nestle writes in *A Restricted Country.* In her late teens and early twenties, Nestle participated in the gay and lesbian scene in Greenwich Village, New York City. This lifestyle was still illegal, and generally centered around bars such as the Stonewall, the site of a later police raid which prompted a riot. During this time, Nestle witnessed the courage of people who openly expressed their homosexuality despite the repression of and violence against gay men and lesbians.

After graduating from high school, Nestle attended Queens College and earned a bachelor's degree in 1963. She would later return to the school as an instructor. Nestle then turned her attention to events in the South. In 1965, she traveled to Alabama to participate in the civil rights march from Selma to Montgomery. She worked with the Congress of Racial Equality (CORE) and in registration drives to bring out black voters. After returning to New York, Nestle earned a master's degree in English from New York University in 1968, then pursued doctoral studies for two years.

In 1971, Nestle once again acted on her political and social convictions by joining the Lesbian Liberation Committee. The following year, she helped form the Gay Academic Union, an organization known as the GAU. Through the efforts of the GAU, gay and lesbian speakers such as Nestle speak at the campuses of colleges and universities across the United States. Nestle met other lesbians with similar social and political concerns through the GAU, and in 1973, they began a collaborative project to assemble historical information about lesbianism in America before the development of the feminist movement. This project became known as the Lesbian Herstory Archives.

*A Restricted Country,* Nestle's autobiography, was published in 1987. As she writes in the book's preface: "I would like this book to be read as history, these stories and essays to be documents of a flesh and a spirit that lived through and were changed by their times: the

McCarthy fifties, the activist sixties, the institution-building of the seventies, and the renewed social struggle of the eighties." *A Restricted Country* represents the synthesis of Nestle's experiences as an activist against prejudice, an educator, and a writer, all within the story of her life and sexual development. She discusses the "butch" (masculine) and "femme" (feminine) labels within lesbianism and their implications, allegations that her work is pornographic, her relationship with her mother, and her lovers.

*A Restricted History* "is a perfectly wonderful book: brilliant, wise, and audacious. It made me cry and it made me hot. In a collection of stories from her own life, political essays, and sex fiction, the author offers us a complex politics of sex, of gender, of class," wrote Rebecca Gordon in the *Women's Review of Books.* A *Booklist* contributor also praised *A Restricted History,* calling it "an amazing book."

With Naomi Holoch, Nestle edited *Women on Women: An Anthology of American Lesbian Short Fiction* (1990). A compilation of material by lesbian authors, its selections exhibit the range and diversity of the available material, its subject matter, and its authors. According to *Booklist* contributor Ray Olson, this diversity gives the volume "sociological interest" and makes the book a valuable addition to public libraries. Holoch and Nestle also edited *Women on Women 2* (1993) and *Women on Women 3* (1996).

In between the second and third installments of *Women on Women,* Nestle edited a project with her longtime friend John Preston. The book, *Sister and Brother: Lesbians and Gay Men Write about Their Lives Together,* is a collection of pieces describing various relationships between gay men and lesbians. "Each story is illuminating, showing lesbians and gay men playing indispensable roles in each other's lives as mentors, muses, best friends, families, even lovers," stated a *Kirkus Reviews* contributor, who also called *Sister and Brother* "richly rewarding." Amber Hollibaugh, writing in the *Women's Review of Books,* observed that *Sister and Brother* "never loses its larger intention: to expose the essential bridges we have built across the great faultlines of gender and class," and described it as "a gift too long in coming," while a *Publishers Weekly* reviewer deemed the book to be an "engaging collection."

Nestle's *A Fragile Union: New and Selected Writings* includes a series of portraits of working-class lesbians and Nestle's account of her bout with colon cancer. Discussing *A Fragile Union* in *Publishers Weekly,* a critic noted that "Nestle is by turns earnest, pedantic, funny, bold, and courageous; her collection is, clearly, the work of an irrepressible, principled woman." In *A Restricted Country,* Nestle presents the text of one of her speeches, a piece that addresses the importance of history. Its closing lines seem to summarize Nestle's life and work: "[History] is always a collective memory as complicated and as contradictory as the people who lived it, but it is always a people's story. Let our tale be marked by our knowledge of what had to be done, and let it shine with the passion of our attempt."

*BIOGRAPHICAL/CRITICAL SOURCES:*

*BOOKS*

Davidson, Cathy N., and Linda Wagner-Martin, editors, *The Oxford Companion to Women's Writing in the United States,* Oxford University Press (New York City), 1995.

*Gay and Lesbian Biography,* St. James Press (Detroit, MI), 1997.

*Gay and Lesbian Literature,* St. James Press, 1994.

Hogan, Steve, and Lee Hudson, *Completely Queer,* Holt (New York City), 1998.

Nestle, Joan, *A Restricted Country,* Firebrand Books, 1987.

Pollack, Sandra, and Denise D. Knight, *Contemporary Lesbian Writers of the United States,* Greenwood Press (Westport, CT), 1994.

Summers, Claude, editor, *The Gay and Lesbian Literary Heritage,* Holt, 1995.

*PERIODICALS*

*Advocate,* June 2, 1992, p. 39.

*Belles Lettres,* spring, 1990, p. 29.

*Booklist,* November 15, 1987, p. 517; May 15, 1990, p. 1782; July, 1992, p. 191; October 1, 1994, p. 216; May 15, 1996, p. 1571.

*Choice,* July/August, 1991, p. 1749.

*Kirkus Reviews,* September 15, 1994, p. 1251.

*Lambda Book Report,* November/December, 1994, p. 17; July, 1996, p. 12; October, 1998, p. 7.

*Library Journal,* June 15, 1992, p. 78; October 1, 1994, p. 102.

*Progressive* (Madison, WI), August, 1989, pp. 16-17.

*Publishers Weekly,* September 26, 1994, p. 49; May 20, 1996, p. 252; November 9, 1998, p. 65.

*Women's Review of Books,* April, 1988, pp. 15-16; December, 1992, pp. 11-12; November, 1995, pp. 19-20.*

## NEUMANN, Robert G(erhard)   1916-1999

*OBITUARY NOTICE*—See index for *CA* sketch: Born January 2, 1916, in Vienna, Austria; died of cancer, June 18, 1999, in Bethesda, MD. Academic, ambassador, and author. Neumann was serving as ambassador to Saudi Arabia in 1981 when he was fired by then-Secretary of State Alexander Haig after only two months on the job. Several theories circulated about his firing, a popular one being that Haig let him go because he had criticized Haig to a senator. After leaving his appointed post he joined the Georgetown University Center for Strategic and International Studies. Neumann was an expert on international affairs and had previously served on the faculty of the University of California at Los Angles and directed the school's Institute of International and Foreign Studies. He was a guest lecturer at several schools including the University of Vienna and the University of Munich. His knowledge of foreign policy resulted in three books: *European and Comparative Government, The Government of the German Federal Republic,* and *Toward a More Effective Executive-Legislative Relationship in the Conduct of America's Foreign Policy.* Neumann also contributed work to *American Government Annual, Collier's Encyclopedia* and to professional journals in Europe.

*OBITUARIES AND OTHER SOURCES:*

*PERIODICALS*

*Los Angeles Times,* June 23, 1999, p. A16.
*New York Times,* June 25, 1999, p. B9.

\*      \*      \*

## NEWHOUSE, John

*PERSONAL: Education:* Duke University, A.B., 1950.

*ADDRESSES: Agent*—c/o Pantheon Books, 201 East 50th St., New York, NY 10022.

*CAREER:* Journalist, specializing in Western Europe, East-West relations, national security, and foreign policy. Bureau of European Affairs, U.S. Department of State, senior policy advisor; Former assistant director of U.S. Arms Control and Disarmament Agency during the Carter administration; Brookings Institution, Washington, DC, former guest scholar in foreign policy studies.

*WRITINGS:*

*Collision in Brussels: The Common Market Crisis of 30 June 1965,* Norton (New York City), 1967.

*De Gaulle and the Anglo-Saxons,* Viking (New York City), 1970.

(With Melvin Croan, Edward R. Fried, and Timothy W. Stanley) *U.S. Troops in Europe: Issues, Costs, and Choices,* Brookings Institution (Washington, DC), 1971.

*Cold Dawn: The Story of SALT,* Holt (New York City), 1973.

*The Sporty Game,* Knopf (New York City), 1982.

*War and Peace in the Nuclear Age,* Knopf, 1988, published as *The Nuclear Age: From Hiroshima to Star Wars,* M. Joseph (London), 1989.

*Europe Adrift,* Pantheon (New York), 1997.

Contributor to *New Yorker.*

*SIDELIGHTS:* Journalist and former political appointee John Newhouse has written widely about U.S. foreign affairs in Europe as they relate to such subjects as economics, politics, and military relations. Several of his early works deal with the politics of former French statesman Charles De Gaulle. In *Collision in Brussels* Newhouse explains the deliberations and political wrangling of the European Common Market, particularly the position of France under De Gaulle—when the British applied to join the fledgling European economic union. Although a critic for *Kirkus Reviews* found Newhouse's effort to be "quite special," and *Library Journal* reviewer Judah Adelson deemed it "fine work," a reviewer for the *Times Literary Supplement* cited important omissions, such as not quoting "the seven-point agreement that settled the crisis" that occurred in 1966.

Newhouse's next work, 1970's *De Gaulle and the Anglo-Saxons,* is a "readable, informative, well-documented work," to quote a *Booklist* reviewer. In this volume Newhouse assesses the relations between the United States, Great Britain, and France during the De Gaulle era, studying in particular such subjects as nuclear policy, the Common Market, and NATO in what a *Publishers Weekly* critic called an "extremely well-written book." Also focussing on European affairs is Newhouse's *Europe Adrift.* In this 1997 book, Newhouse highlights contemporary events based largely on his own work as a journalist, and he proposes a multifaceted strategy for economically and politically strengthening Great Britain, France, and Germany as the core of the European Union. In reviewing *Europe Adrift,* a critic for *Publishers Weekly* called the book's author a "provocative writer," adding that Newhouse

"provides much controversy." A *Kirkus Reviews* writer similarly called the work "illuminating," while contributor Kent Worcester noted in *Library Journal* that the volume "clearly presented" information on its timely subject.

An expert in political and military affairs, Newhouse has published a trio of works on the military in the nuclear age. As a member of the Brookings Institution, he jointly published a study of the U.S. military presence in Europe. Released in 1971, *U.S. Troops in Europe* presents the various arguments for and against the policy of deploying American troops in Europe at an annual cost of ten billion dollars to the United States while the country was suffering from trade deficits. While a *Choice* reviewer applauded the authors' "solid, well-researched" analysis, and the "clear" and "objective" nature of the discussion, *Library Journal* contributor Robert T. Redden found the writing to be "turgid" and the discussion overly speculative.

In *Cold Dawn* Newhouse explains the Strategic Arms Limitation Talks (SALT) of the late 1960s and early 1970s to the general reader. The military and political strategies of the United States and the Soviet Union, the difficulties of surviving a nuclear conflict, and the negotiation of the first stage agreement signed in May of 1972 are each discussed in depth. This work elicited praise from critics. Writing in *Library Journal,* Robert F. Delaney called *Cold Dawn* "absorbing" and "well written" with "perceptive insight." A *Choice* critic likewise described the work as an "excellent journalist account" that is carefully crafted and very approachable.

Newhouse's *War and Peace in the Nuclear Age* is a companion volume to the thirteen-part Public Broadcasting Service television series of the same name that aired in the late 1980s. This work considers the repercussions the creation of the atomic bomb had on world peace. "In clear, elegant prose, Newhouse has brought us a vivid account of American and Soviet behavior in the nuclear epoch," according to Michael R. Beschloss in the *Chicago Tribune.* Newhouse interprets how U.S. presidents from Harry Truman through Ronald Reagan approached the nuclear issue and what consequences resulted. Recommending the work in *Library Journal,* contributor Jack W. Weigel called Newhouse "even-handed and nonpartisan" while at the same time criticizing the presidents with well-reasoned arguments. Calling *War and Peace* "an excellent introduction to the nuclear age," Beschloss concluded that Newhouse presented conclusions "so sensible and persuasive that they are likely to win wide acceptance . . . Newhouse has succeeded in the difficult task of conveying complicated issues to the general reader without oversimplification."

In a different arena all together is *The Sporty Game,* Newhouse's "perceptive, inside view," to quote a *Booklist* critic, of the commercial aircraft manufacturing industry. Focussing on the development and construction of wide-body aircraft by McDonnell-Douglas, Boeing, Lockheed, and European Airbus Industrie, Newhouse analyzes the economic and political aspects of such high-risk enterprises. The work garnered the praise of several commentators, including a *Choice* reviewer who called *The Sporty Game* "very readable" and a "valuable supplement" to other works on the topic, recommending it "most highly." Likewise, Mel D. Lane, in a review for *Library Journal,* found the work to be insightful and predicted that it would appeal to a broad spectrum of readers.

*BIOGRAPHICAL/CRITICAL SOURCES:*

*PERIODICALS*

*American History Illustrated,* summer, 1989, p. 16.
*Booklist,* September 15, 1970, p. 71; July, 1982, p. 1404; November 15, 1988, p. 515; September 15, 1997, pp. 185-186.
*Business Week,* October 6, 1997, p. 18.
*Chicago Tribune,* January 8, 1989, section 14, p. 5.
*Choice,* July-August, 1972, p. 718; December, 1973, p. 1629; November, 1982, p. 475.
*Commonweal,* October 6, 1989, pp. 533-537.
*Economist,* November 15, 1997, p. 7.
*Foreign Affairs,* fall, 1982, p. 223; November-December, 1997, pp. 146-151.
*Journal of American History,* March, 1991, pp. 1419-1420.
*Kirkus Reviews,* September 15, 1967, p. 1182; August 1, 1997, pp. 1194-1195.
*Library Journal,* November 1, 1967, p. 3994; February 1, 1972, p. 506; June 1, 1973, p. 1802; July, 1982, p. 1339; January, 1989, p. 96; September 1, 1997, p. 201.
*New Leader,* March 20, 1989, pp. 17-18.
*New Republic,* June 12, 1989, pp. 38-40.
*Newsweek,* August 9, 1982, p. 63.
*New Yorker,* December 3, 1973, p. 192; December 18, 1989, p. 114.
*New York Times Book Review,* October 5, 1997, p. 17.
*Progressive,* November, 1982, p. 61.
*Publishers Weekly,* February 16, 1970, p. 69; August 11, 1997, p. 394.
*Times Literary Supplement,* April 11, 1968, p. 364; June 30, 1972, pp. 732-733.
*Washington Monthly,* September, 1997, pp. 58-59.

*OTHER*

*Brookings Institution: John Newhouse,* http://www.brook.edu/scholars/jnewhous.htm (November 17, 1999).*

\*   \*   \*

## NEWSOME, (Mary) Effie Lee   1885-1979
## (Mary Effie Lee)

*PERSONAL:* Born January 19, 1885 in Philadelphia, PA; daughter of Benjamin Franklin (a clergyman, chief editor of the *Christian Recorder,* and former president of Wilberforce University) and Mary Elizabeth (Ashe) Lee. *Education:* Attended Wilberforce University, Oberlin College's Academy, 1904-05, the Academy of Fine Arts, 1907-08, and the University of Pennsylvania, 1911-14. *Religion:* African Methodist Episcopal.

*CAREER:* Children's poet, short fiction writer, librarian, and illustrator.

*WRITINGS:*

*Gladiola Garden: Poems of Outdoors and Indoors for Second Grade Readers,* Association for the Study of Negro Life and History (Washington, DC), 1944.

Contributor of poems, sometimes under name Mary Effie Lee, to periodical publications, including *Brownies' Book, Crisis, Opportunity,* and *Phylon.*

*SIDELIGHTS:* Mary Effie Lee Newsome was born in Philadelphia on January 19, 1889, one of five children of Benjamin Franklin Lee and Mary Elizabeth Lee. Her father was a prominent member of the African American community; he was a professor of homiletics at Wilberforce University, and became the University's president in the 1870s and 1880s. Later, he went on to become editor of the *Christian Record,* the official organ of the African Methodist Episcopal Church, and was later elected as the Church's twentieth Bishop. Benjamin Lee and his wife Mary Elizabeth both had a love of literature and the arts, and they made sure their daughters were inducted into the riches to be found there. Newsome was particularly drawn to the visual arts, a love, that would resurface later in the sketches which she drew to accompany her poems in *Brownies'*

*Book* and *Crisis.* Her family moved to Waco, Texas, in 1892 when her father was named bishop of the African Methodist Episcopal Church; Newsome drew pictures of the local landscape and animals, and she also began writing poems that, much like her drawings, were miniature descriptions of her observed world.

Newsome attended Wilberforce University (as had both of her parents), and then went on to study at Oberlin College and the University of Pennsylvania, where she furthered her training as an artist. She began publishing her stories and poems in 1915, in *Crisis,* and later went on to publish in magazines like *Opportunity* and *Phylon.* She was also a major contributor to *The Brownies' Book,* a magazine published by W.E.B. Du Bois for young black children; the magazine contained a variety of features, including biographies of prominent black achievers. The magazine folded after four years, but not before Newsome had a chance to see eleven of her poems published.

In 1924, Newsome began writing "The Little Page" for *Crisis,* another Du Bois venture, and she continued writing for the magazine until 1925. "The Little Page" was like a miniature version of *Brownies' Book,* and included poems, illustrations and short prose writing. "Calendar Chat" was one section, consisting of a short description of an aspect of nature related to a particular month. The "Chat" was designed to both entertain and educate, a common theme throughout her work. Newsome also penned several prose pieces for "The Little Page" that treated race relations, an especially difficult topic for those times, and one that she generally avoided in her writings for children, believing that children's' concerns were generally more immediate. Her sketches highlighted the history of Africa and the black diaspora, and were intended to encourage blacks to feel a sense of pride in their history. It was through this writing that she acquired her reputation as a children's writer.

Newsome's most well known poem is "Morning Light: The Dew-drier," first published in 1918 in *Crisis.* Interest in black literature of the time—1918 was the beginning of the Harlem Renaissance, a flowering of black literature and arts—has led to the poem being frequently anthologized since. In simple, direct language the poem describes the "dew-drier." "Dew-driers" were African boys used to clear a path for white explorers and hunters on safari; defenseless, they frequently faced grave danger as they led the procession through the tall grasses. Newsome makes a connection between this role and the role of African Americans in the struggles for world peace. In 1920, Newsome married a min-

ister in the African Methodist Episcopal Church, the Reverend Henry Nesby Newsome. Prior to this she had written under the name Mary Effie Lee, but dropped the Mary out of consideration for length when she took Newsome's name. Together they moved to Birmingham, Alabama where he was given a congregation; during this time she taught elementary school and acted as the school librarian. They soon returned to Wilberforce, Ohio, however, where Newsome worked first as a librarian at Central State College, and finally at Wilberforce where she remained until she retired in 1963.

In 1944, *Gladiola Garden: Poems of Outdoors and Indoors for Second Grade Readers* was published by the Association for the Study of Negro Life and History, founded by Carter Woodson to promote black culture. The poems in *Gladiola Garden* are spoken through the eyes of a child narrator who notices and describes what she sees in nature, much like the young Mary Effie Lee did in Waco. The poems frequently take birds, flowers, and insects as their subject: there are sixteen kinds of birds and nearly thirty names of flowers in the collection. Newsome's poems also rely heavily on visual images, and the juxtaposition of human elements and closely observed description. Her work is also notable for its balanced rhyme and meter. Since her poetry was aimed at children, it was generally simple and direct. A writer for the 1947 *Negro History Bulletin* says of Newsome that her "aim is not only to help children to appreciate the good and the beautiful but to express themselves accordingly." Donnarae MacCann in the *Oxford Companion to American Literature* describes Newsome's achievement as "giving youngsters two great gifts: a keen sense of their own inestimable value and an avid appreciation of the natural world." Above and beyond her literary achievements, she is an important figure in the larger African American culture in the first half of the century.

*BIOGRAPHICAL/CRITICAL SOURCES:*

*BOOKS*

*Dictionary of Literary Biography,* Volume 76: *Afro-American Writers, 1940-1955,* Gale Research (Detroit, MI), 1988.
*Notable Black American Women,* Gale Research, 1992.
*Oxford Companion to African American Literature,* Oxford University Press, 1997.

*PERIODICALS*

*Negro History Bulletin,* February, 1947, pp. 99-100, 108.*

## NING, Pu 1917-

*PERSONAL:* Born January 1, 1917, in Nanjing, China; son of Shanfun Pu and Suzheng Lu; married Fumei Ma May 15, 1983. *Citizenship:* Taiwanese. *Ethnicity:* "Han nationality." *Education:* Graduated from Russian Language College of Beijing, 1935. *Politics:* Nonpartisan. *Avocational interests:* Calligraphy and writing poems.

*ADDRESSES: Home*—Mu Shang, P.O. Box 00265, Taipei, Taiwan. *Agent*—c/o Homa and Sekey Books, P.O. Box 103, Dumont, NJ 07628. *E-mail*—wenye@aol.com

*CAREER:* Newspaper reporter in Xian, Chongqin, China, 1939-44; editor-in-chief at a publishing company in Shanghai, China, 1947-49; writer and newspaper adviser, Taiwan, 1987-93.

*MEMBER:* China Literature Association, Taiwan.

*AWARDS, HONORS:* Literature awards of Sun Yat-Sen, Taiwan, 1985; National Literature Awards, Taiwan, 1987; Social Meritorious Awards, Taiwan, 1989; "Mighty Dragon Award" of China, Outstanding Personages in 20th Century, Taiwan, 1997; honorary professor of Sun Yat-Sen, San Francisco.

*WRITINGS:*

*Red in Tooth and Claw: Twenty-six Years in Communist Chinese Prisons* (Han Wei-tien's memoir), translated by Tung Chung-Hsuan and others, Grove/Atlantic, 1994.
*Flower Terror: Suffocating Stories of China,* translated by Richard J. Ferris Jr. and Andrew Morton, Homa & Sekey (Dumont, NJ), 1998.

Also author of *A Romance in the North Pole* (novel), 1943, *The Lady in the Pagoda* (novel), 1945, and *Book Without a Title,* six volumes with more than 2.6 million words of fiction.

*ADAPTATIONS: A Romance in the North Pole* is being adapted into a movie.

*WORK IN PROGRESS:* A memoir.

*SIDELIGHTS:* Pu Ning is said to be among the most influential writers in modern China. The Chinese writer refused to work for the government, even though it cost him his freedom on more than one occasion; he was imprisoned. In secrecy he created a large amount of fiction, using thousands of disguised letters to smuggle the text out of his country. His millions of words were collected and published in six volumes known as *Book Without a Title.* When living in Taiwan, Ning met Han Wei-tien and agreed to write his memoir *Red in Tooth and Claw: Twenty-six Years in Communist Chinese Prisons,* a work "[crisp] . . . in its indictment of the Communist system that made Han's long nightmare possible," assessed Jonathan Spence in *New York Review of Books.* "Similar though all labor camp experiences may be in their broadest outlines, each one carries within its own daily agonies, and occasional small triumphs. Especially," maintained Spence, "during the great famine years between 1959 and 1962. . . . As they struggled for their own survival, they watched countless unknown prisoners, and some who had briefly become their friends, die slowly and mainly silently; sometimes they speeded the process by using their last ounce of strength to commit suicide."

"Han Wei-tien, a former Kuomintang army officer who spent twenty-four years in Communist camps before being repatriated to Taiwan, compiled 'a sort of journal' after his release in order to preserve his experiences," explained Spence. "As Pu Ning revised or rewrote Han's words, the two talked often by telephone and also saw each other regularly. . . . The publishers do not even list Han Wei-tien as the book's author, and Pu Ning receives all the credit, leaving the lingering impression—despite the 'chronology' of Han's experiences at the end of the book—that Pu Ning is writing as novelist more than as amanuensis. If that is so perhaps it accounts for the book's moments of insincerity and superficiality." *Publishers Weekly* referred to *Red in Tooth and Claw* as an "extraordinary book [by] the distinguished Chinese author Pu Ning." Mary Ellen Sullivan, who noted in *Booklist* that Pu Ning is "a pseudonym that translates as 'Mr. Anonymous,' " complimented the work, stating that it shows "the extraordinary resiliency of the human spirit."

In 1998, Ning's *Flower Terror: Suffocating Stories of China,* translated by Richard J. Ferris Jr. and Andrew Morton, was released in the United States. The work is comprised of twelve short stories that are primarily composed in the first person and are autobiographical in nature. Exposing life in Communist China from about 1950 through the 1970s, Ning presents the oppression that existed in his homeland, specifically the troubles that intellectuals faced. "Pu," praised a *Publishers Weekly* critic, " . . . writes of his embittering experiences clearly and fluently, without sentimentality or self-pity." *Flower Terror* is "well-written," declared Shirley N. Quan in *Library Journal.* However, cautioned Quan, the volume is best suited "for the informed reader" because the book's structure is laden with "the depressingly heavy political climate."

*BIOGRAPHICAL/CRITICAL SOURCES:*

PERIODICALS

*Booklist,* April 15, 1994, p. 1502.
*Christian Science Monitor,* June 24, 1994, p. 15.
*Current History,* September, 1994, p. 289.
*Library Journal,* April 1, 1994, p. 119; December, 1998, p. 160.
*New York Review of Books,* August 10, 1995, p. 15-18.
*Publishers Weekly,* March 14, 1994, p. 58; November 2, 1998, p. 72.

\*    \*    \*

**NORMAN, Lisanne**

*PERSONAL:* Children: one son. *Education:* Studied teaching in college. *Avocational interests:* Paleontology, genetics, history of religion, cats.

*ADDRESSES: Home*—England. *Agent*—c/o DAW Books, 375 Hudson St., 3rd Floor, New York, NY 10014-3658.

*CAREER:* Writer.

*MEMBER:* The Vikings, N.F.P.S. (English Dark Ages reenactment group), Norvik Hrafnswyrd (local reenactment group; head).

*WRITINGS:*

NOVELS

*Turning Point,* DAW Books (New York), 1993.
*Fortune's Wheel,* DAW Books, 1995.
*Fire Margins,* DAW Books, 1996.
*Razor's Edge,* DAW Books, 1997.
*Dark Nadir,* DAW Books, 1999.

*SIDELIGHTS:* "I began writing when I was eight years old because there weren't enough of the books around that I liked to read," Lisanne Norman told an *Amazon.com interviewer.* "My first influence was the children's writer . . . Enid Blyton. She wrote stories of magic and elves and fairies." Norman also enjoyed reading Angus McIver, who wrote stories about schoolchildren on Mars, Rudyard Kipling's *Jungle Book,* and

books by Gore Vidal, Anne McCaffrey, Jennifer Roberson, C. J. Cherryh, and other science-fiction and fantasy writers. Interestingly enough, she noticed, most of her favorite authors were published by DAW Books, which has published all of Norman's books.

Norman's novels are complex; she told *Amazon.com,* "The only way I've found to keep all the intricate threads of my novels and the time scales straight is to mind-map them. That's a kind of flow chart using bubbles and radiating lines and key phrases. I do this on paper and it really frees my imagination." She has a son and avoids distractions by writing when he is in school or asleep.

*Turning Point,* Norman's first effort, is the story of a human colony in a world that is cut off from Earth by alien conquerors, and of one young woman, Carrie, who becomes telepathically linked with Kusac, a catlike alien from a crashed starship. The two must convince their races to unite against the conquering Valtegans, and they must also deal with the increasing passion they feel for each other—despite being from two different species. "Overall," wrote Carolyn Cushman in *Locus,* "this is fun escapist fare." *Kliatt* critic Susan Cromby called the book "interesting as well as fun," and liked the "realistic" characters.

*Fortune's Wheel* continues Carrie's story, following her and the catlike aliens to their world, where she has been taken. Her telepathic powers, so unusual among humans, are encouraged in the Sholan world, and her bond with Kusac can only intensify. It is a bond they will need as their world enters interstellar conflict, and factions on both worlds try to use their powers for their own ends.

In *Fire Margins* Carrie finally mates with her catlike telepathic lover, and their children's telepathic powers will be even greater than their own. This makes the new race a threat to the traditional Sholan guilds and clans; and the two lovers are forced to set out for a new life, and find answers to the question of how peace can be preserved and the survival of both races assured. *Kliatt* reviewer Judith H. Silverman called the book "a gripping story" written by "a masterful storyteller."

Norman is full of ideas for future books in her series, saying on her web site: "By profession, I trained as a teacher so I'm interested in everything. Learning is an ongoing experience for me. . . . My main interests are in paleontology, ancient civilizations, particularly the Minoans and Ancient Egyptians, and the history of the Old Testament times." She is also a Dark Age reenactor, and has learned how to fight with a double-handed sword, engage in archery battles, and use a sword, spear, Dane axe, and quarterstaff. She runs a local group of re-enactors, and has been a member of the Vikings society since the 1970s.

*BIOGRAPHICAL/CRITICAL SOURCES:*

PERIODICALS

*Analog: Science Fiction and Fact,* May, 1994, pp. 160-63.
*Kliatt,* March, 1994, p. 20; November, 1995, p. 18.
*Locus,* November, 1993, p. 29.
*Science Fiction Chronicle,* January, 1994, p. 32.

OTHER

Lisanne Norman's Web Site, http://www.sff.net/people/Lisanne/.
*Amazon.com,* http://www.amazon.com/.*

\*   \*   \*

**NUGENT, J. O.**
    **See BARR, Amelia Edith (Huddleston)**

\*   \*   \*

**NWANKO, Agwuncha A.**
    **See NWANKWO, Arthur Agwuncha**

\*   \*   \*

**NWANKWO, Arthur Agwuncha    1942-**
    **(Agwuncha A. Nwankwo)**

*PERSONAL:* Born in Nigeria.

*ADDRESSES: Agent*—c/o Fourth Dimension Publishing Co. Ltd., House 16, Fifth Ave., City Layout, Enugu, Nigeria.

*CAREER:* Author, publisher, and political figure; participated in Biafran Propaganda Directorate during Nigerian Civil War, c. 1967-70.

*WRITINGS:*

(With Samuel Udochukwu Ifejika) *The Making of a Nation: Biafra,* C. Hurst (London), 1969, pub-

lished as *Biafra: The Making of a Nation,* Praeger (New York), 1970.
*Nigeria: The Challenge of Biafra,* R. Collings (London), 1972.
*Nigeria: My People, My Vision,* Fourth Dimension Publishing (Enugu, Nigeria), 1979.
*Can Nigeria Survive?,* Fourth Dimension Publishing (Enugu, Nigeria), 1981.
*After Oil, What Next?: Oil and Multinationals in Nigeria,* introduction by Mokwugo Okoye, Fourth Dimension Publishing (Enugu, Nigeria), 1982.
*How Jim Nwobodo Rules Anambra State,* Fourth Dimension Publishing (Enugu, Nigeria), 1982.
*Corruption in Anambra State: The Jim Nwobodo Legacy,* Fourth Dimension Publishing (Enugu, Nigeria), 1983.
*Justice, Sedition Charge, Conviction & Acquittal of Arthur Nwankwo, Author of "How Jim Nwobodo Rules Anambra State,"* Fourth Dimension Publishing (Enugu, Nigeria), 1986.
*Civilianized Soldiers: Army-Civilian Government for Nigeria,* Fourth Dimension Publishing (Enugu, Nigeria), 1984.
*National Consciousness for Nigeria,* introduction by S. G. Ikoku, Fourth Dimension Publishing (Enugu, Nigeria), 1985.
*The Igbo Leadership and the Future of Nigeria,* Fourth Dimension Publishing (Enugu, Nigeria), 1985.
*Thoughts on Nigeria,* Fourth Dimension Publishing (Enugu, Nigeria), 1986.
*The Military Option to Democracy: Class, Power, and Violence in Nigerian Politics,* Fourth Dimension Publishing (Enugu, Nigeria), 1987.
*The Power Dynamics of the Nigerian Society: People, Politics, and Power,* Fourth Dimension Publishing (Enugu, Nigeria), 1988.
*Before I Die: Olusegun Obasanjo,* Fourth Dimension Publishing (Enugu, Nigeria), 1989.
*African Dictators: The Logic of Tyranny and Lessons from History,* Fourth Dimension Publishing (Enugu, Nigeria), 1990.
*Retreat of Power: The Military in Nigeria's Third Republic,* Fourth Dimension Publishing (Enugu, Nigeria), 1990.
*Perestroika and Glasnost: Their Implications for Africa,* Fourth Dimension Publishing (Enugu, Nigeria), 1990.
*Political Danger Signals: The Politics of Federalism, Census, Blanket Ban, and National Integration,* Fourth Dimension Publishing (Enugu, Nigeria), 1991.
*Nigeria: The Political Transition and the Future of Democracy,* Fourth Dimension Publishing (Enugu, Nigeria), 1993.

*Incarnation of Hope,* Fourth Dimension Publishing (Enugu, Nigeria), 1993.

(As Agwuncha Arthur Nwankwo) *Season of Hurricane,* Fourth Dimension Publishing (Enugu, Nigeria), 1993.

(As Agwuncha A. Nwankwo) *Shadows over Breaking Waves,* Fourth Dimension Publishing (Enugu, Nigeria), 1993.

(As Agwuncha A. Nwankwo) *Sand Dunes and Windblows,* Fourth Dimension Publishing (Enugu, Nigeria), 1994.

*The African Possibility in Global Power Struggle,* Fourth Dimension Publishing (Enugu, Nigeria), 1995.

*SIDELIGHTS:* Through the medium of the printed word, Arthur Agwuncha Nwankwo has been trying to help guide the nation of Nigeria through a succession of political and military upheavals, and toward a hoped-for democracy, since the Biafran rebellion of the late 1960s. At times his writings have reflected his own deep personal involvement in the political affairs of his homeland, as can be seen in the title of his 1984 book, *Justice, Sedition Charge, Conviction & Acquittal of Arthur Nwankwo, Author of "How Jim Nwobodo Rules Anambra State."*

Nwankwo's first book was *The Making of a Nation: Biafra,* co-written in 1969 with Samuel Udochukwu Ifejika when both were young academics who had been hurled into the midst of a civil war that was marked by the starvation or near-starvation of vast numbers of civilians. Biafra, a region of eastern Nigeria, proclaimed its independence in May, 1967; the crisis lasted until the collapse of the rebellion in January, 1970. *The Making of a Nation* delineated the problems that led to the secession, including the unifying of disparate Nigerian regions by the British in 1914, the liberation from colonial rule in 1960, a crisis in western Nigeria in 1962, a bitter controversy over the census, a crisis at the university, and two military coups, the second of which occurred in 1966.

Nwankwo and Ifejika wrote from the standpoint of those who had not only witnessed but also experienced the national crisis, and thus provided, for Western readers, a novel perspective, one which attempted to be both scholarly and impassioned. As a *Times Literary Supplement* writer put it, "They look at the issues with a scholarly eye, but their scholarship is tempered by their own basic sympathies." Although the critic found the authors' accounts of events sometimes "oversimplified," the reviewer continued, "At the same time, it is difficult to question the reality of the circumstances." Admitting

that true objectivity was probably impossible in the midst of the war, the reviewer concluded that the authors had helped readers to understand the crisis in historical perspective. *Saturday Review* contributor Stephen Jervis, although commenting on the "subjective" and "propagandistic" slant of the book, applauded it for being "abundantly documented." Particularly useful, Jervis noted, were the appendices containing official documents of aborted peace talks, and the "vivid postcript" by Nwankwo describing the wartime suffering of the Biafran populace. For Auberon Waugh, writing in the *Spectator,* the book was "a work of extraordinary erudition and moderation" in which "[e]veryone's motives are most scrupulously and critically examined." Waugh asserted, "One is happy to see this record of events bound between hard covers, before the Foreign and Commonwealth office machine can distort or suppress what so many Africans know to be the truth." In the *Listener,* Richard West wrote that, considering the authors' Biafran sympathies, they were "commendably fair to their present Nigerian enemies" and that they showed "a spirited, very Biafran disregard for authority." A *Choice* reviewer called the book "excellent," praising its "reasonably balanced evidence, perceptive questions, and . . . scholarly approach." The reviewer indicated that the book was useful as a political record in spite of its subjectivity.

After the civil war, Nwankwo offered the world a retrospective look at the origins, conduct, and aftermath of the rebellion in his 1972 book, *Nigeria: The Challenge of Biafra.* As summarized in the *Times Literary Supplement,* Nwankwo listed three stages in the Biafran rebellion: " 'the period of blunders' . . . [,] the period of adaptation and maturity . . . [,] and finally a period of retrogression, of 'decay and death.' " Declared the *Times Literary Supplement* critic, "All this is well, if over-consciously, told. We have for the first time an insider's insight [into many of the details of the Biafran crisis]. . . . Indeed in the central chapters, the best part of the book, much of Mr. Nwankwo's information is either new in the literature or confirms what hitherto was nothing more than a surmise." Praising the author's "successful achievement of objectivity," the reviewer declared that Nwankwo's study attained "an authenticity and value that no outsider's account can ever hope to surpass or even equal."

Nwankwo did not publish another book until *Nigeria: My People, My Vision* in 1979. After that, he published approximately one book per year on various aspects of the developing situation in his country, as the Buhari junta was followed by the military administration of Babangida and a putative attempt to transfer power from military to civilian hands. In two books from the mid-1980s, *How Jim Nwobodo Rules Anambra State* and *Corruption in Anambra State: The Jim Nwobodo Legacy,* Nwankwo risked a direct confrontation with a powerful state leader in Nigeria, during a period when the banning of politically controversial views was widespread.

Undeterred by a conviction on a sedition charge, Nwankwo proceeded to turn out book after book in which he forcefully examined political, social, and economic problems in Nigeria. In his 1990 work *African Dictators: The Logic of Tyranny and Lessons from History* he went beyond the borders of Nigeria to explore the history of dictatorships in a number of post-colonial African nations, such as Togo. The book is, in the view of Alfred Nhema, writing in the *International Journal of African Historical Studies,* intended as a warning that dictatorships are historically doomed and that democracy is the true goal of African nationalism. Nhema took issue with this view on the grounds that a preference for democracy over dictatorship was an unproven assumption. Nwankwo, Nhema remarked, "simply chooses not to develop [the] important conceptual issue of what comes first, democracy or development." Further, Nhema believed, the "democracy debate" concerning Africa required distinctions to be made among several types of democracies: "liberal, statist or popular." Nevertheless, wrote Nhema, the presentation of the rise and fall of dictatorships was "inspiring in its own way" and contained "some interesting accounts." The book, the reviewer stated, "has fulfilled its stated mission of warning African dictators of the futility of excluding the majority of the people from the political process."

In his 1993 book *Nigeria: The Political Transition and Future of Democracy,* Nwankwo analyzes the theoretical and historical underpinnings of the difficulties in transferring power from the military to civilians under Babangida's rule, a process which led, in the assessment of *African Studies Review* contributor Emmanuel Nnadozie, to "systematic social, political and economic disaster." Although criticizing Nwankwo's apparently socialist views as "obsolete," Nnadozie called the volume a "brilliant book" which "exposes and articulates Babangida's fraudulent attempts to politically and economically reform Nigeria."

*BIOGRAPHICAL/CRITICAL SOURCES:*

*PERIODICALS*

*African Studies Review,* April, 1995, pp. 164-166.
*Choice,* September, 1970, p. 914.
*International Journal of African Historical Studies,* Volume 25, number 1, 1992, pp. 176-177.
*Library Journal,* July, 1970, pp. 2473-2474.
*Listener,* July 10, 1969, p. 55.
*Saturday Review,* January 16, 1971, p. 28.
*Spectator,* June 14, 1969, pp. 790-791.
*Times Literary Supplement,* July 31, 1969, p. 863; December 21, 1973, p. 1556.*

# O

## OCHS, Adolph S(imon) 1858-1935

*PERSONAL:* Born March 12, 1858, in Cincinnati, OH; died following a cerebral hemorrhage, April 8, 1935, in Chattanooga, TN; buried in Temple Israel Cemetery, Mt. Hope, NY; son of Julius and Bertha Ochs; married Effie Miriam Wise (daughter of Isaac M. Wise, leader of the Reform Jewish movement in the United States), February 28, 1883; children: Iphigene Bertha. *Education:* Attended Hampden-Sydney Academy; left school at the age of fifteen.

*CAREER:* Journalist and newspaperman, c. 1868-1935. Owner and publisher, *Chattanooga Times,* 1878-1935; owner and publisher, *The Tradesman,* 1879-99; general manager and chairman of the executive committee, Southern Associated Press, 1891-94; owner and publisher, *New York Times,* 1896-1935; owner and publisher, *Philadelphia Times* (merged with *Philadelphia Public Ledger*), 1901-13; director and executive committee member, Associated Press, 1908-35.

*AWARDS, HONORS:* M.A. Yale University, 1922; LL.D., Columbia University, 1924; Litt.D., University of Chattanooga, 1925; Litt.D., New York University, 1926; Litt.D., Lincoln Memorial University, 1928; LL.D., Dartmouth College, 1932; Chevalier of the Order of the Legion of Honor, France, 1919, Officer, 1924; National Institute of Social Science gold medal, 1929; American Philosophical Society member, 1931; Tennessee Newspaper Hall of Fame, 1969.

### WRITINGS:

*Address by Adolph S. Ochs before the Pulitzer School of Journalism, Columbia University*, privately printed (New York City), 1925.

*Adolph S. Ochs*

*A Memoir of Julius Ochs: An Autobiography,* Privately printed (New York City), 196?.

Contributor to periodical publication *Journal of the National Institute of Social Sciences.*

*SIDELIGHTS:* Best known as owner and publisher of the *New York Times,* Adolph S. Ochs began his career in journalism as an office boy. He went on to take over and revitalize, first the *Chattanooga Times,* and later the *New York Times* in August of 1896. The same year, he introduced the *New York Times*'s motto, "All the News That's Fit to Print." He became the majority stockholder of the *New York Times* in 1900 and continued to serve as its owner and publisher until his death in 1935.

Ochs was born on March 12, 1858, in Cincinnati, Ohio, to Julius and Bertha Ochs. The family moved to Knoxville, Tennessee, in 1864, where Julius opened three dry-goods stores. The businesses earned a considerable profit, but collapsed in the 1867 postwar financial panic that swept the nation, and in 1868, Julius declared bankruptcy. With little business acumen, Julius was never able to recover financially form the loss and the family suffered considerable financial hardships. Out of financial necessity, Adolph Ochs began working, delivering the *Knoxville Chronicle* and earning just $1.50 per week. Ochs kept the job for two years, and then moved in with relatives in Providence, Rhode Island, to help ease his parents' financial burdens. He stayed for only a few months before returning to Knoxville where he found a job as an office boy for Captain Rule's *Chronicle,* again earning just $6 a month. The experience turned out to be invaluable to his career as journalist as he soon began to learn the printing trade, and became a printer's devil at the age of fifteen.

After three years with the *Chronicle,* Ochs decided to move to California, though he only got as far as Louisville, where he found a job as a typesetter for the *Courier-Journal,* and soon became assistant composing-room foreman, and shortly thereafter, reporter. After writing a story about the burial of Andrew Jackson, Ochs realized that his talents lay more in the actual printing process and business side of journalism, than in reporting. Less than a year after he had left, Ochs returned to Knoxville. Ochs found a position as assistant to the composing-room foreman at the *Knoxville Tribune,* and soon became assistant to the *Tribune*'s business manager, Frank M. Paul. In 1876, he moved to Chattanooga with Paul, and editor, J. E. MacGowan, to work as the advertising manager for the failing *Daily Dispatch,* which folded a few months after his arrival. He was appointed receiver for the bankrupt newspaper and soon paid off all of the paper's outstanding debts.

Left without a source of income, Ochs and a fellow *Dispatch* printer, David Harris, decided to put the still-operable printing press into use and print the Chatta-nooga City Directory. The directory served several purposes. As Susan Barnes stated in *Dictionary of Literary Biography,* "The directory served two purposes: it revealed new avenues for expansion in the city that old-line Chattanoogan's had overlooked, and it introduced an enterprising young printer to some of the most influential businessmen and financiers of the city." In addition, Ochs and Harris earned enough money to survive during the six month period.

The *Chattanooga Times,* the only paper remaining in the city, seemed to be following the ill fate of the *Dispatch.* Circulation had dropped and the paper was losing money. When S. A. Cunningham put the paper up for sale, Ochs jumped at the opportunity. He convinced MacGowan and four other out-of-work printers to purchase the paper. With loans he secured though contacts he and Harris had made with the directory, a loan from the First National Bank of Chattanooga, and clever negotiations with Cunningham, Adolph Ochs secured half interest and became the new publisher and part owner of the *Chattanooga Times.*

Within the first year, circulation of the *Times* rose dramatically from the 250 subscribers the paper had when it went up for sale. Local advertisers clamored for space within the paper's pages, but the paper was far from making a sizable profit. Ochs put whatever profit was gained after paying his staff back into the operation of the paper. Through his determination, the *Times* became the voice of the area. As Barnes noted: "He advocated a nonpartisan city government, which became a reality He pushed for the building of a new sewer system, the founding of the University of Chattanooga, improvement of schools and theaters, and later the establishment of Chickamauga and Lookout Mountain National Parks. He sang the praises of the area in the columns of the Times and attracted new business, becoming recognized as a leader in the postwar South's Reconstruction." Finally, the paper became a huge financial success and Ochs bought the remaining half of the paper from Cunningham. Additional money was spent on buying a large house for his parents and siblings and relocating them to Chattanooga.

The *Times,* called "the Builder of Chattanooga," brought a great deal of commerce and outside investments to the city and land values soared. Hoping to make a fortune, Ochs invested heavily in large tracts of land around the city. The land he purchased, however, was full of sulfurous iron ore deposits and unsuitable to produce high-quality steel. Prices plummeted and Ochs ended up in debt.

Though he lost a significant amount of money in the land purchases, Ochs built a new plant for the *Times* on borrowed money. He was determined to buy and turn around the financial losses of a small, failing paper as he did with the *Chattanooga Times,* and began looking in New York. He attempted to buy the *New York Mercury,* but rescinded his offer over a moral disagreement with the papers partners, and focused, instead, on the *New York Times,* which a friend and *New York Times* reporter, Harry Alloway, told him may be for sale. Ochs immediately arranged to interview with Charles R. Miller, the editor of the *New York Times,* who had purchased the paper after co-owner George Jones's death.

With recommendations from such notable figures as President Grover Cleveland, Melville E. Stone of the Associated Press, W. B. Summerville of Western Union and Clark Howell of the *Atlanta Constitution,* among many others, Ochs took over the *Times* on August 18, 1896. He relocated with wife Effie and daughter Iphigene to New York, leaving the *Chattanooga Times* under management of his brother George and under editorial management of his brother Milton.

Ochs kept Miller on as editor and introduced the "All the News That's Fit to Print" motto in October 25, 1896, determined to separate the *Times* from the more sensationalist newspapers that were more popular in New York. Under Ochs's leadership, circulation doubled during the first year. The newspaper's $1,000 a day losses were reduced to just $200 a day and the public and competitors began to respect the paper's new personality. Ochs revamped the entire paper, leaving a signature that remains: he insisted the paper no longer print cartoons, and in the funnies' place, began a Sunday magazine. The book review, which formerly appeared on Saturdays, began to be a regular feature on Sundays, and eventually became a separate publication. On July 1, 1900, Ochs became the majority stock holder of the *Times.*

Much of the *Times*'s success can be attributed to Ochs's keen business acumen and to his ability to intuit the talents of his staff. He kept Charles Miller as editor-in-chief and hired Carr V. Van Anda as managing editor in 1904. Van Anda seemed to have an innate talent for gathering groundbreaking news and was integral to the *Times*'s success. Other important figures in the *Times*'s success were reporters William C. Reick, Arthur R. Greaves, and Henry Lowenthal, and business manager Louis Wiley.

Ochs was as well known for his charity work as he was for his dedication to the *Times.* In 1926, he chaired a committee to raise $4,000,000 for Hebrew Union College in Cincinnati; in 1911, he began appeals in his columns for donations to New York City's six most prominent charities, netting $3,000,000 over the next twenty years; and he contributed $400,000 for the building of the Julius and Bertha Ochs Memorial Building in Chattanooga.

Ochs died in Chattanooga on April 8, 1935, of a cerebral hemorrhage. He was buried April 12 in Temple Israel Cemetery, Mount Hope, New York. Long ranked as one of the world's best newspapers, the *Times* continued to carry on in the tradition of Ochs after his death. His daughter Iphigene, son-in-law, son, and grandson would each succeed Ochs as publisher of the *Times.*

*BIOGRAPHICAL/CRITICAL SOURCES:*

BOOKS

Berger, Meyer, *The Story of the New York Times, 1851-1951,* Simon & Schuster (New York City), 1951.
*Dictionary of American Biography,* Supplement 1, *New York,* Scribner, 1944.
*Dictionary of Literary Biography,* Volume 25: *American Newspaper Journalists, 1901-1925,* Gale (Detroit, MI), 1984.
Talese, Gay, *The Kingdom and the Power,* World (New York City), 1969.*

\* \* \*

## O'CONNOR, Geoffrey

*PERSONAL:* Male.

*ADDRESSES: Agent*—c/o Dutton, 375 Hudson St., New York, NY 10014.

*CAREER:* Documentary filmmaker, including films *At the Edge of Conquest: The Journey of Chief Wai-Wai* and *Amazon Journal,* and writer.

*AWARDS, HONORS:* Academy Award nomination, 1993, for documentary film *At the Edge of Conquest: The Journey of Chief Wai-Wai.*

*WRITINGS:*

*Amazon Journal: Dispatches from a Vanishing Frontier,* Dutton (New York), 1997.

*SIDELIGHTS:* Documentary filmmaker Geoffrey O'Connor is the author of *Amazon Journal: Dispatches from a Vanishing Frontier,* a book that complements his film by the same name. In *Amazon Journal* O'Connor chronicles his experiences during the seven years he spent filming in the rain forests of Brazil. With irony he describes the activities of indigenous Yanomani and Kayapo tribes and such caucasian outsiders as environmentalists, government officials, land grabbers, gold prospectors, and himself as a representative of the media. He discusses the consequences of the water and air pollution brought on by the gold rush and deforestation by ranchers and loggers, and the epidemics among native peoples caused by interactions with outsiders, foreseeing an ecological tragedy.

*Amazon Journal* fared well with critics. A *Kirkus Reviews* commentator praised O'Connor's depictions of his subjects and asserted that he demonstrates "considerable talent as a writer." The critic added that the work itself is a "literate, unexpectedly funny, and ultimately alarming book." Similarly, in *Publishers Weekly* a commentator called the overall work "engrossing" and the portraits in particular "riveting." According to Gilbert Taylor, writing in *Booklist, Amazon Journal* is valuable because it presents the true picture of life in the Brazilian rain forest. Taylor further predicted that the journal will become more valuable as the reality it presents is lost to development.

*BIOGRAPHICAL/CRITICAL SOURCES:*

PERIODICALS

*Booklist,* August, 1997, p. 1857.
*Kirkus Reviews,* May 15, 1997, p. 781.
*Library Journal,* September 15, 1997, p. 81.
*New York Times Book Review,* October 12, 1997, p. 38.
*Progressive,* October, 1993, p. 16.
*Publishers Weekly,* July 7, 1997, p. 57.*

\*　　\*　　\*

## O'DWYER, (Peter) Paul 1907-1998

*OBITUARY NOTICE*—See index for *CA* sketch: Born 29, 1907, in Bohola, Ireland; immigrated to United States, 1925; naturalized citizen, 1931; died June 23 (some sources say June 24), 1998, in Goshen, NY. Attorney and author. O'Dwyer was known in New York City as a man willing to take on the case of the oppressed, no matter how unwinnable it may have

seemed. A champion of the underdog, he represented unionists, civil rights activists, desegregationalists, and those with sympathy for the Irish Republican Army. O'Dwyer came to the United States as a young man, following in the steps of his older brother, William, searching for a better life. After graduating from St. John's University with a law degree in 1929, O'Dwyer was hired as a clerk by attorney Oscar Bernstein. He eventually was named a principal in the firm, which was later known as O'Dwyer & Bernstien. His law practice allowed him time to become active in, or at least attempt to take part in, politics. O'Dwyer's brother, William, was mayor of New York from 1946 to 1950, but he quit while a scandal brewed. O'Dwyer ran for political office six times and was successful in his bids only twice, serving as city councilman from 1963 to 1965 and as council president from 1973 to 1977. He lost contests twice for the U.S. Senate, once for the House and a mayoral primary. However, he seemed to work well from the outside and never let his campaign failures keep him from participating in the political arena. Some of his best-known cases were politically charged. O'Dwyer pushed for the creation of Israel and represented the American contingent of the Irgun Zvai Leumi, which later resulted in him being honored by former Israeli prime minister Menachem Begin. He also won a case against Metropolitan Life Insurance that led to blacks moving into a housing complex in Manhattan. Along the way he campaigned against the Vietnam War and British rule of Ireland. Some people characterized O'Dwyer's rebelliousness as a result of living in British-occupied Ireland as a youth. O'Dwyer was a national coordinator for the American League for an Undivided Ireland, founder of the American Committee for Ulster Justice, and founder and first president of New York City's Irish Institute. He wrote his autobiography, *Counsel for the Defense,* and planned a biography of his brother William. O'Dwyer stayed active in the city well into his eighties and was appointed by former New York mayor David Dinkins as liaison to the United Nations in 1990.

*OBITUARIES AND OTHER SOURCES:*

BOOKS

*Political Profiles: The Johnson Years,* Facts on File, 1976.

PERIODICALS

*Chicago Tribune,* June 25, 1998, sec. 3, p. 12.
*New York Times,* June 25, 1998, p. B9.
*New Republic,* January 5-12, 1980, pp. 37-38.
*Washington Post,* June 26, 1998, p. C8.

## O'FLYNN, Criostoir 1927-
### (Criostoir O Floinn)

*PERSONAL:* Born December 18, 1927, in Limerick, Ireland; son of Richard (a coal seller and deliveryman) and Elizabeth (Connolly) O'Flynn; married Rita Beegan, 1952; children: Colm, Ruairi, Raoimhe, Rionach, Eanna, Niamh, Ciaran. *Education:* Qualified as teacher at St. Patrick's Teacher Training College; received degrees from National University and Trinity College, Dublin.

*ADDRESSES: Home*—47 Pairc Arnold, Dun Laoghaire, County Dublin, Ireland.

*CAREER:* Poet, playwright, and writer, 1967—. Worked as a teacher, broadcaster, journalist, lecturer and in public relations, in England and Ireland.

*MEMBER:* Aosdana (Irish government-sponsored allegiance of artists and writers).

*AWARDS, HONORS:* Awarded bursary by Abbey Theatre, 1973; Oireachtas drama prize; Douglas Hyde Memorial Award, for *Cota Ban Chriost, or, The Order of Melchizedek.*

*WRITINGS:*

POETRY

(Editor) Michael Hogan, *Drunken Thady and the Bishop's Lady: A Legend of Thomond Bridge, by Michael Hogan, the Bard of Thomond,* Dun Laoghaire, 1977.
*Aisling dha abhainn,* Naisiunta Tta (Dublin), 1977.
*Summer in Kilkee,* Treaty Press (Limerick), 1984.
*"Hunger Strike" and Other Poems,* Foilseachain Naisiunta Teoranta (Dublin), 1984.
*Centenary: A Poem,* Foilseachain Naisiunta Teoranta, 1996.

Also author of *Banana, A Poet in Rome, The Obelisk Year, O Fhas go hAois, Aisling Dha Abhainn, Seaclaidi Van Gogh,* and *Eiri Amach na Casca.*

PLAYS

*Is e a duirt Polonius: drama tri mhir,* Oifig an tSolathair, 1973.
*Cluichi cleamhnais,* Foilseachain Naisiunta (Dublin), 1978.
*Cad d'imigh ar Fheidhlimidh?: drama tri mhir,* Oifig an tSolathair, 1978.
*Lamh dheas, lamh chle,* Oifig an tSolathair, 1978.

*Solas an tSaoil: Mair, a chapaill!,* Oifig an tSolathair, 1980.
*A Man Called Pearse: A Play in Three Acts,* Foilseachain Naisiuenta (Dublin), 1980.
*Homo Sapiens: Drama dha mhir,* An Gum (Dublin), 1985.

Also author of *In Dublin's Fair City, Land of the Living* (also known as *Romance of an Idiot*), *The Order of Melchizedek* (produced at the Dublin Theatre Festival), *Cota Ban Chriost, An Spailpin Fanach, Mise Raifteiri an File, Saint Hubert's Day, Is Fada Anocht, Taibhsi na Faiche Moire, Ficheall na Feile, Mair a Chapaill,* and *Aggiornamento.* Also author of the radio plays *One-Night Stand, The Price of a Father, Just Another Fairy Fort, Damascus, County Kildare, Na Cimi, Escape,* and *Cloch ar Charn.* Author of the teleplays *The Lambs, Oilean Tearmainn,* and *Legion of the Rearguard.*

TRANSLATOR

(Contributor of translated poems) *sruth na Maoile: Modern Gaelic Poetry from Scotland and Ireland,* compiled by Michael Davitt and Iain MacDhomhnaill, Conongate Press (Coisceim) 1993.
(Also editor) *The Maigue Poets; Fili ne Maighe,* Obelisk Books, 1995.
*Irish Comic Poems,* 1995.
*Blind Raftery: Selected Poems,* 1998.

Also translator of Dante's *Divine Comedy,* as *Tri Gheata na Sioraiochta,* and of *When Dasher Died (Six Poems on the Death of a Horse).*

OTHER

*Ticiti agus an fainne draiochta,* Oifig an tSolathair (Dublin), 1967.
*Scealta si/[maeve Costello a mhaisigh an leabhar seo],* Oifig tSolathair, 1975.
*An poc ar buile,* Foilseachain Abhair Spioradalta (Dublin), 1993.
*The Poets of Merry Croom* (biograpy), Obelisk Books (Dublin), 1994.
*There Is an Isle: A Limerick Boyhood* (autobiography), Irish-American Book Co. (Boulder, CO.), 1998.
*Consplawkus: A Writer's Life* (autobiography), Mercier Press (Dublin), 1999.

Also author of *An Poc ar Buile* and *Cead Cainte.* Author of the novels *La Da bhFaca Thu* and *Learairi Lios an Phuca.* Author of short story collections, including *Sanctuary Island* and *Oineachlann.* Author of books for junior readers and books in Irish for children. Contributor to the Irish quarterly *An Timire.* Author of weekly column for *Irish Press,* 1969-78.

*WORK IN PROGRESS: Final Pages,* an autobiography, expected in 2000.

*SIDELIGHTS:* Noted for his original insights into Irish life, Criostoir O'Flynn is fluent in both Gaelic and English. He has published several plays, short stories, and books of poetry. Born in Limerick, his interpretation of life in Ireland is generally considered more positive than that of other modern Irish writers. O'Flynn has published many works in English, and many more in Gaelic. Two of his best-known English works are *Sanctuary Island,* a short story collection, and his plays *Land of the Living* and *The Order of Melchizedek.* The *Dictionary of Irish Literature* notes that O'Flynn's themes focus "most notably upon a coalescence of realism and fantasy," and calls his *A Poet in Rome* "casual, curious, and uneven" but also "chatty and companionable" collection of poetry. This may be due in part to his bilingualism, as his work is peppered with idioms and expressions that show, according to a reviewer in the *Library Journal,* writing of *There Is an Isle: A Limerick Boyhood,* that the Irish language "is still alive in the West of Ireland."

A *Publishers Weekly* reviewer, writing about *There An Isle,* observes that the book offers a "conservative, positive and nationalistic view of the Limerick City of bygone days." O'Flynn's father was emloyed throughout O'Flynn's childhood in the 1930s, and while the family was still poor, this detail provides a decisive contrast between O'Flynn and other Irish authors who write of deserted or unambitious fathers during the same time period. Calling *There Is An Isle* "somewhat defensive," the reviewer for the *Ireland at Home Cafe* Web page praises the memoir as "a balanced view of life" in Limerick at that time, and praises O'Flynn for writing with realism and humor.

*BIOGRAPHICAL/CRITICAL SOURCES:*

*BOOKS*

Hogan, Robert, editor, *Dictionary of Irish Literature,* Greenwood Press, 1996.
*Leactai CholmCille X,* Maynooth University, 1979.
O'Flynn, Criostoir, *There Is an Isle: A Limerick Boyhood,* Irish-American Book Co. (Boulder, CO.), 1998.

*PERIODICALS*

*Library Journal,* September 1, 1998, p. 182.
*Publishers Weekly,* August 17, 1998, p. 62.

*OTHER*

*Ireland at HomeCafe,* http://www.emigrant.ie/newiah/tuesday/30.html (January 8, 1999).

\*   \*   \*

## OJO-ADE, Femi

*PERSONAL:* Born in Africa.

*ADDRESSES: Agent*—c/o Greenwood Publishing Group, Box 5007, 88 Post Rd. W., Westport, CT 06881.

*CAREER:* Writer.

*WRITINGS:*

*Analytic Index of Presence Africaine, 1947-1972,* Three Continents Press (Washington, DC), 1977.
*Rene Maran: Ecrivain Negro-Africain,* F. Nathan (Paris), 1977, translated as *Rene Maran, the Black Frenchman: A Bio-critical Study,* Three Continents Press, 1984.
*Colour and Culture in Literature: An Inaugural Lecture Delivered at the Obafemi Awolowo University, Ile-Ife on Tuesday, June 5, 1984,* Obafemi Awolowo University Press (Ile-Ife, Nigeria), 1987.
*Home, Sweet, Sweet Home,* University Press (Ibadan), 1987.
*On Black Culture,* Obafemi Awolowo University Press, 1989.
*Leon-Gontran Damas: The Spirit of Resistance,* Karnak House (London), 1993.
(Editor) *Of Dreams Deferred, Dead or Alive: African Perspectives on African-American Writers,* Greenwood Press (Westport, CT), 1996.

*SIDELIGHTS: Presence Africaine,* a journal of black culture launched by Alioune Diop in 1947, contains essays, studies, papers, poems, plays, and short stories by Africans and non-Africans, including Aime Cesaire, Julius Nyerere, Sekou Toure, Sartre, Gide, Leroi Jones, and Malcolm X. It contains information about the culture, development, and status of African people worldwide. Femi Ojo-Ade's *Analytical Index of Presence Africaine, 1947-1972* includes over 4,700 entries, nearly equally divided by author and subject. The author section also includes anonymous and corporate headings. The index is a valuable tool for those interested in black studies.

*Of Dreams Deferred, Dead or Alive: African Perspectives on African-American Writers,* which Ojo-Ade edited, is a collection of explorations by African critics of the connections between African and African-American poets and writers, including Langston Hughes, W. E. B. Du Bois, Richard Wright, James Baldwin, Gloria Naylor, Toni Morrison, Alice Walker, and Paule Marshall.

*BIOGRAPHICAL/CRITICAL SOURCES:*

PERIODICALS

*Choice,* March, 1978, p. 46.*

\* \* \*

**OLIVER, Reggie**
    **See OLIVER, Reginald Rene St. John**

\* \* \*

**OLIVER, Reginald Rene St. John   1952-**
    **(Reggie Oliver)**

*PERSONAL:* Born July 7, 1952, in London, England; nephew of Stella Gibbons (a writer). *Education:* Oxford University, B.A. (with honors), 1975.

*ADDRESSES: Home*—The Bothy, Wormington Grange, Broadway, Worcester, England. *Agent*—Margaret Ramsay Ltd.

*CAREER:* Actor and playwright. Arts Council of Great Britain, literary consultant to drama panel, 1983-86; Seeds Ltd., director of publications, 1986—.

*MEMBER:* British Actors' Equity Association, Theatre Writers Union, Dramatists Club (honorary president).

*AWARDS, HONORS:* International Theatre Awards, 1985; Time Out Award, for best fringe play.

*WRITINGS:*

UNDER NAME REGGIE OLIVER

*Imaginary Lines: A Comedy,* Samuel French (New York City), 1987.
(Author of adaptation) *Put Some Clothes on, Clarisse! A Farce,* Samuel French, 1990.
*Out of the Woodshed: A Portrait of Stella Gibbons,* Bloomsbury, c. 1998.

Also author of *Zuleika,* 1975; *Interruption to the Dance,* 1977; *You Might as Well Live,* 1978; *The Shewstone,* 1981; *Passing Over,* 1982; *Absolution,* 1984; *Back Payments,* 1985; *Rochester: A Dramatic Biography,* 1986; and *A Portrait of Two Artists,* 1986. Contributor to periodicals.

*BIOGRAPHICAL/CRITICAL SOURCES:*

PERIODICALS

*Times Literary Supplement,* August 21, 1998, p. 27.*

\* \* \*

**ORTEGA, Rafael Enrique   1952-**

*PERSONAL:* Born January 8, 1952, in New York, NY; son of Enrique and Josefina (Nieves) Ortega; married Guadalupe Cervantes; children: Gabriela Danielle. *Education:* Fordham University, B.A., 1974; University of Minnesota—Twin Cities, M.S.W., 1981.

*ADDRESSES: Home*—557 Gorman Ave., St. Paul, MN 55107. *Office*—Chicano Latinos Unidos en Servicio, Westport Bldg., Suite 103, 220 South Robert St., St. Paul, MN 55107.

*CAREER:* Chicano Latinos Unidos en Servicio, St. Paul, MN, executive director. Minneapolis Foundation, member; Coalition of Hispanic Health and Human Services Organizations, member.

*MEMBER:* National Organization of Social Workers.

*AWARDS, HONORS:* Nonprofit Excellence Award, Wilder Foundation, United Way; Coalition Builder Award, St. Paul Urban Coalition.

*WRITINGS:*

*Liberando la Teologia de la Liberacion: Aporte Biblico a la Teologia de la Liberacion,* Ediciones Paulinas (Bogota, Colombia), 1978.

*El Toreo Puro,* Diputacion Provincial de Valencia, 1986.

(With Juan de la Fuente and Miguel Samano) *Agricultura y Agronomia en Mexico: 500 Anos,* Universidad Autonoma Chapingo (Chapingo, Mexico), 1993.

*Ganoteros, Egipcios y Sobrecogedores,* Incipit Editores, 1994.*

\* \* \*

## ORVELL, Miles   1944-

*PERSONAL:* Born January 9, 1944, in New York, NY; son of Samuel (a commercial artist) and Mary (Bass) Orvell; married Gabriella Ibieta, May 31, 1987; children: Ariana, Dylan. *Education:* Columbia University, B.A., 1964; Harvard University, M.A., 1965, Ph.D., 1970.

*ADDRESSES: Office*—Anderson Hall, Department of English, Temple University, Philadelphia, PA 19122; fax 801-383-6186. *E-mail*—orvell@unix.temple.edu.

*CAREER:* Temple University, Philadelphia, PA, professor of English and American studies, 1969—. National Endowment for the Humanities, director of summer seminar for schoolteachers, 1991, 1993-95, and 1999.

*MEMBER:* American Studies Association (member of national council, 1996-98).

*AWARDS, HONORS:* Fulbright fellow in Denmark, 1988; shared John Hope Franklin Prize, American Studies Association, 1990, for *The Real Thing.*

*WRITINGS:*

*Invisible Parade: The Fiction of Flannery O'Connor,* Temple University Press (Philadelphia, PA), 1972, published with new preface as *Flannery O'Connor: An Introduction,* University Press of Mississippi (Jackson, MS), 1991.

*The Real Thing: Imitation and Authenticity in American Culture, 1880-1940,* University of North Carolina Press (Chapel Hill, NC), 1989.

*After the Machine: Visual Arts and the Erasing of Cultural Boundaries,* University Press of Mississippi, 1995.

(Editor with wife, Gabriella Ibieta) *Inventing America: Readings in Identity and Culture,* St. Martin's (New York City), 1996.

*WORK IN PROGRESS:* Senior editor, *Encyclopedia of American Studies,* four volumes, completion expected in 2001; *John Vachon: The FSA Years,* for University of California Press (Berkeley, CA), 2001; a history of U.S. photography, Oxford University Press, 2002.

\* \* \*

## ORWIN, Clifford   1947-

*PERSONAL:* Born February 9, 1947, in Chicago, IL; son of Franklin B. (a businessman, community leader, and philanthropist) and Gloria (Klopot) Orwin; married Donna Tussing (a scholar of Russian literature), 1969; children: Alexander Israel, Ethan Mordechai. *Education:* Cornell University, A.B. (history), 1968; Harvard University, M.A. (political science), 1972, Ph.D. (political science), 1976. *Religion:* Jewish. *Avocational interests:* journalism; participation in Toronto Jewish life, including a program to aid the homeless; various outdoor activities.

*ADDRESSES: Office*—University of Toronto, Department of Political Science, Toronto, Ontario M5S 3G3, Canada. *Agent*—c/o University of Chicago Press, 5801 Ellis Ave., Chicago, IL 60637. *E-mail*—corwin@ chas.utoronto.ca.

*CAREER:* University of Toronto, Toronto, Ontario, lecturer, 1973-75, assistant professor, 1975-79, associate professor, 1979-89, professor of political science, 1989—. Visiting professor at Michigan State University, 1980, Harvard University, 1982-83, University of Chicago, 1991-92, and Ecole des hautes etudes en sciences sociales, Paris, 1993.

*MEMBER:* American Political Science Association, Canadian Political Science Association, National Association of Scholars.

*AWARDS, HONORS:* National Endowment for the Humanities grants, 1986-87, for work on *The Humanity of Thucydides,* and 1996, for work on a book about compassion.

*WRITINGS:*

NONFICTION

*The Humanity of Thucydides,* Princeton University Press (Princeton, NJ), 1994.

(Editor with Nathan Tarcov) *The Legacy of Rousseau,* University of Chicago Press, 1997.

Also contributor to journals, including *American Political Science Review, American Scholar, Public Interest, National Interest, Jewish Political Thought,* and the *Journal of Politics.*

*WORK IN PROGRESS:* A book for the general public on the role of compassion in political life; a scholarly book on the problem of compassion in the thought of Rousseau; a series on articles on the Hellenistic Jewish writer Flavius Josephus.

*SIDELIGHTS:* Clifford Orwin, a professor of political science, broadened his coverage in his published works to address not only politics but also history and philosophy. Orwin's book *The Humanity of Thucydides* takes a look at that Athenian historian, who was responsible for writing about the conflict between Athens and Sparta in the later part of the fifth century, B.C. (the Peloponnesian War). Thucydides saw the Peloponnesian War as a good example of ineffective political leadership, misplaced imperialism, and stressed democracy. Orwin's focus on Thucydides, however, is more directed toward the title character's humanity and not necessarily his interpretation of history.

The book's central theme questions whether Thucydides' work was motivated by necessity or by justice. Orwin's analysis of Thucydides' work includes a look at famous speeches by leaders of the times, speeches which Thucydides wrote as an interpretation of what might have occurred at a particular event. One such speech is the Funeral Oration of Pericles, which was delivered over the dead soldiers' bodies after the first year of the conflict. The speech is one of the most famous of Thucydides' work, and has been compared to the Gettysburg Address by Orwin and others. J. A. S. Evans, writing in the *Virginia Quarterly Review,* appreciated Orwin's unique treatment of the subject, calling Orwin's position "refreshing." Evans concluded that the volume is "well worth reading." But *Choice* contributor R. P. Legon argued against the author's focus on Thucydides' approach, stating that an analysis of a historian should be treated in an historical context. According to Legon, Thucydides "should be judged by how well his ideas explain and draw inferences from the events themselves," otherwise Thucydides might as well have be a philosopher.

*Review of Politics* writer Laurie M. Johnson Bagby thought that Orwin's work provides an interesting context with which to consider contemporary political situations. In particular, Bagby found Orwin's argument that "Sparta's piety holds a regime together better than Athenian rationalism" a relevant lesson for twentieth-century political systems. In Bagby's opinion, the questions that Orwin's book raises about methods of governance may be its most significant offering.

Orwin, with Nathan Tarcov, has also edited a collection of essays on the thoughts of French philosopher Jean Jacques Rousseau. Rousseau wrote about a number of issues, including man's increasing alienation and split from nature, the bourgeois segment of society (which Rousseau found unsatisfactory and unattractive), evolution, ethnic conflict, the alienation of the artist in society, and compassion. Rousseau had a major impact on the evolving thought process regarding ethnic conflict, and he also influenced both left and right wing interests with the results of his thoughts on issues. Many of the contributing authors have a high regard for Rousseau's thoughts and contributions, but did not feel that his successors made any progress on the issues raised by Rousseau. *Choice* critic C. H. Zuckert called the collection's content "of uniformly high quality" and praised its "clarity of presentation."

Orwin told *CA:* "Everything I know I owe to my study of the great political philosophers from Thucydides onward and of the Biblical tradition; in my writing both scholarly and journalistic I try to apply their insights to contemporary problems."

*BIOGRAPHICAL/CRITICAL SOURCES:*

*PERIODICALS*

*Choice,* March, 1995, p. 1191; September, 1997, p. 214.
*Library Journal,* December, 1996, p. 97.
*Review of Politics,* spring, 1995, pp. 342-344.
*Virginia Quarterly Review,* autumn, 1995, pp. 747-749.

*OTHER*

*University of Toronto: Political Science Faculty,* http://www.chass.utoronto.ca/polsci/M-P.html (November 17, 1999).

*       *       *

## OUTLAND, Orland

*PERSONAL:* Male.

*ADDRESSES: Agent*—c/o Putnam Berkley Group, Inc., 200 Madison Ave, New York, NY 10016.

*CAREER:* Novelist; journalist with *Bay Area Reporter* and *Frontiers.*

WRITINGS:

*Death Wore a Smart Little Outfit,* Berkley (New York City), 1997.
*Death Wore a Fabulous New Fragrance,* Berkley (New York City), 1998.
*The Principles: The Gay Man's Guide to Getting (and Keeping) Mr. Right,* Kensington (New York City), 1998.
*Every Man for Himself,* Kensington (New York City), 1999.

*SIDELIGHTS:* Orland Outland said in an interview with Russell Rottkamp of *Q San Francisco* that he wrote his first published novel *Death Wore a Smart Little Outfit* to entertain himself, having given up the idea of seeing his book in publication because he was sick with AIDS. The mystery introduces the well-dressed detective and drag queen Doan McCandler and his straight female pal Binky van de Kamp, a woman living on a trust fund of thirty thousand dollars a year. She and Doan are forever broke, and each has a middle-class relationship—Doan with Stan, a struggling artist, and Binky with Luke, a policeman. When four artists are murdered, Stan is arrested as the suspect, and Doan, Binky, and Luke scour San Francisco to find the real killers. Rottkamp called the writing "wildly creative" with "outrageous and likable characters. . . . Always humorous, especially for those readers who desire a sharp edge to their humor." Rottkamp asked Outland why a drag queen made a good detective; Outland replied it is because "no one cares what a man in a dress thinks. They're obviously just a harmless lunatic."

Doan and Binky return in *Death Wore a Fabulous Fragrance.* The pair now have a detective agency, and their first client is a friend who has been accused of murdering a gay actor. Doan and Binky go to Los Angeles to work on the case where "they quickly find themselves surrounded by human piranhas," wrote Harriet Klausner in *Feminist Mystery Corner.* Klausner called the series "pure fun" with "campy characters" that give it "quirky charm." Klausner said Binky and Doan's "constant zings and witty ripostes are priceless. . . . A new series clearly on the cutting edge." Outland's third book, a nonfiction work, is *The Principles: The Gay Man's Guide to Getting (and Keeping) Mr. Right,* a guide to dating, filled with sound advice for the gay man seeking romance.

BIOGRAPHICAL/CRITICAL SOURCES:

PERIODICALS

*Advocate,* June 24, 1997, p. 109.

OTHER

*Feminist Mystery Reviews,* http://www.feminist.org/arts/mys—revfragrance.html.
*Q San Francisco* online, http://qsanfrancisco.com/qsf/guide/review-3.html.
*Under the Covers,* http://www.silcom.com/manatee/outland—death.html.*

\* \* \*

## OZEKI, Ruth L.
### (Ruth Ozeki Lounsbury)

*PERSONAL:* Female. *Ethnicity:* Japanese-American. *Education:* Smith College, graduated summa cum laude with degrees in Asian studies and English literature; did graduate work on classical Japanese literature.

*ADDRESSES: Home*—New York City and New Brunswick, British Columbia. *Agent*—c/o Viking, 375 Hudson St., New York, NY 10014.

*CAREER:* Documentary and dramatic filmmaker for television and the theater; films have been shown on PBS and at the Sundance Film Festival. Kyoto Sangyo University, former faculty member; worked as production designer for horror movies, beginning 1985; later worked for Japanese television and directed and produced documentary programs for network television.

*AWARDS, HONORS:* Japanese Ministry of Education fellowship; New Visions winner, San Francisco Film and Video Festival, 1995, for *Body of Correspondence;* Kiriyama Pacific Rim Book Prize, 1998, for *Halving the Bones;* also recipient of other awards and grants.

WRITINGS:

(As Ruth Ozeki Lounsbury) *Body of Correspondence* (film), c. 1994.
(As Ruth Ozeki Lounsbury) *Halving the Bones* (film), 1995.
*My Year of Meats* (novel), Viking (New York City), 1998.

*SIDELIGHTS:* Filmmaker and author Ruth L. Ozeki's documentary and dramatic films have been shown on

PBS, at the Sundance Film Festival, and at universities and colleges across the country. Ozeki's first novel, *My Year of Meats,* was described by Darcy Lockman in *Entertainment Weekly* as "juicy as a good burger." In the book, Jane Takagi-Little is the daughter of a Midwestern father and a Japanese mother. She is hired by BEEF-EX, a lobbying group in the United States, to work on the production of a television series, *My American Wife,* that promotes the sale of American meat in Japan. The series features a different, ideal, middle-class American family each week, and the episodes are dubbed for their Japanese audience. Each show features a recipe made with American beef, such concoctions as "Coca-Cola Roast," "Texas-style Beefy Burritos," and "Beef Fudge." In Japan, Akiko Ueno, wife of the promoter of the series, prepares the dishes for her abusive husband. Akiko, who is unable to conceive, eats large amounts of meat at his insistence. He feels the diet will increase her fertility, but Akiko becomes bulimic to keep her weight down and prevent pregnancy.

As Jane travels the United States looking for guest families, she begins to question the image of Americans that is being presented. When she is asked to take over for the Japanese director, she films a Mexican family, a large biracial Louisiana family, and a lesbian, interracial, vegetarian couple to portray a more accurate vision of the diversity of America. When Jane's more human episodes appear, Akiko begins to have hope of a better life away from her husband.

Jane learns of the chemicals and pesticides used in the raising of cattle and becomes uncomfortable with her job of promoting beef. "After years of coping with gynecological problems, she stumbles upon the knowledge that she is a DES daughter," wrote Nora Cody in *In Motion Magazine.* Cody said the descriptions of a slaughterhouse and feedlot "are truly harrowing. Ozeki has clearly done her research and manages to make the complex subject of hormone exposure both clear and compelling." *Booklist* reviewer Joanne Wilkinson, on the other hand, felt Ozeki "overloads her narrative with too many issues." "*My Year of Meats* deals with the cross-pollination of people and values, toxicity in meat, synthetic estrogens, camera angles, and the ever-pertinent issue of perspective and reliability in the media," wrote Nina Mehta for *Salon* online. "The only problem is that Ozeki's novel sometimes feels as much like a Lifetime movie as a complex, hard-hitting expose." *New York Times Book Review* reviewer Lise Funderburg called *My Year of Meats* "a cunning burlesque" and felt that the concerns raised are often "seamlessly incorporated into the plot; at other times,

Ozeki . . . allows her fiction to be overshadowed by her message."

At the novel's end, Akiko, inspired by her images of America, flees to the United States where she is warmly received by the vegetarian lesbians who help her overcome cultural discrimination. Hannah Beech wrote in *Time International* that although her "place in the world is determined by genetics, Akiko's positioning is driven by her own will. It is with this force, and with the hope that Akiko can find a home in the diverse patchwork of American states, that Ozeki hits her stride and allows her novel to leave the pessimistic realm of satire for the more uplifting world of parable."

*Library Journal* reviewer Shirley N. Quan called Ozeki's work "unique in presentation, yet moving and entertaining." "Character gems and exquisite plotting make this a treasure to read, but the real sizzle is in the take on beef: grilled between Oprah and Ozeki, every burger now deserves a long, hard look," said a *Kirkus Reviews* writer. "Wonderfully wild," was Laura Shapiro's description of the book in *Newsweek,* adding that the book "could be called a screed, and probably will be by the beef industry. But this is a genuine novel, and a deft one. . . . Funny, charming, and yes, political . . . a feast that leaves you hungry for whatever Ozeki cooks up next."

## BIOGRAPHICAL/CRITICAL SOURCES:

### PERIODICALS

*Booklist,* April, 1998, p. 1278.
*Entertainment Weekly,* June 26, 1998, p. 120.
*Kirkus Reviews,* April 1, 1998, p. 431.
*Library Journal,* May 1, 1998, p. 139.
*Newsweek,* August 10, 1998, p. 65.
*New York Times Book Review,* July 26, 1998, p. 19.
*Publishers Weekly,* October 27, 1997, p. 25; March 30, 1998, p. 65.
*Time International,* September 14, 1998, p. 48.

### OTHER

*In Motion Magazine,* http://www.inmotionmagazine.com/ozeki.html.
*Salon,* http://www.salon1999.com/books/sneaks/1998/07/01.
*Sundance: Festival,* http://www.sundancechannel.com/festival/films/txt/halvingb.html (November 17, 1999).
*Women of Color Film and Video Festival: About the Artist,* http://www2.ucsc.edu/woc/artists.html (November 17, 1999).*

# P-Q

## PADILLA, Ernesto Chavez 1944-

*PERSONAL:* Born March 9, 1944, in Las Cruces, NM; son of Vidal Eduardo (a migrant worker) and Tomasa (a migrant worker) Padilla. *Education:* Sacramento State College (now California State University, Sacramento), graduated, 1968; earned Ph.D., 1986.

*CAREER:* California State University, Bakersfield, assistant professor of English. Lalo Press, La Jolla, CA, publisher and editor.

*AWARDS, HONORS:* Ford Foundation fellow.

*WRITINGS:*

(With Reymundo Gamboa) *The Baby Chook and Other Remnants,* Other Voices (Tempe, AZ), 1974.

*Cigarro Lucky Strike,* MidiammiX (San Francisco, CA), 1986.

(Contributor) Cesar A. Gonzalez-T., editor, *Rudolpho A. Anaya: Focus on Criticism,* Lalo Press (La Jolla, CA), 1990.

(Contributor) Evelyn F. Brod and Carol J. Brady, editors, *Viajemos 2001,* Macmillan (New York City), 1990.

(Contributor) Catherine Kohler, editor, *What Yellow Is,* Chard (Bakersfield, CA), 1991.

Contributor to periodicals, including *Imagine, Officio, Orpheus,* and *Quinto Sol.*

*SIDELIGHTS:* The literary output of Ernesto Chavez Padilla is relatively modest in quantity, but his poems and short stories have attracted the praise of critics. His first published work was the poem "The Ohming Instick," which appeared first in the Chicano literary jour-nal *Quinto Sol* and later in several anthologies. In an interview for the *Dictionary of Literary Biography,* Padilla explained that the poem was conceived originally as an alternative for a college dissertation on the education of the disadvantaged. It is the story of a Mexican boy in an American school who is asked to speak in class about homing pigeons. He knows a great deal about homing pigeons because he has one of his own, but his English fails him, and he is punished. In the office of the vice principal, angry and humiliated, the boy determines that he will leave school and, like the homing pigeon, will return to the source of his comfort. He will work with his father in the cotton fields, where he will be loved and appreciated.

Another poem, "Darkness on the Delta," revolves around what *Dictionary of Literary Biography* contributor Edwin John Barton described as "shards of light that manage to penetrate an immense darkness"—shards of "[i]nsight and hope . . ., vision and belief," and optimism, fragments of "[t]hat which is worth living for . . . the faces in a crowded room, a visit with old friends, the preservation through performance of a musical tradition."

The success of his poems inspired Padilla to attempt short fiction. In his stories, Barton wrote, Padilla "recalls what it was like to be a Chicano in California in the 1950s and 1960s" in "semi-autobiographical account[s] of life in the barrio and of the cross-cultural struggles that attend those who escape." As a boy in the San Joaquin Valley, the author had lived in the barrio of Tulare and spent summers in the fields with his parents. Barton commented that the series "The Santiago Stories" (not yet published) "are not intended to explore and define the unique properties of Chicano experience so much as to express the sense in which the Chicano's struggle is parallel to all struggles." Barton found the stories "vivid and entertaining," but he observed that another story, "Fina, I Am Fina," represents an even more impressive achievement: "In this story Padilla finds an authentic voice in the person of a retired letter carrier who feels compelled to tell a story of petty sin, guilt, and despair before he dies." The achievement is that "[t]he teller of the tale here . . . can speak of the small comedies as well as the minor tragedies of ordinary life."

Padilla became an assistant professor of English at California State University in Bakersfield. He also created Lalo Press to promote the work of other Chicano writers. These endeavors, Barton observed, "reflect his commitment to furthering the cause of Chicano literature." It is a cause about which Padilla is firmly optimistic. He told Barton, "After all, it wasn't but thirty years ago when the majority of Chicanos were migrant farm workers (as I was) or exploited factory workers in the cities. The talent is here. . . . Let's give them another fifty years. We'll have a Pulitzer prize winner. Give us eighty years, and we'll have a Nobel prize winner."

*BIOGRAPHICAL/CRITICAL SOURCES:*

*BOOKS*

*Dictionary of Literary Biography,* Volume 122: *Chicano Writers, Second Series,* Gale (Detroit, MI), 1992.*

\*    \*    \*

**PARK, Therese   1941-**

*PERSONAL:* Born February 15, 1941, in Taegu, Korea; immigrated to United States, 1966; daughter of Chung Ho Suh (an export/import business owner) and Jee Ja Chung; married Bong Soon Park (a civil engineer), July 22, 1967 (divorced, 1987); married Bruce Hansen (a computer analyst), October 12, 1990; children: Susanne, Irene, Christine. *Citizenship:* United States. *Ethnicity:* "Asian (Korean)." *Education:* Seoul National University School of Music, B.A., 1964; Ecole Normale de Musique de Paris, France, M.A., 1966; studied creative writing at the University of Missouri. *Religion:* Catholic.

*ADDRESSES: Home*—10500 Lee Blvd., Leawood, KS, 66206. *Agent*—Publicity Director, Spinsters Ink, 32 East First St., Ste. 330, Duluth, MN 55802. *E-mail*—Theresepark@MSN.com.

*CAREER:* Cellist with the Kansas City Symphony/Philharmonic, 1966-96. Nazarene College, Graceland College, instructor of cello, 1982-84; private cello teacher for fifteen years.

*MEMBER:* Korean Institute for Human Rights, Kansas City Chapter, Toastmasters Club.

*AWARDS, HONORS:* Women's National Book Association, Reading Group Choices for 1998.

*WRITINGS:*

*A Gift of the Emperor,* Spinsters' Ink (Duluth, MM), 1997.

Contributor of articles to publications such as *Seoul National University Press, Maryknoll Magazine, Our Family in Canada, Best Times in Johnson County, Kansas,* and *The Kansas City Star.*

*WORK IN PROGRESS: Migrating Bird,* the sequel to *A Gift of the Emperor.* As Park told *CA:* "In my new book, Soon-ah's main focus is self-discovery and self-restoration. . . . Returning home in North Korea from a Japanese military brothel, Soon-ah finds her townspeople judgmental about her abduction and sex-slavery. Besides dealing with her tormenting memories of abuse and rape. . . . The Korean war breaks out. In the South, while working as a laundry-room attendent in an American army base, Soon-ah meets an American pilot, who, in the beginning of the war, had mistakenly dropped a bomb on South Korean school children, but later singlehandedly rescued nearly a thousand war orphans from the ruined cities. After learning that his plane was shot down on another mission in the North, she commits her entire life to the orphans, reasoning, 'I must teach these children about those who saved their lives while endangering themselves.' "

*SIDELIGHTS:* Therese Park was born in Taegu, Korea, in 1941, and moved to Seoul when she was a teenager. She studied music at Seoul National University and continued her study of the cello in 1964 at Ecole Normale de Musique de Paris, France, where she earned a master's degree in performance. Park immigrated to the United States in 1966 after successfully auditioning for the Kansas City Philharmonic, now the Kansas City Symphony. Therese Park, a professional cellist for thirty years, was moved to write her first novel, *A Gift of the Emperor,* after watching a documentary film about Asian women forced into sexual servitude by the Japanese government during World War II. "It is about time for Westerners to know the truth about Hirohito's Reunification Policy of Asia," Park told *CA*.

The novel details the life of Soon-ah, a seventeen-year-old Korean schoolgirl, whose life is torn apart by the abuses her family suffers at the hands of the Japanese. In the course of the novel, "a horrible story beautifully told," according to Eleanor J. Bader in *Sojourner,* Soon-ah's family experiences grave brutality. Her father, a Presbyterian minister, is murdered by Japanese police, her mother is raped, and her brother is conscripted into the Japanese army. Soon-ah is abducted after being deceived by the Japanese, who promise her wartime service as a nurse. Instead, as one of "the Emperor's special gifts to the soldiers," she is sent to a military "comfort house" in the South Pacific, where she is forced to work in a brothel. Sadamu, a Japanese war correspondent who has become horrified by the war crimes committed by his countrymen, falls for Soon-ah, orchestrates her placement to a brothel for officers and eventually escapes with her to a tropical island. "I suppose we are meant to see Sadamu as a romantic figure . . . but his character unsettled me," noted reviewer Chris Leidig in the *American Reporter.* "He professes to care about Soon-ah and yet he does not help [her] to escape her life as a prostitute." However, "Soon-ah comes to the realization that even the tender Sadamu has control over her life," Leidig observed.

*Booklist*'s Mary Carroll described the novel as "a vivid re-creation of a devastating tragedy." Leidig commended the "wonderful sense of place" and characters of "dimension and subtlety." *Kirkus Reviews,* however, faulted "characters that seem more like one-dimensional witnesses than vibrantly complex fictional creations," but noted that "war crimes against women are memorably described here." Leidig found that Park "controls the story with a magnificent restraint that never allows the story to wander from its tight focus."

Park decided against a nonfiction approach to depicting the ordeals of the comfort women. "As a woman I wanted to express how they *felt,*" Park told Jeannette Batz in the *Riverfront Times.* "It's not the same physical thing we went through, but the comfort women symbolize a nation called Korea, and we are all connected." Speaking about her primary motivation for writing *A Gift for the Emperor,* Park told *CA*: "Writing deals with one's inner voice. After spending thirty years as a cellist with the Kansas City Symphony, I decided to let my inner voice resound. . . . As a woman born in the strictly male-dominated society of Korea, I learned that,

if a woman wants to be heard or seen, she must be as strong as a bull and as wise as a snake."

*BIOGRAPHICAL/CRITICAL SOURCES:*

PERIODICALS

*American Reporter Book Review,* September 20-21, 1997.
*Booklist,* September 15, 1997, p. 210.
*Kirkus Reviews,* July 15, 1997, p. 1056.
*Sojourner,* January, 1998.
*Riverfront Times,* October 22-28, 1997, p. 10.

\* \* \*

**PARSSINEN, Terry Mitchell 1941-**

*PERSONAL:* Born August 18, 1941, in Savannah, GA; married, 1963; children: two. *Education:* Grinnell College, B.A., 1963; Brandeis University, Waltham, MA, M.A., 1965, Ph.D., 1968.

*ADDRESSES: Office*—University of Tampa, Department of History, 401 West Kennedy Blvd., Tampa, FL 33606. *E-mail*—tparssinen@alpha.utampa.edu.

*CAREER:* Grinnell College, instructor, became assistant professor, 1966-73; Temple University, Philadelphia, PA, associate professor, beginning 1974; University of Tampa, FL, dean of College of Liberal Arts and Sciences, 1992-95, and professor.

*MEMBER:* American Historical Association.

*AWARDS, HONORS:* Institute for the Study of Human Issues, senior research fellowship, 1976; National Institute for Drug Abuse, grant, 1977-79.

*WRITINGS:*

*Secret Passions, Secret Remedies: Narcotic Drugs in British Society, 1820-1930,* Institute for the Study of Human Issues (Philadelphia, PA), 1983.
(With Kathryn Meyer) *Webs of Smoke: Smugglers, Warlords, Spies, and the History of the International Drug Trade,* Rowman & Littlefield, 1998.

Also contributor to numerous scholarly publications, including *English Historical Review, Journal of Social History, Victorian Studies, International Review of So-*

*cial History, Sociology Review, Medical History,* and *Journal of Drug Issues.*

SIDELIGHTS: Social historian Terry Parssinen, a professor of history at the University of Tampa, has specialized in the history of narcotics and their effects on society. His two books explore this subject, in particular as it pertained to nineteenth-century Britain. In *Secret Passions, Secret Remedies: Narcotic Drugs in British Society,* Parssinen traces the changes in British attitudes toward narcotic drugs from 1820 to 1930. In the early 1800s, such drugs were tolerated relatively casually in British society, as evidenced by the easy reception of Thomas de Quincey's *Confessions of an English Opium-Eater* in 1821. Within a few decades, however, such attitudes had given way to more serious concern, fueled by stereotypes of Chinese opium "dens." In the early 1900s, drug control policies were introduced—ironically, at a time when the numbers of addicts was actually declining. Despite some attempts to copy the America policy of making drug abuse a criminal offense, the British implemented a medical system of control.

Critic Virginia Berridge, in *History Today,* observed that Parssinen's study offers little new information on the subject of British drug policy, but added that his "analysis of the involvement of British firms in illegal morphine smuggling in the early 1900s is interesting and original." Berridge also commended Parssinen's review of data from convictions under the 1920 Dangerous Drug Act, from which he draws an "addict profile" for the period. Pointing out that Parssinen writes "with an eye on the continuing debate on U.S. drug policy," Berridge concluded that his suggestions in that area are "also eminently sensible." Similar praise was expressed by H. Wayne Morgan, who commented in the *Journal of Interdisciplinary History* that *Secret Passions, Secret Remedies* is "an informative and useful general account" that offers a "thoughtful, well-written, and concise overview" of its subject.

Parssinen's second book on the history of narcotic drugs, co-written with Kathryn Meyer, also drew some good reviews. *Library Journal*'s Philip Young Blue found *Webs of Smoke: Smugglers, Warlords, Spies, and the History of the International Drug Trade* an "authoritative and well-documented account" of illegal drug trafficking history in the early twentieth century. Blue considered the book "essential" for readers looking for "historical insight into the current narcotics debate." A reviewer for *Publishers Weekly,* however, complained that, though the book is well-researched and covers a fascinating topic, "the final result is disjointed." Both-

ered by the way in which the book digresses from the topic, the reviewer noted writing that was "more coherent" writing could have made the study more relevant.

BIOGRAPHICAL/CRITICAL SOURCES:

PERIODICALS

*Choice,* June, 1984, p. 1542.
*History Today,* September 1984, pp. 53-54.
*Journal of Interdisciplinary History,* autumn, 1984, pp. 329-330.
*Library Journal,* November 15, 1998, p. 79.
*Publishers Weekly,* November 2, 1998, pp. 57-58.

OTHER

University of Tampa faculty profile, http://www.utampa.edu/acad/clas/histpol/tpars.html (February 3, 1999).*

\*    \*    \*

**PARVIN, Roy**

PERSONAL: *Education:* Attended Swarthmore College.

ADDRESSES: *Home*—Slayer, CA. *Agent*—c/o Chronicle Books, 85 Second St., San Francisco, CA 94105.

CAREER: Freelance writer, c. 1997—.

WRITINGS:

*The Loneliest Road in America* (short stories; includes "The Loneliest Road in America," "Smoke," "The Ames Coil," "Trapline," "It's Me Again," "Ice the Color of Sky," and "A Dream She Had"), Chronicle (San Francisco, CA), 1997.

Contributor of short stories to *The Quarterly* and *Northwest Review.*

SIDELIGHTS: Roy Parvin's first book, a collection of short stories titled *The Loneliest Road in America,* saw print in 1997. The tales within are bound together by their setting in the Trinity mountain range in Northern California—the region where Parvin himself lives. As Michael Harrington reported in the Philadelphia *Inquirer,* "this is [acclaimed short fiction author] Raymond Carver country, an audacious choice of locale for a contemporary short story writer." Harrington went on to observe that "Parvin's characters are even more marginalized and lost than Carver's. Their lives are no less desperate."

The characters include, in the title story, an ex-minor league baseball player and lumberjack, maimed and mentally affected by a lightning strike, who befriends an adolescent who killed his abusive foster father; in "Trapline," a closeted homosexual game warden who also secretly poaches while mourning the death of a man he loved; in "Smoke," a Vietnam veteran with a marijuana farm who goes to extreme lengths to protect his crop from theft; and in "The Ames Coil," readers meet a woman who abandons a drug-addicted husband and an autistic son only to take up with a crazy inventor hiding out in the desert who thinks he is the successor to Nikola Tesla. Other stories in *The Loneliest Road in America* feature more conventional characters and situations, such as "Ice the Color of the Sky," in which a famous writer living in Alaska has to return and preside over the funeral of an older brother he has always disliked. In "A Dream She Had," a couple moves to Northern California from San Francisco—more to see if their relationship can survive her casual affair than for the ostensible reason of escaping his unhealthy work environment. According to Jim Shepard in the *New York Times Book Review*, the narrator of "It's Me Again" endures "some forced camping in an Army surplus tent, thrown out of the house by his second wife."

Critics have been overwhelmingly positive in their remarks about *The Loneliest Road in America*. Shepard praised the fact that "part of nearly all the stories' pleasure involves the amount of practical information they convey. We become privy to such occupations as setting choker cable and chip sealing; we learn . . . that painting the top leaves of your marijuana crop with watercolors may fool airborne observers into believing they're flying over wildflowers." Joanne Wilkinson in *Booklist* cited Parvin's "dreamy, seductive language," and lauded his knack for "revealing people at their core, in all their strangeness and vulnerability." A *Publishers Weekly* reviewer hailed *The Loneliest Road in America* as "an unforgettable collection, an awe-inspiring debut," while in the *Library Journal* Vicky J. Cecil applauded the author's "rhythmic prose" and declared that "Parvin effectively captures the inhabitants of Trinity Mountains." Harrington pointed out that in these stories "Parvin uses the sound of the fairy tale and American Indian legend," and concluded that the volume as a whole "is marvelous, a pure pleasure."

*BIOGRAPHICAL/CRITICAL SOURCES:*

*PERIODICALS*

*Booklist,* December 15, 1996, p. 709.
*Inquirer* (Philadelphia), February 2, 1997.
*Library Journal,* February 1, 1997, p. 110.
*New York Times Book Review,* March 2, 1997, p. 12.
*Publishers Weekly,* November 11, 1996, pp. 70-71.*

\*        \*        \*

## PASZTORY, Esther

*PERSONAL: Education:* Columbia University, Ph.D., 1971.

*ADDRESSES: Office*—613 Schermerhorn Hall, Columbia University, 1190 Amsterdam Avenue, New York, NY 11027. *E-mail*—ep9@columbia.edu.

*CAREER:* Art historian. Columbia University, New York City; professor.

*WRITINGS:*

*The Iconography of the Teotihuacan Tlaloc,* Dumbarton Oaks, Trustees for Harvard University (Washington, DC), 1974.
*The Murals of Tepantitla, Teotihuacan,* Garland Publishers (New York City), 1976.
(Editor) *Middle Classic Mesoamerica, A.D. 400-700,* Columbia University Press (New York City), 1978.
*Aztec Art,* H. N. Abrams (New York City), 1983.
(Editor with Kathleen Berrin) *Teotihuacan: Art from the City of the Gods,* Fine Arts Museum of San Francisco (San Francisco, CA), 1993.
*Teotihuacan: An Experiment in Living,* University of Oklahoma Press (Norman, OK), 1997.
*Pre-Columbian Art,* Weidenfeld & Nicolson (London), 1998, Columbia University Press, 1999.

*SIDELIGHTS:* Art historian Esther Pasztory, who specializes in the art of Mesoamerica and the ancient Andes as well as art theory, has written and edited several well-regarded studies in the field of pre-Columbian art. Pasztory's first two books explored art from the city of Teotihuacan, which flourished from approximately 450 to 650 A.D. but was destroyed around 700 A.D. Relatively little is known about the people who built this city, and their art differs in significant ways from that of most other Mesoamerican cultures. In *The Ico-*

nography of the Teotihuacan Tlaloc and *The Murals of Tepantitla, Teotihuacan,* Pasztory considered a topic of great interest to specialists in Mesoamerican art and culture.

Pasztory's third book is a compilation of essays from a 1973 symposium on pre-Columbian art history at Columbia University. *Middle Classic Mesoamerica, A.D. 400-700* argues for "a three-fold rather than a two-fold division of the Mesoamerican Classic" period, in effect creating a "Middle Classic" period. Critics viewed the volume as a work that was certain to generate much debate. Michael D. Coe, in *Archaeology,* noted that some scholars would, like him, reject the contributors' argument for a "Middle Classic" period. Coe observed that this argument would survive only if it were confirmed by radiocarbon dating at the sites in question. Yet Coe pointed out that the book would be useful to specialists, and that it was generally well edited.

A reviewer for *Choice* also considered *Middle Classic Mesoamerica* a work that would generate debate, but found more to praise in its collection of articles, including "some exceedingly interesting new ideas about the origins of both the Maya and the Teotihuacan empires." Adrian Digby, in *The Antiquaries Journal,* expressed a similar view, noting that several of the book's essays were "controversial," but not all were fully convincing, although the book's "basic conception is sound and is a big step forward."

In her next book, Pasztory shifted focus slightly to concentrate on the Aztec empire. In *Aztec Art,* she argues that Aztec culture generated art works that were much more than expressions of mere violence, as was commonly believed. Discovering that certain deities appear exclusively in certain art forms, Pasztory theorized that this occurred because of cultural conflicts between the strictly defined classes: elites, priests, and common people. This highly stratified society, in Pasztory's view, contributed to an artistic culture that was vigorous and extremely complex. A reviewer for *Publishers Weekly* found this argument fascinating and supported with an abundance of detail, and concluded that Aztec Art is "a beautiful and indispensable survey." A contributor to *Library Journal* also gave the book high praise, citing its "fine text" that is "of interest to professional scholars" and "accessible to students and general readers" as well.

In *Teotihuacan: An Experiment in Living,* Pasztory puts forth a thesis critics found original and intriguing. Studying artifacts from what had been the largest, most organized city in ancient America, she found evidence of mass-produced ornaments that she theorized were evidence of a culture that celebrated collective values and avoided elitism. Because the inhabitants of Teotihuacan did not use their art to record historic events or to make representations of their leaders, their culture has remained mysterious to scholars; Pasztory used artistic artifacts to develop a comprehensive theory of Teotihuacan society. Some readers considered this a brilliant analysis. *Choice* reviewer C. C. Kolb wrote that Pasztory's thesis was innovative, written in an "engaging style," and was "argue[d] cogently." A *Publishers Weekly* reviewer, however, felt that Pasztory's argument was based too much on "educated guesswork" and that "too many of the ideas the book supports are based on feelings rather than solid scholarship."

In another critically respected overview, Pasztory deals with the entire subject of pre-Columbian art. *Library Journal* reviewer Sylvia Andrews found *Pre-Columbian Art* "beautifully illustrated," clearly written, and filled with "intriguing conclusions." Andrews especially admired Pasztory's comparison of different Mesoamerican cultures, and her use of artistic evidence to theorize about the beliefs of these cultures. Andrews "highly recommended" *Pre-Columbian Art* as a comprehensive introduction to the subject.

*BIOGRAPHICAL/CRITICAL SOURCES:*

PERIODICALS

*Antiquaries Journal,* January 10, 1986, pp. 160-62.
*Archaeology,* September/October, 1979, pp. 67-68.
*Ceramics Monthly,* June-August, 1997, p. 87.
*Choice,* September, 1978, p. 918; December, 1983, p. 564; July/August, 1997, p. 1843.
*Library Journal,* August, 1983, p. 1473; September 1, 1993, pp. 182-83; January 1999, p. 91.
*Publishers Weekly,* May 13, 1983, p. 46; March 17, 1997, pp. 69-70.

OTHER

Columbia University faculty profile for Esther Pasztory, http://www.columbia.edu/cu/arthistory/pasztory.html (March 5, 1999).*

*          *          *

**PATTERSON, Gardner   1916-1998**

*OBITUARY NOTICE*—See index for *CA* sketch: Born May 13, 1916, in Burt, IA; died of lymphoma, June 26,

1998, in Washington, DC. Economist and author. Patterson was a representative for the U.S. Treasury in Africa and the Middle East in the early 1940s, then was tapped to serve on the Greek Currency Committee in Athens in 1946, when he was only thirty years old. Upon returning in 1948 he served briefly on the economics faculty at the University of Michigan but left in 1949 for Princeton University, where he was a professor and director of the International Finance section. He moved through the Princeton ranks until he departed in 1966 to serve as deputy director general for the General Agreement on Tariffs and Trade (GATT, now the World Trade Organization), in Switzerland. He returned briefly to Princeton before heading back to GATT in 1969 and staying until his retirement in 1981. Patterson helped negotiate international treaties as well as resolve trade disputes. Along the way he wrote *Survey of United States International Finance, A Critique of the Randall Commission Report on United States Foreign Economic Policy, NATO: A Critical Appraisal,* and *Discrimination in International Trade: The Policy Issues, 1945-1965.*

*OBITUARIES AND OTHER SOURCES:*

*BOOKS*

*International Who's Who,* 60th edition, Marquis, 1996-1997.

*PERIODICALS*

*New York Times,* July 4, 1998, p. D6.

* * *

## PAVAROTTI, Luciano 1935-

*PERSONAL:* Born October 12, 1935, in Modena, Italy; came to the United States; son of Fernando (a baker) and Adele (a cigar-manufacturer worker; maiden name, Venturi) Pavarotti; married Adua Veroni, 1961 (separated, 1996); companion of Nicoletta Mantovani; children: Lorenza, Christiana, Guiliana. *Education:* Instituto Magistrale Carlo Sigonio, Diploma magistrale (teaching degree); studied voice with Arrio Pola and Ettore Campogalliani.

*ADDRESSES: Agent*—c/o Crown Publishers, 201 East 50th St., New York, NY 10022.

*CAREER:* Taught mathematics and gymnastics, 1955-57; insurance salesman in the late 1950s; debuted as a professional operatic tenor, April 29, 1961.

*AWARDS, HONORS:* Concorso Internazionale, 1961; Grammy Awards for best classical vocal soloist in 1978, 1979, 1981, 1988, and 1990; Emmy Award for Primetime Programming Individual—Outstanding Individual Achievement—Classical Music/Dance Programming, 1985; People's Choice Award for Music, 1986.

*WRITINGS:*

(With William Wright) *My Own Story,* Doubleday (New York City), 1981.
(With Wright) *Pavarotti: My World,* Crown, 1995.

*SIDELIGHTS:* One of the world's most popular and successful recording artists, Luciano Pavarotti has been acclaimed as one of the greatest operatic tenors of all time. William Wright, co-author of both *My Own Story* and *Pavarotti: My World,* says in his preface to the latter: "Opera gave the world Enrico Caruso and Maria Callas. Now there is Pavarotti." Critics have marveled not only at his bell-like clarity of tone and his unmatched ability to achieve exceptionally high notes, but also at his professional longevity and the nearly perfect preservation of his voice through almost forty years of singing. In addition, Pavarotti's popular success and international recognition are unrivaled by any other opera singer; his influence in the maintenance and promotion of interest and support for opera throughout the world is paramount.

Pavarotti was born on October 12, 1935, in Modena, Italy. His mother worked in a local cigar factory and his father, who was a baker, often sang in the chorus of a Modena opera house as well. Pavarotti quickly manifested a love of music to match his father's, joining the church choir at only five years of age, and mimicking the voices on his father's opera records at home. When he was twelve, Pavarotti contracted a blood infection and was taken to the hospital, where he lapsed into a coma lasting twenty hours. Despite the severity of this episode, he nevertheless made a full recovery and went on to play soccer throughout his teenage years. In his late teens, he met Adele Veroni, and they became engaged in 1954.

During this period, Pavarotti participated in an international music festival in Wales as part of the chorus of the Modena opera, which won first prize. This success, and the encouragement of both his parents, prompted him to continue his pursuit of singing. When the time came to select a career, however, Pavarotti turned his attention away from music, at least at first. He took a degree in education and became a mathematics and gymnastics teacher for a time, but eventually the attraction of opera proved impossible to ignore, and Pavarotti, with the blessing (and partial financial support) of his parents, began studying voice with Poli and Campogalliani. Pavarotti worked as an insurance salesman while training his voice.

1961 proved to be the pivotal year in Pavarotti's life. As the year opened, he was awarded the prestigious Concorso Internazionale prize, which included a leading role in an opera to be performed that year. On April 29, Pavarotti made his professional debut in Reggio Emilia, playing the part that would become his hallmark role: Rodolfo, in Puccini's story of impoverished artists, *La Boheme.* His performance generated considerable interest in the opera world, and brought the possibility of a career as an operatic tenor within reach. 1961 was also the year in which Pavarotti married his fiancee of seven years, Adua Veroni. One of the more long-lived unions among opera singers, the couple remained together for another thirty-five years before separating in 1996.

In 1963, Vienna had its first opportunity to witness Pavarotti's Rodolfo. As interest in him continued to grow, he performed Donizetti's *Lucia di Lammermoor* in the Netherlands, Austria, and Switzerland. His next "big break" came that same year, when Giuseppe di Stefano, who was playing Rodolfo at Covent Garden, became too physically depleted to perform and Pavarotti was asked to substitute for him. These shows were not only his first at England's Royal Opera House, they were his first televised performances. While television had been generally available in western countries since the early fifties, it was only in the early sixties—when television sets were cheaper and more reliable, and there was more programming for them—that it began to realize its potential influence as a medium for the general public. Just as prominent Shakespearean actors were using television to reach masses of viewers who had never been to the theatre, so classical musicians of all sorts were bringing full-scale concerts into people's living rooms; and Pavarotti was one of the most successful "ambassadors" of a classical mode to a popular audience.

By the time 1963 came to a close, Pavarotti had appeared in Spain, Czechoslovakia, Poland, and Hungary. He later joined opera legend Joan Sutherland on a tour of Australia over more than three months—this, after coming to the attention of Sutherland's husband, conductor Richard Bonynge. It was in the company of Joan Sutherland that Pavarotti made his American debut in 1965, with a return to *Lucia di Lammermoor.* He made

his first appearance at the New York Metropolitan Opera, the "Met," in 1968; it proved to be his foremost repeat venue or artistic "home."

In 1972, Pavarotti returned to take the Met by storm in the role of Tonio in *La Fille du Regiment,* delivering nine consecutive high Cs in the course of a single performance. This in turn led to an appearance on *The Tonight Show,* and a further increase in his notoriety and popularity. On February 1 of the following year, Pavarotti gave his first formal recital, in Liberty, Missouri, thrilling audience and critic alike. From this point on, Pavarotti's career continued steadily to gather momentum; he was singing to capacity crowds and breaking sales records with his albums. *O Holy Night,* his 1976 LP, became the first classical release to earn a platinum record. His 1979 collection, *Hits from Lincoln Center,* won him the first of many Grammy awards, and he became the main attraction (with a long-term contract) of London's Decca Records.

It was also during this period, however, that Pavarotti suffered his second brush with death, this time in an airplane crash near Milan in 1975. Exhibiting the resilience that has always been associated with him, Pavarotti claimed that the experience had primarily served to break a long-standing depression and revive his love of life. By the early 1980s, Pavarotti was a household name and international superstar. In response to the considerable clamoring after information about him and his life, he collaborated with writer William Wright on his biography, *My Own Story,* which appeared in 1981. The book consists of twelve short chapters by Pavarotti and Wright, interspersed between twelve testimonials by Pavarotti's friends and colleagues, including Adua Pavarotti, Joan Sutherland, and his first voice teacher. The following year, Pavarotti made his film debut as the star of *Yes, Giorgio.* By this time, Pavarotti was beginning to slow the pace of his performance and recording schedule, and, when the film failed to generate good reviews, many critics began to regard Pavarotti as "washed up" or "sold out." However, Pavarotti did not retire or stop performing throughout the 1980s, and made a comeback of sorts, given that his popularity never greatly diminished, in the 1990s as one of the "Three Tenors."

In 1995, Pavarotti and William Wright resumed their partnership to produce a second biographical volume, *Pavarotti: My World.* In his preface, Pavarotti wrote: "When I was a boy growing up, books were for me very serious, important things. Writing one myself, I feel I must say something profound, something that will change the world. But that is not me. I am a very simple person. In spite of all that has happened to me, I have tried to remain the simple person I started out. Maybe I have no choice."

*BIOGRAPHICAL/CRITICAL SOURCES:*

*BOOKS*

*Baker's Biographical Dictionary of Musicians,* Macmillan, 1984, 1992, 1997.
*Biographical Dictionary of American Music,* Parker Publishing Company, 1973.
*Contemporary Musicians,* Gale, 1998.
*Dictionary of the Arts,* Facts on File, 1994.
*Dictionary of Twentieth-Century Culture,* Gale, 1994.
*Encyclopedia of World Biography,* Gale, 1998.
Ewen, David, *The New Encyclopedia of the Opera,* Hill and Wang, 1971.
*International Dictionary of the Opera,* St. James, 1993.
*Legends in Their Own Time,* Prentice Hall, 1994.
*Metropolitan Opera Encyclopedia,* Simon and Schuster, 1987.
Morehead, Philip D., and Anne MacNeil, *The New American Dictionary of Music,* Dutton, 1991.
May, Robin, *A Companion to the Opera,* Hippocrene, 1977.
*New Grove Dictionary of Opera,* Macmillan, 1992.
*Newsmakers,* Gale, 1998.
*Oxford Dictionary of Opera,* Oxford University Press, 1992.
Pavarotti, Luciano, *Pavarotti: My World,* Crown, 1995.
Pavarotti, Luciano, *My Own Story,* Doubleday, 1981.
*Tenors,* Macmillan, 1974.

*PERIODICALS*

*American Record Guide,* January-February, 1994; March-April, 1994; May-June, 1994; September-October, 1994; November-December, 1994; January-February, 1995; March-April, 1995; July-August, 1995; September-October, 1995; November-December, 1995; March-April, 1996; July-August, 1996; November-December, 1996; May-June, 1997; January-February, 1998; March-April, 1998; November-December, 1998; January-February, 1999.
*Billboard,* February 26, 1994; April 9, 1994; September 10, 1994; October 1, 1994; November 16, 1985; April 9, 1994; May 13, 1995; March 23, 1996; September 20, 1997.
*Booklist,* September 1, 1995.
*Commentary,* October, 1996.
*Cosmopolitan,* November, 1980; November 16, 1996.
*Downbeat,* May, 1994.
*Economist,* May 30, 1981.

*Entertainment Weekly,* July 29, 1994; September 9, 1994; November 10, 1995; December 8, 1995; April 19, 1996; December 13, 1996; September 4, 1998; October 30, 1998; November 6, 1998.
*Harper's Bazaar,* September, 1988.
*Information Please Almanac,* 1995.
*Kirkus Reviews,* August 15, 1995.
*Knight-Ridder/Tribune News Service,* January 22, 1995; January 25, 1995; March 8, 1997.
*Library Journal,* March 1, 1981; October 15, 1995.
*Life,* October, 1980.
*Los Angeles Magazine,* May, 1994.
*Maclean's,* April 1, 1996; January 13, 1997; January 1, 1999.
*Multichannel News,* July 29, 1996.
*Newsweek,* March 5, 1973; March 15, 1976; March 7, 1977; March 25, 1996; June 22, 1998.
*New York,* May 18, 1981; November 13, 1995.
*New Yorker,* June 21, 1993.
*New York Times,* October 13, 1976; January 20, 1980; March 15, 1981.
*Opera News,* September, 1982; March 29, 1986; September, 1993; January 8, 1994; January 22, 1994; April 16, 1994; May, 1994; August, 1994; September, 1994; September-October, 1994; December 24, 1994; January 7, 1995; October, 1995; January 20, 1996; February 3, 1996; April 13, 1996; August, 1996; September, 1996; October, 1996; December 14, 1996; June, 1997; November, 1997; December 6, 1997; January 17, 1998; August, 1998; February, 1999.
*People,* November 17, 1980; September 29, 1986; March 11, 1996, October 3, 1994; November 6, 1995; March 11, 1996; December 7, 1998; December 21, 1998.
*Publishers Weekly,* August 14, 1995.
*Spectator,* November 25, 1995.
*Time,* March 26, 1984; July 18, 1994; April 17, 1995; March 4, 1996; October 28, 1996; December 28, 1998.
*Travel Weekly,* February 13, 1997.
*Wall Street Journal,* January 23, 1997.*

\*　　　\*　　　\*

## PEARS, Charles　1873-1958

*PERSONAL:* Born September 9, 1873, in Pontefract, Yorkshire, England; died in January, 1958.

*CAREER:* Artist, illustrator, and writer. Served as official war artist to British Admiralty during World War

I and World War II. Worked as magazine illustrator; painted posters for government agencies; served as president of Society of Marine Artists; work represented in exhibitions at museums, including Imperial War Museum, Victoria and Albert Museum, and Royal Academy.

*WRITINGS:*

*From the Thames to the Seine,* self-illustrated, G. W. Jacobs (Philadelphia, PA). 1910.

*From the Thames to the Netherlands: A Voyage in the Waterways of Zealand and down the Belgian Coast,* self-illustrated, Chatto & Windus (London, England), 1914.

(Illustrator) Mrs. Alfred Baldwin, *The Pedlar's Pack,* Frederick A. Stokes (New York City), 1925.

*(And illustrator) South Coast Cruising: From the Thames to the Penzance,* Edward Arnold (London), 1931.

Other self-illustrated books include *Yachting on the Sunshine Coast,* 1932, and *Going Foreign.* Illustrator of works by other authors, including *Two Years before the Mast,* John Masefield's *Salt-Water Poems and Ballads,* and *The Complete Works of Dickens.* Contributor to periodicals.

*BIOGRAPHICAL/CRITICAL SOURCES:*

*PERIODICALS*

*Saturday Review,* April 4, 1914.
*Spectator,* April 4, 1931.
*Times Literary Supplement,* July 9, 1931, p. 539.

*OBITUARIES:*

*PERIODICALS*

*London News,* February 8, 1958.
*New York Times,* January 30, 1958.*

\*    \*    \*

**PENN, Arthur**
   **See MATTHEWS, Brander**

**PEREZ, Raymundo   1946-**

*PERSONAL:* Born March 15, 1946, in Laredo, TX. *Education:* Attended Laredo Junior College, Metropolitan State College, Denver, CO, and University of Colorado; Oberlin College, B.A. (political science).

*ADDRESSES: Agent*—c/o Mexican American Cultural Center, 3019 West French Place, San Antonio, TX 78228.

*CAREER:* Poet, c. 1970—. Minority Mobilization Vista Program, community organizer in Texas. *Military service:* Served as gunner's mate in Vietnam.

*WRITINGS:*

*Free, Free at Last* (poems), Barrio (Denver, CO), 1970.

(With Abelardo Delgado, Ricardo Sanchez, and Juan Valdez) *Los Cuatro* (poems; title means "The Four"), Barrio, 1970.

*Phases* (poems), [Corpus Christi, TX], 1971.

*The Secret Meaning of Death* (poems), Trucha (Lubbock, TX), 1972.

(Contributor) Philip D. Ortego, editor, *We Are Chicanos,* Washington Square (New York City), 1973.

(Contributor) *El Quetzal Emplumece,* Mexican American Cultural Center (San Antonio, TX), 1976.

Editor of the newspapers *Los Muertos Hablan* (title means "The Dead Speak"), *Valley of the Damned,* and *Tierra Caliente* (title means "Hot Earth").

*SIDELIGHTS:* Raymundo Perez has been called a poet of social protest, "both a reflection and outgrowth of the Chicano movement," as Arcadio Morales commented in the *Dictionary of Literary Biography.* "Perez . . . sought to capture and interpret the social, political, and cultural anxieties of Chicanos through verse. . . . During his peak years as a poet . . . Perez advocated revolution." The rebellious nature of his poetry was reflected in Perez's behavior from an early age. He grew up in the notoriously tough streets of Laredo, attended four colleges before acquiring a degree in political science, and served in the armed forces in Vietnam. He was opposed to United States involvement in Vietnam and to the inequitable treatment that he believed Chicanos received there, treatment that was only one facet of the exploitation of Chicanos in the general population. In his first civilian job as a veteran, Perez worked as a community organizer for an affiliate of the Mexican American Youth Organization. His experience there did nothing to dispel his outrage at the social injustice to which Chicanos were subjected.

The early poetry collection *Free, Free at Last* exemplifies Perez's outrage, his defiance, and a style of writing that Morales claimed "did not comply with the way established poets wrote," a characteristic that is present in all of the poet's work. He added: "His poetry is primitive in the sense that it is stylistically raw and unrefined, and also because Perez's concern is less with fancy poetic devices: his primary focus is the message not the mode. His intention, then, is to awaken the reader with the sobering language of cold realities. He is a poet grasping for urgent answers to solve the suffering of his people."

In *Free, Free at Last* Perez rails against the cruelty of the military establishment and the exploitative nature of farmers and operators of labor camps. He defends his Chicano brethren and documents the history of the Chicano movement so that Chicanos will always remember their origins. "The message conveyed by the poet in this collection," wrote Morales, "is that a strong sense of self-awareness and identity is the key to individual freedom."

In the 1970s Perez was affiliated with Chicano underground publications. His newspapers castigated the political establishment, and the ruling powers of Texas retaliated with political repression and police harassment that escalated into beatings and at least one Chicano death. The poems included in the collection *Los Cuatro* reveal Perez as a bitter, truculent spokesperson for Chicano revolution. At the same time, they reflect what Morales called "the existential anxieties of loneliness and hopelessness." Despite the melancholy tone of some poems, Perez nonetheless promotes the revolution in such a hostile and insistent voice that some readers have inferred a concrete threat against the safety of the white opposition.

Perez's collection *Phases* explores poetically the plight—and the perseverance—of the Chicago farm worker. The plight he portrays in vivid, emotional images, Morales observed: "Readers are introduced to the issues of exploitation and injustice. . . . In this collection Perez wastes little time in striking out against farmers who hire and exploit workers, treating them like human machines"; he sees the farm worker "as a leaf, trodden upon and smashed into the furrow of the earth by the oppressor farm owner, until other, newer leaves inevitably fall and replace the dead ones." Perez uses the historical perseverance of the farm worker to assail the Chicano movement itself, which he portrays as weakened by internal conflict and diluted by increasing complacence. Perez still hears the workers' call for rev-

olution, but Morales suggested that the poet's "voice is less idealistic than in his earlier collections."

*The Secret Meaning of Death,* the last major collection, "represents a symbolic death for Perez as a poet," Morales wrote: "Despair and isolation are apparent." Yet Morales reported: "The collection as a whole is much better than any of his previous works. It is more refined, and Perez's ideas are crisper. . . . [R]eaders get a more powerful picture of what he was hinting at in *Phases*." The critic concluded: "Perez is best when he is introspective—probing deep into his heart for answers to questions wrought by his troubled psyche."

*BIOGRAPHICAL/CRITICAL SOURCES:*

*BOOKS*

*Dictionary of Literary Biography,* Volume 122: *Chicano Writers, Second Series,* Gale Research (Detroit, MI), 1992.

\*     \*     \*

## PERRY, Mark   1950-

*PERSONAL:* Born in 1950. *Avocational interests:* Reading, volunteer work.

*ADDRESSES: Agent*—c/o Viking Penguin USA, 375 Hudson St., New York, NY 10014. *E-mail*—markperry@msn.com.

*CAREER:* Journalist, beginning in the 1970s; *Nation,* correspondent in Washington, DC; *Veteran* magazine, editor.

*WRITINGS:*

*Four Stars: The Inside Story of the Forty-Year Battle between the Joint Chiefs of Staff and America's Civilian Leaders,* Houghton Mifflin (Boston, MA), 1989.
*Eclipse: The Last Days of the CIA,* William Morrow (New York City), 1992.
*A Fire in Zion: The Israeli-Palestinian Search for Peace,* William Morrow, 1994.
*Conceived in Liberty: Joshua Chamberlain, William Oates, and the American Civil War,* Viking (New York City), 1997.

*SIDELIGHTS:* Journalist Mark Perry has written histories that have received critical praise for their thorough research and balanced analysis of complex subjects. His book *Four Stars: The Inside Story of the Forty-Year Battle between the Joint Chiefs of Staff and America's Civilian Leaders* is a history of the Joint Chiefs of Staff, an elite military group that contains the Chiefs of Staff of the United States Army, Air Force, and Marines, the Chief of Naval Operations of the United States Navy, and a Chairman of the Joint Chiefs of Staff. In *Four Stars,* Perry focuses on the conflicts during the Cold War era between civilian political leaders and military officials who wanted more of a voice in policymaking. According to Perry, these tensions were at their peak in 1967, when the Joint Chiefs considered resigning *en masse* to protest the Vietnam War strategies of the administration of United States president Lyndon B. Johnson.

Discussing *Four Stars* in the *New York Times Book Review,* Russell F. Weigley observed that Perry provides "thoughtful analysis" and "a wealth of historical detail." *Choice* contributor E. Lewis called the work an "exhaustively researched book," while *Booklist* contributor Roland Green labeled it "a well-written, thoroughly researched account." Richard B. Finnegan, writing in the *Library Journal,* commented that *Four Stars* would be "of great value to readers, whether they are armchair strategists or walk the corridors of power."

Perry conducted numerous interviews with Central Intelligence Agency (CIA) officials and staff members and obtained information from classified documents to produce *Eclipse: The Last Days of the CIA.* In *Eclipse,* Perry focuses on the management of the CIA from 1987 to 1991. Like *Four Stars,* the book garnered positive reviews from critics. *Library Journal* contributor Frank Kessler called *Eclipse* a "monumental work" as well as "eye-opening and provocative," while a reviewer in *Publishers Weekly* deemed the book to be "the most revealing inside look at the Central Intelligence Agency to date." *Eclipse* is "an evenhanded audit of the CIA's recent history" and "a first-rate briefing," observed a critic in *Kirkus Reviews. Choice* contributor P. H. Melanson labeled the book a "critical but balanced analysis" and "a vivid and disturbing analysis of politics and power within the CIA."

In *A Fire in Zion: The Israeli-Palestinian Search for Peace,* Perry provides an account of the 1993 peace accord between Israel and the Palestine Liberation Organization (PLO). To research his subject, the author interviewed PLO chief Yasser Arafat, then-Israeli prime minister Yitzhak Rabin, and other people involved in the events. A *Publishers Weekly* reviewer praised the book as "a major entry in the literature of modern diplo-

macy" and called Perry "a talented historian with a narrative gift." While a *Kirkus Reviews* contributor found that Perry's "ideas are not original," the critic conceded that *A Fire in Zion* is "an objective, well-researched historical backdrop to the Israeli-Palestinian peace accord."

*Conceived in Liberty,* Perry's study of the United States Civil War, compares the experiences of two officers who fought against each other at the Battle of Gettysburg. Joshua Chamberlain commanded the Maine regiment defending Gettysburg's Little Round Top against the attack of the Alabama regiment led by William Oates. "Perry's study of two lives of the war and its aftermath will definitely engage the buffs," wrote Gilbert Taylor in *Booklist.* While *Library Journal* contributor Robert A. Curtis found that the book's war sections are "somewhat weak," he called Perry's descriptions of Chamberlain and Oates's lives before and after the war "strong and gripping." A *Publishers Weekly* reviewer noted that Perry "is evocative and convincing in his presentations of backcountry Alabama and respectable Maine" as well as "lucid and perceptive in describing their battles."

## BIOGRAPHICAL/CRITICAL SOURCES:

### PERIODICALS

*Annals of the American Academy of Political and Social Science,* January, 1991, pp. 185-186.
*Booklist,* March 15, 1989, p. 1228; September 15, 1992, p. 106; November 15, 1997, p. 540.
*Choice,* October, 1989, p. 392; January, 1993, p. 883.
*Journal of American History,* June, 1990, p. 365.
*Kirkus Reviews,* August 15, 1992, p. 1046; April 15, 1994, p. 534.
*Library Journal,* April 1, 1989, p. 101; September 15, 1992, p. 79; August, 1994, p. 104; December, 1997, p. 122.
*New Yorker,* October 19, 1992, p. 127.
*New York Review of Books,* May 13, 1993, pp. 49-55.
*New York Times Book Review,* March 12, 1989, p. 9.
*Publishers Weekly,* August 10, 1992, p. 63; May 16, 1994, p. 55; October 13, 1997, pp. 62-63.
*Washington Post Book World,* April 9, 1989, p. 8; December 20, 1992, p. 9; August 7, 1994, p. 8.*

\*    \*    \*

## PETERSEN, Wolfgang 1955-

*PERSONAL:* Born in 1955.

*ADDRESSES: Agent*—c/o Columbia Pictures.

*CAREER:* Director and screenwriter, c. 1977—.

*WRITINGS:*

(Director) *Die Konsequenz* (title means "The Consequence"), Solaris Film (West Germany), 1977.

(Director and screenwriter) *Einer Von Uns Beiden* (title means "One or the Other"), Roxy-Film (Munich), 1978.

(Director and screenwriter) *Das Boot* (title means "The Boat"), Columbia Pictures, 1981.

(Director and screenwriter) *The Neverending Story,* 1984.

(Director and screenwriter) *Shattered,* Capella Films, 1991.

(Director) *In the Line of Fire,* Columbia Pictures, 1993.

(Director) *Outbreak,* Warner Bros., 1995.

(Director) *Air Force One,* Beacon Pictures and Columbia Pictures, 1997.

Also director of several films made in the 1970s for German television.

*SIDELIGHTS:* Wolfgang Petersen is a famous director of films who has also written his share of screenplays. Petersen first earned a place in cinematic history for writing and directing the critically acclaimed *Das Boot,* a movie about a Nazi submarine crew. Petersen directed television movies and at least two films for the big screen before making *Das Boot,* but it was the story of the Nazi U-boat that propelled him to stardom and established him as one of Hollywood's most sought-after directors.

*Einer Von Uns Beiden* ("One or the Other" is a 1974 film directed by Petersen. The taut thriller follows different lives until they intersect, and the characters play one-upmanship games that last beyond death. *Die Konsequenz* ("The Consequence") is a 1977 film about a sexual relationship between an imprisoned young man, Martin, and Thomas, the teenage son of a jailer. Martin is in prison for having homosexual relations with a minor, and his relationship with Thomas lengthens his prison stay. Thomas, for his part, is sent to a reformatory. According to Martyn Auty of the British Film Institute's *Monthly Film Bulletin,* Petersen captures "German cinema's preoccupation with homosexual tragedy in a prison setting that serves as a cogent metaphor for socio-sexual repression."

The 1981 film *Das Boot* ("The Boat") is considered by many critics to be one of the finest war movies ever made. The movie depicts German Nazi submariners on a patrol during World War II. Petersen manages to portray notoriously unpopular Nazis as human beings and almost lures the audience into the grimness of the Nazis' lives. Jeanine Basinger of Wesleyan University said that *Das Boot* contains "tense realism, tight quarters, and total desperation for both sub crew and audience." Owen Gleiberman of *Entertainment Weekly* called *Das Boot* a "quintessential movie experience" with "realism unmatched by that of any other war film."

Petersen followed *Das Boot* by writing and directing *The Neverending Story,* based on a novel by Michael Ende. In the film, a boy named Bastian enters a magical kingdom called "Fantasia" when he reads a special book. In Fantasia, Bastian meets Etreyu, a boy who must save Fantasia's empress by stopping an evil force called The Nothing. There are "gentle lessons about the value of hope, courage and love" in *The Neverending Story,* said Ralph Novak of *People,* "and a fair share of plain old fantasy adventure."

*Shattered* signalled a return to adult themes for Petersen. Released in 1991, *Shattered* is Petersen's adaptation of Richard Neely's novel *The Plastic Nightmare.* *People* magazine reviewer Mark Goodman said that by the time "Petersen gets through wringing you dry in this sleek, storm-tossed thriller, you may lose confidence in *everybody.*" Petersen did not write the script for *In the Line of Fire,* but he did direct the film. The movie, released in 1991, is a fictional account of Secret Service agent Frank Horrigan, an agent who was in the President's car when John F. Kennedy was shot dead in Dallas. Horrigan is haunted by his felt failures, and he is also vexed by a new killer who seeks to kill the present-day President. Stanley Kauffmann, writing for *The New Republic,* declared that Petersen "tackles familiar material with a vigor that makes it fresh."

*Outbreak,* released in 1995 and directed by Petersen, is a story about a deadly virus called Motaba, which is contained in a monkey that has been smuggled from Africa to Cedar Creek, California. In this film, as in others, Petersen "knows how to make a pleasurable wreck of your nervous system," proclaimed Jack Kroll of *Newsweek.* Petersen also directed the 1997 release *Air Force One,* a thriller largely set on the president's private jet. The president, who has just delivered a speech in Moscow, is forced to fend for himself when Russian revolutionaries who seek the resurrection of Communism in Russia take over Air Force One. Petersen "turns the plane into a maze," wrote *New York* reviewer David Denby, and "the picture is beautifully choreographed."

## BIOGRAPHICAL/CRITICAL SOURCES:

### PERIODICALS

*American Film,* September 1985, p. 66.
*American Spectator,* December 1991, p. 38.
*British Film Institute Monthly Film Bulletin,* October 1980, pp. 196-197.
*Entertainment Weekly,* April 18, 1997, p. 45.
*Maclean's* July 23, 1984, p. 47.
*National Review,* August 23, 1993, p. 61.
*New Republic,* August 9, 1993, p. 28; April 10, 1995, p. 30.
*New Statesman,* September 3, 1993, p. 35-36.
*Newsweek,* March 20, 1995, p. 65; July 21, 1997, pp. 66-67.
*New York,* July 30, 1984, p. 47; August 4, 1997, pp. 55-56.
*New Yorker,* March 20, 1995, pp. 105-107.
*New York Times Book Review,* July 25, 1997, p. C1.
*People,* August 13, 1984, p. 16; November 4, 1991, pp. 17-18.
*Variety,* February 2, 1977, p. 22; January 24, 1979, p. 23; October 14, 1991, p. 244.*

* * *

## PHILIP, John Robert    1927-1999

OBITUARY NOTICE—See index for *CA* sketch: Born January 18, 1927, in Ballarat, Australia; died after being hit by a car, June 26, 1999, in Amsterdam, Netherlands. Physicist, mathematician, and author. Philip received numerous fellowships for his work in the sciences and his research on how water, energy and gases move. He helped edit two books, *Salinity and Water Use* with Tjeerd Talsma, and *Science and the Polity* with T. J. Conlon, and contributed nearly two hundred articles to scientific journals. Philip joined the research staff of the Commonwealth Scientific and Industrial Research Organization (CSIRO) in Canberra in 1951. He continued in a variety of positions until being named chief of the Division of Environmental Mechanics in 1971. Philip stayed with the organization until he retired in 1992 as the group's first fellow emeritus. During his career he was a visiting faculty member at several universities, including Cambridge, Harvard, and Cornell. He twice was recognized with the Horton Award from the American Geophysical Union, once for a paper on thermally induced water transport in porous media and then for outstanding contributions to the geophysics of hydrology. He received the CSIRO

David Rivett Medal in 1966 for best publications of a scientist under forty and the Thomas Ranken Lyle Medal from the Australian Academy of Science for distinguished contributions to mathematical and physical sciences.

## OBITUARIES AND OTHER SOURCES:

### PERIODICALS

*New York Times,* July 14, 1999, p. A21.

* * *

## PHILLIPS, Robert H.   1948-

*PERSONAL:* Born in 1948.

*ADDRESSES: Agent*—c/o Avery Publishing Group, 89 Baldwin Terrace, Wayne, NJ 07470.

*CAREER:* Center for Coping, Long Island, New York, founder and director.

## WRITINGS:

*Coping with Lupus: A Guide to Living with Lupus for You and Your Family,* Avery (Wayne, NJ), 1984.
*Coping with an Ostomy: A Guide to Living with an Ostomy for You and Your Family,* Avery, 1986.
*Coping with Kidney Failure: A Guide to Living with Kidney Failure for You and Your Family,* Avery, 1987.
*Coping with Rheumatoid Arthritis,* Avery (Garden City Park, NY), 1988.
(With Thomas W. McKnight) *Love Tactics,* Avery, 1988.
*Coping with Osteoarthritis,* Avery, 1989.
*Rising to the Challenge: Celebrities and Their Very Personal Health Stories,* Avery, 1990.
*Coping with Mitral Valve Prolapse: A Guide to Living with MVP for You and Your Family,* Avery, 1992.
(With Harlan M. Krumholz) *No If 's, And's, or Butts: The Smoker's Guide to Quitting,* Avery, 1993.
(With Thomas W. McKnight) *More Love Tactics,* Avery, 1993.
*Coping with Prostate Cancer,* Avery, 1994.
(With Larry Glanz) *How to Start a Romantic Encounter: Where to Go to Find Love and What to Say When You Find It,* Avery, 1994.
(With Odeda Rosenthal) *Coping with Color Blindness: Sound Helpful Information for Those Who Must*

*Deal with Inherited or Acquired Color Vision Confusion,* Avery, 1997.

(With Robert G. Lahita) *Lupus: Everything You Need to Know,* Avery, 1998.

(With Paula Goldstein) *Coping with Breast Cancer: A Practical Guide to Understanding, Treating, and Living with Breast Cancer,* Avery, 1998.

*SIDELIGHTS:* Psychologist Robert Phillips has written extensively about emotional issues affecting patients with serious diseases. His books are generally considered approachable, informative, and reassuring resources that aim to help patients cope with their diseases and improve their quality of life.

In separate volumes covering such conditions as ostomies, kidney failure, lupus, rheumatoid arthritis, osteoarthritis, prostate cancer, breast cancer, and mitral valve prolapse, Phillips focuses on issues that can help patients maximize control of their lives. As he emphasized in an interview with Dr. Kan Keller, founder of *Wellness Web,* Phillips believes communication skills and pain management techniques can greatly improve patients' abilities to participate in treatment of their diseases and to enjoy their lives. "The motto I use all the time with my patients," he told Dr. Keller, is " 'Regardless of any problem you may face, you can always improve the quality of your life.' "

Reviewers have consistently praised Phillips's books for their friendly tone and useful information. *Coping with an Ostomy, Coping with Kidney Failure, Coping with Rheumatoid Arthritis,* and *Coping with Osteoarthritis* all received highly favorable reviews and were especially commended for their sensible advice and their sensitivity to emotional issues affecting both patients and families. Compared to the high standard set in these volumes, however, Phillips's first book, *Coping with Lupus,* was a disappointment to some critics when it was reissued in a paper edition. *Library Journal*'s Ruth Amernick felt the book presented only a "superficial overview" of its subject and complained that its section on new treatments was not up-to-date. Furthermore, she added that the book "adds very little psychological and medical insights for those coping with lupus." Tracie Richardson, however, commended the title in *Booklist* as a "useful" guide with especially helpful advice on causes of the disease and necessary lifestyle changes. Phillips's second book on lupus, *Lupus: Everything You Need to Know,* co-written with physician Robert G. Lahita, was hailed as a comprehensive, clear, and useful resource.

*Coping with Breast Cancer,* which Phillips co-wrote with social worker Paula Goldstein, did not receive the accolades given many of his earlier titles. *Library Journal* reviewer Bette-Lee Fox found that the book's advice general enough to apply to any serious illness, and objected to its "cutesy" chapter headings. Though she found *Coping with Breast Cancer* basically useful, Fox felt that many better books were available to newly-diagnosed breast cancer patients. Phillips's other coping guides include *Coping with Prostate Cancer, Coping with Mitral Valve Prolapse,* and *Coping with Color Blindness.*

Though Phillips earned much esteem for his guides to living with illness, his *Rising to the Challenge: Celebrities and Their Personal Health Stories* was considered a misstep at best. The book contains interviews with thirty-four celebrities who suffer from a variety of ailments from cerebral palsy to allergies. A *Publishers Weekly* reviewer expressed distaste for the book's concept, noting that physical advice does not gain new authority merely because it is dispensed by a celebrity. The reviewer faulted Phillips for "questions [that] are often insipid" and "advice [that] is 'limp,' " as well as sloppy editing of his subjects' rambling comments in a book that the reviewer felt contained "few articulate voices."

*BIOGRAPHICAL/CRITICAL SOURCES:*

*PERIODICALS*

*Booklist,* April 15, 1988, p. 1380; March 15, 1991, p. 1443; February 1, 1998, p. 888.

*Contemporary Psychology,* February 1985, p. 163.

*Library Journal,* April 1, 1986, p. 157; October 1, 1987, p. 102; June 15, 1988, p. 65; May 15, 1989, pp. 82, 84; March 1, 1991, pp. 108, 110; July, 1997, p. 116; January, 1998, p. 126; May 1, 1998, p. S3; October 1, 1998, p. 126.

*Publishers Weekly,* March 18, 1988, p. 77; March 23, 1990, p. 77.

*OTHER*

*Wellness Web,* http://www.wellweb.com/pain/dan—phillips.html (March 5, 1999).*

## PONCE-MONTOYA, Juanita 1949-

*PERSONAL:* Born in 1949, in Raton, NM; married Juan Lorenzo Montoya (a pipefitter), c. 1960 (died, 1974); children: Anita (deceased), Juan, Jose.

*ADDRESSES: Agent*—c/o Exposition, Hicksville, NY.

*CAREER:* Poet, c. 1978—. Children's Psychiatric Hospital, Albuquerque, NM, worked as a nurse until 1983; also worked as a farm laborer, real estate investor, and home renovator.

*WRITINGS:*

*Grief Work* (poems), Exposition (Hicksville, NY), 1978.

Contributor to *Del Sol New Mexico.*

*SIDELIGHTS:* The poetry of Juanita Ponce-Montoya was born of a grief that is universal to the human experience. The poet is often categorized as a Chicano writer because of her origins, but she records feelings and a journey of spiritual growth that strike familiar chords in readers everywhere. She is classified as a poet, but in the *Dictionary of Literary Biography,* Wolfgang Binder described her as "a Chicano who in writing [her] book *became* a poet."

In *Grief Work,* Ponce-Montoya explores a healing journey that began after the accidental death of her husband in 1974. She had already lost a daughter and persevered through her grief, but now she was faced with the intimidating financial and emotional responsibilities of a single parent with two small sons. Ponce-Montoya met the economic challenge by attending college, working at multiple odd jobs, nursing part-time at a children's hospital in Albuquerque, and eventually buying and remodeling houses for profit. She faced her grief in poems that she wrote—and dated—for approximately two years in the mid-1970s.

Binder commented: "*Grief Work* must be viewed as an extended chronicle—almost all the poems are dated—recording feelings of extreme despondency, but moving toward a cathartic affirmation of self." The poems correspond naturally to a series of healing phases: denial, loss, anger, acknowledgment, acceptance, and freedom.

The first part of the chronicle deals with, according to Binder: "a strong death wish in the survivor, the refusal to believe the sad fact of the loved one's death; feelings of an existential void, of the meaninglessness of life,"

[but also] "the frail beginnings of the concept that the memory of a past love enables a person to walk on." The first feelings to seep into the void are negative, he continued: "a rebellious attitude against the many daily demands and against real and so-called friends, family, and outsiders; expressions of low self-esteem, of loneliness." Then, Binder stated, Ponce-Montoya reaches an emotional turning point: "the admission, hitherto concealed, of her love for her parents; the recognition of her son John-John (Juan) as a life force; and the realization of the importance of friendship." At the end of Part One, the author is able to bid her husband a symbolic farewell and step resolutely, if cautiously, into the future.

The poems in Part Two focus on recovery, including a passionate love affair, according to Binder, "which, because of its urgency, is rendered in religious terminology. Love becomes, in its newly felt ecstasy, almost unnameable; it means 'unison with God.' It ultimately will make a rebirth possible." The affair turns out to be short-lived, but such is the poet's strength, resilience, and self-confidence at this point that the new loss serves only to validate her renewed vitality.

"Ponce-Montoya's range of emotions proves remarkably large," Binder remarked, "offering a highly varied reading of the human condition and thus reaching beyond the undeniably close, direct autobiographical link between author and text." Additionally, he observed that "many of the poems transcend this expediency [of self-catharsis] by their forcefulness, honesty, and power."

*BIOGRAPHICAL/CRITICAL SOURCES:*

BOOKS

*Dictionary of Literary Biography,* Volume 122: *Chicano Writers, Second Series,* Gale (Detroit, MI), 1992.*

*        *        *

## PORTER, H(arry) Boone 1923-1999

*OBITUARY NOTICE*—See index for *CA* sketch: Born January 10, 1923, in Louisville, KY; died of pneumonia, June 5, 1999, in Bridgeport, CT. Theologian and author. Porter grew up in a wealthy family which owned the Porter Paint Company, but rather than go into the family business he made his mark as the person mainly responsible for revising the Book of Common Prayer in 1979. Porter graduated from Yale, Berkeley Divinity School, General Theological Seminary and Oxford University, the last from which he received his doctorate in 1954. After completing Oxford, Porter was hired as an assistant professor at Nashotah House in Wisconsin but left in 1960 for a post in liturgics at General Theological Seminary. While there he designed the country's first doctoral program in liturgical studies. During those years he was a member of the Standing Liturgical Commission, which worked to make the holy communion service more easily understandable for the general servicegoer. The committee's work was not always viewed favorably due to its extensive changes to the Book of Common Prayer, which had not been altered since 1928. The book had been basically unchanged since the 1600s. Porter worked mainly on the Eucharistic Prayer A and part of Prayer B, which provided a choice of prayers for parishes. In addition, Porter wrote numerous books of his own including *The Day of Light, Growth and Life in the Local Church,* and *Keeping the Church Year.* He contributed articles to religious publications and in 1977 was named editor at *The Living Church* magazine, a weekly publication of the Episcopal Church. After retirement in 1994 he went back to Yale, receiving a master's in environmental studies the next year.

*OBITUARIES AND OTHER SOURCES:*

*PERIODICALS*

*Los Angeles Times,* June 13, 1999, p. B5.
*New York Times,* June 11, 1999, p. A31.
*Washington Post,* June 13, 1999, p. C5.

\*　　\*　　\*

**POWERS, J(ames) F(arl)   1917-1999**

*OBITUARY NOTICE*—See index for *CA* sketch: Born July 8, 1917, in Jacksonville, IL; died June 12 (some sources say June 14), 1999, in Collegeville, MN. Teacher and author. National Book Award recipient Powers was admired by fellow writers but not known for a prodigious output of work. His first novel, *Morte d'Urban,* won the prize in 1963 but his next work, a collection of short stories called *Look How the Fish Live,* was not published until 1975. Other works include *Prince of Darkness and Other Stories, The Presence of Grace* and 1988's *Wheat That Springeth Green,* which was a finalist for the National Book Award. Much of

Powers' work centered on priests and Catholicism, which drew kudos and complaints from different corners. Those who liked his work viewed him as a satirist who perfectly captured the day-to-day clerical life, speech patterns and responsibilities. Critics believed he focused too much on a few negatives in the church. Powers' first important work, *Lions, Harts, Leaping Does,* was published in 1943. Shortly after he received the O. Henry Award for *The Valiant Woman.* In 1948 he received a National Institute of Arts and Letters grant, as well as a Guggenheim fellowship in creative writing. Three Rockefeller fellowships followed, although Powers' body of work was small. The characterization of priests was so accurate that one could think Powers had been a member of the clergy, some said. Although he had studied with Franciscan friars as a child, Powers said he never seriously considered entering the priesthood. While developing his writing style he worked a variety of jobs including book store clerk, chauffeur and selling insurance. Although Powers never graduated from Northwestern University, he did teach writing at several schools including St. John's University, Marquette University, the University of Michigan and Smith College. He contributed stories to numerous periodicals like *New Yorker, Nation* and *Collier's* but reportedly slacked on completion of more work due to disappointment over his first novel's lack of sales and what he called innate laziness.

*OBITUARIES AND OTHER SOURCES:*

*PERIODICALS*

*Chicago Tribune,* June 16, 1999, sec. 2, p.11.
*Los Angeles Times,* June 18, 1999, p. A30.
*New York Times,* June 17, 1999, p. C23.
*Washington Post,* June 17, 1999, p. B5.

\*　　\*　　\*

**PROCTOR, Geo(rge W.)**
**(John Cleve, a joint pseudonym; Zach Wyatt, a pseudonym)**

*PERSONAL:* Male.

*ADDRESSES: Agent*—c/o Bantam Books, 1540 Broadway, New York, NY 10036-4094.

*CAREER:* Has worked as a journalist; freelance writer and editor, c. 1976—.

*AWARDS, HONORS: Before Honor* was nominated for a Spur Award.

*WRITINGS:*

SCIENCE FICTION AND FANTASY

(Editor with Steven Utley) *Lone Star Universe: The First Anthology of Texas Science Fiction Authors,* Heidelberg (Austin, TX), 1976.

*The Esper Transfer,* Major (Canoga Park, CA), 1978.

*Shadowman,* Fawcett (New York City), 1980.

*Fire at the Center,* Fawcett, 1981.

(Editor with Arthur C. Clarke) *The Science-Fiction Hall of Fame, Volume 3: Nebula Winners 1965-1969,* Avon (New York City), 1982.

(Under joint pseudonym John Cleve, with Andrew J. Offut) *Master of Misfit* ("Spaceways" series), Playboy Paperbacks (New York City), 1982.

(As Cleve, with Offut) *The Manhuntress* ("Spaceways" series), Playboy Paperbacks, 1982.

(As Cleve, with Offut) *The Yoke of Shen* ("Spaceways" series), Berkley (New York City), 1983.

*Starwings,* Ace (New York City), 1984.

*V: The Chicago Conversion,* Pinnacle (New York City), 1985.

*V: The Texas Run,* Pinnacle, 1985.

(With Robert E. Vardeman) *To Demons Bound* ("Raemllyn" series), Ace, 1985.

(With Vardeman) *A Yoke of Magic* ("Raemllyn" series), Ace, 1985.

(With Vardeman) *Blood Fountain* ("Raemllyn" series), Ace, 1985.

(With Vardeman) *Death's Acolyte* ("Raemllyn" series), Ace, 1985.

(With Vardeman) *The Beasts of the Mist* ("Raemllyn" series), Ace, 1986.

(With Vardeman) *For Crown and Kingdom* ("Raemllyn" series), Ace, 1987.

*Stellar Fist,* Ace, 1989.

UNDER PSEUDONYM ZACH WYATT; "THE TEXIANS" SERIES

*The Texians,* Pinnacle, 1984.

*The Horse Marines,* Pinnacle, 1984.

*War Devils,* Pinnacle, 1984.

*Blood Moon,* Pinnacle, 1985.

*Death's Shadow,* Pinnacle, 1985.

*Comanche Ambush,* Pinnacle, 1985.

OTHER NOVELS

*Enemies,* Doubleday (New York City), 1983.

*Ride for Vengeance,* Pageant (New York City), 1989.

*Walks without a Soul,* Doubleday, 1990.

*Comes the Hunter,* Doubleday, 1992.

*Before Honor,* Doubleday, 1993.

*Blood of My Blood: A Novel of Quanah Parker,* Bantam (New York City), c. 1996.

*SIDELIGHTS:* Geo W. Proctor began his writing career as a newspaper journalist, then became involved with writing and editing science fiction and fantasy during the 1970s. His first book-length title was 1978's *The Esper Transfer.* Since then he has penned numerous other works of science fiction and fantasy, sometimes with a co-author, and sometimes under the joint pseudonym John Cleve. With Robert E. Vardeman he created the "Raemllyn" fantasy series, most of which saw print during the mid-to late 1980s. With Andrew J. Offut, Proctor concocted the "Spaceways" series, using the Cleve name. In the 1980s, Proctor branched out into the western genre, producing "The Texians" series under the pseudonym Zach Wyatt, and also being responsible for several distinguished westerns under his own name. Among these are *Walks without a Soul, Before Honor,* and *Blood of My Blood: A Novel of Quanah Parker.*

Vardeman, who co-authored the "Raemllyn" titles with Proctor, pointed out in an entry for *Twentieth-Century Science-Fiction Writers* that Proctor's major theme in their science-fiction and fantasy stories is that of communication. In novels such as *The Esper Transfer, Shadowman,* and *Starwings,* the characters often employ telepathy in order to speak to one another. In the last example, the protagonist is separated from his love by a time machine, but still manages to make love to her using his mind. In another novel, 1981's *Fire at the Center,* Vardeman reported that the story's heart "isn't the technology of time travel or even the hopes of the protagonists journeying to the past, but how Nils Kendler and Caltha Renent communicate psionically [a psychic phenomenon ostensibly using mind 'power' employing shortened or altered word forms] and the personal challenges they face through the relationship this situation affords." Later in his entry on his co-author, Vardeman declared: "This focus on male-female, human-alien communication extends beyond Proctor's science fiction and into his fantasy novels." He went on to observe also that "while the structure and tone of his fantasy work is strongly influenced by Fritz Leiber's Fafhrd and the Gray Mouser stories, the basic themes are easily identifiable as belonging to Proctor."

Proctor also penned two titles for the *V* series, one of them being 1985's *V: The Chicago Conversion.* Though Michael Klossner in the *Fantasy Review* did not think much of the novel, recommending it "only for the least fussy fans," Vardeman spoke highly of the bulk of Proctor's work in the two related genres, concluding that "the nucleus of Geo W. Proctor's science fiction and fantasy works is both simple and beguiling: communication."

*Walks without a Soul,* a Proctor western which was published in 1990, draws readers into the plight of Nate Wagoner, a slave who lives and works in antebellum East Texas. When the plantation he is chained to is raided by Native Americans of the Comanche tribe, one of Nate's daughters is killed, and his wife and other children taken prisoner by the raiders. Even though a slave, he shares a similar predicament to that of his master and the neighboring whites, and because of this, is allowed to go with the party formed to search for those captured. Not surprisingly he is treated with contempt by the party because of his race and his status as a slave, however, he discovers an advantage over the others in dealing with the Comanches, who in this tale are unfamiliar with people of African descent. The Indians allow him to travel freely among them, and give him the name, "Walks without a Soul." Critics responded well to *Walks without a Soul.* Robert Jordan in the *Library Journal* praised it as "well researched, well paced, and compelling reading." Wes Lukowsky, opining in *Booklist,* also enjoyed *Walks without a Soul,* and praised the way in which Proctor presented the racism of the period in a "realistic, gritty novel" with "an exciting, action-packed plot."

*Before Honor,* Proctor's 1993 effort, takes place in a more modern-day western setting. This novel concerns a small-time rancher named Clint Wayford, who is clinging to his family ranch in South Texas despite competition from corporate ranchers. *Before Honor* was nominated for a Spur Award, one of the western genre's most prestigious honors, and a 1996 review in *Roundup Magazine* praised the paperback reissue of the novel, celebrating the fact that it was "finally available for those who missed it the first time around."

Proctor returned to explore the world of the Comanches once more in his 1996 volume, *Blood of My Blood: A Novel of Quanah Parker.* Though a novelization, *Blood of My Blood* tells the story of a real historical figure, Parker, who was half-Comanche and half-white. As readers meet the Parker of the novel, it is 1875 and the Battle of the Palo Duro has just taken place. Flashbacks are utilized, however, to reveal the trials and tribulations of Parker's Texas boyhood. He and his brother Pecos are born to a captive white woman named Cynthia Ann Parker, and are discriminated against by both their mother's and their father's peoples. When their father dies, Quanah and Pecos are cut off by their Comanche tribe, and told to seek a life among the whites. Their mother is forced to return to the white world, but know-

ing this to be impossible for himself, Quanah instead manages to prove his value to his Comanche people by demonstrating himself to be a brave warrior. As time goes on, he becomes a leader among them, and is especially important as a liaison with the whites as the Comanches are forced to move onto reservations. As a *Roundup Magazine* essayist observed, Parker "was a man uniquely suited to lead the Comanches into the twentieth century, to ensure their survival in an alien white world." The stipend Parker received from the government for helping keep his Native American people from rebelling and to persuade them to let ranchers graze their cattle on Comanche land, however, brought him criticism from some Comanches. As Proctor paints him, Quanah Parker is a man of paradox—for instance, though he claims to hate whites throughout his life, he never ceases to revere the memory of his white mother, and eventually has her disinterred and reburied upon reservation lands.

*Blood of My Blood* met with praise from literary critics. John E. Boyd in *Kliatt* noted the tragic aspects of Parker's life story, and the fact that "although suspected of having great wealth," Proctor's protagonist "dies close to poverty—a sad ending for a great leader" in 1911. Boyd went on to use words such as "interesting," "sensitive," and "realistic" to praise the author's efforts in *Blood of My Blood.* The *Roundup Magazine* reviewer concluded *Blood of My Blood* to be "an eloquently written, meticulously researched novel about a man whose vision bridged two worlds."

*BIOGRAPHICAL/CRITICAL SOURCES:*

*BOOKS*

*Twentieth-Century Science-Fiction Writers,* third edition, St. James Press, 1991.

*PERIODICALS*

*Booklist,* August, 1990, pp. 2155-2156.
*Fantasy Review,* March, 1985, p. 12.
*Kliatt,* September, 1996, p. 13.
*Library Journal,* June 15, 1990, p. 136.
*Roundup Magazine,* August, 1996, pp. 31-32; October, 1996, p. 32.*

\*     \*     \*

**PRUITT, David B(urton)  1948-**

*PERSONAL:* Born in 1948. *Education:* University of Texas Medical School, M.D., 1974. Certification includes ABPN, general psychiatry, 1979, child psychiatry, 1981.

*ADDRESSES: Home*—Memphis, TN. *Agent*—c/o HarperCollins Publishers, 10 East 53rd St., New York, NY 10022.

*CAREER:* University of Texas Houston Affiliate Hospital, Houston, TX, intern, 1974-75; University of Pennsylvania Affiliate Hospital, Philadelphia, PA, general psychiatric resident, 1975-78; Philadelphia Child Guidance Center, Philadelphia, PA, child psychiatric resident, 1978-79; University Physicians, Division of Child Psychiatry, Memphis, TN, director, beginning in 1979, Department of Psychiatry, vice chair, beginning in 1983; Le Bonhemn Child Medical Center, Memphis, TN, chief of child psychiatry, beginning in 1983; University of Tennessee, Memphis, TN, associate professor of psychiatry and pediatrics then professor of psychiatry, 1983—. Affiliated with Le Bonhemn Child Medical Center and St. Judes Child Hospital, both in Memphis, TN.

*MEMBER:* American Academy of Child and Adolescent Psychiatry (AACAP) (president; past chair of Workgroup on Consumer Issues, 1985), American Medical Association.

*WRITINGS:*

(Editor) *Your Child: What Every Parent Needs to Know About Childhood Development from Birth to Preadolescence,* HarperCollins (New York City), 1998.
(Editor) *Your Adolescent: What Every Parent Needs to Know: What's Normal, What's Not, and When to Seek Help,* HarperCollins, 1999.

Also author of articles and book chapters.

*SIDELIGHTS:* Child psychiatrist David B. Pruitt is the editor of 1998's *Your Child: What Every Parent Needs to Know about Childhood Development from Birth to Preadolescence* and 1999's *Your Adolescent: What Every Parent Needs to Know: What's Normal, What's Not, and When to Seek Help.* Reviewers have praised these books, calling them very helpful resources for caregivers.

The first publication, *Your Child,* is "a comprehensive behavioral guidebook" which, complimented a *Publishers Weekly* contributor, "offers a clear and straightforward examination of issues of development behavior and psychological growth." Critical commentaries of

*Your Child* posted on the Amazon.com Web site included a quote from *Parenting Magazine* labeling the book "trustworthy"; a statement from Fred Rogers, of *Mister Rogers' Neighborhood,* in which he exclaimed "Bravo"; and a commendation by Bill Cosby, who praised its "state-of-the-art advice." Presenting information for each age, the four sections of *Your Child* educate caregivers on general medical concerns, common behavioral problems and tips to deal with those problems, and more severe problems and the appropriate time to seek out professional help at various locations. *Your Adolescent,* the follow-up to *Your Child,* addresses similar issues, but focuses on the older child. *Publishers Weekly* called *Your Adolescent* "an invaluable reference for anyone who has close contact with adolescents."

*BIOGRAPHICAL/CRITICAL SOURCES:*

*PERIODICALS*

*Publishers Weekly,* August 3, 1998, pp. 80-81.

*OTHER*

*Amazon.com,* http://www.amazon.com (March 11, 1999).*

\* \* \*

**PUDOVKIN, V(sevolod) I(llarionovich) 1893-1953**

*PERSONAL:* Some sources transliterate middle name as Illareonovitch or Illationovich; born in 1893, in Penza, Russia; died c. July 1, 1953, in Riga, USSR (now Latvia); married Anna Zemtsova (an actress and journalist), 1923. *Education:* Attended State Cinema School, 1920; studied with Lev Kuleshov, beginning in 1922; also attended Moscow University.

*CAREER:* Soviet film director, actor, and writer. Worked as writer and chemist, 1919-20; filmmaker, 1920-21; Kuleshov's Experimental Laboratory, member, beginning in 1923; collaborator with cinematographer Anatoly Golovnia and writer Nathan Zarkhi, beginning in 1925; VGIK, teacher of theoretical studies, 1935; joined Mosfilm Studios, 1938. Director of films, including *Mother,* 1926; *The End of St. Petersburg,* 1927; *The Heir to Genghis-Khan: Storm over Asia,* 1928; and *The Deserter,* 1933; appeared in films, including *The Extraordinary Adventures of Mr. West in* the Land of the Bolsheviks, 1924; *The New Babylon,* 1929; and *Ivan the Terrible,* 1944. *Military service:* Russian Army, Artillery, 1914, prisoner of war, 1915.

*AWARDS, HONORS:* Order of Lenin, 1950 (some sources cite 1935).

*WRITINGS:*

On Film Technique: Three Essays and an Address, translated by Ivor Montagu, Gollancz (London, England), 1929, enlarged edition published as *Film Technique: Five Essays and Two Addresses,* translated by Montagu, G. Newnes (London), 1933.

*Akter v fil'me,* Sektsiia Kinovedeniia (Leningrad, USSR), 1934.

Film Acting: A Course of Lectures Delivered at the State Institute of Cinematography, Moscow, translated by Montagu, G. Newnes, 1935.

"Film Technique" and "Film Acting:" The Cinema Writings of V. I. Pudovkin, translated by Montagu, Lear (New York City), 1949, enlarged edition, Grove (New York City), 1960.

Film e fonofilm: Il soggetto, la direzione artistica, l'attore, il film sonoro, translated by Umberti Barbaro, 3rd edition, Bianco e nero (Rome, Italy), 1950.

*Textes choisis,* [Moscow, USSR], 1955.
*Izbrannye stat'l,* Iskusstvo (Moscow), 1955.
*Sobranie sochinenii v trekh tomakh,* [Moscow], 1974.

Author of other works published in Russian. Contributor to periodicals, including *Sight and Sound* and *Hollywood Quarterly.*

*BIOGRAPHICAL/CRITICAL SOURCES:*

BOOKS

A Biographical Dictionary of Film, Morrow (New York City), 1976.

Drummond, Philip, *Makers of Modern Culture,* Facts on File (New York City), 1981.

PERIODICALS

*Christian Science Monitor,* September 8, 1949, p. 11.
*Library Journal,* June 15, 1949.
*New Republic,* September 26, 1949.

OBITUARIES:

PERIODICALS

*New York Times,* July 2, 1953.*

---

**PUTZ, Louis J. 1909-1998**

*OBITUARY NOTICE*—See index for *CA* sketch: Born June 1, 1909, in Simbach, Germany; immigrated to United States, 1923; died June 24, 1998, in South Bend, IN. Theology professor and author. Putz spent his first fourteen years in Germany before coming to America and enrolling at Notre Dame University, from which he eventually graduated. He continued his theological studies in France and was ordained in Paris. Putz returned to the United States during World War II and took a teaching post at his alma mater. From 1966 to 1972 he served as rector of Moreau Theological Seminary but left there to direct Family Life Services for the diocese of Fort Wayne and South Bend. He wrote books, including *The Modern Apostle* and *The Lord's Day,* and was working on a piece about the spirituality of aging at the time of his death. Notre Dame recognized him with an honorary degree in 1988.

*OBITUARIES AND OTHER SOURCES:*

PERIODICALS

*Chicago Tribune,* June 26, 1998, sec. 3, p. 12.

\*　　\*　　\*

**QUINTANA RANCK, Katherine 1942-**

*PERSONAL:* Born October 4, 1942, in Santa Fe, NM; daughter of Ramon Trujillo and Lebradita (Romero) Quintana; married James Phillip Ranck, 1960; children: Kimberly, Lance. *Education:* Southwestern College, Chula Vista, CA, A.A., 1978; additional study at National University, San Diego, CA. *Avocational interests:* Visiting galleries of southwestern art, reading.

*ADDRESSES: Home*—National City, CA. *Agent*—c/o Tonatiuh-Quinto Sol, Berkeley, CA.

*CAREER:* Worked as bilingual clerk in the medical field; National City Public Schools, National City, CA, began as child development specialist, became director of child development programs. Also worked as a classroom teacher.

*WRITINGS:*

Portrait of Dona Elena (novel), Tonatiuh-Quinto Sol (Berkeley, CA), 1982.

Contributor to magazines and newspapers, including *Grito del Sol.*

*SIDELIGHTS:* According to *Dictionary of Literary Biography* contributor Diana Gonzalez, "Narrative description is Katherine Quintana Ranck's greatest asset as a writer." Whereas many novelists create images to support their plots, Quintana Ranck typically uses a very simple plot as a device upon which to build her descriptions. The novel *Portrait of Dona Elena,* Gonzalez observed, "has a minimum of locales, few characters, and little dialogue to distract the reader from the feelings conveyed via narrative description," yet "[Quintana] Ranck's poetic prose tends to charm the reader into continuing with the work despite the lack of action, movement, or intricate story line."

In the novel, a midwestern artist visits New Mexico to explore her Hispanic roots. While there she encounters Dona Elena, an ancient resident of the village of Nambe, and receives permission to paint her portrait. The artist describes her initial discomfort with the traditional Hispanic environment and her gradual assimilation. Gonzalez explained: "Her emotional conflicts are resolved through the compassion of Dona Elena's family and the artistic and emotional support of grandson Roberto, a fellow artist and kindred spirit who leads her to a sense of completion and personal well-being. The story is told through the eyes of an artist, thus conveying picturesque descriptions of the land itself and of the traditional types who sit for portraits." The story itself is simple; it is the wealth of description that absorbs the reader into the novel, as if to transform observer into participant.

The character Dona Elena is modeled after Quintana Ranck's grandmother, Sofia Madrid Romero (c. 1878-1967), and inspired by the author's childhood memories of family visits to Nambe. The story began as an assignment for a college creative writing class and was expanded, at the insistence of her family, into a short novel. In it, Gonzalez reported: "[Quintana] Ranck re-called sensory impressions of her grandmother's wooden stove, water well, the homemade pies and freshly baked bread in the old family home, as well as the warmth of an extended family living under the gentle protection of a revered monarch." The author told Gonzalez: "Images were what I wrote, a portrait of the land and people I loved."

Quintana Ranck has also written short fiction, though little of it has been published. Many of her stories are used in local school and day-care centers. One story, "Relics," appeared in the periodical *Grito del Sol* in 1984. As in *Portrait of Dona Elena,* narrative description provides sensory orientation for a simple story about what Gonzalez called "internal conflict and a sense of incompleteness." In this instance, Quintana Ranck tipped the balance between narrative and action even farther. She told Gonzalez: "In the short story 'Relics' I provide only the images; the reader is free to provide his own story. Perhaps that is why it took five years to find a publisher for it."

Overall, Gonzalez reported, Quintana Ranck's "works powerfully preserve a fast-disappearing traditional lifestyle once typical in the villages of rural New Mexico." The author's productivity has been hampered over the years by career and family responsibilities, but Quintana Ranck has expressed a desire to focus more intently on her writing, and she hinted at several works in various stages of completion.

*BIOGRAPHICAL/CRITICAL SOURCES:*

*BOOKS*

*Dictionary of Literary Biography,* Volume 122: *Chicano Writers, Second Series,* Gale (Detroit, MI), 1992.*

# R

**RAMON RIBEYRO, Julio 1929-**

*PERSONAL:* Born August 31, 1929, in Lima, Peru; children: one son. *Education:* Studied law at Catholic University of Lima; studied journalism in Spain.

*ADDRESSES: Agent*—c/o University of Texas Press, Box 7819, Austin, TX 78713-7819.

*CAREER:* Universidad Nacional de San Cristobal de Huamanga, Ayacucho, Peru, director of cultural affairs, 1958; France-Presse (news agency), journalist, 1960-70; as member of Peruvian diplomatic corps, served as cultural attache at a Peruvian embassy, 1970-80, then as ambassador to UNESCO.

*WRITINGS:*

*Los Gallinazos sin Plumas* (stories; title means "The Featherless Buzzards"), Circulo de Novelistas Peruanos (Lima, Peru), 1955.

*Cuentos de Circunstancias,* Nuevos Rumbos (Lima), 1958.

*Cronica de San Gabriel* (novel; title means "Chronicle of San Gabriel"), Tawantinsuyu (Lima), 1960.

*Tres Historias Sublevantes* (title means "Three Rebellious Stories"), Mejia Baca (Lima), 1964.

*Las Botellas y los Hombres,* Populibros Peruanos (Lima), 1964.

*Los Geniecillos Dominicales* (novel; title means "Geniuses of Sunday"), Populibros Peruanos, 1965.

*El Ultimo Cliente,* Teatro Universitario de San Marcos (Lima), 1966.

*Vida y Pasion de Santiago el Pajarero,* Universidad Nacional Mayor de San Marcos (Lima), 1966.

*La Palabra del Mudo: Cuentos 52/72* (title means "The Word of the Mute: Stories 52/72"), two volumes, Milla Batres (Lima), 1973, enlarged edition published as *La Palabra del Mudo: Cuentos 52/77,* 1977, 3rd edition published as *La Palabra del Mudo: Cuentos 52/92,* four volumes, 1992.

*Antologia,* Peisa (Lima), 1973.

*La Juventud en la Otra Ribera,* Mosca Azul (Lima), 1973.

(With Emilio Adolfo Westphalen) *Dos Soledades,* Instituto Nacional de Cultura (Lima), 1974.

*Cuentos,* edited by Pedro Simon, Casa de las America (Havana, Cuba), 1975.

*Teatro* (collected plays; title means "Theater"), Instituto Nacional de Cultura, 1975.

*Prosas Apatridas* (title means "Prose of a Man without a Country"), Tusquets (Barcelona, Spain), 1975, revised edition published as *Prosas Apatridas/ Aumentadas,* edited by Carlos Milla Batres, Milla Batres, 1978, 3rd edition published as *Prosas Apatridas (Completas),* Tusquets, 1986.

*La Caza Sutil: Ensayos y Articulos de Critica Literaria* (title means "The Subtle Hunt: Essays and Articles of Literary Criticism"), Milla Batres, 1975.

*Cambio de Guardia* (novel; title means "A Change of Guard"), Milla Batres, 1976.

*Atusparia,* Rikchay Peru (Lima), 1981.

*Solo para Fumadores,* El Barranco (Lima), 1987.

*Dichos de Luder* (prose; title means "Luder's Sayings"), Jaime Campodonico (Lima), 1989.

*Silvio en el Rosedal,* Tusquets, 1989, translation by Maria Rosa Fort and Frank Graziano published as *Silvio in the Rose Garden,* introduction by Jose Miguel Oviedo, Logbridge-Rhodes (Gettysburg, PA), 1989.

*La Tentacion del Fracaso I: Diario Personal, 1950-1960,* Jaime Campodonico, 1992.

*La Tentacion del Fracaso II: Diario Personal, 1960-1974,* Jaime Campodonico, 1993.

*Marginal Voices: Selected Stories,* translated by Dianne Douglas, foreword by Dick Gerdes, University of Texas Press (Austin, TX), 1993.

*SIDELIGHTS:* Julio Ramon Ribeyro has produced a prolific and wide-ranging body of literature as an adjunct to a successful career in journalism and diplomacy. Though his work has not been widely translated, the sheer volume of it and the craftsmanship of his fiction, in particular, have earned Ramon Ribeyro a prominent position among contemporary Peruvian writers.

"[Ramon] Ribeyro has been considered by many critics the Peruvian master of the short story," reported Efrain S. Kristal in the *Dictionary of Literary Biography.* The "stories show a wide thematic and geographic diversity: he has written tales about traveling circuses in the cities of the jungle, military skirmishes on the border between Peru and Ecuador, Indian oppression in the Andes, and the justice system in military outposts." A recurrent theme, however, is what Kristal called "the literary exploration of Peruvian urban life" which focuses on "the muted, tragic lives of marginalized or pauperized urban dwellers in the midst and on the fringes of self-complacent, well-to-do urban society." In this context, Kristal declared, Ramon Ribeyro is a pioneer; he writes about Peruvian people whose stories have never been told because they are not able to speak for themselves.

Ramon Ribeyro's stories can be read in Spanish in at least eight collections, including the four-volume work *La Palabra del Mudo.* One story that has been translated into English is *Silvio in the Rose Garden,* about a violinist who struggles with the realization that his quest for understanding has failed. It typifies "[Ramon] Ribeyro's most characteristic stories," observed Kristal, stories that "occur in a fatalistic atmosphere in which the narrator describes a world he cannot explain and the characters are invariably involved in situations that lead to calamity, failure, or incomprehension. . . . His characters tend to enter into frustrating situations in which things go wrong."

Similar circumstances occur in Ramon Ribeyro's novels, but many of the characters have not yet completed their descent to oblivion. Kristal noted that Ramon Ribeyro is "a novelist who has explored, better than anyone else in Peruvian literature, the experience of those members of the old quasi-feudal order who lost their political power and personal influence when their old ways became archaic and obsolete." *Cronica de San Gabriel* is the story of Lucho, a lazy, unruly youth who is sent to the ancestral home to be reformed by the head of the family. The respect of the family for its patriarch is undeserved; the boy's uncle is a hopeless libertine, and the boy goes home "unchanged, undaunted, and oblivious to the fact that he has witnessed the collapse of the family dynasty," according to Kristal. *Los Geniecillos Dominicales* chronicles the misadventures of Ludo, a mediocre young man from an aristocratic family in decline. Kristal noted: "The novel tells of his successive mishaps in love, sex, business, and literature"; no matter what he tries, "Ludo's hopes are continually raised and relentlessly dashed." Both characters are failures, one because he is caught up in events beyond his control and understanding, the other because of self-delusion and false optimism.

Ramon Ribeyro also wrote several plays, some of which are more political in nature than his fiction is. He has also published collections of literary articles and other nonfiction pieces that reveal his personal views on a wide range of topics, including a description of himself as an optimistic skeptic, or as defined by Kristal, "a man able to recognize problems but unable to give solutions he nonetheless hopes exist."

*BIOGRAPHICAL/CRITICAL SOURCES:*

*BOOKS*

*Dictionary of Literary Biography,* Volume 145: *Modern Latin-American Fiction Writers, Second Series,* Gale (Detroit, MI), 1994.*

\*    \*    \*

## RAYNOLDS, John F(iske III) 1929-

*PERSONAL:* Born in 1929.

*ADDRESSES: Home*—Riverside, CT. *Office*—National Peace Garden Foundation, 1800 Diagonal Rd., Suite D, Alexandria, VA 22314; fax: 703-684-4382. *E-mail*—0pgarden@celebratepeace.org.

*CAREER:* Outward Bound USA, past president and chief executive officer; Ward Howell International (executive search firm), New York City, chairperson, 1993-97; National Peace Garden Foundation, Alexandria, VA, president and chief executive, 1997—. Also worked as investment banker, president of a venture capital company, and construction equipment manufacturer. Harvard University, member of advisory board, John F. Kennedy School of Government; member of board of directors, International Executive Service

Corps., Shackleton Schools, and Achilles Track Club. *Military service:* U.S. Navy, officer with an underwater demolition team and participant in the founding of the SEALS; served in Korea.

*WRITINGS:*

(With Elanor Raynolds) *Beyond Success: How Volunteer Service Can Help You Begin Making a Life Instead of Just a Living,* MasterMedia (New York City), 1988.

(With Glen Stone) *The Halo Effect: How Volunteering Can Lead to a More Fulfilling Life—and a Better Career,* Golden Books (New York City), 1998.

*BIOGRAPHICAL/CRITICAL SOURCES:*

PERIODICALS

*Publishers Weekly,* August 3, 1998, p. 69.*

\*     \*     \*

**REEDY, Pat**
   **See REEDY, Patricia M.**

\*     \*     \*

**REEDY, Patricia M.   1940-**
   **(Pat Reedy)**

*PERSONAL:* Born May 1, 1940, in Mount Vernon, NY; daughter of William Valentine and Gertrude E. (a business executive; maiden name, Mongarell; later surname, Zaffino) Reedy. *Education:* Berkeley School of Business, graduated, 1960; Y & R School of Advertising, certificate, 1961; attended Hunter College of the City University of New York, Art Students League, State University of New York College at Purchase, and Fairfield University; trained for the stage with Michael Shurtleff, Julie Bovasso, Bob Gorman, Charles Regan, Hubert Whitfield, Judy Murray, and David Cohen.

*ADDRESSES: Home*—P.O. Box 77, West Mystic, CT 06388.

*CAREER:* Actress under name Pat Reedy, director, stage manager, designer, and playwright. Appeared on stage as Fran, *Promises, Promises,* produced in Norfolk, VA, at Tidewater Dinner Theater, 1973; as Anita, *Black Mountain,* produced in New York City at Lincoln Center Library, 1973; as Wonder Woman, *Paranoia Party,* produced in New York City, at Theater for the New City, 1974; as Maggie, *It's Only Temporary,* produced in New York City, at Gate Theater, 1976; as Delores, *Sisters and Brothers,* produced in New York City, at Women's Interart Theater, 1978; as Irma, *Bagging It,* produced in New York City, at American Theater of Actors, 1981; as the queen of France in *Cordelia;* and as the wife in *Tynside;* also performed as a singer, including appearances at U.S. military bases. Television appearances include the movie *Stage Struck,* CBS-TV, 1978; and appearances in episodes of *The Dick Lamb Show,* 1973, *Blankedy Blanks,* ABC-TV, 1977, *Another World,* NBC-TV, 1978, *Hotline,* 1979, *The Joe Franklin Show,* 1979, and *Go for It,* 1983. Director of the stage plays *A Bundle for Brunch,* produced at American Theater of Actors, 1979; *Trapped in the Basement,* American Theater of Actors, 1983; *A Step Beyond* and *The Pond,* both produced in New York City, at New York University, 1987; and *Terror Brokers,* American Theater of Actors, 1988. Stage manager and designer of light and sound for the play *Legend of the Sword,* Outdoor Theater, American Theater of Actors, 1982. Director of the radio presentation *Ebbanflo Duo,* broadcast by KBCS-FM Radio.

*MEMBER:* American Federation of Television and Radio Artists, Actors' Equity Association, Screen Actors Guild, Dramatists Guild, National Organization for Women, Smithsonian Institution.

*WRITINGS:*

PLAYS

*It's Only Temporary,* produced in New York City at Gate Theater, 1976.

*A Bundle for Brunch,* produced in New York City at American Theater of Actors, 1980.

*The Stop Over,* produced at American Theater of Actors, 1981.

*A Step Beyond,* produced at American Theater of Actors, 1981.

*Bagging It,* produced at American Theater of Actors, 1981.

(Composer) *Ever Wake Up,* produced in New York City, at New York University, 1987.*

## REID, Gavin 1950-

*PERSONAL:* Born January 21, 1950, in Aberdeen, Scotland; son of George and Catherine (McIntosh) Reid; married Lorraine Beattie, 1972 (died, 1990); children: Christopher. *Education:* University of Aberdeen, B.Ed. (with honors), M.Ed.; University of Glasgow, M.App.Sci., Ph.D.; Open University, M.A. *Religion:* Church of Scotland. *Avocational interests:* Hill walking, cycling.

*ADDRESSES: Home*—7 Blinkbonny Ave., Edinburgh, EH4 3HT, Scotland. *Office*—Holyrood Campus, University of Edinburgh, Edinburgh EH8 8AA, Scotland; fax: +44-131-651-6511. *E-mail*—gavin.reid@ed.ac.uk.

*CAREER:* Teacher at an academy in Aberdeen, Scotland, 1979-85; Fife Regional Psychological Service, Kircaldy, Scotland, psychologist, 1985-90; University of Edinburgh, Edinburgh, Scotland, senior lecturer, 1990—.

*MEMBER:* British Psychological Society (associate fellow), British Dyslexia Association (associate member).

*WRITINGS:*

*Dimensions of Dyslexia,* two volumes, Muray House, 1996.
*Dyslexia: A Practitioner's Handbook,* Wiley (New York City), 1998.
(With Barbara K. Given) *Learning Styles,* Red Rose Publications, 1999.
(With Jane Kirk) *Dyslexia in Adults,* Wiley, 2000.

*WORK IN PROGRESS:* Developing a "listening and literacy index" with which to assess children between the ages of six and nine; research on dyslexia in the prison population.

*SIDELIGHTS:* Gavin Reid told *CA:* "My motivation for writing emerges from my experiences as a psychologist and teacher when I was required to teach and assess children who were not coping with learning in the conventional manner. It was clear to me that these students had considerable abilities but were prevented from fulfilling their potential because many were, in fact, dyslexic. With appropriate provision, recognition of their learning styles, and the use of individualized learning programs, the evidence suggests that dyslexic students can succeed and excel.

"My work and writing therefore involves the dissemination and analysis of the research and teaching and learning suggestions for dyslexic students and professionals. Additionally, my research with colleagues has confirmed the high percentage of undiagnosed adults with dyslexia, and my book with Jane Kirk highlights this. The book makes suggestions for adults and professionals which we hope will help those with dyslexia, whether in employment or in study, fulfill their potential.

"I was further inspired to write on dyslexia by the commitment and the need shown by parents and teachers. My work involves travel and talking to teachers and parents in many countries, and I find the dedication of these people quite staggering. Publications in the area of dyslexia and learning styles are usually warmly welcomed by parents, teachers, psychologists, and adults with dyslexia."

*   *   *

## RIVERA, Marina 1942-

*PERSONAL:* Born February 9, 1942, in Superior, AZ. *Education:* Northern Arizona University, B.A. (summa cum laude), 1964; University of Arizona, M.A., 1966, M.F.A., 1981.

*CAREER:* Teacher of English, speech, and creative writing at high schools in Phoenix and Flagstaff, AZ, in Hayward and Santa Ana, CA, and in Alpine, TX; Tucson High School, Tucson, AZ, English teacher at Special Projects High School for Advanced Studies, until 1982; founder of an upholstery business; language tutor for the families of corporate executives transferred to the United States from Spain. Gives readings from her works.

*WRITINGS:*

*Mestiza* (poems), Grilled Flowers (Tucson, AZ), 1977.
*Sobra* (poems), Casa Editorial (San Francisco, CA), 1977.
(With Will Inman, Sheila Murphy, Burgess Needle, and David Chorlton) *Fingers of Silence* (poems), Brushfire, 1981.

Work represented in anthologies, including *I Had Been Hungry All the Years: An Anthology of Women's Poetry,* edited by Glenna Luschei and Del Marie Rogers, Solo (San Luis Obispo, CA), 1975; *Southwest: A Contemporary Anthology,* edited by Karl and Jane Kopp, Red Earth (Albuquerque, NM), 1977; and *Beyond Rice, a Broadside Series,* edited by Terrence Ames, Lorna Dee Cervantes, and Geraldine Kudaka, Mango & Noro (San Francisco), 1979. Contributor to periodicals, including *Revista Chicano-Riquena, Palabra, Caracol,* and *Denver Quarterly.*

*SIDELIGHTS:* Marina Rivera is not only a poet of the Chicana experience, but of the universal human condition. *Dictionary of Literary Biography* contributor Elaine Dorough Johnson called her "a mature, highly skilled poet who writes . . . as a Chicana—coping with poverty and surviving in an Anglo-American world." In her poems, however, Rivera demands to be perceived, not only as a Chicana, or even a women, but as a human individual independent of ethnicity or gender. Intensely private in her personal life, Rivera uses poetry to communicate her perspectives on life, death, and a wide range of human emotions. Johnson noted: "In the inner space of her artistic consciousness, personal experience is transformed into a poetry of unusual depth and honesty."

Despite her insistence on individualism and independence, Rivera's work resonates with pride in her Hispanic heritage. In the collection *Mestiza,* the title poem contains tributes to her parents: a father who fled from Pancho Villa as a baby in his mother's arms and dedicated his life to fighting tenaciously for the future of his family in a white world, and a mother who transcended poverty by the sweat of her brow. Other poems describe what it was like for Rivera and her brother to grow up in a housing project where they were never fully accepted. Johnson wrote: "Many poems in *Mestiza* address the experience of living simultaneously in two cultures and coping with the tensions that this split produces in the psyche . . . [yet while] the question of racial identity is explicit . . . it is interwoven with intensely personal concerns and is rarely the primary theme." The personal concerns include the traumatizing death of Rivera's beloved brother, the unforgivable violent behavior of adults toward children, the social injustice faced by Chicanos in the United States, and—always—the need to be treated as a unique individual.

Rivera's second poetry collection is *Sobra,* "a much more private, personal, encoded work than *Mestiza*" in Johnson's view. The themes are often similar, Johnson observed: "navigating in the Anglo-American world . . . the effect of an adult's anger on children . . . an older relative overcome by the brutal circumstances of his life . . . the fusion of human beings with nature . . . and the devastation of death." One difference that Johnson noticed is that "[t]he reader of *Sobra* is confronted with an introspection so intense that it is more

anguish than reflection. Similarly the examination of personal relationships is more probing." Another difference is reflected in the poem "Dream," described by Johnson as "clearly surrealistic in its depiction of an inside-out world where trees are bent ceilings and vegetables enter a person's system from the stomach's surface."

A collection-in-progress is *The Celia Poems,* a few of which have appeared singly in various periodicals. According to Johnson, these reveal "the artist in a period of recovery, hibernation, and regeneration, accompanied by an intense concentration of creative energy"; they also reflect a "sense of alienation combined with a defiant independence." This spirit of alienation and independence, which recurs throughout Rivera's poetry, may explain the relative lack of critical attention generated by her work, Johnson suggested: the woman who prefers individual affirmation over approval based on ethnic heritage, gender, political views, and affinity with a specific literary movement "runs the risk of being overlooked." Yet Johnson is convinced that "Rivera speaks to any audience appreciative of serious poetry."

*BIOGRAPHICAL/CRITICAL SOURCES:*

*BOOKS*

*Dictionary of Literary Biography,* Volume 122: *Chicano Writers, Second Series,* Gale Research (Detroit, MI), 1992.*

\*　　\*　　\*

## ROBINSON, Joseph 1927-1999

*OBITUARY NOTICE*—See index for *CA* sketch: Born February 23, 1927, in Lancashire, England; died June 21, 1999. Priest and author. Robinson was born in the north of England and graduated with first-class honors from King's College of the University of London, from which he received both bachelor's and master's degrees. He was ordained a deacon of the Church of England in 1952 and a priest the following year. Robinson worked in three of England's greatest churches, St. Paul's, Canterbury Cathedral and Temple Church, of which he served as master. He contributed essays to church periodicals, edited *Bible Readings Fellowship Notes* and authored one book, *The Cambridge Bible Commentary on the New English Bible: I Kings.* For most of the 1960s he also served on the University of London faculty, where he lectured in Hebrew and Old Testament studies.

*OBITUARIES AND OTHER SOURCES:*

PERIODICALS

*Times* (London), July 9, 1999.

\* \* \*

## ROBOTHAM, Rosemarie 1957-

*PERSONAL:* Born in 1957.

*ADDRESSES: Agent*—c/o Three Rivers Press, Crown Publishing Group, 201 East 50th St., New York, NY 10022.

*CAREER: Essence* (magazine), editor-at-large.

*WRITINGS:*

*Spirits of the Passage,* Simon & Schuster, (New York City), 1997.
*Zachary's Wings* (novel), Scribner (New York City), 1998.
(Editor) *The Bluelight Corner: Black Women Writing on Passion, Sex, and Romantic Love,* Three Rivers Press (New York City), 1999.

*SIDELIGHTS: Zachary's Wings,* Rosemarie Robotham's debut novel, tells about the relationship between Zachary, a social worker from an African-American working-class family living in Philadelphia, and Korie, a reporter recently dismissed from her job who hails from a professional, prosperous Jamaican family. In order to nurse Sam, her gay, almost-ex-husband who suffers from AIDS, Korie and her then sort-of-resident housekeeper Zachary, have Sam live with them. Following Sam's death, Korie become a drug addict, and finally finds salvation when she returns to her family and home in Jamaica. *Zachary's Wings* seemed to *Library Journal* contributor Ellen Flexman like it was written by "an inexperienced romance writer, with contrived situations and characters and language that is unrealistic." A *Publishers Weekly* critic described *Zachary's Wings* as "a sometimes awkward and sometimes moving debut . . . that sensitively tackles issues of class and cultural differences." The critic went on to opine that the novel might have benefited from a faster pace and "more local color about Jamaica."

Robotham is the editor of 1999's *The Bluelight Corner: Black Women Writing on Passion, Sex, and Romantic Love.* The anthology includes "wildly uneven" works, featuring fiction by well-known writers such as Alice Walker and bell hooks, as well as "lesser known writers," according to a contributor to *Publishers Weekly.* Although many of the works in *The Bluelight Corner* had been previously presented to the public, "most retain their freshness and power, and gain resonance in this new context," maintained the *Publishers Weekly* critic, who noted that among the contents of "this rich and very varied collection" may be found a Jamaican island affair, a relationship with a ghost, the family concerns of a prostitute, homosexuality, and teenage pregnancy. A reviewer for *Ebony* indicated that the various stories are commonly connected by their ability to conjure "strong feelings" and "their attention to detail."

*BIOGRAPHICAL/CRITICAL SOURCES:*

PERIODICALS

*Ebony,* December, 1998.
*Essence,* May, 1995.
*Library Journal,* October 1, 1998.
*Publishers Weekly,* September 7, 1998, p. 63; November 9, 1998, p. 59.\*

\* \* \*

## ROMERO, Leo 1950-

*PERSONAL:* Born September 25, 1950, in Chacon, NM; son of Ortencia Romero; married Elizabeth Cook (a partner in the family book store). *Education:* University of New Mexico, B.A., 1973; New Mexico State University, M.A., c. 1981.

*ADDRESSES: Home*—34 Calle el Cancho, Santa Fe, NM 87501.

*CAREER:* Los Alamos National Laboratory, Los Alamos, NM, worked as technical writer in the computing division, and in the science outreach program; Books and More Books (book store), Santa Fe, NM, co-owner. Conducted poetry workshops in northern New Mexico. Also worked for the Social Security Administration in Clovis, NM, c. 1975.

*AWARDS, HONORS:* Resident artist fellow, Wurlitzer Foundation, 1979; creative writing fellow, National Endowment for the Arts, 1981; national Hispanic scholarship, 1981; Pushcart Prize, 1982, for *Agua Negra.*

*WRITINGS:*

*During the Growing Season* (poems), Maguey (Tucson, AZ), 1978.

*Celso* (poems), Tonatiuh-Quinto Sol International (Berkeley, CA), 1980.

*Agua Negra* (poems), Ahsahta (Boise, ID), 1981.

*Celso: Voices of New Mexico* (play), produced in Las Cruces, NM, at Readers Theater, 1982.

*Celso* (poems), Arte Publico (Houston, TX), 1985.

(With Jorge A. Huerta and Ruben Sierra) *I Am Celso* (play), produced in Seattle, WA, by Group Theatre Company, 1985.

*Desert Nights* (poems), Fish Drum (Santa Fe, NM), 1989.

*Going Home Away Indian* (poems), Ahsahta, 1990.

*Rita and Los Angeles,* Bilingual Press (Tempe, AZ), 1995.

Work represented in anthologies, including *We Are Chicanos: An Anthology of Mexican-American Literature,* edited by Philip D. Ortego, Washington Square Press (New York City), 1973; *For Neruda, for Chile,* edited by Walter Lowenfels, Beacon Press (Boston, MA), 1975; *Reality in Conflict: Literature of Values in Opposition,* Scott, Foresman (Glenview, IL), 1976; *Southwest: A Contemporary Anthology,* edited by Jane Kopp and Karl Kopp, Red Earth (Albuquerque, NM), 1977; *The Pushcart Prize VII: Best of the Small Presses,* edited by Bill Henderson, Pushcart (Wainscott, NY), 1982; *Voices: An Anthology of Nuevo Mexicano Writers,* edited by Rudolfo Anaya, Norte/Academia (Albuquerque), 1987; *New Worlds of Literature,* edited by Jerome Beaty and J. Paul Hunter, Norton (New York City), 1989; *Currents from the Dancing River: Contemporary Latino Poetry,* Bamberg (Germany), 1994; *The Floating Borderlands: Twenty-Five Years of U.S. Hispanic Literature,* University of Washington Press, 1998; and *Real Things: An Anthology of Popular Culture in American Poetry,* Indiana University Press, 1998. Contributor to periodicals, including *Fish Drum Magazine, Frank: An International Journal of Writing and Art, L'Ozio, Northwest Review, Americas Review, South Dakota Review, Floating Island, Sonora Review, Bilingual Review,* and *Revista Chicano-Requena.* Poetry editor, *Puerto del Sol.*

*WORK IN PROGRESS:* Novels *Crazy for Fabiola,* "a novel that largely takes place in Las Cruces (Los Nueces) and Albuquerque (Burque)" and *Michael and Los Angeles* (a continuation of *Rita and Los Angeles*); poetry collections *San Fernandez Beat, Ravens Are Real, The God of Oranges,* and *At Dusk Through the Canyon.*

*SIDELIGHTS:* Leo Romero has been identified as one of the most prolific poets of New Mexico. Romero was born in Chacon, a village in the northern part of the state, but he grew up in and around Las Vegas, raised from age four by a single mother in a largely Spanish-speaking community, though he grew up speaking English. It was a return to Chacon in 1975 that inspired the poetic depictions of village people for which he is best known.

In Chacon, Enrique R. Lamadrid reported in the *Dictionary of Literary Biography,* "Time passed in conversation with his grandmother and in simple activities like sitting on the portal and chopping wood. . . . Back in Chacon, Romero came to terms with his past: the uprooting from the rich village culture at such an early age, the deprivation of a paternal history, and the alienation from Spanish, his childhood tongue." There he uncovered his roots within a traditional culture that had eluded him for many years. Lamadrid observed: "What appear in Romero's poetry are the familiar themes, motifs, and voices from the oral traditions of New Mexican folklore, not reported in the manner of a folklorist, but lyrically recounted in new poetic creations."

One of Romero's most popular and well developed characters is the picaro known as Celso. "As a social and literary type," Lamadrid reported, "Celso is part of a millennial tradition of tricksters, outcasts, and rogues that dates back to the picaresque animal fables of both Europe and America." Romero commented in the *Dictionary of Literary Biography:* "To some people Celso would be just a drunk and a bum, but there's a little bit of Celso in everyone. . . . He's free of all the meaningless things we take so seriously. He jokes. He tells stories. He doesn't care about getting a car or getting a house. He doesn't care what people think of him. It takes great courage to live that way. It's a hard life."

Through Celso, Romero explores some themes that are common to picaresque poetry: alienation, magic, and ecstasy. Lamadrid explained, "A basic characteristic of picaros is their social alienation: some begin life as orphans," as Celso did, and "[t]he alienation and bitterness Celso experiences in his youth follow him into old age. . . . But alienation from society is the most important prerequisite for unfettered criticism of it, for the picaresque genre has been the main vehicle for social criticism (in print) for centuries in the Hispanic world." A counterbalance for the bitterness is represented by the magic Celso experiences in the poem "Dancing with Moonlight" and the ecstasy he derives from red wine in "The Sermon of the Grape." Lamadrid observed, "Celso's delirium gives Romero access to lyrical moments of surrealism, and access to the folk realm of legend or supernatural belief."

Celso first appeared in the collection *During the Growing Season* in 1978. Since then, two book-length collections have been devoted to Celso, and he appears in other books and periodicals as well. Romero has earned many awards and honors for his work. Lamadrid noted: "The critical reception of Romero's poetry has been consistently enthusiastic since the appearance of his first book." Denise Chavez wrote in the *Rio Grande Writers' Newsletter:* "The ongoing cyclical movements of Romero's poems are strong, blinding—as sharp knocks on the skull." Lamadrid attributed the poet's popularity to multiple factors: "In his poems Romero has successfully brought the magic of his regional culture to a national audience, not by merely describing its traditions, but rather by evoking the complex and lyrical orality which lies so close to its collective soul."

Romero told *CA:* "For a long time I haven't taken my writing too seriously. I've been quick to jump at a variety of distractions. As an example, I've spent countless hours during the past six years building rock walls and doing a tremendous amount of landscaping on my property which is almost three acres. Those were countless hours I could have spent writing. Rocks, dirt, and plants called to me more than did words. And owning a bookstore has been a major distraction. At first I thought it would be good for my writing. And in many ways it has been. I am continuously coming across books I never would have suspected were out there. That has fed my writing to a certain extent. But on the other hand, I have seen so many books in the past twelve yeras that sometimes I can't help wondering if the world needs another book. But as I scan book after book, I realize how few really good books there are, even with as many mind-boggling books as are being published each year, and I regain my faith in writing, in being a writer. I have yet to take writing seriously. I sometimes think that New Mexico is too sunny and dry and that I need to move somewhere cloudy and rainy. I feel my spirits life when the weather is overcast. I think I would take writing more seriously in such a place, gray, stormy, an ocean not too far away."

*BIOGRAPHICAL/CRITICAL SOURCES:*

*BOOKS*

*Dictionary of Literary Biography,* Volume 122: *Chicano Writers, Second Series,* Gale Research (Detroit, MI), 1992.

*PERIODICALS*

*Rio Grande Writers' Newsletter,* winter, 1981.

\*　　\*　　\*

## ROSEN, Bernard Carl   1922-

*PERSONAL:* Born July 1, 1922 in Philadelphia, PA; son of Morris and Sophie (Slaviter) Rosen; married Shirley Rosenbluth, September 10, 1950; children: Michele. *Education:* Temple University, B.A., 1948; Columbia University, M.A., 1950; Cornell University, Ph.D., 1952.

*ADDRESSES: Home*—895 Highland Rd., Ithaca, NY 14850. *Office*—Cornell University, Department of Sociology, 344 Uris Hall, Ithaca, NY 14853.

*CAREER:* Yale University, New Haven, CT, instructor, 1952-53; University of Connecticut, Storrs, assistant professor, 1953-61; University of Nebraska, Lincoln, associate professor to full professor, 1961-66; Cornell University, Ithaca, NY, professor, 1966-93, professor emeritus, 1993—; also served as visiting professor at University of Sao Paulo, Brazil, 1960-61; Escola Sociologia and Politica, Sao Paulo, 1963-64; Department of Social Relations, Harvard University, 1966; the London School of Economics, 1973-74; and Institute of Social Psychology, University of Padua, Italy, 1983-84; associate editor, *Sociometry;* editorial board, *Luso-Brazilian Review;* consultant to National Science Foundation, National Institute of Health, Upjohn Institute for Employment Research. *Military Service:* U.S. Army, 1943-46, active duty in France and Germany, two battle stars.

*MEMBER:* National Committee for Visiting Scientists Program; chairman, Social Psychology Section, Midwest Sociological Society.

*AWARDS, HONORS:* Recipient of research grants from the National Science Foundation and the National Institute of Mental Health; work featured as Citation Classic in *Current Contents,* August 1, 1983.

*WRITINGS:*

*Adolescence and Religion,* Schenkman Publishing Company (Cambridge), 1965.
(Editor, with H. Crockett and C. Nunn) *Achievement in American Society,* Schenkman, 1969.
*The Industrial Connection,* Aldine Publishing Company (New York City), 1982.

(With A. M. Manganelli Rattazzi, A. Comucci Tajoli, and D. Capozza) *Aspettative Di Istruzione E Occupazione Nei Giovani,* Patron Editore (Bologna, Italy), 1988.

*Women, Work and Achievement,* St. Martin's Press (New York City), 1989.

*Winners and Losers of the Information Revolution: Psychosocial Change and Its Discontents,* Praeger Publishing Company (Westport, CT), 1998.

Contributor to numerous scholarly publications, including *American Sociological Review, Sociometry, Merril-Palmer Quarterly, Sociologica, Child Development, Sociological Inquiry, America Latina, Demography, Journal of Marriage and the Family,* and *Social Forces.* Contributor of chapters to books, including *Motives in Fantasy, Action and Society,* edited by J. W. Atkinson, Van Nostrand, 1958; *Race, Class and Power,* edited by R. W. Mack, American Book Company, 1963; *Readings in Reference Group Theory and Research,* edited by H. Hyman and E. Singer, Free Press, 1968; *Adolescents and the High School,* edited by R. Purnell, Holt, Rinehart & Winston, 1970; *Sociological Observation: A Strategy for New Social Knowledge,* edited by M. Riley and E. Nelson, Basic Books, 1974; *Influences on Human Development,* edited by U. Bronfenbrenner, Dryden Press, 1975; *Foundations of Sociology,* edited by R. D. Shapiro, Rand-McNally, 1978 and others.

*WORK IN PROGRESS:* A book about Generation X, scheduled for completion in 2002.

*SIDELIGHTS:* Sociologist Bernard Rosen, professor emeritus at Cornell University, has focused in his work on what he considers the "quintessential American question: who is destined to be a winner, who a loser, and why?" From his childhood, Rosen felt destined to become a loser. Born in 1922 in Philadelphia, he was raised in a family that lacked the resources to send him to college, and he took several unskilled jobs after high school before becoming a skilled machinist. This experience with blue-collar work, he noted, served him well when he later began to write about the influence of class on values, personality, and achievement.

During World War II, Rosen enlisted in the U.S. Army and saw active combat in France and Germany. He remembers entering the Dachau concentration camp soon after it was liberated by the Allies, and taking care of some of the inmates. He said that "one of the more satisfying experiences" of his military career was his capture of a hidden Nazi prison guard, whom he turned over to the military police. After the war, Rosen took advantage of the G.I. Bill to attend Temple University, where he earned a B.A. in history in 1948. He earned a M.A. in sociology from Columbia University in 1950, and a Ph.D. in sociology and social psychology from Cornell University in 1952. He has held teaching positions at Yale University, the University of Connecticut, the University of Nebraska, and Cornell University, where he was a professor from 1966 to 1993. In 1993, he became professor emeritus.

At Cornell, Rosen held graduate professorships in the psychology, human development, family studies, and Latin American studies departments. He has held editorial positions at *Sociometry* and *Luso-Brazilian Review,* and has served as consultant to the National Institute of Health and the Upjohn Institute for Employment Research. He has been a member of the National Committee for Visiting Scientists Program and was chair of the Social Psychology Section of the Midwest Sociological Society. Rosen has accepted posts as a visiting professor at the University of Sao Paulo, Brazil, the Escola Sociologia and Politica (Sao Paolo), the Department of Social Relations at Harvard University, the London School of Economics, and the Institute of Social Psychology at the University of Padua, Italy. He has received research grants from the National Science Foundation and the National Institute of Mental Health.

Throughout his work, Rosen has explored issues relating to minorities, class, and achievement—subjects of increasing interest and concern through the 1950s and 1960s as postwar demographic shifts caused great social change throughout the United States and other parts of the world. At Yale, Rosen became interested in David C. McClelland's work on achievement motivation, and began to research the possible effects group differences in motivation might have on individual achievement. Rosen traveled to Brazil, Italy, Portugal, and England to conduct field research. He enjoyed learning other languages and experiencing other cultures first-hand, especially Brazil, where he was suspected of being a CIA agent but which he found generally welcoming.

Rosen has written six books and numerous scholarly articles, which have been reprinted as chapters in over thirty textbooks. His overseas fieldwork was especially pertinent in his third book, *The Industrial Connection,* a cross-cultural study of how industrialization's effects on the family can influence individual achievement and personality. In this work, Rosen used Brazil as a model of transitional societies, and found that the Brazilian extended family was strengthened, rather than weakened, by urban-industrial conditions. Using a macrosociological approach, Rosen compared his findings with data from other cities in Brazil and other developing cultures, as well as the United States. Critics considered the book well researched and convincingly argued. It received a respectful review in *Choice,* as well as praise from Robert C. Williamson in *Social Forces.* David O. Hansen, in *Luso-Brazilian Review,* called *The Industrial Connection* "a classic in the comparative family literature and a valuable source book on the Brazilian family."

Another cross-cultural study, *Women, Work and Achievement,* dealt with the complex subject of industrialization's effect on traditional sex roles. Using data from the United States, England, and Italy, Rosen presented an overview of adolescents' behavior and attitudes toward themselves, their parents, and their peers. He then developed his argument that industrialization and urbanization have effected changes in the traditional roles of men and women to the extent that equality between genders in the workplace is almost complete. *Choice* reviewer M. M. Ferree found Rosen's data "impressive," but pointed out that his emphasis on theory weakened the book's effectiveness. "Points are selectively emphasized to give a picture of uniform linear change (progress)," wrote Ferree, "even when his asides suggest that he realizes there is more complexity." The reviewer noted that much of Rosen's research has been presented more thoroughly in journal articles.

Rosen told *CA:* "It was [my] good fortune to study the linkages between race, gender, childrearing, personality and achievement just as international and national forces converged to heighten interest in these topics. . . . Field research is a social as well as an intellectual challenge. But writing is a private, uniquely absorbing task that isolates one from the world. It is this isolation that [I have] always found especially satisfying. (In addition, of course, there is the pleasure of lining up words and ideas in an intrinsically meaningful and esthetically pleasing way.) The isolation that writing brings was to some extent lessened by the public reception [my] work has received."

*BIOGRAPHICAL/CRITICAL SOURCES:*

*PERIODICALS*

*Choice,* January, 1983, p. 770; March, 1990, p. 1402; May, 1999, p. 1696.
*Contemporary Sociology,* November, 1990, p. 808.
*Current Contents,* August 1, 1983, p. 22.
*Luso-Brazilian Review,* winter, 1983, pp. 285-286.
*Social Forces,* September, 1984, p. 299.
*Sociology,* August, 1990, p. 550.

## ROSS, David William 1922-

*PERSONAL:* Born in 1922.

*ADDRESSES: Agent*—c/o Simon & Schuster, 1230 Avenue of the Americas, New York, NY 10020.

*CAREER:* Author.

*WRITINGS:*

*Beyond the Stars,* Simon & Schuster (New York City), 1990.
*Eye of the Hawk,* Simon & Schuster, 1992.

*SIDELIGHTS:* The American West has served as a central theme in David William Ross's two epic novels, *Beyond the Stars* and *Eye of the Hawk.* In these books, Ross explores the epic conflicts that engulfed the region when competing groups such as European Americans, Indians, and Mexicans encountered one another in the late 1800s.

*Beyond the Stars* (1990), Ross's first novel, earned generally respectful reviews. Critics admired its sympathetic treatment of the Plains Indians and its exciting plot. The novel, which a *Kirkus Reviews* contributor called "a great, grasping Western," focuses on the clash between European Americans and the Sioux in the 1870s, the period just before these tribes were confined to reservations. The plot involves a frontiersman raised by Indians, a search for a lost gold mine, and a Crow chief's search for his son's grave in the territory of the enemy Sioux. Though reviewers pointed out that much of this material was typical of the genre, they appreciated Ross's ability to interject new life into it and to create characters that transcended stereotypes. A reviewer for *Publishers Weekly* deemed the book an "engrossing saga" that was especially effective in its treatment of cultures at a turning point. A *Kirkus Reviews* contributor also appreciated Ross's cultural sensitivity, but felt that the author was more sympathetic to the Indians than to the European Americans, which made the novel "ponderous and unwieldy." When *Beyond the Stars* was published in a paperback edition, a contributor to *Kliatt* recommended the book as a "bone-chilling saga" in which "the story is absorbing, the characters are human, and the bloodshed is unrelenting."

Critics were less enthusiastic, however, about Ross's second novel, *Eye of the Hawk.* Another Western epic, the novel tells a complex story of Texas cattle ranchers, skirmishes with Indians and Mexican bandits, fighting for the Confederacy, rape, marital strife, and ill-starred romance. The book, in the opinion of a *Kirkus Reviews* contributor, "juggles too many characters to treat any of them in depth" and never communicates a true sense of the land. But the reviewer praised Ross's writing, noting that the author "moves from the brink of one disaster to another" in the manner of a romance writer. Robert Jordan, in *Library Journal*, likened *Eye of the Hawk* to John Jakes's *North and South*, observing that Ross creates "sympathetic" characters and spins "a good yarn." Yet Jordan also found flaws in the book, noting that Ross "often yields to hyperbole" and makes occasional factual errors. A *Publishers Weekly* reviewer also noted Ross's penchant for exaggeration in this novel, observing that "plot and character development give way to relentless bloodshed and stereotypes" and that the characters "lead soap-opera lives." The reviewer concluded that the "hefty saga" might "leave readers exhausted."

*BIOGRAPHICAL/CRITICAL SOURCES:*

PERIODICALS

*Kirkus Reviews,* March 15, 1990, p. 375; April 15, 1992, p. 494.
*Kliatt,* September, 1991, p. 16.
*Library Journal,* June 1, 1992, p. 180.
*Publishers Weekly,* March 16, 1990, p. 62; May 4, 1992, p. 40.*

\*     \*     \*

**ROSS, Hugh (Norman) 1945-**

*PERSONAL:* Born July 24, 1945 in Westmount, Canada; immigrated to United States, 1973; son of James Stewart Alexander and Dorothy Isabel (Murray) Ross; married Kathleen Ann Drake, July 30, 1977; children: Joel Stephen, David Michael. *Education:* University of British Columbia, B.S. (physics), 1967; University of Toronto, M.S., 1968, Ph.D. (astronomy), 1973. *Ethnicity:* "Scots." *Politics:* Non-partisan. *Religion:* Evangelical Christian. *Avocational interests:* Mountaineering, hiking, bicycling, roller blading, home improvements.

*ADDRESSES: Office*—Reasons to Believe, P.O. Box 5978, Pasadena, CA 91117-0978. *E-mail*—reasons@reasons.org.

*CAREER:* Astronomer. California Institute of Technology, Pasadena, research fellow in radio astronomy, 1973-78; Sierra Madre Congregational Church, Pasa-

dena, CA, minister of evangelism, 1975-86, minister of apologetics, 1986—; Reasons To Believe, Inc. (Progressive Creationist ministry), Pasadena, CA, president, 1986—. Has lectured and appeared on radio and television, as well as in video and audio tapes.

*MEMBER:* American Institute of Physics, American Science Affiliation, American Astronomical Society, American Association for the Advancement of Science.

*AWARDS, HONORS:* Murdock Charitable Trust grantee, 1990.

*WRITINGS:*

*The Fingerprint of God,* 1989, 2nd edition, Promise (Orange, CA), 1991.
*The Creator and the Cosmos: How the Greatest Scientific Discoveries of the Century Reveal God,* NavPress (Colorado Springs, CO), 1993, 2nd edition, 1995.
*Creation and Time: A Biblical and Scientific Perspective on the Creation-Date Controversy,* NavPress, 1994.
*Beyond the Cosmos: The Extra-Dimensionality of God; What Recent Discoveries in Astronomy and Physics Reveal about the Nature of God,* NavPress, 1996.
*The Genesis Question: Scientific Advances and the Accuracy of Genesis,* NavPress, 1998.
*The Genesis Debate,* Crux Publications (Orange County, CA), 2000.
*How to Think about UFOs,* NavPress, 2001.
*Origin of Humanity,* NavPress, 2001.

Also author of articles.

*SIDELIGHTS:* The titles given to Hugh Ross's books, such as *The Fingerprint of God, The Creator and the Cosmos: How the Greatest Scientific Discoveries of the Century Reveal God,* and *Creation and Time: A Biblical and Scientific Perspective on the Creation-Date Controversy,* clearly indicate his long-standing focus. A lecturer who has a appeared on numerous television and radio programs, Ross has earned a doctorate in astronomy and is a trained minister who has spent much of his professional career trying to prove religious teachings with scientific discoveries. Somewhat radical in both religious and scientific domains, he posits that even a literal reading of the Bible coincides with scientific truths.

In his fifth book, *The Genesis Question: Scientific Advances and the Accuracy of Genesis,* Ross examines the

Genesis Question "in the light of its purpose and the original Hebrew," noted Eugene O. Bowser in *Library Journal.* According to Bowser, Ross maintains that ancestry, not directly biological families (i.e., mother, father, and siblings), is the true history addressed in the first chapter of the Bible. As such, thousands of years can be accounted for by what many Bible readers interpret to be very small units of time. Adam and Eve were real people, according to Ross, but they lived around 24,000 years ago. In contrast to the beliefs of some people in the scientific community, they, as people, did not originate from "tool-using, relatively large-brained hominids," which Bowser stated Ross classified as "preadamic" (existing before Adam).

Critical reaction to Ross's books has been mixed. Bowser called *The Genesis Question* a "blueprint" that some people of faith may find fascinating. "Others," declared a *Publishers Weekly* reviewer, "may wonder why he is trying so hard to turn faith into science."

*The Creator and the Cosmos,* in which Ross claims that the universe was specifically made for human beings and would not exist if there was a slight difference in any one of a number its characteristics, is an "interesting," thorough, and "easily understood" work that gives readers "well presented . . . well explained" science, according to Peter F. Arvedson in *Science Books & Films.* Arvedson judged that the book "is not likely to convince" non-believers of God. Ross deduces that proof of God as the creator is found in the understanding that universe has such particular factors conducive to human life. Arvedson was critical of the book's "overuse of probability," its occasional reliance on the Bible as evidence, and its "sketchy" presentation of evolution.

With *Beyond the Cosmos: The Extra-Dimensionality of God; What Recent Discoveries in Astronomy and Physics Reveal about the Nature of God,* Ross approaches the notion that science presents more than supporting evidence of God's existence; Ross suggests that it gives a more convincing case than religion itself. According to Pius Murray in *Library Journal,* Ross's defense of this belief pales in comparison to works by other people. Murray declared: "he weakens his argument by trying to interpret scripture in terms of science." Another of Ross's publications was more positively judged by *Booklist* contributor Patty O'Connell, who praised *Creation and Time: A Biblical and Scientific Perspective on the Creation-Date Controversy* as "extremely well documented . . . more than a good read. It is a call for action. A relevant addition to any library."

Ross told *CA:* "Our focus at Reasons to Believe is not to provide all the reasons to believe in the God of the Bible, but rather the new reasons. Presently, our scientific team digests over 600 research papers per year that provide additional evidences for the Bible's God. It is our goal in producing books and videos to explain to lay people what these new discoveries mean scientifically, philosophically, and theologically. We maintian a daily hotline for fielding questions on science and faith issues and we publish a news magazine, *Facts for Faith,* amd a free newsletter, *Connections,* to keep people up to date on new evidences for God."

*BIOGRAPHICAL/CRITICAL SOURCES:*

*PERIODICALS*

*Booklist,* April 1, 1994, p. 1409.
*Library Journal,* August, 1996, pp. 78-79; December, 1998, p. 115; January, 1999, p. 106.
*Publishers Weekly,* November 9, 1998, p. 71.
*Science Books & Films,* April, 1995, p. 74.

\*    \*    \*

**ROTHAFEL, Roxy**
  **See ROTHAFEL, Samuel L(ionel)**

\*    \*    \*

**ROTHAFEL, Samuel L(ionel)    1881(?)-1936(?)**
  **(Roxy Rothafel)**

*PERSONAL:* Original surname, Rothapfel; born July 9, 1881 (some sources cite 1882), in Stillwater, MN; died of a heart attack, January 13, 1936 (some sources cite 1931), in Philadelphia, PA; buried in Linden Hills Cemetery, Brooklyn, NY.

*CAREER:* Theater manager, radio broadcaster, and writer. Roxy Theater, New York City, manager, beginning in 1927. Radio broadcaster, including presenter of the program *Roxy and His Gang.*

*WRITINGS:*

(With Raymond F. Yates) *Broadcasting: Its New Day,* Century Co. (New York City), 1925, published as *History of Broadcasting: Radio to Television Series,* 1971.

*SIDELIGHTS:* Popularly known as Roxy, Samuel L. Rothafel was renowned for his phenomenal success as a theater manager. His nickname became synonymous with the luxuriously decorated motion-picture palaces of the 1920s, and his pioneering theatrical efforts—he showcased prominent orchestras, famous singers, and precision dancers in addition to feature films—earned him acclaim as the father of the super-cinema. In 1927 the Roxy Theater, built specifically for Rothafel—and managed by him—opened in New York and became known as the Cathedral of the Motion Picture. He later opened the world's largest cinema, New York's Radio City Music Hall, in 1932. Rothafel was also a radio broadcaster whose program *Roxy and His Gang* became popular during the middle to late 1920s and was the first to be broadcast live from the stage.

### BIOGRAPHICAL/CRITICAL SOURCES:

#### PERIODICALS

*Boston Transcript,* May 20, 1925, p. 4.
*Cleveland,* September, 1925, p. 97.
*Literary Review,* July 18, 1925, p. 5.
*New York Times,* April 12, 1925, p. 10.
*Outlook,* June 24, 1925.
*Saturday Review of Literature,* June 20, 1925.*

\*    \*    \*

## ROY, Jules  1907-

*PERSONAL:* Born October 22, 1907, in Rovigo, Algeria; son of Henri Dematons (a schoolteacher) and Mathilde (Paris) Roy; married Mirande Grimal, 1927 (divorced, late 1940s); married Tatiana Soukhoroukoff (a journalist), 1965.

*ADDRESSES: Agent*—c/o Editions Albin Michel, 22 rue Huyghens, 75680, Paris Cedex, Cedex 14, France.

*CAREER:* Novelist, essayist, and playwright, 1942—. *Military service:* French army, 1927-37, air force, 1937-53; earned Distinguished Flying Cross for missions against Germany during World War II.

*MEMBER:* Ecole diAlger (Algiers School).

*AWARDS, HONORS:* Prix Theophraste Renaudot, for *La Vallee heureuse,* 1946; Prix de Monaco, for *Le Navigateur,* 1954; Grand Prix d'Art Dramatique, for *Les Cyclones;* Prix Pelman, for *Le Fleuve rouge,* 1957; Grand Prix de l'Academie Francaise, 1958; Grand Prix National des Lettres, 1969; Grand Prix de la Ville de Paris, 1971.

### WRITINGS:

*Trois Prieres pour des pilotes,* Charlot (Algiers), 1942, revised edition, 1944, bilingual edition, with translation by George Ellidge, published as *Three Prayers for Pilots,* Charlot, 1944.

*Chants et prieres pour des pilotes,* Charlot, 1945, revised edition, Gallimard (Paris), 1952.

*Ciel et terre,* Charlot, 1943.

*L'Oil de loup du roi de Pharan* Setif, 1945.

*La Vallee heureuse,* Charlot, 1946, translation by Edward Owen Marsh published as *The Happy Valley,* Gollancz (London), 1952.

*Comme un mauvais ange,* Charlot, 1947.

*Le Metier des armes,* Gallimard, 1948.

*Passion de Saint-Exupery,* Gallimard, 1951, revised edition published as *Passion et mort de Saint-Exupery,* Julliard (Paris), 1964.

*Retour de l'enfer,* Gallimard, 1951, translation by Mervyn Savill published as *Return from Hell,* Kimber London, 1954.

*La Bataille dans la riziere,* Gallimard, 1953.

*Le Navigateur,* Gallimard, 1954, translation by Savill published as *The Navigator,* Knopf (New York City), 1955.

*La Femme infidele,* Gallimard, 1955, translation by J. Robert Loy published as *The Unfaithful Wife,* Knopf, 1956.

*Nico a la decouverte du ciel,* Calmann-Levy (Paris), 1956.

*Les Flammes de l'ete,* Gallimard, 1956.

*L'Homme a l'epee,* Gallimard, 1957, enlarged edition, Julliard, 1970.

*Les Belles Croisades,* Gallimard, 1959.

*La Guerre d'Algerie,* Julliard, 1960, translation by Richard Howard published as *War in Algeria,* Grove Press (New York City), 1961.

*Autour du drame,* Julliard, 1961.

*La Bataille de Dien Bien Phu,* Julliard, 1963, translation by Robert Baldick published as *The Battle of Dienbienphu,* Harper & Row (New York City), 1965.

*Le Voyage en Chine,* Julliard, 1965, translation by Francis Price published as *Journey Through China,* Harper & Row, 1967.

*Le Grand Naufrage,* Julliard, 1966, translation by Baldick published as *The Trial of Marshal Petain,* Harper & Row, 1967.

*Les Chevaux du soleil,* Grasset (Paris), 1968, revised edition, Club Francais du Livre Paris, 1969, republished as *Chronique d'Alger,* Livre de Poche (Paris), 1975.

*Une Femme au nom d'etoile* (Volume 2 of *Les Chevaux du soleil*), Grasset, 1968, enlarged edition, Tallandier (Paris), 1971.

*Les Cerises d'Icherridene,* (Volume 3 of *Les Chevaux du soleil*), Grasset, 1968.

*La Mort de Mao,* Christian Bourgois (Paris), 1969.

*Le Maitre de la Mitidja,* (Volume 4 of *Les Chevaux du soleil*), Grasset, 1970.

*La Rue des Zouaves, precede de S. M. Monsieur Constantin,* Julliard, 1970.

*L'Amour fauve,* Grasset, 1971.

*Les Ames interdites* (Volume 5 of *Les Chevaux du soleil*), Grasset, 1972.

*J'accuse le general Massu,* Seuil (Paris), 1972.

*Le Tonnerre et les anges* (Volume 6 of *Les Chevaux du soleil*), Grasset, 1975.

*Danse du ventre au-dessus des canons,* Flammarion (Paris), 1976.

*Turnau,* privately printed (Sienne), 1976.

*Pour le lieutenant Karl,* Christian Bourgois, 1977.

*Le Desert de Retz,* Grasset, 1978.

*Concerto pour un chien,* Grasset, 1979.

*Les Chevaux du soleil,* revised and abridged edition, 1 volume, Grasset, 1980.

*Eloge de Max-Pol Fouchet,* Actes-Sud (Le Paradou), 1980.

*Etranger pour mes freres,* Stock (Paris), 1982.

*A propos d'Alger, de Camus et du hasard,* Haut Quartier (Pezenas), 1982.

*La Saison des za,* Grasset, 1982.

*Une Affaire d'honneur,* Plon (Paris), 1983.

*Beyrouth viva la muerte,* Grasset, 1984.

*Priere a Mademoiselle Sainte Madeleine,* Haut Quartier, 1984.

*Guynemer, l'ange de la mort,* Albin Michel (Paris), 1986.

*Chant d'amour pour Marseille,* Editions Jeanne Laffitte (Marseilles), 1988.

*Memoires barbares,* Albin Michel, 1989.

*La vallee heureuse: Roman,* Michel, 1989.

*Saint-Exupery,* La Manufacture, 1990.

*Amours barbares,* Michel, 1993.

*Un apres-guerre amoureux,* Michel, 1995.

*Mort au champ d'honneur: theatre,* Michel, 1995.

*Adieu ma mere, adieu mon cur,* Michel, 1996.

### PLAYS

*Beau Sang* (produced in Paris at Theatre de l'Humour, 1952), Gallimard, 1952.

*Les Cyclones* (produced in Paris at Theatre de la Michodiere, 1954), Gallimard, 1954.

*Le Fleuve rouge* (produced in Paris at Theatre en Rond, 1960-61), Gallimard, 1957.

### OTHER

(Contributor) Peter Henn, *La Derniere Rafale,* translated by Henry Daussy, Julliard, 1952.

(Contributor) Michel Mohrt, *Marin La Meslee,* Editions de Flore (Paris), 1952.

(Contributor) *Saint-Exupery,* R.-M. Alberes, editor, Albin Michel, 1961.

(Contributor) Claude Dufresnoy, *Des Officiers parlent,* Julliard, 1961.

(Contributor) *Djamila Boupacha,* Simone de Beauvoir and Gisele Halimi, editors, Gallimard, 1962, translated by Peter Green, Macmillan (New York City), 1962.

(Contributor) *Camus,* Alberes, editor, Hachette (Paris), 1964.

(Contributor) Martine Lyon, *Les Chinois,* Julliard, 1965.

(Contributor) Gabriel Audisio, *L'Opera fabuleux,* Julliard, 1970.

(Contributor) *Chant de pierre: Dodeigne,* Centre Culturel de l'Yonne Auxerre, 1983.

*D'une amitie: Correspondence Jean Amrouche-Jules Roy,* Edisud Aix-en-Provence, 1985.

Contributor to periodical publications, including *Confluences, Nouvelles Litteraires, Monde, Etudes Mediterraneennes, Figaro,* and *Nouvel Observateur.* Also author of *Sept Poemes de tenebres,* privately printed, 1957.

*SIDELIGHTS:* Born in Algeria, Jules Roy intended as a young adult to become a priest. However, before completing seminary school, he exchanged one life of discipline for another when he decided to join the French military in 1927. Stationed in France in the 1930s, Roy became part of the military's aviation branch in 1937. When France fell during World War II, Roy returned to Algeria along with most of the air force. For a time, Roy remained true to the French government headed by Philippe Petain to which he had sworn an oath of service. But gradually he realized that his loyalty meant serving the Germans whom occupied France. Finally he pledged his allegiance to the Free French, a group organized by Charles de Gaulle that was fighting against the Germans in aerial campaigns with the Royal Air Force between 1944 to 1945. This difficult period was recorded in an essay Roy wrote, *Le Metier des armes* ("The Profession of Arms"), published in 1948. After the war, Roy returned to France to resume the writing career he had briefly begun in the early 1940s. The novel *La Vallee heureuse* (*The Happy Valley*) was published in 1946 and won him the Prix Theophraste Renaudot. During this period he also became part of a literary circle of Algerian writers that became known as the Ecole d'Alger (Algiers School). Among the group was Albert Camus with whom Roy became a close friend.

During this literary period, Roy also continued his military work by maintaining a desk job with the air force while he wrote. But in 1953, war between France and Indochina escalated and Roy was sent as an observer, upon his own request, into the fray. What he discovered was that not only did the French people at home have misgivings about the conflict, but the Indochinese, on whose behalf this war was supposedly being fought, didn't support it either. He also witnessed French officers applying brutal force, not unlike the Nazis had done, and using napalm in their campaigns. These experiences caused him to resign from military service. Upon returning home, Roy began writing about the conflict in articles and the essay, *La Bataille dans la riziere* ("The Battle in the Rice Paddy"), published in 1953. The play *Le Fleuve rouge* ("Red River"), published in 1957, was even more critical of the French government's position and was followed by the equally harsh novel *Les Belles Croisades* ("Fine Crusades"), published in 1959.

Roy's motivation for being openly critical of French policies and his ability to stand up for what he believed were traits he probably learned in his childhood. Writing in *Dictionary of Literary Biography*, Catharine Savage Brosman remarks, "Over Jules Roy's birth and childhood there lay a shadow of scandal and personal shame—of which he was not aware until his teens, and did not grasp wholly until years later, when he recognized and accepted what it meant to be the son of two rebels. This is the central fact of his life, playing a crucial role in what he has done and written."

The scandal and shame to which Brosman refers was a result of his mother's affair with Henri Dematons despite her marriage to Louis-Alfred Roy. Jules Roy was a product of this affair, which is a detail of his life that he retold in several of his later books. The elder Roy sent his wife and illegitimate son away soon after the birth, and they went to live with Mathilde's parents. But in 1910, Louis-Alfred Roy died, and Mathilde was free to marry Dematons. Although Jules lived with his natural parents for the rest of his childhood, he never came to feel that Dematons was his real father.

Roy's experience in the military made its way into his fiction as well as his critical nonfiction. The aviation story, *Le Navigateur* (*The Navigator*), was published in 1954 and won the Prix de Monaco. The story centers on a young French Air Force pilot who survives a mid-air collision. Afterwards, he is afraid to go up in the air again. Getting over this fear, he then develops a fervent death wish, taking unnecessary risks in the air. This and Roy's other aviation novels won him a reputation rivaling that of the famed Antoine de Saint-Exupery. Reviewing a 1955 English translation of *The Navigator*, Henri Peyre wrote in the *Saturday Review,* "With this artistic short novel, Jules Roy, after Saint-Exupery and the Belgian Closterman, shows that the writers in the French language, perhaps because of their bent as grave moralists and of their sense for artistic restraint, have remained without peers in a new literary realm: that of aviation."

The same year Roy's play *Les Cyclones* was published and produced. Another work dealing with aviation, this one focuses on the military testing of planes. In it the author considers the moral dilemmas officers face when they have to give orders that affect the lives of the men under their command. The stage production won the Grand Prix d'Art Dramatique. Roy's criticism of the French government picked up again when conflict arose in his homeland of Algeria in 1954. He discussed his theories on war in a 1955 article, "Dans une juste guerre" ("In a Just War"), the point of which was explained by Brosman: "When the people are against the war, it is no longer just."

A more extensive assessment of the conflict was published in 1960. *La Guerre d'Algerie* ("War in Algeria") resulted from firsthand research and visits to the war-torn area. The war was resolved finally in 1962 when Algeria achieved its independence. Roy's reaction to this development inspired a series of historical novels called "Les Chevaus du soleil" ("The Horses of the Sun"), published from 1968 to 1975. The six novels touch on the subjects of Roy's own past and the story of his parents set against a political backdrop of France's involvement in Algeria.

Roy continued to publish nonfiction works on political topics that interested him. A documentary of the end of France's battle in Indochina, *La Bataille de Dien Bien Phu* (*The Battle of Dienbienphu*), was published in 1965. Following a visit to China, Roy articulated his opinions on the country's government in *Voyage en Chine* (*Journey through China*) published in 1965. *Le Grand Naufrage* (*The Trial of Marshal Petain*), an account of the famous court proceeding in which Petain was tried for treason, was published in 1966. This book raises the same kinds of questions that Roy asked throughout his career as a writer and soldier. Oscar Handlin, a reviewer for the *Atlantic* wrote, "As [Roy] reviews the judgment of the court and the testimony of the witnesses, he searches his own conscience. Given the circumstances of 1940, was the armistice in the interest of France? What were the demands of loyalty at the moment?" During the 1970s and into the 1980s, Roy continued to travel and write about the places he visited as well as develop his discussions about his native land of Algeria. He also wrote many works of fiction, such as the autobiographical novel *Le Desert de Retz* ("The Retz Desert") published in 1978.

## BIOGRAPHICAL/CRITICAL SOURCES:

### BOOKS

Brosman, Catharine Savage, *Art as Testimony: The Work of Jules Roy,* University of Florida Press, 1989.

Brosman, *Jules Roy,* Celfan Monographs, 1988.

Camus, Albert, *Lyrical and Critical Essays,* Knopf, 1968.

*Dictionary of Literary Biography,* Volume 83: *French Novelists Since 1960,* Gale (Detroit, MI), 1989.

*Dictionary of Twentieth Century Culture,* Volume 2: *French Culture 1900-1975,* Gale, 1995.

Obuchowski, Chester W., *Mars on Trial,* Jose Porrua Turanzas, 1978.

### PERIODICALS

*America,* April 6, 1968.
*Atlantic,* March 1968.
*Aurore,* April 1, 1975, p. 2.
*Best Sellers,* March 1, 1968.
*Booklist,* July 15, 1955.
*Book World,* February 25, 1968, p. 4.
*Chicago Tribune,* July 24, 1955, p. 4.
*Choice,* July 1968.
*Christian Science Monitor,* July 28, 1955, p. 5.
*Combat,* July 10, 1969, p. 9.
*Kirkus,* May 15, 1955; July 15, 1956.
*Library Journal,* June 1, 1955; September 1, 1956; January 1, 1968.
*Livres et Lectures,* 5, 1960, pp. 455-459.
*Manchester Guardian,* May 10, 1955, p. 4.
*New Statesman,* May 14, 1955.
*New Yorker,* August 27, 1955; November 17, 1956.
*New York Herald Tribune Book Review,* July 31, 1955, p. 2.
*New York Review of Books,* May 5, 1968, p. 14.
*New York Times,* July 31, 1955, p. 4; December 23, 1956, p. 10.
*San Francisco Chronicle,* August 14, 1955, p. 17.
*Saturday Review,* July 30, 1955.\*

---

## ROZOVSKY, Mark (Grigorievich) 1937-

*PERSONAL:* Born in 1937, in Petropavlovsk, Kazakh Republic, USSR (now Petropavlovsk, Kazakhstan). *Education:* Attended Moscow University.

*ADDRESSES: Office*—Theatre-Studio U Nikitskikh Vorot, Gertsena Str., 23/9, 103009 Moscow, Russia.

*CAREER:* Our Home (amateur theatre), Moscow, USSR (now Russia), cofounder, 1958, manager, 1958-70, became the Theatre-Studio U Nikitskikh Vorot (professional theatre), manager, beginning in 1987; affiliated with the Gorky Theatre, Leningrad, USSR (now St. Petersburg, Russia). Director of stage productions in Leningrad and Moscow, 1970—, director of stage productions in Riga, Latvia, 1970—. Director of the rock opera *Orpheus and Eurydice,* 1975; and (with Georgii Tovstonogov) the musical adaptation of Leo Tolstoy's *Strider: The Story of a Horse,* produced in Leningrad; director of the play *Amadeus,* produced in Moscow.

*AWARDS, HONORS:* Theatre of Nations Prize, Hamburg, West Germany (now Germany) and Avignon, France, 1979; namesake of Mark Rozovsky Theatre in Moscow, Russia.

*WRITINGS:*

### WRITINGS FOR THE STAGE

(With Georgii Tovstonogov) *Strider: The Story of a Horse* (based on a story by Leo Tolstoy; produced in Leningrad, translated into English by Tamara Bering Sunguroff and adapted by Robert Kalfin and Steve Brown, produced at the Chelsea Theatre Center, New York City, 1979), Samuel French (New York City), 1979.

*Kafka: Father and Son* (based on *Letter to His Father* and *The Judgement,* both by Franz Kafka), produced at La MaMa, Etc., New York City, 1991-92.

*Romances with Oblomov,* produced at the Alexandrinsky Theatre, St. Petersburg, Russia, 1992.

Wrote works for the Gorky Theatre, Leningrad; the Theatre of Russian Drama, Riga, Latvia; and the Theatre-Studio U Nikitskikh Vorot, Moscow. Wrote a libretto for an opera about the Russian poet Vladimir Vladimirovich Mayakovsky. Author of books about the theatre.

### TELEPLAYS

Teleplays include documentaries.

*BIOGRAPHICAL/CRITICAL SOURCES:*

*PERIODICALS*

*Nation,* April 13, 1985, pp. 444-445.
*New York Times,* January 29, 1992, p. C17.
*Soviet Life,* April, 1987, pp. 46-55; January, 1991, pp. 52-54.*

\* \* \*

## RUSSO, Gus

*PERSONAL: Education:* University of Maryland, B.A. (political science), 1972. *Avocational interests:* Guitar, bass, and keyboard playing, tennis, travel.

*ADDRESSES: Agent*—(Literary) Noah Lukeman Literary Management, Ltd., 501 Fifth Ave., New York, NY 10017; (film and television) Infinity Management International, 425 North Robertson Blvd., Los Angeles, CA 90048.

*CAREER:* Investigative journalist and author. Campaign advance man for presidential candidate Senator George McGovern, 1972; public relations director for Baltimore entry in World Tennis League, 1973-74; composed and taught music in New York City, including composing for radio jingles and low-budget movies, 1975-89; received grant to do research on President John F. Kennedy's assassination, 1990, for PBS president Jennifer Lawson; assistant to Congressman Lee Hamilton and Senator John Glenn to draft 1992 Assassination Records Collection Act, 1991; research assistant to author Gerald Posner, 1992; reporter for PBS's *Frontline* television program, 1991-93; presidential primary delegate for Democratic candidate Jerry Brown, 1994; researcher for author Anthony Summers, 1995-96; chief investigative reporter for ABC producer Mark Obenhaus, 1996-97.

*MEMBER:* Association of Former Intelligence Officers, United States Tennis Association.

*AWARDS, HONORS:* Pulitzer Prize nomination and Missouri School of Journalism prize nomination, both 1999, both for *Live by the Sword;* best local nonfiction writer award, Baltimore *City Paper.*

*WRITINGS:*

*Live by the Sword: The Secret War against Castro and the Death of JFK,* Bancroft Press (Baltimore, MD), 1998.

*WORK IN PROGRESS:* Working as a consultant and co-producer on a television miniseries version of *Live by the Sword;* researching a book on organized crime.

*SIDELIGHTS:* Gus Russo, like many politically minded journalists and historians of the John F. Kennedy era, has made a life's work of investigating the incidences that surrounded the assassination of President Kennedy. His work has included magazine articles and television documentaries, such as *Frontline*'s "Who Was Lee Harvey Oswald?" and ABC's "Dangerous Worm." In *Live by the Sword: The Secret War against Castro and the Death of JFK,* Russo pursues his theory that, as the Warren Commission concluded, Lee Harvey Oswald was the lone killer of Kennedy. But delineating Oswald's motives is Russo's real project here: Russo believes Oswald killed Kennedy because he had an inkling of the Kennedy administration's "Secret War" against communist dictator Fidel Castro and Kennedy's own desire to assassinate the Cuban leader. Although, according to Russo, one member of the Warren Commission, Allen Welsh Dulles, "knew of a potential Cuban motive to encourage Oswald," Dulles kept any such information under wraps.

Russo points out that Kennedy expected a less-than-warm reception in Dallas, "the virtual capital," according to Max Holland, who reviewed Russo's book for an extended article in the *Nation,* "of his right-wing opponents and the one large municipality that had chosen Nixon over Kennedy in 1960 and was predicted to favor Goldwater in 1964. Not coincidentally, Dallas was also a fount of anti-communist paranoia and the wellspring for some of the ugliest anti-Kennedy bile in circulation." Russo provides evidence that Kennedy was aware that the trip could pose dangers. According to a reviewer writing in *Publishers Weekly,* Kennedy's brother Robert had "received threatening notes at home," and Adlai Stevenson, then representing the United States to the United Nations, "faced a hostile Dallas crowd who spit on him." But Kennedy could not have anticipated that Oswald, a member of the Communist Party who had spent time in the Soviet Union, would be the source of his destruction in this fiercely anti-communist city.

Much of the new material on which Russo's book is based comes out of the 1992 creation of the Assassination Records Review Board (ARRB), a citizens' panel whose existence, said Holland, resulted in the "release of an archival-quality collection that totaled more than 4 million pages at last count . . . including records in state, municipal, and private custody." These previously classified documents include records from the

CIA's Directorate of Operations, the National Security Agency, and Kennedy's little-known Interdepartmental Coordinating Committee on Cuban Affairs. The last group met, Holland explained, to consider "how to create a real or simulated incident—blowing up vessels, shooting down an airliner—that would provide Washington with the pretext necessary to invade Cuba in 1962. . . . Apparently, the entire national security apparatus went mad with near-criminal schemes to get rid of Castro after the Bay of Pigs."

Reviewers were generally impressed with the depth of Russo's knowledge and the accuracy of his documentation. More controversial is the question of whether Russo proves his theory that Oswald sought to protect Castro's life by killing JFK. The *Publishers Weekly* reviewer extolled Russo's research and documentation, but did not presume that his book is "the final word on the assassination." And Gary D. Barber of *Library Journal* called the book "speculative" but recommended it "for most libraries" on the basis of its "new insights."

*BIOGRAPHICAL/CRITICAL SOURCES:*

PERIODICALS

*Kirkus Reviews,* November 1, 1998.
*Library Journal,* October 1, 1998, p. 114.
*Nation,* December 7, 1998, p. 25.
*New York Times Book Review,* May 23, 1999.
*Publishers Weekly,* October 26, 1998, p. 50.*

\*    \*    \*

**RYAN, Oscar   1904-**
   **(Martin Stone)**

*PERSONAL:* Born June 27, 1904, in Montreal, Quebec, Canada; son of Adolph Weinstein (a bookkeeper and peddler of small wares and religious sundries) and Sarah (worked in tobacco and clothing factories; maiden name, Rein); married Toby Gordon (an actress and cofounder of Workers' Theatre, Theatre of Action, and the Toronto Play Actors), 1941; children: Sandy Ellen.

*ADDRESSES: Home*—Toronto, Canada. *Agent*—c/o New Star Books Ltd., 2504 York Ave., Vancouver, British Columbia V6K 1E3, Canada.

*CAREER:* Activist and author. As a youth worked variously, including jobs in a hotel, grocery story, country

club, factories, as well as in the fur industry and as a shipper. Later worked variously, including jobs in a wood-working shop, with pulp-magazine publishers, and in freelance advertising and copywriting for retail stores. Associated with the Young Communist League, speaker at numerous events, c. 1928-29. Canadian Labour Defence League, publicity director, c. 1930; Progressive Arts Club, founder, 1931, cofounder and editorial board member of publication *Masses,* 1932-33; staff member of *Worker* and *Daily Clarion,* all located in Toronto, c. 1930s. *Military service:* Queen's Own Rifles (reserve battalion), served in Toronto during World War II.

*WRITINGS:*

*Deported!* (booklet), Canadian Labour Defence League (Toronto), 1932.
*The Story of the Trial of the Eight Communist Leaders* (booklet), Canadian Labour Defence League, 1932.
*The "Sedition" of A. E. Smith* (booklet), Canadian Labour Defence League, 1934.
*Tim Buck: A Conscience for Canada* (biography), Progress (Toronto), 1975.
*Soon to be Born: A Novel,* New Star (Vancouver), 1980.

PLAYS

*Unity* (produced by Progressive Arts Club in Toronto at Hygeia Hall, May, 1933), first published in *Masses,* later distributed as a mimeographed booklet by International Labor Defense, New York, 1933, then published in *Eight Men Speak and Other Plays from the Canadian Workers' Theatre,* edited by Richard Wright and Robin Endres, New Hogtown (Toronto), 1976.
(With Ed Cecil-Smith, Frank Love, and Mildred Goldberg) *Eight Men Speak* (produced by Progressive Arts Club in Toronto, at the Standard Theatre, December 4, 1933, adapted and performed by Popular Projects Society in Halifax, Nova Scotia, 1982), published in *Eight Men Speak and Other Plays from the Canadian Workers' Theatre,* edited by Wright and Endres, New Hogtown (Toronto), 1976.

OTHER

Creator and author of "Footlight Footnotes" column (stage news and commentary) in *Clarion,* then *Canadian Tribune,* beginning 1983. Also, reviewer of theater and, occasionally, books for the *Worker, Daily Clarion,* and *Canadian Tribune.* Editor, in the 1920s and 1930s, of *Young Worker, Always Ready, Canadian Labour Defender,* and *Winnipeg Voice of Labour.* Author of poetry published in various leftist publications.

*WORK IN PROGRESS:* Another novel.

*SIDELIGHTS:* "Although Oscar Ryan has been known for over fifty years as a theater critic," wrote Rose Adams in *Dictionary of Literary Biography,* "it is as playwright and social activist that he has earned a unique place in Canadian cultural history." During the Great Depression, Ryan helped found the Canadian workers theater movement, which revolutionized Canadian theater arts and created, according to Adams, an "indigenous working-class theater of protest." "In addition," the *Dictionary of Literary Biography* contributor explained, "he has been a biographer, novelist, reporter, poet, editor, activist, and organizer,"

Ryan was raised in a working-class French-Canadian neighborhood. "During the 1920s," Adams continued, " . . . he became politically active, working for civil rights in Canada and writing to express concerns engendered by the political struggles of the day." Ryan published poetry and began to edit various publications, including *Young Worker,* the children's magazine *Always Ready, Canadian Labour Defender,* and the *Winnipeg Voice of Labour.* During the 1930s he began a column on stage news and commentary called "Footlight Footnotes" that published in the *Clarion;* it was revived in 1983 by the *Canadian Tribune.* Ryan also used his working-class background and his leftist politics to form the basis for a theater of political protest in Canada—a theater that diverged from both U.S. and British models. The group he founded, the Progressive Arts Movement, also "felt that too few artists were engaged in social questions," the *Dictionary of Literary Biography* contributor concluded, "and that many ignored their role as cultural workers in relation to social struggles."

"The organ of the Progressive Arts Club was *Masses* . . . [which] united the Progressive Arts Clubs across Canada and disseminated information on how to form a club or a workers' theater group; it also offered criticism, short stories, poems, original plays, and woodcut illustrations," said Adams. "The writers of the Progressive Arts Club, including Ryan, offered to write scripts for the troupe to perform on picket lines and at mass rallies, union meetings, and so on," relayed Adams, specifying: "Ryan wrote a one-act play entitled *Unity* to be performed by the group." "*Unity* is classic agitprop," Adams explained. "It represents a conflict between capitalists and workers, ending in a roaring call for Canadian workers to unite and join in unity with the working classes of Germany, Great Britain, China, and the Soviet Union."

Perhaps Ryan's most famous politically oriented play, however, was *Eight Men Speak* (1933). The play was written in response to the events surrounding the arrest, conviction, and incarceration of Tim Buck, the general secretary of the Communist Party of Canada. Buck and seven other men were jailed under Canada's Section 98. Ryan, who was reporting for the Canadian Labour Defence League, attended Buck's trial. "Thus," stated Adams, "it was he who conceived of *Eight Men Speak* as a mock trial drama . . . [aiming] to rouse public opinion for the repeal of Section 98 and to fight for the release of the jailed men."

"The plot of *Eight Men Speak,* however, goes much further than the actual circumstances of the trials in the range of issues that it succeeds in addressing," remarked Adams, detailing: "*Eight Men Speak* talks about workers' history, the unemployed, and immigrants in Canada. . . . [and also] exposes the media as a source of distortion and accuses government of being removed from the lives or ordinary people." "The play is compelling," judged Adams, "and engages its audience through its use of many different styles and techniques. . . . Reviews of the play in the mainstream press were scant, while its success with its intended audience was unmistakable. . . . *Eight Men Speak* had played an active role . . . in the class politics of its country. . . . [I]n 1982 when it was revived by Popular Projects Society in Halifax, Nova Scotia . . . [it] spoke of a period in Canadian history often ignored."

*BIOGRAPHICAL/CRITICAL SOURCES:*

*BOOKS*

*Dictionary of Literary Biography,* Volume 68: *Canadian Writers, 1920-1959,* Gale Research (Detroit, MI), 1988.
Ryan, Toby Gordon, *Stage Left: Canadian Theatre in the Thirties,* CTR (Toronto), 1981.*

# S

## SADLIER, Mary Anne 1820-1903

*PERSONAL:* Born December 31, 1820, in Cootehill, County Cavan, Ireland; immigrated to Canada, c. 1843; died April 5, 1903, in Montreal, Canada; daughter of Francis Madden (a merchant); married James Sadlier (a book publisher), 1845; six children. *Religion:* Roman Catholic.

*CAREER:* Writer; editor of *McGee's American Celt* and the New York *Tablet;* involved in the management of her late husband's publishing firm, c. 1870-85.

*AWARDS, HONORS:* Laetare Medal, Notre Dame University, late 1890s.

*WRITINGS:*

*Tales of the Olden Times: A Collection of European Traditions,* Lovell (Montreal), 1845.

*The Red Hand of Ulster; or, The Fortunes of Hugh O'Neill,* Donahoe (Boston), 1850.

*Willy Burke; or, The Irish Orphan in America,* Donahoe (Boston), 1850.

*Alice Riordan; The Blind Man's Daughter,* Donahoe (Boston), 1851.

*New Lights; or, Life in Galway,* Sadlier (New York), 1853.

*The Blakes and the Flanagans: A Tale Illustrative of Irish Life in the United States,* Duffy (Dublin), 1855, Sadlier (New York), 1858.

*The Confederate Chieftains: A Tale of the Irish Rebellion of 1641,* Sadlier (New York), 1860.

*Julia; or, The Gold Thimble: A Drama for Girls,* Sadlier (New York), 1861.

*Elinor Preston; or, Scenes at Home and Abroad,* Sadlier (New York), 1861.

*Bessy Conway; or, The Irish Girl in America,* Sadlier (New York), 1862.

*The Lost Son,* Sadlier (New York), 1862.

*Old and New; or, Taste versus Fashion,* Sadlier (New York), 1862.

*The Daughter of Tyrconnell: A Tale of the Reign of James the First,* Sadlier (New York), 1863.

*The Fate of Father Sheehy: A Tale of Tipperary Eighty Years Ago,* Sadlier (New York), 1863, enlarged edition, [Dublin], 1881.

*The Hermit of the Rock: A Tale of Cashel,* Sadlier (New York), 1863.

*The Talisman: A Drama in One Act; Written for the Young Ladies of the Ursuline Academy, East Morrisania,* Sadlier (New York), 1863.

*Con O'Regan; or, Emigrant Life in the New World,* Sadlier (New York), 1864.

*Confessions of an Apostate,* Sadlier (New York), 1864.

*The Old House by the Boyne; or, Recollections of an Irish Borough,* Sadlier (New York), 1865.

*Secret, A Drama Written for the Young Ladies of St. Joseph's Academy, Flushing, Long Island,* Sadlier (New York), 1865.

*Aunt Honor's Keepsake. A Chapter from Life,* Sadlier (New York), 1866.

*A New Catechism of Sacred History,* Sadlier (New York), 1866.

*The Heiress of Kilorgan; or, Evenings with the Old Geraldines,* Sadlier (New York), 1867.

*MacCarthy More; or, The Fortunes of an Irish Chief in the Reign of Queen Elizabeth,* Sadlier (New York), 1868.

(Editor) *The Poems of Thomas D'Arcy McGee,* Sadlier (New York)/Brady (Boston), 1869.

*Maureen Dhu, the Admiral's Daughter,* Sadlier (New York), 1870.

*The Invisible Hand: A Drama in Two Acts,* Sadlier (New York), 1873.

(Editor) *The Young Ladies' Reader,* Sadlier (New York), 1875.

*Purgatory: Doctrinal, Historical and Poetical,* Sadlier (New York), 1886.

*Catholic School History of England,* Sadlier (New York), 1891.

(With daughter, Anna Teresa Sadlier) *Stories of the Promises,* Sadlier (Montreal), c. 1895.

*The Minister's Wife, and Other Stories,* Wildermann (New York), 1898.

*O'Byrne; or, The Expatriated,* Wildermann (New York), 1898.

*Short Stories,* Wildermann (New York), 1900.

Contributor to *Literary Garland;* letters to Sadlier from Thomas D'Arcy McGee are in the Sadlier Papers at the National Archives of Canada.

*SIDELIGHTS:* Immigrant writer Mary Anne Sadlier penned over thirty novels, plays, and other works related to Irish-Catholic life in North America during the latter half of the nineteenth century. Her fiction was characterized by a romanticization and sentimentalization of this diaspora, and was infused with its author's devout Roman Catholic values. Some of Sadlier's success was related to the fact that the man she married had founded a publishing firm that specialized in Catholic titles, but the popularity of her novels also brought profit to the Sadlier firm for many years.

Sadlier was born Mary Anne Madden on New Year's Eve in Ireland in 1820. Her family was a well-to-do one, headed by a merchant father, but Francis Madden's death when his daughter was in her early twenties ended this era of prosperity. As a result, Sadlier and some other siblings sailed for New Brunswick, Canada in 1843. Sadlier had already found publishing success with her poetry in Ireland, and after settling in Montreal she continued in her literary pursuits. The Literary Garland accepted her contributions, and her first book appeared in 1845, *Tales of the Olden Times: A Collection of European Traditions.*

In 1846 the young writer married James Sadlier, and thus freed from financial worries, began devoting more time to her fiction. Over the next fourteen years Sadlier gave birth to six children, but also wrote the same number of novels, beginning with *The Red Hand of Ulster; or, The Fortunes of Hugh O'Neill* in 1850. *New Lights; or, Life in Galway,* from 1853, was the first to be issued by the Sadlier house, which her husband had founded in Montreal with his brother in 1837. These novels

proved a lucrative success for the firm, and were a favorite of Irish immigrants homesick for sentimental fiction that reminded them of the hardships of life back in Ireland and yet at the same time romanticized their fortitude and heritage.

The Sadlier family moved to New York City in 1860, where she continued to enjoy success as an author. One novel from this period was the 1861 work *Elinor Preston; or, Scenes at Home and Abroad. Dictionary of Literary Biography* writer Michle Lacombe termed it "probably the most autobiographical of Sadlier's works, and one that offers a telling commentary on the plight of the genteel lady immigrant." The work is set in Canada, and told in the first person through an unmarried middle-class young woman from Ireland who dies an early death far from her beloved homeland. Another of Sadlier's books, *Bessy Conway; or, The Irish Girl in America,* appeared in 1862. Its heroine is a farm girl from Tipperary who sails alone to New York and finds work as a maid.

Sadlier continued to write books such as *The Daughter of Tyrconnell: A Tale of the Reign of James the First* and *Con O'Regan; or, Emigrant Life in the New World* during the 1860s. Upon the death of her husband in 1869, she became involved in the daily business of the Sadlier house until 1885, when her brother-in-law also passed away. That same year, Sadlier grieved the death of her son, who had become a Jesuit priest and lived in Rome. These circumstances, combined with unexpected financial difficulties, caused her to move to Montreal to be near her daughter, Anna Teresa Sadlier, who was also a novelist.

Sadlier, now in her sixties, became quite active in Catholic charitable organizations, and wrote almost no new fiction. She bestowed money to causes that helped young immigrant women in Montreal, and even founded an orphanage. Firmly committed to the cause of educational opportunities for young women, Sadlier had written a number of didactic plays for female students at convent schools over the years, such as the 1865 work *Secret, A Drama Written for the Young Ladies of St. Joseph's Academy, Flushing, Long Island.* She also served as editor for *The Young Ladies' Reader,* published by Sadlier in 1875.

One of the last titles she penned that was issued by the Sadlier house was *Catholic School History of England,* published in 1891. When a nephew seized control of the family firm in 1895, Sadlier lost the copyrights to her books, and with that all source of income. She died in Montreal in April of 1903. In the critique of *Bessy Con-*

*way* for *Dictionary of Literary Biography,* Lacombe stated succinctly the appeal of Sadlier's novels for her contemporaries, devout Irish immigrants like herself experiencing the trials and tribulations of life on a new continent. "Sadlier offers a moral rather than a political allegory of the contradictory experience of immigration and acculturation experienced by the least privileged of Sadlier's generation of Irish Catholics in the new world, rather innocently claiming to offer her reader sanctity rather than suspense," assessed the critic. "Simple, working-class women and their shared values are celebrated."

*BIOGRAPHICAL/CRITICAL SOURCES:*

BOOKS

Blain, Virginia, Patricia Clements, and Isobel Grundy, *Feminist Companion to Literature in English,* Yale University Press, 1990.
*Dictionary of Irish Literature,* revised and expanded edition, edited by Robert Hogan, Greenwood Press, 1996.
*Dictionary of Literary Biography,* Gale, Volume 49: *American Literary Publishing Houses, 1638-1899,* edited by Peter Dzwonkoski, 1986, Volume 99: *Canadian Writers Before 1890,* edited by W. H. New, 1990.
O'Ceirin, Kit, and Cyril O'Ceirin, *Women of Ireland,* Irish Books and Media, 1996.

PERIODICALS

*Essays on Canadian Writing,* summer, 1984, pp. 96-116.*

\*   \*   \*

**SANCHEZ, Philomeno   1917-**

*PERSONAL:* Born November 20, 1917, in San Luis, CO; married Elsie Arguello, c. 1947 (died, c. 1974). *Education:* Adams State College of Colorado, M.A., 1952.

*ADDRESSES: Home*—Denver, CO. *Agent*—c/o Sangre de Cristo, San Luis, CO.

*CAREER:* Civilian Conservation Corps, laborer, 1935-37; amateur boxer, 1938-43; insurance sales representative in Pueblo, CO, beginning in 1946; teacher at public schools in the San Luis valley of Colorado, 1952-75. *Military service:* U.S. Army, 1943-46.

*WRITINGS:*

*Don Phil-o-meno si la Mancha* (novel; title means "Don Philomeno on the Spot"), Sangre de Cristo (San Luis, CO), 1977.

*SIDELIGHTS:* Philomeno Sanchez has published only one book, in Spanish, but that single accomplishment inspired Nasario Garcia to declare in the *Dictionary of Literary Biography:* "The ease with which he manipulates the Spanish language . . . is clearly an anachronism in the modern Southwest and is not only due to his cultural perspicacity but is a tribute to his poetics" The novel *Don Phil-o-meno si la Mancha* has been compared to Miguel de Cervantes' *Don Quixote,* and the author has been praised for his understanding and accurate use of the literary devices and motifs that were popular in medieval Spanish literature when *Don Quixote* was penned.

*Don Phil-o-meno si la Mancha* is an autobiographical novel relating the adventures of Sanchez as he chased his own seemingly impossible dream. Sanchez describes a poor but happy life in Colorado's Valley of Tears, yet life was not without its share of tragedy. Garcia recorded: "In 1975, at fifty-eight years of age, he had a heart attack, which forced him to retire [from teaching]. One year earlier his wife . . . succumbed to cancer. He continued to live in San Luis until 1979, when his house burned down. Having lost all his possessions, he moved to Denver, where he lives alone, but quite content." Remarkably, perhaps, the character Don Phil-o-meno emerges as an amiable, whimsical fellow with an irrepressible air of mischief and an unflagging sense of humor.

Don Phil-o-meno's partner in adventure is Senor Bigotudo, who has been compared to Quixote's Sancho Panza and likened to Sanchez's own father. Bigotudo is a wise old man, full of proverbs and advice, who, according to Garcia, "also serves as a balance between the outrageous and the rational, the frivolous and the prudent." The two characters complement each other, Garcia suggested, as Senor Bigotudo seems to symbolize Don Phil-o-meno's alter ego: "In the final analysis, the mentor learns as much from his disciple, if not more [than the reverse]." He also noted: "Those who have read *Don Quixote* and appreciate Sancho Panza's repertoire of proverbs will also enjoy Sanchez's wit and wry humor."

The proverbs are one element of the novel that evoke the spirit of medieval Spanish literature, Garcia asserted; others include "Bigotudo's wisdom . . . [,] reminiscent of the exempla that swept Europe and Spain," the father-son relationship that recalls "the *disciplina clericales* literature also popular in medieval Spain," and "the acknowledgment of fugacity coupled with a nostalgic desire for the past." Garcia also noted Sanchez's familiarity with "folklore, such as *entriegas* (poetic renditions of marriage), *dichos* (sayings), *remedios* (remedies), *corridos* (ballads), *posadas* (ritualistic reenactments of Joseph and Mary seeking refuge), and other traditional customs that are fading further into the past and getting lost in the modern technological era."

Sanchez has reportedly begun another manuscript, a memoir for his children in the form of a poem. Garcia explained: "It is intended to be a parody on his own life following the structure of the Stations of the Cross," with no disrespect implied for the religious ritual itself. The critic predicted: "If the use of the Spanish dialect that has typified northern New Mexico and southern Colorado for several centuries . . . is as vibrant in this last work as in his first one, then he will have left a linguistic treasure."

*BIOGRAPHICAL/CRITICAL SOURCES:*

*BOOKS*

*Dictionary of Literary Biography,* Volume 122: *Chicano Writers, Second Series,* Gale (Detroit, MI), 1992.\*

\*        \*        \*

**SANDERS, Winston P.**
 **See ANDERSON, Poul (William)**

\*        \*        \*

**SCHOFIELD, Roger Snowden   1937-**

*PERSONAL:* Born August 26, 1937, in England; son of Ronald Snowden and Muriel Grace (Braime) Schofield; married Elizabeth Mary Cunliffe, 1961 (divorced, 1999); children: Melanie. *Education:* Clare College, Cambridge, B.A., 1959, Ph.D., 1963.

*ADDRESSES: Home and Office*—Clare College, Cambridge CB2 1TL, England. *E-mail*—rssl@cus.cam.ac.uk.

*CAREER:* Fellow of Clare College, Cambridge, 1969—; University of Cambridge, Cambridge, En-

gland, Honorary Reader in Historical Demography, 1991-97. Senior research associate, Cambridge Group for the History of Population and Social Structure, Economic and Social Research Council, 1994-97, director, 1974-94. Sherman Fairchild Distinguished Scholar in the Social Sciences, CIT, 1984-85; visiting professor of Humanities and Social Sciences, CIT, 1992-94. SSRC, member of computing committee, 1970-75, and statistics committee, 1974-78; UK Computer Board, member of software provision committee, 1977-79, population investigation committee, 1976, and treasurer, 1987-97.

*MEMBER:* British Academy (fellow, 1988—), Royal Statistical Society (fellow, 1987—), Royal Historical Society (fellow, 1970—), British Society for Population Studies (member of council, 1979-87, treasurer, 1981-85, president 1985-87).

*WRITINGS:*

(With E. A. Wrigley) *The Population History of England 1541-1871: A Reconstruction,* Edward Arnold, 1981.
(Editor with David Coleman) *The State of Population Theory: Forward from Malthus,* Blackwell, 1986.
(Editor with John Walter) *Famine, Disease, and the Social Order in Early Modern Society,* Cambridge University Press, 1989.
(Editor with David Reher and Alain Bideau) *The Decline of Mortality in Europe,* Clarendon Press (Oxford), 1991.
(With Wrigley, R. S. Davies, and J. E. Oeppen) *English Population History from Family Reconstitution, 1580-1837,* Cambridge University Press, 1997.

Also contributor to *Population Studies, Journal of Interdisciplinary History,* and *Journal of Family History.*

*WORK IN PROGRESS: Taxation under the Early Tudors,* for Blackwell.

*SIDELIGHTS:* Roger Schofield has made his reputation in population studies through his joint development of a process that takes data on births, deaths, and marriages collected from parish registers (which began to be kept by law in England in 1538) and ties it together with economic variables "such as wages, food prices and inflation rates" to produce "an interpretation of the dynamics of population change which has since won almost universal acceptance," states Ray Porter in the *London Review of Books. The Population History of England,* written with Tony Wrigley, was Schofield's first book to manipulate this data, collected and processed by the Cambridge Group for the History of Population and Social Structure. Schofield's statistical analyses helped overturn one of the Malthusian models of population, which suggested that population inevitably outruns food resources, and thus is kept in check primarily through starvation and epidemics. His group found that, in fact, the English birth rate and death rates were much more moderate, and that deferment of marriage was a much greater check on population growth in the period before the Industrial Revolution than had previously been thought. Schofield and Wrigley showed that the population rise that accompanied the Industrial Age was linked more closely to fertility than to mortality, because in that period people married earlier and produced more children.

Schofield's next book to receive widespread critical attention was *The Decline of Mortality in Europe,* which he co-edited with David Reher and Alain Bideau. Schofield and his colleagues provide introductory essays on the current state of population studies as demonstrated within the essays collected in the book and in their own work. To an extent, the essays point toward correction of an influential book by Thomas McKeown called *The Modern Rise of Population* (1976), states Etienne van de Walle in the *Journal of Interdisciplinary History,* in which the author posited that "the decline in mortality in Europe since the eighteenth century was, for the largest part, caused by improved nutrition," and not by improved medical intervention or other factors. Essays in Schofield's book provide evidence that "public health measures and the changing standard of living, particularly in housing and occupation, . . . affected people's exposure," writes Gretchen A. Condran in *Contemporary Sociology,* and that some of the elements McKeown based his study on, such as height as an indicator of nutritional health, are faulty. Other essays provide more accurate background facts on Europe's mortality shifts. The book was well received, although Condran pointed out that, while appealing, the multivariate emphasis of many of its essays "may preclude the kind of analysis that this volume sets out to do." Schofield's introductory essay (co-written with Reher) was especially mentioned in a number of reviews for, in the words of van de Walle, "its masterful summary . . . of trends and patterns."

In 1998, Schofield's *English Population History from Family Reconstitution, 1580-1837* was published. Its authors had held forth the promise of this book in their introduction to their 1981 *The Population History of England,* explains Porter, "to be based on even more sophisticated demographic techniques . . . known as 'family reconstitution' . . . [which] aims to exploit to the full the fact that parish registers record baptisms, marriages and burials. . . . [I]n other words, one could move from mere aggregates to a reconstruction of the demographically significant moments in the lives of actual people." The limitations of the technique are not insignificant, wrote Porter, quoting Schofield and his co-authors: "Since it would have required an army of historians to gut all ten thousand English parish registers, the team has limited itself to 24. These were obviously chosen because they were well kept, but even they have their lacunae. Parish records in any case tell only about baptisms, marriages, and burials, not about birth, copulation and death. And they provide information only about Anglicans, not the whole nation." But Porter readily admitted that "they have given us the best body of data we are ever likely to see."

*BIOGRAPHICAL/CRITICAL SOURCES:*

*PERIODICALS*

*Contemporary Sociology,* March, 1993, pp. 216-218.
*Journal of Economic History,* March, 1993, pp. 165-66.
*Journal of Interdisciplinary History,* winter, 1994, pp. 523-525.
*London Review of Books,* March 5, 1998, pp. 18-19.

\*      \*      \*

## SILLIKER, Bill, Jr. 1947-

*PERSONAL:* Born September 25, 1947, in Medford, MA; son of Bill, Sr. and Ruth L. (a writer) Silliker; married Maryellen Montouri, March 22, 1969. *Education:* Nasson College, B.A., 1969. *Politics:* Independent. *Religion:* Protestant. *Avocational interests:* Music.

*ADDRESSES: Office*—P.O. Box 7106, Ocean Park, ME 04063. *Agent*—Orion Literary Agency, Memphis, TN. *E-mail*—mooseman@lamere.net.

*CAREER:* Wildlife and nature photographer. Broadcaster. Also worked as professional musician (drummer).

*MEMBER:* North American Nature Photography Association (member of board of directors), Outdoor Writers Association of America.

*WRITINGS:*

*Maine Moose Watcher's Guide,* R. L. Lemke, 1993.
*Moose: Giant of the Northern Forest,* Firefly Books (Willowdale, Ontario), 1998.

*Uses for Mooses* (humor), Down East (Camden, ME), 2000.

Author and co-producer of videotape series *Maine's Magnificent Moose* and *Loons of the Northern Forest,* for Down East and Maine's Public Broadcasting System.

*SIDELIGHTS:* Bill Silliker Jr. told *CA:* "I've always loved writing. I tried my hand at short stories and even have an unpublished novel or two in the attic, but writing about nature—my experiences while in the woods with a camera—has proven to be more publishable. The pursuit of photographing wildlife forces one to learn about the species one seeks to capture on film. Combining that learning—information obtained from reading books, research reports, scientific journals, and magazine articles—as well as that most valuable information—the things an attentive person learns while in the field—has proven to be a great way to put to use my writing desires."

\*   \*   \*

## SNOW, Vernon F.   1924-1998

*OBITUARY NOTICE*—See index for *CA* sketch: Born November 25, 1924, in Milwaukee, WI; died of cancer, June 24, 1998, in Jamesville, NY. Professor and author. Snow was a lifelong educator and after getting bachelor's, master's and doctoral degrees he worked at a variety of schools including the universities of Oregon, Wisconsin, Montana, and Nebraska. He taught mostly history classes at those schools in the 1950s and 1960s before joining the Syracuse University faculty in 1974. While in New York he took over the John Ben Snow Foundation and served as its president. The foundation was organized in 1948 by Snow's cousin, who operated several hundred F. W. Woolworth stores overseas. The foundation provided college scholarships and money for cultural activities. Snow also was a trustee of the John Ben Snow Memorial Trust, which provided funding for activities related to higher education. Snow put his knowledge of philanthrophy to work in the classroom and designed a course on the topic while teaching at Syracuse. During his career he wrote several books including *Essex the Rebel: The Life of Robert Devereux, Third Earl of Essex, 1591-1646, Parliament in Elizabethan England,* and *JBS: The Biography of John Ben Snow.*

*OBITUARIES AND OTHER SOURCES:*

*PERIODICALS*

*Chicago Tribune,* July 5, 1998, sec. 4, p. 6.
*New York Times,* July 5, 1998, p. A21.

\*   \*   \*

## SOBEL, Robert   1931-1999

*OBITUARY NOTICE*—See index for *CA* sketch: Born February 19, 1931, in New York, NY; died of brain cancer, June 2, 1999, in Long Beach, NY. Business history professor and author. Although a university professor by trade, Sobel's written works were aimed at the average reader rather than the scholarly set. His way of writing helped readers understand business and companies without the academic jargon some colleagues and critics might have preferred. Born and raised in the Bronx, Sobel was a lifelong New Yorker and graduated from City College (now City University of New York) with a bachelor's and received master's and doctoral degrees from New York University. He joined the U.S. Army in 1953 and served two years. When he was discharged Sobel joined the staff at New York University and stayed there for a year as an instructor before moving to Hofstra University in 1957. He stayed at Hofstra for the next forty years. As he moved from assistant professor to eventually being named Lawrence Stetson Distinguished Professor in business history, Sobel wrote furiously. He contributed articles to journals and periodicals, ghost-wrote business books, edited numerous books and wrote more than thirty-five of his own. His subjects ranged from the history of the stock exchange to profiles of financiers and histories of corporations such as RCA, IBM and the tobacco industry. His first book was *The Origins of Interventionism: The United States and the Russo-Finnish War,* published in 1961, but other titles included *The Big Board: A History of the New York Stock Market, The Age of Giant Corporations: A Microeconomic History of American Business, 1914-1970, The Last Bull Market: Wall Street in the 1960s* and his last book, *When Giants Stumble.* He also wrote a fake textbook, *For Want of a Nail,* about the history of North America if the Revolutionary War battle at Saratoga had gone the other way. He was a contributing editor to *Barron's* magazine when he died.

*OBITUARIES AND OTHER SOURCES:*

PERIODICALS

*Los Angeles Times,* June 6, 1999, p. B5.
*New York Times,* June 4, 1999, p. C18.
*Washington Post,* June 5, 1999, p. B4.

\*     \*     \*

## SOKAL, Alan D. 1955-

*PERSONAL:* Born January 24, 1955, in Boston, MA; son of Nathan (an electronics engineer) and Zelda (an editor; maiden name, Kaufman) Sokal; married Marina Papa (an archaeologist), January 22, 1996. *Education:* Harvard University, B.A. (physics), 1976; Princeton University, Ph.D. (physics), 1981. *Politics:* "Left." *Religion:* Atheist. *Avocational interests:* Music (jazz, choral).

*ADDRESSES: Office*—New York University, Department of Physics, Meyer Hall of Physics, 4 Washington Place, New York, NY 10003. *Agent*—Brockman, Inc., 5 East 59th St., New York, NY 10021. *E-mail*—sokal@nyu.edu.

*CAREER:* New York University, New York City, professor of physics.

*AWARDS, HONORS:* DOE Outstanding Junior Investigator Award, 1990; Golden Dozen Award, New York University, for excellence in teaching, 1996.

*WRITINGS:*

(With Juerg Froehlich and Roberto Fernandez) *Random Walks, Critical Phenomena, and Triviality in Quantum Field Theory,* Springer-Verlag, 1992.
(With Jean Bricmont) *Impostures Intellectuelles,* Odile Jacob (Paris), 1997, published as *Fashionable Nonsense: Postmodern Intellectuals' Abuse of Science,* Picador (New York City), 1998.

Contributor to many periodicals and scientific journals.

*SIDELIGHTS:* Physicist Alan Sokal's research interests include computational, mathematical, and statistical physics, as well as quantum field theory. He has received, however, a great deal of publicity and reaction to his article, "Transgressing the Boundaries: Toward a Transformative Hermeneutics of Quantum Gravity,"

printed in the spring/summer 1996 issue of the journal *Social Text;* the article was submitted as a hoax. "The purpose of his hoax," reported Jim Holt in a *New York Times Book Review* assessment of *Fashionable Nonsense: Postmodern Intellectuals' Abuse of Science,* "was to reveal the fraudulence of much post-modernist thought, especially as it abused science."

"Encouraged by the success of [his] masterly and now notorious experiment . . . [he undertook] a much more thorough exercise in intellectual and moral hygiene," began Kevin Mulligan's *Times Literary Supplement* review of *Impostures Intellectuelles,* the earlier edition of *Fashionable Nonsense* that was first published in France. In the words of *New Scientist* contributor Mike Holderness: "[Sokal] set out with Jean Bricmont, physics professor at the University of Louvain, [Belgium], to show that the emperors of French philosophy have no clothes." "Dismayed by postmodernism's popularity, especially in North America," described Mulligan, "they concentrate in their book *Impostures Intellectuelles,* on two aspects of the phenomenon. First, the extraordinary level of misuse of science and scientific terminology in recent Parisian thought. Second, relativistic currents in analytic philosophy." Their "philosophical case against what they call post-modern relativism," was defined by Holt as their attack on "the notion that physical reality is nothing but a social construct and that science, despite its pretensions to truth, is just another 'narration' that encodes the dominant ideology of the culture that produced it."

Mulligan noted that the Sokal and Bricmont almost entirely, and "wisely[,] do not delve into the background of the abuses they bring into sharp focus. . . . Sokal and Bricmont are, by and large, content to accuse most of their Parisian targets of impostures and deliberate obscurantism. They do not consider the more sever verdict envisaged by Bertrand Russell in a passage they quote, in which Russell predicted that to give up the conception of truth as something which depends on facts largely beyond our control would be to take a step down the road which leads to a sort of madness." In an earlier *Times Literary Supplement* review, Clive James recognized that Sokal and Bricmont's claims had been made before. The critic complained: "the only new element Sokal and Bricmont have brought to the job of dispelling the miasma is their impeccable scientific qualifications." Speaking to the same point, Mulligan wrote: "Sokal and Bricmont have some predecessors—Benda, Louis Rougier, Jean-Francois Revel and Jacques Bouveresse. But their detailed focus on just one aspect of recent French though is new and has, I suspect, provoked more and more violent reactions than other contributions to the genre."

A *Publishers Weekly* review of *Fashionable Nonsense* recommended the book, declaring: "The authors fervor and the precision of their writing makes this a most engaging read." Similarly, *Library Journal* contributor H. James Birx promoted the work as "a bold, engaging, and necessary book that is highly recommended for all large science and philosophy collections." Other critics, sung less overwhelming praises, indicating what Holt stated was "a certain confusion about the gravity and nature of the sins of their targets."

Sokal told *CA:* "I'm pleased by the debate that my parody article, and then our book, succeeded in sparking; but right now my priority is to return to my first love, which is mathematics and physics."

*BIOGRAPHICAL/CRITICAL SOURCES:*

*PERIODICALS*

*Library Journal,* November 1, 1998, p. 122.
*New Republic,* October 12, 1998.
*New Scientist,* February 14, 1998, p. 146.
*New York Times Book Review,* November 15, 1998.
*Publishers Weekly,* October 26, 1998, p. 58.
*Times Literary Supplement,* December 5, 1997, p. 14; May 1, 1998, pp. 13-14.

*       *       *

## SOLDATI, Mario   1906-1999

*OBITUARY NOTICE*—See index for *CA* sketch: Born November 17, 1906, in Turin, Italy; died June 19, 1999, in Tellaro, Italy. Film director, screenwriter, and author. Soldati's work was prodigious in output and although he was well known in the cinema, he said writing was his strong suit. He claimed he only ended up in film because the pervading fascism in Italy prevented him from writing or teaching. Soldati rebelled against the restrictive upbringing of his mother and Jesuit priests who educated him and, after receiving his degree from the University of Turin in 1927, immigrated to the United States. There he taught at Columbia University and found plenty of inspiration for his writing in Times Square. The book *America primo amore,* based on his time in New York, brought him critical and popular acclaim. He returned to Italy with an American wife and began writing screenplays such as

*Gli uomini, che mascalzoni* ("The Men, What Idiots!") and *Giallo* ("Yellow"), but soon was directing pictures. He made nearly thirty films. Some, like *La Provinciale,* were successful, others were not, but it did not affect the amount of his offerings. He lived luxuriously in some of Rome's best hotels but eventually moved to the Ligurian coast and continued writing there. Soldati was intrigued by television when it was new and became involved in documentaries filmed for that medium. One of his best-known works of that type was *Travels Along the Po Searching for Genuine Food.* He work in television led many to view him as the originator of television criticism. Soldati continued working and writing well into his eighties, even covering the 1982 World Cup in Spain. He wrote numerous plays, short stories, novels, and screenplays, and at the time of his death was a contributor to a newspaper in Milan. He last work, *Un Viaggio a Lourdes,* a study of faith, was published weeks before his death.

*OBITUARIES AND OTHER SOURCES:*

*PERIODICALS*

*Los Angeles Times,* June 22, 1999, p. A24.
*New York Times,* June 23, 1999, p. C27.
*Times* (London), June 22, 1999.
*Washington Post,* June 24, 1999, p. B6.

*OTHER*

*CNN Interactive,* June 20, 1999.

*       *       *

## STEWART, John L.   1925-

*PERSONAL:* Born April 19, 1925, in Pasadena, CA; son of John P. (a food company executive) and Edith Irene (a homemaker and writer; maiden name, Lichty) Stewart; married Rita Greenberg, September 15, 1951; children: Bradley C., Mark R. *Education:* Stanford University, B.S., 1948, M.S., 1949, Ph.D., 1953. *Ethnicity:* "White." *Politics:* Independent. *Religion:* "None (humanist)." *Avocational interests:* Hiking, flying, scuba diving, exploring.

*ADDRESSES: Home and Office*—3205 Southeast Spyglass Dr., Vancouver, WA 98683; fax: 360-260-1660. *E-mail*—lstewart@e-z.net   and   http://www.math-2000.com.

*CAREER:* Jet Propulsion Laboratory, Pasadena, CA, research engineer, 1949-51; Hughes Aircraft Co., worked on mathematical and statistical theory, 1951; University of Michigan, Ann Arbor, assistant professor of electrical engineering, 1953-56; University of Southern California, Los Angeles, associate professor of electrical engineering, 1956-59; University of Arizona, Tucson, professor of electrical engineering, 1959-62; Santa Rita Technology, Inc., founder and president, 1962-72; Av-Alarm Corp. (makers of acoustic pest repelling equipment), founder and president, 1972-82; Covox, Inc., founder and president, 1982-90; SET, Inc., president, 1990-92; professional engineer and consultant, 1992—. California Institute of Technology, associate professor, 1956-59. Vancouver Airport, member of advisory board; SCORE, vice chairperson and counselor. *Military service:* U.S. Army Air Forces, 1943-45; served in England; became first lieutenant; received Air Medal with oak leaf cluster.

*MEMBER:* Institute of Electrical and Electronics Engineers, Publishers Marketing Association, APS, PNBA, Sigma Xi, Tau Beta Pi, Eta Kappa Nu.

*WRITINGS:*

*Circuit Theory and Design,* Wiley (New York City), 1956.
*Circuit Analysis of Transmission Lines,* Wiley, 1958.
*Signal Theory,* McGraw (New York City), 1960.
*The Bionic Ear,* Covox, 1979.
*The Forbidden Diary: A B-24 Navigator Remembers* (memoir), McGraw, 1998.
*Fremont's Greatest Western Exploration,* Volume I: *The Dalles to Pyramid Lake,* SET Inc., 1999.

*SIDELIGHTS:* John L. Stewart told *CA:* "My greatest pleasures come from exploring. What I call exploring is not quite conventional. It is done in order to discover something new, whatever may be the field of endeavor-math, science, human affairs, evolution, et cetera. I like to write because I want to tell the world about the things that I have discovered or am trying to discover.

"My principal sources of influence have related to forms of applied mathematics. My general interest in all forms of exploring as well as the mathematical background to navigation have been important in the writing task about John C. Fremont. Another source of inspiration for this particular book was that I inherited an original copy of his report to the congress and found it most enjoyable. A real diary from many years ago caused me to write my war memoirs.

"My Web site allows me full range of expression because articles can deal with virtually any form of ap-plied mathematics. I emphasize that it is the applied form of math that leads to discoveries, including those in geology and even population dynamics.

"Somewhere along the line I became interested in the population problems in the world. This began with a reading of the original works of Thomas Malthus (very dry and tedious stuff). What he observed and what Fremont reports were so similar that I connect the two and say so in the last chapter of my book on Fremont. A future writing effort, after 'Fremont Volume Two,' may be a study of population trends and dynamics combined with economics and sociology as pioneered by a trio of remarkable men—Adam Smith, then Thomas Malthus, then Charles Darwin. Perhaps a major reason for interest in this field is a terrible fear that our world will succumb to universal poverty from far too many inhabitants. I am too old to be around when it happens, but my grandchildren might suffer the consequences.

"How do I write? In the old days, an old Underwood typewriter with little key caps to print special math characters was used. I benefitted greatly from once taking a high school typing course (now called 'keyboarding'). Now I use a word processor, sometimes a very simple one that works on an old PC without a hard drive, but more and more with Word 97. As a publisher I try to get printing done at the lowest possible cost, so I provide camera-ready copy. If photographs are included, or even maps, halftones are made of these and submitted along with the text. I work from a general outline, but not a very detailed one. With everything saved to disk, going back and forth is not difficult.

"There is one more passion that I have. That is to bring back simple old BASIC so that the commoner can calculate business or other applied math problems without first going through the pain of programming classes. Without this capability, the typical citizen gets further and further out of tune with the modern world and must thus feel less and less important as an individual, and ever less likely to want to be an explorer."

*       *       *

## STONE, Lawrence   1919-1999

*OBITUARY NOTICE*—See index for *CA* sketch: Born December 4, 1919, in Epsom, Surrey, England; died of Parkinson's disease, June 16, 1999, in Princeton, NJ. Professor, historian, and author. Stone concentrated much of his work on the changing social order and looked at how society evolved over centuries. He began his career in education by attending the Sorbonne and graduating from Christ Church College, Oxford, from which he received both bachelor's and master's degrees. Before he could get a teaching position, however, World War II intervened and he served in the Royal Navy from 1940 to 1945. After being discharged Stone lectured at both Oxford University and University College until 1950. He then joined the faculty of Wadham College and began working on his first book, *An Elizabethan: Sir Horatio Palavicino,* which was published in 1955. He wrote several books in his lifetime, including *The Crisis of the Aristocracy 1558-1641, Social Change and Revolution in England 1540-1640,* and *The Family, Sex and Marriage in England, 1500-1800.* His research took in a long period of English history and did not concentrate on just a few historical figures, but rather on entire families or populations. He moved to Princeton University as the Dodge Professor of History in 1963 and chaired the department from 1967 to 1970. He also served as founding director of the Shelby Cullom Davis Center for Historical Studies, which promoted new research methods. Stone retired from Princeton in 1990 and around that time he authored a trio of books about English divorce proceedings that had gone undiscovered until 1937. When the records were to be put on microfilm Stone took advantage of their availability and produced the books, which considered sexuality and the patriarchal basis of marriage.

*OBITUARIES AND OTHER SOURCES:*

PERIODICALS

*New York Times,* June 19, 1999, p. A16.
*Times* (London), June 21, 1999.
*Washington Post,* June 20, 1999, p. C6.

\*     \*     \*

**STONE, Martin**
   **See RYAN, Oscar**

\*     \*     \*

**STROHM, Reinhard   1942-**

*PERSONAL:* Born August 4, 1942, in Munich, Germany. *Education:* Attended the University of Munich, studied with Georgiades; Technical University, Berlin, studied with Dahlhaus, Ph.D., 1971. *Avocational interests:* Travel, mountaineering.

*ADDRESSES: Office*—Faculty of Music, St. Aldate's, Oxford OX1 1DB, England.

*CAREER:* Richard-Wagner-Ausgabe, assistant editor, 1970-81; King's College, University of London, lecturer, then reader in music, 1975-83, reader, 1990-91, professor of historical musicology, 1991-96, director of Institute for Advanced Musical Studies, beginning 1991; Yale University, professor of music history, 1983-89; Oxford University, Heather Professor of Music and Fellow of Wadham College, 1996—.

*AWARDS, HONORS:* Edward J. Dent Medal, Royal Musical Association, 1977.

*WRITINGS:*

*Italienische Opernarien des fruehen Settecento: 1720-1730, Volume I: Studien, Volume II: Notenbeispiele und Verzeichnisse,* Volk (Koeln), 1976.
*Die italienische Oper im 18 Jahrhundert,* Heinrichshofen (Wilhelmshaven), 1979, second edition, 1991.
*Music in Late Medieval Bruges,* Clarendon (Oxford), 1985, second edition, 1990.
*Essays on Handel and Italian Opera,* Cambridge University Press (New York City), 1985.
*Giustino by Antonio Vivaldi: Introduction, Critical Notes, and Critical Commentary,* Ricordi (Milano), 1991.
*The Rise of European Music, 1380-1500,* Cambridge University Press, 1993.
*Dramma Per Musica: Italian Opera Seria of the Eighteenth Century* (essays and studies), Yale University Press (New Haven, CT), 1997.

Also author of *Music in Late Medieval Europe,* 1987. Associated with Richard Wagner's *Tannhaeuser und der Saengerkrieg auf Wartburg: grosse romantische Oper in 3 Akten: 1845, mit Varianten bis 1860;* B. Schott's *Soehne (Mainz), 1980-85;* Giovanna Gronda's *La carriera di un librettista: Pietro Pariati da Reggio di Lombardia,* Mulino (Bologna), 1990; and Wagner's *Rienzi, der Letzte der Tribunen: grosse tragische Oper in 5 Akten: WWV 49;* B. Schott's *Soehne, 1974-1991.* Also, contributor to books and journals.

*SIDELIGHTS:* In a *Times Literary Supplement* review of Reinhard Strohm's *Dramma Per Musica: Italian Opera Seria of the Eighteenth Century,* published in 1997, Jonathan Keates said of Strohm: "[O]f all those urging us towards a more rationally comprehensive grasp of the genre [of musicology], none has been more persuasive than Reinhard Strohm. By insisting that we search out these operas in their wider contexts—the fortunes and aspirations of the composer, the nature of the original *mise-en-scene,* the political undertones of the text and the moral expectations of the audience—he has created for eighteenth-century Italian opera a series of unfolding perspectives as vivid and elaborate as those which opened before their entranced [original] audiences."

Strohm's debut book, *Italienische Opernarien des fruehen Settecento: 1720-1730,* appeared in 1976 and "[made] an important contribution to opera of the *primo settecento,*" appraised Sven Hansell, claiming in a *Notes* review that "it belongs with the best writing of the twentieth century. . . . Strohm establishes himself as a leader in eighteenth-century studies." Hansell praised the study, noting that "Strohm uses a resourceful imagination informed by admirable scholarly caution to come to grips with the early eighteenth-century Italian aria. By paying closest attention to textual details such as syntax, meter and, of course, the meaning of individual words, he throws wide the door to a flood of intriguing observations that let him deal with the organization of arias on all levels."

"Strohm's knowledge of early eighteenth-century Italian opera," continued Hansell, "is very broad, although he cites no more than thirty composers in his discussions." In addition to early eighteenth-century composers Vinci and Hasse, who consume the majority of *Italienische Opernarien des fruehen Settecento*'s pages, Strohm addresses Vivaldi, F. Gasparini, Leo, Orlandini, A. Pollarolo, Porpora, Sarri, and A. Scarlatti. Hansell indicates that because the book does not include and index of "key words or topics," readers must read the entire work to locate specific information. However, Hansell believes that readers will already be internally motivated to fully read *Italienische Opernarien des fruehen Settecento,* enjoying the work's two volumes— *Volume I: Studien,* and *Volume II: Notenbeispiele und Verzeichnisse.*

Strohm again addressed the Italian opera in a number of essays written from 1975 to 1984 and collectively published in his 1985 book *Essays on Handel and Italian Opera.* "In his pleasant and modest Preface to these essays . . . Strohm remarks that he feels a sense of gratitude for having been a witness to the great advances made in Handelian research during recent years. But he is far more than a 'witness.' These essays . . . presented here for the first time in English, demonstrate

that he belongs among those who created this flourishing of scholarship," commended Paul Henry Lang in *Musical Quarterly.* Martin Cooper translated the essays; however, his translations were edited by Strohm before being published. Lang remarked that Strohm's final input may account for why the "few and unimportant [flaws]" in the translation of *Essays on Handel and Italian Opera* "are mostly Germanisms."

"Though each piece [in *Essays on Handel and Italian Opera*] is independent," explained Lang, "there are leitmotifs that go through all of them and bind them together. The first thing one notices is the author's intimate familiarity with the cultural and political history of all areas his researches touch upon. The introductory essay deftly sketches the scene Handel encountered during his nearly four-year sojourn in Italy, which was one of political chaos because of the German occupation and the rivalries of the various cities. Handel was always alert to local conditions and tastes, but the extent of his political awareness is a new aspect of his character." Lang continued: "Professor Strohm's 'political reading' of the librettos Handel selected to use casts a new light on what we may call his topical dramaturgy, and shows how historical and dynastic references in the old librettos were altered to suit the political demands of the occasion. Usually Handel had a part in these updatings. Strohm comes to the conclusion that 'as operatic producer Handel seems to have followed public taste rather than his own ideal as a composer.' " "One of the interesting findings of the author," believed Lang, "is the tension between the clerical patrons and the professional opera entrepreneurs; when the situation became unsettling, the Vatican simply forbade opera performances in public theaters."

*Dramma Per Musica* is a collection of previously published essays and studies. As such, it is similar to *Essays on Handel* and *Italian Opera* in its structure, but with "a more obvious sense of purpose," determined Keates. The volume, according to Keates, gives readers "a sense of eighteenth-century opera seria as something suspiciously like a *Gesamtkunstwerk,* in which co-cooperation between musicians, poets, scenic artists, audiences and even singers was, if not deliberate, then often profoundly intuitive."

*The Rise of European Music, 1380-1500* "deserves the attention of any serious historian of the period," asserted Michael Eckert in an *Antioch Review* assessment that noted that Strohm "incorporate[s] much recent research in considerable detail, though at the cost of some unevenness." Adelyn Peck Leverett, writing in *Speculum,* was disappointed that Strohm's text excludes some readers from information that they probably would have enjoyed had the book not been written at the author's own unparalleled level. However, Leverett, in general, was extremely favorable in review which concluded: "*The Rise of European Music* stands as a major and thought-provoking contribution to historical writing on music." "A major theme of his book," detailed Leverett, "is the vast 'new publicity' of polyphonic art in this age, when the increasing wealth of cities and of their individual middle-class denizens brought composed music." "Strohm's coverage of polyphonic practice in the Germanic and central European countries expands greatly that of previous survey histories," reported Leverett, believing that "perhaps the strongest portion of the book is part 3 [of 4], entitled 'The Common Traditions.' Here the author draws upon his own rich archival experience . . . along with other crucial scholarship of the 1980s to present a new picture of the social functions of polyphony in the era just before the advent of music printing."

## BIOGRAPHICAL/CRITICAL SOURCES:

### PERIODICALS

*Antioch Review*, winter, 1995, p. 114.
*Choice*, October, 1994, p. 296.
*Musical Quarterly*, winter, 1986, pp. 119-123.
*Notes*, June, 1978, pp. 859-862.
*Speculum*, October, 1995, pp. 971-973.
*Times Literary Supplement*, May 29, 1998, p. 24.*

\*    \*    \*

## SUSKO, Mario 1941-

*PERSONAL:* Born December 17, 1941, in Sarajevo, Yugoslavia (now Republic of Bosnia and Herzegovina); wife's name, Maria; children: Klea, Alexandria. *Education:* University of Sarajevo, B.A., 1965; State University of New York at Stony Brook, M.A., 1969, Ph.D., 1973. *Ethnicity:* "Croat." *Religion:* Catholic.

*ADDRESSES: Office*—Department of English, Nassau Community College of the State University of New York, Garden City, NY, 11530-6793.

*CAREER:* Nassau Community College of the State University of New York, Garden City, English teacher. New York University, adjunct professor; also taught at University of Sarajevo.

*MEMBER:* Croatian Writers' Union (elected 1968); Scientific Committee, Istituto Italiano di Cultura di Napoli (Italy).

*AWARDS, HONORS:* Telegram Award for poetry, 1965; A. B. Simic Award for an essay, 1970; B. H. Literary Translators' Union Annual Award, 1983; Veselin Maslesa Publishing House Award, for *Saul Bellow: Works,* 1991; Council of Europe Grant/Award for Literary Translators, 1993-94; *Nassau Review* Poetry Award, 1997; Premio Internazionale di Poesia e Letteratura "Nuove Lettere," 1998.

*WRITINGS:*

*Mothers, Shoes, and Other Mortal Songs* (poems), Yuganta (Stamford, CT), 1995.
*Versus Exsul* (poems), Yuganta, 1998.

Poetry published in various periodicals, including *Nassau Review, Seneca Review,* and *Potato Eyes.*

### UNTRANSLATED WORKS

*Prvo putovanje* (poems), Svjetlost (Sarajevo), 1965.
*Drugo putovanje ili patetika uma* (poems), Mladost (Zagreb), 1968.
*Fantazije* (poems), Svjetlost (Sarajevo), 1970.
*Ispovijesti,* Veselin Maslesa (Sarajevo), 1976.
*Skladbe i Odsjevi,* Svjetlost (Sarajevo), 1977.
*Duh i Glina,* Veselin Maslesa, 1978.
*Prezivljenje* (poems), Alfa (Zagreb), 1980.
*Gravitacije, 41,* (poems), Svjetlost (Sarajevo), 1982.
*Izabrane Pjesme; Ilija Ladin: Poezija,* Svjetlost, 1984.
*Savremena Britanska Poezija,* Medunarodna Knjizevna Manifestacija (Sarajevo), 1988.
*Physika Meta* (poems), ICR (Rijeka), 1989.
*Savremena Americka Poezija,* Medunarodna Knjizevna Manifestacija, 1990.
*Knjiga izlaska* (poems), Graficar (Tuzla), 1991.
*Prirucnik za poeziju* (poems), ICR (Rijeka), 1994.
*Buduca Proslost* (poems), Egzil-abc (Ljubljana), 1996.
*Majke, cipele I ine smrtne pjesme* (poems), Hrvatska sveucilisna naklada (Zagreb), 1997.
*Versus Exsul* (poems), Meander (Zagreb), 1999.

Translator of numerous works into Croatian, including *Saul Bellow: Works* (7 volumes), Veslin Mastesa, 1990; and Kurt Vonnegut's *Galapagos,* GZH (Zagred), 1990.

*SIDELIGHTS:* Poet Mario Susko told *CA:* "I am . . . an author who is displaced and fights literally for his literary survival. One cannot be really accepted as a writer in another language, but one can surely try to remain faithful to one's own beliefs that language is a creative force, whether it be English, Italian, or Croatian."

*BIOGRAPHICAL/CRITICAL SOURCES:*

PERIODICALS

*Library Journal,* October 1, 1998, p. 94.
*Slobodna Dalmacija,* July 2, 1996; April 22, 1997; December 15, 1998; June 8, 1999.
*World Literature Today,* winter, 1998, pp. 166-167.

\*    \*    \*

**SUTHER, Judith   1940-**

*PERSONAL:* Born February 18, 1940 in Lawton, OK; daughter of Robert and Audie West. *Education:* University of Missouri, Columbia, B.A., 1960, Ph.D. 1967; University of Michigan, M.A., 1961; University of Grenoble, France, CAPES, 1962.

*ADDRESSES: Office*—Department of Languages and Culture Studies, University of North Carolina, Charlotte, NC 28223.

*CAREER:* Randolph-Macon Women's College, instructor, 1962-64; University of Missouri, Columbia, assistant professor, 1967-68; Texas Christian University, assistant professor and professor, 1968-78, chair of modern languages, 1972-74; University of North Carolina, Charlotte, professor and chair of foreign languages, 1978-82, professor 1982—, director, Master of Arts in Liberal Studies, 1993—.

*MEMBER:* American Association of Teachers of French, Modern Language Association, American Literary Translators Association, Institute Jacques Maritain.

*AWARDS, HONORS:* Elizabeth Stanton Michaels Fellow, American Association of University Women, 1975; American Philosophical Society research grant, 1978; French Cultural Service grants, 1979, 1981, and 1997.

*WRITINGS:*

(Editor) *Essays on Camus's Exile and the Kingdom,* Romance Monographs, Inc. (University, MS), 1980.
*Raissa Maritain: Pilgrim, Poet, Exile,* Fordham University Press (New York City), 1990.

*Slow Branches Burning: Listening to the Lives of Virginia Whitchurch Southwood,* Missouri Association for Social Welfare (Jefferson City, MO), 1994.
(Translator) Elisabeth Manuel, *Cette ombre familiere,* Starbooks (Charlotte, NC), 1995.
(Editor) Kay Sage, *China Eggs,* translation of *Les oeufs de porcelaine,* by Elisabeth Manuel, Starbooks, 1996.
*A House of Her Own: Kay Sage, Solitary Surrealist,* University of Nebraska Press (Lincoln, NE), 1997.

Co-translator, *Three Plays of Andre Obey: One for the Wind, Noah, and the Phoenix,* Texas Christian University, 1972, and *Three More Plays of Andre Obey: The Reunion, Moses and the Mountain, and The Window,* Texas Christian University, 1977. Contributor to scholarly publications, including *French-American Review, Explorations in Renaissance Culture, French Review, Studies in Comparative Literature,* and *Kentucky Romance Quarterly.* Editor, *French-American Review,* 1976-84.

*SIDELIGHTS:* Judith Suther, a professor of French at the University of North Carolina at Charlotte, has written several scholarly studies and translations of French literature. She has attracted broader critical notice, however, for a somewhat controversial biography of poet and religious philosopher Raissa Maritain, wife of philosopher and political activist Jacques Maritain. She has also written a biography of American surrealist Kay Sage.

Born in Lawton, Oklahoma, on February 18, 1940, Suther received a B.A. from the University of Missouri, Columbia, and went on to earn an M.A. from the University of Michigan. Suther then went to France, where she studied at the University of Grenoble. She returned to the University of Missouri for her Ph.D., which she received in 1967. Suther began her teaching career at Randolph-Macon Woman's College, where she was an instructor in French from 1962 to 1964. She also held teaching positions at the University of Missouri and Texas Christian University before joining the faculty at the University of North Carolina, Charlotte. She has specialized in twentieth-century French literature, French-American comparative literature, and translation theory and practice.

Suther's first book is a compilation of essays on Albert Camus's work *Exile and the Kingdom,* for which Suther wrote the introduction and selected bibliography. Intended for nonspecialist students, the volume drew modest praise from Rosemarie Jones in the *Modern Language Review.* Though Jones was not convinced that all the essays in the book were essential to a complete understanding of Camus, she found the collection a "useful, conservative" addition to Camus scholarship.

Suther has translated several plays by Andre Obey, and has written articles for academic journals on such figures as Marguerite de Navarre, Eugene Ionesco, and Thomas Merton. But her two biographies have brought her attention from outside the confines of academia. In *A House of Her Own,* the first biography of American artist Kay Sage, Suther argued that the surrealists' intense dislike of Sage, one of the few women admitted to their exclusive circle, stemmed from the deeply patriarchal attitudes of the group. A reviewer for the *Times Literary Supplement* found Suther's subject interesting, but her thesis not fully convincing. "Try as she might," the reviewer wrote, "she never dispels the impression that Sage's haunting images of bare scaffolds and hooded figures in empty landscapes were derivative from de Chirico and others." The reviewer noted that Suther paid disproportionate attention to Sage's poetry and to her medical problems and domestic situation, and ended the book with her subject as much an enigma as she was at the beginning.

Suther's study of Raissa Maritain received similar criticism. Born to Russian-Jewish parents in 1883, Maritain moved to France with her family and became an impassioned convert to Catholicism. With her husband Jacques Maritain and her sister Vera, she lived a celibate life dedicated to prayer, meditation, and writing. Jacques Maritain became a prominent figure in the American academic world, taking positions at Columbia, Princeton, Chicago, and Notre Dame and later becoming French Ambassador to the Vatican. Raissa, however, who suffered from repeated vague illnesses, lived a secluded life; scholars doubt that her writings would ever have been published if not for the prominence of her husband.

Suther's biography of Maritain received mixed reviews from various critics. Though Suther's biography argued that patriarchal structures prevented Raissa from achieving her due recognition, two critics did not agree that Raissa's work was important enough to warrant this study. Neither Denis J. M. Bradley in *America,* nor Madeline Marget in *Commonweal,* believed Suther succeeded in proving her thesis. But, although Bradley viewed Suther's writing as "sometimes syntactically and psychologically opaque," Marget considered her book "elegantly constructed, thoroughly researched, meticulously annotated, and completely readable." "One can but approve [Suther's] deep motivation and her methodological decision," explained Edouard Morot-Sir, in the *South Atlantic Review,* "Suther's is a serious and carefully written work," stated J. Pierre N. L'Abbe and Kristan A. L'Abbe in the *Maritain Newsletter,* "with detailed analysis of Raissa's poetry and other writings and a deep searching of her character."

## BIOGRAPHICAL/CRITICAL SOURCES:

### PERIODICALS

*America,* February 23, 1991, pp. 214-216.
*Commonweal,* October 12, 1990, pp. 586-587.
*Maritain Newsletter,* May 1, 1991.
*Modern Language Review,* July 1983, pp. 723-724.
*Notes et documents,* September-December, 1990, pp. 98-100.
*South Atlantic Review,* September, 1991, pp. 132-134.
*Times Literary Supplement,* May 29, 1998, p. 36.
*Women's Review of Books,* March, 1998, p. 4.*

# T-U

## TAKAGI, Akimitsu 1920-1995

*PERSONAL:* Born September 25, 1920, in Aomori, Japan; died in 1995.

*CAREER:* Writer.

*AWARDS, HONORS:* Japan Mystery Writers Club Award, 1949, for *Irezumi satsujin jiken* (also known as *Shisei satsujin jiken*).

*WRITINGS:*

*SELECTED NOVELS*

*Irezumi satsujin jiken* (also known as *Shisei satsujin jiken*), Iwaya Shoten (Tokyo, Japan), 1949, translated into English and adapted by Deborah Boliver Boehm as *The Tattoo Murder Case,* Soho Press (New York City), 1998.
*Mikkokusha,* [Japan], 1965, translated into English by Sadako Mizuguchi and published as *The Informer,* Anthos Publishing (Queensland, Australia), 1971.
*Zero no mitsugetsu,* [Japan], 1965, translated into English by Sadako Mizuguchi and published as *Honeymoon to Nowhere,* Soho Press, 1999.
*Kokui no majo,* Kaiseisha (Tokyo, Japan), 1968.
*Shisso,* Nihon Bunkasha (Tokyo, Japan), 1968.
*Yurei basha,* Kaiseisha, 1968.
*No Patent on Murder* (originally published in Japan), translated into English by Sadako Mizuguchi, Playboy Press, 1977.

*NONFICTION*

(With Horiyoshi and Fukushi Katsunari) *Nihon shisei geijutsu Horiyoshi,* Ningen no Kagakusha (Tokyo, Japan), 1983.

*Japanese Tattoo Ladies,* [Tokyo, Japan], 1988.

*SIDELIGHTS:* According to a *Publishers Weekly* contributor, Akimitsu Takagi was "one of Japan's leading suspense writers." Takagi won the 1949 Japan Mystery Writers Club Award for *Irezumi satsujin jiken,* a novel also known as *Shisei satsujin jiken.* Deborah Boliver Boehm translated this novel into English as *The Tattoo Murder Case.*

*The Tattoo Murder Case* is set in Tokyo, Japan, after World War II. Kinue Nomura, a woman with a tattooed torso (forbidden in Japan at the time), has been murdered. Kinue's lover, young medical student Kenzo Matsushita, searches for her murderer. Kenzo discovers Kinue's severed head, arms, and legs in the locked bathroom of her own home, but cannot find Kinue's tattooed torso. Kenzo's suspects include Kinue's husband, that man's boss and his nephew, and a professor. Yet each of Kenzo's suspects has an alibi.

Kenzo must enlist his young friend, Kyosuke Kamizu, to help investigate Kinue's murder. Kyosuke is only nineteen years old but knows six languages and forensic medicine. He finds the murderer and figures out how Kinue's dismembered body ends up in a locked room. While a *Publishers Weekly* contributor observed that "there's a restrained formality to the dialogue and exposition" in the English translation of *The Tattoo Murder Case,* the critic noted that the book offers "an intriguing picture of postwar Japan."

Sadako Mizuguchi translated Takagi's novel *No Patent on Murder.* In this novel, someone kills a man on his wedding night. State prosecutor Kirishima investigates the death of the newlywed husband. This proves to be a difficult task, because many of the victim's relatives have shady histories, providing the prosecutor with a number of suspects. Kirishima must solve an extremely complicated mystery which may involve a valuable patent.

*BIOGRAPHICAL/CRITICAL SOURCES:*

PERIODICALS

*Publishers Weekly,* January 10, 1977, p. 71; December 22, 1997, p. 41.

OTHER

*Soho Press,* http://www.sohopress.com/informer.html (November 4, 1999).*

\*     \*     \*

## TARBELL, Ida M(inerva)   1857-1944

*PERSONAL:* Born November 5, 1857, in Erie County, PA; died of pneumonia, January 6, 1944, in Bridgeport (one source says Bethel), CT; buried in Woodlawn Cemetery, Titusville, PA; daughter of Franklin Sumner and Esther Ann (McCullough) Tarbell. *Education:* Studied French revolutionary history and related subjects at the Sorbonne and College de France, Paris, 1891-94; Allegheny College, A.B., 1880, A.M., 1883, L.H.D., 1909, LL.D., 1915; Knox College, L.H.D., 1909.

*CAREER:* American educator, journalist, historian, biographer, and lecturer. Poland Union Seminary, teacher, 1881-82; *The Chautauquan* (monthly magazine published by the Methodist Church), Chautauqua, NY, writer, associate editor, then managing editor, 1883-1901; *McClure's* Magazine, editor on staff, then associated editor, 1894-1906; *American* magazine (purchased with Finley Peter Dunne and William Allan White, and *McClure's* colleagues Lincoln Steffens, Ray Stannerd Baker, and John S. Phillips), associate editor, 1906-15. Member of women's committee, Council of National Defense; President Harding's Unemployment Conference, 1919; National Women's Committee. Mobilization for Human Needs, 1933-38.

*MEMBER:* American Historical Association, American Economic Association, English Society of Women Journalists, American Woman's Association; Barnard Club, Colony Club, National Arts Club, Cosmopolitan Club, Pen and Brush Club.

*WRITINGS:*

NONFICTION ASSOCIATED WITH ABRAHAM LINCOLN

(With assistance from J. McCan Davis) *The Early Life of Abraham Lincoln, Containing Many Unpublished Documents and Unpublished Reminiscences of Lincoln's Early Friends,* S. S. McClure (New York City), 1896.

*The Life of Abraham Lincoln, Drawn from Original Sources and Containing Many Speeches, Letters and Telegrams Hitherto Unpublished,* two volumes, Doubleday & McClure (New York City), 1900, special illustrators' edition, May, 1900, new edition published as *The Life of Abraham Lincoln, Drawn from Original Sources and Containing Many Speeches, Letters, and Telegrams Hitherto Unpublished, and Illustrated with Many Reproductions from Original Paintings, Photographs, et cetera,* four volumes, Lincoln Historical Society (New York City), 1906, new two volume edition, Macmillan (New York City), 1917, new edition, 1923, four volume Sagamon edition, Lincoln Historical Society (New York City), 1924.

*He Knew Lincoln,* McClure, Phillips (New York City), 1907.

*Boy Scouts' Life of Lincoln,* Macmillan, 1921.

*He Knew Lincoln, and Other Billy Brown Stories,* Macmillan, 1922.

*In the Footsteps of the Lincolns,* Harper (New York City), 1924.

*A Reporter for Lincoln: Story of Henry E. Wing, Soldier and Newspaperman,* Macmillan, 1927.

*Abraham Lincoln and His Ancestors,* University of Nebraska (Lincoln), 1997.

OTHER NONFICTION

*Madame Roland: A Biographical Study,* Scribner (New York City), 1896.

*McClure's Biographies: Napoleon, Gladstone, Bismarck, Grant, Dana, Stevenson and Others,* Volume I: *A Short Life of Napoleon Bonaparte, illustrations from the Hon. Gardiner G. Hubbard's collection of Napoleon Engravings, Supplemented by Pictures from the Collections of Prince Victor Napoleon, Prince Roland Bonaparte, Baron Larrey and Others,* Volume II: *Human Documents: Portraits and Biographies of Eminent Men: Articles by Robert Louis Stevenson, Herbert Spencer, Professor Drummond, Edward Everett Hale, H. H. Boyesen, Gen. Horace Porter, Hamlin Garland, Robert Barr and Others,* S. S. McClure (New York City), 1896, Volume I enlarged for new edition published as *A Life of Napoleon Bonaparte; With a Sketch of Josephine, Empress of the French* (originally appeared in *McClure's* magazine, November 1894-April 1895), McClure, Phillips (New York City), 1901.

*The History of the Standard Oil Company,* two volumes, McClure, Phillips, 1904.

*The Tariff in Our Times,* Macmillan, 1911.

*The Business of Being a Woman,* Macmillan, 1912.

*The Ways of Woman,* Macmillan, 1915.

*New Ideals in Business, An Account of Their Practice and Their Effects Upon Men and Profits,* Macmillan, 1916.

*Peacemakers—Blessed and Others; Observations, Reflections and Irritations at an International Conference,* Macmillan, 1922.

*The Life of Elbert H. Gary; The Story of Steel,* D. Appleton (New York City), 1925.

*Owen D. Young, a New Type of Industrial Leader,* Macmillan, 1932.

*The Nationalizing of Business, 1878-1898,* Macmillan, 1936, reprinted as Volume IX in "History of American Life" series, Arthur M. Schlesinger Sr. and Dixon Ryan Fox, editors, Quadrangle, 1971.

*All in the Day's Work: An Autobiography,* Macmillan, 1939.

Robert C. Kochersberger Jr., editor, *More Than a Muckraker: Ida Minerva Tarbell's Lifetime in Journalism* (published and unpublished works), University of Tennessee Press (Knoxville), 1995.

Contributor of articles to periodicals, including Boston *Transcript, Scribner's,* and *McClure's,* and to McClure Syndicate.

*FICTION*

*Father Abraham,* illustrated by Blendon Campbell, Moffat, Yard (New York City), 1909.

*The Rising of the Tide; The Story of Sabinsport,* Macmillan, 1919.

*In Lincoln's Chair,* Macmillan, 1920.

Also author of short stories.

*SIDELIGHTS:* In *All in the Day's Work: An Autobiography* (1939), Ida M. Tarbell records her youth and journalistic career. Following its republication in 1985, Karen Sue Smith assessed the book for *Commonweal,* beginning her review with the exclamation "Jackpot!" According to Smith the biography presents a wealth of information, including details of wars, railroads, Wall Street, the League of Nations, and popular periodicals of the times. After reading *All in the Day's Work,* Smith

believed that, rather than Tarbell's praised accomplishments, "it is her personal integrity as a rather private woman in public life and as a journalist that [is impressive]." "Both the palpable concern for the common good and the civility evident in the book make a reader mourn for what our society has lost so quickly," Smith declared in 1990. In 1910, during the midst of Tarbell's career, a writer for the *National Cyclopaedia of American Biography* complimented both Tarbell's accomplishments and characteristics, declaring her "one of the foremost historical and biographical writers of the day."

Before becoming involved in journalism, Tarbell taught for two years at Poland Union Seminary. In 1883 she began writing for the *Chautauquan,* eventually becoming its managing editor, and ten years later she began her association with *McClure's.* While an editor for *McClure's* magazine, the foremost muckraking journal at the turn of the twentieth century, Tarbell established her reputation as a trustbuster with her revealing series on the Standard Oil Company, later published as the two-volume *The History of the Standard Oil Company* (1904). In it she exposed the monopoly Standard Oil had on its market, as well as some of the means the company used to achieve its monopoly. The book warned of the threat that big business posed to equal opportunity and democracy, and led to the Supreme Court's decision in 1911 to break up Standard Oil. Of interest was the fact that Tarbell's father had made a fair living manufacturing wooden barrels for oil in the great Pennsylvanian oil strike of 1859 before he was forced out of business by Standard Oil.

One of Tarbell's first assignments for *McClure's* was to write a serialized biography of Napoleon, which ran from November 1894 to April 1895. The articles proved so popular that the magazine's circulation doubled. In 1895, her biographical text on Napoleon was joined and published with another volume of biographies; collectively both volumes were called *McClure's Biographies: Napoleon, Gladstone, Bismarck, Grant, Dana, Stevenson, and Others.* The section on Napoleon was later enlarged and published independently as *Life of Napoleon Bonaparte; With a Sketch of Josephine, Empress of the French* (1901).

Another assignment for *McClure's* directly lead to the publication of her biographies on Abraham Lincoln, perhaps her most highly esteemed books. Among them was the two-volume *The Life of Abraham Lincoln: Drawn from Original Sources and Containing Many Speeches, Letters, and Telegrams Hitherto Unpublished* (1900). For nearly a quarter of a century following its first publication, the work was reprinted in a number of different editions, including Doubleday & McClure's May, 1900 special illustrators' edition, which totaled only 75 copies. In 1974 Barnes reprinted one of Tarbell's earliest biographical works on Lincoln, *The Early Life of Abraham Lincoln: Containing Many Unpublished Documents and Unpublished Reminiscences of Lincoln's Early Friends.* Almost seven decades after its original publication in 1896, a *New Yorker* critic praised the *The Early Life of Abraham Lincoln:* "It remains an excellent introduction to Lincoln as well as an authentic picture of rural and small-town life in the heartlands in the first half of the nineteenth century."

Tarbell was criticized late in her career for her biographies *The Life of Elbert H. Gary; The Story of Steel* (1925) and *Owen D. Young, a New Type of Industrial* (1932), in which she seemingly reverses her earlier antibusiness stance. Responding to the criticism, she claimed it was not her sentiments that had changed, but the nature of big business. With *The History of the Standard Oil Company,* Tarbell's attention shifted to depicting the practices of American big business. Critics observe, however, that in contrast to the muckrakers, with whom she is usually grouped, her politics were basically conservative. She often defended the businesses she described, championing the American capitalist system. Tarbell's conservatism [surfaced in] her criticism, toward the end of her life, of the women's suffrage movement and of women's involvement in politics and business. In such works as *The Business of Being a Woman,* she urged women to remain at home and raise children, arguing, to the disappointment of many of her admirers, that women could be more influential as mothers than as career professionals.

Published more than a half of a century past the death of Tarbell in January 1944, Robert C. Kochersberger Jr.'s *More Than a Muckraker: Ida Minerva Tarbell's Lifetime in Journalism* presents Tarbell as "a probusiness woman who as also concerned with the welfare of the worker," stated Beverly G. Merrick in *Journalism & Mass Communication Quarterly. More Than a Muckraker* is collection of both unpublished and published works by Tarbell, including essays, speeches, and articles. "It is an enjoyable read because the editor is a good writer as well. . . . [His introduction] goes a long way in explaining the life of a writer with a social conscience," noted Merrick, continuing: "He takes great care in explaining the genre of muckraking in the historical context of the turn of the [twentieth] century. In his introduction, he is painstakingly thorough in pro-

viding information upon which any student of history thrives."

*BIOGRAPHICAL/CRITICAL SOURCES:*

*BOOKS*

*American Decades: 1900-1909,* Gale (Detroit), 1996.
Brady, Kathleen, *Ida Tarbell: Portrait of a Muckraker,* Putnam (New York City), 1984.
*Dictionary of Literary Biography,* Volume 47: *American Historians, 1866-1912,* Gale (Detroit, MI), 1986.
*Encyclopedia of World Biography,* 2nd edition, Gale Research, 1998.
*National Cyclopaedia of American Biography,* James T. White (New York City), 1910.
Tomkins, Mary E., *Ida M. Tarbell,* Twayne (Boston), 1974.
*Twentieth-Century Literary Criticism,* Volume 40, Gale, 1991.
*Who Was Who among North American Authors, 1921-1939,* Gale, 1976.
*Who Was Who in Literature, 1906-1934,* Gale, 1979.
*Woman's Who's Who of America,* Gale, 1976.

*PERIODICALS*

*American Heritage,* April, 1970.
*Bookman,* November, 1917.
*Choice,* February, 1972.
*Commonweal,* December 7, 1990.
*Craftsman,* April, 1908.
*Dial,* January 11, 1917; February 14, 1918; August 9, 1919.
*Journal of Mass Communication Quarterly,* winter, 1996.
*McClure's,* no. 2 (Christmas), 1904.
*Nation,* March 1, 1900; January 5, 1905; December 5, 1936.
*New Yorker,* December 2, 1974.
*North American Review,* September, 1905.
*Saturday Review,* November 26, 1966.
*Vanity Fair,* May, 1998.
*Western Pennsylvania Historical Magazine,* winter, 1956.*

\*     \*     \*

## TAYLOR, Telford   1908-1998

*OBITUARY NOTICE*—See index for *CA* sketch: Born February 24, 1908, in Schenectady, NY; died of a stroke, May 23, 1998, in New York, NY. Lawyer, prosecutor, and author. Taylor will be remembered for prosecuting Nazi war criminals after World War II and for believing governments must not be allowed to mistreat the citizens they represent. Taylor was studying law at Harvard and made it onto *Law Review* his last year of studies and clerked for Judge Agustus Hand. From there he became part of President Franklin Delano Roosevelt's administration, helping to draft the Securities Exchange Act. Taylor moved on to the Justice Department and served as general counsel to the Federal Communications Commission. He joined Army intelligence when the United States entered World War II and helped decipher Nazi codes. He was recruited in 1945 to help with the Nuremberg trials.

A top assistant at the trial, Taylor took over the prosecution after he was made a brigadier general. From 1946 to 1949 nearly two hundred Nazis were tried for their roles in the war and Taylor won convictions for about one hundred and fifty. When the trials concluded he returned to the United States and a post in the Truman administration. His first book, *Sword and Swastika,* was published in 1952 and examined the newly appearing apologist writings of German army officials. During the 1950s Taylor raged against Senator Eugene McCarthy and the investigation he instigated, then found himself targeted by McCarthy. McCarthy implied Taylor was less than loyal to his country because he represented people suspected of communism. The attacks did not impact Taylor's career and he responded with the book *Grand Inquest: The Story of Congressional Investigations,* which pointed out McCarthy's flaws.

From 1957 and continuing into the 1970s Taylor served on the law school faculties at Yale University, Columbia University, and Cardozo Law School. Throughout the years he continued writing, eventually completing about a dozen books. Titles include *The March of Conquest, Guilt, Responsibility, and the Third Reich,* and *The Anatomy of the Nuremberg Trials: A Personal Memoir.* He was critical of the war in Vietnam and wrote *Nuremberg and Vietnam: An American Tragedy.* Taylor never lost interest in human rights issues and took on the cause of Jews imprisoned in Russia for wanting to immigrate to Israel and said the behavior exhibited in the Bosnian War should result in criminal indictments. Taylor was honored with many awards, including the Order of the British Empire and the Legion of Honor from France. His book *Munich: The Price of Peace* received the National Book Critics Circle Award in 1980.

*OBITUARIES AND OTHER SOURCES:*

PERIODICALS

*Chicago Tribune,* May 24, 1998, sec. 4, p. 7.
*Los Angeles Times,* May 27, 1998, p. B8.
*New York Times,* May 25, 1998, p. A13.
*Times* (London), May 25, 1998.

OTHER

*CNN Interactive* (electronic), May 23, 1998.

\* \* \*

## THOMS, Peter 1960-

*PERSONAL:* Born August 17, 1960, in Huntsville, Ontario, Canada; son of Gordon William and Maxine (Hanes) Thoms; married Lisa Zeitz, June 17, 1989. *Education:* University of Toronto, B.A., 1983; Queen's University, Kingston, Ontario, M.A., 1985, Ph.D., 1989.

*ADDRESSES: Home*—London, Ontario, Canada. *Office*—Department of English, University of Western Ontario, London, Ontario, Canada M6H 3K7. *E-mail*—pgthoms@julian.uwo.ca.

*CAREER:* University of Western Ontario, London, adjunct assistant professor of English, 1992—.

*AWARDS, HONORS:* Fellow, Social Sciences and Humanities Research Council of Canada, 1990-92; John Charles Polanyi Prize in Literature, 1992-93.

*WRITINGS:*

*The Windings of the Labyrinth: Quest and Structure in the Major Novels of Wilkie Collins,* Ohio University Press (Athens, OH), 1992.
*Detection and Its Designs: Narrative and Power in Nineteenth-Century Detective Fiction,* Ohio University Press, 1998.

\* \* \*

## THURLO, David
## (Aimee Duvall, Aimee Martel, joint
## pseudonyms)

*PERSONAL:* Married Aimee (a writer), c. 1970. *Education:* Attended the University of New Mexico.

*ADDRESSES: Office*—P.O. Box 2747, Corrales, NM 87048. *E-mail*—72640.2437@compuserve.com.

*CAREER:* Mathematics, science, and technology teacher; writer.

*AWARDS, HONORS:* RITA Award nomination, best romantic suspense novel, 1989; *Romantic Times* Reviewer's Choice Award nominations, best Harlequin Intrigue, 1992-93, for *Shadow of the Wolf,* and 1994-95, for *Fatal Charm; Romantic Times* Career Achievement Award nominations, series romantic mystery, 1992-93 and 1996-97.

*WRITINGS:*

NOVELS; WITH WIFE, AIMEE THURLO

*Second Shadow,* Forge (New York City), 1993.

*"ELLA CLAH" SERIES OF NOVELS; WITH AIMEE THURLO*

*Blackening Song,* Forge, 1995.
*Death Walker,* Forge, 1996.
*Bad Medicine,* Forge, 1997.
*Enemy Way,* Forge, 1998.
*Shooting Chant,* Forge, 2000.
*Red Mesa,* Forge, 2001.

*"FOUR WINDS" TRILOGY OF NOVELS; WITH AIMEE THURLO*

*Her Destiny,* Harlequin Intrigue (New York City), 1997.
*Her Hope,* Harlequin Intrigue, 1997.
*Her Shadow,* Harlequin Intrigue, 1998.

*"ROCK RIDGE" SERIES OF NOVELS; WITH AIMEE THURLO*

*Redhawk's Heart,* Harlequin Intrigue, 1999.
*Redhawk's Return,* Harlequin Intrigue, 1999.

*"BLACK RAVEN" SERIES OF NOVELS; WITH AIMEE THURLO*

*Christmas Witness,* Harlequin Intrigue, 1999.
*Black Raven's Pride,* Harlequin Intrigue, 2000.

*NOVELS; WITH AIMEE THURLO; UNDER NAME AIMEE THURLO*

*Ariel's Desire,* Dell Candlelight Ecstasy (New York City), 1987.
*The Right Combination,* Harlequin Superromance (New York City), 1988.

*Expiration Date,* Harlequin Intrigue, 1989.
*Black Mesa,* Harlequin Intrigue, 1990.
*Suitable for Framing,* Harlequin Intrigue, 1990.
*Night Wind,* Harlequin Intrigue, 1991.
*Strangers Who Linger,* Harlequin Intrigue, 1991.
*Breach of Faith,* Harlequin Intrigue, 1992.
*Shadow of the Wolf,* Harlequin Intrigue, 1993.
*Spirit Warrior,* Harlequin Intrigue, 1993.
*Bearing Gifts,* Harlequin Intrigue, 1994.
*Timewalker,* Harlequin Intrigue, 1994.
*Fatal Charm,* Harlequin Intrigue, 1995.
*Cisco's Woman,* Harlequin Intrigue, 1996.

*NOVELS; WITH AIMEE THURLO; UNDER JOINT PSEUDONYM AIMEE MARTEL*

*Secrets Not Shared,* Leisure (New York City), 1981.
*The Fires Within,* Silhouette Desire (New York City), 1984.
*Hero at Large,* Silhouette Desire, 1985.

*NOVELS; WITH AIMEE THURLO; UNDER JOINT PSEUDONYM AIMEE DUVALL*

*Halfway There,* Second Chance at Love, 1982.
*Lover in Blue,* Second Chance at Love, 1982.
*Too Near the Sun,* Second Chance at Love, 1982.
*The Loving Touch,* Second Chance at Love, 1983.
*After the Rain,* Second Chance at Love, 1984.
*One More Tomorrow,* Second Chance at Love, 1984.
*Brief Encounters,* Second Chance at Love, 1985.
*Spring Madness,* Second Chance at Love, 1985.
*Kid at Heart,* Second Chance at Love, 1986.
*Made for Each Other,* Second Chance at Love, 1987.
*To Tame a Heart,* Pageant Romance, 1988.
*Wings of Angels,* Pageant, 1989.

*OTHER WRITINGS; WITH AIMEE THURLO*

Contributor to periodicals, including *Grit, National Examiner,* and *Popular Mechanics.*

*NONFICTION*

Author of *Hands-On Science, Math, and Technology,* Franklin Schaffer Publications (New York City).

*WORK IN PROGRESS:* With Aimee Thurlo, another novel in the Ella Clah series.

*SIDELIGHTS:* David and Aimee Thurlo have produced over forty novels and a number of pieces for periodicals. The novels have appeared under Aimee's name and under the joint pseudonyms of Aimee Martel and

Aimee Duvall. Using their own names, they have penned novels set in the American Southwest featuring Native American characters.

The Thurlos' novel *Second Shadow* was published in 1993. It features Irene Pobikan, a Tewa Indian. An architect, Irene is commissioned to restore a hacienda owned by the Mendoza family. But soon after the work begins, Irene spots an owl—an omen of bad luck among the Tewa. Several strange accidents then occur, and Irene finds a long-dead murder victim. The murderer is still at large, and Irene, who has fallen in love with Raul Mendoza, must summon the help of her guardian spirit, the mountain lion, to help her and those around her. While *Library Journal* contributor Marion F. Gallivan observed that the thoughts of character Raul Mendoza "seem out of place," the suspense in *Second Shadow* "builds effectively to the finale."

*Blackening Song* (1995) is the first of the Thurlos' series of novels featuring Navajo Federal Bureau of Investigation (FBI) agent Ella Clah. Ella lives in San Francisco, California and no longer follows Navajo ways. She learns that her Christian minister father has been murdered at the reservation she left at the age of eighteen. The mutilation of his body suggests a ritual killing. When Ella returns to the reservation, she discovers that her older brother Clifford is the prime suspect. Clifford is a *hataali* (medicine man) who had angrily opposed his father's plan to build a church on the reservation. Clifford has gone into hiding and uses a go-between to contact Ella to claim his innocence and claim that the skinwalkers, black magic devotees, are responsible for the murder.

As Ella pursues the investigation, she finds herself caught in the Navajo reservation's bitter conflict between traditionalists and reformers. Some reservation residents have trouble accepting Ella and view her as a person who has abandoned the reservation to join the white world. The appearance of supernatural occurrences and more mutilated bodies force Ella to rethink her views on Navajo teachings. "The Thurlos ratchet up a lot of suspense" in *Blackening Song,* wrote a critic in *Publishers Weekly.* "The murderer is chosen believably, but characters are thinly sketched," wrote a *Kirkus Reviews* contributor discussing *Blackening Song,* who added that "the real pleasure here is in the complex depiction of cultural conflict and assimilation." Maria A. Perez-Stable, reviewing the novel in the *Library Journal,* commented that "the action moves swiftly in this well-written mystery," and called protagonist Ella Clah "strong" and "independent."

In the 1996 Thurlo novel *Death Walker,* Ella has left the FBI and joined the Navajo tribal police as a special investigator. When several tribal elders are murdered and investigators find religious objects at the crime scenes, it appears that the skinwalkers have returned to threaten the safety of the reservation. Ella must again grapple with the tension between her Navajo background and her training in science and logic to solve the case. *Death Walker* features female characters who "are particularly well drawn" and "tend to steal the show," wrote Mitzi M. Brunsdale in the *Armchair Detective.* These characters include Justine Goodluck, Ella's cousin and assistant, and Ella's gifted mother, Rose Destea.

*Death Walker* is "a satisfying combination of a right-now heroine and an age-old culture," stated *Armchair Detective* contributor Brunsdale. A *Publishers Weekly* contributor judged Ella to be "a tough, appealing heroine," but added that the novel contains a "loose plot" hampered by slow-moving interview scenes, an investigation that does not progress until the novel's second half, and an "anticlimactic" conclusion. Reviewing *Death Walker* in the *School Library Journal,* Pam Johnson deemed it to be "a fast-paced, intriguing novel" and observed that it offers "strong females in contemporary settings."

## BIOGRAPHICAL/CRITICAL SOURCES:

*BOOKS*

Heising, Willetta L., *Detecting Women 2: A Reader's Guide and Checklist for Mystery Series Written by Women,* Purple Moon Press (Dearborn, MI), 1996.

*PERIODICALS*

*Armchair Detective,* summer, 1996, pp. 361-362.
*Kirkus Reviews,* May 1, 1995, p. 586.
*Library Journal,* October 15, 1993, p. 91; July, 1995, p. 124.
*Publishers Weekly,* May 1, 1995, p. 46; April 22, 1996, p. 62.
*School Library Journal,* March, 1997, pp. 216-217.

*OTHER*

*Aimee and David Thurlo,* http://www.comet.net/writersm/thurlo/home.htm (November 5, 1999).*

## TORME, Mel(vin Howard)   1925-1999

*OBITUARY NOTICE*—See index for *CA* sketch: Born September 13, 1925, in Chicago, IL; died of complications from a stroke, June 5, 1999, in Los Angeles, CA. Singer, songwriter, musician, and author. Torme, known by legions of fans as the "Velvet Fog" for his smooth voice, was a gifted child who began singing professionally at age four. He also did radio work as a youth on soap operas like *Song of the City.* When he was a teenager he tasted his first success as a songwriter when Harry James made a hit out of his song "Lament to Love." Perhaps the best-known song he co-wrote was "The Christmas Song" ("Chestnuts Roasting on an Open Fire"), which was a smash for Nat (King) Cole in 1946 when Torme was twenty-one years old. Torme's fan base grew and he recorded for Decca, Musicraft, and Capitol, among others. Although he recorded constantly, his only No. 1 hit was "Careless Hands." Other favorites include "Again" and "Blue Moon," and over his career he wrote about three hundred songs and recorded close to fifty albums. Torme acted in several movies and made his debut opposite Frank Sinatra in *Higher and Higher.* Other pictures include *Words and Music* and *The Land of No Return.* As he matured Torme moved away from his teenage fans and began recording songs more in a jazz, rather than pop, style. His music was not the type sought when rock and roll took over but he scored a minor hit in 1962 with "Comin' Home Baby." He continued working the clubs and built a larger and larger audience as his song repertoire grew to about five thousand tunes. He became better known as a jazz singer and believed that a turning point of his career was a 1977 concert at Carnegie Hall with George Shearing and Gerry Mulligan. His professional relationship with blind pianist Shearing resulted in a Grammy Award for jazz recording in 1982 for the record *An Evening with George Shearing and Mel Torme.* Another Grammy followed in 1983 for "Top Drawer." Around that time he could be seen on television periodically on the show *Night Court,* where character Judge Harry T. Stone was an unabashed fan. Many fans and critics viewed him as one of the finest vocal artists for his scat improvisations and ability to move from style to style smoothly and always with a sense of swing. He frequently played drums at his gigs, showing off his skill on other instruments such as the piano as well. He was such a good drummer that Tommy Dorsey, Gene Krupa, and Stan Kenton had all tried to hire him at one time. His high baritone voice and ability as an entertainer helped him to draw fans of all ages and his career lasted more than 65 years. Torme wrote a few books, including *The Other Side of the Rainbow: With Judy Garland on the Dawn Patrol,* a look at his years working with Judy Garland on her television show; the novel *Wynner; Traps, the Drum Wonder: The Life of Buddy Rich;* and the autobiography *It Wasn't All Velvet.* He also contributed scripts to television series such as *The Virginian* and *Run for Your Life.*

*OBITUARIES AND OTHER SOURCES:*

*PERIODICALS*

*Los Angeles Times,* June 6, 1999, pp. A1, A20, A21.
*New York Times,* June 6, 1999, p. A50.
*Times* (London), June 7, 1999.
*USA Today,* June 7, 1999.
*Washington Post,* June 6, 1999, p. C6.

*OTHER*

*CNN Interactive* (electronic), June 6, 1999.

\*     \*     \*

## TRAPNELL, Coles   1911(?)-1999

*PERSONAL:* Born c. 1911; died of coronary thrombosis, January 29, 1999, in Los Angeles, CA; children: Sarah Trapnell Byrne, Jane Trapnell Marino. *Education:* Attended New York University.

*CAREER:* Television writer and producer. *Glen Cove Record,* Glen Cove, NY, worked as journalist; RKO Radio Pictures, reader, beginning in 1936; Twentieth Century-Fox, story editor and associate producer until 1953; *Four Star Playhouse,* editor, 1954-56; Universal Studios, story editor, 1962-75; retired, 1975. Also produced episodes of the television series *Maverick.* Los Angeles Valley College, teacher of script writing.

*WRITINGS:*

*Teleplay: An Introduction to Television Writing,* Chandler Publishing (San Francisco, CA), 1966.

Writer of episodes of the television series *Maverick,* between 1959 and 1962; writer for other television series, including *Lawman* and *Yancy Derringer.*

*BIOGRAPHICAL/CRITICAL SOURCES:*

*PERIODICALS*

*Choice,* January, 1967, p. 1032.
*Quarterly Journal of Speech,* December, 1966, p. 407.

*OBITUARIES:*

*PERIODICALS*

*Los Angeles Times,* February 4, 1999, p. A21.

*OTHER*

*Chronicle,* http://www.chronicle-online.com (February 4, 1999).*

\*   \*   \*

## TRIPPETT, Frank   1926-1998

*OBITUARY NOTICE*—See index for *CA* sketch: Born July 1, 1926, in Columbus, MS; died of heart failure, June 18, 1998, in New Rochelle, NY. Journalist. Trippett grew up in the south and attended Mississippi College, Duke University, and the University of Mississippi during the mid-1940s. He was hired as a reporter and wire editor at the *Meridian Star* and moved to the *Fredricksburg Star* in 1948, where he stayed for six years before moving to the *St. Petersburg Times.* He eventually joined the staff at *Newsweek* magazine where he was associate editor of national affairs and then moved to *Look* magazine as a senior editor. Trippett became a freelancer in 1971 and wrote several books during his career, including *The States: United They Fell, The First Horseman,* and *Child Ellen.* His reporting resulted in him receiving an American Political Science Association citation and twice sharing the National Headliner Award for Distinguished Journalism.

*OBITUARIES AND OTHER SOURCES:*

*BOOKS*

James B. Lloyd, editor, *Lives of Mississippi Authors, 1817-1967,* University Press of Mississippi, 1981.

*PERIODICALS*

*New York Times,* June 22, 1998, p. A17.

\*   \*   \*

## TURNER, George E(ugene)   1925-1999

*OBITUARY NOTICE*—See index for *CA* sketch: Born September 30, 1925, in Burkburnett, TX; died June 20, 1999, in Pasadena, CA. Illustrator and author. Turner graduated from West Texas State University in 1950 after studying illustration at the Art Institute of Chicago and the American Academy of Art. Turner was intrigued by natural science but made his living with his artistic skills. He moved to Hollywood, where he was a special effects illustrator. Turner worked on the television series *Zorro* as well as several Ray Bradbury films. In addition to his work in cinema, Turner wrote or co-wrote more than a dozen books, including *George Turner's Book of Gunfighters, Murder in the Palo Duro,* and *Secrets of Jesse James.* He illustrated Air Force Jet Training Schools textbooks and books, including *More than Brick and Mortar* and *The LX Brand.* He wrote the cartoon series *The Ancient Southwest* and *Sodbuster Sam* and in 1983 he joined the staff of *American Cinematographer* magazine, staying until 1991 when he retired as editor.

*OBITUARIES AND OTHER SOURCES:*

*PERIODICALS*

*Chicago Tribune,* June 29, 1999, sec. 2, p. 8.
*Los Angeles Times,* June 24, 1999, p. A28.
*Washington Post,* June 28, 1999, p. B7.

\*   \*   \*

## TYREE, Omar (Rashad)

*PERSONAL:* Born in Philadelphia, PA; children: Ameer. *Education:* Attended University of Pittsburgh; Howard University, B.S. (with honors; print journalism), 1991.

*ADDRESSES: Home*—New Castle, DE. *Agent*—c/o Simon & Schuster, 1230 Avenue of the Americas, New York, NY 10020.

*CAREER:* Author, publisher, lecturer, and performance poet. *Capital Spotlight* (weekly newspaper), Washington, DC, reporter, assistant editor, and advertising salesperson; *News Dimensions* (weekly newspaper), chief reporter; freelance writer; founder of MARS Productions, began full-time work beginning in 1993. Has lectured to organizations, at colleges, high schools and community events; appeared on the television talkshow pilot *For Black Men Only,* Black Entertainment Television, fall 1992; and on television's *America's Black Forum.*

*WRITINGS:*

*Colored, on White Campus: The Education of a Racial World* (novel), MARS Productions (Washington, DC), 1992, republished as *Battlezone: The Struggle to Survive the American Institution,* MARS Productions, 1994.
*Flyy-Girl* (novel), MARS Productions, 1993.
*Capital City: The Chronicles of a D.C. Underworld,* MARS Productions, 1994.
*A Do Right Man* (novel), Simon & Schuster, 1997.
*Single Mom* (novel), Simon & Schuster, 1998.

Contributor to periodicals, including *Washington View Magazine* and *Washington Post,* and to *Testimony: Young African-Americans on Self-Discovery and Black Identity,* Beacon Press, 1995.

*WORK IN PROGRESS:* "Sweet St. Louis," fiction; "Explosion, Black Books & Publishing; The New Renaissance of the 1990s," expected to be published in 1999.

*SIDELIGHTS:* Omar Tyree seems to have been persistent, and successful, in his efforts to become a published author and messenger for the experience of black America. He has lectured to organizations, at colleges, high schools and community events; and his commentaries have been televised—Tyree appeared on the Black Entertainment Television fall 1992 talkshow pilot *For Black Men Only.* His writing has appeared in periodicals such as *Washington View Magazine* and the *Washington Post,* and in works of fiction. Tyree's text is focused on sharing his beliefs and the realties associated with being a black person in the United States. For example, *Library Journal* contributor Shirley Gibson Coleman stated that Tyree's novel *A Do Right Man* "gives an honest if tiring interpretation of a black man struggling to do right. . . . [A] rare view of the true-to-life emotions of black males." Another of Tyree's novels, *Single Mom,* "reads mostly like an impassioned essay or sociology textbook," according to Nancy Pearl's *Library Journal* assessment. Of *Single Mom,* a *Publishers Weekly* writer declared: "In one way or another, each of the figures is a mouthpiece for responsible fatherhood or the difficulties of single motherhood."

Through a publishing company he founded, MARS Productions, Tyree was able to release some of his first books. He published a number of novels, among them *Flyy-Girl,* which was later republished by Simon & Schuster. Critics unenthusiastically greeted *Flyy-Girl,* which follows a middle-class Philadelphian through her adolescence. *Publishers Weekly* described the novel as an "unremarkable African American coming-of-age story. . . . [with] a crucial lack of depth." According to the *Publishers Weekly* critic, "teenage chatter" overwhelms the few "soul-searching questions . . . [and] answers" which are also "trite and superficial." Despite a "mildly rushed ending," Shirley Gibson Coleman, writing in *Library Journal,* much more positively judged the work to be "entertaining," displaying "conversation true to life." In stark contrast to the *Publishers Weekly* critic's contention that Tyree's novel was "unremarkable," Coleman asserted that *Flyy-Girl* "is some of the best [of coming-of-age African American stories] . . . read in a long time." However, *Kirkus Reviews* reported some of the same criticisms as *Publishers Weekly,* referring to *Flyy-Girl* as a "morality tale" and a "shapeless docudrama," and indicating that it "is much longer than a [young adult] novel, and far more vulgar, but the subject is pure teen. . . . [and it contains] some silly Afrocentric theorizing."

The critical reception of Tyree's 1997 novel, *A Do Right Man,* is similarly mixed, but with remarks that seem to suggest improvement. *Kirkus Reviews* maintained that "Tyree [is] in a new, more subtle mode" with *A Do Right Man.* "Fortunately," proclaimed the writer for *Kirkus Reviews,* "focusing less on Afrocentric theorizing and more on character—resulting in a good deal more engaging read." The "hip-to-the-punch," "feel-good" *A Do Right Man* was saved from sinking to "fairy tale" status, concluded a *Publishers Weekly* reviewer, by "Tyree's good humor and ear for dialogue." Stronger criticisms, however, were made of Tyree's next book, *Single Mom.* Pearl faulted Tyree's "didactic writing and one-dimensional characters" when denouncing the work. And, according to a *Publishers Weekly* judgment, *Single Mom* is boring, despite its "endearing earnestness."

*BIOGRAPHICAL/CRITICAL SOURCES:*

*PERIODICALS*

*Kirkus Reviews,* August 1, 1996, pp. 1090-1091; October 1, 1997, pp. 1481-1482.
*Library Journal,* September 15, 1996, p. 98; November 15, 1997, p. 78; September 15, 1998, pp. 114-115.
*Publishers Weekly,* August 26, 1996, p. 76; October 6, 1997, p. 74; August 17, 1998, p. 46.*

## URREA, Luis Alberto 1955-

*PERSONAL:* Born August 20, 1955, in Tijuana, Baja California, Mexico; son of Alberto and Phyllis de Urrea; divorced. *Education:* University of California at San Diego, B.A., 1977; University of Colorado at Boulder, M.A., 1994.

*ADDRESSES: Office*—1630 30th St., No. 332, Boulder, CO 80301. *E-mail*—Luisurrea@luisurrea.com.

*CAREER:* Did relief work on the Mexican Border for about ten years, including with San Diego's Spectrum Ministries (a Protestant organization), 1978-82; Harvard University, taught expository writing, 1982-86; Massachusetts Bay Community College, associate professor of liberal arts, 1986-90; writer, c. 1994—.

*AWARDS, HONORS:* Christopher Award, The Christophers, 1994, and *New York Times* Notable Book of the Year, both for *Across the Wire;* Western States Book Award, 1994.

*WRITINGS:*

*In Search of Snow* (novel), HarperCollins (New York City), 1994.
*The Fever of Being,* West End (Albuquerque, NM), 1994.
*Ghost Sickness,* Cinco Puntos (El Paso), 1997.
(Editor with Gregory McNamee) *A World of Turtles: A Literary Celebration,* Johnson (Boulder, CO), 1997.
*Wandering Time: Western Notebooks,* University of Arizona Press (Tucson), 1999.

*"BORDER" TRILOGY*

*Across the Wire: Life and Hard Times on the Mexican Border,* photographs by John Lueders-Booth, Anchor (New York City), 1993.
*By the Lake of Sleeping Children: The Secret Life of the Mexican Border,* photographs by Lueders-Booth, Anchor, 1996.
*Nobody's Son: Notes from an American Life* (memoir), University of Arizona Press, 1998.

*SIDELIGHTS:* Luis Albert Urrea, born in Mexico but raised from the age of three in San Diego, is the author of a critically acclaimed trilogy of books focusing on the life and people at the United States-Mexican border. The series of books—*Across the Wire: Life and Hard Times on the Mexican Border, By the Lake of Sleeping Children: The Secret Life of the Mexican Border,* and

*Nobody's Son: Notes from an American Life*—has been praised by critics for its brutally honest portrait of the struggles experienced by Mexican people on the fringes of the United States. *Across the Wire,* the first in the series, "speaks of the tenacity of these people," informed Kathryn L. Havris, singing praises in *Kliatt* of the work which "gives a graphic picture of the grinding poverty and lives of desperation these people live." Proclaiming the book "testimonial literature at its best," *New York Times Book Review* contributor David Unger wrote: "Thankfully, *Across the Wire* is organized as a series of linked vignettes: after 10 pages, you can take time out to hug your child, call a friend, stroll in the sun. But we keep returning to Mr. Urrea's prose because it is startling, poetic and razor-sharp; in the midst of the most brutal sequences, we are informed and shaken, made to feel the pain of others as if it were our own." Urrea, a Mexican-border relief worker for nearly ten years, "wrote these fragmentary, evocative tales of heartbreak and hope for the *San Diego Reader* after he returned to the region in 1990," noted *Publishers Weekly's* Peggy Kaganoff.

In 1996, remembering NAFTA and California's Proposition 187, a writer for *Kirkus Reviews* stated that *By The Lake of Sleeping Children* "is a stinging and impassioned answer to the anti-immigration wave cresting in American politics today." As Judy Maloof related in *Bloomsbury Review,* Urrea employs "gripping investigative reporting combined with vibrant, poetic description" to create "unforgettable portraits of people struggling to survive—amid abject poverty, unsanitary living conditions, violence, gangs, and lack of opportunities along the Mexican side of the border—offer[ing] North American readers an understanding of the compelling reasons why tens of thousands of men and women are forced to make the dangerous, illegal journey 'across the wire' into the United States." "Urrea movingly retells the stories of the people. . . . stories [that] are painfully realistic," declared Ronald Takaki, quoting in the *Washington Post Book World* a statement Urrea once made: " 'If, as some have suggested lately, I am some sort of "voice of the border," it is because the border runs down the middle of me. I have a barbed-wire fence neatly bisecting my heart.' " Urrea's father, a Mexican, raised him to be entirely "Mexican," while Urrea's mother, an American, raised him to be entirely "American."

In a review of *Nobody's Son,* Urrea's memoir and third installment in his "Border" trilogy, Grace Fill lauded in *Booklist:* "Urrea is not simply a great writer and a wonderful storyteller; he is completely enamored with words and language." "Passion and understanding," "brisk [pacing]," "tender" and "brutal" content, and an "essential tone . . . of self-deprecating humor," are descriptions that Rebecca Martin uses in her complimentary *Library Journal* review of *Nobody's Son*. The "elegant, painful memoir" is comprised of "meandering, discursive portraits" which "chronicles [Urrea's] growth," praised a *Publishers Weekly* reviewer believing that *Nobody's Son* is "not . . . just a book about race." "In fact," specified the reviewer, "it's just as much about writing, and at its best Urrea's staccato phrases build up to a vivid, often brutal image."

## BIOGRAPHICAL/CRITICAL SOURCES:

### BOOKS

*Who's Who among Hispanic Americans,* 3rd edition, Gale (Detroit, MI), 1994.

### PERIODICALS

*Bloomsbury Review,* January, 1995, p. 20; January, 1997, p. 5.

*Booklist,* September 1, 1998, p. 57.

*Kirkus Reviews,* February 15, 1994, pp. 174-175; September 1, 1996, p. 1312.

*Kliatt,* May, 1993, p. 31.

*Library Journal,* February 15, 1994, p. 186; October 1, 1998, p. 88.

*Nation,* July 18, 1994, p. 98; December 26, 1994, p. 810.

*New York Times Book Review,* February 21, 1993, p. 9.

*Publishers Weekly,* December 7, 1992, p. 59; August 10, 1998, p. 381.

*Washington Post Book World,* December 15, 1996, pp. 1, 8.

*Western American Literature,* November, 1996, p. 279.*

# V

## VALDES, Gina 1943-

*PERSONAL:* Born June 6, 1943, in Los Angeles, CA; daughter of George Valdes and Mary Escobar; married Tadashi Hayakawa; children: Rosalia. *Education:* Attended Palomar College, between 1976 and 1978; University of California, San Diego, B.A., 1981, M.A., 1982. *Ethnicity:* " Mexican-American."

*ADDRESSES: Office*—Department of Literature, University of California, San Diego, 9500 Gilman Dr., La Jolla, CA 92093-0410.

*CAREER:* Has taught literature and creative writing at several universities, including University of California, Los Angeles, University of California, San Diego, University of Washington, Colorado College, and University of California, Davis. Gives numerous readings from her works, including a reading recorded on the videotape *Rasgado en Dos* (title means, "Ripped in Two"), released by Public Broadcasting Service.

*WRITINGS:*

*There Are No Madmen Here* (includes stories and a novella titled "Maria Portillo"), Maize (San Diego, CA), 1981.
*Puentes y Fronteras: Coplas Chicanas* (poems), Castle (Los Angeles, CA), 1982, translation by Valdes and Katherine King published as *Puentes y Fronteras; Bridges and Borders,* Editorial Bilingue (Tempe, AZ), 1996.
*Comiendo Lumbre; Eating Fire* (poems), Maize (Colorado Springs, CO), 1986.

Has published poems and short stories in numerous journals and anthologies in the United States, Mexico, Europe, and Asia.

*WORK IN PROGRESS: English Con Salsa,* a book of poetry; and *Spirit Women,* short fiction.

*SIDELIGHTS:* It is "a tension between her social concerns and a strong metaphysical current" that place Gina Valdes "at an important crossroads within Chicano letters," declared Rosaura Sanchez in the *Dictionary of Literary Biography.* "She is fusing trends that have been central to Chicano literature." Sanchez attributed some of this creative tension to the time that Valdes has spent in her husband's homeland of Japan, where she delved into Asian traditions that include the occult, and to the author's own experiences of moving from Los Angeles, where she was born, to Mexico and back again.

Valdes' first book, *There Are No Madmen Here,* contains the novella "Maria Portillo," a work inspired by the time the author spent in Mexico. Maria Portillo is a single parent who comes to Los Angeles from Mexico to earn enough money to support her family. Unable to succeed legitimately, she joins a brother in his smuggling operation. The larger issues in this story, wrote Sanchez, are "the socioeconomic dilemma of Mexican immigrants in the United States" and the "illusory support system [of the family], for the extended family provides more grief and despair than comfort."

The novella is accompanied by several other short stories about Maria and her family, also published in *There Are No Madmen Here.* These stories explore similar themes, Sanchez observed, as well as the author's "concern with additional external forces that restrict and control the lives of the poor." In the title story, for example, Maria is in a mental institution, where she notices that the very bureaucracy which purports to help the helpless in fact creates the policies that are harmful to the patients, notes Sanchez.

Valdes' subsequent work demonstrates a maturing commitment to social themes. "[T]he feminist struggle, the plight of the undocumented worker, the border conflict, consumerism, and the alienation of the Chicano in the United States" are some that attracted Sanchez's notice. Another is the "functions and meanings" of language, which in literature can serve to heal, to explore, and to transform. *Puentes y Fronteras: Coplas Chicanas* is a collection of poems in the form of four line stanzas typical of Mexican folk poetry, with a distinctive difference: the traditional male point of view has been reversed to a female one, and the male has become an object of erotic desire. Many of the poems allude to the traditional wailing woman, represented here as "Mother Earth," Sanchez explained, "wailing for her Mexican children who are forced to cross the border to work, even while facing beatings, death, and deportation at the hands of the . . . Immigration and Naturalization officers." The erotic poems identify the female as an explicitly vocal subject, Sanchez observed, but are ambivalent in depicting the extent of her domination.

Similar themes reappear in *Comiendo Lumbre; Eating Fire,* but, at this point, Sanchez suggested that Valdes "no longer sees words as immanently meaningful; she is aware of distortion and of the ideological nature of language." This distortion can also be applied to words and what they represent. In the poem "Working Women" Valdes relates the words and concepts associated with prostitution to the workplace at large and to the field of education in particular. Without answering the questions she raises, Valdes wonders if the teacher is a "working woman," too. Is the writer a "working woman" hustling words instead of sex? Are all exploited for the product they "sell"? Sanchez remarked: "The voice is distinctive; it is soft yet critical; it is sensual yet social. The social criticism gives [Valdes'] poetry a dynamic quality, a cutting edge, a strength that puts it ahead of other poetic works that fail to go beyond sentimental trivialities or feminist harangues."

Valdes told *CA:* "In my recently completed book of poetry, *English Con Salsa,* I continue to explore the themes of identity, immigration, cultural synthesis, and spirituality, as I grapple with the intricacies of two languages. And in a short fiction book in progress, *Spirit Women,* I explore the lives of women at peak moments of awareness and transformation."

*BIOGRAPHICAL/CRITICAL SOURCES:*

BOOKS

*Dictionary of Literary Biography,* Volume 122: *Chicano Writers, Second Series,* Gale (Detroit, MI), 1992.

\*    \*    \*

## VAN ANDEL, Jay   1924-

*PERSONAL:* Born June 3, 1924, in Grand Rapids, MI; son of James (ran an automobile agency) and Nella (Vanderwoude) Van Andel; married Betty J. Hoekstra, August 16, 1952; children: Nan, Stephen, David, Barbara. *Education:* Studied at Pratt Junior College, 1945, Calvin College, 1942, 1946, Yale University, 1943-44, and Morningside College. *Religion:* Christian Reformed Church (elder).

*ADDRESSES: Home*—7186 Windy Hill Drive SE, Grand Rapids, MI 49546-9745. *Office*—Amway Corporation, 7575 Fulton St. E., Ada, MI 49355-0001.

*CAREER:* Founder and operator, with Richard Marvin DeVos, of flying school and commerical air charter service, Comstock Park, MI, 1945-48, also built and operated associated restaurant; Ja-Ri Corporation (import and distribution business), MI, founder and operator with DeVos, beginning 1949, became chair of board; also founded, then sold a mail order business, c. 1949; Amway Corporation (direct selling), Ada, MI, co-founder with DeVos and senior chair, beginning 1959; Van Andel Education and Medical Research, Grand Rapids, MI, founder; Van Andel Foundation, president. Chair of the board of Amway International, Amway Hotel Corporation, Amway Environmental Foundation, and Nutrilite Products, Inc. Exchange Club, Grand Rapids, director, 1958-60; John Ball Zoological Society, director and treasurer, 1960-61; Ada Township Planning Commission, commissioner, 1964-72; member of Governor Romney's "Operation Europe" travel group to Europe, 1965; Grand Rapids Council of Churches, member of board and finance chair, 1969-70; Youthpower, member of advisory board, 1969; Michigan State Chamber of Commerce, chair of board, 1970-71; Lotus Club, director and vice president, 1970-72; participant White House Conference Industrial World Ahead, 1972; Michigan Republican Finance Committee, chair, 1975-81; Michigan State Officers Compensation Committee, 1975-81; Grand Rapids

Chamber of Commerce, director, 1977-79; Chamber of Commerce of the United States, chair of board, 1979-80; Netherlands Bicentennial Commission, chair, 1982; National Endowment for Democracy, Washington, DC, treasurer and trustee, 1983-93; director of Direct Selling Association of USA, 1984-88, Business-Industry Political Action Committee, Washington, DC, Center for International Private Enterprise of the USCC, Washington, DC, 1985-88, Ferguson Hospital, Michigan National Bank, and Van Andel & Flikkema Motor Sales, Inc.; Commissioner General and U.S. ambassador, Genoa Expo '92, 1992 World's Fair; Right Place Committee, Grand Rapids, MI, founding chair; Grand Rapids United Way, chair of de Tocqueville Society; director of Jamestown Foundation; director of Gerald R. Ford Foundation; member of advisory council, National 4H Foundation; member of advisory council, American Private Education; Heritage Foundation, Washington, DC, board of directors, trustee, treasurer; Citizen's Research Council of Michigan, trustee; Hudson Institute, trustee; co-chair of Michigan Botanical Garden Capital Campaign; Metropolitan YMCA, Grand Rapids, MI, director; USO, served on World Board of Governors. Evangelical Literature League, director, 1964-71; Ada Christian School Board, president, 1966-69; Grand Rapids Christian School Development Council, president, 1969-73; Grand Rapids Central Council of Christian Schools, vice president, 1968-69; Michigan State Chamber of Commerce College—Business Symposiums, lecturer, 1969-70; Calvin College Business Solicitation Drive, chair, 1969; Calvin College Business Advisory Council, 1969-70; American Management Association Camp Enterprise, lecturer, 1970-72; LaGrave Christian Reformed Church, chair of finance committee, 1970-73; Grand Rapids Association of Christian Schools Fund Drive, general chair, 1968-70; Education Voucher Institute, director. *Military service:* U.S. Army, 1942-45, became first lieutenant; served as reserve officer, 1945-50.

*MEMBER:* Soap & Detergent Association of the United States (chair of board, 1977-78), Direct Selling Association (board of directors, hall of fame), U.S. C. of C. (past chair of board), American Management Association, Duke of Edinburgh's Award World Fellowship, National Chamber Foundation (director), MENSA Society USA, Peninsular Club, Cascade Hills Country Club, Lotus Club, Capitol Hill Club (Washington, D.C.), Macatawa Bay Yacht Club (Holland, MI), Le Mirador Country Club (Switzerland), Economics Club (Grand Rapids), Omicron Delta Kappa (honorary member).

*AWARDS, HONORS:* DBA, Northern Michigan University, 1976, Western Michigan University, 1979, Grand Valley State University, 1992; LL.D. Ferris State College, 1977, Michigan State University, 1997; knighted Grand Officer of Orange-Nassau, the Netherlands; Distinguished Alumni award, Calvin College, 1976; Golden Plate award, American Academy of Achievement; Great Living American award and Business and Professional Leader of the Year award, Religious Heritage of America; George Washington medal of Honor, Freedom Foundation; Gold Medals, Netherlands Society of Philadelphia and New York City; Distinguished Citizen award, Northwood Institute; Patron award, Michigan Foundation for the Arts, 1982; Achievement award, UN Environment Programme, 1989; UN Environment Achievement award, Amway, 1989; Business Person of the Year, Economic Club of Grand Rapids, 1990; Adam Smith Free Enterprise award, American Legislative Exchange Council, 1993; Distinguished Service award, Grand Rapids Rotary; Gold Medal, Netherlands Society of New York; Edison Achievement award, American Marketing Association, 1994; named Business Person of the Year, Economic Club of Grand Rapids; Clare Booth Luce award, Heritage Foundation, 1998; Junior Achievement National Business Hall of Fame, 1998; named to Greater Grand Rapids Business Hall of Fame and Direct Selling Association Hall of Fame; World fellow Duke of Edinburgh's award; Donald Porter Humanitarian Award, YMCA Heritage Club, 1999; recipient of honorary doctorates.

*WRITINGS:*

*An Enterprising Life: An Autobiography,* HarperBusiness (New York City), 1998.

*SIDELIGHTS:* The relationship teen-aged Jay Van Andel formed with his neighborhood friend Richard DeVos led both men to become among the richest people in the United States. The co-founders of the successful Amway Corporation, a direct sales company established in 1959, parlayed their teenage business ventures into a corporation selling more than 7,000 products whose sales amounted to more than six billion dollars in 1995, according to Ann Marsh's *Forbes* article listing Americans with a net worth between $3 and $4 billion. In a 1998 review of Van Andel's *An Enterprising Life: An Autobiography,* John Corry stated in the *American Spectator* that "the Michigan-based direct-sales giant started as a modest venture selling liquid soap, and is now a $7 billion consumer-products company with some 3 million distributors in 80 countries."

"Throughout [*An Enterprising Life*] is [Van Andel's] emphatic acknowledgment of the role that God and the Bible have played in his life," remarked *Booklist* contributor David Rouse. "It is . . . a tribute to Van Andel that you believe him. . . . However fashionable (and politically expedient) it has now become to flaunt religious belief, the faith here lives and pulsates," maintained Corry. "In the last sentence of *An Enterprising Life,* Van Andel says he hopes that he somehow has made other people's lives a little better, and you are quite sure that he has," concluded Corry. "A less sincere and humble person might have written a more exciting autobiography," maintained a critic for *Publishers Weekly,* who nevertheless referred to *An Enterprising Life* as offering a "clearly and simply spun . . . prose" with "a rhythm that sustains interest in the absence of drama."

*BIOGRAPHICAL/CRITICAL SOURCES:*

*BOOKS*

Conn, Charles Paul, *The Possible Dream: A Candid Look at Amway,* Revell (Old Tappan, NJ), 1977.
Ingham, John N., and Lynne B. Feldman, *Contemporary American Business Leaders,* Greenwood Press (New York City), 1990.

*PERIODICALS*

*American Spectator,* October, 1998, pp. 82-83.
*Booklist,* September 15, 1998.
*Forbes,* October 14, 1996, p. 116.
*Publishers Weekly,* August 3, 1998, pp. 68-69.

\*   \*   \*

## VAN DYCK, Karen (Rhoads)   1961-

*PERSONAL:* Born January 25, 1961, in New York, NY; daughter of Nicholas (a pastor) and Marian (a teacher; maiden name, Perera) Van Dyck; married Nelson Moe (a professor); children: Jacob Tanner, Benjamin Elias. *Education:* Wesleyan University, B.A.; Aristotelian, Thessaloniki, M.A.; Oxford University, D.Phil.

*ADDRESSES: Home*—401 West 118th St., #52, New York, NY 10027. *Office*—Department of Classics, 515 Hamilton Hall, Columbia University, Box 2873, New York, NY 10027; fax: 212-854-7856. *E-mail*—vandyck@columbia.edu.

*CAREER:* Columbia University, Classics Department, New York City, associate professor of modern Greek.

*MEMBER:* Modern Language Association, MGSA.

*AWARDS, HONORS:* Marshall grant, 1985-88; ACLS grant, 1992; Stavros Papastavrou Award for best doctoral thesis in UK in modern Greek studies, 1992; National Endowment for the Arts translation grant, 1996.

*WRITINGS:*

(Editor) *Greece,* Houghton (Boston, MA), 1995.
(Translator) Margarita Liberaki, *Three Summers,* Paul and Co. (New York City), 1995.
*Kassandra and the Censors: Greek Poetry since 1967,* Cornell University Press (Ithaca, NY), 1998.
(Translator and author of introduction) *The Rehearsal of Misunderstanding: Three Collections by Contemporary Greek Women Poets* (bilingual edition), University Press of New England (Hanover, NH), 1998.

*BIOGRAPHICAL/CRITICAL SOURCES:*

*PERIODICALS*

*Kirkus Reviews,* April 15, 1998, p. 531.
*Times Literary Supplement,* May 29, 1998, p. 35.

\*   \*   \*

## VIALLANEIX, Paul   1925-

*PERSONAL:* Born July 4, 1925, in Gumont, Correze, France; son of Baptiste (a school teacher) and Yvonne (a school teacher; maiden name, Rioux) Viallaneix; married Nelly Roux, August 18, 1951. *Education:* Attended Lycees Edmond-Perrier, Tulle, France; Louisle-Grand, Paris; Ecole normal superieure; Fondation Thiers, Cambridge University; Agrege des lettres; Docteur es lettres, M.A.

*ADDRESSES: Home*—Residence Europe, 95 av. De Royat, 63400 Chamalieres, France.

*CAREER:* L'Ecole normal superieure, lecturer, 1952; University of Clermont-Ferrand, assistant, 1953, senior lecturer, 1959, tenured professor and chair of modern French literature, 1961—; directeur du centre de recherches revolutionnaires et romantiques, 1967—. *Mil-*

*itary service:* Served in the French Resistance during World War II; received two combat medals.

*AWARDS, HONORS:* Overseas fellow, Churchill College, Cambridge University, 1969; overseas fellow, St. Antony's College, Oxford University, 1975; Officier des Palmes academiques et des Arts et des Lettres; Croix du combattant; crois du combattant voluntaire de la Resistance (military combat medals).

*WRITINGS:*

NONFICTION

*Vigny par lui-meme,* 1964.
*La "Voie royale," essay sur l'idee de peuple dans l'oeuvre de Michelet,* 1959, Flammarion (Paris), 1971.
*Le Hors Venu ou le personnage poetique de Supervielle,* 1972.
*Le Premier Camus: Suivi de Ecrits de jeunesse d'Albert Camus,* Gallimard (Paris), 1973.
*Michelet, les travaux et les jours: 1798-1874,* Gallimard, 1998.

EDITOR

Jules Michelet, *Ecrits de jeunesse,* 1959.
Jules Michelet, *Journal,* Volume I, 1959, Volume II, 1962.
Alfred-Victor Vigny, *Oeuvres Completes,* 1965.
Jules Michelet, *La Sorciere,* 1966.
Jules Michelet, *Quinet,* 1966.
Jules Michelet, *Oeuvres Completes,* Flammarion, Volume I, 1971, Volume II, Volume III, 1972, Volume IV, 1974, Volume V, 1975, Volume VI, 1977.
Jules Michelet, *Le Peuple,* Flammarion, 1974.
*Michelet cent ans apres: etudes et temoignages,* University of Grenoble Press (Grenoble), 1975.
*Le Preromantisme: hypotheque ou hypothese?,* Klincksieck (Paris), 1975.
Albert Camus, *Ecrits de jeunesse,* translated from the French by Ellen Conroy Kennedy as *The First Camus: An Introductory Essay,* Knopf, 1976.
*Les Fetes de la revolution,* Societe des etudes robespierristes (Paris), 1977.
(With Simone Bernard-Griffiths) *Edgar Quinet, ce juif errant,* Association des publications de la Faculte des lettres (Clermont-Ferrand), 1978.
(With Marie-Claude Chemin) Jules Michelet, *La Mer,* L'Age d'homme (Lausanne), 1980.
*Nos ancetres les Gaulois,* Association des publications de la Faculte des lettres, 1982.
Alfred de Vigny, *Les Destinees: Poemes Philosophiques,* Impr. Nationale (Paris), 1983.

(With Jean Ehrard) *La Bataille, l'armee, la gloire, 1745-1871: actes du colloque international de Clermont-Ferrand,* Associations des publications de al Faculte des lettres, 1985.
(With Jean Bauberot) *Reforme et revolutions: aux origines de la democratie moderne,* Reforme (Paris), 1990.
*Michelet Ecrit l'Histoire de la Revolution: actes du colloque de Vascoeuil, 30 juin-ler juillet 1989,* Diffusion Les Belles Lettres (Paris), 1993.
(With Oscar A. Haac and Irene Tieder) Jules Michelet, *Cours au College de France (1838-1851),* Gallimard, 1995.
(With Rosette Elmoznino, Etienne Guyon, and Jacques Lautman) *L'apprentissage du savoir vivant: fonction des grands colleges europeens: bicentenaire de la fondation de l'Ecole normale superieure,* Presses Universitaires de France (Paris), 1995.
(With Simone Bernard-Griffiths) *Dialogues autour de Vascoeuil: Dumesnil et Michelet,* Centre de recherches revolutionnaires et romantiques, Universite Blaise-Pascal (Clermont-Ferrand), 1995.

Contributor of chapters to texts, including *Pascal present,* 1962; *Delille est-il mort?,* 1967; and *Livre du centenaire de Lamartine,* 1970; contributor of numerous articles on French romantic and modern writers, including Chateaubriand, Lamartine, Vigny, Michelet, Mickiewiez, Quinet, Musset, Verlaine, Apollinaire, Camus, and Saint-John-Perse.

*SIDELIGHTS:* Scholar Paul Viallaneix has had a distinguished academic career and has written extensively on French literature of the Romantic and modern periods. He has authored books on such major figures as Jules Michelet, Alfred de Vigny, and Albert Camus, has edited the complete works of Michelet and the works of de Vigny, and has contributed numerous articles to scholarly publications.

Viallaneix, the son of schoolteachers, was born on July 4, 1925 in Gumont, Correze, France. During World War II, he was active in the French Resistance, for which he received two military combat medals, the Croix du combattant and the Croix du combattant voluntaire de la Resistance. Viallaneix studied at the Lycees Edmond-Perrier in Tulle, Louis-le-Grand in Paris, Ecole normale superieure, Fondation Thiers, and Cambridge University. He became a lecturer at the Ecole normale superieure in 1952, and joined the faculty at the University of Clermont-Ferrand in 1953. He has served as chair of the department of modern French literature at Clermont-Ferrand since 1961, and has served as director of the Centre de recherches revolutionnaires et romantiques since 1967. In 1969, Viallaneix was named overseas fellow at Churchill College, Cambridge University. In 1975, he was named overseas fellow at St. Antony's College at Oxford University.

Though he has written about such various figures as Chateaubriand, Lamartine, Mickiewiez, Quinet, Musset, Verlaine, Apollinaire, Camus, and Saint-John-Perse, Viallaneix has specialized in the works of French Romantic writers Alfred de Vigny and Jules Michelet. He has written monographs on these writers, and has edited numerous volumes of their works as well as collections of scholarly articles. For nonspecialists, however, his best-known work is probably his study of the early works of existentialist writer Albert Camus. In *Ecrits de jeunesse,* published in English as *The First Camus: An Introductory Essay,* Viallaneix presents selections from Camus' adolescent writings, with an introductory essay analyzing the formative effects of Camus' poverty, physical environment, and literary and philosophical models. *The First Camus* was hailed by Ellen Kennedy in *Booklist* as a "penetrating" analysis of Camus' apprentice years. A contributor to *Choice* also praised the book as "a most interesting and penetrating introduction" to Camus' early work. First translated into English in 1976, *The First Camus* was reissued in 1977, 1980, 1984, and 1990.

Viallaneix has been honored for his services to education by being named an Officier des Palmes academiques et des Arts et des Lettres.

## BIOGRAPHICAL/CRITICAL SOURCES:

### PERIODICALS

*Booklist,* November 15, 1976, p. 446.
*Choice,* May, 1977, p. 383.
*French Review,* February, 1992, pp. 492-493; May, 1996, pp. 1004-1005.*

\*       \*       \*

## VIGIL-PINON, Evangelina 1949-

*PERSONAL:* Born November 29, 1949, in San Antonio, TX; daughter of Juan (a shoe repair shop operator ) and Maria Soto (a homemaker; maiden name, Evangelina) Soto Vigil; married Mark Anthony Pinon (a musician/artist), February 14, 1983; children: Marc Antony. *Education:* Attended Prairie View A & M (business administration); University of Houston (English),

B.A., 1974; graduate studies, St. Mary's University and University of Texas—San Antonio, 1977. *Ethnicity:* "Hispanic."

*ADDRESSES: Office*—c/o Arte Publico Press, University of Houston, 4800 Calhoun-2L, Houston, TX 77204. *E-mail*—evangelina.vigil-pinon@abc.com.

*CAREER:* Writer, c. 1978—. Community newscaster, *Reflejos del barrio,* KPRC-TV, Houston, TX, 1974-76; producer and host, *Radio Jalapeno,* KEDA-AM, San Antonio, TX, 1976-82; arts administrator and writer-in-residence, Galveston, TX 1976-82; paralegal, victim/witness assistance and management, 1982-89; Cultural Arts Council of Houston and Harris County, newsletter editor and public relations/multicultural affairs handler, 1989-95; host, public affairs director, and producer, *Viva Houston,* KTRK-TV (Houston ABC affiliate), 1995—; editor, Arte Publico Press.

*MEMBER:* National Association of Hispanic Journalists, Hispanic Women in Leadership, Houston Association of Hispanic Media Professionals.

*AWARDS, HONORS:* Coordinating Council of Literary Magazines, First Place, national literary competition, 1976; National Endowment for the Arts fellowship for creative writers, 1979-80; Before Columbus Foundation, American Book award, 1983.

*WRITINGS:*

### BOOKS

*Nade y Nade,* M & A Editions (San Antonio, TX), 1978.
*Thirty An' Seen a Lot* (poems), Arte Publico Press (Houston, TX), 1985.
*The Computer Is Down* (poems), Arte Publico Press, 1987.
(Translator) Tomas Rivera, *Y no se lo trago la tierra* (*And the Earth Did Not Devour Him*), Arte Publico Press, 1987.
(Editor) *Woman of Her Word: Hispanic Woman Write,* Arte Publico Press, 1987.
(Editor with Julian Olivares) *Decade II: An Anniversary Anthology,* Arte Publico Press, 1993.
*Nalina's Muumuu* (children's book), Arte Publico Press, 2001.

Also contributor to numerous anthologies and literary periodicals.

*TELEPLAYS; AND NARRATOR AND PRODUCER*

*Night Vigil,* De Colores Productions (Houston, TX), 1984.

*El Diez y Seis de Septiembre,* KTRK-TV, 1995.

*La Familia: Strength and Struggle,* KTRK-TV, 1996.

*Viva la Raza: Lation Diversity in Houston,* KTRK-TV, 1996.

*Texas Chicano Soul: Little Joe y la Familia,* KTRK-TV, 1998.

(Co-author with Regina Hall) *Portrait of a People: Houston's Asian American Community,* KTRK-TV, 1998.

*The Hispanic Century,* KTRK-TV, 1999.

Also author of short features, including *Siquieros,* 1996, *Tina Midotti,* 1996, *Stan Natchez: Native American Artist,* 1997, *Hombres de Valor: Veterans of War,* 1997, and *Gato Barbieri,* 1999.

*WORK IN PROGRESS: Aura of Inertia,* a book of poems.

*SIDELIGHTS:* Evangelina Vigil-Pinon was the second child in a family of ten children and grew up speaking both Spanish and English. Her mother's family came from Mexico to San Antonio, Texas in the early 1900s, and her father's family came from the area of Seguin, Texas. In her later childhood, she lived with her maternal grandmother's extended family and heard her great-uncle tell many stories about life growing up in Parras, Coahuila, Mexico, during the Mexican Revolution and about the struggles making a new life in the United States at the turn of the century. According to Elaine Dorough Johnson in the *Dictionary of Literary Biography,* she learned from her maternal grandmother "to observe and listen for words of wisdom which come only with experience." Her great-uncle, who was a father figure to her during her teenage years, gave her a sense of independence and self-reliance. Through her mother, who read the *San Antonio Light* daily, page to page, she developed a love of reading.

Even as a small child, Vigil-Pinon was sensitively aware of her environment; she recalls wandering in a rose garden, savoring the flowers' fragrance and the distant music of a neighbor's radio. She was talented in art, and in sixth grade was one of only two grade school students who attended the Inman Christian Center, a private art school in San Antonio. According to Johnson, she recalled, "The art studio was a wonderful place—I loved the smell of oil paints and inks and art supplies all around, the students' canvases on ea-sels. . . . My teacher's name was Mrs. Burk. She was the most inspiring teacher I've ever known."

Like her father, a shoe repairman who occasionally picked up the guitar and sang to friends and family, Vigil-Pinon loved music. She sang with the radio and in the school choir, and formed a neighborhood combo with her cousins. In high school, she told Johnson, "Music became central to my existence. But then music had really been in the center of my soul, nurtured by the culture of San Antonio, where people 'live' music." She wrote her first poem when she was eight years old, winning third place in a national poetry contest sponsored by Dreamside Ice cream, and her love of music and words intertwined as she grew older; she wrote down the lyrics of her favorite songs, filling in the lines she didn't know with her own words. Poetry, she told Johnson, is "the rhythm of time, the ticking of clocks, hearts beating. To me poetry is music. It is the song in our hearts. Life is the dance to that music."

Vigil-Pinon might have studied art or music had she not been railroaded into secretarial classes in high school. She then received a scholarship to study business administration at Prairie View A & M University, one of the country's historically black colleges. The exposure to the African-American culture and heritage increased her awareness of her own Mexican American identity, coinciding with the late sixties social climate of civil rights struggles. In her junior year, she transferred to the University of Houston, where she changed her major from business to English with a minor in political science. Although she studied classical writers as well as "beat" and counterculture poets, she told Johnson that the writers who influenced her the most were African American, particularly Frederick Douglass, James Baldwin, Nikki Giovanni, and Ntozake Shange.

In 1978, Vigil-Pinon decided to devote more time to her writing; most of the poems in her collection *Thirty An' Seen a Lot* were written between 1976 and 1979, and *Nade y Nade* was published in 1978. *Nade y Nade* is a collection of thirty poems on the topics of sadness, the passage of time, self-knowledge, and communication with others. Johnson wrote, "In spite of the weighty sound of these themes, the poems in this volume are neither ponderous not bitter in tone. In fact many are characterized by gentleness and a contemplative spirit." The poems often combine Spanish and English and accurately portray Hispanic dialogue, but their subjects are universal.

*Thirty An' Seen a Lot* is a collection of poems written during a six-year period in Houston, San Antonio, and

Galveston, where Vigi-Pinon moved in 1981. The poems praise simple pleasures, celebrate the wisdom passed down by elders in the barrio, portray Hispanic culture, and show her relationship with nature. Vigil-Pinon loved living in Galveston, on the coast of the Gulf of Mexico, and told Johnson, "If there is one single element that has inspired me the most to write, it has to be the ocean, the sea, the surf, beaches and breezy umbrella skies." In 1983, she married her husband. She told Johnson that married life gave her less time to write, but she did not mind this, saying, "Ensconced in a warm, loving relationship, I don't feel the solitude and sense of isolation which I experienced in my younger years. The transformation has been from the single, carefree writer, to the full-time professional, and mother and wife. . . . Yet, the creative process never remains the same, so I don't long for the inspirational elements of my past."

Vigil-Pinon told *CA:* "I look to the future and the magic of time passing and of life in a state of flux, the catch in the moment. I'm very intensively working on my music, with a serious intent, like never before. It's exciting and scary because for me, making music means risk to fail or succeed and means cutting the edge."

### BIOGRAPHICAL/CRITICAL SOURCES:

*BOOKS*

*Dictionary of Literary Biography,* Volume 122: *Chicano Writers, Second Series,* Gale (Detroit, MI), 1992.
Garcia, Juan A., Theresa Cordova, and Juan R. Garcia, *The Chicano Struggle: Analysis of Past and Present Efforts,* Bilingual Press, 1984.

\*   \*   \*

## VILLAS, James  1938-

*PERSONAL:* Born February 10, 1938, in Charlotte, NC; son of Harold and Martha Pearl (a cook and writer; maiden name Pierson) Villas. *Education:* University of North Carolina, B.A. (with honors), 1960, M.A., 1961, Ph.D., 1966.

*ADDRESSES: Home and Office*—160 East 74th St., New York, NY 10021. *Agent*—Robin Straus, 229 East 79th St., New York, NY 10021.

*CAREER: Town and Country,* food and wine editor, 1972—.

*AWARDS, HONORS:* Fulbright Scholar, 1961-62; James Beard Award nominee.

*WRITINGS:*

*American Taste: A Celebration of Gastronomy Coast-to-Coast,* Arbor House (New York City), 1982, Lyons Press, 1997.
*The Town & Country Cookbook,* illustrations by Catherine Kanner, Little, Brown (Boston), 1985.
*James Villas' Country Cooking,* Little, Brown, 1988.
*Villas at Table: A Passion for Food and Drink,* Harper & Row (New York City), 1988.
*The French Country Kitchen: The Undiscovered Glories of French Regional Cuisine,* Bantam Books (New York City), 1992.
(With mother, Martha Pearl Villas) *My Mother's Southern Kitchen: Recipes and Reminiscences,* Macmillan (New York City), 1994.
*Stews, Bogs, and Burgoos: Recipes from the Great American Stewpot,* Morrow (New York City), 1997.
(With Martha Pearl Villas) *My Mother's Southern Desserts: More than 200 Treasured Family Recipes for Holiday and Everyday Celebrations,* Morrow, 1998.
(With Martha Pearl Villas) *My Mother's Southern Entertaining,* Morrow, 2000.

Also contributor to periodicals, including *Food & Wine, New York Times, Gourmet, Esquire, Bon Appetit, Travel & Leisure,* and *Cuisine.*

*WORK IN PROGRESS: The Last Greyhound,* a novel; *I Saw the Elephant,* memoir/portraits.

*SIDELIGHTS:* James Villas, food and wine editor of *Town and Country* magazine, has expressed his enthusiasm for American and French cuisine in several well-received books of essays and recipes. His broad knowledge of food traditions and his personable prose have led him to be favorably compared, in *Publishers Weekly,* to such noted food writers as James Beard and Evan Jones.

Villas's first volume focuses on regional American cuisine. *American Taste: A Celebration of Gastronomy Coast-to-Coast,* which a reviewer for *Publishers Weekly* considered "refreshingly well-written," with diverse articles covering such seemingly mundane items as southern barbecues, hamburgers, and fried chicken. The personal touch Villas brings to this material prompted mixed reviews. "Villas is witty and highly opinionated," enthused *Publisher Weekly*'s Genevieve

Stuttaford, and offers "a lively, freewheeling account" of native American cooking. *Library Journal*'s Johanna Ezell found *American Taste* informative, but noted that the book was "not so much fun as sardonic." Ezell complained about Villas's "less-than-exciting style" and his "dull" commentary.

*The Town & Country Cookbook* drew more consistent praise. This volume includes almost six hundred recipes, most from the magazine but some from Villas's personal files, for foods that reflected the author's wide-ranging cosmopolitan tastes, from peanut butter sandwiches to fiddlehead ferns with mushrooms. Even the most everyday dishes in the collection, noted Karen Gray for *Publishers Weekly,* contained a distinctive elegance, and the recipes avoided fussiness or elaborate cooking skills. Robert Donahugh, in *Library Journal,* commented that though some of Villas's material here was chic, "generally his recipes show a nice balance between classics and well-conceived newer ideas."

Such "literate coherence and acerbic wit," as Florence Fabrican of the *New York Times Book Review* put it, quickly became trademark features of Villas's books. Also characteristic is Villas's unabashed enthusiasm for two particular gastronomic traditions: American Southern country cooking and French country cooking. A native of rural North Carolina, Villas grew up in a family with Greek, Swedish, and Southern roots, and had a mother who was a renowned country cook. He developed a soft spot for such homey masterpieces as his mother's flaky biscuits, Southern fried chicken, and cholesterol-rich desserts. Villas pays homage to some of these dishes in *Villas at Table: A Passion for Food and Drink,* a collection of forty-three essays that, like those in his first collection, run the gamut from the mundane to the more exotic. But he has gone on, in two more recent books, to focus exclusively on the Southern country table. *My Mother's Southern Kitchen: Recipes and Reminiscences,* which Villas wrote with his mother, Martha Pearl Villas, presents not only Mrs. Villas's recipes, but also a spirited reminiscence of her approach to food. "Villas . . . pays homage to his mother with such intensity—sometimes bordering on defensiveness—that you have to pay attention," wrote *New York Times Book Review* contributor Richard Flaste, who vacillated between finding the book's mother-and-son banter either "cute or dysfunctional." Noting that the book is filled with recipes calling for such health-conscious taboos as lard, bacon grease, and heavy cream, Flaste also found lighter alternatives included, and pointed out that several recipes sounded quite appealing.

Even heavier on the rich ingredients is *My Mother's Southern Desserts: More than 200 Treasured Family Recipes for Holiday and Everyday Celebration.* A reviewer for *Publishers Weekly* found the book a "winsome repertoire" of calorie-laden delights, enhanced by Villas's entertaining anecdotes about such subjects as "Cuddin' Berta's Georgia Kiss Pudding" or the origins of Blueberry Flummery. Mrs. Villas, noted *Library Journal*'s Judith C. Sutton, "really knows her sweets."

Villas's other passion, French country cuisine, serves as the focus for *The French Country Kitchen,* a book that Barbara Jacobs, in *Booklist,* found "as informative as it is mouthwatering." In this volume, Villas presents one hundred and seventy-five recipes from several regions of France, and tackles such subjects as authentic French bread and "la salade verte." Many recipes, reviewers found, were based on everyday ingredients and are easy to follow. A *Publishers Weekly* reviewer appreciated the "loving commentary" with which Villas describes each region's traditions.

*BIOGRAPHICAL/CRITICAL SOURCES:*

*PERIODICALS*

*Booklist,* April 1, 1992, p. 1421.
*Cuisine,* September 1980, p. 20; October 1982, pp. 10-11.
*Library Journal,* July, 1982, p. 1326; September 15, 1985, p. 81; October 15, 1998, p. 92.
*New York Times Book Review,* December 4, 1985, p. 85; December 8, 1985, p. 21; December 4, 1988, p. 85; December 4, 1994, p. 24.
*Publishers Weekly,* May 21, 1982, pp. 67-68; August 12, 1983, p. 64; September 20, 1985, p. 97; October 21, 1988, p. 57; March 30, 1992, p. 102; August 17, 1998, p. 67.
*Town & Country,* November, 1988, p. 207.

\*       \*       \*

**VIVIERS, Jacobus Cornelius   1938-1999**

*PERSONAL:* Born January 31, 1938, in Vereeniging, South Africa; died of cancer, February 2, 1999, in Johannesburg, South Africa; son of Pieter L. (a police officer) and Maria Magdalena (a teacher; maiden name, Erasmus) Viviers; married Marjorie Maureen Laatz. *Education:* Attended school in Heidelberg, Germany. *Avocational interests:* Painting, conservation of game animals.

*CAREER:* Journalist and editor.

*WRITINGS:*

*Rand Daily Mail,* Johannesburg, South Africa, journalist, 1955-59; United Press International, journalist, 1960-61; *Rand Daily Mail,* journalist, 1962-71, news editor, 1971-74, assistant editor, 1974-77; *Sunday Express,* Johannesburg, deputy editor, 1977-81; *Eastern Province Herald,* Port Elizabeth, South Africa, editor, 1982-84, editor-in-chief, 1984-87; *Cape Times,* Cape Town, South Africa, editor, 1987-95. *Evening Post* and *Weekend Post,* editor-in-chief, 1984-87.

*OBITUARIES:*

*PERIODICALS*

*Washington Post,* February 10, 1999, p. B7.

# W-Z

## WALKER, Alice 1900-1982

*PERSONAL:* Born December 8, 1900, in Lancashire, England; died of liver cancer, October 14, 1982, in Bude, Cornwall, England; daughter of George Edward (practiced law) and Mary Alice (Cort) Walker. *Education:* Royal Holloway College, B.A. (with first-class honors), 1923, Ph.D., 1926; studied at Girton College.

*CAREER:* Royal Holloway College, Egham, Surrey, assistant lecturer in English, three-year term ending in 1932, librarian, 1939-41, secretary and registrar, 1941-44.

*AWARDS, HONORS:* Martin-Holloway Prize, 1924, "for the most intellectually outstanding member of the year"; Christie Prize for Italian, 1925; postgraduate traveling scholarship, University of London, 1927-28; Rose Mary Crawshay Prize, British Academy, 1954, for *Textual Problems of the First Folio: Richard III, King Lear, Troilus and Cressida, 2 Henry IV, Hamlet, Othello;* Readership of Textual Criticism, Oxford, 1960-67; professorial fellow, St. Hilda's College, 1964; Reader Emeritus, 1972.

*WRITINGS:*

*The Life of Thomas Lodge,* Sidgwick & Jackson (London), 1933.
*Textual Problems of the First Folio: Richard III, King Lear, Troilus and Cressida, 2 Henry IV, Hamlet, Othello* ("Shakespeare Problems" series), Cambridge University Press (Cambridge), 1953.

*OTHER*

(Editor with Gladys Doidge Willcock) George Puttenham, *The Arte of English Poesie,* Cambridge University Press, 1936.
(Editor with John Dover Wilson) *Othello,* in *The Works of Shakespeare,* edited by Dover Wilson, Cambridge University Press, 1957.
(Editor) *Troilus and Cressida,* in *The Works of Shakespeare,* edited by Dover Wilson, Cambridge University Press, 1957.
(Contributor) *Studies in Shakespeare: British Academy Lectures by H. S. Bennett,* edited by Peter Alexander, Oxford University Press (London), 1964.

Also contributor to periodicals, including *Review of English Studies, Modern Language Review, Library, Shakespeare Survey, Studies in Bibliography,* and *Times Literary Supplement.*

*SIDELIGHTS:* Alice Walker was a noted scholar, editor, and bibliographer, associated with the bibliographical movement of the twentieth century referred to as "new bibliography." This movement sought a more scientific approach to bibliography. As well as a proponent of the movement, Walker worked closely with one of its leaders, R. B. McKerrow, on editing an Oxford old-spelling Shakespeare edition—a project that was never published. Walker would achieve success with her 1953 *Textual Problems of the First Folio: Richard III, King Lear, Troilus and Cressida, 2 Henry IV, Hamlet, Othello,* which was part of the "Shakespeare Problems" series, edited by John Dover Wilson. Following this project, Wilson commissioned Walker to edit two Shakespearean plays, *Othello* (which she coedited with Wilson) and *Troilus and Cressida,* for his Cambridge edition of *The Works of Shakespeare.* This volume, containing Walker's editions, was published in 1957.

From a young age, Walker had developed a propensity for English studies. She attended the Royal Holloway College, where she excelled as a student. The principal of the college, in a reference letter, proclaimed she was "perhaps the most brilliant student who has passed through the English department of this college." Following her undergraduate studies, Walker went on to obtain a Ph.D. Her thesis expounded on the works of Thomas Lodge, and she hoped she could shape it into a published work. In 1927, the publishing house Sidgwick and Jackson, of which McKerrow was a managing director, took notice of Walker's work on Lodge and published, in 1933, some of Walker's research as *The Life of Thomas Lodge.*

Having made the acquaintance of McKerrow through her work for Sidgwick and Jackson, Walker would continue the relationship by contributing to the periodical, *The Review of English Studies,* which he edited. Impressed by Walker's editorial skills, McKerrow requested that Walker help him with the proposed Oxford old-spelling Shakespeare edition. She worked diligently for about four years on this edition under McKerrow's direction until he passed away in 1940. Following McKerrow's death, Walker was considered to take over the doomed project. However, World War II averted attention from the project, and by the time the project was reexamined-some years after the war, the interest was no longer there to continue with it. Walker would also continue her association with Royal Holloway College long after she graduated from there. In 1939, she took a position as a librarian and, in 1941, she would become the secretary and registrar under the principal, Janet R. Bacon. The latter position, however, proved tumultuous, for Bacon was not well liked. Thus, Walker and Bacon decided to leave the college in 1944. This freed Walker's time so she could focus more on her scholarly research. In 1950, she began publishing articles on Shakespearean plays, focusing on textual problems. This led to her celebrated and award-winning publication, *Textual Problems of the First Folio: Richard III, King Lear, Troilus and Cressida, 2 Henry IV, Hamlet, Othello.* Philip Williams of *Shakespeare Quarterly* deemed it "one of the few important textual studies in Shakespeare."

In honor of her vast achievements in textual studies, Walker was awarded the Readership of Textual Criticism at Oxford in 1960. This post kept her very busy as a teacher of graduate students. To Walker's dismay, she could not find time for her own research. Thus, in 1965, Walker requested a sabbatical, and in 1968, when her post ended, she retired. In retirement, Walker only wrote two more essays. Despite the almost twenty-year lull in publishing a work toward the end of her life, Walker was remembered as "a great bibliographer and editor," as heralded by T. H. Howard-Hill of *Dictionary of Literary Biography.*

*BIOGRAPHICAL/CRITICAL SOURCES:*

BOOKS

Bingham, Caroline, *The History of Royal Holloway College, 1886-1986,* Constable, 1987.
*Dictionary of Literary Biography,* Volume 201: *Twentieth-Century British Book Collectors and Bibliographers,* Gale, 1999.
Thompson, Anne, *The Margins of the Text,* edited by D. C. Greetham, University of Michigan Press, 1997.

*PERIODICALS*

*Shakespeare Quarterly,* 1953.*

\* \* \*

## WALKER, Roger (Michael) 1938-1999

*PERSONAL:* Born July 25, 1938; died January 11, 1999; married Patricia Eccles, 1960 (divorced, 1980); children: one daughter, one son. *Education:* Victoria University of Manchester, graduated (first class honors), 1960; earned Ph.D., 1970.

*CAREER:* University of Bristol, Bristol, England, faculty member, c. 1961; University of London, Birkbeck College, London, England, faculty member, 1963-80, professor of Spanish, beginning in 1980, department head at Centre for Language and Literature, also served as vice-master of the college.

*WRITINGS:*

(Compiler with Brian Dutton and L. P. Harvey) *Cassell's New Compact Spanish-English, English-Spanish Dictionary,* Funk (New York City), 1969.
*Tradition and Technique in El Libro del Cavallero Zifar,* Tamesis Books (London, England), 1974.
(Editor) *Estoria de Santa Maria Egicciaca,* University of Exeter (Exeter, England), 1977.
(Editor) *El Cavallero Placidas,* University of Exeter, 1982.

Contributor to scholarly journals. *Modern Language Review,* Hispanic editor, beginning in 1980, general editor, 1983-93.

*OBITUARIES:*

*PERIODICALS*

*Times* (London), February 11, 1999.*

\* \* \*

## WARNER, Brian 1969(?)- (Marilyn Manson)

*PERSONAL:* Born January 5, 1969 (some sources say 1970), in Canton, OH; son of Hugh (a furniture salesperson) and Barb (a nurse) Warner; companion of Rose McGowan (an actor). *Religion:* Episcopalian. *Avocational interests:* Painting and writing.

*ADDRESSES: Office*—Nothing Records/Interscope Records, 10900 Wilshire Blvd., Suite 1230, Los Angeles, CA 90024.

*CAREER:* Musician and music producer using the name Marilyn Manson. Founder of the bands Marilyn Manson and Marilyn Manson and the Spooky Kids. Using the name Marilyn Manson, actor in films, including *Lost Highway,* PolyGram/October Films, 1997; (and soundtrack producer) *Jawbreaker* (also known as *Hard Candy*), Columbia/TriStar, 1999; and *Holy Wood,* New Line Cinema, 2000. Appeared on episodes of the television series *The Howard Stern Show,* E! Entertainment Television and simulcast on radio; and *Havoc,* [New Zealand]. Also worked as a photojournalist.

Numerous albums, including as Marilyn Manson with band Marilyn Manson, *Portrait of an American Family,* Nothing Records/Interscope Records, 1994, *AntiChrist Superstar,* Nothing Records/Interscope Records, 1996, *Mechanical Animals,* Nothing Records/Interscope Records, 1998, *Last Tour on Earth,* Nothing Records/ Interscope Records, 1999; EPs with band Marilyn Manson, *Smells Like Children,* Nothing Records/Interscope Records, 1995; singles with band Marilyn Manson "Get Your Gunn," Nothing Records/Interscope Records, 1994, "Lunchbox," Nothing Records/Interscope Records, 1995; imported singles with band Marilyn Manson, "Remix & Repent," Nothing Records/Interscope Records, 1997, and other imported singles include "The Beautiful People," "The Dope Show," "I Don't Like the Drugs (But the Drugs Like Me)," "Long Hard Road Out of Hell," "Marilyn Manson," "Rock Is Dead," "Sweet Dreams," and "Tourniquet"; video recordings with band Marilyn Manson, *Dope Hat,* 1995, (with others) *Alleys and Motorways* (also known as *Bush: Alleys and Motorways*), 1997, *Closure* (also known as *Halo 12* and *Nine Inch Nails: Closure*), Nothing Records/Acme Filmworks, 1998, *Dead to the World,* Universal Music and Video Distribution, 1998, *Marilyn Manson Gift Set,* Nothing Records/Interscope Records, 1999, also appeared in *Demystifying the Devil.* Music videos by the band Marilyn Manson include "The Beautiful People," "Dope Hat," "The Dope Show," "Get Your Gunn," "Long Hard Road Out of Hell," "Lunchbox," "Man That You Fear," "Sweet Dreams," and "Tourniquet."

Other works with band Marilyn Manson include *The Marilyn Manson Star Profile* (audio documentary), 1999; also appeared on recordings, including *All Talk, Chatback Interviews, Interview, An Interview With, Maximum Manson,* and *Rockaview Interviews;* soundtracks with others include (and producer, with others) *Lost Highway,* Nothing Records/Interscope Records, 1997, (and producer, with others) *Nowhere,* PGD/PolyGram, 1997, *Private Parts,* Warner Bros. Records, 1997, (and producer, with others) *Spawn,* Sony Music, 1997, *Dead Man on Campus,* 1998, *Strange-Land,* TVT Records, 1998, (and producer, with others) *Detroit Rock City,* Nothing Records/Interscope Records, 1999.

*AWARDS, HONORS:* All with the band Marilyn Manson: Jammy Award, entertainer of the year, 1992; SLAMMIE Awards, band of the year, 1993 and 1994, best band, best video, and best record, all 1996, and best hard alternative band; MTV Video Music Award nomination, best hard rock video, 1996, for "Sweet Dreams"; Music Video Production Awards, best art directing, best editing, and best styling, and three MTV Video Music Award nominations, all 1997, for "The Beautiful People"; KERRANG Award, "best band in the world"; SLAMMIE Award nominations.

*WRITINGS:*

*MEMOIRS*

(With Neil Strauss) *The Long Hard Road Out of Hell* (autobiography), HarperCollins (New York City), 1998.

*SCREENPLAYS*

*Holy Wood,* New Line Cinema, 2000.

*SIDELIGHTS: New York* magazine contributor Chris Norris has described controversial musician Brian Warner's alter ego, Marilyn Manson, as "crass, witty, and repellent." Norris also observed that "Marilyn Manson has taken the tradition of dark and joyfully depraved pop statement to a new level." As Manson, Warner penned the autobiography *The Long Hard Road Out of Hell* (1998). He chronicles his path from an ordinary kid to a rock star, describing his childhood, drug use, and his emergence as Manson, a self-proclaimed "Anti-Christ Superstar."

Originally from Canton, Ohio, Warner is the son of a furniture salesperson and a nurse. He became interested in rock and roll while attending a Christian grammar school where the school's teachers played records backward and examined them for Satanic messages. Warner admitted that as a student, he was terrified of the concept of the Antichrist. Later, he began to view the Antichrist in a different light. As Warner told Chris Willman in *Entertainment Weekly:* "When I got older, I realized that it was something that I wanted to become, not something I was afraid of."

As Manson, Warner presents an eerie figure, performing in heavy makeup, vividly colored contact lenses, women's clothing, and "body accouterments that look like medieval prostheses," wrote Lorraine Ali in *Rolling Stone.* Warner's songs with the band Marilyn Manson celebrate pain, death, Satanism, and sexual perversity and often use profanity. This music "mixes the compressed rage of death metal with the electro-sonic fascination of techno and industrial," observed *New York* contributor Chris Norris. According to Ali, Manson's look and music create a phenomenon that "is sure to terrify impressionable children, scare the bejesus out of their concerned parents and, most important, attract disgruntled teens like moths to a porch light." As Manson, Warner has a legion of hard-core fans, and an equally large—if not larger—group of detractors. These detractors include parents, local governments, and Christian organizations.

Some critics have wondered if Warner is more concerned with showmanship than with music. "Manson is a great American pop huckster, in the tradition of P. T. Barnum, Gene Simmons, and Larry Flynt," stated *New York* contributor Norris, comparing Warner/Manson to a circus founder, another rock star, and a pornography publisher. "What Manson is about on a deeper level is our culture's premiere value: hype. The old injunction to 'shock the bourgeois' long ago was amended to 'shock the bourgeois—and sell millions of dollars worth of albums to their children,' " wrote Rich Lowry

in the *National Review.* Regardless, Marilyn Manson fans remain loyal, as Lowry discovered when he attended one of the band's concerts. As Lowry observed: "The kids love it."

*BIOGRAPHICAL/CRITICAL SOURCES:*

*PERIODICALS*

*Entertainment Weekly,* November 24, 1995, p. 104; December 15, 1995, p. 72; October 11, 1996, p. 90; April 11, 1997, p. 85; July 25, 1997, pp. 36-39; March 6, 1998, p. 74.
*National Review,* June 30, 1997, pp. 53-54.
*Newsweek,* September 21, 1998, p. 99.
*New York,* January 13, 1997, pp. 48, 62, 79.
*People Weekly,* September 22, 1997. p. 29.
*Rolling Stone,* November 28, 1996, pp. 129-130; January 23, 1997; May 28, 1998, pp. 106-107; September 17, 1998, pp. 23-24; October 15, 1998, pp. 36-44.
*Time,* September 28, 1998, p. 90.

*OTHER*

*Amazon.com,* http://www.amazon.com/exec/obidos/quicksearch-query/002-4885682-5135820 (May 6, 1998).
*Dead Souls,* http://www.deadsouls.com/mm/ (November 4, 1999).
*Marilyn-manson.com,* http://www.marilyn-manson.com/press/rs1.htm (October 16, 1998).
*Marilynmanson.net,* http://www.marilynmanson.net (October 15, 1998).
*Rolling Stone Network: Magazine,* http://www.rollingstone.com/sections/magazine/text/excerpt797.asp?afl=rsn (December 1, 1998).
*Spookhouse,* http://www.spookhouse.net/faq/ (November 4, 1999).*

\*    \*    \*

## WEEKS, Kent R.

*PERSONAL:* Married; wife's name Susan Howe. *Education:* University of Washington at Seattle, M.A., 1965; Yale University, Ph.D., 1970.

*ADDRESSES: Agent*—c/o William Morrow & Co. Inc., 1350 Avenue of the Americas, New York, NY 10019.

*CAREER:* American University in Cairo, Egyptologist and professor 1988—. Worked on archaeological projects in Egypt and Nubia in 1960s; two years at the Metropolitan Museum of Art's Egyptian Department; Queens College, CUNY, taught in History Department; American University in Cairo, Department of Anthropology, 1972-74; University of Chicago Oriental Institute's Epigraphic and Architectural Survey at Chicago House, Luxor (Egypt), field director; University of California, Berkeley, associate professor, then professor of Egyptian archaeology, 1977-88; started Theban Mapping Project, 1978, to survey and map the Theban West Bank.

*WRITINGS:*

*The Classic Christian Townsite at Arminna West,* Volume 3, Publications of the Pennsylvania-Yale Egyptian Expedition (New Haven, CT), 1967.
(With James Harris) *X-Raying the Pharaohs,* Scribner's (New York City), 1973.
(Editor) *Egyptology and the Social Sciences: Five Studies,* American University in Cairo Press (Cairo), 1979.
*The Berkeley Map of the Theban Necropolis: Preliminary Report,* [Berkeley], 1979.
*KV5: The Lost Tomb,* William Morrow (New York City), 1998.

Also author of *An Historical Bibliography of Egyptian Prehistory,* 1985. Author and field director for report "The Temple of Khonsu, II: Scenes and Inscriptions in the Court and the Hypostyle Hall," *Publications of the Oriental Institute,* University of Chicago Press (Chicago), 1982. Contibutor to numerous magazines, journals, encyclopedias, and books, including *National Geographic, Oxford Encyclopaedia of Egyptology, Encyclopaedia of the Archaeology of the Ancient Near East, A History of Ancient Egypt,* by Nicolas Grimal, 1994, and "The Work of the Theban Mapping Project and the Protection of the Valley of the Kings," in *The Valley of the Kings,* edited by Richard Wilkinson, 1996.

*SIDELIGHTS:* Kent Weeks's interest in ancient Egypt started as a child and has resulted in a career that has taken him all over the globe. As a student of the University of Washington at Seattle, Weeks met his wife, fellow student Susan Howe, while both were working on archaeological projects in Nubia, Egypt. In 1966, Weeks started working with Dr. James E. Harris, and their project enabled them to X-ray mummies in the Egyptian museum. The two then collaborated on *X-raying the Pharaohs,* published in 1973. While teaching at the American University in Cairo in the 1970s, Weeks documented a group of mastabas—ancient flat,

oblong structures built over entrances of mummy chambers or burial pits—west of the Great Pyramid.

Weeks worked as field director of the University of Chicago Oriental Institute's Epigraphic and Architectural Survey at Chicago House in Egypt at Luxor, a city on the Nile near the ancient ruins of Thebes. He found that there were no reliable atlases that documented the large number of monuments in the region. As a result, the Theban Mapping Project was started after Weeks returned to the United States in 1978. The project was designed to survey and plot the ancient structures in the Theban necropolis area. Weeks has published several reports of the Theban Mapping Project since the original *The Berkeley Map of the Theban Necropolis: Preliminary Report* in 1979.

In 1987, the Theban Mapping Project began searching an area in the Valley of the Kings northeast of the entrance to the tomb of King Ramses IX. Weeks, drawing from earlier expedition reports, remote sensing surveys, and ancient texts, believed a forgotten tomb may have been in that area. The "rediscovery" of the entrance to KV5 in 1987 touched off a media frenzy. In 1995, the media and the academic community was much more interested to learn that the tomb was many times larger than previously thought. In *The Lost Tomb,* Weeks draws from his diaries, and those of his wife and site foreman, to explain to the world at large the trials and tribulations of rediscovering and exploring what he believes to be the burial site for the sons of Ramses II. Edward K. Werner, in a *Library Journal* review of *The Lost Tomb,* calls Weeks's rediscovery "by far the most significant" Egyptological find of the second half of the century. The book does not focus on the technical, purely scientific side of the discovery, but instead "documents the excitement, challenges, and frustrations of modern archaeological investigation," according to Werner. John Ray, the Herbert Thompson Reader in Egyptology at Cambridge University, wrote in the *New York Times Book Review* that "KV5 is to the ordinary tomb in the Valley of the Kings . . . what a supermarket is to the corner shop."Although Weeks's tale is a little repetitious and loosely organized, according to Ray, the account itself is "readable." Weeks relays his personal feelings to the reader. Ray notes that much of Weeks's affection for his Egyptian workmen, the citizens of Luxor, and their ancestors comes across in his writing. A *Publishers Weekly* review of the book proclaims that "Weeks gives a sense of immediacy in the reconstruction of a fascinating story that fully conveys the thrill of discovery after years of painstaking work."

*BIOGRAPHICAL/CRITICAL SOURCES:*

PERIODICALS

*Library Journal,* October 1, 1998, p. 114.
*New York Times Book Review,* October 18, 1998, pp. 32-33.
*Publishers Weekly,* September 7, 1998, p. 76.

OTHER

*Theban Mapping Project Home Page,* http://www.kv5.com (January 11, 1999).*

\*　　\*　　\*

## WEINER, Myron   1931-1999

*OBITUARY NOTICE*—See index for *CA* sketch: Born March 11, 1931, in New York, NY; died of brain cancer, June 3, 1999, in Moretown, VT. Professor and author. Weiner helped raise awareness in India and elsewhere that decreasing illiteracy and improving education could have a positive economic impact on that country's economy. Weiner graduated from City College (now City College of the City University of New York) and received advanced degrees from Princeton. In 1953 he received a Fulbright award for research in India and he followed that as a Social Science Research Council fellow in India in 1957 and 1958. His interest in India led him to compare economic, social and political issues there with developing countries in Africa as well as with China. Weiner worked at numerous schools while doing his research, among them Princeton, the University of Chicago, and the Massachusetts Institute of Technology, where he stayed for nearly forty years until retiring in 1998. Weiner wrote more than thirty books, including *Party Politics in India, India at the Polls: The Parliamentary Elections of 1977,* and *The Global Migration Crisis: Challenge to States and to Human Rights.* He also edited several books, among them *Threatened People, Threatened Borders: World Migration and U.S. Policy* and *The State and Social Transformation in Afghanistan, Iran, and Pakistan.* His 1991 work *The Child and the State in India* is believed by many to have had a strong impact on discussions about child labor.

*OBITUARIES AND OTHER SOURCES:*

PERIODICALS

*New York Times,* June 9, 1999, p. A27.

## WHITE, Jane
## See BRADY, Jane

\*　　\*　　\*

## WHITE, Joan   1909-1999

*OBITUARY NOTICE*—See index for *CA* sketch: Born December 3, 1909, in Alexandria, Egypt; died June 8, 1999. Actress and director. White was known to audiences on both sides of the Atlantic due to the length of her career. Her first appearance on stage was in Cambridge when she was twenty years old and appearing in *Tobias and the Angel* and she continued acting well into her eighties. White was a familiar face to West End theater-goers and performed in plays such as *Love's Labours Lost* and others by Shakespeare before embarking on a career as a stage director. She directed plays that included *Flat Spin, The Queen's Husband,* and *The Hollow Crown.* White toured the United States in 1958 with the cast of *My Fair Lady* and in 1960 was hired, with her third husband Robert Grose, to run the Berkshire Playhouse Drama School in Stockbridge, Massachusetts. They stayed until 1965, offering conferences on playwriting and presenting more than fifty productions. White acted on Broadway in 1962 in *A Passage to India* but returned to England in the late 1960s. In 1969 she joined the faculty in the University of Washington's drama school where she stayed for six years, directing and acting in productions around Seattle. She founded a theater school there and connected with American universities to take students and their productions to the United Kingdom. She maintained the school until 1990, while also running the Next Stage Company in London. White retired in 1994.

*OBITUARIES AND OTHER SOURCES:*

BOOKS

*Who's Who in the Theatre,* 17th edition, Gale, 1981.

PERIODICALS

*Times* (London), June 17, 1999.

\*　　\*　　\*

## WHITNEY, Ruth Reinke   1928-1999

*OBITUARY NOTICE*—See index for *CA* sketch: Born July 23, 1928, in Oshkosh, WI; died of amyotrophic lateral sclerosis (Lou Gehrig's disease), June 4, 1999, in Irvington, NY. Editor. Whitney never attended journalism school but became an influential member of the publishing world for her work at *Glamour* magazine, where she served as editor for more than thirty years. Whitney grew up in Wisconsin and graduated from Northwestern University in 1949, the same year she married her husband, Daniel. She began her career as a promotional copywriter at *Time* magazine but was eventually fired due to, she claimed, her support of Adlai Stevenson. Unable to get a job at a general interest magazine because of her gender, Whitney moved into women's magazines and was hired at *Better Living* in the mid-1950s. Within two years she was named editor-in-chief, a post she kept until 1956 when she moved to *Seventeen*. Whitney stayed with *Seventeen* until taking over at *Glamour* in 1967, where she immediately drew attention for putting a black model on the cover in 1968 and being the first women's magazine to do so. She continued running copy on once-scandalous subjects such as feminism, rape, and abortion. The magazine won accolades such as the 1992 National Magazine Award under her direction and she increased circulation to more than two million readers. Whitney retired as editor-in-chief in 1998.

*OBITUARIES AND OTHER SOURCES:*

PERIODICALS

*Chicago Tribune,* June 7, 1999, sec. 2, p. 6.
*Los Angeles Times,* June 7, 1999, p. A18.
*New York Times,* June 5, 1999, p. C16.
*Washington Post,* June 8, 1999, p. B5.

\*  \*  \*

**WILSON, Jean Moorcroft**

*PERSONAL:* Married; children: five.

*CAREER:* Lecturer at University of London. Also runs a publishing house with her husband.

*WRITINGS:*

*Isaac Rosenberg, Poet and Painter: A Biography,* C. Woolf (London), 1975.
*I Was an English Poet: A Critical Biography of Sir William Watson (1858-1936),* C. Woolf, 1981.
(Editor with Cecil Woolf) *Authors Take Sides on the Falklands: Two Questions on the Falklands Con-*

*flict Answered by More Than a Hundred Mainly British Authors,* C. Woolf, 1982.
*Virginia Woolf, Life and London: A Biography of Place,* illustrated by Leonard McDermid, C. Woolf, 1987, W. W. Norton (New York City), 1988.
(Editor) *The Collected Letters of Charles Hamilton Sorley,* C. Woolf, 1990.
*Siegfried Sassoon—the Making of a War Poet: A Biography (1886-1918),* Routledge (New York City), 1999.

*SIDELIGHTS:* Jean Moorcroft Wilson is noted for her biographies of Virginia Woolf, Isaac Rosenberg, Charles Hamilton Sorley, and William Watson, and for producing the first full-length biography of World War I poet Siegfried Sassoon. Her biography of her husband's aunt, Virginia Woolf is, according to one reviewer, "as much literary companion as critique." The reviewer, J. K. L. Walker, writing in the *Times Literary Supplement,* concludes the review by citing the book as a "pleasant and useful literary guide to an enduring London myth." Indeed, a *Kirkus Reviews* commentator praises *Virginia Woolf, Life and London: A Biography of Place* as "part biography, part travel guide, a slight but charming book rich in conception and successful in execution." The book offers readers a list of walks for the fan who wants to travel London in light of Virginia Woolf.

Wilson's biography of Charles Hamilton Sorley, another World War I poet, was not as warmly received by critics. Neal Philip of *British Book News* was not convinced by Wilson's assertion that Sorley's poetry has been unduly neglected. Philip claimed that the biography was really too long, but that the research was "admirable." Neil Corcoran, of the *Times Literary Supplement,* wondered "whether a well-edited selection of the letters and war poems would not have made a better book." Corcoran did praise Wilson's research, writing, "What is most interesting in Jean Moorcroft Wilson's biography is its account of what provoked, in this superficially unexceptional career, such an exceptional response" to battle encountered in World War I.

*BIOGRAPHICAL/CRITICAL SOURCES:*

PERIODICALS

*British Book News,* March 1986, p. 179.
*Kirkus Reviews,* August 1, 1988, p. 1140.
*Times Literary Supplement,* February 28, 1986, p. 214; August 12-18, 1988, p. 894.\*

## WING, Donald G(oddard)   1904-1972

*PERSONAL:* Born in 1904, in Anthol, MA; died in 1972; son of Frank and Edith Wing; married Charlotte Farquhar, June 28, 1930; children: Robert and Cathy. *Education:* Yale University, B.A., 1926; attended Trinity College, Cambridge, 1926-27; Harvard University, M.A., 1928; Yale, Ph.D., 1932.

*CAREER:* Bibliographer, librarian at Yale University, 1928-70: assistant reference librarian, 1930-39; head of accessions, 1939-45; associate librarian, 1945-65; associate librarian for collections of the libraries, 1966-70.

*AWARDS, HONORS:* Guggenheim fellowship for study in Great Britain, 1935; first Yale librarian to be awarded a sabbatical, 1967-68.

*WRITINGS:*

*Short-Title Catalogue of Books Printed in England, Scotland, Ireland, Wales, and British America and of English Books Printed in Other Countries, 1641-1700,* three volumes, Columbia University for the Index Society (New York City), 1945-51, second edition, Volume 1, revised, Modern Language Association (MLA) (New York City), 1994, Volume 2, revised, MLA, 1982, Volume 3, revised, MLA, 1988.
*A Gallery of Ghosts: Books Published Between 1641-1700 Not Found in the Short-Title Catalogue,* Index Committee of the MLA (New York City), 1967.

Also contributed articles to scholarly journals.

*SIDELIGHTS:* Donald G. Wing's *Short Title Catalog of English Books, 1641-1700,* referred to simply as "Wing's *STC,*" has been an indispensable aid to scholars of English and American history and literature. Wing, a librarian at Yale University, made it his life's work to catalogue in detail all the previously uncatalogued works from the period. William Baker in the *Dictionary of Literary Biography* called Wing's compendious catalogue "the great work of enumerative bibliography by which [Wing] will be remembered."

Wing was born in Anthol, Massachusetts, and attended public schools before entering Yale University. Even as a child he was interested in cataloguing things, creating several detailed notebooks about movie actors of his time. After graduating from Yale in 1926, Wing went to Trinity College, Cambridge, earned a master's degree at Harvard, and completed a Ph.D. at Yale. He began working at the Yale library in 1928, where he would stay for four decades.

In the process of moving early books to a new library building at Yale, Wing began to put together a catalogue of the books Yale possessed in 1742. In his research he discovered that very little bibliographical information was available on books in English published from the 1640s to 1700. Taking on this challenge, Wing won a Guggenheim fellowship in 1935 to search British libraries for books published in this period. The story was told that he sailed with thirty-six shoe boxes full of bibliographical slips and returned with fifty-one boxes after searching libraries at Oxford and Cambridge, as well as collections in Scotland, France, and Holland.

Upon Wing's return to Yale, each of the slips was painstakingly converted into typescript, and a prospectus for a catalogue appeared. Other libraries, hearing of his project, checked their collections, and a network of collectors and scholars interested in the mid-seventeenth century developed. In the pre-computer days when Wing was working on his project, he continued to file his bibliographical notation in rows of shoe boxes.

In his dual position as acquisitions librarian and bibliographer, Wing was in a special position to develop the library collection at Yale. He also attracted interest in books of the period and gained the respect of antiquarian book dealers. The historical period he chose was of particular interest to scholars, encompassing the English Civil War, the Cromwellian period, the Restoration, and the ascent of the American colonies.

The first volume of Wing's *STC* was published in 1945; Volume II, in 1945; and Volume III, in 1951. The volumes were revised several times, the last, as of this writing, in 1994. As word spread about the comprehensive nature of the catalogue, scholars, booksellers, and librarians around the world flooded Wing with enough information to fill seventy drawers in a card catalogue. In 1967 he published his second work, *A Gallery of Ghosts,* in which he lists 5,000 titles he had found listed in bibliographies but had never seen. Titles subsequently located were included in a revised *STC.* Although Wing died before the later revisions were done, his work was continued by other dedicated scholars.

The immense project that was Wing's *STC* was admired by most observers. Still, some critics found some faults in the book. Non-English and non-American critics faulted him for not including more sources from

Australia and New Zealand. A contributor to the *Times Literary Supplement* felt that some of Wing's many abbreviations were confusing and found the rearrangement of the 1972 edition awkward; the reviewer added, "[T]his revision is far from comprehensive, and additions are haphazard while the concealment of so many changes in unnoted renumeration is, at the very least, disconcerting and inconvenient."

No one, however, could discount the importance of Wing's *STC* to the world of seventeenth-century studies. The *Times Literary Supplement* reviewer called it "an indispensable tool of scholarship." Today's computerized methods have made the task of coordinating bibliographies much easier. At the time of Wing's death in 1972, he could not have foreseen that his shoe boxes and card catalogues could now be compressed onto CD-ROMs. Those working on or using revisions of the STC, however, will not forget the pioneering work of Donald Wing. As A.N.L. Munby, another bibliographer, remarked about Wing's STC in the *Book Collector,* "Whatever its defects, our indebtedness to Wing remains."

*BIOGRAPHICAL/CRITICAL SOURCES:*

*BOOKS*

Rosenblum, Joseph, editor, *Dictionary of Literary Biography,* Volume 187: *American Book Collectors and Bibliographers,* 2nd series, Gale Research (Detroit, MI), 1997.

*PERIODICALS*

*Antiquarian Bookman,* October 16, 1972.
*Bookman,* autumn, 1974.
*New York Times,* October 11, 1972.
*Times Literary Supplement,* January 26, 1973.*

\*   \*   \*

## WOLSELEY, Roland E. 1904-1998

*OBITUARY NOTICE*—See index for *CA* sketch: Born March 9, 1904, in New York, NY; died May 31, 1998, in Syracuse, NY. Teacher and journalist. Wolseley began his career as a journalist in the early 1920s at a number of papers in Pennsylvania, including the *Herald-Telegram, News-Times,* and *Tribune.* He graduated from Northwestern University in 1928 and followed with a master's degree in 1934. He worked at a few papers in Illinois before joining the faculty at Northwestern University in 1938. Wolseley stayed until 1946, when he left for Syracuse University where he was on the faculty and chaired the magazine department for more than twenty years. Wolseley was book review editor for *Quill and Scroll* magazine for more than six decades and wrote furiously, completing about one thousand magazine articles. He also wrote numerous books and journalism texts including *Critical Writing for the Journalist, Understanding Magazines, Still in Print,* and *Courage and Enterprise: A Gallery of Black Journalists.* His best-known book was *Black Press U.S.A.,* an overview of black journalism that received a Kappa Tau Alpha citation. He received an award from the Association for Education in Journalism and Mass Communication's magazine division in 1985 for distinguished service as an educator. Wolseley retired from Syracuse as professor emeritus in 1972.

*OBITUARIES AND OTHER SOURCES:*

*PERIODICALS*

*New York Times,* June 29, 1998, p. B9.

\*   \*   \*

## WROTH, Lawrence C(ounselman) 1884-1970

*PERSONAL:* Born January 14, 1884; died December 25, 1970, in Providence, RI; son of Peregrine (a clergyman) and Mary Augusta (Counselman) Wroth; married Barbara Pease (a teacher), December 27, 1930; children: three sons. *Education:* Private preparatory school, Baltimore; Johns Hopkins University, A.B., 1905.

*CAREER:* American bibliographer, librarian, and historian of printing and the book trades. Librarian, Maryland Episcopal Diocesan Library, 1905-12; editor, *Maryland Churchman,* beginning 1908; assistant librarian, Enoch Pratt Free Library, Baltimore, 1912-17, 1919-23; managing editor, Johns Hopkins alumni magazine, beginning 1912; librarian, John Carter Brown Library, Providence, RI, 1923-57; columnist, *New York Herald Tribune,* 1937-47; consultant, Pierpont Morgan Library, New York City, beginning 1938; consultant, rare books, Library of Congress, Washington, DC, to 1951; librarian emeritus, John Carter Brown Library, 1957-64, librarian emeritus, 1964-70. *Military service:* Maryland National Guard, 1917-19; served in World War I in France with the U.S. Army, 110th Field Artillery.

*MEMBER:* Bibliographical Society of America (president, 1931-33).

*AWARDS, HONORS:* Named Honorary Secretary for America, Bibliographical Society of London; Rosenbach Fellow in Bibliography, University of Pennsylvania, 1934(?); honorary D. Litt., Brown University, 1932; honorary title of Research Professor of American History, Brown, 1932; gold medal, American Institute of Graphic Arts, 1948; *festschrift* in his honor, edited by Frederick Goff, 1951; gold medal, Bibliographical Society of London, 1957.

*WRITINGS:*

*Parson Weems: A Biographical and Critical Study,* Eichelberger (Baltimore), 1911.

*A History of Printing in Colonial Maryland, 1686-1776,* Typothetae of Baltimore (Baltimore), 1922.

*The John Carter Brown Library: Report to the Corporation of Brown University,* 34 volumes, John Carter Brown Library (Providence, RI), 1924-57.

*William Parks: Printer and Journalist of England and Colonial America; with a List of the Issues of His Several Presses and a Facsimile of the Earliest Virginia Imprint Known to Be in Existence,* William Parks Club (Richmond, VA), 1926.

*The Colonial Printer,* Grolier Club (New York City), 1931, 2nd edition, Southworth-Anthoensen Press (Portland, ME), 1938.

*An American Bookshelf, 1755,* University of Pennsylvania Press (Philadelphia), 1934.

*The Way of a Ship: An Essay on the Literature of Navigation Science,* Southworth-Anthoensen, 1937.

*The First Century of the John Carter Brown Library: A History with a Guide to the Collections,* Associates of the John Carter Brown Library (Providence), 1946.

*Typographical Heritage: Selected Essays,* Anthoesen Press for the Typophiles (Portland, ME), 1949.

*The Voyages of Giovanni da Verrazzano, 1524-1528,* Yale University Press for the Pierpont Morgan Library (New Haven, CT), 1970.

Also contributor to periodicals, including "The Wickedest Book in the World," *Dial,* May 16, 1909; "Recent Bibliographical Work in America," *Library,* June, 1928; "The Indian Treaty as Literature," *Yale Review,* July, 1928; "Career in Books," *Johns Hopkins Alumni Magazine,* April, 1938; and "The Chief End of Book Madness," *Library of Congress Quarterly Journal of Current Acquisitions,* October, 1945.

Contributor to anthologies, including "North America (English-Speaking," in *Printing, A Short History of the Art,* edited by R.A. Peddie, Grafton (London), 1927; "Book Production and Distribution from the Beginning to the War Between the States," in *The Book in America: A History of the Making, the Selling, and the Collecting of Books in the U.S.,* edited by Wroth, Hellmut Lehmann-Haupt, and Ruth Shepard Granniss, R.R. Bowker (New York City), 1939, revised edition, 1951; "Good Booksellers Make Good Libraries," in *To Dr. R.: Essays Here Collected and Published in Honor of the Seventieth Birthday of Dr. A. S. W. Rosenbach, July 22, 1946,* compiled by Percy E. Lawler, (Philadelphia), 1946; and *In Retrospect, 1923-1949. An Exhibition Commemorating Twenty-six Years of Service to the John Carter Brown Library by Lawrence C. Wroth, Librarian,* compiled by Wroth and the staff of the library (Providence), 1949.

*SIDELIGHTS:* Lawrence C. Wroth fulfilled a number of roles in his career, all related to his love of books. He was a librarian and author who contributed voluminously to scholarship on the history of printing and book publication. He also was in demand as a consultant to a number of libraries and organizations that valued his bibliographical skills. For many years he headed the prestigious John Carter Brown Library at Brown University in Providence, Rhode Island.

Wroth's career path was set soon after he graduated in 1905 from Johns Hopkins University in Baltimore, when he took a position as librarian at the Maryland Episcopal Diocesan Library in Baltimore. He also began editing a monthly diocesan newspaper, the *Maryland Churchman,* and in 1911 published his first book, *Parson Weems, A Biographical and Critical Study.* This work was a critical examination of the life of Mason Locke Weems, who had come to public attention for his story of George Washington and the cherry tree. In 1912 Wroth began working as assistant librarian at the Enoch Pratt Free Library in Baltimore. During this time he also taught at Johns Hopkins, published books and articles on the history of Maryland, and became managing editor of the alumni magazine at the university. He entered military service in 1917, serving in France during World War I, before returning to the Pratt Library and his scholarly pursuits.

Wroth's interests were increasingly focused on the history of the book. He revised some earlier scholarly assumptions on early printers in Maryland, producing *A History of Printing in Colonial Maryland, 1686-1776* in 1922. In this book he deals with not only the printed materials themselves, but how printers interacted with the politics and the business conditions of their time. In 1923 Wroth moved to the John Carter Library, whose specialized collection began with many of the primary sources which influenced the early Western Hemisphere explorers and extended through eighteenth-century publications. Wroth developed the collection, adding some 5,500 books by the end of his tenure at the library. According to a profile of Wroth by Carolyn Smith in the *Dictionary of Literary Biography,* "The books he discovered in the library, or added to it, ranged from obvious high spots to works which could be appreciated best with imagination and sympathy." Examples of Wroth's interesting acquisitions are the early accounts recorded by Richard Hackluyt of the first explorations of the North American coast and transcripts of speeches given by Native Americans meeting with colonists. Wroth routinely went over his acquisitions budget and spent a great deal of time soliciting funds from alumni and other contributors.

Wroth's 1931 volume *The Colonial Printer* is a compendious work chronicling the history of printing in Maryland. He covers not only the early printers, but the ways in which they interacted with their contemporaries and the printing techniques and equipment they used. In addition, he discusses early industries who supplied printers, the aesthetic qualities of their books, and other interesting topics.

Wroth was active in many professional organizations, including the Bibliographical Society of America and the Bibliographical Society of London. His book *An American Bookshelf, 1775,* published in 1934, was a compilation of three lectures he gave as a Rosenbach Fellow in Bibliography for the University of Pennsylvania. In this book he discusses intellectual activity in America prior to the American Revolution as evidenced through many publications of the day.

Wroth's writing was, of course, mostly for a specialized audience. For the ten years after 1937 he also reached a wider readership through a column he edited in the *New York Herald Tribune.* He also expanded his responsibilties by agreeing to be a consultant to the Pierpont Morgan Library in New York City in 1938, and later to the Library of Congress. After receiving a number of honors from graphic arts and bibliographical societies in the late 1940s and early 1950s, Wroth retired from the Library of Congress in 1954 and from the John Carter Brown Library in 1957. He stayed on in Providence as librarian emeritus, however, for several more years. Asked to edit a manuscript account of explorer Giovanni da Verrazzano's voyages along the east coast of North America in 1524, Wroth eventually expanded that project into a full-scale book, *The Voyages of Giovanni da Verrazzano, 1524-1528,* published in 1970

just before his death. This work is an exhaustive look at all the available sources and an attempt to put Verrazzano's explorations into their social and cultural contexts. Smith said that Wroth, though a specialist, was able to communicate well with non-specialists in his writings: "Wroth was a conscious stylist and a lover of formal English; he wrote without affectation and with absolute clarity. . . . His best writing has a smooth flow and elegant finish, and he has the gift of meeting his reader directly and almost personally," Smith added that "he made an original and permanent contribution to the history of the book in America."

*BIOGRAPHICAL/CRITICAL SOURCES:*

*BOOKS*

*Dictionary of Literary Biography,* Volume 187: *American Book Collectors and Bibliographers, 2nd Series,* Gale (Detroit, MI), 1997.

*PERIODICALS*

*Antiquarian Bookman,* January 18, 1971.
*Proceedings of the American Antiquarian Society,* Volume 81, 1971, pp. 37-39.
*Publishers Weekly,* January 11, 1971.
*Quarterly Journal of the Library of Congress,* Volume 30, 1973, pp. 211-227.*

\*       \*       \*

**WYATT, Zach**
   **See PROCTOR, Geo(rge W.)**

\*       \*       \*

**WYDEN, Peter H.   1923-1998**

*OBITUARY NOTICE*—See index for *CA* sketch: Born October 2, 1923, in Berlin, Germany; immigrated to United States, 1937; naturalized citizen, 1943; died of a stroke and subdural hematoma, June 27, 1998, in Danbury, CT. Journalist. Wyden came to the United States at age thirteen and started his journalism career at the *Daily Metal Reporter* in New York City. He was on staff at newspapers in Kansas and Missouri during the late 1940s and early 1950s before joining *Newsweek* as its Washington, D.C., correspondent. He stayed in magazines for the next decade, working as senior editor at *McCall's,* executive editor for *Ladies' Home Journal,* and associate editor for the *Saturday Evening Post.* Along the way he wrote several books, the first of which was *Suburbia's Coddled Kids.* Other titles include *The Overweight Society: An Authoritative, Entertaining Investigation Into the Facts and Follies of Girth Control, Bay of Pigs: The Untold Story,* and *Day One: Before Hiroshima and After,* which won an Overseas Press Club Award and was the basis for the 1989 television movie *Day One.* Other books he wrote studied Berlin, the Spanish Civil War and Hitler's Germany. His most recent book, 1998's *Conquering Schizophrenia: A Father, His Son and a Medical Breakthrough,* chronicled Wyden's struggles with his son, Jeff, who was mentally ill.

*OBITUARIES AND OTHER SOURCES:*

PERIODICALS

*New York Times,* June 29, 1998, p. B9.
*Washington Post,* June 29, 1998, p. D8.

OTHER

*CNN Interactive* (electronic), June 29, 1998.

\*   \*   \*

## Y. Y.
### See LYND, Robert

\*   \*   \*

## YAN, Geling

*PERSONAL:* Name is pronounced "*Ge*-ling Yen;" born in Shanghai, China; daughter of Xiao Ma (a writer); married Lawrence A. Walker, 1992. *Education:* Wuhan University, B.A., 1989; Columbia College, Chicago, IL, M.F.A., 1999.

*ADDRESSES: Home*—Alameda, CA. *Agent*—Dijkstra Literary Agency, 1155 Camino del Mar, Suite 515, Del Mar, CA 92014.

*CAREER:* Writer. Guest on media programs in the United States, China, Taiwan, and Hong Kong. *Military service:* People's Liberation Army of China; became major.

*MEMBER:* Chinese Writers Association.

*AWARDS, HONORS:* First Prize, best novel, and Ten Year Prize, soldier's favorite novel, both from People's Liberation Army Publishing House, 1987, for *Green Blood;* first prize, *Central Daily News* (Taiwan), 1991, for the novella *Siao Yu,* and 1992, for the story "The Landlady;" *China Times* (Taiwan), Critics Prize, 1993, for the story "Red Silk Dress," and Million Yuan Literature Prize, 1998, for *Inner Space; United Daily News* (Taiwan), first prize, 1993, for the story "Across the Ocean," and Best Novel Award, 1995, for *Fusang;* Golden Horse Award, best script adaptation, Taiwan Academy of Motion Pictures, 1998, for *Xiu Xiu: The Sent-Down Girl;* first prize, National Students and Scholars Literary Contest (Taiwan) and prize for best experimental fiction, Columbia University Scholastic Press Association, both 1998, for the story "Celestial Bath."

*WRITINGS:*

*White Snake and Other Stories,* Aunt Lute (San Francisco, CA), 1999.

Works in Chinese include the novels *Green Blood, Whispers of a Woman Soldier, Female Grasslands, Straw-Sandaled Nobility, Fusang,* and *Inner Space;* the novella *The River Flows Backwards;* the short story collections *Siao Yu, Across the Ocean, The River Flows Backwards,* and *Kite Song;* an essay collection, *Bohemian Towers;* and the biography *Joan Chen: The Early Years.* Author of the film script for *Xiu Xiu: The Sent-Down Girl* (based on her short story "Celestial Bath"), 1998, and the script for the film *Siao Yu* (based on her short story). Writer for a radio series on American life, Voice of America, 1997. Contributor to periodicals, including *Hair Trigger.*

*ADAPTATIONS:* Yan's story "Nothing Other than Male and Female" was adapted as a screenplay and released by Yen Ping Co. of Taiwan in 1995; it was also broadcast as a television series by China Central Television, 1995.

*WORK IN PROGRESS:* An English-language translation and a film script of the novel *Fusang;* a television series on the lives of Chinese immigrants to the United States in the 1920s and 1930s, for China Central Television.

*SIDELIGHTS:* Geling Yan told *CA:* "I was born in Shanghai and attended primary school there until the Cultural Revolution closed down all schools. I entered the People's Liberation Army at age twelve and served in ballet and folk dance troupes. I was stationed in Chengdu, Sichuan Province, but I spent most of the time on the road, performing at various military installations. I spent a total of eighteen months in Tibet.

"The daughter of a writer, I began writing in the late 1970s as a war correspondent covering the Sino-Vietnamese border war. After being discharged from the army with the rank of major, I moved to Beijing and published my first novel, *Green Blood,* about my experiences as an adolescent girl soldier. I earned a bachelor's degree in Chinese literature from Wuhan University in 1988. That same year, I was invited to visit the United States under the auspices of the U.S. Information Agency's International Visitors' Program. In 1989, I went to the United States again and studied at Columbia College in Chicago. I now live in the San Francisco Bay area."

*     *     *

## YOUNG, Dick  1917(?)-1987

*PERSONAL:* Born in 1917 (some sources say 1918), in New York, NY; died August 31, 1987, in New York, NY; married; wife's name Jay; children: seven daughters, one son. *Education:* Attended George Washington High School, New York City. *Ethnicity:* Russian, Jewish. *Politics:* Conservative. *Religion:* Catholic.

*CAREER:* Sportswriter, sports editor, *New York Daily News,* 1936-81; *New York Post,* 1982-87; columnist, *The Sporting News,* late 1950s to 1985.

*AWARDS, HONORS:* Inductee, National Baseball Hall of Fame, 1978; J.G. Taylor Spink Award, National Baseball Hall of Fame, 1979; President, Baseball Writers' Association of America; James J. Walker Award, Boxing Writers Association of America, 1987.

*WRITINGS:*

*Roy Campanella,* Barnes & Noble (New York City), 1952.

Also author of articles contributed to periodicals and books, including "Battle on the Plains," in *Best Sports Stories (BSS) of 1944,* edited by Irving T; Marsh and Edward Ehre, Dutton (New York City), 1945; "The Outlawed Spitball," in *BSS: 1956,* edited by Marsh and Ehre, Dutton, 1956; "He Walked with the Stars," *Coronet,* July, 1959, pp; 25-28; "The Big Leagues' Iron Curtain," in *BSS: 1964,* edited by Marsh and Ehre, Dutton, 1964; "The Joe Namath System," in *BSS: 1971,* edited

by Marsh and Ehre, Dutton, 1971; "It's Religion, Baby, Not Show Biz," *Sports Illustrated,* April 9, 1973; "The Barbie Doll Soap Opera," in *BSS: 1977,* edited by Marsh and Ehre, Dutton, 1977; "Muhammad Ali," *Sport,* December, 1986; and "1947: Brooklyn Dodgers 3, New York Yankees 2," in *The Baseball Reader,* edited by Charles Einstein, Bonanza Books (New York City), 1989.

*SIDELIGHTS:* Dick Young, longtime sports journalist for the *New York Daily News* and the *New York Post,* was dubbed "the world's most controversial sportswriter" by Douglas A. Noverr in the *Biographical Dictionary of American Sports.* In his 1987 book about the Brooklyn Dodgers in the 1950s, *The Boys of Summer,* Roger Kahn called Young "spiky, self-educated, and New York." His column in the *Daily News,* "Young Ideas," delighted and enraged readers for more than forty-five years. Young spent nearly his entire career at the *Daily News,* eventually becoming sports editor, until he left that newspaper for the *Post* in 1982, just five years before his death.

According to Jack Ziegler in the *Dictionary of Literary Biography,* Young was a "key transitional figure" between the "gentlemanly" sports reporting of old-time writers like Grantland Rice and Arthur Daley. Young had a longtime feud with Red Smith of the *New York Times,* whom Young considered an old-fashioned sentimentalist. Young's style was streetwise, often abrasive, and direct. Ziegler said that "he wrote authentic, accurate accounts of games and players."

Young was unhesitatingly frank in his opinions of sports figures, managers, and other sports commentators. He called sportscaster Howard Cosell "Howie the Shill." He was never politically correct, telling Harry Waters in a 1973 *Newsweek* article that many African-American athletes "believe that everything bad that is happening to them is happening because of their blackness. It's a terrible crutch."

Ziegler noted that Young never let go of the values he developed in the 1930s and 1940s—a high level of patriotism, conservative political and social views, a no-nonsense attitude toward hard work and achievement, a loathing for drug abuse among players, and a disdain for the younger players who did not meet his high standards. For many years, for example, he was unsympathetic toward the draft-resisting of Muhammad Ali, whom he persistently called by his pre-Islamic name, Cassius Clay. In 1971, in an article called "The Joe Namath System," he all but called the New York Jets quarterback a spoiled brat who made unreasonable demands on his managers. Instead, Young reserved his respect for older athletes, like Roy Campanella, the longtime catcher for the Brooklyn Dodgers who was paralyzed in an accident. Young wrote a biography of Campanella in 1952.

Young may have developed his crusty attitudes from his hardscrabble childhood. Born in the Bronx, he was farmed out to an Italian Catholic family in the Washington Heights section of Upper Manhattan from the ages of six to twelve. Poor but ambitious, he went with his father to California after high school, then worked for thirty dollars a month at Civilian Conservation Corps projects in upstate New York during the Great Depression. He hitchhiked to New York City, landing a job at the *Daily News* as a messenger boy. There he stayed, working as a tabulator, a beat reporter, a columnist, and finally sports editor, until he moved to the *Post*. At his peak he earned around $150,000, probably the highest salary earned by any sportswriter during his time.

By 1944 Young was already approaching legendary status in the sportswriting field. With what Ziegler called his "superb sense of narration," he riveted readers with his stories of subjects like illegal betting in the sports arena, Jackie Robinson's entry into the major leagues, and Happy Chandler's suspension of Dodger manager Leo Durocher in 1947. He disliked the abrasive Durocher personally but defended him as the victim of a hypocritical owner. Young had few kind words for Durocher's mild-mannered successor, calling him "Kindly Old Burt Shotton," often shortened to "KOBS." Young deeply regretted the departure of the New York Giants and the Dodgers and began to campaign fiercely for a new National League franchise. Suffering with the fans through the early, somnolent days of the New York Mets, he praised them for their comeback when they won the National League East championship in 1969. Yet he castigated fans for the poor sportsmanship they exhibited toward the rival Montreal Expos.

Mellowing somewhat in his latter years, Young often lionized older sports figures like Babe Ruth in his columns. Minimizing Ruth's known alcoholism, he still saw him as a hero, compared to a young star like Namath, whom he frequently castigated. Young also admired baseball commissioner Ford Frick, who had a major role in desegregating the game. Young's longstanding dislike for Muhammad Ali came to an end when he reconciled with the fighter around 1986. According to Ziegler, "[He] realized that beneath his slick

surface, Ali was a decent man, devoted to his family and possessed of courage and athletic skill."

Young was a complicated mixture of bravado, coarseness, sensitivity, belligerence, practicality, intelligence, and idealism. Other writers praised the breezy style which often masked profound thinking. In an *Esquire* article, Randall Poe found Young's writing style "coarse and simpleminded, like a cave painting. But it is superbly crafted." Young often applied higher moral standards to others than he adopted in his own life; he was known for womanizing and heavy drinking. At the same time, he had an extremely demanding work ethic. He wrote as many as seven "Young Ideas" columns in a week and routinely covered a baseball team six days a week. Revealing some of his writing secrets to Kahn in *The Boys of Summer*, he said, "Now you're gonna write the game most of the time. Nothing you can do about that and it ain't bad. But anytime you . . . can get your story off the game you got to do it. Because that's unusual and people read unusual things. Fights. Bean Balls. Whatever. Write them, not the games." In the end, Young succeeded in becoming the kind of sportswriter he dreamed of being. As he told Ross Wetzsteon in an article published in *Best Sports Stories: 1986*, "I wanted to be a stop-the-presses guy, competing with the other paper for the scoop and for the girl."

## BIOGRAPHICAL/CRITICAL SOURCES:

### BOOKS

*The Ballplayers: Baseball's Ultimate Biographical Reference,* edited by Mike Shatzkin, Morrow (New York City), 1990.
*Best Sports Stories: 1986,* Sports Network (St. Louis), 1986.
*Biographical Dictionary of American Sports, 1989-1992 Supplement,* edited by David L. Porter, Greenwood Press (Westport, CT), 1992.
*Dictionary of Literary Biography,* Volume 171: *Twentieth-Century Sportswriters,* Gale (Detroit, MI), 1996.
Kahn, Roger. *The Boys of Summer,* Harper & Row (New York City), 1987.
Kahn, Roger, *The Era,* Ticknor & Fields (New York City), 1994.

### PERIODICALS

*Esquire,* October, 1974, p. 173.
*Journal of American Culture,* fall, 1984, pp. 31-37.
*Newsweek,* May 21, 1973, p. 60.
*Sport,* December, 1986, p. 18.

*OBITUARIES:*

PERIODICALS

*Newsweek,* September 14, 1987.
*New York Times,* September 2, 1987.
*Time,* September 14, 1987.
*Washington Post,* September 2, 1987.*

\* \* \*

## ZAND, Herbert   1923-1970

*PERSONAL:* Born November 14, 1923; died of kidney failure, July 14, 1970; son of Adolf (a farmer) and Aloisia Zand; married Minnie (Mimi) Gutjahr, June 16, 1953. *Education:* Attended schools in Bad Aussee, Austria, 1934-38. *Ethnicity:* Austrian.

*CAREER:* Austrian novelist, poet, essayist, and translator, c. 1947-70. Publisher's reader, post-World War II; began writing novels after being wounded in the war; worked for the literature division of the Austrian radio network, beginning 1968. *Military service:* German army, radio operator in the infantry in World War II.

*AWARDS, HONORS:* Austrian State Prize for Literature for *Letzte Ausfahrt;* Prize of the City of Vienna, 1957; Peter Rosegger Prize of Styria, 1957; prize from the Theodor Korner Foundation, 1961; Anton Wildgans Prize of Austrian Industry, 1966; year's stipend from the Gerhard Fritsch Foundation for Austrian authors, 1970.

*WRITINGS:*

FICTION

*Die Sonnenstadt: Roman,* Schonleitner (Vienna), 1947.
*Letzte Ausfahrt: Roman der Engekesselten,* Donau (Vienna), 1953, translation by C. M. Woodhouse published as *The Last Sortie: The Story of the Cauldron,* Hart-Davis (London), 1955.
*Der Weg nach Hassi el emel,* Donau, 1956, translation by Norman Denny published as *The Well of Hope,* Collins (London), 1957.
*Erben des Feuers: Roman,* Muller (Salzburg), 1961.
*Demosthenes spricht gegen die Brandung: Erzahlungen,* edited by Wolfgang Kraus, Europa (Vienna), 1972.

POETRY

*Die Glaskugel: Gedichte,* Donau, 1953.

*Aus zerschossenem Sonnengeflecht: Gedichte,* Europa (Vienna), 1973.

ESSAYS

*Traume im Spiegel: Essays,* edited by Kraus, Europa, 1973.

COLLECTION

*Kerne des paradiesischen Apfels: Aufzeichnungen,* edited by Kraus, Europa, 1971.

SELECTED TRANSLATIONS

Henry Miller, *Symbole und Signale: Fruhe Dokumente der literarischen Avantgarde,* edited by Kraus, Lehunemann (Bremen, Germany), 1961.
Lawrence Durrell, *Die schwarze Chronik: Roman,* Rowohlt (Hamburg, Germany), 1962.
Durrell, *Leuchtende Orange, Rhodos-Insel des Helios,* Rowohlt, 1964.
Anais Nin, *Tagebucher, 1930-1934,* Rowohlt, 1966.
Nin, *Tagebucher, 1934-1939,* Wegner (Hamburg), 1967.

*SIDELIGHTS:* The small country of Austria was very proud of its native son, Herbert Zand, who began writing novels after he was severely wounded in World War II. Although not privileged to have a higher education, Zand produced a number of works of fiction, essays, poetry, and translations of the works of other major writers. He is not a major author, but, according to Pamela Saur in the *Dictionary of Literary Biography,* "the enduring literary merit and historical relevance of Zand's writings will ensure him a place in Austrian literary history."

Zand was born in a small Austrian village in the region of Styria, the son of uneducated farmers. Sent to the Eastern Front after being drafted by the German army, he experienced the horrors of war, which he portrayed later in his 1953 novel *Letzte Ausfahrt* ("The Last Sortie"). Prior to that effort he had published *Die Sonnenstadt* in 1947; this novel tells the story of a woman who makes her castle into a hotel after the war—and of her son, who attempts to create an artists' colony there after her death.

*Letzte Ausfahrt* gave Zand his greatest public acclaim and won a literary prize. Its philosophy has been called "existentialist humanism," which attempts to find meaning in even the most horrible of circumstances. The novel concerns a company of advancing German soldiers, and at the same time, the inhabitants of a besieged East German city. Both groups witness the nightmares of war, when traditional religion and morality seem to have lost relevance. Ludwig Hohn, the protagonist of the story, wrote Saur, is transformed "from a sensitive, cultivated piano player into a crude, foulmouthed killer." Despite the depressing plot, however, Saur said that the book "also portrays hope and freedom that existentialism cherishes as possible even in the midst of unspeakable guilt and suffering."

In 1953 Zand produced a book of poems, *Die Glaskugel* ("The Glass Sphere"), and in 1956 he published a novella, *Der Weg nach Hassi el emel* ("The Well of Hope"). Said to be a perfectionist, Zand burned one manuscript and left others unfinished. The last book to appear in his lifetime was *Erben des Feuers* ("Inheritors of Fire"), a mystery novel published in 1961. The convoluted plot of the book reveals more than just a mystery story, however: Saur said that the villain's misdeeds in the story, "like those of Austria during World War II, are . . . smoothed over with a veneer of prosperity."

Despite his increasing bad health, the direct result of his war wounds, Zand continued to write creatively almost until his death of kidney failure in 1970. A collection of his essays, sketches, interviews, and diary entries was brought out by his friend Wolfgang Kraus in 1973. Saur said that the collected pieces are particularly noteworthy for their stark portraits of rural life during Zand's youth. "Despite his . . . admiration for [his parents]," Saur asserted, "Zand asserts that they are guided by a philosophy of slavery, an attitude characterized by resignation, suspicion, the overvaluation of physical strength and labor, and a lack of interest in luxury, beauty, success, or even rest."

In 1972 a collection of Zand's stories, *Demosthenes spricht gegen die Brandung* ("Demosthenes Orates Against the Waves"), was published. Saur said that the stories were written "with a light touch" but that many have "a menacing undertone." The essays in *Traume im Spiegel* ("Dreams in the Mirror") concern daydreams which artists turn into artistic creations. In 1980 additional material left in Zand's literary estate appeared in the journal Literatur und Kritik.

In the short span of his life, Zand went far beyond his early postwar literary efforts. According to Saur, he was "a captivating storyteller who knew the appeal of suspense and adventure, mystery and romance" who also "confront[ed] the modern problem of finding meaning and identity in an apparently senseless universe." Saur concluded, "Zand's writings convey his fundamental vision of human beings drawing sustenance and a sense of permanence from the land, however bloodstained that land may be."

*BIOGRAPHICAL/CRITICAL SOURCES:*

*BOOKS*

*Dictionary of Literary Biography,* Volume 85: *Austrian Fiction Writers After 1914,* Gale (Detroit, MI), 1989.

*PERIODICALS*

*Die Neue Rundschau,* Volume 84, 1973, pp. 545-550.
*Literatur und Kritik,* July, 1971, pp. 340-347; May, 1974, pp. 229-241.
*Wort in der Zeit,* Volume 6, 1960, pp. 13-17.*

\*　　\*　　\*

## ZECH, Paul 1881-1946
### (Timm Borah)

*PERSONAL:* Born on February 19, 1881, in Briesen near Thorn (later Torun, Poland); died following a stroke, September 6, 1946; married Helene Siemon 1904; children: two. *Education:* Attended Zurich, Bonn, and Heidelberg Universities.

*CAREER:* Novelist, playwright, and lyricist, 1909-46. Local official, librarian, and dramatic adviser, Berlin, 1910-33; arrested, 1933; exiled, 1934-46. Miner, early 1900s. *Military service:* Served in Russia and France, 1915-17; injured by grenade and gas poisoning.

*AWARDS, HONORS:* Received Kleist Prize for young writers, 1918.

*WRITINGS:*

*Das schwarze Revier,* Elberfeld, 1909, revised edition, Meyer (Berlin-Wilmersdorf), 1913, new revised edition, Musarion (Munich), 1922.
*Waldpastelle: Sechs Gedichte,* Meyer, 1910, revised and enlarged edition published as *Der Wald,* Sibyllen (Dresden), 1920.
*Gedichte: Paul Zech, August Vetter und Friedrich Kerst,* Bergische Druckerei und Verlagsanstalt (Elberfeld), 1910.
(With Christian Grunewald, Ludwig Fahrenkrog, and Julius August Vetter) *Das fruehe Gelaeut: Gedichte,* Meyer, 1911.

*Rainer Maria Rilke,* Borngraeber (Berlin), 1912, revised and enlarged edition published as *Rainer Maria Rilke: Der Meusch und das Werk,* Jess (Dresden), 1930.

*Schollenbruch: Gedichte,* Meyer, 1912.

(With Richard M. Caben, Johannes Kublemann, Paul Mayer, Bruno Quandt, and Robert R. Schmidt) *Fanale: Gedichte der rheinischen Lyriker,* Saturn (Heidelberg), 1913.

*Schwarz sind die Wasser der Ruhr: Gesammelte Gedichte aus den Jahren 1902-1910,* Druckerei der Bibliophilen (Berlin-Wilmersdorf), 1913.

*Die Sonette aus dem Exil,* Officina Serpentis (Berlin-Steglitz), 1913, enlarged edition, Zech (Berlin), 1948.

*Die eiserne Bruecke: Neue Gedichte,* WeiBen Buecher (Leipzig), 1914.

*Der schwarze Baal: Novellen,* WeiBen Buecher, 1917, revised edition, 1919.

*Helden und Heilige: Balladen aus der Zeit,* Drugulin (Leipzig), 1917.

*Gelaudet: Ein dramatisches Gedicht,* Revillon-Presse (Laon), 1918, revised edition, Roland (Munich), 1919.

*Vor Cressy an der Marne: Gedichte eines Frontsoldaten namens Michel Michael,* Revillon-Presse, 1918.

*Der feuerige Busch: Neue Gedichte (1912-1917),* Musarion, 1919.

*Das Grab der Welt: Eine Passion wider den Krieg auf Erden,* Hoffmann & Campe (Hamburg), 1919.

*Die Gedichte an eine Dame in Schwarz,* Musation (Munich), 1920.

*Das Ereignis: Neue Novellen,* Musarion, 1920.

*Golgatha: Eine Beschwoerung zwischen zwei Feuern,* Hoffman & Campe, 1920.

*Das Terzett der Sterne: Ein Bekenutnis in drei Stationen,* Wolff (Munich), 1920.

*Verbruederung: Ein Hochgesang unter dem Regenbogen in fuenf Statione,* Hoffmann & Campe, 1921.

*Omnia mea mecum porto: Die Ballade von mir,* Rowohlt (Berlin), 1923.

*Die ewige Dreieinigkeit: Gedichte,* Greifenverlag(Rudolstadt), 1924.

*Das Rad: Ein tragisches Maskenspiel,* Schauspiel-Verlag (Liepzig), 1924.

*Die Reise um den Kummerberg: Erzaehlung,* Greifenverlag, 1924.

*Das trunkene Schiff: Eine szenische Ballade,* Schauspiel-Verlag, 1924.

*Steine: Ein tragisches Finale in sieben Geschehnissen,* Schauspiel-Verlag, 1924.

*Der Turm: Sieben Stufen zu einem Drama,* Schauspiel-Verlag, 1924.

*Erde: Die vier Etappen eines Dramas zwischen Rhein und Ruhr,* Schauspiel-Verlag, 1925.

*Die Geschichte einer armen Johanna,* Dietz (Berlin), 1925.

*Peregrins Heimkehr: Ein Roman in sieben Buechern,* Dietz, 1925.

*Das toerichte Herz: Vier Erzaehlungen,* Dietz, 1925.

*Die Mutterstadt: Die unterbrochene Bruecke: Zwei Erzaehlungen,* Koesel & Pustet (Munich), 1925.

*Ich bin Du, oder, Die Begegnung mit dem Unsichtbaren: Roman,* Wolkenwanderer-Verlag (Leipzig), 1926.

*Rainer Maria Rilke: Ein Requiem,* Officina Serpentis (Berlin), 1927.

*Das Baalsopfer,* Deutsche Dichter-Gedaechtnis-Stiftung (Hamburg), 1929.

*Rotes Herz der Erde: Ausgewaehlte Balladen, Gedichte, Gesaenge,* edited by Walther G. Oschilewski, Arbeiterjugend-Verlag (Berlin), 1929.

*Morgenrot leuchtet! Ein Augsburger Festspiel fuer Einzelstimmen, Sprech, Tanz-und Bewegungschoere,* Heber (Augsburg), 1930.

*Neue Balladen von den wilden Tieren,* Jess (Dresden), 1931, revised edition published as *Balladen von den Tieren,* Zech, 1949.

(Under pseudonym Timm Borah) *Berlin im Licht, oder, Gedichte linker Hand,* Rabenpresse (Berlin), 1932.

*Terzinen fuer Thino,* Rabenpresse, 1932.

*Das Schlotz der Brueder Zanowsky: Eine unglaubwuerdige Geschichte,* Rabenpresse, 1933.

*Baeume am Rio de la Plata,* Transmare-Verlag (Buenos Aires), 1935.

*Neue Welt: Verse der Emigration,* Quadriga (Buenos Aires), 1939.

*Ich suchte Schmied . . . und fand Malva wieder,* Editorial Estrellas (Buenos Aires), 1941.

*Stefan Zweig: Eine Gedenkschrift,* Quadriga, 1943.

*Die schwarze Orchidee: Indianische Legenden,* Zech, 1947.

*Occla, das Maedchen mit den versteinerten Augen: Eine indianische Legende,* Schauer (Frankfurt am Main), 1948.

*Paul Verlaine und sein Werk,* Zech, 1949.

*Kinder vom Parana: Roman,* Greifenverlag (Rudolstadt), 1952.

*Das rote Messer: Begegnungen mit Tieren und seltsamen Menschen* Greifenverlag (Rudolstadt), 1953.

*Die Voegel des Herrn Langfoot: Roman,* Greifenverlag, 1954.

*Die gruene Floete vom Rio Beni: Indianische Liebesgeschichten,* Greifenverlag, 1955.

*Die Ballade von einer Weltraumrakete* Trias (Berlin-Friedenau), 1958.

*Abendgesaenge und Landschaft der Insel Mara-Pampa,* Zech, 1960.

*Die ewigen Gespraeche: Deutsche Variationen nach Themen von Charles Peguy,* Zech, 1960.

*Die Sonette vom Bauern,* Zech, 1960.

*Venus Urania: Sieben Gesaenge fuer Mirjam,* Daphnis-Presse (Berlin), 1961.

*Hymnen von den zwoelf Fenstern: Gedichte,* Zech (Berlin-Friedenau), 1965.

*Die Haeuser haben Augen aufgetan: Ausgewaehlte Gedichte,* edited by Manfred Wolter, Aufbau (Berlin), 1976.

*Deutschland, dein Taenzer ist der Tod: Ein Tatsachen-Roman,* edited by Helmut Nitzschke Greifenverlag (Rudolstadt), 1980.

*Menschen der Calle Tuyuti: Erzaehlungen aus dem Exil,* edited by Wolfgang Kieztling, Greifenverlag, 1982.

*Vom schwarzen Revier zur Neuen Welt: Gesammelte Gedichte,* edited by Henry A. Smith, Hanser (Munich), 1983.

*Michael M. irrt durch Buenos Aires: Aufzeichnungen eines Emigranten. Roman,* edited by Nitzschke, Greifenverlag, 1985.

*Von der Maas bis an die Marne: Ein Kriegstagebuch,* Greifenverlag, 1986.

*OTHER*

(Translator) Leon Deubel, *Die rot durchrasten Naechte: Gedichte,* Officina Serpentis (Berlin), 1914.

(Translator) Stephane Mallarme, *Nachmittagstraum eines Fauns,* privately printed (Berlin), 1914.

(Translator) Emile Verhaeren, *Die wogende Saat,* Insel (Leipzig), 1917.

(Translator) Mallarme, *Herodias: Ein Fragment,* privately printed, 1919.

(Translator) Honore de Balzac, *Tante Lisbeth,* 2 volumes, Rowohlt (Berlin), 1923.

(Editor), *Der Mann am Kreuz: Geschichten zeitgenoessischer Erzaehler von Rhein und Ruhr,* edited by Zech, Zentralverlag (Berlin), 1923.

(Translator) Arthur Rimbaud, *Erleuchtungen: Gedichte in Prosa,* Wolkenwanderer-Verlag (Leipzig), 1924.

(Editor) Christian Dietrich Grabbe, *Werke in Auswahl,* 2 volumes, Volksbuehnen-Verlag, 1925.

(Translator) Henry-Marx, *Triumph der Jugend: Ein Schauspiel in drei Akten,* Schauspiel-Verlag (Leipzig), 1925.

(Translator) Rimbaud, *Das Werk,* Wolkenwanderer-Verlag, 1925, revised edition published as *Das gesammelte Werk,* 1927.

(Translator) Rimbaud, *Das trunkene Schiff: Ballade,* Schacht (Bochum), 1928.

(Translator) Francois Villon, *Die Balladen und lasterhaften Lieder des Herrn Francois Villon,* translated by Zech, Lichtenstein (Weimar), 1931.

(Translator) Friedrich Hoelderlin, *Hiperion, o, Eleremita en Grecia,* introduction by Zech, Emece Editores (Buenos Aires), 1946.

(Translator) Louise Charly Labe, *Die Liebesgedichte einer schoenen Lyoneser Seilerin namens Louize Labe,* Zech, 1948, revised edition, Greifenverlag (Rudolstadt), 1956.

(Translator) Rimbaud, *Das Herz unter der Soutane,* Buerger (Lorch & Stuttgart), 1948.

(Translator) Jorge Icaza, *Huasipungo: Ruf der Indios,* Greifenverlag, 1952.

(Translator) Balzac, *Gesammelte Werke,* Rowohlt (Hamburg), 1952.

(Translator) Rimbaud, *Saemtliche Dichtungen,* Deutscher Taschenbuch (Munich), 1963.

(Translator) *Altfranzoesische Liebesieder,* Friedenauer (Berlin), 1965.

*Stefan Zweig/Paul Zech: Briefe 1910-1942,* edited by Donald D. Daviau, Fischer (Frankfurt am Main), 1986.

Also co-editor of *Das neue Pathos,* 1913-1920; editor of *Das dramatische Theater,* 1924.

*SIDELIGHTS:* Paul Zech is best known as a lyrical prose writer who told of the worker's plight. His dense descriptions of the physical difficulties and pleasures of working life are believed to be informed by his own widely varied experiences: Zech himself labored as a miner and flourished as an acclaimed editor and writer; he was beloved by his countrymen and he subsisted on charity in exile. His writing relates not only his varied experiences, however, but also his deep sense of natural social rectitude. As Mary Garland writes in the *Oxford Companion to German Literature:* "A worker's poet without party political commitment but with strong religious convictions, he was concerned with brotherhood and the rebirth of man through the contact with nature." Ward B. Lewis, writing for the *Dictionary of Literary Biography* concurs: "Zech's socialistic impulses were infused initially with a Christian religiosity that was associated with vitalism and a reverent awe of nature. These attitudes evolved as did his writing, reflecting at turns his pastoral inclinations, the features of Workers' Poetry, the styles of expressionism and the New Objectivity, and various combinations of all of these."

Zech was born in Briesen near Thorn (later Torun, Poland) on February 19, 1881. His father was a local schoolmaster, who insured that Zech was well taught. As a youth, he studied at Wuppertal-Eberfeld, and then attended the Universities of Bonn, Heidelberg, and Zurich. After school, however, Zech took two years to work in the coal mines and steel mills in Belgium and France. The experience was apparently one of the most powerful of his life; as Lewis explains: "In the early days his prose depicted aspects of the existence he had known in the mills and mines; but even in his advanced years, when the author found himself encapsulated in an alien culture, his sympathies continued to be expressed for the subjects of exploitation."

Following his experiences in the mines, and his 1904 marriage to Helene Siemon, Zech turned to more literate expressions of his love of work. In 1909 he published his first poems, *Das Schwartze Revier* (1909) and *Waldpastelle: Sechs Gedichte* (Forest Pastel, 1910). In these volumes, Zech extols the beauty of the countryside as a healing force in men's lives. Following the publication of these verses, Zech was able to assume editorial positions in Berlin, at magazines such as *Das neue Pathos*. But by 1915, Zech was sent to war, where he was wounded in battle.

Back in Germany, Zech turned back to his discussions of nature and workers, now in a lyrical prose style that he would maintain for the rest of his career. Of his first prose work, *Der schwartze Baal: Novellen* ("Black Baal," 1917), Lewis remarks: "Borrowing for the title image of a Semitic deity favored by the expressionists, [Zech] describes the industrial scene—cables, chains, rails, cogged wheels, the humming of belts, the whine of drills, sparks, smoke, and steam from engines and chimneys. This kind of language is usually associated with the genre of Worker's Poetry, where it constitutes a paean to the joy of labor. Here Zech employs the vocabulary in prose; there is not a hint of joy, however, in *Der schwartze Baal: Novellen.*"

Despite the relatively grim tone of his work, this period of Zech's career proved successful with critics. In 1918, he received the Kleist Prize for young authors. And though Zech would attempt plays and other forms throughout the years, it was really the prose writing from this period that is most associated with his work. Lyrical, dense, almost prose poetry, Zech's style would suit the kinds of novels and prose collections for which he was later known. As Lewis describes Zech's later work: "Profuse and lyrical descriptions of the country—the music of the wind in the treetops, apple picking in gardens, views along the roadside—suggest that nature's beauty continues eternally despite the ravages of war. The author borrows from the palette of van Gogh to juxtapose vivid swatches of color, setting the black of a roof against the blue of the sky, the white of a gable before the yellows and vermillions in the background."

In many of Zech's works, he used this dense prose style in a collected series of related sketches—for example, in *Das Ereignis: Neue Novellen* ("The Event," 1920) or *Die Reise um den Kumerberg: Erzahlung* ("Travels about the Mountain of Grief," 1924). In these works, Zech links brief snapshots, rich with language, in order to give a more subtly varied sense of emotional presence. In *Das Ereignis,* he offers nine different sketches, each reflecting on the sexual potency of women. In *Die Reise um den Kummerberg,* Zech lines up twenty-six pieces, each told in the first person. Lewis details the style used in this text: "Employing a sparse, direct style consisting of short sentences and sentence fragments to achieve a staccato effect, Zech writes in language which the critics characterized variously as boldly original or insufferably affected . . . A lyrical outpouring of joy and vitalism in the style of expressionism celebrates a country landscape and its creatures in the summer."

Zech also developed for himself a following among novel readers, particularly with his popular book, *Die Geschichte einer armen Johanna* ("The Tale of Poor Johanna," 1925). The novel recalls the romantic novels of fallen women popular in the eighteenth and nineteenth centuries: in it, a plain seamstress becomes a demimondaine, acting as a high-class harlot to the wealthy. Nevertheless, she grows ill and tired, and dies melodramatically. Of this novel, Lewis remarks: "The wide audience reached by this novel felt that the work was a profound expression of the author's love and sympathy toward a victim of society. Less gracious voices characterized the work as sentimental kitsch." Nevertheless, the novel was beloved by Zech's readers and helped to make him famous in his own land.

Though Zech continued to lead the life of a successful writer, he was soon caught up in the political struggles of Germany. Though he had never affected any particular political leaning, he often wrote in a "social democratic" tone, according to Lewis. For this, Zech was arrested in 1933; after a brief incarceration, he fled into exile, leaving behind his family and lover, the actress Hilde Herb. He seems to have traveled throughout South America and the United States, and often wrote about these travels in his later work. During this period, he published several volumes of "exile writing," in which he describes exotic travels he may have taken. None of these works were well received, however, and his literary reputation suffered immeasurable damage from his loss of a national readership. Zech died of a stroke on September 7, 1946.

Zech wrote prolifically for most of his life, attempting several different styles but generally offering a lyrical prose style shot through with blissful reflections on nature and sexual pleasure. His politics, which were always more social-leaning than dogmatic expressions of party allegiance, unfortunately cost him the means of expressing himself to his own countrymen.

*BIOGRAPHICAL/CRITICAL SOURCES:*

*BOOKS*

*Dictionary of Literary Biography,* Volume 56: *German Fiction Writers, 1914-1945,* Gale (Detroit, MI), 1987.
*Oxford Companion to German Literature,* Oxford University Press (Oxford), 1997.

*PERIODICALS*

*South Atlantic Bulletin,* November, 1973, p. 54.*